The Beatles
Volume 2
After The Break
1970–2001

CW00482451

BOOKCASE

CENTRE COUR... ... ...CE
LSU2 LOWER M...
M54345703145140411016167
427
AID : A000000031010
VISA DEBIT

VISA DEBIT

4543 1302 1830 6828
EXP 09/04
ICC

SALE

CUSTOMER COPY

AMOUNT   £14.98

THANK YOU
PLEASE KEEP THIS RECEIPT
FOR YOUR RECORDS
16:17 16/10/03
COMPLETED
RECEIPT 3564

HSBC <☒>

HSBC <☒>

VISA DEBIT

HSBC <☒>

VISA DEBIT

ICC

SALE

HSBC <☒>

AMOUNT   £??.98

HSBC <☒>

COMPLETED
RECEIPT 3564

The Beatles Years
Volume 2:
After The Break-Up
1970–2001

Keith Badman

OMNIBUS PRESS

Edited by Chris Charlesworth
Cover & Book designed by Pearce Marchbank
Picture research by Nikki Russell & Keith Badman

ISBN: 0.7119.8307.0
Order No: OP48189

Exclusive Distributors
Book Sales Limited
8/9 Frith Street
London W1D 3JB, UK

Music Sales Corporation
257 Park Avenue South
New York, NY 10010, USA

The Five Mile Press
22 Summit Road
Noble Park
Victoria 3174, Australia

To the Music Trade only
Music Sales Limited
8/9 Frith Street
London W1D 3JB, UK

Printed by Creative Print & Design (Wales) Ltd
Typeset by Galleon Typesetting, Ipswich

A catalogue record for this book is
available from the British Library.

www.omnibuspress.com

Foreword

by Miles

One of the more predictable questions at Beatles press conferences was, "What will you do when the bubble bursts?" They always answered, just as predictably, "We'll burst with it! Ha! Ha!" But it was not the case. Twenty-five years after the group broke up, The Beatles were once more the biggest earning entity in show business, more than the Stones, more than Michael Jackson, more than Bill Cosby or Oprah Winfrey. This was of course because of the *Anthology* television series, the video set and the three double CDs. But in the intervening years The Beatles had never really gone away: they and their fans behaved as if they still existed. There were none of the usual signs of a long disbanded group: all of their catalogue was always readily available, almost always at full price, and only rarely did their songs appear on Sixties compilations.

When the band broke up there were only one or two books available about them. Now there are more than 400 and new ones are published on an average of one every two weeks. On the Internet there are more Beatles sites than any other music group with over 40,000 pages devoted to them. There are annual Beatles weekends in London, Liverpool, San Diego, Orlando, Los Angeles and other cities. The Beatlefests in Liverpool, New York and Chicago attract more than 10,000 people to watch film clips, hear pundits pontificate and to buy Beatles memorabilia, most of which has been produced since the group broke up. Beatles merchandising has become an industry in itself, with hundreds of dealers doing nothing else but buy and sell the detritus of marketing campaigns, old copies of *Radio Times* and the occasional rare picture sleeve. Blue chip Beatles memorabilia, especially handwritten lyrics and items relating directly to John, always fetches the highest prices at auction sales.

In America there are a number of 24-hour Beatles stations, playing nothing but songs by the collective and solo Beatles, endlessly, month after month. Hundreds of stations have weekly Beatles shows or Beatles request shows. 'Yesterday' is the world's most popular song: in 1993, it passed the six million airplay mark in the USA, followed at second most popular by 'Michelle' at four million. 'Yesterday' has also been covered by more than 2,300 other artists. Just one copy of each version would fill a wall of shelves. How can anyone compete with that? Well, Paul McCartney can, of course. At the height of the punk movement, McCartney calmly released 'Mull Of Kintyre', a sentimental ballad which immediately became the biggest selling single in Britain up to that time – selling more than any Beatles' record.

There was a time when they hated to be called "ex-Beatles"; usually stressing the fact that The Beatles was just a band they were once in, and now they were doing something else. Time passed and now they are just 'The Beatles' again. They may have had enormous success with solo careers, but they are Beatles and always will be as long as they live. At Apple and in Beatles circles there was a saying: "Nothing is safe from Beatlification" and it turns out that The Beatles themselves aren't immune from it either.

In the Seventies, the image of The Beatles was frozen in time: the long-haired bickering Beatles of *Let It Be* and the Saville Row rooftop concert. This gradually changed, as images from all periods of The Beatles' career, from the Fab Four, the Four Mop Tops, the Lords of Psychedelia and Sgt. Pepper's Lonely Hearts Club Band all intermingled to a composite Beatles, like a collage image of the Sixties from the Kennedy Assassination through Christine Keeler to Man landing on the Moon and a Technicolor Jimi Hendrix playing the guitar with his teeth. The Beatles are a passage from black and white to glorious colour; from the cheeky Northern lads of *A Hard Day's Night* to the sublime psychedelic John Lennon singing 'I Am The Walrus' in *Magical Mystery Tour*. Not surprising then that they had a bit of an influence over the music scene.

The Beatles sit like a monolith in the middle of popular music history, you can't avoid them. In the early days of pop music there was only one hit parade and they dominated it, year in, year out. These days with the hip-hop charts, the house music and techno charts, charts for rappers and charts for sensitive Canadian lady folk singers it is hard to imagine any one group ever having that dominance again. These days someone can be number one for months and half the record buying public will never have even heard of them because they buy a different type of record.

The Beatles introduced the singer-songwriter, they did the first "concept album", they were the first to print their lyrics on the sleeve, they invented stadium rock, they not only had the John Lennon-Paul McCartney songwriting team on board but, astonishingly, had George Harrison as well. George's 'Something' was described by Frank Sinatra as "the greatest love song of the past fifty years" and has been covered by such greats as Ray Charles, James Brown and Smoky Robinson. In The Beatles George had to fight to even get a B-side.

They broke up and all went solo. George's career was the first to take off with the release of his box set *All Things Must Pass*, the first triple album in rock'n'roll. Unfortunately for him, in 1976 the big hit single from the set, 'My Sweet Lord', was deemed (unfairly) by the courts to have more than a passing similarity to The Chiffons' 'He's So Fine' and he forfeited the royalties on that song. In the early Seventies, however, George was riding high, he was the coolest man in rock. He even brought Bob Dylan out on stage for the first time in several years at a benefit concert for the refugees of Bangladesh which George organised at Madison Square Garden. The problem was that George is a slow writer and with his triple album set, he had put all his eggs in one basket. There wasn't much left for the next album – or the one after that – and his recording career never reached such heights again. George turned instead to films – not acting, but producing. His company Handmade Films put £2,000,000 into the Monty Python team's *Life Of Brian* and made a massive profit. Suddenly George had another career.

John was also fast off the mark. Whereas Paul got married in the full glare of publicity, but honeymooned in private, John had a secret wedding but invited the world press to attend the honeymoon, first at the Amsterdam Hilton then, as he was unable to enter the States, in Montreal where he wrote the memorable peace anthem 'Give Peace A Chance'. John made his private life public, just as in his songs he expressed his most intimate private feelings. He recorded *Imagine*, an album which is in part hauntingly beautiful – John had a fantastic voice – and also deeply flawed with its vicious attack on McCartney, 'How Do You Sleep?'. Then in 1971 John moved to New York City, never to set foot in England again. (Even when he obtained a green card and was able to travel again, Yoko was opposed to him returning to Britain.) In New York he fell in with media hucksters and self-styled revolutionaries Jerry Rubin and Abbie Hoffman which resulted in the terrible *Some Time In New York City*. For the first time John was writing about things people told him, rather than writing from personal experience, and it showed. His career in the UK effectively ended with that album until his work was reassessed at his death. The album also attracted the attention of Richard Nixon and John soon found himself under FBI surveillance as a dangerous revolutionary when all he really wanted was his green card so he could stay in the country.

Ringo also started well; 'It Don't Come Easy' in 1971 was followed a year later with 'Back Off Boogaloo', both fine singles which indicated a solid solo career. In addition, his acting improved with each film he appeared in, beginning with the dismal *Candy* (now a cult movie, so bad it's good), faring much better in *The Magic Christian* and peaking with *That'll Be The Day* where he was finally given the right role. His album *Ringo* in 1973 was better than any the other ex-Beatles had made in years and his singles 'Photograph' and 'You're Sixteen' both reached number one in the States. Ringo joined the jet set and became a tax exile in Monte Carlo with houses in Amsterdam and Los Angeles. A generation of children grew up thinking of him as the voice of *Thomas The Tank Engine and as the narrator on Nilsson's animated cartoon The Point*.

Paul, the most likely Beatle to succeed as a solo artist, got off to a very slow start. He had been badly affected by the break-up of the group and the subsequent legal wrangles. *McCartney* and *Ram* were slated by the critics, as were the early efforts by Wings. Then in 1973 he had his own TV special, wrote the theme to *Live And Let Die* and released *Band On The Run*. This was followed by a massive 1975–76 world tour and from then on he never looked back.

Perhaps goaded by Paul's success, John returned to the recording studio. He took his famous eighteen-month long weekend with May Pang in Los Angeles and recorded 'Whatever Gets You Through The Night', his first solo number one in America. Then he returned to Yoko and in 1975, Sean was born, John got his green card and became a "house husband", bringing up their son while Yoko got on with making money.

The Beatles, meanwhile, were not forgotten. In 1976 EMI re-promoted all The Beatles' singles – these were not re-issues because they were never off the catalogue – and they immediately charted. All of them; taking up about a quarter of the Top 100. There was a new Beatles single among them. 'Yesterday' had never been issued as a single in the UK, though it had been a huge hit in the USA. Now it had its own turn at the top of the UK charts.

1980 was a bad year. First Paul was busted at Narita airport, Tokyo, trying to take pot into Japan and spent ten anxious days in jail before being released. Then on December 8, 1980, John was senselessly murdered outside his home at the Dakota in New York, and nothing was ever the same again. The remaining Beatles hunkered down, surrounded by bodyguards and security systems, and effectively disappeared from sight. Records continued to appear from them all but it was not until the late Eighties that they took on a public presence again. In 1989 both Paul and Ringo planned tours: Ringo put together his All-Starr Band and Paul went for something rather more ambitious: a world tour of stadiums lasting 11 months to promote his *Flowers In The Dirt* CD and, much to the audiences' delight, play Beatles songs again. George popped up in The Traveling Wilburys and toured in Japan.

Then came the *Anthology* series: a worldwide multi-part television series, eight videos, three double CDs, two new Beatles singles (there would have been three but George didn't like John's tape). All that was missing at the time was the book, which eventually surfaced in the autumn of 2000, followed by *1*, the first single CD of Beatles greats which music industry insiders predict will become the best-selling album ever. The Beatles were back and it seemed that Paul, George and Ringo didn't mind at all being Beatles again. They had never really been away.

As the world moves into the third millennium, the enormous celebrity of The Beatles remains firmly intact. Their status as the greatest pop group ever remains unchallenged as each new generation of bands acknowledges their influence. Paul is now firmly established as a sort of elder statesman of British pop, its senior figure who is invariably invited to top the bill at prestigious charity events, much as he did at Live Aid. He is now Sir Paul McCartney, an accolade that was long overdue considering those knighthoods bestowed upon other, lesser, figures from the world of entertainment. No matter how you measure success in the entertainment world, Paul is on top: the most number one records, the most air-plays, the fastest selling tickets, the biggest paying audience, and of course, the most money. He is unquestionably the wealthiest of British rock stars, his fortune generally estimated to be in the region of £500 million whenever broadsheet newspapers and music magazines discuss such matters. A great wave of public sympathy was extended towards Paul when Linda died, and for some time afterwards he maintained an uncharacteristically low profile. He's since re-emerged in the company of the handicapped model Heather Mills, a relationship the Great British Public seems to have gladly countenanced. Paul is a grandfather now, daughter Mary having presented him with a grandson, while his youngest daughter Stella has found fame in her own right as a fashion designer.

Low profiles come naturally to George. The quiet Beatle has become ever more silent over the years, dry of wit and content to potter around in his garden and indulge his love of automobiles and Formula One racing. He remains a deeply private and quietly religious man. The break-in at Friar Park over Christmas 1999, with its eerie echoes of John's murder, will likely push him yet further away from the limelight. As a Beatle he never much liked having his photo taken and he probably never will. Relations between George and Paul fluctuate with the tides. They haven't performed together since the Apple rooftop show in January 1969, and it's unlikely they ever will again.

Ringo remains, indubitably, Ringo, the all-smiling, all-singing, all-dancing ex-Beatle whose run of luck goes on forever. He was never taken very seriously when he was a member of The Beatles and he's never been taken very seriously since, although his problems with alcohol and drugs put a dent in the lovable image created by his deadpan rendering of *Thomas The Tank Engine*. Ringo presents no threat to anyone and as such he remains the bridge between Paul and George, and probably also Yoko, John's widow and the fourth, ever-intriguing factor in the ongoing saga of the greatest pop group the world has ever known.

Miles, April 1999 & November 2000.

Author's Notes

After The Break-Up is an attempt to list chronologically all the facts relating to the lives of John Lennon, Paul McCartney, George Harrison and Ringo Starr after they ceased to be a working group in the early months of 1970. They were still Beatles, of course, and will always remain so, but this book lists all those events, crucial and otherwise, that occurred in their lives once they ceased to make music together on a regular basis.

A compilation of this kind has not been attempted before and I am the first to admit that no matter how hard I try I cannot hope to list absolutely everything that happened in the lives of these four remarkable men from 1970 to the present day. By far the most interesting events are those that involve a combination of two or more former Beatles, be it recording sessions, live performances, business meetings or casual get-togethers. Meetings between the two principal former Beatles, John and Paul, virtually stopped at the beginning of the Seventies but became more common around the middle of the decade, only to cease completely thereafter. I believe that every such meeting is logged here, including a few unreported elsewhere. John's final meetings with George, Ringo and, most importantly, Paul are confirmed here for the first time.

Naturally the book hinges upon their professional lives. I believe it contains the most comprehensive accounts ever published of John's activities during his final decade and Paul's adventures with Wings. For the sake of space and time, I have included only those records released in the UK and USA, unless releases elsewhere in the world are especially noteworthy, as in the case of Paul's Russian rock'n'roll album. I have included every known public performance, every film appearance, every recording session, almost every TV and radio appearance and every substantial magazine and newspaper interview that has come to my attention in the 20 years or more that I have taken a close interest in The Beatles. The text is therefore liberally enhanced by extracts from those interviews that I felt contained illuminating opinions from the former Fabs.

Also in amongst these pages are details of every known court case involving The Beatles, be they civil cases involving disputes over millions of pounds in royalties, Paul's heavily reported drug busts or George getting yet another rap on the knuckles for speeding. And I have included as many social occasions as I know about, including births, marriages and deaths, as well as holidays, parties and nights out on the town.

All the thousands of entries that I have listed herein pale into insignificance compared with the tragic events of December 8, 1980. John Lennon's murder remains the single most tragic event in the history of popular music.

That a book of this kind can find a publisher 37 years after the release of their first record is a remarkable tribute to the group which John assembled and led. Long live The Beatles!

I would like to acknowledge the following individuals who have greatly assisted me with my research over the last ten months: John Bloomfield (for his most invaluable perusal of the text), Mike Dalton (for additional research and photography), Steve Holmes (Beatles For Sale) for supplying no end of source material, Pete Nash (for his hospitality and allowing me unlimited access to one of the greatest Beatles collections in the world), Terry Rawlings (my former writing partner in crime), Steve Vallis (a tower of strength and a great friend for over 25 years), Peter and Fenella Walkling (for their hospitality and allowing me unlimited access to one of the greatest private George Harrison collections in the world).

In addition, very special thanks go to the following individuals: Jason Hobbs, Neil Sommerville (BBC), Andy Davis, Peter Doggett, Martin O'Gorman, Andy Neill, Stephen Rouse, Tony Rouse, Robert Batchelor, Miles, Simon Rogers, Jean Catherall (Liverpool Beatlescene), Spencer Lloyd, Bob Gruen, Frieda (Kelly) Norris, Tetsuo Hamada (Produce Centre, Japan), Greg Schmidt (USA), Jos Remmerswall (Holland), Andy Brooks, Rene Van Haarlem (Holland), Matt Hurwitz (USA), Dirk Van Damme (Belgium), Bob Boyer (USA), Carole Ann Lennie, Debbie Wakeford, Dawn, Mel (and all the other LIPA Scruffs, too many to mention), Paul Wayne at Tracks, Jack Douglas, Leslie Benson, Brian Durrant, Dave Ravenscroft, Mark Paytress, Dave McGlynn, Dave Carter, Janice Wallis, Dave Withers, Joerg Pieper (Germany), Paul McEvoy (MC80), Mark Saunders (for Princess Diana information), Marc Roberty (for Eric Clapton information), John Homer (Beach Boys), Dan Matovina (Badfinger), Lou Maloney (VH-1), John Hellier, the staff at Run Print Run and the staff of Upton Lea postal services.

Beatles books & magazines: The Beatles Book Monthly, Beatles Unlimited (Holland), Beatlefan (USA), Good Day Sunshine (USA), Working Class Heroes (Neville Stannard), The Beatles – The Ultimate Recording Guide (Allen J. Wiener), All Together Now (Castleman & Podrazik), The Beatles – A Diary (Miles), Many Years From Now (Miles), The Beatles Chronicles (Mark Lewisohn), Loving John (May Pang), Living On Borrowed Time (Fred Seaman), Lennon (John Robertson) and Waiting For The Beatles (Carol Bedford).

General newspapers & magazines: Melody Maker, New Musical Express, Playboy, Newsweek, Record Collector, the Liverpool Echo, Q, Mojo, The Times, the Sun, Daily Mirror, New York Times, Rolling Stone, Daily Star, Sotheby's auction house (London).

TV and Radio libraries around the world: Apple, MPL, BBC TV, LWT, BVL Enterprises, ABC TV, NBC TV, CBS TV, NHK (Japan), Veronica TV (Holland), RKO Radio, VH-1, MTV, Radio Bremen, Pathe, Movietone, E Network (USA). Also the many wonderful Beatles/solo Internet sites that are available on the worldwide web (notably the most informative Abbey Road page) who have all been a most invaluable source of information.

Other sources of information: The BBC Written Archives, Slough Public Library, Colindale newspaper library, and the Westminster reference library. Thanks to all the respective staff.

Special inspirational thanks must go to Arsene Wenger, the finest football manager in the world, who has made Arsenal FC, once again, the greatest club in the land; and United Nations goodwill ambassador Geri Halliwell, one of the most fascinating and kind-hearted people in the world.

Last but by no means least, a very special thanks goes to: Kathleen, Sheila, Pauline, Michael, and everyone else who's assisted me in my madness to create a (hopefully) definitive book on the solo years of The Beatles (sorry if I've missed anyone out!). My occasional, but reliable, assistant Caroline, who continues to pop in and out of my life at a most alarming rate.

And to Bob Wise, Nikki Russell and Chris Charlesworth, of Omnibus Press, who commissioned this book and agreed with me that a tome like this is long overdue. Special thanks also to Chris, for sharing with me (and now the world) his most precious memories of John Lennon and being an absolute tower of strength as we pieced this huge book together. I just hope you all think it was worth it!

Keith Badman, May 1999.

The Beatles Years
Volume 2:
After The Break-Up
1970–2001

1970

"I woke up and didn't have a job anymore! Oh Jesus! No band. What do I do? I've got to work out something for myself now."

– Paul

"Big bastards, that's what The Beatles were. You have to be a bastard to make it, that's a fact, and The Beatles are the biggest bastards on earth!"

– John

Wednesday April 1

 Ringo becomes the last Beatle to play at a Beatles recording session at EMI's Abbey Road Studios in London when, working with Phil Spector in studio one, he overdubs his drum parts on the tracks 'Across The Universe', 'The Long And Winding Road' and 'I Me Mine'.

 John and Yoko issue a hoax press release announcing that: "They have both entered the London clinic for a dual sex-change operation." In truth, the couple enrol themselves in a four-week course of Primal Therapy with the American psychologist Dr. Arthur Janov at his private London hospital at 20 Devonshire Place. At John's invitation Janov met John and Yoko at the Lennon's Tittenhurst Park mansion in Ascot the previous day. John was greatly impressed by Janov's book *The Primal Scream – Primal Therapy: The Cure Of Neurosis*, which had been sent to him in an unsolicited package in the middle of March. The Lennons decide to attend treatment in his clinic because their Ascot mansion is full of builders who are currently renovating the place. Meanwhile, the John Lennon Lithographs, seized by police at the London Arts Gallery in New Bond Street on January 16, are produced at Marlborough Street Magistrates' Court where they are compared to similar works by Picasso. Mr David Napley, defending Mr Eugene Shuster, a director of London Arts Incorporated who ran the exhibition, hands over a set of John's lithographs to the court and says: "I hope the officer will not mark them because, no doubt, by the end of the case they will be worth more than £550!" When Mr Napley said that the prints appear to depict the marriage and honeymoon of John Lennon and his wife, Inspector Cliff of Scotland Yard replies: "Only if they were described and introduced that way!"

Thursday April 2

 Phil Spector's final task on the *Let It Be* album is to mix the tracks into stereo and edit those recordings on which Ringo overdubbed his drum tracks yesterday.

 In an interview with the *Evening Standard*, Paul states: "We all have to ask each other's permission before any of us does anything without the other three. My own record (*McCartney*) nearly didn't come out because Klein and some of the others thought it would be too near to the date of the next Beatles album . . . I had to get George, who's a director of Apple, to authorise its release for me. We're all talking about peace and love but really, we're not feeling peaceful at all."

Sunday April 5

 Ringo appears live on the BBC Radio One programme *Scene And Heard* broadcast between 3:01 and 3:59pm where he is interviewed by the host Johnny Moran.

Monday April 6

 Allen Klein arrives in London to conclude the business deals for the United Artists film *Let It Be*.

Thursday April 9

 The Beatles' Apple organisation denies that Paul McCartney has left the group. Mrs Mavis Smith, Derek Taylor's assistant and head of Apple's public relations office, states, "This is just not true. Although it is true that there are no plans at the moment for more Beatles recordings, this is quite normal. Next month, their new LP will be issued. It has already been recorded so, consequently, as there is already material available, there are no plans for more recordings. I hope that The Beatles will get together for another recording session after the summer." Mavis reveals that Paul has not been seen at Apple's HQ in Saville Row since before Christmas, but adds, "He communicates by telephone and, as he has got recording studios at his home, it is not necessary for him to come in. Paul will issue a statement today with the release of his new album, but any critical statements do not mean a real break-up of the group!"

 Meanwhile, aware of the contents of the interview enclosed within advance copies of his *McCartney* album due for release tomorrow, Paul phones John at Janov's clinic to inform him of its release but shies away from telling John he is leaving The Beatles. As John recalls, "Paul said to me, 'I'm now doing what you and Yoko were doing last year. I understand what you were doing', all that shit. So I said to him, 'Good luck to yer.'" The first that John hears of Paul's split from the group is when news breaks in the media the following morning.

● The *Daily Mirror* newspaper receives an advance copy of Paul's statement and uses this to form the basis of tomorrow's world-shattering front-page story.

Friday April 10

● The *Daily Mirror*'s front-page story is headlined: Paul Is Quitting The Beatles.
● Paul publicly announces the break-up of The Beatles and says that the band will never work together again. His announcement takes the form of a printed "self-interview" sent out to the national press, various broadcasting organisations and included within advance promotional copies of his *McCartney* album. In it, he explains why he has broken with The Beatles, claiming it is down to "Business and musical differences, but most of all, because I have a better time with my family." He adds, "I do not know whether the break will be temporary or permanent" and in conclusion states, "I do not foresee a time when the Lennon & McCartney partnership will be active again in songwriting."
● Later, Paul admits that he didn't really consider this "self-interview" to be an official announcement of The Beatles split; instead he claims that he simply filled in the answers to questions that had been prepared by the Apple assistant Peter Brown. Apple's press officer Derek Taylor announces from his Saville Row office: "They do not want to split up, but the present rift seems to be part of their growing up . . . at the moment they seem to cramp each other's styles. Paul has called a halt to The Beatles' activities. They could be dormant for years." He also explains Klein's business relationship with Paul: "It is no secret that Klein and Paul have never hit it off. Paul has been into this building just twice since Klein came here. He opposed the appointment of Klein and wanted to make his father-in-law John Eastman, a New York lawyer, manager."
● Fans distressed by the news of the split begin to converge outside the offices at 3 Saville Row. Among those present are the Apple Scruffs, a small group of girls who, for years, have been regularly hanging around the Apple offices and Abbey Road studios just to get a brief meeting with a Beatle. A reporter asks Carol Bedford, a member of the Scruffs, "Will anyone ever replace The Beatles for you?" She replies, "No! It's just one Beatles group. That's it! We don't want there to be another. We grew up with them. When they started, they were younger when we were younger, and all through the years we've just developed!"
● A news team from CBS in America has arrived and proclaims on its evening news broadcasts, "The small gathering in Saville Row is only the beginning. The event is so momentous that historians may, one day, view it as a landmark in the decline of the British Empire . . . The Beatles are breaking up!"
● Meanwhile, as news of Paul's split from the group spreads like wildfire round the world's media, top-level business meetings involving the various factions of The Beatles, are being held in the Apple offices. Asked about Paul's now obvious dislike of him, Klein remarks to journalists, "It's never pleasant when someone appears not to like you!"
● George is also to be found in Saville Row, away from the bedlam, being interviewed for the religious programme *Fact Or Fantasy?* subtitled *Prayer And Meditation*. This filmed appearance will be first transmitted on BBC1 on Sunday April 26 and then repeated the following day. He ends the day alone in his Saville Row office watching an early version of *The Long And Winding Road*, the official history of The Beatles' career. A close friend of George remarks, "George doesn't want to talk about it (the split). He just wants to be left alone."
● John, still with Arthur Janov, is preparing more lithographic artwork displays. When asked about Paul's departure, he says enigmatically, "You can say I said jokingly, he didn't quit, he was fired."
● Ringo, staying aloof, remarks, "This is all news to me."
● Paul, Linda, Heather and Mary leave their home in Cavendish Avenue for Scotland. A close friend of the family tells reporters outside the house: "He's not giving any interviews at the moment. In fact, fans and other people have been making his life a bit of a misery lately by picketing his pad. I wish they'd leave him alone to live his life now."

Saturday April 11

"I woke up and didn't have a job anymore! Oh Jesus! No band. What do I do? I've got to work out something for myself now." – Paul
● Respected *Times* columnist William Mann writes on Paul's decision to leave The Beatles. "If The Beatles were just another pop group there would be no cause for alarm

in Paul McCartney's suggestion, announced yesterday, that he may never work with them again. The others would simply find another bass guitarist and lead singer and go on roughly as before. But The Beatles' image, and influence on pop culture in the last ten years has depended on four distinctive personalities working well together." Mann concludes: "They would not be the same without Paul."

● As The Beatles single 'Let It Be' reaches number one in the American charts, John and Yoko, even though they are in London, partake in the two-month Fluxus Group Arts Festival in New York. Subtitled *Fluxfest*, the event takes place at the Greenwich Village store in Canal Street owned by the Fluxus member Joe Jones, the founder of the Tone Deaf Music Company. The first week of the festival, which runs until April 17, features *Do-It-Yourself By John And Yoko*. Also on display is *Two Eggs By John Lennon*.

● Meanwhile in England, Paul's first duty after leaving The Beatles is to purchase the film rights to the cartoon character Rupert The Bear. The transaction is handled by his new company, McCartney Productions Ltd (originally Adagrove Limited, formed on February 12, 1969).

Friday April 17

● The album *McCartney* is released in the UK. (The American release takes place on April 20.) The track listing is: side one: 'The Lovely Linda', 'That Would Be Something', 'Valentine Day', 'Every Night', medley: 'Hot As Sun – Glasses – Suicide', 'Junk', 'Man We Was Lonely'; side two: 'Oo You', 'Momma Miss America', 'Teddy Boy', 'Singalong Junk', 'Maybe I'm Amazed' and 'Kreen-Akrore'. (Recordings begin in December 1969, utilising several locations which include Paul's home, EMI's Abbey Road Studio 2 and at Morgan Studios in Willesden, London.)

● Sir Lew Grade, the head of Associated Television (ATV), the company which in 1969 acquired the publishing rights to The Beatles' songs, describes Paul's album as "absolutely brilliant".

● George is asked about the album: " 'That Would Be Something' and 'Maybe I'm Amazed' I think are great and everything else I think is fair, you know. It's quite good, but a little disappointing, but maybe I shouldn't be disappointed, it's best not to expect anything, then everything's a bonus. I think those two tracks are very good and the others just don't do anything for me. The arrangements for 'Teddy Boy' and 'Junk', with a little bit more arrangement could have sounded better. Me, Ringo and John, not only do we see each other, but we see so many musicians and other bands, maybe Paul does too. But I just get the impression that he doesn't. That he's so isolated from it, he's out on a limb. The only person he's got to tell him if the song's good or bad is Linda. In the Beatle days, if someone came in with a song that had a corny line and some of the others got a bit embarrassed by it, we'd say it!"

● Today, in the American *Rolling Stone* magazine, John announces: "I'm telling you what's going on. It's John, George and Ringo as individuals. We're not even communicating with or making plans about Paul. We're just reacting to everything he does. It's a simple fact that he couldn't have his own way, so he's causing chaos . . . Paul was the same with Brian (Epstein), at the beginning. He used to sulk and God knows what. It's always been the same, only now it's bigger because we're all bigger."

Saturday April 18

● Arthur Janov suggests to John that he should pay a visit to his first wife Cynthia and their son Julian. But the family get-together is halted when Cynthia's housekeeper informs the party that, "Yoko has just called and is threatening to commit suicide unless John returns home immediately!" Meanwhile in America, *Fluxfest* continues, where this week, until the 24, John and Yoko offer two New York bus tickets to the show *Tickets By John And Yoko*.

● Today's *Melody Maker* prints an article entitled "Paul – The Truth", in which they describe his decision to leave The Beatles as "possibly the non-event of the year". Alongside it is Richard Williams' review of *McCartney*. He describes it as containing . . . "the best and worst of an extraordinary talent . . . 'Maybe I'm Amazed' would have been a classic had it been included on say, *Abbey Road* . . . 'Man We Was Lonely' is sheer banality. If it had been sung by Dave Dee, Dozy, Beaky, Mick and Tich, I (and you) would've sneered and turned it off. It's the worst example of his music-hall side."

Sunday April 19

In an unprecedented move for a pop-promotional film, the London area of ITV, London Weekend Television, screen in its own 6:00–6:04pm slot, Paul's promotional clip for 'Maybe I'm Amazed', produced by the film director David Putnam. It features a montage of still photographs of Paul, Linda, and her daughter Heather. A further screening occurs in America, on CBS Television's *The Ed Sullivan Show*, between 8:00 and 9:00 EST.

Tuesday April 21 & Wednesday April 22

London's *Evening Standard* newspaper publishes a two-part interview with Paul, where he goes to great lengths to explain his problems with the Phil Spector arrangement of 'The Long And Winding Road': "A few weeks ago I was sent a re-mixed version of my song 'The Long And Winding Road' with harps, horns, an orchestra and women's choir added. No one had asked me what I thought. I couldn't believe it. I would never have female voices on a Beatles record . . . anyway, I've sent a letter asking for some of the things to be altered, but I haven't received an answer yet."

Thursday April 23

Taking advantage of his recently acquired brief US visitor's visa, George, along with Patti and Derek Taylor, depart from London's Heathrow Airport en route to New York where George starts work on producing Billy Preston's Apple album *Encouraging Words* and spends time checking out Apple's new New York offices at 1700 Broadway.

Apple Corps in London release the following press statement: "The film *Let It Be* will, in Britain, be simultaneously premiered in both London and Liverpool on May 20, and, under the distribution agreement with United Artists, the film will open in New York on May 13 and will be shown in 100 cities all over the world! *Let It Be* is described by United Artists as a 'Bioscopic Experience'."

Friday April 24

Ringo's album *Sentimental Journey* is released in America and within two weeks will sell over half a million copies. (The album was released in the UK on March 27.)

Saturday April 25

The *Fluxfest* festival continues with the exhibition of *Measure By John And Yoko*, in which the vital statistics of the viewing public are the centre of attraction. Further *Fluxfest* fun and games take place between May 2 & 8, with an exhibition called *Blue Room By John And Yoko*, which features *Three Spoons By John Lennon* and *Needle By John Lennon*. Between May 9 & 15 *Fluxfest* features *Weight And Water By John And Yoko*, which involves the flooding of the Canal Street exhibition room. Between May 16 & 22 the festival features *Capsule By John And Yoko*, and between May 23 & 29 *Portrait Of John Lennon As A Young Cloud*, where the exhibition room is filled with 100 drawers, 99 of which are empty. The other contains John's smile. Between May 30 & June 5 it focuses on a collection of New York ticket machines, which are presented as *The Store By John And Yoko*, and during the final week, June 6–12, patrons are tested on what they have learnt over the previous nine weeks, in a piece entitled *Exam By John And Yoko*.

Monday April 27

In a dramatic London High Court ruling, summonses against the London Art Gallery of Bond Street, and its director Eugene Schuster, over John's Bag One lithographs, are dismissed and ruled not to be obscene by Marlborough Street magistrates' court. Mr Schuster, who was forced to make two journeys from America for the case, says after the hearing, "We shall try to get the prints on view again tomorrow morning. We shall hang the prints in the gallery as soon as we get them back. They are still in police custody. Mr Lennon, who is working in London now on his second set of prints, will be immediately told about the case." Schuster adds, "The first set of John's prints are on view in America. I think they have already sold out in New York."

Tuesday April 28

During his visit to the Apple offices at 1700 Broadway, George gives an interview to the WPLJ Radio reporter Howard Smith.

Wednesday April 29

🍎 Following twenty-eight straight days of shouting, screaming, sketching and eating 28 different colours of ice cream, John and Yoko's therapy sessions with Arthur Janov at his London offices are concluded. He recommends that the Lennons fly out to Los Angeles and resume their treatment at his Primal Institute clinic in California.

🍎 George and Derek meet Bob Dylan at his MacDougal Street townhouse in Greenwich Village, New York.

Thursday April 30

🍎 John and Yoko depart from London's Heathrow Airport en route to Janov's Primal Institute in Los Angeles. They will stay in California for four months at a rented accommodation in Bel Air.

🍎 Paul appears on the front page of *Rolling Stone* magazine in America. Inside is an in-depth interview with the former Beatle, carried out by Jann Wenner. The issue also features a report on George acquiring his Friar Park mansion.

🍎 George, meanwhile, joins Bob Dylan for an informal jam session in Dylan's MacDougal Street townhouse. They perform the tracks 'When Everybody Comes To Town' and 'I'd Have You Anytime', which are recorded by Dylan on his home recording equipment. (Columbia acetates cut from the tape of this session are later sold by the auctioneers Galston & Co. and subsequently find their way, in the late Seventies, on to various bootleg records incorrectly dated as May 1.) George and Derek are invited by Bob to attend his recording sessions tomorrow.

May

🍎 Mr. Richard Dunn of the Linguaphone Group reveals that John has recently taken out an audiocassette course on "How to speak Japanese".

Friday May 1

🍎 In Studio B at the Columbia Recording Studios in New York City, George joins Bob Dylan in a recording session for his album *New Morning*. George picks up a guitar and jams with Bob, Charlie E. Daniels (on bass), Russ Kunkel (drums) and Bob Johnston (piano), who also serves as producer, on the following tracks: 'Sign On The Window', 'If Not For You', 'Time Passes Slowly', 'Working On The Guru', 'Went To See The Gypsies', 'Song To Woody', 'Mama, You've Been On My Mind', 'Don't Think Twice, It's Alright', a cover of The Beatles' 'Yesterday', 'Just Like Tom Thumb's Blues', 'Da Doo Ron Ron', 'One Too Many Mornings', 'Ghost Riders In The Sky', 'Cupid', 'All I Have To Do Is Dream', 'Gates Of Eden', 'I Threw It All Away', 'I Don't Believe In You (She Acts Like We Never Have Met)', 'Matchbox', 'Your True Love', 'Las Vegas Blues', 'Fishin' Blues', 'Honey, Just Allow Me One More Chance', 'Rainy Day Women Nos. 12 & 35', 'It Ain't Me Babe' and 'Tomorrow Is A Long Time'. Some of the songs, in true *Get Back* sessions style, are only 17 seconds in duration. The recordings, which include overdub sessions, take place between 2:30–5:50pm, 6:30–9:30pm and 10:30pm–1:30am on the morning of May 2. (Note: A take of 'If Not for You' with George on slide guitar is released in 1991 on Dylan's *The Bootleg Series Volume 1–3 (Rare and Unreleased) 1961–1991*. (In order not to upset Apple, George's appearance at this session is not logged in the CBS recording contracts.)

Saturday May 2

🍎 *Melody Maker*'s Mailbag section publishes a letter under the headline: "Who Does Paul McCartney Think He Is?" It reads: "Who does Paul McCartney think he is? We don't see anything of him for a year, and then out he pops from his mysterious hermit like existence, advertising his new record in a publicity-crazed manner. Does he really think we'll believe that he played all the instruments? Let's face it, Mailbag, we're not suckers. It's obvious George Martin had a lot to do with it. In fact if you listen carefully to the end of the third track played backwards, you can almost hear him whistling." The letter is signed Paul McCartney.

Tuesday May 5

🍎 George and Derek Taylor return home to England.

Friday May 8

🍎 The album *Let It Be* is released in the UK as a deluxe box set, which also contains the book *Get Back*, a wonderful photographic record of the January 1969 *Get Back/Let It Be* sessions. The album will be re-released in the UK on November 6 in a regular sleeve and without the book. (A standard version of the *Let It Be* album, this time in a gatefold sleeve, is released in America on May 18.)

Saturday May 9

🍎 At the annual Cannes Film Festival in the South of France, Ringo and Maureen are guests of honour at the screening of *Woodstock*, the big-screen film record of the outdoor festival held in upstate New York in August 1969. Clips of their visit are featured in a report on the festival, included in the bi-weekly London Weekend Television arts show *Aquarius*, transmitted across the ITV network on Friday May 22 between 11:01 and 11:44pm.

🍎 Richard Williams ends his in-depth *Melody Maker* review of the *Let It Be* album by writing: "The Beatles are dead – Long live The Beatles."

Monday May 11

🍎 In America, the single 'The Long And Winding Road'/'For You Blue' is released. The single will sell 1,200,000 copies within two days.

Wednesday May 13

🍎 Contrary to the original intentions of both Apple and United Artists, the New York premiere of the film *Let It Be* does not take place today. The date for the film's release has now been set for Thursday May 28.

Thursday May 14

🍎 In America, *Rolling Stone* magazine publishes a report on John and George's brief US visas, stating that, although they can now enter America, they do so on the condition that they must leave the country within a short space of time, usually 30 days.

Friday May 15

🍎 Reports in America announce that Paul's solo album *McCartney* has sold over 1,000,000 copies in its first four weeks of release.

Monday May 18

🍎 At 10:30am, two days before the UK premiere, *Let It Be* receives its first ever public screening, for the benefit of the press and close friends, at the London Pavilion in Piccadilly Circus. When asked about the film, George later admits that the film does not bear well with him. "There are scenes in it like the roof top concert that was good, but most of it makes me so aggravated . . . I can't watch it, 'cos it was a particularly bad experience that we were having at that time and it's bad enough having it, let alone having it filmed and recorded so you've got to watch it for the rest of your life. I don't like it!"

Wednesday May 20

🍎 The *Let It Be* film opens today in Britain with special simultaneous Gala North–South premiere events. In the South, crowds surge upon the London Pavilion where guests include Spike Milligan, Mary Hopkin, Julie Felix, Sir Joseph Lockwood, Richard Lester, Simon Dee, Julie Edge and Lulu. Not to mention fifty dancing members of the Hare Krishna group and various members of The Rolling Stones and Fleetwood Mac pop groups. Most noticeable in the crowd are women no longer involved with The Beatles, John's ex-wife Cynthia Lennon and, two years after her split from Paul, the actress Jane Asher. Before entering the cinema, Spike is playfully pictured by the press, alongside the police, trying to hold back the large excited crowds. At the conclusion of its first week at the 1,004-seat cinema, where *Let It Be* was screened a total of 41 times, the film nets approximately £6,229. Brian Millwood, on behalf of UA, announces: "We're happy with the start made by the film. It's by no means the biggest take for the house, but it's nevertheless good." *Let It Be* will run at the London Pavilion for five weeks until Tuesday June 23, when it is replaced by the Mick Jagger film *Ned Kelly*. Meanwhile in Liverpool, the northern premiere takes place with a comparatively quiet, invitation only, event at the

Gaumont in Camden Street, London Road. (The screenings at both cinemas commence at 8:45pm.) *Let It Be* will eventually go on to be released in 100 major cities around the world.

Thursday May 21
💷 The day after the official northern premiere, Tom Hutchinson of the Liverpool *Daily Post* scathingly reviews *Let It Be*. He describes the film as: "An occasion for sadness." He continues by writing: "Watching this 81-minute long U-certificated account of The Beatles making their latest LP, I felt that I was sitting at the deathbed of one of the greatest group talents ever to escape from the trivial treadmill of so much pop music." He concludes: "So, I regret the passing of an institution: as I regret that this film should be judged as the most suitable hearse for that institution." Even so, *Let It Be* opens to the general public today at the Gaumont in Liverpool where, alongside *Yellow Submarine*, it can be seen three times a day, at 2:45pm, 5:55pm and 9:05pm.

Friday May 22
💷 Workmen renovating John and Yoko's eighteenth century Georgian mansion in Ascot call out the bomb disposal squad when they discover an unexploded incendiary shell. The Lennons had purchased the estate from a football pools magnate for £150,000 during May 1969.

Saturday May 23
💷 BBC Radio One in the UK transmits a 44-minute reflective programme on The Beatles. Suitably called *Let It Be*, the show (transmitted between 5:00 and 5:44pm) features the *Scene And Heard* presenter Johnny Moran talking individually (using pre-recorded tapes) to all four Beatles about their futures with particular reference to the possibilities of them ever working together again. Paul is asked about the *Let It Be* film: "It's like a documentary, it's like a film say of a painter who comes in and sets up a canvas, puts one brush mark on, then eventually you see him finish the painting. It's all that he goes through to finish the painting. Well, with us, someone walks in, 'Twang, G and C, this is how the song goes' and eventually you see us finish the record. It's the stages, it's a good film though, it's interesting."
💷 George too gives his personal feeling on the movie: "The Beatles' film is just pure documentary of us slogging and working on the album really. We were thinking of how to do a TV show, but really, it was much easier just to make it into a film. It's very informative, but it's not really nice for me, I can't stand seeing it, but for other people who don't know really what we're about, who like to go in and see our warts, it's very good. You can see us talk, you can hear us playing, you can hear us coughing, it's the complete opposite to the clinical approach we normally have, you know. Studio recordings, you know, the balance and everything is just right, the silence in-between tracks, well, this is not really like that. There's a nice song of Paul's, which is one of those that probably hundreds of people will record. Somebody's gonna have a hit with it. It's called 'The Long And Winding Road', it's one of those ballad, standard sort of things."
💷 Ringo, in the briefest of the interviews, talks about John as his "soul brother", his wife Maureen, his future in acting and his album *Sentimental Journey*.
💷 To conclude the show, John is asked: "Are The Beatles going to record again?" He replies: "I've no idea if The Beatles will work together again, or not. I never really have. It was always open. If somebody didn't feel like it . . . that's it! It could be a rebirth or death. We'll see what it is. It'll probably be a rebirth."
'My Bonnie', 'The Ballad Of John & Yoko', 'Act Naturally', 'Instant Karma', 'Govinda', 'Sentimental Journey' and a selection of tracks from the *Let It Be* album accompany the interviews on the show. Significantly, the original unreleased version of 'Dig It' is also played on the programme.
💷 Reports from America indicate that the *Let It Be* album has advance orders of 3,700,000 (worth $25,900,00), the largest initial sale in the history of the American record industry. Although *Let It Be* reaches number one in the UK album charts today, reviews of the album are not good. *New Musical Express* describes it today as "a cardboard tombstone" and a "sad and tatty end to a musical fusion".
💷 Paul's first solo album *McCartney* reaches number one in the American album charts.

Tuesday May 26 (until early November)

🍏 At the EMI Abbey Road Studios in London, George, working with Phil Spector, begins recording tracks for his three-album set *All Things Must Pass*. The sessions, which feature Ringo on drums, produce the following: 'My Sweet Lord', 'Isn't It A Pity' (two versions), 'I'd Have You Anytime', 'Wah-Wah', 'What Is Life', 'If Not For You', 'Behind That Locked Door', 'Let It Down', 'Run Of The Mill', 'Beware Of Darkness', 'Apple Scruffs', 'Ballad Of Sir Frankie Crisp (Let It Roll)', 'Awaiting On You All', 'All Things Must Pass', 'I Dig Love', 'Art Of Dying', 'Hear Me Lord' and *Apple Jam*, a bonus album that features 'Out Of The Blue', 'It's Johnny's Birthday', 'Plug Me In', 'I Remember Jeep' and 'Thanks For The Pepperoni'. At one point during the recordings, the musicians break into a brief version of Cliff Richard's 1968 chart-topper 'Congratulations', thus earning a royalty claim for its songwriters Bill Martin and Phil Coulter. George also records demo versions of 'Everybody, Nobody', 'Window, Window', 'Beautiful Girl' (a version later to appear on his 1976 album *Thirty Three And A Third*), 'Tell Me What Has Happened To You', 'Nowhere To Go', 'Cosmic Empire', 'Mother Divine', 'I Don't Want To Do It', a track he will not release until 1985 as part of the film soundtrack to *Porky's Revenge*, 'Gopala Krishna', 'Going Down To Golders Green', 'I Live For You' and several versions of 'Dehra Dun', a track written in India in 1968 which was not publicly unveiled by George until the 1995 *Anthology* TV series. George and Pete Drake also record a snippet of Paul Simon's 'Bridge Over Troubled Water' and The Beatles' 'Get Back'. (Recordings on the album shift to EMI's Trident Studios in London in early June and will continue right through until early November. Producer Alan Parsons is called in by George to briefly assist with the production.)

Thursday May 28

🍏 With no grand premiere and all of sixteen days after it was originally scheduled, *Let It Be* (rated G for general audiences) finally opens in America as a United Artists Premiere Showcase with simultaneous screenings in various New York cinemas. These include venues in Manhattan, The Bronx, Staten Island, Brooklyn, Queens, Nassau, Westchester and the Victoria Walter Reade Theaters. Supporting The Beatles' film, is a short featurette entitled *What Is Happening To Our Oceans?* subtitled *Crisis On The Coast*, narrated by Arthur Godfrey. (Incidentally, *Let It Be* was originally scheduled for release in America during February; to be launched with a special New York premiere screening, an event which John, on more than one occasion, said he would be attending.)

Friday May 29

🍏 Following its opening yesterday, *Let It Be* is unfavourably reviewed in the *New York Times*. "The documentary is none too artfully made . . . somebody must have grabbed a camera fast, for it jerkily hovers over The Beatles' playing and informal chatting." In conclusion, the paper writes: "The most intriguing figure of the film is Yoko Ono, Lennon's Japanese-born wife. Except for one playful twirl with him, Mrs. Lennon remains at her husband's side, expressionless and silent, her eyes never leaving him . . ."

June

🍏 At Twickenham film studios in London, Richard Lester pays a visit to the film library to re-acquaint himself with the 'out-takes' from the films *A Hard Day's Night* and *Help!* To his dismay, he discovers that all the footage not included in the original films has been "junked" under the studio's policy of keeping the 'out-takes' for "five years after the completion of the original film".

Thursday June 4

🍏 Apple band Badfinger travel to Hawaii to appear at the Capitol Records convention. Following this, they immediately fly to Italy for concerts in Rome.

Monday June 8

🍏 As part of their primal therapy treatment, Arthur Janov instructs John to go to see The Beatles' film *Let It Be*. This he does, where besides Yoko, he joins Jann Wenner, the editor of *Rolling Stone* magazine, and his wife Jane for an afternoon screening of the film in an otherwise empty San Francisco theatre.

Thursday June 11
🍎 John and Yoko announce to the Californian press today that they intend to make New York their home.

Saturday June 13
🍎 In America, the single 'The Long And Winding Road' and the album *Let It Be* both reach number one on the same day. In the bottom end of the charts, the compilation album of early Polydor tracks recorded in Germany entitled *The Beatles Featuring Tony Sheridan – In The Beginning* (Circa 1960) makes number 117.

Monday June 15
🍎 Paul's father-in-law Lee Eastman drafts a letter to Allen Klein in New York, insisting that The Beatles be officially dissolved immediately. Klein does not reply.

Friday June 19
🍎 The George produced Doris Troy album *Ain't That Cute* is released by Apple. Both George and Ringo feature on some of the tracks.

Saturday June 20
🍎 Mavis Smith, Derek Taylor's assistant for the last eighteen months, officially resigns from the Apple press office.

Saturday June 27
🍎 Beatles fans begin scouring round London record stores when it's announced in the music press that a good quality stereo album, released by IFP Records, entitled *Get Back To Toronto*, is to be found in certain music shops. The bootleg record contains alternative recordings from the 1969 *Get Back* sessions, including the unreleased tracks 'Teddy Boy' and 'The Walk', as well as Christmas and peace messages from John and Yoko.

Sunday June 28
🍎 "The Beatles . . . rehearsing . . . recording . . . rapping . . . relaxing . . . philosophising . . . creating. The Beatles live in a new motion picture. Ten new songs. An intimate experience with The Beatles. A new motion picture . . . The Beatles . . . *Let It Be*." (The original cinema trailer – June 1970.)
🍎 The Beatles' final film *Let It Be* goes on release in the UK at selected Odeon and other important theatres. (For its release, the original 16mm colour film is blown up to 35mm.) Supporting *Let It Be* is the 1968 animated fantasy *Yellow Submarine*.

Monday June 29
🍎 Ringo leaves London Airport for Nashville to begin recording tracks for a new album and to negotiate a deal for a 12-part American TV series due to be transmitted at the end of the year. (The series never materialises.)

Tuesday June 30 & Wednesday July 1
🍎 At the Music City Recorders studio in Nashville, Tennessee, Ringo begins recording tracks for his album *Beaucoups Of Blues*. The two-day sessions produce the following songs: 'Beaucoups Of Blues', 'Love Don't Last Long', 'Fastest Growing Headache In The West', 'Without Her', 'Woman Of The Night', 'I'd Be Talking All The Night', '$15 Draw', 'Wine, Women And Loud Happy Songs', 'I Wouldn't Have You Any Other Way', 'Loser's Lounge', 'Waiting' and 'Silent Homecoming'. Ringo also records the track 'Early 1970', as well as 'Coochy-Coochy', which originally featured a running time of approximately 28 minutes. This song later appears in America only, on a single with the title track 'Beaucoups of Blues'. For the recordings, Ringo uses twenty-one of Nashville's top country musicians under the production guidance of Pete Drake. Scotty Moore, Elvis' first guitarist and early manager, engineers the sessions. Ringo returns home to Britain on July 2 clutching the studio master tapes.
  Ringo recalls the recording of the album: "I was trying to get it together over here in Britain, which is really silly. I was trying to fly in 12 guys from Nashville and all that rubbish and suddenly I was playing on George's album and Pete Drake was there and I was talking to him about it and he said, 'Look here son, why don't you come over to Nashville? – I'll get it together in a week', and I said, 'Come on . . . you can't get an album

together in a week, it's impossible!' He said, 'But Dylan's only took two days!' I said, 'OK, you go back and fix it up and I'll fly out a few days later'. We did the album in two nights. I did a few other tracks that we didn't put out. I was only there three days recording. I'd learn five songs in the morning and I'd go and record five songs that night. It was really good!"

(Note: Acetates of alternative versions of some of the released tracks and some of the songs that Ringo referred to as we "didn't put out" are sold at a Sotheby's auction in London during August 1992. Entitled *Ringo In Nashville*, the two 12-inch discs feature Apple custom recording labels and boast an alternative running order of tracks than featured on the released version, many of which contain additional sounds and various count-ins.)

July
🍎 John's treatment with Janov continues. He also begins recording several demos of songs that will later appear on the album *John Lennon/Plastic Ono Band*. With no reply from Allen Klein to Lee Eastman's letter on June 15, Paul decides to write to John in LA, asking him about dissolving The Beatles. He replies: "I will only consider it when George and Ringo have had their say."

Friday July 3
🍎 The three-day Peace and Poetry Festival, planned for today, tomorrow and Sunday at Mosport Park in Toronto, Canada, announced by John and Yoko at their press conference at Ontario's New Science Center on December 17, 1969, fails to materialise.

Saturday July 4 & Sunday July 5
🍎 George aborts work on *All Things Must Pass* and returns home to Liverpool to see his ailing mother Louise. Meanwhile, on a happier note today George's song 'Something' wins an Ivor Novello award for 'The Best Song Musically and Lyrically of the Year'.

Tuesday July 7
🍎 In Liverpool, George's mother Louise Harrison, dies of cancer.

Friday July 10
🍎 BBC Radio One's only female disc-jockey Anne Nightingale arrives at Apple's headquarters in Saville Row to conduct interviews for an article. Her shocking report on the decline of The Beatles' empire appears in *The Sketch* newspaper on Monday July 13. The article is suitably titled, "Apple Coming Apart At The Core."

Sunday July 26
🍎 Today, at the Primal Institute in Los Angeles, John records several demos of the track 'God', which significantly feature the lyric "I don't believe in Beatles".

August
🍎 During a break from the *All Things Must Pass* sessions at Abbey Road, Ringo and George record a special unreleased song for John, celebrating his 30th birthday on October 9. Also, according to the Apple Scruffs, George is annoyed to discover that one of the American Beatles fan clubs has started to advertise trips to England to see the grave of his late mother. He immediately takes action to close the fan club down.
🍎 At the end of the month, feeling cleansed and invigorated, John and Yoko leave the Primal Institute and head for New York.

Saturday August 1
🍎 John's first wife Cynthia marries the Italian hotelier Roberto Bassanini at Kensington register office in London. Julian, her son with John, serves as the page boy. The show business world is represented only by Twiggy and Justin de Villeneuve.

Tuesday August 4
🍎 Apple's press office in London closes down, with the two remaining employees being fired. From now on Apple Corps Ltd's only task is to collect the ever-flourishing Beatle royalties and deal with the numerous unfinished Beatles problems.

Saturday August 15

 Melody Maker prints the results of a question and answer session between reporter Chris Charlesworth and Apple spokesman Peter Brown at Saville Row.

MM: "Is there any recorded (Beatles) material still unreleased?"

Apple: "No. Even if there were it would never be issued. The group are always very conscious of keeping up with the current tastes."

MM: "Are there plans for a (Beatles) recording session in the future?"

Apple: "There are no plans at all."

MM: "Are there any plans for any kind of performances whatsoever?"

Apple: "None at all. There are no plans for any shows or tours."

MM: "Have The Beatles finished as a group?"

Apple: "That is a question I cannot answer . . ."

Saturday August 29

 Melody Maker publishes a letter from Paul in response to the question and answer story two weeks ago: "Dear Mailbag, In order to put out of its misery the limping dog of a news story which has been dragging itself across your pages for the past year, my answer to the question, 'Will The Beatles get together again?' . . . is no."

September

 During the middle of the month, the legendary Sixties record producer Mickie Most arranges to fly to Paul's Scottish farmhouse to discuss with him a possible film part. Mickie hopes to persuade Paul to appear as the poet Lee Simons in *The Second Coming Of Suzanne*. Michael Barry, the son of the actor Gene Barry, writes the script. Mickie remarks: "Paul's a hard guy to contact, but Apple are trying to get him for me. The chances are if he likes the script, he'll do it. Paul once told me that every film script offered to The Beatles was another *Help!* and that he wanted to do something different. This film is different."

Tuesday September 1

 Twenty-year-old Brett Solaries appears in court charged with being found unlawfully in the grounds of Paul's home in Cavendish Avenue, in St. John's Wood, London. He is remanded in custody until September 8 by Marylebone magistrates. Solaries, of no fixed address, protests at the remand, pleading: "I am a member of a religious sect known as The Iskow."

Monday September 14

 In Las Vegas, the American Vice President Spiro Agnew publicly attacks The Beatles over references to drug taking in some of their lyrics. For example, Spiro recites two lines from 'With A Little Help From My Friends' ("I get by with a little help from my friends, I get high with a little help from my friends . . ."). "It's a catchy tune," he remarks, "but until it was pointed out to me, I never realised that the 'friends' were assorted drugs!"

 Meanwhile in Sweden, the film *Let It Be* goes on general release.

Saturday September 19

 George, alongside Ravi Shankar, makes a rare public appearance at the *Festival Of Arts Of India* concert at the Royal Festival Hall in London. George is there to promote the festival, which includes Indian music and dancing by a dozen performers. The show later moves on to Birmingham, Manchester and Leeds and is organised by Birenda Shankar, Ravi's nephew.

Tuesday September 22

 Contrary to popular belief, John and Yoko do not appear with Arthur Janov today on the ABC TV talk show *The Dick Cavett Show*. The Lennons' first appearance on the show actually takes place on September 8, 1971 (see entry).

Thursday September 24

 John and Yoko, after five months out of the country, arrive back in Britain at Heathrow Airport and travel immediately to their Ascot mansion to prepare for recording sessions due to start on Saturday at Abbey Road. He is now 28 lbs heavier than when he left England last April. When asked about this, John put this down to "eating 28 different colours of ice-cream" during his course of treatment with Janov.

Friday September 25
◖ Ringo's album *Beaucoups Of Blues* is released in the UK. (The American release takes place on September 28.)

Saturday September 26
◖ At the Abbey Road Studios, working with Phil Spector, John begins committing to tape proper studio recordings of the demos he recorded while undergoing his primal therapy treatment in Los Angeles. The songs are: 'Mother', 'Hold On (John)', 'I Found Out', 'Working Class Hero', 'Isolation', 'Remember', 'Love', 'Well Well Well', 'Look At Me', 'God' and 'My Mummy's Dead'. The tracks will form the basis of his album *John Lennon/Plastic Ono Band*. Joining John and Yoko at the session are Ringo on drums and Klaus Voorman on bass. In between takes, the group finds time to jam tracks such as 'When A Boy Meets A Girl', 'That's All Right (Mama)', 'Glad All Over', 'Honey Don't', 'Don't Be Cruel', 'Hound Dog' and 'Matchbox'. (The sessions will conclude on the morning of October 27, with the final three days spent mixing the album with Spector.) This period of recording also produces the album *Yoko Ono/Plastic Ono Band*. This features the tracks: 'Why', 'Why Not', 'Greenfield Morning I Pushed An Empty Baby Carriage All Over The City', 'Touch Me' and 'Paper Shoes'. (The track 'AOS' which also appears on the album, was recorded by Yoko back in February 1968.) Also recorded are: 'Don't Worry Kyoko (Mummy's Only Looking For Her Hand In The Snow)' (released on Yoko's 1971 *Fly* album) and 'Between The Takes' (unreleased until it appears as a bonus track on the Ryko *Fly* CD issue in 1998). During early October, Abbey Road is the setting for both the recording of this album and the mixing of George's *All Things Must Pass*. (See entry for October 9.)

October
◖ Paul, Linda and family depart from England on board the luxury liner SS *France*, en route to New York. They return to England just before Christmas.
◖ At 214 Oxford Circus in London, George Martin's new £400,000 recording studio AIR (Associated Independent Recording) Studios opens for business. One of the first to take advantage of its modern day equipment is Ringo, who re-mixes some private recordings.
◖ Apple opens an account at the Lasky's electrical store in Tottenham Court Road, London. George has so far spent thousands on hi-fi equipment, usually comprising set-ups as presents for close friends. The shop's proprietor remarks: "He usually rings me at lunchtime and asks me to make up a £200 system and, usually at tea-time, someone calls in with the money."

Thursday October 1
◖ At the BBC Television Theatre in Shepherd's Bush, London, Ringo records his second solo appearance for Cilla Black on her BBC1 Saturday night variety show, *Cilla*. For his slot, he sings a duet with the host, and the 30-piece BBC orchestra, a live version of 'Act Naturally'. With an ex-Beatle present, Cilla also takes the opportunity to perform two Beatle covers, 'Don't Pass Me By', with the actor Richard Harris and the resident orchestra, and 'Back In The USSR', again with the orchestra, but this time she is accompanied by the ten-piece resident dance group The Breakaways. The 44-minute programme, which also features Stanley Holloway and John Clive, who was responsible for the voice of John in the film *Yellow Submarine*, is transmitted for the first time on BBC1 on February 13, 1971 between 7:41 and 8:24pm. For his services, Ringo is paid the handsome sum of £750. A short clip of his appearance on the show is repeated in the children's TV request show *Ask Aspel* on BBC1 on February 19, 1971, hosted by the television personality Michael Aspel. (This edition of *Cilla*, which does not survive in the BBC archives, has long been incorrectly listed as being originally transmitted on April 24.) As usual, the theme tune for the programme, and indeed her entire BBC series, is Paul's 1968 composition 'Step Inside Love'.

Monday October 5
◖ Ringo's single 'Beaucoups Of Blues'/'Coochy-Coochy' is released in America.

Thursday October 9
◖ On John's 30th birthday, he takes a break from his recordings to join George and Ringo in an adjacent Abbey Road Studio where they present him with their special recording of 'It's Johnny's Birthday'.

Tuesday October 13
🍎 Paul's Shetland wool jumper fetches $95 (approximately £39) at a New York auction. The item is among a collection of rock memorabilia sold at the Fillmore Theater. Proceeds from the sale are being used to finance peace campaigns during next month's American elections.

Thursday October 15
🍎 Apple denies a rumour that George and Ringo have been working with The Bee Gees on their first album since their reformation. Meanwhile, George, along with Phil Spector, begins the final mixing of the album *All Things Must Pass* in a studio near Marylebone Station on the same street immortalised at the start of The Beatles' 1964 film *A Hard Day's Night*. During this two week period, they are joined by Mal Evans and 'Magic' Alex Mardas.

Friday October 23
🍎 George announces to the press that his next release will be the single 'My Sweet Lord'.

Saturday October 24
🍎 George takes a break from mixing his album by visiting London's Lyceum to watch the band The Incredible Stone Ground. He is accompanied by a French underground musician who plays in the group Slow Death. Meanwhile, it is reported that George still donates £5,000 a year to the charity fund Release.

Monday October 26
🍎 Three days after announcing its release, George changes his mind and announces that 'My Sweet Lord' will not, after all, be issued. He says, "I don't want the single to detract from the impact of the *All Things Must Pass* triple album."

Tuesday October 27
🍎 With the sessions for *John Lennon/Plastic Ono Band* now concluded at Abbey Road, John and Yoko board a plane to New York for the first time as a couple. During their visit they arrange to meet Jonas Mekas and some old friends, do some publicity on Primal Scream, begin work on two new films, *Up Your Legs Forever* and *Fly* and also to promote their new albums. (They will not return to England until Thursday December 24.)

Wednesday October 28
🍎 While in America, John is sought by the defence as a witness at the Sharon Tate murder trial in Los Angeles. They wish to ask him whether or not a song could have inspired Charles Manson to violence. Manson believes that The Beatles, in their 1968 recording 'Helter Skelter', predicted a race war.
🍎 George and Patti arrive in New York where, along with Phil Spector, work concludes on the album *All Things Must Pass*. (The master tapes have been brought from England by George personally on his flight.) Also joining George on his visit is Pete Bennett, The Beatles' record promotions manager.

November
🍎 While George and Patti are in the city, they visit the group Badfinger backstage in their dressing room at the Ungano's Club. He asks the group if he can introduce them on stage, to which they agree. George also records their performance on a portable tape recorder and plays the results back to them in their dressing room following the show.
🍎 The 1966 film *The Family Way*, featuring soundtrack music written by Paul, is re-released to selected cinemas in the UK alongside the comedy film *Till Death Us Do Part*, starring Warren Mitchell and Dandy Nichols. Paul, meanwhile, is to be found in New York starting work on his second solo album. During this time, George phones him and arranges to meet up. Rumours begin to circulate in the American music press that Paul is to tour with the Sixties pop group The Rascals, a rumour that Paul quickly denies.

Friday November 6
🍎 An exhibition of Yoko's work, entitled *Happening And Fluxus*, takes place at the Kolnischer Kunstverein in Cologne, West Germany. The show runs until January 6, 1971.

Wednesday November 11
 Ringo and Maureen's daughter Lee Parkin is born at Queen Charlotte's Hospital in Hammersmith, London.

Sunday November 15
 Through his solicitors, Paul files the lawsuit against John, George, Ringo and Apple in the High Courts of London to dissolve 'The Beatles'.

Monday November 23
 George's single 'My Sweet Lord'/'Isn't It A Pity' is released in America. (The UK release does not take place until January 15, 1971.)

Thursday November 26
 At Abbey Road studios, the four-track tapes from John and Yoko's Lyceum Ballroom, London performance on Monday December 15, 1969, are prepared by engineers and immediately dispatched to the Lennons in New York. John, though, will not begin the final mixes of the tapes until the sessions at the Record Plant in New York which run during the first three weeks of January 1972. The recordings (which contain: 'Cold Turkey' and 'Don't Worry Kyoko') will ultimately appear on side three of the *Sometime In New York City* double album, released on June 12, 1972 in America and on September 15, 1972 in the UK.

Friday November 27
 George's *All Things Must Pass* triple album is released in the US. (The UK release takes place on November 30.)

December
 At the start of the month, Paul and George's planned social meeting in New York takes place, but the meeting does not go well. This merely furthers Paul's desire to dissolve The Beatles' partnership.

Tuesday December 8
 Jann Wenner of *Rolling Stone* magazine conducts a remarkably candid interview with John in his rented New York Greenwich Village apartment. Among his many controversial remarks, he describes his former group as:"Big bastards, that's what The Beatles were. You have to be a bastard to make it, that's a fact and The Beatles are the biggest bastards on earth!"

On George's album *All Things Must Pass*: "I think it's all right, you know. Personally, at home I wouldn't play that kind of music; I don't want to hurt George's feelings; I don't know what to say about it."

On Paul's *McCartney* album: "I thought Paul's was rubbish! I think he'll make a better one when he's frightened into it."

On Ringo's *Beaucoups Of Blues*: "I think it's a good record. I wouldn't buy it, you know. I was glad and I didn't feel as embarrassed as I did about his first record."

On the break-up of The Beatles, implying that he was the first to leave: "We were discussing something in the office with Paul, and Paul said something or other about The Beatles doing something and I kept saying, 'No, no, no' to everything he said. So it came to a point where I had to say something, of course, and Paul said, 'What do you mean?' I said, 'I mean the group is over. I'm leaving.'

"I don't know whether Paul said, 'Don't tell anybody', but he was darned pleased that I wasn't going to. He said, 'Oh, that means nothing really happened if you're not going to say anything.' It's like he knew really that this was the final thing; and six months later he comes out with whatever."

The lengthy interviews will feature over two parts of *Rolling Stone* magazine on January 21 and February 4, 1971. The entire interview will later be reprinted in the form of the book *Lennon Remembers*. John later criticises Wenner for publishing the interview in book form without his consent.

Thursday December 10
 In England, tonight's edition of *Top Of The Pops* (show number 355, hosted by Tony Blackburn and transmitted on BBC1 between 7:05 and 7:44pm), features in its album

slot, George's *All Things Must Pass*. Set to BBC film, showing seal lions at play, the two minute two second sequence includes excerpts from 'Let It Down' (11 seconds), 'Art Of Dying' (18 seconds), 'I Remember Jeep' (25 seconds), 'Wah-Wah' (35 seconds) and 'Plug Me In' (33 seconds).

Friday December 11

 John's album *John Lennon/Plastic Ono Band* is released simultaneously in the US and UK (featuring Ringo on drums). Yoko's matching album *Yoko Ono/Plastic Ono Band* is also released today in the US and the UK and features John prominently on guitar. (The album is co-produced by both John and Yoko.) John's use of the word "fucking" on his song 'Working Class Hero' causes much hysteria in the music press. A spokesman for Apple defends John's controversial lyric by remarking: "We don't think it will effect sales or the dealers' options to stock the records. I don't think there will be a problem with it." But a spokesman for EMI takes a different attitude: "This matter is under discussion with The Beatles' management. There will be a definitive statement next week and some action may be taken." When *Melody Maker* writer Michael Watts hears the *John Lennon/Plastic Ono Band* album, he remarks: "The album is not going to convert anyone who does not already like Lennon's musical approach. Melodically there is nothing earth-shattering but then, Lennon has never set out to become another Cole Porter."

Sunday December 13

 From his Greenwich Village apartment, John gives an interview to Howard Smith of the American radio station WABC.

Monday December 14

 In New York, on a seventh-floor sound stage on West 61st Street, John and Yoko begin filming their latest adventure in cinéma vérité, a new movie entitled *Up Your Legs Forever*. Lacking work permits, the Lennons are obliged to merely observe the proceedings behind a screened off enclosure, while the seemingly endless parade of male and female volunteers stand on a podium with their bare bottoms faced towards a colour 16mm film camera. In charge of the filming is Dan Richter, the man responsible for the choreography of the ape sequences at the start of the 1968 Stanley Kubrick space epic *2001: A Space Odyssey*. Richter plays the part of the lead ape in the film and is memorably seen throwing the animal bone into the air, which then symbolically turns into the image of a spaceship. This fact greatly impresses John, as *2001* was one of his all-time favourite films. Another of the people assisting John and Yoko with the filming is May Pang, an employee of Klein's who is based at his ABKCO offices in Broadway, New York. For the filming of *Up Your Legs Forever*, the actors, for a fee of just one-dollar, are required to stand motionless while the camera pans up their bare legs from the toes to the hips. When John and Yoko announce that they are happy with the results, the volunteer signs a release permitting his or her name to be used for publicity and advertising in connection with the exploitation of the film. John also takes a Polaroid instamatic record of the proceedings for his photo album. Among them is Larry Rivers, the press agent for Jim Rivers, Pete Bennett, The Beatles' record promotions man, *Rolling Stone* editor Jann Wenner and even Don (D.A.) Pennebaker, the director of the film of the Monterey pop festival, who supplied the movie camera. Filming continues tomorrow, Tuesday December 15.

Wednesday December 16

 Filming of *Up Your Legs Forever* is concluded in New York with almost 300 bare bottoms having been committed to both film and snapshots. Recent additions include the actor George Segal and even, after much persuasion, The Beatles' manager Allen Klein. A reporter asks John: "Haven't you seen enough of these (bottoms) yet?" To which he replies, "No, but I'm getting cured." The journalist asks again: "What are you going to do next, John?" He thinks for a moment and then says: "I dunno . . . there must be something else." (The film *Up Your Legs Forever*, featuring an original running time of 80 minutes, will receive its premiere as part of the London Art Spectrum festival, which runs between August 11 and 13, 1971.) With filming of the first film completed, John and Yoko concentrate on *Fly*, their second film production.

Thursday December 17
🍎 Back in England, Lucille Iremonger, the writer and Member of Parliament for Ilford North, admits that she has recently received through the mail from John and Yoko, a copy of the *Primal Scream* book by Dr. Arthur Janov. They had sent it to her after John had read Lucille's latest book *The Fiery Chariot*.

Friday December 18
🍎 *The Beatles Christmas Album* (UK title *From Then To You*) is released officially to paid-up members of The Beatles fan club. The disc features the seven Beatles Christmas flexi-disc records, released to its members between 1963 and 1969. Because the original studio master tapes for the album had been mislaid, the record was compiled from the original flexis owned by the fan club secretary Freda Kelly.

Saturday December 19 & Sunday December 20
"Let a fly walk on a woman's body from toe to head and then fly out of the window." – Yoko
🍎 In a top floor loft in a derelict building on the Bowery in New York, again working with Dan Richter and Steve Gebhardt, John and Yoko conduct auditions for their film *Fly*. Actresses are requested to lie motionless while a fly crawls over their naked body. Eventually, a young lady by the name of Virginia Lust is chosen for the lead role. Incidentally, the camera tests for each model are preserved on 16mm film by the Lennons and excerpts of these are scheduled to appear in the original version of the 1988 film *Imagine: John Lennon*. They do not make the finished version. Filming of *Fly* is scheduled to begin on Monday.

Monday December 21 & Tuesday December 22
🍎 In the loft of the Bowery, the two-day filming of *Fly* gets underway but, as one might imagine, they soon run into the problem of how to keep the fly on the naked woman and stop it from flying away. Dan comes up with a solution where the flies should be gassed with carbon dioxide. This way, when the fly wakes up, it will remain long enough on the body for John and Yoko to get the shot they require. As expected, the supply of flies for the film runs out, so six college students are sent out with fly nets to neighbouring Greenwich Village kitchens to obtain a fresh supply. After two long days, ending in the early hours of the morning, shooting is finished and John and Yoko prepare to head back to England.

Due to the amount of people involved in trying to catch the flies for the film, John remarks: "The credits will almost be as long as the film!" Incidentally, the original running time to *Fly* (film no. 13) is 50 minutes, but will be trimmed down to 25 minutes for its limited screenings. The first public screening of *Fly* will take place at the Filmmaker's Fortnight Festival in Cannes, France on May 15, 1971.

Thursday December 24
🍎 In order to avoid any problems with overstaying their welcome in America, John and Yoko return to England to celebrate Christmas at home, arriving back this evening at London's Heathrow Airport.

Friday December 25
🍎 Ringo's friend, the already established art designer Robin Cruikshank, presents to Maureen as a Christmas present a few mercury filled perspex dishes. This Yuletide gift will plant the seed of an idea that will eventually manifest itself in the shape of their design company Ringo O'Robin Ltd.

Saturday December 26
🍎 George's single 'My Sweet Lord' reaches number one in America.
🍎 *Melody Maker* reports that The Beatles are searching for a new bass player to replace Paul, with Klaus Voorman on a short list of three candidates.

Sunday December 27
🍎 George and Patti are among the guests present at the London wedding of Tony Ashton, of the pop group Ashton, Gardner and Dyke.

Monday December 28
 John's single 'Mother'/'Why' (by Yoko) is released in America.
 The Beatles' 1964 big screen début *A Hard Day's Night* receives its British television premiere on BBC1 today between 4:05 and 5:29pm. John watches the film at home in Ascot and is inspired to write 'I'm The Greatest'.

December
 At the end of the month at John's Ascot home studios (December 28 and 29), he records the first demos of the tracks 'I'm The Greatest' (a reflective song about his life which also expresses how pleased he is with what he and Yoko have achieved at the end of his first year away from The Beatles) and 'Make Love Not War', later re-recorded as 'Mind Games' in 1973.
 Paul gives a phone interview from America to Alexis Korner on BBC Radio One in which he discusses the tragic death of Jimi Hendrix.

December 31
 For the individual members of The Beatles, the year ends on a very low point, with Paul filing a suit against John Ono Lennon of Ascot, Berkshire, George Harrison of Henley-on-Thames, Berkshire, Richard Starkey of Highgate, London, and Apple Corps of Saville Row in London, in London's High Court, seeking an end to The Beatles & Company. The writ, issued in the Chancery Division, seeks: "A declaration that the partnership business carried on by the plaintiff and the defendants under the name of The Beatles & Co., and constituted by a deed of partnership dated 19 April 1967 and made between the parties hereto, ought to be dissolved and that accordingly the same be dissolved." Paul's suit also requests that a receiver for Apple be appointed until the case is settled, and that Allen Klein is formally charged with the mismanagement of the Apple funds. Both George and Ringo decline to comment on Paul's action. To all intents and purposes, Paul had decided that the group was finished. He remarks: "For me, I want to get out of the contract. I think the group is finished. We've split and everything that we've ever earned should now be split. They don't agree. They think it should continue exactly as planned. But if the three of them want to, they could sit down today and write a little bit of paper saying I'll be released . . . that's all I want!"
 (Note: A reading of the draft balance sheet up to today's date, reveals that the total credit of the four individual Beatles, excluding the Apple company, stands at £738,000. Of that sum, it is calculated that £678,000 is still owing in income tax.)
 Ringo meanwhile gets away from this bombshell by Paul by holding a New Year's Eve party at Ronnie Scott's Club in London. He joins in on an all-star "jam" session which features Charlie Watts (sharing drums with Ringo), Eric Clapton, Bobby Keys (on sax), Klaus Voorman, Maurice Gibb (both sharing bass) and Georgie Fame (organ). The gathering all drink champagne until the early hours of 1971.

"I just want the four of us to get together somewhere and sign a piece of paper saying it's all over. No one would be there, not even Linda or Yoko or Allen Klein. That's all I want now. But John won't do it. Everybody thinks I am the aggressor but I'm not you know . . . I just want out."

– Paul

January
 Time magazine in America votes John Lennon "a bore".
 A full-page advert appears in the UK music trade papers depicting, what we are led to believe, John and Yoko. The couple is actually Paul and Linda in costume.
 In New York, Allen Klein is asked about Paul's attempts to appoint a receiver for Apple. "It doesn't accomplish anything," Klein states, "except bringing out into the public a lot of dirty laundry within the life that they live. Because of the financial and tax structures, which had gone before I came, they cannot just simply write a piece of paper and say 'Goodbye' without horrendous tax problems. You can understand distinctly that they entered into a 10-year arrangement that they would, in effect, split the money. They don't ever have to work together if they don't want, they don't even have to see each other. It's a financial arrangement and the question really comes down to what the understanding was. It's very clear. Would the four of them divide equally the moneys, which were earned either on a collective or individual basis? Paul McCartney was the only one of the four on 'Yesterday'. He sang, he was the player and performer, yet all four shared the money on that record equally. The other three had always understood that they always shared everything. It is whether or not they should share the money equally . . . nothing more. That is the bone of contention . . . plus the tax problem!"

Saturday January 2
 George's album *All Things Must Pass* reaches number one in the US charts.
 At their Scottish farmhouse, Paul and Linda shoot some 'wild' footage (i.e. miscellaneous film with no acting or miming) which includes them riding horses, paddling in the sea and playing in the sand. Then, following a five-month gap, this 16mm colour film is edited by Ray Benson, who previously worked with Paul on *Magical Mystery Tour*, to accompany the tracks '3 Legs' and 'Heart Of The Country'. Finished versions of which are completed just prior to a rare television screening, taking place on BBC1's *Top Of The Pops* (between 7:35 and 8:14pm on June 24) during the short-lived album slot on the programme. A 20-second colour excerpt of '3 Legs' will appear, two decades later, during the American VH-1 *One To One* programme, transmitted on May 3, 1993.

Sunday January 3
 Paul, Linda and family head off to New York to work on the album *Ram*. Before sessions can begin, and with an eye for getting a new band together, Paul arranges for four days of auditions to find the best musicians in town.

Tuesday January 5
 The three-day audition to find a guitarist for Paul is held in a dirty loft on 45th street. The 21-year-old ace session guitarist David Spinoza had been invited to the auditions by Linda.

Wednesday January 6 (until Wednesday January 20)
 Driven by their personal assistant Anthony Fawcett, John and Yoko head to Liverpool docks in order to depart from England by boat en route to Japan, arriving firstly in Miami, Florida. Prior to their departure and still in their white Rolls Royce, John gives Yoko a guided tour of his Liverpool hometown, which includes his original home and many historical sites relating to The Beatles, including the Cavern Club in Mathew Street. Once in Miami, John and Yoko fly to Toronto, Canada, where they are interviewed for the CBC (Canadian Broadcasting Corporation) programme *Weekend*. Appearing primarily to promote their forthcoming "pop peace festival" at the Mosport auto racetrack, near Toronto, this July (which again fails to materialise), the Lennons also take the opportunity to warn teenagers away from drugs. During the broadcast John remarks: "My time on drugs was when I had no hope, and when a person is on drugs it is harder to find hope." The couple also describe Canada as the first country to help with their peace movement, adding: "We were astonished when Canadian reporters treated me and Yoko like human beings." The couple then return by plane to Miami, where they resume their journey to Japan, taking up residence at the Hilton Hotel where they register under the names of Mr and Mrs Gherkin. John and Yoko make their exits and entrances via a fire escape in order to avoid the persistent journalists.

Friday January 7

 Paul holds auditions for a drummer in a seedy basement where eventually he discovers the much-in-demand and experienced session man Denny Seiwell. According to Paul, he found him "lying on a mattress one day in The Bronx. You know how all those people pass them by in *Midnight Cowboy*? Well, we thought we'd better not, so we picked him, put him up on a drum kit, and he was alright!" Denny remembers the audition: "A lot of the boys (the other drummers) were really put out at being asked to audition. Paul just asked me to play, he didn't have a guitar, so I just sat and played. He had a certain look in his eyes . . . he was looking for more than a drummer, he was looking for a certain attitude too. I just played . . . I always say that if you can't get it on by yourself you can't get it on with anyone." Paul invites Denny to join the sessions which are scheduled to begin the following Monday January 10.

Monday January 10 (periodically until Monday March 15)

 The recording sessions for *Ram* begin at the former Columbia Studios of A&R in New York (work begins at 9am each morning and continues until 4am the following morning). During this period, Paul records the tracks 'Another Day', 'Oh Woman, Oh Why', 'Too Many People', '3 Legs', 'Ram On' (two versions at 2:30 and 0:55 in duration), 'Dear Boy', 'Uncle Albert – Admiral Halsey', 'Smile Away', 'Heart Of The Country', 'Monkberry Moon Delight', 'Eat At Home', 'Long Haired Lady' and 'Back Seat Of My Car'. For the songs 'Uncle Albert – Admiral Halsey', 'Long Haired Lady' and 'The Back Seat Of My Car', Paul conducts the New York Philharmonic Orchestra, while on the song 'Monkberry Moon Delight', Heather, Linda's daughter from her first marriage, sings backing vocals. Session musicians Dave Spinoza and Hugh MacCracken provide additional guitar work. These sessions also produce the first version of Linda's 'Seaside Woman', the song 'Dear Friend' (which later appears on the album *Wild Life*), 'Get On The Right Thing', (which later appears on *Red Rose Speedway*) plus several other unreleased tracks such as 'A Love For You' and 'Rode All Night'. Controversy follows from the other ex-Beatles over the tracks that Paul recorded for the *Ram* album. John interpreted 'Too Many People' and 'Dear Boy' as personal attacks on him, while John, George and Ringo all view the song '3 Legs' as personal attacks on them. John will later retaliate with 'How Do You Sleep?' and 'Crippled Inside' on his 1971 album *Imagine*.

 Denny Seiwell recalls the first sessions with Paul: "When we made *Ram*, Paul would run through a song a couple of times, we'd check out a couple of parts and do takes in a few minutes. It's a nice way to work." Paul too is impressed with Seiwell's work on the album and, at the conclusion of the sessions, invites him to join his new group on a more permanent basis. Seiwell jumps at the chance and, along with his French wife Monique, they immediately pack their bags in New York and head off to a house near Paul's Scottish farm in Campbeltown. Denny becomes the first recruit of what will eventually become Wings. During early January, Paul is also saddened to hear that a London High Court date has been set for the court case to officially dissolve The Beatles' partnership.

Saturday January 9

 Paul, through his company, purchases another 400 acres of land next to his farm at High Park, in Campbeltown, Scotland.

Friday January 15

 After British disc jockeys continually play the song, great public demand forces the release of 'My Sweet Lord' as a single. (The song was written during the December 1969 Delaney & Bonnie tour with Eric Clapton. George admits that he was inspired to write this classic after first hearing 'Oh Happy Day' by the Edwin Hawkins Singers in July of that year.)

"The only purpose for being alive is to get yourself straight. Each soul is potentially divine. That goal is to manifest that divinity and what I believe in is liberation. That's what I really want to do, is liberate myself from this chaos and of this body. I want to be free of my body; I want to be God conscious. That's really my own ambition and everything else is incidental." – George, January, 1971.

 Contrary to earlier claims that The Beatles' finances were in a terrible state, a letter from the bank (dated today) which handles Apple's financial accounts, reveals that the group has over £2 million on deposit.

Saturday January 16
 Due to the December 28, 1970 screening of *A Hard Day's Night* by BBC TV, The Beatles' 1964 album of the same name re-enters the UK charts at No.30. Also today, the BBC reveals that they have just acquired the broadcast rights to The Beatles' second film *Help!* and they will shortly be re-screening *A Hard Day's Night* because "many people missed it the first time round".

Tuesday January 19
 The Beatles & Company partnership case opens in the Chancery Division of the London High Court in front of the Judge, Mr. Justice Stamp. Today Mr David Hurst QC, representing Paul, reveals that the financial affairs of The Beatles' partnership are in a "grave state", adding: "The latest accounts suggest that there probably is not enough in the kitty to meet even the individual Beatles income and surtax liability. On a conservative estimate, the four's surtax liability must be £500,000." Counsel gives three reasons why Paul is claiming the dissolution of the group:

1. The Beatles had long since ceased to perform together as a group, so the whole purpose of the partnership had gone.

2. In 1969, McCartney's partners, in the teeth of his opposition and in breach of the partnership deed, had appointed Mr. Klein's company, ABKCO Industries Ltd., as the partnership's exclusive business managers.

3. Mr. McCartney had never been given audited accounts in the four years since the partnership was formed.

"Until 8:15pm yesterday," Mr. David Hurst revealed, "the only accounts we had received of the partnership were draft accounts for the 16 months up to March 31, 1968. A receiver should be appointed because the partnership assets and income should be safeguarded to meet the potential tax liability. The partnership agreement was entered into in April 1967, before the death in August of The Beatles' manager, Mr. Brian Epstein. The next year, and early in 1969, disagreements began to occur.

"Artistic differences arose, particularly between Paul McCartney and John Lennon, who had written most of the songs. In January 1969, Mr. Klein was introduced by John Lennon who proposed that he be appointed manager. George Harrison and Ringo Starr also became keen. Mr. McCartney did not trust Mr. Klein and wanted a New York law firm, Eastman and Eastman, partners in which were his father-in-law and brother-in-law. In May 1969, the other three insisted on appointing Mr. Klein, or rather ABKCO Industries Inc., as exclusive director. Mr. McCartney opposed and protested strongly. But ABKCO was appointed manager, at a fee of 'no less than 20 per cent of the gross income'. McCartney has never accepted, and does not accept Mr. Klein as manager."

Mr. David Hurst, QC, continued: "Up to 1965, Mr. Epstein had run their business affairs, selected their professional advisers and been completely trusted by The Beatles. In 1966, the four decided to abandon touring and make records instead. That increased their financial success because of the enormous worldwide market. On tour they had a close personal relationship. Once they switched to recording they began to drift apart. After The Beatles partnership deed was signed in 1967, the group activities began to decline. They made their last record in the summer of 1969, and that in September John Lennon announced that he was leaving the group. Since then, each Beatle had increasingly gone his own way. Last Spring Paul McCartney decided that he, too, should leave the group. Mr. McCartney's first solo record was released last April in spite of efforts by Mr. Klein, Mr. Harrison and Mr. Starr to postpone its release. In June 1968, Mr. McCartney's accountant was told by the partnership accountants that the combined net profits of the partnership for the year to March 31, 1968 and for Apple Corps, for the year to December 31, 1967, were about £1.5 million.

"In December 1969, other figures were given. Beatles royalties to December 1968, £3.5 million; due from Capitol Records Inc. for three months United States record sales $2.5 million; Apple Corps' net income for 1969, about £2 million; Beatles share of United States record royalties from September 1969 to June 1970, $7,815,628. The rate of partnership income in the middle of last year was between £4 million and £5 million. By last September, Paul McCartney's royalties from his solo record last year amounted to £487,000.

"A quick reading of the draft balance-sheet up to December 31, 1970, showed the total credit of the four individual Beatles, excluding the company, as £738,000. But based on the figures produced by the partnership's accountants, £678,000 is owing in income tax. The four Beatles must be liable for at least £500,000 surtax. There was a tax deficiency of about £450,000. The net current assets of the partnership as a whole were shown as £1.56 million, of which £1.55 million were said to be owed by Apple Corps Ltd. The partnership's solvency would appear to depend on the ability of Apple Corps to pay. It manifests that Apple Corps must owe very large sums in corporation tax."

After further discussions between counsel, Mr. Hurst announced that acceptable undertakings to Mr. McCartney have been offered, to last until the full hearing of the motion. Mr. Harrison, Mr. Starr and Apple Corps will undertake that Apple Corps will procure payment into solicitors' joint account of money due to The Beatles. (Mr. Lennon could not agree to this as he was reported to be "on the high seas".) This will include $3 million from their associated companies: about £100,000 owed by associated companies to the partnership: 25 per cent of all the group's gross receipts: and £487,000 McCartney royalties held by EMI. It is further agreed that no payment will be made out of the joint account without instructions from both sides' solicitors."

In conclusion, it is mutually agreed that evidence is to be completed within a month, and a date for the full hearing is to be fixed as soon as possible after that. The judge, Mr. Justice Stamp, sums up: "It is obviously an urgent matter."

🍎 While John is visiting Japan, he gets his first calls from a solicitor in London who is trying to track him down regarding Paul's High Court actions. He does his best to avoid them but soon faces the inevitable, as he recalls: "I got to Japan and I didn't tell anybody I'd arrived. Then suddenly I got these calls from the lawyer. Fucking idiot! I didn't like his upper class Irish-English voice as soon as I heard it. He insisted that I come home. I could have done it all on the fucking phone!" He and Yoko had no alternative but to return home to England on January 21.

🍎 Meanwhile in Los Angeles at the Sharon Tate murder trial, the jury spends more than 90 minutes listening to all four sides of The Beatles' 1968 *White Album* to "learn if the songs could have influenced Charles Manson and his followers to go on a killing spree."

Wednesday January 20
🍎 Following the accusations made in the High Court, Allen Klein issues a statement from his New York office: "I wish to make it clear that the (Beatles) partnership is solvent and has more than sufficient net current assets to meet all income tax and surtax liabilities."

🍎 In Japan, John meets Yoko's parents for the first time. Yoko's mother, Mrs. Isako Ono, remarks of John: "My husband and I found Lennon very nice and gentle." John and Yoko return to England at Heathrow Airport the following day.

Thursday January 21
🍎 An interview with John and Yoko is carried out at Tittenhurst Park with prominent left-wing activists Tariq Ali and Robin Blackburn for their underground magazine *Red Mole*, excerpts of which reappear in *The Sun*.

Friday January 22
🍎 Enthused by the interview yesterday, John goes into his Ascot studios and records the track 'Power To The People'.

Saturday January 23
🍎 Richard Williams of *The Times* reviews the album *All Things Must Pass*. "Of all The Beatles' solo albums to date, George Harrison's *All Things Must Pass* makes far and away the best listening, perhaps because it is the one which most nearly continues the tradition they began eight years ago." He concludes by saying: "Harrison's light has been hidden under the egos of McCartney and Lennon. But from time to time there have been hints on several of their albums that he was more than he was being allowed to be."

Monday January 25
🍎 At the Wells Street Magistrates Court in London, George, through his solicitor, pleads guilty to 'driving without reasonable consideration' in the West End of London on September 3, 1969, when he drove his Mercedes car against the legs of a policeman who was signalling him to stop. The magistrate, Mr. Iain McClean, postponed sentencing until February 23 because Mr. Harrison had "lost his driving licence".

✦ At Pinewood Studios in Iver, Buckinghamshire, Ringo begins five days of rehearsals for the surreal Frank Zappa movie *200 Motels*. The cast includes Keith Moon, the drummer with The Who, in the role of The Hot Nun. Ringo has been cast as Larry the Dwarf, who just happens to resemble and dress like Frank Zappa! Rehearsals are concluded the following Friday (January 29) with the shooting for the film scheduled to begin on Monday February 1.

Tuesday January 26
✦ During a 10-minute court hearing, the matter of The Beatles' assets is further discussed. The latest difficulty is over implementing the undertakings on which last week's case was adjourned. New undertakings given today mean that money can be paid into a joint account in New York instead of London. Mr. David Hurst QC tells the judge: "Alternative undertakings have been agreed." (This revised undertaking concerns the opening of a second solicitor's joint account in New York and the payment into it of certain money owed by The Beatles.) The Judge concludes by saying he will hear the case again on February 19.

Saturday January 30
✦ George's single 'My Sweet Lord' and his album *All Things Must Pass* both reach number one in the UK charts on the same day. By the end of the month, figures reveal that the single has passed the 200,000 sales mark, with around 30,000 copies being sold a day. In America, the sales have gone past the two million mark. In Britain, sales figures for the album are now approaching 60,000 copies.

February
✦ Plans are announced for Paul to record an American TV special in California featuring the musicians who are currently recording with him in Los Angeles on the album *Ram*.

Monday February 1 (until Friday February 5)
✦ Over several sound stages at Pinewood Studios, Ringo begins shooting the bizarre Associated Company/Lion TV Services production of *200 Motels* starring (the real life) Frank Zappa and The Mothers of Invention. Based on "an account of what it is like to be a pop musician on the road in 1971", Frank's original plan to produce the show for Dutch television is scuppered when a large enough sound stage for the shooting could not be found. Problems again occur when filming is originally scheduled to begin in late January at Shepperton Studios, but, due to every inch of studio space being taken, mainly by Roman Polanski's production of *Macbeth*, shooting is switched at short notice to Pinewood. Using a new technique where the action is shot directly onto videotape and transferred onto 35mm film (by Technicolor-England) for cinema release, each day's work is concluded at 5:20pm due to a strict union ruling. During a break from the five-day taping, Ringo brings in a specially prepared birthday cake for Zappa's drummer Jimmy Carl Black and is seen chatting to Hollywood actor Tony Curtis who is at the studios filming a second series of The Persuaders with Roger Moore. *200 Motels* also features a cameo appearance by Ringo's 22-year-old chauffeur Martin Lickert who will quit Ringo's employment in April and join Frank Zappa and The Mothers for a tour of America. Filming is concluded on Friday February 5, when at 5:20pm precisely, the cast and crew attend a party celebrating the conclusion of the production. The director Tony Palmer will edit the 24 hours of videotape at Europe's largest VT facility, Television Recordings, in London the following week, using three VTR machines and just one vision-mixer. (The 95-minute film will premiere in London on Thursday December 16 at the Classic Cinema in Piccadilly Circus.)

Tuesday February 2 & Wednesday February 3
✦ At Abbey Road Studios, over this two-day period, Leon Russell and Badfinger's Pete Ham join George recording tracks for a proposed album by Phil Spector's wife Ronnie. The sessions produce 'Try Some, Buy Some' but George will later remove Ronnie's vocals, slow the tempo down and add his own vocals and use the track on his 1973 album *Living In The Material World*. Other tracks recorded are 'You' (the backing tracks of which are retained and will appear featuring George's new vocals on his 1975 album *Extra Texture (Read All About It)*), 'Tandoori Chicken', 'A Bit More Of You' and the unreleased 'Loverly Laddy Day'. On the second day of the sessions, John joins in playing

piano. (A Ronnie Spector single comprising 'Try Some, Buy Some'/'Tandoori Chicken' is released in the UK as Apple 33 on April 16, 1971, while in America the two tracks appear as Apple 1832 on April 19.)

Monday February 8

☕ With work on *200 Motels* now completed, Ringo departs with Maureen for a holiday in Switzerland. He is forced to abandon the vacation early after solicitors in London request him to return to England to deal with Paul's High Court action.

Tuesday February 9

☕ In Liverpool at the Cavern Club in Mathew Street, fans celebrate the tenth anniversary of The Beatles' début there.

Friday February 12

☕ While The Beatles' trial is due to start in one week, Klein submits his affidavit to the High Courts of London.

Monday February 15

☕ George's single 'What Is Life'/'Apple Scruffs' is released in America.

Wednesday February 17

☕ From his Tittenhurst Park mansion, John gives a live radio interview to the American DJ Scott Muni.

Thursday February 18

☕ One day before the trial officially opens; papers released privately give three further reasons why Paul wishes to leave The Beatles:

    1. Allen Klein had tried to delay the release of Paul's album *McCartney*.

    2. Klein's company ABKCO altered Paul's song 'The Long And Winding Road' without consulting him first.

    3. ABKCO, without any authority from Paul, had transferred the film rights of *Let It Be* from Apple to United Artists.

☕ Paul and Linda return to England from New York this morning. They return to America the following day to resume work on *Ram*.

Friday February 19

Beatles High Court Case – Day One:

☕ The trial opens with Paul (now sporting a heavy beard) and Linda sitting in the front row of the court to watch the proceedings. (He wins a two-shilling bet with the courtroom attendant who says that John and Yoko will also be there in court to "settle old scores" in public.) Paul's QC, Mr David Hurst, begins by telling the judge, Mr Justice Stamp, that Allen Klein has been convicted of tax offences in New York. Announcing that, "On January 29 last, he was convicted of ten tax offences by a jury in New York's Federal District Court, even though they are effectively under appeal. It has obviously not enhanced Mr. McCartney's confidence in Mr. Klein." (The case is adjourned until Monday February 22.) The excitement of a Beatle appearing personally in court is reflected in the number of photographers and TV crews who shoot the couple leaving the building.

☕ Also on this day, Paul's single 'Another Day'/'Oh Woman, Oh Why' is released in the UK (the American release takes place on February 22). Maclen Music Ltd, the first assignees of the copyright to all Lennon and McCartney compositions, claim half of the copyright to 'Another Day', and the other half is claimed by a company called McCartney Inc.

☕ An unscheduled two-minute clip of Ringo, appearing on the BBC programme *Cilla* on February 13, is repeated during the children's television show *Ask Aspel* on BBC1.

☕ Today heralds the start of many London meetings between John, George, Ringo and three counsels. As John recalls: "It went on for weeks and weeks. George and Ringo were getting restless and didn't want to do it anymore. George eventually said, 'I've had enough, I don't want to do it anymore. Fuck it all! I don't care if I'm poor. I'll give it all away.'"

Monday February 22
Beatles High Court Case – Day Two:
 Today, Mr. Morris Finer QC, on behalf of the defence, declares in the High Court: "Allen Klein has saved The Beatles from almost total bankruptcy." He continues: "Mr. Klein largely left accountants to sort out the mess. He considers his main job was to try and get money to rescue the group from the dreadful situation in which he found them. And in that, he was very successful!" Later, Mr. Finer points out: "The Beatles, other than Mr. McCartney, had always counted their individual earnings as group assets. This arrangement would not necessarily be disadvantageous to Mr. McCartney, who claims that the royalties from his solo record belong to him alone. Mr. Harrison's royalties on 'My Sweet Lord', his individual record this year, are going to be nearly twice as much as Mr. McCartney's – nearly £1 million!" (The hearing is adjourned until tomorrow.)

Tuesday February 23
Beatles High Court Case – Day Three:
 The case for the defence continues today, when their QC, Mr. Morris Finer, reads out to Mr. Justice Stamp, affidavits by John, George and Ringo.
 John, in his long and detailed affidavit, writes: "After the death of Brian Epstein, The Beatles' company Apple was full of 'hustlers' and 'spongers'. The staff came and went as they pleased and were lavish with money and hospitality. We have since discovered that around that time, two of Apple's cars had completely disappeared and that we owned a house which no one can remember buying. But a few weeks after Mr. Klein had been authorised by me to make changes in the organisation of Apple the effects were felt. Early in 1969, Mr. Klein dismissed incompetent or unnecessary staff; the 'hustling' and lavish hospitality ended; discipline and order appeared in the Apple offices. The four of us started to receive monthly accounts of their personal spending, copies of bills and, where necessary, explanations. We also received regular bank statements and statements of our income and investments. It was true, that when the group was touring, their work and social relationships were close, but there had been a lot of arguing, mainly about musical and artistic matters. I suppose Paul and George were the main offenders in this respect, but from time to time we all gave displays of temperament and threatened to 'walk out'. Of necessity, we developed a pattern for sorting out our differences, by doing what any three of us decided. It sometimes took a long time and sometimes there was deadlock and nothing was done, but generally that was the rule we followed and, until recent events, it worked quite well. Even when we stopped touring, we frequently visited each other's houses in or near London and personally we were on terms as close as we had ever been. If anything, Paul was the most sociable of us. From our earliest days in Liverpool, George and I, on the one hand, and Paul, on the other, had different musical tastes. Paul preferred 'pop-type' music and we preferred what is now called 'underground'. This may have led to arguments, particularly between Paul and George, but the contrast in our tastes, I am sure, did more good than harm, musically speaking, and contributed to our success.

"If Paul is trying to break us up because of anything that happened before the Klein–Eastman power struggle, his reasoning does not make sense to me. After Mr. Epstein's death, Mr. McCartney and me, in particular, tried to be businesslike over Apple's affairs, but we were handicapped by our ignorance of accounting, business practice and our preoccupation with our musical activities. Above all, although royalties were coming in, none of us had any idea at all about the state of our finances or our liabilities. We decided that we must find a new manager and we interviewed several people, but none seemed to have any idea of what was needed. I arranged to see Mr. Klein, whom I had heard about from Mr. Epstein. He was tough but he knew the entertainment business. I then introduced Mr. Klein to the other Beatles. If Paul is suggesting that I was trying to rush him and the others into engaging Klein or pushing him down their throats, that is a wrong impression. At all times, Mr. Klein had shown himself on top of the job. The only other major contenders for the manager's job were the Eastmans – father of McCartney's wife Linda, and her brother. I had opposed the idea of having as manager anyone in such a close relationship with any particular Beatle.

"Paul's criticism of Mr. Klein was not fair. Klein is certainly forceful to an extreme, but he does get results. So far as I know, he has not taken any commission to which he was not entitled."

❤ Mr. Morris Finer, QC, then reads out an affidavit written by George: "The only serious row was between Paul and me. In 1968 I went to the United States and had a very easy co-operation with many leading musicians. This contrasted with the superior attitude which, for years past, Paul has shown towards me musically. In January 1969, we were making a film in a studio at Twickenham, which was dismal and cold, and we were all getting a bit fed up with our surroundings. In front of the cameras, as we were actually being filmed, Paul started to 'get at' me about the way I was playing. I decided I had had enough and told the others I was leaving. This was because I was musically dissatisfied. After a few days, the others asked me to return and since I did not wish to leave them in the lurch in the middle of filming and recording, and since Paul agreed that he would not try to interfere or teach me how to play, I went back. Since the row, Paul has treated me more as a musical equal. I think this whole episode shows how a disagreement could be worked out so that we all benefited. I just could not believe it when, just before Christmas, I received a letter from Paul's lawyers. I still cannot understand why Paul acted as he did."

❤ Ringo, in his submitted affidavit, optimistically states: "The Beatles might yet stay together as a group. Paul is the greatest bass player in the world. He is also determined. He goes on and on to see if he can get his own way. While that may be a virtue, it did mean that musical disagreements inevitably rose from time to time. But such disagreements contributed to really great products." The affidavit continues: "I was shocked and dismayed, after Mr. McCartney's promises about a meeting of all four Beatles in London in January, that a writ should have been issued on December 31. I trust Paul and I know he would not lightly disregard his promise. Something serious, about which I have no knowledge, must have happened between Paul's meeting with George in New York at the end of December." He optimistically concludes by saying: "My own view is that all four of us together could even yet work out everything satisfactorily."

Mr. Morris Finer finishes by reading evidence provided by accountants who estimate that: "Apple Corps's liability for corporation tax for the period April 1967 to December 31, 1970 was £1,935,000. The total surtax liability of the four individual members of the partnership was estimated at £630,000."

The hearing is adjourned until tomorrow.

❤ Meanwhile, while an affidavit by George is being read out in the High Courts, George's solicitor Mr. Martin Polden is representing him at the Wells Street Magistrates Court in London, concerning the charge of 'driving without reasonable consideration', postponed from January 25. At the end of the hearing George is fined £35 and banned from driving for a month. He is also ordered to pay £15 costs. Polden later lodges an appeal against the disqualification.

Wednesday February 24
Beatles High Court Case – Day Four:

❤ The accountant Mr. John Darby reads out an affidavit from Allen Klein, which states that: "The group's partnership assets are not now in jeopardy." The day begins with claims by Klein, in submitted written evidence, that he had: "more than doubled The Beatles' income in the first nine months after I took over as manager in May 1969. In 1970, I had increased it fivefold. Furthermore, as a result of my efforts, The Beatles' partnership income increased from £850,667 for the year ended March 31, 1969 to £1,708,651 in the nine months ended December 31, 1969. In the year to December 31, 1970, the income was £4,383,509." Mr. Morris Finer, QC, then reads out another affidavit from Klein: "I deny that The Beatles have been prejudiced by having me as their manager. On the contrary, they have greatly benefited. Mr. McCartney has made attacks on my commercial integrity in general and, in my dealings with The Beatles in particular, Mr. McCartney had also declared that the assets of The Beatles partnership were in jeopardy. I am concerned to answer these attacks and to rebut this allegation."

The submitted evidence continues: "I appreciated before I became The Beatles' manager that I was taking over a very perilous situation which, according to the auditors, involved solvency. I made this position clear to The Beatles at many meetings and my first task was to help them to generate enough income to alleviate this situation. The largest potential source of income was from royalties on records and I wanted to negotiate a new arrangement with EMI. Discussions were held with The Beatles and with John Eastman as to how EMI should be approached and who should go to a meeting with them. It was decided by all four Beatles that I alone should go with them and have authority to negotiate. McCartney was anxious that Mr. Eastman should attend, but McCartney went along with the collective decision. A meeting was held on May 7, 1969, attended by Mr. McCartney, Mr. Lennon, Mr. Harrison, Yoko Ono, myself and three representatives of EMI. Ringo Starr was not there, as he was making a film. No conclusion was reached at that meeting, but EMI made it clear that they were not prepared to negotiate any new arrangements so long as the NEMS claim was outstanding. I had arranged for my company ABKCO to take over from NEMS at considerable profit to The Beatles. Notwithstanding, on July 8, 1969, Mr. John Eastman saw fit to write to each of The Beatles criticising the settlement and alleging I cost them £1.5 million."

Referring to Paul's claim that he sold, without authority, the film rights to *Let It Be* from Apple to United Artists, Klein remarks: "It made an absolute fortune for all four Beatles. The film's profits will be absolutely enormous, but Mr. McCartney, his advisers or Mr. Eastman will not concede that I have done something that was entirely proper."

The case is adjourned until the following day.

Thursday February 25
Beatles High Court Case – Day Five:
 Further High court evidence by Allen Klein read out to the court by Mr. Morris Finer, QC: "Paul McCartney never accepted me as his manager, but the partnership did, and I have continued as manager of the partnership. McCartney has accepted the benefits, which I have negotiated in that capacity. As regard to my ability to make deals, I am content to be judged on my record."

At that point, Mr. Finer, representing John, George and Ringo, produces a schedule which claims to show the total income received by The Beatles from June 1962 until December 1968, but not including the income from songwriting which has never been part of the joint activities. In that six and a half years the total income of The Beatles, from tours, films, record royalties and other sources, was £7,864,126. By comparison, for the 19 months between May 1969, when the Klein management agreement was made, and December 1970, the total income was £9,142,533, more than £8 million of that sum coming from record royalties.

To this evidence, Mr. Finer again returns to Klein's affidavit: "I deny ever having been untruthful, that I was unscrupulous or that I had ever held myself out as Mr. McCartney's manager. It was not true that any of The Beatles had told him that the Capitol agreement was a tricky one. This is the big agreement that has been so responsible for the increase in income. Still less did I advise The Beatles to enter into an agreement on a false basis. The agreement makes specific provision for records, which might be made by The Beatles individually and expressly provides for the contingency that they might not perform as a group at all. In spite of Mr. McCartney's reluctance, it was a fact that he signed it!

"Your Lordship may think it is pretty unlikely that EMI, which has been for years in such close association with the group, were under any kind of misapprehension at any time as to what the facts were regarding these young men and their relationship with each other. EMI has acted as father and mother to these young men for years. Everybody knew it."

The judge replies: "Well, I think not."

Mr. Finer responds: "That is why I am trying to bring these matters home to your Lordship." He continues: "It seemed obvious that Mr. Klein had been advising John Lennon and Paul McCartney in relationship to Maclen (Music) Ltd., the music company in which Mr. McCartney and Mr. Lennon each hold 40 per cent holdings and Apple Corps 20 per cent. Maclen consisted of valuable rights and potentials and had to be managed. Mr. Klein gets, I think it's clear from the evidence, no management fee from Maclen, but Maclen pay a management service fee to Apple Corps, and Mr. Klein gets a proportion of that fee through Apple. Under the ultimate agreement, Mr. Klein gave up his claim to commission that arose under the original management agreement and said that if he did not get his commission under that arrangement, then Apple would manage the affairs of Maclen which had to be managed and obtain remuneration for doing so. The effect was that Apple got a gross commission of 20 per cent, which came back to McCartney and the other Beatles. Royalties from Mr.McCartney's solo record *McCartney* was 'Beatle money'. The same applies to Mr. Harrison and the record he made three months ago which was making double the money. No one is getting at Mr. McCartney on this."

- The case is adjourned until tomorrow when Paul and Linda will again appear in court. They arrive back from New York later this evening.
- Meanwhile, George's 'My Sweet Lord', currently number one in the UK singles chart, appears at the end of tonight's edition of *Top Of The Pops* (transmitted between 7:05 and 7:39pm on BBC1). With no promotional film to show, the song plays to an accompaniment of the studio audience dancing.

Friday February 26
Beatles High Court Case – Day Six:

- Paul, alongside Linda, returns to the High Courts in London. This time, Paul stands in the witness box to give evidence where, in particular, he responds to John's statement, read out on February 23, that said: "We always thought of ourselves as Beatles, whether we recorded singly or in twos or threes."

   Paul denies that claim, saying: "Since The Beatles stopped making group recordings, we have stopped thinking of ourselves as Beatles. One has only to look at recent recordings by John or George to see that neither thinks of himself as a Beatle. On his recent album, John Lennon has listed things he did not believe in. One was 'I don't believe in Beatles.'

   "When the four of us entered into our partnership agreement in 1967, we did not consider the exact wording or give any thought to the agreement's legal implications. We had thought that if one of us wanted to leave the group he would only have to say so. On the way in which the four of us had sorted out our differences in the past, I deny that it had been on a three-to-one basis. If one disagreed, we discussed the problem until we reached agreement or let the matter drop. I know of no decision taken on a three-to-one basis. I deny that the Eastmans and I obstructed Mr. Allen Klein in the preparation of accounts. Nor had the Eastmans been contenders for the job of manager for the group. I wanted them as managers but when the rest of the group disagreed, had not pressed the matter. Mr. Lennon had challenged my statement that Mr. Klein had sowed discord within the group, but I recall a telephone conversation in which Mr. Klein had told me, 'You know why John is angry with you? It is because you came off better than he did on *Let It Be*.' Mr. Klein also said to me, 'The real trouble is Yoko. She is the one with ambition.' I often wonder what John would have said if he heard the remark. When the four of us had talked about breaking up the group, Mr. Harrison had said, 'If I could have my bit in an envelope, I'd love it.' "

   Paul then recalled the negotiations by Klein to acquire one of the NEMS companies for Apple. "He told us, 'I'll get it for nothing'. That was a typical example of the exaggerated way in which Mr. Klein expressed himself to us. I became more and more determined that Klein was not the right man to be appointed manager."

   Paul concludes his evidence by saying: "None of the other three Beatles seemed to understand why I had acted in the way I did. The short answer is that the group had broken up, each now had his own musical career, there were still no audited accounts and they still did not know what their tax positions were. None of these points, I add, had been denied by the other Beatles."

   The case is adjourned until Monday.
- Paul and Linda return to their St. John's Wood home, before returning to New York on March 1, and the final recording sessions for *Ram*.

March

- Following their chance idea on Christmas Day, Ringo and Robin Cruikshank begin formulating ideas for their range of exclusive furniture designs. They call the company Ringo O'Robin Ltd, but will not officially form the company until September 3.
- The American publishers Bright Tunes instigate legal action against George and Apple over the unauthorised plagiarism of The Chiffon's track 'He's So Fine'. (The case will go on until 1976 – see entries for September 7 and November 8.) George receives the news of the plagiarism case while he is recording with Phil Spector and a huge orchestra.

Monday March 1
Beatles High Court Case – Day Seven:

- Mr. David Hurst, QC, representing Paul, begins his final summing up, by saying: "It was quite plain that The Beatles had irretrievably broken up." (Counsel's summing up and arguments on the legal position take up the next two days.)

Tuesday March 2

Beatles High Court Case – Day Eight:

🍎 David Hurst continues with his summing up in court: "When Mr. Allen Klein came on the scene, The Beatles were on the crest of a wave. He could claim no credit for the wave, let alone the ocean across which it moved! The group had broken up and there was no prospect of its reconstruction. Whichever version of the disputed facts one accepted, it would manifest there was disharmony. Four aspects had been clearly shown in support of Paul McCartney's case: jeopardy of the assets, exclusion of a partner, lack of good faith towards a partner by other partners and the likelihood of eventual dissolution."

Mr. Morris Finer, QC, on behalf of John, George and Ringo, replies by saying: "There is a rule of democracy in partnerships, as in other aspects of life, and the law enshrines it – the will of the majority should prevail. Mr. McCartney, through his Counsel, seems to live in a world where everyone is either a seraphin or angel, ape or viper . . . where there is precious little room for the intermediate atmosphere in which most people live. This partnership has got a manager – Apple Corps Ltd. But it has proven itself in the past, both as an organisation and a company, as being incapable of properly managing the affairs of the partnership. One thing which is manifest is that if the interests of the partnerships are properly to be looked after between now and the trial of this action, it is vital that any order your lordship makes – I shall ask you to make no order – must provide for management. The effect otherwise would give rise to loss and, indeed, chaos."

"I am inclined to agree with you on that point," replies Mr. Justice Stamp. (The hearing is adjourned until tomorrow.)

Wednesday March 3

Beatles High Court Case – Day Nine:

🍎 The final arguments continue with Mr. Morris Finer, QC, continuing his summing up: "In practice, the appointing of a receiver of the group's business affairs would be a disaster! The appointment of a receiver would give the impression that the business had stopped, and the reputation of The Beatles would be damaged."

Mr. Justice Stamp then asks: "Can you say that The Beatles' reputation is such a delicate blossom?"

Mr. Finer replies: "The reputation of Apple Corps, which is an active business, includes a lot more business than dealings with Beatles' records."

The hearing is adjourned until tomorrow.

🍎 Meanwhile, the South African Broadcasting Company lifts its 1966 ban on Beatles records. A ban on John's solo recordings, however, remains.

Thursday March 4

Beatles High Court Case – Day Ten:

🍎 The final arguments continue. Mr. William Forbes, the other solicitor representing John, George and Ringo, tells the court: "Before Mr. Allen Klein took over the management of The Beatles, the four partners had been drawing from the partnership account at the rate of £6,000 a month. In the 28 months before the Klein era, The Beatles had drawn a total of £272,000 from the account, although the combined net profit available to them was only £122,000! In the pre-Klein era, the four of them were drawing an average of £10,000 a month, an overdrawing of £6,000 a month. But after Klein took over their management, The Beatles' drawings continued at £11,000 a month, but the money available to them increased to £40,000. For the year ended December 31, 1970, the net profit available for them was £840,000, out of which they drew £184,965. The basic objection was that the proposals should leave Mr. Klein as manager."

🍎 Meanwhile, this evening at Abbey Road Studios, Yoko re-records her vocals for 'Open Your Box' due to the insistence of EMI who demand that the lyrics be cleaned up. Philip Brodie, the managing director of EMI Records, was reported as saying he thought the "original lyrics were distasteful". Due to this unscheduled Yoko session, the release of the single (originally scheduled for tomorrow) is delayed by one week.

Friday March 5

Beatles High Court Case – Day Eleven:

🍎 A judgement in the trial is expected today but fails to materialise. Instead, another judge in the High Court, Mr. Justice Plowman, grants an application in the High Court by Northern Songs Ltd. for temporary orders banning Maclen Music Ltd. (John and

Paul's company) from publishing or causing to be published, compositions by Mr. Lennon and Mr. McCartney and from asserting on sheet music or record labels any rights to the copyright.

Saturday March 6 & Sunday March 7
❦ Staff at the EMI factory in Hayes, Middlesex work overtime to press a "cleaned up" version of the 'Power To The People' / 'Open Your Box' single. A spokesman for Apple explains why 'Open Your Box' had to be re-recorded. "The original lyrics said 'Open your trousers, open your skirt, open your legs and open your thighs.' The last words in each case have now been changed, with the consent of John and Yoko, to 'houses, church, lakes and eyes'. He is asked, "Did John and Yoko object to the censorship?" "No", the spokesman replied. "They just wanted to get the record out." Interestingly, Apple had mistakenly sent out advance copies of the single, featuring the uncensored version of Yoko's track to UK DJs.

Monday March 8
❦ The Apple single 'Power To The People'/'Open Your Box' (aka 'Hirake') performed by Yoko, is released in the UK only.

Friday March 12
Beatles High Court Case – Judgement Given In Favour Of Paul:
❦ In the High Courts of London, Paul wins the first stage in his battle to dissolve The Beatles' partnership. Today, Mr. Justice Stamp announces that Mr. James Spooner, a partner in a city firm of chartered accountants, has been appointed as receiver and manager of The Beatles' business interests, pending trial of the main action. Mr. Spooner's appointment is postponed for seven days pending a possible appeal against the judgement by John, George and Ringo. On hearing of the verdict, Mr. Andrew Leggatt, representing Paul announces: "My client's worst fears about the financial position of the partnership have been proven right."

When John, George and Ringo are told of the result they leave the court and head back to Saville Row in John's white Rolls Royce, telling reporters in their trail, "No comment!" According to the Apple Scruffs, the three ex-Beatles then drive to Paul's home in Cavendish Avenue in St. John's Wood where John grabs two bricks from his car, scales the wall of Paul's home and proceeds to throw them through his windows. John, George and Ringo return to Apple's headquarters where again they face a barrage of questions from the press waiting outside their offices.

Monday March 15
❦ Following the final sessions on the *Ram* album, Paul and Linda depart for California where they have rented a house for several months.

Tuesday March 16
❦ In Los Angeles, The Beatles' *Let It Be* album receives a Grammy Award for the 'Best Original Score Written For A Motion Picture or Television Special in 1970'. Paul and Linda, who only arrived in LA this morning, collect the award from the Hollywood legend John Wayne. As Paul leaves the building, a reporter asks him if he is in America to record an album. Paul replies by saying: "I have a knife and a fork and I'm here to cut a record" before escaping in a Cadillac amid screams from waiting Beatles fans. The couple depart into the night and remain unseen for months, even failing to show for a concert by Santana, for which they had booked (and received) two front row tickets. Prior to his departure, Paul had given his name to protesters demonstrating against the proposed building of a 200-room hotel in Cavendish Avenue, London. Westminster Council eventually scraps the idea.

Wednesday March 17
❦ In the *New Musical Express* singles chart, Paul's 'Another Day' reaches number one, while in the other charts, the record reaches only number two.

Saturday March 20
❦ The *Daily Mirror* reports of a meeting held the previous night at Apple involving John, George, Ringo and Klaus Voorman, to discuss future recording plans. When told of this

meeting, Apple publicist Les Perrin denies that the meeting ever took place. Klaus meanwhile, with news spreading through the media that he is to become the new Beatle, vanishes from his Hampstead home with his wife Christine and takes up residence with George at his Friar Park mansion.

Monday March 22
 John's single 'Power To The People'/'Touch Me' (performed by Yoko), is released in America only.

Saturday March 27
 In the early hours of the morning (between 1:00 and 2:00am), John gives a live interview to Kenny Everett for his programme on Radio Monte Carlo. During the one-hour slot, conducted from John's Ascot home, the complete *John Lennon/Plastic Ono Band* album is also played. The station's broadcasts to the UK, which had begun transmission on December 1, 1970, comes to an abrupt halt this evening due to the exceptionally poor reception which, in turn, has resulted in the withdrawal of essential advertising revenue.

Tuesday March 30
 John and Yoko are in attendance at The Rolling Stones' farewell party, held at the Skindles nightclub in Maidenhead, Berkshire, before the group leave to become tax exiles in the South of France.

Wednesday March 31
 Paul submits his first year-end accounts, covering the years 1970-71, of his new company McCartney Productions Ltd. The figures reveal modest sales figures, accounted to the company, of £3,017, while outgoing expenses run up a bill for £5,417, resulting in a first-year loss to Paul of £2,400. (Of course, Paul's main source of income at this point is coming through The Beatles' crumbling Apple empire.)

April
 In an interview for *Life* magazine, Paul reveals the problems of the break-up of his former group: "I do think if it were just up to the four of us we would have picked up our bags – these are my shoes, that's my ball, that's your ball – and gone. And I still maintain that's the only way, to actually go and do that, no matter what things are involved on a business level. But, of course, we aren't four fellows. We are part of a big business machine, so that's why I've had to sue in courts to dissolve The Beatles, to do on a business level what we should have done on a four fellows level. I feel it just has to come."

Paul goes on to say he searched his soul before deciding to take the other three Beatles to court. "People said, 'It's a pity that such a nice thing had to end.' I think that too. It is a pity. I like fairy tales, but you realise that you're in real life and you don't split up a beautiful thing with a beautiful thing."
 An abridged version of Ringo's 1968 film *Candy* is re-released to selected UK cinemas alongside the controversial Beryl Reid film *The Killing Of Sister George*.

Friday April 9
 Ringo's single 'It Don't Come Easy' (produced by George)/'Early 1970' is released in the UK. (The American release takes place on April 16.) George also played guitar on the A-side. (The final recording sessions for 'It Don't Come Easy' took place at Trident Studios in London over a year previously on March 8, 1970, with Ron Cattermole on saxophone.)

Thursday April 15
 Even though The Beatles are no longer together as a performing or recording unit, the group still continues to pick up awards. This time, in Hollywood at the Dorothy Chandler Pavilion in Los Angeles, California, just one month after the Grammys, they receive an Oscar from the US Academy Of Motion Picture Arts And Sciences for '1970 Best Original Song Score', with their music for *Let it Be*. During this 43 Oscar celebration they beat stiff competition from the films *The Baby Maker*, *A Boy Named Charlie Brown* and *Darling Lili*, starring Julie Andrews.

Thursday April 22

🍎 John and Yoko fly from Madrid to Palma airport in Spain on their private jet. They tell waiting journalists their journey is for "business and a rest".

🍎 Meanwhile, back in England, tonight's edition of *Top Of The Pops* (show number 371 and broadcast on BBC1 between 7:04 and 7:39pm) features the Apple promotional film for Ringo's 'It Don't Come Easy'. This features clips such as Ringo on the set of his first solo film *Candy*, on December 15, 1967, various shots of him playing drums with large table tennis bats in fast motion, playing billiards, pulling faces at the camera and even home movies of his kittens.

Friday April 23

🍎 In Palma, Majorca in Spain, John and Yoko are taken into police custody and questioned regarding their alleged abduction from a playground of Yoko's seven-year-old daughter Kyoko. The child's father, Anthony Cox had, somewhat ironically for John, been attending a meditation session by the guru Maharishi Mahesh Yogi, at the Cala Murada, the Majorca home of the Maharishi for the last eighteen months. John and Yoko had taken the child and looked after her at their hotel, the Melia in Madrid. In court, Yoko claims that she had been awarded custody in the US when she and Cox were divorced. Following the hearing, the judge listens to evidence behind closed doors and rules that Kyoko should return to Cox. The judge had asked Kyoko: "Which parent would you like to be with?" She replied: "My daddy." Outside the courthouse, a tearful, yet defiant Yoko tells waiting reporters: "We will be back for her . . . wherever she is!" Taking further legal advice, British lawyers inform the Lennons that their best attempt for obtaining custody of Kyoko is to get a custody order from the authorities in the US Virgin Islands, where Yoko and Anthony Cox were officially divorced.

Saturday April 24

🍎 John and Yoko attempt to leave Palma airport en route to the Virgin Islands but are stopped by police for further questioning over the abduction. Their departure is delayed by several hours.

Monday April 26

🍎 Through their solicitor, John, George and Ringo admit that they have accepted Paul's decision to leave The Beatles and will not appeal against it.

Tuesday April 27

🍎 At the Camden Cinema in London, during the week-long Camden Arts Festival '71, *Let It Be* is screened in the afternoon and *Help!* is screened in the evening.

🍎 Ringo, meanwhile, is to be found in snow-covered Norway shooting a special film clip of 'It Don't Come Easy' for inclusion in this Thursday's edition of *Top Of The Pops*. (Transmitted only once on the show on BBC1 between 7:05 and 7:39pm on Thursday April 29.) Working with the show's producer Michael Hurll, the clip features Ringo singing the song at a piano outside in the snow wearing a pair of mittens and dark glasses. The footage, intercut with scenes of the former Beatle skiing and riding a ski-mobile, will receive a welcome repeat during the UK Gold *Top Of The Pops* re-runs on August 2, 1993.

May

🍎 At Tittenhurst Park in Ascot, John cuts a studio demo of the track 'God Save Us'.

🍎 Paul and Linda issue a special limited-edition version of the *Ram* album, entitled *Bring To Ewe By Hal Smith*. This features 15 short sketches by Paul and Linda, all including Paul singing the recurring song 'Now Hear This Song Of Mine', which also features recorded bleats from their sheep. Intended purely for radio broadcasts, the disc features lead-in tracks and conversations with the couple. Only 1,000 copies are pressed by Apple and distributed. The McCartneys spend the rest of the month writing at their farmhouse in Scotland.

🍎 Ringo is seen working with the recording engineer Andy Hendricksen at the Command Studios in London.

Wednesday May 5

🍎 Zarach, an exclusive modern design company, opens a new shop at 183 Sloane Street, London SW3, and features amongst its headline items, the first piece of Kinetic sculpture designed by Ringo and Robin Cruikshank. Described as a "rich man's plaything", the item comprises a "mercury filled object containing zigzagging discs powered by a small motor which sits in the opaque light box underneath and all housed in a transparent perspex case". The price of this item is a most reasonable £60.

Monday May 10
 The South African government opposes the idea of a nude statue of John, as immortalised on the *Two Virgins* sleeve, being erected in a township.

Wednesday May 12
 Paul, Linda and their children, as well as Ringo and Maureen, fly in a specially chartered plane to St. Tropez in France to attend Mick Jagger's wedding to Bianca. Later, both Paul and Ringo, with respective partners, attend the reception which is held at the nearby Café Des Arts. The celebrations continue until 4am. This is the first time that Paul and Ringo have socialised since the split of The Beatles over a year ago.

Friday May 14
 John and Yoko are pictured at Heathrow Airport before their departure to Cannes in the South of France.

Saturday May 15
 Even though John and Yoko are scheduled to appear in court in Majorca charged with trying to abduct Kyoko, they instead attend the annual Cannes Film Festival where two of their films, *Apotheosis (Balloon)* and *Fly*, are being screened during the Filmmaker's Fortnight Festival. The audience reportedly boos during the screening of *Apotheosis*, while *Fly* receives a standing ovation. John and Yoko, who appears sporting a fashionable pair of black hot pants, arrive at the screening with fellow film maker Louise Malle. For the programme of the event, Yoko writes a piece entitled: "What is the relationship between the world and the artist?" The article concludes by saying: "There are only two classes left in our society. The class who communicates and the class who doesn't. Tomorrow, I hope there will be just one." A report on John and Yoko at the festival, entitled: John And Yoko At Cannes: I Made A Glass Hammer, appears in the American newspaper *The Village Voice* on June 24. Meanwhile, the judge in Majorca excuses the Lennons for their non- appearance in court.
 Nearby, in a luxury yacht called SS *Marala*, hired for the duration of the festival, Ringo, who remained in France following Mick Jagger's wedding, is to be found with Maureen, George, Patti and Cilla Black. It was during one of these get-togethers that the song 'Photograph' comes about, with all the guests chipping in lyrics to the song. During her stay, Cilla invites Ringo to appear on her BBC TV special, soon to be filmed in Scandinavia. (See entry for June 24.)
 Meanwhile, *Melody Maker* reports on its front page, that "The Beatles are bootlegged again", revealing that: "A Beatles' double album containing new original material not previously issued by the group may soon be released as a bootleg album in Britain. A tape, featuring about 30 unreleased songs by the group, is circulating in London at present. The holder of the tape is searching for a pressing plant to convert the tapes into albums and a distributor to handle the heavy demand that there is likely to be." Apple announces that: "Such tapes could be in existence – but they (The Beatles) have no idea how they could come into the hands of a would-be bootlegger." Meanwhile EMI flatly reveal: "We know nothing about it." (The album referred to in the article is in fact the single album *Live At Shea '65*.)

Monday May 17
 Paul and Linda's album *Ram* is released in America. (The album is released in the UK on May 21.) EMI report 100,000 advance orders for the record and within one week of its release, the album will be named as the 'Best Selling Album of the Month'. On the right hand side of the front album cover there is a zigzag design which reads 'Lily' (Linda I Love You?) while on the back there is a curious picture of two beetles copulating! Paul spoke about the album: "Linda was present all the way through. We've been writing many more songs together and we're developing as a harmony team . . . I found this New York drummer named Denny and we just went to work the following Monday."
 Meanwhile in the States, John remarks about the track 'Uncle Albert – Admiral

Halsey': "I liked the beginning . . . I liked the little bit of 'Hands across the water', but it just tripped off all the time. I didn't like that bit."

Saturday May 22
 Chris Charlesworth, in his *Melody Maker* review of *Ram*, writes: "A good album by anybody's standards and certainly far better than the majority released by British groups and singers. Trouble is you expect too much from a man like Paul McCartney. It must be hell living up to a name . . ."

Thursday May 27
 It is announced today that Ringo is to star in the spaghetti western film *Blindman*, to be shot on location in Italy and in Almeria, Spain. The movie is produced by Allen Klein's ABKCO organisation and Ringo has been cast in the role of a vicious bandit. During the shooting, he is asked about the part: "I wanna be, like in this film, a crazy cowboy or whatever part I get. We're talking about me being an actor now, not being used for the name like I have been. In this film I really feel as if I'm acting."

June
 George visits Los Angeles to help Ravi Shankar record his album. It is during these sessions that the idea for the Bangladesh concert is conceived and by the end of the month plans for the show are nearly in place. During George's period in LA at Nichols Canyon, he writes the songs 'Miss O'Dell', influenced by the Apple employee Chris O'Dell, 'Be Here Now' and the track 'Tired Of Midnight Blue', recalling a visit to a seedy Los Angeles nightclub.

Tuesday June 1
 John records 'Do The Oz', released on a single with Bill Elliot's 'God Save Us'. The recording is credited to The Elastic Oz Band. For the latter, Elliot merely recorded his own vocal track over John's Ascot studio demo. Later in the day, John and Yoko board a plane to New York in an attempt to gain custody of Kyoko. "We're trying to locate her," Yoko hurriedly tells reporters at Heathrow Airport.

Thursday June 3
 For the first time in many years, without Yoko or any friends or groupies, John ventures out completely on his own at New York's 5th and 6th Avenue.

Sunday June 6
 At the start of the day, John and Yoko give an interview to the freelance American journalist Alex Bennett and then make a guest appearance on Howard Smith's radio talk show on station WPLJ. Then, at the insistence of the artist Andy Warhol, the Lennons perform live with Frank Zappa and The Mothers of Invention at New York's Fillmore East. Prior to their performance, the Lennons keep security tight by clearing the backstage area completely. Kip Cohen, the manager of the Fillmore, remarks: "It was like the Jews being driven from Amsterdam." Within ten minutes, the wings have cleared and the place is like a tomb, except for the second-floor dressing room where John and Yoko briefly rehearse with Zappa and his band, watched by the privileged few Fillmore 'hangers-on'. Then, coming on stage as part of the Zappa/Mothers encore, John and Yoko perform 'Well (Baby Please Don't Go)', 'Jamrag', 'Scumbag' and 'Au'. (Yoko arranges to have a movie camera capture the unique performance on 16mm colour film.) A member of the audience is heard to remark at the end of the show: "When The Mothers were on it was just another stage. With Lennon on it . . . the stage became something else; it became like a visitation!"

An audio of the performance is later released on the double-album *Sometime In New York City*. For the release, Klaus Voorman is later required to overdub the bass parts. (Incidentally, on October 27, 1992, re-mixed versions of these tracks, plus unreleased recordings such as: 'Say Please' and 'Aaawk' appear on the Frank Zappa CD album *Playground Psychotics*.)

Monday June 7
 In Italy, at the Cinecitta Studios in Rome, the ABKCO movie *Blindman*, co-starring Tony Anthony, begins production. (Ringo does not join the crew until June 17.) During

the ten-week shooting schedule, further location work will be carried out in Spain. The director of the western is Ferdinando Baldi.

Tuesday June 8 (until June 16)
🍎 Ringo joins an all-star cast that assembles in London to record with the American blues legend B.B. King who is visiting Britain. Other music luminaries present include Peter Green, Gary Wright, Bobby Keys, Jim Keltner and Alexis Korner. John, if he arrives back in the UK in time, has promised to join in on the recordings. (Unfortunately he does not.) The sessions continue until Wednesday June 16, when a crew from the BBC arrives to shoot film for a television documentary. (The recordings are later released on an album entitled B.B. King In London, released in the USA on October 11 this year and in the UK on November 19. Ringo appears on only three of the released tracks.)

Thursday June 10
🍎 Late this night, a strange unmarked parcel addressed to Paul McCartney is found at the BBC Bush House studios in Aldwych in London. Fearing it to be a bomb, BBC staff call out Scotland Yard who carefully open the parcel to find that it is none other than a present for Paul's upcoming birthday. The package contains crockery, wine glasses and a letter written in Spanish saying, "I love you".

Saturday June 12
🍎 The bootleg king of Britain, Jeffrey Collins, who runs a record shop in Chancery Lane, London, admits in the music press that he intends to issue a Beatles' double album entitled *Rock 'N' Roll*, featuring 20 tracks comprised mainly from the Sixties BBC radio series *Saturday Club*.

Wednesday June 16
🍎 In New York at Klein's offices at 1700, Broadway, John and George have a brief jam session during which John invites George to play on his next album, due to start recording in a week at his Tittenhurst Park mansion. The album will be called *Imagine*. George accepts the invitation and puts a phone call through to Klaus Voorman asking him if he too would like to play on the sessions.

Thursday June 17
🍎 John and Yoko arrive back in Britain at Heathrow Airport in London.

Monday June 21
🍎 John and Yoko, along with Led Zeppelin, Deep Purple, Jethro Tull and T.Rex among many others, lend their support to Edgar Broughton's Save A Life, an appeal in aid of the East Pakistani refugees in Bangladesh, which is launched in the *Daily Mirror* newspaper today.

Wednesday June 23
🍎 At his Tittenhurst Park studios in Ascot, John begins recording tracks for his new album *Imagine*. On the first morning he plays his new song to the other musicians which will turn out to be the title track of the album. Then, using an eight-track machine which the Lennons affectionately call ASS (Ascot Sound Studios), the recording sessions produce the following songs: 'Crippled Inside', 'Jealous Guy', 'It's So Hard', 'I Don't Want To Be A Soldier, I Don't Want To Die', 'Gimme Some Truth', 'Oh My Love', 'How Do You Sleep?', 'How' and 'Oh Yoko!'. (The sessions, which also include the unreleased track 'San Francisco Bay Blues', will continue until July 2.) Fearing legal problems with Paul, Klein advises John to severely tone down the lyrics to 'How Do You Sleep?'. During the recordings, an American man called Claudio has been seen hanging around the grounds surrounding the mansion and sleeping at night in the trees on the estate. John and Yoko, taking pity on him, invite him in for something to eat. This, as with most of John and Yoko's activities during the Seventies, including the *Imagine* recording sessions themselves, is captured on 16mm colour film. A documentary on the making of the *Imagine* album, entitled *Working Class Hero*, is proposed but is never released, although some of the footage is utilised in the 1988 documentary film *Imagine: John Lennon*.
  Incidentally, during the early stages of the *Imagine* recordings, John records the

earliest known demo of the track 'Aisemussen', while at the end of the sessions, on Friday July 2, John records a further demo of the track 'I'm The Greatest'. (A report on the *Imagine* recording sessions, written by Steve Peacock and Kieron Murphy, appears in an issue of the music paper *Sounds*.) This period of recording also produces tracks for Yoko's album *Fly*. These include: 'Airmale', 'Don't Count The Waves', 'Mrs. Lennon', 'O' Wind', 'Midsummer New York', 'Mind Train', 'Mind Holes', 'You' and the title track 'Fly'. To promote both the *Imagine* and *Fly* albums, John and Yoko produce, from 40,000 feet of film, a 70-minute film entitled *Imagine*, which features, on its soundtrack, a selection of tracks from both records. The completed film will be premiered on American TV on December 23, 1972, although the first clip from the film ('Gimme Some Truth') will actually be seen in Britain during an episode of BBC2's *The Old Grey Whistle Test*, transmitted on December 12, 1972. The first piece of shooting for the film takes place on July 6, (see entry).

"Did you know that George wanted to redo his guitar solos on 'Gimme Some Truth' and 'How Do You Sleep?' That's the best he's ever fucking played in his life! He'd never get that feeling again. He'd go on for ever if you let him." – John Lennon, June 1971.

Thursday June 24

🍎 While two of his former colleagues are at work on *Imagine* in England, Ringo is to be found in Scandinavia where he shoots his third and final appearance with Cilla Black for her Saturday night BBC1 variety show. Instead of her usual programmes, set in the confines of the BBC Television Theatre in London, the setting is Stockholm for her special production of *Cilla In Scandinavia*. Ringo is seen performing a unique version of 'It Don't Come Easy' (backed on the soundtrack by the 29-piece Ronnie Hazelhurst orchestra) up on the peak of a mountain. The programme, a joint production by the BBC in England and the European stations Sveriges-Radio-TV2, Norsk Riksringkasting and Oy Yleis Radio ABTV1, also features the unusual sight of Ringo singing the 'Snowman Song' with Cilla and Basil Brush, the puppet fox. With Ringo as a major guest on the show, Cilla gives the programme a Beatles flavour. She performs, in various locations in Norway, Sweden and Finland, covers of 'Norwegian Wood' with Marvin, Welch and Farrar, the new group featuring two of the former members of The Shadows, 'Drive My Car', and the perennial 'Step Inside Love'. The 45-minute programme is first transmitted on BBC1 over five months later on Saturday November 27 (between 9:04 and 9:49pm). Incidentally, Ringo's brief period filming the programme is marred when a chance conversation with Professor Thorolf Rafto is turned, without Ringo's knowledge or permission, into a major exclusive interview for a Norwegian newspaper.

July

🍎 George and Patti begin renting a house in Los Angeles, California, for a six month period, even though most of this time is spent in New York.

Saturday July 3

🍎 John and Yoko fly to New York where they conclude work on *Imagine* at the Record Plant. (The sessions resume tomorrow, July 4.)

🍎 Paul's album *Ram* reaches number one in the UK album charts.

🍎 George visits a New York television station to watch the recordings of an Ike and Tina Turner special featuring as special guests The Beach Boys. Strange rumours begin to circulate in the press that George, along with Keith Moon of The Who, will be joining The Beach Boys on their UK tour in November.

Sunday July 4 & Monday July 5

🍎 At the Record Plant in New York, working with Phil Spector and Allen Klein, John finishes 'It's So Hard', 'I Don't Want To Be A Soldier' and 'How Do You Sleep?' Joining them at the session is legendary sax player King Curtis who will be killed in a street fight just six weeks later. (These final recordings for *Imagine* are also mixed into quadraphonic sound.)

🍎 On the 4th, George and Patti attend a concert by Leon Russell at the Inglewood Forum, and on the 5th, George begins recording his next single 'Bangla Desh', coupled with 'Deep Blue'. He also spends time during the following week completing the soundtrack to the Apple film *Raga*. (George returns to Britain on July 12.)

Tuesday July 6

 The Beatles' second film *Help!* receives its British television premiere on BBC1 between 7:32 and 8:59pm. The screening is the first in a series of six Sixties pop films to be broadcast on the station. The weekly series, titled *Pop Go The Movies*, also includes: The Dave Clark Five in *Catch Us If You Can*, Freddie and The Dreamers in *Every Day's A Holiday*, Frank Ifield in *Up Jumped A Swagman*, Joe Brown in *What A Crazy World* and Billy Fury in *I've Gotta Horse*.

 In America celebrating both the end of the *Imagine* recording sessions and the birthday of Allen Klein's wife Betty, John and Yoko attend a garden party thrown by Klein at his New York home. Also present are Andy Warhol and Jonas Mekas, who captures the event on his home movie camera. (Excerpts appear accompanying 'Crippled Inside' in John and Yoko's 1972 film *Imagine*.) Miles Davis also attends, meeting John and Yoko for the first time. Miles asks him if Yoko is Japanese? "No", he replies. "She's a New Yorker." "Why didn't you marry a nice white bride?" Miles asks again. "That's what I thought she was!" John retorts. "They all said I was blind!" (Further filming for *Imagine* takes place on July 15.)

Friday July 9

 George and Patti visit Ike and Tina Turner in their dressing room after a Schaeffer Music Festival show in New York's Central Park.

Saturday July 10

 John, Yoko and Jerry Rubin visit a New York cinema on 3rd Avenue where they watch the Mike Nichols' film *Carnal Knowledge* starring Jack Nicholson, Art Garfunkel and Ann-Margaret. In the lobby at the theatre, they bump into Jonathan Cott of *Rolling Stone* magazine.

Sunday July 11

"I'll be in a group with John and George and Klaus and call it the Ladders or whatever you want to call it, but I don't think it would be called The Beatles." – Ringo.

 During a break from the filming of *Blindman* in Almeria, Spain, *Melody Maker* interviews Ringo for a three-part feature. Relaxing by the side of the hotel swimming pool, he talks frankly about a number of topics including The Beatles' unreleased music, their split, drugs and his thoughts on the current music of his three former colleagues.

MM: "Who's got all that (Beatles) stuff that wasn't released?"

Ringo: "It's around. Apple's got most of it. They can't release it unless we say. They can't just shove it out."

MM: "How much stuff would you say there was? How many tracks? Fifty or less?"

Ringo: "No, no, nowhere near that. I'd say there'd be 20 or 30 tracks at the most. I heard that there's enough material for another 25 years and all that, but you mustn't believe that rubbish."

MM: "What do you think of John's last album?"

Ringo: "Some of the tracks are just incredible."

MM: "What about *All Things Must Pass*?"

Ringo: "Well, George is sensational. There are so many great tracks on it, good tracks and so much work."

MM: "What about Paul's?"

Ringo: "I feel sad with Paul's albums because I believe he's a great artist, incredibly creative, incredibly clever but he disappoints me on his albums. I don't think there's one tune on the last one *Ram* . . . I just feel he's wasted his time, it's just the way I feel . . . he seems to be going strange."

MM: "Can you say when the first cracks appeared in The Beatles' set-up?"

Ringo: "I think on the *White* album. I left on the *White* album; I had to leave. I thought that the other three were together and I wasn't one of them, I was separate . . ."

MM: "How many (LSD) trips did you take in all?"

Ringo: "About nine . . . they were good and bad, some extremely bad, some extremely good."

(The interviews are published in *Melody Maker* on July 31, August 7 and 14.)

Monday July 12

 George calls a meeting at Apple in Saville Row and informs the members of Badfinger that he is returning to New York immediately to arrange a concert for the people of Bangladesh. He arrives in New York on Tuesday July 13 and meets up with John. As a favour for playing on his *Imagine* album, George asks John to appear at the concert. John agrees to think about it and returns immediately to England.

Wednesday July 14
 After flying into Heathrow Airport, John and Yoko attend a press conference in support of the *Oz* magazine obscenity trial. His brief version of 'The End Of The Road' during the conference is released as a flexi-disc included in the *Oz* magazine. John signs off as "Radio Free Widnes". Accompanying the Lennons on their journey is May Pang.

Thursday July 15
 Yoko signs copies of her book *Grapefruit* at Selfridges store in London. John is naturally in attendance. The event is filmed and excerpts will appear accompanying 'Gimme Some Truth' in their 1972 film *Imagine*. (The main bulk of filming for *Imagine* will begin on Wednesday July 21.)

"*Grapefruit* is a beautiful and profound book from the genius of one of the world's most important artists. In future, it will be used widely by people with time on their hands. It will help them to live." – John on Yoko's book *Grapefruit*.

Saturday July 17
 Today, in studio 1 at the BBC Television Centre in Wood Lane, London, John and Yoko make a guest appearance on the fifth edition of the late-night BBC1 chat show *Parkinson*, hosted by Michael Parkinson. For the benefit of the Lennons' private film archive, an aide takes film of John and Yoko arriving and entering the BBC building. Prior to the afternoon recording of the show, used primarily as a promotional vehicle for the book *Grapefruit*, the Lennons agree with Michael that if he mentions "The Beatles", he will have to conduct the rest of the interview inside a black bag! With that agreed, John and Yoko arrive on stage to an accompaniment of 'Help!' as performed by the resident studio house band, the Harry Stoneham Five.

From the start, Michael freely admits that he finds the *Grapefruit* book "incomprehensible!" Even though a large part of the early interview is directed towards Yoko, John naturally makes no end of attempts to join in. The conversation continues about Yoko's avant-garde work and their recent films.

Parkinson: "You've made a film about a fly crawling up a woman's body, you've made your famous *Bottoms* film and there's also been a film made of your penis, isn't there John?"

John: "That was a joke really." (Roars of laughter from the audience.) "I made a film called *Self Portrait*, you know, and at that time I was a bit of a prick!" (More laughter and this time applause, from the studio audience.)

Yoko reads extracts from her *Grapefruit* book before Michael asks about the alienation of the couple in England.

John: "The British press actually called her ugly. I've never seen that about any woman or man, even if the person is ugly. You don't normally say that in the papers. She's not ugly, and if she were you wouldn't be so mean! They even say attractive about the most awful looking people to be kind . . ."

Parkinson: "Recently, another reason for people taking a dislike to you, is because you're known again through the newspapers, as the woman who broke up The Beatles."

John (interrupting): "But that's not true! Listen, I tell ya, people on the streets and kids do not dislike us . . . It's the media; I'm telling ya. We go on the streets and the lorry drivers wave. 'Hello John, hello Yoko', all that jazz, and I judge it by that. My records still sell well. Her records sell all right."

Parkinson: "Did Yoko's presence put tension on the group?"

John: "The tension was already there you see . . . after Brian died."

With that, as he threatened, John instructs Michael to go inside a black bag.

"What do you want me in the black bag for, John?" Michael asks inquisitively.

"Because," John replies, "then it's total communication if you're in the black bag. Are you going to do that? And then we'll talk about The Beatles."

"Oh! All right, fine." Parkinson reluctantly agrees.

After a round of applause, the interview continues with Michael, completely out of sight from everyone, inside a large black bag!

John: "Imagine if a coloured guy, or a black guy went for a job, or that anybody who went for a job at the BBC had to wear a bag, then they wouldn't know what colour people were, and there'd be no prejudice for a kick-off."

"I'll tell you what," Parkinson replies, gasping for air, "they'd all fritter away 'cos it's red hot inside this bag!"

The "Beatles" conversation then resumes. Anticipating this, John is heard to mumble, "Big deal!"

Parkinson: "Why did you break up? What were the real reasons?"

(With Michael doing his best to ask the questions seriously in his own inimitable style, the audience again breaks out laughing at the bizarre events unfolding before their eyes.)

Yoko (interrupting): "The Beatles are four very talented young men and they're four very strong people, so I don't think I could have tried even to break them up."

John: "We broke ourselves up, you know."

Michael (himself now interrupting, hearing that John and Yoko were lighting up a cigarette): "I smoke too!" (He retorts!)

(Again the audience reacts by laughing uncontrollably.)

John: "When we was 28 or 29, it began to be 'What's the goal?' you know. We've made it! We'd become more talented and George began to write more songs. He was lucky to have a track on an album. The personalities have developed. They were a bit stifled in The Beatles. Between us now, we sell ten times more records than The Beatles did. Individually, if you add them all together we're doing far better than we were then."

John then allows Michael out of the bag . He is worried about the state of his hair.

"Your hair's fine," John remarks.

"One thing," Parkinson replies, "it proves it's not a wig!" Michael was now enjoying the fun of a most unusual interview.

John: "I never wanted them (The Beatles) to slide down and sort of make comebacks and things like that. I said, when I was 20 in The Beatles, that 'I'm not going to be singing 'She Loves You' when I'm 30!' Well, I was 30 this year and I didn't force it to happen. It just happened naturally. I guessed that by the time I was 30 I would have just grown out of it. And I have, you know . . ."

The 18-minute interview is followed by Marion Montgomery who, backed by the Harry Stoneham Five, performs a moving version of John's composition 'Love'. At the conclusion, John signals his approval by winking and giving her an "OK" sign. Although the broadcast still survives, the programme is no longer in the BBC film and VT library. The first repeated excerpts, albeit 13 seconds only, appear in the Lennons' 1972 *Imagine* film. Further clips reappear in America on Monday July 30, 1973, during the ABC TV programme *Geraldo Rivera: Goodnight America*, and then again during the 1988 Warner Brothers film *Imagine: John Lennon*. John and Yoko request their £100 appearance fee on *Parkinson* be made payable to "The *Oz* obscenity fund." The show (watched by Paul and Linda in their Cavendish Avenue, London, home) will be John's last ever interview for a UK TV show.

Monday July 19

 John and Yoko hold a press conference at Apple's headquarters in Saville Row, talking about Yoko's book *Grapefruit*. He informs reporters that: "The book was first published in a limited edition in 1964 and was republished last year. It sold 2,000 copies here and 50,000 in America." He adds, as a dig to some of the reporters who are smirking at the book, that . . . "it was taken seriously in the United States!" John then shifts tack by talking personally: "In England I'm regarded as the guy who won the pools. She's regarded as the lucky Jap who married the guy who won the pools. In America, we are both treated as artists." Yoko is then asked about the publication: "The idea of the book is that anyone can be an artist. The artist is a frame of mind. In New York they call it a toilet reading book." John then quips: "Yeah, that's the best place to read it!"

Tuesday July 20

 John and Yoko face the world's media in another press conference for *Grapefruit*, this time at the Lennon's spacious Tittenhurst Park mansion in Ascot. Due to the sheer volume of people present at this unique event, John and Yoko stipulate that, at the very most, they will spend no more than 15 minutes with each reporter/journalist.

Wednesday July 21 (until Friday July 23)

 Imagine filming – day one:
John and Yoko begin shooting the main bulk of footage for their 70-minute film Imagine, later described by critics as: "One of the most expensive home movies ever produced." With the aid of a helicopter whose rotor-blades touch tree tops, John and Yoko film scenes in their Ascot grounds involving their car and their boat on the lake. Also captured today, filmed at the house in the middle of the lake, is the unusual sequence where the couple are seen playing chess. Yoko flashes her leg and John eats the chess pieces.

Thursday July 22

 Imagine filming – day two:
The day begins very early with John and Yoko filming one of the most memorable sequences in their movie-making career. With the early morning mist still swirling round their Tittenhurst Park mansion, the Lennons are filmed walking up their path towards the entrance of the house, which has "This Is Not Here" written above the door. This scene will feature at the very start of the Imagine film and will serve as a wonderful opening to the 'Imagine' song itself. After four retakes, John and Yoko then film scenes, still in the mist, of themselves wandering around in their Ascot grounds. This sequence will be used to accompany the track 'Mrs. Lennon'. Later this afternoon, this time inside the mansion, film is taken of John seated at his white piano singing 'Imagine', while Yoko goes around opening the shutters of his music room, letting in the daylight. In the afternoon, filming of Imagine continues with John, wearing a blindfold, and Yoko playing billiards. Then, film is shot of Yoko during a photo session. Later, with most of the shooting now complete, John sits for the photograph, which will appear on the Imagine album cover, an event also included in the film. The day ends with Yoko giving John a haircut which, somewhat surprisingly, is not captured on film.

Friday July 23

 Imagine filming – day three:
The final day of the Imagine/Ascot filming begins with Yoko sitting up in bed reading the morning papers while John is seen going to the toilet. Respecting no limits to what they can or cannot film, the Lennons leave the cameras rolling while they have fun in the bathtub. (The next scenes for Imagine are filmed on Wednesday August 11.)

Saturday July 24

 Denny Laine, currently working on a solo album of his own and contemplating going back on the road, receives a phone call from Paul asking if he would be interested in working with him. Paul: "I remembered Denny Laine, ex-Moody Blues and Balls. I'd known him in the past and I just rang him and asked him, 'What are you doing?' He said, 'Nothing', so I said, 'Right. Come on then!' " Denny immediately scraps plans for his album and heads for London.

 John and Yoko again travel to the Virgin Islands where a judge grants them an order giving them the right to bring up Kyoko, on the provision that they allow Anthony Cox reasonable access to the child. One problem still remains: John and Yoko do not know where Kyoko is. Private investigators, hired by the couple, inform them they believe she is currently in America.

Sunday July 25 (until Wednesday July 28)

 Paul holds a top-secret session in studio two on July 27. Security on the first night is so strict that he even forbids EMI staff entry to the building. When the music press find out about these get-togethers, Shelley Turner, Paul's assistant, briefly remarks: "Paul is very happy with the band and with the tapes they made." Following the conclusion of the recordings on the evening of the 28th, Paul and Linda prepare to take a three-day holiday in the Mediterranean. But in New York there's bad news for the couple when they are told, shortly before their departure, that Northern Songs Ltd, of Great Britain, and MacLen Music Inc, of New York, are suing the couple for $1,050,000 (approximately £437,000). They claim that the McCartneys have violated an "exclusive rights agreement" for their song 'Another Day'.

Monday July 26
In New York, the first rehearsals for the Concert For Bangla Desh take place at the Nola Studios facility on West 57th Street. Scheduled to appear so far are just George and Klaus Voorman, but during the day Badfinger fly into New York's Kennedy Airport from London and join in on the rehearsals. Eric Clapton, meanwhile, already invited by George to appear, is feeling none too well and asks Ringo if he will be willing to deputise for him in case he is forced to drop out. As the days progress, George spends hours constantly phoning other musicians, hoping to persuade them to appear in the show.

Tuesday July 27
George and Ravi hold a press conference to announce the Concert For Bangla Desh this Sunday at New York's Madison Square Garden. Before a large crowd of journalists and reporters, George tries to tell them of his nervousness about performing solo at the concert. But this is quickly dismissed when a reporter asks him about The Beatles: "Are there ever times when you wish you were back together again as a group?" "Yeah," he replies, "there are times. But there are times also when we all appreciate not being together." The reporter asks why? But George is having none of this Beatles talk and retorts, "Shouldn't we talk about the (Bangla Desh) concert?"
An interview with John and Yoko by Sue Faulconbridge, carried out in Ascot on July 20, is published in today's *Liverpool Echo*. "You can no longer consider John Ono Lennon apart from Yoko Ono Lennon – they are, if you like, one person . . ."

Wednesday July 28
George's single 'Bangla Desh'/'Deep Blue' is released in America. (The UK release takes place on July 30.) The B-side is about the death of George's mother a year ago.

Friday July 30
Former Apple employee Richard DiLelo, author of the book *The Longest Cocktail Party*, visits George at the Park Lane Hotel in New York and informs him that he is writing a book about The Beatles. George replies: "Well, it's only just the beginning!" Later, only two days before the Bangla Desh concert, Leon Russell arrives.

Saturday July 31
John tells *New Musical Express*: "The thing with Paul is he wants all the action. He wants it all. It's not just the money; it's the principle. I think, for instance, that Paul's cost us probably over a million since he started this thing . . . It's like Monopoly, only with real money . . . and costing us a fortune."
George meanwhile is proceeding with the Bangla Desh show, happy in the knowledge that Bob Dylan has agreed to perform. Later this night, at Madison Square Garden, the final rehearsal for tomorrow's concert takes place.

August
John asks the photographer Iain MacMillan to begin taking regular still photographs of the construction of the London International Hotel, near Heathrow Airport, from one location only. These pictures will be compiled to form the 17-minute film *Erection*. Featured on the soundtrack is Yoko's track 'Airmale'. One of its first screenings, albeit brief, will take place on *The Dick Cavett Show*, transmitted by ABC TV in America on September 12.
Short clips of Paul performing 'Bip Bop' and 'Hey Diddle' are filmed during this period. They will first be seen in the 73-minute *Wings Over The World* 1979 television special, first broadcast on CBS TV in America on March 16, 1979.
During the month, Ringo completes the filming of *Blindman*, which is premiered in Rome on November 15. Unfortunately, due to its excessive violence, the film will run into problems with the British film censors. This month, also in Rome, Ringo records the title track of the film.

Sunday August 1
George and Ringo appear twice (afternoon and evening) at the Concert For Bangla Desh, held at Madison Square Garden in New York in front of two capacity 20,000 crowds. Also appearing are Bob Dylan, Eric Clapton, Billy Preston, Klaus Voorman, Leon Russell, Ravi Shankar and members of Badfinger. During the concert George performs:

'Wah-Wah', 'My Sweet Lord', 'Awaiting On You All', 'Beware Of Darkness' (with Russell), 'While My Guitar Gently Weeps', 'Here Comes The Sun', 'Something' and 'Bangla Desh'. Ringo performs 'It Don't Come Easy'. Outside the venue, touts are seen getting between $50 and $600 for one single $7.50 ticket.

"There was no rioting. Not one policeman was allowed in there . . . Zero! I would allow none. No one was allowed backstage, nobody, no hangers-on, nothing. It was the best show that there ever was!" – Allen Klein, following the Bangla Desh concert.

"I thought the beauty of the concert was that it was so rushed and so spontaneous . . ." – George, following the concert.

Following the concert, a celebrity party is held at the New York City night spot Ungano's. Also in attendance are The Who, currently in the city and two dates into their 1971 American tour. The star-studded line-up is treated to a live performance by George and Billy Preston and then Phil Spector, who delivers a unique version of 'Da Do Ron Ron'. This features Keith Moon on drums who, at the conclusion of the song, spectacularly kicks the drum kit (belonging to Badfinger) into the crowd.

First estimates predict that a total of £100,000 will be raised from the two Bangla Desh concerts and that four times this figure will be made from sales of the concert record alone. Most of the evening concert will appear on the album *The Concert For Bangla Desh*, released in America on December 20 and in the UK on January 7, 1972. Phil Spector carries out recordings with 44 microphones, using a Wally Heider sixteen-track machine borrowed from the nearby Record Plant Studios. The film version of the concert, directed by Sol Swimmer, who previously directed the ABKCO films *Come Together* and *Blindman*, is suitably titled *The Concert For Bangla Desh* and will premiere in New York on March 23, 1972 and in the UK on July 26, 1972. Incidentally, Peter Frampton, the former lead singer of the Herd, takes a private colour 8mm film of the shows.

George recalls the concerts this day, in particular the fact that Bob Dylan almost didn't appear: "It took me three months on the telephone really, day and night, just trying to con everybody into doing it, like Dylan. He was very difficult to get because he had been laid up for years and he had just done the one show, in the Isle of Wight in 1969. He was not feeling that strong about doing it (the Bangla Desh show), because he had been out of it so long. In fact, right up until the moment he stepped on stage I was not sure that he was coming! I had a little list on my guitar which had a point where it said . . . after 'Here Comes The Sun', just Bob with a question mark. And when it got to that point I turned round to see if Bob was coming, because the night before, we went to Madison Square Garden and he freaked out. He saw all these cameras and microphones and this huge place and he was saying, 'Hey man, this isn't my scene. I can't make this.' And I was saying, 'Look, it's not my scene either man. I don't do this every day . . . this is the first time I have ever done anything on my own. You, at least, have been a solo artist for years.' I was just tired of trying to organise the whole thing. He was saying, 'I've got to get back to Long Island. I've got a lot of business to attend to.' So, on stage, I just looked round to see if there was any indication if Bob was going to come on, or not, and he was already there. He was so nervous and he had his harmonica on and his guitar in his hand and he was walking right onto the stage. It was like now or never, and so I had to say, 'Like to bring on a friend of us all . . . Mr. Bob Dylan.'"

Later Ravi Shankar tells the story behind the shows: "It was completely my idea. I was very disturbed about the happenings, because I am a Bengali, and my father and family came from that area and I was getting a lot of sad news. I told George that I wanted to do something in a big way so that we could raise a lot of money. I knew he wouldn't be able to participate himself, but I thought he could ask some of his friends. He was very moved at that moment and so he also wrote the song 'Bangla Desh' and said he would participate himself, which was a great surprise and made me very happy. It was a historic evening!"

When asked about the shows, Ringo said: "I enjoyed playing immensely. It was a bit weird, because it was the first time I had been on stage for about three years. I was crazy with nerves beforehand. But if you have done your job, it's okay. You soon relax. It was nice, anyway, because we had a lot of good pals around. We weren't out just to entertain each other, we wanted to entertain the twenty five thousand who had paid to come in. It is no good just standing there with your guitar and freaking yourself out. What is the point?"

A subsequent rumour concerning John's non-appearance at the Bangla Desh concert suggests that George didn't want Yoko to sing, so John replied by saying, 'If Yoko can't play neither can I' and that when John tells Yoko of George's decision, the couple had a row. John then flew to Paris while Yoko returned to England.

However, only a few weeks after the show, John told a different story: "Allen Klein was putting it around that I had run off to England so I couldn't be there for the concert. But I told George a week before the show that I wouldn't be doing it. I just didn't feel like it. We were in the Virgin Islands and I certainly wasn't going to be rehearsing in New York, then going back to the Virgin Islands, then coming back up to New York and singing."

Incidentally, a plan by Lord Harlech, the British politician, to stage a Bangla Desh style concert at Wembley Stadium is soon quashed by both George and Klein, but on Saturday September 18 at the Oval Cricket Ground in Kennington, South London, an all-day English concert to raise money for the Bangladesh relief fund is staged before a crowd of 30,000 fans. It features performances by Cochise, The Grease Band, Lindisfarne, Quintessence, Mott The Hoople, America, Atomic Rooster, The Faces and, topping the bill, The Who.

Monday August 2
🍎 Paul and Linda's single 'Uncle Albert – Admiral Halsey'/ 'Too Many People' is released in the US. Meanwhile, the second rehearsals for Paul's new band take place today at his farmhouse in Campbeltown, Scotland, where they begin recording songs intended for the album *Wild Life*. The sessions produce the following tracks: 'Mumbo', 'Bip Bop', 'Love Is Strange', 'Wild Life', 'Some People Never Know', 'I Am Your Singer', 'Tomorrow' and 'Bip Bop' (reprise). They also record the unreleased tracks 'Tragedy' and 'Breakfast Blues', a blues instrumental that will receive a rare airing on the New York radio station WCBS-FM during December.

🍎 In New York, still enthused by the previous evening's performance, George writes the song 'The Day The World Gets Round' and Ravi gives an interview in his hotel room to *Rolling Stone* magazine. Later in the day, George and Phil Spector begin a week of all-night sessions on the *Bangla Desh* album. At this stage, the proposed release date of the record is August 15.

Tuesday August 3
🍎 Pleased by the sessions with his new group, Paul announces to the press that he has formed a new band consisting of himself, Linda, drummer Denny Seiwell and the former Moody Blues guitarist Denny Laine. They still do not have a name.

Saturday August 7
🍎 *NME* describe The Concert For Bangla Desh as "The Greatest Rock Spectacle Of The Decade!"

🍎 In the *Melody Maker*, Norman Wright of Hull writes: "I have purchased a copy of the bootleg *Live At Shea '65* Beatles album and for £3.00 I received less than 29 minutes of playing time which by normal standards is of dismal quality. It's about time The Beatles swallowed their pride and allowed the release of material not yet available – no matter what the standard of their playing or recording quality." (The letter is read in New York by John who promptly puts pen to paper.)

Wednesday August 11
🍎 John and Yoko are among 1,000 protesters taking part in a demonstration march past the Ulster Offices in London. The protest is against British policy towards Northern Ireland and the prosecution of the editors of *Oz* magazine on obscenity charges. (Footage from this demonstration later appears during the 'Power To The People'/ 'Gimme Some Truth' sequence in the 1972 *Imagine* film.) Meanwhile, back in England, five of John and Yoko's films are screened during the London Art Spectrum at the Alexandra Palace. They are *Cold Turkey* (1969), *The Ballad Of John And Yoko* (1969), *Give Peace A Chance* (1969), *Instant Karma* (*Top Of The Pops* – transmitted February 12, 1970) and *Up Your Legs Forever* (1970). (The show runs until August 13.)

Thursday August 12
🍎 A cheque to the value of just over $243,418, covering the proceeds from the Bangladesh concerts on August 1, is sent by Madison Square Garden Inc. to UNICEF.

🍎 Meanwhile in England, John and Yoko are also handing out money, this time a donation of £1,000 towards the UCS (United Clyde Shipbuilders) Fighting Funds in York. The shipbuilders are currently fighting a pay dispute. As a goodwill gesture, last week John and Yoko had sent a bunch of flowers.

Friday August 13

🍎 Paul and Linda's single 'Back Seat Of My Car'/ 'Heart Of The Country' is released in the UK, where it reaches number 39 in the singles charts.

🍎 John and Yoko return to New York and again take up residence at the St. Regis Hotel. They return to England on the 16th. Meanwhile in London, at the NFT (the National Film Theatre) on the South Bank, the films of John and Yoko are featured in a special presentation.

Saturday August 14

🍎 *Melody Maker* publishes a letter by John, replying to last week's letter regarding the *Live At Shea '65* bootleg album: "Dear Norman Wright, c/o *MM*, Why buy the bootleg in the first place? You must have read how bad they are before now. Anyway, the reason we haven't released the old stuff is because we haven't got round to remixing it yet. That's all folks. Love John & Yoko, in lieu of Beatles . . . LP winner (I'd like Chuck Berry, please.)"

Thursday August 19

🍎 Another Beatles related bootleg album appears on the market, this time *Gulp!*, featuring, among many other highlights, John's performance of 'Yer Blues' at the 1968 *Rolling Stones Rock 'N' Roll Circus*. The album retails at £2.75.

Saturday August 21

🍎 *Melody Maker* publishes the first part of a two-part interview with The Beatles' producer George Martin.

MM: "What was wrong with Pete Best?"

Martin: "He never joined in with the others. He was always a bit quiet, almost surly. But the basic thing was that I didn't like his drumming. It wasn't very sound and he didn't bind the group together."

🍎 Martin's recollection of the song 'Please Please Me' does not please John, and again he is forced to put pen to paper. (See entry for August 28.)

Monday August 23

🍎 The release of the *Concert For Bangla Desh* live album is delayed by various legal problems. The title for the record being brandished about now is *George Harrison And Friends*.

Saturday August 28

🍎 Scribbled on the back of one of Yoko's "A hole to see the sky" postcards, *Melody Maker* publishes John's reply to the George Martin article in the previous week's edition of the paper.

"Dear George Martin (Richard Williams), I wrote 'Please Please Me' alone. It was recorded in the exact sequence in which I wrote it. Remember?
Love John & Yoko. LP winner!"

🍎 Meanwhile, the paper continues unperturbed with the second part of the exclusive George Martin interview.

MM: "John recently said something about you: 'Show me some of George Martin's music. I'd like to hear some.' How do you feel when one of them says something like that about you?"

Martin: "That's silly of course. I guess I feel sorry for him, because obviously he's a schizophrenic in that respect. He must have a split mind . . . either he doesn't mean it, or if he does mean it he can't be in a normal state of mind at the time."

MM: "Could you tell me what you think of what each one has done since the last Beatles record?"

Martin: "I have admiration for George. He's done tremendously because it's a sort of devotion to duty as far as he's concerned. We forced him into being a loner I guess . . . John's become more obvious in a way . . . 'Power To The People' is a rehash of 'Give Peace A Chance' and it isn't really very good. It doesn't have the intensity that John's capable of. Paul, similarly, with his first album. It was nice enough, but very much a home-made affair . . . I don't think Linda is a substitute for John Lennon, any more than Yoko is a substitute for Paul McCartney."

Again, John reads the article and is enraged by Martin's comments. Another letter is duly sent in reply and is published on September 25 – see entry.

Sunday August 29

◄ An article entitled *Yoko: The Film Maker*, by Henry Edwards, appears in today's edition of the paper *Crawdaddy!*

Monday August 30

◄ John invites the *Sounds* journalist Kieron Murphy back to Tittenhurst Park to hear the finished version of the album *Imagine*.

Tuesday August 31

◄ John and Yoko depart from London's Heathrow Airport en route for America and take up a more permanent residence on the 12th floor in rooms 1701, 1702 and 1703 of the St. Regis Hotel in New York. Again, their aim is to gain custody of Kyoko and, should they be unsuccessful, pursue Anthony Cox through the US courts. Lawyers representing Yoko suggest to her that to secure her custody rights, she and John must take up permanent residence in the States. Although he wasn't to know it at the time, John would never again return to his native country.

John: "Yoko and I were forever coming and going to New York, so finally we decided it would be cheaper and more functional to actually live here . . . so that's what we did!"

September

◄ Paul's brother-in-law John Eastman negotiates with both CBS and NBC for an American TV musical special featuring Paul.
◄ Ringo records the song 'Back Off Boogaloo'.

Wednesday September 1

◄ Earlier this morning, Paul and Linda, now heavily pregnant, come out of hiding and are seen walking in Carlisle Street in West London.

Friday September 3

◄ Ringo and Robin Cruikshank officially form the furniture Design Company Ringo O' Robin Ltd.

Saturday September 4

◄ Paul and Linda's single 'Uncle Albert – Admiral Halsey' reaches number one in the US charts.

Sunday September 5

◄ Still in their St. Regis Hotel room, the Lennons give an interview to Peter McCabe and Robert Schonfeld.

Question (about George): "He's perhaps the most enigmatic Beatle. Are you saying George is more conventional than he makes himself out to be?"

John: "There's no telling George. He always has a point of view . . . you can't tell him anything. He's very trendy and he has the right clothes and all that . . ."

Yoko (interrupting): "But he's not sophisticated, intellectually."

John: "No. He's very narrow-minded and he doesn't really have a broader view. Paul is far more aware than George, one time in the Apple offices in Wigmore Street, I said something to George and he said, 'I'm as intelligent as you, you know.'"

Peter McCabe and Robert D. Schonfeld will later write the 1972 book *Apple To The Core*. John's complete interview with McCabe and Schonfeld will not be published until 1984 when it appears in the book *John Lennon: For The Record*.

Monday September 6

◄ In their St. Regis Hotel room, John and Yoko continue with their *Imagine* filming activities by shooting scenes with the legendary Hollywood dancer Fred Astaire, the American actor Jack Palance and the American chat show host Dick Cavett, who all just happen to be staying in the hotel. Invited along to appear by May Pang, they all happily participate in scenes which include them individually, arm in arm with Yoko, entering their hotel room and walking over to the window. (Although a quite simple piece to act out, Astaire, a true professional, insists that he "can do the scene better", and requests a retake.) George, back in New York for work on the Bangla Desh concert film, is also beckoned up to the room to shoot the scene. (Much of the *Imagine* filming had already been completed in England during July. See entries for July 21-23.) Following his brief scene, Cavett requests that the couple join him as guests on his talk show. A recording date is immediately arranged for September 8.

Wednesday September 8

◆ In New York, at the television studios of ABC TV, John and Yoko record their first appearance on *The Dick Cavett Show*. (The programme will be transmitted on September 12.) The Lennons chain-smoke throughout the 90-minute interview where, at one point, John looks up to the camera and jokes: "Didn't work did it, Arthur?" This was a reference to the fact that their four-month primal scream therapy last year with Janov was supposed to cure their addiction to nicotine. The general light-hearted conversation contains some unique play-offs between John and the host.

John: "Ella Fitzgerald dear Watson . . . that's a pun on elementary."
Cavett: "That's known as word play."
John: "Yes, I'm always playing with myself!"
Then on a more serious note . . .
Cavett: "Yoko, you've even been called the dragon lady who broke The Beatles apart."
Yoko: "Yes."
John (instantly defending): "Well, if she took us apart, can we please give her the credit for all the nice music that George made, Ringo made, Paul made and I've made since they broke up!"
Yoko: "It turned out all right, didn't it?"
John (continuing): "Anyway, she didn't split The Beatles. How can one girl split The Beatles, or one woman, y'know? The Beatles were drifting apart on their own!"
Cavett: "Can you remember when you realised it was inevitable that you thought that you'd split up?"
John: "No. It's just like saying do you remember falling in love. It just sort of happens."

The "black bag" idea is resurrected when two friends (one of which is May Pang) appear on the set. This prompts John to recall the incident when the black bag conception was used on BBC TV's *Parkinson* in July.

"We did a talk show in England and every time the man wanted to talk about 'Beatles', because I'm fed up talking about them, I asked him to go in a bag and he did it. The interviewer, the Dick Cavett of England, he was in the bag all the time, so every time the cameras panned to him, the audience broke up, so he could never get the questions out. It was a very good show!"

To compensate for the fact that John and Yoko will not be performing on the show, they bring along with them excerpts from the film *Imagine* ('Mrs. Lennon' and 'Imagine' itself), *Erection* and *Fly*. John concludes the show by announcing that they will be going out on the road next year with a band. One viewer of the show in New York is George Harrison. (The Lennons will return to *The Dick Cavett Show* on May 5, 1972.)

After the final credits for the programme roll, and the audience stop clapping, John and Yoko decide that they would like to carry on talking. Besides resuming a conversation with Cavett, John and Yoko also take questions from the studio audience, on topics including John's songwriting and whether or not drugs effected it. Yoko is also asked her opinions about the overpopulation of the world. This sequence is included in the show transmitted on September 19.

Following the broadcast, critics are quick to attack the show, saying John and Yoko "annoyed most of the watchers by spending 90 minutes plugging everything they had ever done or ever hoped to do. There was very little conversation; instead viewers were treated to excerpts from films and albums the couple have done separately and together." The controversy continues the following day when American radio airs complaints about the show. Listeners voice their opinions, saying that the constant plugging of the Lennons' products made them feel that they were "being taken for a ride".

Incidentally, a clip from the show where John recalls the writing of the song 'Imagine' later appears in the 1994 Tom Hanks film *Forrest Gump*.

Thursday September 9

◆ John's album *Imagine* is released in America. (The UK release takes place on October 8.)

John answers questions about 'How Do You Sleep?':

"The song isn't only about Paul, it's a song in its own right anyway, you know . . ."

Reporter: "Paul said, 'How can he make the quarrel so public?' "

John: "Oh hells, bells . . . listen to *Ram* folks! The lyrics weren't printed, just listen to it. I'm answering *Ram*. When I heard *Ram*, I immediately sat down and wrote my song which is an answer to *Ram*. It's as simple as that. It's also a moment's anger. But it was written down on paper and when I sang, it wasn't quite as angry as when I sang it in the studio, because it was four weeks later and we were all writing it, you know. It was like a joke. 'Let's write this down.' We didn't take it that seriously."

🍎 Meanwhile in England, due to a last minute problem with clearance, a clip of George performing 'Bangla Desh' during the August 1 show, is not included in tonight's edition of *Top Of The Pops* on BBC1. The show's producer Stan Appel announces: "We only heard from Apple yesterday morning saying that we couldn't use it." PR Les Perrin, on behalf of George, reveals: "He didn't want the film of the concert going out before it is properly edited." The song is still included in the broadcast, however, accompanied by BBC film of an Indian dancer.

Friday September 10

🍎 The Lennons begin recording the soundtrack for their unreleased film *Clock* in their room at the St. Regis Hotel in New York. The short film includes on the soundtrack John's unreleased versions of 'Glad All Over', 'Heartbeat', 'Honey Don't', 'J.J. (Angela)', 'Lend Me Your Comb', 'Mailman, Bring Me No More Blues', 'Maybe Baby', 'New York City', 'Not Fade Away', 'Peggy Sue' (2 takes),'Peggy Sue Got Married', 'Send Me Some Lovin' ', and 'Shazam!' The film is premiered at Yoko's Syracuse art exhibit on October 9, John's 31st birthday. He also commits to tape a demo of the song 'Just Give Me Some Rock 'n' Roll'.

Saturday September 11

🍎 George's single 'Bangla Desh' reaches number 10 in the UK charts and number 23 in America.

Monday September 13

🍎 Paul and Linda's second child, Stella Nina McCartney, is born at the King's College Hospital in London. As with the birth of Mary a year previously, Paul had moved into the hospital to be at Linda's side. Unfortunately, due to slight complications, Stella has to be delivered by Caesarean section and Paul is naturally barred from the operating theatre. Paul recalls the time: "I sat next door in my green apron praying like mad . . . the name Wings just came into my head." Linda maintains he was thinking about "Wings of an angel". Paul had briefly toyed with the idea of calling his new group Turpentine, but was persuaded from doing so by a 79-year-old Beatles/McCartney fan.

🍎 At the opening of Liberty's new "modern-day" furniture department, on the third-floor of their store in Regent Street, London, a new range of Ringo O'Robin designs is unveiled. These include a stainless steel dining table (costing £45), a Cylinder of Sound, containing hi-fi equipment (£2,000), Ringo's own design for a fireplace (£350) and two Rolls Royce radiators used as supports for a stainless steel table top (£1,200).

Wednesday September 22

🍎 George and Patti return from New York aboard the *QE2*. Joining them on the journey is their musician friend, Gary Wright.

Saturday September 25

🍎 Another of John's letters responding to the two-part George Martin interview in *Melody Maker* (published on August 21 and 28) is published.

From his St. Regis Hotel room, John rants: "I don't see anything 'schizoid' in having more than one emotion though you obviously do. When people ask me questions about, 'What did George Martin really do for you?' I have only one answer, 'What does he do now?' "

In addition, on the subject of 'Revolution 9', John states: "It was purely my concept, fully. For Martin to say that he was 'painting a sound picture' is pure hallucination. Ask any of the other people involved. The final editing Yoko and myself did alone (which took four hours). Of course, Martin was a great help in translating our music technically when we needed it, but for the cameraman to take credit from the director is a bit too much . . ."

John then turns his attentions to the song 'Eleanor Rigby': "At least 50 per cent of the lyrics of 'Eleanor Rigby' were written by me in the studios and at Paul's place, a fact never clearly indicated in your previous article.

"PPPPPS 'LP winner'. Right on Johnnie Boy!"

Thursday September 30

🍎 George is the only ex-Beatle in attendance at a party to celebrate the opening of Apple's new £500,000 recording studio based at their headquarters at 3 Saville Row in London. Again, outside the building, the ever-faithful Apple Scruffs are in attendance. At the gathering, George tells journalists of how this grand opening is tinged with sadness: "It's a bit sad now that Apple is in the position all four of us planned three years ago. I just wish Paul would use the studio if he wants to. It's silly not to." But he admits: "I can't see the four of us working together again, but I'd like us to be friends. We all own the business and it's doing well. I'd like all four of us to enjoy it now."

During the first month of business at the studio, Ringo plays drums on sessions for the new Apple duo Lon and Derek Vaneaton, and George produces albums for Badfinger and Fanny. Promotional brochures, given away at the launch, indicate that the studio is available at £37 per hour for 16-track recording and £31 an hour for 8-track.

October

🍎 During the first part of the month, still in residence at the St. Regis Hotel, John again spends time committing to tape various demos. This month he is quoted as saying: "I keep reading about Paul being the brilliant melody writer and George being the philosopher. So where does that leave me? Yes, that's right . . . the nut!"

Friday October 1

🍎 In London, George meets Patrick Jenkins MP, the Chancellor of the Exchequer, in an effort to try to get the purchase tax due on every copy of the *Bangla Desh* album sold scrapped. But the meeting does not go well, when Jenkins tells George: "Sorry! It is all very well for your high ideals, but Britain equally needs the money!"

Saturday October 2

🍎 George and Patti return to New York, sailing aboard the luxury liner SS *France*, as used by Paul last October.

Tuesday October 5

🍎 To combat the bootleg albums of the Bangla Desh concert currently appearing in New York, George, in a statement to the press, announces that Apple will now release the triple-album next month, a month ahead of schedule. Meanwhile in protest at the bootleg copies of the *Bangla Desh* album, posters are being put up in record shops proclaiming: "Save A Starving Child, Don't Buy A Bootleg!"

Friday October 8

🍎 At 2pm, John and Yoko hold a press conference at the Everson Museum of Art in Syracuse, New York, to announce Yoko's art exhibition This Is Not Here which is due to open to the public tomorrow and will run until October 27. (As per normal, the Lennons film the press conference.) Even before the show had opened, New York critics were sharpening their knives in anticipation of what Yoko has to offer, writing unflattering lines like: "Yoko's exhibits promise to be about as artistic as a rusty piece of plumbing in the sodden debris of the city dumps." Knowing that she would be in for a torrid time with the notoriously hard to please New York art critics, John and Yoko go to the extraordinary length of chartering a plane to carry an assortment of 65 critics, journalists and members of the avant-garde circle from New York City to Syracuse to preview the show. As the conference gets under way, Yoko explains: "In this show, I'd like to prove you don't need talent to be an artist. Artist is just a frame of mind. Anybody can be an artist. Anybody can communicate if they're desperate enough."

🍎 Besides Yoko's pieces, a number of celebrities contributed exhibits to be put on display. Ringo sent a green plastic bag, the size of two pillows, that looks as if it is filled with green water. George's piece, entitled Milk Bottle, is listed in the show's catalogue but fails to be put on display. Bob Dylan sent over a copy of his 1969 *Nashville Skyline* record minus the sleeve, and John's piece is a strange pink mass inside a plastic bag, curiously called Napoleon's Bladder. The museum's bookshop offers for sale souvenir *Imagine* and *Fly* T-shirts, John and Yoko albums and copies of the *Grapefruit* book.

Saturday October 9

🍎 On John's 31st birthday, Yoko's art exhibition This Is Not Here opens to the general public at the Everson Museum. The show, a 10 year retrospective look at her career which is billed as "A show of unfinished paintings and sculpture", is taped and broadcast on American TV on May 11, 1972, as a programme suitably called *John And Yoko In Syracuse, New York*. (The show runs until October 27.) Guests in attendance include Ringo and Maureen, Allen Klein, Phil Spector, Dick Cavett, John Cage, Bob Dylan, Dennis Hopper, Spike Milligan, Jack Nicholson, Andy Warhol and Frank Zappa. Even though it was his birthday, John gives everyone a silver zodiac necklace as a present. The Lennons make a seven-minute feature of the exhibition entitled *The Museum Of Modern Art Show*.

Later this night, in a Syracuse hotel room, an all-star jam session celebrating John's birthday takes place. They are joined by Klaus Voorman, Allen Ginsberg, Jim Keltner, Mal Evans, Neil Aspinall and Eric Clapton. A tape of the party is made which features the group performing: 'What'd I Say', 'Yellow Submarine' (naturally sung by Ringo), 'On Top Of Old Smokey', 'Goodnight Irene', 'Take This Hammer','He's Got The Whole World In His Hands', 'Like A Rolling Stone', a medley of 'Twist And Shout', 'Louie, Louie' and 'La Bamba', 'Bring It On Home To Me', 'Yesterday', 'Tandoori Chicken', 'Power To The People', 'Maybe Baby', 'Peggy Sue', 'Bring Out The Joints' (a Lennon/Spector original), 'My Baby Left Me', 'Heartbreak Hotel', 'Blue Suede Shoes', 'Crippled Inside', 'Give Peace A Chance', 'Crippled Inside' (reprise), Paul's 'Uncle Albert – Admiral Halsey', George's 'My Sweet Lord','Imagine' and 'Oh Yoko'. During the party, a Japanese journalist interviews John and Yoko, part of which is aired on *The Lost Lennon Tapes* American radio series. The item is aptly called *The Argument Interview*, due to an unusual degree of acrimony between the two during the proceedings.

🍎 In Britain, the music press finally reveals that Paul's new band will be called Wings. Reports also suggest that the group are "rehearsing for live appearances later this year".

Monday October 11

🍎 John's single 'Imagine'/'It's So Hard' is released in America.

Thursday October 14

🍎 John and Yoko appear on the public broadcast television show *Free Time,* transmitted on the New York public TV station WNET TV.

🍎 In the UK, it is announced that a documentary on The Beatles, tracking the group's history from the Cavern Club in Liverpool to their eventual break-up, is to be made for BBC Radio One and scheduled for transmission next March.

Saturday October 16

🍎 John and Yoko take up residence at their new New York premises, a two-room apartment at 105 Bank Street in Greenwich Village, owned by Joe Butler, the former drummer with the sixties American group The Lovin' Spoonful. There are two large rooms, one of which is bought while the other is rented, and a wrought-iron staircase, which runs up to a small roof garden. Their neighbours include John Cage, Bob Dylan and Jerry Rubin.

Soon after taking up residence John and Yoko purchase a couple of bicycles. (John's is English, while Yoko's is Japanese. They are quick to point out that this was not intended.) Asked about this form of transport, John replies: "Everybody cycles round the village. Dylan goes on his all the time, chaining it to the railings when he stops and nobody ever recognises him. I can't wait to get out on mine."

A reporter naturally asks why he and Yoko decided to live there: "It's the best place to live in the world," John explains. "Every time the car leaves the village, I feel sick. Going back to England is like going to Denmark – and I don't want to live in Denmark!"

Sunday October 24
🍎 In America, a special 90-minute retrospective look back at the history of CBS Television's *The Ed Sullivan Show* features Beatles' performances of 'She Loves You' (from 1964) and 'Yesterday' (from 1965).

Monday October 25
🍎 In his new apartment, David Wigg interviews John for the BBC Radio One series *Scene And Heard*. The recordings will be transmitted over three parts in the UK, on November 13, 20 and 27. Later, in 1976, they will form a part of the Polydor double album *The Beatles Tapes*.

Tuesday October 26
🍎 John and Yoko, at their Greenwich Village apartment, record a home demo version of 'Happy Christmas (War Is Over)'.

Thursday October 28
🍎 This evening, at the Record Plant studios, based at West 44th Street in New York, John and Yoko begin the recording sessions for 'Happy Christmas (War Is Over)'. The first part of the evening is spent with John teaching the chords of the song to five guitarists, Chris, Teddy, Bob, Stu and Hugh. The Hugh in question is the session guitarist Hugh McCracken who, earlier this year, played on Paul's *Ram* album, but John, at this point, is unaware of this. Before recordings officially begin, John leads them through a medley of rock 'n' roll numbers, including 'Too Much Monkey Business', 'Rock Island Line' and 'Slippin' And Slidin' '. Phil Spector, wearing his trademark "Back To Mono" badge, produces the sessions. The musicians present also include Nicky Hopkins on piano and Jim Keltner on drums. Impressed by his work on *Imagine*, John had requested Klaus Voorman to join them, but because his flight from Germany had been delayed, Klaus will not join them until tomorrow. The first night of recordings goes on until 4am and is mainly taken up with recording the backing tracks.

Friday October 29
🍎 Back at the Record Plant, recording begins on Yoko's 'Listen, The Snow Is Falling', one of the very first tracks that Yoko showed to John back in 1968. As scheduled, Klaus is now present at the session. This track will become the B-side to the 'Happy Christmas' single.

Saturday October 30
🍎 John and Yoko are most pleased when they are told that John's album *Imagine* has reached number one in the American charts.

Sunday October 31
🍎 The recording sessions for 'Happy Christmas (War Is Over)' continue at the Record Plant where the musicians are joined by the Harlem Community Choir. Unusually for John, the sessions are held in the afternoon because the 30-piece choir, aged between 4 and 12, will have to leave in the early evening to make sure they are in bed on time. Their mothers join them at the recordings to make sure these requests are suitably adhered to. The final sessions begin with John teaching the choir, whom he affectionately calls "The Supremes", the lyrics to the song from a blackboard in the studio. At the conclusion of the taping, John, Yoko, the band, the children, the engineers, secretaries, Phil Spector and his brother-in-law Joe, all gather round a plastic Christmas tree which had been erected in the studio, to have a picture taken together for use on the single's picture sleeve. (Additional work on the song, an overdubbing of strings, take place the following day.) Incidentally, a single film camera shoots these activities for a promotional film to accompany the single's release. The only UK TV transmission of this occurs on BBC 1's *Top Of The Pops* on Thursday December 14, 1972, transmitted between 7:25 and 7:59pm.

November
🍎 At their Greenwich Village apartment, John and Yoko record the track 'Will You Touch Me', unreleased until it appears as a bonus track on the 1998 Ryko CD issue of Yoko's album *Fly*.

Saturday November 6
◆ The BBC Radio One programme *Scene And Heard* begins broadcasting (between 4:00 and 4:59pm) the first of a four-part interview with John carried out in New York by David Wigg. Part two is transmitted one week later on November 13, part three on November 20 and part four on November 27. Today's *Melody Maker* features an exclusive report by Richard Williams on the recording of 'Happy Christmas (War Is Over)'.

Sunday November 7
◆ Paul and Linda, along with their children, leave the seclusion of their Scottish farmhouse and board a second class train compartment en route to London to launch Wings.

Monday November 8
◆ A party to celebrate the launch of the group Wings and their album *Wild Life* is thrown at the Empire Ballroom in Leicester Square, London W1. Paul personally hand writes all the invitations to the costumed gala event which features music by Ray McFall and his band, a performance by the Frank and Peggy Spencer Formation Dance Team, a bumper prize raffle, food, drink and music from the Wings album played over the P.A. The 800 guests include Elton John, Keith Moon and John Entwistle of The Who, Ronnie Lane, Ronnie Wood, Ian McLagen and Kenny Jones of The Faces, various top DJs and Jimmy Page of Led Zeppelin. The ever-reliable *Melody Maker* is there to cover the event.

MM: "Why the Empire Ballroom on a Monday night?"

Paul: "Why not?"

Linda: "We thought it would be a nice idea to invite a whole lot of our friends to a big party where they could bring their wives."

Paul: "EMI are paying for it."

MM: "When will we hear Wings live?"

Paul: "Well, it should be soon now. We want to start in a very small way, maybe do some unadvertised concerts or something."

Melody Maker reporter Chris Charlesworth requests from Paul a more in-depth interview for the paper. A session is granted for Wednesday, November 10. Meanwhile, Paul and Linda's children have been left with child minders at his home in Cavendish Avenue, London.

Tuesday November 9
◆ A most unusual interview with John and Yoko is broadcast today on BBC Radio Two, when, between 2:01 and 2:59pm, the couple are featured in a *Woman's Hour* special, dealing with the exploitation of sex in books, films and magazines. The Lennons again film the interview, which was pre-recorded back in August at their Tittenhurst Park mansion. (A 6-second excerpt appears in the 1972 *Imagine* film.)

Wednesday November 10
◆ The Ringo/Frank Zappa film *200 Motels* opens in New York.
◆ As arranged, *Melody Maker*'s Chris Charlesworth interviews Paul at the Abbey Road studios. The result is published in the paper on Saturday November 20 (see entry).

Friday November 12
◆ At their Greenwich Village apartment, John records several demos of the song 'Luck Of The Irish'. The proceedings are privately captured on a black & white 'open-reel' Sony video recording machine. Several versions of the song find their way onto this 17-minute recording which is suitably titled *Luck Of The Irish – A Videotape By John Reilly*. The item shows John discussing how to spell the lyrics to the song, venting his anger at the way electrical currents and film running speeds vary between England and America and announcing that John and Yoko had friends coming to dinner tonight at 6 o'clock. The footage, in which John refers to himself as Sean O'Leaharn and Yoko as Mrs. O' No No, ends with the couple listening to the finished version of the song.

Saturday November 13
◆ The very first picture of Paul's group Wings appears on the front page of this week's *Melody Maker*.

Monday November 15

 The spaghetti-western film *Blindman*, starring Ringo as a vicious gun-toting bandit, has its world premiere in Rome. For the screening, the entire movie is naturally dubbed into Italian.

Saturday November 20

 Melody Maker publishes the exclusive interview with Paul carried out by Chris Charlesworth in the control room at EMI's Studio 2 at Abbey Road on November 10. The article is titled: "Why Lennon Is Uncool."

During the piece, Paul exclaims his current feelings about The Beatles: "I just want the four of us to get together somewhere and sign a piece of paper saying it's all over, and we want to divide the money four ways. No one would be there, not even Linda or Yoko, or Allen Klein. We'd just sign the paper and hand it to the business people and let them sort it out. That's all I want now. But John won't do it. Everybody thinks I am the aggressor but I'm not you know, I just want out.

"John and Yoko are not cool in what they're doing. I saw them on television the other night and thought that what they were saying about what they wanted to do together was basically the same as what Linda and I want to do. John's whole image now is very honest and open. He's all right is John, I like his *Imagine* album but I didn't like the others . . . there was too much political stuff on the other albums. You know I only listen to them to see if there is something I can pinch . . ."

Paul then touches on the song 'How Do You Sleep?': "I think it's silly. So what if I live with straights? I like straights. I have straight babies . . . he says the only thing I did was 'Yesterday' and he knows that's wrong . . ."

Paul gives his own version on why he didn't play at the Bangla Desh concert this August: "You know I was asked to play at George's concert in New York for Bangladesh and I didn't. Klein called a press conference and told everyone I had refused to do so for the Pakistani refugees – that's what he called them. It wasn't so. I said to George the reason I couldn't do it was because it would mean that all the world's press would scream that The Beatles had got back together again, and I know that it would have made Klein very happy. It would have been an historical event and Klein would have taken the credit. I didn't really fancy it anyway. If it wasn't for Klein I might have had second thoughts about it, but I don't know really."

Asked about The Beatles' live shows – or rather lack of them – Paul remarks: "I just wanted to get into a van and do an unadvertised Saturday night hop at Slough Town Hall or somewhere like that. We'd call ourselves Ricki and The Red Streaks or something and just get up and play."

 Meanwhile in New York at Greenwich Village, John is infuriated by Paul's accusations and again he immediately prepares a reply. (See entry for December 4.)

Monday November 22

 The first screening of the 96-minute Apple film *Raga* takes place with a press screening at New York's Carnegie Hall cinema. George and Patti and John and Yoko are in attendance. The film includes George receiving sitar tuition from Ravi Shankar at Big Sur, south of San Francisco, California, back on June 10, 1968.

Tuesday November 23

 The *Raga* film receives its premiere this evening at the Carnegie Hall cinema. Earlier in the day, George videotapes an appearance, for the one and only time, on the ABC Television programme *The Dick Cavett Show*, accompanying Gary Wright and Wonder Wheel on slide guitar for the song 'Two Faced Man'. In complete contrast to John and Yoko's September 12 appearance on the show, George, besides plugging the Lennons' new single 'Happy Christmas', makes no attempt to hide his displeasure of doing television interviews.

Cavett: "Is there a slight undercurrent of hostility between you and the other members (of The Beatles)? Are you, in any sense, in contact with each other?"

George: "I saw John last night actually at the premiere of *Raga* . . . which is what we should talk about maybe." (The audience breaks into a rather subdued round of laughter.)

Cavett: "OK . . . But what did you say?"

George: "Hi . . . Hello."

Cavett: "Do you get writers who say these sort of things? What did he (John) come back with?"

George: "Hi." (The audience again breaks into laughter.)

Cavett: "Was there more?"

George: "You don't need boring people to talk to on your show. I'm most probably the biggest bore you've had on your show!"

Cavett: "Really . . . you think?"

George: "They asked me, 'Do you want to come on *The Dick Cavett Show*' and I said 'I've got nothing to talk about really' and they said 'Well, think of something . . . anything.' So I thought, 'OK, I'll go and talk about *Raga*.'"

Cavett: "You mean, that's it! When we're done talking about that . . ."

George (interrupting): "Then I'll go."

Cavett: "You don't like to talk then?"

George: "Well . . . not really. Sometimes, if there's something to say. But there's really nothing to say these days."

When George is finally prompted to speak, he talks about recording his songs, drugs, alcohol, heroin, the comedian Jack Benny, his inability to recall his Beatles days and his displeasure towards American TV:

"It's such a load of rubbish," he admits. "But not *The Dick Cavett Show* of course." (Further laughter and applause from the studio audience.)

George continues: "It just drives you crazy, you know. The commercials . . . you're just getting into something and they'd say, 'Sorry, now another word from . . . and another word from.' They just put on commercials all the time. You don't know if it's the commercials or the show!"

George also goes on to plug the BBC TV comedy series *Monty Python's Flying Circus*, and recalls the infamous 1967 interview with Paul for ITN about taking LSD. Naturally, the Concert For Bangla Desh and Indian music come into the conversation. Ravi Shankar joins George and Cavett during the latter half of the interview. George also recalls the troubles that ensued from the revenue from their Bangla Desh concert and the reasons why the album has still not appeared. "We'll get it out," George says defiantly. "I'll even put it out with CBS. Bhaskar (Menon, head of Capitol) will then have to sue me!" George says raising a defiant fist towards the cameras, adding: "We're going to play the sue me, sue you blues. Sue me Bhaskar!" Then, apparently out of reach from the studio microphones, George mutters: "It's none of your business to fuckin' be in . . . Bleep!" realising that his expletive has indeed been heard. (The outburst, for the first transmission tonight and again during the 1996 VH-1 Archive re-run, is indeed censored. Another similar "F-word" outburst by George during the show falls to an identical censored airing.)

As it happened, once George got into the mood for talking he actually gave more than enough interview material for the 90-minute show which also includes an excerpt of 'My Sweet Lord' from the *Concert For Bangla Desh* film.

Tuesday November 30
🍎 John's album *Imagine* reaches number one in the UK charts.

December
🍎 During further home demo tape recordings this month, John records the track 'Call My Name'.

🍎 By telephone from the States, Paul and Linda record a 30-minute interview feature for Radio Luxembourg. Shortly after arriving in New York, Paul and Linda, at the A&R Studios, mix the instrumental 'Breakfast Blues'.

Wednesday December 1
🍎 John and Yoko's single 'Happy Christmas (War Is Over)'/'Listen The Snow Is Falling', performed by Yoko, is released in America, but due to a problem with Yoko's songwriting credits, the UK release is delayed for almost a year. (The eventual release takes place on November 24, 1972.) This becomes Lennon's first solo single not to feature the Apple logo on the label.

Friday December 3
🍎 George happily accepts another invitation to appear with Ravi Shankar, this time

giving a sitar demonstration on the American Westinghouse Group television programme *The David Frost Show*. For the past two years, Frost has been presenting his own American television chat show.

Saturday December 4

 Melody Maker publishes a stinging letter from John, attacking Paul over his interview published in the paper on November 20. John's lengthy reply, which he insists is published on the grounds of "equal time", includes a seven part attack on Paul, including an accusation that his "politics are very similar to Mary Whitehouse's". On the grounds of potential libel action, *Melody Maker* is forced to edit from publication nine lines of John's original letter.

"Dear Paul, Linda, et all the wee McCartneys,Thanks for your letter . . .

1. We give you money for your bits of Apple.

2. We give you more money in the form of royalties, which legally belong to Apple. (I know we're Apple, but on the other hand, we're not.)

For the millionth time in these past few years I repeat, what about the tax? It's all very well playing simple honest ole human Paul in the *Melody Maker*, but you know damn well we can't just sign a bit of paper.

You say, 'John won't do it'. I will if you'll indemnify us against the taxman. Anyway, you know that after we have our meeting, the fucking lawyers will have to implement whatever we agree on – right?

It's up to you, as we've said many times – we'll meet you whenever you like. Just make up your mind. Eg. Two weeks ago I asked you on the phone 'please let's meet without advisors etc. and decide what we want.' I especially emphasised Maclen which is mainly our concern; but you refused – right? You said under no condition would you sell to us, and if we didn't do what you wanted, you'd sue us again, and that Ringo and George are going to break you John etc. etc.

One other little lie in your 'It's only Paulie' *MM* bit. *Let It Be* was not the 'first bit of hype' on a Beatle album. Remember Tony Barrow? And his wonderful writings on *Please Please Me* etc. etc. The early Beatle Christmas records . . .

And you gotta admit that it was a 'new phase Beatle album', incidentally written in the style of the great Barrow himself. By the way, what happened to my idea of putting the parody of our first album cover on the *Let It Be* cover?

Listen, my obsessive old Paul, it was George's press conference – not 'dat ole debbil Klein' – he said what you said – 'I'd love to come, but . . .'

Wanna put your photo on the label like uncool John and Yoko, do ya? (Ain't you got no shame?) If we're not cool what does that make you?

P.S. The bit that really puzzled us was asking to meet without Linda and YOKO. I thought you'd have understood by now, that I'm John and Yoko.

P.P.S. Even your own lawyers know you can't 'just sign a bit of paper' (or don't they tell you?)."

Sunday December 5

 The London High Court appoints a receiver for Maclen (Music) Ltd.

Monday December 6

 The President of Capitol Records, Bhaskar Menon, replies publicly to George's outburst against him over the *Bangla Desh* album on *The Dick Cavett Show* (transmitted November 23). "Harrison is clearly not in possession of all the facts," he remarks.

Tuesday December 7

 The first Wings album, *Wild Life*, is released simultaneously in America and in the UK. A proposed first single off the album, 'Love Is Strange'/'I Am Your Singer' (Parlophone R5932), is cancelled by Apple and Parlophone due to the disappointing sales of the album.

Thursday December 9

 John and Yoko fly from New York to Ann Arbor, Michigan in preparation for tomorrow's concert in aid of the jailed John Sinclair.

Friday December 10

 This morning in his Michigan hotel room, John is joined by singer Phil Ochs. A tape is made by Lennon of the two performing the song 'Chords Of Fame'.

"We're playing acoustic tonight, you might call us the Quarry Men . . . I haven't done this in years."

Later this evening, John and Yoko are among a line-up of musicians performing at a benefit concert in the Chrysler Arena in Ann Arbor, Michigan, for the radical activist John Sinclair, who had been sentenced to 10 years imprisonment for attempting to sell two marijuana joints. Their acoustic performance includes: 'Attica State' (which suffers badly from feedback), 'The Luck Of The Irish', 'Sisters O Sisters' and 'John Sinclair' and is featured in the film of the event entitled *Ten For Two*, which is premiered in Ann Arbor during December 1972. A full American release will not take place until April 1, 1989, more than 17 years after the event. The John and Yoko produced film also features contributions from Bobby Searle, Allen Ginsberg, Jerry Rubin and David Dellinger. (Incidentally, Sinclair is released on December 13, three days after the concert.) The Detroit television station WTVS also covers John and Yoko's performance. Their uncut videotape footage runs to almost 19 minutes, four minutes longer than the official *Ten For Two* film version. Scenes where John's guitar string breaks prior to the start of 'Luck Of The Irish' are consigned by the Lennons to the cutting room floor. Following the performance, the Lennons are approached to appear as co-hosts on the Emmy Award-winning afternoon talk show, *The Mike Douglas Show*. (See entries for January 31, 1972.)

Monday December 13

 From the Lennons' Bank Street, Greenwich Village apartment, John and Yoko again write to *Melody Maker*, this time addressing a reply to Simon and Gill Frith's letter of December 11 expressing their concern over the Lennons' involvement in the capitalist system. On Apple-headed notepaper, the letter read:

"Simon and Gill and *MM* Readers.

"Apple was/is a capitalist concern. We brought in a capitalist to prevent it sinking (with The Beatles on board). I personally have had enough of Apple/Ascot and all other properties which tie me down, mentally and physically. I intend to cash in on my chips as soon as I can – and be free. John/Yoko intend to do all performances around the world FREE and/or whatever we've earned will go e.g. to prisons to release people who can't afford bail, etc. – and many other ways of getting money back to the people. This is one way of paying the people back."

They end their letter with Yoko saying: "P.P.P.P.S. I personally have had enough of Apple/Ascot long before John has and I'm very happy that John's coming round – and not only 'Imagine no possessions' but wanting to get rid of it – the things that interfere with our work and life.

P.P.P.P.P.S. Please stop attacking John for 'How Do You Sleep?', it happens to be a good song (very powerful and full of pathos) and also, it happens to be an answer to Paul's *Ram*. Listen to *Ram* carefully and you'll see".

(The letter is published in *MM* dated December 25.)

Tuesday December 14

 At their Greenwich Village apartment, John, Yoko and Jerry Rubin give an interview to Jean François Vallee for the French INA television programme *Pop 2*, which is transmitted during January of 1972. (John will again be interviewed by Vallee on March 18, 1975 for the French television programme *Un Jour Futur* – see entry.)

Wednesday December 15

 John and Yoko attend a reception in New York honouring U Thant, the retiring United Nations Secretary General.

 Paul and Linda appear on the New York radio station WCBS-FM, where Paul plays the unreleased track 'Breakfast Blues', promotes his new group Wings and discusses the new album *Wild Life*.

Thursday December 16

 The 95-minute Ringo/Frank Zappa film *200 Motels* opens at the Classic Cinema in Piccadilly Circus, London.

In New York, John and Yoko record an appearance on the Westinghouse Group's programme *The David Frost Show*. They appear at the very start of the show backing Apple artist David Peel as he sings 'The Ballad Of New York', with John happily plucking on a tea-chest bass. The Lennons reappear in the show backed by members of the group David Peel and The Lower East Side, performing 'Attica State', 'Luck Of The Irish' (short version), 'Sisters O Sisters' and 'John Sinclair'. Other highlights of the show, first transmitted in America on January 13, 1972, include a screening of a silent home movie of John and Yoko recently visiting the American Indian Chief Lion and his tribe. The Lennons, who first met the Chief during Yoko's Syracuse exhibition in October, are now actively involved in his campaign to stop the construction of a freeway through his tribe's reservation. The Chief himself also guests on the show. Another most memorable sequence occurs when John and Yoko get involved in a heated discussion with two members of the studio audience, who accuse the Lennons of "making it sound as if the only worthwhile people in this world are people who have committed crimes". This was, in fact, John and Yoko's second US TV appearance with David Frost. (The first was transmitted in America on July 10, 1969.) It is clear that John does not enjoy this further encounter. He refuses to take a bow to the audience at the end of part one of the programme, and reappears later only to perform. This leaves Yoko to face questions from Frost on her own. During the Lennons' appearance on *The Dick Cavett Show*, John had sarcastically referred to David Frost as "Fravid Drost".

Friday December 17

John appears at another benefit concert, this time at the Apollo Theater in Harlem, New York, to perform for the families of the victims of the riot at New York's Attica State Prison. During the show, which is captured on 16mm film, John performs acoustic versions of both 'Imagine' and 'Attica State' while Yoko sings 'Sisters O Sisters'.

Saturday December 18

John and Yoko visit Houston, Texas, in order to gain access to see Kyoko and take her to the hotel where they are currently staying. Again Anthony Cox denies them, and due to his breaking a previous court order, the Lennons decide to inform the authorities. Also today, *Melody Maker* publishes its report on the recording sessions for 'Happy Christmas (War Is Over)'.

Monday December 20

The album *The Concert For Bangla Desh* is released in America. (The UK release takes place on January 10, 1972.) At first Capitol Records in America refuse to release the album unless it is financially rewarding for them, which greatly aggravates George. He argues that with Phil Spector agreeing to mix the album for free, Apple supplying the booklet and album at no cost and all the other record companies allowing their artists to appear, Capitol must give up something. George then threatens to take the album to CBS if Capitol will not budge. This they eventually do and Capitol present Apple with a cheque for $3,750,000 as payment for advance record sales. The only label to actually make money from the album is Columbia, who, for the privilege of Bob Dylan's appearance, receive 25 cents on every copy sold, although Bob will receive none of that himself. George also expresses his dislike at the high retail price of the package, which in the UK sells for an unusually high price of £5.50.

Wednesday December 22

Following Anthony Cox's refusal to allow Yoko access to her daughter Kyoko on Saturday, a Houston civil court judge, after a two-hour hearing, jails Cox for five days for contempt of court. During the sitting, Yoko is horrified to be told that, due to neglect of schooling by Cox, Kyoko is three years behind in her studies.

Saturday December 25

On Christmas Day, Radio Luxembourg votes *Imagine* 'Album of the Year' and 'My Sweet Lord' as 'Best Single of the Year'.

Monday December 27

For the second successive year, The Beatles' 1964 film *A Hard Day's Night* is shown by BBC1 over the Christmas period. Today's screening occurs between 9:40 and

11:04am. The corporation will continue to screen "Boxing Day With The Beatles" movies right up until 1975.

🍎 Later this evening, and again on BBC1, *Best Of Top Of The Pops '71 – Part 2* is screened (between 4:35 and 5:14pm) and features the five-piece dance troupe Pan's People dancing to George's number one 'My Sweet Lord'. The show is hosted by Tony Blackburn and also features music by the New Seekers, Slade, Rod Stewart & The Faces, T.Rex, Diana Ross and The Tams.

Thursday December 30
🍎 At 10:30am, a trade screening of *200 Motels*, for the purpose of registration, takes place at the private United Artists theatre in Wardour Street, London.

December
🍎 At the end of the month, John and Paul meet in New York to try to sort out their business difficulties, after which Paul returns home to Scotland, where he produces an instrumental version of his album *Ram*. On release it is entitled *Thrillington*, and credited to his pseudonym Percy Thrills Thrillington. (Paul's home studio recordings will continue early into the next year.)

🍎 To close the year, the magazine *Record & Tape Retailer* reveal that 'My Sweet Lord' was the top selling single of the year. Beatle related honours continue in the American publication *Record World*, when *Imagine* is voted 'Album of the Year' and 'My Sweet Lord' is voted 'Best Single Disc of the Year'. George himself receives the honour of being voted 'Top Male Vocalist of 1971'. Paul and Linda are not forgotten – they are recognised as the 'Top Duo of the Year'.

Q: "Have you seen your former Beatles mates recently?"
Paul: "No, I've got no particular reason to, and I don't really want to. They're into their things and I'm into mine."

January
 In Scotland, Paul's home studio sessions continue. This month he records 'Little Woman Love' and unreleased versions of '1882' and 'Soily' (see entry for January 13). Towards the end of the month (around the 25th), the former Grease Band guitarist Henry McCullough becomes the latest addition to join Wings, having left his previous group in December. Meanwhile at the very last minute, a planned visit by Paul to tout his new group Wings and their music at the 6th Annual Midem Music Trade Festival in Cannes in the South of France, is scrapped because Paul felt that "it was not worth doing".
 John spends most of the month at the Record Plant (until January 21), mixing the (soon to be titled) *Sometime In New York City* album. He also spares time to mix (for release as proposed EPs) the audio tapes from the John Sinclair Benefit Concert, on December 10, the Apollo Theater concert from December 17 and the Lyceum Ballroom concert from December 15, 1969. (The latter eventually appears on side three of the *Sometime In New York City* album.) This month, John also gives approximately 25 hours of unreleased Lennon music to Bruce Bierman during the sessions for David Peel's album *The Pope Smokes Dope*, which John produced. Also this month, the magazine *Arts And Artists* features an article entitled Yoko Notes by Michael Benedikt.
 George, meanwhile, finds the grounds of his Friar Park mansion overrun with a film crew. They are there to shoot the exterior scenes for the Kenneth Shipman produced soft-porn movie *Au Pair*, starring the British comedy actor Richard O'Sullivan and Gabrielle Drake. (The completed film, sporting the new title of *Au Pair Girls*, will be released to UK cinemas in July and follows the sexual exploits of four au pair girls who have just arrived in England.)

Thursday January 6
 John and Yoko announce the formation of Joko Films Ltd.

Monday January 10
 John assists Yoko during her concert at the Alice Tully Hall in New York's Lincoln Center. Due to their failure to obtain US work visas, their performance has to be carried out from seats in the audience.

Wednesday January 12
 While the film crew continues to work on Friar Park, George is forced to record interviews for inclusion in four programmes of the upcoming BBC Radio One series *The Beatles Story* at 3 Buregate Road in Felixstowe, Suffolk. For his services, he is paid £20.
 Ringo's film *Blindman* receives its American premiere in Chicago.

Thursday January 13
 John and Yoko guest with David Peel and The Lower East Side Band on *The David Frost Show* on American TV (see entries for Thursday December 16, 1971, for further details).
 Still in Scotland, Paul begins the recording sessions for 'Mary Had A Little Lamb'. During the rehearsals, a team from RKO Radio in America arrives to record an interview for their programme *Paul McCartney Now*. Sessions are concluded on Saturday (the 15th) and, following a break on Sunday, the group head down to London on Monday (see next entry).

Monday January 17 (until Friday January 28)
 Paul begins a mammoth 12-day period of rehearsals at London's Scotch of St. James club, all arranged so that he can decide on his final line-up of Wings. Henry McCullough is invited down by phone on the 24th. After playing with Paul, Linda, Denny Laine and Denny Seiwell, McCulloch is invited to join the group full-time. McCulloch recalls the event to the press: "I had a call asking me to come down for a blow with the band and Paul asked me to join after the rehearsal. All we have played so far has been rock and roll, and I am a good rock and roll guitarist." Asked about his role in the group, he replies: "I will be doing some vocals and hope to do some songwriting." Meanwhile, Paul's assistant, Shelley Turner, throws some light on their rehearsals: "They are getting a show together and doing material for the next album. They are getting ready for live appearances, but it won't be before April."

Friday January 28
In Studio C at the BBC TV Centre, Wood Lane, London, Ringo videotapes a most unusual television appearance, guesting in a non-speaking role at the tail end of an edition of *Monty Python's Flying Circus*. This clip features Ringo, alongside the singer Lulu, sitting on a large couch waiting to be interviewed by the host of a television chat show. Underneath a large "It's" sign, Ringo and Lulu wait patiently until the host arrives. It turns out to be a scruffy tramp, portrayed by Python member Michael Palin, who regularly appears in this guise to open and close each *Monty Python* episode. The tramp enters and sits between them and begins his introduction, in David Frost style: "Hello, good evening, welcome . . . It's . . ." a cue for the closing titles of the programme to run. While Lulu gets up and storms off stage in a huff, Ringo (still not uttering a single word) becomes involved in a skirmish with the tramp (Palin). This one-minute sketch is first transmitted on BBC1 on Saturday October 26, 1972 (between 10:17 and 10:47pm), at the very end of episode six in the third series.

Saturday January 29
Henry McCullough's first interview since becoming the new full-time member of Wings appears in today's *New Musical Express*.
Paul and Linda leave London's Heathrow and head to New York where they have arranged to meet John and Yoko. During dinner John and Paul agree to stop "slagging off each other in the press".

Sunday January 30
During Paul's stay in the city, he is interviewed about Wings for the radio station KHJ, but because of Paul's strong language during a discussion on the shootings in Ireland today, the recording has to be severely edited prior to the broadcast. The following day Paul and Linda return to London where he immediately arranges a recording session for February 1 to record his new song 'Give Ireland Back To The Irish', hastily written about the Irish troubles.

Monday January 31
During the morning, at a press conference in New York to announce their appearances on *The Mike Douglas Shows*, Yoko announces to the world: "We tried to show that we're working to change the world, not with dollars, but with love. We're not just freaks shouting and screaming about it, but we're thinking in terms of a balanced life – changing it gradually through our daily lifestyle. We're saying to older people, let's work it together, because we have to work it together."

*   *   *

John & Yoko on *The Mike Douglas Show*

Monday January 31 (until Monday February 7)
In New York, John and Yoko begin taping five programmes as the week's co-hosts on the prestigious Emmy award-winning WBC (Westinghouse Broadcasting Corporation) afternoon talk show *The Mike Douglas Show*. The shows are transmitted in two weeks time, between February 14 and 18. The line-up and highlights of the week's shows (transmitted daily between 4:30 and 6:00pm) are as follows:

Monday February 14 (show 1, recorded Monday January 31)
John informs Douglas that he had written the middle eight of 'Michelle', which was used as the show's introduction, adding, "Normally they play 'Yesterday' which was Paul's song." John & Yoko (with The Plastic Ono Band and the New York group Elephant's Memory) perform live: 'It's So Hard'. Guests on the show include the comedian Louis Nye, Attorney Ralph Nader and The Chamber Brothers. Yoko begins the reconstruction of a broken china cup.

Tuesday February 15 (show 2, recorded Tuesday February 1)
'With A Little Help From My Friends' is used as the show's introduction, together with 'Oh My Love' (excerpt from *Imagine* film). Yoko, John, Plastic Ono Band and Elephant's Memory perform live: 'Midsummer New York'. Guests on the show include US Surgeon

General Dr. Jesse Steinfield, the outspoken radical Jerry Rubin, the actress and film maker Barbara Loden and, making their television début, the two-piece folk duo Yellow Pearl.

Wednesday February 16 (show 3, recorded Wednesday February 2)
After Yoko and John perform 'Sisters O Sisters' with John on acoustic guitar, he remarks: "Some people thought she was singing about nuns!" The 'Crippled Inside' excerpt from the *Imagine* film is aired. John, Yoko, Chuck Berry, Plastic Ono Band and Elephant's Memory perform 'Memphis, Tennessee' and later, 'Johnny B. Goode' live. The Lennons, Berry and Douglas take part in a cookery demonstration by the macrobiotic food expert Hilary Redleaf. At one point, John and Chuck share the same apron! Other guests on the show include Joseph Blatchford, the head of Action Corps For Peace and David Rosenbloom, the musician, composer and computer scientist.

Thursday February 17 (show 4, recorded Friday February 4)
John, Plastic Ono Band and Elephant's Memory perform 'Imagine' live. Yoko gives Douglas a Box Of Smile (from 1967) which reflects his smile back at him. The 'Mrs. Lennon' excerpt from *Imagine* film is aired. Guests on the show include the actress/singer Vivien Reed, the four-piece comedy routine act Ace Trucking Co., the President of the Black Panther Party Bobby Searle, Marsha Martin, the student body President and Donald Williams, a medical student.

Friday February 18 (show 5, recorded Monday February 7)
Yoko concludes her china cup reconstruction. John & Yoko take questions from the studio audience in a segment called "Everything you've always wanted to know". John & Yoko perform an acoustic (censored) version of 'Luck Of The Irish'. The 'How' excerpt from the *Imagine* film is aired. The show ends with Yoko performing a Japanese folk song and then Mike Douglas sings 'Thanks To John & Yoko' for being his co-hosts for the week, to an accompaniment of a visual record of the five days by the resident Douglas photographer Michael Leshnov. Guests on the show include the comedian George Carlin, biofeedback expert Dr. Gary E. Schwartz and the New York appeals attorney Rena Uviller.

(Note: For several years after their original transmissions, the five 73-minute shows languished, untouched, in a film and video archive in Pennsylvania. Yoko rescued them for clips to be inserted into her 1984 *Milk And Honey* videos. All five shows appear officially in America on home video on May 19, 1998.)

* * *

Also during this period:

February
During the month, Ringo records at the Record Plant in New York City.

Tuesday February 1
Henry McCullough is quickly thrown into a political controversy when today at Island Studios in London, Wings record vocal and instrumentation versions of the controversial track 'Give Ireland Back To The Irish'. (ABC TV of America videotape Wings in the studio rehearsing the song.) The track is Paul's heartfelt reaction to the events of only two days previous when, on January 30, British paratroopers shot dead thirteen Catholics after a civil rights demonstration in Londonderry. The troops claim that they were replying to sniper fire. The tragedy will soon become known in Northern Ireland as Bloody Sunday. The ABC TV London reporter George Watson asks Paul about his political stance: "As an entertainer, it doesn't worry you about getting a bit into politics?"

Paul: "No. You can't stay out of it, you know, if you think at all these days. We're still humans, you know, and you wake up and you read your newspaper, it affects you. So I don't mind too much, it doesn't worry me, like I say. I don't now plan to do everything I do as a political thing, you know, but just on this one occasion I think the British Government overstepped their mark and showed themselves to be more of a sort of a repressive regime than I ever believed them to be."

The clip reappears in the ABC TV programme *David Frost Salutes The Beatles*, transmitted on May 21, 1975 (see entry for more information on the programme).

Wednesday February 2 (until Monday February 7)

 Wings resume rehearsals for their upcoming college appearances by assembling at the ICA (Institute Of Contemporary Arts) on the Mall in London. Tyncho Films capture the sessions for a production Paul will suitably call *The ICA Rehearsal*. The *Let It Be* style production features performances of 'The Mess', 'Wild Life', 'Bip Bop', 'Blue Moon Of Kentucky', 'Maybelline', 'Seaside Woman', 'My Love', 'Give Ireland Back To The Irish' and 'Lucille'. In between takes, the group is seen relaxing, puffing on cigarettes and drinking cans of Coke. To date, just 50 seconds of this film has been seen publicly, forming a short piece in the 1979 MPL documentary *Wings Over The World*.

Friday February 4

 A secret memo addressed to the US Attorney General, John Mitchell from Senator Strom Thurmond, suggests that John Lennon should be deported as an "undesirable alien", due to "his political views and activism".

Saturday February 5

 In temperatures well below freezing, John and Yoko are among 400 protesters outside the offices of the British Overseas Airways Corporation in New York. The protest is against the New York union leaders, Thomas Gleason and Matthew Guennan, who announce they will boycott all British exports into America. Their action is aimed towards the British policy in Northern Ireland.

Tuesday February 8

 Paul and Linda, the band, wives, girlfriends, children and even pets, climb into a caravan and head onto the motorway, stopping at whichever university town takes their fancy. Their musical instruments along with two roadies follow in a van. Once there, Paul will send in an assistant to ask if they can put on a show for the students the following day. Once agreed, word is spread around the campus and posters are put up. This scenario occurs today at Nottingham University. The road manager for this tour, Trevor Jones, remembers the historic first concert: "We went into Nottingham University Students' Union at about five o'clock and fixed it up for lunchtime the next day. Nottingham was the best because they were so enthusiastic. No hassles. No one quite expected it or believed it. We went down there at half-past eight the next morning with the gear. We threw up a few posters and put the word out on the tannoy."

* * *

Wings University Tour Of The UK
February 9–23

Paul and Wings, anxious for live concert experience without generating the massive media exposure an ex-Beatle in concert would naturally attract, play a string of small low-key unannounced UK University dates. Their repertoire of songs during this 11-date tour consists of 'Blue Moon Of Kentucky', 'Help Me', 'Say Darling', 'Wild Life', 'Bip Bop', 'Henry's Blues', 'My Love', 'Long Tall Sally', 'Seaside Woman', 'Some People Never Know' and 'Smile Away'. 'Give Ireland Back To The Irish', 'The Mess' and 'Lucille' will sometimes be reprised due to the lack of sufficient songs fully rehearsed by the band. Occasionally the group will drop into their set 'mock' portions of the songs 'Turkey In The Straw' and 'The Grand Old Duke Of York'. The running order of songs for the tour will vary from one night to the next, with the tracks 'Lucille' and 'Wild Life' alternating as the opening number of the show. Their unscheduled shows include performances at the following venues:

Nottingham University (Wednesday February 9)
York's Goodridge University (Thursday February 10)
Hull University (Friday February 11)
Newcastle-Upon-Tyne (Sunday February 13)
Lancaster University (Monday February 14)

Leeds Town Hall (Wednesday February 16)
Sheffield (Thursday February 17)
Manchester (Friday February 18)
Birmingham University (Monday February 21)
Swansea University (Tuesday February 22)
Oxford University (Wednesday February 23)

Some universities they approach are unable to accommodate Paul's concert offer as exams are being held or the halls at the venues simply aren't big enough to cater for the audience Paul and his band will attract. Linda, with absolutely no previous musical experience, tells *The Sunday Times* how she came to be involved in this tour. "Paul went on and on about it, saying he was dying to get back to performing, but wanted me to join in. 'Can you imagine,' he said, 'standing on the stage, the curtain going up, the audience all waiting.' He made it sound so glamorous that I agreed to have a go."

Wednesday February 9
With 18 hours notice, the tour kicks off at Nottingham University. The lunchtime audience comprises 700 curious students who file in to see this new band. Paul remembers the first gig: "It was a spur of the moment thing. One of the group said he had played at Nottingham University and liked it so that's where we ended up. It was 50p at the door, and a guy sat at the table taking the money. The kids danced and we all had a good time. The Students' Union took their split and gave us the rest. I'd never seen money for at least ten years. The Beatles never handled money . . . we (Wings) walked around Nottingham with £30 in coppers in our pockets."

After the concert, Paul, having just made his first live scheduled performance since The Beatles' final show at Candlestick Park on August 29, 1966, is reluctant to say much about the group's performance but he is obviously relieved by the tremendous response from the audience. He tells *Melody Maker*: "It was very good for us. We will go on touring the country for a while, playing more of these concerts when we feel like it." He also remarks to another journalist: "All I'm doing now with Wings is rehearsing . . . the main thing for me is I don't want to do old Beatle numbers. The obvious connection is like trying to live off your old records!"

Thursday February 10
A proposed concert today at Leeds University is cancelled at short notice when Paul discovers that there has been some major advance publicity. Instead, he drives out of the venue and at short notice books the group into the dining room at York's Goodridge University. Unfortunately the show doesn't go quite as smoothly as the opening concert as Linda suffers her first attack of stage fright. Paul recalls: "She was paralysed by fear and quite unable to put her hands on the keyboards." Paul immediately goes to her rescue and discovers that he has forgotten the chords to their opening song 'Wild Life'. The lunchtime crowd cheer enthusiastically. Another 300 fans are locked outside, unable to enter. From her office in London, Paul's assistant Shelley Turner, somewhat oblivious to his recent concert appearances, tries to explain to journalists on the phone the current university tour: "They are on the road at the moment and have taken a lot of sandwiches with them. They could turn up anywhere and play this week. I don't know exactly where they are."

Meanwhile, there is further bad news for Paul today when the BBC announces that, due to its political nature, they have banned the single 'Give Ireland Back To The Irish'.

Saturday February 12
With the controversy growing over 'Give Ireland Back To The Irish', Shelley Turner announces: "EMI are 100 per cent behind it and are very keen to put it out. As soon as they have got the final lacquer, they will put it out. It will probably be in the shops by next week. Paul has strong feelings about the Irish situation."

Taking a night off from the university gigs, Paul makes a live appearance with Kid Jensen on his Radio Luxembourg show tonight between 10:30 and midnight. He takes phone questions from listeners and uses the opportunity to vent his feelings towards the BBC banning 'Give Ireland Back To The Irish'. One cheeky caller rings in to ask Paul if he can release, as a bootleg single, The Beatles' version of 'How Do You Do It?'

Monday February 14

In an interview for *Melody Maker*, Linda talks about how pleased she is with the tour so far: "We've only been playing together for five days and already I have confidence in the band. So far audience response has been good. Surprisingly perhaps, I am enjoying these one-night appearances – it's like a touring holiday, and the children love it too." Again she is asked why they are doing the unscheduled concerts: "We just don't want to be tied down. If we wake up one morning and decide that we don't want to go to Hull, we don't have to. With an organised tour your freedom is limited. This is the only way to do it."

Thursday February 17

While Wings are preparing for a concert in Sheffield, the High Courts of London dismiss an application by Northern Songs to put in a counter claim in the proceedings originally started by Paul back in December of 1970. Paul wants a ruling that any songs he composes in collaboration with anyone other than John is not bound by the 1965 agreement giving copyright benefits to Northern Songs, as under the terms of the original agreement. (This agreement is scheduled to terminate in February of 1973.)

In America, at the annual meeting of stockholders in New York, Allen Klein announces that the other three Beatles are to make an offer to Paul for his 25% interest in Apple within the next weeks. It is reported that the offer will be made because of the recent improvement in the relationship between John and Paul.

Monday February 21

In London, Paul's assistant Shelley Turner announces that: "Paul is interested in the proposed offer by John, George and Ringo to buy his 25% share of Apple, but he has seen no statement yet."

Tuesday February 22

At 5pm, Paul rings Swansea University to ask them if Wings can play there. Within 75 minutes a queue of 800 students has built up outside the university hall to watch the performance.

*   *   *

Also during this period:

Thursday February 17

 In England, John and Yoko's gift to the Hanratty family, a 40-minute colour film of the campaign into the enquiry of the hanging of James Hanratty, charged with the A6 motorway murder in 1961, is shown in the crypt of St. Martin-in-the-Fields Church, London. This is the only public screening of the complete Lennon film, although a short clip from the production later appears in the UK during a Channel 4 television programme on the subject. (John and Yoko had first discussed the idea of the film with Hanratty's parents at an Apple press conference in Saville Row, London on December 10, 1969.)

Saturday February 19

 Allen Klein is quoted as saying: "I have the ability to think like a thief!"

Friday February 25

 In the UK, Wings release their first single, 'Give Ireland Back To The Irish'. (The American release occurs on February 28.) An Apple produced 30-second television commercial for the release, featuring Paul, is immediately banned by the ITA (Independent Television Authority, the controller of the ITV network) because it contains "political controversy" canned under the ITA Act. ATV, Radio Luxembourg and the GPO also announce that they too have banned the single. When Paul is told of the ban by the BBC, he retorts: "Up them! I think the BBC should be highly praised . . . preventing the youth from hearing my opinions." One station that doesn't ban the single is Thames, the TV station that serves the London and South-East region of the ITV network. For the next six weeks they, albeit unsuccessfully, try to lure Paul on the weekday news programme *Today* for an interview with Eamonn Andrews.

Saturday February 26
🍎 Linda tells the *Melody Maker* about the low-key Wings university concerts: "Eric Clapton once said that he would like to play from the back of a caravan, but he never got around to doing it. Well – we have! We've no managers or agents – just we five and the roadies. We're just a gang of musicians touring around." Radio One DJ John Peel comments on the BBC ban of 'Give Ireland Back To The Irish': "The ban disturbs me – the act of banning it is a much stronger political act than the contents of the record itself. It's just one man's opinion."

Sunday February 27 & Monday February 28
🍎 In Hungary, Ringo and Maureen attend Elizabeth Taylor's two-day 40th birthday party, held at the Intercontinental Hotel in Budapest. Fellow celebrities in attendance include the comedian Frankie Howerd and the former actress Grace Kelly, now Princess Grace of Monaco.

Monday February 28
🍎 In New York at their Greenwich Village apartment, John and Yoko are visited by a two-man crew from London Weekend Television in England who are there to shoot film of the Lennons for an *Aquarius* documentary on the theme of "The Pursuit Of Happiness in Modern-day America". For their three-minute 13-seconds appearance, John is seen performing (on a steel guitar) a version of the song 'Attica State', which breaks down one minute 14 seconds into the song because, in his words: "I've forgotten the last verse . . . I've forgotten the rest." John spends the rest of the time explaining his and Yoko's attempt to change the apathy of the youth in America.

John optimistically announces: "Our job now is to tell them there is still hope and we still have things to do and we must get out now and change their heads and tell them it's OK. We can change it! It isn't over just because flower power didn't work. It's only the beginning; we're just in the inception of revolution."

With Yoko sitting by his side, he goes on to say: "That's why we are going out on the road. All our shows we do will be for free. All the money will go to prisoners or to poor people, so we'll collect no money for the performance. We hope to start touring in America and then eventually, go around the world and go possibly to China too. For instance, we'd go to, say, Chicago and then, in the Chicago prison, half or quarter of the money earned will go towards releasing the first 500 people alphabetically who couldn't get bail to get out of prison. So, wherever we go, the show will arrive and we will release people in each town. So possibly when the Stones are touring America for money, we'll be touring for free!" John concludes by cheekily looking into the camera and, laughing, asks: "What are you going to do about that Mick?"

The feature is included in the 53-minute, Tony Palmer directed, *Aquarius* special, which is transmitted for the only time across the ITV network on Saturday March 11, between 10:10 and 11:08pm. The show, taking in locations from New York to Los Angeles, also includes an all-female roller derby, a male film star called Candy Darling and an experimental theatre group called the Liquid Theater.

🍎 Still in New York, Allen Klein announces that he is suing the magazine *New York* for $150 million for libel. The article claimed (last month) that from each copy of the *Bangla Desh* album: "$1.40 of the proceeds from each record sold could not be accounted for in the production and distribution costs." As Klein angrily points out: "This implies that ABKCO Industries have received the money. Based on the present figure of 568,000 copies sold, we will make a loss of more than a dollar on each copy sold!"

🍎 Paul, Linda, their family and Wings depart for Los Angeles to begin work on their next album.

🍎 George and Patti Harrison, on their way to London from their Friar Park mansion, are involved in an accident on the M4 motorway near Maidenhead in Berkshire. Around midnight, during an electrical blackout in the area, their 6-litre Mercedes car approached a recently opened roundabout and collided with a lamppost on a centre barrier. (The bright fluorescent lighting on the road had been extinguished just 75 minutes before the accident occurred.) George, with blood streaming down his face, and Patti, are immediately transferred by ambulance to Maidenhead Hospital where they are treated for their head injuries in the casualty department. George is discharged but has to return later to the hospital to have his stitches removed. He returns to his Henley mansion while Patti is taken to the nearby Nuffield Nursing Home in Fulmer, Slough, suffering from concussion. She is detained for observation and the following morning the hospital announces that she is "quite comfortable". (George is ordered to appear before magistrates over the incident on July 12 – see entry.)

Tuesday February 29
 John and Yoko's original US visa expires. They are immediately granted a 15-day extension. This sees the beginning of a three-and-a-half-year struggle by John to reside in America. The government's opposition to his request is apparently based on his 1968 UK drug conviction.

March
 In Los Angeles, Wings enter the studios to begin recording tracks for the album *Red Rose Speedway*. The first period of sessions produce the following tracks: 'Big Barn Bed', 'One More Kiss', 'Little Lamb Dragonfly', 'Single Pigeon', 'When The Night', 'Loup (1st Indian On The Moon)', medley: 'Hold Me Tight – Lazy Dynamite – Hands Of Love – Power Cut'. He will also produce the first recording of the song 'I Would Only Smile', which Wings member Denny Laine will later release as a solo recording. Paul also records 'My Love' and the track 'Mama's Little Girl', which will not appear until February 5, 1990 when, in the UK, it is released as a bonus track on the CD and 12-inch single of 'Put It There'. (The recording sessions for the album *Red Rose Speedway* will move to the Olympic Studios in Barnes on Monday, March 19, and will continue off and on until October this year.)
 Apple recording artist Mary Hopkin quits the record label and is therefore currently without a recording contract. Mary's manager Jo Lustig says: "I have had offers from three major companies but haven't made a deal yet."

Wednesday March 1
 In New York, at the Record Plant, John and Yoko begin recording tracks for the album *Some Time In New York City*. The sessions, which are co-produced by Phil Spector, feature the following songs: 'Woman Is The Nigger Of The World', 'Sisters O Sisters', 'Attica State', 'New York City', 'Sunday Bloody Sunday', 'Luck Of The Irish', 'John Sinclair' and 'Angela'. (The sessions continue until March 20.) Unreleased "jam" tracks from this period, featuring John and Elephant's Memory, include 'Don't Be Cruel', 'Hound Dog', 'Send Me Some Lovin' ', 'Roll Over Beethoven', 'Whole Lotta Shakin' Goin' On', 'It'll Be Me', 'Not Fade Away', 'Ain't That A Shame' and 'Caribbean'. John and Yoko also spend some of this time, again at the Record Plant, producing an Elephant's Memory album. The photographer Bob Gruen captures the Lennons at work and playing host to celebrities, including Mick Jagger, Rudolph Nureyev, Andy Warhol and Jerry Rubin, who all drop in to see the couple.

Friday March 3
 Legal custody of her daughter Kyoko is again granted to Yoko, but the girl's father, Anthony Cox, has again fled with the child. The situation is one of John's main reasons for wishing to remain in America, so that he and Yoko can try and find the girl.

Saturday March 4
 In the American albums charts, George's *Concert For Bangla Desh* album sits at number two, while in the UK singles charts, Badfinger's 'Day After Day' is at number nine and Wings' 'Give Ireland Back To The Irish' enters at number 28.

Monday March 6
 Just five days after being granted an extension, the American Immigration and Naturalisation Services cancel John and Yoko's extensions on their US visas. Even though the Lennons are currently in America legally, this cancellation means that they are now, by a technicality in the States, "overstays". This problem will soon come to haunt John in his battle to obtain a 'green card' and thus remain in the US legally.

Monday March 13
 The BBC's ban on The Beatles' 1967 track 'A Day In The Life' is finally lifted. Hardly anyone notices when a portion of the song is played today on BBC Radio Four's long-running show *Desert Island Discs*, where it is chosen by the novelist David Storey.

Tuesday March 14
 In America, at the 14th annual Grammy Awards ceremony, The Beatles are honoured, receiving a NARAS Trustee Award for their "outstanding talent, originality and music creativity that have done so much to express the mood and tempo of our times to bridge the culture gap between several generations".

Thursday March 16
 In New York, John and Yoko persuade the US Immigration Authorities to let them stay for another four weeks. The couple are called to explain why they should not leave the country. They are granted a further temporary extension to their stay in America and told to reappear in court on April 18. Afterwards, outside the court, John tells the waiting reporters: "We want to stay permanently because New York is the centre of the earth and also because we want to find Yoko's daughter Kyoko."

Friday March 17
 Ringo's single 'Back Off Boogaloo' (produced by George, on which he plays guitar)/'Blindman' (co-produced by Ringo and Klaus Voorman) is released in the UK. (The US release takes place on March 20.) As part of the special UK promotions, EMI set up a special London phone line for advanced hearing of the song. 'Boogaloo' has long been cited as Paul's nickname from the other Beatles, but on VH-1 *Storytellers*, recorded in May, 1998, Ringo announces that the song was influenced by Marc Bolan, when he came to dinner one night. "He was an energised guy. He used to speak 'Back off boogaloo . . . ooh you, boogaloo.' 'Do you want some potatoes?' 'Ooh you, boogaloo!' "

The middle section of the song ("Get yourself together now and give me something tasty") was inspired by the English football presenter Jimmy Hill, who Ringo just happens to be watching one Sunday afternoon on London Weekend Television's soccer show *The Big Match*. Hill remarks that a particular footballer's playing was very "tasty".

Saturday March 18
 Filming begins on the Marc Bolan and T.Rex Apple movie *Born To Boogie* during Bolan's two performances this evening at the Empire Pool, Wembley. Ringo, sitting in the photographers' pit below the stage, directs the shooting of both concerts, although only footage from the second show will appear in the finished film. (Additional scenes of Bolan at the afternoon soundcheck and brief shots of his first Wembley show, again directed by Ringo, can be seen during the final credits of the *Born To Boogie* film.) Additional scenes for *Born To Boogie* are arranged for Tuesday March 21 (see entry).

Monday March 20
 Work on *Red Rose Speedway* resumes at the Olympic Sound Studios in Barnes, where Paul enlists the assistance of producer Glyn Johns.
 Meanwhile in Ascot, during one of Ringo's frequent "house-sitting" stints at John's Tittenhurst Park mansion, Ringo films a unique promotional film for 'Back Off Boogaloo', which features him wandering aimlessly around the vast grounds looking for his creation, a Frankenstein monster. This image is reused on the picture sleeve of the single and suitably ties in with the advertising slogan for the release "Another monster from Apple". Surprisingly enough, Apple does not finance the clip. Instead, the production is carried out by Caravel Films, the Slough based company regularly employed by BBC TV to produce for *Top Of The Pops* the amusing short films that accompany the various songs on the programme when an artist cannot appear or no promotional film clip was available. The camera work for 'Back Off Boogaloo' is by Alan Taverner with direction by Tom Taylor.

Tuesday March 21
 During the afternoon, the full line-up of Marc Bolan and T.Rex join Ringo at John's Tittenhurst Park mansion to film additional scenes for *Born To Boogie*. Joining T.Rex and Elton John in Lennon's ASS (Ascot Sound Studios), Ringo joins in on an all-star jam to perform, before the cameras, versions of 'Tutti Frutti', 'Children Of The Revolution' and 'The Slider', with only the first two tracks appearing in the finished version of the film. An additional day's filming is set for tomorrow.

Wednesday March 22

 Apple's film *The Concert For Bangla Desh* is previewed in New York at The DeMille Theater with John, Yoko, Jerry Rubin and Nino Tempo in the audience. John is reported to have enjoyed the screening but is seen leaving the theatre during Bob Dylan's segment.

 Meanwhile back in England, the final piece of shooting for *Born To Boogie* is completed this afternoon, when Ringo supervises the filming of the Mad Hatter's Tea Party sequence on the grounds of John's vast estate. This scene features disgusting table manners from Micky Finn, Bolan's right-hand man from T.Rex. (The *Born To Boogie* film will premiere in London on December 14.)

Thursday March 23

 The film *The Concert For Bangla Desh* officially opens in New York. The movie is presented in 70mm film with six-track sound. (The UK release will not take place until Thursday July 27 – see entry.)

Tuesday March 28

 In the UK, the ITV network transmits (between 10:32 and 11:28pm) the ATV (Associated Television) documentary entitled *Whatever Happened To Tin Pan Alley?* a 50-minute examination into the changing face of popular music. The show also features a three-minute retrospective look at The Beatles, and includes an interview with their producer George Martin. He remarks: "I think the four of them are greater than the individuals and obviously each individual album that has been produced is good because they're all very talented people, but I still don't think they're as great as they were when they were Beatles together."

A clip of 'Twist And Shout' from Granada Television's *Scene At 6:30* (originally transmitted in June 1963) along with a medley of Beatles hits (from 1962–1967) set to a collage of Beatles photographs, accompany their part of the show. The programme also includes contributions from modern day pop contemporaries, including singers Mick Jagger, Paul Jones, record producer Mickie Most, Marc Bolan & T. Rex, The Who, Cliff Richard and Jonathan King.

Friday March 31

 The official Beatles' Fan Club in England is closed. Freda Norris (nee Kelly) who has been running the club for 11 years remarks: "Paul pulled out of the fan club last August and John, George and Ringo in January. So there was no point in keeping the project running as a corporate Beatles fan club with the four principals shooting off in different directions." She goes on to reflect on the declining popularity of the club. "Around 1965 the membership was 80,000 . . . the membership now is down to 11,000."

 Meanwhile, the second year of McCartney Productions Ltd. accounts reveal sales figures of £4,234, while outgoing expenses have increased to a hefty £13,446, meaning a loss of £9,212 for the tax year ending March 31, 1972.

April

 In an interview, Ravi Shankar is asked about George: "To me, he is like a son, like a younger brother, like a disciple all combined together. I have a very great love and affection for him."

 The first edition of the politics and arts magazine *Sundance* features an article by Yoko entitled "What A Bastard" describing how different women suffer when they have a job. Meanwhile, also this month, the Lennons are requested to join two respected US anti-drug organisations, the American Bar Association Council Against Drug Abuse and the Presidents Commission Against Drug Abuse.

 Possibly in a turmoil becuase the company has made a loss for the second consecutive year, callers to the McCartney Productions office in Soho Square London hear a recording of 'Give Ireland Back To The Irish'.

Saturday April 1

 John writes again to *Melody Maker*, this time in response to the March 18 claim that: "Marc Bolan was now as important as Lennon or Dylan and that people like Lennon and Jagger were now checking him out." John writes: "I ain't never heard 'Jeepster', tho' I heard and liked 'Get It On' and his first hit. Anyway, we all know where all these 'new licks' come from – right, Marc? . . . By the way, Marc's checking us out not vice-versa! He's called us babe! Anyway, he's ok – but don't push yer luck. Love Lennon, Ono."

🍎 A quick look at the UK charts reveals that 'Give Ireland Back To The Irish' is placed at number 23 (down from number 20) and 'Back Off Boogaloo' has entered at number 30 in the singles charts. While in the album charts, *Imagine* is at number 11 and *Bangla Desh* is at number 15.

Saturday April 8
🍎 In the UK singles chart, 'Back Off Boogaloo' has risen to number 16, while Wings' 'Give Ireland Back To The Irish' has slipped to number 30.
🍎 George and Patti are present at a London party honouring the composer Jim Webb. Also in attendance are Harry Nilsson, Alan Price and Dudley Moore.

Monday April 17
🍎 Producer Glyn Johns reveals that he has walked out of the sessions for Paul's latest album at the Olympic Studios in Barnes. They part company due to a "disagreement" over the recordings. "Now we have respect for each other," Glyn announces.

Tuesday April 18
🍎 An Immigration and Naturalisation Service hearing is held in New York regarding deportation proceedings against John. Immediately following the brief trial, John and Yoko meet, for the first time, with Geraldo Rivera who interviews the Lennons about the case for ABC TV Channel 7's *Eyewitness News*. When John and Yoko leave the Immigration and Naturalisation building they face an army of newspapers and TV reporters. Asked why is it so important for him and Yoko to stay in America, John states: "Well . . . the judge who gave us temporary custody of Kyoko said we must bring the child up in the continent of America, and we're quite happy with that. Yoko has been here half her life. She was educated here . . . fifteen years she's lived here. She has an American child, she was married to an American citizen and now she is married to an English citizen . . . and that's caused all the trouble. But we love to be here."
Further hearings for the case occur on May 12 and 17. (Incidentally, evidence revealed much later shows that the Nixon administration feared Lennon would lead demonstrations at the upcoming 1972 Republican National Convention in Miami, Florida, but in fact John never even went near the convention site.)

Saturday April 22
🍎 In New York, John and Yoko address the National Peace Rally in Duffy Square. They are seen leading a chorus of 'Give Peace A Chance'.
🍎 Ringo and Maureen are in the audience for Jerry Lee Lewis' concert at the London Palladium.

Monday April 24
🍎 John's single 'Woman Is The Nigger Of The World'/'Sisters O Sisters', performed by Yoko, is released in America only. A large number of US radio stations refuse to play the record but, nevertheless, it still manages to reach number 57 in the *Billboard* charts.

Thursday April 27
🍎 John publicly states that "deportation proceedings against him are politically motivated".

Saturday April 29
🍎 John Lindsay, The Mayor of New York, asks the Federal Authorities to allow John and Yoko to remain permanently in America and to quash the deportation proceedings against them. He announces: "A grave injustice is being perpetrated!"

May
🍎 Early this month, John, in an interview with Ray Connolly, is quoted as saying about Paul: "I went through a period of saying things that I thought would spur him on, but I think they were misunderstood. That's how 'How Do You Sleep?' was intended. Although I suppose it was a bit hard on him. But that was just how I felt when I wrote and recorded it."
🍎 Paul takes possession of his new car, a brand-new Lamborghini.

 Ringo, for the third year running, attends the Cannes Film Festival in the South of France.

 Allen Klein denies alleged mismanagement of The Beatles' finances: "Under Brian Epstein, the group made six and a half-million pounds in six years; under me and my ABKCO Industries, they earned £9 million in 19 months – that's a published fact!"

On the break-up of the group, Klein states: "One of the things that has always concerned me is that so much emphasis is put on 'Oh! The Beatles have broken up.' I don't think it was a tragedy. They haven't died! Maybe it was time they had a chance to live their own lives. It's almost like saying that every time a child leaves home it's a tragedy. But why? Doesn't he grow, isn't it time he started his own life?"

Tuesday May 2
 In America, the New York Times runs an editorial supporting John and Yoko's bid to remain in the States. To support the campaign, the National Committee for John and Yoko is formed.

Friday May 5
 John and Yoko make their second, and final, appearance during the second half of ABC TV's *The Dick Cavett Show*. Unlike their first appearance last year, John and Yoko perform live in the studio. Along with Elephant's Memory, they sing 'Woman Is The Nigger Of The World' and 'We're All Water'. Besides the songs, John also takes the opportunity to again express his feelings against television in England and announces that he and Yoko watched George's appearance on the programme last November where he plugged the Lennons' single 'Happy Christmas (War Is Over)'. "That was nice of him," John adds. The couple also uses *The Dick Cavett Show* to explain, in great detail, the history of the problems they've faced trying to regain custody of Kyoko. In addition, Yoko uses the show as a launch pad for her new appeal, a campaign for Children's Medical Relief International to help raise money for a hospital in Saigon called The Centre for Plastic and Reconstructive Surgery. This is a modern facility designed to treat children directly and indirectly injured during the Vietnam war, whose financial support is currently being stripped by the US government. During their interview, John also claims to Cavett that his phones are being tapped and that he is being followed.

"Intellectuals? They can't hear or feel anything!" – John on *The Dick Cavett Show*, May 11, 1972.

Joining the Lennons on the show is the actress Shirley MacLaine. Incidentally, before the broadcast on Thursday May 11, the bosses at the ABC television station had decided to cut the performance of 'Woman Is The Nigger . . .' from the broadcast completely, fearing that it might upset some viewers. Cavett objected to the cut and insisted that the song remain and, prior to the telecast of the programme, inserted a brief videotape of him explaining why the song must be shown. Critics and viewers rate the show a success, a response particularly pleasing to Cavett who is now facing a possible axe from the station due to a "lack of audience response". By the time of this programme, a National Committee acting for both John and Yoko had collected a petition urging the US government to halt deportation proceedings against him.

Friday May 12
 Originally scheduled for the 5th, the Wings' single 'Mary Had A Little Lamb'/'Little Woman Love' is released in the UK. Described by Paul and Linda as "A song for spring to make people happy", its EMI release number comes exactly 1,000 singles after The Beatles' début 'Love Me Do' in October 1962. (The American release takes place on May 29.)

When Paul is asked why he recorded the track he said it was because . . . "my daughter Mary liked hearing her name sung. It's the one song people seem to think is a bit daft. I don't regret writing it, 'cos I wrote it for her." The song, in complete contrast to the controversial slant of his previous A-side, naturally confuses the music press. The paper *Sounds* ask Paul about this. "I'm crazy. I've always been crazy from the minute I was born . . . Geminis are supposed to be changeable and I don't know if that's true or not but I'm a Gemini and I know one minute I might be doing 'Ireland' and the next I'll be doing 'Mary Had A Little Lamb'. I can see how that would look from the sidelines, but the thing is we're not either of those records, but we are both of them. 'Mary' is just a kids' song. It was written for one of our kids, whose name is Mary and I just realised if I sang that, she'd understand." With retrospect, Paul admits that 'Mary' was not "a great record", but points out that "it goes down well at live shows". In conclusion, Paul remarks: "The quote that sums up that song for me is I read Pete Townshend saying that his daughter had to have a copy . . . I like to keep in with the five year olds!"

Saturday May 13
🍎 Meanwhile in America, John and Yoko, along with Elephant's Memory, appear in Washington Square at the benefit concert held in the Methodist Church. Backstage at the concert John gives an exclusive interview to KUPS Radio.

Monday May 15
🍎 Back in England, at the Manor Studios in Oxfordshire, Paul begins the first mixing of tracks intended for the album *Red Rose Speedway*.

Sunday May 21
🍎 Two months after it was originally scheduled, due to a clearance problem with Apple, BBC Radio One broadcast the first part of *The Beatles Story* (between 5:00 and 5:55pm). The opening show is called *The Birth Of The Liverpool Sound*. (The series, written and produced by Johnny Beerling and narrated by Brian Matthew, will run weekly, for 13 parts, until Sunday August 13.) To celebrate the series, originally titled *The Lives And Music Of The Beatles*, models of the group adorn the cover of the BBC listings magazine *Radio Times*, covering the week May 20-26. Inside this edition, there is an interview with John by Ray Connolly and Paul by Pete Matthews. Paul is not impressed with the idea of the series, saying: "It's like an obituary for me, I don't like these old 'Remember them' things; you know, one of them's a bin man . . ."
  To trace the initial idea for the series we have to go right back to October 1965, when D.H. MacLean, of BBC Radio, first approached Brian Epstein with the view to telling, in their own words, the story of the group. In January of 1966 the plans were put on hold because, amazingly, they felt that there was not enough pre-taped material of the group from both England and America. With the split in 1970, the idea to resurrect the series came full circle and production on the series began towards the end of 1971 when a number of Beatles connected people, besides the fab four, were interviewed for the series, including George Martin (interviewed in London at his AIR Studios), Anne Nightingale (interviewed at her home in Brighton, Sussex) and Radio One presenter David Wigg (at his home in London). To help ease the burden of the high production costs, a rushed sale of the series on 13 BBC Transcription Disc records goes ahead to America at a cost of (for the time) an amazing $100,000.
  Paul makes no secret of his distaste for the programmes so no specific pieces by him appear throughout the entire series. The BBC instead have to be content with pre-recorded material, such as the interview by Michael Wale conducted backstage at Wings' first European concert in France on July 9 which is included in the thirteenth and final part transmitted on August 13.

Monday May 22 (with a break on Thursday May 25)
🍎 Paul and Wings return to London's Scotch of St. James where they rehearse for their upcoming tour, although the details of this will not be released until the following Monday, May 29.

Thursday May 25
🍎 At the BBC Television Studios in Wood Lane, London, Wings take a break from rehearsals to record their first studio appearance on *Top Of The Pops* where they mime a live performance of 'Mary Had A Little Lamb'. The show, which is transmitted later this night on BBC1 between 7:25 and 7:59pm, is hosted by Ed "Stewpot" Stewart and also features studio performances by The Move, John (formerly Long John) Baldry and Friends, T. Rex and Elton John. The BBC reach a separate agreement with Paul to use, on future radio broadcasts, the live performance used on this broadcast. Unfortunately the Wings' videotape clip is wiped during the year.
  Paul: "I hear people knocking *Top Of The Pops*, but I'm telling you, I watch *Top Of The Pops* just because it is pop. In Britain you just do not have anything, and I'd rather watch that than the news any day. *Top Of The Pops*, Tom & Jerry; they may be for kids, but I'm a kid then, because I dig that stuff. I think rather than don't do *Top Of The Pops*, you

should do *Top Of The Pops*. Rather than drop a show like that, there should be five more like that!"

Sunday May 28
 BBC Radio One transmits part two of *The Beatles Story* (between its regular 5:00 to 5:55pm slot). The show is called *Getting It Onto Wax.*

June
 George and Ringo fly to New York together. George is there to collect an award (see June 5) and to oversee the latest matters involving money raised from his Bangla Desh concert. To date, money raised from the album stands at $1,320,000 (and rising) and $255,000 from the concert. The film has just begun to show a profit.

Saturday June 3
 Melody Maker announces: "Wings To Play 'Official' Tour", revealing that: "Paul McCartney's Wings will be playing British dates in London, Manchester and Glasgow during July – and also making an extensive tour of the Continent." The report adds: ". . . they will visit France, Germany, Italy, Scandinavia, Belgium and Holland."

Sunday June 4
 Part three of *The Beatles Story (Chart Success And The Package Tours)* is transmitted on BBC Radio One.

Monday June 5
 Following their fundraising efforts for the people of Bangladesh, UNICEF, the United Nations children's fund, award George, Allen Klein and Ravi Shankar, its "Child Is The Father Of The Man" award at its annual luncheon.

Tuesday June 6
 Wings shoot a new videotape clip for 'Mary Had A Little Lamb' at the BBC Television Theatre in Shepherds Bush, London. This clip, which features the band miming the song at what is supposed to be the bottom of a hill with Paul playing the piano, all intercut with animated sequences to illustrate the lyrics, is inserted into programme eight of the latest series of the long-running children's programme *The Basil Brush Show*, transmitted on BBC1 on Saturday June 24 between 5:00 and 5:29pm. Hosted by Derek Fowlds, the comedy show also features contributions by The Roger Stevenson Marionettes and The Bert Hayes Sextet. During the taping session, Paul is informed by a member of the Joe Lights lighting company that the lyrics to the 'Mary Had A Little Lamb' song were the first words ever recorded by Thomas Edison when he invented the phonograph back in 1877.

To aid with the promotions for 'Mary Had A Little Lamb'; Wings appear in two further video clips. The first features the group miming the song in a barnyard setting. Paul is seen playing the song on the piano while a hen perches on top of it. Linda is seen cuddling a lamb and then singing the song while playing bongos. The second performance, affectionately called the "psychedelic version", features Wings performing the song in matching orange T-shirts and dungarees, with strikingly bright blue, yellow, black and red colours appearing in the background. Incidentally, Nicholas Ferguson, who first met Paul on the set of *Ready Steady Go!* in the sixties, directs all three of the above versions. He also directed The Beatles Intertel studio promotional films on November 23, 1965. (Paul will appear in another taped version of 'Mary Had A Little Lamb' during the 1973 TV special *James Paul McCartney*, see entry for March 10, 1973.)

Wednesday June 7
 A month before its UK premiere, Apple's film *The Concert For Bangla Desh* opens in Sweden at selected cinemas.

Saturday June 10
 It is announced that Paul and Linda, as composers and owners, are continuing their association with the ATV group with a seven-year agreement. All differences between them and Sir Lew Grade have been, according to an ATV spokesman, "amicably settled". The agreement is in the form of a co-publishing deal.

Sunday June 11
🍎 Part four of *The Beatles Story (The Start Of Beatlemania)*, is transmitted on BBC Radio One.

Monday June 12
🍎 The album *Sometime In New York City*, by John, Yoko and Elephant's Memory, is released in America. (The UK release takes place over three months later on September 15 due to copyright problems over the songs.) Also on the 12th, as part of promotions for the album, John records an interview with the freelance American radio journalist Scott Johns at his Greenwich Village apartment, during which he discusses his relationship with the musician David Peel. In 1980, the tape is subsequently released on the limited edition disc *The David Peel Interviews*.

Sunday June 18
🍎 Part five of *The Beatles Story (The World Surrenders)* is transmitted on BBC Radio One.

Sunday June 25
🍎 Part six of *The Beatles Story (The Life And Rewards Of Success)* is transmitted on Radio One.

Wednesday June 28
🍎 In London, at the annual Ivor Novello Awards luncheon, George wins two awards for his song 'My Sweet Lord'.

Thursday June 29
🍎 In England, the "barnyard" version of the MPL promotional film-clip of Wings performing 'Mary Had A Little Lamb' is broadcast on BBC1's *Top Of The Pops* between 7:25 and 7:59pm, and introduced by Jimmy Savile.

Friday June 30
🍎 Another exhibition of Yoko's work this time entitled Documenta 5, opens in Kassel, West Germany. The show runs until October 8.

July
🍎 At the start of the month, George finally takes delivery of his brand new BMW 3.0 litre CSA Coupe, having purchased it on June 26. He will keep the car for five years until July 1977, when he will sell it to a dealer in Suffolk.

Sunday July 2
🍎 In New York, lawyers representing John and Yoko prepare a final brief for the United States Immigration and Naturalisation Service outlining the reasons why they should be allowed to stay in the United States. The special inquiry officer Mr. Ira Fieldsteel holds the case over until the following day.
🍎 In the UK, BBC Radio One transmits part seven of *The Beatles Story*. This week's show is called *When The Touring Had To Stop*.

Monday July 3 (to July 6)
🍎 Wings hold their final rehearsals in preparation for their European tour at the ICA on The Mall in London.

Friday July 7
🍎 Wings leave England en route to France to begin their Wings Over Europe tour. This is in fact the first pre-planned tour by any Beatle since 1966 and the longest itinerary by any member of the group since they stopped touring that year. For the next seven weeks Wings will travel through France, Germany, Switzerland, Denmark, Finland, Sweden, Norway, Holland and Belgium, using as their base a specially converted, gaily painted London Transport double-decker bus, rented from a company in Hounslow and driven by Pat Puchelli, which had its roof removed and will be affectionately nicknamed Silverline Tours by Paul. It reaches a top speed of only 38 mph, and its fridge contains cheese, steaks and beer. Paul also takes with him the Rolling Stones Mobile Recording Unit, which he will use to professionally record five of their shows in Holland and

Belgium (only 'The Mess' will see the light of day). Paul reveals to waiting journalists, who are there to cover their departure: "When we were on holiday recently I was rediscovering the song 'Yesterday', playing it on an acoustic guitar. I love 'em . . . I enjoyed it all. Fantastic thing (The Beatles) while it lasted!"

* * *

'Wings Over Europe' tour 1972
July 9 to August 24

On Sunday July 9, Wings perform an open-air concert at the Théâtre Antique, Chateau Vallon in France, marking the start of the Wings Over Europe 1972 tour, which extends through until August 24. Songs performed during the tour include: 'Smile Away', 'The Mess', 'Hi Hi Hi', 'Mumbo', 'Bip Bop', 'Say You Don't Mind' (performed by Denny), 'Seaside Woman' (performed by Linda), 'I Would Only Smile' (Denny), 'Blue Moon Of Kentucky', 'Give Ireland Back To The Irish', 'Henry's Blues' (by Henry McCullough), '1882', 'I Am Your Singer', 'Eat At Home', 'Maybe I'm Amazed', 'My Love', 'Mary Had A Little Lamb', 'Soily', 'Best Friend', 'Long Tall Sally', 'Wild Life' and 'Cottonfields' (a cover of The Beach Boys' hit). The repertoire varies slightly from one concert to the next, an exercise to sharpen up the Wings live act. Paul produces a film of this tour called *The Bruce McMouse Show*. This features animated footage, intercut with live Wings concert film, of a cartoon character called Bruce McMouse along with his wife Yvonne and their children Soily, Swooney and Swat who travel with Wings and live beneath the stage while the band perform. To date, this MPL film, edited down to 50 minutes, has never been released. The only public screening from the film occurs when a short clip of 'Hi Hi Hi' is included in the 1986 BBC/MPL programme *McCartney* (first screened on BBC1 in England on August 29 1986).

The full Paul and Wings European concert tour includes shows at:

Théâtre Antique, Chateau Vallon, Toulon, France (Sunday July 9)
Juan Les Pins in France (Wednesday July 12)
Théâtre Antique, Arles, France (Thursday July 13)
Arles, France (Friday July 14 – Cancelled due to poor ticket sales)
Olympia Hall, Paris, France (Sunday July 16 – 2 shows)
Circus Krone, Munich, Germany (Tuesday July 18)
Offenbach Halle, Frankfurt, Germany (Wednesday July 19)
Kongresshaus, Zurich, Switzerland (Friday July 21)
Pavilion, Montreux, Switzerland (Saturday July 22 & Sunday July 23)

Then, following a few days rest, the tour resumes with shows at:

K.B. Hallen, Copenhagen, Denmark (Tuesday August 1)
Messuhalli, Helsinki, Finland (Friday August 4)
Idraets, Kupittaan Urheiluhalli, Turku, Finland (Saturday August 5)
Tovoli Gardens, Kungliga Hallen, Stockholm, Sweden (Monday August 7)
Idretis Halle, Oerebro, Sweden (Tuesday August 8)
Oslo, Norway (Wednesday August 9)
Scandinavium Hall, Gothenburg, Sweden (Thursday August 10)
Olympean, Lund, Sweden (Friday August 11)
Fyns Forum, Odense, Denmark (Sunday August 13)
Wejlby Risskov Hallen, Arkus, Denmark (Monday August 14)
Hanover, Germany (Wednesday August 16)
Evenementenhal, Groningan, Holland (Thursday August 17 – Cancelled/redated August 19)
De Doelan, Rotterdam, Holland (Thursday August 17)
De Doelan, Rotterdam, Holland (Friday August 18 – Cancelled/redated August 17)
Turschip, Breda, Holland (Saturday August 19 – Cancelled)
Evenementenhal, Groningen, Holland (Saturday August 19)
Concertgebouw, Amsterdam, Holland (Sunday August 20)
Congresgebouw, The Hague, Holland (Monday August 21)
Cirque Royale, Brussels, Belgium (Tuesday August 22 – Cancelled)
Borgerhout (originally Cine Roma), Antwerp, Belgium (Tuesday August 22)
Deutschlandhalle, Berlin, BRD (Thursday August 24)

The former *Rainbow Theatre* manager John Morris handles the tour. He announces to the music press: "We have no specific plans to play Britain. Paul wants to play small halls and most of the capacities here are less than 3,000. He wasn't interested in playing the monstrous places which he probably could have filled." The concerts, which feature no support act and no encore, are divided into two sets. The second set is accompanied by a movie (which includes clips of the countryside, flying birds, waves crashing against rocks and astronauts landing on the moon) which is flashed onto a screen behind the group as they perform.

Sunday July 9
Backstage prior to the opening concert at the outdoors Théâtre Antique in Chateau Vallon, Paul is asked about the tour: "We wanted to start at quite a smallish place. We're going to appear in England but if you go and play Britain or America with a very new band you're really put on the spot. You've got to be red hot, and it takes a little time for a band to get red hot!" Interestingly, he then reveals that George had invited him to appear in last year's Concert For Bangla Desh in New York. He tells reporters why he turned George down: "If I'd gone there I know for certain it would have been played up as 'Hey! The Beatles are back together again!' It may have only been for one night, but the whole world would have taken it as the truth. But it's ended! The Beatles have definitely ended. The man from the record company (EMI) said, 'Would you play just once a year lads?' like a sort of memorial tribute. Well, I'm not going to get into that because I'm not dead yet. You can get into all that when I'm dead if you want to, but it's no good for me now."

The attendance for this opening concert is approximately 2,000. The top ticket price was 20 francs, approximately £1.25. Following a triumphant show, Paul enthusiastically offers his view on the tour to *Melody Maker* reporter Chris Charlesworth, who naturally begins by asking him "why no British dates?" Paul optimistically replies: "We will play there sometime or other, but not right now. The audiences are very critical in Britain and we're a new band just starting out – no matter what we've been through before. We have to get worked in before doing any big shows in Britain or America." Paul's mood characteristically changes when he is asked: "Have you seen your former Beatle mates recently?" Paul bluntly replies: "No, I've got no particular reason to, and I don't really want to. They're into their things and I'm into mine."

On a lighter note, another reporter asks Paul why Wings are travelling around in a double-decker London bus. "It mainly came about when we were on holiday and we were trying to get healthy before a tour," he explains. "We suddenly thought 'Wait a minute', if we're gonna be in Europe in summer going to places like the South of France, we thought it'd be silly to be in some box all day gasping for air. So we came up with this idea to have an open deck. We've got mattresses up there so we can just cruise along – fantastic! Just lie around, get the sun and keep healthy."

Linda is asked if she was nervous during the concert: "I was nervous in the first half. We had no soundcheck, no rehearsal, no nothing. We had to go out cold, so I had to warm up a bit. We were very hot in the second half."

Friday July 14
A Wings concert, scheduled for today in Lyons, France, is cancelled due to poor ticket sales, so instead Wings, comprising of Paul, Linda and Denny, hastily assemble at the EMI Pathe Marconi Studios in Paris, to record the first version of Linda's 'Seaside Woman'.

Saturday July 22
The single 'Mary Had A Little Lamb' reaches number 28 in the American charts. (The song will reach number nine in the UK charts.)

Thursday August 10
Following their performance at the Scandinavium Hall in Gothenburg, Sweden, the P.A. system is abruptly cut off by the police who are waiting to question Paul, Linda and Denny Seiwell about seven ounces of marijuana that customs officials had intercepted. Amidst scenes of confusion backstage, caught in pictures by the tour photographer Joe Stevens, the three, along with Paul's secretary Rebecca Hines, are taken away for questioning at police headquarters. They are later arrested on charges of drug possession and fined the equivalent of $1,000, $200 and $600 respectively.

After three hours of questioning, they confess to the police that the cannabis they smoke is sent to them daily by post from London. Paul, Linda and Denny admit, according to the authorities, they smoke hash every day and are almost addicted to it. But, according to John Morris, a different set of events took place at police headquarters. "Paul, Linda and Denny did admit to the Swedish police that they used hash. At first they denied it but the police gave them a rough time and started threatening all sorts of things. The police said they would bar the group from leaving the country unless they confessed. The drugs were found in a parcel addressed to Paul by customs men. Lots of people send drugs to the band. They think they are doing them some kind of a favour, instead it causes all this kind of trouble. It was simply a case of pleading guilty, paying the fine and getting out of the city. As far as we are concerned, the whole business is finished." An unnamed member of Wings though is heard to playfully remark: "The police acting against us was an excellent advertisement . . . our name now flies all over the world."

Throughout the duration of the tour, the European press continues to snipe at Paul and his new band, blowing even the most trivial matter out of proportion. As one leading tabloid reports: "At virtually every hotel there have been tantrums because the McCartneys will not accept the conventional Scandinavian single beds. Their attitude seems to be, 'I want it, therefore it must happen.' "

Sunday August 20
During their seven-day stay in Holland, Wings appears today on the VPRO radio programme *Popsmuk*, the highlight of which is when the group gathers round Henry McCullough, seated at the piano, who plays the improvised tune 'Complain To The Queen' which features a vocal by Paul.

Monday August 21
An extra date to the tour is added tonight at the Congresgebouw, The Hague, in Holland, where Paul and Wings are recorded singing 'The Mess'. Their performance is later released on a single as the B-side to 'My Love'.

At the conclusion of the European tour, Paul sums up: "The main thing I didn't want was to come on stage, faced with the whole torment of five rows of press people with little pads, all looking at me and saying, 'Oh well, he is not as good as he was.' So we decided to go out on that university tour which made me less nervous, because it was less of a big deal. So we went out and did that, and by the end of that tour I felt ready for something else, so we went into Europe. I was pretty scared on the European tour, because that was a bit more of a big deal. Kind of, 'Here he is, ladies and gentlemen. Solo!' I had to go on there, with a band I really didn't know much about, with all new material. We had decided *not* to do Beatle material, which was a killer of course. We had to do an hour of other material, but we did not have it then. I didn't even have a song then that was mine. I felt that everybody wanted Beatle stuff, so I was pretty nervous about that. By the end of the European tour I felt a bit better. By then, there was enough of a repertoire to do it. I wouldn't mind doing Beatle songs, but it's a bit funny when you feel that people want to hear certain Beatle songs, just through nostalgia, and yet you don't want to live on your laurels. You want to try and create a whole new thing, so that you say, 'Well, this is me.' Then you do the Beatle stuff, once you've established yourself. That's the way I felt really."

* * *

Sunday July 9
 In the UK, BBC Radio One transmits part eight of *The Beatles Story*, entitled *The Psychedelic Chapter*.

Wednesday July 12
 George appears before the magistrates in Maidenhead, Berkshire, to explain his car crash on February 28. He tells the court: "I hit a motorway interchange crash barrier because I did not see the warning sign." George is later found guilty of careless driving and is fined £20. In addition, his licence is endorsed for the second time, the first being on Tuesday February 23, 1971 (see entry).

Sunday July 16
 The Beatles Story part nine, *Meditation And Corporation*, is broadcast.

Sunday July 23
 The Beatles Story part ten, *Hello Goodbye Or Come Together*, is broadcast.

Wednesday July 26
 At 11:30am, a special preview screening of *The Concert For Bangla Desh* takes place at the Rialto cinema in Coventry Street, London.
"The Greatest Concert Of The Decade. Now You Can See It And Hear It . . . As If You Were There!" – Advertising slogan for the film.
George recalls the problems with the *Concert For Bangla Desh* film: "I put all the expense to Apple at the time, and the only way Apple could break even was if the film came out any good. And the film wasn't that good! The cameramen were crazy and it took Dylan and I months to try to make it into something decent. All the cameras had cables hanging in front of them, and another camera was out of focus all the way through so we couldn't use that one. The film finally shows what the concert was about. I said to the artists, 'Look, we are recording and filming it, but if it turns out lousy, I promise you we are not going to put it out. I want you to see it and hopefully you will agree to let us do it.'
"Bob (Dylan) came down to the editing of the film, but he didn't really want to. I mean if you look at Bob's section, there is one single camera shot all the way through. Which, in a way, you can get into. It is funny, once you realise it is not changing camera angles and it is all grainy. But that was because Bob wanted it like that, he's a bit of a funny little fellow! But he wanted it like that, so I am not going to argue. It was great to have him in it at all!"

Thursday July 27
 The Apple film *The Concert For Bangla Desh* opens to the general public at The Rialto cinema in Coventry Street, London. Over its first twelve days of business the movie will take £12,979 at the box office, smashing the ten previous daily records. The figures are the best for the theatre in two years. Continuous round-the-clock screenings take place between 10am and 4am on July 27, 28 and 29.

Sunday July 30
 The Beatles Story part eleven, *The End Of The Beatles?* is broadcast on BBC Radio One.

August
 At the start of the month in his Friar Park studios, George records, with Cilla Black on vocals and Eric Clapton on guitar, the tracks 'You've Gotta Stay With Me' and 'When Every Song Is Sung', a song that in 1976, will be re-recorded by Ringo as 'I'll Still Love You' for his *Rotogravure* album. Also this month, George is seen socialising with Joe Cocker and is present in the audience at the CBS annual dinner, held at the Grosvenor Hotel in London. Towards the end of the month, George takes a summer holiday without Patti, spending a week in Portugal at a villa rented by his musical friend Gary Wright and his wife Christina. Wright remarks about the former Beatle: "George is just driving around Portugal and the South of France, staying with friends and at hotels. He seems to be enjoying himself. He's writing lots of new things and he seems to be having a good time." (Patti, incidentally, is to be found back home at Friar Park, while renovation work is being carried out.) Summing up, Wright adds: "Sometimes, George goes off on his own. Sometimes he takes Patti with him but I think he just felt like a holiday and wanted to get away."
 Ringo begins filming *Count Downe* on location around London. Billed as a "comedy rock-horror flick", the film features the direction of Freddie Francis, best known for his low-budget British horror and science fiction films of the sixties. Although production is completed in November, the film will not premiere until April 19, 1974, when by then, it will be retitled *Son Of Dracula*. Some of Ringo's dialogue and the songs 'Daybreak' and 'At My Front Door' from the film, appear on the soundtrack album *Son of Dracula*. In total, it is estimated that Ringo is investing some $800,000 in the picture. (See further entries for the film, listed August 15, 16 and November 25.)

Thursday August 3 (until Sunday August 6)
 In a further attempt to find Kyoko, John and Yoko travel to San Francisco. Geraldo Rivera covers their journey for an ABC TV Channel 7 *Eyewitness News* special programme

concerning the Lennons' constant attempt to find Yoko's child. Film footage (on Saturday August 5) taken by Geraldo includes him travelling through the city with John and Yoko in a car, aboard a tram car and braving extremely windy conditions to pay a visit to the Golden Gate Bridge. Later this night, back at the Lennons' hotel, and for the benefit of the *Eyewitness News* cameras, John (on acoustic guitar) and Yoko perform a medley of the tracks including: 'Well (Baby Please Don't Go)', 'Rock Island Line', 'Maybe Baby', 'Peggy Sue', 'Woman Is The Nigger Of The World', 'A Fool Like Me' and 'The Calypso Song'.

It is during this weekend that the idea for the One To One concerts for the benefit of the Willowbrook School for Children is conceived. John enlists the assistance of Elephant's Memory and the first rehearsals for the show are arranged for Friday August 18. John and Yoko return to New York, again without Kyoko, on Monday August 7.

🍎 Meanwhile, back in England on Sunday August 6, *The Beatles Story* part twelve, *The John, Paul, George and Ringo Show*, is broadcast on BBC Radio One.

Friday August 11
🍎 In London, George hires a small Mayfair cinema, behind the Hilton Hotel, to show selected guests the Apple film *Raga*. One of those invited is the star of the film Ravi Shankar, who is currently in Britain for a concert at Southwark Cathedral in London on Tuesday August 15.

Sunday August 13
🍎 The final part of *The Beatles Story*, *John, Paul, George And Ringo Today*, is transmitted on BBC Radio One in the UK.

Tuesday August 15 & Wednesday August 16
🍎 At the Surrey Docks, Ringo, along with Harry Nilsson, Keith Moon, Peter Frampton, Klaus Voorman, Rikki Farr, Bobby Keyes and Jim Price, who are collectively known as The Count Downes, begin filming three tracks intended for the next Apple film production *Count Downe*. Songs shot over these two days include 'At My Front Door', 'Jump Into The Fire' and 'Daybreak'. (For the second day's shoot, scenes are filmed with Led Zeppelin's drummer John Bonham, replacing Keith Moon who has flown to Belgium to rejoin The Who on their current European tour.) Ringo attends the filming but does not appear in the two concert sequences.

Thursday August 17
🍎 George returns to Liverpool to witness a performance by Ravi Shankar at the Philharmonic Hall.

Friday August 18
🍎 In America, John, Yoko and Elephant's Memory begin rehearsals for the One To One concerts at the Butterfly Studio at West 10th Street in New York City. During the three days of rehearsals (days two and three take place on August 20 and 22), the group rehearses the following tracks: 'Cold Turkey', 'Give Peace A Chance', 'Come Together', 'Well Well Well', 'Mother', 'New York City', 'Instant Karma', 'It's So Hard', 'Sisters O Sisters', 'Woman Is The Nigger Of The World', 'Don't Worry Kyoko', 'It's Only Make Believe', 'Open Your Box', 'We're All Water', 'Tequila', 'Move On Fast', 'Roll Over Beethoven', 'Unchained Melody', 'New York City', 'Long Tall Sally', 'Hound Dog', 'Mind Train', a short burst of Ringo's 'Back Off Boogaloo' and a jam entitled 'Bunny Hop'. Taking a break from the sessions, the group takes time out in Chinatown. (The rehearsals usually continue until the early hours of the morning.)

Sunday August 20 – Tuesday August 22
🍎 Additional One To One concert rehearsals are carried out by John, Yoko, and Elephant's Memory. But this time, the sessions move across to the Fillmore East Theater in New York.

Wednesday August 23
🍎 Following a late night of rehearsals, a rather exhausted looking John (wearing a black beret) and Yoko announce their One To One concert plans in a press conference at the blue room in New York's city hall. Accompanying them is John V. Lindsay, the mayor of New York City, Geraldo Rivera and a young girl who is a resident of the Willowbrook

School; a home for retarded children. The day of the concert, August 30, will also be, as John and Yoko reveal, "One To One Day". As a preview to the shows, this week John records some One To One concert radio commercials.

Tuesday August 29

 During the afternoon and early evening, the final rehearsals for the One To One concerts again take place at the Fillmore East Theater in New York.

Wednesday August 30

"Good evening ladies and gentlemen, from Madison Square Garden in New York, John Lennon and Yoko Ono present the One To One concert . . ." – The MC's announcement at the start of the show.

 John and Yoko perform two One To One benefit concerts (one in the afternoon and one in the evening) at Madison Square Garden in New York with The Plastic Ono Elephant's Memory band, performed for the benefit of the Willowbrook School for Children. Before the concerts rumours circulate in the press to the effect that the money raised from the shows will actually be going to the artists and not the children, a story which prompts one unnamed top recording group to drop out of the show.

John and Yoko's set-list for the two shows is as follows: Afternoon: 'Power To The People', 'New York City', 'It's So Hard', 'Move On Fast', 'Woman Is The Nigger Of The World', 'Sister O Sisters', 'Well Well Well', 'Born In A Prison', 'Instant Karma', 'Mother', 'We're All Water', 'Come Together', 'Imagine', 'Open Your Box', 'Cold Turkey', 'Don't Worry Kyoko (Mummy's Only Looking For Her Hand In The Snow)' and 'Hound Dog'; Evening: 'Power To The People', 'New York City', 'It's So Hard', 'Woman Is The Nigger Of The World', 'Sisters O Sisters', 'Well Well Well', 'Instant Karma', 'Mother', 'We're All Water', 'Come Together', 'Imagine', 'Cold Turkey', 'Hound Dog' and 'Give Peace A Chance', where John and Yoko are joined on stage by the stars and organisers of the shows.

The shows, organised by the ABC TV reporter Geraldo Rivera, also feature the legendary *Motown* recording star Stevie Wonder, Roberta Flack and Sha Na Na. Prior to the concerts, John purchases $60,000 worth of tickets for the show and gives them away to volunteer fund-raisers. The event will raise over $1.5 million for the Willowbrook School. As the sell-out crowd enters the building, they are handed a tambourine and asked to shake it during the concert. (A live radio broadcast of the evening show appears on the programme *The King Biscuit Radio Hour*.)

A selection of the songs performed at the concerts, are later released on the album *John Lennon: Live in New York City* (released in America on January 24 1986 and in the UK on February 24), namely 'Cold Turkey', 'Hound Dog', 'Give Peace A Chance' (clip) from the evening show; and 'New York City', 'Come Together', 'Imagine', 'Instant Karma', 'Mother', 'It's So Hard', 'Well Well Well', and 'Woman Is The Nigger Of The World' from the afternoon performance. A short clip of 'Give Peace A Chance' also appears on the 1975 John Lennon compilation LP *Shaved Fish*.

Both concerts are professionally filmed, and a version featuring seven of the songs performed at the evening concert ('Imagine', played to scenes of the One To One Day fun activities in Central Park this afternoon, 'Come Together', 'Instant Karma', 'Sisters O Sisters', 'Cold Turkey', 'Hound Dog' and 'Give Peace A Chance') is transmitted on ABC TV in America as a 53-minute special on December 14 1972.

Incidentally, the afternoon performance of Yoko's 'Move On Fast' will receive a rare one-off screening in England during the January 30, 1973 edition of BBC2's late night rock show *The Old Grey Whistle Test* (see entry). Meanwhile, a one-hour videocassette, suitably titled *John Lennon: Live in New York City* is released at the same time as the LP, and features different edits of some of the songs and adds some of Yoko's numbers. (The recording supervisor for the shows is Phil Spector.) Following the successful concerts, John, Yoko, and the other artists on the bill attend a celebratory party at the Tavern In The Green in Central Park.

Thursday August 31

 In America, an interview carried out with Paul backstage at the Théâtre Antique concert in France on Sunday July 9, is published in today's *Rolling Stone* magazine.

September
♣ At the Olympic Sound Studios in London, with the London Symphony Orchestra and Chamber Choir, Ringo records 'Fiddle About' and 'Tommy's Holiday Camp' for inclusion on the album of Lou Reizner's production of Pete Townshend's rock-opera *Tommy*. The all-star cast also includes The Who, Steve Winwood, Richie Havens, Rod Stewart, Maggie Bell, the actor Richard Harris, Graham Bell, Sandy Denny and Merry Clayton. (The album is released in the UK on November 24.)

Saturday September 2
♣ George is rumoured to be appearing today at Crystal Palace's Garden Party Concert alongside his friend Gary Wright. He fails to show.

Wednesday September 6
♣ In New York, John and Yoko appear live with Elephant's Memory towards the end of the all-day annual American TV special *Jerry Lewis Labor Day Telethon,* an event to raise money for the illness muscular dystrophy. They perform live versions of 'Imagine', 'Now Or Never' and a reggae version of 'Give Peace A Chance'.

Saturday September 9
♣ In England, an exclusive interview with Ringo, carried out by Ray Connolly, is published in tonight's *Evening Standard*.

Tuesday September 12
♣ The *Daily Mirror* publishes a report on the making of Ringo's film *Count Downe*.

Saturday September 16
♣ John and Yoko travel to Far Hills in New Jersey, to attend the memorial celebrations for Ken Dewery.

Tuesday September 19
♣ Following a routine surveillance, police raid Paul's Scottish farm in Kintyre, Argyll, where they find cannabis plants in a greenhouse. The plants are analysed by police chemists the following day (see entry for Friday, December 22).

Wednesday September 27
♣ In a bizarre double suicide, Rory Storm, the leader of Ringo's old group, The Hurricanes, is found dead with his mother in their beds at their Stormsville home in Liverpool. They had died from barbiturate and alcoholic poisoning. Two empty whisky bottles are found in the house. Rory, aged 33, had been depressed for a very long time because he had not reached the big time like The Beatles. His mother, meanwhile, had not recovered from the death of her husband. Allan Williams later asks Ringo why he never went to the funeral. "I wasn't at his birth either, was I?" he replies.

Saturday September 30
♣ *Melody Maker* publishes its annual readers' poll. Amongst the results in the British Section: Male Singer – John no. 9 and Album – *Imagine* no. 5; in the International Section: Best International Composer – John no. 3. Drums – Ringo no. 9. Bass – Paul no. 7. Album – *Bangla Desh* no. 2 and *Imagine* no. 7. In the *NME* musicians' poll, John is named as the world's no. 1 singer.

October
♣ At the Morgan Studios in Willesden, London, Paul and Wings record 'Hi Hi Hi', 'C Moon', 'Country Dreamer', 'Live And Let Die' and 'I Lie Around'. During the evening they record 'C Moon' and jam with Led Zeppelin drummer John Bonham. Meanwhile, the recordings for *Red Rose Speedway,* which had begun in March, are later this month moved to London's Abbey Road studios.
♣ Ringo flies to Hollywood to screen *Born To Boogie* to prospective film buyers.
♣ Rumours fly about this month that: "John and Elephant's Memory will be joined for a Madison Square Garden charity concert by Wings and a special group comprising of George and Ringo." Apple reply: "It ain't so . . ." But what does happen this month is that, again at the Record Plant, John co-produces with Yoko, her album *Approximate Infinite*

Universe. At the conclusion of the sessions in December, the Lennons participate in an episode of the Marks/Avcoin produced music series *Flipside.* The 22-minute show, which is primarily a promotional tool for Yoko's new album (which is released in America on January 8 1973 and in the UK on February 16 1973) features studio performances of four tracks from the album, 'Shirankatta (I Didn't Know)', 'Death Of Samantha', 'Catman (The Rosies Are Coming)' and 'Winter's Song'. Although John is not seen performing, he does contribute lengthy interviews in between the tracks. (The first public airing of this programme occurs on February 16 1973.)

🍎 Back in England, during a mammoth three-month Abbey Road recording session, George records tracks intended for *The Light That Lightened (sic) The World* album (later re-titled *Living In The Material World*). Working with Phil Spector, he first produces: 'Give Me Love (Give Me Peace On Earth)' and 'Miss O'Dell' which will be released the following year as a single, the latter featuring George bursting into laughter several times. The sessions, which feature Ringo alternating with Jim Keltner on drums, Nicky Hopkins (piano), Klaus Voorman (bass) and Gary Wright (keyboards), also produce the following: 'Sue Me, Sue You Blues', 'The Light That Has Lighted The World', 'Don't Let Me Wait Too Long', 'Who Can See It', 'Living In The Material World', 'The Lord Loves The One (That Loves The Lord)', 'Be Here Now', 'Try Some, Buy Some' (originally started during February of 1971), 'The Day The World Gets Round' and 'That Is All'. At this stage, the album is scheduled for a January/February 1973 release. (The recordings ultimately continue through into January 1973.)

🍎 Sgt. Pilcher, in charge of the drug squad at Scotland Yard in London, is jailed for six years on corruption charges. John has long claimed that Pilcher was responsible for planting the illegal substances in his flat when he was busted in 1968.

Wednesday October 11
🍎 Paul, through the British media, issues an appeal for the return of a stolen guitar he used on stage with The Beatles. He says: "If the thief stole it to sell it, he can sell it back to me!"

Thursday October 12
🍎 The promotional film clip of Wings performing 'Mary Had A Little Lamb' (the psychedelic version) is transmitted on *The Flip Wilson Show* on American TV.

Monday October 23
🍎 Ringo travels to Butlins holiday camp based on the Isle of Wight to begin filming the Goodtimes Enterprises' production of *That'll Be The Day* for Anglo-EMI. The film co-stars David Essex, who leaves his current role as Jesus in the musical *Godspell*, Billy Fury, and Keith Moon, the drummer with The Who. Based on a screenplay by the *Evening Standard* writer Ray Connolly, the seven-week shooting will be completed on December 14, although Ringo completes his scenes two weeks previous to that and returns home to London. The London premiere takes place on April 12, 1973. (For an interview on the set of *That'll Be The Day,* see entry for November 25.)

November
🍎 The Record Plant recording studio opens its third location in Sausalito, a small community across the bay in San Francisco. John and Yoko are among those attending the grand opening. During the middle of the month, Mick Jagger drops by to visit the Lennons at the New York Record Plant studio. He plays piano and guitar on some tracks.

🍎 Apple announce that they are now compiling for cinema release a film entitled *Ten Years In The Life Of The Beatles*. Ringo announces: "We are getting together all the clips we own to show the change in our music and our attitudes to life. It's a kind of *All Our Yesterdays*." Original plans reveal that the film is scheduled to be released to coincide with a proposed Beatles greatest hits package early next year.

🍎 Ringo completes the shooting of the film *Count Downe*.

Thursday November 2
🍎 A copyright is registered for the track 'You've Gotta Stay With Me', written by Paul L. Woodall (responsible for the words, music and the arrangement) and George Harrison (music and arrangement).

Sunday November 12
♣ At his Friar Park mansion, George begins drilling 200-feet deep holes, not for oil, but for water. His quest is to find 500,000 gallons of the stuff to cater for the needs of his vast ornamental lakes, based in the grounds of his mansion in Henley-on-Thames.

Monday November 13
♣ In America only, Apple releases the Yoko Ono/Elephant's Memory single 'Now Or Never' b/w 'Move On Fast'.

Friday November 24
♣ The album *Tommy*, featuring the two songs by Ringo, is released in the UK. (The American release takes place three days later, on November 27.)

Saturday November 25
♣ On the set of *That'll Be The Day*, Ringo gives an interview to *Cinema & TV Today* to promote the completion of his first feature, the Apple film *Count Downe*. Directed by Freddie Francis, the film is a musical with horror overtones and stars Harry Nilsson, Freddie Jones and Susannah Leigh. Ringo also appears, this time in the role of a wizard. He explains the film's story: "I just think that if Dracula were around today he would be into rock. We've got the whole family in this one – Frankenstein, the Mummy, Dracula, the Wolf Man, and me as Merlin. On *Count Downe* I went through everything – casting, meetings with actors, electricians, the lot. I wanted to make the film here in England because it's easier to learn at home." *Count Downe* is Apple's fifth full-length film, the others being *The Concert For Bangla Desh, Raga, El Topo* and *Born To Boogie*. (*Count Downe* will not see the light of day until April 19, 1974 when it receives its premiere in Atlanta, Georgia, where, by then, it appears under the different title of *Son Of Dracula.*)

Monday November 27
♣ Paul and Wings work on 'Seaside Woman' at AIR Studios in London.

Tuesday November 28
♣ Wings travel to the Southampton based studios of Southern ITV, at Northam in Hampshire, to shoot two promotional film clips, one for either side of their new single 'Hi Hi Hi' and 'C Moon'. Directed by Steve Turner, best remembered for his work on the award-winning BBC2 late-night 1968/1969 music show *Colour Me Pop*, these straightforward performance films feature the group miming on a low three-step stage. For 'C Moon', Paul plays the piano while sporting a pink sweatshirt emblazoned with the song's logo. Though shot on tape, the clips are subsequently transferred onto 16mm film for distribution to television, not yet utilising the convenient videotape process. Paul oversees the tape-to-film transferring process immediately after shooting and leaves the Southern ITV studios later this evening clutching the 16mm film masters. 'Hi Hi Hi' will receive a screening on LWT's *Russell Harty Plus* on Saturday December 16. While in Europe, amongst many screenings, the ZDF German music show *Disco 73* belatedly screens the clip during March of the following year.

Thursday November 30
♣ To celebrate the release of 'Hi Hi Hi'/'C Moon', Paul throws a lunchtime party at the Village Restaurant near London's Charing Cross Station.

December
♣ George, at his home studios in Friar Park, Henley, records an unreleased demo version of 'Sue Me, Sue You Blues'. He will return to the song again during January 1973.
♣ With the shooting now complete on *Count Downe* (*Son Of Dracula*) the Apple film undergoes sound dubbing at the World Wide Studios in St. Anne's Court, London.

Friday December 1
♣ The Wings double A-side single 'Hi HI Hi' / 'C Moon' is released in the UK. (The American release takes place on December 4.) The record is released purely because of the tremendous response the songs have received during the last tour. BBC Radio One and Two immediately ban 'Hi Hi Hi'. BBC publicity officer Rodney Collins explains the ban: "The ban has nothing to do with drugs," he remarks. "We thought the record unfit

for broadcasting because of the lyrics. Part of it goes: 'I want you to lie on the bed and get you ready for my body gun and do it, do it, do it to you'. While another part goes: 'Like a rabbit I'm going to grab it and do it till the night is done.'" The irony of the story is that Paul did not write 'get you ready for my body gun'. The lyrics, as he wrote, go 'get ready for my polygon'. He admits that it was intended to be suggestive "in an abstract way". While the BBC ban on the song has taken an immediate effect, someone at the Corporation had unfortunately forgotten to tell DJ Tony Blackburn who had already spun the track on his radio show last week.

The flip side, 'C Moon', is inspired by the 1965 hit 'Wooly Bully' by Sam Sham and The Pharaohs, which features the line "Not to be L7", in other words "square". So Paul made up 'C Moon' which makes a circle, the opposite of square. The single reaches number five in the UK charts. Paul explains the story behind the songs on the single:

"We wrote 'Hi Hi Hi' in Spain, because we had this tour coming up. Purposely as a nice easy rocker . . . it's basically a rock and roll thing written on three rock and roll chords to give us something aside from the rest of our material. The general reaction is that 'Hi Hi Hi' is kind of the strong side, but the reason we made it a double A is that 'C Moon' is one of those songs that catches up on you after a while. I can hear 'C Moon' in a year's time, people saying, 'Yeah! I like that one'. There's things to listen to on that one, put it on headphones and it's quite a trip."

Linda chips in: "Especially if you've just come home from work, that's the side to get into." Paul also explains the recordings on the track: "We left all the little bits in that you'd normally clean up for the record. There's the intro., the bit 'is this the intro.' that was for real. I missed the intro. and the song has changed because of it."

Saturday December 2
🍎 "'Mary Had A Little Lamb' . . . those lyrics are a heavy trip. Anyway, it sold as many as 'Tumbling Dice', so there! There was a critical thing about it, but listen, the point is we were all babies once and there are still a lot around who like to sing the song." – Paul, being interviewed by Mark Plummer in today's *Melody Maker*.

He continues his discussion of 'Mary Had A Little Lamb': "For me there were lots of silly little interesting things about the song, like I never knew beyond the first verse before. I knew 'Mary had a little lamb and its feet were white as snow, and everywhere that Mary went the lamb was sure to go' and I knew they sang the la las. Then after that I knew it followed her to school, but I never knew that the whole story was about the teacher chucking the lamb out of class. I thought it was just a great end where it gets chucked out. Everyone's wondering why this lamb is hanging about 'cause Mary loves the lamb. To me that's like a heavy trip those lyrics. It's very spiritual when someone hangs around because it's loved. I'm sure no one ever thinks about those kind of things."

🍎 Fresh from the filming of *That'll Be The Day*, Ringo and Maureen attend the London premiere of Josef Shaftel's production of *Alice In Wonderland* starring Fiona Fullerton at the Odeon Marble Arch in the presence of Her Majesty The Queen. Also in attendance are the celebrities Spike Milligan, Peter Sellers and Michael Crawford. Following the screening, Ringo and Maureen are among those attending a party at the Inn On The Park hotel.

Tuesday December 5
🍎 The proposed release today of John's single 'Woman Is The Nigger Of The World' (Apple R5953) is cancelled.

Tuesday December 12
🍎 Ringo appears live, promoting the film *Born To Boogie,* on the Thames/ITV children's television show *Magpie*. Meanwhile a clip of 'Children Of The Revolution' from the *Born To Boogie* film appears on tonight's edition of *The Old Grey Whistle Test*, broadcast on BBC2 between 10:35 and 11:20pm. The show also features 'Gimme Some Truth', extracted from John and Yoko's film *Imagine*.

Wednesday December 13
🍎 This morning, Ringo attends the *Born To Boogie* press screening at the Oscar One cinema in London. Whilst there he undertakes a few brief question and answer sequences with members of the British press.

Reporter: "How did you come to be filming Marc Bolan?"
Ringo: "I telephoned him one day and said, 'Come and see me. I've got this idea. See

what you think. Yes or no.' And on that particular thing it was 'no'. But through that meeting we got to know each other and became friendly. Then I heard he was going to be filmed at his Wembley show. Well, Apple has a film company so I said, 'Why don't you let me do it? I'm your pal.' And he said, 'Okay. We'll do it together.' After the show we looked at the footage we had got and decided to add to it. You see, my theory about filming concerts is that you cannot create the atmosphere that was in the hall. So I needed to do more. We got him to write a few things and set up a couple more days shooting."

Reporter: "What about the 'Some people like to rock. Some people like to roll' sequence?"
Ringo: "Oh yes! It was so messy that it had to be included!"
Reporter: "Was the Wembley show in any way a nostalgic experience for you?"
Ringo: "Very much so. They were screaming and shouting and I love that."
Reporter: "So you enjoy the screams then?"
Ringo: "Oh yeah. If they had been quiet when I played I would have died. I wouldn't have known what to do."

Thursday December 14
🍎 At 7pm, Ringo's film on Marc Bolan and T.Rex, *Born to Boogie,* premieres in London at the Oscar One cinema in Brewer Street, just off Shaftsbury Avenue. In attendance is Ringo with Maureen, plus Marc Bolan, Micky Finn and Elton John. During its opening two weeks at the cinema, the film will net approximately £1,613.

🍎 In America, ABC TV broadcasts the film version of John and Yoko's *One To One Concert,* which took place on August 30. While in England, this evening's *Top Of The Pops* (transmitted on BBC1 between 7:25 and 8:00pm) includes the promotional clip for 'Happy Christmas (War Is Over)', filmed at the recording sessions on October 31, 1971 (see entry for further details).

Saturday December 16
🍎 In the UK, the London Weekend Television chat-show series *Russell Harty Plus* transmits the Wings promotional film for 'Hi Hi Hi' during tonight's broadcast in the London region of ITV only. (The screening occurs between 10:41 and 11:39pm.)

Thursday December 21
🍎 *The Times* book review section Quick Guide, unfavourably reviews the new Beatles publication *Apple To The Core*, which sets out to chart the slow decline and disintegration of the group.

Friday December 22
🍎 It is announced that Paul is to face trial on March 8, 1973, accused of growing cannabis on his farm near Campbeltown, Kintyre, in Scotland. Paul does not appear to face the three charges at the Campbeltown sheriff court today. Through his solicitor, Paul pleads not guilty. Two of the three charges allege that he possessed cannabis at High Park farm and Low Ranachan farm, and the third charge alleges that he cultivated five plants of the drug.

Saturday December 23
🍎 The world premiere of John and Yoko's 70-minute film *Imagine* takes place on American television. (An edited 60-minute version, omitting Yoko's tracks, will be released on PMI [Picture Music International] home video in 1985.) The final version is an edit from more than 40,000 feet of film taken by the Lennons and is meant to serve as an accompaniment to John's *Imagine* album and Yoko's *Fly,* but unfortunately, by the time of this release, both albums had been freely available for over a year.

Monday December 25
🍎 Keith Moon, dressed as Father Christmas and accompanied by a sleigh pulled by several reindeers, appears unannounced at Tittenhurst Park in Ascot, as a Christmas Day surprise for Ringo and Maureen. Unfortunately, Keith hasn't got the money to pay for the prank so he asks Ringo to pay the bill, which he does.

Tuesday December 26
🍎 This afternoon on BBC1, between 3:31 and 4:59pm, during the corporation's annual "Boxing Day With The Beatles" slot, *Help!* receives its second TV broadcast. Later this evening, the BBC2 rock music programme *The Old Grey Whistle Test* broadcasts

(between 11:15 and 12:04am) a 16mm film supplied by Granada Television, of The Beatles at the Cavern Club in Liverpool on August 22, 1962, performing 'Some Other Guy'. (This is only its third ever TV screening.)

December
 Denny Laine remarks: "The next year is really going to be exciting for Wings. A lot of amazing stuff is bound to happen!"

"Just like that . . .
no planning. The
three ex-Beatles
recorded one of
John's songs.
Everyone in the
room was just
gleaming. It's
such a universal
gleam with The
Beatles."
– *producer Richard Perry*

January
 Extended recordings on George's album *Living In The Material World* (as it's now titled) continue at the Apple Studios' basement at 3 Saville Row in London.

Monday January 1
 The *Liverpool Echo* publishes a recent interview with Ringo, carried out by Rex Reed, aboard an aeroplane. The ex-Beatle discusses being a businessman, his thoughts on forming his own band and the current *Son Of Dracula* film.

Wednesday January 3
 Ringo is interviewed by David Wigg for the BBC Radio One programme *Scene And Heard,* which is transmitted on January 6 and will later form a part of the 1976 Polydor double-album of interviews entitled *The Beatles Tapes.*

Thursday January 4
 This afternoon, in Studio 8 at the BBC Television Centre in Wood Lane, London, Wings videotape their second studio appearance on *Top Of The Pops.* Their mimed performance of 'C Moon' is included in tonight's show, transmitted on BBC1 between 6:45 and 7:14pm. As with their May 25, 1972, appearance, the corporation, for a fee of £50, acquires the live audio soundtrack of tonight's clip for future foreign radio broadcasts. (Unfortunately, the appearance is later wiped by the BBC.)

Saturday January 6
 "Yoko Goes It Alone" – Yoko Ono appears on the front cover of today's *Melody Maker.* Inside the paper is a review of her new album *Approximate Infinite Universe* and an exclusive interview with her, carried out over the phone to New York, by *MM* reporter Michael Watts. Another Yoko feature, again by Watts, appears in *Melody Maker* on January 27 (see entry).

Wednesday January 10
 In New York, and with John nowhere in sight, Yoko performs a solo concert during a meeting for the *Organisation Of Women.*

Saturday January 13
 George and Ringo are seen in the audience at the Rainbow Theatre in London for Eric Clapton's concert this evening. Later, during the after show party, the two former Beatles are seen having a drink at the bar, with George having a pint of Guinness.

Monday January 22
 A law suit, seeking more than $1 million (approximately £400,000) in actual and punitive damages, is being sought by Northern Songs Ltd. and Maclen Music Ltd., both of London and New York, against John and Yoko. In papers, filed today in Manhattan Supreme Court, the plaintiffs charge that John has violated a songwriters' agreement of February 1965 in which he granted the plaintiffs exclusive rights to his compositions. The suit charges that John and Yoko have recently collaborated in writing a series of songs, and that each claims one half interest in the copyright to each composition. The songs in dispute are 'Sunday Bloody Sunday', 'Luck Of The Irish', 'Angela' and 'Woman Is The Nigger Of The World'. The suit also charges that Yoko and Allen Klein "intentionally and unlawfully induced John to violate the February 1965 agreement".

Thursday January 25
 A pre-recorded interview with Paul, carried out by the DJ Peter Price, is transmitted this evening on his BBC Radio Merseyside programme *Twice The Price.*

Saturday January 27
 "Lady Of Pain" – *Melody Maker* concludes the interview with Yoko Ono, carried out by Michael Watts. During the article, she claims: "They were pretty hard on me, you know."

Tuesday January 30
 As by way of a 10th anniversary celebration since The Beatles had their first number one hit single (depending, that is, on which chart you read), tonight's *Old Grey Whistle Test*

(transmitted on BBC2 between 10:45 and 11:14pm) features three complete tracks ('Please Please Me', 'From Me To You' and 'I Saw Her Standing There') from The Beatles' February 11, 1964, concert at the Washington Coliseum in America. The programme also includes the first screening of 'Move On Fast', an unbroadcast clip from John and Yoko's August 30, 1972, One To One concert at Madison Square Garden, which, for this transmission, has been intercut with various scenes from the *Imagine* film. During Bob Harris's introduction to the clips, he announces that he was in the audience during The Beatles April 26, 1964, *NME* Poll Winners concert at the Empire Pool, Wembley. Also on tonight's *Whistle Test* programme, is a mimed studio performance by The Who.

February
🍎 Rumours begin to circulate in the press that John and Yoko's marriage is in trouble.
🍎 Ringo's film *That'll Be The Day* is edited and dubbed at the Pathe/EMI studios in London.
🍎 Paul's UK tour with Wings is delayed so that he can begin work on his ATV/ITC TV special *James Paul McCartney*, which begins shooting on Monday February 19 (see entry). He spends the first two weeks of the month rehearsing with Wings in Marrakesh in Morocco.
🍎 EMI Records in Britain announce that the forthcoming Beatles greatest hits packages will most probably be titled *The Best Of The Beatles*.

Saturday February 3
🍎 'Hi Hi Hi' reaches number 10 in the American singles chart. While in the UK, the single will reach number five.
🍎 In Liverpool, at the world-famous Cavern Club in Mathew Street, it is announced that, following last orders this evening, the club will close for business. Its manager Roy Adams announces: "We've got to go – there's nothing we can do about it!" (However, following a last minute reprieve from the local council, the Cavern Club continues for business until May 27, when its fate is finally decided – see entry.)

Sunday February 4
🍎 As reports circulate that the Cavern Club in Liverpool has closed and is to be torn down, today's *Sunday Times* reveals that, when asked, the individual Beatles were uninterested in the club's fate.

Monday February 5
🍎 In Lancashire in the North of England, work commences on the George Harrison produced Apple film *Little Malcolm*. The shooting will last six weeks and be concluded on Friday March 23.

Monday February 19
🍎 At the ATV Television Studios, at Elstree in Borehamwood, Hertfordshire, Paul begins work on his television special *James Paul McCartney*. It is the first time that a major pop or rock 'n' roll star has starred in a prime-time television show aimed for both UK and USA TV audiences.

Monday February 26
🍎 In America, Apple releases the Yoko Ono/Elephant's Memory single 'Death Of Samantha' b/w 'Yang Yang'. (The UK release is on May 4.)

Tuesday February 27
🍎 In a small, low key, brief press conference today during the taping of *James Paul McCartney,* Paul announces to the press: "I am to stage my first tour of Britain with my new group Wings, during two weeks in May. We will visit twelve large towns."

March
🍎 In Los Angeles, at the Capital Records tower in Hollywood, a series of important meetings are held with John, George and Ringo. At the top of their agenda are two urgent points.
1. To put a stop on the two forthcoming pirate Beatles retrospective double albums *Alpha Omega*.

2. The postponement of the two official EMI/Capitol Beatles retrospective greatest hits packages *1962–1966* and *1967–1970*, formerly titled *The Best Of The Beatles*.

🍎 The Beatles, most notably John and Paul, are not happy with the official compilations. This factor is a major worrying point for EMI and Capitol as a large consignment of the printed and packaged *1962–1966* and *1967–1970* double albums has been sitting in warehouses awaiting distribution.

🍎 Their time in Los Angeles is not all doom and gloom for the three ex-Beatles. During their stay, Ringo, Maureen, John, Yoko and Ringo's producer, Richard Perry, all attend a screening of the controversial sex film *The Last Tango In Paris*, starring Marlon Brando. George had been invited along but declined the offer, admitting to the others: "I've already seen it in New York."

Saturday March 3

🍎 In America, the triple album *The Concert For Bangla Desh* is awarded a Grammy as 'Album of the Year for 1972'.

Monday March 5

🍎 At the Sunset Sound Recorders Studios in Los Angeles, California, Ringo begins the recording sessions that will produce the *Ringo* album. The tracks recorded during this first period (which lasts until March 27) include: 'I'm The Greatest' (written by John), 'Have You Seen My Baby', 'Sunshine Life For Me (Sail Away Raymond)', 'You're Sixteen', 'Oh My My', 'Step Lightly', 'Devil Woman', 'You And Me (Babe)', 'Photograph' and 'Down And Out'. Additional work on the *Ringo* album takes place in California at the Burbank Studios, the Sound Labs and at the Producers Workshop. Further work in England, which starts on April 16 when Paul returns from his holiday in North Africa, is carried out at the Apple Studios in Saville Row, London (see entries for March 10, 12 and 13).

Thursday March 8

🍎 Paul and Linda are both fined £100 after pleading guilty to a charge of growing five cannabis plants on their farm at Campbeltown in Scotland, following a raid by police on September 19 last year.

The court hears that a crime prevention officer visited the McCartneys' estate (two farms called High Park and Low Ranachan) to check that it was secure while unoccupied and noticed five plants growing in the greenhouse along with tomatoes. He became suspicious and, on returning to the police station, consulted a reference book that identified them as cannabis. As a result, three charges are brought against Paul: one for knowingly cultivating cannabis plants, to which he pleads guilty, and two others of possessing and having control of cannabis to which he pleads not guilty, and which are subsequently withdrawn.

Following the hearing at the Campbeltown sheriff's court, Paul pleads his case: "I don't think cannabis is as dangerous as drink. I'm dead against hard drugs. It should be like homosexuality; legal amongst consenting adults . . . but the magistrate was sweet. I must admit though, I did expect my fine to be worse." He then goes on by saying jokingly: "I was planning on writing a few songs in jail."

His solicitor continues pleading Paul's case, by telling the waiting reporters again that, "The plants had been grown from seeds sent through the post by a fan." He also admits that this charge, as with John's case from 1968, could have a serious effect on Paul's career in America. Later, the McCartneys hire a jet and fly back to London to resume work on his television special *James Paul McCartney*.

Friday March 9

🍎 This evening, George leaves England from Heathrow Airport en route to Los Angeles to attend a Beatles related meeting.

Saturday March 10

🍎 Paul and Wings assemble on Hampstead Heath, London, to continue work on *James Paul McCartney*. Shooting today is for the song 'Mary Had A Little Lamb' (see entry for April 16 – part three).

🍎 While in America, during a break from the *Ringo* sessions at the Sunset Sound Recorders Studios in Los Angeles, Ringo records an anti-drug commercial called 'Get Off', which is later distributed to American radio stations by the National Association of Progressive Radio Announcers.

♠ This afternoon during the sessions, George arrives in Los Angeles and heads to see Ringo at the Sunset Sound Studios. Upon his arrival, George is played some of the recordings already completed for the record and announces, "I'm knocked out by what you've done" and excitedly tells everyone he would like to play on the album. He will return to the studio on Monday.

♠ Today's *Melody Maker* carries a two-page article by Chris Charlesworth, celebrating ten years since The Beatles topped the UK singles charts for the first time. The piece, suitably entitled "Ten Years After", ends by saying, "Yes John, you've passed the audition."

Monday March 12

♠ At the Sunset Sound Recorders Studios, work resumes on the album *Ringo*. Today, George assists Ringo by providing backing vocals to some of the tracks.

Tuesday March 13

♠ Work again continues on the *Ringo* album, with George and Ringo both in attendance, but also present today are John and Yoko who just happen to drop by the studios. It is during this session that the three ex-Beatles record ten (including breakdown) versions of John's 'I'm The Greatest'. (Their session lasts approximately 18 minutes.)

Ringo's producer, Richard Perry, recalls the day: "Just like that; no planning. The three ex-Beatles recorded one of John's songs. Everyone in the room was just gleaming . . . it's such a universal gleam with The Beatles."

Almost immediately, word is leaked out to the media that three former Beatles have been recording again. But, the session musician Nicky Hopkins, who was present at the session, is quick to play down this "Beatles reunion" rumour, as he recalls: "All it was, was all the people turned up, which has happened many times before in England. For example, Ringo worked on George's upcoming album and Harrison helped out on my own forthcoming solo LP."

Also arriving today are Klaus Voorman and Billy Preston, who summed up the session by simply saying, "They (John and George) were just looking for something to do, just playing together and having a good time."

John and Yoko return to New York on March 14, while work continues in America on the *Ringo* album until March 27, when production shifts to England (see entry for April 16). Incidentally, John will not see George again until Saturday December 14, 1974.

Thursday March 15

♠ In England, work resumes on the ATV/ITC TV special *James Paul McCartney*. Today, at the ATV studios in Borehamwood, Hertfordshire, Paul performs an unreleased acoustic medley of 'Bluebird'/'Mama's Little Girl'/'Michelle' and 'Heart Of The Country' which does not appear in the finished version of the special. A similar medley, but this time without 'Mama's Little Girl', is included in the show.

♠ In America, the four album set *Alpha Omega* (Volume One) and (Volume Two) is released. The two volumes each contain 60 tracks, predominantly randomly selected Beatles material with up to a dozen solo tracks mixed in among them. These releases, sold through TV and radio advertising, promptly push Apple to compile and rush release its own Beatles "greatest hits" packages on two double albums, namely *The Beatles 1962–1966* and *The Beatles 1967–1970*.

♠ John begins recording several unreleased demos prior to the commencement of his *Mind Games* album sessions in New York. Tired of living in Greenwich Village, he and Yoko visit Connecticut with Bob Gruen and his wife, John and Yoko's assistant Nadya, with a view to buying a quiet place to live.

Saturday March 17

♠ "Beatles To Record Again!" – The news of John, George and Ringo playing together in Los Angeles this week reaches England, when a story appears on the front page of today's *Melody Maker*. The story continues: "Rumours flashed through Los Angeles this week that three of The Beatles have again teamed up for recording purposes. John Lennon, George Harrison and Ringo Starr are all in Los Angeles with Klaus Voorman, the bassist rumoured to replace Paul McCartney after his departure from the group . . ."

 Meanwhile, interest in The Beatles continues unabated when tonight's edition of the BBC1 programme *The Sound Of Petula*, hosted by the singer Petula Clark, pays tribute to the music of the fab four and also ventures into the streets where she asks passers-by, "What do you think of The Beatles?"

Sunday March 18
 At 4:45pm, by way of a finale on the TV special *James Paul McCartney*, Paul and Wings record a special live concert on a soundstage at the Elstree TV Studios in Borehamwood, Hertfordshire. After arriving on stage, the group opens up with 'The Long And Winding Road', Paul playing piano while Linda takes photographs of the Wings' performance. This is immediately followed by 'Maybe I'm Amazed', 'When The Night' (from *Red Rose Speedway*), 'The Mess' and 'My Love'. Denny then takes over lead vocals to perform 'Go Now', his number one hit single during his time with the Moody Blues. At its conclusion, Paul returns to the microphone to take lead on 'Hi Hi Hi' and then 'Long Tall Sally', which closes the show.

Fifteen minutes later, and with the audience thinking there will be no encore, Paul returns to the stage to inform everyone that, due to the lacklustre audience response, the entire repertoire must be repeated for the benefit of the television cameras. Of the eight tracks performed again, 'Hi Hi Hi' is played twice, the latter version being delivered at a much slower tempo. (For details of the final transmissions, see April 10 – part ten.) Immediately following the taping, Wings, in front of an audience of 200 people who had paid £5 a head, perform at the Hard Rock Cafe in London's Park Lane in Piccadilly for the benefit of *Release*, a charity that helps drug-takers and other young people in trouble.

Monday March 19 (periodically until the end of the month)
 During breaks from work on *James Paul McCartney*, Wings continue recording their second album *Red Rose Speedway* at Abbey Road studios.

 While in America on the 19th, at a press conference at the Capitol Records tower in Hollywood, Capitol vice-president Brown Meggs announces to the press news of the impending release of *The Beatles 1962–1966* and *The Beatles 1967–1970* double albums. His statement reads: "We will be issuing, on Apple, a two-record set of vintage Beatle songs in an effort to counteract the sale of the bootleg Beatles records, called *Alpha Omega*, which are currently being blatantly advertised on television and in newspapers across the country. We feel it will be easier to fight the bootleg product with a rival package than through the courts. It's appropriate and right that The Beatles have, on Apple, the official authorised collection put together by themselves." (In fact, Allen Klein compiled the track-by-track line-up for both *1962–1966* and *1967–1970* albums, which are set for release in America next Monday, March 26.)

Friday March 23
 Wings release in England the single 'My Love'/'The Mess'. (The American release takes place on April 9.)

 While in America, US Immigration and Naturalisation Service Judge Ira Fieldsteel rules that John has to leave America within 60 days or face deportation. He also makes the decision to grant Yoko permanent residency. Supporting John in his case is John Lindsay, the Mayor of New York, Lord Harlech, the former British Ambassador in Washington, plus various artists and academics across the country. Judge Fieldsteel, following his decision, announces that one single fact prevents John from being accepted as a permanent resident in America . . . his conviction in London in November of 1968. John immediately files an appeal.

Outside the court, he tells the waiting press, "Having just celebrated our fourth wedding anniversary, we are not prepared to sleep in separate beds. Peace and love, John and Yoko."

Monday March 26
 The original release date for both *1962–1966* and *1967–1970* passes without a *Red* or *Blue* double album in sight. When asked about this, a spokesman for Capitol Records in America replies: "The delay is down to an unspecified snag." But sources close to Capitol suggest that the delay is, in fact, down to Paul who has obtained an injunction against their worldwide release.

Wednesday March 28

 Ringo and his producer Richard Perry fly back to England. Ringo heads to Saville Row to resume work on *Ringo* and to appear with Russell Harty tomorrow, while Perry meets up with Paul, who has requested his services for help on the soundtrack of *James Paul McCartney*. Under his arm, Perry is also clutching some of the tapes from the recent sessions with Ringo in Los Angeles, some of which, of course, include recordings with John and George.

Thursday March 29

 At the London Television Studios on the South Bank, Ringo videotapes an appearance for the top-rated London Weekend Television ITV Saturday night chat show *Russell Harty Plus*, produced as a direct attack on the prestigious BBC1 rival show *Parkinson*. Ringo, dressed in a Teddy boy outfit, is there obviously to promote his new film *That'll Be The Day*. (The interview is transmitted across the London region of ITV only on Saturday March 31 between 11:01 and 11:49pm.)

Saturday March 31

 Today, Allen Klein's management contract with John, George and Ringo expires and is not renewed. (The three ex-Beatles will not formally fire Klein until November of this year.) He publicly announces that his ABKCO company is "cutting its links with Apple and with the former Beatles, John Lennon, George Harrison and Ringo Starr on Monday April 2."
 For the third consecutive year, Paul's McCartney Productions Ltd. company shows a loss in its end of year tax returns. For the period 1972/1973, sales total £5,783 while outgoing expenses reach a hefty £57,616, resulting in a loss of £51,833.

April

 During the month, John and Yoko begin moving from their Greenwich Village apartment and into their new dwelling, a 12-room luxury apartment in the Dakota building, based on the upper West Side of New York. The property, which five years before had been the setting for the Mia Farrow horror film *Rosemary's Baby*, is purchased off the legendary American film actor Robert Ryan following the death of his wife through cancer. Apparently, soon after the Lennons move in to the apartment, they hold a seance to contact the spirit of Mrs. Ryan. Yoko, the story goes, then contacts Ryan's daughter Lisa, to inform her how her mother is doing "on the other side". Lisa, apparently, is none too pleased to be told this. Following the Lennons' move into the Dakota, an event covered by the magazine *New York* for its May edition, John wistfully tells their reporter: "The Sixties are finally over."
 Meanwhile, news of John, George and Ringo's get-together in a Los Angeles recording studio on Tuesday March 13 has forced some LA pop stations to begin issuing daily news update bulletins on their re-formation and even a major national news magazine to write a story, under the banner of: "Come Together."

Sunday April 1

 Most fittingly on April Fool's Day, John and Yoko, along with his attorney Leon Wildes, hold a press conference at the New York Bar Association announcing the birth of their conceptual country Nutopia. John, before a host of TV camera crews and reporters, reads through the country's "constitution": "We announce the birth of a conceptual country – Nutopia. Citizenship of the country can be obtained by declaration of your awareness of Nutopia. Nutopia has no land, no boundaries, no passports, only people."
John announces that the national flag will be a tissue. (Parts of this are aired years later on the American Westwood One radio series *The Lost Lennon Tapes*..) During this period, John records another demo version of 'I'm The Greatest'.
 Paul and Wings conclude the shooting of *James Paul McCartney* at the Elstree Studios in Hertfordshire, taping today performances of a 'Little Woman Love – C Moon' (medley), 'My Love' and 'Live And Let Die'. (See entries for April 16 – parts four and eight.)
 At the A&M Studios in Los Angeles, George begins producing Ravi Shankar's latest album.

Monday April 2

To combat the brisk sales of *Alpha Omega*, the two official Beatles' greatest hits double albums, namely *The Beatles 1962–1966* and *The Beatles 1967–1970* are finally released in America by Apple. They will soon become fondly referred to as the *"Red"* and *"Blue"* albums respectively. (They are released in the UK on April 19.)

🍎 Shortly after their release, producer Richard Perry recalls talking about the records with George. "I was talking to George the other night about the four-record set; the first two records cover the period 1962 to 1966 and the last cut on the second record is 'Yellow Submarine'. The third record begins with 'Strawberry Fields Forever', through 'Sgt. Pepper' and 'Magical Mystery Tour', and really, that's the meat of their career. Then we were looking at the fourth record and George said, 'It seems like the career took a little turn here, because it's like, all of a sudden, there's some great stuff, but it seems incomplete. It doesn't seem right that it should or could end there!'"

Tuesday April 3
🍎 At a press conference in New York City, John and Yoko discuss their appeal, filed this day, to the March 23 decision by the US Immigration and Naturalisation Service to deport John. Even though the deportation order is the top priority for John, journalists still ask him about his separation from Klein.

"We separated ourselves from him," John replies.

"Why?" asks the reporter.

"Why do you think?" John snaps. "We will go into that next time!"

The conference ends abruptly and the Lennons head to the airport where they board a plane for Los Angeles.

Wednesday April 4
🍎 Meanwhile in England, at the BBC Television Centre, in Wood Lane, London, Wings record their third appearance on *Top Of The Pops*. Their mimed performance of 'My Love', alongside studio performances by Gary Glitter, Frank Hardcastle, Stuart Gilles and Pan's People is transmitted the following night on BBC1 (between 6:45 and 7:15pm) and is introduced by Tony Blackburn. Also performing on tonight's show, is Hurricane Smith, previously known as the EMI recording engineer Norman "Normal" Smith, with whom Paul previously worked at Abbey Road during The Beatles' sessions in the sixties. (A further screening of the 'My Love' clip appears during the *Top Of The Pops* broadcast on Thursday May 11.)

Friday April 6
🍎 Five days after it is announced publicly that John, George and Ringo have split with Allen Klein, the Lennons drop into the Los Angeles offices of ITN to videotape an interview on the subject with John Fielding for London Weekend Television's political and current affairs show *Weekend World*. During the 10-minute feature, John, dressed in a matching light blue casual shirt and trousers and a pair of sandals, is first asked:

"Can you tell me what happened with Allen Klein? Why did you and the other two decide finally to get rid of him?"

John: "There are many reasons why we finally gave him the push, although I don't want to go into the details of it. Let's say possibly Paul's suspicions were right . . . and the time was right."

Fielding: "His contract was coming up for renewal anyway . . . wasn't it?"

John: "The contract expired I think in February, and we were extending it at first on a monthly basis and then finally on a two-week basis, and then finally we pushed the boat out."

Fielding: "When did you personally decide that Klein probably wasn't the man you thought he was?"

John: "Well, you're concluding that I thought he was something. My position has always been a 'Devil and the deep-blue sea', and at that time I do whatever I feel is right. Although I haven't been particularly happy personally for quite a long time with the situation, I didn't want to make any quick moves and I wanted to see if maybe something would work out."

Lennon is naturally asked if, due to the present situation, the chance of The Beatles performing again as a group is enhanced. Slightly agitated, he replies, "With or without the present situation, the chances are practically nil! Although I hate to say 'definitely' to anything, because, every time, I change my mind. But I don't have a feeling about it and I don't think any of the others really do. If any of you actually remember when we were together, everybody was talking about it as though it was wonderful all the time. All the press and all the people, all saying how great and how wonderful . . . but it wasn't like that at all! And imagine *if* they did get together, what kind of scrutiny would they be under? Nothing could fit the dream people had of them. So forget it, you know, it's ludicrous!"

Following the split from Klein, John admits that a number of people have been calling him, coming out of the woodwork and asking, "Can I help you?" and going as far as to leave bottles of champagne in his hotel room. Yoko, besides puffing away on cigarettes, sits beside John throughout the interview and barely says more than a handful of words. The piece is concluded by John waving into the camera saying: "Hello Aunt Mimi, how are you? We're OK! We're eating well, and I haven't given up my British citizenship . . . I just want to live here, that's all."

(The item, alongside reports on the footballer Nat Lofthouse, children's truancy and the introduction in the UK of VAT [Value Added Tax], is transmitted across certain ITV regions, two days later, on Sunday April 8 between 11:31am and 12:28pm.)

Thursday April 12
◆ The film *That'll Be the Day* receives its world premiere at the ABC2 cinema in Shaftsbury Avenue, London. Special guests in attendance include Keith Moon and Pete Townshend of The Who and Ronnie Wood of The Faces. Also present are Radio One DJs Tony Blackburn, Alan Freeman, Johnny Walker and Dave Lee Travis plus the film's writer Ray Connolly and the director Claude Whatham. (The registration for the film will not take place until the following Thursday April 19 at 10:30am at Metro House.) *That'll Be The Day* will receive its American premiere when it opens in Los Angeles on October 29.
◆ Paul, Linda and their family take a vacation in the Caribbean. They return on Sunday April 15. One of Paul's first assignments when he returns to England is to assist Ringo with the recording of 'Six O'Clock' for his *Ringo* album. Work begins on April 16 (see entry).

Friday April 13
◆ In America, the double albums *The Beatles 1962–1966* and *The Beatles 1967–1970* are certified by the RIAA (Record Industry Association of America) as having sold enough copies to qualify for a gold record.

Sunday April 15
◆ Ringo's film on T.Rex, *Born To Boogie*, goes on general release across Britain.

Monday April 16
◆ Paul's ATV special *James Paul McCartney,* receives its television premiere on ABC-TV in America. To coincide with its screening, a still from part four of the programme adorns the cover of the prestigious American TV listings magazine *TV Guide*. (The UK TV premiere of the show occurs across the ITV network on May 10 between 9:01 and 9:59pm.) The show is broken down into eleven different segments:

Part one: 'Big Barn Bed' – Stage performance by Wings, who play in front of an audience comprising a row of television sets. During the song, each band member spells out, using captions on the screen, their likes and dislikes. Paul notes that his favourite kind of music was "good" and that the loves of his life were "Linda and kids".

Part two: 'Acoustic Medley' – Paul performs a medley of 'Blackbird', 'Bluebird', 'Michelle' (featuring a new arrangement, emphasising the French lyrics) and 'Heart Of The Country'. As he sings, sitting on a stool surrounded by an array of photographic lights and umbrellas, Linda is seen taking photographs of his performance.

Part three: 'Mary Had A Little Lamb' – The group, dressed all in white, perform the song at an outside location. This comprises Paul sitting at the piano and Linda playing the tambourine, sitting in a tree swing while the other band members sit under it. These shots are inter-cut with footage of miscellaneous horse-riding sequences and, not surprisingly, some cameo appearances by some sheep!

Part four: 'Wings And An Orchestra' – The group, now back in a studio setting backed by an orchestra, perform a medley comprising 'Little Woman Love' and 'C Moon' and then a complete version of 'My Love'.

Part five: 'Uncle Albert' – Paul is seen sitting in an armchair doing a crossword puzzle while Linda is seen pouring out a cup of tea. The scene then cuts to a bizarre spectacle of a row of identically dressed typists, among which is a pipe smoking Paul and Linda dressed in a secretarial outfit. The "we're so sorry, Uncle Albert" section is portrayed by a group of elderly people using the telephone. Additional scenes for the 'Admiral Halsey' part of the song, using extra scenes from the above, are cut prior to transmission.

Part six: 'Chelsea Reach' – Introduced by a voice-over from Paul, this part of the programme features a McCartney family and friends get-together at the *Chelsea Reach* public house near Liverpool. Those present include Paul's father Jim, who is seen giving Paul money to help pay towards the drinks, plus Paul's Auntie Gin (whose fondness for the 1965 Beatles track 'I've Just Seen A Face' inspired the original working title for the song, 'Auntie Gin's Theme'), Auntie Dilys and fellow Liverpudlian Sixties musician Gerry Marsden. Not to mention, Paul's brother Mike (McCartney) McGear and many others. This lengthy sequence features basic reminiscent chatter between the guests and then a participation in a pub singalong, which includes 'April Showers', 'Pack Up Your Troubles' and 'You Are My Sunshine'.

Part seven: 'Gotta Sing, Gotta Dance' – Paul's tribute to the great Busby Berkeley musicals of the Thirties. He sings the song, originally written for Twiggy to perform, dressed in a pink tuxedo, gold high-heeled shoes and wearing a moustache. Accompanying him is a large female dance troupe that is split, costume-wise, into two camps. One in blonde wigs and silver leotards, the other dressed as men in black suits. The spectacular foot-tapping and tap-dancing, excellently choreographed by Rob Iscove, ends in a flurry of glitter cascading from the ceiling. (A planned sequence where Paul was to appear in the scene dressed in "drag" is scrapped due to a fear of upsetting the lucrative American television sponsors.)

Part eight: 'Live And Let Die' – Paul and Linda open this sequence seated in an empty cinema eating popcorn. (In fact, this is an empty viewing room at Elstree studios.) He provides the voice-over: "You know, American movies have got better popcorn than European movies – but that's only an opinion. I go to the films to hear the soundtrack; the picture becomes a background. They've just filmed a background to some music I wrote. It's the new James Bond film, *Live And Let Die*, and I must admit that the film helps the music work. So does the popcorn." Shot in the same studio as used in part four of the programme, Wings are seen miming 'Live And Let Die' inter-cut with scenes from the new United Artists James Bond film. The scene ends with a "baddie" dressed in a hat and cloak setting off a bomb which explodes inside Paul's piano. He later reveals that this special effect had actually hurt his hand, a result of the flying wooden piano debris.

Part nine: 'Beatles Medley' – A humorous scene where passers-by in a street near ATV's Borehamwood Studios, are asked to sing a Beatles song. Various off-key Beatles classics such as 'When I'm 64' and 'She Loves You' are delivered to the camera. Most memorable is the man who decides to deliver his own version of 'Yesterday'. His lyrics go as follows: "I said wait for me, if you go, you mustn't stay. I said wait for me, how I long for yesterday." Strangely, when *James Paul McCartney* is transmitted in the States, certain affiliated stations decide to omit this sequence.

Part ten: 'Wings In Concert' – At the ATV Studios in Borehamwood, Wings are seen performing live (from the second afternoon show) 'The Mess', 'Maybe I'm Amazed' and (for American viewers only) 'Long Tall Sally'. (For the UK and European transmissions, the latter track is replaced by the fast/normal version of 'Hi Hi Hi'.) For full details of the recordings that day, see entry for March 18.

Part eleven: 'Yesterday' – For the eleventh and final sequence of the 50-minute show, with Linda and the other members of Wings sitting around him, Paul performs a solo acoustic guitar version of 'Yesterday'. This is his first rendition of the track since The Beatles acrimonious split almost three years earlier, played as a personal request to his fellow band members. The song concludes with the end of show credits running over the screen.

Paul retains full artistic control, and following the first transmissions, he is asked about the Busby Berkeley Hollywood musical routine. "I suppose you could say it's fulfilling an old ambition. Right at the start I fancied myself in musical comedy. But that was before The Beatles. But don't get me wrong. I'm no Fred Astaire or Gene Kelly and this doesn't mean the start of something big. I don't want to be an all-rounder. I'm sticking to what I am." As for the show in general, he adds, "I do not want to take up acting seriously, but I'd like me and Linda to be seen riding into the sunset at the end of a western with Henry of Wings sitting asleep under a tree."

Critics, though, are not too kind about the TV special. *Melody Maker*, in particular, gives a somewhat sour view about the show: "McCartney has always had an eye and ear for full-blown romanticism, and nothing wrong with that, but here he too often lets it get out of hand and it becomes overblown and silly."

‡ While in New York, John catches the show and later remarks, "I liked parts of Paul's TV special, especially the intro. The bit filmed in Liverpool made me squirm a bit. But Paul's a pro. He always has been."

Aside from *James Paul McCartney*, today, April 16, the American TV presenter Elliot Mintz records a lengthy interview with John and Yoko, excerpts from which are transmitted throughout the *Lost Lennon Tapes* U. S. radio series.

‡ While in London, sessions for the album *Ringo* continue at the Apple Studios in Saville Row. Ringo works with Paul and Linda on the track 'Six O'Clock'. Ironically, the final recording sessions for the song (which include 15 takes) take place at 6 o'clock in the morning, with both Ringo and Paul the worse for wear. At the completion of the song, Ringo sends his chauffeur out to find some tap dancing shoes. On his return, Ringo puts on the shoes, and whilst clutching a microphone stand, records the step dancing tracks used on the song 'Step Lightly'.

‡ The finished *Ringo* album features all four of the ex-Beatles. John writes 'I'm The Greatest', (both he and George participate during the final recording of the song). Paul also plays on 'You're Sixteen'; George co-wrote 'Photograph' with Ringo and 'You And Me (Babe)' with The Beatles' former road manager Mal Evans. George also composes 'Sunshine Life For Me' and performs on each of these recordings. (The recordings continue until April 30, though additional overdubbing back in America at the Sunset Sound Studios will carry on until July.)

‡ With so many solo Beatle contributions on the album, Paul is quick to fend off rumours that this is the start of a reunion for the group: "The others did some tracks for it in Los Angeles and then the material was brought over here for me," he remarks. "I worked on a track called 'Six O'Clock' . . . so in a way there's been some collaboration already and I think that kind of thing might happen more often. I'm happy to play with the other three and I'm sure they are too if it is physically possible but more important for me is the new thing (Wings) because I really get turned on by new ideas."

‡ Even if The Beatles had decided to play together, the problems over John and Paul's previous drug convictions meant it was nigh impossible to meet in the first place. John is fighting to remain in America, while Paul cannot enter the country until he obtains his entry visa. A tongue-in-cheek suggestion circulates in the music industry whereby, to get round this rather delicate situation, John and Paul could meet in a Canadian border town, each keeping to his own side of the frontier, to discuss any future Beatles plans.

Saturday April 21
‡ As a prelude to the forthcoming UK tour, a two-page article on Wings by Mark Plummer, entitled "Wings – Anatomy Of A Hot Band", appears in today's *Melody Maker*. During the feature, band member Henry McCullough announces, "I don't suppose we'll be together forever. I'm sure Paul's got more of a tie to The Beatles than to Wings . . . Wings has all the makings of a great group, but our battle is to keep it as a band and not let it fall apart as it could so easily do."

Thursday April 26
‡ George founds The Material World Charitable Foundation Trust.
‡ *Rolling Stone* magazine in America features a report entitled: "John & Yoko Fight Deportation: Hard-hats Join Appeal."

Friday April 27
‡ The double album *The Beatles 1967–1970* reaches the UK number two position.

Sunday April 29
‡ Taking a break from producing Ravi Shankar's latest album, George and Patti briefly attend the seven-day Columbia Records *A Week To Remember* party, held on the 16th floor of the Los Angeles Hilton Hotel. Following a brief pose for the press and the Columbia photo archives, George returns to the A&M Studios where recordings resume with Ravi, while Patti stays behind, partying with stars such as the singer Cat Stevens.

Monday April 30
‡ The Wings album *Red Rose Speedway* is released in America. (The UK release takes place on May 4.) The title of the album is inspired by the name of Paul's housekeeper, Rose. On the back cover of the album, in the top left-hand corner, there is a Braille

message to Stevie Wonder, which reads "We Love You". (In November of 1980, John will admit that this was the last album by Paul he ever listened to.)

May
 John and Yoko finally take up residence at the Dakota building, adjacent to Central Park and home to some of the richest people in the city and therefore the world. The Dakota had become known as the first block of flats in the city to incorporate a lift into its building. Also this month, Yoko announces that she plans to do another interview for the BBC Radio Two programme *Woman's Hour*, in which she will be talking about the independence of the female. (The feature fails to materialise.)
 Allen Klein's company ABKCO announces plans to buy Apple.

Saturday May 5
 Melody Maker writes: "So good old George Harrison is co-producing the new Ravi Shankar album. We think George has a nerve taking such credit. It's not that he's not a fine musician – just that Shankar has probably forgotten more about sitar playing than George can ever know . . ."

Monday May 7
 Today, George releases his first single since 1971, 'Give Me Love (Give Me Peace On Earth)'/'Miss O'Dell'. (The UK release takes place on May 25.) Paul is asked about the A-side: " . . . the single is very nice. The guitar solo is ace and I like the time changes."

*   *   *

Wings First Tour Of Britain
May 11 – July 10

After a three-month delay, Paul and Wings begin their first major British tour – the first scheduled UK tour by an ex-Beatle since their last appearance together back in 1966. During the two month tour their repertoire includes: 'Big Barn Bed', 'Soily', 'When The Night', 'Wild Life', 'Seaside Woman' (performed by Linda), 'Go Now' (Denny Laine), 'Little Woman Love', 'C Moon', 'Live And Let Die', 'Maybe I'm Amazed', 'Say You Don't Mind' (Denny Laine), 'My Love', 'The Mess', 'Hi Hi Hi' and 'Long Tall Sally'. The support acts for the tour are Brinsley Schwarz and, during the interval just prior to Wings appearing on stage, a juggler who throws around large hoops. The tour, including all its spectacle and splendour, includes performances at:

Bristol's Hippodrome (Friday May 11)
Oxford's New Theatre (Saturday May 12)
Cardiff Capitol (Sunday May 13)
Bournemouth Winter Gardens (Tuesday May 15)
Manchester's Hard Rock (Wednesday May 16 and Thursday May 17)
The Liverpool Empire (Friday May 18 – two concerts. 6:15 and 9:00pm)
Leeds University (Saturday May 19)
Preston's Guildhall (Monday May 21)
Newcastle Odeon (Tuesday May 22)
Edinburgh Odeon (Wednesday May 23)
Green's Playhouse, Glasgow, Scotland (Thursday May 24 –
    a date added to the tour itinerary in early April)
Hammersmith Odeon, London (Friday May 25 and Saturday May 26)
Hammersmith Odeon, London (Sunday May 27 – extra night added due to an
    overwhelming demand for tickets and the cancellation of the show in Birmingham at
    the Hippodrome.)

The following concerts are added due to an excessive amount of fans wishing to see the group:

Sheffield's City Hall (Wednesday July 4)
Trentham Gardens, Stoke-on-Trent (Thursday July 5 – concert cancelled –
    due to its clashing with the *Live And Let Die* premiere)
Birmingham's Odeon (Friday July 6)

Leicester's Odeon (Monday July 9)
Newcastle City Hall (Tuesday July 10)

Note: The *original* dates for some of the shows, announced to the press in early February, were:

Edinburgh Odeon (Tuesday May 22 – two concerts at 6:15 and 9:00pm)
Newcastle City Hall (Wednesday May 23)
Birmingham Hippodrome (Sunday May 27)

Saturday May 12

Prior to the start of the concert at Oxford's New Theatre, Paul and Wings hold a press conference for 40 journalists, some from as far away as New Jersey, many of whom had been specially ferried in on buses from London at the expense of EMI. Instead of the evening becoming, for the journalists, just another job, Paul has invited them to bring along their wives or girlfriends. Besides ducking from the tiresome "When are The Beatles going to get together again?" questions, Paul is asked, "Why did you do the Ringo song?" a referral to the track 'Six O'Clock' on the *Ringo* album. "I would do it for any friend," Paul replies. "I would do it for Rod Stewart if he rang up . . ." (When Rod is told of this quote, he promptly rings Paul, and asks him to "write me a song then!" The song will become 'Mine For Me', released in 1974 – see entry for November of this year.)

Immediately following tonight's concert in Oxford, Paul is interviewed backstage by David Symonds for his BBC Radio One show, suitably titled, *The David Symonds Show*. David humorously tells Paul that his daughter refers to him as "Paul McCarpet"! Following the show, a party is held for the press at a nearby hotel. Reporters from the UK music newspapers are forced to hang their heads in shame when reporters from the continent keep asking Paul: "Will The Beatles get back together again?"

Sunday May 27

The final night of the first part of the Wings concert tour is scheduled to take place with a performance at the Birmingham Hippodrome. But the show is cancelled by MAM, the tour's promoters, because of the electrical danger posed by a 15-ton water tank built into the stage and currently being used as a part of the American revue *Pyjama Tops*, which is currently running at the theatre. Following the additional concert at London's Hammersmith Odeon, Wings hold a party in the reception hall of the Café Royal in Regent Street, London, to celebrate the completion of the first leg of the tour. Paul gives an impromptu performance, alternating between piano, lead guitar and drums. Elton John, who also performs, is among the star-studded audience.

June

With their next concert appearance not scheduled until July 4, Wings spend most of the month rehearsing in Scotland at Paul's private studio. It is during these rehearsals, on June 29, that the film *Live And Let Die* will receive its American premiere with a screening in New York. (The UK premiere takes place on July 5 – see next entry.)

Thursday July 5

Paul and Linda take a break from the tour to join a star-studded line-up present at the London premiere of the new James Bond film *Live And Let Die* at the Odeon cinema in Leicester Square, London. Paul arrives wearing a tuxedo and bow tie, but *without* a shirt. The gala gathering is in aid of the National Playing Fields Association and the Stars Organisation for Spastics. To attend the screening, Paul cancels this evening's scheduled Wings concert in Stoke-on-Trent at the Trentham Gardens.

Friday July 6

Backstage at Birmingham, Paul tells *Melody Maker*, "After we've finished the tour, we're going to take a small break and get some material together. I've written a few new songs. I've got about four, a couple half-finished and we'll put that all together for the next LP." He is asked if Wings have benefited from the tour? "We've learned lots from it. Just kind of working with an audience. You can get a bit rusty, you know, if you lay off for a while. I laid off for about six years in front of an audience and the enjoyment of playing to an audience is something you get into after a while." *Melody Maker* asks Paul if the other Beatles are missing out by not touring. He nonchalantly replies, "It's up to them what they fancy doing. It just depends if they'd enjoy it. If they enjoy it, yes, they're missing out . . . I know Ringo said he just wouldn't ever consider touring again. I don't know if he ever will." (The interview is published on July 14.)

Paul turns his attention to David Bowie's recent decision to disband his group The Spiders From Mars, a move interpreted by many to mean he is quitting touring. "I don't know why he is giving it up. I should have asked him. I met him last night at the premiere of *Live And Let Die* . . . I think it's a pity. I'll tell you why it's a pity; it's because I haven't seen his show yet! I'd like to see it. So come on David. Just do a quick one for me!"

Monday July 9
Backstage at the Odeon in Leicester Paul is interviewed for a piece that appears on a *Band On The Run* promotional album in December.

Tuesday July 10
Backstage in Newcastle, Paul tells a reporter from *Melody Maker*: "The way we tour now, it seems easier. Its not actually more organised, but we get days off every now and then, so it's quite good. It hasn't ground me into the ground, anyway."

* * *

Saturday May 12
🍎 The double album *The Beatles 1962–1966* reaches number three in the UK charts.

Sunday May 13
"Unusually Entertaining . . . Ringo . . . A Splendid Performance!" – The *Daily Express*.
🍎 The film *That'll Be The Day* goes on general release around the UK at ABC and other leading Cinemas. Prior to the film's release, Paul revokes the verbal agreement between him and the film's producers, allowing them to use Buddy Holly songs on the soundtrack.

Monday May 14
🍎 In Houston, Texas, Yoko is awarded permanent custody of her daughter Kyoko. But one problem remains; the child still cannot be traced.

Saturday May 19
🍎 In the UK, the double album *The Beatles 1967–1970* reaches number one in the UK charts. A similar success occurs in America when, on May 26, it also reaches number one in the album charts, a record breaking 15th consecutive US chart topping album for the group. Meanwhile, *1962–1966* reaches number three in the American charts.

Tuesday May 22
🍎 Yoko performs another solo concert, this time during a WBAI Benefit concert in New York.

Friday May 25
🍎 Wings' album *Red Rose Speedway* is acknowledged for a gold record by the RIAA (Record Industry Association of America).

Sunday May 27
"Yoko doesn't need excuses any longer . . . she has her three chords together, and more. She can write real songs about things that matter. John Lennon is married to her you know, remember him?" – *Melody Maker*.
🍎 At the Town Hall, just off-Broadway in New York, Yoko performs another solo concert for the benefit of WBAI Radio, an event sponsored by Capitol Records. Wearing a white suit, white shoes and a white T-shirt sporting the *Approximate Infinite Universe* emblem, Yoko tells the audience, "You probably know me as the actress who married a public John, or as mad Jack the screamer, or something."

The show opens with the group Weather Report, who are followed by Elephant's Memory. Yoko arrives on stage to perform 'Looking Over From My Window', backed by Elephant's Memory who remain on stage following their brief set. Yoko's performance continues with 'What A Bastard The World Is' and 'Catman (The Rosies Are Coming)' where, at the conclusion of the song, she begins her auction. First up for grabs is a sheet she slept on with John during their 1969 Bed-In events in Amsterdam. (Featuring both John and Yoko's signatures, it sells to a man in the audience for just $10.) She then offers her panties and then the T-shirt she is currently wearing. "No, I don't come with it!" she screams to a man in the audience, adding, "I'm too experienced for you." The potential buyer insists that he will purchase the garment only if she takes the T-shirt off in front of him. "Okay," she replies, "only if you give me $30." He agrees and, as promised, Yoko removes the shirt, only to reveal another white shirt underneath. "Ha! The jokes on you," she screams at the buyer. "You male pig! You've seen me nude before, haven't you? *Two Virgins?*"

Yoko's performance continues with 'Death Of Samantha'. At its conclusion, she summons two blindfolded young girls from the wings of the stage and tells them to go searching in the audience for a guy who's had a tail pinned to his bottom. Then, while the girls start touching up the men in the audience, Yoko and Elephant's Memory begin performing 'Kite Song'. To close the show, sitting cross-legged on a stool, she performs the song 'Is Winter Here To Stay', a track which features the same three lines repeated over and over again.

🍎 In Liverpool, to make way for a ventilation shaft to the city's new underground railway station, the original Cavern Club in Mathew Street finally closes for good at the end of the evening, after a four-month reprieve. For posterity, the last night of the Cavern Club is filmed and recorded for an album. Booked to appear on this historic last night are the groups Hackensack and, from America, The Yardleys. But all is not lost for the Cavern, when plans announced shortly after reveal that the club will now move across the road and continue business in the disused fruit exchange building. A re-opening of the Cavern Club is set for the end of June. (Incidentally, in the Eighties, with plans for the station long since scrapped, the site is eventually turned into a car park. While in 1984, a shopping centre called Cavern Walks opens on the site and includes, below ground, a new replica of the Cavern Club, designed to look like the original and built from some of the club's original bricks.)

Monday May 28
🍎 BBC Radio broadcast the first in a short series of exclusive pre-recorded tapes by George on the series *Radio One Club*, daily between 5:00pm and 6:59pm until May 31. Further pre-recorded *Radio One Club* tapes by George are played on the shows transmitted on June 18–21, June 25–28 and July 9 (see entry). For each session tape played, George commands a fee of £25.

Wednesday May 30
🍎 The American release of George's album *Living In The Material World*. (The UK release takes place on June 22.)

Thursday May 31
🍎 In Los Angeles, during the birthday celebrations of Led Zeppelin's John Bonham, George and Patti are thrown, fully dressed, into the hotel swimming pool. Reports suggest that "George loved every minute of it!"

June
🍎 Yoko, strangely without John by her side, performs another solo concert at the New York radio station WBAI. Following her performance, she is asked if she will do anymore. "I wouldn't mind," she remarks, but adds "they'd have to include some jokes, I just couldn't do it straight-faced." John and Yoko begin to discover, to their detriment, that the cost of running their new Dakota apartment is proving rather costly, with their outgoing expenses far exceeding their income. For example, Yoko's phone bill, per month, averages $3,000.
🍎 While researching his book *The Man Who Gave The Beatles Away*, the group's former manager Allan Williams acquires the infamous but historical reel-to-reel tapes of The Beatles' live performance at the Star Club in Hamburg, recorded by Ted Taylor of King Size Taylor and The Dominoes, on December 31, 1962. Williams bumps into a Liverpool recording engineer who, at his studios in Hackins Hey back in 1963, had been given the task of editing the tapes by Taylor who had a view to releasing them. Williams and the engineer discuss the tapes, whereupon he tells Allan that the tapes may still be in his old Hackins Hey offices, which have remained derelict for years. Then, after a Sunday lunchtime drink, they go to the old offices where, amazingly enough, they find the original 1962 Hamburg 'reel-to-reel' audio tapes still languishing under a pile of rubbish. Sensing the significance of

the recordings, Williams contacts the press. Articles soon begin appearing in, amongst others, *Melody Maker* (see entry for August 4) and the *Daily Mirror* in a report by Bill Marshall. (Apple and the individual Beatles are offered the tapes in the middle of July.)

Friday June 1
 Wings' single 'Live And Let Die'/'I Lie Around' is released in the UK. (The American release takes place on June 18.) Interestingly, when the producer of the A-side, George Martin, plays the track to James Bond music producer Harry Saltzmann, he presumes that this version is no more than a demo recording and instantly suggests that Thelma Houston should record the track for the film. Martin embarrassingly insists that this is actually the finished article by the ex-Beatle! The song remains, but a new version, recorded by Brenda J. Arnau, also appears on the film's soundtrack.
 George's *Living In The Material World* album is awarded a gold record by the RIAA.

Saturday June 2
 The Wings single 'My Love' and the album *Red Rose Speedway* both reach number one in the US record charts. 'My Love' will be replaced at the top spot by George's 'Give Me Love (Give Me Peace On Earth)'.

Sunday June 3
 John and Yoko attend the International Feminist Planning conference at Harvard University where they give an interview to Danny Schechter. Portions of this interview reappear on *The Lost Lennon Tapes* radio series.

Saturday June 9
 The double album *The Beatles 1962–1966* reaches number one in the UK album charts.

Monday June 11
 The first in a short run of George's pre-recorded musical sessions are broadcast on the *David Hamilton Show*, transmitted weekdays on BBC Radio One between 2:00pm and 4:59pm. The dates for the first broadcasts are June 11–15, then repeated June 18–22, then again on July 9–13 and finally on July 16–20.

Saturday June 23
 George's album *Living In The Material World* reaches number one in the US album charts.

Thursday June 28
 On the day that John and Yoko take part in protest demonstrations at the South Vietnamese Embassy in Washington, DC, John along with Apple Films Ltd. and Apple Records of New York, are sued by ABKCO Industries for a total of $508,000 (approximately £203,000). ABKCO claim that, on John's behalf, they paid various persons, corporations and government bodies a total of $126,894 (£48,000) which still has not been repaid. The charge is answerable within 28 days.

Friday June 29
 The eighth James Bond film *Live And Let Die,* featuring the title track by Paul and Wings, opens in New York. (The London premiere takes place on July 5.)
 For two days (June 29 & 30), John and Yoko attend the Senate Watergate hearings in Washington, D.C. John sports a close cropped haircut and Yoko, inspired by the excitement of the court room, writes 'Men Men Men'.

Saturday June 30
 George's 'Give Me Love (Give Me Peace On Earth)' reaches number one in the American singles chart and number eight in the UK chart.

July
 Towards the end of the month, the Apple offices in New York close down. Apple Corps Ltd announces that they may open a replacement office in Los Angeles soon. George and Ringo, meanwhile, are more than happy to run the Apple premises at St. James Street in London, where Allan Williams has just made contact with them regarding some 1962 Beatles home audio recordings (see entry for August 15).

🍎 Yoko is asked about her two months of living at the Dakota. "John and I are living like bums up here!" she replies.

Sunday July 1

🍎 At the Record Plant studios in New York, Yoko begins recording tracks for her next album, provisionally titled *Straight Talk*, but ultimately released as *Feeling The Space* on November 2 in America and on November 23 in the UK. Meanwhile John is also recording there, producing songs intended for his album *Mind Games*. Yoko announces that John is somewhat apprehensive about the sessions. "He hasn't been in the studio for a long time," she reveals, "and I think he's nervous about it." During the John sessions, which finally begin on July 4, he records the track 'Rock 'n' Roll People' which does not make the final version of the album and is released posthumously on the 1986 compilation album *Menlove Ave.* (John will later give the song to Johnny Winter, who releases his version on the album *John Dawson Winter 111.* Winter will also release a live concert version of the number on *Johnny Winter Captured Live.*) Further work by John on 'Rock 'n' Roll People' takes place the following day, July 5. John also records the title track 'Mind Games', which was started back in December 1970 as 'Make Love Not War'. (*Mind Games* recordings will continue into August when the sessions produce 'Meat City', 'Tight A$', 'Aisumasen (I'm Sorry)', 'One Day (At A Time)', 'Bring On The Lucie (Freeda People)', 'Nutopian International Anthem', 'Intuition', 'Out The Blue', 'Only People', 'I Know (I Know)' and 'You Are Here'.) Incidentally, a planned musical by John, Yoko and Shirley MacLaine on the Watergate scandal is finally scrapped this month due to the Lennons' heavy recording commitments. John and Yoko also turn down interviews with crews from both BBC radio and TV.

🍎 Meanwhile, also in New York, rehearsals are held for the Robert Stigwood produced Beatles musical stage-play, provisionally titled *Sgt. Pepper's Lonely Hearts Club Band With The One And Only Billy Shears*. The show is directed by Tom O'Horgan and is scheduled to open in Chicago at the Auditorium Theater on August 17 before moving to the Felt Forum in New York on September 18.

Monday July 2

🍎 The soundtrack album to the film *Live And Let Die* which includes the title track by Paul and Wings, is released in America. (The UK release takes place on July 6.) The album also features a version of the track as performed by Brenda J. Arnau and features twelve George Martin orchestrations recorded under his direction.

Tuesday July 3

🍎 At the Hammersmith Odeon in London, Ringo attends the farewell performance of Ziggy Stardust and The Spiders From Mars, a character created by David Bowie. Ringo's brief appearance with Bowie, backstage in his dressing room, later appears in the 90-minute D.A. Pennebaker documentary of the show, called *Ziggy Stardust And The Spiders From Mars*. The film will not be officially released until 1982.

Friday July 6

🍎 In America, Wings' single 'My Love' is awarded a gold record by the RIAA.

Saturday July 7

🍎 An alternative pre-recorded version of 'Give Me Love (Give Me Peace On Earth)' is transmitted by BBC Radio One during today's *Alan Freeman Show*, between 3:00 and 4:59pm. The tape is repeated again on Monday July 9 during the *Radio One Club* programme (between 5:45 and 6:59pm). Joining George on this session are Jim Keltner on drums, Nicky Hopkins on piano, Klaus Voorman on bass and Gary Wright on guitar. For the tape, the corporation pays George a £5 fee. Meanwhile George visits Heathrow Airport to personally welcome to Britain, his guru, A.C. Bhoktivedanta Swami, the leader of the *Hare Krishna* religious sect. During his stay in the country, he will reside in the 10-bedroom mansion at Letchmore Heath in Watford, Hertfordshire, which George had purchased for the sect in 1972.

Sunday July 8

🍎 George and A.C. Bhoktivedanta Swami take part in a religious procession from London's Marble Arch to Piccadilly.

Saturday July 14
🍎 A quick check on the record charts reveals a host of activity. In the UK albums chart, *The Beatles 1967–1970* is still at number one, *Living In The Material World* is at number five (up from number 11), *The Beatles 1962–1966* is at number six (down from number three) and *Red Rose Speedway* which is placed at number 10 (up from number 11). Not to mention the Ronco soundtrack album *That'll Be The Day*, which is placed at number four (up from the previous week's number eight). While in the UK singles charts, 'Give Me Love' is at number nine (down from number seven) and 'Live And Let Die' is at number 11 (down from the previous week's number eight). Stateside listings reveal that in the singles chart, George's 'Give Me Love' has dropped from number one to number four and that two Wings singles are in the charts. 'My Love' is at number six (from last week's number 11) and 'Live And Let Die' is a new entry at number 28. In the US album charts *Living In A Material World* is still at number one, *Red Rose Speedway* at number five (down from number three), *The Beatles 1967–1970* at number 15 (down from number 13) and *The Beatles 1962–1966* up to number 18 from number 20.
🍎 In London, at the Classic Cinema in Piccadilly, The Beatles' films *A Hard Day's Night, Help!, Yellow Submarine* and *Let It Be* are screened for seven days, through the night, between 11:30pm and 7:00am. (The successful run ends on Friday July 20.) Also a part of the screenings is a short film on the group Fairport Convention.

Thursday July 19
🍎 In America, *Rolling Stone* magazine publishes an exclusive interview with Yoko, carried out by B. Hendel.

Friday July 20
🍎 After almost two months of work, the sound dubbing on the Apple film *Little Malcolm* is completed at the Gate Recording Theatre in London.

Tuesday July 24
🍎 At the Sunset Sound Recorders Studios in Los Angeles, mixing continues on the *Ringo* album, with Ringo personally overseeing the proceedings.

Wednesday July 25
🍎 George, with great displeasure, writes out a personal cheque for £1 million to the British Government for taxes owed on revenues from the 1971 *Bangla Desh* concert and album.

Thursday July 26
🍎 Ringo forms *Wobble Music Ltd.*

Friday July 27
🍎 Denny Laine and Henry McCullough travel to Paul's Scottish farm to begin a five-week period writing tracks for the next Wings album.

Monday July 30
🍎 In America, the ABC TV programme *Geraldo Rivera: Goodnight America* transmits a short illustrated history of The Beatles entitled *Braverman's Condensed Cream Of Beatles* (aka *Braverman's Time Capsule*). The Braverman in question is the film director Richard Braverman. The feature, which runs for approximately 14 minutes, contains an animated whistle-stop journey through the career of the group from 1962 with live concert clips, TV appearances, newsreels and interviews right through to the break-up in 1970. The show then carries on to the present day with recent newsreels and live clips, including 'Instant Karma' (from the *One To One* concerts) and 'Bangla Desh' (from the 1971 show of the same name). Geraldo Rivera, who has now become a close friend of the Lennons, also introduces on his show tonight excerpts from Carole King's recent appearance in Central Park.

August
🍎 Paul admits this month that he is none too pleased with Robert Stigwood's plan to stage the musical *Sgt. Pepper* . . .

❧ The legendary Motown recording artist Martha Reeves, formerly with The Vandellas, comes to London to record her long-awaited solo album with the producer Richard Perry. For some strange reason, rumours appear in the music press that all four Beatles will perform (individually) on the tracks.

❧ Reports in the music press suggest that George is to form his own independent record label with Bob Dylan, Paul Simon and Joan Baez. Apparently, Clive Davis, the sacked ex-President of Columbia Records, has been approached by the artists to head their label. The idea is soon scotched by Baez herself in Los Angeles, but adds: "It seemed like a good idea!"

Saturday August 4
❧ *Melody Maker* breaks the story on the discovery of the 36–track Beatles' Star Club in Hamburg tapes. The report goes into how determined Ted Taylor and Allan Williams are to get the tapes released. "(I'll release it) even if it's a bootleg," Williams remarks, admitting that their best bet for a release is EMI. He goes on, "It's been two weeks now and I've still had no joy from Apple . . . maybe they just want the background of The Beatles completely forgotten." He also reveals that he has just found amongst his belongings an IOU for £15 signed by Paul and Stuart Sutcliffe.

Wednesday August 8
❧ In England, *Punch* magazine prints Paul's review of the recently published *Paul Simon Songbook*.

Saturday August 11
❧ 'Live And Let Die' reaches number two in the American singles chart, kept from the top spot by Diana Ross's 'Touch Me In The Morning'.

Wednesday August 15
❧ With no offer forthcoming from Apple, Allan Williams, clutching the 1962 Star Club tapes meets George and Ringo at the Apple offices at 54 St. James Street, London SW1, and asks them to pay £5,000 for the tapes. They are uninterested, but request that four copies of the tape be made, two for John and two for Paul. As part of a proposed deal, George also requests copies of Williams' old Hamburg Beatles contracts for their own private archives. Williams, wanting a straight cash deal, will have none of it. So, as a departing gift, George gives Williams a small pouch containing 16 uncut rubies, which Allan is instructed by George and Ringo to give to his wife Beryl for a birthday present. Attached to the small package is a note which reads, "Dear Beryl, happy birthday (give Allan a kick) – God bless! George H. Ringo S." Following the meeting, an optimistic Williams is heard to remark, "The Beatles blow hot and cold but they appeared to be genuine, they liked the idea."

❧ (Note: Apple's offices are now based at 54 St. James Street, having moved from Saville Row in 1972. They will remain here until 1975 when Apple will move across the road into nos. 29 and 30 St. James Street. Meanwhile, 3 Saville Row will continue to be used for its basement recording studios, and will ultimately close down during May of 1975. While in October 1976, The Beatles connection to the famed building is finally relinquished when Apple Corps Ltd. will sell its freehold interest.)

Friday August 17
❧ In America, the Tom O'Horgan produced stage musical *Sgt. Pepper's Lonely Hearts Club Band* opens at the Auditorium Theater in Chicago for a six-day run.

Thursday August 23
❧ The *New York Times* publishes an exclusive interview with Yoko to promote her latest, but as yet unreleased, album *Feeling The Space*.

Saturday August 25
❧ Excitement surrounding the Star Club tapes mounts when *Melody Maker* reports that the Star Club tapes: " . . . may be released by Apple next year." The article concludes by revealing that Paul is expected to leave Apple following recent meetings between lawyers representing the four Beatles.

Wednesday August 29

 Reporter Barb Fenick arrives for an interview at Paul's Scottish farm. Meanwhile, on the eve of Wings' departure for recording sessions in Lagos in Nigeria, Henry McCullough and Denny Seiwell phone Paul to inform him that they will not be coming. Paul is not greatly distressed, and instead expresses his pleasure that he . . . "can now play drums on the album".

Thursday August 30

 Paul, Linda and Denny Laine travel to Lagos where they begin the recording sessions for *Band On The Run* at EMI's 8-track studio. It was chosen by Paul not because of the sun but because . . . "it just happened to be the only EMI studio available during this three-week period."

Paul: "We thought 'Great – lie on the beach all day, doing nothing. Breeze in the studios and record.' It didn't turn out like that. One night Linda thought I had died. I was recording and suddenly I felt like I had a lung collapse. So I went outside to get some air, and there wasn't any. It was a humid, hot tropical night. So I collapsed and fainted."

Linda takes over the story: "I laid him on the ground and his eyes were closed and I thought he was dead! We went to the doctor's and he advised Paul that he was smoking too much."

Following all the problems, *Band On The Run* will eventually become Wings' most popular and successful album. Meanwhile, as the new line-up of Wings land in Lagos to begin their adventure, a spokesman for Wings in London states: "I have no idea what Henry (McCullough) is doing. He left Wings due to usual musical differences and by mutual agreement. Everybody thinks it's for the best and wishes each other well in the future."

Friday August 31

 While in America, a further award is bestowed on Paul when the 'Live And Let Die' single is awarded a gold disc by the RIAA.

September

 Back home in Campbeltown in Scotland, prior to his departure, Paul places a newspaper advert in his local paper which reads: "Anybody caught on my High Oak of Low Rannoch farm will be prosecuted." He makes it clear that the farms are "not for the killing of wild life".

 Plans are revealed for a follow-up to *That'll Be The Day*. Entitled *Stardust*, the film will again star David Essex, but Ringo declines to play the part of a road manager. "I just don't think it is right for me," he says. "The follow-up is David Essex making it as a star. I have done that in reality and I do not want to go through all that torment again. Also, in *That'll Be The Day*, I was just an actor. People tended to forget about Ringo and The Beatles, and all that. I don't think that would happen with the follow-up because it is a musical. People will keep relating to the musical situation."

Saturday September 1 (until September 22)

 The *Band On The Run* recordings begin in Lagos, Nigeria. The sessions produce the following tracks: 'Band On The Run', 'Jet', 'Bluebird', 'Mrs. Vanderbilt', 'Let Me Roll It', 'Mamunia', 'No Words', 'Picasso's Last Words', 'Nineteen Hundred And Eighty Five', 'Helen Wheels' and, the instrumental, 'Zoo Gang'. In America only, the released album includes 'Helen Wheels', as indeed did the compact disc version many years later. During the sessions, the three-piece Wings line-up also record the track 'B-Side To Seaside' (later issued as the B-side to the single 'Seaside Woman' in 1977) and 'Oriental Nightfish', featuring lead vocals from Linda and used in the May 1978 animated cartoon of the same name.

During their stay in Lagos, Paul is accused of "exploiting" African music and that during the sessions there has been "considerable tension" between him and the Nigerian musicians. The trouble begins when Paul insists on playing congas! He even finds himself in the *Lagos Evening Times* in a report about the scandal headlined: "Step Softly, This Town Is Jinxed." If this wasn't enough, Paul and Linda are even robbed. Dressed like typical tourists, armed with tapes and cameras, they set off on a 20-minute walk to Denny Laine's rented house. During their journey, a mysterious kerb-crawling car stops in front of them and six men jump out, one clutching a knife. Paul remembers Linda screaming, "He's a musician, don't kill him!" He wisely hands over his money and Paul and Linda are allowed to resume their walk.

Monday September 10

🍎 In England, working on orders given over the phone by John in New York, estate agents in Ascot put his Tittenhurst Park mansion up for sale.

Tuesday September 18

🍎 Just over a week after going on the market, Ringo purchases the 26-room Georgian Tittenhurst Park mansion in Ascot, reportedly as part of an out-of-court settlement regarding John's unpaid loans with Allen Klein. The ASS studio that John installed is duly renamed *Startling Studio* and is immediately opened for hire. A report announcing Ringo's acquisition of the Tittenhurst Park property appears in tonight's *Evening Standard*.

🍎 Today, John moves out of the Dakota apartment in New York and heads off to Los Angeles. In 1980, he recalled this fateful day: "Yoko kicked me out! I didn't go off on a 'I'm gonna be a rock and roll bachelor' thing. She literally said, 'Get out!' I said 'OK, OK, I'm going . . . bachelor free.' I've been married all my life and I thought whoooo – whoooo-yippee! But it was *god awful!*"

John's new constant companion is Yoko's secretary May Pang. John begins telling everyone he has gone to LA to . . . "put the finishing touches to *Walls And Bridges*." On his arrival, he checks into the Beverly Hills Hotel under the name of Mr. Corey. During his first few weeks away from Yoko, John is also seen socialising in LA at the Rainbow Bar & Grill, watching an act at the Roxy and spending a weekend in Vegas where he sees Fats Domino. Because he is living off just a few thousand dollars a month (his allowance from The Beatles' receiver in London), John is forced to borrow $10,000 from Capitol Records, a sum advanced against his forthcoming record royalties. "Never in a million years would I have thought I'd be romantically linked to John Lennon," says May Pang.

Saturday September 22

🍎 In an interview to promote her forthcoming album *Feeling The Space, Melody Maker* publishes an interview with Yoko. "He was a male chauvinist when I met him, and I think he was rather surprised," she says of John. "He didn't expect that he'd have to change so much but it wasn't like I tried to sort of force him into it. He's a sensitive character, and he sort of immediately picked up, so he started to get aware of what was going on . . . he had never really lived with somebody who was actually working in society. He said he started to compare me with him, and of course, I had more difficulty than he had. He began to see what kind of handicap all women have."

The conversation turns sad when she talks about her daughter Kyoko. "She's ten now and when I saw her last she was five. I don't even know how she looks now. It's like five years is a long time."

Sunday September 23

🍎 Wings leave Lagos and return home to England, happy with their completed recordings for *Band On The Run*. They had been scheduled to arrive back at 6pm on September 22 but their plane was delayed at Lagos due to a brake failure. (Many fans who turned up at the airport the previous day were disappointed.)

Monday September 24

🍎 Ringo's single 'Photograph' (co-written by George and Ringo and featuring George on guitar and backing vocals)/'Down And Out' (co-written by George) is released in America. (The single is released in the UK on October 19.) To accompany the release, Ringo shoots an unusual promotional film clip at his recently acquired Tittenhurst Park estate in Ascot. To comply with the BBC miming ban for shows like *Top Of The Pops*, he is seen wandering aimlessly round the grounds singing (or rather miming) the first verse of 'Photograph' with his hand covering his mouth, trying his best not to be seen singing the song, yet at the same time giving the impression that he *was* performing. Ringo later reveals that the 35mm film, produced by *Top Of The Pops* producer Michael Hurll, had no script and was "made up as they went along". Except for one screening on the show, the clip has since remained unscreened anywhere in the world.

🍎 A rumoured appearance by George and Mick Jagger at a recording of BBC2's *In Concert* at the Television Centre in London featuring Billy Preston fails to materialise.

🍎 In America only, Apple Records release the Yoko Ono single 'Woman Power' b/w 'Men Men Men'.

Sunday September 30
🍎 Still in America, seven weeks after *Punch* magazine had published a review by Paul, the *New York Times* publish John's favourable review of Spike Milligan's book *The Goon Show Scripts*.

October
🍎 The Faces' guitarist Ronnie Wood and his wife Chrissie are invited by George and Patti to stay at their Friar Park mansion for a month, with three of the four weeks spent recording in FPHOTS (Friar Park Henley-On-Thames Studios). Among the tracks recorded is 'Far East Man', a song inspired by the T-shirt Ronnie was wearing, acquired on the recent Faces tour of the Far East. Also present at these sessions are Jean Rousell and Ian McLagan (piano/keyboards), Mick Taylor (bass) and Andy Newmark (drums). (The track will ultimately appear on Ronnie's album *I've Got My Own Album To Do*, released by Warner Brothers in America on September 23 and in the UK on September 27, 1974.) George will re-record 'Far East Man' during the September–October 1974 sessions for the album *Dark Horse*.

During the month, a romantic liaison develops between Ronnie and Patti, details of which are not revealed publicly until November 26 (see entry).

Monday October 15 (until Friday October 19)
🍎 Paul spends the week at Abbey Road studio 2, mixing tracks for the album *Band On The Run*.

Friday October 19
🍎 During one of John's frequent visits to the Rainbow Bar & Grill on Sunset Boulevard, he meets Chris Charlesworth, now *Melody Maker's* American correspondent based in LA. Chris recalls the meeting: "I went upstairs into the VIP area of the Rainbow where I met Tony King, who I knew because he used to work for Elton John. He told me he was now working for John Lennon and he asked me, 'Do you want to meet him?' 'Of course I want to meet John!' I replied. Tony led me over to where John was sitting drinking, talking with some friends. Following the introductions, John began quizzing me about life in London, what was happening on the London rock scene, how Paul (McCartney) was, what the weather was like, what the government was like, how much a pint of milk cost and what the royal family was doing. I got the impression that he seemed to be very isolated; or rather he had chosen to isolate himself. It was almost as if he was homesick, though he would later deny that. He was just curious about what was going on back home." After sharing a few drinks with John, Chris requested a formal interview. He tells Chris to ring him in the morning and, over the phone the following day, an interview is arranged for Monday October 22 (see entry), at Lou Adler's Bel Air mansion where John is staying with May Pang.

Saturday October 20
🍎 Even though George is back at home in Friar Park recording with Ronnie Wood, a long lease for him begins on an apartment in Hollywood where he is scheduled to reside while writing tracks for a new Barbra Streisand album. The sessions are soon to begin at the Gamble and Huff studios in Philadelphia.

Monday October 22
🍎 In Los Angeles, at Lou Adler's Bel Air Mansion, John is interviewed by *Melody Maker's* Chris Charlesworth outside by the pool. The result of this 90-minute session, which is continually interrupted by the sound of low flying aeroplanes, is published in *Melody Maker* on November 3 (see entry).

🍎 Back in England, it is announced that Ringo has joined a consortium hoping to win a radio licence up for grabs in Liverpool. He joins a team, which includes the singer Cilla Black, and the comedian Arthur Askey.

Tuesday October 23
🍎 Under the American Freedom of Information Act, John sues the US Immigration and Naturalisation Service in an attempt to obtain documentary evidence that will show prejudgement in his deportation case and prove the illegal wiretapping of his phones. (An appeal hearing is set for October 31.) Later this night, Yoko begins a five-night string of low-key New York club dates, beginning at *Kenny's Castaways*. For the first time in a long while, John is conspicuous by his absence.

Wednesday October 24
 In Los Angeles, John films a television commercial for *Mind Games* with Tony King, who plays the part of the Queen of England. Elton John is present at the sessions. Later, John and King record two radio commercials for the album. While, back in New York, Yoko is found in performance again at *Kenny's Castaways*.

Friday October 26
 Wings release in the UK the single 'Helen Wheels'/'Country Dreamer'. (The American release takes place on November 12.) The A-side is a song written about the McCartney's trusty old Land Rover.

Saturday October 27
 Today's *Melody Maker* reports that Paul is writing the music for a forthcoming 90-minute television special entitled *Gotta Sing, Gotta Dance* starring Twiggy. The shooting is scheduled to begin in California next February.

Monday October 29
 John's single 'Mind Games'/'Meat City' is released in America. (The UK release takes place on November 16.)
 The film *That'll Be the Day* opens in Los Angeles, California.

October (until December)
 In Los Angeles, at the Record Plant and at the A&M Studios, John begins work on the *Rock 'N' Roll* album, originally titled *Oldies But Mouldies*, with Phil Spector. The first sessions produce John's versions of such well-known tracks as 'You Can't Catch Me', 'Sweet Little Sixteen', 'Bony Moronie', 'Just Because', 'My Baby Left Me', 'To Know Her Is To Love Her', 'Angel Baby', 'Be My Baby' 'Ya Ya' and 'That'll Be The Day'. Another track recorded by John during these sessions is 'Here We Go Again', which was co-written with Spector and which will ultimately appear on the 1986 compilation album *Menlove Ave*. An atmosphere of chaos pervades the sessions and only the first four tracks listed will eventually see release on the *Rock 'N' Roll* album released by Apple on February 1, 1975, in America and on February 21 in the UK.

Following these inaugural Los Angeles sessions, Spector vanishes with the tapes. They will eventually be returned to John on Friday June 14, the following year. John's recordings of 'Angel Baby' and 'Be My Baby' will not feature on the official Apple *Rock 'N' Roll* album but appears on the unauthorised LP *John Lennon Sings The Great Rock And Roll Hits,* most commonly known as *Roots,* which was released in the US by mail order only (see entry for February 1975). 'Angel Baby' is officially released on the compilation album *Menlove Ave.* and also on the official *Lennon* CD box set. Also appearing on the *Menlove Ave.* album are John's versions of 'My Baby Left Me' and 'To Know Her Is To Love Her' from these LA sessions.

The tracks 'Angel Baby', 'Ya Ya' and the offending 'You Can't Catch Me' are recorded by John as an out of court settlement between him and Chuck Berry's publisher Morris Levy, who accused John of plagiarising Berry's song 'You Can't Catch Me' on The Beatles' 1969 recording 'Come Together'. All three songs are taken from Levy's Big Seven catalogue.

November
 At EMI's Boulogne-Billancourt Studios near Paris, Wings record further versions of 'Seaside Woman', 'B-Side To Seaside', 'Oriental Nightfish' and 'Wide Prairie'. Paul also records a short ditty entitled 'Luxi', a jingle intended for the station Radio Luxembourg. Towards the end of the month, Wings are busy at Wembley completing the shooting of a TV film, and reporter Chris Welsh interviews Paul at his London offices for a *Melody Maker* article published on Saturday December 1.
 George is invited to appear on a new solo album by former Ten Years After guitarist Alvin Lee. The two met in their local pub the Row Barge in Henley-On-Thames. Lee lives at Woodcote, about three miles from George's Friar Park mansion.
 Yoko appears for three days at New York's Bitter End club. Opening for the estranged Mrs. Lennon is Dory Previn. John meanwhile is seen out socialising with Phil Spector, Lou Adler and the actor Jack Nicholson. They attend the opening night concert of Bobby Blue Bland at the Whiskey-A-Go-Go. Also this month, John busies himself with various

promotional activities for the album *Mind Games*, including a four-part interview on Malibu Beach, California, with Elliott Mintz of Channel 7's ABC *Eyewitness News*.
🍎 Rumours this month suggest that Paul and Ringo will tour America together in the coming year.

Friday November 2
🍎 John, George and Ringo, together with Apple Corps Ltd., and thirteen other companies in the group, issue a high court writ against Allen Klein and his ABKCO company over payments that are due to The Beatles and for damages for alleged misrepresentation. Immediately, Klein counter sues them for $19 million, claiming that he is due unpaid fees. An attempt by Klein to sue Paul for a total of $34 million is thrown out of court.
🍎 Ringo's album *Ringo* is released in America. (The UK release takes place on November 13.)
🍎 John's album *Mind Games* is released in America. (The UK release takes place on November 16.)

Saturday November 3
John: "I don't miss England like I didn't miss Liverpool when The Beatles moved to London. England will always be there if I choose to go back . . . I love New York. It's the hottest city on earth. The difference between New York and London is the difference between London and Liverpool. If I feel homesick for England, I feel homesick for Cornwall or Ireland or Scotland where I went on holidays."
🍎 *Melody Maker* publishes an exclusive interview with John carried out by the paper's American correspondent Chris Charlesworth by the side of the pool at Lou Adler's Bel Air mansion. The wide-ranging ninety-minute conversation includes talk about his new record, his love for America, his immigration problems, his thoughts about the recent Beatles greatest hits packages, his lack of live appearances, his views on the current music scene and, of course, his relationship with the other ex-Beatles.

John is first asked about his new album. "It's finished," he replies. "I'm out here in LA to sit on Capitol, to do the artwork and to see things like radio promotion. The album's called *Mind Games*, and it's, well . . . just an album. Someone told me it was like *Imagine* with balls, which I liked a lot." He admits that Yoko is not on the album and reveals that the two of them have decided to keep their careers separate for a while. "Now that she knows how to produce records and everything about it, I think the best thing I can do is keep out of her hair. We get a little tense in the studio together, but that's not to say we won't ever do another album . . . it's just the way we feel at the moment. We're just playing life by ear and that includes our careers. We occasionally take a bath together and occasionally separately, just however we feel at the time. Yoko has just started a five-day engagement in a club in New York, and I ain't about to do five days. She's over there rehearsing and I'm letting her get on with it her own way." The current separation between John and Yoko is the longest there has ever been, but John is quick to deny the inevitable rumours that they have parted. "We have been apart more than people think, for odd periods over the years, and now I know people are calling from England suggesting we've split up. It's not so."

John then talks about the sessions for the *Ringo* album, which brought together three ex-Beatles – almost four – for the first time since the split. "Yeah, the three of us were there and Paul would most probably have joined in if he was around, but he wasn't. I just got a call from Ringo asking me to write a track so I did. It seemed the natural thing to do . . . For the track I was on piano, Billy Preston was on organ, Ringo was on drums, George was on guitar and Klaus Voorman was on bass."

John announces that he talks to at least one of the other ex-Beatles every two weeks: "I've talked to Ringo a lot recently because he's just moved into my house at Ascot, which is nice because I've always got a bedroom there. I haven't talked to Paul since before he did the last tour with Wings, but I heard *Red Rose Speedway* and it was all right.

"I had a ticket for The Rolling Stones on the East Coast but at the time I was in Los Angeles, so I never got to see them. I haven't seen the Stones since the *Rock and Roll Circus* which was the film that never came out . . . people are saying the Stones are getting too old to appear now but that's bullshit. Mick'll never be past it. I saw the show on TV they did over here and it was fantastic. It was a master performance and that's what Mick is, a master performer."

About a return to live concerts . . . "Another thing that puts me off playing live – the fact that you've got to do the same thing over and over again every night, and the audience wants to hear the songs you're associated with. I remember I sang 'Imagine' twice in one day when I was rehearsing it and that bored me. I've nothing against the song, in fact I'm quite proud of it, but I just can't go on every night singing it. I'd try and vary it, but then I don't like to see that myself. If I go to watch an artist I'd expect to hear the things I know. I understand it from both points of view. Actually I have trouble remembering the lyrics. I sang 'Come Together' at Madison Square Garden for a TV show and really I sang 'She Got Hairy Arseholes' instead of what it should have been, and it was never noticed."

John then talks about his new project, an album of rock and roll oldies with Phil Spector: "Phil and I have been threatening to do this for years. I want to go in and sing some 'Ooh eeh baby' type songs that are meaningless for a change. Whenever I'm in the studio, between takes, I mess around with oldies. I even used to do it in the Beatle days, so now I'm finally getting round to doing a John Lennon sings the oldies album. This will be my next album. I hope people won't think I've run out of ideas, but sod it, I just want to do it."

Conversation turns to the recent double Beatles (*1962–66* and *1967–70*) compilations. "George (Martin) controlled the choice of the material on those albums more than any of us. They sent me lists and asked for my opinion, but I was too busy at the time. I think it was the pressure of the bootlegs that finally made us put them out after all this time. Did you know that there's a bootleg out now of the Decca audition which The Beatles did? I have a copy of it, but I'm trying to find the tape. It's beautiful. There's us singing 'To Know Her Is To Love Her' and a whole pile of tracks, mostly other people's but some of our own. It's pretty good, better than that Tony Sheridan thing. Every time I go on TV here somebody tapes it and within a week it's in all the shops. In a way I dig it because it's good for your ego, but I know I'm not supposed to because it's against the business. I got copies made from this Decca audition and sent it to them all (the bootleggers)! I wouldn't mind actually releasing it."

Chris tells John that he has obtained a copy of the album *The Beatles Live At Shea Stadium 1965*. "Yes, I've got that one," John replies. "I think I've got them all. There's one of a Beatles show at the Hollywood Bowl which was an abortion, and there's others from everywhere we played, obscure places here in the States. It seemed someone was taping it everywhere."

The final question from Chris, inevitably, is, "Any chance of us seeing the four Beatles on a stage or record again?"

John grins and glances down at Chris's tape recorder. The 90-minute tape has almost run out. He makes as if to switch it off but Chris stops him, grabbing his hand and moving the recorder out of his reach. "There's always a chance," says John. "As far as I can gather from talking to them all, nobody would mind doing some work together again. There's no law that says we're not going to do something together, and no law that says we are. If we did something, I'm sure it wouldn't be permanent. We'd do it just for that moment. I think we're closer now than we have been for a long time . . ." The tape runs out before John can say any more.

Thursday November 8
In America, Ringo's album *Ringo* receives a gold record from the RIAA (Record Industry Association of America).

Friday November 9
In the UK only, Apple 48 is released, featuring Yoko's 'Run Run Run' b/w 'Men Men Men'.

Monday November 12
John gives a transatlantic phone call interview to Kenny Everett at *Capital Radio* in London, the first Independent radio station in the UK, serving the London and South East region of the country, which had been broadcasting for a month.

Friday November 23
In New York, twenty-one months after appearing on the show with John, Yoko, backed by Elephant's Memory, appears on the Westinghouse Group television programme *The Mike Douglas Show*. John, meanwhile, gives an interview about the *Mind Games* album to the US radio programme *Rockspeak*.

Saturday November 24
 Ringo's single 'Photograph' reaches number one in the American charts. (The single will reach number eight in the UK charts.)
 Paul becomes the second ex-Beatle to give an interview for the new Independent London station *Capital Radio*.

Monday November 26
 In England, from his home on Richmond Hill, Surrey, Faces' guitarist Ronnie Wood issues the following statement: "My romance with Patti Boyd is definitely on. Things will be sorted out in a few days. Until then, I naturally can't say very much. We're going to talk it out between us and hope to get a happy arrangement. Meanwhile, Patti has gone back to her home and will be talking to George about it. I won't be seeing her today."

Later in the day, George reads Ronnie's statement at Friar Park. He replies by saying: "Whatever Ronnie Wood has got to say about anything, certainly about us, it has *nothing* to do with Patti or me! Got that? It has *nothing* to do with us – her or me!"
 Paul, Linda and Denny travel to Paris to work on more recordings, notably another version of Linda's 'Seaside Woman', 'Wide Prairie' and 'I Got Up'. Sessions at the Pathe Marconi Studio last from 12.45am to 5.30am, the first time that the studios had been used throughout the night. Following the all night recording, the group return to the George V Hotel to get some sleep. They awake at 5.30pm to do interviews for the French magazines *Paris Match* and *Français*. Joining them at the session is Davy Lutton, the ex-drummer of the sixties chart group Love Affair, and the guitarist Jimmy McCulloch. (Paul, Linda and Denny return home later the same evening.) Prior to their departure, Paul gives an interview at his offices in Soho Square, London, to BBC Radio One.

Tuesday November 27
 Rumours naturally persist in the media that George's marriage to Patti is on the point of breaking up.

Friday November 30
 A pre-recorded interview with Paul is transmitted on the BBC Radio One programme *Rockweek*. Also today, in England, Wizard Records release the Denny Laine record *Ahh . . . Laine*, the album that he was recording in July of 1971 before Paul invited him to join his new group.
 In America, John's *Mind Games* album receives a gold record from the RIAA.

December
 John spends time recording at the A&M Studios in Los Angeles.

Sunday December 2
 While in LA, John, feeling somewhat depressed, writes a most poignant postcard to Derek Taylor at his home in Ascot, England. It reads, "I'm in *Lost Arseholes* for no real reason . . . Yoko and me are in hell, but I'm gonna change it . . . probably this very day. Anyway, I'm still famous. He who laffs last is often hard of hearing."

Monday December 3
 Ringo's single 'You're Sixteen'/'Devil Woman' is released in America. (The UK release takes place on February 8. It will reach number four in the UK charts.)

Wednesday December 5
 The Wings album *Band On The Run* (featuring 'Helen Wheels') is released in America. (The UK release, without that track, takes place on December 7.) Paul explains: "Al Corey, the man from the American record company, rang me up one day and said, 'Hi Paul, transatlantic call. I just did the Pink Floyd thing and we took a single off that and we increased the sales by two hundred thousand units. I think you should do it in America, especially as 'Helen Wheels' is going great guns over here. Put it on the album!' So I said, 'I'll ring you back tomorrow.' And I rang him back and said, 'You have got it. Sounds good to me!' "

Paul also reveals how the song 'Drink To Me (Picasso's Last Words)' came about: "We were on holiday, near the place where Steve McQueen and Dustin Hoffman were filming their new film called *Papillon* about Devil's Island. We went round to Dustin's one evening. We were having dinner there, and he was talking about writing songs. He said, 'Can you just write them about anything?' I said, 'Well, you know, pretty much. It's like acting. You are given a script and you go and do it.' He said, 'Well, I have got these words here, out of a magazine.' It was a news story about Picasso having died and it was the last words that he said. Dustin thought they were very poetical words, and he thought they would really suit being a song. The words went: 'Picasso that evening toasted his friends, and he said to them, "Drink to me. Drink to my health. You know I can't drink anymore." Then he went to his studio, he painted a little bit more, and he died the next morning.' So these were his famous last words. Dustin showed me these and I had a guitar with me. I plonked a few chords and did the tune. He leapt out of his chair, and he runs to get his wife and he says, 'Annie! Annie! Come here! This is the most fantastic thing that has ever happened to me. I have got thrills all up my backbone.' He was well chuffed and kept jumping up and down. So that was where that one started from."

Paul on the writing and recording of 'Let Me Roll It': "I wrote that up in Scotland one day. It was a nice day. I was just sitting outside, plonking my guitar and I got this idea for a song. We took it off to Lagos and put down a backing track with Linda playing organ, me playing drums and Denny playing guitar. Then we overdubbed the big guitars you can hear right the way through it, going through a PA amp, not a guitar amp, but a vocal amp, which was a big powerful amp."

The *Band On The Run* album will soon reach number one on both sides of the Atlantic and will be voted album of the year by *Rolling Stone* magazine in America. One critic goes as far as to say " . . . the best thing any of The Beatles have done since *Abbey Road!*" The cover, shot at the stately home at Osterley Park, features various media personalities – the actors James Coburn, and Christopher Lee, the chef and MP Clement Freud, the singer Kenny Lynch, the Liverpudlian boxer John Conteh and the chat show host Michael Parkinson – crouching with Paul, Linda and Denny as escaped convicts caught in a searchlight. In exchange for appearing on the sleeve, Parkinson requests that Paul appears as a guest on his BBC1 Saturday night chat show. Paul agrees but the interview doesn't take place until October 12, 1997 (see relevant entry).

Paul commissions Gordon House and Storm Thorgerson, from the Hipgnosis design team, to shoot a promotional film for the album. With a total running time of 7' 35", it features behind the scenes footage of the preparations for the album cover, set to the tracks '1985' and 'Mrs. Vanderbilt', and a series of shots of seagulls in flight superimposed with images of Paul, Linda and Denny set to 'Bluebird'. The complete MPL film is never released but a short clip from the film is seen on the back-projection video screen during the performance of 'Band On The Run' on the American leg of the Wings 1975/1976 world tour, also seen in the 1979 MPL *Wings Over The World* and *Rockshow* documentaries.

Friday December 7
 In America, the Wings album *Band On The Run* receives a gold record from the RIAA.

Saturday December 8
 A quick perusal of this week's record charts reveals . . . in the UK singles charts – 'Photograph' is at number seven, 'Helen Wheels' is number 13 and 'Mind Games' is a new entry. In the UK album listings, *Ringo* is at number two, and *Mind Games* is at number nine. While in the States, the US singles charts reveal that 'Photograph' is at number six, 'Mind Games' is at number 16 and 'Helen Wheels' is a new entry at number 23.

Sunday December 9
 Radio Luxembourg organises a national petition to gain a pardon from the Queen for John's 1968 drug offences. Over the phone, the DJ Tony Prince interviews John who appeals for "clemency and the right to travel freely between America and Britain." Following the transatlantic phone conversation, Tony remarks, "I believe there is a terrible injustice taking place with regard to John Lennon. When found guilty of drug possession back in 1968 his sentence was a fine, which he paid, but the sentence hasn't stopped at this. Lennon misses Britain but he can't come home."

Monday December 10
 John donates £1,000 to the ailing American 'underground' magazine, the *International Times*.

Sunday December 16

🍎 At Paul and Linda's home at St. John's Wood, London, the McCartneys record an appearance for the traditional BBC1 festive holiday programme *Disney Time*. During the show, which features a running time of 42 minutes, the couple introduce clips from past *Disney* classic films such as *Pinocchio, Mary Poppins, Wild Geese Calling, Run Cougar Run, Bambi, The World's Greatest Athlete, 101 Dalmatians, Snow White & The Seven Dwarfs, Herbie* and, *Disney*'s latest, *Robin Hood*. Paul, who is dressed in emerald trousers, a red, blue and white sweater and red and yellow 'two-tone' shoes, almost resembles a cartoon character himself. Throughout the show, flanked by daughters Heather, Mary and Stella, Paul and Linda are visited on set by a procession of cartoon characters including Goofy, Pluto, and a larger than life Robin Hood. The programme is first transmitted on the station on Boxing Day, December 26, between 6:16 and 6:58pm. Off-camera, Paul gives an interview, where he admits that he did the show because he was "knocked out by cartoons", revealing "we're working on a little production of our own at the moment, an animated film for TV, about a family of mice from an original drawing of mine". The production in question is *The Bruce McMouse Show*, originally started during the *Wings Over Europe* tour of 1972.

Wednesday December 19

🍎 In studio 6 at the Granada Television studios in Quay Street, Manchester, Paul and Wings assemble to perform a mimed version of 'Helen Wheels' in today's edition of *Lift Off With Ayshea*, hosted by Ayshea Brough, and transmitted live across the ITV network between 4:21 and 4:49pm. The show also features musical performances by Marc Bolan & T.Rex and Freddie Garrity, the former lead singer of Freddie and The Dreamers.

Tuesday December 25

🍎 On Christmas Day, Yoko performs a special solo concert in New York at the Cathedral of St. John the Divine, backed by the guitarist David Spinoza.

Wednesday December 26

🍎 This morning, in its traditional "Boxing Day With The Beatles" slot BBC1 transmits the 1964 film *A Hard Day's Night* (between 10:33 and 11:56am). It is the third UK television screening following its premiere broadcast, also on BBC1 on December 28, 1970. Later in the day, the station also broadcasts *Disney Time*, introduced by Paul and Linda (see entry for December 16).

Thursday December 27

🍎 Ringo's film *Blindman* finally receives its UK premiere with a screening this evening at the Astoria in Charing Cross Road, London.

Friday December 28

🍎 In America, Ringo's single 'Photograph' receives a gold record from the RIAA.

December

🍎 At the end of the month, at the Record Plant West Studios in Los Angeles, John produces an unreleased recording of 'Too Many Cooks', featuring Mick Jagger on lead vocals.

🍎 Ringo is asked, "Are you still a vegetarian?" He replies, "Yes. I eat meat twice a year. On Bonfire night I have a sausage and Christmas I have a turkey with the festivities, because it is exciting. I am getting excited over Christmas. So they are the only two days I have it."

"It's all a fantasy putting The Beatles back together again. If we ever do that it's because everyone is broke. I'd rather have Willie Weekes on bass rather than Paul McCartney. Paul is a fine bass player but he's a bit overpowering. I'd join a band with John Lennon any day, but I couldn't join a band with Paul McCartney."

– George

January
🍎 In Los Angeles, John records an acoustic demo of 'What You Got'. On the subject of a Beatles reunion, he remarks, "Nobody would mind doing some work together."
🍎 Eric Clapton tells George about his close relationship with Patti. Shortly after this, Patti moves out of Friar Park and takes up residence with Eric at his Hurtwood Edge home in Surrey.

Tuesday January 1
🍎 Ringo starts the New Year by announcing, in the press, why he turned down a role in the new David Essex movie *Stardust*, the sequel to the highly successful film *That'll Be The Day*. "I couldn't face Beatlemania again," he states.

Thursday January 4
🍎 With the tour of Australia now long since postponed, Paul begins a four-month on-and-off stint in 10cc's Strawberry Studios at Stockport producing his brother Mike's album *McGear*. He contributes two songs and co-writes a further five with Mike and one with the Liverpool poet Roger McGough. During this period, Mike's group Scaffold records the single 'Liverpool Lou', which Paul produces, and features, on the B-side, 'Ten Years After On Strawberry Jam', a track written by him and Linda. During the sessions the American brother and sister act The Carpenters, currently on tour of Britain, pay a visit to see Paul at work. He greets the duo by singing a brief snippet of the chorus of their hit 'Top Of The World'. Also this month, Wings are rumoured to be appearing alongside Stevie Wonder and Tony Orlando & Dawn at this year's Midem Music Business Fair, opening in Cannes in the South Of France later this month. They fail to show.

Saturday January 5
🍎 In England, *Melody Maker* publishes the results of its "Top Albums Of '73" poll. *The Beatles 1967–1970* is placed at number six, *The Beatles 1962–1966* – number eight, the *That'll Be The Day* Ronco film soundtrack album – number 19 and Wings' *Red Rose Speedway* is placed at number 36. (Voted number one in the poll carried out by *MM* readers is Pink Floyd's *Dark Side Of The Moon*.)

Tuesday January 8
🍎 In America, the Capitol compilation album *The Early Beatles* receives a gold record from the RIAA.

Saturday January 12
🍎 'Helen Wheels' reaches number 10 in the American singles chart. (The track will reach number 12 in the UK charts.)
🍎 Today's *Melody Maker* features, on its front page, a story headlined, "Beatles To Get Back?" The report reads, "The Beatles back together again? It could happen, according to Paul McCartney. Commenting in New York, he says: 'We have broken up as a band, but I'd like to see us work together on a loose basis – and I think we will.' "

Monday January 14
🍎 Ringo's film *That'll Be The Day* goes on general release in Sweden.

Saturday January 26
🍎 Ringo's single 'You're Sixteen' reaches number one in the US singles charts.

Monday January 28
🍎 Paul shelves plans to release, as the next Wings single, 'Jet'/'Mamunia' in America. (The next US release instead takes place on February 15.)

Thursday January 31
🍎 Ringo's 'You're Sixteen' receives a gold record from the RIAA.

February
🍎 John spends a part of the month on holiday in Miami, Florida with his son Julian. Their activities include a visit to *Disneyworld*.
🍎 George spends the month in India where again he visits Ravi Shankar.

Wednesday February 6

Brian Matthew: "What about the business side of things. You're in charge of Apple these days aren't you?"

Ringo: "No, no . . . I'm not even in charge of myself these days!"

◾ In England at BBC Broadcasting House, Portland Place, London, Ringo records an appearance with Brian Matthew for the BBC Radio One programme *My Top Twelve*, which is transmitted on Sunday April 7, between 5:01 and 5:59pm. Among his choice of twelve tracks to make up an imaginary album, Ringo chooses: Cream – 'Strange Brew', Stevie Wonder – 'You Are The Sunshine Of My Life', Elvis Presley – 'Heartbreak Hotel', Eddie Cochran – 'Something Else' and Leo Dorsey – 'Everything I Do Has Got To Be Funkin''. During the programme, Brian plays a tape of the two of them talking back in 1966 and Ringo admits: "I am not keen on a Beatles reunion!"

Saturday February 9

◾ In the second part of the weekly *Melody Maker* tribute series "Rock Giants – From A–Z", John comes under the spotlight.

Friday February 15

◾ The Wings single 'Jet'/'Let Me Roll It' is released in the UK. (The American release takes place on February 18.) Paul's Labrador puppy inspires the A-side.

"What with the energy crisis, vinyl squeeze and shortage of radio air space, we sent a top executive to Strawberry Studios, Stockport, to ask Paul and Wings to prepare a specially edited version of their new single 'Jet' (lifted from *Band On The Run*), losing about one minutes playing time. Their reply was: 'We'd love to cut it, but we don't know how.' We now agree with them." – Advertising slogan for Wings' news single.

Saturday February 16

◾ The music industry is thrown into chaos when the *Melody Maker* publishes on its front page: "Beatles Get Together!" The report reads: "The Beatles are back together again! That was the strong report which swept through the American music business last week, adding fuel to the speculation which has been rife in London for the past few weeks. Informed sources in New York suggest that the four of them are preparing a joint statement to be released in the next few days, revealing their plans for a new Beatles album. *Melody Maker* understands all four ex-Beatles have been in New York during the last weeks for legal talks. Ringo Starr, indeed, is still believed to be in America. The New York reports suggest that financial reasons lie behind any decision to reform the band. Since the legal dispute started, it is believed that both Lennon and McCartney's songwriting royalties have been frozen. Only Harrison and Starr have benefited from publishing royalties during the past four years."

Interestingly enough, in light of these bold claims, spokesmen on behalf of Apple or the four ex-Beatles do not make any attempt to deny or confirm this story.

Sunday February 17

◾ The newspaper the *New York Sunday News*, prints an interview with Yoko conducted by Mary Heinholz.

Monday February 18

◾ Ringo's single 'Oh My My'/'Step Lightly' is released in America.

◾ On Yoko's birthday, John and May Pang briefly visit the Dakota to help celebrate the event.

Wednesday February 20

◾ John and May depart for Los Angeles. On their arrival, they meet up with The Beatles' former roadie Mal Evans. Later, they take up residence at the home of the record executive Harold Seiders.

Saturday February 23

◾ Ringo is seen hanging out with Harry Nilsson down in Allman country, Macon, Georgia. Rumours persist in the industry that John, George and Paul will shortly join Ringo and Harry in the town's Capricorn studios to cut an album.

⚫ Meanwhile back in England, today's *Melody Maker* profiles Paul in today's "Rock Giants – From A–Z".

Monday February 25

⚫ In London at the High Court, Judge Megarry approves a scheme to help the receiver carry on running The Beatles' partnership affairs. On hearing this news, Paul releases the statement: "As soon as things are sorted out we can all get together again and do something. We've talked about it, but haven't been able to do anything because this has been going on and on."

Thursday February 28

⚫ From her Dakota apartment, Yoko drafts a letter to *Rolling Stone* magazine.

March

⚫ In the States, the music magazine *Crawdaddy!* publishes an interview with John carried out by Patrick Synder-Scrumpy and Jack Breschard. John is asked about his songwriting: "Do you ever sit down and decide, 'I want to write a song about such and such' and then do it?" John replies: "No. Sometimes I'll want to express something, like an emotion but that's about as far as it goes. Generally, it's whatever comes out, like diarrhoea. I try to sneak up on myself so I'm not too conscious of what I'm doing. If I can just open the plug it will do itself for good or for bad but then I don't have to sweat over it. But I do sweat a lot, usually over trying to do something, then I book the session and then, bam, there it is."

⚫ Paul and Wings spend the first part of the month rehearsing for their upcoming visit to Los Angeles. Prior to his departure, Paul gives an interview, carried out at his London offices, to NBC News, in which he discusses The Beatles, his desire to be a teacher, how young he still feels, the 1969 death hoax and his rebirth as a person. (The interview is transmitted on the station on June 12, 13 and 14.) Also this month, Paul is nominated for an Oscar and a Grammy award for his title track of the James Bond film *Live And Let Die*.

Friday March 1

⚫ In the US district court, John asks for a temporary restraining order of the Immigration and Naturalisation Service appeal ruling on his deportation case. (John's request is denied on May 1.)

Monday March 4

⚫ Apple Corps of London confirm in a brief statement that George is to tour America this year.

Tuesday March 5

⚫ In England, the *Evening Standard* gets Apple's statement yesterday slightly wrong by reporting that "George and Ringo are to join forces for a giant tour of America this year."

Friday March 8

⚫ At his MPL offices in London, at the end of the current Wings rehearsals, Paul gives a two-part interview to ABC TV of America to celebrate the fifth anniversary of his marriage to Linda. He also talks about writing 'Eleanor Rigby' and how he came to write 'Picasso's Last Words (Drink To Me)' for Dustin Hoffman.

Paul is also asked: "Can The Beatles be recreated again?" To which he replies: "They might do bits together again, we don't know yet. Every time I say that, some paper prints a headline saying 'The Beatles To Reform', so I'm a bit cautious about saying anything . . . I don't think we'll get together as a band again, I just don't think it'll work actually, it might not be as good. I just saw Jerry Lewis talking the other day about Dean Martin, it's a little bit like that."

Clips from 'My Love', 'Maybe I'm Amazed' and 'Mary Had A Little Lamb' accompany the feature. (The interview is transmitted in America on March 12 and 13.) Even though Linda sits besides her husband throughout the 15-minute interview, her participation in the piece is minuscule.

⚫ Apple 49 (featuring Badfinger's 'Apple Of My Eye' b/w 'Blind Owl') is released as a single in the UK, and thus becomes the last of the non Beatles-related singles released on the label. (The single had been released in America on December 17, 1973.)

Saturday March 9

🍎 Paul, Linda, their family and Wings head for Los Angeles for more rehearsals. Shortly after their arrival, Paul is interviewed at the Beverly Hilton Hotel for the LA radio station KHJ. Rumours in the music industry begin suggesting that Paul's flight to Los Angeles is primarily to meet John. In fact, there is some truth to this rumour as both John and Paul are seen during the annual Academy Awards ceremony, where they meet up backstage for a chat. Paul and Linda watch the show from the audience.

Monday March 11

🍎 One week after Apple's statement comes a press release from George concerning his forthcoming American tour. This shows that the finalised details of the tour are far from concluded. The release reads: "Although I have been considering a US tour for the autumn of 1974, and although several promoters have been approached on my behalf with regard to a possible tour, no decisions have been taken either with respect to the tour itself, the promoters or the band." Unofficial sources in America suggest that the shows will encompass 25 concerts in 15 American cities and that Ravi Shankar will also be on the bill.

Tuesday March 12

🍎 John and Harry Nilsson watch a performance by the comedy duo The Smothers Brothers at the Troubadour Club in LA. During the show, John and Harry heckle the performance and, at about 12:20am, are thrown out. Witnessing John's drunken escapades in the star-studded audience are Paul Newman, his wife Joanne Woodward, TV personality Flip Wilson, singer Helen Reddy, porn star Linda Lovelace, comedy actress Lily Tomlin, actors Peter Lawford and Jack Hayley Junior and the actress Pam Grier. As John is escorted to his car, he tells the car park attendant, "Don't you know who I am? I'm Ed Sullivan!"

Things turn worse for John when a club waitress claims that Lennon assaulted her, but the charge is later dismissed, and a photographer, 51-year-old Hollywood Matron Brenda Parkins, files a complaint against John, at the West Hollywood Sheriff's department, claiming he hit her. (The case is settled out of court.) The incident draws public attention to the current drinking and carousing binge by John, Ringo, Harry, Keith Moon and various other "wild" rock stars.

In 1975, during an *Old Grey Whistle Test* interview, John recalls the event: "I got drunk and shouted. It was the first night I drank Brandy Alexanders, which is brandy and milk, folks. I was with Harry Nilsson, who didn't quite get as much coverage as me, the bum! He really encouraged me, you know. I usually have somebody there who says, 'Okay Lennon. Shut up.' And I take it. But I didn't have anybody round me to say 'Shut up', and I just went on and on. There was some girl who claimed that I hit her, but I didn't hit her at all, you know. She just wanted some money and I had to pay her off because I thought it would harm my immigration. She said she was a press photographer and she had an Instamatic! She didn't even have any pictures. I was saying: 'If I hit her, why isn't there pictures of me like that?' They said, 'Okay, you'd better leave, Mr. Lennon.' And they took me out.

"Okay, so I was drunk. When it's Errol Flynn, all those showbiz writers say, 'Those were the days, when we had Sinatra and Errol Flynn socking it to the people. You know, they were real men.' I do it, I'm a bum! So it was a mistake, but hell, I'm human. I was drunk in Liverpool and I smashed up phone boxes, but it didn't get into the papers then. I didn't hit a reporter. She got one thousand dollars or some crap, because I had to pay her off. That's what it was. She wasn't a reporter, in fact."

🍎 Meanwhile in England, George puts a damper on the recent rumours that he and Ringo are going to get together for a major tour of America. "There will be no link-up," he states. "It is all speculation!"

Wednesday March 13

🍎 John appears on the front page of newspapers around the world following the incident at the Troubadour. Evidently overcome with remorse, a new clean and sober looking John is seen arm in arm with May Pang, attending the televised *American Film Institute* tribute dinner to the legendary film actor James Cagney at the Century Plaza. Earlier in the day, as an apology, John and Harry Nilsson send flowers to The Smothers Brothers with a note of apology for the whole incident. The short note reads: "With Love &

Tears!" On receiving this, they announce to the press that . . . "the incident was partly our fault as we had engaged in banter with an already quite drunken John, and that the newspaper reports have blown the whole incident completely out of proportion." Asked her opinion in New York, Yoko sternly replies: "No Comment!"

Thursday March 14
 John and Harry Nilsson return to the Troubadour Club to personally apologise to the club's manager, Doug Weston.

Wednesday March 20
 Meanwhile, back in the relative tranquillity of Friar Park, where George is to be found contemplating the Universe and denying rumours of a US tour with Ringo, insiders suggest that his estranged wife Patti is returning briefly to her role as a fashion model.

Friday March 22
 John, along with May Pang, takes up residence at new rented premises, a beach house in Santa Monica. Over the next two weeks, the place becomes a Mecca for local musicians and celebrities. Ever present during this month of frequent comings and goings are Ringo, his manager Hilary Gerrard, Keith Moon, Harry Nilsson, Klaus Voorman, his girlfriend Cynthia Webb, and many other top musicians.

Sunday March 24
 At his beach house, John hosts the first of his planned weekly Sunday night musical get-togethers, open to any of his musical friends who just want to drop in and have a friendly jam session.

Wednesday March 27
 Meanwhile in England, a petition from Beatles' fans containing over 60,000 signatures requesting a pardon for John from his 1968 drugs conviction, is delivered to Prime Minister James Callaghan at 10 Downing Street, in London today.

Thursday March 28
 At Burbank Studios in California, John starts producing the Harry Nilsson album *Pussycats,* for which he writes the track 'Mucho Mungo' and records several demos of the song. John recalls the problems recording the album with Harry: "He'd lost his voice and I don't know whether it was psychological or what. You know, he was going to doctors and having injections and he didn't tell me till later that he was bleeding in the throat, or I would have stopped the session. But he had no voice. So what do you do? I'm saying: 'Well, where is all that yoooooo-deeeee-dooooo-dahh stuff?' and he's going 'croak'. Someone writes a story saying that he's imitating me. He wasn't imitating me. He *couldn't* . . . he had *no* voice. But we were committed.

"The main thing was we had a lot of fun. There was Keith Moon, Harry, Ringo and me all living together in the house and we had some moments. But it got a little near the knuckle. That's when I straightened out. In the middle of that album. That's when I realised: 'There's something wrong here. I mean, this is crazy, man!' I was suddenly the straight one in the middle of all these mad, mad people. I suddenly was not one of them. I pulled myself back and finished the album the best I could. I mean we'd already spent the money. Everything was booked in. We had the tapes. So me and Harry had the best out of it, you know, because we spent a few good nights together."
 Paul and Linda drop by to watch the recording, and Paul joins in a jam session with John and the other musicians on the track 'Midnight Special', joining John for the first time in a musical environment since the split of The Beatles some four years ago. At the end of the day, John invites Paul to his beach house music session on Sunday (see entry).
 Ringo features on drums on the *Pussycats* album, which is released on August 19 in America and on August 30 in the UK.
 In London today, March 28, George registers his new company. It will be entitled *Oops Publishing Ltd.*

Friday March 29 & Saturday March 30
 Additional recording sessions for *Pussycats* (one day only) take place at the Burbank Studios in California.

 On Saturday, 'Jet' reaches number seven in both the American and UK singles charts. Also today, Paul and Linda, currently staying with the Eastman family in New York, take their children to the Ringling Brothers and Barnum & Bailey circus at Madison Square Garden. Afterwards, the McCartneys board a plane at Kennedy Airport and return to Los Angeles.

Sunday March 31

"Don't get too serious, we're not getting paid. We ain't doing nothing but sitting here together, and anybody getting bored with me – take over!" – John Lennon.

 With no recordings planned at the Burbank Studios, John spends the day relaxing by the pool and, later this evening, holds the second of his Sunday night music jam sessions at his beach house. Those in attendance include Paul.

"Just turn the fucking vocal mike up . . . McCartney's doing the harmony on the drums," says John Lennon during the all-evening session, which is recorded for posterity on equipment borrowed from Burbank Studios.

Alongside the two former Beatles (John on guitar, Paul on drums and both often sharing vocals) are Linda, Stevie Wonder, Jesse Ed Davis and others. The session is recorded and among the songs they haphazardly perform are versions of: 'Never Trust A Bugger With Your Mother', 'Little Bitty Pretty One', 'I Left My Home And I Was Movin' Around', 'Lucille', 'Nightmares', 'Stand By Me', 'Cupid', 'Chain Gang' and 'Take This Hammer'. At the end of the session, in the early hours of April 1, Paul, Linda and family depart for their nearby hotel. During his 1975 BBC2 *Old Grey Whistle Test* interview, John briefly recalled the all-evening session: "I did actually play with Paul. We did a lot of stuff in LA. But there was fifty other people playing, and they were all just watching me and Paul!"

 Ringo meanwhile is to be found out socialising in LA with Keith Moon and Harry Nilsson.

 In London, there's bad news for Messrs Starkey and Moon when the *Playboy* club announces that they have banned them from using the club. The decision comes after a guardrail was smashed during a party they held there recently. A spokesman for the *Playboy* club announces: "It was decided to withdraw their membership because damage by Mr. Starr and Mr. Moon came to an amount totalling almost £30!"

 Still in England, tax returns for the years 1973/1974 show all is not well with Paul's McCartney's Productions Ltd. company. Sales for the period total £39,142, while outgoing expenses reach £154,751, resulting in a loss of £115,609 – a loss for the fourth consecutive year.

April

 After many refusals following his 1973 English drug conviction, Paul finally gets his American visa.

 A statue of The Beatles by the sculptor Arthur Dooley, erected on the wall of the new Cavern Club in Mathew Street, Liverpool, is unveiled. The piece, produced from funds raised by the people of Liverpool and fans throughout Britain, features a Madonna holding three babies with the fourth (Paul) flying away. A plaque underneath reads: "Four Lads Who Shook The World".

Monday April 1

 In the early hours of the morning and shortly after Paul and Linda had left, Ringo, along with Keith Moon and Harry Nilsson, arrive at the beach house. Noticing that someone had been playing his kit, Ringo asks: "Who's been fiddling with my drums?" John and the others reply, "Paul. Paul's been here." Later this morning, Paul and Linda return to the beach house, only to find John still in bed. Paul immediately heads for the piano and, along with Moon and Nilsson, performs a medley of Beatles tunes, with all three musicians happily joining in. Afterwards, Paul is offered some angel dust by Nilsson, which he refuses. John wakes from his slumber around 3pm and joins the other musicians and friends who are relaxing, sitting by the swimming pool. Keith Moon's friend and assistant, Dougal Butler, snaps pictures of Paul performing a Beatles' medley on the piano as well as John and Paul together by the pool. (This Polaroid snapshot will turn out to be the last ever picture taken of John and Paul together.)

 The soundtrack album *Son Of Dracula* is released in America and contains excerpts from Ringo's film dialogue, and the Harry Nilsson songs 'Daybreak' (featuring Ringo on drums and George on cowbell) and 'At My Front Door', with Ringo on drums. (The album is released in the UK on May 24.)

Tuesday April 2
🍎 Ringo again visits the beach house; accompanied by Keith Moon and Harry Nilsson. The Beatles' former confidant and roadie Mal Evans is also present.

Wednesday April 3
🍎 Sessions for *Pussycats* take place at Burbank Studios (also on April 4, 6, 8, 10 & 11).

Thursday April 4
🍎 While still in Los Angeles on holiday, Paul and Linda decide to pay a visit to Brian Wilson, the now reclusive member of The Beach Boys, at his Bel Air home. The McCartneys bang on the door for over an hour, but Wilson refuses to let them in. Paul and Linda know Brian is there, because they can hear him inside quietly crying to himself. With no alternative, Paul and Linda depart from the house and head on their way.

Monday April 8
🍎 The Wings' single 'Band On The Run'/'Nineteen Hundred And Eighty Five' is released in America only.

Tuesday April 9
🍎 John records his second radio interview with Capital Radio in England on the transatlantic phone, talking with DJ Nicky Horne for the programme *Your Mother Wouldn't Like It* (transmitted the following night, April 10, between 9:00 and 10:59pm).

Wednesday April 10
🍎 Just over two weeks after moving in, John and May Pang again pack up their bags and move out of their rented beach house and into new rented premises, this time a house nearby in Santa Monica that once belonged to the film actor Peter Lawford. The rent on this Pacific Coast Highway house is $5,000 a month (approximately £2,500). Just over two weeks later (on April 27), with the *Pussycats* album sessions descending into chaos and with John fearing that his life is going nowhere, he and May head back to New York.

Saturday April 13
🍎 *Band On The Run* tops the American album charts. It will go on to sell over 6,000,000 copies worldwide and spend over two years on both the US and UK charts. Meanwhile, it is reported that Paul's former girlfriend, the actress Jane Asher, has given birth to a baby girl at the Middlesex Hospital. Wishing privacy, Jane tells the staff "not to release any details"!

Sunday April 14
🍎 In California, just before midnight, a somewhat intoxicated Ringo appears as a guest on Flo and Eddie's Sunday night radio phone-in show on the small Pasadena based station KROQ. (Flo and Eddie are Mark Volman and Howard Kaylan, formerly with the American sixties pop group The Turtles, and more recently members of Frank Zappa's Mothers Of Invention.) Arriving with Keith Moon moments before the station ceased broadcasting for the night, Ringo is in no condition to be interviewed. During the first 90 seconds of his interview, as Volman recalls, he uses the word "fuck" no less than 14 times. Because of this, Volman, Kaylan and their producer are all sacked by the radio station shortly after transmission. Following several complaints from listeners, investigators from the Federal Communications Commission are called in to investigate Ringo's actions as well as the station and the programme itself.

Monday April 15
🍎 Meanwhile back in England on Easter Monday, The Beatles' 1968 animated fantasy film *Yellow Submarine* receives its UK TV premiere on BBC1, between 7:40 and 9:04pm. The BBC's weekly listings magazine *Radio Times* describes the film as: "The best full-length cartoon since the golden age of Disney!"

Friday April 19

🍎 The 91-minute Cinemation distributed Apple film *Son Of Dracula,* starring Ringo and Harry Nilsson, is premiered in Atlanta, Georgia, an amazing year and a half after filming was completed. Both Ringo and Keith Moon attend the premiere.

🍎 In New York, Yoko makes her second solo performance on *The Mike Douglas Show.* Backed again by Elephant's Memory, she performs the track 'Shirankatta'.

Saturday April 20

🍎 Beatles reunion rumours continue to dominate the music press around the world. Rumours suggest that John, Paul, George and Ringo are all gathered for a business meeting today in Los Angeles' Beverly Wiltshire Hotel.

Friday April 26

🍎 With the McCartneys now back in England, Paul holds auditions for a new drummer at the Albery Theatre in St. Martin's Lane, London. From fifty hopefuls, he eventually chooses Geoff Britton. Geoff recalls the audition: "You should have seen the people there. It was like a *Who's Who* of the music industry. But I was a bit disappointed actually because I thought it would be a chance to play with McCartney, but they'd hired session men to play with us instead. Wings just sat out in front of the audience and watched. I wasn't really nervous. I'm never nervous, although I might be a bit apprehensive. We had to play about four numbers – some of it quite advanced stuff for an ordinary rock and roll number. Anyway, I got up there and did my stuff . . . A few days later I got this phone call and they said I was on the short-list of five, and this time it would be Paul and the group playing. That time I had a 20 per cent chance, yet I felt it was more hopeless than ever. I met Paul and the group and they were really nice. After that I got a phone call saying they'd narrowed it down to two geezers. Each of us spent a whole day with the group and had dinner with them. Then one day the phone rang. It was Paul. He said, 'Well, we've decided' and he was mucking about, geeing me up . . . In the end I said: 'Well, who's it gonna be?' and he said: 'You got the job.'"

Saturday April 27

🍎 John decides that he is tired of the crazy wild LA lifestyle and decides to return to New York, accompanied by May Pang and Harry Nilsson, where work resumes, on recording the RCA album *Pussycats.*
John: "What do you think, Ringo?"
Ringo: "I don't know John – I'll ask George. What do you think George?"
George: "I don't know Ringo, I'll ask Paul. What do you think Paul?"
Paul: "Our Linda says I've got to stop at home and prune the roses, George!"
(A cartoon from today's *Melody Maker.*)

🍎 With no sign of a let-up in the interest concerning the rumoured Beatles reunions, *Melody Maker* publishes the article: "Should The Beatles Come Back Together?" Among those offering their opinion on the matter is The Beatles' original manager Allan Williams, who says: "I don't think there's even a chance of The Beatles reforming. But if they did, I'd certainly offer my services as manager!"

Sunday April 28

🍎 With Beatles reunion nonsense whirling its way across the music press around the world, John appears briefly with Harry Nilsson at the March Of Dimes benefit concert, in New York's Central Park, at the start of the "walkathon" rally organised by a local radio station. They are joined on stage by local New York radio DJ Cousin Brucie. Besides ad-libbing their own 'March Of Dimes' song, dancing, signing autographs for the crowd and taking time to hold a baby, John is asked by Brucie about the latest news on the other Beatles. He also asks Harry about the recently released film *Son Of Dracula.* Their stint on stage goes largely unnoticed on the TV news and in local newspapers. WABCTV is there to shoot a two-camera 15-minute report on the proceedings. Unfortunately many of the teenagers in the 20-mile walk are taken to the nearby Roosevelt Hospital suffering from exhaustion. Now being back in New York, John and May Pang have taken up residence at the luxurious Pierre Hotel on Fifth Avenue. Soon after arriving back in the city John is visited by Derek Taylor.

Monday April 29

🍎 Catching up with old friends in New York, John drops into the Record Plant and meets up with Mick Jagger. Totally off-the-cuff, John produces the track 'Please Don't Ever Change', with Jagger singing lead vocals.

🍎 Meanwhile, Beatles reunion rumours continue unabated. The latest reads: "Beatles business meetings in Los Angeles are still going on. Sources close to the group suggest that the reformed Beatles' tour will open in Monticello, near New York, in June or July." (The journalist, who instigated this, fails to report that John, in fact, is *no longer* in Los Angeles.)

May

🍎 During John's absence, Yoko employs the Tarot card reader John Green to read her cards for the first time.

🍎 It is revealed that Paul and Linda are now *not* too strong in their vegetarian beliefs.

Friday May 17 & Saturday May 18

🍎 John donates two days of his time acting as a guest disc jockey for the Philadelphia based radio station WFIL's Helping Hand Marathon fundraising drive.

Thursday May 23

🍎 George launches his own record label Dark Horse Records. He also signs a worldwide distribution deal in Paris with A&M Records. Its first signing is Ravi Shankar, but the group Splinter turns out to be the only success for the label, other than George himself, when 'Costafine Town' reaches number 17 in the UK and number 77 in the US singles charts.

Friday May 24

🍎 In the UK, one month before the release of Wings' version, Pye-Bradley Records release 'Zoo Gang' as a single, as performed by Jungle Juice.

June

🍎 During the early part of the month, John records several demos prior to the start of the *Walls And Bridges* sessions, including the song 'What You Got'. Also this month, the controversial 1972 movie *Oh Calcutta!* based on the successful theatre production, featuring an all-nude cast and a scene scripted by John back in 1969, goes on general cinema release in America.

🍎 Paul produces 'Liverpool Lou' for his brother Mike's group Scaffold. The single reaches number seven in the UK charts.

🍎 Also this month at the annual Berlin Film Festival in Germany, the Apple film *Little Malcolm And His Struggle Against The Eunuchs* wins the Silver Bear Award. The film features the Dark Horse signed duo Splinter performing the Mal Evans song 'Lonely Man'.

Tuesday June 4

🍎 In America, Paul's 'Band On The Run' single is awarded a gold record by the RIAA (Record Industry Association of America.)

Saturday June 8

🍎 The Wings single 'Band On The Run' reaches number one in America.

Thursday June 13

🍎 After The Who's concert at Madison Square Garden this evening, John and May are visited in their Pierre Hotel suite by Keith Moon, Moon's assistant Dougal Butler and Chris Charlesworth, *Melody Maker*'s American correspondent. Keith being Keith, he suggests to John that they all have a drink, assuming, wrongly as it turned out, that John would have a huge bar stocked with drink. In the event, all he had was a bottle of expensive red wine, a very fine red wine, given to him by Allen Klein. Chris takes up the story: "John was a bit spooked that he got this bottle and mentioned that he was, at present, involved in a lawsuit with Klein who might have a good reason to poison him. John suggested that someone in the company should taste the wine. He said, 'Well Keith, you can't taste it because you're the drummer with The Who, you're doing a show tomorrow night and we don't want you to die. I'm John Lennon, the famous Beatle, and I can't die. I'm in love with May Pang, she's my companion at the moment and I don't want her to die, therefore the only person left to taste the wine is you Chris . . . so here you are mate.' The bottle is duly opened, the wine is poured into my glass and I sampled it as the others all stared at me. To this day, that was the finest glass of wine I've ever had in my entire life . . . it was so rich, full-bodied, it was just so fine. I said to everyone, 'It's absolutely beautiful,' and it was duly shared, but once the drink had gone, Keith was not keen to overstay his welcome and was eager to move on." (Their visit lasted less than an hour.)

Friday June 14
🍎 During a *Walls And Bridges* album planning session at the Record Plant Studios in New York, Al Coury, Capitol's head of promotions in California, informs John he's retrieved Phil Spector's *Rock 'N' Roll* album tapes, Capitol having handed over $90,000 to Spector.
🍎 Reports today indicate that *Band On The Run,* besides being number one in America, has also reached the top spot in Australia, Norway and Sweden, earning a gold disc in each country.

Saturday June 15
🍎 Following the split of the group Stone The Crows, the guitarist Jimmy McCulloch joins Wings. (He had first played with Paul and the group in Paris, back in 1972 on the sessions that produced the first version of 'Seaside Woman'.) Paul is reacquainted with him when he asks him to play on the album *McGear,* which Paul produced for his brother.

Monday June 17
🍎 At the Record Plant, John starts the recording sessions for *Walls And Bridges.* Joining him are the musicians Jesse Ed Davis, Kenny Ascher, Nicky Hopkins, Eddie Mottan and Arthur Jenkins. Work soon begins on 'Whatever Gets You Through The Night' (with Elton John on organ, piano and harmony vocals), 'Beef Jerky' (instrumental) and 'Bless You'. Later this night, Ringo phones John at his hotel asking him to write a new song for his next album. John will write (and demo record) the track 'Goodnight Vienna'.
🍎 Meanwhile, Paul, Linda, their family and Wings depart from Heathrow Airport en route to a 133-acre ranch in Nashville, USA, the home of the songwriter Curly Putnam, who, in 1966, had written the Tom Jones hit 'The Green Green Grass Of Home'. During their seven-week stay, Wings will record at the nearby Sound Shop Studios where, working between 6pm and midnight, they produce 'Junior's Farm', a song inspired by Curly and the place that Wings are currently renting, 'Sally G', and the instrumental 'Walking In The Park With Eloise'. The latter, written many years ago by Paul's father, James McCartney, will later become a choice of Paul's during his January 30, 1982, BBC Radio Four *Desert Island Discs* appearance.
Linda tells the story behind the song and how it came to be recorded during these sessions: "When Paul was a little boy, about 10 . . . he remembers sitting at the foot of the piano while his dad was playing the song. We were having dinner with the guitar player Chet Atkins and Paul had been playing a lot of his music to him and Paul said, 'Here's one that my dad wrote a long time ago' – and he started playing it.' Chet suggested that the song should be recorded and that it would be nice for his dad . . . so we got Chet playing on it and Floyd Cramer, the piano player, and we got together a nice little band called Country Hams with lots of Nashville people."
Paul later reveals to *Disc* magazine that his father was extremely touched by the gesture: "He loved having his record out – but he's very shy . . . and he didn't like all the publicity. He was very emotional about it when I first played it to him – he said I really shouldn't have bothered, but I know he enjoyed it. And do you know what? My Uncle Joe has now written some words to go with it . . ."
The line-up also records 'Bridge Over The River Suite'. During these sessions Paul also records the unreleased tracks 'Hey Diddle', 'Send Me The Heart' (a track Denny will re-mix for his album *Japanese Tears*), 'Proud Mum' and demos of songs that will appear on the album *Venus And Mars*. Linda also records the song 'Wide Prairie', which will not see the light of day until October 26, 1998, when it appears on the album of the same name. Paul breaks from Wings' duty to spend time producing the Peggy Lee album *Let's Love*. (Paul will affectionately call these sessions *The Peg 'N' Paul Show.)* Linda surprises

Paul by purchasing for him the original double bass as used on Elvis Presley's recording of 'Heartbreak Hotel'.

It is reported (incorrectly) that both McCulloch and Britton have left the group after recording only a handful of tracks. The story makes a headline in the *New Musical Express* during August that reads "Wings Upheaval". The report states: "The existing line-up of Paul McCartney's Wings appeared this week to have broken up, following what is understood to have been a major internal policy disagreement. Sources close to the band suggest that Denny Laine and the two unofficial members, guitarist Jimmy McCulloch and drummer Geoff Britton, are no longer working with Wings. A spokesman for Laine confirms that there had been 'personal difficulties', while another contact stated emphatically: 'Wings have split, the old band doesn't exist any more.'"

Meanwhile in a further *NME* report, sources close to the band reveal that Denny Laine has also just "fallen out with Paul and Linda over personal difficulties". The story adds a statement from a Wings spokesman who stipulates that: "Wings members are free to pursue their own musical careers. This will enable them to develop working relationships free of contractual ties. In future Wings will have a fluid concept, which will be adapted to suit current and future projects." When the spokesman is pressed by the paper to confirm or deny the split in Wings, he gave this response: "It is wrong to say that Wings are no more, because Wings are Paul and Linda McCartney."

Denny later gave his side of the story: "We went to Nashville with the idea that we'd get this group together and we'd all sign contracts and be Wings as a business thing . . . but then it seems as if it was being a bit rushed. I thought 'hang on – let's make sure that this is the right group.' Then I started thinking about contracts and I decided that I could be in any group without signing a contract. It just didn't seem necessary to me, and the minute I said this to Paul he said, 'Great, that's the way I want it too', and then I realised that we were only going through this thing with contracts because we'd all been advised to do it. It wasn't what we wanted."

Regardless of all this speculation, the Wings line-up of Paul, Linda, Denny, Jimmy and Geoff remain together, for the time being. The group returns home to England on Wednesday July 17.

Tuesday June 18
 Paul celebrates his five-year marriage to Linda by telling the *Daily Express*: "I've discovered I'm rather old-fashioned – I believe in the marriage contract." Further comments from Paul during this period continue to appear in the music press, many of which stem from a press conference that took place in the front yard of Putnam's Nashville ranch.

Wednesday June 19
 A copyright is registered for the unreleased track 'Where Are You Going?' co-written by Ringo and Billy Lawrie.

Friday June 28
 During a break from the *Walls And Bridges* sessions, John records a demo version of 'Goodnight Vienna' for Ringo.
 In the UK only, Wings release the single 'Band On The Run'/'Zoo Gang'. The B-side will later appear as the theme tune to the ITV UK action series of the same name, starring Brian Keith and John Mills. The first episode is transmitted across the ITV network on April 5 this year and will run to only six episodes with the final show being transmitted on May 10.

July
 Towards the end of the month, on returning from Nashville, Paul commissions the director Jim Quick to produce an animated promotional film for the song 'Mamunia'. In a style reminiscent of the Sixties children's TV series *Ivor The Engine*, the clip features animated sequences that recreate the song lyrics. The short item, save for one isolated ITV screening late in the year, will remain unscreened. Incidentally, the popularity of Paul's group Wings is proven when the *Wings Fun Club* in London announces that they currently have a membership base of around 8,000 people, with some subscribers as far away as America, Japan and Australia.
 This month, George spends time recording in his Friar Park studios in Henley.

The film *Little Malcolm And His Struggle Against The Eunuchs* receives its premiere at the Berlin Film Festival, where it wins the Silver Bear award.

Friday July 5
 In America, the first US television screening of The Beatles' 1968 film *Yellow Submarine* is transmitted as CBS TV's *Friday Night Movie*, between 8:01 and 9:28pm. As expected, the clip of 'Hey Bulldog' is not part of this broadcast.

Saturday July 6
 The Wings *Band On The Run* album reaches number one in the UK.

Thursday July 11
 In London, George invests £5,000 in a new business venture with the fashion designer Ossie Clarke.

Saturday July 13
 Band On The Run continues to top the UK album charts.

Sunday July 14
 Julian flies from England to visit John in New York.
 Today, at his private studio in Scotland, Paul records what is soon known as his "Piano Tape", comprising a number of somewhat uninspiring tunes, ditties and improvised songs on his studio piano. Among the highlights of the 61-minute recording are: 'Million Miles', 'Mull Of Kintyre', 'I'll Give You A Ring', 'Baby, You Know It's True', 'Women Kind', 'Getting Closer', 'I'm In My Dreams', 'Rockestra Theme', 'Letting Go', 'Call Me Back Again', 'Lunch Box/Odd Sox', 'Treat Her Gently/Lonely Old People', 'You Gave Me The Answer', 'Waiting For The Sun To Shine', 'She Got It Good', 'Blackpool', 'Sunshine In Your Hair', 'Girl Friend', 'I Lost My Little Girl', 'Upon A Hill', 'Sea', 'Love Is Your Road, Love Is My Road', 'Sweet Little Bird', 'Partners In Crime', 'Suicide' and 'Dr. Pepper'.
 Jonathan Clyde takes up his appointment as director of *Dark Horse* records in America.

Monday July 15
 In New York, at the Record Plant, work continues with John recording a version of 'Move Over Ms. L', a track originally written for Keith Moon. He also writes the song 'Incantation' with Roy Cicala, but no recording of the song has yet surfaced. (Even though a copyright for the song is registered on November 15.)
 Paul and Linda head out of Heathrow en route to New York to see John and his new companion May Pang at their new apartment.

Tuesday July 16
 John and May Pang take up residence in a small apartment at Eddie Germano's two-storey building at East 52nd Street, in New York. Two of their first visitors are Paul and Linda. According to John, they spend a couple of . . . "Beaujolais evenings, reminiscing about the old times." Sharing the apartment with John and May are two kittens, one black, one white, named Major and Minor respectively. A seven-inch single often played on John's record player is a bootleg disc of 'How Do You Do It?', as recorded by The Beatles back in 1962. (Paul and Linda return to England on Sunday July 21, and return to New York on August 1.)

Wednesday July 17
 The US Immigration and Naturalisation Service Board deny John's October 31, 1973, appeal against the deportation order that he leave America within 60 days. John files a further appeal.

Sunday July 21
 Work on *Walls And Bridges* shifts to the more familiar surroundings of the Record Plant. Here John begins work on the following songs: 'Going Down On Love', 'Old Dirt Road', 'What You Got', 'Scared', 'No. 9 Dream', 'Surprise, Surprise (Sweet Bird Of Paradox)' (featuring Elton on backing vocals), 'Steel And Glass' (believed to be an attack on Allen

Klein), 'Nobody Loves You (When You're Down And Out)' and 'Ya Ya', featuring John's son Julian on drums. (Alternative versions of several of these songs appear on the compilation album *Menlove Ave.* in 1986.) Elton John extracts from John a promise to appear with him at his Thanksgiving concert at New York's Madison Square Garden in November if 'Whatever Gets You Through The Night' should reach number one. John agrees to this, feeling certain that the song would not reach number one "in a million years!"

Wednesday July 24
In the UK, the *London Evening News* publishes an interview with Denny Laine, who boasts of his trusting relationship with Paul. "I have signed so many contracts that have got me into trouble that I never want to sign anything again!"

Friday July 26 – Sunday July 28
A three-day Beatles convention called *Strawberry Fields Forever* opens in Boston, Massachusetts.

August
Ringo records songs for his album *Goodnight Vienna* at the Sunset Sound Studios and Producers Workshop in Los Angeles, California. The sessions produce the following tracks: 'Call Me', 'Goodnight Vienna', 'Occapella', 'Oo Wee', 'Husbands And Wives', 'Snookeroo', 'All By Myself', 'No No Song', 'Skokiaan', 'Easy For Me' and 'Goodnight Vienna' (reprise). The title track is written by John, who recorded a demo of the track for Ringo and supervised the recording of the song. While there, John also cuts a studio demo of 'Only You'. Then, at John's suggestion, Ringo re-records his vocals over the top for a version to appear on the album.

On his way home from Los Angeles, John stops at the Caribou Ranch in Colorado to do back-up work on Elton John's recording of 'Lucy In The Sky With Diamonds'. With John still away with May Pang, Yoko prepares for her most testing concert tour in years, a six-date tour of her homeland, Japan.

Further awards are heaped on the film *Little Malcolm*, this time a gold medal at the annual Atlanta Film Festival. This month, George announces at a press conference that he has now opened Dark Horse offices in Los Angeles, London and Rotterdam. Also during this month, George is seen on holiday in Grenada, Spain, accompanied by his new female companion, 24-year-old Kathy Simmons. On his return to England at the end of the month, he takes time to promote his new Dark Horse Records signing, the unknown duo Splinter – Bobby Purvis and Billy Elliott. At a press gathering in London, George is asked why he signed the group. "When making *Little Malcolm And His Struggle Against The Eunuchs*," George recalls, "big Malcolm Evans (Mal Evans, The Beatles' former roadie) materialised the ideal song required for a certain part of said film, and thinking it was a potential hit that may help to get the film noticed by the controllers of the film industry, I thought I'd try to produce a hit single by Splinter."

George introduces Ravi Shankar on stage at the Albert Hall in London. After a few words about Lord Krishna, George greets Ravi's appearance by kissing his feet.

Sunday August 1
Paul, Linda and the family arrive back in New York City.

Tuesday August 3
Yoko and her six-piece Plastic Ono Super Band leave New York en route to Tokyo, Japan.

*   *   *

Yoko Ono & The Plastic Ono Super Band
Tour Of Tokyo, Japan:
August 5 – August 16

With John still in Los Angeles with May Pang, Yoko sets out on her six-date tour of Tokyo, Japan, where she is accompanied by the six-piece group The Plastic Ono Super Band. This comprises a line-up of David Spinoza (guitar), Sneaky Pete (steel guitar), Ken

Asher (keyboards), Michael Brecker (tenor sax), Gordon Edwards (bass guitar) and Jim Keltner (drums). Their concert appearances are as follows:

Kaiseizan Stadium, Koryama (Monday August 5)
Koseinenkin Hall, Osaka (Tuesday August 6)
Nagoya City Hall, Nagoya (Friday August 9)
Sun Plaza, Tokyo (Sunday August 11)
Koseinenkin Hall, Tokyo (Monday August 12)
Hiroshima Prefectural Gymnasium, Hiroshima (Friday August 16)

To coincide with her visit, Apple in Japan released a very limited editon promotional album featuring a selection of her best solo work to date.

Monday August 5
Yoko and The Plastic Ono Super Band perform on the second day of the two-day One Step Festival, an event organised by the locally published magazine *One Step*. Joining Yoko on the bill today is the singer Yuya Uchida.

* * *

Thursday August 15
🍎 At London's EMI Abbey Road Studios, working again with the director David Litchfield, Wings record songs for a proposed live studio album and an MPL documentary, entitled *One Hand Clapping*. The ambitious 50-minute programme includes live studio performances of 'Jet', 'Soily', 'C Moon', 'Maybe I'm Amazed', 'My Love', 'Bluebird', 'Band On The Run', 'Live And Let Die', '1985' and, to conclude the show, a solo piano performance by Paul of 'Baby Face'. Of most significance are the unreleased performances of 'Suicide', a track first "jammed" by The Beatles during the January 1969 *Get Back/Let It Be* sessions, a song he claims to have written for Frank Sinatra. Also, 'I'll Give You A Ring', which remains unreleased until June 1982 when it appears on the B-side to 'Take It Away'. *Let It Be* style behind the scenes footage of the group at work and at play is also included, such as Geoff Britton performing a drum solo and practising karate, as well as Paul and Jimmy jamming a version of Paper Lace's recent hit 'Billy, Don't Be A Hero'. Joining Wings at the sessions are the orchestral arranger/conductor Del Newman, and the Liverpool saxophone player Howie Casey, a veteran of the Liverpool music scene who first teamed up with Paul when he played in Hamburg with The Beatles in the early Sixties. Following this session, Paul invites Howie to join the group on a more permanent basis, later appearing on the Wings 1975/1976 and 1979 concert tours. The *One Hand Clapping* film again remains unreleased save for a brief snippet of 'Jet' being broadcast on Capital Radio in London during Christmas of 1976. Tracks recorded during this all day session which fail to make the finished *One Hand Clapping* edits include 'Let Me Roll It', 'Little Woman Love', 'Junior's Farm' (this will receive limited screenings on European television as a promotional clip to accompany the release of the single), 'Wild Life', 'Hi Hi Hi', Denny Laine's 'Go Now' and 'Blue Moon Of Kentucky' (see entry for Monday, September 9).

One segment from these sessions is later edited into another unreleased MPL film, this time entitled *The Backyard*. This 9-minute short film, features Paul alone with his acoustic guitar, seated on a stool in the gardens of Abbey Road studios where he performs a version of the unreleased track 'Blackpool' as well as four rock 'n' roll classics, 'Twenty Flight Rock' (which is interrupted at the end by the sound of a siren from an ambulance rushing past the studios), 'Peggy Sue', 'I'm Gonna Love You Too' and 'Sweet Little Sixteen'. The tracks 'Blackbird', 'Country Dreamer', 'Loving You', 'We're Gonna Move' and 'Blue Moon Of Kentucky' are also filmed, but fail to make the final edit. To date, only 75-seconds of 'Peggy Sue' has been seen in public, transmitted as part of the 1986 *McCartney* TV special, originally broadcast on BBC1, in England, on August 29 1986.

🍎 Meanwhile, today at the Lyric Theatre in Shaftesbury Avenue, London, Robert Stigwood's production of *John, Paul, George, Ringo and Bert,* written by Liverpool schoolmaster Willy Russell opens. The play, originally presented for six weeks in Liverpool at the Everyman Theatre, tells the story of The Beatles from the days of the Cavern club to their break-up in 1970. The character Bert is the fictional Beatle who is booted out before the group became famous. He narrates the story in the guise of a fan who watches The Beatles develop and progress. George is the only Beatle to attend the opening but he leaves during the intermission. Paul reads the original script and decides it falsely portrays him as the villain and therefore denies Stigwood the film rights to the story. Coincidentally, Paul's brother Mike feels the play is "worthwhile!" Trouble occurs over rights to use Beatles music in the play when George orders Stigwood to remove the song 'Here Comes The Sun'. It is replaced by the Lennon & McCartney track 'Good Day Sunshine'.

Paul is forthcoming about his views on the play: "I certainly appear to come out as the one saying, 'No. No. Don't do Klein, and don't do this . . .' I think I did have a good idea of what was going on there, because no one seemed to spot the Klein thing, and there was me left in a big bad situation. In fact, I'd like to use this interview to say that Willy Russell in his *George, Bert and Thingy* thing . . . he's got me saying, 'I'm leaving. I'm leaving the group' and the rest of the group saying, 'Oh no . . . come on Paulie. It's the group. Let's stick together.' In fact, that is physically wrong. I was actually the last to leave the group!"

Friday August 16
 Reports today indicate that both John and Paul have signed co-publishing agreements with ATV music. Experts predict this deal will "bolster Lennon's bank account by a sum in excess of £1,000,000!"

Friday August 23
 On the roof of Eddie Germano's apartment at 9pm this evening, John, standing completely naked, witnesses his first UFO. As the object flies away, John screams out, "Take me with you!" Weeks later, he is still protesting that he saw the object and it was not something he imagined. "They all thought I was potty," John recalls. "It was there! I didn't believe it either. It was an oval shaped object, flying left to right with red lights on top. After about two minutes, the object disappeared over the East River and went behind the United Nations building. I hadn't been drinking. This is the God's honest truth. I only do that at weekends or when I see Harry Nilsson."

Saturday August 24
 John and May fly out to California to supervise the recordings of 'Goodnight Vienna' and 'Only You' with Ringo (see August entry above for more information). John and May return to New York on August 28.

Saturday August 31
 John testifies in the US Federal Court that officials of the Nixon administration sought to deport him on trumped-up charges strictly because of John's anti-Vietnam war activities and fears that he would lead anti-war demonstrations in Miami at the 1972 Republican National Convention. Following the hearing, John spoke to reporters about his 1968 drugs conviction in England, one of the stumbling blocks in his quest to stay in America: "I thought it would just go away, it'd be like a parking fine, you know. I was living with Yoko and she was pregnant and I thought they'd let her off if I pleaded guilty."

September
 At Germano's apartment in New York, John and May play host to guests including Paul, Linda, Mick and Bianca Jagger, Glyn Johns and David Bowie. This month, John is also interviewed by Tom Donahue on the San Francisco based radio station KSAN-FM. Excerpts from this interview reappear on the American *The Lost Lennon Tapes* radio series.

Friday September 6
 At a London press conference, George launches his own record label Dark Horse and announces plans for a Ravi Shankar concert tour of Europe through September and October. Meanwhile, the first release on the Dark Horse label is to be the album *The Place I Love* by Splinter. Harrison also appoints Jonathan Clyde as a director of the company.

Saturday September 7
 Melody Maker publishes the three-page article: "Do We Still Need The Beatles?" As part of the feature, Derek Taylor is quoted as saying, "I'm not interested in them getting together again."

Monday September 9
 At EMI's Abbey Road Studios, in preparation for a proposed *Wings Live In The Studio* EP, a 6-track acetate is cut from Wings' *One Hand Clapping* session on Thursday August 15 (see entry). Songs featured are: 'Jet', 'Let Me Roll It', 'Junior's Farm', 'My Love', 'Little Woman Love – C Moon – Little Woman Love' (medley) and 'Maybe I'm Amazed'. (The release fails to materialise.)

Friday September 13
 In America, Screen-Gems prepare for distribution of a 30-second *Pussycats* television commercial which features various animated stills of Ringo, Nilsson, Keith Moon and others, taken during the recording of the album, alongside images of the participants playing pool, relaxing and generally fooling about.
 In England, Dark Horse records the Ravi Shankar & Friends single 'I Am Missing You' b/w 'Lust'. (The US release takes place on November 6.) This same day, Dark Horse also release the Splinter single 'Costafine Town' b/w 'Elly-May'. (The US release takes place on November 7.)

Saturday September 14
 In today's *Melody Maker*, the American guitarist Todd Rundgren writes: "John Lennon ain't no revolutionary, he's a fucking idiot, man. Shouting about revolution and acting like a cunt, it just makes people feel uncomfortable. All he really wants to do is get attention for himself and if revolution gets him that attention, he'll get attention without revolution. Hitting a waitress in the Troubador. What kind of revolution is that? He's an important figure, sure, but so was Richard Nixon. Nixon was just like another generation's John Lennon. Someone who represents all sorts of ideals, but was out for himself underneath it all. Like The Beatles had no style other than being The Beatles. So the Nazz used to do, like heavy rock, and also these light, pretty ballads, with complex ballads."

John catches sight of this rant and, inevitably, drafts a reply on September 30 (see entry). *Melody Maker* publishes his reply on October 12. Today's issue of *MM* also features a lengthy article on John under the headline: "Lennon – A Night In The Life" which features an interview with John conducted by Ray Coleman during the recording sessions for the album *Walls And Bridges*. Coleman asks John: "Do you resent being a Beatle and having to live with it for ever?"

John replies: "No, no, no. I'm going to be an ex-Beatle for the rest of my life, so I might as well enjoy it."

Coleman: "Are The Beatles going to get together?"

John: "No! What for? We did it all. Christ, we can't even get the four of us together for a meeting, let alone play! The other month Paul and Ringo and me met in Los Angeles and we wanted George to be there but they wouldn't let him in at that time. So there was three of us and everybody says, 'Beatles getting back together'. Hey, hey, we can't even *meet* man!"

 The first *Beatlefest '74* event is staged over this weekend in New York at the Commodore Hotel. The brainchild behind this event is 26-year-old record shop assistant Mark Lapidos. "I first had this idea when I bumped into John in Central Park earlier this summer and I decided to do something about it," says Mark. "He really liked the idea and put me in touch with people who'd be able to help. From that point on, it was on the road."

The two-day event receives the blessing of the BBC TV and Apple in London, who both send over Beatles films from their libraries, including footage previously unseen in America. (Apple sends over a 16mm film print of the documentary *The Beatles Live At Shea Stadium*.) False rumours suggest that John, in heavy disguise, attends the New York event but May Pang *is* there, sent by John to acquire interesting Beatles memorabilia. *Melody Maker*'s American correspondent Chris Charlesworth advises her on what to buy. She returns to John with some unique original pictures of The Beatles in Hamburg, taken in 1960 by Jurgen Volmer. (John will later use one of these for the front of his 1975 Apple album *Rock 'N' Roll*.) For the *Beatlefest '74* auction, John and Paul supply guitars, George sends over a table while Ringo sends over some autographed drumsticks. From the sales, 10% of all money raised goes directly to charity (the sum actually donated totals $3,000). For a total of 24 hours of Beatles entertainment, including guest speakers and a non-stop film show, the admission price is only a very reasonable $10.

Tuesday September 17
🍎 In Los Angeles, Ringo announces that over the next twelve months he is to campaign against drug taking by young people.

Friday September 20
🍎 Two weeks after the launch of George's new label comes the news that Polydor Records will, in the future, be distributing records released on Ringo's new label *Ringo O'Records*. Also today, Dark Horse records release the Splinter album *The Place I Love* (US release on September 25) and Ravi Shankar's *Shankar Family & Friends* (US release on October 7).
🍎 While in America, further promotions for *Walls And Bridges* continue when John is interviewed on the radio station KHJ.

Monday September 23
🍎 John's single 'Whatever Gets You Through The Night'/'Beef Jerky' is released in America. (The single is released in the UK on October 4.)
🍎 Ravi Shankar's Music Festival From India, produced by George, takes place at the Royal Albert Hall in London. The concert is filmed and recorded by Dark Horse Records (the film, though, remains unreleased). The tour also takes in Paris, Brussels, Frankfurt, Munich and Copenhagen.

Wednesday September 25
🍎 John gives a 70-minute interview to RKO Radio.

Thursday September 26
🍎 John's album *Walls And Bridges* is released in America. (The UK release takes place on October 4.) As part of a huge advertising campaign on both sides of the Atlantic, items bearing the "Listen to this . . ." slogan (featuring John's eyes) appear on press kits, billboards, matchbooks, T-shirts, cash registers, badges etc. The elaborate cut-up interchangeable headshots for the album sleeve, based on John's idea, are designed by Roy Kohara. To also help promote the release, the Californian based *Vidtronics Co. Inc.* prepare, on behalf of Capitol, a 30-second 16mm colour TV commercial for the album. The advert features a voice-over by Ringo, who tells viewers to "Listen to this television commercial," accompanied by an animated sequence of the interactive album cover. Tracks from the album, such as 'Whatever Gets You Through The Night', 'Nobody Loves You When You're Down And Out' as well as John's version of 'Oo-wee' are featured on the soundtrack. The latter is dropped from the line-up of the album at the last minute and subsequently given to Ringo for inclusion on his album *Goodnight Vienna*. The item concludes with Ringo announcing: "You've been listening to John Lennon's album *Walls And Bridges*."
John replies: "Thank you, Ringo."
Ringo: "It's a pleasure John."
John gives another interview, this time to CHUM Radio.
🍎 Paul is asked about the album: "It's a very good, great album, but I know he can do better. I heard 'I Am The Walrus' today for instance, and that is what I mean. I know he can do better than *Walls And Bridges*. I reckon 'Walrus' is better. It's more adventurous. It's more exciting."

Friday September 27
🍎 Between 6am and 8am John appears on the breakfast show as a special guest DJ on the Los Angeles radio station KHJ-AM. Whilst at the studios, he also records a 58-second radio "spot" for *Walls And Bridges* to be played by the giant record store Tower Records as well as a 61-second *Listen To This Radio Spot* commercial for broadcast on the KHJ-AM station. John also reads out commercials for Tobias Casuals. Following the

broadcast, John records a telephone interview for a Detroit radio station then boards a plane and flies back to New York.

Saturday September 28

♣ At just before 4pm, John makes another radio appearance, this time on the New York radio station WNEW-FM, where Denis Elsas interviews him. Among the many topics of conversation, John and Denis discuss The Beatles' original recordings, in particular the recent EMI greatest hits compilations:

Denis: "Many of these things have been re-mixed into stereo."

John: "Oh! It was awful!"

Denis: "I think the original monaural recordings are better."

John: "I didn't think it'd happen when they put out that package last year."

Denis: "The *Blue* and *Red* albums?" (*1967–1970* and *1962–1966* respectively.)

John: "I just thought, or rather presumed, they'd just copy them off the masters and put them out. I didn't even listen to it, until it was out and I took it back and listened to it and I played it and it was embarrassing! Some of the tracks survive but it was embarrassing. Some fool had tried to make it stereo and it didn't work!"

Denis: "People should stay with the mono."

John: "Yeah, because there's a difference between mono and stereo obviously, and if you mix something in mono and try to fake it, you lose the guts of it. The fast version of 'Revolution' was destroyed! I mean it was a heavy record, but they made it into a piece of ice-cream!"

During his stint on the show, John acts as the DJ, reads out the weather forecast and even delivers, in his own unique style, the various radio advertisements, one of which is for a local nightclub: "Tonight at the *Joint In The Woods*, guess who's there? It's ladies night, featuring the eight-piece all female group *Isis*. All females admitted at half-price . . . ah good! Bowie can get in! Also dance and party with *Lock, Stock And Barrel*, that probably is a group because it's in inverted commas, coming next Wednesday October 2 to the *Joint In The Woods*. Nothing like a joint in the woods . . . he says losing his green card possibility in one blow! T.Rex on Friday. That's a good band. Buy a couple of his records . . . he's getting fat with worry!"

Monday September 30

♣ From his New York apartment, John types a letter of reply to Todd Rundgren against his outburst against him in *Melody Maker* on September 14. John writes:

An Open Lettuce To Sodd Runtlestuntle. (from dr. winston o'boogie). Couldn't resist adding a few "islands of truth" of my own, in answer to Turd Runtgreen's howl of hate (pain).

Dear Todd, I like you, and some of your work (including 'I Saw The Light', which is not unlike 'There's A Place' (Beatles), melody wise).

1. I have never claimed to be a revolutionary. But I am allowed to sing about anything I want! Right?

2. I never hit a waitress in the Troubador. I did act like an ass, I was drunk. So shoot me!

3. I guess we're all looking for attention Rodd, do you really think I don't know how to get it, without "revolution"? I could dye my hair green and pink for a start!

4. I don't resent anyone but my SELF. It sounds like I represented something to you, or you wouldn't be so violent towards me. (Your dad perhaps?)

5. Yes Dodd, violence comes in mysterious ways, it's wonders to perform, including verbal. But you'd know that kind of game, wouldn't you? Of course you would.

6. So the Nazz used to do "Like heavy rock" then suddenly a "light pretty ballad". How original!

7. Which gets me to The Beatles, "who had no other style than being The Beatles"!! That covers a lot of style man, including your own, To Date . . .

Yes Godd, the one thing those Beatles did was to affect Peoples' Minds.

Somebody played me your rock and roll pussy song, but I never noticed anything. I think that the real reason you're mad at me is cause I didn't know who you were at the Rainbow (LA). Remember that time you came in with Wolfman Jack? When I found out later, I was cursing, cause I wanted to tell you how good you were. (I'd heard you on the radio.)

Anyway, however much you hurt me darling; I'll always love you,

J.L. 30th Sept. 1974.

September – October
 George begins work on his album *Dark Horse.* The four-week sessions, carried out at his Friar Park studios in Henley, produce the following tracks: 'Dark Horse', 'I Don't Care Anymore', 'Ding Dong, Ding Dong', 'Hari's On Tour (Express)', 'Simply Shady', 'So Sad', 'Bye Bye Love', 'Maya Love', 'Far East Man' and 'It Is He (Jai Sri Krishna)'. (Additional recording and overdubbing on one track is carried out in Los Angeles.) George's laryngitis mars the recordings. By the end of October, his voice has deteriorated further and his North American tour in November and December is thrown into grave doubt.

It is also reported that George has had an affair with Ringo's wife, Maureen. By now, George and Patti's marriage has ended and Patti has settled in with George's close friend Eric Clapton. George writes new lyrics to the old Everly Brothers recording 'Bye Bye Love', in which he publicly criticises Eric and Patti and then, cheekily, asks them to take part on the recording of the song for his album. George will soon find a new girlfriend, the 26-year-old Olivia Trinidad Arias, a secretary from Dark Horse Records in Los Angeles, whom he will eventually marry.

October
 The New York Yankees baseball team adopts the track 'Band On The Run' as their theme tune.
 This month in Los Angeles, Ringo and Harry Nilsson begin shooting the half action/half animation film *Ringo And Harry's Night Out,* a comedy which centres around the pair's wild nights in LA and which also features a cameo appearance by Keith Moon. The film is being co-financed by Ringo and Mike Viners, the president of Pride Records in the States. (The film is neither completed nor released.)
 In America, Dark Horse records release to US radio stations the *George Harrison Interview Record*, a special promotional disc to accompany the first distributed copies of the new George Harrison album *Dark Horse*. The American DJ Chuck Cassell conducted the interview, which was recorded at George's home in Los Angeles during August.

Tuesday October 1
 In England, Paul and Linda are at the Wembley ringside to watch 23-year-old boxer John Conteh become the world light heavyweight boxing champion, the first British boxer to do so in a quarter of a century. Before the fight, the McCartneys had sent John a telegram, which reads: "You Made Me Number One. Now *You* Be Number One!" (A reference to Conteh's appearance on the *Band On The Run* record sleeve which, of course, had gone on to be a number one album in charts around the world.) The McCartneys will go on to play an integral part of Conteh's setup for the programme *This Is Your Life* (see entry for November 6). In America, the Peggy Lee album *Let's Love*, featuring production by Paul, is released. (The UK release takes place on November 8.) Shortly afterwards, Paul, Linda and Wings head off to the States to announce the details of their forthcoming US tour.
 While in America, Alan Stone interviews John for the KWRS Radio station in Indianapolis.

Saturday October 5
 The solo album from Paul's brother Mike, entitled *McGear* is released by Warner Brothers and features Wings playing on the backing tracks and production from Paul himself.

Monday October 7
 In the States, the Peggy Lee single 'Let's Love', featuring Paul's production and taken from the album of the same name, is released. (The UK release takes place on October 25.)

Wednesday October 9
 John celebrates his 34th birthday at an exclusive New York club with his close friends.

Saturday October 12
 John tells the *NME:* "When we (The Beatles) see each other, there's no tension. We get on fine . . . but I'm sure if we ever did anything it would be in 1976, when the (EMI) contract runs out . . . together we would sound exactly the same, only better – 'cos we're all better now, y'know." In today's *Melody Maker,* the paper prints John's reply to Todd

Rundgren's previous outburst (see entry for September 30).

🍎 Also today at 4pm, outside The Beatles' offices at 3 Saville Row in London, The Beatles Fan Club International hold their first annual meeting. Those in attendance are given a free Beatles Fan Club International magazine and various free Beatles pictures.

Sunday October 13

🍎 In New York, the legendary American showbiz personality Ed Sullivan dies of cancer of the oesophagus. He was 72 years of age and is survived by one daughter. Friends of the legendary newspaper reporter and television personality say he never fully recovered from the death of his wife, Sylvia Weinstein, who died last year. He was responsible for giving The Beatles their live US TV début on his long running CBS TV show *The Ed Sullivan Show* back on February 9, 1964. Sullivan is later buried at the Ferncliff Cemetery and Mausoleum, in Hartsdale, New York.

Friday October 18

🍎 The Country Hams single 'Walking In The Park With Eloise'/'Bridge Over The River Suite' is released in the UK. (The American release takes place on December 2.)

Monday October 21

🍎 At the Record Plant, John resumes work on the ill-fated *Rock 'N' Roll* album. With John now back in possession of the original 1973 Los Angeles/Phil Spector produced tapes, this four-day session (which continues until the 25th) largely consists of John re-recording new vocals over the inadequate takes from 1973. The new tracks recorded for the album include 'Be-Bop-A-Lula', 'Stand By Me', a medley of 'Rip It Up' and 'Ready Teddy', 'Ain't That A Shame', 'Do You Want To Dance', 'Slippin' And Slidin'', 'Peggy Sue', a medley of 'Bring It On Home To Me' and 'Send Me Some Lovin'' and 'Ya Ya' (featuring John's son Julian on drums). Also recorded during these sessions are versions of 'Thirty Days' and 'C'Mon Everybody', as well as a brief 44-second burst of Link Wray's 'Rumble' and nine seconds of Led Zeppelin's 'Whole Lotta Love'. Apple releases the *Rock 'N' Roll* album in America on February 17, 1975, and in the UK on February 21.

Tuesday October 22

🍎 John's album *Walls And Bridges* is awarded a gold record by the RIAA.

🍎 In America, Paul, Linda and Wings hold a press conference to announce the details of their forthcoming 1975/1976 Wings world tour.

Wednesday October 23

🍎 Today in America at the Beverly Wiltshire Hotel in California, George conducts a press conference to finally confirm his forthcoming North American tour. He announces to the waiting press: "I tried to squeeze in some concerts before Christmas, although all the places were booked out. Really, the feeling in the band was that we should do a gig in London."

He also touches upon his good friend Eric Clapton, who is now living with George's wife Patti: "Eric's been a close friend for years. I'm very happy about it. I'm still very friendly with him . . . he's great. I'd rather she was with him than with some dope."

Naturally, George is faced with the inevitable Beatles questions, and, as we've come to expect, his replies are honest and forthright.

Question: "What's your relationship like with John and Paul now?"

George: "It's very good. I haven't seen John since he's been in the States (Tuesday March 13, 1973, during a brief rehearsal of 'I'm The Greatest' at the Sunset Sound Recorders Studios in Los Angeles). I spoke to him a lot on the telephone. He's in great shape. I met Paul recently, and everything is very friendly. It doesn't mean everybody is going to form a band."

Question: "Are you amazed about how much The Beatles still mean to people?"

George: "Not really. I mean it's nice. I realise that The Beatles did fill a space in the Sixties. All the people that The Beatles meant something to have grown up. It's like anything you've grown up with; you get attached to things. I understand The Beatles, in many ways, did nice things and it's appreciated that the people still like them. They want to hold on to something. People are afraid of change. You can't live in the past."

Question: "Are you involved with any serious negotiations to get The Beatles back together for one night?"

George: "It's all a fantasy, putting The Beatles back together again. If we ever do that, it's because everyone is broke. I'd rather have Willie Weekes on bass rather than Paul McCartney. With all respect to Paul, since The Beatles I've been in a box, taking me years to be able to play with other musicians. Paul is a fine bass player, but he's a bit overpowering at times. I'd join a band with John Lennon any day, but I couldn't join a band with Paul McCartney. That's not personal, but from a musical point of view."

Friday October 25
🍎 The first Wings single to feature Geoff Britton and Jimmy McCulloch, 'Junior's Farm'/ 'Sally G', is released in the UK. (The American release takes place on November 4.) On February 7, 1975, the single is re-issued with the sides reversed, as Paul reveals: "We flipped the single and I thought it might seem like we were trying to fool the public, but it isn't. It's only to get a bit of exposure on that song. Otherwise, it just dies a death, and only the people who bought 'Junior's Farm' get to hear 'Sally G'. I like to have hits, that is what I am making records for." This will be the last single to appear on the original Apple label.

Monday October 28
🍎 In the London High Courts today, Allen Klein loses his legal case against John, George, Ringo, Yoko and 28 English and American companies associated with The Beatles. The vice-Chancellor, Sir Anthony Plowman, gives Klein and his ABKCO companies leave to appeal.

Wednesday October 30
🍎 The famous picture of John, taken by Bob Gruen, giving a "peace" sign in front of the Statue of Liberty, is taken this morning.

November
🍎 At her bungalow in Poole in Dorset, John's Aunt Mimi meets up with Rudi Kamphausen, the president of the International Beatles Fan Club.
🍎 In the Kings Road, London, Paul and Linda purchase a brass bedstead from the antiques shop *And So To Bed*.

Friday November 1
🍎 John requests court permission to question the Immigration and Naturalisation Service regarding its motivation for deporting him and the former US Attorney General John Mitchell's role in the proceedings.

*   *   *

George's 'Dark Horse' North American Tour
November 2 – December 20

Even though George is suffering from laryngitis, his tour of North America still takes place. Accompanying him are Ravi Shankar, Billy Preston, Tom Scott, Jim Horn, Chuck Findley, Robben Ford, Andy Newmark, Emil Richards and Willie Weeks. George's repertoire includes 'The Lord Loves The One (That Loves The Lord)', 'Who Can See It' (both dropped after the opening show), 'Hari's On Tour (Express)', 'For You Blue', 'Something', 'Sue Me, Sue You Blues', 'Maya Love', 'Sound Stage Of Mind', 'Dark Horse', 'Give Me Love (Give Me Peace On Earth)', 'In My Life', 'While My Guitar Gently Weeps', 'What Is Life' and 'My Sweet Lord'. Controversy follows George on the tour when he decides to re-write some of the lyrics for the 1965 Lennon/McCartney track 'In My Life'.

The tour includes performances at:

The Pacific Coliseum, Vancouver (Saturday November 2)
Seattle, Washington (Monday November 4)
The Cow Palace, San Francisco (Wednesday November 6 and Thursday November 7)
Oakland Coliseum (Friday November 8 – 2 shows)
Long Beach Arena (Sunday November 10)
Los Angeles Forum (Monday November 11 – 1 show)
Los Angeles Forum (Tuesday November 12 – 2 shows)
Tucson Community Center, Arizona (Thursday November 14)

Salt Palace, Salt Lake City (Saturday November 16)
Denver Coliseum (Monday November 18 – 2 shows)
St. Louis Arena (Wednesday November 20)
Tulsa Assembly Center, Oklahoma (Thursday November 21)
Fort Worth, Texas (Friday November 22)
Houston's Hofheinz Pavilion (Sunday November 24)
Baton Rouge, Louisiana (Tuesday November 26)
Mid-South Coliseum, Memphis (Wednesday November 27)
The Omni, Atlanta (Thursday November 28 – 2 shows)
Chicago, Illinois (Saturday November 30 – 2 shows)
Olympia Stadium, Detroit (Wednesday December 4 – 2 shows)
Toronto Maple Leaf Gardens (Friday December 6 – 2 shows)
Montreal Forum (Sunday December 8 – 2 shows)
Boston Garden (Tuesday December 10 – 2 shows)
Providence Civic Center, Rhode Island (Wednesday December 11)
Capitol Center, Largo, Maryland (Friday December 13 – 2 shows)
Nassau Coliseum, Uniondale, Long Island (Sunday December 15 – 2 shows)
Philadelphia Spectrum (Monday December 16 – 1 show)
Philadelphia Spectrum (Tuesday December 17 – 2 shows)
New York Madison Square Garden (Thursday December 19)
New York Madison Square Garden (Friday December 20 – 2 shows)

Prior to the start of each concert on the tour, George plays over the PA speakers Monty Python's 'The Lumberjack Song'. Also, George writes the song 'It's What You Value', inspired by drummer Jim Keltner who requests a Mercedes 450SL car in lieu of money for working on the shows.

Wednesday November 6 & Thursday November 7
George gives $66,000 in proceeds from today's concerts in San Francisco to the Haight Ashbury Free Medical Clinic. The money had been collected in a large box in the theatre's lobby underneath a huge sign, which requests the audience to "Put In Here All Your Loose, Dirty And Filthy Money!" Noting George's very weak voice at his first concert in San Francisco, one critic writes: "With a tour dictating 44 cities in 47 days, it isn't likely that he'll have much time to rest it and help it heal. There is talk that, by the time he hits New York, he'll be entirely mute! This, however, isn't much worse than what he's doing now!"

Monday November 25
During a break from the tour, George appears on the Houston radio station KLOL-FM, where he takes the opportunity to talk about Paul's law suit against him and to express his passion for the English comedy team Monty Python.

Saturday November 30
Things continue to go wrong on the tour when in Chicago, at the conclusion of tonight's performances, Ravi Shankar, still wearing his stage costume of Indian gowns, is rushed to hospital with a suspected heart attack. His coronary turns out to be nothing more than a bout of serious indigestion, possibly caused by over-exertion. Ravi is forced to miss the next concerts, and will not return to the tour until December 19.

Friday December 6
Back in England on BBC Radio One, as promotion for the album *Dark Horse*, George's 30-minute interview with the DJ Alan Freeman, recorded at Apple's offices at 54 St. James's Street, is transmitted on the FM stereo programme *Rockspeak* between 10:00pm and midnight. (For his services, George is paid £22.) The interview is first aired in America, syndicated across the country during September 1975, re-titled *Rock Around The World* and re-cut to be used as a promotional interview to coincide with the release of George's follow-up album *Extra Texture (Read All About It)*. Played during the American version of the interview are unreleased versions of the songs 'Dark Horse', 'I Don't Care Anymore', 'Far East Man' and 'Awaiting On You All' which were given personally to Freeman by George on October 18, specifically to play during the American broadcasts. The interview itself throws up some candid remarks from the "quiet Beatle" . . . his

feelings on John: "He was both a saint and a bastard"; on Paul: "He ruined me as a guitar player"; and of his former group: "I'm ready for The Beatles to reform and kick down some doors!"

Friday December 13
While in America, George, his father Harry, his girlfriend Olivia, Ravi Shankar and Billy Preston, visit US President Gerald Ford for lunch at the White House, at the invitation of the President's son John, whom they met on tour. Harrison announces later that he senses "good vibes" coming from President Ford's administration.

American news cameras and reporters are present to capture the party arriving. One of them asks George: "Do you think The Beatles will ever get back together for a concert?"

George: "I don't know . . . I don't know."

Reporter: "Would you like to?"

George: "Well . . . I'm having more fun with this band to tell you the truth. We (The Beatles) all grew up, lived in a room together for years and years, and it's a natural thing for each one of us to develop individually. Individually speaking, I'm having more fun doing this sort of thing . . . I've never been so happy in my life as with this band."

'For You Blue' from today's concert at the Capitol Center in Largo, Maryland, is officially released on February 15, 1988, as part of the limited edition CD and vinyl EP contained in the book *Songs By George Harrison*. Also, the live version of 'Hari's On Tour (Express)', also from today's Largo concert, is officially released as part of the CD contained in the 1992 limited edition book, *Songs By George Harrison 2*.

Saturday December 14
George, fresh from Washington, arrives with Olivia Arias at the Plaza Hotel in New York where he has arranged to meet John and May Pang. They all spend the night at the hotel and the following day (December 15), George invites the couple to his concert in Nassau.

Sunday December 15
As planned, John and May attend George's second concert this evening at the Nassau Coliseum. John remarks that he is pleased that "he doesn't have to sit through Ravi's bit!"

Monday December 16
George's album *Dark Horse* receives a gold disc from the RIAA.

Thursday December 19
In New York, George and his band turn up at the NBC TV studios where they record a short live version of the track 'Dark Horse' for inclusion in a future edition of the comedy programme *Saturday Night Live* which is currently in the planning stages. George's live performance, which lasts just 1' 52", is never screened and *Saturday Night Live* fails to reach the American TV networks for another year.

The opening night at Madison Square Garden fails to sell out, leaving ticket touts outside the venue with red faces. They had originally planned to sell the $9.50 tickets for $25; instead, they are forced to virtually give the tickets away, making a loss of almost $5 on each. Ravi Shankar returns to the show. Paul and Linda, currently in town for the dissolution of The Beatles' business entanglements, watch the show in heavy disguise. John's son Julian also attends the show, accompanied by Ringo's manager Hilary Gerrard. A planned appearance on stage by John fails to materialise because, earlier in the day, he refused to sign the "Famous Beatles Agreement" forms, which were due to be signed by all four ex-Beatles at midnight tonight. According to May Pang in her book *Loving John*, George, over the phone, tells May to tell John: "I started the tour without him and I'll finish it without him." (Ringo, meanwhile, remains in London to sign the papers, refusing to come to America and therefore avoiding a subpoena from Klein.)

Friday December 20
Hilary Gerrard again takes Julian to see George's concert at Madison Square Garden and John meets with Lee Eastman to discuss the "Famous Beatles Agreement". Later, John, along with May Pang and Neil Aspinall, attends a party celebrating the end of

George's tour at New York's Hippopotamus Club. Yoko, arriving separately, is among the guests in attendance.

● John recalls: "George and I are still good pals and we always will be, but I was supposed to sign this thing on the day of his concert. He was pretty weird because he was in the middle of that tour and we hadn't communicated for a while because he doesn't live here. I've seen Paul a bit because he comes to New York a lot, and I'm always seeing Ringo in Los Angeles. Anyway, I was a bit nervous about going on stage, but I agreed to because it would have been mean of me not to go on with George after I'd gone on with Elton. I didn't sign the document on that day because my astrologer told me it wasn't the right day, tee hee! (John will finally sign the papers on Friday December 27 at Disneyworld in Florida – see entry.)

"George was furious with me at the time because I hadn't signed it when I was supposed to, and somehow or other I was informed that I needn't bother to go to George's show. I was quite relieved in the end because there wasn't any time to rehearse and I didn't want it to be a case of just John jumping up and playing a few chords. I went to see him at Nassau and it was a good show. The band was great but Ravi wasn't there, so I didn't see the bit where the crowd is supposed to get restless. I just saw a good tight show. George's voice was shot but the atmosphere was good and the crowd was great. I saw George after the Garden show and we were friends again. But he was surrounded by the madhouse that's called 'touring'. I respect George but I think he made a mistake on the tour. Mistakes are easier to spot if you're not the person making them, so I don't want to come on like 'I know better', 'cos I haven't done that . . . one of the basic mistakes seemed to be that the people wanted to hear old stuff. George wasn't prepared to do that, and I understand him. When I did that charity concert at Madison Square Garden, I was still riding high on 'Imagine' so I was OK for material. But when I did 'Come Together' the house came down, which gave me an indication of what people wanted to hear."

● Following the Hippopotamus Club party, John visits George in his hotel room where they are interviewed separately by the KHJ Los Angeles radio station for a one-hour special.

* * *

November
● Paul begins the recording sessions with Wings for his album *Venus and Mars* at Abbey Road Studios in London. The sessions are due to continue in New Orleans during January.

Friday November 1
"I would like," said John Lennon, drawing deeply on his cigarette, "The Beatles to make a record together again."
● An exclusive interview with John, carried out by John Blake in New York, is published in the *Liverpool Echo*.

Monday November 4
● While George is performing in Seattle, Washington, the stage show *Sgt. Pepper's Lonely Hearts Club Band On The Road,* opens in Hartford, Connecticut.
● Still in America, Mercury Records release the Rod Stewart single 'Mine For Me', a track written by Paul.

Tuesday November 5
● At his Tittenhurst Park mansion, Ringo celebrates Guy Fawkes (Bonfire) Night with specially invited guests including Eric Clapton and Patti Harrison.

Friday November 8
● Ringo makes a pre-recorded appearance on the BBC Radio One programme *Rockspeak*. Meanwhile in America, he joins Keith Moon to videotape an appearance on the USTV show *ABC In Concert*. (The programme is first transmitted on November 11 between 11pm and midnight.)

Saturday November 9

✦ Today's *Melody Maker* pre-empts the other music tabloids by announcing: "Elton And Lennon On Stage." The report continues: "When Elton John plays giant concerts in New York later this month, John Lennon is expected to join him for some songs on stage." In the same issue, Todd Rundgren concludes his feud with John by writing: "First, I would like to extend my apologies to John Lennon for the extreme nature of my remarks. I am often reputed to be over critical, and my comments do not reflect my personal respect for him. I would like to dissipate the idea that I am involved in a feud with anyone, as our prime interest, I'm sure, is the same, that being a little honest communication. Thank you."

Monday November 11

✦ Ringo's single 'Only You (And You Alone)'/'Call Me' is released in America. (The UK release takes place on November 15.) 'Only You', written by Buck Ram and Ande Rand, dates back to 1955 when it was originally recorded by The Platters, who were then managed by Ram.

Wednesday November 13

✦ In England, Paul and Linda, as part of a setup for John Conteh's appearance on the Thames/ITV Network programme *This Is Your Life*, invite the boxer to Abbey Road for a "supposed" celebratory snap shot after winning the world light-heavyweight boxing title at Wembley on October 1. With the picture taken, the show's host Eamonn Andrews pounces, to say "John Conteh, this is your life" while Paul and Linda stand laughing and applauding. The 26-minute show, the first in the latest series, is transmitted across the ITV network this evening between 7:00 and 7:28pm. Earlier in the day, Paul and Wings record a jingle intended for the soundtrack of a 30-second *Mother's Pride* bread commercial. Unfortunately, due to a controversy over increases in the price of a loaf of bread, the TV commercial is never screened and remains un-transmitted to this day.

Thursday November 14

✦ The stage play *Sgt. Pepper's Lonely Hearts Club Band On The Road*, directed by Tom O'Horgan, opens in New York at the Beacon Theater with John and May Pang in attendance. Later this evening, John and May attend a party celebrating the opening at New York's Hippopotamus Club where they mingle with guests, including Ronnie Spector and Mick and Bianca Jagger.

✦ At the Capitol Records tower in Hollywood, Ringo shoots a commercial to accompany his album *Goodnight Vienna*. Produced by the Californian based Vidtronics Company Inc., he is seen banging a drum amongst a marching band in the street when a flying saucer lands which subsequently captures and bundles him inside the craft which flies onto the roof of the Capitol Records tower. The 60-second (and re-edited 30-second) clip ends with Ringo, alongside the ship, waving from the top of the tower. To an accompaniment of the tracks 'Goodnight Vienna' and 'Only You', John assists Ringo with the narration of the commercial.

John: "Is that Ringo Starr advertising his new album *Goodnight Vienna* on Apple Records and tapes?"
Ringo: "It certainly is, John."
John: "My, you look so wonderful!"
Ringo: "Thank you!"
The commercial ends with the following banter:
John: "*Goodnight Vienna* on Apple Records and tapes."
Ringo: "Thanks John."
John: "It's a pleasure, Ringo!"

With shooting of the advert completed, work immediately begins on the promotional film for 'Only You'. Directed by the BBC *Top Of The Pops* and *In Concert* director Stanley Dorfman, the clip retains the flying saucer, which again lands on the Capitol tower where Ringo mimes the song alongside a cigarette smoking Harry Nilsson, who wears headphones and a peaked cap and is reading a copy of the music paper *Radio & Records*. The only UK TV screening of the film occurs on BBC1's *Top Of The Pops*, transmitted on Thursday December 19. Incidentally, at the end of the day's shoot, Ringo, still in his space suit, treats the neighbouring streets to a free laser show from the tower, when beams of lights are projected onto a star shaped mirror attached to his chest. The lights, reportedly, are visible for hundreds of miles beyond the Los Angeles city limits.

Friday November 15

🍎 With a two-man BBC film crew in tow (dispatched from the corporation's offices in the city), John ventures out in New York to shoot a 16mm colour promotional film for the song 'Whatever Gets You Through The Night'. For this wonderful piece of cinéma vérité, John wanders aimlessly round the city and sets about capturing on film whatever comes his way. Dressed all in black with a large floppy hat, long coat, flared trousers and platform shoes, John supervises the filming of street beggars, truck drivers, a father carrying his small child on his back and even the city's 25-cent adult peep shows at 42nd Street. John is also seen signing autographs, imitating a street puppeteer, playing a large church-style organ and, at a hot-dog stand in Central Park, performing an impromptu magic trick involving tin cans and paper bags to a small bemused looking crowd of onlookers. Memorable, brief, ad-libbed shots include John outside the Beacon Theater where, the previous night, he had seen the opening of the *Sgt. Pepper's* musical play. Outside the theatre, he takes a close-up of the musical's poster, and points at the words "John Lennon & Paul McCartney". As his personal tribute to the 1961 Audrey Hepburn and George Peppard film *Breakfast At Tiffanys*, John recreates the start of the picture by panning down the front of the Tiffany & Co. building. But instead of going to the side window, as Hepburn did to gaze adoringly at the expensive jewellery, John, in front of further bemused onlookers, enters the building only to reappear clutching and eating a hot-dog. Footage from this session will be seen for the first time in the UK on BBC1's *Top Of The Pops* (transmitted on Thursday February 27, 1975, between 7:20 and 7:59pm), where an alternative two minutes 25 seconds edit is compiled to promote the 1975 single issue of 'No. 9 Dream'.

🍎 Meanwhile, also today in the States, a copyright is registered for the unreleased song 'Incantation', co-written by John and Roy Cicala during John's Los Angeles 1974 *Walls And Bridges* sessions.

🍎 Ringo's album *Goodnight Vienna* is released in the UK. (The American release takes place on November 18.) A planned American TV special utilising four tracks from the album fails to appear, even going so far as to have a US TV transmission date arranged for 1975. The sleeve of the *Goodnight Vienna* album, which features a still from the 1951 Michael Rennie Science-Fiction film *The Day The Earth Stood Still,* with Ringo's head superimposed over the top of Rennie's, curiously contains the word KLAATU, which was the name of the alien played by Rennie in the film. (Promotional posters for the album feature the cryptic slogan "Don't forget: Klaatu Barada Niktu", which was Klaatu's secret instructions to his robot Gort.) In 1976, a Canadian group adopts this name and releases an album on Capitol Records. The album, following rumours that Klaatu is in fact the reformed Beatles under an alias, will go on to sell a million copies.

Saturday November 16

🍎 John's single 'Whatever Gets You Through The Night' reaches number one in the US charts. This is his first American solo number one. The album *Walls And Bridges* also reaches number one in the US album charts on this date. Tonight, John is in the audience of Elton John's concert at the Boston Gardens. Immediately following the performance, John flies back to New York.

Sunday November 17

🍎 Late this afternoon, John spends time at the Record Plant mixing his *Rock 'N' Roll* album.

Monday November 18

🍎 George's single 'Dark Horse'/'I Don't Care Anymore' is released in America.

Wednesday November 20

🍎 Back in England, in Studio 8, at the BBC TV Centre in Wood Lane, London, Wings record their fourth studio appearance on *Top Of The Pops*, videotaping a performance of 'Junior's Farm' for inclusion in tomorrow night's show. The programme, hosted by Noel Edmonds, also features studio performances by The Rubettes, Queen, Alvin Stardust, Hot Chocolate, Hello, Lulu and Carl Douglas and is transmitted on BBC1 between 7:20 and 7:59pm. At the conclusion of the recordings, Paul, Linda and Denny reappear unannounced, miming backing vocals to David Essex's number one song 'I'm Gonna Make You A Star'. For the Wings' mimed performance of 'Junior's Farm', which is no longer in the BBC VT library, they command a fee of £170.

Saturday November 23

🍎 Today's *Melody Maker* publishes an interview with Ringo.

MM: "I know you've been asked this question 100 times, but is there any chance of you getting together as The Beatles?"

Ringo: "No! How can we get together if George won't play with Paul!"

On the subject of John's US green card problem, he states: "I think he should be able to stay. Give the guy a break! What's he done to anybody?"

Sunday November 24

🍎 John joins Elton John in rehearsals at the Record Plant studios in New York, for Elton's November 28 Thanksgiving concert at Madison Square Garden.

Wednesday November 27

🍎 In England, Paul and Linda turn up unannounced to provide backing vocals on the McCartney penned song 'Mine For Me' during a live concert performance by Rod Stewart and The Faces at the Odeon Cinema, in Lewisham, South London. Paul later reveals that they intended only to go and *watch* The Faces in performance and *never* had the slightest intention of appearing on stage with the group. Paul later admitted doing so because "the ham in him rose to the occasion" as Rod called them to the stage, helped of course by a bit of Dutch courage induced by the alcoholic drinks in The Faces' dressing room. The McCartneys' appearance with The Faces is filmed and broadcast in America on the music programme *Midnight Special,* transmitted on April 25, 1975. An excerpt is also scheduled to appear in the 1975 Rod Stewart documentary *Smiler,* but the programme is never released. Asked why he wrote the song for Rod, Paul replies, "It was just the result of another drunken night, I suppose! It's nice to write for someone like Rod, because he's got such a distinctive voice. You can hear him singing it as you are doing it. Certain people . . . well, they are just a bit boring, and you write boring songs for them."

🍎 In America, on the eve of the Thanksgiving concert, John and May visit Elton at the Sherry Netherlands hotel in New York.

Thursday November 28

🍎 Just one day after Paul and Linda made an impromptu appearance during a concert, John keeps his promise and also performs unannounced. Joining Elton John and his band at their Thanksgiving Concert at New York's Madison Square Garden, John performs 'Whatever Gets You Through The Night', 'Lucy In The Sky With Diamonds' and 'I Saw Her Standing There'.

John recalls the event. "It was great. He was more nervous than I was, because he was nervous for me as well. Elton used to be in the Dick James office when The Beatles sent in their latest demos, so he had a real emotional feeling for The Beatles. I went to see Elton at Boston and I was nervous just watching him. I was thinking 'Thank God it isn't me', as he was getting dressed to go on. I went through my stage fright at Boston so by the time I got to Madison Square I had a good time, and when I walked on they were all screaming and shouting. It was like Beatlemania. I was thinking 'What is this?' 'cos I hadn't heard it since The Beatles. I looked round and saw someone else playing the guitar. It brought the house down. It was deja vu for me, not like The Beatles screaming bit, but the place was really rocking.

"We'd had a rehearsal but we weren't that together. By the time we got to 'I Saw Her Standing There' Elton's piano was jumping off the floor. It was his idea to do that song. We had to do 'Whatever Gets You Through The Night' because of a bet we had . . . and naturally we did 'Lucy In The Sky With Diamonds' because I did that with him at Caribou. That's me out of tune in the background, doing the reggae bit. I got it wrong just like I did the original on *Pepper.* Elton wanted me to do 'Imagine', but I didn't want to come on like Dean Martin doing my classic hits. I wanted to have some fun and play some rock and roll and I didn't want to do more than three because it was Elton's show after all. He suggested 'I Saw Her Standing There' and I thought 'great', because I never sang the original of that. Paul sang it and I did the harmony. When I came off stage I said to the waiting journalists, 'It was good fun, but I wouldn't like to do it for a living.' I'm not against live performances, but I haven't got a group and I haven't put a stage show together. I'm just not keen on it right now, but I may change my mind."

🍎 It is estimated that some 30,000 counterfeit tickets for the show had been circulated, resulting in thousands of disappointed fans being turned away from the venue. Following the show, John and May attend a special party at the Pierre Hotel, where guests are treated to mind-bending illusions by Uri Geller. Incidentally, John and Yoko have always insisted that John did not know that Yoko was in the audience. However, according to May Pang in her book *Loving John*, not only did John know well in advance that Yoko was attending but he had also reserved Yoko's tickets and that she had phoned him more than once to complain about the location of her seats.

Saturday November 30
🍎 While George is currently on a two-month tour of North America, an interview with Paul appears in today's *Melody Maker* in which he announces that his next tour with Wings will be a massive outing, taking in the world and is scheduled to last through 1975 and 1976. Also today, at the Michael Sobell Sports Centre in Islington, London, Wings' drummer Geoff Britton lines up for the Amateur Karate Association of Great Britain team in their competition against the World Karate Union of Japan, fighting in two bouts, losing the first but winning the second. Paul captures the event for the unreleased 32-minute MPL documentary *Empty Hand*. The production, featuring incidental music by Paul and a mix of black & white and colour sequences, is directed by David Litchfield, who previously worked with Paul in August during the also unreleased MPL film *One Hand Clapping*.

December
🍎 Paul, Linda and their family fly to the States for a short holiday. They return to England on December 22 to spend Christmas at home in Scotland.
🍎 George and Olivia spend Christmas in Hawaii. During their stay he writes the song 'This Guitar (Can't Keep From Crying)'.

Thursday December 5
🍎 *Rolling Stone* magazine reproduce a secret memo, dated February 4, 1972, to former US Attorney General John Mitchell from Senator Strom Thurmond, which charges that John's deportation case is political.

Friday December 6
🍎 George's single 'Ding Dong, Ding Dong' (featuring Ringo on drums)/'I Don't Care Anymore' is released in the UK. The release makes number 38 in the singles chart. George talks about the A-side: "It's very optimistic. Instead of getting stuck in a rut, everybody should try ringing out the old and ringing in the new. I mean, they all hold hands and dance about, doing 'Knees Up Mother Brown' every New Year's Eve but they never apply it. They sing about it, but they never apply it to their lives. I mean, it is comical, but at the same time it is pretty good. I was just sitting by the fire, playing the guitar and I looked up on the wall, and there it was written, carved into the wall in oak: 'Ring Out The Old. Ring In The New' on the left and on the right of the fire: 'Ring Out The False. Ring In The True'. I thought 'God, it took me five years of looking at that, before I realised it was a song.' A loony, who used to own the house, he built it, and it has got all these great things written all over the place. 'Yesterday, Today Was Tomorrow' was written in the stone on a window in the garden buildings, and on the other window 'Tomorrow, Today Will Be Yesterday'."

Saturday December 7 & Sunday December 8
🍎 John visits Los Angeles where he spends the weekend hanging out with Ringo.

Monday December 9
🍎 Once again, John appears unannounced, this time following Ronald Reagan on the ABC TV sports programme *Monday Night Football,* where he is briefly interviewed by the host Howard Cosell during the intermission in a game between the Los Angeles Rams and the LA Redskins at the Los Angeles Coliseum. John tells the viewing public what he thinks of the American professional football scene: "It's an amazing event and sight," he announces. "It makes rock concerts look like tea parties." John also reveals that when he arrived at the stadium, the first thing he heard being played was The Beatles' tune 'Yesterday' which "cheered me up no end!" Of course, no interview will be complete without the perennial question, this time from Cosell: "Will The Beatles ever

reunite?" John replies by saying: "You never know, you never know. I mean, it's always in the wind. If it looked like this (referring to the stadium and crowd), it might be worth doing, right?" John finishes off by plugging his own album *Walls And Bridges* and Ringo's latest *Goodnight Vienna* and then returns to watch the game.

 George's album *Dark Horse* is released in the US. (The UK release takes place on December 20.) Besides 'Ding Dong, Ding Dong', Ringo plays drums on the track 'So Sad'.

 Still in America, Ringo's album *Ringo* receives a gold disc by the RIAA.

Wednesday December 11
 In the States, Ringo officially changes the name of his company from *Reckongrade Ltd.* to *Pyramid Records Ltd.*

Sunday December 15
 Following almost three years of fighting to remain in the United States, reports published today offer further proof that the Immigration and Naturalisation services responded to political pressure in deciding to press its case against John. The report goes on: "They claim that John is unable to remain in the States due to his minor drugs offence in 1968, but today in Washington, records show that some 118 other offenders with more serious narcotics backgrounds have been allowed to live in the country."

Monday December 16
 John's single 'No. 9 Dream'/'What You Got' is released in the US. (The UK release takes place on January 31, 1975.) To coincide with its release, John makes the first of four scheduled American television interviews, in a period that will last until April 28, 1975. The first is for the NBC TV breakfast show *Today*. Introduced by the host as "John Lennon from The Beatles", he appears primarily to promote his latest single, but the continuing problem over his America residency is uppermost in the programme's agenda. John's lawyer, Leon Wildes, also appears. At 7:31am John sits smiling at the camera, giving a "V" (peace) sign while the host continues with his lengthy prologue. "John will not be singing for us this morning. He is deeply involved in trying to prevent himself from being deported," says the host. "The United States Immigration Department know that a drug violation for which he was found guilty, or pleaded guilty in 1968 in England, is grounds for his deportation . . ." Following cutaways to a news-break and a check on the latest weather, John takes his first question:

Host: "Do you get tired of people introducing you as the 'former Beatle'?"

John: "It's an improvement on ex. I like former better. In England I'm an expatriate and an ex-Beatle. Former looks nicer."

Host: "Do The Beatles still exist? When you disband, does the name go somewhere, and the whole thing just go off into oblivion?"

John: "The Beatles name will continue, because it's 'Beatles Limited' you know, and there's lots of Beatles products that are repackaged. For instance, last year, there were two sets of double-albums (*1962–1966* and *1967–1970*) that did as well as anything that we put out when we were together. And there's a film in the offing that's comprised of all the films we've collected from all the tours and all the interviews over the world . . . which will be called *The Long And Winding Road*, no doubt. So they exist, but they don't work together anymore."

Host: "You haven't worked together in three or four years?"

John: "Well, let me say, I've worked with Ringo and George on Ringo's album. I worked with George on an album of mine. I worked with Ringo about two months ago and I might be working with George on Friday night, folks!"

Host: "What's happening?"

John: "Well, he's in town performing and we're still friends, you see, so we might have a laugh. It's the last night of the tour and (turning to the camera with a big smirk on his face) . . . see you Friday!" *

Host: "Will The Beatles ever play together again as a group?"

John: "It's quite possible, but it's a question even cab drivers ask me. They ask me two things – 'Are you going to play together again?' and 'How's your immigration?' In what form we play together again I don't know. It's been a psychical impossibility for the four of us to be in one place at one time. I couldn't leave here because I couldn't get back in and George and Paul also have problems coming in and out. There's probably three here now, or by the end of the week, but Ringo's gone back. So it's really been an immigration problem that's kept us from even sitting in a room together to decide or saying, 'Hello', although we've done it in different combinations of the four."

Host: "So if the immigration problems were solved, you're saying there's nothing personal between the four of you that would prevent you someday playing again or making music albums or so on."

John: "For us to do that, we'd have to do it more than just to resurrect what went on in the Sixties. Whatever format, it's not in the offing but it's quite possible. Whatever format we did together, it would have to be interesting to us musically, as otherwise they'd be no point. We don't want to just do it for old times sake, you know."

(* Within days of this interview, John's planned concert appearance on Friday is changed to Thursday, a date John fails to keep. See prior entry – dated Thursday December 19.)

Today, in England, the *Daily Mail* reports that "a secret and near hysterical" White House report lies behind John's dispute with the US immigration authorities and that President Nixon had personally ordered officials to "harass Lennon and kick him out of America"!

Thursday December 19

🍎 Meanwhile, back in England, Ringo's promotional film for 'Only You' receives its UK TV premiere on tonight's edition of *Top Of The Pops*, transmitted on BBC1 between 7:19 and 7:59pm.

Saturday December 21

🍎 Full-page advertisements appear in the UK music papers announcing that Paul and Wings have been awarded a platinum disc for over 500,000 sales in Britain for their album *Band On The Run*.

Monday December 23

🍎 George's single 'Ding Dong, Ding Dong'/'Hari's On Tour (Express)' is released in the US. To coincide with the release, George, at his Friar Park mansion, shoots a 16mm colour promotional clip for the A-side where he is seen wandering (and tripping) around his vast land and pointing (with a false hand) at various bushes and twigs. Additional scenes shot include, this time inside the Friar Park mansion, George miming the song, dressed satirically to represent chronologically The Beatles years. He first appears sporting a Beatles mop-top wig, a collarless Beatles suit and playing a Rickenbacker guitar. (Still in this garb, George nips outside into the grounds of Friar Park to film a brief exterior shot.) Later, George dresses in his *Sgt. Pepper* outfit and films scenes with midgets miming the song wearing false hats, beards and eye patches. Retaining The Beatles' retrospective idea, George recreates John's *Two Virgins* cover by appearing naked save for a pair of large furry boots and a guitar to hide his modesty. The clip ends with George up on the roof of his mansion lowering a Pirates flag, replacing it with a flag bearing a Hare Krishna symbol.

Thursday December 26

🍎 For the fourth successive year, BBC1 transmits a Beatles film over Christmas. Today, in its traditional "Boxing Day With The Beatles" slot, this time between 10:28 and 11:55am, *Help!* receives its third television screening.

Friday December 27

🍎 John, May Pang, and his son, Julian spend the day at Disneyworld in Florida. "We went to Disneyland on what must have been the most crowded day of the year," John recalls. "It's funny, I was sitting on the monorail along with everyone else, not being recognised, and I heard someone with his back to me say that 'George Harrison was there today'. The guy was leaning on me at the time and he'd heard that a Beatle was there somewhere. He couldn't see the wood for the trees."

Today, in the Hawaiian Village hotel adjoining Disneyworld, John finally signs the papers dissolving The Beatles' partnership, the last ex-Beatle to do so. Thus, the end of The Beatles, as both a group and as a company, officially occurs in, of all places, Disneyworld.

Sunday December 29
 John gives another radio interview, this time appearing on the CKLW station in Detroit.

Tuesday December 31
 In London, the year-end financial reports for Apple Corps Ltd reveals a turnover of £3,759,127 which, after tax and expenses, results in a profit of £261,075.
 Later in the day, at Tittenhurst Park in Ascot, Ringo hosts a New Year's Eve party for close friends including Eric Clapton and Patti Harrison.

December (until February 1975)
 Back in New York, John records several demos of the song 'Tennessee', a track that will undergo a number of progressive changes, including the lyrics and even the working titles, later becoming 'Memories' and 'Howling At The Moon'. (A portion of 'Memories' *will* eventually form the basis to the 1980 *Double Fantasy* track 'Watching The Wheels'.) According to May Pang, during this period John also wrote a catchy tune entitled 'Popcorn'. During the month, John gives another transatlantic phone call interview to Kenny Everett on the London based station Capital Radio in the UK.

1975

"I've lost all that negativity about the past and I'd be happy as Larry to do 'Help!' I've just changed completely in two years. I'd do 'Hey Jude' and the whole damn show, and I think George will eventually see that."

— *John*

January

🎶 John records 'Across The Universe' and 'Fame' with David Bowie at the Ladyland Studios in New York. John remembers this session: "David rang and told me he was going to do a version of 'Across The Universe' and I thought 'great' because I'd never done a good version of that song myself. It's one of my favourite songs, but I didn't like my version of it. So I went down and played rhythm on the track. Then he got this lick, so me and him put this together in another song called 'Fame' . . . I had fun!"
(John first met Bowie at Elizabeth Taylor's birthday party in Los Angeles in February 1974.)

🎶 This month, John also receives an invitation from Paul to join him in New Orleans on the sessions for his new album *Venus And Mars*. Meanwhile, it seems that Los Angeles has become the residence of choice for ex-Beatles. Paul has just instructed his representatives to look for a property in Beverley Hills and George has just purchased a property belonging to the comedian Dan Rowan, of *Rowan & Martin's Laugh-In* fame. Ringo, meanwhile, is about to go looking for a home while John has revealed that he aims to keep his in Hollywood Hills . . . provided he is allowed to stay in the country.

🎶 The musical *Sgt. Pepper's Lonely Hearts Club Band*, which only opened last November, collapses before it can even leave New York. Law suits and counter lawsuits are to blame.

Thursday January 2

🎶 The US district court judge Richard Owen rules in New York City that John and his attorney, Leon Wildes, are to be permitted access to US Immigration and Naturalisation Service files that deal with John's ongoing deportation case. John is also permitted to question the INS officials. This decision is designed to give John the opportunity to determine whether or not the deportation order against him is really based on his 1968 UK drug conviction or because of his opposition to certain US political activities.

Thursday January 9

🎶 The last remaining links which still legally bind the four Beatles together are finally severed when the April 1967 The Beatles & Company partnership is formally dissolved at a private hearing in London's High Court. The ruling comes just over four years after Paul had originally requested that The Beatles' partnership be dissolved. (Even so, following various last minute hold-ups, the ultimate absolution of their partnership will not take effect until April 9.)

Friday January 10

🎶 Paul, Linda and family leave Heathrow Airport en route to New York. In light of yesterday's High Court judgement, Paul remarks to the waiting reporters: "I'm relieved that the legal links between The Beatles have been separated!"

Saturday January 11

🎶 'Junior's Farm' reaches number three in the American singles chart. (The flip-side 'Sally G' makes number 39 on February 22.)

🎶 'Dark Horse' reaches number 15 in the American singles chart.

Thursday January 16 (until Monday February 24)

🎶 Wings assemble at Allen Toussaint's Sea Saint Studios in New Orleans where they begin recording songs for the album *Venus and Mars*. Paul reveals that he is recording there to . . . "achieve an even greater flexibility with the blues-rock sound". The sessions produce the following tracks: 'Venus And Mars', 'Rockshow', 'You Gave Me The Answer', 'Magneto And Titanium Man', 'Letting Go', 'Venus And Mars (reprise)', 'Spirits Of Ancient Egypt', 'Medicine Jar', 'Call Me Back Again', 'Treat Her Gently – Lonely Old People', 'Listen To What The Man Said', 'Love In Song' and 'Crossroads Theme'. They also record the tracks 'Karate Chaos' and an instrumental piece entitled 'Sea Dance'. Although they remain unreleased, Paul will copyright these two tracks on June 16. During the recordings, Geoff Britton mysteriously quits the band after playing on only two *Venus And Mars* album tracks. Paul calls on the services of the New York drummer Joe English.

Paul is asked at a press conference in New Orleans why he recorded the 'Crossroads Theme': "It's a joke! It's after 'Lonely Old People', you see. They are sitting there in the park, saying, 'Nobody asked us to play'. It's a poignant moment. Then there's a little break and then 'Crossroads' starts up. It's lonely old people. It's just the kind of thing that lonely old people watch. It could just as easily have been *Coronation Street*, but we knew the chords to *Crossroads*. I just thought that it would be nice to do it." (*Crossroads* was a soap-opera set around a fictional hotel in "Kings Oak". Produced by ATV in the British midlands, it ran for 4,510 episodes on the ITV network between November 1964 and April 1988.)

Wings hold a press conference aboard the boat *Voyager* while sailing through Bayou country down the Mississippi River, and Paul and Linda visit the annual Mardi Gras festival where he performs on stage with The Tuxedo Jazz Band. This will inspire Paul to record the song 'My Carnival' on February 12 but it will not see the light of day until 1985, when it appears on the B-side to 'Spies Like Us'. A local news team, for their evening programme *News Scene 8,* is present in the studio to capture the recordings of 'My Carnival'. The recordings for the album *Venus And Mars* will be concluded at the end of the month in Los Angeles at the Wally Heider Studios where they also record the instrumental 'Lunch Box'/'Odd Sox'. (See entry for February 25.)

When Geoff Britton returns to the UK, he is extremely evasive over the events that led to his departure from the group. All he will reveal is: "I completed half the tracks on the album and then a local drummer called Joe English did the rest." Britton, who is considering an offer to appear in an Italian spaghetti–kung fu film, concludes: "It's a funny band, Wings. From a musician's point of view, it's a privilege to do it. From a career point of view, it's madness! No matter how good you are, you're *always* in the shadow of Paul."

Monday January 27
🍎 Ringo's single 'No No Song'/'Snookeroo' is released in America.

Friday January 31
🍎 John pays a visit to Yoko at the Dakota. To friends, he gives his reason for the visit as: "Yoko has a cure for my smoking". Later in the year, John recalls this day: "I was just going over for a visit and it just fell in place again. It was like I'd never left. I realised that this was where I belonged. I think we both knew we'd get back together again sooner or later, even if it was five years, and that's why we never bothered with divorce. I'm just glad she let me back in again. It was like going out for a drink, but it took me a year to get it!"

As John will later recall in 1980, the reasons behind his return ran a lot deeper. "I really needed to be with her," John freely admits. "I wanted to be with her and could not literally survive without her. As a functioning human being I just went to pieces. I didn't realise that I needed her so much. I was haunted all right, because I needed her *more* than she needed me and I always thought the boot was on the other foot. That's as honest as I can get."

John moves back into the Dakota apartment over the coming weekend.

February
🍎 George's Apple film *Little Malcolm And His Struggle Against The Eunuchs* premieres in London at the West End, where it will soon sink without trace. George and Olivia are present at the first screening. Also, early in the month to coincide with the film's premiere, Sarah Dickinson of LBC (London Broadcasting Company) station interviews George to help promote the film.

Monday February 3
🍎 Ringo begins shooting the Warner Brothers film *Lisztomania*, starring Roger Daltrey, of The Who, at Shepperton Studios, Middlesex and on location, working with the controversial director Ken Russell. The movie has an 11 week schedule, which will eventually run to 15 weeks, but Ringo is only present this month and in March. The film, in which the former Beatle is cast in the role of The Pope, is premiered in New York on October 10 and in London on November 13.

Tuesday February 4
🍎 In New York, John bumps into May Pang at a dentist's surgery. He informs her, "I've now gone back to live with Yoko."

Wednesday February 5

 In England, Terry Doran, George's long time personal assistant, resigns from Oops Publishing Ltd., one of George's publishing companies. Doran, a Liverpudlian who had been responsible for maintaining The Beatles' cars for many years, was immortalised as "the man from the motor trade" in 'She's Leaving Home'.

Friday February 7

 Ringo and 24-year-old American Nancy Andrews leave Heathrow Airport en route to California. This visit to England had been Miss Andrews' first visit to Europe and Ringo had been serving as her guide around the sites of London.

 In England, Dark Horse records release the George produced Splinter single 'Drink All Day (Got To Find Your Own Way)' b/w 'Haven't'.

 Also today, Warner Brothers release the Paul produced Mike McGear single 'Sea Breezes' b/w 'Givin' Grease A Ride', co-written by Paul and Mike.

Saturday February 8

 The album *John Lennon Sings The Great Rock & Roll Hits (Roots)* is released in America via heavy television and radio mail-order advertising. The record, which depicts a picture of John from 1968, features the following tracks: side one: 'Be-Bop-A-Lula', 'Ain't That A Shame', 'Stand By Me', 'Sweet Little Sixteen', 'Rip It Up', 'Angel Baby', 'Do You Want To Dance' and 'You Can't Catch Me'; side two: 'Bony Maronie', 'Peggy Sue', 'Bring It On Home To Me', 'Slippin' And Slidin' ', 'Be My Baby', 'Ya Ya' and 'Because'.

The album had been produced by Morris Levy, without John's permission, from an early mixed tape of his *Rock 'N' Roll* oldies recording sessions. John promptly sues Levy, rightfully claiming that this release is illegal. (See entries for January 23 and February 20, 1976.) John later states that when *Roots* first became available, he had to wait some three weeks for its delivery! This could well have been due to its scarce availability, with a reported 2,500 copies of the album and only 500 copies of an 8-Track cartridge, being produced.

 Meanwhile, George's 'Ding Dong' makes number 36 in the US singles chart. Also today, George boards a plane at Heathrow Airport and heads for Los Angeles.

Thursday February 13

 John (totally uninvited) gives another radio interview to Scott Muni, on his WNEW-FM New York show. He brings with him an early copy of the *Rock 'N' Roll* album. (The 90-minute broadcast is repeated in its entirety on the Cleveland station WGCL on December 11, 1983.)

Monday February 17

 To combat the sales of *Roots*, John's official Apple album *Rock 'N' Roll* is rush-released in America. (The UK release takes place on February 21.) "You Should'a Been There . . ." is the record's advertising slogan.

The cover features a picture of John taken in a doorway in Hamburg in 1960. The shot re-emerged at the Beatlefest convention held in New York last September where the original photographer, Jurgen Volmer, was holding an exhibition of his early Beatles photographs. The three blurred figures walking in front of John in the snap are, from left to right, George, Stu Sutcliffe and Paul. Coincidentally, through his purchase of the Buddy Holly song catalogue, Paul receives royalties from the album because of John's recording of 'Peggy Sue', and Allen Klein receives money from John's recording of 'Bring It On Home To Me', of which Klein owns the publishing.

At the time of its release, John reflects on the history of the recordings of the *Rock 'N' Roll* album: "The LA sessions gradually collapsed into mania. That's one way of putting it. It definitely got crazy, you know. There are twenty-eight guys playing a night and fifteen of them are out of their minds . . . including me! The sessions broke down. We broke them down pretty well, me and Phil. They got really barmy! I'm not even going to say what happened. There are about eight tracks, half of them you couldn't use for one reason or another . . . 'Angel Baby' is a phenomenal track. Some of it was ridiculous. That's the first time I let an album out of my control, since the first Beatle album. I'll never do it again! Phil had the tapes and I waited for eight months in LA for him to recover. I came home to New York and the day before we go in to record *Walls And Bridges,* I get the tapes back. So I did the rest of it myself using the basic unit that I usually use of about eight guys. I did it in five days, three tracks a night. I just said: 'Rock'n'roll, okay, rock!' And we just went in . . . I'd rehearsed them a couple of days beforehand, so they were loose. Then we just went in and: 'Okay, take one, "Stand By Me". Take two – "Be-Bop-A-Lula".' You know. The opposite of what was going on down on the West Coast and this was a year later.

"It was a choice of either just leaving it forever and never putting it out, or trying to find some format for four or five Spector tracks, which I didn't think were singles. I was so sick of it. So I thought: 'Now what can I do? Leave it in the can?' I *hate* leaving stuff in the can. I've got no stuff in the can, neither have The Beatles!* And I thought: 'Okay, finish it off and see what it is. Then once it went out I felt great! It's out, it's out. I've never been so long on an album in my life! It was longer than *Sgt. Pepper* and I normally only take eight weeks to make an album from start to finish and out in the shops, you know, otherwise I get bored."

(* John's comment comes just under 21 years before the release of the official Beatles six-CD *Anthology* series!)

Friday February 21
 Ringo's single 'Snookeroo'/'Oo Wee' is released in the UK. (Promotional pictures for the release feature Ringo and the robot, as featured on the *Goodnight Vienna* album sleeve, pasted over the top of his 1952 half-yearly school report.)
 In the UK, just two weeks after their last single, Dark Horse records release the George produced Splinter single 'China Light' b/w 'Drink All Day (Got To Find Your Own Way)'.

Monday February 24
 DJM release (simultaneously in both the UK and the US) the Elton John single 'Philadelphia Freedom' which features on the B-side 'I Saw Her Standing There', as performed by John and Elton, live at Madison Square Garden in New York on November 28, 1974. The track is credited to John Lennon and The Muscle Shoals Horns.

Tuesday February 25
 A happy looking John is pictured outside the Dakota building wearing a large silver *Elvis* badge.
 Wings move on to Los Angeles to resume recordings for *Venus And Mars*. On the way to the studios in their car, Paul invites Joe English to become a permanent member of Wings. During their stay in Los Angeles, Paul and Linda will attend the annual Grammy Awards ceremony on March 1 (see entry), where they receive awards for the album *Band On The Run*. (Incidentally, the *Venus And Mars* album will become Paul's first release for Capitol Records in America under his new contract.)

Thursday February 27
 In England, tonight's edition of *Top Of The Pops* (transmitted on BBC1 between 7:20 and 7:59pm) features the first UK screening of the film shot by the BBC of John wandering around New York on Friday November 15 last year. Originally filmed to accompany 'Whatever Gets You Through The Night', the film was re-edited (lasting two minutes 25 seconds) to accompany John's latest single 'No. 9 Dream'. Incidentally, some of the film unveiled tonight receives its worldwide television premiere, as some scenes were not included in the original 'Whatever Gets You Through The Night' promotional film. Introduced by Dave Lee Travis, tonight's *Top Of The Pops* also features music by The Rubettes, Showaddywaddy, Mud, The Hues Corporation, The Shadows, Cockney Rebel and Duane Eddy and The Rebellettes.

Friday February 28
 George's single 'Dark Horse'/'Hari's On Tour' is released in the UK.
 A copyright for the instrumental version of Paul's 'Tomorrow' is registered. A vocal version has originally appeared on the Wings album *Wild Life* in August 1971.

March
 Ringo is frequently seen out socialising in LA. This month, alongside Alice Cooper, Harry Nilsson, Keith Moon, Bernie Taupin, Richard Perry and Stevie Wonder, he attends an Arista Records party in Bel Air.

Saturday March 1

🍎 At the annual Grammy Awards show, televised live from New York, John puts in a guest appearance as an award presenter. He is seen with Paul Simon and Andy Williams presenting the award for 'Records Of The Year – Artist & Producer'. The three singers, standing at the podium, before the presentation, partake in a cleverly scripted comedy routine, which pokes fun at their three respective former partners.

John (wearing his trademark beige cap and scarf): "Thank you mother, thank you . . . Hello, I'm John. I used to play with my partner Paul."

Paul Simon: "I'm Paul. I used to play with my partner Art (Garfunkel)."

Andy Williams: "I'm Andy. I used to play with my partner Claudine (Longet, his former wife)." (The audience breaks into laughter.)

With spontaneous applause, Andy continues with another swipe at his former wife. Turning to John and Paul, he continues: "The music that you fellows wrote, though, really did influence my life. As a matter of fact, it helped tell the story of me and my partner."

John asks: "Any song in particular Andy?"

He replies: "Well, let's see. It started off with 'I Want To Hold Your Hand' and finished off with 'Bridge Over Troubled Water'."

John replies: "Touching, touching." Then, in an attempt to get things back on track, he continues: "Shall we get on with it? My God, so this is what dawn does, is it?" (Producing more laughter from the star-studded audience.)

John gives out a loud cheer when it's announced, by Simon, that Elton John's 'Don't Let The Sun Go Down On Me' is one of the nominees for the award. At this point television cameras catch sight of Yoko sitting in the front row of the audience, clearly enjoying the antics of her husband. As if this ceremony wasn't chaotic enough, humour continues when, of all people, Art Garfunkel appears from the audience to receive, on behalf of Olivia Newton-John, an award for the song 'I Honestly Love You'. With Art now standing on the podium, John introduces him to his former partner Paul, adding: "Which one of you is Ringo?", following this with: "Are you ever getting back together again?" Simon retorts by asking John: "Are you guys getting back together again?" With a sigh, John replies: "It's terrible, isn't it?"

With that, a rather serious Art Garfunkel leans towards the microphone and asks Paul: "Are you still writing?" To which, Simon replies: "I'm trying my hand at a little acting Art." John chips in by enquiring: "Where's Linda?" The joke is somewhat lost, prompting him to add: "Oh well, too subtle that one," before handing the award to Art with the words: "There you are my dear." Then, at the conclusion of a rather passive acceptance speech by Art, John remarks: "You're so serious."

🍎 During the extravaganza, Paul wins two 1974 Grammys for his Wings album *Band On The Run*, one for 'Best Pop Vocal Performance by a Group' and the other for 'Best Produced Non-Classical Recording'. The Beatles are also given a special 'Grammy Hall Of Fame Award'.

After the ceremony, John attends an after-show party with some of the other guests, which include Roberta Flack and David Bowie. Yoko Ono is seen chatting with John backstage and is later pictured with him leaving the event. This is big news back in England, making the front page of the *Daily Mirror* on Monday March 3.

🍎 Meanwhile in today's *Melody Maker*, in a story entitled "John's No. 1 Dream", Chris Charlesworth reports that John's negotiations to remain in America will reach a climax within the next three months. His lawyer, Leon Wildes, says that he has " . . . information that shows that the Government deliberately ignored his application, actually locking the relevant document away in a safe. This was because of a memorandum which was circulated by an unknown Government agency to other Government agencies which stated that John and Yoko were to be kept under physical observance at all times because of possible political activities." Wildes goes on to add that he is currently trying to find the source of this document and if he does it will "break the case wide open and prove that there has been a miscarriage of justice".

Monday March 3

🍎 In Los Angeles, Paul, Linda and the three children are driving out of Los Angeles, heading back to their temporary base in Malibu, when Linda is arrested on suspicion of possessing marijuana. Police had only stopped Paul and Linda's car for running through a red traffic light. The California Highway Patrol announces later: "Mr. McCartney and his wife Linda and their three children were driving along Santa Monica Boulevard when the car went through a traffic light soon after midnight. While a patrolman was writing a traffic ticket, he said he smelt the odour of marijuana in the car and ordered the McCartneys out. He found a plastic bag containing a quantity of marijuana which Mrs. McCartney had allegedly carried in her purse." Linda insists that the drug is hers alone and is detained for two hours while Paul is freed to drive the children back to their hotel. Linda is subsequently charged with possession of marijuana and released on $500 (£200) bail. She is ordered to appear in Municipal Court on March 10.

Thursday March 6
🍎 John's single 'Stand By Me'/'Move Over Ms. L.' is released in America. (The UK release takes place on April 18.) John also issues a press release, officially announcing that he has now returned to Yoko, adding that "our separation hadn't worked out".

Friday March 7
🍎 John is sued for $42 million (£18 million) by the Big Seven Music Corporation of America on the grounds that he has "monopolised the sale and distribution of his records and tapes". The suit results from the Morris Levy publishing case.
🍎 Still in America, Dark Horse records release the George produced Splinter single 'China Light' b/w 'Haven't Got Time'.

Saturday March 8
🍎 *Melody Maker* published an interview with John undertaken by Chris Charlesworth at the Capitol Records offices on 6th Avenue in New York. Before their chat, a buoyant John talks on the telephone to no less than 35 different disc jockeys simultaneously across America. "I like 'Stand By Me' and 'Be-Bop-A-Lula' is one of my all-time favourites," he says. "There's been more trouble with this album than soft mick." John discusses the chequered history of this infamous album: " . . . I just finished *Mind Games* when I started the new album and I just wanted to have some fun. It was so soon after *Mind Games* that I didn't have any new material. I wanted to just sing and not be the producer. I thought, 'Who's the one to do it with?' and I thought of Phil Spector. We went down to the Record Plant and started cutting and, well, it got pretty crazy . . . it really got wild at times. But we managed to cut seven or eight in the end before it collapsed . . . which is the only way to put it.

"Next thing Phil had apparently had an auto accident. Only he knows whether he did or didn't, but that's what the story said. That was the end of it then, because he'd got the tapes and I didn't get them back until two days before I went into the studio to cut *Walls And Bridges*. I went on to do the Harry Nilsson thing (*Pussycats*) and I tried everything to get them (the *Rock 'N' Roll* album tapes) back, even just hanging around LA to see if Phil would get better. I couldn't think what to do, so I did the album with Harry while I was waiting. When I got the tapes, I couldn't get into them because I was all geared to *Walls And Bridges*. When I did get into them, I found that out of the eight, there were only four or five that were worth using. The sessions had twenty-eight guys playing live and a lot of them out of tune, which is too much, even for rock and roll. So I didn't know whether to forget it or carry on, but I hate leaving stuff in the can. I thought about putting out an EP – remember them? But they don't have them in America, and thought about a maxi-single. In the end I decided to finish it off and produce the rest myself.

"I did ten tracks in three days in October, all the numbers that I hadn't got around to with Phil. I had a lot of fun and mixed it all down in about four or five days. My one problem was whether it sounds weird going from the Spector sound to my sound from twenty-eight guys down to eight. But they match pretty well I think. So there it was, I suddenly had an album."

Chris mentions to John how Paul will profit from the album. "What a clever move that was," he replies. "I hope he gives me a good deal. I don't care who gets the money. With Paul it's cool, 'cos we're pals, and even Klein's all right really. I'm not gonna get much money from this album anyway."

John seems happier with his past than at any time since 1970. "I've lost all that negativity about the past and I'd be happy as Larry to do 'Help!' I've just changed completely in two years. I'd do 'Hey Jude' and the whole damn show, and I think George will eventually see that. If he doesn't, that's cool. That's the way he wants to be."

John also announces that he is now back with Yoko. "I'm happy as Larry," he beams, "and she is . . . I hope. We've known each other for nine years. I met her in 1966. We had a sort of breakdown last year, one way or another, but we called each other often even when I was going crazy out on the West Coast, and I probably said a lot of barmy things to her which I'll regret."

Monday March 17

🍎 In preparation for his new series of *The Old Grey Whistle Test* for BBC2, Bob Harris and its producer Michael Appleton travel to America to conduct various interviews with contemporary rock and pop stars, one of whom is John at his Dakota apartment. For the first day, after being given a box of Chocolate Olivers (part of the deal for doing the show), he gives a fascinating interview on all manner of subjects. These include living in New York, the recording studios there, missing England, the recording of *Sgt. Pepper* and the putting together of a TV show around a new album. Harris asks John about the green card situation.

John: "Well, the situation is that I'm still appealing. Like every now and then they'll say, 'You've got thirty days to get out', and my lawyer will appeal and we'll go to another court, or something like that. It'll just go on forever."

Bob: "Do you think they are kind of picking on you?"

John: "Oh yeah, they picked on me. I'm telling you, when it first started I was followed in a car and the phone was tapped. Now we lost the phone tapping case, because how do you prove that your phone was tapped? At that time it was pre-Watergate, so you can imagine! It was: 'John Lennon says his phone was tapped and there were men following him in a car.' I went on a TV show here, a talk show (*The Dick Cavett Show* – September 12, 1971), and I said that this was happening to me, and it stopped the next day. I think they wanted me to know to scare me. And I was scared! Paranoid! People thought I was crazy then. They do anyway! But I mean more so, you know? 'Lennon, you're a big-headed little maniac. Who's going to follow you around?' Well, what do they want? That's what I'm saying. What do they want? I'm not going to cause them any problems."

Bob: "Presumably, when the green card comes through, we will see you in England."

John: "Oh you bet! Of course! I've got family in England. I've got a child who has to keep travelling over. Hello Julian. I've got my Aunty Mimi. Hello Mimi! And all my other relatives, who are furious with me, but I won't tell you why. But I'll tell you Mimi isn't."

Bob: "The inevitable question. Are they . . ."

John (interrupting): "Are they ever going to get back together again?"

Bob: "Yeah. But first of all, is there any possibility? But secondly, more important, do you think it's a good idea?"

John: "Well, that's another point altogether, whether it would be a good idea or not. You see it is strange, because at one point, when they were asking me, I was saying, 'No, never. What the hell. Go back? Not me?' And then came the period when I thought, 'Well, why not? If we felt like making a record or doing something.' Everybody always envisaged the stage show, but to me, if we worked together . . . studio again, you know. The stage show is something else. If we'd got something to say in the studio, okay. Now, when I'm saying that I am keen to do it, I turn the paper and George is saying: 'Not me!' Right? It's never got to the position where each one of us wants to do it at the same time. I think that over the period we've been apart, we've all thought, 'Oh that would be nice. That wouldn't be bad.' And the other question is: 'Would it be worth it?' But that is answered by if we wanted to do it. If we wanted to do it, then it would be worth it. If we got in the studio together and we thought we turned each other on again, then it would be worth it, again. And sod the critics, you know. They've got nothing to do with it. The music is the music. If we made a piece that we thought was worthwhile, it goes out. But it's such a pie in the sky, you know. I don't care either way. If someone wants to pull it together, I'll go along. I'm not in the mood to pull it together that's for sure!"

(The show is edited for transmission on Tuesday April 15, and then first broadcast on Friday April 18 on BBC2 in a special early-evening slot between 8:09 and 8:59pm to coincide with the release of the 'Stand By Me' Apple single. John's piece totals 29 minutes 36 seconds, with the rest of the show being made up of a studio performance by A Band Called O and music by Emmylou Harris. Due to the success of the show, a repeat screening, albeit edited, occurs between 10:20 and 10:59pm on September 30, when it is screened as a prelude to the fifth series of *The Old Grey Whistle Test*. A third screening, repeating the edited version, occurs on October 11, 1980, between 10:30 and 10:59pm and again on BBC2, when it is because John is again recording and the Suntory

World Matchplay International Golf Championship had been postponed due to bad weather. Immediately following this rebroadcast, the promotional clip for 'Stand By Me' reappears as part of the 350th *Old Grey Whistle Test* programme celebrations on BBC2.)
 Keith Moon's album *Two Sides of the Moon* is released in the US. Ringo is featured as the announcer on 'Solid Gold' and on drums and "rap" on the track 'Together'. (The album appears in the UK on May 23.)

Tuesday March 18
 At the Dakota, John records his second interview with the journalist Jean-François Vallee (his first being on December 14, 1971), this time for inclusion in the French television programme *Un Jour Future*. His piece, entitled *Il Etait Une Fois John Lennon (Once Upon A Time There Was John Lennon)*, is produced by Michael Lancelot and features John, besides speaking on the telephone, being interviewed while sitting on the floor. Among many topics of conversation, he discusses Paul's drug taking admission to ITN news in 1967, The Beatles as "world leaders", his visit to Paris in 1961 and the trademark Beatle haircut and collarless jacket. He also reveals how he incorporated reggae into the 1964 Beatles tune 'I Call Your Name'. At one stage, he goes out onto the balcony and performs a mock magical trick with a handkerchief, which appears from the bottom of his trousers. Inside his apartment again, this time solo on the piano, John performs a unique version of Labelle's hit 'Voulez Vous Coucher Avec Moi, Ce Soir (Lady Marmalade)'. (John appears in the interview wearing a T-shirt that has that logo stamped on to it.) For its first television broadcast, on Saturday June 28, and for the benefit of the non-English speaking French viewers, Lancelot strangely dubs John's answers with two separate male/female French voices. Sections of the interview where John speaks frankly about sex and drugs are deemed too risky for transmission and are never screened. Following the French TV filming, John records another transatlantic telephone conversation with the Capital Radio DJ Nicky Horne for his programme *Your Mother Wouldn't Like It*. A planned meeting between John and Ringo, who is scheduled to appear in Capital's US studio to ask John some questions, fails to materialise as Ringo fails to show because he had to return to England for additional work on *Lisztomania* at Shepperton Studios.

Later in the day, the concluding part of the *Old Grey Whistle Test* show takes place at the Hit Factory studios in New York, where John and his band film studio performances of 'Slippin' And Slidin'' and 'Stand By Me'. The production of these are carried out by Apple and subsequently licensed to the BBC for inclusion in the programme. ('Slippin' And Slidin'' is filmed because, at this stage, this is the choice for the second single from the *Rock 'N' Roll* album.)

Monday March 24
 Paul holds a party celebrating the end of the recording sessions for *Venus And Mars* aboard the ocean liner *Queen Mary,* which is permanently docked in Long Beach, California, and converted into a hotel. Among the 200 guests present to wave goodbye to Paul, Linda and Wings after two months of recording are former Monkees Micky Dolenz and Davy Jones, Joni Mitchell, Carole King, Marvin Gaye, The Faces, Rudy Vallee, Phil Everly, The Jackson Five, Bob Dylan, Ryan and Tatum O'Neal, Dean Martin, Tony Curtis, Paul Williams, Cher, David Cassidy, members of Led Zeppelin and their manager Peter Grant, Mal Evans, Derek Taylor and George Harrison. This marks the first time that George and Paul are seen socialising together since the break-up of The Beatles five years earlier. As the guests file into the Grand Saloon, they are greeted by large posters which read: "Venus & Mars Are All Right Tonight". Paul, dressed in a silk shirt and slippers, spends the evening greeting guests while music is provided by The Meters and Professor Longhair, aka Henry Bird. His performance is recorded by Paul and released on the MPL album *Live On The Queen Mary*, which Paul co-produces. (Although this party serves as their farewell to America, Paul and Linda will not actually leave America until April 2.)

Wednesday March 26
 Paul and Linda remain in America to attend the Los Angeles film premiere of *Tommy,* the big-screen version of Pete Townshend's rock-opera, which stars Ann-Margaret, Oliver Reed and Roger Daltrey in the title role. David Frost, who covers the event for his ABC TV show *Wide World Of Entertainments,* interviews the McCartneys for the programme.

Saturday March 29
Ringo attends the European premiere of the film of Pete Townshend's rock opera *Tommy* at the Leicester Square Theatre in London. The former Beatle, wearing a top hat adorned with a Tommy badge, joins members of The Who, Elton John, Rod Stewart and Brit Ekland, Andy Fairweather-Low and David Essex. Capital radio DJ Nicky Horne broadcasts his whole *Your Mother Wouldn't Like It* show from the theatre's lobby, intercut with interviews, including one with Ringo. Following the screening Ringo attends a party for 800 at the Inn On The Park hotel. A torrential downpour soaks both stars and waiting fans.

Monday March 31
In London, the financial returns for McCartney Productions Ltd. reveal, for the year 1974/1975, sales of £473,576, while outgoing expenses are £231,324, resulting in a first time profit for the company of £196,631 after the company is liable for a tax bill of £45,621.

April
The Beatles' former personal assistant Peter Brown arrives in London from New York to oversee plans for the £1 million production of Robert Stigwood's big screen version of *John, Paul, George, Ringo . . . And Bert*. Shooting is scheduled to begin in July.

Wednesday April 2
Paul, Linda and the family arrive back in England at Heathrow Airport. Reporters at the airport remark somewhat unkindly that Paul, who is carrying a large portable radio, is wearing the exact same outfit, suit, shirt and shoes, that he wore when he left the country on January 10 earlier this year.

Friday April 4
Ringo forms a new record label called Ring O'Records, a name suggested by John. To promote the label, he begins a heavy round of promotional interviews, one of which is for *Melody Maker*. The feature is published on April 12 (see entry). During his interview for BBC Radio One, he puts a damper on The Beatles reunion rumours by announcing: "I am not keen on reforming The Beatles!"

Saturday April 5
Ringo's 'No No Song' peaks at number three in the US singles chart.

Tuesday April 8
In New York, it is reported that Linda will not fight a charge of marijuana possession against her. She reveals that she is "ready to attend a class on the evils of drug abuse in expiation".

Wednesday April 9
In London, one day short of five years since Paul announced that he had quit The Beatles, the partnership of The Beatles & Co. is finally dissolved at a private hearing before a High Court. Solicitors announce: "All matters in the dispute between Mr. McCartney and John Lennon, George Harrison and Ringo Starr have been fully settled."

Thursday April 10
Pre-recorded interviews with John, recorded in New York to promote the album *Rock 'N' Roll*, form the basis of a Capital Radio special, transmitted tonight, entitled *An Evening With John Lennon*.

Saturday April 12
Melody Maker publishes an interview with Ringo, carried out by Steve Lake, entitled "Why I Don't Want To Play Drums Like Buddy Rich". The feature is by way of a promotion for his new record label called Ring O'Records. *Melody Maker* naturally asks: "What will Ring O'Records do that Apple couldn't?"

Ringo: "What people don't realise is that Apple was never really much more than an extension of Parlophone."

The conversation shifts to Ringo – the drummer. "Nothing is more satisfying than playing the kit. I prefer studios to being on the road, mostly because it's so much more relaxed . . ." On his drumming style . . . "Buddy Rich might be the fastest thing on two feet, but I've got no interest in trying to play like him, not that I could anyway." On his songwriting: "I only know three chords, and when I'm writing, I use three guitars, one tuned to each chord . . ."

Friday April 18

 On the day that BBC2 transmits John's *Old Grey Whistle Test* interview (see entries for March 17 and 18) for the first time in England, Lennon himself is to be found in the Grand Ballroom of the Hilton Hotel in New York City, recording an appearance for the ATV/ITC TV special *Salute To Sir Lew – The Master Showman*. This is a star-studded cabaret event to celebrate the distinguished career of Sir Lew Grade, the former tap-dancer and now the cigar-puffing head of Associated Television (ATV), who had recently been honoured by the National Academy of Television and Sciences. John's appearance is also part of a belated settlement, arising from a publishing dispute over material co-written by him and Yoko, which caused the delay of John's UK release a few years earlier.

For tonight's show, John, sporting a pair of dark round glasses, appears with his long hair tied back into a ponytail and is dressed in a bright red boiler suit covered in zips. Clutching an acoustic guitar, he performs live vocal versions of 'Slippin And Slidin' ', 'Stand By Me' and, rather nervously, 'Imagine', in which John changes the lyrics to "brotherhood and sisterhood of man", a reference to his espousal of feminist politics. He is joined by the eight-piece band Etcetera, who appear dressed in matching boiler suits and, rather strangely, face masks attached to the back of their heads. John is naturally asked about the significance of these masks. He replies: "It was a sardonic reference to my feelings on Lew Grade's personality!" (His resentment stems from Grade's ATV company taking control of The Beatles' Northern Songs in 1969. The Beatles, most significantly John and Paul, were forced to sell their remaining stock in Northern Songs to ATV for a sum reputed to be in excess of $5 million.)

Incidentally, John's backing band, Etcetera, is actually the group BOMF, which stands for Brothers Of Mother Fuckers, a name still visible on the bass drum during their performance. (BOMF had actually originated from the group Community Apple, whose previous lead singer Joey Dambra sang backing vocals on John's track 'No. 9 Dream'. At John's suggestion, BOMF will later change their name to Dog Soldier – the words from one of his songs.)

John returns at the very end of the *Salute To Sir Lew* show to take a bow with the rest of the cast, this time dressed in a more formal blue shirt and white trousers, plus, of course, his trademark cap and scarf. Joining him on the star-studded bill tonight is the host, the Irish comedian Dave Allen, plus singing stars Tom Jones and Julie Andrews, comic genius Peter Sellers and the Dougie Squires Second Generation dance group. The show is watched by an equally star-studded audience, which includes from the world of American entertainment, George Segal, William Conrad, Shirley MacLaine, Kirk Douglas, Gene Kelly, Goldie Hawn and Lauren Bacall. The 52-minute videotaped show is first transmitted in America on June 13, 1975, while the UK TV screening takes place one week later, across the ITV network on June 20 at different times throughout the evening. Both US and UK versions of the show cut 'Stand By Me' from John's three-track live performance which will turn out to be John's last. (Incidentally, Sir Lew Grade died in London, aged 91, during the early hours of December 13, 1998, following complications with a heart operation.)

Saturday April 19 & Sunday April 20

 At his home in Los Angeles, George records a two-hour radio interview with Dave Herman of the New York radio station WNEW. The DIR syndication network in America transmits the interview on May 24, with a further airing taking place on August 17 as part of the *King Biscuit Flower Hour*.

Thursday April 24

 In England, Badfinger's Pete Ham is found hanged at his home in Woking, Surrey. He was only 27 years of age.

Monday April 28

❆ Since the demise of The Beatles five years previously, the appearance of an individual Beatle on a nationwide television programme is a guaranteed audience puller. However, tonight, on Channel 4, WNBC TV in America, the station manages to pull off a major scoop by screening separate appearances by two former Beatles on the one channel. Firstly, almost seven years since The Beatles appeared on the show by way of a pre-taped video, Ringo reappears solo to perform again on the top-rated variety show *The Smothers Brothers Show* (transmitted between 8:00 and 9:00pm ET), hosted by Tom and Dick Smothers. The pair, of course, were infamously involved with John during the Troubadour Club fracas on March 12, 1974. On tonight's show, Ringo performs, with The Smothers Brothers, a rendition of 'No No Song', at the end of which, as part of the act, a US policeman appears to arrest whoever is carrying the "substance" outlined in the song they've just sung. A member of the studio audience shouts out, "Share it!" to which they cry out the lyrics of the song, "No, no, no, no, we don't smoke it no more!" Also shown is the rarely screened promo film for 'Snookeroo'. Joining Ringo on tonight's show is the comedy actress Lily Tomlin.

Later in the evening, (between 1:00 and 2:00am ET), John is interviewed by Tom Snyder for the programme, *The Tomorrow Show*. Such is the importance of an appearance by John that the entire 50-minute programme is given over to him and, during the final part of the show, his lawyer Leon Wildes. Snyder begins the interview recalling The Beatles' impact in America during their first visit in 1964, and visiting a concert in Philadelphia in 1965 where, he remembers: "So much screaming and so much carrying on." He asks John, "Did this bother you at all while you were doing these concerts, that people couldn't hear your music and that all they could hear was themselves screaming?"

John replies: "It got a little boring. It was great when it first happened, when you first come on, all you got was 'wah!' But then it became lip-synching, miming, sometimes things would break down and no one would know . . . It wasn't doing the music any good."

Tom: "As I recall, there were fan clubs or clubs of followers for each of the individuals in the organisations . . ."

John (interrupting): "Well, it was mainly a 'Beatle-Club' but they fanned it out a little just to keep a . . ."

Tom (interrupting): "Now, I'm just wondering just how unified any group can be when the audience have certain favourites. Maybe they like Paul more than they like John . . ."

John (breaking into laughter): "That's true."

Tom: "I just wondered if it's awfully difficult to be friends. And do you really care about whether or not you're friends when you are a group such as The Beatles, or whether you are The Rolling Stones or whatever?"

John: "We didn't break up because we weren't friends. We just broke up out of sheer boredom, you know, and boredom creates tension."

Tom (naively): "How can you get bored doing what you did?"

John: "Because it wasn't going anywhere, you know. We'd stopped touring and we'd just sort of say, 'Time to make an album'. You know, go into the studio, the same four of us, be looking at each other and be playing the same licks . . ."

Tom (interrupting): "In those silly haircuts."

John: "Those silly haircuts that you have now. If you notice, he's got his now." (John points to Tom's haircut, reminiscent of The Beatles, circa 1964.)

Tom continues the conversation by asking John about his 1969 *Bed-Ins* with Yoko.

John: "What we virtually had was a seven-day press conference in bed. The first day they fought at the door to get in, thinking there was something sexy going on."

Tom: "Like sensuous."

John: "That was the word I was looking for, and they (the reporters) found two people talking about peace. Reporters always have about five minutes with you, ten minutes with you. We'd let them ask anything for as long as they wanted for seven days, and all the time we just kept on plugging peace."

The exchange continues with Tom asking about people in the public eye not being able to enjoy their privacy.

John replies: "I can walk down the street and somebody'd say, 'Hi John' or 'How's your immigration?' They don't hassle me. I might sign one autograph – I don't get hassled. I actually went through that period when I couldn't go anywhere. We go and eat, we go to the movies, we go wherever we want . . . but if we decide to go and eat, it's cool. We're probably less recognisable than you."

Snyder moves on to talk about drugs in the music business.

John: "There's as much dope in the music business as there is in virtually every other business now. Dope is so out in the open that you can go anywhere and it's there. There's no underground movement of people taking dope. The most extraordinary straight people are taking dope, including cocaine, anywhere and at any time. If you want it, you can have it."

This leads to John recalling his infamous 1968 drugs bust when he, along with fellow pop stars were targeted by the late Sgt. Pilcher of Scotland Yard in London, and the subsequent difficulties these stars encountered when trying to get in and out of America. "That's why Leon is here," says John, introducing his lawyer Leon Wildes.

Wildes: "John was charged as being deportable in the United States, for being an over-stay. The IS (Immigration Service) created the very status that they charged him with being deportable for. We fought that deportation case, and a decision was finally rendered, after about a year, that he was, an over-stay." (In 1973, the IS revoked a two-week extension at the end of the first week, and thus cited that John had been an over-stay for a week.)

Tom turns to John and says: "When all of us were little, we were told, 'Why try to be some place when they tell you you're not wanted.' You could live anywhere you want in this world. If you're getting hassled this way, why put up with it?"

John: "Because I'd like to live in the land of the free, Tom and also, if it's up to Joe Doe on the streets, he doesn't care about it, or would be glad an 'El Beatle' is living here. If I get in the cab, he says, 'How's it going? I hope you can stay.' I like to be here, because this is where the music came from; this is what influenced my whole life and got me where I am today, as it were. I love the place, I like to be here, I've got a lot of friends here, and it's where I want to be. Statue of Liberty . . . welcome!"

(Repeat screenings of the show are suitably renamed *The John Lennon Show*.)

(The day after John's assassination in 1980, the *Tomorrow Show*, accompanied by studio interviews with journalist Lisa Robinson and Jack Douglas, the producer of *Double Fantasy*, is re-broadcast. In 1983, this re-broadcast is released on Star Box home video sporting the suitable title *The John Lennon Interview*.)

May

🍎 Rumours circulate in the music industry that Wings is to play at this year's Knebworth Festival. The group spend most of this month rehearsing and recording, alternating between Abbey Road Studios and a soundstage at Elstree Film Studios in Hertfordshire.

🍎 In Los Angeles, George records songs for his album *Extra Texture (Read All About It)*. The sessions produce the following tracks: 'You', 'World Of Stone', 'The Answer's At The End', 'This Guitar (Can't Keep From Crying)', 'Ooh Baby (You Know That I Love You)', 'A Bit More Of You' (continued from the Abbey Road February 1971 sessions), 'Can't Stop Thinking About You', 'Tired Of Midnight Blue', 'Grey Cloudy Lies' and 'His Name is Legs (Ladies And Gentlemen)'. (The recordings continue into June.)

Friday May 2

🍎 In London, at 3 Saville Row, the end of an era dawns when Apple's basement recording studios officially close down.

Monday May 5

🍎 An interview with Paul is transmitted on BBC Radio One.

Friday May 9 (until Sunday May 11)

🍎 As part of a succession of high-profile appearances, John travels to Philadelphia where, for three days and nights, he helps out for the second successive year on the *WFIL Helping Hand Radio Marathon*, an event to raise money for multiple sclerosis. John talks on the phone and even does a short stint reading the weather. He was invited to do the shows by the DJ Larry Kane, whom John met during The Beatles first visit to the States in February of 1964.

Friday May 16

🍎 The Wings single 'Listen To What The Man Said'/'Love In Song' is released in the UK. (The American release takes place on May 23.) This is the first release to include the MPL logo on its label.

Wednesday May 21

 In one of the very first "Beatles History" type show, the ABC TV programme *David Frost Salutes The Beatles* is transmitted in America. The 60-minute special tells the story of the group from 1962 through to the current day, using film clips (usually from ABC's own archive) and recent exclusive interviews with Beatle associates George Martin, Derek Taylor, Peter Brown and Mal Evans, in one of his very rare personal appearances. The Beatles' influence on contemporary musicians is featured in interviews with David Essex, Bobby Vinton, Chuck Berry and Andy Williams. The archive clips include 'Some Other Guy', from the Cavern in August 1962 and, receiving its first airing in a decade, The Beatles' January 1965 appearance on *Shindig!* Representing The Beatles as they are now, the show includes clips from the February 1, 1972 Wings rehearsal for 'Give Ireland Back To The Irish', Ringo in *That'll Be The Day* and John during his Malibu Beach *Eyewitness News* interview with Elliott Mintz during November, 1973.

Tuesday May 27

 The Wings album *Venus And Mars* is released in America. (The UK release takes place on May 30 where it will win 'Album Cover Of The Year' for 1975 from *Music Week* magazine.) This becomes the first Beatles-related album since 1968 not to feature the Apple logo. (See entry for June 26.)

Saturday May 31

 To promote *Venus And Mars, Melody Maker* publishes an interview with Wings carried out by Chris Welch at Paul's London offices in Soho, London. The piece is entitled: "McCartney: 'Abbey Road' Revisited".

Paul talks about recording the album: "I'd never been to New Orleans, except on tour when we never saw anything except the inside of a trailer. The only thing I remembered about New Orleans was the vibrator bed in the motel and it was sweating hot. So we went down to New Orleans in search of a musical town and the weather. Then we found out Mardi Gras was on while we were there. I'd written most of the stuff before we got there and Jimmy had written one of the tracks with a mate of his. We'd been in Jamaica before we went to New Orleans and for the first time ever, I'd got all the songs together like a scroll that went from here to the end of the room. So I had all that together and we just went and turned up and started recording. With this new album I did this scroll thing and sat down and put one song there, and another song here. Fiddle about. Fiddle about. The only time I've done this before was on the mini-opera on *Abbey Road*, the only time I've sat down with four sheets of paper and put them in order."

MM: "Does *Venus And Mars* have any astrological or astronomical significance?"

Paul: "It's really a total fluke. I was just sitting down and started to sing anything and some words came out. And I got this whole idea . . . well, the bit on the second side came first . . . and I got this idea about a fellow sitting in a cathedral waiting for this transport from space that was going to pick him up and take him on a trip. The guy is a bit blotto and he starts thinking about a 'good friend of mine studies the stars. Venus and Mars are all right tonight'. And the next bit was 'your ruling star is in ascendancy today', but 'Venus and Mars are all right' was better, it flipped off the tongue. I thought, well I know Venus and Mars are planets so I can't go wrong there. But afterwards somebody said to me, 'Did I know that Venus and Mars are our closest neighbours' and I said 'wow' . . . you live and learn. And then somebody told me, 'Venus and Mars have just eclipsed the sun', or something, I'm not exactly sure, you'll have to check up with Patrick Moore. But they did something and aligned themselves exactly for the first time in 2,000 years. I swear I had no idea about all this going on. It was just stuff that happened afterwards."

Paul talks about his plans for *Rupert The Bear*. "I've got a big plan to do Rupert. I've been saying this for years unfortunately, but I would like to get together a big *Bambi* if you like. A Disney style cartoon – which will be the first actual film score I've bothered to try and get into, and I'd really love to do that . . . I did a couple of the main themes in *The Family Way* (1966) and then handed them over to George Martin."

June

 John pops up again on the radio, this time being interviewed by the DJ Scott Muni. With his spate of promotional appearances concluded, he and Yoko move to a house on Long Beach for the summer.

 In England, at Abbey Road studios, Paul records the instrumental track 'Rudolph The

Red Nosed Reggae'. Meanwhile, following their holiday in the South of France, Paul, Linda and the family take up residence in a two-bedroom cottage called Waterfall near Rye in Sussex. The property, with over 160 acres of farmland, is purchased from Mr. Jim Huggs for £40,000. Their farmyard includes 11 horses and ponies, 10 sheep, 18 pheasants, ducks and hens, three dogs and an aviary of budgerigars. Also, unconfirmed reports in the music press reveal that Wings will be touring America at the end of the year and that Wings have been invited to appear at this year's Reading Festival in Berkshire, scheduled for the weekend of August 22-24. (The offer is ultimately rejected.)

Monday June 2
🍎 In the States, the Wings album *Venus And Mars* is awarded a gold disc by the RIAA.
🍎 Still in America, Ringo releases the medley single 'It's All Down To Goodnight Vienna' – 'Goodnight Vienna' (reprise)/'Oo-Wee'.

Monday June 9
🍎 George signs a second rock group to his Dark Horse label. They are called Jiva, a four-piece band that originate from America. Also today, BBC Radio One transmits the pre-recorded interview with George carried out by the DJ Paul Gambaccini for his programme *Rockweek*.

Thursday June 12
🍎 Tonight's edition of *Top Of The Pops* (broadcast on BBC1 between 7:10 and 7:40pm) features the popular all-female dance troupe Pan's People dancing to the Wings track 'Listen To What The Man Said'.

Friday June 13
🍎 John's pre-recorded appearance on the ATV/ITC television special *A Salute To Sir Lew Grade* is aired on American TV. (The UK transmission, featuring the alternative title of *Salute*, occurs across the ITV network on June 20, at different times throughout the evening. See entry for April 18.) One of John's three songs, 'Imagine', is later released in 1992 on the PMI home video *The John Lennon Video Collection*.

Saturday June 14
🍎 *Venus And Mars* tops the UK album charts. (It will reside in the charts for a total of 22 weeks.)

Thursday June 19
🍎 At the Federal Court in Manhattan, John files a suit against the former Nixon administration attorneys General John Mitchell, Richard Kleindienst and officials of the US Immigration and Naturalisation Service. The suit charges that John had been singled out for selective prosecution because of his political views and that he was not being deported, as previously stated by the US government, because of his 1968 drug conviction in England.

Saturday June 21
🍎 At Wembley Stadium in London, Ringo is to be found backstage in the VIP area at the concert by The Beach Boys and Elton John.

Thursday June 26
🍎 A 60-second TV commercial to promote the *Venus And Mars* album begins transmissions across the UK ITV network tonight and tomorrow. The piece, made by Karel Reisz at a private house in Holland Park, London last month, features the band playing a light-hearted game of snooker, accompanied by a soundtrack featuring excerpts of 'Venus And Mars', 'You Gave Me The Answer', 'Listen To What The Man Said', 'Treat Her Gently', 'Medicine Jar' and 'Venus And Mars' (reprise). Also this evening (in most ITV regions), Paul's version of the *Crossroads* theme appears for the first time closing tonight's edition of the soap opera. (It will subsequently run at the end of each edition for the next four years.) The star of the serial, Noelle Gordon, who plays Meg Richardson, the owner of the *Crossroads* motel, is asked about the introduction of Paul's music: "I am in favour of the switch," she replies. "After all, we're eleven years on and it's time for something a little more advanced."

Saturday June 28

- The Wings album *Venus and Mars* reaches number one in the UK.

July

- At his Dakota apartment, John shaves off all his hair, thereby becoming the first totally bald Beatle!
- Paul and Linda return to Nashville, this time purely for a holiday. They go to see the critically acclaimed film *Nashville* starring Lily Tomlin and Shelley Duvall, but find it not to their liking.
- Shooting begins on Robert Stigwood's *John, Paul, George, Ringo . . . And Bert* at several key locations in Liverpool and London. Shooting is eventually scrapped and filming will not resume until 1977 by which time it will have a completely new story and cast.

Friday July 4

- In the UK, Warner Brothers release the Mike McGear single 'Dance The Do', a song co-written by Paul (who also produces) and Mike. Promotions for the single involve the participation of the *Top Of The Pops* dance troupe Pan's People.

Saturday July 5

- A scheduled interview with Paul by Charles Shaar Murray, due for publication in the *NME* today, fails to materialise due to industrial action.

Monday July 7

- As a special surprise for Ringo's 35th birthday, Keith Moon arranges for a skywriter to write in the sky "Happy Birthday Ringo". Later, a birthday party is held at the Beverly Wiltshire Hotel in Los Angeles. Among those in attendance are The Rolling Stones.

Saturday July 12

- Ringo's 'Goodnight Vienna' reaches number 31 in the US singles chart.

Thursday July 17

- In London, a decree nisi, based on the grounds of adultery, is granted to Maureen Starkey against Ringo. He does not fight the action.

Saturday July 19

- The Wings single 'Listen To What The Man Said' and the album *Venus and Mars* both reach number one today in the American charts.

August

- George spends time in Los Angeles, where he sees shows by The Rolling Stones and Carlos Santana and socialises with Ringo.
- Also this month, Ringo, accompanied by his new companion Nancy Andrews, attends the first annual *Rock Music Awards* in Santa Monica, California.

Saturday August 16

- The musical *John, Paul, George, Ringo . . . And Bert* closes at the Lyric Theatre in London's Shaftesbury Avenue after running for a year.

Saturday August 23

- To preview the upcoming British tour by the new-look Wings, *Melody Maker* publish, on its front, a picture of Linda during the *Venus And Mars* recording session. "Linda McCartney," the report reads, "faces her sternest test this autumn when Wings start a major British tour, the opening part of a mammoth world-wide trek . . ."
- Meanwhile in Los Angeles at the Cherokee Studios, Ringo plays drums with Eric Clapton, joining him on guitar for a promotional appearance by Mac Rebennack (aka Dr. John). For the show, United Artists turn the studio into an imaginary night-spot, all to celebrate the fact he has just been signed to their label.

Monday August 25 (until August 29)

- During his time in Los Angeles, George drops in to play slide guitar on the Tom Scott track 'Appolonia (Fostrata)', which will appear on Scott's album *New York Connection*, which is released in America on December 8 and in the UK on April 2, 1976.

September

🍎 An interview with John, carried out by the reporter Penny Grant, is printed in the American magazine *Game*.

🍎 The legendary sax player Bobby Keys signs a long time contract to Ring O'Records. His first release is the single 'Gimme The Keys'/'Honky Tonk'.

🍎 George grants another interview to the DJ Paul Gambaccini for his BBC Radio One programme.

Friday September 5

🍎 The Wings single 'Letting Go'/'You Gave Me The Answer' is released in the UK where it will reach the number 41 position. (The American release takes place on September 29.) On the same day, the single 'Listen To What The Man Said' is awarded a gold disc by the RIAA in America.

Saturday September 6

🍎 At 7:45pm, prior to the start of the Wings 1975/1976 world tour, the group performs live on Stage 5 at the Elstree Film Studios in Hertfordshire for 1,200 EMI employees, tour associates, and 100 members of the Wings fan club, randomly chosen from those who live within the greater London area. Also present are 100 specially invited guests including Ringo (who arrived late from Los Angeles and missed chatting with Paul and Linda at the start of the concert), Victor Spinetti, Twiggy, Elton John, Harry Nilsson, the actor Richard Chamberlain, Dave Mason, Long John Baldry, all four members of the group Queen and even a real life Womble. Following their performance, the Wings troop across to Studio 8 at Elstree where Elton John's manager John Reid is having a birthday party. On the wall is a fifty-foot high tapestry design of Elton. The setting for the party is an old western town, which had been constructed earlier by the studio stagehands.

🍎 Meanwhile, "George Bounces Back!" George appears on the front page of *Melody Maker* to promote his latest album *Extra Texture (Read All About It)*. Inside, he breaks his long silence to talk exclusively to the paper about Bob Dylan, the sitar, the play *John, Paul, George, Ringo . . .. and Bert*, California, The Bay City Rollers, Bob Marley, his new album and, of course, The Beatles.

"I'd rather be an ex-Beatle than an ex-Nazi!" he exclaims.

"George Harrison went to see the celebrated play *John, Paul, George, Ringo . . . And Bert* in London last week. He left the theatre at the interval. He could not stand the pain of seeing himself and the Beatle years being re-enacted so uncannily, and he questioned the fundamental need for the show," the *Melody Maker* report states. "He had been persuaded to go by close friend Derek Taylor. 'George found it hard work to watch, and I found it hard work sitting with him. It was a genuine form of suffering for him.' It was hardly surprising that George didn't enjoy it – after all, he was hardly in love with The Beatles story while it was happening."

"In some ways I feel like I'm out of touch!" says George.

On Bob Marley, whom George has seen perform three times in Los Angeles at the Roxy Theatre: " . . . best thing I've seen in ten years. Marley reminds me so much of Dylan in the early days, playing guitar as if he's so new to it. And his rhythm is so simple yet so beautiful. I could watch The Wailers all night."

On the sitar: "I haven't played the sitar since 1968 or '69, and the funny thing is that I keep winning the *Playboy* polls for playing it . . . I'm still trying to master the guitar!"

MM: "Do you ever play Beatles albums, George?"

George: "No, I haven't played one for years."

MM: "How do you remember them when you look back?"

George: "Oh, I think The Beatles were, or are . . . very good. After all, we went through it all together and we were all very young when The Beatles happened. We've still got plenty in common even though we're different people – naturally, we're about ten years older!"

On Bob Dylan: " . . . he is still the most consistent artist there is. Even stuff which people loathe, I like . . . I've seen him quite a bit recently – he's the looniest person I've ever met."

" . . . To tell you the truth, I've still never heard The Bay City Rollers."

♦ Later this evening, BBC Radio One broadcast the programme *Rockweek*, where George discusses the *Extra Texture* album track by track.

Sunday September 7
♦ Paul and Linda pay a visit to the Hammersmith Odeon in London to see Dave Mason in concert. Following the show, they join the former Traffic guitarist backstage for a chat.

*   *   *

Wings World Tour 1975/1976
Part One - Britain and Australia
September 9 – November 14

Paul and Wings begin a thirteen-month tour of ten countries, beginning with Britain and Australia. Their repertoire, which will ultimately be played to over two million people, consists of the following: 'Venus And Mars', 'Rock Show', 'Jet', 'Let Me Roll It', 'Spirits Of Ancient Egypt', 'Little Woman Love', 'C Moon', 'Maybe I'm Amazed', 'Lady Madonna', 'The Long And Winding Road', 'Live And Let Die', 'Picasso's Last Words', 'Richard Cory', 'Bluebird', 'I've Just Seen A Face', 'Blackbird', 'Yesterday' (the last two featuring Paul solo on acoustic guitar), 'You Gave Me The Answer', 'Magneto And Titanium Man', 'Go Now', 'Call Me Back Again', 'My Love', 'Listen To What The Man Said', 'Letting Go', 'Medicine Jar', 'Junior's Farm' and 'Band On The Run'. The encores are 'Hi Hi Hi' and 'Soily'.

The UK dates kick off with shows at:

Southampton Gaumont (Tuesday September 9)
Bristol Hippodrome (Wednesday September 10)
Cardiff Capitol (Thursday September 11)
Manchester Free Trade Hall (Friday September 12)
Birmingham Hippodrome (Saturday September 13)
Liverpool Empire (Monday September 15)
Newcastle City Hall (Tuesday September 16)
Hammersmith Odeon (Wednesday September 17 and Thursday 18)
Edinburgh Usher Hall (Saturday September 20)
Glasgow Apollo (Sunday September 21)
Aberdeen Capitol (Monday September 22)
Dundee Caird Hall (Tuesday September 23)

Prior to the start of the tour, Paul and Wings briefly record at Abbey Road. Meanwhile, footage of Paul, Linda and Wings departing from their home in London on Monday September 8 to start their tour is filmed and included at the start of the 'Letting Go' promotional film. Accompanying Wings on their trip is a special tutor for Paul and Linda's children, Mary and Heather. Ticket prices for the Wings' provisional concerts cost between £1 and £2.50, while for the London dates, tickets cost between £1 and £2.80. Every night, for the benefit of the group's entourage, Paul lays on a film show, which usually includes the 1972 Woody Allen film, *Play It Again, Sam,* Mel Brooke's *Blazing Saddles* and *French Connection 11.*

The concerts at Elstree (September 6), Liverpool (September 15), Newcastle (September 16) and Glasgow (September 21) are all filmed for Paul by the London based Production Company Tyncho Films. To date, only clips of 'Venus And Mars', 'Rock Show' and 'Letting Go' from the Glasgow Apollo show have seen the light of day.

Thursday September 11
The morning after the concert at the Hippodrome in Bristol, Wings give a press conference at the Post House hotel, situated just outside the town. Paul is asked: "Just what keeps you going?"
"Drugs" he jokingly replies. "No. I just like the music."
Reporter: "Have you seen The Beatles lately?"
Paul: "We run into each other and stuff – we're just good friends."
Reporter: "Is Wings really a logical development from The Beatles?"
Paul: "Well, I've always written songs, but with The Beatles we only ever rehearsed for three days at the most. With this band we rehearse a lot."

Reporter: "Are you looking forward to playing in Cardiff?" (The show scheduled for tonight.)

Paul: "Of course."

Reporter: "Why did you decide to go back on the road?"

Paul: "Well, either we sit at home and do it, or we play in front of people. Now it's a pleasure to do it and we want to keep on working."

Reporter: "Will Wings ever become as big as The Beatles?"

Paul: "I think it could be, funnily enough. The whole thing is bigger now. We're having a great time – we like to play music and people like to come and hear it."

Reporter: "How different is Wings from The Beatles?"

Paul: "They scream at our concerts, but they don't scream as much. People used to come and scream and didn't hear any of the music. Now they can."

Reporter: "Do you want to bring back The Beatles?"

Paul: "It wasn't within my power to bring back The Beatles. It was a four way split and we all wanted to do different things. We're all very good friends. John is keeping very quiet at the moment, while unfortunately I'm out working . . . I like it."

Before departing for Cardiff, Paul and Linda give interviews to news crews from BBC TV and Harlech ITV. As the entourage head off up the motorway, a camera team zooms up alongside Paul and Linda's car, filming the couple in the back of their black Rolls Royce.

Monday September 15

During tonight's concert at the Liverpool Empire, the song 'Soily' is temporarily forgotten by the band and has to be inserted into their encore, where it will stay for the remainder of the tour.

Wednesday September 17 & Thursday September 18

♣ To promote the two Hammersmith Odeon concerts, Paul commissions a special 30-second television commercial which is screened across the South East areas (Thames and Southern) of the ITV network only days before the shows are scheduled to take place. The irony is that the adverts are selling a concert that have long since been a sell-out. During Wings' second concert at the Hammersmith Odeon in London (September 18), a fan shouts from the audience: "What about John Lennon?" Paul quickly replies: "What about him?"

Following the show, Paul throws a party, which is attended by Ringo, Alice Cooper, Harry Nilsson, Lynsey De Paul, David Frost and various members of Pink Floyd and Queen.

Friday September 19

A pre-recorded interview with Paul on the tour is transmitted on Capital Radio in London.

Saturday September 20

Linda remarks: "They'll keep asking about The Beatles forever . . . all four of them get so bored with it."

With Wings in the middle of their UK tour and about to prepare to take to the road in Australia, *Melody Maker* publishes the first of a two-part report on the group by Chris Welch. (The second part, which features an interview with Linda, is printed on September 27.)

Sunday September 21

For their encore tonight at the Glasgow Apollo, the group reappears on stage wearing kilts.

Saturday September 27

Melody Maker publishes the second part of its two-part feature on Wings, focusing entirely on Linda. She discusses her love for British football. "I love it. Manchester United – and Everton. Everton were good last year. I love watching *Match Of The Day*. I've always loved sports and football is the game to watch on a Saturday night on telly, y'know."

She is asked if she ever saw herself becoming a musician? "Not even when I married Paul I didn't. It never entered my mind. If he hadn't said anything I wouldn't have done it.

It was his idea – it wasn't like me saying, 'Listen I can do this . . .' I never tried to sing or play or anything."

Chris Welch points out that she seems very relaxed and competent on this tour: "I never was on any of the other tours. But I think that's 'cos I like it now and know a few chords. Last night a few things kept going out of tune, like the Moog bit on 'Band On The Run' and the Mellotron went out a bit – that sort of thing. It happened on 'Live And Let Die'. During rehearsals I used to get really really nervous when a solo bit came up because it all depended on me, but it's funny in front of an audience, I feel more relaxed."

Wednesday September 17

Chris Charlesworth, in his *Melody Maker* review of Wings' opening night concert at the Hammersmith Odeon in London, concludes by writing, "An excellent concert, and one which must surely go to America soon. After George Harrison's dismal tour in the States last year, Paul will reawaken Beatlemania should he choose to take Wings across the Atlantic."

October

Meanwhile in Australia, one month before the Wings concerts at the Melbourne Myer's Music Bowl are scheduled to take place, tickets for the two shows on November 13 and 14 go on sale in the city at the Tivoli Arcade. Approximately 1,500 fans queue through the night and endure thunder, lightning and heavy rain in order to get the best seats for the shows. The box office finally opens at 8am, and within two hours 2,000 seated tickets, priced at $10, are sold and by noon 11,000 lawn seats, priced at $6.80, are sold to fans.

Following Paul and Linda's two-week holiday, Wings, and half of their entourage, arrive in Perth on Tuesday October 28. Even though an official press conference had been arranged for the following Sunday (November 2), Paul still finds time to speak to a small cluster of reporters who are standing on the tarmac to greet him. The Australian leg of the Wings World Tour, before crowds totalling 60,000, goes as follows:

Perth Entertainment Centre (Saturday November 1)
Adelaide Apollo Stadium (Tuesday November 4 and Wednesday November 5)
Sydney Horden Pavilion (Friday November 7 and Saturday November 8)
Brisbane Festival Hall (Monday November 10 and Tuesday November 11)
Melbourne Myers Music Bowl (Thursday November 13 and Friday November 14)

During the tour . . .

Saturday October 25

'Letting Go' reaches number 41 in the UK and number 39 in the US singles charts.

Monday October 27

The start of the Australian leg of the world tour begins shakily when Paul, Linda and their family oversleep, forcing the passengers already seated on the Qantas Jumbo jet to Australia to wait for 45 minutes while the McCartneys rush to London's Heathrow airport. Paul's fine works out at $200 a minute.

Wednesday October 29

Following a lengthy Wings rehearsal in Perth, Denny is presented with a huge cake to celebrate his 31st birthday. Later in the day, the group travel to Rottnest Island and return to their base by hydrofoil.

Saturday November 1

A 12-minute interview with Wings, carried out backstage this afternoon at the Entertainment Centre in Perth, is transmitted later this evening on the Channel 7 programme *The Mike Walsh Show*. Tonight's Wings concert at the Entertainment Centre is recorded by the Australian radio station 3XY and transmitted the following evening.

Sunday November 2

Still in Perth, Wings give a press conference in front of over 200 reporters and photographers, one of which is with the top Australian comedian Norman Gunston, who flies in especially to interview Paul and Linda for his Channel 9 programme, *The Norman*

Gunston Show. Chaos ensues as Wings arrive. In the room, primarily to greet the Australian press and to receive some gold records acknowledging vast record sales in the country, the group find Gunston asleep in their chairs. Amid the scenes of pure chaos, Gunston (real name Garry McDonald) first asks Linda:

"It must be difficult, Mrs. McCartney, being married all day, you know the two of you, and then at night having to perform together on stage."

Linda: "We're about to have a fight on stage one night."

Gunston: "Do you ever feel like sometimes saying, 'Not tonight, thanks darling. I've got a headache?' They'd slow hand clap you if you did."

After a break to allow the laughter from around the room to die down, Gunston continues: "Would you coax one of your children to go into the 'overnight sensation' world of the music industry?"

Paul: "Well, if they wanted to, Norman, I'd let them."

Gunston: "I suppose anyway, if they didn't do too good they could always open up a sandwich shop using your name, you know, something like *Paul McCartney's Son's Take Away Foods* . . . except that fruit shop of yours didn't do too good in London did it?"

Paul (rather bemused, asks inquisitively): "The McCartney fruit shop? (Then, with the joke suddenly dawning on him) . . . Apple! . . . oh Apple!"

Gunston: "That didn't do too good!"

Paul: "Give that man a drink."

Gunston: "Was that one of John's ideas?"

Paul: "It was, Norm, yes."

Gunston: "There are two sides to every story, but I've heard the other Beatles used to get a bit annoyed because Mrs. McCartney used to invite them over for long boring slide evenings all the time . . ." (He pauses again while another round of laughter fills the small room.)

Gunston: "When you did that LP *Abbey Road*, was there any truth in the rumour that you were dead?"

Denny Laine: "He's not really here." Paul refuses to comment.

Gunston: "Did you have any Beatlemania Mrs. McCartney?"

Linda: "Constantly."

Gunston: "Which one was your favourite, before you was related?"

Linda: "Er . . . Mick Jagger!"

Gunston (whispering towards his television camera): "I think she got him (Paul) on the rebound!" Then returning to his questions directed at the couple: "Er . . . the marriage is OK? The marriage is OK?" (He asks desperately.)

Paul: "It's all right, but you're not helping it, Norm!"

Gunston: "It's funny, you know (looking towards Linda), you don't look Japanese!"
(A 1' 28" excerpt from this press conference reappears in the 1979 MPL documentary *Wings Over The World*.)

Tuesday November 11

Bad news reaches Paul when the Japanese government ban him and Linda from entering Japan for a series of concerts. They cite the British drug conviction of March 8, 1973. Paul remembers the problem: "It was the Minister of Justice's fault. I suppose he'd say it was my fault for having smoked some of the deadly weed. But we had our visas signed by the London Embassy. Everything had been cleared and David Bailey was coming over to do a film. We were in Australia, just about a week from going to Japan when a little note arrived saying the Japanese Minister of Justice says 'No' . . . It was just one of those things but we felt a bit sick about it. They're still old fashioned over there. There's a generation gap and the wrong end of the gap is in the Ministry of Justice, as it is here."

Thursday November 13

Wings arrive at Melbourne's Myers Music Bowl for an afternoon rehearsal where Paul and Linda's arrival is covered by Channel 9 news. Due to the incredible demand for tickets in Australia, this evening's concert at the Bowl in Melbourne is taped for an Australian TV special. Paul dedicates the show to "all the people who couldn't get in to see us".

For the transmission, the show includes the following songs: 'Venus And Mars', 'Rock Show', 'Jet', 'Let Me Roll It', 'Maybe I'm Amazed', 'I've Just Seen A Face', 'Blackbird', 'Yesterday', 'Listen To What The Man Said', 'Call Me Back Again', 'Letting Go', 'Band On The Run' and 'Hi Hi Hi' (for the encore).

Aware now that he cannot enter Japan, Paul requests a copy of the Melbourne television show be sent to the country to compensate disappointed fans. (Paul also videotapes a special 30-second message of apology to be shown on Japan's NHKTV channel.) To accompany the Wings live broadcast on Japanese TV, a programme is tagged onto the show which discusses the merits and demerits of marijuana. Wings return home early to England on November 15. With extra time on their hands, Paul, Linda and their family then take a vacation in Hawaii.

* * *

Friday September 12
 George's single 'You'/'World Of Stone' is released in the UK. (The American release takes place on September 15.) In the UK on BBC Radio One, the single becomes the *David Hamilton Record Of The Week* for the period Monday September 8 to Friday September 12. This evening, George makes a somewhat late live appearance on Nicky Horne's Capital Radio show *Your Mother Wouldn't Like It* (broadcast between 9:00 and 11:00pm, with George scheduled to appear at approximately 9:30). Horne covers the countdown to George's arrival at the Capital studios in London as the former Beatle battles his way through the heavy traffic. Shortly after this show, George will return to Los Angeles.

Saturday September 13
 In England, the UK music newspaper *Record Mirror & Disc* publishes an interview with Paul.

Wednesday September 17
 From his LA home, by way of a promotion for the new album *Extra Texture (Read All About It)*, George is interviewed by the US DJ Dave Herman.

Monday September 22
"Ohnothimagen".
 George's album *Extra Texture (Read All About It)* is released in America. (The UK release takes place on October 3.)

Tuesday September 23
 In Washington, the American Justice department delays a deportation order against John. Mr. Oswald Kramer, the acting commissioner for the Immigration and Naturalisation Service in the north eastern States, says: "Mr Lennon is entitled to a delay on humanitarian grounds because of his wife's pregnancy."

Friday September 26
 In the UK, Island Records release the Peter Skellern album *Hard Times*, which features George playing guitar on the track 'Make Love Not War'.

Saturday September 27
 In South Africa, at Ellis Park in Johannesburg, Ringo takes part in an all-star celebrity tennis tournament.

October
 In Los Angeles, following his recent visit to South Africa, Ringo attends the opening night concert performance by Dr. John at the Roxy club.

Saturday October 4
 Melody Maker publish: "Just An Ordinary Superstar – Fresh from a highly successful Wings tour, Paul McCartney talks to Chris Welch."
 " . . . It occurred to me the other day I can now afford to sit down and see what everyone else has been doing all these years instead of doing it myself. We came back with Wings and proved we could still play. 'He's proved he can still sing, pull an audience and sell out – what more do you want? So he's proved that – now good night!' "

On George seeming to be the most anti-press: "Oh no he isn't. George is so straight. He's so straight and so ordinary and so real. And he happens to believe in God. That's what's wrong with George, to most people's minds. He happens to believe in God, y'know which is a terrible crime and that's so mad. There's nothing freaky about George at all. Some people think he's freaky because he's grown a beard . . . all George is – he's a grown-up teenager, and he refuses to give in to the grown-up world. He won't do it – just because everyone says: 'You're a freak, you're a recluse.' "

On John: "John's supposed to be a loony according to some people and I know he isn't. If you ask me, The Beatles are very sane but they're cheeky with it. With The Beatles our great 'in-joke' was always that whenever we split up we'd do a Wembley concert and John was gonna do this big thing like: 'Fuck the Queen!' We were really going to blow it. It was a beautiful dream."

Why didn't you do it? "You're joking, aren't you? Up on the roof at Apple was probably the last time we played together. I can't remember. I'm not a great Beatle-ologist. The Sixties for me are a blur. Sixty-three is the same as sixty-seven. It was all one big time. I read the Hunter Davies book and bits of the Allan Williams book too, which John gave me a copy of the last time I saw him. That's a laugh that one. I mean blimey, that's slightly exaggerated to put it mildly. *The Man Who Gave The Beatles Away*, eh? My brother was thinking of writing one called *The Man Who Couldn't Give The Beatles Away*."

Sunday October 5
🍎 With Wings now most definitely a force to be reckoned with, BBC Radio One finally dedicate a whole show to the group. The show, transmitted today between 5:00 and 5:59pm as part of the *Insight* documentary series, is titled *Wings – The Birth Of A Band*, and features Paul discussing the current Wings tour, their music and their plans for the future with Paul Gambaccini.

Monday October 6
🍎 In America, Dark Horse Records release the Splinter album *Harder To Live*, featuring production by George and Tom Scott. The record also features the Mal Evans track 'Lonely Man', which appeared in the Apple film *Little Malcolm And His Struggle Against The Eunuchs*.

🍎 In England, the hit musical *John, Paul, George, Ringo . . . And Bert*, starts a tour of the provinces featuring a different cast to that of its year long London run. Tonight the musical play opens at the Ashcroft Theatre in Croydon, with its tour ending at the Rex in Wilmslow on December 20.

Tuesday October 7
🍎 John wins a further victory in his three-and-a-half-year battle to remain in America, when a three-judge US court of appeal in New York City overturns (by a two to one decision) the order to deport him. The court ruling states that John's 1968 UK drug conviction was contrary to the US understanding of due process of law and therefore did not justify deportation. The ruling notes that: "Lennon's four-year battle to remain in our country is a testimony to his faith in the American dream." The court orders the Immigration and Naturalisation Service to reconsider John's request for permanent resident status and rules that his 1968 drug conviction in England did not make him an "excludable alien".

Thursday October 9
🍎 Two days after winning another significant point in his fight to remain in America, John becomes a father for the second time, when Yoko, through caesarean section, gives birth to their son, Sean Taro Ono Lennon at the New York hospital. He weighs in at 8 pounds 10 ounces. John is quoted as saying: "I feel higher than the Empire State Building!" Elton John becomes the child's godfather.

Friday October 10
🍎 The Warner Brothers film *Lizstomania,* featuring a cameo by Ringo in the role of the Pope, premieres in New York. It will open in London on November 13, and becomes the top grossing film of the week, beating strong competition from Walt Disney's *Jungle Book* and a re-issue of the classic *Gone With The Wind. Lisztomania* takes in £13,240.

Friday October 24
 John's compilation album *Shaved Fish* is released simultaneously in the UK and the US. The album features the following tracks: side one: 'Give Peace A Chance', 'Cold Turkey', 'Instant Karma', 'Mother', 'Woman Is The Nigger Of The World'; side two: 'Imagine', 'Whatever Gets You Through The Night', 'Mind Games', 'No. 9 Dream', 'Happy Christmas (War Is Over)', 'Give Peace A Chance'. (Note: The first and last track, 'Give Peace A Chance', are short extracts from the August 30, 1972 One To One Concert performance at New York's Madison Square Garden.) Also today in the UK, John's single 'Imagine'/'Working Class Hero' is released for the first time.

Monday October 27
 The Wings single 'Venus And Mars', 'Rock Show'/'Magneto And Titanium Man' is released in the US. (The UK release is on November 28.)

Saturday November 1
 George's 'You' reaches number 38 in the UK and number 20 in the US singles charts.

Friday November 7
 In the UK, Atlantic Records release the Steve Stills album *2 Originals Of Steve Stills (1 & 2)*, featuring Ringo drumming on the tracks 'To A Flame' and 'We Are Not Helpless'.

Tuesday November 11
 George's album *Extra Texture* receives a gold disc from the RIAA, representing the high record sales in America.

Friday November 14
 In the UK, Charisma Records release the George Harrison produced Monty Python single 'The Lumberjack Song'.

Sunday November 16
 Ringo's film *That'll Be The Day* is reissued to London cinemas, playing as a support to its follow-up movie *Stardust,* also starring David Essex. The double-bill goes on general release the following day.

Thursday November 20
 In Los Angeles, Judge Brian Cahan dismisses marijuana charges against Linda after she completes a psychiatric and drugs counselling course in London.

Saturday November 22
 In the UK charts, John's *Shaved Fish* reaches number eight while the single 'Imagine' hits number six.

Monday November 24
 The pre-fab four, The Rutles, enter our story when today, at Denham's Memorial Hall in Buckinghamshire, rented for a fee of £6.75, the group is filmed performing the Neil Innes song 'I Must Be Love' for inclusion in the BBC2 comedy series *Rutland Weekend Television*. (Innes, of course, was a member of the sixties comical-musical act The Bonzo Dog Doo Dah Band, who recorded 'I'm The Urban Spaceman', which was produced by Paul, using the alias of Apollo C. Vermouth.) The three-minute item features the group miming the song, inter-cut with scenes filmed in the style of 'Can't Buy Me Love' as it appeared in *A Hard Day's Night*. Although intended for the *Rutland Weekend Television* series, the clip actually first appears in America where it is transmitted on WNBC (between 11:30pm and 1:00am) during NBC TV's *Saturday Night Live* on October 2, 1976 (see entry). The first UK TV airing of the clip takes place, as intended, during the first show of the second series of *Rutland Weekend Television,* which is transmitted (between 9:01 and 9:29pm) on November 12, 1976. Incidentally, at this stage, the line-up for The Rutles is Dirk, Stig, Nasty and Kevin, with Eric Idle in the role of the George character. (Idle, of course, moves to the Paul role, Dirk McQuickly, in the full-length 1978 TV version of *The Rutles*.) George will also appear personally on *Rutland Weekend Television* (see entry for December 13).

Tuesday November 25
 Ringo's compilation album *Blast From Your Past* is issued in America. (The UK release, with a Red Apple label, takes place on December 12. This is the last original album to appear on the Apple label in Britain.) The tracks include on side one: 'You're Sixteen', 'No No Song', 'It Don't Come Easy', 'Photograph', 'Back Off Boogaloo'; side two: 'Only You (And You Alone)', 'Beaucoups Of Blues', 'Oh My My', 'Early 1970' and 'I'm The Greatest'.

December
 During the first part of the month, Paul and Linda are seen briefly in Los Angeles, between flights from Hawaii to New York, where they also visit the Starwood Club to check out the latest rock & roll talent. On returning home to England at Christmas, Paul spends time recording in his Scottish studios the unreleased songs 'Thank You Darling', 'When I Was In Paris' and 'The Great Cock And Seagull Race'.
 ABC Records in America is set to conclude a $5,000,000 recording deal with Ringo which will tie him to their label for five years. At this point, for tax purposes, Ringo officially moves to Monte Carlo, to live with his girlfriend Nancy Andrews, although he returns to England to spend Christmas at his Tittenhurst Park mansion in Ascot in Berkshire.

Monday December 8
 George's single 'This Guitar (Can't Keep From Crying)'/'Maya Love' is released in America today. (The UK release takes place on February 6, 1976.)

Thursday December 11
 The photographer Bob Gruen is invited to the Dakota apartment by John and Yoko to take Sean's first official baby snaps. For the occasion, John, Yoko and Sean dress up in Japanese kimonos and John ties his long hair into a ponytail.

Saturday December 13
 Today, at the BBC Television Centre in Wood Lane, London, George, as pirate "Bob", records a special Boxing Day edition of *Rutland Weekend Television*, featuring his exclusive performance of the Harrison/Eric Idle composition 'The Pirate Song' which appears at the very end of the show with the credits running over the top. George also makes further cameo appearances in the 31-minute programme, including one where he is dressed as a pirate. The show, which also features such comic delights as *How To Ski In Your Own Home* and the Christmas play entitled *Santa Doesn't Live Here Anymore*, is broadcast for the first time on BBC2 on December 26 between 10:55 and 11:26pm. (*Rutland Weekend Television*, besides being the show that first introduced The Rutles to the nation, is a comedy series centred around a small TV station in Rutland and was created by Eric Idle, one of the brains behind The Rutles and a founder member of the Monty Python comedy team.)
 The Wings single 'Venus And Mars' – 'Rock Show' reaches number 12 in the American singles chart, but fails to crack the UK charts, Paul's first ever chart miss.

Sunday December 14
 Shortly after his return from the tax haven of Monte Carlo, Ringo is present in the audience at Queen's concert tonight at the Hammersmith Odeon in London.

Thursday December 18
 At the Odeon Theatre in London, Ringo, joined by the singer Lynsey De Paul, keeps up his high profile by attending the Royal European Film Premiere, in the presence of Princess Anne, of *The Man Who Would Be King*, starring Michael Caine and Sean Connery.

Christmas Week
 John, Yoko and Bob Gruen are enjoying a quiet drink at the Dakota Building when they hear a loud knock on the door, followed by carol singing. Bob opens the door to discover that the carol singers are none other than Paul and Linda, currently in New York to visit Linda's family. The Lennons and McCartneys, together with Gruen, spend the next few hours relaxing together.

Thursday December 25 & Friday December 26
 The Beacon Theater in New York presents a two-night film presentation entitled *Celebration Of The Beatles*, featuring archive newsreels, live clips and excerpts from BBC TV and US TV specials. There are different clips on both nights, repeating the successful *Beatles Festival* that took place in New York last year. Meanwhile on Boxing Day back in the UK, The Beatles' 1970 film *Let It Be* receives its British TV premiere on BBC1 between 10:55 and 12:13pm. This is the last of six successive years of BBC1 Christmas screenings of Beatles' movies, although *"The Beatles At Christmas"* theme will be resurrected in some style for Christmas 1979. (See entry for December 21 of that year.)

Saturday December 27
 The year ends with good news for John when his attorney Leon Wildes tells *Melody Maker*: "As far as the case is concerned, we are just about through. In two or three months I estimate the whole thing will be over and John will be free to remain in the US and travel abroad."

Monday December 29
 Michael Abdul Malik, better known as Michael X, is executed by hanging in Trinidad for the murder of Joseph Skerritt. John and Yoko had, for some years, worked for a reversal of his conviction to prevent his execution.

Wednesday December 31
 In its annual report for the year, Apple Corps Ltd reveals a turnover of £2,540,979 which, after tax and expenditure, results in a profit of £261,075.

December (into early 1976)
 In his Dakota apartment, John records a number of acoustic home demos, one of which is 'Mucho Mungo', the track he wrote for Harry Nilsson in 1974.

"Beatles reunion? The only way we could come together would be if we wanted to do something musically, not lukewarm just to get the money. I'm not going to be blackmailed into going. It would ruin the whole Beatles thing for me."

– Paul

January
◉ At the second of Bonhams musical instruments sales in London, John's 1958 Epiphone guitar, as used on the original 1962 Abbey Road recording of 'Please Please Me', is sold to *The Sun* newspaper for £280, who bought it to offer in a competition. The story goes that, following the session, John handed the guitar to the songwriter Al Stewart who, after playing it for years, then gave it to a Mr. Bridges who subsequently put it into the auction. Mystery soon surrounds the guitar, questioning whether or not John had actually owned it. When asked about the guitar, Stewart denies ever being given a guitar by John and ever knowing a Mr. Bridges.

Thursday January 1
◉ At his Dakota apartment, John gives a 60-minute *Earth Day Interview* to Elliott Mintz and records a home demo tape featuring a performance of 'As Time Goes By'. Later in the day, Bob Gruen is invited to the apartment to take more pictures of the family, one of which is a picture of John which will later appear on his infamous "green card". (See entry for July 27.)

Sunday January 4
◉ At his Los Angeles motel apartment at 8122 West 4th Street, Mal Evans, The Beatles' long time friend and roadie, is shot and killed with a 30.30 rifle fired by Lieutenant Charles Higbie, of the LAPD robbery and homicide division. In a drunken stupor, Mal had become uncontrollably violent, appeared to be attempting suicide and pointed a loaded rifle at the policeman who, in self-defence, then shot him six times, four bullets hitting Mal. He was living with his new girlfriend Fran Hughes, having recently separated from his wife Lili Evans, who had reportedly asked him for a divorce just before Christmas. Mal was working on a book about his time with The Beatles, entitled *Living With The Beatles Legend*, which was scheduled to be delivered to the American publishers, Grosset & Dunlap, on January 12. He was just 40 years of age. When John is told of his death, he breaks down in tears.

Wednesday January 7
◉ The body of Mal Evans is cremated in Los Angeles. The urn carrying his ashes back to England gets lost in the post and is subsequently recovered in a lost letter office.

Friday January 9
◉ Ringo's single 'Oh My My'/'No No Song' is released in the UK.

Saturday January 17
◉ Ringo's greatest hits album *Blast From Your Past* reaches number 30 in the US charts.

Friday January 23
◉ In New York, Judge Thomas Grisea declares a mistrial in the Morris Levy publishing rights case against John when a lawyer shows the jury a copy of the 1968 *Two Virgins* sleeve. The judge calls this "purely prejudicial" and demands that the case continue without a jury. (See entry for February 20.)

Saturday January 24
◉ John and Yoko are seen in public, for the first time since Sean's birth, at Ashley's Club in New York. They are seen chatting with Mick Jagger and guitarist Jesse Ed Davis.

Sunday January 25
◉ Ringo makes a surprise guest appearance with Bob Dylan and The Band at an all-star benefit concert called *Night Of The Hurricane's II*, arranged for the convicted murderer and ex-boxer Rubin "Hurricane" Carter at Houston's Astrodome in Texas.

Monday January 26
◉ The Beatles' nine-year contract with EMI expires. While Paul will re-sign with the company, Ringo signs with Atlantic in America and Polydor elsewhere while John does not sign any new contract, electing to remain a free agent. George, now also a free agent, heads for Cannes in France, and the annual Midem music trade fair, where he announces that his next album will be on his own Dark Horse label. He wastes no time in signing to the label, doing so on Tuesday January 27. A&M will continue to distribute the label

throughout the world. George reveals that his next album will be released in late spring and tells *Melody Maker*: "I'd like someone to produce me, either that or a co-producer or just a friend working with me. I've found there's no way that you can judge your own work. It's always useful to have a friend around. Maybe I should get Ry Cooder to produce me. I've always liked his work. But the nearest I've got to him was waving to him when we were watching Bob Marley and The Wailers." George goes on to say that he would like to play in Britain this year, although he wants to avoid difficulties in a big tour operation. "England makes me guilty," he remarks. "I even got a postcard from someone saying how much they enjoyed *Extra Texture* but why don't I play in England. I'd really like to play. It's just a question of how I'd do it."

⬥ During his stay in Cannes, George takes up residence in a suite at the Carlton Hotel, where he plays host to an avalanche of reporters all keen to know more about his signing to Dark Horse. Away from business, he seldom leaves the building.

January (through into February)

⬥ Wings return to the Abbey Road recording studios in London where they begin recording tracks intended for the album *Wings At The Speed Of Sound*. The sessions produce the following tracks: 'Let 'Em In', 'The Note You Never Wrote', 'She's My Baby', 'Beware My Love', 'Silly Love Songs', 'Cook Of The House', 'Must Do Something About It', 'San Ferry Anne', 'Warm And Beautiful', 'Time To Hide' and 'Wino Junko'. When asked about the recordings, Wings' manager Brian Brolly excitedly claims that: "The new album will be better than *Venus And Mars*."

February

⬥ At the start of the month, Bill Sargent, a Los Angeles pop promoter, offers The Beatles a guaranteed $50 million to perform one reunion concert, which will be televised on closed circuit television throughout the world. His basic plans are laid out as follows:

1. All four Beatles will perform live at any location of their choice, anywhere in the world, and that they may perform individually but they *must* play together for a minimum of at least 20 minutes.

2. Bill Sargent will retain all rights and all interests in the show in all media in perpetuity.

He estimates that the cost of putting on the concert will be about $68,000,000 but, by charging $50 a seat at all cinemas showing the closed circuit broadcast, he believes he can gross approximately $150,000,000 in one single night. First reports suggest that The Beatles are keen on the idea, although there are complications that stand in their way. Sargent reveals that he has met with lawyer David Braun, who represents George, and that John is "keen on the idea", having suggested a reunion some weeks before the news of Sargent's offer broke.

⬥ Ringo, meanwhile, is noncommittal; instead he is still seen partying throughout the month in Los Angeles. This month, alongside Alice Cooper, Carly Simon, Rod Stewart, Flo & Eddie and members of the Electric Light Orchestra. He also attends the David Bowie reception at the Forum Club.

⬥ Beatles hysteria continues to sweep the States when the group is honoured at the Santa Monica Civic Auditorium in Los Angeles. The film show, arranged by the production company Moonstar Euphoria, contains freshly printed copies of the group's promotional films and performances in Washington from February 1964 and Tokyo from July 1966. The frenzy gets so far out of hand that, according to American showbiz reporters, "every time Paul McCartney is shown on the screen, hysteria breaks out in the audience." This leads other American media commentators to write: "There is no doubt that when McCartney tours the US, he will eclipse all existing attendance marks, especially in LA, where he could sell out for two weeks . . ."

⬥ In England, EMI International makes available on import the following American Beatles Capitol albums: *Magical Mystery Tour, The Beatles Beat, Beatles Greatest, Something New, Beatles VI, Beatles '65, Help!* (soundtrack album), *The Beatles Second Album, Yesterday . . . And Today* and *The Beatles Story*. Prices range from £2.99 to £3.40.

Wednesday February 4

⬥ At the Southport Arts Centre in England, over 300 Beatle fans cram in to watch the programme *The Man Who Gave The Beatles Away*, featuring a nostalgic talk by The Beatles' one-time manager Allan Williams. The evening's entertainment also features screenings of the 1963 BBC TV documentary *The Mersey Sound* and the Pathe Newsreel

The Beatles Come To Town, also from 1963. In addition, fans are treated to a public relations film made for Liverpool council entitled *And The World Listened*, various original Merseybeat footage including The Spinners, The Searchers and a live concert performance of Beatles numbers by brothers Pete and Mick Rimmer. The highlight of the evening is a rare public airing of the legendary 1962 tapes of The Beatles live at the Star Club in Hamburg, Germany.

Saturday February 7 & Sunday February 8
🍎 Amid waves of hysteria concerning the possible Beatles reunion concert, a two-day *Beatlefest* convention takes place this weekend in Philadelphia.

Friday February 20
🍎 In New York, John's case against Morris Levy concludes with the judge ruling in favour of the former Beatle, and awards him the sum of $144,700 in damages.

March
🍎 In America, the show business magazine *Variety* claims that in the summer: "John Lennon, George Harrison and Ringo Starr will team up with Harry Nilsson and Klaus Voorman for concerts," adding: "Paul McCartney is still expected to tour the States with Wings . . . but no firm dates have yet been released."
🍎 Towards the end of the month, George arrives in the States to begin arrangements to record his next album.
🍎 Ringo visits Hamburg in Germany, where he shoots an interview with Horst Konigstein for the 1977 film *Ringo Und Die Stadt Am Ende Des Regenbogens*, which tells the story of Ringo's career to date.
🍎 Meanwhile, all is not well with Allen Klein's ABKCO company, when accounts reveal that they have showed a loss of $140,679 during the first quarter of 1976.
🍎 In England, Willy Russell's hit musical play *John, Paul, George, Ringo . . . And Bert* is set to go out on its second national tour next month. Due to its success, the singer Barbara Dickson is now a household name in the UK. The tour, featuring Joy Askew in Dickson's role, will open in Birmingham on March 1 and will run until April 24 with a show at the Wimbledon Theatre.

Friday March 5
🍎 The Beatles' entire 22 singles, released in the UK between 1962 and 1970, are reissued by EMI. In addition, the company releases the Parlophone single 'Yesterday' coupled with the 1964 recording of 'I Should Have Known Better'. Although the company has never deleted the singles, few record shops carry a complete stock. An EMI spokesman talked about the reasons behind the reissues. "We continually get orders from dealers for The Beatles' singles, so it seemed like a good idea to re-promote all of them this way." The singles come in special green bags featuring the old Parlophone sleeve on the front and a picture of The Beatles, taken from the respective period, on the back. The Apple singles will still feature the company's logo and label. To display the collection in record stores, EMI send out special Beatles "browser boxes". Some fans are annoyed to discover that to buy all 23 singles will cost them a staggering £11!

Wednesday March 10
🍎 Ringo signs a long-term recording contract with Polydor International in the UK and Atlantic in the US and Canada. As part of the deal, he is obligated to deliver seven albums in the next five years. His first is scheduled for a June release.

Monday March 14
🍎 Wings begin a week-long series of rehearsals at Elstree studios north of London.

Tuesday March 16
🍎 With The Beatles not responding to his original offer, the American promoter Bill Sargent doubles his bid for a reunion concert. In a statement, Sargent promises the group: "As soon as I get an official okay from you, the money will be made available to all four of you within 24 hours." He also announces that the proposed date for the show is America's Bicentennial Day, July 4, with plans to broadcast the show on closed circuit throughout the world and, in addition to the money, Sargent offers The Beatles a stake

in the profits from the promotion. Jonathan Clyde of Dark Horse records tells *Melody Maker*: "We don't know anything about this – certainly George has said nothing to us. And until he says something concrete, I can't comment." Meanwhile, a spokesman for Paul announces a terse: "No comment!"

Wednesday March 17
🍎 The American industrialist Mike Mathews, head of the Electro-Harmonix electrical equipment manufacturers, gets into the Beatles reunion circus by offering the group a meagre £3 million, to be split between them, for a one-off concert appearance. He further tempts the band by giving them a share of profits from the closed circuit broadcasts, which, he anticipates, should boost their income by a further £30 million.

Thursday March 18
🍎 Paul's father, James McCartney dies, aged 73, of bronchial pneumonia at his home in Gayton, in the Wirral on Merseyside. Among the first to hear the news is John in New York, whom Paul calls personally with the sad news.

* * *

Wings World Tour 1975/1976
Part 2 – Europe
March 20 – 26

Wings undertake a short five-date European tour, where they are accompanied by a brass section. They perform shows at:

The Falkoner Theater in Copenhagen (Saturday March 20 & Sunday March 21)
Deutschlandhalle, Berlin, Germany (Tuesday March 23)
Ahoy Sport Paleis, Rotterdam, Holland (Thursday March 25)
Pavillion Du Paris, France (Friday March 26)

Friday March 19
Prior to their departure to Copenhagen, Wings undertake a massive press conference at Paul's Soho offices in London.

Tuesday March 23
Lee Eastman, Linda's attorney father who is working for Paul, ends speculation of a Beatles reunion when he publicly announces that, "The offer isn't even being considered!"

Thursday March 25
The album *Wings At The Speed Of Sound* is released in America where it receives its airplay premiere on the New York radio station WNEW. In Los Angeles, controversy reigns when the radio station KHJ-FM plays the album 24 hours before the other LA stations had received their copy. As a result, some of these stations refuse to play the record, citing that KHJ-FM received preferential treatment. (The UK release of the album will take place on April 9.)

Away from the controversy, at a low-key press conference prior to their London departure, Paul is asked about two tracks appearing on the album:

Reporter: "What is the origin of the doorbell used to introduce 'Let 'Em in'?"

Paul: "Well, as it happens, it is our actual doorbell which our drummer bought us, so it has a group significance, and it seemed a good introduction to the album."

Reporter: "What was the origin of 'Cook Of The House'?"

Paul: "Well, we were in Adelaide and rented a house to stay at rather than a hotel, and after the gig each night, Linda and I would get dropped off and sit up in the kitchen and have a late night bite. They had these pots of sage and onion – all the condiments of the season – that's a joke that, condiments of the season. Well all this stuff was lined up and it was a kind of freak song and I took everything I saw and tried to work it into a song. Every line in the song was actually in the kitchen."

Reporter: "What were the sizzling noises heard in the introduction?"

Paul: "We went round to our house with the mobile unit and Linda decided to cook a meal and get cooking sounds recorded and then fed the meal to us and the engineers.

We all had a laugh and a drink. The mobile was outside the house and we just ran wires into the kitchen. Take one. Bacon frying. The first British cooking on record. There are chips at the end, which is great because it sounds like applause. If you get any questions you can tell them it was an E flat bacon pan and Selmer chips!"

Also today, Veronica Television films Wings' arrival in Holland for a special documentary to be transmitted on May 12. Later this evening, backstage at the Rotterdam venue, Paul, wearing a *Mersey Beat* T-shirt, is asked about the Bill Sargent Beatles reunion offer: "Well that's a big offer," he replies.

"I don't mind pretending I'm John Lennon!" Denny Laine says, interrupting.

Paul continues by being rather indecisive: "The thing is, nobody, as yet, has spoken about it. We've talked to each other. We've talked about ordinary things, you know, but no one has actually said, 'Do you want to do it?' None of the other three has asked me. We might do it, and if we did, we'd try and make it good, you know. But then again, we might not do it. But, then again . . . we might!"

Linda: "It's a yes, no, maybe."

Paul: "It's a positive, maybe."

Friday March 26

During the show in Paris, on the final night of the tour, Jimmy McCulloch fractures a finger on his left hand after slipping in the bathroom. This naturally causes a three-week postponement of their American tour, due to start at Fort Worth, Texas on April 8. Meanwhile, back in England, a live interview with Paul is transmitted on Capital Radio.

Monday March 29

With the brief tour now concluded, Paul and Linda stay in Paris where they appear on the French Television show *Number One*, interviewed by the host Michael Drucker.

*   *   *

Saturday March 27

🍎 Paul: "Beatles reunion? The only way we could come together would be if we wanted to do something musically, not lukewarm just to get the money. I'm not going to be blackmailed into going. It would ruin the whole Beatles thing for me . . . I'd read the papers which said John Lennon was the hottest on this. I spoke to the bugger and he didn't even mention it. Where do you go from there?"

Melody Maker publishes another exclusive interview with Paul by Chris Welch. Getting away from Beatles talk, Paul remarks: "We had fab fun in Australia. It was the first real tour we'd done for a while. The audiences were great and we just dug playing . . . It was more like a holiday."

Wednesday March 31

🍎 Back in England, McCartney Productions Ltd. financial returns for the year 1975/1976 reveal sales figures of £466,867 while outgoing expenses have reached a hefty £426,202, largely due to the costs of the current Wings concert tour. After a tax bill of £19,800, Paul's company sees a profit of £20,865 for the year. This, incidentally, will be the final year of McCartney Productions Ltd., as, from April 7, the organisation changes its name to MPL.

April

🍎 At their Dakota apartment, John and Yoko go on a fast to cleanse their bodies, electing not to eat solid food for forty days. This sees the beginning of an era where he takes an increased interest in food, immersing himself in cookbooks and books on nutrition. John also begins to read the George Ohsawa publication *You Are All Sanpaku*, featuring a translation by William Dufty, the man responsible for starting him on a macrobiotic diet.

🍎 *The Beatles Book Monthly* in England returns with the first of the original magazine reprints, naturally starting with issue No. 1, first published back in August of 1963. Surrounding the issue is eight pages of news covering the recent activities of the solo Beatles.

⚫ At the Sunset Sound Studios in Los Angeles, with assistance from Paul who is waiting for his American tour to begin, Ringo begins recording tracks intended for his album *Ringo's Rotogravure*. The sessions, which during June move to the Cherokee Studios in Hollywood, produce the following tracks: 'A Dose Of Rock And Roll', 'Hey Baby', 'Pure Gold', 'Cryin'', 'You Don't Know Me At All', 'Cookin' (In The Kitchen Of Love)', 'I'll Still Love You' (originally called 'When Every Song Is Sung'), 'This Be Called A Song', 'Las Brias', 'Lady Gaye' and the instrumental track 'Spooky Weirdness'. He also records the unreleased songs 'Where Are You Going', 'All Right' and 'It's Hard To Be Lovers'. Incidentally, while Ringo is recording the album, George Martin, producing an album by a new band who call themselves American Flyer, is in the studio next door. Their paths do not cross as George is recording during the day while Ringo, in typical Beatles fashion, records through the night.

⚫ During the sessions in Hollywood on June 12, John assists by playing piano on the recording of 'A Dose Of Rock And Roll' as well as on his own composition 'Cookin' (In The Kitchen Of Love)'. On June 19, Paul and Linda, during a break from their American tour, join Ringo at Cherokee for a four-hour recording session for Paul's track 'Pure Gold'. Sadly, George fails to make this an album featuring musical contributions from all four ex-Beatles as he is unable to attend any of the sessions. His typical guitar sound, on his own composition of 'I'll Still Love You', is recreated by Lon Van Easton. George is in New York working on his next album. Rumours circulate this month that he is to tour America at the end of the year, anxious to make amends for his disappointing 1974 concert appearances.

Thursday April 1
⚫ The Wings single 'Silly Love Songs'/'Cook Of The House' is released in America. (The UK release takes place on April 30.)
⚫ John's father, Alfred "Freddie" Lennon, dies in England. John never enjoyed much of a relationship with his father, who deserted him as a young boy and reappeared in his life only after The Beatles had gained worldwide fame and wealth in the mid-Sixties. By all accounts, the two had settled their differences during the final days of Freddie's life.

Saturday April 3
⚫ In the UK, The Beatles again hit the single charts when 'Yesterday' reaches number eight. Other chart placings from the re-issues include: 'Hey Jude' (number 12), 'Paperback Writer' (number 23), 'Get Back' (number 28), 'Penny Lane'/'Strawberry Fields Forever' (number 32) and 'Help!' (number 37).
⚫ Also in the UK, *Wings At The Speed Of Sound* reaches number two. Paul is unimpressed by the resurgence of The Beatles' back-catalogue, saying: " I don't fancy 'Silly Love Songs' being kept from the number one spot by 'Love Me Do' ."

Wednesday April 7
⚫ In London, at the start of the new tax year, Paul officially changes the name of his company from McCartney Productions Ltd. to MPL Communications Limited.

Thursday April 8
⚫ Due to Jimmy McCulloch's accident in Paris, the first Wings tour of America, originally scheduled to begin today in Fort Worth, Texas, is rearranged to start on May 3. Some original dates of the tour will remain but there are serious doubts over the shows at Madison Square Garden in New York. Experts predict that the tour, which will play to approximately 500,000 people, has the potential to gross more than $4 million. With a couple of weeks spare time on their hands, Paul and Linda spend time relaxing, socialising and helping out Ringo at the start of his *Ringo's Rotogravure* recording sessions.

Friday April 9
⚫ In the UK, in response to The Beatles hysteria currently sweeping the country, *Reveille* magazine publishes on its front page the headline: "Beatles Boom", over a report which predicts: "They will fill the top ten in May!" (At the time of his writing, The Beatles are occupying 23 places in the top 100 singles. 'Yesterday' is placed at number six while 'Something' is the lowest, at number 89.) Inside the paper, an EMI spokesman talks about the current Beatles revival. "The new Beatles boom is amazing, particularly when you

consider that some of their records are more than ten years old!" The spokesman continues: "The nostalgia boom is one thing, but The Beatles are recent history. Kids of 13 and 14 who never knew the group in its heyday, are now being wowed by the Beatle sound." The newspaper runs a competition to win the complete set of 23 Beatles singles. Those entering must state their own personal choice of top ten best Beatles singles, the results of which will be featured in a special *Reveille/Radio Luxembourg* radio programme to be broadcast next month. Beatlemania in *Reveille* continues the following week (April 16) when the newspaper begins a three-part series on the history of the group.

Sunday April 11
 To coincide with the resurgence of The Beatles in the UK singles chart, BBC Radio One transmits (between 5:00 and 5:59pm) the programme *The Beatles Again*, which focuses on the importance and influence of the group's music. The show, hosted by Brian Matthew, also features interviews with people who were closely associated with The Beatles during the Sixties and serves as a prelude to a tribute to the group by Radio One, which features The Beatles throughout the schedules the following weekend. (See next entry.)

Friday April 16
 BBC Radio One begins a special Easter Holiday weekend of Beatles programming, featuring all of their music released between 1962 and 1970 played in chronological order. The bonanza commences today at 11am with Tony Blackburn and finishes, with their final recordings, during the *Dave Lee Travis Show*, which starts at 4:30pm on Easter Monday, April 19. (For the trivia buffs among you, the first track played is 'Love Me Do', and the last track played, by Travis, is 'Get Back'.)

Monday April 19
 In America, today's Wings shows at the LA Forum are rearranged for June 21 to 23. In the run-up to the ticket availability, long lines of sleeping bags are seen on the pavement outside the venue. The allocation for tickets is a disappointing two per person.

Tuesday April 20
 Still in America, George, wearing the uniform of the Royal Canadian Mounted Police, appears unannounced with his friends the Monty Python comedy team at New York's City Center, at West 55th Street, during their performance of 'The Lumberjack Song'. He had, in fact, been watching the first half of the show from the audience and went backstage at the interval. The Python team, starting a three-week run at the venue, invited him to join the cast during the song. "George is a lumberjack freak. He used that song on his tour to introduce the show," says Nancy Lewis, Monty Python's American manager. (Incidentally, the former Beatle is such a fan of the song that, when George and Olivia go on holiday during the late Seventies and early Eighties, he will use the name "Jack Lumber" as an alias.)

Saturday April 24
 The album *Wings At The Speed Of Sound* reaches number one in the American charts. Paul, happy with the news, makes an evening visit to John and Yoko's Dakota apartment. By chance, John, eager to watch appearances by Raquel Welch and John Sebastian, the former front man for The Lovin' Spoonful, is watching the NBC TV comedy show *Saturday Night Live* (transmitted on Channel 4, WNBC between 11:30pm and 1:00am ET), and which also just happens to feature the famous Lorne Michaels' "Beatles Reunion" offer. With both John and Paul watching, Lorne Michaels delivers his legendary speech, unbeknownst to him that two of the ex-Beatles are actually tuned in:

"Hi, I'm Lorne Michaels, the producer of *Saturday Night*. Right now, we're being seen by approximately 22 million viewers, but please allow me, if I may, to address myself to four very special people . . . John, Paul, George and Ringo . . . The Beatles. Lately, there have been a lot of rumours to the effect that the four of you might be getting back together, that would be great. In my book, The Beatles are the best thing that ever happened to music. It goes deeper than that, you're not just a musical group, you're a part of us, we grew up with you. It's for this reason that I'm inviting you to come on our show. Now, we've heard and read a lot about personality and legal conflicts that might prevent you guys from re-uniting, that's none of my business. You guys will have to handle that. But it's also been said that no one has yet come up with enough money to satisfy you. Well, if it's money you want, there's no problem here. The National Broadcasting Company authorises me to authorise you a cheque for $3,000. Here can you get a close-up of this?" (Michaels holds a cheque, made payable to 'The Beatles', close up to the camera.) "As you can see, verifiably, a cheque made out to you . . . The Beatles for $3,000. All you have to do is sing three Beatle tunes. 'She Loves You, Yeah, Yeah, Yeah', that's $1,000 right there. You know the words, and it'll be easy. Like I said, this cheque is made out to 'The Beatles'. You divide it anyway you want, if you want to give Ringo less that's up to you. I'd rather not get involved. I'm sincere about this. If it helps you to reach a decision to reunite well, it's a worthwhile investment. You have agents, you know where I can be reached. Just think about it, OK? Thank you."

🍎 John recalls the evening: "Paul was visiting us at our place in the Dakota with Linda. He and I were watching it and we went ha-ha, wouldn't it be funny if we went down and we almost went down to the studio, just as a gag. We nearly got into the cab, but we were actually too tired."

🍎 Paul and Linda leave the Dakota apartment as John and Yoko begin watching the 1960 science-fiction film *The Time Machine* starring Rod Taylor.

Sunday April 25

🍎 Pleased by how well the two of them got on together last night, Paul returns to John's Dakota apartment this evening. Unfortunately, the welcome is not so warming, as John recalls in the September 1980 *Playboy* interviews: "That was a period when Paul just kept turning up at our door with a guitar. I would let him in, but finally I said to him, 'Please call before you come over. It's not 1956, and turning up at the door isn't the same anymore. You know, just give me a ring.' That upset him, but I didn't mean it badly. I just meant that I was taking care of a baby all day, and some guy turns up at the door with a guitar." Paul departs, unaware that he will never see John again. Paul immediately heads for Dallas, Texas and some Wings rehearsals.

Monday April 26

🍎 In Dallas, Wings begin rehearsals for their upcoming American leg of their world tour.

May

🍎 George attends the annual Cannes Film Festival in the South of France.

* * *

Wings World Tour 1975/1976
Part 3 – America
May 3 – June 23

With Jimmy McCulloch now recovered, the American leg of Wings' world tour finally takes place. Their repertoire includes the following: 'Venus And Mars', 'Rock Show', 'Jet', 'Let Me Roll It', 'Spirits Of Ancient Egypt', 'Medicine Jar', 'Maybe I'm Amazed', 'Call Me Back Again', 'Lady Madonna', 'The Long And Winding Road', 'Live And Let Die', 'Picasso's Last Words', 'Richard Cory', 'Bluebird', 'I've Just Seen A Face', 'Blackbird', 'Yesterday', 'You Gave Me The Answer', 'Magneto And Titanium Man', 'My Love', 'Listen To What The Man Said', 'Let 'Em In', 'Time To Hide', 'Silly Love Songs', 'Beware My Love', 'Go Now', 'Letting Go', 'Band On The Run', 'Hi Hi Hi' and 'Soily'.

The tour includes performances at:

Fort Worth Tarrant Country Convention Center, Texas (Monday May 3)
Houston Summit, Texas (Tuesday May 4)
Detroit Olympia, Texas (Friday May 7 and Saturday May 8)
Toronto Maple Leaf Gardens, Canada (Sunday May 9)
Cleveland Richfield Coliseum, Ohio (Monday May 10)
Philadelphia Spectrum (Wednesday May 12 and Friday May 14)
Largo, Maryland Capitol Center, Washington (Saturday May 15 and Sunday May 16)
Atlanta Omni (Tuesday May 18 and Wednesday May 19)
Long Island Nassau Coliseum (Friday May 21)
Boston Garden (Saturday May 22)
New York Madison Square Garden (Monday May 24 and Tuesday May 25)

Cincinnati Riverfront Coliseum (Thursday May 27)
Kansas City Kemper Arena (Saturday May 29)
Chicago Stadium, Illinois (An extra date is added for Monday May 31. Scheduled
  concerts: Tuesday June 1 and Wednesday June 2)
St. Paul, Minnesota Civic Center (Friday June 4)
Denver McNichols Arena (Monday June 7)
Seattle Kingdome (Thursday June 10)
San Francisco Cow Palace (Sunday June 13 and Monday June 14)
San Diego Sports Arena (Wednesday June 16)
Tucson Community Center (Friday June 18)
Los Angeles Forum (Monday June 21, Tuesday June 22 and an extra date on
  Wednesday June 23)

Wings' equipment on the tour is carried around in three articulated lorries, on the roof of
each are the words "Wings", "Over" and "America". The publicity for the tour was
originally going to be undertaken by the firm Solters & Roskin, but Paul fires them when
he discovers they are also handling the publicity for the International Committee To
Reunite The Beatles campaign. Coverage of the tour reaches England, with reports
appearing regularly on Capital Radio. The most detailed of which appear on the show
Rock Around The World.

Monday May 3 – Wednesday June 23 (duration of tour)
The following songs from the American concert tour appear on the triple album *Wings Over
America,* (released simultaneously in America and the UK on December 10): 'Lady
Madonna', 'The Long And Winding Road', 'I've Just Seen A Face', 'Blackbird', 'Yesterday',
'You Gave Me The Answer', 'Live And Let Die', 'Picasso's Last Words', 'Richard Cory',
'Bluebird' , 'Venus And Mars', 'Rock Show', 'Jet', 'Let Me Roll It', 'Spirits Of Ancient Egypt',
'Medicine Jar', 'Maybe I'm Amazed', 'Call Me Back Again', 'Magneto And Titanium Man',
'Go Now', 'My Love', 'Listen To What The Man Said', 'Let 'Em In', 'Time To Hide', 'Silly
Love Songs', 'Beware My Love', 'Letting Go', 'Band On The Run', 'Hi Hi Hi' and 'Soily'.
  Many of these live recordings are actually taped at the final show on June 23 at the Los
Angeles Forum. (Prior to the album's release, the group carry out extensive musical
overdubs.)

Monday May 3
The excitement of Paul's first American concert in ten years produces newspaper stories
such as this in the *Los Angeles Times*: "When the house lights dimmed . . . virtually
everyone in the arena stood in anticipation of what was clearly the most notable return to
rock concerts since Bob Dylan's 1974 appearance in Chicago."
  The attendance at Forth Worth tonight is a sell-out 14,000 crowd where, before Wings
had even played one single note, they are given a 15-minute standing ovation.

Tuesday May 4
During tonight's concert at the Summit, in Houston, Texas, Paul escapes serious injury –
by a matter of inches – when a large piece of scaffolding falls from above the stage.
Unfortunately, the pole hits Wings' road manager Trevor Jones, who is rushed to
hospital and given 13 stitches.

Wednesday May 5
During a day off from the tour in Texas, Paul, Linda and their family spot an Appaloosa
stallion standing aimlessly by the roadside and stop to enquire whether they can buy it.
After little persuasion they purchase the horse from its owner for a small fee.

Friday May 7
Following the third show on the tour at Detroit's Olympia, Paul gets annoyed with an
American journalist who repeatedly asks questions about The Beatles. He angrily snaps:
"Look mate, it's 1976 and I don't think most of the people here care about what happened
ten years ago. All they're interested in is what I'm doing now. The past is gone and it
won't come back!" Another reporter, this time from England, asks: "Will John Lennon be
appearing with you at Madison Square Garden in New York next week?" Paul replies:
"Well, I know he wants to come to the show, but I don't know whether he'll play . . . just

wait and see." As for tonight's concert itself, Paul is annoyed when the PA keeps feeding back throughout the show and is frustrated when his acoustic guitar work is restricted due to a cut finger. He injured himself the previous day while slicing up a pizza. Worst to suffer is his version of 'Blackbird'.

Sunday May 9
George and Ringo are seen among the 18,000 strong audience at tonight's concert at the Maple Leaf Gardens in Toronto.

Monday May 10, Wednesday May 12 & Friday May 14
Following performances in Cleveland and Philadelphia, Wings fly back to their base in New York. To help with the boredom of the flights, Paul arranges for a home video machine to be placed on board their customised 24-seater private plane, a BAC1–11. Among the films they watch are *Next Stop, Moses, Greenwich Village* and *Dog Day Afternoon*. The group also takes aboard the plane their own sports equipment, which includes a table tennis set. Meanwhile, seen in the audience at the show at Philadelphia's Spectrum on May 12 are Peter Frampton and The Beatles' first manager Allan Williams, who meets Paul backstage at the gig and promises to send him a copy of the 1962 Star Club tapes.

Saturday May 15
The opening night's performance at the Capitol Center in Largo, Maryland, before a capacity 22,000 fans, is attended by The Eagles, as well as Linda Rondstadt and Peter Asher, formerly of Sixties chart stars Peter & Gordon, and now a successful LA based record producer. Following the show, Linda and Peter go backstage to chat with Paul.

Wednesday May 19
In Atlanta, the *Peaches* record store invite Wings to put their hands and footprints into their 'Pavement of Stars' walkway outside their store. However, the local police thought that if the group go downtown to do it, they would cause a major traffic jam. So instead, the shop arranges for the concrete to be brought to them, where Paul, Linda and Wings climb aboard the van to leave their marks and, once the concrete is set, their prints are returned to the pavement outside the store.

Saturday May 22
The Wings single 'Silly Love Songs' reaches number one in the American singles chart. (It will reach the number two position in the UK on June 12.)

Monday May 24 & Tuesday May 25
Following just one radio announcement, the 40,000 tickets for both Madison Square Garden performances sell out in just 24 hours. Many of the fans camped outside the venue overnight in order to be sure of getting their seats. In attendance at both of the shows are British members of the Wings Fun Club, who flew out on a specially chartered plane arranged by the *Daily Mirror* Pop Club. Speculation is rife over who will be the special guest to join Wings on stage at these venues. The name of John Lennon is heard on many occasions . . . At the conclusion of the show on the first night, Paul, Linda and Wings, once the venue had cleared, come down into the hall to be pictured with the Wings Fun Club and *Daily Mirror* Pop Club members. Following the show on Tuesday May 25, Wings give an interview to the New York radio station WNEW. Later this evening, to celebrate the two sell-out shows at the Garden, a party is held at the venue but there is a strict rule of "no press allowed". This is because of a request from Jackie Onassis, who will attend only if there are no members from the press present. Jackie is photographed backstage with Paul and Linda.

Due to the success of the tour, Wings add two additional concerts to their itinerary, at Chicago on Monday May 31 and the Los Angeles Forum to wrap up the tour on Wednesday June 23.

Monday May 31
At the Chicago Stadium, Wings are interviewed backstage before the show by the Chicago radio station WLS.

Friday June 4
Wings performance in Minnesota today is shot for a television programme called *Wings Over St. Paul.*

Thursday June 10
A large part of the officially released 1980 MPL concert film *Rockshow* is shot today at Seattle's Kingdome. A selection of tracks from the show are videotaped directly off the in-house video feed. The audience at tonight's performance numbers 67,100, this being 11,000 over the fixed-seat capacity of the Kingdome venue and in doing so sets a new world record for a single act. Meanwhile, backstage before the show, Wings are interviewed for the US TV programme *Monday Night Special*, which is transmitted the following Monday June 14.

Saturday June 12
'Silly Love Songs' reaches number two in the UK singles chart, kept off the top spot by EMI stable mates The Wurzels and their song 'Combine Harvester'.

Friday June 18
In Tucson, Arizona, Linda, the other members of Wings and their entourage throw a surprise 34th birthday party for Paul.

Saturday June 19
During a break from the tour, Paul and Linda meet up with Ringo at the Cherokee recording studios in Hollywood for a four-hour recording session of the McCartney penned track 'Pure Gold'.

Sunday June 20
In Los Angeles, during a further break from the tour, Paul and Linda are invited to attend the birthday party of Beach Boy Brian Wilson. The event is filmed and will later appear on an edition of NBC TV's *Saturday Night Live* and later as part of the 1986 American documentary *The Beach Boys – An American Band.*

Monday June 21 & Tuesday June 22
The hysteria surrounding Wings' American Tour rolls on, when the Los Angeles Ticketron headquarters sell 2,000 seats in just nine minutes. At the LA Forum itself, 40,000 tickets are sold in less than four hours! In attendance at both concerts is a planeload of Japanese Wings Fun Club members. On the opening night at the Forum, at the conclusion of the Wings' second encore performance of 'Soily', Ringo appears on stage to present Paul with a bunch of flowers and then playfully picks up Paul's guitar to play. Ringo was watching the show from an audience that also includes Diana Ross, Harry Nilsson, Robbie Robertson, Elton John, Jack Nicholson, Cher, Jesse Ed Davis, Candy Clark, Dustin Hoffman, Leo Sayer, Adam Faith, Dennis Wilson of The Beach Boys and John Bonham of Led Zeppelin. Following the concert, Ringo joins Paul and Wings backstage, an event also captured for the documentary *Wings Over The World.*

Thursday June 24
At 8pm, in California's Benedict Canyon, at the Harold Lloyd Estate, Wings hold a party to celebrate the completion of the tour. The party costs the band over $75,000 and all the guests are instructed to wear white, thus providing an appropriate canvas for the Hawaiian painters who spray the clothes of the guests. These include Rod Stewart, Jack Nicholson, Tony Curtis, David Cassidy and, amongst others, members of The Beach Boys. Food is served at 10pm and following this, guests are entertained at the poolside with The Nelson Riddle Orchestra providing the music.

Paul: "After The Beatles, you would have thought it would have been pretty much impossible for me to follow that and to get anything else going. At least I thought that . . . This tour has convinced us that we're a group and I think it has convinced audiences too. This wasn't just a one-time trip. This is going to be a working band." He triumphantly concludes: "We'll be back!"

* * *

Saturday May 8

♣ With the results now in and the complete set of 23 Beatles singles collections now received by the lucky participants, Radio Luxembourg broadcasts (between 11:00 and 11:45pm) the results of the "Beatles Top Ten Readers Poll" conducted in the recent *Reveille* Beatles competition. The outright winner, as one may imagine, is Paul's 1965 classic 'Yesterday'.

Saturday May 22

♣ With no Beatles reunion forthcoming, Lorne Michaels puts out another appeal on tonight's edition of *Saturday Night Live* (transmitted on Channel 4, WNBC between 11:30pm and 1:00am ET). This time, he ups the offer to $3,200 and cheekily agrees to throw in some "hotel accommodation".

Monday May 24

♣ George begins recording his album *Thirty Three And A Third* at his Friar Park Studios. The four-month sessions produce the following songs: 'This Song', 'Learning How To Love You', 'Woman Don't You Cry For Me', 'Dear One', 'Beautiful Girl', 'See Yourself', 'It's What You Value', 'True Love', 'Pure Smokey' and 'Crackerbox Palace', which was the name of Lord Buckley's house in Los Angeles. The song was originally written back in 1975 after meeting George Grief, a man who reminded George of Buckley. (The sessions on the album will continue until September 13.)

Monday May 31

♣ Capitol Records in America release The Beatles' single 'Got To Get You Into My Life'/ 'Helter Skelter'.

June

♣ In America, George becomes a part of the Warner Communications Inc., *Big Button* promotional campaign. He appears in a promotional picture which runs until December in various US trade papers, as well as in *Cashbox* magazine and the *Hollywood Reporter*.
♣ Still in America, in the grounds of his Los Angeles home, Ringo gives a 31-minute interview for the Australian television programme *Magic Camera*.

Monday June 7

♣ The Beatles' double album compilation, *Rock 'N' Roll Music,* is released by Capitol in America, where they announce that the double-album will be backed by "the largest selling campaign" in the history of the music business. In England, where the compilation is released on Friday June 11, a rather evasive EMI spokesman announced: "I can tell you nothing about the album's release because I am sworn to secrecy under the pain of direst consequences. A statement will be released and there'll be no information until then."

The full 28-track listing, featuring previously released recordings is: side one: 'Twist And Shout', 'I Saw Her Standing There', 'You Can't Do That', 'I Wanna Be Your Man', 'I Call Your Name', 'Boys' and 'Long Tall Sally'; side two: 'Rock 'N' Roll Music', 'Slow Down', 'Kansas City', 'Money (That's What I Want)', 'Bad Boy', 'Matchbox' and 'Roll Over Beethoven'; side three: 'Dizzy Miss Lizzy', 'Any Time At All', 'Drive My Car', 'Everybody's Trying To Be My Baby', 'The Night Before', 'I'm Down' and 'Revolution'; side four: 'Back In The USSR', 'Helter Skelter', 'Taxman', 'Got To Get You Into My Life', 'Hey Bulldog', 'Birthday' and 'Get Back'.

The album retails in the UK for £4.50. Fifteen thousand copies of the album are shipped out from EMI's factory in Hayes, Middlesex, to meet the heavy demand for the release in Japan.

Saturday June 12

♣ John and Yoko join Ringo at the Cherokee Studios in Hollywood, where he is currently recording his latest album *Ringo's Rotogravure*. John plays piano on the tracks 'A Dose Of Rock 'N' Roll' and on his own composition 'Cookin' (In The Kitchen Of Love)', which will be John's last studio recording session until August 4 1980 when he begins work, with Yoko, on the album *Double Fantasy* (see entry).

Saturday June 19

♣ *Rock 'N' Roll Music* reaches number 11 in the UK album charts.

Wednesday June 23
 During a press conference at the World Trade Center in New York, Radio Caroline DJ Ronan O'Rahilly introduces a new four-piece band comprising of Mickey Gallagher, Charlie Charles, John Turnbull and Norman Wattroy who call themselves Loving Awareness. The reason for the press conference? They are intending to change their name to The Beatles! The four lads announce to open-mouthed reporters: "We have written to John, George, Paul and Ringo suggesting that, since they no longer use the name, they relinquish it to Loving Awareness, who will be happy to carry on in their tradition." When asked about the name change, famed New York promoter Sid Bernstein remarks: "I believe the boys are sincere about their music but the new name's got to go!"

Friday June 25
 In England, to further promote the *Rock 'N' Roll Music* album, Parlophone release the 24th official Beatles single, coupling 'Back In The USSR' with 'Twist And Shout'. (It will reach number 19 in the UK chart.) EMI compile a promotional film for the A-side, featuring miscellaneous clips of The Beatles' visits to Holland in 1964 and Germany in 1966.

Monday June 28
 Geraldo Rivera interviews Paul, Linda and Wings about the success of their American tour on his American late-night ABC TV show *Goodnight America*. During the course of the interview, excerpts from the Wings June 10 Seattle concert ('Band On The Run' and 'Yesterday') are shown for the first time. The group also take the opportunity to promote their new single 'Let 'Em In'/'Beware My Love', which is released today. (The UK release takes place on July 23. The single will reach number one in America and number two in the UK. It is also worth noting that a special 12" version, housed in a leopard skin cover and featuring a disco version of the B-side, is released in France.)

Tuesday June 29
 Further excerpts from Wings' Seattle concert on June 10 are transmitted on the ABC TV breakfast show *Good Morning America*.

July
 Ringo shows off his new look, appearing bald after visiting a barber's shop in Monte Carlo. His new companion during this period is actress Vivienne Venturi.
 An exhibition of Stuart Sutcliffe's paintings, organised by his mother Millie, is put on display at a South London art gallery.

Saturday July 10
 In the US album charts, *Rock 'N' Roll Music* reaches number two.
 Paul and Linda, as well as Rod Stewart, Jesse Ed Davis, Jan and Dean, Tony Kaye and Leo Sayer, are among the celebrities in attendance at The Beach Boys' concert tonight in Anaheim, California. The performance has great historic significance as Brian Wilson, the genius behind the group, is performing live with The Beach Boys for the first time in 12 years.

Saturday July 17
 In the UK music press, EMI Records reveal that, due to the success of the *Rock 'N' Roll Music* album, they intend to release further Beatles compilation albums in the future, although, according to EMI bosses, they "do not intend to saturate the record buying public."

Saturday July 24
 In the singles charts, 'Back In The USSR' reaches number 19 in the UK, while in America, 'Got To Get You Into My Life' reaches number seven.

Monday July 26
 While Paul revels in the success of a sell-out American tour and constant hit records with Wings, George fails to deliver an album due to A&M Records under the terms of his original contract. George cites a serious bout of hepatitis as the reason for the delay in the completion of *Thirty Three And A Third*.

Tuesday July 27

 John finally wins his five-year battle against the Immigration Authorities, when his American application for a 'green card' is approved (no. 17-597-321). Effectively, this allows him to remain permanently in the US and, most importantly, leave and re-enter the country without any problems. John is also able to apply for full American citizenship in 1981. The 90-minute hearing takes place at the downtown New York offices of the US Immigration and Naturalisation Service, where Judge Ira Fieldsteel officially hands John the green card. Ironically, it was Fieldsteel who had handed down the decision ordering John to leave America on March 23 1973. When the verdict is announced, John embraces Yoko and the packed courthouse bursts into spontaneous applause. The celebrities present who testify for John include the American news reporter Geraldo Rivera, the actress Gloria Swanson, the sculptor Isamu Noguchi and the writer Norman Mailer, who describes John as "one of the great artists of the Western world". Close friends of the Lennons, Peter Boyle and John Cage are also present in the courthouse.

The day begins with the judge reading a brief résumé of the history of the case, which had begun on August 31, 1971 when John last entered America. He has remained in the country ever since, refusing to leave in case he is not permitted to return.

John, wearing a white shirt, black suit and tie, cowboy boots and sporting a short-cropped haircut, is called to give evidence, answering questions from his attorney Leon Wildes:

"Have you ever been convicted of any crime anywhere in the US?"

John: "No."

"Have you ever been a member of the Communist Party or any other organisation that may seek to overthrow the US Government by force?"

John: "No."

"Do you intend to make the US your home?"

John: "I do."

"Will you continue your work here?"

John: "Yes. I wish to continue to live here with my family and continue making music."

Wildes then asks John if there is anything he has to add in connection with his request to be granted permanent residency.

John: "I'd like to publicly thank Yoko, my wife, for looking after me and pulling me together for four years, and giving birth to our son at the same time. There are many times that I wanted to quit, but she stopped me. I'd also like to thank a cast of thousands, famous and unknown, who have been helping me publicly and privately for the last four years. And last, but not least, I'd like to thank you, my attorney, Leon Wildes, for doing a good job well, and I hope this is the end of it."

Leon Wildes then calls the first of several witnesses to speak on behalf of John. The first is Mr. Sam Trust, President of ATV Music Corporation, which owns the rights to John's compositions. He says: "There are two very positive reasons why Mr. Lennon should be allowed to remain in the US. The music scene in the US is in the doldrums right now, and the current resurgence of interest in The Beatles and their material proves that they are the most powerful source of music in the last 30 years. I believe we can look forward to many new innovations in music if Lennon is allowed to remain in this country. The second point is that Lennon is a tremendous revenue generator. The US will be the scene for the reception of that revenue if he is allowed to remain."

Next is the writer Norman Mailer: "I think John Lennon is a great artist who has made an enormous contribution to popular culture. He is one of the great artists of the Western world. We lost T.S. Eliot to England and only just got Auden back . . . it would be splendid to have Mr. Lennon as well!"

Next up is the broadcaster, lawyer and close friend of the Lennons, Geraldo Rivera. He, of course, was involved with John and Yoko on the 1972 *One To One Concert* at Madison Square Garden, which raised $90,000 for the Willowbrook School, a home for mentally retarded children in New York. To help the cause, John and Yoko donated a further $50,000 from their own money. (See entry for August 30, 1972 for full details of the show.) For his testimony on behalf of John, Geraldo continues on this point: "This money liberated at least 60 retarded children from the pits of hell and set them up in small residences where they could be cared for on a 'one-to-one' basis. I believe that what was started by John and Yoko and other artists in 1972 was a turning point in the care of the mentally retarded, and if there ever was a person who deserved to stay in this country it is John Lennon."

Leon Wildes then reads a letter from the Bishop of New York, the Rt. Rev. Paul Moore, which emphasises Lennon's contribution to the culture of New York and praises him as being a "gentleman of integrity".

The final witness is Gloria Swanson who, despite her advancing years, takes to the stand appearing to be in perfect mental and physical strength. She says: "For many years I have been actively interested in the physical fitness of the youth of New York. My husband met John Lennon in a health food store in this city, and we found we had feelings in common on this subject. We feel that good food is essential to physical wellbeing and we are anti-junk food. I hope very much that he will help us in this sphere. We must educate the country and the Lennons will help to do something about it."

After a short deliberation, the Judge returns to enquire whether or not John will become a state charge (i.e. draw welfare benefit or its equivalent). The packed courthouse breaks into a subdued round of sniggers. John's attorney rises from his seat to answer this question: "On the contrary, your Honour. Mr. Lennon was a member of The Beatles, and has substantial earnings every year. It is therefore *most* unlikely. He is also the owner of several valuable copyrights, properties and such like."

Mr. Wildes retakes his seat and, almost immediately, the Judge speaks again to deliver this short sentence: "I find him (John) statutorily eligible for permanent residence."

John's five-year fight was over.

Leon Wildes stands up and says: "Your honour, this is one decision that I won't appeal against."

Following the hearing, John, Yoko, their friends and an army of reporters and cameramen are ushered into another room where an immigration official hands John his "green card" where he is pictured with Yoko, accepting it. The card had already been prepared, which suggests that John's fate had been decided prior to today's hearing. (Bob Gruen took the picture on the card on New Year's Day this year.)

Outside the building, surrounded by the large crowd, a happy and relieved looking John says: "It's great to be legal again. I'll tell my baby. I thank Yoko and the Immigration Service who have finally seen the light of day. It's been a long and slow road, but I am not bitter. I can't get into that. On the contrary, now I can go and see my relations in Japan and elsewhere. Again I thank Yoko, I've always thought there's a great woman behind every idiot."

As the Lennons again pose for the army of photographers and television crews, with the "green card" proudly held aloft, *Melody Maker*'s Chris Charlesworth, who was present at the hearing, remarks to John: "Hey John, well done! I'll tell you something . . . have you noticed? Your green card is actually *blue!*" (Ironically, after years of searching for the elusive green card, John now realises, to his amusement, that it is actually blue.)

A reporter then asks John: "Will you now apply to become a full US citizen?" John replies: "I will first enjoy the advantages of holding a green card before making up my mind on that point. The main thing is that I can travel now. Until today my attorney wouldn't even let me go to Hawaii for a vacation in case I couldn't get back. Whenever I flew to Los Angeles I was paranoid in case the plane was diverted to Toronto on the way." He is then asked, considering the previous five years of turmoil, why do you still want to live in America? John replies: "If I had lived 2,000 years ago I would have wanted to live in Rome. New York is the Rome of today. Now I'm going home to crack open a tea-bag and start looking at some travel catalogues."

In fact John and Yoko do not do that. Instead they visit the well-known Upper East Side ice cream parlour Serendipity's where, for this time only, John breaks his "no sugar" diet and indulges in some chocolate.

Friday July 30

🍎 In England, despite a last minute attempt by George and Ringo to halt the release, the Polydor double album *The Beatles Tapes* is released in the UK featuring David Wigg's individual interviews with the four Beatles, originally broadcast on the BBC Radio One series *Scene And Heard*. George and Ringo base their bid for a High Court injunction on the point that the views expressed then do not necessarily hold true now. Mr. Justice Rubin unfortunately sides with Polydor and rejects their injunction.

August

🍎 Meanwhile, at Paul's private studios in Scotland, during a break from Wings activities, Denny Laine records the album *Holly Days*, which features Paul playing most of the instruments on the album and providing backing vocals. During the month, Paul records demo versions of the following songs: 'Heartbeat', 'Moondreams', 'Rave On', 'I'm Gonna Love You Too', 'Fool's Paradise', 'It's So Easy – Listen To Me' (medley) and 'Look At Me'.

Tuesday August 3
⚫ BBC1 transmits, for the fourth time in the UK, The Beatles' 1964 film *A Hard Day's Night* (between 6:45 and 8:09pm) and thus launches a four-week series of their films on a Tuesday night. Unfortunately, the corporation announces that *Shea Stadium* and *Magical Mystery Tour* do not figure in these plans.

Saturday August 7
⚫ A quick look at the UK singles charts reveal 'Back In The USSR' at number 26, 'Here Comes The Sun' by Steve Harley and Cockney Rebel at number 27 and 'Let 'Em In' at number 30. In the album charts, *Wings At The Speed Of Sound* is at number 14, *Rock 'N' Roll Music* is at number 20 and *The Beatles Tapes* reaches number 45. In the American singles listings 'Got To Get You Into My Life' is at number three and 'Let 'Em In' is at number four, while in the album charts, *Wings At The Speed Of Sound* is placed at number three and *Rock 'N' Roll Music* is at number six.

Tuesday August 10
⚫ In the second of this four-week series, BBC1 broadcasts The Beatles' 1965 film *Help!* (between 6:45 and 8:09pm). This is its fourth UK TV transmission on the station.

Saturday August 14
⚫ 'Let 'Em In' reaches number three in the US singles chart.

Monday August 16
⚫ The Wings album *Band On The Run* is issued in the Soviet Union on the Melodiya label.

Tuesday August 17
⚫ The Beatles' 1968 film *Yellow Submarine* is transmitted, for the second time, on BBC1 tonight between 6:46 and 8:09pm.

Saturday August 21
⚫ Paul and Linda attend the annual Knebworth Festival in Hertfordshire, not to perform but to watch performances by Lynyrd Skynyrd and The Rolling Stones.

Tuesday August 24
⚫ Eight months after receiving its British television premiere, The Beatles' 1970 film *Let It Be* is transmitted again on BBC1 (between 6:51 and 8:09pm) thereby concluding the month-long run of Beatle movies on the station. Asked again why they did not show *Shea Stadium* or *Magical Mystery Tour*, the BBC respond by repeating: "We could not obtain the broadcasting rights." (Incidentally, the TV rights for *MMT* at this stage are held by Japanese Television.) Beatles fans around the country are incensed with the non-appearance of *Magical Mystery Tour* and begin putting pen to paper.

Saturday August 28
⚫ 'Let 'Em In' makes number two in the UK charts.
⚫ At 1pm today, Britain's first Beatles convention takes place at St. Andrews Hall in Norwich. Amongst the highlights of this 12-hour event is an exhibition of Beatles memorabilia, an auction, a flea market, a talk by Allan Williams and another public airing of the legendary Star Club tapes from 1962. The promoter is Dave Chisnell, who, a month prior to the convention, announces that he anticipates up to 2,000 people to attend. He adds: "If this one goes well we may take the whole convention on the road and set it up in the major cities around the country. We are certainly hoping that there will be enough interest to make it an annual event. I got the idea for it when I met Paul McCartney in New York on the Wings tour. I mentioned it to him and he thought it was great. It is inspired by the American conventions they had and I really do not know why Britain has not done it before. We have sold 1,000 tickets already, including 400 in Liverpool. We have also invited The Beatles to attend, but I cannot say I am all that confident they will turn up." But things turn sour for Chisnell when, just a week before the convention, he is threatened with legal

action if he continues with a plan to show the film of the 1965 *Shea Stadium* concert. "We were told by Suba Films, which is a subsidiary of Apple, that they will sue us if the film went on because of copyright and permission to use it," he remarks. "This is a blow because it was something a lot of people were looking forward to. We have some legal people working for us investigating some loopholes which may allow us to go ahead, but it is all very complicated." The convention, with a suitable replacement for the *Shea Stadium* film, is a great success with an attendance totalling 2,000 fans. Extra exhibits on the day include a display of paintings by Stuart Sutcliffe, which sell between £50 and £150, while at an auction, a set of American bubblegum cards go for £8 and a single cartoon drawing by Sutcliffe realises only £7. Due to the success, Chisnell announces plans to stage a similar two-day event in London towards the end of the year.

September
🍎 Following the recent run of Beatles movies on BBC1 (August 3 to 24 – see entry), Beatles fans in England begin petitioning the Corporation demanding a repeat screening of the 1967 film *Magical Mystery Tour*. Their pleas go unheeded for a further three and a quarter years.

Tuesday September 7
🍎 With Paul having now owned Buddy Holly's song publishing since 1971, he stages the first Buddy Holly Week, a 7-day extravaganza celebrating the 40th anniversary of Holly's birth. On the opening day, Norman Petty, Holly's manager, co-writer and producer, is a guest of honour at a special luncheon hosted by McCartney. The event is also attended by Elton John, Queen, Roger Daltrey, Steve Harley, 10cc, Eric Clapton and Patti Boyd. During the get-together, Petty makes a speech, at the conclusion of which he presents to Paul the cuff links worn by Holly during his fateful air crash. Celebrations continue on September 9, when a special Buddy Holly night is held at London's Lyceum featuring music from three bands, Mike Berry and The Outlaws, Flight 56 and Flying Saucers. Buddy Holly Week will become an annual event. To coincide with it, Paul releases three Buddy Holly maxi-singles.
🍎 Today, George is found guilty of "subconscious plagiarism" of the 1963 Chiffons' hit 'He's So Fine' composition royalties. The late composer Ronnie Mack composed the song, but Bright Tunes pressed ahead with the case. During trial testimony, George maintains that he never intended to plagiarise 'He's So Fine' and actually had the spiritual 'Oh Happy Day' in mind when he composed the song 'My Sweet Lord'. The case resumes on November 8 (see entry).

Wednesday September 8
🍎 Capitol Radio in London broadcast a real scoop by playing, for the first time on any radio station in the world, The Beatles' version of 'Love Of The Loved' as recorded by the group during their Decca Records audition from New Years Day 1962.

Friday September 17
🍎 Sid Bernstein, the promoter of The Beatles' New York concerts in 1964, 1965 and 1966, takes out a full-page advert in today's *New York Herald Tribune* requesting that "The Beatles reunite for a one-off charity concert."
🍎 Meanwhile, Ringo's album *Ringo's Rotogravure* is released in the UK. (The American release takes place on September 27.) The title is inspired by the Judy Garland and Fred Astaire 1948 film *Easter Parade*, that Ringo had enjoyed on TV some three years earlier. Besides John's contribution on 'Cookin' (In The Kitchen of Love)', Paul writes 'Pure Gold' (on which he contributes backing vocals) and George writes 'I'll Still Love You'. The album makes number 28 in the US charts. Ringo is naturally asked how he received contributions from John, Paul and George.
    "Well, Paul asked to write a song. I asked John and he worked on it and worked on it and eventually he came up with 'You Got Me Cooking' (sic). You know he's really into that now – cooking! I also asked George to write one, but there was an old one of his that was never released by anybody that I always loved. I was on the session when it was recorded so, in the end, I asked him if instead of writing one, could I have that old one? He said fine; it saved him a job. It's called 'I Still Love You', a big ballady thing."
(Note: Although George allows Ringo to record the song, he is not pleased with the result and takes legal action against Ringo. The action is resolved later this year.)

Ringo is asked if he has seen Sid Bernstein's latest advertisement asking The Beatles to reform for one more concert? "I haven't read it properly," he replies. "But if it is another one of those things that offers us the moon to do one concert – as of now, it is *out!* Look, people have been asking us to do this thing for so long and offering us God-knows how much, but they don't seem to realise – we didn't start doing it for money, and we ain't going to end it that way. The Beatles were formed because four guys wanted to get together and play. Now those four guys are going their separate ways. I can't speak about what might happen in five years time, but as of now – *no* Beatles! We just don't need it."

"But", the reporter insists, "John and Paul both appear on your new album."

"Well, look", replies an irritated Ringo, "we are brothers. We will be close forever. You do not come through all we did and not have love for each other and occasionally we drop in on each other's albums."

"George didn't appear though," the reporter asks again, "was that to avoid the album being called 'By The New Beatles'?"

"No," Ringo insists. "George was in London. The album was recorded in Los Angeles."

◀ Today, George arrives in Los Angeles for a meeting with A&M executives over the non-delivery of his latest album.

* * *

Wings Short European Tour:
September 19 – 27

Wings return to live performances with a four-date tour of Europe, which includes performances in:

Vienna, Austria (Sunday September 19)
Zagreb, Yugoslavia (Tuesday September 21)
Venice, Italy (Saturday September 25)
Munich, Germany (Monday September 27)

Saturday September 18
Paul, Linda and Wings arrive in Austria to be greeted by an official EMI welcoming committee and a huge banner, which reads "EMI Records In Austria Welcomes Paul McCartney + Wings In Vienna". Then, after posing for a handful of photographers, Paul tells the waiting reporters that the first thing he is going to do in this beautiful city is "get some sleep!"

Monday September 20
Paul is given an American record industry award for being voted Top Male Vocalist of the Year.

Friday September 24
Wings arrive in Venice, Italy. Paul, Linda and the kids spend this first day sightseeing the beautiful town and taking a ride on a gondola.

Saturday September 25
Wings perform a UNESCO (United Nations Educational, Scientific and Cultural Organisation) benefit concert in St. Mark's Square, Venice, where they help raise $50,000 towards restoring the historic city and help stop it from sinking. The show, part of a week of concerts in the city, which features Ravi Shankar, Peter Ustinov and Mort Schuman, is a great success but unfortunately the weight of the equipment used by the group causes subsidence damage in the area. As part of the deal, Wings perform free of charge and Paul agrees to pay for transport of their equipment, but the organising committee foot their hotel bills and the cost of erecting the stage and seating in the Piazza. To offset the massive investment for this one concert, Paul arranges for the other concerts (on September 19, 21 and 27) to take place on either side of the Venice concert. It is attended by approximately 15,000 people, all paying around £10 a head.

* * *

Monday September 20

 Ringo's single 'A Dose Of Rock And Roll'/'Cryin'' is released in America. (The UK release takes place on October 15.) Because he is currently a tax exile, all promotional interviews for the release of this and the *Rotogravure* album are carried out in his room at the George V Hotel in Paris, France. Capitol Radio DJ Tony Prince is among those present today, and he asks Ringo if he has seen the Sid Bernstein Beatles reunion offer?

Ringo replies in no uncertain terms: "I think Sid Bernstein is trying to get his name in the papers. When I got up someone said, 'Have you seen this?' But I hadn't, it was too long to read. I realised the whole gist of the situation is that he wants to give us $230 million. I don't know how long he wants us to play, it's good for five minutes, but I don't know why all this pressure is on us. We're busy all the time. I'm here promoting this album and he's put that out and all I'm gonna get from you and everyone else is 'Sid Bernstein said this'. I *don't care* about Sid Bernstein; I'm promoting my record. I don't know what the others (John, Paul and George) are gonna say about it, but it won't be now. Next week someone's gonna come in with $500 million. It annoys me because I have to spend all this energy all the time talking about it when we should be talking about something else. That's when it annoys me. If that hadn't been in the papers we would have passed right over it. We've just spent ten minutes talking about this guy who writes to a newspaper." (The interview is transmitted on Capitol Radio the following Friday October 1.) Ringo also records an interview with Radio Luxembourg, which is transmitted in two parts, the first part on October 2, with the second transmitted on October 10. Further promotions for the album also include an interview for the Dutch station AVRO Radio, which is transmitted on October 4.

Thursday September 23

 Further European promotions for his *Rotogravure* album take place today, when Ringo holds a press conference in Milan, Italy.

Friday September 24

 During an evening out at a New York restaurant, John and Yoko are briefly interrupted at their table by the roving reporter Ugly George from the local subscription channel Manhattan Cable. Ugly George is possibly best remembered for persuading attractive young females off the street to remove their clothes for his late night TV show. With that in mind, it is hardly surprising that George asks John: "How much of the dialogue that you wrote as a part of The Beatles in the Sixties and today, is associated with sex?" John replies by saying how "fish and finger pie", as used in The Beatles' track 'Penny Lane', was "an old colloquial Liverpool saying for frigging!" In response to Ugly George's question about Manhattan Cable's policy of cutting back on sex on the TV, John replies: "Tits and arse is good here, they should show more!"

Tuesday September 28

 In Los Angeles, A&M Records sue George for $10 million, claiming that he has failed to comply with the terms of his original contract by not completing an album by the July 26 deadline and for not returning the £588,000 advance. The company also seeks a court injunction preventing George from making any more records until the case is heard. Asked about the action by A&M, George says he is "astonished and saddened" by the move. Both parties mutually agree to terminate the contract and swiftly resolve the matter. George subsequently retains Warner Brothers services to distribute his Dark Horse label.

Later, George reflects on the trouble: "When you hear about somebody getting sued for something, all it gets down to is the first press release seems to be the good guy. And that's the case, as it happened. It came in the papers about A&M suing me because I didn't deliver an album, but it goes much deeper than that. What happened was, we had a deal for Dark Horse and I had a deal for myself, which didn't happen until this year because I was with EMI and Capitol. They were trying to get together over the two years to finalise all the details. The attorney who was with them when they made the deal was not the one with them when they were filling in the details. He read the deal and he said they were going to use my money to offset Dark Horse. We said, 'No. No. It's in the contract. It has been there for two years. You don't cross-collateralise me and Dark Horse.' And the attorney said, 'I can't believe the other attorney did this to you.' So, in effect, what happened was they realised they had not made themselves such a good deal.

Instead of phoning me up and saying, 'Now look George, we have made ourselves a bad deal. Let's talk about it and work it out', they found the only legal grounds they had was that I had had hepatitis, so my album was two months delayed. We had, in the original contract, that I would give it to them around the 25 of July. And so they picked on that legal point and said, 'Okay, we'll get him on that.' I arrived in LA with my album under my arm, all happy, and I was given this letter saying, 'Give us back the million dollars', which was an advance, 'and give us the album, and when you give us the album, you don't get the million back.' Now, I turned down a great deal from Capitol and EMI which was of more value, from the money point of view, and guarantees, than what I took with A&M. But I took that because of the relationship we were, supposedly, going to have, which it turned out we never did. And that was it. I couldn't live with that sort of situation, so I left. We backed the truck up to the office and filled it with our stuff and we went off. But, almost overnight, me and Dark Horse Records were transferred from A&M on one side of the Hollywood Hills to Warner Brothers on the other, and a new album, *Thirty Three And A Third,* was soon in the racks in the record stores."

Wednesday September 29
 Ringo flies in to Copenhagen to undertake further promotions for *Ringo's Rotogravure*. From this country, he will fly into Holland for *Rotogravure* promotions in early October.

October
 A pair of Paul's old leather trousers are taken to America by Allan Williams to be auctioned. They had belonged to the singer Faron Rufley and were left by mistake in his suitcase during 1962. Rufley's mother later found the trousers in the attic of their home and subsequently gave them to Williams to sell.

Paul spends most of the month at Abbey Road studios listening to over 90 hours of tapes recorded during Wings' tour of America, with the intention of selecting material for the triple *Wings Over America* album, scheduled for release at the end of the year.
 Apple Corps Ltd. sell its freehold interest in their four-storey Georgian building at 3 Saville Row, London.

Saturday October 2
 On the American NBC TV show *Saturday Night Live*, host Lorne Michaels revisits the sketch involving an appeal for The Beatles to get back together . . .

"Hi, I'm Lorne Michaels. Several months ago I made a bona-fide offer of $3,000 to The Beatles to perform on *Saturday Night*. For months there was no response and then about two weeks ago, I got a long distance phone call from Eric Idle, tonight's host, in London saying that if I would let him come over and host the show, he would bring The Beatles with him. Well, in my excitement, I agreed and foolishly sent him the cheque for $3,000. You see, he said The Beatles wanted the money in advance so that they could buy some new clothes to wear on the show. Well, when I met Eric at the airport last Monday, I noticed that he was alone. So I said, 'Where are they, I mean The Beatles.' He said, 'Well, their new clothes weren't ready yet, so they were going to catch a later flight.' I still didn't think anything was wrong, until yesterday, when a telegram arrived saying, 'Can't come now. Ringo's pants too long . . . Stop . . . Please send more money for alterations . . . Stop . . . Signed The Beatles.' When I showed the telegram to Eric, he said he would call London immediately and did, and convinced John, Paul, George and Ringo to send over a film instead. Well, 20 minutes ago, the film arrived from England. I just saw it and it's . . . quite good, only it's *not* The Beatles, it's The Rutles. Evidently, Eric had a bad phone connection to London and, well, anyway . . . it's halfway through the show and Eric's already spent the $3,000, so ladies and gentlemen, here are The Rutles . . .

"The fabulous Rutland sound, created by the fab-four, Dirk, Stig, Nasty and Barry . . . who created a musical legend that will last a lunchtime."

With that, *The Rutles* are launched in America. The success of this early film sequence leads to the full-blown *Rutles* TV special entitled *All You Need Is Cash,* which will premiere in America on March 22 and in the UK on BBC2 on March 27, 1978. (The 75-minute film continues to be shown around the world, with one of its most recent screenings occurring on the Paramount Comedy Channel as part of a *Monty Python Weekend* on Sunday October 25, 1998, and then, more recently on the station on Friday February 5, 1999.)
 In the UK, *Melody Maker* publishes an exclusive interview with Ringo carried out with Ray Coleman in Paris at the George V Hotel.

Ringo takes a swipe at EMI over their policy of repackaging vintage Beatles recordings without consulting any former members of the group. In particular, he is angry over the cover design for the compilation album *Rock 'N' Roll Music*. "I'd like some power over whoever is at EMI who's putting out these lousy Beatles compilations. They can do what they like with all our old stuff, we know that. It's theirs. But Christ man, I was there. I played on those records and you know how much trouble we used to go to just getting the running order right, so those tempos of songs are nicely planned and everything? And the album covers! John rang them up and asked them if he could draw them one . . . John told me he was told to 'piss off'. All of us looked at the cover and could hardly bear to see it. It was terrible! So listen EMI, if you're reading this – please let us know what you're doing with the records we made. We'd like it done, how do I say, nicely!"

(Note: When told of Ringo's reaction, EMI gave this reply: "It is a little bit difficult to comment directly on this as (the *Rock 'N' Roll Music* album) was generated from Capitol in America. But every step was taken to involve all The Beatles in the project. We gather that at the crucial time, when the design for the cover had to be in hand, the Capitol people were unable to contact John for a final meeting. We are very concerned that in repackaging and re-promoting, we maintain the artistic integrity of the catalogue and the more involvement that we can have with any of The Beatles we would welcome.")

Ringo is also asked why he lives in Monte Carlo? "It's the tax thing. If you want to keep any of your bread, it seems that you've got to stay out of England . . . I'd rather live in England, but, well, I want some bread."

The reason for the magnifying glass with each copy of his new album *Ringo's Rotogravure*? "So that the album buyers would have no problem in reading the graffiti on the back." (This depicts a picture of the front door at Apple's now derelict headquarters at 3 Saville Row in London, which now carries inscriptions from Beatles fans, saying, amongst many things, that John should get his green card.)

Ringo is asked: "But yet, how come you picture it and highlight it, with a magnifying glass on the back of your album which purports to establish Ringo as a personage beyond Beatlemania?"

"Couldn't resist it," he replies. "Anyway, I knew that if I didn't put it on the cover of my album, John'd have it on his and as he's not got a record coming out, I thought I'd get in fast."

Ringo is asked: "How did you feel about George's 'My Sweet Lord' episode?"

He replies: "George was very unlucky. There's no doubt that the tune is similar but how many songs have been written with other melodies in mind? George's version is much heavier than The Chiffons – he might have done it with the original in the back of his mind, but he's just very unlucky that someone wanted to make it a test case in court. If I'd written 'He's So Fine', I guess I'd have sued if I'd wanted some money."

Finally, Ringo is asked why he shaved his head bald recently?

"To see what it looked like and to make sure I didn't have boils or anything on my scalp."

Ringo's final words to Ray Coleman? "Hey, we haven't talked much about the new album . . ."

🍎 Later this evening, Paul is interviewed by Tony Prince for the 60-minute Radio Luxembourg programme, suitably called *A McCartney Special*.

Monday October 4
🍎 At 4pm, in the Okura Hotel in Amsterdam, Holland, Ringo gives an interview for the Dutch fanzine *Beatles Unlimited*.

Tuesday October 5
🍎 During his stay in Holland, Ringo makes a 15-minute live appearance on the AVRO NED2 programme *Voor De Vuist Weg*, hosted by Williem Duys, the highlight of which occurs when Ringo proceeds to cut off the tie of the host. To conclude the appearance, the promotional clip of 'You Don't Know Me At All' is transmitted. Shortly after the interview, Ringo returns to the States.

Saturday October 9
🍎 As a present for his 36th birthday, Ringo sends Cherry Vanilla over to John and Yoko's Dakota apartment, where she delivers her own special version of *Romeo & Juliet!* John

and Yoko announce plans to release a book entitled *365 Days Of Sean*, which consists of photographs of Sean, taken by Bob Gruen, from every day of Sean's first year.

* * *

Wings Live At The Empire Pool in Wembley, London, England
Tuesday October 19 – Thursday October 21

To climax their massive world tour, Wings perform three sell out concerts at the Empire Pool in Wembley, with tickets priced between £1.80 and £3.50. The shows begin at 8pm each night. Problems occur when some fans, who had bought expensive £3.50 tickets, are unable to see Wings on stage. This is caused by a huge loudspeaker gantry, which blocks the view for several hundred seats. One concertgoer Martin Griffiths complains: "I paid £14 for four tickets but none of my party could see a thing! It ruined what could have been a great concert." A spokesman for the Empire Pool announces: "Anyone disappointed with their seats should apply to the promoter Harvey Goldsmith for refunds."

Tuesday October 19
Wings are featured live, backstage at the Empire Pool with Eamonn Andrews, during the Thames ITV regional programme *Today* (transmitted in the London region of ITV only between 6:00 and 6: 34pm). Eamonn talks to the group about their world tour and the Wembley concerts. Joining Wings are two members of the Wings Fun Club, Alan Springate and Debra Enderby, who travelled to America with the *Daily Mirror* Pop Club to see Wings perform at Madison Square Garden.

Thursday October 21
Following the show, Wings attend a special party, organised and paid for, by EMI Records in London. Amongst the guests are 10cc, Kiki Dee, *Old Grey Whistle Test* presenter Bob Harris and the *Supersonic* ITV music show producer, Mike Mansfield.

* * *

Friday October 29
 In Atlantic's New York studios, Ringo records the unreleased track 'I Can Hear You Calling'.

October & November
 The Warner Brothers promotional films to accompany the songs 'Crackerbox Palace', 'True Love' and 'This Song' are distributed to selected TV stations around the world. During November, George records an interview for Granada ITV's *Granada Reports* programme, to promote his new album, which is transmitted only in the northern region of England.
 In November, the *Star Trek* producer Gene Rodenberry approaches Wings, while they are working at Abbey Road Studios on their new live album, to appear in his new science-fiction musical concerning "an invasion from space". The original proposal is for Wings to simply play themselves. Work is scheduled to commence in January. (The film fails to materialise.)
 Also in November, it's announced that filming is scheduled to begin early next year on the big-screen film version of *Sgt. Pepper's Lonely Hearts Club Band*, starring Peter Frampton and The Bee Gees.

Friday November 5
"The world's greatest recording artists, perform Lennon & McCartney's greatest songs on the greatest album ever."
 The all-star soundtrack album *All This And World War II* is released. The double album features Elton John, Rod Stewart, David Essex, The Bee Gees, Bryan Ferry, Roy Wood, Keith Moon, Jeff Lynne, The Four Seasons, Helen Reddy, Richard Coctaine, Peter Gabriel and Tina Turner and others all performing covers of well-known Beatles songs. There is also an 88-minute black and white Fox/Lou Reisner film featuring the covers of Beatles songs interwoven with clips from World War II newsreels, including one of 'The Fool On The Hill' – accompanying shots of Hitler at his mountain retreat in Berchtesgaden, Germany.

Saturday November 6
🍎 'A Dose Of Rock 'N' Roll' reaches number 26 in the American charts.

Monday November 8
🍎 George's album *The Best Of George Harrison* is released in America. (The UK release takes place on November 20.) The track listing for the record is as follows: side one: 'Something', 'If I Needed Someone', 'Here Comes The Sun', 'Taxman', 'Think For Yourself', 'For You Blue' and 'While My Guitar Gently Weeps'; side two: 'My Sweet Lord', 'Give Me Love (Give Me Peace On Earth)', 'You', 'Bangla Desh', 'Dark Horse' and 'What Is Life'.

George is asked about the release. "Well, I did have a suggestion – which I made to Capitol early in the year – as to a title and a format of songs."

Did they take your suggestion? "No. What they've done is take a lot of songs which happen to be me singing lead on my songs which were Beatles songs, when there was really a lot of good songs they could have used of me separately. Solo songs. I don't see why they didn't do that. They did that with Ringo's *Blast From Your Past* and John's *Shaved Fish*. It was just John's. It wasn't digging into Beatles records."

🍎 Also today, in the case over George's plagiarism over the song 'He's So Fine', damages totalling $587,000 are awarded to Bright Tunes. The damages are eventually paid on February 26, 1981, ironically to former Beatles' manager Allen Klein's company ABKCO, which had purchased the rights to 'He's So Fine' in 1980.

🍎 Also today, Capitol release The Beatles' single 'Ob-La-Di Ob-La-Da'/'Julia'.

Friday November 12
🍎 Tonight, on BBC2 in England (between 9:01 and 9:29pm), the first-ever clip of The Rutles, performing the Neil Innes song 'I Must Be In Love', is screened during episode one of series two of *Rutland Weekend Television*. (The three-minute clip was filmed on Monday November 24, 1975, and premiered in America on October 2 earlier this year. See relevant entries.)

Monday November 15
🍎 George's single 'This Song'/'Learning How To Love You' is released in America. (The UK release takes place on November 19.)

Wednesday November 17
🍎 In Los Angeles, George attends a special dinner at Chasen's on Hollywood Boulevard, arranged by Warner Brothers to announce a worldwide distribution deal with Dark Horse records. (Currently on their books are Splinter, Attitudes, Kenny Burke and Stairsteps.) Before entering the restaurant, George chats briefly to waiting reporters.

Reporter: "Are you going to expand the Dark Horse roster?"

George: "No. I'm not interested in signing a lot. I made up my mind over the last year what we've got, and basically I'll keep it at that and see how it goes. I don't want to get into a big deal. It's too time-consuming. But if we do well we'll see how things go. If we don't do well I'll just keep it small."

Reporter: "What about a tour?"

George: "I had some dates planned for this year but I became sick halfway through the album and had to stop. I was sick in bed for two and a half months with hepatitis so I had to cancel the dates. It was going to be Germany, Amsterdam, London, Paris and Japan, which was the first part of the tour, so I'm going to do that next year. I'm going to India for Ravi Shankar's niece's wedding and I'll stay in India for a while and be back here around January and maybe make a new album and then go on the road next summer. An American tour would probably be next summer. It takes such a long time to organise things like that."

Reporter: "What about a band?"

George: "No, not at the moment. But I'd try and keep it real simple and have to wait and see how that will evolve."

Reporter: "What did you learn from your first solo tour?"

George: "I learned that I should make sure that I have plenty of rest before it. Because last time I had such a heavy work schedule that I did myself in right before the tour. I just had no throat. I learned a lot of things. Possibly I'll do a Dark Horse tour this time and take some of the other Dark Horse acts. A special show."

🍎 During the luncheon, a short colour film of George performing Fleetwood Mac's 'Go Your Own Way' on an acoustic guitar is shown to the Warner Brothers personnel. Derek Taylor, the former Beatles' press officer, also attends.

Friday November 19

 In New York, in Studio 8-H at 30, Rockefeller Plaza in New York City, George and Paul Simon record several songs for the NBC TV show *Saturday Night live*. The broadcast, which takes place the following day, includes acoustic performances of 'Here Comes The Sun' and 'Homeward Bound', as well as the promotional films for 'Crackerbox Palace' (directed by Eric Idle) and 'This Song' (directed by George). Also rehearsed (and taped) by George and Paul are performances of 'Bye, Bye, Love', a brief snippet of 'Don't Let Me Wait Too Long', 'Yesterday', 'Bridge Over Troubled Water', 'Rock Island Line', a brief 'Flight Of The Valkyries' and a reprise of 'Here Comes The Sun'. (Their performance of 'Homeward Bound' will appear on the charity album *Nobody's Child: Romanian Angel Appeal,* which is released on July 24, 1990.)

 At the start of tonight's *Saturday Night Live* show, which is neatly arranged to coincide with the November 24 release of George's much delayed album *Thirty Three And A Third*, George is seen asking Lorne Michaels if he can have the promised $3,000 Beatles reunion money. Michaels insists, "If it was up to me, you could have the money. But NBC wouldn't agree." (Incidentally, the UK release for the album *Thirty Three And A Third* takes place today.) Promotional adverts for the album feature George's original birth certificate underneath the headline: "1943 Was A Great Year For Music."

 The Beatles album *Magical Mystery Tour*, originally released in America by Capitol Records in 1967, finally appears in the UK on Parlophone featuring the exact same track listing.

Monday November 22

 Ringo's single 'Hey Baby'/'Lady Gaye' is released in America. (The UK release takes place on November 29.)

Wednesday November 24

 Ringo appears on drums with The Band during the performance of 'I Shall Be Released' at their farewell performance at the Winterland in San Francisco, California. This concert is filmed by United Artists and later released to the cinema as *The Last Waltz*.

Tuesday November 30

 This afternoon, at 40 Royal Avenue, London SW3, George records (on 16mm film) an interview with Bob Harris for inclusion in this evening's edition of the late night rock music programme *The Old Grey Whistle Test*, transmitted on BBC2 between 23:19pm and 00:01am. The feature lasts for 10 minutes and 58 seconds and includes the promotional films for 'This Song' and 'True Love'.

December

 A new big glossy book is published by Jonathan Cape, entitled *Linda's Pictures*, which features work from her early days on *Rolling Stone* through her days at New York's Fillmore East Theater to her portraits of Paul and their family. The respected photographer Terry O'Neill reviews the book in *Melody Maker*. "I fully expected this book to be an unmitigated disaster. However, I was very pleasantly surprised and can only take my hat off as one professional to another. Well done!"

 Rumours fly around in the music industry that Eric Stewart, currently playing with the chart-topping group 10cc, will soon replace Jimmy McCulloch in Wings.

 Meanwhile, *Music Week* magazine publishes an article under the headline: "Worldwide Release For Pre-EMI Beatles Set." It refers to the proposed issue of the Star Club tapes and an alleged letter from The Beatles' first manager Brian Epstein, which states that: "Mr. Ted Taylor owns the tapes and is allowed to release them."

Friday December 10

 The Wings triple album *Wings Over America* is released simultaneously in the UK and America. The album retails in the UK for £6.80. During the run-up to the final mastering of the album, Paul is reported to have spent 14 hours a day, seven days a week for six weeks working on the release. Paul prepares a special 30-second television commercial to coincide with the album's release, featuring highlights of the songs 'Live And Let Die', 'Soily', 'Yesterday' and 'Maybe I'm Amazed'.

 In England, George drops into the *Seven O Sound* hi-fi shop in London, where he requests a copy of each of his six BBC2 *Rutland Weekend Television* videotapes. His £194 bill remains unpaid until October 30, 1980.

Saturday December 11

◆ The single 'Ob-La-Di, Ob-La-Da' reaches number 49 in the American charts.

Saturday December 18 & Sunday December 19

◆ London's first Beatles convention takes place over two days at Alexandra Palace in North London. Among the highlights is the auction of George's original suit worn at Salisbury Plain during the filming of *Help!* in 1965. It sells for £200! A scheduled screening of *Shea Stadium* again fails to materialise, as does a planned transatlantic phone call with John in New York, due to be carried out with the Radio Luxembourg DJ Tony Prince. Other events, which do go ahead, include a Beatles quiz, a Beatles karaoke sound-alike competition, an exhibition of paintings by Stuart Sutcliffe which are available to buy, the price depending on the size of the picture, and four giant Beatle effigies which, due to an unfortunate accident, sadly deflate. There is also a performance by fellow Liverpudlian chart-toppers Gerry and The Pacemakers. The event is not a success as only a few hundred fans turn up instead of the expected 4,000. Dejected organiser Dave Chisnell remarks: "I'm disappointed that a lot more fans didn't turn up but I think we did quite well considering the weather which was miserable. You've got to remember that this is the first major Beatles' convention and I think people have got to get used to the idea of having them." The event runs between 10am and 2am on the Saturday and from 12 noon until midnight on Sunday. A report on the first day of the convention appears on the BBC1 evening news.

Monday December 20

◆ Hampshire Police in the UK announce that they are to question the staff of John Lennon in connection with the Watership Down murder of 1975. This follows a new breakthrough after a Reading taxi driver tells police that he picked up a young German girl named Richter who informed him that she "once worked for Mr. Lennon". (The original murder was of a young German girl who was found in an orchard on Watership Down on the Hampshire-Berkshire border the previous year.)

Friday December 24

◆ George's single 'My Sweet Lord'/'What Is Life' is released in the UK.
◆ Paul and Linda attend the opening night concert by Rod Stewart at London's Olympia. Following the show they are seen chatting backstage with Marc Bolan, Alvin Stardust, Status Quo's Rick Parfitt, Liberal leader David Steel and the actress Susan George. Paul's brother Mike and Denny Laine are also in attendance.

Saturday December 25

"Live Beatles At Star Club To Be Released."
◆ *Melody Maker* reports: "The Beatles' Hamburg tapes, recorded 15 years ago in the famed Star Club, will be released as a live double album early next year. The album includes an early version of 'I Saw Her Standing There' plus 'Roll Over Beethoven' and 'Long Tall Sally'. The tapes were subsequently lost and then rediscovered by The Beatles' first manager Allan Williams while he was researching his book *The Man Who Gave The Beatles Away*."

Monday December 27

◆ A further meeting is held between lawyers representing George and Bright Tunes Inc.

Friday December 31

◆ John and Yoko spend New Years Eve at the Shun Lee Dynasty restaurant in Manhattan alongside friends including the singer Carly Simon and her husband James Taylor.

"It's a joke! I mean it needs a joke when the last offer was for $50 million. It's trying to put the responsibility of making the world a wonderful world again onto The Beatles. I think that's unfair."

– George, on another Beatles reunion offer

January
🍎 At the Capitol Radio Music Awards show in London, Wings collect the accolade for Best Live Show in London with their 1976 Wembley performances. The group appears personally to collect the award. In the *NME*, the album *Wings At The Speed Of Sound,* comes second, behind Abba, in the Most Popular Record of 1976 chart.

🍎 Ringo is cast in the role of a temperamental European movie director and ex-husband of Mae West in the film *Sextette*, which also stars Keith Moon of The Who.

🍎 George and Olivia travel to India where they attend the wedding of Ravi Shankar's niece. The Harrisons then travel on to Mexico for a holiday. In 1979, George will recall 1977 as . . . "The year I took off from music," revealing that he didn't write one single song between January and December. "I went to the races," said George, who became a regular fixture at Formula 1 motor races around the world.

🍎 On a beach in the Bahamas, Eric Idle and former Beach Boys sideman Rikki Fataar begin writing the script for the full length television comedy programme *The Rutles.*

🍎 The new English Tourist Board guidebook called *Discover Merseyside* describes Liverpool as "The home of The Beatles," but adds, "We cannot find one single relic of the group!"

Saturday January 8
🍎 In England, at the *Daily Mirror Pop Club Readers Poll Concert*, held at the Bingley Hall in Staffordshire, further awards are bestowed on Wings when they arrive to collect their awards for Best Pop Group and Best Rock Group. In addition, Paul is voted by *Daily Mirror* readers as the Best Group Singer. Joining Paul, Linda and Denny at the ceremony are fellow poll award winners, including David Essex, The Rubettes, The Real Thing and John Miles.

Monday January 10
🍎 A statement issued today reveals Apple Corps Ltd. has finally settled their dispute with Allen Klein. The settlement will cost Apple $5,009,200 (approximately £2.9 million). John signs his "release from Klein" papers in New York at the Plaza Hotel, where The Beatles first stayed after arriving in America on February 7, 1964. In his statement, Klein praises the "tireless efforts and Kissinger-like negotiating brilliance of Yoko Ono Lennon". This result gives Paul some satisfaction – knowing that Klein is now out of the way – but the fact that Apple has to pay him this sum clearly rankles, as some of this cash was legally his since all of the money Paul had earned up to *Band On The Run* was paid directly into Apple's account. News that The Beatles are now legally free to reunite produces worldwide speculation. Paul, though, will have none of it. In preparation for the inevitable "When will The Beatles get together again?" question, he prepares a rhyme, a parody of those penned by heavyweight boxing champion Muhammad Ali:
"The Beatles split in '69,
And since then they have been doing fine.
And if that question doesn't cease,
Ain't no one gonna get no peace.
And if they ask it just once more,
I think I'll have to bash them on their jaw."

Wednesday January 19
🍎 John and Yoko are among an abundance of celebrities attending Jimmy Carter's Presidential Inauguration Ball, held at the Kennedy Center for the Performing Arts in Washington DC. Performing at the televised event are Paul Simon, Aretha Franklin, Linda Rondstadt and Stevie Wonder, although his appearance does not make the transmitted CBS TV show. Carter is inaugurated as the 39th President of the US the following day.

Friday January 21
🍎 The Beatles' solicitors Frere Cholmeley, of London, enquire of Paul Murphy of Lingasong Ltd., about the 1962 Star Club tapes. They are informed, over the phone, that "the records will be released shortly".

Saturday January 22
🍎 *Wings Over America* reaches number one in the American album charts.

Monday January 24
❧ George's single 'Crackerbox Palace'/'Learning How To Love You' is released in America.

Wednesday January 26
❧ John writes a postcard to Chris Charlesworth, *Melody Maker*'s American editor, declining an interview request. Says Charlesworth: "I'd got to know John quite well by this time and instead of going through PRs whenever I wanted to interview him, I simply sent a telegram to the Dakota building. If he was in New York he'd ring me back within 24 hours and we'd make arrangements to meet or just chat on the phone. This was the last time I requested an interview and, of course, he'd gone into hiding, so he wrote, 'No comment, was the stern reply. Am invisible.' I never saw or spoke to John again."

Saturday January 29 & Sunday January 30
❧ In America, based on an idea from BBC Radio One (see entry for Friday April 16, 1976), the entire Beatles recording output from 1962 to 1970 is transmitted in alphabetical order over the weekend on the New York radio station WNEW. During the six hours of programming, the first to be aired is 'Across The Universe' and the last, late on Sunday night is 'You Really Got A Hold On Me'.

February
❧ It is reported that Linda is expecting a baby in September. Meanwhile, the former Wings guitarist Henry McCullough travels to Liverpool and promptly gets involved in a fight while drinking in a wine lodge. Reports suggest that he had been saying "not too kind a word" about Paul, one of Liverpool's favourite sons!

Tuesday February 1
❧ At BBC Broadcasting House in Portland Place, London, George records a lengthy interview with Anne Nightingale of Radio One, to be broadcast on her show over two parts (Saturday February 5 and 12. See entry for February 5 for details of the interview.) Immediately following the afternoon taping, George boards a flight to Holland to undertake some brief European promotional appearances.

Thursday February 3 (until Sunday February 6 and through February)
❧ At Dam Square in Amsterdam, Holland, George films an interview for Veronica Television. During the short 11-minute feature, which also includes the promotional films for 'Crackerbox Palace' and 'True Love', George talks about his new album, his work for the third world and goes into detail about his first LSD trip. Naturally he is asked about The Beatles getting together again. Even though the problem with Klein has now been resolved, he dismisses the possibility of anything happening with the group again. "Physically we're all in different places and we don't spend time together any more. That's the problem," he states. "We'd have to get to know each other again, everyone's into their own lives. It seems very difficult, the idea of trying to get together."

He is then asked about the recent huge-money Beatles reunion offers. "It's a joke!" says George. "I mean it needs a joke when the last offer was for $50 million and it's just crazy, you know. It's trying to put the responsibility of making the world a wonderful world again onto The Beatles. I think that's unfair. I know a lot of people like The Beatles but it's like eight years ago we split up and it's different you know. It's like we all grew up and left home. It's like trying to get the family back again or trying to get us to go back to school again!" (The interview was last repeated in Holland on February 24, 1988.)

George's next European port of call is Germany, where (on Saturday February 5) he mimes 'This Song' on the ZDF TV music show *Disco '77*. Besides taking part in a brief conference to promote the album *Thirty Three And A Third*, George visits Hamburg's Grosse Freiheit, the area of the famous Star Club, Indra and the Kaiserkeller night clubs where The Beatles played during the early Sixties. George next travels to France where he is interviewed for the Sunday night (February 6) programme TFI-TV show *Les Rendezvous Du Dimanche*. During his 16-minute studio appearance, he talks with host Michael Drucker (with questions translated into English via his earpiece) and introduces the promo film for 'This Song'. Other guests on the show include the heavyweight Greek singer Demis Roussos. When his European duties are completed, George and Olivia fly on to Acapulco in Mexico, where they attend a press party. (Surprisingly, George appears at the gathering wearing a Beatles T-shirt). Later, the Harrisons return to their home in Los Angeles.

 Also on February 4, the Wings single 'Maybe I'm Amazed' (live version)/'Soily' is released in the UK, where it will reach number 28. (The American release takes place on February 7.)

Saturday February 5

 BBC Radio One transmits (between 1:30 and 2:29pm) the first of two hour-long conversations between George and Anne Nightingale at BBC Broadcasting House, London, on Tuesday February 1. He discusses a wide range of subjects including the *Bangla Desh* concert, the break-up of The Beatles and his solo recordings. Firstly, Anne asks about recording 'My Sweet Lord' and the troubles that followed with the song.

George: "The first version of that was recorded with Billy Preston with the Edwin Hawkins Singers . . . that was good because the idea for the song came to me anyway based upon 'Oh Happy Day'. I was on the road with Delaney & Bonnie and Eric (Clapton) at the time in Sweden and I was just thinking of a way of how to combine Halleluja and Hare Krishna which is just simplistically the West and the East . . . how to get everybody singing 'Halleluja Halleluja Halleluja' and then suddenly shove 'Hare Krishna' in and catch them before they realised! That was really the idea, based upon 'Oh Happy Day' by The Edwin Hawkins Singers. As it happened, they came to town and phoned up and said, 'Do you want us to do any dates?' So we got them down to Olympic Studios. The original version of 'My Sweet Lord' is with The Temptations, so we had their drummer, bass player and guitar, Billy (Preston) on piano and organ and The Edwin Hawkins Singers. If you listen to that one, there is a point where I was trying get The Edwin Hawkins Singers to sing 'Hare Krishna'. They are a funny group of people. They were saying, 'What? What is this Hare Krishna?' Luckily, there was one young guy in there and he said, 'You know, Hare Krishna. You have seen them out there, dancing in the street.' And so, if you listen to that version, there is one place where they are going 'Halleluja. Hare Krishna.' So I was happy. I got in twice actually.

"It wasn't until my own version had been released and it was a hit, that trouble loomed large. The first thing I knew was when Klein said something. He said, 'Somebody has made a recording.' It was the company Bright Tunes; they had got this version recorded by Jodie Miller of 'He's So Fine' which was really like, you know, putting the screws in. What they did was to change the chords of 'He's So Fine' and make them completely into the same chords as 'My Sweet Lord' because there is actually a slight difference and then also put on top of it the slide guitar part. So it was really trying to rub it in, and I thought 'God!' So then, all the people started hustling each other and the guy from Bright Tunes was demanding money and various things. I really didn't hear anything about it for years. The attorneys were supposedly settling the thing and in the end I said, 'Look, it is just a lot of aggravation. Just give the guy some money.' And so they were going to give him two hundred thousand dollars. I found out, last week, after it has been to court and has been a big scene, now the guy only gets fifty thousand! The judge made a slip after the court case. He just said to my attorney, 'Actually, I like both of the songs.' My lawyer said to him 'What do you mean, both of the songs? You said, in your decision, that it's the same song.' And he said 'Ooops! Sorry. What I mean is, I like the song with the two sets of lyrics!' "

Anne, being terribly diplomatic and polite, tries to avoid the delicate subject of Patti Harrison going off with George's close friend Eric Clapton. But George is happy to comment on it.

"No. No. You see, ever since 1963 I have not really had a private life. So one thing I found was that if you have got something to hide, you've got all these people buzzing round you, round your front door, all the time. Say, for example, if you split up with your wife and you're trying not to tell anybody, then there's people there who are trying to find something out. But if there's nothing to be known, then it is much easier in the long run. So consequentially, since 1963/1964, The Beatles have been owned by the public, or Fleet Street, and we learnt to live with that. I found that it was much easier just to tell people. What's the point in trying to hide something. It only means that they are going to be crawling around your garden, trying to get pictures of you and stuff. It's easier just to say 'Sure, I'm divorced' or whatever."

Anne: "So that was the way of doing it."

George: "So well, you know, it was public knowledge, at least with the few people I know, and so that was just a little joke . . . 'Bye Bye Love'."

On a trivia note, Anne points out that there are over 120 cover versions of 'Something' in the BBC record library. The interviews are complimented by a wide range of Beatles and solo recordings, plus 'Dispute And Violence' and 'I Am Missing You' by Ravi Shankar, 'Something' performed by The London Symphony Orchestra, 'Costafine Town' by Splinter and versions of 'He's So Fine' by The Chiffons and Jodie Miller. (Part two of this interview is transmitted one week later, on Saturday February 12.)

🍎 Meanwhile, at the Cherokee Studios in Los Angeles, California, Ringo begins working for the first time with the producer Arif Mardin and records the unreleased songs 'Lover Please' and 'Wild Shining Stars'. Towards the end of the month, Ringo records the tracks 'Out In The Streets', 'It's No Secret' and 'Gypsy'.

Monday February 7
🍎 Wings begin recording the tracks 'London Town' and 'Deliver Your Children'. During this period, work commences on the track 'Girl's School', which will appear at the tail end of the year as the B-side (in the UK) to 'Mull Of Kintyre'. (The recordings will continue until March 31.) During the sessions at Abbey Road, a television crew from Australian television's *Countdown* show visits the group to watch them rehearse. (The report is first transmitted in the country on April 3.)

Friday February 11
🍎 George's single 'True Love'/'Pure Smokey' is released in the UK.

Saturday February 12
🍎 Ringo's cover of Bruce Channel's 1962 'Hey Baby' peaks at number 74 in the American singles chart.

Saturday February 19
🍎 In Los Angeles, Ringo, appearing alongside the composer Paul Williams, is a guest presenter on the annual Grammy Awards show, which is televised across America.

Sunday February 20
🍎 Paul and Linda fly off to Jamaica for a fortnight's holiday. Prior to their departure at Heathrow, fans mob Paul.

Saturday February 26 & Sunday February 27
🍎 Another *Beatlefest* convention takes place this weekend in America. This time the two-day event will be staged at the Statler Hilton Hotel in New York. Amongst the promised attractions is the Granada Television film of The Beatles performing 'Some Other Guy' at the Cavern Club on August 22, 1962. Also on February 26, *Melody Maker* writes: "Beatles Set For First Live Album." The report goes: "A Beatles live double album looks set for release later this year – if the former members of the band give their consent. Beatles producer George Martin has put together the album from tapes of a concert at the Hollywood Bowl in Los Angeles in 1964. Martin has already spoken to Lennon about the project in New York." Meanwhile, the paper prints further news on the impending release of the Star Club tapes. "BUK records, reported as planning a release of the album last year, admit that the deal has now fallen through," adding: "The American owner of the 15-year-old tapes, Lee Halpen of New York's Double H Licensing Corporation, is seeking a deal with a British company. He is hoping to set up a contract with one of the television merchandising companies."

March
🍎 John, Yoko and their photographer friend Bob Gruen attend a Broadway performance by the avant-garde Merce Cunningham Dance Company, after which they attend a special reception where they mingle with celebrities such as James Taylor and Carly Simon. Merce Cunningham was an old friend of Yoko's from the Fluxus Art Movement of the late Sixties and early Seventies. Then, within days of the event, and purely as an exercise to see if "the green card works", John ceremoniously packs an overnight bag and travels to Singapore and Hong Kong. From Singapore he sends a postcard to *Melody Maker* editor Ray Coleman, which cryptically reads: "Far East, Man." Later in the month, John, Yoko and George visit another Fluxus Art Movement friend, this time George Maciunas at his New Marlboro farm. The Lennons also pay a visit to Monterey in Canada, where they have their pictures taken at a photo studio in old west costumes. With John spending much of his time away from the Dakota, he fails to receive a written request from the film director Francis Ford Coppola,

asking him to write music for his upcoming film *Apocalypse Now*. Meanwhile, also this month in the States, rumours begin to circulate in the music industry that "Lennon is shopping around for a new record label and may sign with Portrait, run by CBS."

 Paul and Wings are among the artists scheduled to appear at two giant concerts in London in June to celebrate the Queen's Silver Jubilee. Paul and Wings have apparently been approached to perform at the British Night concert at Earl's Court on June 4. Also scheduled to appear is Queen.

 George, eager for more non-music related business ventures, joins the comic Peter Sellers in investing money in a luxury hotel on the Seychelle Islands.

 It is also announced that Derek Taylor, currently the co-deputy-managing director of WEA in England, is shortly to become a vice-president and director of Warner Brothers in California. (He will take up the post in July.)

Saturday March 5
 'Maybe I'm Amazed' (live version) reaches number 28 in the UK singles chart.

Saturday March 12
 Further news of the *Hollywood Bowl* album appears in the *Melody Maker*. The report reads: "Beatles Live LP In May". The short article announces that: ". . . all four Beatles have now given their consent for the release of the album and that it will be in the shops on May 6. EMI are to back the album with a massive advertising campaign on television, similar to the campaign mounted when The Beatles' *Rock 'N' Roll Music* album was released last year." The report concludes by saying: "The album, however, will not, as previously reported, be a double album."

Wednesday March 23
 Following further enquiries, Apple's solicitors again contact Lingasong Ltd. to ask what they intend to do with the Star Club tapes. They are informed that "the records will be in the shops within two or three months," adding "they may not be released in England as an EMI record of The Beatles is due in May."

Tuesday March 29
 With hysteria mounting about the release of a "new" Beatles album, George Martin talks about the *Hollywood Bowl* recordings to an American newspaper: "Although technically they were pretty awful, hearing the boys' voices in those days and the excitement of it all was really amazing." As for the re-mastering of the original tapes: "It was a labour of love, like restoring an antique motor car."

April
 John, Yoko and Sean return to New York where they pay a visit to the circus at Madison Square Garden, an event captured by ABC Channel 7 News where John and Yoko are briefly seen chatting with Mick Jagger.

 The musical *Beatlemania* comes to Broadway's Winter Gardens Theater in New York. The show, produced by David Krebs and Steve Leber, features Murray The K (Kaufman), the original "fifth Beatle", as a special consultant. The Beatles are played by Joe Pecorino (John), Mitch Weissman (Paul), Leslie Franklin (George) and Justin McNeil (Ringo). While in England, Granada television, the ITV station serving the North of England, transmits, for the first time ever in the UK, the Al Brodax cartoon series *The Beatles*. These were produced in America between 1965 and 1967, and feature the animated Beatles in short comedy sketches set to the real EMI recordings, which were usually cut or re-edited. (The first American transmissions were on ABC TV on Saturday September 25, 1965.)

Friday April 1
 In London, Frere Cholmeley, representing Apple Corps Ltd., write to Paul Murphy at Lingasong Ltd., informing them that they will institute proceedings to "Prevent the making, sale or distribution of the Star Club records" unless they receive suitable undertakings this afternoon. No undertakings are forthcoming and a notice of motion against Lingasong Ltd., is served later in the day. This is The Beatles' first legal move against the proposed release of the Star Club tapes, and their delay will ultimately prove to be a major downfall in their defence.

Saturday April 2
🍎 The live version of 'Maybe I'm Amazed' reaches number 10 in the US singles chart.

Monday April 4
🍎 John's 'Stand By Me'/'Woman Is The Nigger Of The World' is released as a single in America.
🍎 George's 'Dark Horse'/'You' is also released as a single in America today.

Tuesday April 5
🍎 Mr. Richard Scott QC, on behalf of The Beatles, applies for a High Court injunction against Paul Murphy and his Lingasong companies releasing the double album *The Beatles Live At The Star Club In Hamburg, Germany 1962*. Due to a loophole in copyright restrictions, the record is still due to go on sale in Germany this Thursday. Asked about the UK release, Paul Murphy, head of BUK Records, a part of Lingasong, announces: "I don't wish to say anything about that until after the question of this injunction is settled. Though I do plan to release the record in one month." A reporter asks him about The Beatles' claims that they never gave permission for the album to be released. "No-one has heard The Beatles deny that they have given permission for the album to be released," he replies, adding: "We feel it is ethical to release it. It's cost us £50,000 to get the album ready for release."

Wednesday April 6
🍎 The Beatles lose in their bid to halt the commercial release of the double album *The Beatles Live! At The Star Club In Hamburg, Germany: 1962*, which contains recordings originally made by Ted "Kingsize" Taylor on a portable tape recorder during their December 31, 1962, shows. High Court Vice-Chancellor Sir Robert Megarry turns down their application after hearing Ted Taylor say: "The Beatles had originally agreed to the tape provided I bought them a beer!" The judge ultimately rules in favour of Paul Murphy and Lingasong due to the: "Inactivity of the plaintiffs (Apple) until Friday April 1. Until then they had given no sign of objection or protest, they had long known of the tapes and of attempts to exploit them commercially."

His Lordship's ruling goes on: "I cannot treat seriously the contention that the plaintiffs had no thought of the possibility of the records being issued in England and contemplated only publication in the United States. Not until the defendants (Lingasong) were far along the road towards issuing the records, and had incurred the expense of processing the tapes to improve the quality, and had manufactured the records, did the plaintiffs strike on the very day when they uttered their first warning. Such inactivity was inequitable enough to make the court reluctant to intervene by granting the equitable remedy of injunction. Furthermore, it was common ground that some sort of oral contract was given to the making of the original tape and that consent might well have been wide enough to authorise all that has been done, which failed to satisfy section 1 of the 1958 act only because the consent was not in writing."
🍎 The result is bad news for EMI, whose own "live" Beatles album, the *Hollywood Bowl* 1964/1965 compilations, is set for release on May 1. As expected, they issue a "no comment" statement from their London headquarters. The *Star Club* album first appears in Germany on Friday April 8, licensed for release from the New York Company Double H Licensing Corporation. For the next two decades, the Star Club tapes become freely available and appear in countless different configurations around the globe. Unbelievably, 21 years and one month after the first case, the tapes will again be the subject of another case in the High Courts of London. (See entry for Tuesday May 5, 1998.)
🍎 Meanwhile, in New York, there is further court excitement when Allen Klein is indicted by a grand jury on charges of failing to report more than $216,000 (approximately £127,000) income from the sale of promotional Beatles records. The indictment claims that Klein, aged 46, schemed to get them sold to wholesalers and distributors at a profit. This follows Klein's previous charge of tax evasion during the years 1970–72.

Friday April 8
🍎 Further problems befall the infamous *Live At The Star Club* record when 100,000 copies of the double album, ready for immediate dispatch to England, are caught up in German airport workers' industrial action.

Saturday April 23
 In tonight's edition of *Saturday Night Live*, *Rutlemania* hysteria continues to grow when "Ron Nasty (played by Neil Innes, wonderfully imitating John circa 1969), now living in seclusion in New York, is invited out of retirement to join in a *Save Britain Telethon*." The story behind tonight's show goes: "During the late Seventies, Great Britain is reported to be going through enormous financial difficulties and Eric Idle is determined to do something about it." Throughout the show, viewers are (jokingly) requested to pledge money to "help keep Great Britain afloat", a cause that inspires Ron Nasty to come on the show to perform the track 'Cheese And Onions', a song re-recorded for *The Rutles* TV special transmitted the following year. The audience response to this and the previous Rutles clip forces Lorne Michaels to contemplate the funding of a full-length Rutles television programme, to be made by Eric Idle and Gary Weiss, the man responsible for the short comedy films on *Saturday Night Live*. (See entry for Monday July 18.)

Friday April 29
 The album *Thrillington*, Paul's instrumental version of his *Ram* album, recorded under the alias of *Percy Thrills Thrillington*, is released in the UK. A single, 'Uncle Albert – Admiral Halsey'/'Eat At Home' is also issued in the UK today. (The album is released in America on May 17.)

Saturday April 30
 Paul and Linda, currently in town on business and to see some Broadway plays, take up residence at the Stanhope Hotel, situated on the east side of Central Park opposite John and Yoko's Dakota apartments on the west side.

May
 Following the McCartneys' return from New York, Wings continue recording their album *London Town,* this time aboard the yacht *Fair Carol* off the Virgin Islands which had been converted, by the Record Plant in New York, into a 24-track studio. (Due to the locality of their base, Paul had briefly toyed with calling the album *Water Wings*.) The idea of recording on a boat came from Rod Stewart and the band America, who had both previously recorded on a sailing vessel. For the duration of the recordings, *McCartney Productions* also hires two other boats, a minesweeper called *Samala*, used to house the band and *El Toro* where Paul stays with Linda and the family. These sessions produce the following: 'With A Little Luck', 'Backwards Traveller'/'Cuff Link', 'Cafe On The Left Bank', 'I'm Carrying', 'I've Had Enough', 'Famous Groupies', 'Don't Let It Bring You Down' and 'Morse Moose And The Grey Goose'. Paul also records various unreleased titles such as 'Boil Crisis', 'After You've Gone', the instrumental 'El Toro Passing' and a Denny Laine track, which features the working title of 'Find A Way'. When not recording, the members of Wings go swimming and "drink swigs of rum", but unfortunately most of the entourage return home with one ailment or another. Paul cuts his knee and bruises a leg, Denny suffers from severe sunburn and Jimmy McCulloch gashes a knee and suffers from temporary deafness. Even Paul's management is in for a rough time, when Alan Crowder of MPL slips down a tight stairway and breaks his heel. Geoff Emerick returns to England suffering from an electrocuted foot! Paul talks further about these sessions for *Melody Maker* (see entry for November 19).
 In New York, John enrols in a Japanese language course. It is here that he again bumps into the world famous Brazilian footballer Pele.
 Neil Innes begins writing the songs intended for *The Rutles* television special. He completes the task in just less than two weeks.

Monday May 2
 The Lingasong double album *The Beatles Live! At The Star Club In Hamburg, Germany: 1962* is released in the UK. The full line-up of tracks on the album is: 'I Saw Her Standing There', 'Roll Over Beethoven', 'Hippy Hippy Shake', 'Sweet Little Sixteen', 'Lend Me Your Comb', 'Your Feet's Too Big', 'Twist And Shout', 'Mr. Moonlight', 'A Taste Of Honey', 'Besame Mucho', 'Reminiscing', 'Kansas City – Hey-Hey-Hey-Hey', 'Nothin' Shakin' (But The Leaves On The Trees)', 'To Know Her Is To Love Her', 'Little Queenie', 'Falling In Love Again', 'Ask Me Why', 'Be-Bop-A-Lula', 'Hallelujah I Love Her So', 'Red Sails In The Sunset', 'Everybody's Trying To Be My Baby', 'Matchbox', 'I'm Talking About You', 'Shimmy Shake', 'Long Tall Sally' and 'I Remember You'. An

alternative album, featuring four different songs, is released in America on June 13. These additional tracks include: 'I'm Gonna Sit Right Down And Cry Over You', 'Where Have You Been All My Life', 'Till There Was You' and 'Sheila'. Incidentally, neither version contains all of the songs originally recorded back on December 31, 1962.

Friday May 6
◆ Four days after an unofficial Beatles live recording reaches the shops, *The Beatles At The Hollywood Bowl,* a selection of tracks, re-mixed by George Martin, recorded during The Beatles' live concerts at the venues on August 23, 1964, and August 30, 1965, is released by EMI. EMI announce that they are anticipating sales close to one million copies and have earmarked up to £300,000 for the *Hollywood Bowl* promotion campaign. £245,000 of that will go towards three weeks of TV commercials comprising vintage footage of The Beatles live at the Hollywood Bowl venue back in 1964, £20,000 going to radio adverts while a further £25,000 has been allocated towards elaborate advertising boards to be displayed in record shops. The full track listing on the album is: side one: 'Twist And Shout', 'She's A Woman', 'Dizzy Miss Lizzy', 'Ticket To Ride', 'Can't Buy Me Love', 'Things We Said Today', 'Roll Over Beethoven'; side two: 'Boys', 'A Hard Day's Night', 'Help!', 'All My Loving', 'She Loves You', 'Long Tall Sally'.

Stories soon surface about how these tapes have languished in the Capitol Records archives in America for well over a decade. At the time of their recording, both the label and The Beatles deemed them unsuitable for release. One of the major reasons was that the unsophisticated Capitol three-track recording equipment was incapable of drowning out the screams of 17,000 hysterical fans. This made balance mixing impossible. Also, The Beatles, performing without any "fold-back" speakers, could not even hear what they were playing. The Beatles' main reason for not allowing these recordings to see the light of day back in the Sixties was because they did not contain any new Beatles' tracks, and instead showcased songs which were readily available on any official Beatles' record. It was agreed to shelve the recordings until the beginning of 1977 when EMI and Capitol, fresh from the successes of *Rock 'N' Roll Music* and the single re-issues in the UK, took a fresh look at the tapes, cajoled into doing so by some American radio stations who had started playing bootleg albums of the *Hollywood Bowl* live tapes, under the guise of playing the "original Capitol tapes".

Beatles producer George Martin takes up the story: "Bhaskar Menon, the president of Capitol Records, mentioned these tapes and asked me whether I'd listen to them because the company was interested in releasing an album. My immediate reaction was that, as far as I could remember, the original 1964 concert tapes had a rotten sound. I told Bhaskar: 'I don't think you've got anything here at all.' There have been an awful lot of bootleg recordings made of Beatles concerts around the world. But when I listened to the *Hollywood Bowl* tapes I was amazed at the rawness and vitality of The Beatles' singing. I'd quite forgotten what impact they had. So I told Bhaskar that I'd see if I could bring the tapes into line with today's recordings."

Working with the studio engineer Geoff Emerick, who had also worked with Martin on many of The Beatles' original sessions, their first task was to transfer the three-track tapes onto modern day 24-track recordings. Once accomplished, Martin's next task was to choose the material for the album. Some tracks were discarded due to the music being completely obliterated by the continuous screaming and, during one part of the show, a microphone packs up completely, rendering the live vocals inaudible for almost five minutes. "Both concerts were fairly identical in performance," Martin adds, "and there was very little variation in repertoire. So rather than try to keep the two performances chronologically separate, I thought the best thing to do was make a complete performance from the two."

Martin's next task was to gain permission from all of the ex-Beatles. "I had to go to New York anyway," he recalls, "so I rang John and told him about the recordings. I told him that I'd been very sceptical at first but now I was very enthusiastic because I thought the album would be a piece of history, which should be preserved. I said to John, 'I want you to hear it after I've gone. You can be as rude as you like, but if you don't like it give me a yell.' I spoke to him the following day and he was delighted with it."

Unsurprisingly, the reaction from both George and Ringo is not so enthusiastic.

Friday May 13
◆ The UK release of Roger Daltrey's album *One Of The Boys,* which includes 'Giddy' written by Paul. (The American release takes place on June 16.)

Saturday May 14

 The Beatles' episode of the Tony Palmer history of popular music *All You Need Is Love* is transmitted across the ITV network between 10:32 and 11:28pm. The show, titled *Mighty Good,* again tells the history of the group and again focuses on their influence on contemporary, mostly American, musicians. The 48-minute show, based on a script by Derek Taylor who is also interviewed, features additional interview material with Allan Williams, Brian Epstein's mother Queenie, George Martin, Murray 'The K' Kaufman, Taylor himself, Roger McGuinn of The Byrds, promoter Bill Graham and, from The Beach Boys, both Mike Love and Carl Wilson. Paul, sporting a tartan scarf, gives an exclusive interview and performs 'Yesterday', recorded during the American tour, which closes the show. Archive film used, most of which derives from Granada TV, together with excerpts from the 'Strawberry Fields Forever' and 'Lady Madonna' promotional films, the 1965 Shea Stadium documentary, 'All You Need Is Love' from the 1967 *Our World* live television broadcast, George receiving sitar tuition from Ravi Shankar during the filming of *Raga* in 1968 and John from the 1975 *Old Grey Whistle Test* interview. (Further Beatles clips, as well as more from the interview with Paul, is included in the series during the show which is dedicated to The Rolling Stones.)

 The music press reveals that George Martin has been named as musical director for the upcoming musical film *Sgt. Pepper's Lonely Hearts Club Band*, which begins shooting in Holland this summer. (This follows on from the previous Robert Stigwood production *John, Paul, George, Ringo . . . And Bert* which, even after filming had begun during July of 1975, was eventually scrapped.)

Thursday May 26

 The musical tribute show *Beatlemania* opens at the Winter Garden Theater in New York.

Saturday May 28

 Melody Maker publishes a fascinating article on Voyle Gilmore, the man responsible for originally producing The Beatles' *Hollywood Bowl* audio tape recordings. Today, Gilmore is to be found running a boatyard and dry dock in Bethel Island, 60 miles outside of the Bay Area. He retired from Capitol in 1969 after 24 years service. At his Farrar Park dry dock home, he is naturally asked:

"Have you heard the recently released Beatles live album yet?"

Voyle: "I haven't had a chance yet . . . I will. George Martin . . . he made such a speech. It sounds like he changed it, but I doubt it. There's not much he could do. It was recorded on three-track machines with half-inch tape. When The Beatles were first coming here, we (Capitol) would love to have a live album. I think Epstein would have gone for it, but the boys didn't go for it. They came from a poor background and they were always conscious of that. They felt a live album would be a rip-off because all the tunes were already recorded. Anyway, we took a sound truck up to the Hollywood Bowl and plugged directly into the soundboard with our mikes. The Bowl has a pretty good stereo sound system. They used to hold those stereo concerts, so we plugged our mikes in right there. George Martin was at the first concert. We parked several blocks away and took a cab up together. He wasn't around the sound truck that much. Oh, I think he stuck his head in and said, 'That sounds terrible', or something like that. He was more interested in hanging out backstage with the boys or going out front to see how it sounded out there, that sort of thing. The results weren't that bad. I kept thinking 'maybe we were going to get permission to release it' so I took it back into the studio and worked on it awhile. I worked with the applause, edited it down, made it play, and EQ'd it quite a bit. The Beatles heard it and they all wanted tape copies. So I had five or six copies made and sent over. That's where the bootlegs must have got out, from The Beatles themselves. We had a system at Capitol and knew where all our copies were. They said they liked it, that it sounded pretty good, but they still didn't want to release it. Capitol called me a few months back and asked if I could help find the tapes in the library. Of course, I knew right where they were."

Tuesday May 31

 George's single 'It's What You Value'/'Woman Don't You Cry For Me' is released in the UK.

 The Suzy And The Red Stripes single 'Seaside Woman'/'B Side To Seaside' is released in America. Linda McCartney writes the A-side, which features Paul and Linda sharing the lead vocal, while Paul composes the B-side, which again features Linda on lead vocal. Paul also produces the record, which was not released in the UK until August 10, 1979. (Incidentally, the name Suzy And The Red Stripes originates from a brand of Jamaican beer.)

June

● George and Olivia visit the Monte Carlo rally where they meet up with Ringo and Nancy Andrews. Also this month, at the Atlantic Studios in New York, Ringo records 'Just A Dream' during the sessions for the album *Ringo The 4th*. This period of recording sees the completion of the following tracks: 'Wings', 'Drowning In A Sea Of Love', 'Tango All Night', 'Gave It All Up', 'Out On The Streets', 'Can She Do It Like She Dances', 'Sneaking Sally Through The Alley', 'It's No Secret', 'Gypsies In Flight' and 'Simple Love Song'. Ringo also records the unreleased song 'By Your Side', as well as private recordings, inspired by his girlfriend Nancy Andrews, which feature the working titles of 'Nancy, Ringo, Vinnie And Friends' and 'Duet – Nancy And Ringo'. Later in the month, Ringo returns to Los Angeles, where he resumes recordings at the Cherokee Studios. These sessions produce the unreleased tracks 'Birmingham' and 'The Party' and another alternative version of 'Just A Dream'. Also this month, Ring O'Records release their début single, 'It's All Over Now, Baby Blue' by Graham Bonnet.

● At the end of the month, John, Yoko and their son Sean begin a four-month visit to Karuizawa in Japan to stay with Yoko's family, stopping over briefly in Hong Kong. During their stay at the Mandarin Hotel, they dine with David Bowie. In Karuizawa the Lennons are typical tourists, visiting temples and Onioshidashi, the popular spot on the Asama Mountain. John, Yoko and Sean take up residence at the Hotel Okura and also play host to Elliott Mintz who stays with them briefly. (They return to New York on October 6.)

Saturday June 4

● The album *The Beatles At The Hollywood Bowl* reaches number one in the UK album charts. It is a record-breaking twelfth UK chart-topping album for the group.

Thursday June 9

● In London, at a private court hearing, George consents to a decree nisi being granted to his wife Patti. (They had been married since January 21, 1966.)

● Meanwhile, to coincide with a surge of Beatlemania currently gripping America, the new musical, suitably titled, *Beatlemania* opens (after a one week delay) on Broadway at the Winter Gardens Theater. The show features 49 Beatle songs lifted directly off the original records, and has been running in Boston for the last three weeks. Outside the theatres, a disclaimer notice is put up announcing: "This is an amazing assimilation of The Beatles – It is *not* the real thing!" A report from the show reads: "The audience went wild after each song and I had an uncanny feeling many times that I was back in time at a real Beatles concert. Mitch Weissman, who is unbelievably like Paul, has been mobbed many times in the New York streets and now has to wear dark glasses. Already the four lookalikes are doing TV and promotion work."

Saturday June 11

● *The Beatles Live At The Hollywood Bowl* reaches number two in the US album charts.

Tuesday June 28

● George is among the 300 guests at London's Savoy Hotel for a special 'Farewell from Britain' luncheon honouring Derek Taylor before he takes up his new post for Warner Brothers in California. The lunch, hosted by George Melly, features George and Kenny Everett recalling the lunacy of Apple in its heyday and, by way of a TV link-up, Ringo appears on screen from Los Angeles to pay his tribute as does Peter Asher and the top hierarchy of the LA music industry. Melly and John Chilton's Feetwarmers provide the music. Derek's wife Joan and their six children accompany him at the bash.

Thursday June 30

● The final British battle over 'My Sweet Lord' against 'He's So Fine' is fought out in London's High Court. Both records are played in court before the judge Mr. Justice Slade, who is then informed that both parties have now agreed on a settlement.

July
 At the Berwick Street Studios in London, working with the producer Hugh Murphy, Ringo records the following songs for the children's album *Scouse The Mouse:* 'I Know A Place', 'S.O.S.', 'A Mouse Like Me', 'Living In A Pet Shop', 'Scouse's Dream', 'Running Free', 'Boat Ride' and 'Scouse The Mouse'. Although originally planned to coincide with an animated *Scouse The Mouse* television special, based on a story by the actor Donald Pleasance, this part of the project never materialises due to trade union problems. (See the album's release details on December 9.)
 During the middle of the month, the New York production of *Beatlemania* is doing great business. In one week alone (ending Sunday July 24), the theatre grosses $110,000 even though the ticket prices have been hiked up to between $12.50 and $13.50. (The average New York ticket prices for the top performers at this time are between $8.50 and $11.) Reviews of the show are also positive, surprising since many of the reviewers have had to pay their own way to get in to see the performance.

Friday July 15
 Back in England, during the practice runs for Sunday's British Grand Prix, George is to be found in the VIP area at Silverstone race track.

Monday July 18 (until Saturday July 30)
 In London, with funding from *Saturday Night Live*'s Lorne Michaels, filming begins on *The Rutles* television special. Amongst the locations utilised is Queen's Park Rangers football ground at Loftus Road in Shepherd's Bush, which is thinly disguised as Che (Shea) Stadium. One week later, on July 25, production moves to Liverpool.

Saturday July 30
 The Beatles Live! At The Star Club In Hamburg, Germany: 1962 reaches number 111 in the American album charts.

Sunday July 31
 Now back in New York, George is interviewed by the radio station WNEW.

August
 At London's Abbey Road Studios, Paul records 'Mull Of Kintyre' and completes the song 'Girls School', originally started back in March. He also returns to the unreleased "daft" punk track 'Boil Crisis', but admits he dare not issue it. "If I release it," Paul claims, "people will only slag me off. It's 'One night in the life of a kid named Sid, he scored with a broad in a pyramid . . .' "

Monday August 1
 Filming on *The Rutles* again returns to London where additional scenes are re-shot. Also filmed this week (on Tuesday August 2) is George's appearance as an ageing television reporter and Rolling Stone Ronnie Wood as a punk rocker! The first batch of filming in the UK is wrapped up on Thursday August 4. (Work on the show will resume on September 5.)

Saturday August 13
 From his hotel room in Japan, John drafts a short postcard to Derek Taylor in England. It reads: "Hello Taylors, am in Alan Waits country, hi mountains, John, Yoko and Sean."
 Inspired by the wonderful sights in Japan, and his freedom from both the confines of his Dakota apartment and a recording contract, John commits to tape a demo of the song 'Free As A Bird'.

Tuesday August 16
 In Japan, following the death of his idol Elvis Presley, John issues a brief statement: "Nothing really effected me until Elvis!" This does not represent his true feelings on Elvis's death (see entry for October 4).
 Around this time at Keith Moon's home at Victoria Point Road, Trancas, in the exclusive area of Malibu Beach, California, Ringo joins Keith to film scenes for inclusion in the film *The Kids Are Alright*, a documentary on the history of The Who, which is premiered at the Cannes Film Festival on Monday May 14, 1979. Ringo will also record several radio spots and appear in a special cinema trailer to promote the film.

Thursday August 25
♪ Ringo's single 'Wings'/'Just A Dream' is released in America.

September
♪ Sometime during this month John inadvertently gives his last public performance before a couple of total strangers in his suite at the Hotel Okura in Tokyo. A Japanese couple enter the room by mistake while John is strumming his guitar and singing 'Jealous Guy'. Because of its size the couple evidently assume that John's suite is a public room, that a waiter will arrive to serve them and that the man in the corner playing guitar is paid by the hotel to entertain guests. They wait politely for a few minutes listening to John but leave when no-one comes to take their drinks or food order.

Sunday September 4
♪ In Los Angeles, Ringo, in another plug for his new single, gives a 60-minute interview to the DJ Dave Herman.

Monday September 5
♪ For three weeks starting today, production on *The Rutles* continues in New York. Besides additional scenes for the programme, comical interviews with Mick Jagger and Paul Simon are also conducted. (Shooting in New York is concluded on September 24.) During one of the weekends in New York, Eric Idle and Basil Pao write the wonderful booklet to be featured inside *The Rutles* soundtrack album. When he is shown the results, George is so impressed that he arranges for them to meet Mo Austin, the head of Warner Brothers. Meanwhile, back in London, the first scenes shot between July 18 and August 4 are being edited.

Thursday September 8
♪ Jimmy McCulloch leaves Wings and joins the reformed group Small Faces whose British tour is scheduled to start at the Birmingham Hippodrome on Monday September 12. Asked about Jimmy's departure, Paul remarks: "Jimmy has been playing some great guitar recently and it is a pity he is leaving, but problems have been building up for quite a while now and so the rest of us are happy to carry on without him."

Jimmy has this to say about his leaving: "I enjoyed playing with Wings and I learned a lot from Paul, but I felt it was time for a change and the ideal change for me was The Small Faces. They are old friends of mine whose music I have always enjoyed."

In a strange twist The Small Faces are supported by Blue, a band that McCulloch played in prior to joining Wings.

Monday September 12
♪ Paul and Linda's son James Louis McCartney is born at the Avenue Clinic in St. John's Wood, London. He weighs 6 pounds 1 ounce.

Wednesday September 14
♪ From his hotel room in Karuizawa, Japan, John scribbles (on American Airlines note paper), a short reply regarding a business proposition to Mike Turner in New York. "Sounds interesting. We'll be back in USA in Oct'. We got court cases, films to edit, and museums to fill, if we think of anything we'll call or write." In conclusion, John writes: "In flight – yes. Attention: Hello New York. Location: Here and there."

♪ Meanwhile back in England, at the Kilburn Gaumont, Mick Jagger and Ronnie Wood are among the all-star guests present at Paul's annual Buddy Holly Week celebratory concerts. Both Paul and Linda are naturally in attendance.

Friday September 16
♪ Ringo's single 'Drowning In A Sea Of Love'/'Just A Dream' is released in the UK. (The American release takes place on October 18.)

Tuesday September 20
♪ Ringo's album *Ringo the 4th* is released in the UK. (The American release takes place on September 26.)

Saturday September 24

- In the annual *Melody Maker* reader's poll, Paul is voted the fifth best bass player of 1977.
- Meanwhile, filming on *The Rutles* moves, for one week, to New Orleans.

Friday September 30

- The production team of *The Rutles* head back to England to resume work on additional scenes that need to be re-shot. Filming officially concludes on Wednesday October 5.

Tuesday October 4

- At the end of their four-month vacation, John and Yoko hold a 45-minute press conference at the Hotel Okura in Tokyo, prior to returning home to New York. John announces that his highest priority for the next several years will be the raising of his son Sean and that his creative endeavours would be secondary. Before a handful of reporters, John thanks the Japanese people for respecting their privacy, and remarks: "We've basically decided, without a great decision, to be with our baby as much as we can until we feel we can take the time off to indulge ourselves in creating things outside the family. Maybe when he's three, four or five, then we'll think about creating something else other than the child."

Wearing an expensive black two-piece suit, with a white and pearl-grey tie, John continues: "We really have nothing to say." Even so, the Japanese press ask John his opinions on the recent death of Elvis Presley, one of his great idols.

"Elvis died when he went into the army," says John. "Up until he joined the Army I thought it was beautiful music, and Elvis was for me and my generation what The Beatles were to the Sixties. I basically became a musician because of Elvis Presley. I never did concerts to influence people. I did them for many reasons, and since 1966 I have not performed for money, only charity."

Another reporter asks the question that everyone present just knew was coming, "Will The Beatles revive?"

"I doubt it very much," is John's simple reply. He then answers questions about punk rock, giving the impression that for the last year he paid little attention to today's music. After questions about his returning to Britain ("at some point" is his reply) and recording again, the press conference concludes. As the journalists get ready to depart, John is asked, "Why do you appear to be so different now?" He replies: "Basically, I'm now a Zen pagan." Yoko sat beside John throughout the conference and translated his words.

When John does return to their Dakota apartment (on October 6), he continues to record various home demos, such as the unreleased 'Mirror Mirror (On The Wall)' and the first version of 'Real Love', tracks that are intended for a planned stage musical, entitled *The Ballad Of John And Yoko*.

Saturday October 8 & Sunday October 9

- A two-day Beatles convention takes place in the UK, this time at Mr. Pickwick's Club in Fraser Street, Liverpool 3. The event, subtitled "24 Hours Of Beatle Happenings" is arranged by Allan Williams and Bob Wooler, the former DJ at the Cavern Club. Amongst the attractions are the latest Liverpool groups, including Black Maria, Glass Roots and the Acme Novelty Band, plus Beatle-Brain and Lookalike competitions, memorabilia displays, guest DJs and film shows. A special guest, for Beatle fans that is, is Raymond Jones, now 37, the man responsible for putting Epstein on to The Beatles when he went into Eppy's record shop asking for a copy of 'My Bonnie'. "No, I had no idea what I started back in '62," he remarks. "The Beatles brought some happiness didn't they?"

Fans are also given the chance (for an extra charge of 50p) to go on a Magical History Tour bus ride around "Beatle Landmarks" in Liverpool on the Sunday morning. This takes in twenty different sites, from Gulliver's nightclub (formerly the Peppermint Lounge) to the now demolished Cavern Club in Mathew Street where dewy-eyed fans stood and stared at the rubble remains of this world-famous club. Richard Quick, of the English Tourist Board, remarks at the spot: "Where the Cavern is, it will probably become another hideous office block once British Rail have used the site for the reason they bought it, which was to make it possible to build an underground railway system." The weekend event, which brought in an attendance of around 2,000, kicks off with an opening speech by the Lord Mayor of Liverpool, Councillor Peter Orr, and runs from 1pm to 1am with tickets costing £3 for both days or £2 for one.

Tuesday October 11
 Back in the States, the New York Federal Court indicts Allen Klein for tax evasion.

Thursday October 13
 At Paul's Scottish farmhouse, working with director Michael Lindsay-Hogg, Paul, Linda and Denny film the first promotional clip for their next single 'Mull Of Kintyre'. Paul is seen climbing off a fence and walking with his acoustic guitar while lip-synching the vocals. Linda, Denny and The Campbeltown Pipes Band join him later in the clip. Additional scenes of local residents joining Wings around a fire to sing along are shot later this evening. In between takes, Linda is on hand to keep everyone warm with a non-stop supply of tea. (The group will record a second clip for 'Mull Of Kintyre' on December 2 – see entry.)

Tuesday October 18
 To celebrate the Queen's Silver Jubilee, the BPI (British Phonographic Industry) hold a ceremony at the Wembley Conference Centre in London to celebrate the best British music since 1952. The Beatles are The Best British Group 1952–1977 and *Sgt. Pepper's Lonely Hearts Club Band* is the Best British Pop Album 1952–1977. Highlights of the event are transmitted across the ITV network on Thursday October 20 between 8:01 and 8:59pm, in a programme called *Britannia Awards For Recorded Music*. A clip from the 'Ticket To Ride' sequence from The Beatles' 1965 film *Help!* is shown during the broadcast.

Wednesday October 19
 By a huge majority vote of 9 to 1, Liverpool City Council reject a plan to build a lasting monument in honour of The Beatles in Liverpool, a decision they will come to regret. Fans in the UK throw up their arms in anguish.

Friday October 21
 The double album Beatles compilation *Love Songs* is released in America. (The release takes place in the UK on November 19.) The track listing is as follows: 'Yesterday', 'I'll Follow The Sun', 'I Need You', 'Girl', 'In My Life', 'Words Of Love', 'Here, There And Everywhere', 'Something', 'And I Love Her', 'If I Fell', 'I'll Be Back', 'Tell Me What You See', 'Yes It Is', 'Michelle', 'It's Only Love', 'You're Gonna Lose That Girl', 'Every Little Thing', 'For No One', 'She's Leaving Home', 'The Long And Winding Road', 'This Boy', 'Norwegian Wood (This Bird Has Flown)', 'You've Got To Hide Your Love Away', 'I Will' and 'P.S. I Love You'.

Tuesday October 25
 Wings hold additional recording sessions for *London Town* at EMI's Abbey Road studios in London. (These will continue until December 14). During this period, Paul also records the unreleased song 'Waterspout', which is originally scheduled to appear on the, ultimately rejected, 1981 *Cold Cuts* album. Incidentally, a release of the song is scheduled on Paul's 1987 *All The Best* greatest hits compilation but, again, this fails to materialise.
 In America, The Beatles' Capitol single 'Girl'/'You're Gonna Lose That Girl', taken from the *Love Songs* compilation, scheduled for release today, is cancelled.

November
 For no apparent reason, Joe English becomes the latest member to leave Wings.

Friday November 11
 The Wings single 'Mull Of Kintyre'/'Girls School' is released in the UK. (The American release takes place on November 14 with the A- and B-sides reversed.) To coincide with its release, Paul, Linda and Denny are presented, at Abbey Road studios, with gold and silver discs for the album *Wings At The Speed Of Sound*. The gathering is also treated to a first showing, on a small television set, of the completed 'Mull Of Kintyre' promotional film (version one, shot at their Scottish farmhouse on October 13).

Reporters also ask Paul about his plans for 1978. "I plan to play a tour of small British clubs next year," he replies. "I also have an ambition to play Joe's cafe and sing requests from the man in the audience. It's the atmosphere of the man in the street."

During the get-together, Linda is presented with a specially made small T-shirt, featuring a picture of Paul and Linda posing in hospital with their new-born child James, shortly after his birth on September 12.

'Mull Of Kintyre', besides its other accolades, will go on to win the prestigious Ivor Novello award for the Best Selling A-Side of 1977 and is also voted by Capitol Radio in London as 'The Best Single Of 1977'. At a luncheon at London's Grosvenor House Hotel, Paul and Linda receive the award from Lord George Brown.

Paul is later criticised in the UK press when it is revealed that, even after all the money the song generated around the world, he paid The Campbeltown Pipes Band only a standard union rate for playing on 'Mull Of Kintyre'.

To promote the single today, Paul gives a live interview in London to Capital Radio.

Saturday November 12
❦ Further promotions for 'Mull Of Kintyre' occur when Paul gives a live interview to BBC Radio One.
❦ *Ringo The 4th* reaches number 162 in the American album charts.

Sunday November 13
❦ In England, an interview with George is published in the *News Of The World* newspaper.

Saturday November 19
❦ To promote his new single 'Mull Of Kintyre', *Melody Maker* publishes an interview with Paul by Chris Welch done in Abbey Road studio number two. Paul talks about the *London Town* album recordings, carried out during May of this year in the Virgin Islands:

"We hired a charter boat that people use for holidays. The captain went spare when he saw all the instruments. We remodelled his boat for him, which he wasn't too keen on. We converted his lounge into a studio and we turned another deck into a sound control room, and it was fantastic! We had a recording boat and two others we stayed on. We didn't have any problems with salt water in the machines or sharks attacking us. At night, there was much merriment, leaping from top decks into uncharted waters and stuff. I had a couple too many one night and nearly broke something jumping from one boat to another. But then you always break yourself up on holiday. The studio worked out incredibly well and the very first day we got a track down. There was a nice free feeling. We'd swim in the day and record at night. We've come back to Abbey Road here to finish it all off. We're overdubbing and putting on main vocals."

On 'Mull Of Kintyre': "It's Scottish. It sounds so different from the songs we did on the boat, we thought it should be a single and it sounds very Christmassy and New Yeary. It's kind of 'glass of ale in your hand, leaning up against the bar' tune. We had the local pipe band join in and we took a mobile studio up to Scotland and put the equipment in an old barn. We had The Campbeltown Band and they were great – just pipes and drums. It was interesting writing for them. You can't just write any old tune, because they can't play every note in a normal scale. It's a double A-side. The other one, 'Girls School', I wrote after reading the back pages of those American entertainment guides. These days there are whole pages of X films, y'know the porn page? It's all titles like *School Mistress* and *The Woman Trainer*. I just put them all together in the lyrics and called it 'Girls School'. It's about a pornographic *St. Trinians*. We made it a double A because the B-sides always get swallowed. You never hear them. At least 'Girls School' will get played a bit. 'Mull Of Kintyre' is different from anything we've done before . . . but sure. It's Wings. It's definitely not punk."

Sunday November 20
❦ At his Friar Park mansion, George writes the lyrics to the song 'Faster'.

December
❦ At the Elite Recording Studios in the Bahamas and the Canadian based premises of The Can-Base Studios and Nimbus 9, the recording sessions for Ringo's next album *Bad Boy* are carried out. The recordings produce the following songs: 'Lipstick Traces', 'Old Time Relovin' ', 'Who Needs A Heart', 'Bad Boy', 'Heart On My Sleeve', 'Where Did Our Love Go', 'Tonight', 'Hard Times', 'Monkey See, Monkey Do' and 'A Man Like Me', a re-recording of the track 'A Mouse Like Me', as previously featured on the *Scouse The Mouse* album. During this period, Ringo also records, with Davy Jones of The Monkees providing backing vocals, the short songs 'Simple Life' and 'I Love My Suit' for inclusion in five different *Simple Life* leisure suits commercials for broadcast on Japanese Television.

 On a back-lot at the Universal Studios in Hollywood, filming begins on *Beatles 4 Ever*, a movie about a group of New Jersey teenagers who travel to New York City to see The Beatles' début on *The Ed Sullivan Show* on February 9, 1964. (The film will be released in the UK during October 1978, sporting the alternative title of *I Want To Hold Your Hand*.)

 As the rush to cash in on anything Beatles' related in America reaches fever pitch, this same month sees the completion, in Los Angeles, of another Beatles flick, this time *Sgt. Peppers Lonely Hearts Club Band*, an all-star musical headed by The Bee Gees and Peter Frampton. The respected *Rolling Stone* magazine in America causes near hysteria when they announce that: "John, Paul, George and Ringo are to make an appearance in the film."

 Meanwhile, the Broadway musical *Beatlemania,* featuring the original New York cast, is booked into the Los Angeles' Shubert Theater for a run of at least 19 weeks. While in New York, in order to keep the stage play running, a new cast is hastily assembled.

 On a sad note, Beatles fans in New York are horrified at the sight of John's famous vintage white Rolls Royce car sitting neglected in an inch-deep pool of oily water in a $100 a month private garage.

Thursday December 1
 Today's ITN News (transmitted across the ITV network between 5:45 and 6:00pm) features Paul at Abbey Road studios talking briefly about 'Mull Of Kintyre' with the reporter Peter Sharp.

Friday December 2
 During a further break from *London Town* recordings in Abbey Road Studio No. 2, Paul films a much lengthier interview, this time with Melvyn Bragg, for inclusion in the very first edition of the new London Weekend Television arts programme *The South Bank Show* (transmitted across the ITV network on Sunday January 14 1978 between 10:16 and 11:13pm). During the course of the 30-minute feature, subtitled *Paul McCartney: Songsmith*, Paul discusses a number of subjects with Melvin including his childhood, his father, early song writing with John, The Beatles not releasing 'How Do You Do It?', making it big in America, writing 'Eleanor Rigby', 'Yesterday' and 'When I'm 64', the break up of The Beatles and the early days of Wings. Music featured in the show includes Paul recording his guitar and vocal parts to 'Mull Of Kintyre', a brief performance on piano of 'I Lost My Little Girl', the first song he ever wrote, an impromptu attempt to write a song called 'Melvin Bragg' and a "jam" of the track 'Lucille' featuring Denny on guitar joining Paul on drums. Archive clips featured in the programme include The Beatles performing 'Love Me Do' from the 1963 BBC TV programme *The Mersey Sound*, 'I Feel Fine' from the 1965 *Shea Stadium* concert and both 'Hi Hi Hi' and 'Maybe I'm Amazed' from the 1973 ATV/ITC special *James Paul McCartney*.

 After Paul has filmed the *South Bank Show* interview with Melvyn Bragg, he joins Linda and Denny to shoot the second promotional clip for 'Mull Of Kintyre'. This bizarre clip features Wings miming 'Mull Of Kintyre' while sitting around a garden patio table, all intercut with scenes from the unreleased 1972 MPL *Bruce McMouse* film. This version is never transmitted and remains unreleased to this day.

Saturday December 3
 On the day that the Wings' single 'Mull Of Kintyre' (co-written by Paul and Denny) reaches number 1 in the UK singles charts, where it will remain for nine weeks, the group begin several additional recording sessions for *London Town,* this time at George Martin's AIR studios in London. (These will continue until December 14.)

Friday December 9
 The various artists album *Scouse The Mouse* is released in the UK only by Polydor. Joining Ringo, who, as Scouse, only sings on eight of the fifteen tracks, are Barbara Dickson as Molly Jolly, Ben Chatterley as Olly Jolly, Adam Faith as Bonce, Lucy Pleasance as Holly Jolly and Rick Jones as Louey The Gull. Inside early copies of the album is an entrance form to a *Scouse The Mouse* colouring and drawing competition, open to children aged between five and ten, with two hundred copies of an illustrated *Scouse The Mouse* book as a prize. This book, published by the New English Library, features the story by Donald Pleasance accompanied by the drawings of Gerry Potterton.

 While the first promotional film clip of 'Mull Of Kintyre' is being transmitted in

America on the programme *Midnight Special*, Wings are to be found on stage two at the Elstree film studios in Hertfordshire, filming a third promotional film clip for 'Mull Of Kintyre'. Often referred to by Beatles collectors as the 'Misty' version, this clip features Paul, Linda and Denny singing the tune against a backdrop of rocks with rolling fog where, towards the end of the clip, The Campbeltown Pipes Band march into shot. Not quite as commonly shown as the first 'Mull Of Kintyre' clip, this version, directed by Nicholas Ferguson, who previously directed The Beatles' Intertel Studio promotional films from November 1965, has endured a quite healthy broadcasting history over the years around the world. (Final editing on the clip takes place on Sunday December 11.)

Saturday December 10

🍏 At the BBC TV Theatre in Shepherd's Bush, London, Wings record an appearance on the BBC1 variety show *The Mike Yarwood Christmas Show*. The group perform in a comedy sketch with Yarwood, who is dressed as a 'Chunky Punky', a punk-rocker version of Dennis Healey, the then Chancellor of the Exchequer. Paul is seen performing at a piano and when Linda informs him that Dennis is dropping in to see him, he promptly hides a bundle of bank-notes in the lid of the piano. Wings return later in the programme to mime a version of 'Mull Of Kintyre' backed by The Campbeltown Pipes Band. The show, which is transmitted on Christmas Day on BBC1 between 8:21 and 8:55, is a great success, with an estimated 40% of the British population tuning in. The audience viewing figures are an estimated 21.4 million! (Incidentally, The Campbeltown Pipes Band, this month, are voted the Top Scots Entertainers of the Year.)

🍏 Today, The Beatles' double album compilation *Love Songs* reaches number 54 in the American charts.

Sunday December 11

🍏 In London, the third 'Mull Of Kintyre' promotional film (the misty version) is edited and prepared today for television distribution around Europe.

Saturday December 17

🍏 The one millionth copy of 'Mull Of Kintyre' is sold to Mr. David Ackroyd, a Green Goddess soldier-fireman, and thus becomes the first ever person to receive a gold disc for a purchase of a standard seven inch single. Ackroyd will receive the disc, as well as a Christmas hamper, from Paul and Wings in a special celebration ceremony at Paul's MPL offices in Soho Square, London. 'Mull Of Kintyre' will go on to sell over 2.5 million copies, replacing 'She Loves You' as the UK's biggest-selling record. In 1985, 'Kintyre's sales will be eclipsed by Band-Aid's 'Do They Know It's Christmas' which will briefly feature Paul on the B-side.

In 1978, Paul remarks about 'Mull Of Kintyre': "I nearly didn't put it out . . . I knew old folks, Scottish people, The Campbeltown Pipers liked it . . . but at that time *everything* was punk. But I checked it with a lotta young kids and they liked it, so we went on with it."

🍏 An exhibition of Linda's pictures opens at the Jan Baum and Iris Silverman Gallery in Los Angeles, California. The show will run until January 28, 1978.

🍏 At the *Row Barge* public house near his home in Henley-on-Thames, George gives an impromptu performance on guitar to various regulars. It is his first live appearance, albeit unannounced, in three years. Shortly afterwards, George and Olivia leave for their two-month Christmas vacation in Hawaii.

🍏 The Beatles' *Love Songs* double album reaches number seven in the UK charts.

December (until Friday December 23)

🍏 Additional recordings take place for the album *London Town*. These sessions produce additional work on: 'Backwards Traveller'/'Cuff Link', 'Children Children', 'Girlfriend' and 'Name And Address', a tribute to the style of Elvis Presley, plus the unreleased track 'Waterspout'.

🍏 In New York, at the Dakota, John is still recording home demos, amongst them the unreleased song 'One Of The Boys'.

December (Christmas)

🍏 Julian visits his father in New York to celebrate the festive period. A picture is taken of them sleighing in the snow in Central Park.

"**The Beatles made a lot of money and we have not seen them since.**"
– A Liverpool city councillor

January
♫ With Julian now returned to England, John, according to Yoko's Tarot card reader John Green, retreats to his Dakota bedroom, where he will stay for a large part of the next fifteen months, spending his time channel hopping on the TV, reading, smoking French cigarettes and sleeping for long periods at a time.

Monday January 1
♫ In Hawaii, George celebrates his year lay-off away from music by composing the songs 'Blow Away' and 'If You Believe', a track co-written with Gary Wright.

Thursday January 4
♫ At EMI's Abbey Road Studios, Wings near completion of the final recording sessions for the album *London Town*. (The recordings are finally wound up on January 23.)

Saturday January 14
♫ The Wings single 'Mull Of Kintyre' becomes the biggest selling single ever in the UK with sales, so far, of over 1,667,000 copies. By the end of January, the single will have sold over two million copies in the UK alone. These sales figures are not matched in America where the track 'Girls School' receives the most exposure and reaches the comparatively low number 33 position.

Sunday January 15
♫ With perfect timing, the first programme in the new London Weekend Television series *The South Bank Show*, entitled *Paul McCartney: Songsmith*, is transmitted across the ITV network later this evening. (See entry for Friday December 2, 1977.) This week's *TV Times*, the ITV listings magazine for the week of January 14–20, profiles Paul and the *South Bank* programme in a feature entitled *Masks Of McCartney*.

Wednesday January 25
♫ At the Thames Television studios in Euston Road, London, George is a surprise guest on the ITV network programme *This Is Your Life* (transmitted between 7:00 and 7:28pm), which tonight honours the motor cyclist Barry Sheene. George appears in the studio where he talks of admiration for Barry, but admits that: "Before I met him, I thought Barry was a bit of a Midland Banker!" Later, at the after-show party, Eamonn Andrews asks the show's researchers why he didn't have any notes on the fact that George had once been employed by Midland Bank. Andrews clearly missed the gist of George's rhyming slang.

Thursday January 26
♫ George and Olivia depart from Heathrow Airport en route to Los Angeles and then Hawaii for a nine-week holiday.

February
♫ George, now in Hawaii with his creative juices flowing, writes the tracks 'Love Comes To Everyone', 'Soft Hearted Hana' (the lyrics of which are started in his local public house *The Row Barge*), 'If You Believe' and 'Here Comes The Moon', a follow-up to his Beatles' track 'Here Comes The Sun'. He also composes (on February 26) 'Dark Sweet Lady' for his girlfriend Olivia Arias and the unreleased humorous song 'Sooty Goes To Hawaii'.

Monday February 4
♫ John and Yoko pay more than $178,000 for several acres of land in Delaware County, New York. They announce that they intend to use the land as a vacation retreat and for raising Regis Holstein cows.

Monday February 11 (until Friday February 22)
♫ In Hollywood, for ten of the next twelve days, Ringo shoots his TV special *Ringo*, sometimes affectionately known as *Ognir Rrats,* after the character in the show. (See entry for Wednesday April 26 for details of the show.) The last few days of the month are spent with various overdubbing requirements.

Tuesday February 19
 The episode of Tony Palmer's TV history of popular music series *All You Need Is Love,* entitled *Mighty Good*, which focuses entirely on The Beatles, is broadcast on American Television. (The UK transmission took place across the ITV network on May 14, 1977.)

March
 From the seclusion of his Dakota apartment, John commits to tape humorous recordings featuring the exploits of the French detective Maurice Dupont.
 With production of *Ringo* now complete, Ringo takes a holiday with Nancy Andrews in Portugal.
 In Liverpool, at the start of the month, the local city council puts forward plans for an alternative Beatles tribute. With the idea of a statue now rejected, committee members suggest a possible "Beatles sports centre" or a "Beatles museum". (See entry for March 21.)

Saturday March 18
 During his Portuguese vacation, Ringo poses for a snap with a young lady who makes large dinosaur monsters out of papier-mâché.

Monday March 20
 The Wings single 'With A Little Luck'/'Backwards Traveller' – 'Cuff Link' is released in America. (The UK release takes place on March 23.)

Tuesday March 21
 An interview with Paul to promote the new single is broadcast on Capital Radio.
 In Liverpool, the city council finally decide that a Beatles statue will serve as a fitting tribute to "their favourite sons" and will be erected in Williamson Square. It's decided that the piece will be cast locally by Brian Burgess, who is to be sponsored to the tune of £25,000. The Beatles' former manager Allan Williams is given the task of raising the money. So far, he has been promised £5,000 by a nostalgic carpet retailer named Spencer Lloyd Mason, who once managed the Sixties group The Mojos. Unfortunately, the scheme does not please some members of the local council. A Labour chairman is heard to remark: "The Beatles made a lot of money and we have not seen them since." A Conservative councillor, also against the statue, states: "The Beatles? They could not sing for toffee." A spokesman for the Liberals disagrees, stating: "Can you imagine Vienna having the same attitude over Strauss?" It's also revealed that the Royal Institute of British Architects has lent its name to a competition to elicit ideas for a redevelopment of an area of Liverpool City centre which includes Mathew Street, the former home of the, now demolished, Cavern Club.

Wednesday March 22
"I think it was the trousers!"
 The Beatles-spoof TV special *All You Need Is Cash* is premiered on NBC TV in America between 9:31 and 10:58pm. The first repeat screening takes place on the same station on December 10 this year, between 11:46pm and 1:13am. (The UK TV premiere, featuring a 64-minute truncated version, takes place on BBC2 on Easter Monday, March 27, between 8:45 and 9:49pm, while a repeated, thankfully longer, version is shown shortly after.) This delightful take-off of The Beatles' career, written by Eric Idle, traces the history of a mythical pop group called The Rutles, portrayed by Neil Innes (as John), Eric Idle (Paul), Rikki Fataar (George) and John Halsey (Ringo). George Harrison, as a grey-haired television reporter, Mick Jagger, Ronnie Wood and Paul Simon all make cameo appearances. The collection of *Beatle-esque* songs, written by Innes, is released on a Warner Brothers soundtrack album. (A copy of both the programme and soundtrack album are sent to John, at the Dakota, for him to give a nod of approval. The former Beatle was so impressed by the results that he refused to send either back to Innes. The guideline for *The Rutles* television show was based on the 1976 version of The Beatles' *The Long And Winding Road* documentary, loaned to Innes by George the previous year.)
 In England, Wings hold a press launch for their new album *London Town* on a boat which sails along the Thames from Charing Cross pier to Tower Bridge and back again. Eating a bag of fish and chips, Paul, Linda and Denny pose for photographers and take all manner of questions from the press. All areas of the media including *Thames At Six* (for London ITV) and BBC Radio One naturally cover the event. Amongst the questions,

Paul is asked his opinion on the imminent arrival of *The Rutles*. "No Comment!" he replies.

Monday March 27
◀ In America John resumes his own private recordings. Today, he commits to tape his 'Mind Movies' series.

Friday March 31
◀ The Wings album *London Town* is released simultaneously in the UK and in America.

April
◀ At Abbey Road Studios, Wings begin recording the track 'Daytime Nightime Suffering'. (They will return to the track in January 1979.)
◀ George and Olivia conclude their nine-week holiday at the Grand Prix at Long Beach, California. The couple return to England via Heathrow Airport on April 4.
◀ Ringo holds a party in New York to celebrate the release of his new album *Bad Boy*.
◀ EMI withdraw their funding of the Monty Python film *Jesus Christ – Lust For Glory*, later to be called *The Life Of Brian*.

Tuesday April 11
◀ Back at Friar Park, George, invigorated by his holiday, records the track 'Flying Hour', originally included on the original, unreleased version of the album *Somewhere In England* but rejected from the released version. (The song will appear in a re-mixed form on the bonus EP and CD, included in the limited edition book *Songs By George Harrison,* released on February 15, 1988.) George also begins recording songs for his album *George Harrison.* As inspiration for the recordings, George listens again to his 1970 album *All Things Must Pass.* During the sessions he records the following tracks: 'Love Comes To Everyone', 'Not Guilty', 'Here Comes The Moon', 'Soft Hearted Hana', 'Blow Away', 'Faster', 'Dark Sweet Lady', 'Your Love Is Forever', 'Soft Touch' and 'If You Believe'. He also resurrects the song 'Circles', which he had composed back in 1968. The track will not see the light of day until 1982, when it appears on the album *Gone Troppo*. (The recordings are concluded on October 12.)

Saturday April 15
◀ At a private London cinema, Paul and Linda attend a special 45th anniversary screening of the 1933 John Barrymore comedy film *Dinner At Eight.*

Monday April 17
◀ Six years after John and Yoko had appeared on the programme, Ringo guests on American television's prestigious afternoon, top-rated talk show *The Mike Douglas Show* (transmitted between 4:30 and 6:00pm ET). Naturally he takes the opportunity to promote his new album, single and his *Ognir Rrats* television special which, coincidentally, also features a cameo appearance by Mike Douglas.

Tuesday April 18
◀ Ringo's single 'Lipstick Traces'/'Old Time Relovin'' is released in America.

Friday April 21
◀ Ringo's album *Bad Boy* is simultaneously released in both the UK and in America. It will only reach number 129 in the American charts.
◀ In New York, today and tomorrow (April 22), a board meeting, featuring representatives from each of The Beatles, is held regarding the reorganisation of Apple Corps Ltd.

Wednesday April 26
◀ Intended as a vehicle for the *Bad Boy* album, Ringo presents his own American TV special, a modern-day comic musical reworking of Mark Twain's *Prince And The Pauper,* titled simply *Ringo* (or sometimes affectionately as *Ognir Rrats*.) The show, narrated by George Harrison who also makes a cameo appearance, features Ringo exchanging his high pressure pop star lifestyle with that of a low-life "Map Of The Stars Home" seller called *Ognir Rrats.* Hank Jones plays the role of Ringo's double. Newly recorded songs performed during the 48-minute special include: 'I'm The Greatest', 'Act Naturally', 'Yellow

Submarine', 'You're Sixteen' (performed as a duet with Carrie Fisher), 'With A Little Help From My Friends' and, as part of a concert sequence at the end of the show, 'Heart On My Sleeve', 'Hard Times' and 'A Man Like Me' on which he is backed by Ringo's Roadside Attraction. The cast also includes Art Carney, John Ritter, Carrie Fisher and, in cameos, Angie Dickinson, Mike Douglas and Vincent Price. In the television ratings revealed the following week, the show finishes 53rd out of 65 programmes aired this evening. (The first UK TV transmission will not take place until Channel 4 on January 2, 1983.)

May

🍎 George's father, Harold Harrison, dies at George's Friar Park mansion in Henley-on-Thames. George later reveals that, the night before his father's death, he had a dream of his father bidding him farewell. This month, the Monty Python team approach George to finance their film *Jesus Christ – Lust For Glory*. He says he will look into it and consults Dennis O'Brien, to whom he was introduced by Peter Sellers in 1973.
🍎 Linda's short animated film *Oriental Nightfish* is shown at the annual Cannes Film Festival in France. (The film is later included on the *Rupert And The Frog Song* home video release.) Also present at the festival is Ringo, accompanied by his girlfriend Nancy Andrews.

Wednesday May 3

🍎 In New York, a fire on one of John's farms in Franklin completely demolishes the barn, garage and tool shed.

Friday May 5

🍎 Wings assemble at the RAK Studios in London to begin recording the guitar, bass, drums and piano tracks for the song 'Same Time Next Year', which later appears on the final credits of the 1985 Ann Margaret film *Twice In A Lifetime*. (It will be released on February 5, 1990 in the UK on the 'Put It There' CD and 12-inch singles.)

Saturday May 6

🍎 Additional work on 'Same Time Next Year' takes place at the RAK Studios, where today Paul supervises the recording of a 68-strong string orchestra, featuring Paul and Fiachra Trench. Meanwhile, at the Baynard Gallery in the Soho section of New York City, an exhibition of Linda's photographs opens. The event runs until June 1.

Tuesday May 9

🍎 In the UK, the promotional film for 'With A Little Luck' is transmitted (between 4:21 and 4:44pm) on the Granada ITV children's television show *Paul*, hosted by Paul Nicholas.

Sunday May 14

🍎 Paul and Linda appear in a 30-minute simultaneous BBC Radio One and Two interview on *The Simon Bates Show* (transmitted between 6:00 and 6:59pm) to promote the release of the album *London Town* as well as the single 'With A Little Luck'.

Saturday May 20

🍎 'With A Little Luck' tops the US singles chart, while in the UK, the single will reach number five.
🍎 A rare archive clip of The Beatles performing 'Can't Buy Me Love', from the March 20, 1964 edition of Associated Television's *Ready Steady Go!,* is transmitted during the first 'Revolver Reviver' slot of the new ATV music series *Revolver*, hosted by Peter Cook, and transmitted across certain ITV regions late this evening. (This is the first airing of the clip since July 15, 1965.) Joining the Fab Four on this first show are Kate Bush and The Tom Robinson Band who perform live in the studio.

June

🍎 Ringo and Polydor announce that 'Lipstick Traces' will be the first single released off the *Bad Boy* album, even going so far as to allot it a catalogue number (Polydor 2001-782). But the single never appears.
🍎 In a brief statement released to the press in New York, John and Yoko announce their next venture. Over a year in the planning, it is a musical entitled *The Ballad Of John And Yoko*. Songs intended for it at this point are 'Real Love' and 'Every Man Has A Woman Who Loves Him'. This month John and Yoko take another holiday in Japan.

Thursday June 1
❡ At the Plaza Hotel in New York, John and Yoko visit Ronnie Wood and Charlie Watts of The Rolling Stones. The Lennons bring along a bottle of Scotch for Ronnie as today is his birthday, but the Stones' guitarist doesn't have a chance to chat with John, as the former Beatle spends most of the evening asleep on the bed.

Friday June 2
❡ George and a heavily pregnant Olivia take another holiday, this time a three-day break in Madrid in Spain. They leave this morning bright and early from London's Heathrow Airport and return to England on June 5.

Sunday June 11
❡ In England, the *News Of The World* newspaper publishes the first part of its exclusive two-part series by John's first wife Cynthia. Primarily serialisations from her new paperback book *A Twist Of Lennon,* it includes accusations that "John introduced me to drugs against my will" and that "Yoko stole John from me". During this period, Cynthia (who since her marriage to John has been married twice more) also undertakes a round of promotional TV and radio appearances, including the BBC1 lunch time show *Pebble Mill At One.*

Monday June 12
❡ The Wings single 'I've Had Enough'/'Deliver Your Children' is released in America. (The UK release takes place on June 16, where it will reach the number 42 position in the charts.)

Tuesday June 13
❡ In New York, John reads the first of Cynthia's *News Of The World* articles and immediately issues a High Court libel writ in an attempt to prevent further extracts from her book being published and alleging that Cynthia is in breach of marital confidence. The case is heard in London's High Court on Friday June 16 (see next entry).

Friday June 16
❡ John's case against Cynthia over her *News Of The World* article last Sunday June 11 is heard at the High Court in London. John loses the case and the second part of the feature, a serialisation of the book *A Twist Of Lennon*, goes ahead on Sunday June 18. (The case immediately goes to the Court of Appeals.) In conclusion, Lord Denning, who presided over the case, remarks: "I cannot see that either of these two parties have had much regard for the sanctity of marriage. It is as plain as it can be that the relationship of these parties has ceased to be a private affair."

Monday June 19
❡ In London, 60 members of the Wings Fun Club attend the Wembley Music Centre to assist with the completion of the *Wings Over America* film. Their task is to help with overdubbing by clapping and singing along with some of the songs in the film. Paul, meanwhile, is to be found with Linda in the 3,000 strong audience at the New York Palladium, watching a live performance by The Rolling Stones. (The McCartneys return home to England on Wednesday June 21.)

Thursday June 29 (until July 27)
❡ At Paul's Spirit Of Ranachan Studios in Scotland, Wings begin recording tracks for inclusion on the album *Back To The Egg*. Songs produced during the first 29-day period include: 'To You', 'Arrow Through Me', Denny's 'Again And Again And Again', 'Winter Rose – Love Awake' (first versions recorded between July 12 and 17), 'Old Siam Sir' and 'Spin It On' (recorded in one day, on July 23), an early version of 'Ballroom Dancing' plus further work on the soundtrack for Paul's *Rupert* film. During these sessions, guitarist Laurence Juber and drummer Steve Holly join the group full time. Unreleased tracks recorded during this time include 'Cage' (later to be dropped from the *Back To The Egg* album in favour of 'Baby's Request'), 'Crawl Of The Wild' (with ex- Traffic member Dave Mason), 'Maisie', which later reappears on the Laurence Juber solo album *Standard Time*, and 'Weep For Love' which Denny Laine will later release on his solo album *Japanese Tears* (aka *In Flight*). The first *Back To The Egg* sessions end on July 27, when the group breaks

for their summer vacation. (Work on the album will resume on September 11.)
Incidentally, Paul will re-title his Ranachan Studios, Rude Studios later in his career.

July
🍎 Doing his best to forget the betrayal of his former wife, John charters a small jet in
Florida where he, Yoko and Sean fly to the Caribbean for a holiday. Reports suggest that
John will spend a large part of the vacation locked in his hotel room.
🍎 After two months of planning, George, a long-time *Monty Python* fan, manages to obtain
the necessary finance and gives the go-ahead for work to begin on the Monty Python film,
The Life Of Brian. Shooting is scheduled to begin in Tunisia on September 16.
🍎 Meanwhile, shooting begins on another Beatles-related film, this time the Dick Clark
produced made-for-TV film *The Birth Of The Beatles*. Filming is scheduled to last for seven
weeks, visiting fifty key locations in Liverpool, London and Germany. The production is
directed by Richard Markland and features Pete Best as the technical advisor.

Thursday July 6
🍎 Ringo's single 'Heart On My Sleeve'/'Who Needs A Heart' is released in America.

Friday July 7
🍎 In London, at the Pavilion cinema, Paul and Linda are present at the premiere of MGM's
new movie *That's Entertainment II*. Following the special screening, the couple attends the
after-show party where they are pictured dancing and smooching to the music.

Saturday July 15
🍎 In England, Ringo attends Bob Dylan's Blackbush concert at the Aerodrome in
Camberley, Surrey, but is annoyed to discover that even though he is seated in a special
reserved section alongside Bianca Jagger, he can neither see nor hear properly.
Immediately following the show, Ringo flies to France where he joins up with the
Australian filmmaker Christian Topps.

Friday July 21
🍎 Ringo's single 'Tonight'/'Old Time Relovin'' is released in the UK. It will be his last
Polydor single. To promote the *Bad Boy* album, Ringo and Nancy Andrews begin work in
the French Riviera on a proposed 30-minute film special based on tracks on the album.
Directed by Christian Topps, the production is never completed. To date only 'Tonight',
which features Ringo and Nancy dancing, has been screened. During Ringo's stay in
France this month, he is involved in some ugly scenes at the *Lido Cabaret Club* when he
thrashes out at a photographer who insists on taking his picture while he is eating a meal.

Saturday July 22
🍎 Ringo, accompanied by Nancy Andrews, flies from France to Copenhagen, Sweden
where, during the Russ Ballard sessions at the Sweet Silence Studios, he records the
unreleased tracks 'She's So In Love' and 'On The Rebound'. Further sessions at the
studio take place tomorrow.

Sunday July 23
🍎 The second day of recording at the Sweet Silence Studios in Copenhagen produces
the unreleased tracks 'One Way Love Affair' and 'As Far As We Can Go'. (The latter
appears as a bonus track on the *Old Wave* CD re-issue.)

Friday July 28
🍎 At the Sweet Sound Studios in Copenhagen, the engineer David Devore begins work
preparing rough early mixes of the four tracks recorded by Ringo on July 22 and 23.

August
🍎 John, Yoko and Sean return to Japan, where again they stay at the Hotel Okura.
Rumours suggest that for the first time in seven years the Lennons intend to visit
England, where they will visit John's Aunt Mimi at her bungalow at Poole in Dorset.
(This fails to materialise.)
🍎 Ringo leaves Sweden and spends this month on holiday in Spain with his children.

Tuesday August 1
 At the Royal Windsor Hospital in Berkshire, Olivia Arias, George's girlfriend, gives birth to their son, Dhani (the Indian word for "wealthy" or a "wealthy person"). He weighs five pounds.

Saturday August 5
 'I've Had Enough' reaches number 25 in the US singles chart.

Monday August 14
 To coincide with The Bee Gees' film, The Beatles' single 'Sgt. Pepper's Lonely Hearts Club Band' – 'With A Little Help From My Friends'/'A Day In The Life' is released in America by Capitol. (The UK release takes place on September 30, where it will reach number 63, staying in the charts for only three weeks.)

Monday August 21
 The Wings single 'London Town'/'I'm Carrying' is released in America. (The UK release takes place on August 26, where it will reach number 60 in the charts.)

Friday August 25
 To ease the strain of childbirth, George takes Olivia away for a short holiday to Amsterdam, Holland. Departing from London's Heathrow Airport, their first class tickets cost £123.

Saturday September 2
 Four weeks after the birth of their son, George and Olivia Arias are married in a secret ceremony at the Henley-on-Thames Register Office. The press are not informed of the marriage until September 8.

Wednesday September 6
"Every Day's A Holly Day"
 In London, Paul and Linda host the third Buddy Holly Week. Special guests at the party on the opening night include Micky Dolenz, formerly of The Monkees, Carl Perkins, George Melly, David Frost and the former Apple artiste Mary Hopkin. At the conclusion of the week, Paul and Linda attend a party at the eatery Peppermint Park, in St. Martin's Lane, London, the same premises where Cynthia Lennon will later open her short-lived, and rather pricey, Lennons restaurant. Among the guests are Paul's brother Mike, Kenny Jones and Keith Moon. Following their meal, guests watch a midnight screening of the new film *The Buddy Holly Story*, starring Gary Busey, at the Odeon Theatre in Leicester Square. Keith Moon leaves before the end and returns to the Mayfair flat he is renting from Harry Nilsson where, the following day, he is found dead in bed. Inside the flat are clothes belonging to Ringo.

Monday September 11 (until Friday September 29)
 Back To The Egg recording sessions resume at Lympne Castle in Kent where Wings record 'We're Open All Night', another version of 'Love Awake' plus 'After The Ball' and 'Million Miles'. The group also record 'The Broadcast', featuring the poems *The Sport Of Kings* by Ian Hay and *The Little Man* by John Galsworthy, both of which are read by Harold Margery, who is not credited on the *Back To The Egg* album.

Friday September 15
 George buys Brundon Mill house, situated a mile from the market town of Sudbury, for Derek Taylor. The property, valued at £67,000, is purchased from Mrs. Beresford Jones.

Saturday September 16
 In the Tunisian Desert, filming begins on the Handmade production of Monty Python's *The Life Of Brian*, featuring a cameo appearance by George. (Shooting will continue until November 12.)

Saturday September 30
 The Capitol single 'Sgt. Pepper's Lonely Hearts Club Band' – 'With A Little Help From My Friends'/'A Day In The Life' reaches number 71 in the American charts on the day that

Robert Stigwood's critically panned big-screen version of the album opens in cinemas. The musical film stars The Bee Gees, Peter Frampton and Earth, Wind And Fire.

October
 The American big-screen movie *I Wanna Hold Your Hand*, which focuses on four teenagers attempting to meet The Beatles as they make their live US TV début on *The Ed Sullivan Show* on February 9, 1964, opens in cinemas across London. Executive producer is Steven Spielberg and there is a cameo appearance by DJ Murray 'The K' Kaufman. The film was originally to have starred Carrie Fisher but she pulled out, to be replaced by Susan Newman. The film was released in the US the previous April.

Tuesday October 3
 Between 10:30am and 6:30pm, *Back To The Egg* recording sessions continue at Abbey Road Studio Two in London. Wings are joined by a large "supergroup" of guest musicians, who are collectively billed as *Rockestra*. (The musical instruments begin arriving at 10:30am and the musicians, as requested by Paul, arrive one hour later.) Those present include Hank Marvin, from The Shadows, Pete Townshend of The Who, Dave Gilmour of Pink Floyd, John Bonham and John Paul Jones of Led Zeppelin, Ronnie Lane and Kenny Jones of The (Small) Faces, Tony Ashton of Ashton, Gardner and Dyke, and Speedy Acquaye, Tony Carr, Ray Cooper, Morris Pert, Howie Casey, Tony Dorsey, Steve Howard and Thaddeus Richard. During the all-day session they record the 'Rockestra Theme' and 'So Glad To See You Here' which both appear on the *Back To The Egg* album. On hand to capture the proceedings is a film crew, using five 35mm Panavision cameras, hired by Paul and featuring the direction of Barry Chattington, who previously worked with Paul on the unreleased 1972 *Bruce McMouse* concert film. In 1980, Paul edits together (from a total of 80,000 feet of film taken on the day), a 40-minute programme comprising 5,500 feet of film from the events, and calls it simply *Rockestra*. This film remains unreleased, save for a brief 15-minute excerpt, which is screened at the *Back To The Egg* launch party on Monday June 11, 1979 (see entry).
 Paul recalls the filming: "I asked the fellow who was going to film (Barry Chattington), if he could film it like they film wild life. You know, they sit back off wild life and just observe it and they just let it go on with its own thing and when you try and film our session it's a bit like the same sort of thing. If everyone notices the cameras and lights, they all freeze up and won't talk naturally and they all get embarrassed. So they (the cameramen) put all the cameras behind a big wall and no one could see the cameras and a lot of them didn't even know it was being filmed. John Bonham had no idea it was filmed . . . in fact he is suing us!" Paul jokingly concludes.
 Further *Back To The Egg* recordings take place on October 10.

Friday October 6
 In America, Ringo makes a guest appearance on the television chat show *Everyday*.

Monday October 9
 To celebrate Sean's third birthday, and of course John's 38th, a party is held at the Tavern On The Green in New York's Central Park.

Tuesday October 10
 Further recordings for *Back To The Egg* take place at Abbey Road Studio Two, where Wings record the first versions of 'Getting Closer' and 'Baby's Request'. (Additional work on the album takes place in November – see entry.)

Saturday October 14
 London Town reaches number 39 in the American album charts, while in the Swiss Alps, Aubrey Powell, of the Hipgnosis design studio, shoots the cover to the album *Wings Greatest*.

Friday October 20
 Five weeks after shooting had started, George flies in to Tunisia to check on how the filming of Monty Python's *The Life Of Brian* is doing. During this 24-hour visit he films his brief role in the film, as "Mr. Papadopoulos". George flies back to his wife and child the following day, October 21.

November (until the end of December)

🍎 Further work on *Back To The Egg* takes place at Paul's recently opened Replica Studios, situated in the basement of his MPL offices in Soho Square, London. It is so called because it is an exact replica of EMI's Abbey Road Studio Two created because Paul's favourite EMI location was unavailable to him on more than one occasion. During this six week period Wings record additional overdubbing on previously recorded tracks, including 'Getting Closer' and 'Baby's Request'. (The group resumes work on *Back To The Egg* in January next year.)

🍎 At the end of the month, in the seclusion of his Dakota bedroom, John ad-libs a Bob Dylan parody while watching a TV news broadcast, using the words of the news reports to create spontaneous lyrics. The track becomes known as the 'News Of The Day (From Reuters)'.

Sunday November 5

🍎 On a yacht on Boston Harbour, Denny Laine marries his long time girlfriend Jo Jo Wood.

Wednesday November 22

🍎 The Wings' compilation album *Wings Greatest* is released in America. (The UK release takes place on December 1.) The tracks for the album are: 'Another Day', 'Silly Love Songs', 'Live And Let Die', 'Junior's Farm', 'With A Little Luck', 'Band On The Run', 'Uncle Albert – Admiral Halsey', 'Hi Hi Hi', 'Let 'Em In', 'My Love', 'Jet' and 'Mull Of Kintyre'. (It reaches number 5 in the UK and number 29 in American charts.) To promote its release, Paul sanctions a 30-second TV advert featuring a man in the bath singing an out-of-tune version of 'Mull Of Kintyre', 'Silly Love Songs' sung by a chef in a busy restaurant and 'Jet', sung by two secretaries, one of which is painting her nails. The final part of the advert sees a dustman sitting at the wheel of a large truck (parked in Abbey Road near the studios), singing a hopelessly bad chorus of 'Band On The Run'. A car containing Paul, Linda and Denny pulls up alongside him, and Paul exclaims, "You're a bit flat mate!" before immediately driving away. Leaning out of his window, the driver replies: "Funny, I only checked them this morning." The advert is screened regularly on the ITV network over the next two weeks.

December

🍎 The rejected first version of the Capitol album *Rarities* is released in America. (A revised edition is released on March 24, 1980.)

🍎 In the village of Pishill in England, George appears with Mick Ralphs, Boz Burrell, Simon Kirke, Ian Paice and Jon Lord. The group naturally bill themselves as The Pisshole Artists.

🍎 Two years on and Beatles fans in the UK again petition the BBC demanding a repeat screening of The Beatles' film *Magical Mystery Tour*. This time, the Corporation takes notice of the demands and looks into the possibility of another transmission.

Thursday December 7

🍎 George attends a concert by Eric Clapton and Elton John at the Guildford Civic Hall in Surrey. He is persuaded to join them on stage, where he performs on the song 'Further On Up The Road'. The surprise appearance is captured on film by Rex Pipe and appears in the 1980 Angle films 70-minute production of *Eric Clapton And His Rolling Hotel,* which has very few airings. These include a screening at the National Film Festival in London and at another in New York. (Incidentally the Rolling Hotel in question is a special train built by Hermann Goering, which will house the musicians and crew of Clapton's 1979 tour of Germany, starting on March 27.)

Thursday December 28

🍎 In Liverpool, at the club Romeo & Juliet's in the St. John's precinct, Bob Wooler and Allan Williams host (between noon and 2am) a *Beatles Christmas Party,* featuring live groups, Beatle quizzes, auctions, and a Beatles disco. Later, across the road at the ABC Theatre in Lime Street, Wooler and Williams present an *All-Night Beatles Film Show,* featuring (between midnight and 7am on the morning of December 29), screenings of *A Hard Day's Night, Help!, Yellow Submarine, Let It Be* and *How I Won The War.* The all-day ticket costs just £5.

"The Beatles are close to reuniting for the first time in ten years to give a concert in aid of the Vietnamese boat people."

– The *Washington Post*

January (into February)
🍎 In London, Wings resume work on *Back To The Egg* at Replica Studios, where work commences on various versions of 'Goodnight Tonight' and 'Daytime Nightime Suffering'. (Further work on the album takes place in March – see entry.)

Wednesday January 31
🍎 George and Olivia, with their friend Gary Wright, fly out from London's Heathrow Airport en route to Rio to watch the Brazilian Grand Prix.

February
🍎 Outside the Dakota building, John and Yoko meet the photographer Paul Goresh for the first time.
🍎 In between appearances on the radio, and having accidents on his tractor, George goes house hunting on the island of Mustique.

Thursday February 8
🍎 George and Olivia fly back (via Paris) to London's Heathrow Airport, where he prepares for various upcoming radio appearances to promote his new single and album.

Friday February 9
🍎 At BBC Broadcasting House, in Portland Place, London, George appears live with Michael Jackson on the BBC Radio One programme *Roundtable,* hosted by David "Kid" Jensen, where they act as judges on this weeks new single releases. The former Beatle also reveals during the interview that he has brought back with him on the flight "a big bag of Brazilian albums". (The show is transmitted on the station between 6:31 and 8:00pm.)

Wednesday February 14
🍎 The album *George Harrison* is released in America. (The UK release takes place on February 16.) George's single 'Blow Away'/'Soft Hearted Hana' is also released today in America.

Thursday February 15
🍎 George is interviewed by Peter Clements of the BBC Wolverhampton based studio Beacon Radio.

Friday February 16
🍎 George's single 'Blow Away'/'Soft Touch' is released in the UK. George recalls the inspiration behind the A-side: "I wrote 'Blow Away' on a miserable day, it was pouring with rain, and we were having a few leaks in the roof. To tell you the truth, I was a bit embarrassed by it! It was catchy and I was embarrassed to play it to anybody, it was too obvious."

Monday February 19
🍎 Outside the London Polytechnic, disc jockey Nicky Horne briefly interviews George getting out of his sports car. Horne asks about the recently released film of *Sgt. Pepper's Lonely Hearts Club Band.* "Have you seen it yet?" asks Horne.
   "No, no," George replies. "I'm not going to see it. Everybody tells me it's awful!"
   "Well," replies Horne diplomatically, "a lot of people have said it's awful. The thing is, how much control, if any, did you have over it?"
   "We didn't have any control," George exclaims. "I mean, there's been a lot of Beatles things, you know, like *John, Paul, Bert, Ringo, Ted . . . And Ringo,* and *Sgt. Pepper,* and all kinds of things like that, because the Fab Four were split and all over the world, then it was pretty easy to go and do things like that. All they needed was the songs, and ATV Music owned most of the songs, so it was pretty easy to do that. But, I don't really think they're supposed to do that and, in fact, we've just got together a group of people to go and sue them all!"
   The three-minute feature is transmitted this evening in the latest edition of *Nicky Horne's Music Scene,* included within the regional news programme *Thames At Six,* transmitted in the London area of ITV region only (between 6:00 and 6:34pm). Shortly after this interview George is involved in an accident driving his tractor on his Friar Park estate. While tending his vast farmland, the brakes of his tractor fail and George is

thrown from the vehicle, whereupon the back wheels drive over his foot. George is immediately rushed to Reading hospital where X-rays reveal that he is bruised but not badly injured. Even so, he uses a walking stick on his upcoming promotional trip to the States. As a tongue-in-cheek gesture, George arrives at Heathrow Airport for his departure in a wheelchair.

🍎 In America Fred Seaman starts work as an assistant for John and Yoko.

Wednesday February 21
🍎 In America, WEA prepare for television distribution the promotional video for 'Blow Away'. The first UK TV screening occurs on March 6 (see entry).

Friday February 23
🍎 As a further promotional activity, George makes another live appearance with Nicky Horne on his Capital Radio programme *Your Mother Wouldn't Like It* (transmitted between 9:00 and 11:00pm).

Tuesday February 27
🍎 At the Dakota, without any great ceremony, John finally shaves off his thick heavy beard.

March
🍎 Recordings for *Back To The Egg* return to Abbey Road Studio Two where vocals are added to the tracks 'Winter Rose' – 'Love Awake'. Further work during these sessions involves synthesiser overdubs being recorded on the tracks 'Getting Closer' and 'Love Awake'. (Further *Back To The Egg* sessions take place on April 1 – see entry.)

🍎 At a little record shop in Greenwich Village, Manhattan, a couple of miles away from the Dakota building, Fred Seaman arranges a standing order for "one copy of *every* bootleg Beatles and Lennon album that should ever come into the shop, to be put to one side, awaiting collection". On a regular basis, over the next 21 months, Seaman will return to the shop, hand over whatever money is owing, no questions asked, and collect whatever the owner has received. Once back at the Dakota, John will lovingly store the albums without opening the sealed sleeves. (As a result, John will soon boast one of the largest Beatles bootleg album collections in the world.)

Tuesday March 6
🍎 George's video for 'Blow Away' is screened on the children's music programme *Pop Gospel*, transmitted across the ITV network between 4:21 and 4:44pm.

Thursday March 15
🍎 The Wings single 'Goodnight Tonight'/'Daytime Nightime Suffering' is released in America on the Columbia label, to which Paul had just signed, thereby becoming the highest paid recording artist in the industry, with an advance of two million dollars per album against a 22 per cent royalty. (The UK release takes place on March 23.)

Friday March 16
🍎 In America, the 90-minute MPL documentary film *Wings Over The World* (originally titled *Paul McCartney Sings His Greatest Hits)*, which features highlights from the Wings 1975/1976 World Tour, receives its premiere on American TV. (The first UK TV screening occurs on BBC2 on April 8 between 8:10 and 9:24pm, with a repeat screening on BBC1 on December 24, between 2:40 and 3:53pm.)

Monday March 26
🍎 Paul's first 12″ extended mix release occurs with the issue of Wings 'Goodnight Tonight'/'Daytime Nightime Suffering' in America. (The UK release takes place on April 3.)

Sunday April 1
🍎 The pre-recorded NBC Radio show *An Afternoon With Paul McCartney*, featuring Paul in conversation with Paul Gambaccini, is broadcast in America. While this is being transmitted, Paul is joined by The Black Dyke Mills Band at Abbey Road, Studio Two where they record their parts for the track 'Winter Rose'. Paul, of course, having worked with the band back in 1969 when he produced their Apple single 'Thingamebob'/'Yellow Submarine'.

♦ Meanwhile in the States, John hires a small yacht for a cruise around Palm Beach in Florida. Accompanying them are Yoko's nieces Reiko, Akiko and Tokato as well as Julian, Sean, Fred's wife Helen Seaman and the 12-year-old daughter of their Palm Beach real estate agent. At the end of the month, Julian returns home to England. (This is the last time he will see his father.)

Tuesday April 3
♦ On the stage of the Hammersmith Palais in London, working again with Keith McMillan's company Keef & Co., Wings video-tape promotional clips for their next single 'Goodnight Tonight'. During this all-day session, which began at 5:30am with the setting up of intricate stage lighting, five different versions are shot. Shooting finally starts at 4pm, but Paul chooses only three of the versions taped today when the clips are edited and prepared for distribution on April 7. (Only versions B and C are ultimately screened, with version D remaining unseen to this day.) For the clips, Paul, Linda and Wings appear dressed in their modern day clothes as well as in the style of the Forties, with greased-back hair and all. With clever editing, version B features the "roll back" technique, which involves cutting the video footage of the band in regular clothes with everything in the same position as when they were in costume. Version C features the same footage, but without the edits back into modern day clothes. In the UK, the clip appears on BBC1's *Top Of The Pops* and on the Thames/ITV network programme *The Kenny Everett Video Show,* one week later, on Monday April 9 (between 7:01 and 7:28pm), where the video is shown in its entirety.

Wednesday April 4
♦ At 12:30pm, a preview screening of the 73-minute MPL film documentary *Wings Over The World* takes place at the Bijou Theatre at 113 Wardour Street, London W1.

Friday April 6
♦ The promotional film clip of George performing 'Blow Away' is broadcast in today's edition of *Midnight Special* on American TV.

Friday April 20
♦ George's single 'Love Comes To Everyone'/'Soft Hearted Hana' is released in the UK where it fails to chart.

Friday April 27
♦ In America, Allen Klein is found guilty on charges of tax evasion and is sentenced to serve two months, out of a two-year sentence, in prison.

Saturday April 28
♦ During his stay in Monte Carlo, Ringo again becomes seriously ill with peritonitis, an illness he suffered as a child. He is transferred to the Princess Grace Hospital in Monte Carlo where he undergoes life-threatening internal surgery for an intestinal blockage. During the operation several feet of intestines are removed from his body.

Friday May 4
♦ EMI release the compilation album *Monument To British Rock*, which features George's 1971 track 'My Sweet Lord'.

Sunday May 6
♦ Capital Radio this morning broadcasts a Beatles feature which includes separate interviews with both George Harrison and The Beatles' producer George Martin.

Friday May 11
♦ George's single 'Love Comes To Everyone'/'Soft Touch' is released in America. To coincide with its release, George gives another interview to London based Capital Radio.
♦ The Beatles' compilation *Hey Jude* (also known as *The Beatles Again*) is released in the UK. (The album was originally released in America on February 26, 1970.)

Monday May 14
♦ At the annual film festival in Cannes, in the South of France, The Who's "rockumentary"

The Kids Are Alright, featuring cameo appearances by Ringo, filmed around the middle of August 1977, receives its worldwide premiere screening.

Saturday May 19
🍎 At his Hurtwood Edge home in Surrey, Eric Clapton throws a party for 200 guests to celebrate his marriage to George's first wife, the former Patti Boyd. (The couple married in Tucson, Arizona, on March 27.) At the end of the evening, Paul, George and Ringo, as well as the other celebrities present, including Mick Jagger, Denny Laine, Ginger Baker and Lonnie Donegan, join Eric for an impromptu concert on a stage set up in a large marquee tent in his grounds. They run through various old rock'n'roll hits and even some Beatles' covers. Friends and family take souvenir pictures of the event, although none have appeared in print.

🍎 'Goodnight Tonight' reaches number five in both the US and UK singles charts.

Thursday May 24
🍎 The Wings' album *Back To The Egg* is released in America. (The UK release takes place on June 8.)

🍎 At 12:15pm, George and Olivia fly out (economy class) from Heathrow to Nice Airport, arriving at 3:05pm.

Saturday May 26
🍎 George, who had just arrived in Monte Carlo, meets Ringo at the Monaco Grand Prix. A roving camera team from ABC America's *Wide World Of Sport* interviews them along with racing driver Jackie Stewart.

Sunday May 27
🍎 The New York Times publish, on page 20E a "Love Letter From John And Yoko To People Who Ask Us What, When And Why". The full-page letter of explanation includes the following:

"The past 10 years we noticed everything we wished came true in its own time, good or bad, one way or another. We kept telling each other that one of these days we would have to get organised and wish for the good things. Then our baby arrived! We were overjoyed and at the same time felt very responsible. Now our wishes would also effect *him*. We felt it was time for us to stop discussing and do something about our wishing process: the spring cleaning of our minds! It was a lot of work. We kept finding things in those old closets in our minds that we hadn't realised were still there, things we wished we hadn't found. As we did our cleaning, we also started to notice many things wrong in our house: there was a shelf which would never have been there in the first place, a painting we grew to dislike, and there were two dingy rooms, which became light and breezy when we broke the walls between them. We started to love the plants, which one of us originally thought were robbing the air from us! We enjoy the drum beat of the city which used to annoy us ..."

It continues: "Many people are sending us vibes every day in letters, telegrams, taps on the gate, or just flowers and nice thoughts! We thank them all and appreciate them for respecting our quiet space, which we need. Thank you for all the love you send us. We feel it every day. We love you, too. We know you're concerned about us. That is nice. That's why you want to know what we are doing. That's why everybody is asking us, 'What, When And Why.' We understand. This is what we've been doing. We hope that you have the same quiet space in your mind to make your own wishes come true.

"If you think of us next time, remember our silence is a silence of love and not indifference. Remember, we are writing in the sky instead of on paper – this is our song. Lift your eyes and look up in the sky. There's our message. Lift your eyes again and look around you, and you will see that you are walking in the sky, which extends to the ground. We are all a part of the sky, more so than of the ground. Remember, we love you."
John Lennon & Yoko Ono, May 27, 1979, New York City
P.S. We noticed that three angels were looking over our shoulders when we wrote this! (The letter is copyrighted *Sprit Music '79*.)

This first public announcement in years from one of the world's most famous couples naturally features prominently in news reports around the globe.

Monday May 28
🍎 Before returning home to England, George persuades Stewart to appear in his

promotional film for 'Faster'. Stewart is filmed chauffeuring George around the Monaco racetrack while he sings the song in the back of the car. George and Olivia, after their four-day stay, head back to England, departing from Nice Airport at 6:35pm, and landing at Heathrow's Terminal 2 at 7:25pm. (Vegetarian meals are served to the couple on the flight.) Ringo, meanwhile, travels to New York to meet John at the Dakota.

Tuesday May 29
🍎 Ringo drops in to meet John at his Dakota apartment. The event is captured with a Polaroid snapshot taken by Fred Seaman.

Thursday May 31
🍎 In England, Paul enlists Keith MacMillan, Phil Davey and Hugh Scott-Symonds to carry out the production for the promotional clips to accompany the *Back To The Egg* album. (The final choice of seven songs to be taped was actually down to MacMillan, Paul having furnished him with an early tape of the album the previous week.) Shooting is scheduled to begin the following Monday June 4.

Friday June 1
🍎 The Wings single 'Old Siam Sir'/'Spin It On' is released in the UK.

Monday June 4 & Tuesday June 5
🍎 As planned, shooting commences on the promotional clips to accompany the seven tracks taken off the album *Back To The Egg*. The first taping occurs in a small hall at Lympne Castle in Kent, where shooting takes place for 'Old Siam Sir'. (This location is familiar to Wings as tracks for the album were recorded there.) On June 5 production shifts to a small private aircraft hangar, about a mile from the castle, where Wings tape 'Spin It On' and 'Getting Closer'. In the best tradition of utilising the best of what's on offer, the crew move outside the hangar to shoot, in the nearby field, Denny's track 'Again And Again'. Shooting continues late into the night with additional hangar scenes for 'Getting Closer' and exterior driving scenes, seen briefly at the very start of the clip.

Tuesday June 5
🍎 Wings' single 'Getting Closer'/'Spin It On' is released in America.

Wednesday June 6
🍎 Taping continues at Lympne Castle where shooting commences, with specially added snow, on the track 'Winter Rose' – 'Love Awake'.

Friday June 8
🍎 While Ringo is getting ready to appear on the American NBC TV show *Midnight Special,* backing Rolling Stone Ronnie Wood on drums for the track 'Buried Alive', Wings are driving the forty miles from Lympne Castle in Kent to Camber Sands, to continue with more work on the *Back To The Egg* promotional clips. Under the spotlight today is the track 'Baby's Request'. In preparation for the launch of the *Back To The Egg* album, Wings return to London the following day.

Monday June 11
🍎 At Abbey Road Studio Two, Wings hold a 12:30pm press launch for their new album *Back To The Egg*. An avalanche of press and TV reporters are treated to the bizarre spectacle of the world famous studio being turned into a giant frying pan (accomplished by blacking out the studio walls with black curtains), with fried eggs sitting within. (These are actually tables with parasols that had been painted to resemble the yolks of an egg.) At these tables a host of guests, including the DJ Kenny Everett, hear Wings' latest offering plus the first ever screening (albeit 15-minutes only) of the MPL *Rockestra* film, recorded on October 3 last year (see entry). The Keef & Co. film crew, who shot the *Rockestra* film, are present and are presented with a specially engraved egg-cup and spoon by Paul and Linda. Clips from the afternoon gathering are featured in a two-minute report on this evening's *ITN News At 5:45* (transmitted across the ITV network between 5:45 and 6:00pm), where the reporter John Suchet is informed by Paul that "I intend taking Wings back out on tour towards the end of the year".

Wednesday June 13
🍎 Work on the *Back To The Egg* promotional films are concluded today when, at Keef & Co.'s London studios, Wings tape a version of 'Arrow Through Me'. Also taped today are additional scenes for 'Getting Closer', where Wings are seen behind the wheel of their van at the very start of the promotional clip.

Friday June 15
🍎 Paul's promotional interview for *Back To The Egg* is broadcast by Capital Radio in London.

Saturday June 30
🍎 Paul gives another interview to promote *Back To The Egg* tonight, this time on Radio Luxembourg.

July (throughout month)
🍎 During extensive solo recording sessions at his private studios in Scotland, working as both engineer and producer, and using such abstract methods as a drum kit balanced in the toilet, Paul records the tracks 'Wonderful Christmastime' and 'Coming Up', during sessions that will form the basis of his 1980 album *McCartney II*. The rest of the home-based recordings will feature the following songs: 'Temporary Secretary', 'Waterfalls' (originally titled 'I Need Love'), 'Nobody Knows', 'On The Way', 'Summer's Days Song', 'Bogey Music', 'Darkroom', 'One Of These Days', 'Check My Machine' and 'Secret Friend' as well as the instrumentals 'Front Parlour' and 'Frozen Jap'. ("Most of the numbers were, in fact, made up as I went along, except for 'Waterfalls', which was a song before I went in to record it," says Paul in May 1980.)
    Paul originally plans the album as a double featuring a total running time of approximately 80 minutes. Among the tracks cut are 'All You Horseriders' (later to appear on the soundtrack of the MPL film documentary *Blankit's First Show*, first transmitted in England on BBC2 on July 12, 1986), 'Blue Swat', 'Mr. H. Atom', 'You Know I'll Get You Baby' and 'Bogey Wobble'. The tracks 'Check My Machine' (featuring a running time of 5' 44") and 'Secret Friend' (10' 20") both officially appear as McCartney B-sides.

Saturday July 14
🍎 In England, George is present at the Silverstone Grand Prix where he is interviewed for ITV's *World Of Sport* programme. George also takes part in a celebrity race on the track but stalls his car at the start of the race, an event captured by television cameras. Shortly afterwards, this time at the Donington Park racetrack, George is seen driving Stirling Moss's car.

Saturday July 28
🍎 'Getting Closer' reaches number 28 in the US singles chart.

Monday July 30
🍎 George's single 'Faster'/'Your Love Is Forever' is released in the UK. (The record also becomes available as a limited edition picture disc, the first such release from any of the ex-Beatles.) The single is released to raise money for the Gunnar Nilsson cancer fund. Nilsson was a Swedish racing driver who had died of the disease.
🍎 A further promotional interview by Paul for *Back To The Egg* is broadcast tonight on Radio Luxembourg.

August
🍎 John and Yoko again visit Karuizawa in Japan for their summer holiday, returning home four weeks later partly by train. This will be their last holiday in Japan as a family.
🍎 The McCartney song 'Did We Meet Somewhere Before', rejected for the Warren Beatty film *Heaven Can Wait*, is featured in the Warner Brothers film *Rock 'N' Roll High School*, starring The Ramones.

Friday August 10
🍎 The UK release takes place of the Suzy And The Red Stripes single 'Seaside Woman'/'B Side To Seaside'. (The single was originally released in America on May 31, 1977.) The single does not chart.

Wednesday August 1
🍎 George, Olivia and Dhani take a holiday in Athens, returning to England on Friday August 17.

Tuesday August 14
🍎 The Wings' single 'Arrow Through Me'/'Old Siam Sir' is released in America.

Thursday August 16
🍎 The Wings' single 'Getting Closer'/'Baby's Request' is released in the UK.

Saturday August 18
🍎 George's promotional film for 'Faster' is screened, most suitably, during the ITV network Saturday afternoon sports programme *World Of Sport,* hosted by Dickie Davies.

Monday September 3
🍎 Live from Superdance in America, Ringo appears as a special guest on the Annual TV fundraising spectacular *The Jerry Lewis Muscular Dystrophy Telethon,* where he joins Bill Wyman, Todd Rundgren, Doug Kershaw and Kiki Dee. Ringo is seen taking pledges over the phone and then joins in on drums for an all-star jam, where they perform the songs 'Money'/'Twist And Shout' and 'Jumpin' Jack Flash'. The promo film clip of Wings' 'Getting Closer' is also screened during the broadcast.
🍎 With The Beatles' legal action against the producers of *Beatlemania,* hinted at by George back on February 19, now gathering momentum, George is forced to fly out to the States for various Apple business meetings. He will return to Heathrow Airport from New York's Kennedy Airport on September 5.

Tuesday September 4
🍎 Still in the States, Ringo gives a radio interview to the DJ Dave Herman.

Wednesday September 5
🍎 In New York, at his Dakota apartment, John begins recording a scathing verbal memoir of his life on his small portable machine. This includes his earliest childhood memories, his reaction to witnessing his mother Julia performing oral sex on "Twitchy" Dykins and considerable criticism of fellow musicians, including Paul McCartney, Mick Jagger and Bob Dylan, whom he labels "company men".

Thursday September 13
🍎 Just a week after a previous flight, George is again obliged to fly to New York, for legal reasons. His 48-hour visit concludes when he returns home to England at 9pm on September 15. (The flights, which serve vegetarian meals, cost £1,027.50.)

Friday September 14
🍎 Back in England, Paul is to be found performing live at the Hammersmith Odeon in London as part of the grand finale of the fourth annual Buddy Holly Week celebration. The 8pm concert, which features amongst others Jerry Allison, Don Everly and Sonny Curtis, is captured on videotape by Paul's MPL Communications company and will form a major part of the short TV documentary, transmitted in America on MTV under the title of *The Music Lives On,* on September 8, 1984. Paul is seen performing 'It's So Easy' and 'Bo Diddley', while Denny is seen singing 'Raining In My Heart' with Don Everly of The Everly Brothers. Guests in the audience include former Monkee Micky Dolenz, Superman actor Christopher Reeve, DJ Alan Freeman, David Frost, former member of The Faces Ronnie Lane, former 10cc drummer Kevin Godley plus Paul's old friend, the actor Victor Spinetti.

Friday September 21
🍎 In America, the United Nations Secretary General Kurt Waldheim asks The Beatles to reunite to aid the Vietnamese boat people. (Again, the offer is declined.) Meanwhile, an optimistic report, on the same lines, appears today in the *Washington Post.* This reveals that: "The Beatles are close to reuniting for the first time in ten years to give a concert in aid of the Vietnamese boat people. Paul McCartney, George Harrison and Ringo Starr have agreed to give the New York concert under the auspices of the United Nations and John Lennon is considering the idea."

Thursday September 27
❡ The Beatles get together, not to perform, but to sue the organisers of the *Beatlemania* stage show. Lawyers representing Apple in New York reveal that The Beatles are seeking, in Los Angeles, $60 million (around £27 million) in actual and punitive damages against the organisers and promoters cashing in on the stage show in London later this year. The Beatles are also seeking to close down the six *Beatlemania* shows that are at present running in various parts of America and to halt attempts to package a *Beatlemania* television show. In reply to this action, Steve Leber, of Leber-Krebs Inc., the man responsible for the shows, says: "My company bought the rights to perform all the old Beatle songs for the show." He adds, "The Beatles are making more money from the show from royalties than I am!"

❡ On a most sombre note, the former Wings guitarist Jimmy McCulloch is found dead from a drug overdose in London. He was only 26 years of age.

Monday October 8
❡ The soundtrack album of Monty Python's *Life Of Brian,* featuring the track 'Always Look On The Bright Side Of Life', which is mixed by George and Phil MacDonald is released in America today. (The UK release takes place on November 9.)

Tuesday October 9
❡ John and Yoko hold a party for Sean's fourth birthday at Le Roy's Tavern On The Green restaurant in New York. Also present are Sean's young friends and their respective parents who also live at the Dakota. John and Yoko give them all a present and arrange for them to be entertained by a magician and a clown. Today, John also turns 39 years of age.

❡ Meanwhile back in England, acting on a request on October 5 from the Clerk of the Justices, in Witham, Essex, George's secretary Cherrie Cowell sends them George's driving licence following his recent ban from driving.

Friday October 12
❡ The album *The Beatles Rarities* is released in the UK, eleven months after EMI announced that the album will *only* be available within the expensive EMI *Beatles Collection* album box set.

Saturday October 13
❡ 'Arrow Through Me' reaches number 29 in the US singles chart.

Monday October 15
❡ In New York, John and Yoko contribute $1,000 to a fund that purchases bullet-proof vests for New York City police officers.

❡ At Friar Park, in response to a request on October 1, George's secretary Cherrie sends to the Reverend Fraser Smith in Nottingham a signed Christmas card for display in their annual Christmas Carol service.

Thursday October 18
❡ Even though they are facing a law suit from the real "Beatles", the "Multi-Media Musical Experience" *Beatlemania* opens at the Astoria Theatre in London's Charing Cross Road, as planned. John is played by Michael Palaikis and Peter McGann, while Paul is portrayed by Tony Kishman and Peter Santora. In the role of George are Jimmy Poe and Peter Santora and playing the part of Ringo are Louis Colucci and Bobby Taylor.

Saturday October 20
❡ Just five weeks after his last visit, George again returns to New York. He will return to England just 24 hours later on October 21.

Wednesday October 24
❡ At a party at the Les Ambassadors Club in Hamilton Place, London, Paul is awarded a rhodium-plated disc by the *Guinness Book Of Records*, recognising his record-breaking achievements in song writing and record sales and named the Most Honoured Man In Music. (The Rhodium disc is made of a metal much shinier than Platinum and twice as expensive. Paul's disc is actually worth an incredible £345 an ounce! Amazingly enough, the Guinness Book people were going to present to Paul a special disc made from Osmium,

one of the world's densest metals. That was until they realised, just in time, that it was highly poisonous!) Paul collects the less-harmful award from Norman St. John Stevas, the Minister for the Arts. He is now included in the *Guinness Book of Records* book as the most successful composer and recording artist of all time, his awards including 43 million sellers, 60 gold records and more total worldwide record sales than any other artist. Also being honoured at the club today is the boxing champion John Conteh, the racing driver David Purley, the lyricist Tim Rice and George Schmidt, a man fluent in 31 different languages. Exclusively available today, within the new 1980 *Guinness Book Of Records* publication, is a special "Paul McCartney Bookmark", limited to only 200 copies. (A special feature on the ceremony is transmitted live today on BBC Radio One.) Immediately following the ceremony, Paul is interviewed at the hotel by Geraldo Rivera for the American TV programme *20/20 Action News* on ABC TV.

Tuesday October 30
 At Friar Park, in a session that will periodically last a full year (until October 30, 1980), George records a vast selection of the songs that will appear on the album *Somewhere In England*. These tracks include 'Baltimore Oriole', 'Hong Kong Blues', 'Unconsciousness Rules', 'Save The World', 'Life Itself' and 'Writing's On The Wall'. The songs 'Sat Singing' (recorded during March of 1980), 'Lay His Head' and 'Tears Of The World' (both recorded during April of 1980), and 'Flying Hour' (recorded back in March of 1978) are rejected by Warner Brothers when presented by George for its original release on November 2, 1980. They demand that these four tracks be replaced before the album is released. (Bootleggers move swiftly to release this original version of the album, although the four rejected songs are eventually released officially.)

Wednesday October 31
 John ventures out of his Dakota apartment to take Sean to see a production of *Peter Pan* on Broadway.

Thursday November 1
 In America, Geraldo Rivera again interviews Paul and Linda for the ABC TV programme *20/20*. (The interview is simultaneously transmitted on the radio station WPLJ.)

Saturday November 3
 The Beatles album *Rarities* reaches number 71 in the UK charts.

Monday November 5
 Ringo again visits John at the Dakota where they celebrate fireworks night. During the visit, John gives him a demo of the song 'Life Begins At 40', a track he wants Ringo to record for his next album.
 The music press reveals that Wings are to perform an 18-date UK tour during November and December.

Monday November 12
 In New York, John writes out his will, which is subsequently filed at the Manhattan surrogate court. On his death, half of his $30 million estate will go to "my beloved wife" and the remainder will go into a trust fund for Sean set up by both John and Yoko.

Friday November 16
 Paul's single 'Wonderful Christmastime'/'Rudolph The Red Nosed Reggae' is released in the UK. (The American release takes place on November 20.) On the release, Paul tells the story of the mystery violinist who plays on the B-side. Apparently, while Paul was rehearsing the song (back in June of 1975), a violin was delivered to the studio and he decided he would like the instrument to appear on the track. Paul asks the delivery man if he would play it, to which he agrees. Even though the man is paid a session fee, no one bothers to take his name and, following his departure, he becomes filed as "unknown". An appeal for the "mystery fiddler" is put out by Paul during Wings' appearance on *TISWAS*, transmitted on Saturday December 1 (see entry). On the day of its release, Wings commandeer the Fountain public house in Ashurst, West Sussex, to shoot a promotional clip for the A-side of their new single. The festivities are later intercut with brief scenes from their upcoming UK tour.

Broadcasts of the clip are plenty, most notably, *Tiswas* (on December 1), *ATV Today* (December 12) and BBC1's *Top Of The Pops* (December 27).

*   *   *

Wings UK Tour
November 23 – December 17

Wings begin a 19-date tour of the UK. Their repertoire consists largely of the following: 'Got To Get You Into My Life', 'Getting Closer', 'Every Night', 'Again And Again', 'I've Had Enough', 'No Words For My Love', 'Cook Of The House', 'Old Siam Sir', 'Maybe I'm Amazed', 'The Fool On The Hill', 'Let It Be', 'Hot As Sun', 'Spin It On', 'Twenty Flight Rock', 'Go Now', 'Arrow Through Me', 'Wonderful Christmastime', 'Coming Up', 'Goodnight Tonight', 'Yesterday', 'Mull Of Kintyre' and 'Band On The Run'. Supporting the group on the tour is the acoustic guitarist/comedian Earl Okin.

The tour visits:

> Liverpool Royal Court Theatre (Friday November 23 until Monday November 26)
> The Apollo in Ardwick, Manchester (Wednesday November 28 and Thursday November 29)
> Southampton Gaumont (Saturday December 1)
> Brighton New Conference Centre (Sunday December 2)
> Lewisham Odeon Theatre, London (Monday December 3)
> The Rainbow Theatre, Finsbury Park, London (Wednesday December 5)
> Empire Pool, Wembley (Friday December 7 until Monday December 10)
> Birmingham Odeon (Wednesday December 12)
> Newcastle City Hall (Friday December 14)
> Edinburgh Odeon, Scotland (Saturday December 15)
> Glasgow Apollo, Scotland (Sunday December 16 and Monday December 17)

Friday November 23

To fulfil a promise, the opening night of the tour is at the Royal Court Theatre in Liverpool. The 5pm concert is a free warm-up show for the benefit of a specially invited 1,500 audience which include handicapped children and the 600 student employees of the Liverpool Institute, Paul's old school. Prior to this evening's concert, the school's art teacher and pupils from the sixth form present him with a large illustration. Then, to celebrate the show and the opening of the tour, Paul and Linda hold a party at the venue for close family and friends. A profile, by Tony Wilkinson, on Paul's return to his home city is included in an 18-minute feature on BBC1's *Nationwide* programme. This includes most of the events in Liverpool, interviews with the band, clips of Wings rehearsing 'Again And Again' from the afternoon rehearsal plus 'Got To Get You Into My Life' and 'Yesterday' from the concert itself. (A 38-second clip of 'Yesterday' reappears during Paul's January, 1982, Abbey Road interview with Sue Lawley for BBC1's *Nationwide* programme.) A further report on Paul's return to Liverpool is broadcast on this evening's *News At Ten*, transmitted across the ITV network between 10:00 and 10:29pm.

Tuesday November 27

Wings take an afternoon boat ride on the *Royal Iris*. The *Liverpool Echo* newspaper is at hand to capture the event.

Wednesday November 28

Just prior to going on stage at the Ardwick in Manchester, Wings consent to two UK interviews. The first is for the Saturday morning children's show *TISWAS*, on which they are interviewed by Sally James, and they then take part in a short comedy sketch, joining Chris Tarrant and John Gorman (formerly of The Scaffold) in a brief performance of the *TISWAS* Christmas single 'The Bucket Of Water Song'. Paul also takes time to appeal for the "mystery fiddler" who appears on the track 'Rudolph The Red Nosed Reggae' (see entry for Friday November 16). This four-minute feature is transmitted the following Saturday December 1, across certain ITV network regions, between 10:30 and 12:28pm. Wings' second interview is for the midlands regional news programme *ATV Today*, where they are briefly interviewed by a young Anne Diamond, later to face Paul on the

ITV breakfast channel TV AM during the Eighties. This 90-second interview with the group is retained back from transmission until December 12, in order to neatly coincide with the group's appearance in Birmingham. The promotional film for 'Wonderful Christmastime' features in both TV appearances.

Wednesday December 5
Just prior to going on stage at the Rainbow Theatre in Finsbury Park, London, Paul and Linda are interviewed via satellite by Tom Snyder for inclusion in the NBC TV programme, the *Tomorrow Show*. (The 45-minute interview will be transmitted on Channel 4, WNBC TV on December 20 between 1:00 and 2:00pm ET.)

Friday December 7
During the opening night at the Empire Pool in Wembley, Wings add to their repertoire the songs 'Cook Of The House' and 'Baby Face'.

Friday December 14
This morning, Wings are interviewed backstage at Newcastle's City Hall by Tyne-Tees Television for the children's programme *Saturday Shake Up*. Clips from 'Old Siam Sir', 'Goodnight Tonight' and 'Wonderful Christmastime' also feature in the 24-minute programme, which is subtitled *Flying With Wings*, and transmitted, only in the Tyne-Tees region of the ITV Network, on Saturday December 22 between 11:46am and 12:19pm.

Saturday December 15
During the performance of 'Spin It On' at the Edinburgh Odeon, Wings suffer a power cut. To keep the audience entertained while technicians rectify the problem, Denny performs some acrobatic tricks and treats everyone to a "Max Wall" funny walk. The brass section join in the fun by coming down to the front of the stage and performing 'When The Saints Go Marching In', while Linda leads an audience sing-a-long to accompany them. After a six-minute break, the electricity is back and the concert resumes.

Monday December 17
The performance of 'Coming Up' tonight at the Glasgow Apollo, is recorded and released officially in 1980 as part of the 'Coming Up' (studio version) single. Also, on this the final night of the tour, Wings later don kilts to be joined on stage by The Campbeltown Pipes Band.

* * *

Friday November 23
 ABC TV in America premieres the Dick Clark made-for-TV production of *The Birth Of The Beatles*. The film, which features The Beatles' former drummer Pete Best in the role of technical advisor, tells the story of the group from their days in Liverpool to when they first arrived in America, appearing on *The Ed Sullivan Show* on February 9, 1964. Aside from claims that the film told them nothing new, fans are in uproar over the number of mistakes that appear in the feature-length film. As one Beatles fan remarks: "After the first ten minutes, I gave up counting the errors!"

Wednesday November 28
 Ringo's Los Angeles home in the Hollywood Hills, rented from close friend Harry Nilsson, is destroyed by fire which causes £67,000 worth of damage. He loses several of his most prized Beatles mementoes, many of which are stored inside the house. Television news crews film the tragic sight of Ringo watching helplessly as the fire rages out of control.

November – December
 The 31-minute Wings TV special *Back To The Egg* (videotaped between June 4 and 13), comprising (in order) the promotional clips for 'Getting Closer', 'Baby's Request', 'Old Siam Sir', 'Winter Rose' – 'Love Awake', 'Spin It On', 'Again And Again', 'Arrow Through Me' and 'Goodnight Tonight', is syndicated across various television stations in America. (The UK TV premiere of the show will not take place until BBC1 screen the show during the evening of June 10, 1981, between 7:45 and 8:16pm.)

December

🍎 Paul and Linda donate $10,000 to the *New York Times* Neediest Fund, a charity set up to help the poor at Christmas.

🍎 Ringo, until recently linked romantically with 20-year-old Stephanie La Motta, an ex of Donny Osmond, returns to Britain to celebrate Christmas. Joining him on the flight home is singer Lynsey De Paul, with whom Ringo will also be linked romantically. All this changes when he meets an actress on the set of his new film, which is due to begin filming in Mexico City on February 18, 1980.

Thursday December 6

🍎 BBC TV announces that this year's festive programming will be called "A Beatles Christmas", and that they will show six Beatles movies over the holiday period, including *Shea Stadium* and *Magical Mystery Tour*, both un-screened since the Sixties. Specially created TV trailers soon begin to appear on both BBC1 and 2.

🍎 George, meanwhile, is to be found with Olivia, attending the Springfield Boys Club Christmas show in Big Hill, Harrow, in north west London.

Friday December 21

🍎 Following much hype, "The Beatles At Christmas" season gets underway tonight on BBC2 with the much-awaited re-screening of *Magical Mystery Tour,* transmitted between 6:11 and 6:59pm. (This is its third television showing and its first broadcast on UK TV since the BBC2 colour screening on January 5, 1968.)

🍎 Meanwhile in Scotland, a pre-recorded interview with Paul is transmitted on Clyde Radio.

Saturday December 22

🍎 The BBC2 "Beatles At Christmas" season continues with *Help!* transmitted between 6:35 and 7:59pm. (This is its fifth British TV screening.)

Sunday December 23

🍎 The BBC2/Beatles season rolls on with *The Beatles At Shea Stadium*, a documentary of their August 15, 1965 concert at the venue, transmitted between 5:31 and 6:19pm. (This is its first British TV screening since the BBC1 broadcast on Saturday August 27, 1966.)

Monday December 24

🍎 The European version of *Yellow Submarine* is transmitted (between 5:40 and 6:59pm) as the fourth film in the BBC2 "Beatles At Christmas" season. Earlier in the day, and this time on BBC1, the documentary *Wings Over The World* receives its second, and final UK TV transmission, between 2:40 and 3:53pm.

Tuesday December 25

🍎 With millions tuning into the James Bond film *Goldfinger*, ITV's big Christmas Day movie, dedicated Beatles fans tune instead into BBC2 to watch the fifth TV screening of *A Hard Days Night* (between 3:00 and 4:24pm), the penultimate film in "The Beatles At Christmas" season.

🍎 As a Christmas present, Paul, at a cost of £40,000, purchases for Linda a ranch set in 80 acres in Arizona. Linda had fallen in love with the place during a stay there in the Sixties.

Wednesday December 26

🍎 Back in England, the BBC2 Beatles season concludes with the 1970 film *Let It Be*. (Transmitted today between 5:51 and 7:09pm. It is the third UK TV screening.)

Saturday December 29

🍎 Amid wild press hysteria that The Beatles are to play together again on stage this evening, Wings perform live as part of a special benefit performance at London's Hammersmith Odeon on the final night of the four *Concerts for Kampuchea*, which had begun on December 26. Proceeds go directly towards the emergency relief work of the United Nations agencies for the civilians in Kampuchea. These shows had come about as a direct result of personal contact last autumn between Paul and the United Nations' Secretary General, Dr. Kurt Waldheim.

Playing a reduced set, Wings drop from their repertoire 'Wonderful Christmastime' and again add 'Cook Of The House', and later appear as part of the "supergroup" *Rockestra*, when they are joined by eleven guest musicians, including Billy Bremner and Dave Edmunds (from Rockpile), James Honeyman-Scott (The Pretenders), Robert Plant, John Paul Jones and John Bonham (Led Zeppelin), Ronnie Lane (ex- Small Faces and The Faces), Bruce Thomas (The Attractions), Gary Brooker (Procol Harum), and Kenny Jones and Pete Townshend (The Who), of whom Paul remarks, "The only sod who wouldn't wear a silver suit!" This was largely because Townshend was totally pissed! He had mistakenly thought that when Paul said there was an "8 o'clock rehearsal", he meant 8 o'clock in the morning. When Pete arrived at the venue at this early time, he was told by security guards to "come back later!" This he did, having spent the time in-between drinking with Ronnie Lane.

The *Rockestra* perform 'Lucille', 'Let It Be' and the 'Rockestra Theme'. These songs, as well as the Wings performances of 'Got To Get You Into My Life', 'Every Night' and 'Coming Up', also appear on the album *Concerts For The People Of Kampuchea,* released in America on March 30, 1981, and in the UK on April 3, 1981, as well as in the Keef & Co. TV presentation, featuring highlights from the four concerts, which are edited into a programme called *Rock for Kampuchea* and transmitted in the UK on ITV on January 4, 1981. Also appearing tonight on the bill with Wings are Billy Connolly, Elvis Costello and Rockpile with Dave Edmunds. This concert will turn out to be Wings' final live performance.

It has long been rumoured that the other Beatles, including John, were sitting in the audience this evening. Tim Smith, a long time Beatles fan, present at the venue tonight, dismisses the story, as he recalls: "On the night of the concert, touts were outside the venue commanding and getting £40 a ticket, because everyone was buzzing with the rumour that The Beatles were going to reform. I was sick to my stomach knowing that The Beatles might be playing and, because I didn't have a ticket, I was going to be standing on the pavement outside the theatre. Anyway, I was standing by the stage door talking to the people I was with, watching the touts get their huge prices for the tickets, when the side door opened and a little dark-haired guy stepped out and started swearing about the touts. I recognised this man as Jake Riviera, Dave Edmunds and Elvis Costello's manager. I told him that I was a big fan of Dave Edmunds and he pulled two tickets from his pocket and said, 'There you go, mate. Go on in.' Resisting the temptation to go and sell them for £80, my mate and I went into the bar, which was full of celebrities. I noticed the singer Lulu, who was wearing a leather cat suit, leaning up against the bar. Also leaning against the bar was Pete Townshend, who was almost legless. He couldn't stand up and was using the bar as a means of support. My mate and I attempted to take pints of beer out of the bar but we bumped into the Police, who were in a humorous mood. I got talking to a Policewoman and while I was chatting to her, I got jogged and accidentally tipped my pint glass of beer all over her shoes. As she thankfully dismissed the situation, I asked her: 'Are The Beatles going to play tonight?' 'I can categorically state,' she replied while mopping the beer from her brand new black leather boots, 'they are not!' 'How do you know that?' I asked, slightly disappointed. 'Because, before we (the police) came out,' she explained, 'we were briefed on what to do and who to expect. All the celebrities here tonight are on this list,' she said and produced the list from her top pocket. This was proof that none of the other Beatles were here tonight. She also told me that if Lennon were here, his name would have been printed in big bold black letters. The celebrities listed were, more or less, those who appeared on stage."

Thus, another long-time Beatles rumour, that "John was seen in the audience watching the show", bites the dust. The nearest the audience got to John this evening was the toy robot, which crawled across the front of the stage during Wings' performance. Noticing it, Paul shouted: "No! It's not John Lennon!"

Monday December 31

 John, meanwhile, is to be found in New York where he and Yoko dissolve their various companies, which include Bag Productions Ltd. and Joko Films Ltd. Later this evening, to celebrate New Year's Eve, John and Elliot Mintz hold their first (and last) Club Dakota meeting at their New York apartment. Dressed in black tie and tails, they request their guests to "join in on an evening of polite entertainment". The only person to receive an invitation is Yoko Ono.

1980

"I haven't seen any of The Beatles for I don't know how long. It doesn't even cross my mind as to whether I've seen them or not. It's just irrelevant. It wouldn't matter to me if I saw them often or if I never saw them again."

– John

January
☙ From his Dakota apartment in New York, John begins the new decade by drafting a most poignant four-page letter to his cousin in England.

"I'm 40 next," he writes. "I hope life begins – ie. I'd like a little less 'trouble' and more – what? I don't know." He touchingly concludes: "I'm almost scared to go to England, 'cos I know it would be the last time I saw Mimi + I'm a coward about goodbyes . . ."

According to Fred Seaman: "Yoko's behaviour became increasingly weird [this month] and was accompanied by a marked deterioration in her physical appearance. Her face was haggard, her eyes glassy around pinned pupils, and she began to spend time in the bathroom making loud snorting noises, frequently followed by frightful retching. I realised she was strung out on heroin." He continues: "On the rare occasions John and Yoko met, they circled each other wearily. John would harangue Yoko about her Vampire hours and her dishevelled, Zombie-like appearance."

John and Yoko bump into record producer Jack Douglas in a health food store on New York's East Side. John asks Jack to give him a call, an offer he does not take up.

(Douglas first met the Lennons back in 1971 when he was the second engineer on the *Imagine* album. He also stayed briefly with John in Los Angeles during the 1973–74 "lost weekend" period.)

☙ George meanwhile starts the Eighties by co-funding, with his Monty Python pals, the expansion of an environmental magazine called *Vole*.

Wednesday January 2
☙ Meanwhile, back in England, work resumes on rehearsals for Wings' impending tour of Japan. Utilising Paul's small Mill studio until January 10, the group performs their repertoire for the best part of a week.

Friday January 11
☙ A pre-filmed cameo appearance by George, at the recent British Grand Prix, appears during the ITV network documentary *Brian Moore Meets Niki Lauda*, a programme on George's motor racing friend, which is transmitted this evening between 9:01 and 9:58pm.

Saturday January 12
☙ Paul, Linda, their children and Wings leave Heathrow Airport in London en route to Japan. During the course of their journey, the entourage stop briefly in New York and take up residence at the Stanhope Hotel, situated on the other side of Central Park to John and Yoko's Dakota residence.

Monday January 14
☙ Late this evening, Paul tries to phone John at his apartment. His aim is to visit John and share some "dynamite weed". Yoko intercepts the call and refuses to allow Paul to speak to John. She becomes alarmed when Paul informs her that he is on his way to Tokyo and intends to stay at the Okura Hotel, John and Yoko's favourite hotel in Japan where they have stayed on each of their last four visits to the country.

☙ Meanwhile, back in England, a controversy of another kind begins when George's Handmade Films produced film Monty Python's *The Life Of Brian,* featuring George in the brief cameo role of "Mr. Papadopoulos", goes on general release across the UK. Within days, there are calls by religious leaders to ban the film.

Wednesday January 16
☙ Paul, Linda, their four children and Wings arrive in Tokyo, Japan, to start an 11 concert tour, scheduled to run from January 21 until February 2. Paul, whose previous application for a Japanese visa was turned down in 1976, is only allowed to enter the country this time because he is only planning to stay for eighteen days before moving on to China, where Wings are planning to play some unscheduled concerts. On their arrival at the Narita International Airport, customs men discover 219 grams (approximately 8 oz) of marijuana, with a street value of 600,000 yen (approximately £1,116) hidden away in Paul's baggage and inside the hood of one of Paul's children. Paul is arrested, handcuffed and questioned for an hour by narcotics control officers who announce that further questioning will take place tomorrow. Though the tour is in jeopardy, the optimistic Japanese promoters announce a decision on the eleven Wings concerts will be made tomorrow. Later this evening, acknowledging the worst, promoters dejectedly tell

reporters: "Almost 100,000 tickets for the concerts have been sold, representing a possible loss of well over 100 million yen (£186,000)."

Paul, now known as prisoner number 22, spends the night in the local jail, while Linda, their four children and Laurence, Steve and Denny of Wings take up residence at the Okura Hotel, where they stand by, waiting for the outcome of Paul's fate. Sources close to those concerned later suggest that Paul's arrest might have resulted from a tip-off from Yoko Ono. With immediate effect, the music of Wings is banned from all radio and TV stations in the country.

Later this evening, in her Tokyo hotel room, Linda remarks: "It's really very silly. People certainly are different over here. They take it so very seriously. Paul is now in some kind of detention place and I have not been allowed to see him. As soon as they get someone nice like Paul, they seem to make a field day of it!" She concludes: "I'll never come back to Japan again. It's my first trip *and* my last!"

Thursday January 17

& Officials question Paul, accompanied by the Japanese lawyer Tasuko Matsuo, for over six hours. He tells them the marijuana he smuggled into Japan yesterday was for his own personal consumption and that he intended to smoke it during the performances. He concludes by saying: "It is less toxic than alcohol." Following the questioning, which was carried out in English, an attempt is made by narcotic agents to escort Paul back to the police detention centre. The plan backfires when 200 fans, screaming "Paul! Paul!", bar their way, forcing Paul and the officials to withdraw back into the building. Riot police are called to the scene, along with two fire engines that answer a hoax telephone call.

Paul spends his second night alone in his cell at the detention centre. The narcotics officials refuse to comment on whether Paul will be referred to the Tokyo district public prosecutor's office for trial or whether he will be deported. Meanwhile, the officials of the Ministry of Justice refuse to exclude the possibility of deporting Paul because, in their opinion: "He had not legally landed when he was seized." They admit though that if prosecuted, Paul could face a prison sentence of up to seven years under Japan's stringent drug laws.

As expected, Wings' 11-date concert tour is cancelled by the disheartened promoters. The shows were to have been at Budo Khan Hall, Tokyo (Monday January 21 to Thursday January 24), Aichi-Ken, Taiiku-Kan, Nagoya (Friday January 25 and Saturday January 26), Festival Hall, Osaka (Monday January 28), Osaka Furitsu-Kan, Osaka (Tuesday January 29), Budo Kan Hall, Tokyo (Thursday January 31 to Saturday February 2).

Friday January 18

& The Tokyo district court grant a request from the prosecutor's office to hold Paul for up to ten more days for questioning. They also announce that if no decision is reached to free him or charge him with possessing marijuana, he may face another ten days in jail. Japanese newspapers suggest he will be expelled without facing formal charges. Paul's Japanese agents also announce today that: "An equivalent of $1.8 million (£800,000) will be returned to the concert ticket holders." Meanwhile, officials at the detention centre where Paul is staying tell reporters: "He slept well in jail, but he is concerned about his wife Linda and four children." He concludes by saying: "His wife will also be questioned." Paul's request for a guitar in his cell is denied.

Sunday January 20

& With Paul still languishing in jail, the 1973 James Bond film *Live And Let Die*, featuring music by Paul and Wings, receives its UK TV premiere at 7:45pm across the ITV network.

Monday January 21

& The other members of Wings, Denny, Laurence and Steve, leave Japan. The latter two head for the States while Denny heads for Cannes, in the South of France, where he catches the end of the annual Midem Festival. It is there that he concludes the publishing deal, with the company Performance Music, for all but two of the tracks that will appear on his forthcoming album *Japanese Tears*. Informed of Denny's actions, Paul becomes annoyed by the fact that while he is languishing in a Japanese cell, Denny is sunning himself in France and concluding business deals behind his back.

& An international telegram addressed to Paul and Linda arrives at the Okura Hotel in

Tokyo. It reads: "Thinking of you all with love. Keep your spirits high. Nice to have you back home again soon. God bless. Love, George and Olivia."

Tuesday January 22
 Linda visits Paul in his cell for the second time, staying for half an hour and bringing science fiction books for him to read. She later reveals that Paul is "laughing his way through his ordeal" in the Japanese jail. "I took some books because he is not allowed a guitar or a tape-recorder. He looks incredibly well. He was managing to smile and crack jokes. In fact, he was laughing so much, he even got me laughing and believe me, I haven't been able to do much laughing during the last week."
 In England, Ringo, who is passing through Heathrow Airport on his way from Los Angeles to Nice, remarks to reporters: "It's the risk you take when you're involved with drugs. He's just been unlucky."
 At Friar Park, George's secretary Cherrie Cowell drafts a reply to Jack Crawshaw of Thames Television, refusing his request for George to appear on the January 30 edition of *This Is Your Life*, honouring George Martin. She writes: "He is just leaving the country for the holidays and, in fact, will not be back in the country again until the middle of March." (A Beatle does appear on the show – see entry for January 30.)

Thursday January 24
 Reports in the Japanese press today reveal that the half-pound of marijuana that Paul tried to smuggle into Japan could cost him £700,000 – nearly £100,000 an ounce! As Linda leaves the cells where Paul is staying, she is asked: "How long do you intend to stay in Japan?"
 She defiantly replies: "I'm prepared to stay in Japan for as long as it takes!"

Friday January 25
 After spending 10 days in a Tokyo jail, Paul is released and promptly deported from Japan. He is ushered to Tokyo airport after the authorities had decided not to press charges. Officials at the prosecutor's office say: "Charges were not brought against Mr. McCartney because he had brought in the marijuana solely for his own use and that he has already been punished enough as a result of the incident."
 As Paul leaves his detention cell, fans shout: "Sayonara, sayonara" (Goodbye, goodbye). Witnessing this, Paul remarks: "Japanese fans are so great. I want to come back again if I'm allowed." The lawyers who negotiated his release admit that this is highly unlikely.
 On board the waiting Jumbo Jet, Paul is reunited with his family for the 12:30pm flight back to England, which includes brief stopovers in Alaska (for refuelling) and then Schipol Airport in Amsterdam, Holland. Fighting back tears, Paul cries: "This is the longest time I have ever been away from Linda and the kids in ten years. I don't ever want a separation like it again."
 Every step of the way home, he faces a scrimmage of cameramen and reporters eager to have a quick word with the "jailbird ex-Beatle". Paul announces: "I have been a fool. What I did was incredibly dumb. My god, how stupid I have been! I was really scared, thinking I might have been imprisoned for so long and now I have made up my mind *never* to touch the stuff again! From now on, all I'm going to smoke is straightforward fags and no more pot!"
 Paul also tells reporters: "I Sang 'Yesterday' to a killer in the bath! I joined my fellow inmates for a dip in the baths and they asked for a sing-song. I gave them the old ones like 'Red Red Robin' and 'Take This Hammer'. Their favourite, though, was 'Yesterday'."
 Paul is naturally asked how he spent his time in jail. "I communicated with other prisoners by knocking on the walls and shouting. I became quite matey with the chap next door. He could speak a bit of English. Funnily enough, he was inside for smuggling pot. We told each other the worst jokes in the world. They were really dreadful, but they helped to relieve the tension. Discipline in the prison was very strict, but I made friends among the prisoners and guards. We sang and laughed together as if we had been mates for ages. But I was never allowed to see sunlight or get a breath of fresh air. That was depressing!"
 Paul also reveals that he lost his wedding ring. "That made me very, very low," he says. "It was confiscated and packed with my luggage to be sent on later. I now wear a ring made from a paper-clip. I just had to have a wedding ring of some sort. It's the sort of gesture that Linda and I will look back on rather romantically."
 Turning to Linda, who sits beside Paul on the journey home, he sums up: "It was terribly hard for Linda – and terribly hard for me!"

Paul arrives back in England at Lydd Airport in Kent (on January 26), and is whisked off into seclusion with his family at his home in Peasmarsh in Sussex.

Denny Laine, in particular, is angry over the incident. His song 'Japanese Tears' is a critical account of this event. Paul is held personally accountable for the losses suffered by the concert promoters and ticket holders. Experts predict this sum will total several million dollars. Due to an oversight, Paul's tour insurance had lapsed just prior to the Japanese visit.

Saturday January 26
♘ "I'll Never Smoke Pot Again!" is the headline in today's edition of *The Sun*, beneath a story relating to Paul.

Sunday January 27
♘ With an army of reporters waiting at his gate, Paul has no alternative but to go and face them. Sitting on the gate, he says: "I'd prefer to forget this incident right now!"

Reporter: "For the next few days, presumably, they'll be a chance for you to get back to the English way of life and particularly to have a break with your family?"

Paul: "Yeah! If you fellows would leave me alone, that *would* be possible."

Meanwhile, at the Rock City Studios at Shepperton, Denny Laine hurriedly completes the recording of his album *Japanese Tears*.

Wednesday January 30
♘ With George having turned down the opportunity, Paul makes his first public appearance since the Tokyo drugs bust by taping a pre-recorded filmed insert for the Thames/ITV network programme *This Is Your Life* which honours his good friend, The Beatles' producer George Martin. The show, transmitted between 7:00 and 7:28pm, is the tenth show in the 20th series of this long-running programme.

February
♘ In America, John and Yoko take a holiday in Palm Beach, Florida with the actor Peter Boyle and his wife, writer Loraine Alterman. During their stay they visit the restaurant La Petite Marmite where a freelance reporter photographs John, now sporting a very thick beard and glasses, sitting peacefully at the table. This annoys John who later protests about the incident to Boyle back at their hotel. The picture is reproduced worldwide, including the *Daily Mirror* in the UK, as part of a feature on Monday March 31, which also features Ringo in his costume on the set of his new film *Caveman*. (See entry.) When the Lennons return to New York at the end of the month, John reveals that he is "revitalised and ready for a period of constant rebirth". A period of home demo taping sees John return to the tracks 'My Life', now titled 'Don't Be Crazy' which in turn becomes 'The Worst Is Over'. It will be released later in the year as '(Just Like) Starting Over'. At the end of the month, John practically completes the tracks 'Beautiful Boy' and 'Watching The Wheels'.

Sunday February 10
♘ In America, Ringo gives another radio interview, this time with the DJ Robert W. Morgan.

Monday February 11
♘ At 8:30am, George, Olivia and Dhani, leave Heathrow Airport for St. Bartholomys, via New York. Asked about his trip, George tells reporters: "I'm going to America to work." Soon after, he flies into a rage when his Concorde flight is delayed due to a wheel fault. As a result his attitude towards the reporters changes. Asked again about his trip. he snarls: "I'm going to mind my own business!" Due to the problems with Concorde, the Harrisons miss their connecting flight to Miami, forcing them to hop on a private jet owned by Bee Gee Maurice Gibb.

Sunday February 17
♘ Possibly as a result of Paul's recent troubles, Ringo is strip-searched by customs as he enters Mexico City to begin filming the United Artists movie *Caveman*.

Monday February 18
♘ In Durango, at the Churubusco Studios in Azteca, Mexico City, Ringo, cast in the role of Atouk, begins filming the United Artists prehistoric caveman slapstick comedy film *Caveman*, directed by Carl Gottlieb and co-starring Dennis Quaid, Shelley Long and Jack

Paul. *(Barry Plummer)*

April 10, 1970: fans gather at Apple's Saville Row headquarters in London after Paul's dramatic announcement that he is leaving The Beatles. *(Associated Press)*

October 28, 1970: George arrives in New York with Patti, bringing with him the master tapes for *All Things Must Pass*. *(Associated Press)*

February 19, 1971: Paul and Linda arrive at the High Court in London, Paul to give personal evidence in his lawsuit to dissolve The Beatles' partnership. *(LFI)*

June, 1971: Ringo in Almera, Spain, on the set of the movie *Blindman*. *(Associated Press)*

May 15, 1971: John and Yoko at the Cannes International Film Festival, where two of their films, *Apotheosis (Balloon)* and *Fly*, are being shown. *(Michael Lipchitz/Associated Press)*

May 12, 1971: Ringo and Maureen leave Gatwick Airport *en route* for the wedding of Mick and Bianca Jagger in St. Tropez in the South of France. *(PA News)*

July 27, 1971: George at the press conference to announce the Concert For Bangla Desh at New York's Madison Square Garden. *(LFI)*

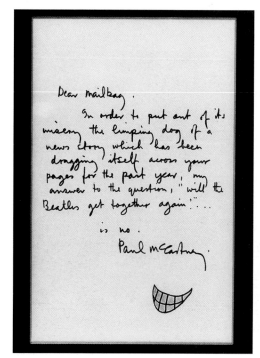

August 29, 1970: Paul's letter published in *Melody Maker* dispelling rumours that The Beatles might reform. *(Sotheby's)*

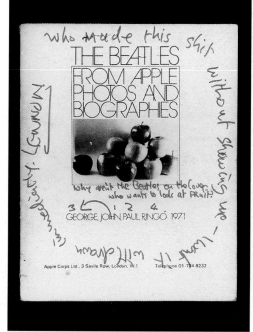

December, 1971: John expresses strong feelings about Apple artwork. *(Sotheby's)*

May 12, 1971: Paul and Linda, with daughters Mary and Heather, arrive in St. Tropez for Mick Jagger's wedding. *(Associated Press)*

July 9, 1972: Paul, on stage at an open-air concert at the Theatre Antique, Chateau Vallon in France, marking the start of the Wings Over Europe tour. *(Rex Features)*

July 23, 1971: John and Yoko at Tittenhurst Park, Ascot, their last home in England before moving permanently to New York. *(Redferns)*

September 13, 1971: Ringo, at the London launch of his R*R steel ornaments business. *(Barry Plummer)*

John. *(Redferns)*

August 1, 1971: George on stage at his Bangla Desh
Concert at New York's Madison Square Garden. *(LFI)*

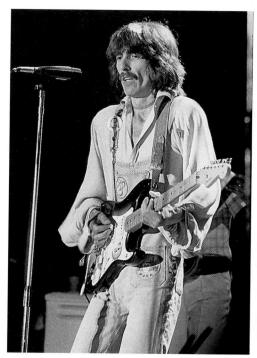

December 19, 1974: George on stage, again at Madison
Square Garden, during his North American tour.
(Rex Features)

March 18, 1972: Ringo filming *Born To Boogie*, the
Marc Bolan/T.Rex documentary movie. *(Rex Features)*

March 21, 1972: Ringo at his drum kit at Tittenhurst Park,
the home he bought from John, during *Born To Boogie*
filming. *(Redferns)*

Summer, 1972: The first five-piece line-up of Wings, left to right: Henry McCullough, Denny Sewell, Denny Laine, Paul and Linda. *(Rex Features)*

July, 1972: Paul and Linda on their début tour with Wings throughout Europe. The bus on which they travelled, rented from a firm in Hounslow, is in the background. *(Rex Features)*

April 1, 1973: John and Yoko hold a press conference at the New York Bar Association announcing the birth of their conceptual country Nutopia. *(Associated Press)*

October, 1974: John with May Pang, with whom he would live during his separation from Yoko in 1973/74. *(Rex Features)*

November 28, 1974: John joins Elton John and his band on stage at their Thanksgiving Concert at New York's Madison Square Garden. *(Rex Features)*

April 18, 1975: John records an appearance for the TV special *Salute To Sir Lew – The Master Showman*, in the Grand Ballroom of the Hilton Hotel in New York. *(Associated Press)*

October, 1972: Ringo and David Essex on location at Butlin's holiday camp on the Isle of Wight filming *That'll Be The Day*. *(Redferns)*

April 4, 1973: Paul appears on *Top Of The Pops*, leading Wings through 'My Love' on the set at the BBC Centre in west London. *(Barry Plummer)*

September 23, 1974: George and Ravi Shankar at London's Royal Albert Hall, before Ravi's Indian Music Festival. *(PA News)*

October 23, 1974: George hosts a press conference at the Beverly Wilshire Hotel in Los Angeles, announcing plans to tour America and Canada. *(Associated Press)*

March 12, 1974: John and Harry Nilsson are thrown out of the Troubadour Club in Los Angeles after heckling a performance by The Smothers Brothers. *(Rex Features)*

April 1, 1974: John and Paul at John's beach house in Malibu, left to right: John, Keith Moon, Paul and Linda. No one knew it at the time, least of all Peter Butler, Moon's assistant, who took this photo with a Polaroid camera, but this was the only time that John Lennon and Paul McCartney would ever be photographed together in the Seventies and the last time they would ever be photographed together. (*Peter Butler*)

March 1, 1975: John and Yoko attend the annual Grammy Awards in New York, left to right: David Bowie, Art Garfunkel, Paul Simon, Yoko, John and Roberta Flack. (*Rex Features*)

Gilford. Set in the year "One Zillion Years B.C." and featuring only fifteen words of dialogue, the former Beatle is cast in the role of a misfit who forms his own tribe from outcasts from nearby caves. During the shooting, he meets fellow co-star Barbara Bach, an ex-James Bond girl. Insiders on the film set notice that their love scenes in the film are turning into the real thing off camera during the evenings. The five-week filming on the 91-minute film is concluded on March 25. During the shooting Ringo and the cast are joined by television news crews from Germany and Mexico and, from America, *The John Davidson Show*, for which they record unique outtake sequences. The film's European premieres included West Germany on June 4, 1981, Sweden on July 31 and Finland August 14.

Tuesday February 19
🍎 Due to some of the worst storms in American history, emergency evacuating workers desperately try to contact George in London to tell him that his home in Beverly Green, off the coast of Malibu, is threatening to break away from its hillside and smash into the houses below. Neighbours of George who have already lost their expensive homes include actors Cary Grant and Rod Steiger and the singers Olivia Newton-John and George's close pal Bob Dylan. After George's recent departure to New York (see entry for February 11), he refused to inform *anyone* of his exact whereabouts.

Wednesday February 20
🍎 In America, Paul gives an interview to *Rolling Stone* magazine.

Tuesday February 26
🍎 Eagerly anticipated by the nation's media, Paul attends the *British Rock and Pop Awards,* held at the Café Royal in London. He is there to receive an award for the Outstanding Music Personality of 1979, as voted by readers of the *Daily Mirror,* viewers of BBC TV's *Nationwide* programme and listeners of BBC Radio One. Paul collects the award from Pauline McLeod of the *Daily Mirror* and Dave Lee Travis of Radio One. (The event is covered by BBC1, highlights of which are transmitted on the station the following evening, Wednesday February 27, between 7:00 and 7:49pm.)

Wednesday February 27
🍎 In Los Angeles, Paul's 'Rockestra Theme' wins a Grammy award for the Best Rock Instrumental Performance.

March
🍎 John and Yoko buy a $1 million beach-side mansion in Palm Beach, Florida.
🍎 At Friar Park, George records the track 'Sat Singing', originally scheduled for the album *Somewhere In England,* but not officially released until 1988.
🍎 Ringo's 1978 American TV special, *Ringo,* is given a new lease of life when it is screened in 650 closed-circuit cinemas in colleges and universities across America.
🍎 In Liverpool, Eric's club in Mathew Street, often referred to as the new Cavern, faces closure following a recent raid by Police. The local council reveal that "their new licence may not be renewed when it has expired!"

Monday March 3
🍎 For three straight weeks (until March 23), Paul buries himself away in recording studios, at the Abbey Road Studios in London and, towards the middle of the month, at his home studios in Sussex.
🍎 In London, one of the first Sotheby's Rock & Pop auctions takes place. Among the Beatle related items on offer are postcards, photos and a signed copy of their Parlophone début release 'Love Me Do' from 1962.

Friday March 7
🍎 George, Olivia and Dhani head back to England from Miami, briefly stopping over in New York, where they occupy two bedrooms at the Waldorf Astoria hotel.

Saturday March 8
🍎 The Harrisons resume their journey back to England, arriving today at London's Heathrow Airport.

Sunday March 16
♣ In preparation for George's recording sessions which are scheduled to resume at FPHOTS tomorrow, Willie Weeks, Neil Larsen and Andy Newmark arrive at Friar Park.

Thursday March 20
♣ John and Yoko celebrate their 11th wedding anniversary by buying each other lavish presents. Yoko splashes out on a Rolls Royce and John returns the compliment by buying her 500 gardenias and a heart-shaped diamond.

Monday March 24
♣ The album *The Beatles Rarities* is released in America. The compilation features the first authorised release of the first version of 'Love Me Do', which features Ringo, instead of Andy White, playing drums.

Wednesday March 26 & Thursday March 27
♣ For two days, at the Ewart Television Studios in London working with the director Keith McMillan, Paul contents himself with the making of what will become one of his most complex, elaborate and memorable promotional videos. To help promote 'Coming Up', Paul and Linda, through the wonders of modern technology, appear in the guises of ten different people. Collectively billed as the twelve-piece *The Plastic Macs*, Paul dresses as Buddy Holly, Frank Zappa, Andy Mackay, Ron Mael (keyboard player from the group Sparks), Ginger Baker (drummer of Sixties supergroup Cream), Hank Marvin and as himself, Beatle Paul, circa 1963, wearing a collarless jacket. The completed clip will appear at the start of the MPL programme *Meet Paul McCartney* (see entry for May 19). Clips from the video also appear in an alternative film for the song which features the footage intercut with various still photographs supplied by the French Beatles fan club, *Les Club Des Quatre De Liverpool*. Released to Gaumont Cinemas in France during June, it starts with gun shots shattering a window where a picture of *McCartney II* is seen. Again, Keith McMillan directs the piece.

Saturday March 29
George and Olivia join in the Friends of the Earth anti-nuclear march through London.

Monday March 31
♣ In what was originally going to be a feature entitled "Ringo Starr: How I Shook Off The Blues And Learned To Live Again", the *Daily Mirror* run the piece (in abbreviated form) but add the recent picture of a heavily bearded John with thick lensed glasses taken last month at the La Petite Marmite restaurant. (See entry for February.)

April
♣ Three months after Paul's problems in Tokyo, commercial TV and radio stations in Japan lift their ban on Wings' music.
♣ Further sessions at George's Friar Park Studios produce the tracks 'Lay His Head' and 'Tears Of The World', both planned for *Somewhere in England,* but they do not see the light of day until 1987 and 1992 respectively.

Wednesday April 9
♣ John, Yoko, Sean and the Seamans depart for Cold Spring Harbor on Long Island for another vacation.

Friday April 11
♣ Wings' single 'Coming Up' (studio version)/'Coming Up' (live version) – 'Lunch Box-Odd Sox' is released in the UK. (The American release takes place on April 15.)

Sunday April 13
♣ John and Fred Seaman drive out on Route 110 to buy Yoko some flowers. During the journey, John hears 'Coming Up' for the first time on the car radio.

Monday April 14
♣ George, along with Olivia and Dhani, are seen nosing around the Falmouth area of Cornwall, looking for a Cornish home.

Sunday April 20
❦ At Cold Spring Harbor, John records his day-to-day activities on his newly acquired video camera. These include playing with Sean, having lunch with Yoko on the lawn overlooking the sea and strumming his guitar. Today, to the camera, John records two versions of 'Dear Yoko', the second being re-recorded after he noticed on playback that he needed to put a light on!

Monday April 21
❦ Yoko having requested John to "clean out his head", John begins a ten day period of silence at Long Island. It ends at noon on April 30 when John shaves off his long thick beard.

Tuesday April 22
❦ In the *Music Week*, BBC/BRMB UK music chart, Paul's 'Coming Up' enters at number seven.

May
❦ Vic Garbarini interviews Paul for the magazine *Musician*. A recording of the interview is later released on the limited edition album *The McCartney Interview*.

May (and June)
❦ Towards the end of the month, John briefly visits South Africa, from where he sends many telegrams to friends and former associates. He stays at the Mount Nelson Hotel in Cape Town between May 23 and May 27, booking in under the alias of John Green, Yoko's Tarot card reader, and then travelled on to Johannesburg. During this period of travelling, John also visits Germany and Spain, the nearest he will ever come to revisiting England.

Thursday May 1
❦ John takes possession of his new sailing boat, called *Royal Isis*, from Tyler Conley. He spends the rest of the month learning how to sail.

Friday May 2
❦ In the UK, Scratch Records release the Denny Laine single 'Japanese Tears'.

Thursday May 8
❦ In England, Ringo and Barbara decline to comment to *Daily Mirror* reporters about their rumoured romance.

Friday May 9
❦ Paul appears in public again to collect the Ivor Novello Special Award For International Achievement at the Grosvenor Hotel in London.

Friday May 16
❦ Paul's second truly *solo* album, *McCartney II* is released in the UK. He and Linda travel to the 33rd annual Cannes Film Festival in the South of France where Oscar Grillo's five-minute animated film *Seaside Woman,* based around Linda's 1973 song of the same title, wins the first prize, the *Palm d'Or*, in the short film category. Paul later reveals that during its screening at the festival, he and Linda sneaked in unannounced to watch their film, and that the applause at the conclusion was one of their fondest memories. The prestigious gathering also serves as a wonderful exercise to promote Paul's latest album, but bosses at EMI make a huge blunder with the promotions at the festival when they accidentally give away to journalists more copies than they intended. They are obliged to buy some of the "free" copies back. Besides facing a lengthy photo call from the press, the McCartneys are briefly interviewed by the American columnist Rex Reed for his ITV programme *Diary Of The Cannes Film Festival*, which is transmitted across the network on Friday July 18, between 9:01 and 9:58pm.

Reed: "Do you think there'll ever be the chance of another Lennon & McCartney song?"

Paul: "Well, I wouldn't say there would be actually, 'cos the last time I spoke to John [1976], I just happened to ask him about whether he was writing songs and stuff, just out of my curiosity, and he told me he was kind of finished doing that and that he's not really into that, which when you say it to people, they say, 'Oh, it's a big disappointment' or 'He must have gone crazy', but if you think about it, most of us do our jobs to arrive at a point where we no longer have to do our jobs and we can put our feet up and we can enjoy life for a change. I think John's probably reached that point."

During their visit to Cannes, Paul and Linda stay at the Montfleury Hotel, where they meet up with Ringo, who asks Paul if he would like to produce and play on his next album. Paul instantly agrees.

Saturday May 17
🍎 The promotional video for Paul's 'Coming Up' receives its American premiere on NBC TV's *Saturday Night Live,* where it is introduced by Paul, Linda and Billy Crystal, the show's resident comic, who is dressed as the character Father Guido Sarducci, via satellite from outside their MPL Soho offices in Soho Square, London. The scenes, which include Sarducci singing a "Beatles Medley" and, in an attempt to get the McCartneys out of bed, starts throwing stones at their windows, were actually taped early in the month, at around 5:30am.

Monday May 19
🍎 Driving to a party in south-west London, Ringo and Barbara Bach escape serious injury when they are involved in a car accident less than half a mile away from where Ringo's friend Marc Bolan had been killed back in 1977. Their 12-year-old Mercedes car was approaching the Robin Hood roundabout on the A3 at Roehampton when it spun out of control, demolishing two lampposts and somersaulting fifty yards before coming to an abrupt halt on its roof.

Ringo drags Barbara from the wreckage and gives her a cigarette. She is later quoted as saying: "He (Ringo) believes that if we could survive that together, we can survive anything. We then decided to make sure we were never apart again. He's the nicest, kindest, funniest and most sensitive man I've ever met!"

An eyewitness reports: "Ringo was pretty cool about it. He got a hell of a shake-up."

Ringo and Barbara are taken to Queen Mary's Hospital in London and released shortly afterwards after treatment. Ringo is found to have slight leg injuries while Barbara has sustained injuries to her back. Police admit that they will not be taking action against Ringo, but reveal that he may face a council bill for repairs to the demolished lampposts.

After a night at London's Dorchester Hotel, they head back to Los Angeles. During the flight, Ringo proposes marriage and Barbara accepts.

🍎 Back in London (on May 19), Paul begins an extremely hectic round of promotional appearances, beginning this morning at the Trilion Studios, where Tim Rice interviews him for a 25-minute programme featuring the curious title of *Meet Paul McCartney.* (Considering the events earlier this year, not to mention Paul's career to date, he certainly needs no introduction.) The show features Paul discussing the recordings for *McCartney II*, but will have very limited UK screenings: a broadcast on the Thames region of ITV during the afternoon of Thursday August 7 between 3:46 and 4:14pm and in the Granada region of ITV on October 27. The video clips for 'Coming Up' and (the yet un-filmed) 'Waterfalls' (version three) top and tail the show. A scene where Paul's friend, the actor Victor Spinetti, arrives on the set dressed as a punk rocker and proceeds to handcuff and arrest Paul, before leading him off and crashing him into the staging is cut from any subsequent broadcasts.

Immediately after the interview Paul dashes across London to film, at the Thames Television Studios in Euston Road, an interview with Nicky Horne for his *Nicky Horne's Music Scene* section, a short 5-minute item encompassed within the Thames regional news programme *Thames At Six* show (transmitted later this evening between 6:01 and 6:39pm in the London and South East region of ITV only).

Besides using the interview to promote his new album, Paul also recalls his drugs bust a few months earlier: "It was very stupid! We'd been in America and the attitude to drugs over there is very different and it led me to take a real casual approach. Most people taking that kind of thing into the country would give it to the roadies, that's the common practice. That just shows that I wasn't really thinking about it. I was taking *my* opinion of it instead of the legal opinion of it, and I just didn't really think much about it, you know till the fellow pulled it out of the suitcase and he looked more embarrassed than me! He wanted to put it back in and forget the whole thing, you know."

Nicky Horne: "What thoughts went through your head when you realised it could be seven years!"

Paul: "The first thing you do is ask to see your British Consul. You always think 'He'll get me out!' Well, he turned up with a flat cap on, he didn't look like a Consul at all, *our man in Havana* or something. He said, 'Well Paul, there's a fellow in here who had a lot less than you had and he's done three months already, so you could have seven years hard labour to look forward to!' I thought 'What?' and my jaw dropped. You're worried about how long it's gonna last; you're not just worried about the immediate conditions. It's not *Bridge On The River Kwai* you know . . . it's not that bad. The immediate worry during the time is what's going to happen to Linda and the kids. Those are the main worrying things."

(Horne will interview Paul again, this time on Capital Radio, on May 23 for his programme *Mummy's Weekly*.)

To conclude the busy day, Paul returns to his MPL offices in Soho Square where he gives an interview to Eddie Blanche of Associated Press.

Tuesday May 20

This afternoon at BBC Broadcasting House in Portland Place, London, Paul records an interview with the radio disc jockey Andy Peebles, which forms part of a special programme devoted to his colourful career. The show is transmitted on BBC Radio One on May 26.

Across London, George and Olivia attend the Chelsea Flower Show.

Wednesday May 21

Paul's album *McCartney II* is released in America. Advance copies include a one-sided 7" promotional copy of 'Coming Up'. This unique disc is not included within the UK release.

To neatly coincide with Paul's album, John releases a statement revealing his plans to cut his last links with The Beatles by selling his quarter share in Apple. His statement jokes: "I have been inundated with calls from investors wishing to buy my quarter share. The phone hasn't stopped ringing." Yoko emphasises the reason behind John's decision: "We are both artists and we are really big into being a family. Those are the things that we care about. We've bought a good-sized boat and we will live comfortably on it." John concludes the statement by saying he wishes to: "Sail off into the sunset with Yoko and Sean." (The boat is their recently acquired 63-foot yacht *Royal Isis*, which is currently moored at Long Island, New York.)

Friday May 23

Further promotions for *McCartney II* continue when Paul gives a live interview on Capital Radio for the programme *Mummy's Weekly*, hosted by Nicky Horne.

Monday May 26

To further promote *McCartney II*, a pre-recorded interview with Paul is transmitted today on BBC Radio One.

Tuesday May 27

Denny Laine breaks from Wings' activities to appear solo on the Children's Thames/ITV Network programme *Magpie* (transmitted between 4:46 and 5:14pm), where he talks to Mick Robertson about his new book *The Denny Laine Guitar Book*.

Saturday May 31

Paul's album *McCartney II* reaches number one in the UK album charts.

The American Beatles album *Rarities* reaches number 21 in the US charts.

June

Featuring production again from Keef & Co., Paul shoots a promotional film for the song 'Waterfalls' on a specially built set in the middle of Wandsworth Common, with additional scenes being shot in a disused aircraft hangar. To assist with the taping, Paul obtains one and a half tons of polystyrene, and an eight-foot Polar bear called Olaf, hired from Chipperfield's Circus. After numerous re-edits of the sequences, a total of six different promotional films are prepared, but only version three will be screened on shows such as *Meet Paul McCartney* (see previous entry for May 19). 'Waterfalls' will receive its first UK screening on the ATV Saturday morning children's show *Tiswas*, transmitted on certain regions of the ITV network on June 14. Unfortunately, due to the current technicians' strike at the BBC, the clip never makes it onto the flagship pop programme *Top Of The Pops*. (See entry for June 3.)

Tuesday June 3
🍎 As a mark of protest against the axing by the BBC of five of their own musicians, Paul requests that his pre-recorded interview, in which he promotes *McCartney II* in tonight's edition of BBC2's *The Old Grey Whistle Test,* be pulled from broadcast. The gesture becomes fruitless when the Musicians Union force the postponement of tonight's show, as well as *Top Of The Pops* on Thursday.

Wednesday June 4
🍎 While in America, John departs from Farmingdale Airport en route to Newport Virginia where he and three others board a sailing boat called *Megan Jaye* that will take them to Bermuda. During the journey, the vessel hits a major storm and John is the only one on board capable of taking control.

John recalls the event during his September *Playboy* interview: "It was my first time at sea, three thousand miles in seven days. I always talked about sailing but my excuse was that I'd never had lessons. Yoko's attitude was 'Put up or shut up'. So she sent me on this trip and I went. She sent me specifically to open up my creativity, though she didn't tell me that. There were four of us on this forty-one-foot boat, and it was the most fascinating experience I had ever had. I loved it!

"A storm started one afternoon and lasted three days. The captain was sick and so were his two cousins, the other guys on the boat. There was no reference point. Wherever you would look we were the centre of the circle. There was no land to be seen. They were throwing up and the captain says to me, 'There's a storm coming up. Do you want to take over the wheel?' I said, 'Do you think I can?' I was supposed to be the cabin boy learning the trade, but he said, 'Well, you'll have to. There's no one else who can do it.' I said, 'Well, you had better keep an eye on me.' He said he would.

"Five minutes later he goes down below to sleep and says, 'See you later.' No one else could move. They were as sick as dogs. So I was there, driving the boat. For six hours keeping it on course. I was buried under water. I was smashed in the face by waves for six solid hours. It won't go away. You can't change your mind. It's like being on stage – once you're on, there's no getting off. A couple of the waves had me on my knees. I was just hanging on with my hands on the wheel – it's very powerful weather – and I was having the time of my life! I was screaming sea chanteys and shouting at the Gods! I felt like the Viking, you know, Jason and the Golden Fleece. The captain found our way with a sextant. He was a great guy, Hank. He looked like the man on the Zig Zag rolling papers, with a beard and a scarf on his head, doing the sextant.

"I arrived in Bermuda. Once I got there, I was so centred after the experience at sea that I was tuned in or whatever, to the cosmos. And all these songs came! (See entry for June 22.) The time there was just amazing. Fred (Seaman) and Sean and I were there on the beach taping songs with this big machine and me just playing guitar and singing. We were just in the sun and these songs were coming out."

Wednesday June 11
🍎 In Los Angeles, Ringo and Barbara announce that they intend to marry in the next few weeks, possibly in America. He also announces to the press: "She's a beautiful, sexy, funny and warm-hearted person." Following the announcement, the happy couple are seen shopping for a wedding ring.

Thursday June 12
🍎 John's nine-day journey aboard *Megan Jaye* comes to an end when they arrive in Bermuda. Sean and Fred Seaman join John on June 16.

Friday June 13
🍎 Paul's single 'Waterfalls'/'Check My Machine' is released in the UK. (The American release takes place on July 22.)

Saturday June 21
🍎 Relaxing in Bermuda, John listens to the Bob Marley album *Burnin'* and is inspired to write the track 'Borrowed Time'.

Sunday June 22
🍎 Stimulated by his writing yesterday, John commits to tape, on a Panasonic boom box,

further versions of 'I Don't Want To Face It', 'Watching The Wheels' and, also during this period, he records demos for 'I'm Stepping Out', 'Dear Yoko', 'Strange Days Indeed', 'Beautiful Boy', 'Borrowed Time', an early slow version of 'Woman' and an unreleased song called 'Welcome To The Bermudas'. Creatively aroused, he will sing his new compositions to Yoko over the phone. Then, later, she will return the call and sing to John her new songs. "It inspired me completely," he recalls. "As soon as she would sing something to me or play a cassette down the phone, within ten or fifteen minutes, whether I wanted to work or not, I would suddenly get this song coming to me. I always felt that the best songs were ones that come to you. I like it to be inspirational from the spirit, and being with Sean and switching off from the business sort of allowed that channel to be freed a bit."

John, as he will put it, "had a diarrhoea of creativity". Later in the year he would recall the result of this period of sudden writing: "I just couldn't wait to get back and start recording. I had all this material after not really trying . . . but not really trying either. For five years I'd been so locked in the home environment and completely switched my way of thinking, so that I didn't really think of music at all. My guitar was sort of hung up behind the bed literally, I don't think I took it down in five years!"

Later this evening, John accompanies Fred Seaman to the local nightclub called *Flavors* where John hears 'Rock Lobster' by the B-52s for the first time. It reminds him of Yoko's work a decade earlier. (Further demos for *Double Fantasy* are recorded when he and Sean return home to the Dakota on July 29.)

Sunday June 23
🍎 Meanwhile, at an auction in Syracuse, New York at the State Fair, the Massachusetts dairy farmer, Steve Potter, purchases from agents working on behalf of John and Yoko, a single Holstein pedigree dairy cow called Daisy, for $265,000 (approximately £132,000). It is the highest sum paid to date for one single cow, one of 250 cows recently purchased from the Bridgewater, Virginia dairy farmer Nelson Gardener. (This record sale gains John his first non-musical entry in the *Guinness Book of Records*.) Within a few days of this sale, agents working on behalf of John and Yoko go on to purchase a further 71 Holstein cows, this time from Kenneth Kibler, another dairy farmer, based in nearby Luray. The money from the sale of the cow will go towards the Lennons' latest venture in New York, the acquisition of an apartment to store their large collection of fur coats. Italian fur specialists have recently installed air-conditioning to keep the coats at a suitable temperature.

Monday June 24
🍎 Back in Bermuda, John visits a botanical garden with Sean and sees a freesia hybrid flower called *Double Fantasy*.

Thursday June 26
🍎 Denny and his wife Jo Jo Laine reveal their plans for a concert tour. He admits: "I was getting bored, so we decided to get out on the road." He adds: "I'm still with Wings though!"

Friday June 27
🍎 Yoko flies to Bermuda to meet John but cannot stand the hot weather and returns to New York alone two days later. John is disgusted by her action.

Saturday June 28
🍎 The Wings single 'Coming Up' (live version) reaches number one on the American charts. Today at Finston Manor, an ancient concert hall just outside Tenterton in Kent, Wings assemble for almost two weeks of rehearsals. On July 9, a camera crew from Southern ITV's *Day By Day* news team visits the final day of the sessions and interviews Paul. The feature is transmitted in the Southern region of ITV only on July 10 between 6:00 and 6:28pm.

July
🍎 In the UK, in *Woman's Own* magazine, Linda reveals that Paul has decided not to make out a will, implying erroneously that should Paul die, his family would not benefit from his vast wealth. This, of course, is not the case since under British law the next of kin inherit automatically, regardless of the wealth of the deceased. "If you put aside a lot for kids when you die," Linda says, "they spend your entire old age looking forward to

what they are going to get and wish that you were dead. So no trust funds for us. We don't want to be lumbered with all that."

Meanwhile in Japan, six months after Paul was thrown out of the country, the music of Wings is still banned on the national radio and TV station NHK.

Tuesday July 1

🍎 In Bermuda, John is unable to contact Yoko during one of his frequent daily phone rituals to her at the Dakota. Expressing his disappointment, he writes 'I'm Losing You'.

Friday July 4

🍎 Fred Seaman arrives back at the Dakota from Bermunda. He learns from Yoko's close circle of friends that she is "planning to divorce John".

🍎 Ringo and Barbara fly to London from Los Angeles, where he confirms that he intends to marry the former James Bond girl. Ringo tells the waiting reporters: "We've still got to finalise details, and it could be in London." (After watching the closing stages of the annual Wimbledon Tennis Championships, they return to Tittenhurst Park in Ascot, then leave for France on Wednesday July 9.)

🍎 George's limited edition book *I Me Mine* is published which controversially sells for £148 per copy, with only 2,000 copies printed worldwide. (A much cheaper version appears later in paperback.) The book includes all of George's music and lyrics to all of his songs.

When he reads the book at his Dakota apartment, John is upset that he receives only the briefest of mentions for his role in the development of George's music. "I was hurt by it," he tells *Playboy*. "By glaring omission in the book, my influence on his life is absolutely zilch and nil. Not mentioned. In his book, which is purportedly this clarity of vision of each song he wrote and its influences, he remembers every two-bit sax player or guitarist he met in subsequent years, yet I'm *not* in the book."

The book's price comes under scrutiny in the *Liverpool Echo* newspaper, where Allan Williams describes it as "unfair to the great majority of the group's fans, who would never be able to afford it. To me, it's just a trendy book for the jet-setting brigade. I can't see any justification for bringing out a book costing this amount of money. He is a hero of the pop world and fans would have given their right arm for a copy of the book, but he has just deprived all the genuine people of it."

In George's defence, his friend Derek Taylor has this to offer: "It's a limited edition. It's not meant to upset anyone."

🍎 A 16mm print of the 1944 Humphrey Bogart film *To Have And Have Not* is delivered to Friar Park (and returned to London on July 8).

Monday July 7

🍎 The Granada Television region of the ITV network begin screening (every Monday morning between 10:00 and 10:14am), the original Beatles cartoon series, produced by Al Brodax in America between 1965 and 1967. It is only the second time it has been seen in the UK.

Tuesday July 8

🍎 George receives a letter from Thames Television requesting his appearance on the station's "Race-A-Thon", a marathon model racing competition, scheduled to take place, between 11pm and midnight, at the Wembley Conference Centre in London on October 2 and 3. George fails to attend or reply.

Thursday July 10

🍎 The general release of the five-minute animated film *Seaside Woman* begins in selected cinemas across the UK, in support to Peter Sellers' final film *Being There*. To coincide with its release, Linda is featured in the *Mirror Woman* section of today's *Daily Mirror*. The piece is entitled: "The Launching Of Linda – Paul's Wife Goes It Alone." She reveals that Paul and Linda's nickname for their son James is Dee-Dee and that they cut each other's hair.

🍎 Meanwhile, at Friar Park in Henley-on-Thames, a proposed new Ravi Shankar album, to be recorded at the FPHOTS with George, is ultimately scrapped.

Friday July 11 (until Monday July 21)

🍎 At the Super Bear Studios in Paris, France, located 2,700 feet up a mountain, Ringo

begins recording tracks for his new album *Can't Fight Lightning* (which will eventually be retitled *Stop And Smell The Roses*, on its 1981 release). The ten-day session produces the following tracks: 'Private Property' and 'Attention' (both written by Paul), plus 'Drumming Is My Madness', 'Stop And Take The Time To Smell The Roses', 'Sure To Fall', 'Back Off Boogaloo' (new version) and 'Nice Way'. Ringo also records several tracks which do not appear on the finished album, including the original title track, 'Can't Fight Lightning', as well as 'Life Begins At 40', a song written for Ringo by John. ('Can't Fight Lightning' was written by Ringo for Barbara after they were almost struck by lightning.) Also present for the sessions are Paul, Linda and Laurence Juber. Breaking away from Ringo's album, the three briefly utilise the studio facilities to record their own track, Linda's unreleased song 'Loves Full Glory'. The *Can't Fight Lightning/Stop And Smell The Roses* sessions resume in North Hollywood on September 4 (see entry).
🍎 At the end of the first sessions, Paul, Linda, their children and Laurence head back to England.

Saturday July 12
🍎 A private helicopter ferries George and Olivia to Brands Hatch to watch the British Grand Prix.

Friday July 18
🍎 In Bermuda, John poses for a painting intended as a present for Yoko. She is in New York, spending the weekend with her art dealer friend Sam Green.

Sunday July 27
🍎 Following a short holiday in France at the conclusion of the *Can't Fight Lightning (Stop And Smell The Roses)* sessions, Ringo and Barbara fly on to Los Angeles, where they stay until early September.

Monday July 28
🍎 In America, Ringo and Barbara appear as TV guests on *The John Davidson Show*.

Tuesday July 29
🍎 John and Sean fly from Bermuda to New York and return home to the Dakota. John and Yoko go out for dinner and return home in a carriage. Back in their apartment, Yoko plays John her new composition, 'I'm Your Angel', on the piano. Close friends of the couple reveal that Yoko has now "abandoned plans to divorce John".

Wednesday July 30
🍎 In London, 23-year-old society beauty Michele Howard appears in court on drug charges. As an 8-year-old in 1965, she had lived briefly with The Beatles in Austria during the filming of *Help!*, and was the inspiration for Paul to write the song 'Michelle'. Her father, Anthony Howard, was responsible for promoting The Beatles' films in the sixties.

Thursday July 31
🍎 Yoko phones record producer Jack Douglas and says: "John's coming back. He wants to talk to you about making this record." Yoko requests that Douglas go to 34th Street, board a seaplane and fly out to the beach "near the big house in Glen Cove", which was Lennon's Long Island mansion. On arrival Yoko hands him an envelope which cryptically reads: "For Jack's eyes only." Inside the envelope is a cassette containing various demos of songs intended for John's forthcoming album and a letter which reads: "I think I want to go back into the studio. Would you be interested in producing my album? Here's a bunch of songs. I think they're the same old shit! Tell me what you think. John."
Douglas: "I listened to these songs and they were just incredible. Fred Seaman was playing pots and pans, and John was either playing piano or acoustic guitar. The whole thing was charming."
Douglas is asked by John to put together a band for the sessions. Douglas agrees to work with them now on the condition that he is the sole engineer. (He will eventually share this role with both John and Yoko.)

August
🍎 Paul, Linda and their children spend most of this month on holiday in the Caribbean.

Friday August 1

 In London, George officially forms his company Handmade Films (Productions) Ltd.
 In New York, John and Yoko finish some last minute songwriting and again meet with Jack Douglas, who books the Hit Factory for some studio recording. Later at the Factory, Douglas conducts the first rehearsals for the *Double Fantasy* sessions, working with hand-picked musicians, including Hugh McCracken, who played with John on his 1971 *Imagine* album, Tony Devileo, Earl Slick, George Small and Andy Newmark, who has just recently finished recording with George at Friar Park. The musicians, who learn the songs from John's demos which Douglas plays them back in the studio, are still none the wiser as to whom they will be recording with. They are informed that all will be revealed tomorrow evening. John, meanwhile, is at the Dakota working on some of Yoko's songs that he feels are still not quite ready.

Saturday August 2

 Acting on instructions from Jack Douglas, the musicians who had rehearsed the previous evening meet up on the corner of 72nd and Central Park West en route to meet this "top secret" musician they will be recording with. By now, with the Dakota apartment building clearly visible, they begin to realise they will be backing John Lennon. Inside the Dakota, in apartment 71, John and Yoko greet the musicians and rehearse the songs to be recorded in the studio on August 4. Among the songs are 'Beautiful Boy', 'Borrowed Time' and Yoko's '(Yes) I'm Your Angel'. Supervising the rehearsal is Jack Douglas. For inspiration, John asks Fred Seaman to go out and buy for him the singles 'Babooshka' by Kate Bush and 'Magic' by Olivia Newton-John, as well as a tape by the singer Lena Lovich. At the end of a successful night, as the musicians leave the apartment, John calls Jack to one side and plays him his new song, '(Just Like) Starting Over'. Douglas loves it, telling John, "It will be the new single." (The track has come through a long line of alternative versions and titles, including 'I Watch Your Face', 'My Life', 'Don't Be Crazy' and 'The Worst Is Over'.)

Sunday August 3 & Monday August 4

 John and Yoko prepare for their studio comeback by relaxing for two days at Sam Green's house on Fire Island. They return to New York during the morning of August 4.

Monday August 4 (until Wednesday September 10)

 Today is a historic day as, for the first time in over four years, John re-enters a recording studio to begin producing some new music. Wearing a large floppy hat and carrying a briefcase, he is photographed by Paul Goresh entering the Hit Factory studio with Yoko. With producer Jack Douglas, John and Yoko begin recording tracks for *Double Fantasy*, which include (recorded by John): '(Just Like) Starting Over', 'Cleanup Time', 'I'm Losing You', 'Beautiful Boy (Darling Boy)', 'Watching The Wheels', 'Woman', 'Dear Yoko', 'Grow Old With Me', 'Borrowed Time', '(Forgive Me) My Little Flower Princess' and 'I'm Stepping Out'. Two further tracks recorded by John during these sessions, 'Everybody's Talking' (later to become 'Strange Days Indeed' and then 'Nobody Told Me') and 'I Don't Wanna Face It', were originally intended as songs for Ringo to record. Recorded by Yoko during this period are 'Kiss Kiss Kiss', 'O' Sanity', 'Every Man Has A Woman Who Loves Him', 'Hard Times Are Over', 'Give Me Something', 'I'm Moving On', '(Yes) I'm Your Angel' and 'Beautiful Boys'. (Note: leftover songs from the *Double Fantasy* sessions were originally planned to be released in the spring of 1981, when John would perform a concert tour. As Douglas recalls: "John pictured a big production tour including performances of Beatles numbers featured with a new arrangement." The eight remaining unreleased tracks will be released posthumously on the 1984 Polydor album *Milk and Honey*. (Incidentally, on Monday September 22, John also records a harmony vocal track for Yoko's song 'Every Man Has A Woman Who Loves Him', also appearing in 1984 as part of the *Every Man Has A Woman* album but without Yoko's lead vocal, therefore appearing, quite incorrectly, to be a solo John Lennon recording.)

*   *   *

Double Fantasy recording day 1
The sessions begin with John and the group rehearsing and then recording '(Just Like) Starting Over'. Throughout the *Double Fantasy* recordings, to achieve John's finished vocal

track, Jack Douglas will generally edit together a combination of five different vocal tracks. Later on day one, work begins on Yoko's 'Kiss Kiss Kiss', 'Every Man Has A Woman Who Loves Him' and 'I'm Moving On'. The musicians at the studio today include Hugh McCracken, Earl Slick, Tony Levin, Arthur Jenkins, Ralph McDonald and Andy Newmark. (Keyboard player Jean Roussell is invited by John to join in on the sessions at a later date.) Douglas informs the musicians, in no uncertain terms, that these are "top secret" recording sessions and if news leaks out, the sessions will end immediately. (Despite this, news of John's return to studio recordings soon becomes a major news story in the press around the world.) At the end of every session, John will sit quietly, his feet up on the console, smoking from a 500-year-old opium pipe and softly ask Jack Douglas: "Is it all over?" Jack would reply: "It's over, John." Douglas recalls that should a Beatles record ever come over the radio which played quietly in the background, John would reminisce about it.

Tuesday August 5 (*Double Fantasy* recordings day 2)
Every morning for the duration of the *Double Fantasy* sessions, John will meet Jack Douglas at the Dakota at 9am, and walk the short distance to the La Fortuna cafe on 71st street for breakfast. At around 11am, while Douglas would return to the Hit Factory to resume work with Yoko, John would return to his Dakota apartment for a short sleep until the early afternoon when he would rejoin Yoko and Jack at the Hit Factory. Today, they begin work on the tracks 'Cleanup Time' and 'Woman'.

Wednesday August 6 (*Double Fantasy* recordings day 3)
At the Hit Factory, work starts on rehearsing John's tracks 'I'm Stepping Out', 'Watching The Wheels' and 'Strange Days Indeed' (later to be titled, on its official 1984 release, 'Nobody Told Me').

Thursday August 7 (*Double Fantasy* recordings day 4)
The Hit Factory sessions continue with John, Tony Levin, Earl Slick, Andy Newmark and Arthur Jenkins recording 'I'm Stepping Out', 'Borrowed Time' and, briefly, the unreleased composition, 'Gone From This Place'.

Friday August 8 (*Double Fantasy* recordings day 5)
Additional recordings for 'Strange Days Indeed' and 'Kiss Kiss Kiss', during which, John is seen openly smoking pot during the session.

Saturday August 9 (*Double Fantasy* recordings day 6)
Recordings for 'Beautiful Boy (Darling Boy)' and Yoko's 'Don't Be Scared'. As she accidentally fluffs her lyrics, John is heard to scream: "Remember the bridge on the River Kwai, you fuck!"

Sunday August 10 & Monday August 11
John, Yoko and Jack Douglas take a break from recordings, with the Lennons spending two days at the Dakota relaxing with Sean.

Tuesday August 12 (*Double Fantasy* recordings day 7)
John and Yoko issue a statement announcing their comeback and that the theme for their next album is the "exploration of sexual fantasies between men and women". Almost immediately, Jack Douglas starts receiving phone calls from record company executives, including one from Bruce Lundvall, of Columbia Records, who tells Douglas, "Whatever John wants for this record, we'll give it to him!" Meanwhile, back at the Hit Factory, shortly after hearing John's demo versions for the first time, work commences with Cheap Trick's Bun E. Carlos (drums) and Rick Nielsen (guitar) on 'I'm Losing You' and 'I'm Moving On'. Their period with the Lennons does not last long, with Yoko telling Douglas to "get rid of them", feeling that they were "getting a free ride on John's coat-tails!". (On Yoko's insistence, the rehearsal version of 'I'm Losing You' is not released on the *Double Fantasy* album, and will not appear officially until 1998 when a version appears on the four-CD *Lennon Anthology* box set.) By way of a strange coincidence, the two members of Cheap Trick had broken off from a recording session produced by George Martin, the famed Beatles producer. Also present at the Hit Factory session today is Tony Levin.

Wednesday August 13 (*Double Fantasy* recordings day 8)
During the sessions for 'Cleanup Time' and 'I'm Losing You', Paul calls John from holiday to suggest a collaboration but, because Yoko does not allow the call to be put through, John is not informed that his former Beatles partner has rung. This event has a touch of irony, as Jack Douglas recalls: "From what I heard from John, he was looking to get hooked up with Paul to do some writing . . ." For the rest of the *Double Fantasy* recordings, John and Yoko are rejoined by the musicians who first played with the couple on August 7.

Thursday August 14 (*Double Fantasy* recordings day 9)
Excited by the sessions, John arrives an hour early. Recordings take place today for 'Forgive Me My Little Flower Princess' and more versions of 'Beautiful Boy (Darling Boy)'. Yoko does not attend the session; instead she spends her time with Sam Green.

Friday August 15 (*Double Fantasy* recordings day 10)
Sessions continue with Yoko's track 'Beautiful Boys'.

(Saturday August 16 & Sunday August 17)
A further break from recordings, where again John and Yoko spend time relaxing at the Dakota with Sean and eating out in local Chinese restaurants.

Monday August 18 (*Double Fantasy* recordings (day 11) and start of week-long videotape shoot – which ends on Friday August 22)
The production team who usually produce the *Crazy Eddie* record store advertisements are invited by Yoko to videotape the sessions at the Hit Factory. During the sessions, primarily to shoot footage to be included in the '(Just Like) Starting Over' promotional video clip, John and his band (on the first day, August 18), perform versions of: 'C' Mon Everybody', 'Rip It Up', 'I'm A Man', 'Be-Bop-A-Lula', '12-Bar Blues', 'Dream Lover', 'Stay', 'Mystery Train', 'I'm Losing You' (two takes), 'Blues In The Night', The Beatles' 'She's A Woman' (four takes), '(Just Like) Starting Over' (two takes) and 'I'm A Man'. (The bootleg audio tapes of this session originate not from the video but from a microphone, which was hidden in the studio.) With videotaping still continuing, John and the band continue with further recordings of '(Just Like) Starting Over' and 'I'm Losing You', using as a guideline the Cheap Trick demo recorded on Tuesday August 12, which is played through their headphones. Due to his extremely thin appearance, John is not happy with the video taken over these five days and, according to Jack Douglas, John either "Tore it up in the bath tub" or "Sunk it in the pool!" The existence or non-existence of this video still remains a mystery.

Tuesday August 19 (*Double Fantasy* recordings day 12)
Recordings for 'Hard Times Are Over'.

Wednesday August 20 (*Double Fantasy* recordings day 13)
Further recording work on 'I'm Losing You'.

Thursday August 21 (*Double Fantasy* recordings day 14)
Further recording sessions for '(Just Like) Starting Over'.

Friday August 22 (*Double Fantasy* recordings day 15)
Further recording sessions for '(Just Like) Starting Over' and the last day of the unreleased *Crazy Eddie* video shoot.

Saturday August 23
Another break from recording spent at their Dakota apartment. After years of seeing his dad hanging out in the apartment, Sean becomes inquisitive about where John is spending most of his days. John suggests Sean visit the studio tomorrow to watch him record.

Sunday August 24 (*Double Fantasy* recordings day 16)
As planned, Sean visits the Hit Factory sessions, where he watches John record additional guitar parts on '(Just Like) Starting Over' and 'Gone From This Place'.

Monday August 25 (*Double Fantasy* recordings day 17)
Recordings resume on the track 'Watching The Wheels'.

Tuesday August 26 (*Double Fantasy* recordings day 18)
Most of the day is spent overdubbing additional guitar work on the track 'Watching The Wheels'.

Wednesday August 27 (*Double Fantasy* recordings day 19)
Additional recordings for the track 'Woman'.

Thursday August 28 (*Double Fantasy* recordings day 20)
Recordings for the track 'I'm Moving On'.

Friday August 29 (*Double Fantasy* recordings day 21)
Recording sessions for 'Dear Yoko' and 'Cleanup Time'.

Saturday August 30
Although there are no recording sessions booked for today, John and Yoko still arrive at the Hit Factory at 2:40pm in their silver limousine, accompanied by a photographer from the *Star* newspaper. At the Hit Factory, a reporter interviews John about his career and captures the events on his RCA home video camera. The soundtrack is marred by the fact that John is sitting in on the overdubbing of the *Star Wars* film *The Empire Strikes Back*. He talks quite candidly about all manner of subjects, including Paul's 'Coming Up' and The Beatles' film *Magical Mystery Tour*, and admits that the last album by Paul he listened to was the one where "he had a rose in his mouth" (*Red Rose Speedway*).
   During conversations with Jack Douglas around this time John revealed plans for a tour in 1981. "He planned tremendous production," Jack recalls, "including his new arrangements of songs he never got right. Like 'She Loves You' and 'I Want To Hold Your Hand'."

Sunday August 31
John and Yoko spend the day in seclusion at the Dakota.

Monday September 1 (*Double Fantasy* recordings day 22)
A new month and a new song to be recorded, this time Yoko's track '(Yes) I'm Your Angel' as well as a studio version of John's 'Grow Old With Me'.

Tuesday September 2 (*Double Fantasy* recordings day 23)
Recordings resume with John's 'I Don't Wanna Face It'.

Wednesday September 3 (*Double Fantasy* recordings day 24)
Recording sessions for Yoko's 'Beautiful Boys'.

Thursday September 4 (*Double Fantasy* recordings day 25)
Further work on 'Watching The Wheels'.

Friday September 5 (*Double Fantasy* recordings day 26)
Additional (horn playing overdubbing) work takes place on 'I'm Losing You' and 'Cleanup Time'.

Saturday September 6 (*Double Fantasy* recordings day 27)
Yoko records her vocals for the track 'Every Man Has A Woman Who Loves Him'.

Sunday September 7 (*Double Fantasy* recordings day 28)
Further work on '(Just Like) Starting Over' and 'Give Me Something'.

Monday September 8 (*Double Fantasy* recordings day 29)
Additional overdubbing on the track 'Woman'.

Tuesday September 9 (*Double Fantasy* recordings day 30)
The first batch of recordings is concluded today with the songs 'Dear Yoko' and 'Every Man Has A Woman Who Loves Him', although additional recordings, upon the insistence of Jack Douglas, take place on September 22, 24, 26 and 29 (see entries) with the very final work on the album being concluded by Douglas on October 20.

Wednesday September 10 (*Double Fantasy* recordings day 31)
Vocal overdubs on Yoko's tracks are recorded with a black teenage choir.

*   *   *

Friday August 8
❦ George goes on holiday with Olivia and Dhani. They return to England on Monday August 18.

Monday August 11
❦ In North Hollywood, at the Devonshire Sound studios, Ringo and his band resume recordings for the album *Can't Fight Lightning*. Among the musicians is Stephen Stills. (Periodical recording will continue until February 12, 1981, with the next sessions booked at the Cherokee Studios in Los Angeles on September 4.)

Monday August 18
❦ At his Friar Park studios, after another lengthy break, George resumes recording his album *Somewhere In England,* almost ten months after the sessions had begun on October 30, 1979. This period of recording will continue until Tuesday September 23.

September
❦ In Australia, 25,000 copies of the boxed set of 13 Beatles albums are sold, thereby qualifying for a "gold box". Reports this month reveal that the BBC and EMI Records in London are currently negotiating for an official worldwide release of The Beatles' BBC studio recordings from the Sixties.

❦ In readiness for Sean's fifth birthday, John and Yoko purchase for him a £62,500 aeroplane, complete with a pilot and stewardess.

❦ Paul is spotted in the audience of Stevie Wonder's concerts at the Wembley Arena. This year, Paul fails to hold his annual Buddy Holly Week celebrations; instead he hosts a Buddy Holly special on London's Capital Radio.

❦ Ringo's central London retail outlet for his *Ringo Or Robin* exclusive furniture and art moves premises.

❦ "In September, when I was just starting my record company, everybody was talking about John and Yoko. I thought, wouldn't it be great to sign them? I sent them a telegram and proceeded to forget about it. An impossible dream." – David Geffen in *Rolling Stone* magazine.

Monday September 1
❦ At Friar Park, George reads a copy of the book *The Beatles A–Z* by Goldie Friede, Robin Titone and Sue Weiner.

Thursday September 4
❦ At the Cherokee Studios in Los Angeles, recording resumes on *Can't Fight Lightning*.

Sunday September 7 (until Sunday September 14)
❦ While John is nearing completion of his comeback album in New York, Paul is busily preparing for the annual Buddy Holly Week celebration.

Wednesday September 10 (until Sunday September 28)
❦ At the conclusion of the recordings for *Double Fantasy,* John agrees to a series of interviews with David Sheff for *Playboy* magazine. John: "I'm going to be forty. Sean's going to be five. Isn't it great? We survived. I am going to be forty and life begins at forty so they promise. Oh, I believe it too. It's like wow. What's going to happen next?"

The first part of these interviews is printed in the December 1980 issue. (Excerpts from these lengthy interviews are later released in 1983, on the album *Heart Play – Unfinished Dialogue,* with additional clips being broadcast in America on *The Lost Lennon Tapes* radio series.) The first day of interviews in the Dakota is concluded at 1:30am in the early hours of Thursday September 11. During the interview sessions, John tells Sheff: "This will be *the* reference book!"

Thursday September 11
❦ Day two of John's *Playboy* interview takes place at his Dakota apartment.

Playboy: "Will you follow the release of the new record with a tour?"

John: "Well, we probably will, you know. I wouldn't have believed it a month ago. But then I thought, what the hell, why not?"

Meanwhile, Yoko has a meeting with David Geffen of Geffen Records.

◆ Back in London, Capitol Radio, broadcasts a Beatles radio special featuring many of their greatest recordings in a show called *Making Waves*.

Friday September 12
◆ On day three of John's *Playboy* interview the venue switches to the La Fortuna coffee-shop on Columbus Avenue in New York, a block and a half from the Dakota building. The conversation resumes back at John's Dakota apartment.

Playboy: "John, do you listen to your own records?"

John: "Least of all my own. For pleasure I would never listen to them. When I hear them, I just think of the session – the forty-eight hours Paul and I sat up putting the *White Album* (The Beatles) in order until we were going crazy; eight hours of mixing 'Revolution 9' – whatever. Jesus, we were sitting for hours doing the bloody guitars. I remember every detail of the work."

Saturday September 13
◆ The *Playboy* interview resumes at the Hit Factory.

John: "I'm always proud and pleased when people do my songs. It gives me pleasure that they even attempt to do them . . . I go to restaurants and the groups always play 'Yesterday'. Yoko and I signed a guy's violin in Spain after he played us 'Yesterday'. He couldn't understand that I didn't write the song. But I guess he couldn't have gone from table to table playing 'I Am The Walrus'."

Monday September 15
◆ Paul's limited edition 12-inch single 'Temporary Secretary'/'Secret Friend' is released in the UK. Shortly after its release, Paul turns down a request from the Alfred Marks Employment Bureau to use the song for advertising purposes.

◆ John continues his interview with *Playboy* magazine.

Playboy: "Why is it so unthinkable that the fab four can get back together to make some music?"

John: "Talking about The Beatles getting back together again is an illusion. That was ten years ago. The Beatles only exist on film and on record and in people's minds. You cannot get back together what no longer exists. We are not those four people anymore. Anyway, why should I go back ten years to provide an illusion I know doesn't exist?"

Playboy: "Forget the illusion. What about just to make some music?"

John: "Why should The Beatles give more? Didn't they give everything on God's earth for ten years? Didn't they give themselves? Didn't they give all?"

Following a lengthy interview session at the Dakota, he joins Sheff on a stroll up 72nd Street, down Columbus Street, around Central Park and back to the Dakota.

Tuesday September 16
◆ Further interviews with John for *Playboy* magazine are carried out at the Hit Factory and his Dakota apartment.

John: "When I was a Beatle, I thought we were the best fucking group in the goddam world, and believing that is what made us what we were, whether you call it the best rock'n'roll group or whatever. As far as we were concerned, we were the best, but we thought that before anybody else had even heard of us. In that respect I think The Beatles are the best thing that ever happened in pop music, but you play me those tracks and I want to remake every damn one of them. I heard 'Lucy In The Sky With Diamonds' last night. It's abysmal, you know? The track is just terrible. I mean, it is a great track, a great song, but it isn't a great track because it wasn't made right. You know what I mean? I feel I could remake every fucking one of them better!"

Unfortunately, throughout the entire interview, John has neglected to inform Sheff that another interview he did with *Newsweek* magazine is about to reach the stands.

Wednesday September 17
◆ Advanced text of John's explosive *Newsweek* article reaches the news wires. This naturally annoys Sheff and G. Barry Golson, the executive editor of *Playboy* magazine, who thought that their interview with John was an exclusive. They confront him this morning. "John, you rat," Barry screams at the Dakota. "You blew our exclusive!" "Well," John humbly replies, realising his mistake, "what can I do to make it up with you boys?" Quick as a flash, Barry decides to ask John to go over his music song by song, to recall

who wrote what and under what circumstances and what memories the songs might inspire. John enthusiastically agrees. "I'm proud of my work, " he remarks. "I'll give you the definitive version, the whole damned thing – at least my version . . . I have a terrific memory. You can do it from the womb to the grave. Boom!"

John: "We (Paul and I) wrote a lot of stuff together, one on one, eyeball to eyeball. Like in 'I Want To Hold Your Hand', I remember when we got the chord that made the song. We were in Jane Asher's house, downstairs in the cellar playing on the piano at the same time. And we had 'Oh you . . . got that something' and Paul hits this chord and I turn to him and say, 'That's it!' I said, 'Do that again.' In those days we really used to absolutely write like that – both playing into each other's noses. We wrote in the back of vans together. We wrote 'She Loves You' in a van on the way to Newcastle."

Playboy: "But what about a complex song like 'Eleanor Rigby'?"

John: "Yeah, 'Rigby'. Ah, the first verse was his but the rest are basically mine. He knew he had a song. But by that time he didn't want to ask for my help, and we were sitting around with Mal Evans and Neil Aspinall, so he said to us, 'Hey, you guys, finish up the lyrics.' Now I was there with Mal, a telephone installer, and Neil, who was a student accountant, and I was insulted and hurt that Paul had just thrown it into the air. He actually meant that he wanted me to do it, and of course there isn't a line of theirs in the song because I finally went off into a room with Paul and we finished the song. I do know that George Harrison was there when we came up with 'Ah, look at all the lonely people.' He and George were settling on that as I left the studio to go to the toilet, and I heard the lyric and turned around and said, 'That's it!' The violin backing was Paul's idea. Jane Asher had turned him on to Vivaldi, and it was very good, the violins, straight out of Vivaldi. I can't take any credit for that, at all."

Later, with Sheff and Golson still in tow, more interviewing takes place at the Hit Factory.

Thursday September 18

& Day eight of John's interview with *Playboy* magazine takes place at the Hit Factory.

John: "I haven't seen any of The Beatles for I don't know how long. It doesn't even cross my mind as to whether I've seen them or not. It's just irrelevant. It wouldn't matter to me if I saw them often or if I never saw them again. Because the whole Beatles message was, as Baba Rama Ding-Dong says, 'Be Here Now'. I don't know what they do now. Somebody asked me what I thought of Paul's last album and I made some remark like I thought he was depressed and sad. But then I realised that I hadn't listened to the whole damn thing. I heard one track – the hit, 'Coming Up', which I thought was a good piece of work. Then I heard something else that sounded like he was depressed. I don't follow Wings, you know. I don't give a shit what Wings are doing, or what George's new album is doing or what Ringo is doing. I'm not interested, no more than I am in what Elton John or Bob Dylan is doing. It's not callousness. It's just than I'm too busy living my own life to follow what other people are doing."

At the conclusion of the interview, John requests a few days breather. Work resumes on Monday September 22.

Friday September 19

& At 9am, because her horoscope reading today is favourable, Yoko meets David Geffen of Geffen Records, who agrees to release *Double Fantasy* without hearing any of the tracks John and Yoko have just recorded. Before this five-year agreement, John had toyed briefly with the idea of selling the completed *Double Fantasy* master tapes in an auction so that they would be released by the highest bidder, thus freeing him from signing any record contract.

Monday September 22

& This morning, after a weekend deliberation, John and Yoko sign a recording contract with Geffen Records. Later, John continues the *Playboy* interview with David Sheff, firstly at the Hit Factory and later at the Dakota apartment.

Playboy: "What about the Bangladesh concert with George and Dylan and others?"

John: "Bangladesh was caca . . . everybody else is getting paid except for the musicians. It's an absolute rip-off, but it makes the artist look good."

Recordings at the Hit Factory today include John re-recording his vocals on 'Woman' and recording his backing vocals on Yoko's 'Every Man Has A Woman Who Loves Him'.

Tuesday September 23
❦ Ringo continues recording *Can't Fight Lightning* at the Cherokee Studios in Los Angeles, where he is joined by Ronnie Wood of The Rolling Stones to record an early version of the track 'Dead Giveaway'.
❦ At Friar Park, George completes his album *Somewhere In England*. Unfortunately, as things turn out, the sessions will have to be resumed in November.

Wednesday September 24
❦ Mixing of *Double Fantasy* moves from the Hit Factory to Record Plant East in New York. John is naturally in attendance. During the session, John gives an interview to Lisa Robinson of the 97-FM Buffalo radio station.

Thursday September 25
❦ At the Dakota, Yoko meets with Sean's bodyguard, Doug MacDougall, to discuss the security surrounding the Lennons. This is in direct response to the number of fans who are beginning to hang around the front of the Dakota building in the hope of catching a glimpse of John leaving to go to the recording studio.
❦ In Los Angeles, at the Cherokee recording studios, Ringo, still with Ronnie Wood, records the track 'Brandy'. A further session is planned for Saturday September 27.

Friday September 26
❦ At the Record Plant East studios in New York, Jack Douglas prepares the mixes for the single '(Just Like) Starting Over' and 'Kiss Kiss Kiss'. Further *Double Fantasy* mixes take place on September 29. Back in England, BBC Radio One transmits a profile on John in Paul Gambaccini's *Appreciation* series.
❦ George leaves Heathrow Airport en route to Montreal in Canada. He will then fly on to Los Angeles on Sunday September 28 where he will meet up with Derek Taylor.

Sunday September 28
❦ The tenth and final day of *Playboy* interviews takes place this morning during breakfast at La Fortuna's coffee shop.
Playboy: "Do you still take LSD?"
John: "Not in years. A little mushroom or peyote is not beyond my scope, you know, maybe twice a year or something."
In total, John and Sheff have recorded over thirty hours of fascinating interview material. Following the session with *Playboy*, John has another haircut and, along with Yoko, boards a plane for Los Angeles where they have arranged to meet George and Derek Taylor at Monty Python's concert at the Hollywood Bowl. George gives John a copy, on audio cassette, of his latest album. Following the show, George remains in LA while John and Yoko return to New York, arriving back in the early hours of September 29.

Monday September 29
❦ As planned, *Newsweek* magazine hits the American news stands and, as expected, carries an exclusive two-page interview with John and Yoko by Barbara Graustark. The article, John's first major interview since the NBC TV's *Tomorrow Show* with Tom Snyder on April 28, 1975, includes questions on a wide range of topics including Yoko's role as John's business manager, whether John stopped listening to music and a typical day in the life of John and Yoko?
Barbara: "Why did you go underground in 1975? Were you tired of making music – or of the business itself?"
John: "It was a bit of both. I'd been under contract since I was 22 and I was always 'supposed to'. I was supposed to write a hundred songs by Friday, supposed to have a single out by Saturday, supposed to do this or that. I became an artist because I cherished freedom – I couldn't fit into a classroom or office. Freedom was the plus for all the minuses of being an oddball! But suddenly I was obliged to a record company, obliged to the media, obliged to the public. I wasn't free at all."
Barbara: "Paul McCartney's theory is that you became a recluse because you'd done everything – but be yourself."
John: "What the hell does that mean? Paul didn't know what I was doing – he was as curious as everybody else was. It's ten years since I really communicated with him. I know as much about him as he does about me, which is *zilch*. About two years ago

(1976), he turned up at the door. I said, 'Look, do you mind ringin' first? I've just had a hard day with the baby, I'm worn out and you're walkin' in with a damn guitar!' "

Barbara: "Why did you decide to record again?"

John: "Because *this* housewife would like to have a career for a bit! On October 9, I'll be 40 and Sean will be 5, and I can afford to say 'Daddy does something else as well.' He's not accustomed to it – in five years I hardly picked up a guitar. Last Christmas our neighbours showed him *Yellow Submarine* and he came running in saying 'Daddy, you were singing . . . were you a Beatle?' I said, 'Well yes, right!' "

Barbara: "People have blamed Yoko for wrenching you away from the band and destroying The Beatles. How did it really end?"

John: "I was always waiting for a reason to get out of The Beatles from the day I filmed *How I Won The War*. I just didn't have the guts to do it. The seed was planted when The Beatles stopped touring and I couldn't deal with not being on stage. But I was too frightened to step out of the palace. That's what killed Presley. The king is always killed by his courtiers. He is overfed, overindulged, overdrunk to keep him tied to his throne. Most people in the position never wake up."

Barbara: "Do you ever yearn for the good old days?"

John: "Nah! Whatever made The Beatles 'The Beatles' also made the Sixties the Sixties, and anybody who thinks that if John and Paul got together with George and Ringo 'The Beatles' would exist, is out of their skulls. The Beatles gave everything they had to give – and more. The four guys who used to be that group can never ever be that group again even if they wanted to be. What if Paul and I got together? It would be boring. Whether George or Ringo joined in is irrelevant because Paul and I created the music, OK? There are many Beatle tracks that I would redo – they were never the way *I* wanted them to be. But going back to The Beatles would be like going back to school . . . I was never one for reunions. It's all over!"

In Honolulu, a 25-year-old long-term Beatles fan reads the article and convinces himself that John is "a phoney". His name is Mark David Chapman.

Mixing work on *Double Fantasy* continues on the tenth floor of the Record Plant in New York. Sound effects, taped in the New York streets by Fred Seaman and engineer Jon Smith, are added to the tracks 'Watching The Wheels' and '(Yes) I'm Your Angel'. For the song 'I'm Losing You', John instructs Jack Douglas to mix into the end of the song a secret message in synthesized Morse code, which reads "I love you Yoko." This afternoon, sporting his new shorter haircut, John is pictured climbing out of his limousine and entering the studios.

Tuesday September 30
 On the suggestion of Yoko, the *Double Fantasy* mixing sessions are moved back to the Hit Factory.

October
 Following another haircut, John is pictured by photographer Lilo Raymond walking around New York with Yoko and at the Hit Factory studios.

 Handmade Films complete the shooting of the film *Time Bandits*, which stars John Cleese, Michael Palin, Sir Ralph Richardson and Sean Connery. In between film duties, George is to be found in the audience of Ravi Shankar's concert at London's Royal Albert Hall.

 With fifteen years having elapsed since the completion of The Beatles' second film *Help!*, the full and complete rights to this and The Beatles' first big-screen adventure *A Hard Day's Night*, automatically revert back to the films' producer Walter Shenson from United Artists. Recognising this fact, Shenson begins restoring the original *A Hard Day's Night* film soundtrack, utilising the latest Dolby sound systems, and contemplates a reissue of the film to American cinemas.

Wednesday October 1
 George is now joined in Los Angeles by Olivia and Dhani. They all return to London on Friday October 24.

Thursday October 2 (until Saturday October 25)
 Paul and Wings, in what turns out to be their final session together as a five-piece, return to Finston Manor in Tenterton, Kent, to record a set of demos in preparation for the proposed *Hot Hits, Cold Cutz,* album as well as initial work on the *Rupert The Bear*

film soundtrack. After the first week, rehearsals shift towards tracks which are scheduled to appear on Paul's next studio album, ultimately to appear on the *Tug Of War* (1982) and *Pipes Of Peace* (1983) albums. Amongst the tracks 'jammed' during this three-week period are: 'Rainclouds', 'Average Person', 'Keep Under Cover', 'Ebony And Ivory', 'Twenty Flight Rock', 'Ballroom Dancing', 'Cage', 'Old Man Lovin'', 'Sure To Fall', 'Movie Magg', 'Blue Moon Of Kentucky', 'Summertime', 'Good Rockin' Tonight – Shake, Rattle And Roll' (medley), 'Cut Across Shorty', 'Stealin' Back To My Same Old Used To Be', 'Singin' The Blues', 'Johnny B. Goode', 'Dress Me Up As A Robber', 'The Pound Is Sinking', 'Sweetest Little Person', 'Wanderlust' and 'Take It Away'. In addition, Wings jam five further tracks, which remain unreleased. These are 'Take Her Back, Jack', 'The Unbelievable Experience', 'Here's The Chord, Roy', 'Seems Like Old Times' and a further version of 'Boil Crisis' first recorded by Wings back in 1977. Due to the largely uninspiring nature of these rehearsals, a planned Wings recording session in December at George Martin's recently opened studio in Montserrat fails to materialise.

◉ During the month, at his Dakota apartment, John records several more demos of the song 'Real Love' which he had originally begun composing in the late Seventies. (Take 6 of the song is released in 1988 on the compilation soundtrack album *Imagine: John Lennon.* Yoko copyrights the song in 1985 under the alternate title of 'Girls And Boys'.) During this month, John also records several more unreleased songs, including many different takes of 'Serve Yourself', a full-blown foul-mouthed parody of Bob Dylan's 'Gotta Serve Somebody', which had been recorded several times throughout 1980, initially in early spring.

Thursday October 9
◉ Yoko hires a skywriter to write: "Happy Birthday John & Sean – Love Yoko" nine times in the sky, an event that makes a major news story on US TV. While John sleeps through the proceedings back at the Dakota, fans gather outside the building in the hope of catching a glimpse of the former Beatle. Later in the day, John and Yoko pose for an official "40th Birthday" snapshot and the Lennons' assistant, Fred Seaman, announces to the press that "next Spring, John and Yoko will be touring Japan, USA and Europe". After an absence of ten years, John will finally be returning to England.

Friday October 10
◉ Paul and Linda donate a £500 cheque to the appeal fund for Johnny Owen, a Liverpool boxer injured in a bout.

Monday October 13
◉ With John about to re-enter the world of record releases, Parlophone/EMI in England waste no time in compiling a new Beatles album, entitled *The Beatles Ballads – 20 Original Tracks.* The line-up of previously released tracks includes: 'Yesterday', 'Norwegian Wood (This Bird Has Flown)', 'Do You Want To Know A Secret', 'For No One', 'Michelle', 'Nowhere Man', 'You've Got To Hide Your Love Away', 'Across The Universe', 'All My Loving', 'Hey Jude', 'Something', 'The Fool On The Hill', 'Till There Was You', 'The Long And Winding Road', 'Here Comes The Sun', 'Blackbird', 'And I Love Her', 'She's Leaving Home', 'Here, There And Everywhere' and 'Let It Be'.
◉ John enjoys a belated official birthday party with Yoko and Sean at their regular birthday venue, the Tavern On The Green in New York's Central Park.

Wednesday October 15
◉ In London, George forms Handmade Films (Distribution) Ltd, to serve his Handmade Production Company.

Thursday October 16 & Friday October 17
◉ Still in the capital, Abbey Road studios hold their "Sale of the Century" auction. Among the historical recording equipment put under the hammer over the two days is the original Struder J37 4-track recording machine as used by The Beatles when they made *Sgt. Pepper* back in 1967, which sells for £500, and a mellotron tape organ, as used on the recordings for *Magical Mystery Tour* and complete with many of The Beatles original tapes still intact, which sells to musician Mike Oldfield for £1,000. Also sold at the auction is a brass ashtray as used by Ringo during various Beatles recording sessions. This fetches £120.

Saturday October 18
♦ In a Honolulu public library, Mark Chapman borrows the Anthony Fawcett book *One Day At A Time*. Chapman, who has been psychologically deranged for more than ten years, somehow further convinces himself that John has become a hypocrite and has now sold out on all his ideals and principles. Reading this book, Chapman suffers serious mental turmoil and decides that the only solution to this problem is to kill John Lennon.

Monday October 20
♦ The final mixes for the album *Double Fantasy* are concluded by Douglas at the Hit Factory. Shortly after their completion and excited by what they've just done, John aborts a planned trip to Bermuda and asks Douglas to rejoin him and Yoko in the studio. He tells him he is keen to continue with more recordings and eager to record some tracks for Ringo's next album. Hit Factory sessions are quickly arranged for November 17, the day that *Double Fantasy* will be released simultaneously around the world.

Thursday October 23
♦ Mark Chapman departs from his post as a Honolulu maintenance man at the Waikiki Condominium, signing off from his employees using the pseudonym "John Lennon".

Friday October 24
♦ With great anticipation, John's comeback single '(Just Like) Starting Over', backed with Yoko's 'Kiss Kiss Kiss' is released in the UK. (The American release takes place three days later, on October 27.)

Monday October 27 (until Monday November 3)
♦ Paul joins George Martin at AIR Studios in London to continue more solo projects, this time the soundtrack for the proposed *Rupert The Bear* film, which includes: 'Rupert Song', 'Tippi Tippi Toes (Parents Theme)', 'Flying Horses', 'Cohen, The Wind Is Blowing', 'The Castle Of The King Of The Birds', 'Sunshine, Sometime', 'Sea-Cornish Water' (medley), 'Storm', 'Nutwood Scene', 'Walking In The Meadow', 'Sea Medley' and 'Rupert Song' (version two). On October 31 and November 3, joined by The King's Singers and the St. Paul's Boys Choir, Paul records both vocal and humming versions of the song 'We All Stand Together', later to appear in the 1984 animated film short *Rupert And The Frog Song* and released as a single in the UK only on November 12, 1984. The most significant of these recordings are 'Sea', which was first demoed by Paul during Sunday July 14, 1974, the so-called 'Piano Tape' (see entry), 'Sunshine, Sometime', which first appeared during the 1971 *Ram* album sessions and 'The Castle Of The King Of The Birds', which was a track first "jammed" by Paul in January 1969 during The Beatles' *Get Back/Let It Be* sessions.
♦ In Honolulu, Mark Chapman purchases a .38 calibre "charter arms undercover" short barrelled revolver. (In English money, the gun costs £75.)

Wednesday October 29
♦ Mark Chapman flies from Honolulu to New York. In his possession on the flight is a handgun, but no ammunition.

Thursday October 30
♦ Chapman arrives at the Dakota in an attempt to meet John. His failure leads him to return for the next five days. An attempt to buy some bullets for his handgun also results in failure.

November (until June 16 1981)
♦ Back in England, at his Friar Park studio, George periodically resumes sessions for *Somewhere In England,* recording four new tracks to replace those rejected by Warner Brothers. One of them, 'Blood From A Clone', is an attack on the company for rejecting his first version of the album. Though George had produced the earlier album recordings, Ray Cooper now becomes the co-producer with George during this period of recordings.
♦ During November at the Dakota, in preparation for further Hit Factory recording sessions, John records a number of demos of unreleased songs, including 'Dear John', one of the last songs he will ever compose. During the recording, he goes into the lyrics of 'September Song', all the more poignant given the events that are soon to follow. Outside the Dakota apartment, John bumps into Mitch Weissman, who plays the role of Paul in the *Beatlemania* stage play. Mitch tells John: "I am hoping to leave the show and do other

things." John replies: "I can feel for you, but once you're a Beatle, it's tough to get out."
 John's return to the world of record releases brings with it renewed appreciation of anything Beatles related. With this in mind, Radio Luxembourg (every Tuesday evening, between 8:00 and 9:00pm) begin broadcasting this month *The Beatles Hour*, a non-stop feast of pure Beatles music.
 A pre-recorded interview with Paul is broadcast on the Irish radio station CBC.

November (first week)
 EMI's budget label MFP (Music For Pleasure) releases, simultaneously worldwide, their first cut-price Beatles albums. The titles include *The Beatles Rock 'N' Roll Music* Volumes 1 and 2 (the 1976 double album split into two single discs but featuring the new, previously unreleased, George Martin remixes), Ringo's 1973 album *Ringo*, John's *Mind Games* and George's *Dark Horse*. In the UK, the records retail for just £1.99.

Sunday November 2
 Back in the States at 8pm this evening, Jack Mitchell photographs John and Yoko for the November 9 edition of the Arts and Leisure section of the *New York Times*.

Monday November 3
 In England, EMI's mail-order division World Records releases the eight album box set entitled *The Beatles Box,* containing 126 original Beatles' recordings, including several rare mixes.

Tuesday November 4 & Wednesday November 5
 In the States, Paul oversees the final edits of the Wings concert film *Rockshow,* being prepared for its New York premiere on November 26. He returns home on Thursday November 6.
 On November 4, a copy of the Gene Kelly musical film *Singin' In The Rain* is delivered to Friar Park. (The print is returned to London on Monday November 10.)

Thursday November 6
 During the sessions still taking place at Cherokee Studios in Los Angeles, Ringo, still accompanied by Ronnie Wood, records a demo of the track 'I Don't Believe You'. At its conclusion, Ringo and Barbara get ready to return home and a further *Can't Fight Lightning* session is booked for Wednesday January 14, 1981.

Sunday November 9
 Chapman flies back to New York. On his flight he reads an *Esquire* magazine article by Laurence Shames which criticises John's radical beliefs and exclusive lifestyle. Once back in New York, Chapman returns to the Dakota and is repeatedly told by 27-year-old doorman Jay Hastings that John and Yoko are "out of town for the week". Hastings, who has been working at the Dakota for the past two years, is a life-long Beatles fan and has regularly greeted John and Yoko when they returned from their late-night Hit Factory recording sessions. As the Lennons return home, John would usually greet him by saying, "Bonsoir, Jay".

Monday November 10 (periodically until Wednesday November 26)
 Back at his home in Rye, Sussex, Paul, continues work with Linda and Denny on demo recordings of tracks intended for the next Wings studio album.
 Ringo also returns from America and, back at his Tittenhurst Park mansion, contacts George to ask if he would like to appear on his next album. George agrees. A date is set for Wednesday November 19.

Tuesday November 11
 In his rented New York apartment, Chapman phones his wife in Hawaii and informs her: "I am planning to murder John Lennon!" She pleads with him to return home, advice he fails to follow.

Wednesday November 12
 Taking a break from the sessions at FPHOTS, George purchases, from Asprey & Company, in Bond Street, London, a musical box costing £295.00, which plays George's

Beatles tune 'Here Comes The Sun'. (Over the years, this fact slowly became distorted, and it is eventually believed that George bought a toilet which, when the seat is lifted, plays John's tune 'Lucy In The Sky With Diamonds'.)

Friday November 14
🍎 At his Dakota apartment, John records, on his final home taping session, demos of 'Pop Is The Name Of The Game', 'You Saved My Soul (With Your True Love)', and a final version of 'Serve Yourself'.

Saturday November 15
🍎 According to Ringo during his interview on the ABC TV *Barbara Walters Special* (transmitted in America on March 31 1981), he and Barbara met John and Yoko tonight at the Plaza Hotel in New York, where The Beatles stayed on their first visit to America in February 1964.

Monday November 17
🍎 "*Double Fantasy* – we feel like this is just the start and this is our first album. I know we've worked together before and we've even made albums before, but we feel like this is the first album. I feel like nothing has happened before today." – John (in an RKO Radio interview recorded on December 8).

John and Yoko's album *Double Fantasy* is released simultaneously in America and in the UK. To celebrate this fact, the Lennons happily pose for the photographer Paul Goresh on their way to the Hit Factory. Back home, the reviews of the album are not very good. *Melody Maker* writes: "The whole thing positively reeks of an indulgent sterility . . . It's a godawful yawn!"

Shortly after the album's release, John sends Aunt Mimi a silver box from Cartier's with a pearl necklace and matching brooch. Inside the box, there is an engraved message which reads: "Double Fantasy – Christmas 1980 – NYC – John and Yoko". After receiving the present, Mimi rings John at the Dakota and tells him: "You're daft!" But John just laughs, saying: "Go on Mimi, spoil yourself . . . just for a change."

Tuesday November 18
🍎 George has a 4pm meeting at the London offices of Frere Cholmeley, the solicitors who represent Apple Corps.

Wednesday November 19 (until Tuesday November 25)
🍎 In England, as scheduled, Ringo joins George for the *Can't Fight Lightning* recording sessions at Friar Park in Henley-on-Thames, where they record the basic guitar and drum tracks on a song that will later form the basis of George's track 'All Those Years Ago'.

Friday November 21
🍎 John, wearing a black beret, and Yoko are photographed walking through Central Park. They return there for more pictures on November 26.

Wednesday November 26
🍎 For the second time in a week, John and Yoko return to Central Park for more pictures. This time they are filmed walking around the park by ABC News for their programme *20/20*. Yoko also arranges for this footage to be re-edited and used in additional scenes for the promotional film to accompany the single '(Just Like) Starting Over'. Unfortunately, this does not happen and, in early 1981, the film will reappear accompanying the song 'Woman'. (Further, unscreened, excerpts appear later in the 1988 film *Imagine: John Lennon*.) Later the couple attend the Sperone Gallery in the Soho area of New York, where a large white bedroom has been specially created for the couple to be filmed undressing, kissing and simulating sex on a bed. (Clips from this are first seen in the video for 'Walking On Thin Ice', premiered in January 1981 at a New York nightclub.)

🍎 "Rockshow . . . Now The Movie . . . Rockshow . . . See The Beatles' Classics . . . McCartney's Greatest Hits . . . All New Sight And Sound Experience. Paul McCartney. Wings – *Rockshow*." – *Rockshow* Film Trailer, November 1980.

Later this evening, the Wings live concert film *Rockshow*, consisting of film shot at the Wings Seattle concert on June 10, 1976, premieres at the Ziegfeld Theater in New York.

Neither Paul nor Linda is present. (The European premiere takes place in the UK on April 8, 1981– see entry.)

🍎 While Paul's latest venture is premiering in town, Ringo and Barbara fly into New York's Kennedy Airport, then head for the Plaza Hotel, where they have arranged to meet John and Yoko. Although a one hour meeting was scheduled, the evening goes so well that they end up staying together almost five hours. At the conclusion of the evening, John agrees to appear on Ringo's *Can't Fight Lightning* album, and a date is arranged for Wednesday January 14, 1981. Reports suggest that John will also join in on Paul's Montserrat recording sessions, which are scheduled to begin on Monday February 2, 1981.

Thursday November 27
🍎 The day after the premiere of the Wings film *Rockshow*, Paul and Linda appear, live by satellite from their Sussex farmhouse, on the ABC TV breakfast show *Good Morning America*, where they are interviewed by the regular host Dan Hartman. During the 10-minute feature, which commences at 7:46am on Thanksgiving Day, Paul is asked whether or not he still enjoys performing 'Yesterday', and the McCartneys reveal that they "have no nanny, Linda takes care of the children and we live in a ridiculously small house with four kids in two bedrooms!" Mysteriously, the lights in their Rye farmhouse keep going out.

Hartman asks Paul about John's apparent resentment towards him, inquiring: "Do you know why?"

Paul: "I don't know. I can guess and stuff. I actually keep a bit quiet now because anything I say he gets a bit resentful of. It's a weird one. I don't quite know why he thinks like that. I really just shut up these days . . . It's the best policy, David." (This final half of Paul's speech is said, somewhat spookily, in near darkness due to the power fluctuations.)

🍎 In New York, Ringo and Barbara are pictured leaving a local restaurant.

Friday November 28
🍎 As part of a legal deposition for Apple Corps against the producers of the *Beatlemania* stage show, John states today that: "I and the three other former Beatles have plans to stage a reunion concert," an event to be filmed and included as the finale to *The Long And Winding Road,* an official Beatles produced documentary to be released in the mid-Eighties. (John's deposition will not be made public until the case is settled on June 4, 1986 – see entry.)

🍎 Paul and Denny join George Martin at his AIR London studios to resume work on the next Wings album. The sessions are scheduled to run until the middle of December.

🍎 Ringo and Barbara fly out from New York and head for the Compass Point Studios in Los Angeles to resume work on the album *Can't Fight Lightning.*

Sunday November 30
🍎 The photographer Allan Tannenbaum visits John and Yoko at the Dakota to show them prints and slides from their last two sessions with him.

🍎 Ringo, along with Harry Nilsson and engineer Paul Jarvis, spends time at the Compass Point Studios listening to the previous *Can't Fight Lightning* session tapes, recorded at the Super Bear studios in France between July 11 and July 21.

December
🍎 From New York, John and Yoko send Aunt Mimi a Christmas card, which reads: "Happy Christmas and a brand new year. We wish you health! Wealth!? Wisdom???! And the time to enjoy it! Love John, Yoko, Sean."

Monday December 1
🍎 At the Compass Point Studios, recordings resume on Ringo's album *Can't Fight Lightning* where he records his vocals for the title track.

Tuesday December 2
🍎 At Compass Point Studios, Ringo, along with his engineer Paul Jarvis, spends time mixing tracks intended for the *Can't Fight Lightning* album. Further mixing takes place on Wednesday December 3.

Wednesday December 3

🍎 A local New York paper *Soho News* publishes a front-page story on Yoko entitled "Yoko Only". John loves this title so much that he decides that this will be the title for Yoko's next record release, to include the track 'Walking On Thin Ice', currently in production at the Hit Factory. Meanwhile, John and Yoko agree to lend their support to a San Francisco demonstration in aid of Japanese workers employed by local food importers who are on strike for better wages, a protest scheduled to take place on December 13. During the late afternoon, *Rolling Stone* photographer Anne Liebovitz visits the Lennons at their Dakota apartment to take photos for the magazine. This evening, at the Hit Factory, Yoko records her master vocal for the track 'Walking On Thin Ice'. John, alongside Jack Douglas, supervises the recordings.

🍎 At Friar Park, another 16mm film is delivered. This time, it's the 1933 musical *42nd Street*, starring Ruby Keeler, Dick Powell and Ginger Rogers. (The print is returned to the British Film Institute in London on Monday December 8.)

Thursday December 4

🍎 The album *The McCartney Interview,* featuring the interview with Paul by Vic Carbarini recorded in May for the *Musician* magazine, is released in America. (The UK release takes place on February 23, 1981.)

🍎 Early this morning, Andy Peebles and BBC producer Paul Williams arrive in New York to carry out their interview with David Bowie for Radio One. Then, with the assistance of WEA Records in Britain and Geffen Records in New York, Peebles and Williams manage to arrange an interview with John and Yoko, which is set for six o'clock on the evening of Saturday December 6, at the Hit Factory. Meanwhile, still in New York, the evening sessions at the Hit Factory continue, with John recording the guitar and keyboard tracks for Yoko's track 'Walking On Thin Ice'.

🍎 At the Compass Point Studios in North Hollywood, Ringo records his vocals for the new version of 'Back Off Boogaloo'.

Friday December 5

🍎 At the start of the day, John begins planning his return to England, an event Aunt Mimi recalls: "He rang and said he was looking out of a window in New York, looking at the docks and ships and wondering whether any of them were going to Liverpool. It made him homesick. He was coming home. He was coming here to Poole, Dorset, and going to Liverpool." John requested that Mimi send him his old school tie. Following the conversation, Mimi begins preparing a bedroom for John to stay in during his visit.

Later in the day at the Dakota, Andy Peebles and Paul Williams of BBC Radio One meet Yoko to outline the following evening's interview with John. Then later, to accompany the snaps of John from December 3, Jonathan Cott visits the Dakota to interview John for *Rolling Stone* magazine. The interview resumes at the Hit Factory where John is currently remixing Yoko's tracks 'Open Your Box', 'Kiss Kiss Kiss' and 'Every Man Has A Woman Who Loves Him' for an EP, now provisionally titled *Yoko Only*. John's interview with Jonathan Cott continues until 4am on the morning of December 6 while Yoko is asleep on the couch in the studio. A fourth track for the EP, 'Walking On Thin Ice', is still not yet concluded, but work on that is scheduled to resume on Monday December 8. (Excerpts of John's interview with Cott will later appear on *The Lost Lennon Tapes* American radio series.)

🍎 In North Hollywood, this period of *Can't Fight Lightning* sessions are concluded and Ringo flies out to the Bahamas to join Barbara on holiday. (The sessions are scheduled to reconvene on Wednesday January 14, 1981.)

🍎 George continues recording at his Friar Park Studios.

🍎 Mark Chapman arrives back in New York and immediately begins looking for somewhere to stay.

Saturday December 6

🍎 *Playboy* magazine, featuring the first part of John and Yoko's interview from September, reaches the magazine stands. Meanwhile at the Hit Factory, John gives another lengthy interview today, this time to the BBC Radio One disc jockey Andy Peebles.

John: "I love *Fawlty Towers*. I'd like to be in that, you know. Part of me would sooner have been a comedian. I just don't have the guts to stand up and do it, but I'd love to be in *Monty Python* rather than The Beatles. *Fawlty Towers* is the greatest show I've seen in years . . .

"I can go right out of this door now and go in a restaurant. You know how great that is? Or go to the movies? I mean, people come and ask for autographs or say 'Hi', but they don't bug you . . ."

Andy finds John in a most optimistic mood and is keen to talk further, so the session continues into the early hours of Sunday December 7, at New York's Mr. Chow's restaurant. (The three and a quarter hour interview later forms the five-hour BBC radio special and book, entitled *The Lennon Tapes*. On November 12, 1990, the interview is released in the UK on an official BBC CD entitled *John And Yoko – The Interview*.)

🍎 Mark Chapman checks into the YMCA on 63rd Street and then heads again for the Dakota building. On his way, he drops by a record store to buy John and Yoko's latest album *Double Fantasy*.

Sunday December 7

🍎 After spending parts of yesterday reading the interview, Yoko phones interviewer David Sheff of *Playboy* magazine to tell him she is pleased with the results of the interview and that John is also pleased and "excited" with the piece. This evening, John rings his Aunt Mimi at her bungalow in Poole, Dorset, and informs her: "I am coming to England and I'm going to Liverpool."

🍎 In the seclusion of his Friar Park mansion, George spends his time recording the track 'Dream Away', intended for the closing credits of the Handmade film *The Time Bandits*. (Ultimately, this track will also appear on his 1982 album *Gone Troppo*.)

🍎 Mark Chapman checks into the relatively expensive ($65 a night) Sheraton Hotel, from where he takes another trip to the Dakota building. He purchases a copy of the January 1981 issue of *Playboy* magazine, which features the lengthy interview with John and, ironically, a set of nude pictures of Barbara Bach who the following year will become Mrs Ringo Starr. On Chapman's back is a rucksack, which contains 14 hours of Beatles music on audio cassette.

Monday December 8

🍎 In the UK, a short excerpt from Andy Peebles interview with John and Yoko on December 6 is transmitted at approximately 8:15am during the Dave Lee Travis show, where the Lennons plug their interview with Andy Peebles, send an exclusive Christmas message to all the BBC Radio One listeners and announce that they "will be coming back to England on the QE2". (This is a unique recording and will *not* feature in the 1981 *Lennon Tapes* Radio One series.) Later, a two minute excerpt appears during the *Andy Peebles Live From New York* show, broadcast on BBC Radio One between 10:32 and 11:30am (New York time: 5:32–6:30am). The song 'Happy Christmas (War Is Over)' accompanies the feature.

In New York, John begins his day shortly before 7:30am (local time) by having breakfast at La Fortuna's and then, at 9am, visiting his local barbers, where his hair is cut into a Fifties style, with a quiff reminiscent of his Beatle days in Hamburg. He returns to the Dakota around 9:45am where, shortly before 10am, Dave Sholin, Laurie Kaye, Ron Hummel and Bert Keane interview John and Yoko, in their Dakota office for an RKO Radio special.

During the lengthy conversation, John remarks: "I was saying to someone the other day, there's only been two artists I've ever worked with for more than a one night stand, as it were. That's Paul McCartney and Yoko Ono. I think that's a pretty damn good choice. As a talent scout, I've done pretty damn well."

Later, he adds: "Maybe in the Sixties we were all naive . . . the thing the Sixties did was show us the possibility and the responsibility that we all had. It wasn't the answer, it just gave us a glimpse of the possibility . . ."

On his relationship with Yoko: "We've been together now longer than The Beatles, do you know that? People always think in terms that John and Yoko just got together and then The Beatles split. We've been together longer than The Beatles!"

John dedicates the album *Double Fantasy* to: "The people who grew up with me. I'm saying 'Here I am now, how are you? How's your relationship going? Did you get through it all? Weren't the Seventies a drag, you know?' Here we are, well, let's try to make the Eighties good, because it's still up to us to make what we can of it. It's not out of our control. I still believe in love, I still believe in peace, I still believe in positive thinking."

Following the 90-minute interview, at just after midday, *Rolling Stone* photographer Annie Liebovitz arrives at their apartment for another photo session, from 2 to 3:30pm.

(Many of these shots appear in the January 22, 1981, edition of *Rolling Stone* magazine, which memorably features, as John had suggested for its cover, the nude shot of John lying across the fully clothed Yoko. This was the last photo taken of the couple together.)

At approximately 4pm, John, Yoko and the RKO team leave the Dakota. The limousine, arranged by the Lennons to pick them up and take them to the Hit Factory, has not arrived so instead they hitch a ride to the studios in the car belonging to the RKO team. Before doing so, John is photographed by Paul Goresh autographing a copy of *Double Fantasy* for Mark Chapman. During the evening session, John again phones Mimi in England. She remembers: "He was so happy, laughing and joking and looking forward to coming over to England . . . it was like a new John." David Geffen drops by to inform John, Yoko and Jack Douglas that *Double Fantasy* has just gone gold, after its first two weeks of release.

At approximately 10:30pm, following four hours of work on Yoko's recording of 'Walking On Thin Ice', John, wearing a new leather jacket he'd bought at the Gap store a week earlier, turns to his producer Jack Douglas and says: "Hey, shall we call it a night? I'm bushed. We'll be back in the morning. Yoko and I want to stop and have a bite to eat on the way home." As Yoko later recalls: "Although we had planned to stop and eat at Stage Deli, we decided not to. We went straight home instead. We were going to check on Sean and then go out for a bite." Sean had been left at the Dakota with Fred Seaman's wife Helen.

On this unusually warm December evening, the streets outside their Dakota residence were almost deserted. John emerges from their limousine and, a couple of paces ahead of Yoko, strolls towards the archway entrance leading into the Dakota's large courtyard. They are surprised to see a man standing in the shadows who says: "Mr. Lennon". The man has a gun and, taking up a combat stance, he fires five shots into John from his .38-calibre Charter Arms five-shot revolver. Yoko remembers: "I didn't realise at first that John had been shot. He kept walking and then he fell and I saw blood." The time is 10:52pm New York time, 3.52am London time.

Aside from Yoko, there are four witnesses to this terrible deed: the Dakota doorman, an elevator operator, a New York taxi driver and a passenger he has just dropped off. John struggles towards the Dakota entrance and manages to climb six short steps to a room used by the concierge. Yoko rushes to his side and cradles his head in her arms. He whispers to her: "Help me!" She begins to scream hysterically, "He's been shot, he's been shot. Somebody come quickly."

The Dakota doorman, Jay Hastings, who had been scheduled to give Yoko a red Plexiglas rain hat, left as a present from an avant-garde clothes designer earlier in the day, recalls the evening: "I had been reading a magazine shortly before 11pm when I heard several shots outside the office, and then the sound of shattering glass. I heard someone coming up the office stairs and John stumbled in, with a horrible confused look on his face. Yoko followed, screaming, 'John's been shot, John's been shot.' At first, I thought it was a crazy joke. But when I saw him collapse to the floor, scattering the cassette tapes of his final sessions that he'd been holding in his arms, I knew it wasn't."

Hastings immediately triggers a police alarm and rushes to help John, gently removing his glasses. Next Hastings takes off his blue Dakota uniform jacket and places it over John's motionless body. Blood is pouring freely from John's mouth. Hastings whispers to John: "It's okay John, you'll be all right."

The first policemen to react to Hastings and the wave of 911 emergency calls, are Officers Steve Spiro and Peter Cullen from the New York Police department who were cruising in their squad car at Broadway and 72nd Street. Their first action at the scene of the crime is to arrest the murderer. "Put your hands up!" they tell Hastings, who is kneeling, covered in blood. "Not him," the other Dakota doorman insists. "He works here. He's the one," he says, pointing to Mark David Chapman who is standing to the left of the archway on West 72nd Street, reading a copy of J.D. Salinger's book *Catcher In The Rye*. The gun had been thrown away, coming to rest in nearby bushes alongside the signed copy of *Double Fantasy* Chapman had obtained earlier in the evening. Spiro and Cullen perform on Chapman the "spreadeagle and patting down" ritual against the Dakota's elegant stone facade. Chapman evidently prepared himself for his arrest. "Don't hurt me. Stay with me," he pleads. "No one's going to hurt you," Cullen says. "Just turn around and place your hands against that wall, your feet apart." Following a search, Cullen says to Spiro, "He's clean, cuff him Steve." The firearm, has been retrieved from the bushes by the elevator operator and is handed over to Spiro. The search of Chapman's person yields just keys, the copy of *Catcher In The Rye* and a wallet, which contains $2,000 in cash. Chapman is heard to say: "I've got a big man inside me and I've got a little man inside me. The little man is the man who pulled the trigger!"

By now, more policemen from the 20th Precinct station house on West 82nd Street have appeared at the scene. Arriving on the heels of Messrs Spiro and Cullen are Police Officers Bill Gamble and James Moran who, seeing that Spiro and Cullen have the situation with the suspect under control, race to John's side. Against Yoko's wishes, Gamble turns over John's body to determine the severity of his injuries and asks: "What is your name?" John hesitantly replies, "Lennon". Due to the obvious seriousness of John's condition, Gamble informs Moran that they cannot afford to wait for an ambulance and decide instead to take John to hospital in their car. Moran grasps John's legs and Gamble grips Lennon by the underarms and they carry him in the crooks of their elbows to their parked car, placing him on the back seat. Gamble takes up a position kneeling at his side while Moran takes to the driver's seat, setting off the roof emergency light panel and sirens. At a speed of 50mph, the car travels through the streets en route to the nearest emergency hospital, St. Luke's Roosevelt Hospital on West 59th Street, a distance of fourteen blocks, the equivalent of more than half a mile.

Gamble keeps up a conversation to keep John conscious. "Are you sure you're John Lennon?"

"I am," he says, becoming increasingly weak.

"How do you feel?" Gamble continues.

"I'm in pain," John replies.

At approximately 11pm (ET), the event reaches the American news feeds. The report reads: "A man, tentatively identified as John Lennon, has been shot."

Moran, meanwhile, has radioed ahead to the hospital to arrange for a rolling stretcher to be in position by the time they arrive. Following their car is another police car, driven by Officer Anthony Palmer, which contains Yoko. She is hysterical and keeps on screaming, "Tell me it's not true . . . please tell me it's not true." When the first car arrives, in less than three minutes, John's body is moved into emergency surgery. Among the first physicians to administer treatment to him is Dr. Stephan Lynn, the medical director of the hospital's emergency room. In the hospital, Yoko puts a phone call through to their Dakota apartment to check that Sean is OK. After coming off the phone she is told that despite all the attempts to save John, including massive blood transfusions and surgical procedures by Lynn and an army of highly trained staff, John has been pronounced dead. "He never stood a chance," he sympathetically tells Yoko. "Nothing we were able to do could revive your husband. We believe the first bullet killed him. It ripped through John's chest causing irreparable damage to a major artery." In complete shock, Yoko asks him hysterically: "Do you mean that he is sleeping?"

John was officially pronounced dead at 11:07pm. Yoko was told at 11:15pm.

The news spreads fast and America first hears about John's murder on WABC TV's *Monday Night Football*, ironically, a show on which John had appeared live one day short of six years ago, where he was seen being interviewed by Howard Cosell. It is Cosell himself who is faced with the unenviable task of revealing the news of John's tragic death when he picks up the news feed originating from the WABC TV station. Cosell recalls: "Near the end of the *Monday Night Football* broadcast, my producer, Bob Goodrich said, 'Roone Arledge just called and told me that John Lennon has been shot and rushed to the hospital. We're waiting for details from ABC News.' I couldn't believe it. Goodrich then told me he was dead on arrival. I was devastated. We were in the midst of a tied football game that was about to go into overtime and I was wrestling with the problem of breaking the news on TV, thinking that, even in this sick, sports-obsessed country, this is far more important than any goddamn football game will ever be. I went on the air and said that it was just a game, and I felt compelled to tell this story."

Back at the Hit Factory, Jack Douglas, still at work on John and Yoko's track 'Walking On Thin Ice', is informed of the tragedy by his wife at 11.35pm. He immediately goes into a state of shock, which, according to Douglas, lasts six months. Douglas immediately recalls some strange things John said in the control room during their final session. He decides it best that the tapes of the studio banter between him and John this evening be wiped. (To this day, Jack Douglas refuses to say exactly what John said to him on this fateful night.)

Tuesday December 9
In New York . . .

✝ At 12:10am, back at the Roosevelt hospital, Dr. Stephan Lynn, the director of the emergency room service and the man responsible for trying to save John, faces the press in a room adjacent to the emergency room. Facing a non-stop strobe light of whirring flash bulbs, Lynn, in his spotless white lab coat, begins: "John Lennon . . . (pausing for twenty seconds in order to regain his composure) . . . John Lennon was brought to the emergency room of the St. Luke's Roosevelt Hospital this evening, shortly before 11pm. He was dead on arrival. Extensive resuscitative efforts were made, but in spite of transfusions and many procedures, he could not be resuscitated. He had multiple gunshot wounds in his chest, in his left arm and in his back. There were seven wounds in his body. I don't know exactly how many bullets there were. I'm certain that he was dead at the moment that the first shots hit his body."

A reporter asks him: "Did you tell Yoko that Mr. Lennon was dead? What did she say?"

Lynn replies: "I did tell his wife that he was dead. She was . . . most distraught at the time and found it quite hard to accept. She is no longer in the hospital."

As the press conference continues, Yoko quietly leaves the Roosevelt hospital to be escorted back to the Dakota by David Geffen, Jack Douglas and the police. A crowd of nearly two hundred has by now gathered outside the apartment block. Within an hour, that figure has reached almost six hundred, all of them chanting Beatles and John Lennon songs, many of them weeping uncontrollably. By now, New York Police had erected wooden barriers in front of the entrance to the building.

At 2:00am, at the Twentieth Precinct on West 82nd Street, the Chief of Detectives, James T. Sullivan, holds another press conference. He begins: "We asked you to come here so we could give you a briefing on what we know at this point in the homicide of John Lennon. We have arrested Mark David Chapman of 55 South Kukui Street, Hawaii, for the homicide of John Lennon. Born May 10, 1955, he has apparently been in New York City for about a week staying briefly at the YMCA. I'm not sure which one." Sullivan concludes by saying: "Mark Chapman behaved very calmly when he was arrested." The final question from the press was answered at 2:24am.

At approximately 3:00am (Eastern Time), with Yoko watching the constant television news reports on the tragedy, Elliot Mintz arrives at the Dakota to comfort her. She then dictates to David Geffen a personal statement to be read out later in the morning. Shortly after 3:30am, she rings Paul at his home in Sussex to tell him the distressing news. At 6:00am, a caller from California rings the main office at their Dakota apartment, saying: "I am flying to New York to finish the job Chapman started. I'm going to get Yoko Ono." Police at the Los Angeles Airport intercepts the call.

At 7:00am ET, Sean wakes up and, for 24 hours, he is not told anything about what has just happened.

Geffen Records release Yoko's first statement, which reads: "There is no funeral for John. Later in the week we will set the time for a silent vigil to pray for his soul. We invite you to participate from wherever you are at the time. We thank you for the many flowers sent to John. But in the future, instead of flowers, please consider sending donations in his name to the Spirit Foundation Inc, which is John's personal charitable foundation. He would have appreciated it very much. John loved and prayed for the human race. Please pray the same for him. Love Yoko and Sean."

The tragedy is naturally the headline on every major TV and radio station across the States. Richard Lester, director of The Beatles' films *A Hard Day's Night* and *Help!*, appears live to talk about the tragedy on the NBC TV breakfast show *Today*. He manages to avoid speaking about John's death in great detail, instead saying: "It seems appalling to me that all this time no one has spoken about the problem of people having guns in America, and the problem that people can just shoot a man on the street . . ."

At 10:30am, an autopsy is carried out on John's body. Yoko is informed that because of John's death one fan has already committed suicide. She immediately issues a statement requesting fans not to turn against themselves in their anguish. Shortly before this, Ringo and Barbara arrive at the Dakota to comfort Yoko and play with Sean, their entrance to the building blocked by hundreds of still hysterical weeping fans.

Yoko records a piano demo of the song 'I Don't Know Why' at the Dakota before going out for dinner with Elliot Mintz and David Geffen.

In England . . .

"Rush . . . New York, Monday – Former Beatle John Lennon Was Shot And Killed Tonight At His Home In New York City, Police Said." Reuters News Copy – 04:55am.

The news of John's death reaches England early in the morning. Disbelief mingles with anger as the country instantly becomes a nation in mourning. The tragedy is the major news headline and the talking point throughout the world. TV and radio stations reschedule their programmes to transmit tributes and non-stop Lennon and Beatles music. These include the *Simon Bates Golden Hour* show (BBC Radio 1, broadcast between 9:32 and 10:30am) and the *Andy Peebles Live From New York* show (11:32 to 12:30pm), which is hastily re-titled *Andy Peebles Tribute To John Lennon*, and features the host, who had arrived back in London from New York at breakfast time, in a state of total shock.

⏺ At Friar Park, George is the first of the ex-Beatles to be told of John's shooting when, at 5am, he receives a phone call from his sister Louise in America. Hearing the news and believing it to be nothing more than a flesh wound, he goes back to sleep. When he awakes a few hours later, he immediately issues a statement to the press from his Friar Park office. His statement, in full, reads: "After all we went through together I had and still have great love and respect for him. I am shocked and stunned. To rob life is the ultimate robbery in life. This perpetual encroachment on other people's space is taken to the limit with the use of a gun. It is an outrage that people can take other people's lives when they obviously haven't got their own lives in order."

Later, at his private Friar Park Studios, George attempts to do more work on the track 'Dream Away' but, overcome with remorse, he aborts the session early and retires to the living quarters of his Henley mansion.

⏺ In Poole, Dorset, Aunt Mimi wakes up after hearing the words "John Lennon" on the BBC World Service radio broadcast. Almost immediately, the phone rings. It is Neil Aspinall, who asks her: "Mimi, have you heard?" She naturally asks: "What are you talking about?" Before Neil can answer, he hangs up. Mimi heard him crying. Her attention is redrawn towards the radio broadcast, from which she learns the shocking news.

⏺ Shortly after 8:45am, while Linda is taking the children to school, Paul rings his brother Mike in Liverpool to inform him of John's death. As Mike recalls in the *Liverpool Echo* newspaper: "Paul was too distressed to talk properly. He just said, 'Keep sending the good vibes down from Liverpool to help him through the day.' It is going to be a busy day for him and he is very, very upset."

At 11:29am, as Paul attempts to leave his Sussex farmhouse, he is greeted by an army of reporters who have been camping outside his home since the news of John's death broke. Still in a complete state of shock, Paul has this to offer: "I can't take it at the moment. John was a great man who'll be remembered for his unique contributions to art, music and peace. He is going to be missed by the whole world."

Paul is driven to London where he joins Denny Laine and George Martin at AIR Studios, where they spend the afternoon recording, to the best of their ability, a small piece of the track 'Rainclouds'. During the afternoon, Paul telephones Yoko at the Dakota to offer his further condolences.

⏺ Meanwhile, a team from the nation's media has gathered outside the studio, all eager to obtain Paul's further reactions. When he finally leaves the studio in the early evening, he is unable to express his feelings towards John's tragic death. Finally confronted, he offhandedly remarks to the reporters: "It's a drag, innit?" The comment is sadly mistaken as being flippant.

⏺ During the morning, Ringo and Barbara, still on holiday in the Bahamas, receive a phone call from Barbara's daughter back in England who tells them that John has been hurt. Instantly dismissing it as exaggeration by the media, she rings through again, informing them that John was, in fact, dead. Ringo then phones his ex-wife Maureen to tell her the news. By coincidence, John's first wife Cynthia hears the news from Ringo at the same time as she is staying with Maureen at her house. Cynthia immediately rings her and John's son Julian at their home in North Wales and informs him of the news, telling him not to leave the house or speak to reporters until she returns. Ringo and Barbara, along with a bodyguard, immediately charter a jet to fly them to New York where they join Yoko and Sean at the Dakota, entering the premises through the back door to avoid the huge throng of people who have gathered at the front of the building. Before they enter the Dakota Ringo calls Yoko from a payphone to alert her of their imminent arrival. As they enter the Lennons apartment, Yoko requests that only Ringo come in but Ringo insists, "Where I go, Barbara goes too!" When Ringo and Barbara eventually leave the Dakota they are forced to face the crowd of near hysterical Beatles fans. As they do so, the fans begin reaching out to Ringo, attempting to touch him. This causes Ringo and Barbara great distress, as he recalls: "I was disgusted, not with the idea that they were there, but with the fact that you had a lot of dummies in the crowd all shouting at Yoko and saying, 'Come to the windows'. She didn't want to deal with it at the time you know, the very next day after

John's death. I also didn't want to hear people saying how much they loved The Beatles. I was there for a friend, not because he was a member of a pop group." As Ringo leaves the Dakota, John's first son Julian arrives, just off a plane from his home in North Wales.

🍎 Paul, meanwhile, retreats to his farm in Sussex where he will quietly celebrate Christmas and the New Year with his family. He will not reappear in public again until February 1 next year.

🍎 UK TV schedules are hastily rearranged to broadcast special tributes to John. BBC1 broadcasts (from 6:00pm) an extended *Nationwide* tribute, hosted by Frank Bough, and The Beatles' 1965 film *Help!* (between 7:31 and 8:59pm). While on BBC2 (between 9:01 and 9:29pm), the Radio One DJ Anne Nightingale presents a special *Old Grey Whistle Test* tribute programme, featuring as special guests the DJs Andy Peebles and Paul Gambaccini, and journalist Michael Watts. Towards the end of the show, an emotionally charged Anne Nightingale reveals that "Paul [McCartney] has just phoned me and said to give you a message which is 'on behalf of Yoko and George and Ringo and Linda, to say thank everybody for their support since this tragedy. It's an incredible drag, and I want to thank you all so very much'." Later in the evening, the same station designates the majority of their *Newsnight* programme to a review of John's life and career. Over on the ITV network, Granada quickly put together a 40-minute tribute programme called simply *Lennon*, which is hosted by Tony Wilson and features among its guests John and Yoko's former assistant Anthony Fawcett, Johnny Hamp, journalist Richard Williams and, in a filmed interview, Beatles' biographer Hunter Davies.

🍎 The picture taken by the photographer Paul Goresh of John signing the *Double Fantasy* album for Chapman will make over $100,000 in sales. The *New York Daily News* paid Goresh $2,000 for full rights to the picture and then joined forces with UPI (United Pictures International) to handle the world syndication.

🍎 In West Germany, orders for *Double Fantasy* begin rising from 10,000 to 50,000 a day. In East Berlin, the radio station DDR-1 broke from its usual ban against the playing of Western rock music by airing a ninety-minute programme featuring nothing but Beatles music.

🍎 From this day forward, all around the world, the image, legend and devotion surrounding The Beatles will never be quite the same.

Wednesday December 10

🍎 John's tragic murder continues to dominate the pages of the morning papers, more so today because the timing of the murder left little time for newspapers to prepare material the previous day. The *Daily Mirror* sums it all up perfectly when they print on their front page: "Death Of A Hero".

🍎 When Sean awakes at 7am (New York Time), Yoko gently informs him what has happened to John. Once dressed, she takes him to the spot where John was killed. Sean naturally asks why this happened. Yoko has no answer. She immediately prepares another press statement. On Lenono, Studio One, 1 West 72nd Street, New York, New York 10023, headed note paper, Yoko and Sean's statement reads as follows:

"I told Sean what happened. I showed him the picture of his father on the cover of the paper and explained the situation. I took Sean to the spot where John lay after he was shot. Sean wanted to know why the person shot John if he liked John. I explained that he was probably a confused person. Sean said he would find out if he was confused or if he really had meant to kill John. I said that was up to the court. He asked what court – a tennis court or a basketball court? That's how Sean used to talk with his father. They were buddies. John would have been proud of Sean if he had heard this. Sean cried later. He also said, 'Now daddy is part of God. I guess when you die you become much more bigger because you're part of everything.'

"I don't have much more to add to Sean's statement. The silent vigil will take place December 14th at 2pm for ten minutes.

"Our thoughts will be with you."

"Love,

"Yoko & Sean

"Dec. 10 '80, N.Y.C."

Later, from the seclusion of her Dakota apartment, Yoko arranges for John's body to be cremated at 2pm (New York Time) today at the Ferncliff crematorium in suburban Hartsdale, north of the city in Westchester County. The cremation is captured on film, and offensive photos of John lying dead on a mortuary slab are sold to a New York newspaper for $10,000. At 9pm this evening (New York Time) Doug MacDougall of the Ferncliff Mortuary delivers John's ashes to Yoko in an urn. Reports later suggest that these are either placed beneath Yoko's bed, on John's side, or sent to "somewhere in England".

In Liverpool, the *Liverpool Echo* newspaper begins printing the series "The Magic Of John Lennon".

Thursday December 11
🍎 The Lennons' personal assistant Fred Seaman requests to be temporarily relieved from his duties at the Dakota. In Florida, a 16-year-old girl takes an overdose of pills, while in Utah a man shoots himself. Both were overcome with remorse following John's death. This prompts Yoko to phone the *New York Daily News*, with a statement that she hopes will stop others from committing suicide.
🍎 At Friar Park, George cancels another recording session.

Friday December 12 & Saturday December 13
🍎 For two straight nights, Yoko joins Jack Douglas at the Record Plant recording studios working on a strange collage featuring John's music and voice. It was, for Yoko, an "exercise in emotional exorcism" but for Douglas, it was "like a funeral service".
🍎 The *Liverpool Echo* (December 12) publishes a tribute to John by Bill Harry entitled "He Only Wanted To Be Himself". The touching piece concludes: "So many dreams were killed with him, so many potential rock masterpieces lost forever, all speculation about a Beatles' reunion finally laid to rest. God bless you, John. We all loved you and will never forget you."

Sunday December 14
🍎 Crowds ranging in size from a few dozen to tens of thousands gather in cities throughout the world to observe a day of mourning for John. At Yoko's request, ten minutes of silence are observed at all of these locations at 2pm EST (7pm UK time). During this period, many radio stations around the world cease broadcasting. Work ceases at Abbey Road Studios in London, where a large crowd has gathered, and studio engineers pump John's music into the car park. Two of the largest gatherings are in New York's Central Park and in Liverpool, where Sam Leach, one of The Beatles' first promoters, leads 25,000 mourners in a seven-hour tribute to John Lennon outside Liverpool's St. George's Hall. Played at the emotional gathering are pre-recorded tapes by Yoko Ono, the boxer Muhammad Ali and the former Prime Minister Harold Wilson. The ceremony ends with the ten-minute silent vigil as requested by Yoko. The Central Park event is covered live by ABC *Eyewitness News* and features interviews with Sid Bernstein and the DJ Cousin Brucie. At the conclusion of the worldwide vigil, Yoko releases the following statement: "Bless you for your tears and prayers. I saw John smiling in the sky. I saw sorrow changing into clarity. I saw all of us becoming one mind. Thank you. Love, Yoko."

Friday December 19
🍎 As part of their Christmas celebrations, a copy of the 1946 film *The Best Years Of Their Life*, starring Myrna Loy and Dana Andrews, is delivered to George at Friar Park. (The print is returned to the BFI on Monday December 22.)

Wednesday December 24
🍎 On Christmas Eve at the Dakota, Sean receives his final festive present from John, an Akita puppy he names Merry. Meanwhile, a gold watch inscribed to Sean from John and Yoko, as well as various other Christmas presents, mysteriously vanish from their apartment.

Saturday December 27
🍎 As the world continues to mourn John's death, his single '(Just Like) Starting Over' and the album *Double Fantasy* both reach number one in the American charts. (They will reach the same position in the UK charts on January 3, 1981.)

"It's more exciting for me to talk about my records than Beatles' records, 'cos we've been talking about them for twenty years."

– Ringo

January
 To escape from the morgue-like surroundings at the Dakota, Yoko packs Sean off to Palm Beach with his nanny. Yoko is now free to resume work on 'Walking On Thin Ice' with Jack Douglas at the Hit Factory. Meanwhile, John's famous psychedelically painted 1956 Bentley S1, previously donated to the Smithsonian Institute in Washington, is sold to an Arizona garage owner for $50,000.
 Due to his life as a tax exile in Monte Carlo, Ringo is only entitled to live six months a year in his rented house in Los Angeles.

Sunday January 4
 In England, the TV presentation of highlights from the *Kampuchea* concerts of December 26–29, 1979, entitled *Rock For Kampuchea,* is transmitted on certain regions of the ITV network and includes footage of Paul and Wings December 29 performance (see entry).

Monday January 5
 Liverpool City Councillors are told that in the two and a half years since the campaign to raise £40,000 to pay for a commemorative statue to The Beatles in Liverpool was started, no more than £300 has been banked.

Saturday January 10
 John's music continues to fill the UK singles charts with 'Imagine' reaching number one. (This version of the single was first released on October 24, 1975, in the UK and has never been deleted.) 'Happy Christmas (War Is Over)' is at number two while 'Give Peace A Chance' reaches number 33.

Monday January 12
 John's single 'Woman', backed with 'Beautiful Boys', performed by Yoko, is released in America. (The UK release takes place on January 16.) To coincide with its release, an interview with Yoko is published in the American *People* magazine. The piece, written by the *Playboy* reporter David Sheff, is entitled "Yoko – How She Is Holding Up", and features the sub-heading, "The eulogies ended, Yoko Ono faces the pain of life without John."

Wednesday January 14 (until Friday January 16)
 With a deep sense of sadness hanging over his head, Ringo reappears at the Cherokee Studios in Los Angeles to conclude the sessions for his *Can't Fight Lightning* album where he is again joined by Ronnie Wood of The Rolling Stones. Recordings resume on Tuesday January 20.

Thursday January 15
 A political party in San Paulo, Brazil, revokes plans for a square to be renamed *John Lennon Square.*

Friday January 16
 Yoko dispatches Fred Seaman off to England to deliver a copy of the 'Woman' promotional film to the BBC for transmission on the next edition of BBC1's *Top Of The Pops.* The clip, version one, is broadcast once only on Thursday January 22, on BBC1 between 7:25 and 8:04pm and is immediately brought back to Yoko in New York. Accompanying Seaman on his journey to England are copies of John's personal diaries between 1976 and 1980 to be presented, in accordance with John's will, to Julian.

Sunday January 18
 BBC Radio One begins broadcasting (between 4:00 and 5:00pm) the five-part radio series called *The Lennon Tapes,* centring around John's interview with Andy Peebles on December 6 last year. The book to accompany the series, also titled *The Lennon Tapes,* featuring a transcript of the interviews, is published by the BBC on February 6. On the same day, January 18, the *Sunday Times* newspaper publishes a special "Open Letter From Yoko Ono".

Tuesday January 20
❦ In the States, Yoko prepares for distribution today a second version of the 'Woman' promotional film, intended for a special one-off American TV screening.
❦ The final period of recordings (which continues until Thursday February 12) for the album *Can't Fight Lightning* sees Ringo complete the songs 'Dead Giveaway', 'Wake Up', 'Brandy', 'You Belong To Me' and 'Wrack My Brian'.

Wednesday January 28
❦ Meanwhile, in preparation for the upcoming Montserrat recording sessions with George Martin, Paul comes out of seclusion by arranging to have his musical equipment flown by Jumbo jet to Antigua.

Sunday February 1
❦ Paul reappears in public when he is seen arriving at George Martin's AIR Studios, on the island of Montserrat, to begin recording. The tracks he records on Montserrat will released on the albums *Tug Of War* and *Pipes Of Peace*.

Monday February 2 (until Tuesday March 3)
❦ Paul's Montserrat recording sessions begin, with George Martin as producer. These early sessions, on which Paul works with the English drummer Dave Mattacks, produce the following tracks: 'Somebody Who Cares', 'The Pound Is Sinking', 'Hey Hey' and further work on the track 'Rainclouds'.

Friday February 6
❦ In the UK, BBC Books publish *The Lennon Tapes,* the transcript of John's conversation with Andy Peebles from December 6 last year.

Sunday February 8
❦ In Montserrat, the highly respected bass guitarist Stanley Clarke arrives from Philadelphia to join Paul at the sessions.

Monday February 9
❦ A day of jamming takes place in Montserrat with Paul, Clarke and, on drums, Steve Gadd. (Paul's previous drummer Dave Mattacks had by now returned to England.)

Friday February 13
❦ At the Compass Point Studios in Los Angeles, California, the final mixes of *Can't Fight Lightning* take place, with ten out of the fifteen recorded tracks being selected to appear on the album.

Sunday February 15
❦ Ringo and Barbara arrive from Los Angeles to join Paul and George Martin at the Montserrat studios to assist with the recordings. Joining Ringo on his flight is his favourite drum kit which he had used during the recent *Can't Fight Lightning* sessions.

Monday February 16 & Tuesday February 17
❦ Recording sessions take place for the track 'Take It Away', featuring Ringo on his favourite drums.

Wednesday February 18
❦ Taking a break from recordings, Paul, Linda and the family are seen relaxing by a pool at their rented house in the West Indies.

Thursday February 19
❦ With his sessions now concluded, Ringo, along with Barbara, flies back to Los Angeles.

Friday February 20
❦ An old friend of The Beatles, Carl Perkins, joins Paul and George Martin on the island.
❦ In England, to cash in on John's death, the album *Hear The Beatles Tell All* is released. (The album was originally released in America on September 14, 1964.)

 In the UK, Yoko releases the single 'Walking On Thin Ice', the track John had been working on the night he died. The B-side, 'It Happened', originally recorded back in 1973 during the sessions for *Feeling The Space*, opens with dialogue between John and Yoko recorded on November 26, 1980, during the Central Park filming of the ABC *20/20* news programme and later used in the 'Woman' promotional film clip. Also today, at her Dakota apartment, Yoko gives her first interview since John's death to Chrissy Smith, a BBC New York producer, a selection of which is exclusively transmitted on the BBC Radio 4 programme *The World This Weekend* on Sunday February 22.

Saturday February 21 (until Wednesday February 25)
 Paul and Carl Perkins begin recording the track 'Get It', plus the unreleased song 'My Old Friend', as well as several other tracks, which include 'Honey Don't', 'Boppin' The Blues', 'Lend Me Your Comb', 'When The Saints Go Marching In', 'Cut Across Shorty' and 'Red Sails In The Sunset'.
 George is seen at his local Friar Park garage, filling up his car with his usual £20 worth of petrol.

Thursday February 26
 Stevie Wonder attends the sessions where, along with Paul, they record their co-written track 'What's That You're Doing?'

Friday February 27 & Saturday February 28
 Paul and Stevie spend time recording different versions of 'Ebony And Ivory'. (The sessions conclude in the early hours of March 1.)
 In America, on February 27, John's will, dated November 12, 1979, is published, revealing that he has left £2,522,317 gross. Experts predict that this figure represents only a fraction of John's true fortune, with conservative estimates putting it at over £125 million, a sum currently growing at £100,000 a day from worldwide record royalties alone. In selected cinemas across Indianapolis (from Friday February 27 until Sunday March 1), the Wings concert film *Rockshow* is playing in a special Miramax Films presentation which, amazingly enough, features The Beatles' 1970 film *Let It Be* as the support.
 In a New York court, on February 27, damages of $587,000 (£267,000) are awarded against George in the plagiarism trial over 'My Sweet Lord' resembling 'He's So Fine'.
 At the New York Metro Convention in Secaucus, New Jersey, the seventh annual *Beatlefest* convention takes place. (The event runs until Sunday March 1.)

March
 In London, rumours circulate in the music industry that a ten-track 1961 Cavern Club performance by The Beatles has been discovered. Within weeks, the supposedly "legendary" tape is revealed to be the January 1, 1962, Decca Records audition tape.

Tuesday March 3
 The sessions in Montserrat completed, Paul and Linda return to England and head for George Martin's AIR Studios in Oxford Street, London for additional recording. During a break from these sessions Paul plays bass for two hours in an adjacent AIR studio with The Michael Schenker Group, having been invited to do so by their drummer Cozy Powell.

Friday March 13
 The EP *The Elton John Band Featuring John Lennon And The Muscle Shoals Horns*, featuring live recordings from the November 28, 1974, concert at Madison Square Garden, is released as a 12" single in the UK. Meanwhile, John's single 'Watching The Wheels'/'Yes, I'm Your Angel', performed by Yoko, is released in America. (The UK release takes place on March 27.)

Monday March 16
 In England, George and Olivia spend the first of three nights at the Birmingham Metropole & Warwick NEC Hotel. On their departure on Thursday March 19, they pay a bill of £165.33.

Saturday March 21
 George, Olivia and Dhani depart from London's Heathrow Airport at 11:20am en route to Copenhagen, arriving at 14:05pm. They will return to London the following day, on Sunday March 22, arriving in England at 10:20am UK time.

Tuesday March 24
 In Chicago, Ringo holds a press conference to launch his forthcoming film, the United Artists comedy *Caveman*.

Sunday March 29
 Liverpool's Anglican Cathedral holds a memorial service to John. Local Conservative politicians boycott the event in protest.

Monday March 30
 The all-star album *Concerts For The People Of Kampuchea*, featuring Paul and Wings live on December 29, 1979, is released in America. (The UK release takes place on April 3.)
 In the UK, Elm Tree Books publish *Shout – The True Story Of The Beatles*, the result of three years of research by journalist Philip Norman. Promoted as a definitive biography of the group and serialised in the *Sunday Times*, Paul is not pleased with the book, and is quick to point out why: "What the book says about me being the great manipulator, simply isn't true! Nothing happened in The Beatles unless everyone wanted it to happen. But when there was a decision to be made, somebody had to say it out loud, and that usually turned out to be my job. I accepted it." Paul will later refer to the book as "Shite".
 George heads off to Rome with Olivia and Dhani, staying for one night at the Ergife Palace Hotel. They return to England the following day.

Tuesday March 31
 In America, Ringo and Barbara make their first television appearance since John's death in a pre-recorded 13-minute feature on the ABC TV show *The Barbara Walters Special*. During the show Ringo is seen in the recording studio teaching Barbara how to play the guitar, and announcing that they will marry this year. Ringo becomes emotional when Barbara Walters asks him about John's death, and he requests that the tape be turned off until he composes himself for the interview to continue. (Incidentally, during this programme, there is a discrepancy over the date as to when Ringo claims that he last saw John. On this show, he said it was on Saturday November 15, but in the *Stop And Smell The Roses* CD booklet, he claims it was Wednesday November 26, 1980.)

April
 Ringo has a disagreement with CBS Records, who distribute Portrait Records in America, and leaves the label. The *Can't Fight Lightning* album is subsequently abandoned and Ringo begins looking for another label. (Eventually he signs for RCA in Britain and Broadwalk in America, whereupon the album will become titled *Stop And Smell The Roses*.)
 In New York at the Hit Factory studios, working with Phil Spector, Yoko completes the recording of the album *Seasons Of Glass*. To coincide with the release, Yoko renames the *Lenono Music* publishing company *Ono Music*.
 George officially becomes a paid-up member of CND, the Campaign for Nuclear Disarmament. Also this month, at Jimmy Page's SOL Studio in Cookham, Berkshire, George, along with Page on guitar, assists Fleetwood Mac's drummer Mick Fleetwood recording his solo album.
 BBC Radio One DJ Mike Read plays a bootleg single of The Beatles 1962 performance of 'How Do You Do It?' at EMI's Abbey Road Studios on his breakfast show. To do so, he has obtained special permission from EMI.

Wednesday April 1
 In America, at the Los Angeles Superior Court, Ringo's former partner Nancy Andrews files a lawsuit against the former Beatle, claiming damages of $5 million and rights to half of the assets they bought while they were together.

Wednesday April 8

🍎 At 8:30pm, the European Charity premiere of the Wings concert film *Rockshow* takes place at London's Dominion Theatre in Tottenham Court Road, in the presence of the Earl and Countess of Snowdon. The event, in aid of the Snowdon Award scheme for physically handicapped children, is attended by a host of star celebrities including Mike Oldfield, Gary Glitter, Steve Strange, Steve Harley, Eric Stewart, Phil Lynott, Kenny Jones, Billy Connolly, Paul Gambaccini and Victor Spinetti. As a prelude to the main attraction, the audience is treated to a screening of the short animated film *Seaside Woman*. At the end of the evening, following the successful screenings, Paul and Linda invite their guests backstage for a celebration party.

Thursday April 9

🍎 In New York, at 6pm, at the Rivoli Theater, at Broadway and 49th Street, Ringo and Barbara's film *Caveman* receives a special press screening. During the first two weeks of the film's screenings in America, patrons receive a special *Daily Caveman* newspaper, which is dated 'Thursday, One Zillion Years B.C.'

Friday April 10

🍎 The world premiere of *Caveman* takes place in New York at the Rivoli Theater. Asked about the film, Ringo replies: "I'm a very visual person, so for me, *Caveman* is a great piece. It's more than dialogue, and it's far more creative to me to transmit those feelings." (The film opens in London on July 23.)

Thursday April 16

🍎 In America, two unauthorised Beatles' albums, *Dawn Of The Silver Beatles* and *Lightning Strikes Twice*, containing recordings from The Beatles' Decca Records audition on January 1, 1962, are released through mail-order.
🍎 In honour of John, Ed Koch, the mayor of New York, signs a city ordinance renaming a designated area of Central Park *Strawberry Fields*.

Monday April 27

🍎 At 3:45pm, Joseph Jevans marries Ringo and Barbara Bach at the Marylebone Registry Office in London, the couple having arrived at the registry office in a London taxi cab. Barbara's dress was specially created by the Emmanuel's design team in London, who are currently hard at work designing the dress for the future Princess Diana's wedding to Prince Charles in July. Mr Jevans was the same registrar who conducted the marriage of Paul and Linda in the same room back on March 12, 1969. Besides the McCartneys and some of their children, those attending include George and Olivia, Neil Aspinall, Derek Taylor, Harry Nilsson, Ray Cooper and Ringo's mother and stepfather (Elsie and Harry). Following the service, the couples pose for official wedding photographer Terry O'Neil, who had flown in especially from New York for the occasion. The 70 guests then attend a reception at the Mayfair club *Rags*, where an all-star jam session takes place, featuring George on guitar, Paul and Nilsson alternating on piano and Ringo sharing teaspoon percussion with Ray Cooper. For their wedding rings, Ringo had two fragments of glass from the shattered windscreen from their May 19, 1980 car crash set into two star-shaped gold rings as a reminder of their good fortune. At the reception, the former Beatles and their partners pose for a group photo, the first time three of The Beatles have been photographed together since August 22, 1969. As a souvenir of the day, Ringo and Barbara give each of their guests a solid silver star.
🍎 In New York, Yoko is asked if she and Sean had been invited. "No," she replies. "My way of taking it now is that, because of what happened to me, they (Ringo and Barbara) felt intimidated about inviting me, because it was really not the right time to encounter people being happy. But it would have been nice to have been told about it!"
🍎 Also today, it is announced that Wings have split up. Denny Laine counters the announcement by revealing it was he who left the group. Denny, who is currently rehearsing his new band at the Rock City Studios at Shepperton, says: "I wanted to go back on the road, but Paul is a studio person."
Reporter: "Reports suggest that he, at times, is a difficult man to get on with. Did you ever find that?"
Denny: "Well . . . I've had my moments!"
A report on his departure, as well as an exclusive interview with Denny is featured on

ATV's *ATV Today*. Following his departure, George Martin naturally suggests to Paul that the albums resulting from the Montserrat sessions earlier this year, are credited to Paul McCartney and *not* Wings.

May
🍎 Ringo talks about his marriage on the Robert Klein radio show in America.

Sunday May 3
🍎 In England, an interview with Yoko is published in *The Times* newspaper.

Thursday May 7
🍎 Ringo and Barbara appear live by satellite from Los Angeles on the ABC TV breakfast show *Good Morning America,* where they are interviewed by the host David Hartman. John's death naturally comes into the conversation.

🍎 Back in England George receives an invitation in the mail to appear on the Scotti Brothers *Legends Within The UK* programme, an English version of the American *Portraits Of A Legend* tribute series. George declines the offer. On May 18, his secretary writes back informing them that: "George is giving no interviews at present."

Monday May 11
🍎 George's tribute to John, the single 'All Those Years Ago'/'Writing's On The Wall' is released in America. (The UK release takes place on May 15.) Using the basic track recorded by George and Ringo during the Friar Park session between November 19 and 25 last year, George removed Ringo's vocals and recorded his own specially rewritten lyrics. To complete the song, Paul and Linda visit Friar Park to record backing vocals. The worldwide exclusive first airing of the track is played on BBC Radio One in the UK. To accompany the release a promotional film, never transmitted in the UK, comprising a dazzling array of archive Beatle footage is compiled.

🍎 In America, Ringo and Barbara appear on the breakfast show *AM Los Angeles*.

Wednesday May 20
🍎 Ringo and Barbara appear on the US TV programme *PM Magazine*.

Friday May 22
🍎 On John's behalf, Yoko accepts a Handel Medallion, New York's highest medal of honour. Receiving the award, she tearfully states: "This city meant a lot to him. This was our town, and it still is."

Sunday May 31
🍎 George and Olivia decline an invitation to the wedding of the American DJ Dave Herman at Drea Beach in the gardens of Billy Acres in Newton, Connecticut. Instead, the Harrisons send a bouquet of flowers.

June (onwards)
🍎 At his private studios in Scotland, Paul records additional songs that will be released on the albums *Tug Of War* and *Pipes Of Peace*. The tracks include: 'Dress Me Up As A Robber', 'Tug Of War', 'Ballroom Dancing', 'Be What You See', 'Wanderlust', 'Here Today', 'I'll Give You A Ring' (originally started back in 1974), 'The Man', 'Average Person', 'Keep Under Cover', 'Sweetest Little Show' and the instrumental 'Ode To A Koala Bear'. During these sessions, Paul is joined by Michael Jackson where they record 'Say Say Say', a track co-written with Jackson.

Monday June 1
🍎 George's album *Somewhere In England* is released in America. (The UK release takes place on June 5.) The issue reaches number 11 in the US and number 13 in the UK album charts.

Saturday June 6
🍎 John's new single '(Just Like) Starting Over'/'Woman' is released in America.

Monday June 8

 In America, Yoko releases *Seasons Of Glass*, her first solo album since 1974. Controversy surrounds the front cover, which depicts John's shattered bloodstained glasses sitting in the window of their Dakota apartment and a track on the album, 'No No No', which begins with the sound of gunshots. (The album is released in the UK on June 12.)

 EMI in the UK reissue all The Beatles' original studio albums (with the exception of *Abbey Road* and the *White Album*) in mono. These monaural versions of the albums were deleted back in 1979.

Wednesday June 10

 In England, the 31-minute MPL programme *Back To The Egg*, containing the eight Wings promotional videos from the album of the same name (taped two years ago, on April 3 and between June 4 and 13, 1979 – see relevant entries), receives its UK TV premiere this evening on BBC1 between 7:45 and 8:16pm.

Friday June 12

 The Wings single 'Silly Love Songs'/ 'Cook Of The House' is re-released in America.

Monday June 15

 Parlophone release the eight-album box set entitled *The John Lennon Boxed Set*, which comprises John's officially released albums from *Live Peace In Toronto* (in 1969) to *Shaved Fish* (in 1975).

 Yoko and her former company *Lenono Music* face a plagiarism charge over the *Double Fantasy* track 'Yes, I'm Your Angel'. Rival publishers cite the similarity between this and the 1928 track 'Makin' Whoopee', originally recorded by Eddie Cantor.

Thursday June 18

 In England, Paul's 39th birthday is celebrated with a 50-minute feature during Simon Bates' BBC Radio One show.

Monday June 22

 In New York, amidst scenes of high security, Mark Chapman pleads guilty to the second degree murder of John. He will be sentenced on August 25.

July

 Jack Douglas files a lawsuit claiming that he has received no royalties for his production work on the album *Double Fantasy*. In turn, Yoko countersues, claiming fraud and misrepresentation.

 The Handmade film *Time Bandits* opens in London and includes George's recording of 'Dream Away' which plays over the closing credits and is later remixed and released on his 1982 album *Gone Troppo*. A planned six-track EP containing 'Dream Away' and excerpts from the film's soundtrack is scrapped on the insistence of both Handmade and George.

Friday July 3

 In the UK, Bob Dylan releases the single 'Heart Of Mine' which features Ringo playing the tom-toms.

Saturday July 4

 'All Those Years Ago' reaches number 13 in the UK and number two in the US album charts.

Thursday July 9

 During tonight's 900th edition of BBC TV's long running *Top Of The Pops* series, short excerpts from The Beatles' 1963 BBC TV show *It's The Beatles* are repeated.

Saturday July 18

 To celebrate his first chart success for a number of years, George pays the final balance of £149 on a pair of silk pyjamas at the shop *After Dark*, based at 64 Pimlico Road, London.

Sunday July 19
🍎 George is seen chatting with some American Beatles fans outside his home at Friar Park.

Tuesday July 21
🍎 Radio Luxembourg celebrates The Beatles by designating the entire evening's broadcasts to their music.

Thursday July 23
🍎 Ringo's latest film *Caveman* opens at the Studio cinema in Oxford Street, London. The film is not well received by the critics. The *Guardian* newspaper's reviewer writes: "Worth about half an hour of anybody's time . . . unfortunately, it runs 97 minutes!"

Friday July 24
🍎 George's single 'Teardrops'/'Save The World' is released in America. (The UK release takes place on July 31.)

August
🍎 In America, the Magnetic Video Company release, on behalf of United Artists, the home video of The Beatles' 1970 film *Let It Be*.
🍎 Paul's Old English sheep dog Martha, immortalised on The Beatles' 1968 *White Album* track 'Martha My Dear', dies at Paul's Scottish farmhouse, aged 15. Paul, along with Linda and his family spends most of the month on Long Island in East Hampton, New York, with his in-laws. Paul tells the waiting reporters outside the house they are currently staying: "I'm out here putting my feet up and relaxing, trying to pretend that I am just a normal person." (Incidentally, Yoko is currently staying in a hotel less than a mile away, also in East Hampton.) This month's Italian magazine *Ciao 2001* features a report on Paul's recent recordings with Stevie Wonder.
🍎 Yoko attends the opening of the *Peking Opera* at the Lincoln Center in New York. It is her first public appearance since John's death last December.
🍎 At Earl's Court in London, George is seen in the audience, alongside Eric Clapton, watching a concert performance by Bob Dylan.

Friday August 7 (until Sunday August 16)
🍎 In America, The Beatles' newsreel compilation film *This Is The Week That Beatlemania Was*, is given a limited ten-day cinema release across America.

Tuesday August 11
🍎 Paul and Linda send a postcard from New York to their MPL staff in Soho Square, London.

Wednesday August 19
🍎 In New York, Yoko writes a letter to friends and possible benefactors about an area of Central Park, which has been honoured to John.
"It will be known as *Strawberry Fields*," she writes. "It happens to be where John and I took our last walk together. John would have been very proud that this was given to him, an island named after his song, rather than a statue or a monument. When we first met over ten years ago, we planted an acorn in England as a symbol of our love. We then sent acorns to all the heads of state around the world inviting them to do the same. So in the name of John and Yoko and the spirit of love and sharing, I would like once again to invite all countries of the world this time to offer plants, rocks, and/or stones of their nations for *Strawberry Fields*."

Monday August 24
🍎 Ringo and Barbara return to England via London's Heathrow Airport.

Tuesday August 25
🍎 George pays an initial deposit of £700 to the Clark Stone Originals firm in Herefordshire for a small replica model of his Friar Park mansion.
🍎 In America, John Lennon's murderer, Mark David Chapman, receives a 20-years-to-life sentence, to be served ironically in Attica State prison.

Wednesday August 26
✦ From the *Seasons Of Glass* album, Yoko releases as an American single, the track 'No No No'.

Saturday August 29
✦ In Liverpool, between 10am and 12 midnight, the first *Annual Mersey Beatle Extravaganza* takes place at the Adelphi Hotel in Lime Street. Originally this Beatles convention was due to take place at the Royal Court Theatre but was switched at the last minute due to a flood. An estimated 1,500 fans are treated to guest appearances by Philip Norman, the author of *Shout!*, the actor Victor Spinetti, and Brian Southall, the publicity executive for EMI Records, who reveals that "EMI has a recording of a song called 'Leave My Kitten Alone', featuring a vocal by John Lennon and recorded in 1963 (sic) which we consider good enough to release as one side of a new Beatles single." He goes on to add: "Apart from the Christmas disc tapes, EMI has *no other* completed issuable material." When he takes questions from the audience, he is asked: "Where then are all the other unreleased tracks?" Brian replies: "It would seem that when a song had been recorded, one or another of The Beatles would take the tapes home, strictly against EMI's wishes, and would only return material they themselves wanted released."
✦ At Sotheby's annual rock and pop memorabilia auction in London, Cynthia Powell Lennon Twist sells, for a record price of £8,800, a Christmas card drawn personally by John.

September
✦ Cynthia Lennon, as she now calls herself, visits New York to promote her 15 caricatures at the crumbling, almost derelict, Tower Gallery in Southampton. Before the opening of her first show, she receives a good-luck telegram from Yoko. During Cynthia's stay in the city, she makes promotional appearances on shows such as ABC TV's *Good Morning America*.
✦ Paul wins a High Court ban on the sale of the 1958 Quarrymen recording of 'That'll Be The Day', put up for auction by original Quarrymen member John 'Duff' Lowe. This month, along with Linda, he travels to New York where he visits Yoko and Sean at the Dakota. The McCartneys reciprocate by inviting her to stay at their Scottish farmhouse.
✦ The *Los Angeles Herald* reports that Yoko has been in her office every morning at 6:30am writing a book on her life with John.
✦ At Carnegie Hall in New York, Frank Sinatra performs the George Harrison song 'Something', dedicating it to "Mr. Lennon and Mr. McCartney". Fans in the audience are in an uproar; not knowing that this has been a staple diet of Frank's great stage act for over a decade.

Thursday September 3
✦ In Mathew Street, Liverpool, a giant glass fibre statue of John, entitled *Working Class Hero*, is put on display. The piece, created by 44-year-old sculptor Alan Curran, is part of a £12,000 appeal, this being the cost of having it cast and preserved in bronze.

Wednesday September 16 (until Friday September 18)
✦ In England, working with Keith MacMillan's Keef & Co. company, Ringo begins three days taping promotional video clips for 'Stop And Smell The Roses' and 'Wrack My Brain'. On the first day at Egham Aerodrome in Surrey (without any rehearsal), Ringo and 59 members of the Wickford Youth Band and Majorettes, tape the clip for 'Stop And Smell The Roses', recreating a mock traffic jam in France caused by the band and majorettes marching. The children, some as young as seven, were given special permission by their schools to appear in the five-hour shoot. Some of the extras, who are wearing striped jerseys and berets, were the children's parents. Ringo, dressed as a traffic cop, appears walking alongside the ranks and majorettes singing his song and, during breaks in the taping, he gives drum lessons to some of the children. For the second day's taping, production moves to Tittenhurst Park where Ringo concludes the scenes for 'Stop And Smell The Roses', as well as the opening shots for the clip to accompany 'Wrack My Brain', in which Ringo is seen getting out of, and subsequently jumping back into, his bed at the end of the clip. On Friday, interior scenes for 'Wrack My Brain' are shot at Keef & Co.'s south west London studios, with Ringo appearing in a horror dungeon with a whole host of creatures, including Dracula and a mummy. Barbara appears dressed in a straitjacket, which upsets many American broadcasters.

Saturday September 19
♣ The promotional video for Ringo's 'Stop And Smell The Roses' is prepared in preparation for television distribution. Some of the scenes, taped at his Tittenhurst Park mansion in Ascot, show Barbara in a cameo appearance hitting Ringo over the head with a bottle. Ringo is criticised over the scene in which Barbara is tied up in a straitjacket, but he is having none of it. Asked about the clip, Ringo replies: "It was the only way to keep her still. We took that home . . . what fun at night folks!"

Sunday September 27
♣ An interview with Paul is published in the *Sunday People* newspaper, where he is asked if he would object if his children went into showbiz, "No, but I wouldn't push them," he replies.

Wednesday September 30
♣ Yoko releases a second single from *Seasons Of Glass*, this time the song 'Goodbye Sadness'. (The promotional video for this track receives its world premiere on the NBC TV show *Saturday Night Live*.)

October
♣ During the month, George and Olivia fly to Hawaii, taking up residence at the Maui plantations to help their good friend Dr. Zion Yo celebrate the opening of his rejuvenation centre. "If I lived here I'd be in twice a week," George tells reporters covering the opening. Later, in conversation over dinner, George explains to Zion who The Harlem Globetrotters are. (The Globetrotters, of course, are the long running showbiz American basketball team.) Following the visit, George flies on to Los Angeles to attend the premiere of Handmade's *Time Bandits*, a charity event to raise money for needy children. He then returns to London.
♣ Eleven years down the line Neil Aspinall, in London, is still working on The Beatles' history documentary film *The Long And Winding Road*. It is now revealed that should Neil finally complete the editing, the chances of it seeing the light of day is pretty slim because he has been unable to get release permission from the three Beatles. Hearing this, *A Hard Day's Night* film producer Walter Shenson remarks: "It is criminal that The Beatles won't allow this footage to be released to the public!"
♣ Paul announces plans to build a £250,000 home on his 150-acre farm in Rye, Sussex.
♣ The Beatles' former drummer Pete Best is a guest on an American ABC TV "where are they are now?" variety show, entitled *Whatever Became of . . .*

Tuesday October 6
♣ In Los Angeles, a pre-recorded interview with Yoko is broadcast on Jim Ladd's radio show, with part two being transmitted one week later on Tuesday October 13.

Friday October 9
♣ In Los Angeles, on what would have been John's 41st birthday, a seven-foot bronze statue of him by the 27-year-old American sculptor Brett Livingstone-Strong, is unveiled outside City Hall. The three-ton piece, costing $75,000, had taken Brett three months to create. After its unveiling, fans begin laying flowers at the plinth of the statue. To coincide with this event, Yoko announces today as International World Peace Day.

Monday October 12
♣ In the UK, Thorn-EMI home video release, on VHS and BETA systems, the tape of Paul's MPL film *Rockshow*. This home video version omits six tracks that appeared during the cinema screenings earlier this year. The tracks to suffer from the cut are: 'Call Me Back Again', 'Lady Madonna', 'The Long And Winding Road', 'Picasso's Last Words – Richard Corey' (medley), 'Blackbird' and 'My Love'.

Friday October 16
♣ In Los Angeles, Ringo shoots promotional pictures to accompany the album *Stop And Smell The Roses*.
♣ To promote the release of the new Handmade film *Time Bandits*, George appears, by satellite from London, on the ABC TV breakfast show *Good Morning America* where he is interviewed by the host David Hartman. It is his first major US TV interview since he

appeared on *The Dick Cavett Show* back on Tuesday November 23, 1971 (see entry). Part two of George's appearance on *Good Morning America* is transmitted on Tuesday October 20.

Sunday October 25 (until Saturday October 31)
☙ Still in the States, with the first anniversary of John's death just six weeks away, a week-long campaign begins to promote an "end to handgun violence". The event, which is sponsored by John's friend Harry Nilsson, is staged across the country and takes the form of public service announcements, including one by Ringo, post mailings and 250 major fundraising events.

Monday October 26
☙ Ringo begins a month-long series of interviews and appearances to promote his new record. Today, he appears on the US KLOS Los Angeles radio show *Rockline,* premiering his *Stop And Smell The Roses* album and taking phone calls from listeners.

Tuesday October 27
☙ Over three years since his last album, Ringo's *Stop And Smell The Roses* is finally released in America, featuring a limited edition "scratch & sniff" sleeve, so that buyers can actually "smell the roses". For the album, Paul writes and produces the tracks 'Private Property' and 'Attention' and features on bass, piano, vocals and percussion. He also plays on the track 'Sure To Fall', which he also produces. George writes and produces 'Wrack My Brain', on which he plays guitar and performs backing vocals. He also produces the track 'You Belong To Me', on which he also contributes lead guitar. (The album is released in the UK on November 20.) To coincide with the US release today, Ringo, just a week after George, appears on the ABC TV breakfast show *Good Morning America.*

Also today in America, a single is taken off the album, coupling 'Wrack My Brain' with 'Drumming Is My Madness'. (The UK release for the single takes place on November 13.) The sessions for *Stop And Smell The Roses* started back on Friday July 11, 1980, when the record was originally titled *Can't Fight Lightning.* Unfortunately, *Stop And Smell The Roses* will not fare well Stateside, where it will be voted as "the worst record of 1981".

☙ Today's edition of *The Sun* newspaper features an exclusive interview with Yoko carried out by Barbara Graustark, in which she reveals: "We are still a duet. John is doing what he can upstairs. I do what I can down here."

Looking at her room full of John's mementos, Yoko remarks: "I don't intend to spend the rest of my life alone, but could I bring another man into all this?"

Wednesday October 28
☙ In Liverpool, a biographical play about John Lennon written by Bob Eaton, titled simply *Lennon,* opens at the Everyman Theatre.

Friday October 30
☙ A promotional interview by Ringo for the *Stop And Smell The Roses* album takes place today on Kevin O'Connell's WBEN Buffalo radio programme.

November
☙ As the first anniversary of John's death approaches, a spate of new single couplings appears in America. This time, 'Happy Christmas (War Is Over)' is paired with 'Beautiful Boy (Darling Boy)'. Meanwhile, from the seclusion of his cell in Attica State prison, Mark Chapman drafts a letter to Yoko informing her that he intends writing a book about his shooting of John. He also asks her to support the project on the condition that he hands over to her all the proceeds for charity.

☙ At the start of the month, Paul, Linda and their family visit New York, where he spends time recording in the studio with Michael Jackson. The McCartneys will return to England on November 10.

☙ This month, in America, the publishers Simon & Schuster release in paperback form George's 1980 book *I Me Mine,* this time at a more reasonable price of $12.95.

☙ Before Ringo commences additional promotional work for the album *Stop And Smell The Roses*, he and his wife Barbara take a belated honeymoon in Rome.

Tuesday November 3
♣ An interview with Ringo plugging his new album is published in the *LA Times*.

Wednesday November 4
♣ George's single 'All Those Years Ago'/'Teardrops' is released in America.
♣ John's single 'Watching The Wheels'/'Beautiful Boy (Darling Boy)' is also released in America.
♣ An interview with Ringo, again promoting his latest album, is published in the *Indianapolis News*.

Thursday November 5
♣ In London, *The Times* newspaper reports that John is to be the subject of a forthcoming book by Elvis Presley biographer Albert Goldman. The report reveals that two American publishers, Morrow and Avon, are expected to pay $1 million for the book.

Friday November 6
♣ The Handmade film *Time Bandits* premieres in most US cities.

Wednesday November 11
♣ In America, CBS TV's *Entertainment Tonight* show reveals that Yoko is writing a book on widowhood and has, allegedly, been offered $5 million as an advance from a London publisher.

Thursday November 12
♣ In the UK, Yoko pops up again when the *Daily Mirror* prints the story: "Yoko And A Man Like John" in which she is pictured strolling arm in arm through Central Park with Sam Havadtoy, a man who strikingly resembles John in likeness. The report adds, "Rumours say Sam and Yoko will marry soon."

Thursday November 19
♣ Ringo guests on the CBS TV show *Entertainment Tonight*, where he is asked: "Is it a burden being a former Beatle?"
    "It's never really a burden. That's the wrong word," he replies. "It used to get in the way sometimes, and still every interview you do people like to ask you about them. There's no madness out there like it used to be. I *was* a Beatle, I'm still Ringo Starr and I'm doing my own records now. It's more exciting for me to talk about *my* records than Beatles records, 'cos we've been talking about them for twenty years!"
♣ John is posthumously awarded with an ASCAP (American Society of Composers, Authors and Publishers) Award, but Yoko and Sean are unable to attend the ceremony personally. Instead, they send a video message of thanks, which requires six re-takes, in which Sean, quite clearly, cannot comprehend why he has to say "thank you" to a piece of paper which Yoko is reading.
♣ Following a secret meeting in New York, Paul offers £21 million for the full control of Northern Songs, the publishing company which owns the prestigious and lucrative Lennon & McCartney song catalogue. Owner Lou Grade insists that he will only sell The Beatles' songs as part of ATV Music and not as a separate entity. Paul maintains: "I'm only interested in The Beatles' tunes!" Asked about the situation, Yoko reveals that she has never been approached and insists that she "does not have an interest in the songs!"

Saturday November 21
♣ Two days after the meeting, now joined by Yoko, Paul announces that he is to sue Lord Grade's ATV Music Corporation for alleged breach of trust, following the failure, two days earlier, of Paul's attempt to buy back the rights to all The Beatles' hits.

Sunday November 22
♣ In England, an interview with Ringo, carried out by Gordon Blair to promote his latest album, is published in today's *Sunday Mirror*.

Tuesday November 24
♣ Ringo appears live in an 11-minute interview on the *Merv Griffin Show*. Immediately afterwards Ringo and Barbara fly back to England to celebrate Christmas in Ascot.

Wednesday November 25
♣ A pre-recorded interview with Ringo and Barbara is transmitted in America on the NBC *Tomorrow* show. During the show, Ringo remarks to the show's host Tom Synder: "I am the best rock and roll drummer in the land . . . I am!"

Friday November 27
♣ In Liverpool, a Wimpey Homes housing estate featuring street names such as John Lennon Drive, Paul McCartney Way, George Harrison Close and Ringo Starr Close is opened by Michael Heseltine, the Minister for the Environment, and councillor Derek Hatton. Three blocks are also added, Epstein Mews, Apple Court and Cavern Court.

December
♣ George, Olivia and Dhani spend their Christmas vacation as virtually the only occupants of Hamilton Island in Australia. They spend their days cruising the barrier reef on a chartered boat. In January 1982, during their two-month break, George consents to a rare interview for *Good Morning Australia*, who ask him: "How would you describe yourself in 1982?"

He replies: "As a middle-aged ex-pop star, peace seeker, gardener, ex-celeb . . . until now again!"

The five-part interview is not transmitted until Monday April 19, to Friday April 23, 1982, due to a stipulation from George that it could only be shown once he and his family had left the island and returned home to Friar Park. On his first day in the country, George gets stopped for speeding in his rented car, as he recalls: "The policeman asked me for my driver's licence, so I opened the back of the car to get it. The cop did a double take when he saw the name, 'George Harrison from London'. He said, studying the English licence, 'You're with The Rolling Stones aren't you?' " Meanwhile this month, the *New York Post* and the *Chicago Tribune* newspapers reveal that George has started recording his new album and that John's eldest son Julian is playing drums on a couple of tracks.

♣ Ringo appears in a Christmas message on *America's Top Ten* with Casey Kasem, then, once back in England, becomes part owner of a cable TV company in Liverpool. With his time spent in England rapidly increasing, practically ending his six-year life as a tax exile in Monte Carlo, a reporter asks Ringo if he has returned to England because of death threats in America, to which Ringo replies: "That is utter rot!" (Ringo and Barbara wait until his Startling Studios recording complex is completely finished and the house renovated before moving in full time, during October 1982.)

♣ Dave Clark, the former drummer with the sixties group The Dave Clark Five, acquires from the estates of Associated-Rediffusion the full copyright to the classic Sixties pop show *Ready Steady Go!* He announces that he intends to release highlights from the series worldwide on home video cassette. (The Beatles naturally figure in these plans.)

Wednesday December 2
♣ Immediately on returning to England, Ringo gives a promotional interview for *Stop And Smell The Roses* to Capital Radio in London. (Excerpts of the interview are repeated on a Capital Radio John Lennon tribute programme, broadcast on December 8.)

Sunday December 6
♣ An interview with Yoko and Sean is published in today's *New York Daily News*, where she discusses John's unreleased music and announces: "I do have plans to go through John's music."

Monday December 7
♣ Today's *Liverpool Echo* publishes an exclusive interview with John's Aunt Mimi in a piece entitled "My Boy John – I Just Want To Put The Record Straight". On the recently opened *Lennon* play at Liverpool's Everyman Theatre, she remarks: "They invited me to the first night. I wouldn't go. I'm glad I didn't. Friends of mine in Liverpool have been and seen it and have come away shocked. Much of how they portray John to be is completely the opposite of what he was!"

Meanwhile, on almost the first anniversary of John's tragic death, a street in Madrid, Spain, is renamed John Lennon Boulevard. Walls on the street feature a large mural inspired by The Beatles' film *Yellow Submarine*.

❧ In America, *People* magazine features Ringo in conversation with Tom Snyder, host of the NBC TV *Tomorrow Show*.

❧ Parlophone EMI in the UK release the 13-disc *Beatles EP Collection* box set, which includes an all-new bonus disc entitled *She's A Woman*. This contains 'This Boy', 'Baby, You're A Rich Man', 'The Inner Light' and the title track, featuring a previously unreleased count-in by Paul, all presented as four rare stereo Beatles recordings. (In fact, due to a mix-up at the mastering stage of the EP, a mono recording of 'This Boy' was accidentally used instead of the planned stereo version.)

❧ Back in Liverpool, it is announced that the original Cavern Club site in Mathew Street may be excavated and a shop and office built above it, with a reconstruction of the original club as a centrepiece. The £7 million project will shortly go before the Liverpool City Council for planning approval. David Beachouse, the architect of the scheme, optimistically says: "I believe some of the structure of the original Cavern Club will be exposed when the site is excavated."

Tuesday December 8

❧ As a Japanese sign of mourning on the first anniversary of John's death, Yoko cuts off 30 inches of her hair and spends the day in seclusion at Cold Spring Harbor. In France, a pre-recorded interview with Yoko concerning the first anniversary is transmitted on the French television station A2.

In England, John's Aunt Mimi Smith gives her first television interview about John to the Southern ITV programme *Day By Day*.

EMI in the UK announce that, in this first year since John's death, a staggering 75 million Beatles records have been sold worldwide.

In Liverpool, an open-air concert and a late night vigil for John takes place at St. George's Hall. At the 400-seat Everyman Theatre in the city, the entire evening's takings from the play *Lennon* are given to a charity of Yoko's choice.

Saturday December 12

❧ Over ten years since John and Yoko appeared on the programme, Ringo and Barbara make a guest appearance on the BBC1 late-night chat show *Parkinson* (transmitted between 10:41 and 11:39pm), hosted by Michael Parkinson and recorded in Studio B at the BBC Television Centre in London. Ringo talks about working at the Butlins holiday camp, filming the "path by the water" scene in *A Hard Days Night* when he had a hangover, working with the film 'greats' such as Peter Sellers and Mae West, and writing songs for The Beatles.

"I used to write all these songs and I used to think 'Wow! I've written another song!' Then, I'd go along where we'd be making another album, or something, and I'd say, 'I've written this song'. I would play them the song I had written and they would all be on the floor laughing, because I had usually re-written another song, usually a Jerry Lee-Lewis B-side."

Parkinson: "When The Beatles were recording you submitted a song? You all did? You all submitted songs when you were making an album?"

Ringo: "Well, it was pretty difficult in the beginning, because, even from the start, Lennon and McCartney were good writers."

Parkinson: "Not bad! Did you feel that was a bit daunting for you?"

Ringo: "To say the least. It's like Emily Brontë. I don't even know what that means! It was a bit heavy, you know. 'Well, I've got this lads'. And they'd say, 'Well, we've got this (singing) 'Yesterday'. So I'd say, 'Okay. We'll do yours!' "

To close the show, he and Barbara join Tim Rice, Jimmy Tarbuck and Michael Parkinson in an impromptu performance of the track 'Singing The Blues', with Ringo briefly playing drums. (Incidentally, 'Wrack My Brain' today reaches number 38 in the American charts.)

Also today, an interview with Ringo plugging the *Stop And Smell The Roses* album appears in the *New Musical Express*.

Thursday December 17

❧ Another interview with Ringo to promote his new album is published, this time in the American newspaper *The Daily Report*.

Tuesday December 22
🍎 At the Sotheby's Rock & Pop auction in London, over £80,000 is spent on Beatles-related items, including £8,000 on a line drawing by John of himself.

Wednesday December 23
🍎 It is reported that Yoko is to finance a centre aimed at improving research and preventive health care for children in Liverpool.

Thursday December 31
🍎 Before celebrating the New Year, an ever business conscious Paul is seen briefly at his MPL offices in Soho Square, London.
🍎 Further bad news for Ringo's *Stop And Smell The Roses* album when the HMV Record Store in London announce that, during the traditionally extremely busy month of December, just thirty copies of the album were sold throughout the entire run-up to Christmas.

1982

There were times when we thought, 'Oh, it would be great. It would be good.' But we generally thought that if we did it, it would be a let-down and we didn't want to come back as decrepit old rockers saying, 'Remember us? Hey, She loves you, yeah, yeah, yeah.'"

– Paul

January
 The year begins badly for Yoko when she is forced to fire her assistant Fred Seaman. He leaves her employment armed with John's diaries, recording equipment and manuscripts.
 At Abbey Road Studios, Paul spends most of the month concluding work on the album *Tug Of War*. Amongst the visitors to the studio this month is Paul Weller, front man of The Jam, who is recording in an adjacent studio. This month, MPL, in association with Thorn-EMI, spend a total of £100,000 for TV advertising of the *Rockshow* home video.

Sunday January 3
 Today's *Sunday Mirror* publishes a report on Paul, his home in Rye, Sussex, and the changes he has made to it.
 In Liverpool, long time Beatles fans Liz and Jim Hughes officially open *Cavern Mecca*, a Beatles museum, in Mathew Street.

Monday January 4
 In England, a profile on Paul is published in *The Times* newspaper. During the piece, which is headlined "Living With The Beatles' Legacy . . . The Smears That Lennon Left Behind . . . And The Battle To Win My Babies Back", Paul is quoted as saying: "If I could get John Lennon back, I'd ask him to undo this legacy and to tell everybody what he told Yoko – that he still liked me after all!"

Friday January 8
 BBC1 in the Southeast transmits a pre-recorded interview with Paul at Abbey Road Studios by Sue Lawley, for the news magazine programme *Nationwide*.

Tuesday January 12
 The Beatles' former drummer Pete Best records an interview for inclusion on the unauthorised Beatles American triple album *Like Dreamers Do*.

Wednesday January 13 (until Friday January 15)
 Ringo's single 'Private Property'/'Stop And Smell The Roses' is released in America. To coincide with its release, Ringo and Barbara join Paul and Linda at the Ewerts Studio in south-west London to appear in a special eleven-minute short film showcasing three tracks from the album *Stop And Smell The Roses*, entitled *The Cooler*. The film, produced by Paul's MPL company, features 'Private Property', 'Attention' and 'Sure To Fall', and receives its premiere at the Cannes Film Festival on May 24. UK cinemagoers have a chance to see the film when it is released as a support to the musical *Grease 2*.

Sunday January 17
 In England, as part of the BBC Radio One series *The Record Producers*, George Martin discusses his early comedy recordings, the early days of The Beatles and recalls the recording sessions for 'Yellow Submarine', 'Strawberry Fields Forever' and 'Being For The Benefit Of Mr. Kite'.

Wednesday January 20
 To celebrate its 40th anniversary, Paul, making his first major media appearance since John's death, becomes the 1,630th castaway on the long-running BBC Radio Four programme *Desert Island Discs*. Hosted by Roy Plomley, and recorded this morning at the BBC Studios at 201 Egton House in London, the 39-minute show is first transmitted on BBC Radio Four between 6:15 and 6:54pm on Saturday January 30, with a repeat transmission, on long wave radio only, the following Friday February 5 between 9:05 and 9:44am. During the conversation with Plomley he reveals that he doesn't own a complete collection of his own records.

Paul's choice of records to take to the mythical island are: 'Heartbreak Hotel' by Elvis Presley, 'Sweet Little Sixteen' by Chuck Berry, 'Dances From Gloriana' written by Benjamin Britten and performed by Julian Bream, 'Be-Bop-A-Lula' by Gene Vincent, 'Beautiful Boy (Darling Boy)' by John Lennon, 'Searchin'' by The Coasters, 'Tutti Frutti' by Little Richard and 'Walking In The Park With Eloise' by The Country Hams, the only song ever written by Paul's father, Jim. The Country Hams, of course, was an alias used by Paul whilst recording in Nashville during June and July of 1974 (see entry for further details on the sessions). Plomley asks Paul if he could only take one disc, which one would he take. He chooses John's 1980 recording of 'Beautiful Boy'. As one luxury item, Paul chooses a guitar and, for a choice of book, he elects his wife's book of photography, *Linda's Pictures*.

The show is also filmed by BBC2 for an *Arena* documentary, first transmitted on Tuesday February 23 between 10:05 and 10:49pm, where he is seen singing along with parts of The Coasters' recording of 'Searchin'' and, in an emotionally charged sequence, he sings along with John's 1980 song 'Beautiful Boy (Darling Boy)'.

Paul's first public appearance since John's untimely death gets off to a bad start when, just as he is about to enter the BBC Studios, he punches the *Daily Star* photographer Paul Massey, who was on his very first assignment. Realising his mistake, Paul apologises to Massey. The incident appears on the front page of the *Daily Star* on Thursday January 21, headlined: "Paul's Latest Hit . . . The Man From The Star." There is further controversy surrounding the *Desert Island Discs* programme when the noted Sixties impresario Larry Parnes sues Paul and the BBC over remarks made during the show.

Monday January 25
🍎 Paul appears briefly in a short videotape introduction for Stevie Wonder during tonight's syndicated ABC TV *American Music Awards* presentation.

February
🍎 The official EMI monthly magazine *Entertainment News* publishes a two-part interview with Paul to promote his forthcoming album *Tug Of War*. (The second part is printed in the March edition.)
🍎 In London, at the Globe Theatre, George is seen in the audience at Eric Idle's new stage play *Pass The Butler*.
🍎 Still in the capital, Ringo and Barbara attend the British Charity Premiere of *Absence Of Malice* at the Odeon in Leicester Square, an event which will raise a record £80,000 to be split between The Variety Club Of Great Britain and the Italian Hospital in London.

Monday February 8
🍎 In England, the Handmade Films production of *Scrubbers* begins filming.

Tuesday February 9
🍎 In Los Angeles, after a wait of ten years, George finally receives, from Hugh Downes, the chairman of the US committee for UNICEF, the UNICEF Award for his work on the 1971 Bangladesh relief concert. George is also honoured with a citation for an 'Outstanding Contribution to the World's Children'. After the ceremony, the former Beatle remarks: "It's nice to know you can achieve these sort of things. Even though the concert was over ten years ago and the public has probably forgotten about the problems of Bangladesh, the children still probably need help and the money will have significant impact." Coverage of his awards presentation will be featured on ABC TV's *Good Morning America* breakfast show tomorrow morning and on the CBS TV *Entertainment Tonight* programme, transmitted on February 11.

Thursday February 11
🍎 At the Old Royal Mint in London, make-believe prison scenes are shot for the second version of the 'Ebony And Ivory' promotional clip. Paul's additional scenes, including the first version with Stevie Wonder, are shot in London the following month.

Saturday February 13
🍎 The Cleveland, Ohio, radio station WZZP causes near hysteria by announcing (unofficially) that Capital/EMI will release The Beatles' single 'Leave My Kitten Alone' backed with 'How Do You Do It?' later this year.

Monday February 15
🍎 Still in Los Angeles for the UNICEF Award, George and Olivia check into L'Ermitage Hotel in Beverly Hills, California, using the alias "Mr. Jack Lumber". The Harrisons leave the hotel on Thursday February 18, paying a bill of $2,308.99.
🍎 Today's planned UK release of Paul's *Tug Of War* album fails to materialise. The release date is now scheduled for Friday March 12.

Wednesday February 24

♣ In Los Angeles, at the 1981 Grammy Awards, *Double Fantasy* is voted 'Album Of The Year'. A tearful Yoko, standing alongside Sean, acknowledges a standing ovation and collects the award in person. In London, at the first annual BRIT Awards held at the Grosvenor House in Mayfair, John is honoured for his 'Outstanding Contribution to British Music'.

Saturday February 27

♣ Ringo and Barbara attend Elizabeth Taylor's 50th birthday party at the London nightclub *Legends*.

March

♣ At Elstree Studios in Hertfordshire, working with the director Barry Myers, Paul films two different promotional clips for the song 'Ebony And Ivory'. For the first version (featuring Stevie Wonder), Paul films his scenes alone with Wonder's scenes (filmed in America) being edited in later. During a break from the sessions, he consents to an interview for the April 11 edition of *Good Morning Australia*, clips of which later form the TV special *Freeze Frame*, which also includes a recent interview with George Martin, also conducted for the *Good Morning Australia* programme. The first version of 'Ebony And Ivory', is premiered in America on *Friday Night Videos* on April 23 (see entry).

Paul's former Wings partner Denny Laine, via his manager Brian Adams, begins touting around to book publishers a "warts and all" exposé on his time with Paul, Linda and Wings.

♣ Reports in the UK and USA press insinuate that Ringo and Barbara's eleven month wedding is already hitting the rocks.

♣ Still in America, Murray "The K" Kaufman, the self-titled "fifth Beatle", dies of cancer, aged 60. As a tribute, BBC Radio One in the UK broadcast a twenty-minute tribute to the man.

Tuesday March 2

♣ In the UK, the *Daily Star* publishes the first of a three-part interview with Paul, conducted by Moira Warren and Jan Bendrick. (Part two is printed on March 3 with part three appearing on Thursday March 4.)

Sunday March 7

♣ To celebrate the 20th anniversary of The Beatles' first BBC radio appearance, Radio One transmits (between 3:00 and 4:59pm) the two-hour special *The Beatles At The Beeb*. The show, introduced by Andy Peebles, features many of the Beatles BBC radio sessions recorded between 1962 and 1965 and an interview with Peter Philbean, the producer of their first radio appearance. (A revised repeat of the show takes place on December 27.)

Friday March 12

♣ Paul's new studio album *Tug Of War* again fails to show. Reports suggest that the delay is due to further remixing. The release, Paul's last under his current US contract with CBS/Columbia, is now re-scheduled for April 19.

Monday March 15

♣ At 1:05pm, at George Martin's AIR Studios in London, Paul gives his first major interview since John's death. The interview, carried out by Freddy Hausser for the French television station A2, is for a 31-minute special entitled *James Paul McCartney*. He talks about his idols, which include the Liverpool footballer Kenny Dalglish, music publishing, and announces that his new album (*Tug Of War*) will be a solo release and not credited to Wings. Paul also performs on the piano a short piece of his first ever composition 'I Lost My Little Girl'. Archive film clips from *Rockshow* and the new video for 'Ebony And Ivory' accompany the feature.

Thursday March 18

♣ In the UK, the paperback version of George's *I Me Mine* is published, brought forward from its planned April 15 release date.

Friday March 19
♣ Yoko and Sean are featured in the German magazine *Horzu*.
♣ In Australia, press reports insinuate that George appeared on stage tonight, at the Horden Pavilion, with Elton John during the performance of 'Empty Garden', a song written by Elton as a tribute to John.

Saturday March 20
♣ Incensed by the perpetual TV, radio and newspaper rumours concerning the apparent breakdown of his marriage to Barbara, Ringo, at his home in Ascot, phones the UK newspaper the *Sunday Mirror*, to tell them that these stories are: "Nonsense," adding, "Barbara is here with me now and I'm telling you in front of her that I am deeply in love with her and we are very much married . . . now and for always!" A story about Ringo's phone call is published the following day, Sunday March 21, while the extremely happy Mr & Mrs. Starr are heading off to Cleveland, Ohio.

Sunday March 21
♣ Hours after arriving in America with Barbara, Ringo gives a live interview to the American radio station WZZP in Cleveland, conducted by the DJ Robert W. Morgan.

Monday March 22
♣ The Beatles' compilation album *Reel Music*, featuring a selection of tracks from their feature films, is released in America. (The UK release takes place on March 29, 17 days after it was originally scheduled for release.) A single to promote the album, 'The Beatles Movie Medley'/'I'm Happy Just To Dance With You' is also released today in America. (The UK release takes place on May 24.) Its original B-side 'The Fab Four On Film', featuring an interview with The Beatles on the set of *A Hard Day's Night*, is pulled off just prior to release, due to a dispute with the producer Walter Shenson.

Monday March 29
♣ Paul's single 'Ebony And Ivory' (performed with Stevie Wonder) and 'Rainclouds', recorded by Paul during the time of John's tragic death, is released in the UK. (The American release takes place on April 2.) The UK 12-inch single (also released on April 16 in America) features Paul's solo version of 'Ebony And Ivory'. To coincide with the release, the promotional video for the solo version of the song is prepared today for worldwide television transmission.
♣ Also today, in London, Handmade films begin production on film *The Missionary,* starring Michael Palin. Further location shooting takes in Scotland and Africa.

April
♣ The Liverpool station Radio City begins transmitting the longest ever Beatles radio special. Entitled *The Beatles – Days In Their Lives*, it lasts almost thirty hours, in 15 two-hour episodes spread over five consecutive weekends. Roger Wilkes, the station's head of programming, says: "It's a monumental piece of history, with a lot of new sidelights on John, Paul, George and Ringo. There are scores of previously unheard interviews with them." Based on an idea by the Canadian broadcaster David Pritchard, the series, already sold to various US stations, covers The Beatles' schooldays right through to the break-up in 1970.

The Liverpool City Council gives a green light to a £7 million redevelopment scheme which will turn Mathew Street into a multi-storey shopping complex.

In the States, The Beatles' film *A Hard Day's Night* is re-released to selected American cinemas, where, during its first week on the circuits, it grosses over $340,000. In Philadelphia it rakes in over $48,742. At the end of the month, at the UCLA in Los Angeles, the film's producer Walter Shenson holds a seminar on The Beatles where he discusses his work with the group. Many fans are outraged to discover that tickets for the event are, in their opinion, an extortionately high $5.50.
♣ At the start of the month, Paul and Linda visit New York where they have lunch at Le Cirque restaurant with Yoko, Sean, Lee and John Eastman and Yanov Collart, who in December will present Linda's pictures at an exhibition in Paris, followed by shows in Amsterdam, Geneva, Milan and Barcelona. The McCartneys then fly on to Tucson, Arizona, for a short holiday and then to Los Angeles, where, on April 16, they visit the Universal Film Studios. Besides taping appearances for the *Today* show (transmitted

between April 26 and 29) and *Entertainment Tonight,* and being interviewed for the *New York Times* (published April 25), Paul also records an appearance for the US TV music show *Friday Night Videos* (recorded on April 16 and transmitted on April 23 – see entry) and spends three days recording at Westlake Studios on April 14, 15 and 16, with Michael Jackson and Quincy Jones, the song 'The Girl is Mine', also written by Jackson. (The track is later released as part of the single 'Can't Get Outta The Rain', appearing also on Jackson's album *Thriller.*) Also this month, Paul becomes the first Beatle to be listed in the prestigious book *Who's Who.*

 At the start of the month, George, and Dennis O'Brien, attend Handmade Films business meetings in New York. George then travels on to Long Beach to watch the Grand Prix and then Nassau, where he and Olivia spend time with his friend, the writer Jerry Kosiuski.

Saturday April 3 & Sunday April 4
 Ringo and Barbara are spotted in New Rochelle, New York, during their weekend stay at the Sheraton Plaza Inn. They are here to attend the wedding of Barbara's brother, Dr. Peter Goodbach, who is marrying Dr. Jo Shapiro on Monday April 5. The following day Ringo and Barbara return to England.

Tuesday April 6 (until Friday April 16)
 At Startling Studios, based at his Tittenhurst Park mansion in Ascot, Ringo, joined by the former Eagles guitarist Joe Walsh, begins recording the first tracks intended for his album *Old Wave,* although the bulk of the sessions will not begin until Friday May 31.

Wednesday April 7
 In the States, Cynthia and her son Julian appear by satellite from London on the ABC TV breakfast show *Good Morning America,* where they are interviewed by the regular host David Hartman.

Thursday April 8
 This evening's *Top Of The Pops* (transmitted on BBC1 between 7:25 and 7:59pm) features the world premiere screening of Paul's promotional film clip (version one featuring Stevie Wonder) to accompany the single 'Ebony And Ivory'.

Sunday April 11
 A pre-recorded interview with Paul, carried out at his MPL offices in Soho Square, to promote *Tug Of War* is transmitted on the German television show *Musicszene.*

Monday April 12
 A pre-recorded interview with Paul to promote *Tug Of War* is transmitted on the German television station WDR 3TV.

Wednesday April 14 & Thursday April 15
 At the Westlake Studios in Los Angeles, Paul begins recording sessions with Michael Jackson and Quincy Jones.

Thursday April 15
 Rolling Stone magazine in America pre-empts the other papers by exclusively revealing that: "Ringo is in London working on a new album with Joe Walsh acting as the producer."

Saturday April 17
 In the UK, the first part of a two-part pre-recorded interview with Paul is featured in *SFX,* the short-lived music magazine on an audio cassette. Part two is included in the edition released May 1. (Copies reach the shops up to three days before the issue date.) Another interview with Paul is broadcast today on BBC Radio One.

Sunday April 18
 Now back in England, BBC Radio One broadcast a pre-recorded interview with Paul conducted by Andy Peebles, to promote the album *Tug Of War.* This same day, a two-part interview with Paul, carried out by Tony Fletcher, is published in the *Sunday Mirror.* (Part two is published on April 25.)

1982

Monday April 19

 With the media awash with pre-recorded interviews, Paul is to be found resting and writing new songs at his Scottish farmhouse.

Tuesday April 20

 A section of New York's Central Park, partly funded by Yoko, is officially dedicated to John as *'Strawberry Fields'*.

 Paul appears in a pre-recorded feature on CBS TV's *Entertainment Tonight*.

Friday April 23

 In America, tonight's edition of *Friday Night Videos* features the first US screening of the 'Ebony And Ivory' promotional film, featuring the specially recorded introduction by Paul who, by now, has returned to London and is spending the day at George Martin's AIR Studios in London. He will leave the studio at 7pm.

Saturday April 24

 Back in England, to coincide with the release of Paul's new album *Tug Of War,* an exclusive interview with the former Beatle is published in the *Record Mirror.*

 Still in London, Ringo, alongside Barbara, is seen socialising at a party with his old flame, the singer Lynsey De Paul and the actor James Coburn.

Sunday April 25

 An interview with Paul to promote *Tug Of War,* carried out by Robert Palmer, is published in today's *New York Times.* During the feature, Paul recalls a previous meeting he and Linda had with John and Yoko at their Dakota apartment. Also today, an interview with Paul is published in the *LA Times.*

Monday April 26

 Paul's album *Tug Of War* is finally released, simultaneously in both America and in the UK. The grunting and groaning at the start of the title track was recorded at the championship meeting of the Tug Of War Association in Huddersfield, while Ringo is featured on drums on the track 'Take It Away'. Another track on the album, 'Here Today', becomes Paul's tribute to John. To coincide with the album's American release, a pre-recorded four-part interview with Brian Gumble is transmitted (daily until April 29) on the NBC TV breakfast show *Today.* Just before he enters the television building for the taping session, which took place at the start of the month, a roving reporter briefly interviews him for the CBS TV programme *Entertainment Tonight.* Paul, meanwhile, is to be found today at AIR Studios in London, where he is seen leaving with Linda and their son James at the usual time of 7pm.

Thursday April 29

 Further promotions for *Tug Of War* takes place when an interview with Paul is published in the Liverpool music newspaper *Scene.*

May

 Ringo asks the Windsor and Maidenhead District Council for permission to build a two-storey building in the grounds of his Tittenhurst Park mansion which he plans to use as a video and sound recording studio.

Saturday May 1

 The single 'Ebony And Ivory' reaches number one in the UK singles chart.

Wednesday May 5

 George begins recording songs for his album *Gone Troppo.* The three-month sessions, carried out at his Friar Park Studios, produce the tracks: 'I Really Love You', 'Greece', 'Wake Up My Love', 'Mystical One', 'Gone Troppo', 'Unknown Delight', 'Baby Don't Run Away' and 'That's The Way It Goes' (which will not appear until 1988 when it is released in the UK as a bonus track on the 'When We Was Fab' 12" and CD singles). The finished album also features the track 'Circles', originally written in India back in 1968 and recorded in 1978 during the April 11–October 12 recordings for the *George Harrison* album. (The sessions continue until August 27.)

Thursday May 6
🎸 At the BBC TV Centre in Wood Lane, London, Paul and Linda appear unannounced following the screening of the 'Ebony And Ivory' promotional clip to send their greetings to their daughter Heather at the end of tonight's edition of *Top Of The Pops*, transmitted on BBC1 between 7:25 and 7:59pm. (Heather McCartney had recently been thrown from her horse and was in traction for a while, having broken both her leg and collarbone.) The McCartneys, making their first studio appearance on the show since November 20, 1974 (see entry), also take part in a short interview with the host Simon Bates. As the final credits run to the accompaniment of 'Really Saying Something' by Bananarama & Fun Boy Three, Paul is seen signing autographs among the audience.

Saturday May 8
🎸 The Beatles' film *Let It Be* receives its fourth UK TV screening this afternoon on BBC2 between 3:11 and 4:29pm. This will be its last television screening in Britain for almost two decades. In the States, 'The Beatles' Movie Medley' reaches number 12 in the American singles charts and *Reel Music* makes number 19 in the US album charts.

Friday May 14
🎸 In New York, Crown International Pictures re-release Ringo's 1978 film *Sextette*, starring Mae West.

Saturday May 15
🎸 There is a double celebration today for Paul, when his single 'Ebony And Ivory', reaches number one in America and his album *Tug Of War* reaches number one in the UK album charts.

Wednesday May 19
🎸 Paul pops into Air Studios in Oxford Street, London where he briefly meets George Martin.

Monday May 24
🎸 The MPL film *The Cooler* (see entry for Wednesday January 13) is entered in the 'Best Short Subject' competition at the annual Cannes Film Festival in the South of France with both George and Ringo in attendance.

Saturday May 29
🎸 The two-hour radio special *The Beatles At The Beeb* is transmitted in America throughout the Memorial Day weekend.
🎸 On the day that the album *Tug Of War* reaches number one in the US charts, Paul is to be found back in Liverpool, attending the wedding of his brother Mike to the former dress designer Rowena Horne at St. Barnabas Church in Mossley Hill. At their service, where Paul serves as best man, the church organist plays The Scaffold hit 'Lily The Pink' to accompany Rowena as she walks up the isle. A reception follows at the McCartneys' home in Rembrandt, Heswall, The Wirral, Merseyside.

Monday May 31 (until Thursday June 10 & Thursday June 24 until early July)
🎸 At Startling Studios in Ascot, Ringo continues recording songs for his album *Old Wave*, which at one stage was to be called *It Beats Sleep*. This month-long (periodically produced) session will include the tracks: 'In My Car', 'As Far As We Can Go', 'Hopeless', 'Alibi', 'She's About A Mover', 'Be My Baby', 'I Keep Forgetting', 'Picture Show Life', 'I'm Going Down' and the instrumental 'Everybody's In A Hurry But Me'. The album will have a very limited release, in Germany on June 16, 1983, where a single, 'In My Car'/'As Far As We Can Go' is also released, and in Canada, where the album is issued on June 24, 1983. *Old Wave* is released in several other countries, namely Australia, Brazil, Mexico, New Zealand and Japan but not in either America or in the UK. Four songs from it do appear in America, when they are released on the Rhino CD *Starr Struck – Best Of Ringo Starr Vol. 2* on February 24, 1989.

June
🎸 A profile of Paul's career is featured in this month's woman's adult magazine *Playgirl*. Paul, though, retains his clothes. This month, even though he is sporting a heavy disguise,

Paul is still recognised at a Ry Cooder concert at the Hammersmith Odeon, London.
🍎 George and Olivia are seen in the audience of Simon & Garfunkel's Wembley Stadium London comeback concerts. Later, the Harrisons attend a gathering at London's Jazz Club in Camden, where they are seen partying until dawn. George continues his bout of concert going by joining Ringo, on a different night to Paul, at a performance by Ry Cooder at the Hammersmith Odeon. Ringo is also seen with Barbara at the opening night of The Rolling Stones' three-night run at Wembley Stadium.

Friday June 11
🍎 Ringo and Barbara depart from Heathrow Airport en route to Los Angeles to deliver sample master tapes of some of the tracks from his latest album *Old Wave*. (The couple return to England on Monday June 14.)

Sunday June 13
🍎 In readiness for Paul reaching his 40th birthday next Thursday, the *Sunday Mail* publishes a two-page article headlined "The Magical Maturity Of McCartney".

Monday June 14
🍎 *The Sun* newspaper reports that Paul has bought an 18th century windmill for his Sussex property. (This will later be turned into a recording studio, located about three miles from his *Waterfalls* home in Peasmarsh.)

Tuesday June 15
🍎 Today's *Daily Mirror* publishes an interview with Yoko Ono, who announces: "I'm very anxious to visit England some day, although no immediate plans have been made."

Friday June 18 (until Wednesday June 23, but excluding Sunday June 20)
🍎 On a set at the Elstree Film Studios in Hertfordshire, working with the director John McKenzie, filming begins on the promotional clip for Paul's new single 'Take It Away'. On the first day, a party is thrown to celebrate Paul's 40th birthday, and among those in attendance, besides Linda, are Ringo and Barbara, George Martin, Eric Stewart and the drummer Steve Gadd. (See entry for June 23.) Paul receives a telegram from Cilla Black which reads: "If life begins at 40, what the 'ell 'ave you been doing all these years?" Paul also receives a birthday "kissogram" from a scantily clad singing telegram girl, who calls herself Susie Silvey. The sight of an attractive, near naked female came as a complete surprise to everyone present, as Susie recalls: "I told a girlfriend I wanted to do a singing telegram for him, but didn't know if I dared. She dared me! So I took all the gear along to the studio where Paul was making 'Take It Away'. Just before lunch, I slipped into my fishnets, suspenders and black lace corset and covered it with a dress I could easily peel off when the moment came. I was shaking like a leaf. As Paul started to leave the set for lunch, I ran after him and shouted, 'Paul!' He spun round and as he did so, I took off my dress and stood there in front of him in my gear, singing a special version of 'All You Need Is Love'. Then I gave him the birthday congratulation telegram. He thought it was amazing."
🍎 *The Sun* newspaper celebrates Paul's 40th birthday by publishing the article "Fab And 40". In America, a pre-recorded three-part interview with Paul, entitled *Paul McCartney Today*, is transmitted on NBC Radio. (Part two is aired on June 19, with the third and final part being aired on June 20.)

Sunday June 20
🍎 The American radio station WMMS-FM in Cleveland, Ohio, broadcasts the audio soundtrack from the complete unedited NBC TV *Today* show interview with Paul, transmitted between April 26 and April 29.

Monday June 21
🍎 Paul's single 'Take It Away'/'I'll Give You A Ring' is released in the UK. (The American release takes place on July 3.)

Wednesday June 23
🍎 On Stage 4 at Elstree Studios in Hertfordshire, on a day that had begun at 10am (brought forward from 12 noon due to the current London tube strike), Paul completes the shooting of 'Take It Away', this time before a live studio audience comprising

members of his UK Wings Fun Club. Many of them are kept waiting on stage 3 until the technicians are ready to shoot their scenes, and the waiting continues when they are told that they will not be needed until 2pm. The disgruntled fans are then told they will not be needed for another two hours. At 4pm the fans are treated to a mini-concert by Paul, including performances of 'Bo Diddley', 'Peggy Sue', 'Send Me Some Loving', 'Reelin' And Rockin'', 'Lucille', 'Twenty Flight Rock', 'Searchin'' and the instrumental theme tune to the American cops drama series *Hill Street Blues*. Before the show begins, Paul introduces the band. "George Martin on electric piano, Richard (Ringo) on drums, a Steve Gadd look-alike butler on drums, Eric Stewart on lead guitar, The Q-Tips brass section, our Lin' on tambourine and my name's Fred." During a break, someone asks Ringo to sing and he delivers a few lines of 'Yesterday'. At this point, George Martin starts to play the tune on his piano but Paul resists all temptations from the excited crowd to join in with the others. Instead, he tells Martin to "carry on entertaining us", and sings a brief snippet of 'Here, There And Everywhere'. At its conclusion, Linda delivers a short version of 'Maybe I'm Amazed'.

The taping concludes at 5:30pm and restarts at 6pm until 7pm. Following another break at 7:45pm the band are moved on to Stage 3 at Elstree in order to make room for more elaborate concert sequences. Then, at 8:15pm, the band return to Stage 4 where scenes involving the actor John Hurt are filmed. Once completed, Paul and Linda hold a signing session for the fans, but due to the number of records, pictures and magazines being presented, fans are asked to sign their name and address on the back of each item handed in and promised that the item will be returned to them once Paul and Linda have signed. By all accounts, Ringo becomes extremely moody, apparently because no one was bothering to try to get his, or Barbara's, signature.

July
- EMI Records in London announce that The Beatles' version of 'Leave My Kitten Alone' will be released as a single before Christmas.
- Rumours fly around the film industry that Ringo is set to play a pirate in Graham Chapman's new comedy film *Yellowbeard*, with the former Beatle replacing the pop singer Adam Ant who has now dropped out of the role.
- Yoko is seen at a matinee screening of the film *Diner* at the Festival Theater in New York.

Saturday July 3
- 'The Beatles' Movie Medley' reaches number 10 in the UK singles chart.

Monday July 5
- Paul's 12-inch single 'Take It Away'/'I'll Give You A Ring' and 'Dress Me Up As A Robber', is released in the UK. (The American release takes place on July 26.)

Thursday July 15
- Paul's promotional film for 'Take It Away' receives its UK TV premiere tonight on *Top Of The Pops*, transmitted on BBC1 between 7:35 and 8:10pm.

Friday July 16
- In London, Capital Radio broadcast the special programme *Cruising – The Early Years Of The Beatles,* which features an examination of The Beatles' music covering the years up to 1963.

Friday July 23
- Philip Norman's best-selling Beatles biography *Shout!* is published in paperback in the UK by Corgi Books.

August
- Paul, Linda and the children spend most of the month on holiday in the West Indies.

Sunday August 1
- WGAR-AM Radio in Cleveland, Ohio, broadcasts a pre-recorded interview with Paul, conducted by David Perry, to promote his new album and single. The show is called *Paul McCartney: The Man & His Music.*

 George visits the Northampton General Hospital to see his motorcyclist friend Barry Sheene, who was recently involved in a nasty motorbike accident.

Thursday August 5
 Yoko and Sean arrive on stage at Elton John's Madison Square Garden concert in New York, following a performance of 'Empty Garden', his tribute to John. Yoko tells the large crowd: "I want to thank you all. I really believe you are all my family."

Sunday August 15
 Ringo and Barbara arrive back in Britain at London's Heathrow Airport, where he announces to the press that he has "changed his mind about appearing in the film *Yellowbeard*", adding, "If it goes ahead I *won't* be in it."

Thursday August 19
 In the shop *Browns*, based at 143 New Bond Street, George buys a medium sized Ralph Lauren shirt and eight pairs of socks. His bill comes to £108.

Saturday August 21
 'Take It Away' reaches number 15 in the UK and number 10 in the American charts.

September
 The Mobile Fidelity Sound Labs release a 13-album box set of original stereo UK Beatles albums on half-speed mastered discs. The special box also includes a half-speed mastered version of the US compilation album *Magical Mystery Tour*.
 Bettina Huebers, a 20-year-old German woman, files a paternity suit against Paul, claiming he is her father. Paul, meanwhile, begins recording songs to be featured on the album *Pipes of Peace* in his Sussex farmhouse studio. These sessions produce the tracks: 'Pipes Of Peace', 'So Bad', 'The Other Me', 'Through Our Love' and 'Tug Of Peace'.
 Yoko sends Sean on a fortnight's holiday to Bermuda, accompanied by three burly bodyguards. Yoko is unable to go due to business commitments.
 Ringo and Barbara spend the first three weeks of the month on a Polynesian holiday.

Wednesday September 1
 Yoko and John's first son Julian are pictured, by Bob Gruen, leaving the Hit Factory recording studio in New York.
 In London, Paul begins a short period of recording and mixing at Abbey Road Studios.

Tuesday September 7
 Paul and Linda, dressed suitably in genuine fifties garb, are present at the Buddy Holly Rock 'n' Roll Championship at London's Lyceum. Described by those present, who include Ringo and Barbara, as "The biggest Rock 'N' Roll Party In The World", the event carries on long into the early hours of September 8, and launches Paul's annual Buddy Holly Week celebration, which concludes on September 13.

Friday September 10
 A selection of tracks from The Beatles' Decca Records audition of January 1, 1962, is released in the UK by Audiofidelity Enterprises as an album entitled *The Complete Silver Beatles*. Fearing legal reprisals, missing are the three Lennon-McCartney numbers recorded that day, namely 'Love Of The Loved', 'Like Dreamers Do' and 'Hello Little Girl'. (The album is released in America by Backstreet Records.)
 In New York, a Manhattan woman whose daughter was allegedly injured by another young girl at Yoko's Long Island estate sues Yoko for more than a million dollars. The injured girl, seven-year-old Caitlin Hair, had her arm broken during a dispute on the front lawn of the Lennon's property. The lawsuit is asking for $1 million for "permanent injury" and $50,000 for medical negligence in expenses and also accuses Yoko of leaving her child in the care of "incompetent, irresponsible, careless and negligent bodyguards, agents, servants and employees." (The case continues.)

Friday September 17 (to Sunday September 19)
 In America, Westwood One syndicates the radio tribute programme *John Lennon: Rock And Roll Never Forgets*.

🍎 Also on September 19, this time in the UK, and as a prelude to his new series, BBC Radio One repeats (between 4:01 and 4:59pm) Paul Gambaccini's profile on The Beatles for his series *Appreciation*. Still in the UK, the *Sunday Mirror* reveals that Paul has taken an interest in the dubious art of body tattooing.

Monday September 20
🍎 Paul's single 'Tug Of War'/'Get It' is released in the UK. (The American release takes place on September 26.)
🍎 *Sextette,* starring Ringo and Mae West in her last ever film, is released on Media home video in the UK. (This becomes the first time this film has been seen outside of America.)

Thursday September 23 & Friday September 24
🍎 Paul shoots a promotional film clip for 'Tug Of War' at George Martin's AIR Studios in Oxford Street, London. The American *Yonkers Herald Statesman* newspaper reveals that, "Paul may sign with RCA instead of resigning with Columbia in America."

Saturday September 25
🍎 Following a night at their Cavendish Avenue home, Paul and Linda are joined by over 80 top recording stars, including The Police and Pink Floyd, at Abbey Road recording studios for a *Guinness Book Of Hits* book launch party. At the end of the evening, Paul and Linda leave the building and sign autographs for fans camped outside the building.

Sunday September 26
🍎 Ringo and Barbara leave Heathrow Airport, en route to Sydney, Australia.
🍎 In the first of a new radio series for BBC Radio One (transmitted between 4:01 and 4:59pm), John is spotlighted in the Paul Gambaccini programme *Appreciation*.

Monday September 27
🍎 In America, the album *The Silver Beatles Volumes 1 & 2* is released by Pheonix Records and contains 12 of the 15 tracks recorded by The Beatles at their Decca audition on January 1, 1962. Seven of the 12 tracks are artificially extended by repeating sections of the recordings.

Tuesday September 28
🍎 Just over nine months after appearing with Michael Parkinson on his show in England, Ringo and Barbara record a television appearance on *Parkinson In Australia,* one of the first shows presented by Michael Parkinson shortly after leaving the BBC. During the Sydney based show, besides being interviewed, Ringo plays drums and performs on the medley of 'Honey Don't'/'Blue Suede Shoes', supporting the vocals of Glenn Shorrock. (The 50-minute programme is broadcast on October 8.)
🍎 Back in the States, Fred Seaman is arrested on charges of stealing some of John's priceless letters, paintings, unreleased music tapes, photographs, videotape recordings, stationery, a sound mixer and an AM-FM radio. The police report that following his arrest virtually all of John's stolen property was recovered.

Wednesday September 29
🍎 Following a night in the cells, Fred Seaman is released without bail from Manhattan's Criminal Court.

October
🍎 A scheduled special Beatles 20th anniversary of 'Love Me Do' edition of the BBC1 Mike Read series *Pop Quiz* is cancelled due to "technical difficulties". To coincide with the celebrations, MGM/UA release on home video worldwide the two-hour documentary *The Compleat Beatles,* which claims to feature an abundance of "previously unseen footage". For once, the hype proves to be true. In England, following the reprint of the 77 original magazines, Beat Publications re-launch the official *Beatles Book Monthly,* which is now devoted entirely to the current activities of the former fab four, and includes archive features and reports on the continual Beatle happenings which regularly take place around the world. In Brazil, EMI Records release a special 20th anniversary (limited edition of 200 copies) disc called *Tudo Comecou Ha 20 Anos Atras,* which roughly translated means *It*

Was All Started 20 Years Ago. The 12-inch single features Lizzie Bravo recounting how she came to sing on the original (February 1968) version of 'Across The Universe', interspersed with snippets of various Beatles songs and an excerpt from The Beatles' 1963 Christmas recording. On the B-side , there is the second version of 'Love Me Do' and the recent compilation song 'The Beatles' Movie Medley'.

🍎 MTV in America reveal that Paul has saved the music magazine *Jamming* from going broke by donating $10,000.

🍎 Ringo finally leaves his tax haven home of Monte Carlo to live back in England at his 17th Century Tittenhurst Park mansion in Ascot, Berkshire, with his wife Barbara.

🍎 Newspaper reports again suggest that Yoko and her interior designer Sam are planning to marry.

🍎 George and Olivia visit New York where they are seen backstage at a taping of NBC TV's *Saturday Night Live*. Later, they are also seen at a party for cast and crew at New York's *Palace Restaurant*.

Sunday October 3

🍎 In America, Yoko officially leaves Geffen Records and signs for Polygram Records. She takes with her the *Double Fantasy* leftover tracks that will (in 1984) form the *Milk & Honey* album.

Monday October 4

🍎 As part of the current EMI Beatles celebrations, Parlophone/EMI issue 7-inch vinyl and picture disc versions of the single 'Love Me Do'/'P.S. I Love You' as a 20th-anniversary commemorative release. Due to an oversight by EMI, the single features the album version of 'Love Me Do' and not the original single version with Ringo playing drums. EMI make amends for this error on November 1 (see entry). To coincide with the anniversary, Paul gives an exclusive interview for BBC TV news, which is included in the late night programme *Newsnight*. He is asked: "Just how likely was it, when John was still alive, that The Beatles would ever play together again?"

Paul: "There *were* times when we thought 'Oh, it would be great, it would be good.' But we generally thought that if we did it, it would be a letdown. One of the things we'd been consciously aware of with The Beatles was to go and have a great career and leave them laughing and we thought we'd done that, you know. We didn't want to come back as decrepit old rockers saying 'Remember us? Hey . . . She loves you, yeah, yeah, yeah!' "

From this point on, right up until 'Let It Be' in 1990, all of the original Beatles UK singles, with the exception of 'I Want To Hold Your Hand' in November 1983, will be reissued on the nearest possible date to the 20th anniversary of their first release.

To celebrate the special 20th anniversary release of 'Love Me Do', BBC Radio 2 broadcast throughout the day both sides of every Beatles single released in the UK between 1962 and 1970. Later this evening Capital Radio throws a special Beatles party at London's Dominion Theatre which features screenings of *Help!* and *Let It Be*, the new stereo version of the film *A Hard Day's Night*, as well as miscellaneous Beatles Movietone newsreels from the Sixties.

🍎 Aside from Beatles activities, Thorn-EMI delay (due to contractual problems) the release on home video in the UK of the 95-minute version of George's *Concert For Bangla Desh* from August 1, 1971 (see entry). This truncated version removes a large portion of Ravi Shankar's performance.

Tuesday October 5

🍎 Paul gives another 'Love Me Do' 20th anniversary interview, this time with DJ Tony Prince for the station Radio Luxembourg which is included in the programme *McCartney Remembers*.

Thursday October 7

🍎 In England, Paul breaks from the fresh round of Beatlemania by giving his time to a matter most dear to him, the current health workers' pay claim. He sends a telegram to Prime Minister Margaret Thatcher, warning her: "What the miners did to Ted Heath, the nurses will do to you." His action angers Tory MPs who tell him to, "Stick to your music and stay out of politics." Paul's brother Mike McGear points out that the reason for Paul's militancy is that their mother Mary, who died in 1956, was a midwife in Speke, Liverpool, and was affectionately called "The Angel" by her patients.

Saturday October 9
As part of a special 'Love Me Do' 20th anniversary feature, Paul's brother Mike McCartney appears as a special guest on the BBC1 Saturday morning children's show *Saturday Superstore*, hosted by the DJ Mike Read. During the interview, during which promotional film clips for 'Love Me Do' and Paul's 'Tug Of War' are transmitted, Mike McCartney reveals that he has a Beatles rehearsal tape, recorded at The Cavern back in 1962. While he is showing Read various Beatles artefacts, he accidentally drops a model of Paul, breaking off one of its hands.

Sunday October 10
The *Los Angeles Daily News* reports that George has purchased a new home in Los Angeles that is so private, it is accessible only by helicopter.

Monday October 11
The EMI TV advertised compilation album *The Beatles Greatest Hits* (Parlophone EMTVS 34) is shelved. It was scheduled to include all 22 singles plus 4 other double A-side tracks. Instead, plans have been shifted towards the Parlophone album *20 Greatest Hits* (see entry for October 15).

Wednesday October 13
At their encore at Shea Stadium this evening, The Who perform 'I Saw Her Standing There' and 'Twist & Shout' as a tribute to The Beatles who played the venue back in 1965 and 1966. Prior to the start of this evening's Who show, excerpts from The Beatles' August 15, 1965, Shea Stadium appearance are flashed on the stadium's video screens.
The Handmade Film production of *Time Bandits* premieres in cinemas in Manila in the Philippines. The film will re-open in US cinemas shortly afterwards.

Friday October 15
With a new wave of Beatlemania currently gripping the world, EMI waste no time in rushing out *The Beatles 20 Greatest Hits*. (The UK release takes place on October 18.) The album reaches number 10 in the UK and number 50 in the US charts.

Sunday October 17
The BFBS (British Forces Broadcasting Services) station in Germany broadcasts the two-hour 'Love Me Do' 20th anniversary show entitled *Beatlemania*, which features interviews with Bob Wooler, Tony Barrow, Norman Smith and Victor Spinetti among others.

Tuesday October 19
In New York Linda McCartney buys a pair of doves at the *Crystal Aquarium*, situated at 93rd Street and Third Avenue.

Saturday October 23
'Tug Of War' reaches number 53 in both the UK and US single charts.

Monday October 25
The Michael Jackson single 'The Girl Is Mine', a duet with Paul, is released in America. (The UK release takes place on October 29.)

Wednesday October 27
George's album *Gone Troppo* is released in America (the UK release takes place on November 8). Also in America, two tracks from the album, 'Wake Up My Love'/ 'Greece', are released as a single. (The UK release of the single, to coincide with the album, occurs on November 8.) George declines to involve himself in any promotional activities for either the album or single, and the sales of the records are poor, with 'Wake Up My Love' only reaching number 53 in the American charts on December 4.

Thursday October 28
With his new album in the American shops, George, Olivia and Dhani fly out on Concorde from London's Heathrow Airport at 11:45am, landing in Washington at 12:05am (local time). On their arrival, they are picked up by the Dav-El Limo Hire

company who transport the Harrisons to the nearby Watergate Hotel, where they have rooms booked (for one night) under the alias of Mr and Mrs Tannerhill.

Friday October 29
 To cash in on the current Beatles hysteria, 'Searchin'' b/w 'Money' and 'Till There Was You', is lifted off the Decca audition album and released as a single in the UK by Audiofidelity Enterprises. In the States, Lyric Art Productions of California release the first "officially licensed" Beatles calendar. The pages feature 'eight days a week' instead of the more regular seven.
 Videoform Pictures release in the UK Ringo's 1969 film *The Magic Christian*, which co-stars Peter Sellers.
 In Washington, a limousine from Dav-El arrives at the Watergate Hotel to take the Harrisons to the airport where they board Lockheed Tristar TWA 891 5:00pm first class flight to Los Angeles, arriving at 7:20pm.

Saturday October 30
 'Love Me Do' reaches number four in the UK singles chart.
 On the WBEN radio station in Buffalo, New Jersey, Ringo takes part in a radio phone-in, taking many Beatles-related questions live on air.

November
 Sources close to MPL suggest that Paul's new album will either be called *Hug Fo' Love* or *Tug Of War II* and is scheduled for release in either late January or early February 1983.
 In Sweden, Polydor records release the six-track EP featuring both the German and English (in stereo) introductions to 'My Bonnie' and the first version of 'Sweet Georgia Brown' as recorded by The Beatles with Tony Sheridan in Germany back in 1961. The EP also features Ringo's 1977 track 'Just A Dream', 'Badge' by Cream (a track co-written by George who also plays rhythm guitar) and 'Giddy', a track composed by Paul for Roger Daltrey.
 An interview with Ringo appears on the GRSS Buffalo radio programme *Soundtrack Of The 60s*.

Monday November 1
 Parlophone/EMI make up for not reissuing the correct version of 'Love Me Do' on October 4 by releasing a 12-inch single coupling both versions of the track, featuring Ringo on drums on one track and Andy White on the other, as well as 'P.S. I Love You'. (Note: The master tape to the original single version of 'Love Me Do', featuring Ringo on drums, was destroyed by EMI back in 1963. To release this new 12-inch version today, a tape is made from a pristine copy of the original single, as supplied from the collection of Mark Cousins, a life-long Beatles fan.)
 Also in the UK today, the compilation album *The John Lennon Collection* is released and contains the following tracks: 'Happy Christmas (War Is Over)', 'Stand By Me', 'Power To The People', 'Whatever Gets You Through The Night', 'No. 9 Dream', 'Mind Games', 'Love', 'Imagine', 'Jealous Guy', '(Just Like) Starting Over', 'Woman', 'I'm Losing You', 'Beautiful Boy (Darling Boy)', 'Watching The Wheels' and 'Dear Yoko'. (The American release, featuring an alternative track listing of: 'Give Peace A Chance', 'Instant Karma', 'Power To The People', 'Whatever Gets You Through The Night', 'No. 9 Dream', 'Mind Games', 'Love', 'Imagine', 'Jealous Guy', '(Just Like) Starting Over', 'Woman', 'I'm Losing You', 'Beautiful Boy (Darling Boy)', 'Dear Yoko' and 'Watching The Wheels', takes place on November 8.)
 Pete Best is a live guest on the ABC TV breakfast show *Good Morning America* where he discusses his departure from The Beatles over two decades ago with the host David Hartman.

Tuesday November 2
 Yoko's album *It's Alright (I See Rainbows)* is released in America. A track on the album, 'Never Say Goodbye', features John shouting.

Friday November 5
 At the Elstree Film Studios in Borehamwood, Hertfordshire, working with a budget of

£1,500,000, Paul begins filming and recording songs for the movie *Give My Regards To Broad Street*. The opening scenes filmed today at Teston Locks on the River Medway include Paul dressed in Dickensian style clothing for the 'Eleanor's Dream' sequences of the film. *Broad Street* production will continue until May 8 next year and will include new song titles such as: 'No More Lonely Nights' (ballad and playout versions), 'Not Such A Bad Boy', 'No Values' and the instrumentals 'Goodnight Princess', 'Corridor Music' and 'Eleanor's Dream' plus new recordings of The Beatles' classics 'Eleanor Rigby', 'For No One', 'Good Day Sunshine', 'Here, There And Everywhere', 'The Long And Winding Road' and 'Yesterday'. Paul also reworks more recent compositions, including 'Wanderlust' and 'Ballroom Dancing'. (These songs will appear on the *Give My Regards to Broad Street* soundtrack album.) The London Weekend Television programme *The South Bank Show* films a documentary, aptly titled *The Making Of Give My Regards To Broad Street*, during this period. The show, hosted by Melvyn Bragg, will be transmitted for the only time across the ITV network on Sunday October 14, 1984, between 10:31 and 11:29pm. (The production on the *Broad Street* film will continue through until July 26, 1983.)

 During the filming of *Broad Street*, Paul and Linda's daughter Heather passes several A level exams with flying colours. Following her success, she requests that her parents buy her a car, which she receives only after Ringo urged Paul to do so. "Give the kid a break," Ringo told him. "All her friends have cars and it's not as if she wanted a BMW or a Roller. We're only talking about a Volkswagen!" The lunch breaks for Paul during the shooting are also quite memorable when, on more than one occasion at the studio canteen, he will bump into the cast of the latest *Tarzan* film, Barbra Streisand (who is there filming *Yentl*) and Steven Spielberg (who is currently filming *Indiana Jones And The Temple Of Doom*). During the filming at Elstree, Paul and Ringo book into the studios using the aliases Mr Manley and Mr Newbury respectively.

 The Handmade Film production of *The Missionary*, starring Michael Palin, opens in Los Angeles cinemas.

Saturday November 6
 The album *The Beatles 20 Greatest Hits* reaches number 10 in the UK and number 50 in the American charts. Today, *Billboard* magazine reports that the temporary restraining order against MGM/UA over the "rockumentary" *The Compleat Beatles* has been lifted, with MGM/UA agreeing to pay Apple Corps a royalty for the use of The Beatles' name, logo and film performances. (The case is settled out of court and the sum involved in the agreement is not disclosed.)

Sunday November 7
 In England, the *Sunday People* newspaper prints a story on the finding of some lost Beatles pictures taken during their first visit to America in February, 1964, recently found by a young man in a junk shop.

Monday November 8
 On the same day in America that *The John Lennon Collection* is released, Yoko releases as a single 'My Man'. (The record is released in the UK on December 3.)

Thursday November 11
 In America, to promote *The John Lennon Collection*, the single 'Happy Christmas (War Is Over)'/'Beautiful Boy (Darling Boy)' is released.

Saturday November 13
 At Surrey University, George Martin presents a cheque for £2,000 to the recipient of the first John Lennon Scholarship, 23-year-old David Wilson. The purpose of this award is to encourage the study of recording techniques.

Monday November 15
 To help promote *The John Lennon Collection*, John's single 'Love'/'Gimme Some Truth' is released in the UK.

Wednesday November 17 (until Sunday December 5)
 The *Beatlemania* stage play opens in Los Angeles at the Beverly Theater for a limited three-week only run.

Sunday November 21
 An interview with Ringo to promote his *Stop And Smell The Roses* album is broadcast on US TV on the Casey Kasem music show *America's Top Ten*.

Tuesday November 23
 A short pre-recorded interview with Paul is transmitted on the BBC Radio One lunch time show *Newsbeat*.

Wednesday November 24
 Paul and Linda arrive in Paris in preparation for Linda's show which opens tomorrow.

Thursday November 25
 In Paris, Paul and Linda attend the opening of a third exhibition of her pictures, this time at La Galerie Ganon.

Friday November 26
 Polydor (UK) release the Yoko Ono single 'My Man' b/w 'Let The Tears Run Dry'.

Monday November 29
 Michael Jackson's album *Thriller* is released in America, and features his duet with Paul on 'The Girl Is Mine'. (The album is released in the UK on December 3.)
 Yoko releases the album *It's Alright* in America. (The UK release takes place on December 10.)

December
 ITV and Channel 4 viewers this month get to see a special 45-second (later trimmed to 30-second) television commercial advertising *The John Lennon Collection* album.
 Following the withdrawal of several Beatles-related items from the Sotheby's Rock & Roll Auction this month, Paul sues the famous auction house for the return of various personal artefacts.
 Over Christmas, in a London vegetarian restaurant, George meets Cilla Black and they decide to finish off their unreleased recordings from August, 1972 (see entry for details).

Friday December 3
 In the UK, Channel 4's tea-time music show *The Tube* broadcasts a previously unscreened 8mm colour film of The Beatles shot by the photographer Dezo Hoffmann in Sefton Park, Liverpool, and on July 22, 1963, while the group was on tour in Weston-Super-Mare. Dezo had actually given Channel 4 all 15 minutes of the film but only two minutes is used. This exclusive is part of a feature to promote Dezo's new book of unpublished Beatles photographs entitled *With The Beatles,* which is published today by Omnibus Press, priced at £4.95. (Also featured in the, so called, *Tube's Beatle Movie,* are colour excerpts from the 'Strawberry Fields Forever' promotional film, a complete version of the film for 'Penny Lane' (in black & white) and clips from the never-before-seen Beatles interviews on the set of *A Hard Day's Night,* shot by HTV Television back in 1964.) Highlights from the feature are repeated in *The Tube's Return Ticket,* a best of the series compilation programme, which is transmitted in certain ITV regions during September, 1983.

Monday December 6
 One year on from the lavish Beatles EPs collection comes *The Beatles Singles Collection* in a box, released today in the UK by Parlophone, which comprise the entire official singles output from 1962 to 1982 in newly designed picture sleeves.

Wednesday December 8
 On the second anniversary of John's death, Paul appears in a Channel 4 tribute programme to the cartoon character *Rupert The Bear*.
 In America Yoko gives a lengthy interview to the New York station WNEW-FM, as well as to Tom Brooke of BBC Television (see entry for December 21). Back in England, the station LBC (London Broadcasting Company) broadcast a special programme looking at the events since John's death. The programme is titled *John – Two Years On.*

 In England, Ringo is accused by a Labour member of the Windsor and Maidenhead District Council of being a scrooge for applying for a £500 grant to help restore his Tittenhurst Park mansion in Ascot, Berkshire.

Thursday December 9
 Shout! author Philip Norman is a guest on the BBC1 lunch time show *Pebble Mill.*

Monday December 13
 Two years after John's death, the American *People* magazine prints another article by *Playboy* reporter David Sheff, this time entitled "Yoko And Sean – Starting Over".

Sunday December 19
 In today's *Sunday Mirror,* Yoko publicly replies to John Green's allegations about her and John in the book *Dakota Days.*

Tuesday December 21
 Yoko and Sean appear on the BBC1 news programme *Nationwide.* Tom Brooke carried out the short pre-recorded filmed six-minute interview in their Dakota apartment on December 8. Accompanying the feature is a report on tomorrow's Sotheby's rock and pop auction in London.

Wednesday December 22
 On the morning of the annual Sotheby's rock and pop auction, Paul drops in to see what is on offer this year. After seeing an American gold record for the album *London Town,* he leaves the premises. Later at the auction, a Japanese businessman, Kosaku Koishihara, outbids a host of Beatles fans by purchasing, on behalf of the Tokyo store Seiku, £50,000 worth of souvenirs. Top price paid is £13,000, for a gold disc presented to The Beatles for the album *Sgt. Pepper.* Among the other lots on offer today is John Lennon's 1964 two-piece olive green suit, which sells to an anonymous buyer.

Saturday December 25
 The Parlophone compilation album *The John Lennon Collection* reaches number one in the UK album charts. Today, Christmas Day, Yoko writes a piece called *Surrender To Peace* in which she recalls her foundation of Nutopia with John on April 1, 1973. (The article is printed a month later in the *New York Times.*)
 In a busy few days involving The Beatles on the radio, Radio Luxembourg transmits *The Paul McCartney Interview* between 6:45 and 7:59pm.

Sunday December 26
 Beatles-related radio shows continue today when BBC Radio London broadcasts (between 3:03 and 4:59pm) the two-hour radio special entitled *The Beatles Revolution,* which features archive Beatles interviews and reports. Later in the day, this time on BBC Radio One (between 4:00 and 4:59pm), Paul is featured in the Paul Gambaccini *Appreciation* series.

Monday December 27
 BBC Radio One and Two simultaneously broadcast (between 2:00 and 3:59pm) a revised repeat of the radio special *The Beatles At The Beeb,* originally transmitted on March 7. This version, features songs from the original broadcast replaced by others not included in the earlier version of the show, for instance, The Beatles' 1962 version of 'Dream Baby'.

Tuesday December 28
 Tonight's special Christmas edition of *Pop Quiz,* hosted by Mike Read and transmitted on BBC1 between 5:25 and 5:54pm, features the belated *Beatles Pop Quiz* section, postponed from October, and includes questions especially set by both Paul and Ringo.

Thursday December 30
 The Beatles pop up again on the radio, this time featured in the Mike Read BBC Radio One programme *A History Of The Abbey Road Studios,* transmitted this evening between 7:01 and 7:59pm.

They're not interested in me as a human being, they are only interested in The Beatles – what guitar I played on *Sgt. Pepper* and all that crap."

– George

January

❦ Linda's touring exhibition of photographs, drawn from her book *Photographs,* opens in Liverpool at the Open Eye Gallery, at 90–92 Whitechapel, where it is visited by over 8,000 people. (The exhibition has previously been seen in Australia and Germany.) To promote her new book and the exhibitions, Linda records an appearance this month for the BBC Radio 4 programme *Woman's Hour.* It is also reported this month that Paul, with most of the film's location work now completed, has spent time at Abbey Road Studios, working with George Martin, re-recording some of The Beatles' classic songs for inclusion in his film *Give My Regards To Broad Street.* Paul is now anticipating a November worldwide release of the cinema film, while his animated short *Rupert And The Frog Song,* is also pencilled in for a cinema release, as support for the third *Star Wars* film *The Revenge Of The Jedi.*

❦ At the end of the month while in Australia, George visits Elton John, who has gone to see the English test cricket team in action.

❦ Ringo arrives to collect his phone purchases at the Dixons electrical store in Bond Street, London, but he is told by the shop assistant that unless he is able to supply some identification, he cannot take the goods. He shows his driving licence and passport. Asked about the incident, a shop assistant says: "Ringo took our actions very well. He certainly has less cheek than the Duchess of Kent, who had been in our shop earlier to *borrow* a pair of headphones."

Sunday January 2

❦ In England, Ringo's American TV special *Ringo* receives its UK premiere on Channel 4, almost five years after its US premiere on April 26, 1978. (See entry for that date for full details on the programme.)

Tuesday January 4

❦ BBC1 screens the 50-minute documentary *Beatlemania* which takes a close look at past and present "Beatlemaniacs", many of whom are seen at the American and Liverpool Beatles fan conventions.

Saturday January 8

❦ 'The Girl Is Mine', a duet by Paul and Michael Jackson, reaches number two in the US chart.

Sunday January 23

❦ While George is on his Australian vacation, a lengthy interview with the former Beatle is published in the *Sunday Times.* A short extract from the piece will appear in the *Sun* on Thursday.

Monday January 24

❦ George, Olivia and Dhani leave Calcutta at 13:45 and arrive in Bangkok at 17:30 on Thai Airlines, flight TG312. Then, on Thai Airlines flight TG401, the Harrisons depart from Bangkok at 19:00 and arrive in Singapore at 22:10, where they stay for one night at the Mandarine Hotel.

❦ In London, a pre-recorded interview with Yoko is transmitted on the Capital Radio programme *Monday Matters.*

Tuesday January 25

❦ Yoko's single 'Never Say Goodbye', briefly featuring John shouting, backed by 'Loneliness', is released in America only.

❦ George, Olivia and Dhani leave Singapore, on British Airways flight BA011 at 18:35 and arrive in Perth, Australia at 23:25.

Thursday January 27

❦ The *Sun* newspaper reproduces an extract from Sunday's *Times* article, headlined: "I'm George, not a Beatle", in which he remarks about the press: "They're not interested in me as a human being, they are only interested in The Beatles – what guitar I played on *Sgt. Pepper* and all that crap!"

Saturday January 29
❦ The 20th anniversary reissue of The Beatles' 'Please Please Me' reaches number 29 in the UK singles chart. Collectors are now on the lookout for a picture disc copy of Hawkwind's single 'Silver Machine', which, due a mix-up at the EMI pressing plant, features The Beatles performing 'Ask Me Why' on the B-side.

February
❦ With the MGM/UA documentary *The Compleat Beatles* doing tremendous business on home video around the globe, sources close to Apple and the individual Beatles announce that their own, long mooted, Beatles history documentary film *The Long And Winding Road,* is now ready for release. In America, the former Beatles' aide Peter Brown, along with writer Steven Gaines, release the book *The Love You Make – An Insider's Story On The Beatles.* It contains several scandalous Beatles-related stories and is soon renamed *The Muck You Rake* by disgusted Beatles fans.
❦ George donates his own private copy of the rarely seen 1974 Apple/George financed production of *Little Malcolm And His Struggle Against The Eunuchs* to a New York company who plan to screen the film at an upcoming New York festival.
❦ Ringo and Barbara take Barbara's son Gianni to the London premiere of the film *The Dark Crystal,* but Gianni is sent home before the party afterwards at Hamilton's Gallery in Mayfair, London, where Ringo parties until way past midnight.

Wednesday February 2
❦ Michael Jackson arrives in London to join Paul in shooting a promotional film clip for the track 'The Man'. During Jackson's visit, he stays with the McCartneys at their Sussex farmhouse.

Monday February 7
❦ George's single 'I Really Love You'/'Circles' is released in America.
❦ Also in America, Yoko releases her latest single, 'Never Say Goodbye'.

Thursday February 10
❦ Paul, Linda and Michael Jackson attend the second annual BRIT Awards, held at the Grosvenor House Hotel in London. Paul receives an award as the 'Best British Male Artist of 1982' from the British Record Industry, an accolade presented to him by George Martin. The Beatles are also honoured for their Outstanding Contribution to British Music. Then, to complete a hat trick of awards, Paul is honoured with the new Sony Award, recognising his Technical Expertise. The evening is topped off with both George Martin and Geoff Emerick collecting awards for their work on Paul's album *Tug Of War.* Highlights of the event are covered by the breakfast station TV AM and are transmitted on the station the following morning.

Wednesday February 16
❦ In London's High Court, a judge rules in favour of ATV Music in the case involving Paul and the executors of John's estate who had been seeking at least £5 million in additional royalties on some of their most famous compositions. A second action, filed today by Paul seeking full rights to ATV Music and therefore the complete Beatles music, is thought unlikely to reach the courts until sometime in 1984.
❦ Ringo's £500 grant towards the repairing of a roof on the stable block and the renovating of statues and ornaments in the gardens of his 79-acre Tittenhurst Park mansion estate, is rejected by the Windsor and Maidenhead District Council. (The claim had been filed on December 8 last year.)

Sunday February 26
❦ The *Sunday Mirror* publishes an interview with Paul in which he denies rumours that his marriage is on the rocks.
❦ The *Sunday Times* publish an article called *The Beatles And Us,* which takes a fond look at fans who reminisce about seeing The Beatles at the Cavern Club in Liverpool.

March
❦ Under a "Freedom of Information Act" request, Jon Wiener of the University of California in Irvine, obtains a series of heavily censored FBI files relating to the agency's

actions against John in 1972. Wiener also receives 26 pounds of immigration data dealing with John's lengthy battle to remain in America, and sues the FBI to obtain the relevant information deleted from the files. The information he uncovers form the basis of his book *Come Together* published in 1984. (In 1991, an American court ruling orders the FBI to turn over the deleted files to Wiener.) Reports released this month indicate that May Pang is writing a memoir about her relationship with John between 1973 and 1975. The book features a provisional title of *Was It Just A Dream?*

🍎 EMI in the UK schedule for release The Beatles single 'How Do You Do It?' backed with 'Leave My Kitten Alone'. (The release fails to materialise.) In Manchester, Granada Television announce that they have completed editing a Beatles documentary, comprising archive Sixties film clips that had been languishing in their film library for almost two decades. The show's producer, Johnny Hamp, who worked with The Beatles at the time, reveals that, "Granada may well transmit the programme later in the year or release it straight to home video," adding that the show will "dispel a few myths". On completion of the production, preview VHS videos of the show are sent out to Paul, George and Ringo for their approval. Granada reveals that its first ITV screening will take place during October. (Its first public airing will actually take place in America on Tuesday July 12 – see entry.)

Saturday March 12
🍎 Ringo goes into a London hospital for a checkup and has to cancel a planned interview with a US TV film crew who are informed that "Ringo is unwell". Shortly afterwards, Ringo's secretary Joan Woodgate reveals: "He has passed his checkup with flying colours."

Friday March 18
🍎 In London, a compulsory winding-up order for *Denny Laine Ltd.* is served.

Wednesday March 23 (until Wednesday March 30)
🍎 The *San Francisco Bay Guardian* newspaper prints a fascinating series of articles entitled *John Lennon And The FBI Files,* in which they look at how the US Government were harassing John in the early Seventies. The reports also include reprints of various Government memos.

Saturday March 26 & Sunday March 27
🍎 George spends two days at the Long Beach Grand Prix.

April
🍎 Paul re-records the 1978 song 'Theme From Twice In A Lifetime', later heard at the close of the 1985 film of the same name starring Ann Margaret. Location filming for *Broad Street* resumes this month, with scenes filmed at an empty Royal Albert Hall in London and at the BBC's London headquarters, at Broadcasting House, in Portland Place. In addition, at a disused warehouse in London's West End, Paul, along with Ringo, Dave Edmunds and Chris Spedding, films an all-day jam session, which includes performances of classic Fifties rock songs as previously performed by Eddie Cochran, Chuck Berry, Buddy Holly and Little Richard. All this extra work means that Paul is forced to delay the release of the album *Hug Fo' Love* until October.

🍎 The American publishers *Simon & Schuster* reveal that Fred Seaman has been paid a $900,000 advance for a "warts and all" exposé book on his working life with John Lennon.

Wednesday April 6
🍎 Paul wins two awards at the first American Video Awards (AVA), one for 'Ebony And Ivory' as the best soul video and a second award for which former Monkee Mike Nesmith inducts him into the Video Hall Of Fame.

In Germany, a court orders Paul to pay the American equivalent of $282 per month to Bettina Huebers, a 20-year-old German woman who had filed a paternity suit in September 1982, claiming that she was Paul's illegitimate daughter. In order to disprove her claim, Paul offers to submit to blood tests or to any other tests determined by the German courts. Although Paul insists that he was not Miss Huebers father, the court orders that he continues to make the payments until the case is settled. Later, Bettina Huebers, besides making lucrative appearances on German TV chat-shows, also poses nude for an adult German magazine, claiming she did so because, in her words, "I needed the money after Paul had not made any payments to me." (See entry for Friday October 14.)

Sunday April 17
 In the UK, following heavy television advertising the night before, the *Sunday People* newspaper prints a three-page article by Denny Laine's wife Jo Jo about her time spent with the McCartneys.

Tuesday April 19
 London's Victoria & Albert Museum write to George at Friar Park expressing their interest in buying a Burne-Jones window they had seen during a recent visit to George's mansion in Henley-on-Thames.

Thursday April 21
 The *Daily Express* reports that, "Ringo turned up at his son Jason's school fete with nothing but £50 notes for the 5p entrance fee. His chauffeur was sent home and found nothing, so instead ended up plundering Jason's money box for the coin."

Wednesday April 27
 At the St. James Club in London, Paul and Linda join Ringo and Barbara to help celebrate the latter's second wedding anniversary.

Saturday April 30
 The 20th anniversary reissue of The Beatles' 'From Me To You' reaches number 40 in the UK singles chart.

May
 The McCartney/Stevie Wonder hit 'Ebony And Ivory' receives the award for International Hit Of The Year at the prestigious annual Ivor Novello Awards ceremony, held at the Grosvenor Hotel in London. This month also sees Paul winning an award for his album *Tug of War* at the German Phono-Academy Awards, called *Bambi*.
 In the English countryside, near Henley, Handmade Films begin shooting the comedy *Bullshot*, starring Billy Connolly.
 At Tittenhurst Park, Ringo completes the two-month periodical taping of the ABC-FM American radio series *Ringo's Yellow Submarine – A Voyage Through Beatles Music*, which is scheduled to begin transmissions on Saturday June 4. This month, the American *National Enquirer* magazine reports: "Ringo Starr ran up a $700 dinner bill for himself and pals at *La Eaterie* and then refused to give a tip. 'I don't believe in tipping,' he told dumbfounded waiters."

Sunday May 8
 Filming concludes at the Elstree Studios in Borehamwood, Hertfordshire, on Paul's film *Give My Regards To Broad Street*. To celebrate, a huge party is thrown on the set for the cast and crew, with everyone present being given a crystal cut glass tumbler inscribed with the recipient's name and the line: "With Love From Paul & Linda". (Additional brief post-production filming on *Broad Street* is still required, and scheduled for July 16 [see entry] and 26.) It is reported that Twentieth-Century Fox will be the distributors for the film, which is scheduled for an America premiere on October 25, 1984, and in the UK in Liverpool on November 28, 1984.

Monday May 9
 The Beatles' producer George Martin, promoting his new book *Making Music*, is a guest on this morning's TV AM breakfast show *Good Morning Britain*.

Wednesday May 11
 In England, the *Daily Mirror* newspaper publishes an exclusive picture of Paul and Ringo, dressed in Fifties style, at a re-creation of London's Lyceum Theatre, performing in concert for the film *Give My Regards To Broad Street*.

Saturday May 14
 George Martin appears on BBC Radio One plugging his new book *Making Music*.

Monday May 16
 In Hollywood, California, Ringo and Barbara are pictured on the set of the made-for-television two-part mini series *Princess Daisy*, based on a story by Judith Krantz. They play the roles of gay fashion designers.
 In England, an interview with Paul is published in the *Daily Mirror* in which he explains how he writes a song.
 George Martin appears on BBC Radio One where he talks about working with Paul on the *Give My Regards To Broad Street* film.

Friday May 27
 In an American courtroom, Fred Seaman pleads guilty to charges of grand larceny. He is sentenced on July 14 to five years probation on the condition that he never reveals the contents of John's documents and manuscripts that have been in his possession.

Sunday May 29
 A revised edition of the two-hour radio special *The Beatles At The Beeb* is syndicated in America. This version features tracks that had not been heard on the original broadcasts.

June
 After much discussion, Paul re-signs with CBS Records in America. The deal includes two more albums, one of which is *Pipes Of Peace*. This month, an interview with Paul is published in the American *Parade* magazine.
 In the States, Johnny Carson's Carson Productions purchase from Yoko the exclusive rights to produce the TV film *Imagine – The Story Of John Lennon & Yoko Ono*. This will not be announced publicly until August.
 Seel Street in Liverpool is chosen as the sight of *Beatle City*, the planned permanent museum dedicated to The Beatles. The provisional opening date is January 1, 1984.

Friday June 3
 It is announced that this summer Abbey Road Studios will be throwing open its doors to the general public for the first time.

Saturday June 4
 In America, Ringo's 26-week ABC Radio Network series, entitled *Ringo's Yellow Submarine*, featuring the former Beatle in the role of DJ reminiscing about The Beatles, begins transmissions. (The DJ links were recorded at his Ascot home during April and May of this year.) One memorable show features Ringo spinning the original Capitol Beatles "open-ended" interview disc from February 1964, while asking the questions himself. (The final broadcast takes place on November 26.)

Sunday June 5
 A live interview with Paul, carried out on the set at Shepperton Studio, is transmitted on MTV in America.

Monday June 6
 George earns praise in the Soviet newspaper *Sovietskaya Rossiya* for his musical abilities and concern for the Third World. The paper notes his 1971 charity concert for the people of Bangladesh.

Tuesday June 7
 As Paul's train pulls into London's Charing Cross station, he spots an elderly woman struggling with a heavy suitcase and volunteers to help. Climbing into his waiting chauffeur driven silver Volvo car, he calls out to her, "You'll be all right now" as the car drives away. The lady, thinking Paul was a porter, had given him a tip.

Thursday June 16
 Ringo's album *Old Wave* is released in Germany. A single featuring the tracks 'In My Car'/'As Far As We Can Go', is also released today in the country. The album is also

released in several other countries as well, including Canada on June 24 but not in the US or UK.

🍎 In England, at BBC Broadcasting House in London, Paul records an interview with Simon Bates for his BBC Radio One show, during which he talks about *Broad Street*, his upcoming *Pipes Of Peace* album and also sings the Radio One jingle. (The feature is transmitted the following day, on Friday June 17.) Paul spends the rest of this month recording in London at George Martin's AIR Studios.

Saturday June 18
🍎 In America, the Westwood One radio station celebrates Paul's birthday by transmitting in its Startrack Profile series, a special programme entitled *Paul McCartney – The Solo Years*.

Monday June 20
🍎 An interview with Yoko is published in the *New York Post*.

Sunday June 26
🍎 An interview with Paul is published in *Parade* magazine.

July
🍎 At the Hit Factory recording studios in New York, Yoko returns to the *Double Fantasy* leftover tracks with a view to issuing them as an album.
🍎 George appears in the American magazine *Ford Times*, in which he is seen sitting on the bonnet of Ford's new 4-wheel drive Bronco II car in Hawaii.
🍎 Paul records an interview intended for airing on London hospital radio stations only. The programme is called *Paul McCartney's Bedside Manners*.

Monday July 4
🍎 Paul is seen at AIR Studios in Oxford Street, London. On the completion of these sessions, he flies off to Montserrat to record at George Martin's studios, where he records a demo of 'My Darkest Hour' for Frankie Miller.

Friday July 8
🍎 In London at 12:30pm , introduced by the Abbey Road Managing Director Ken Townsend, the first public airing of *The Beatles At Abbey Road* video presentation takes place in Studio 2 for the benefit of 200 members of the press and TV. The 75-minute (two-part) show features narration from the Capital Radio DJ Roger Scott, and a host of previously unheard Beatles studio outtakes and rarely seen archive film clips. Among the American television crews invited are MTV and ABC TV. (The show will not open to the general public until Monday July 18.)
🍎 In the UK, Warner Home Video release, on rental only, Ringo's 1981 comedy film *Caveman*.

Monday July 11
🍎 Two days after unveiling the tracks for the press, EMI's Abbey Road Studios in London announces the "finding" of some previously unreleased Beatles recordings, namely 'How Do You Do It?', 'That Means A Lot', 'If You've Got Troubles' and 'Leave My Kitten Alone'. Of course, they had not just been "discovered" at all: this is all part of the promotion for the upcoming *The Beatles At Abbey Road* studio presentations. (See entry for Monday July 18.)

Tuesday July 12 (until September 17 – 3 shows a day)
🍎 Granada Television's Beatles archive clips documentary, now titled, *The Beatles Early Days*, receives its world premiere screening at New York's Museum of Broadcasting, at One East 53rd Street. Accompanying the programme is a compilation of Beatles films from the Museum's own personal collection, such as their *Ed Sullivan Show* appearances (1964–1966), and excerpts from The Beatles performance in Washington on February 11, 1964.

Saturday July 16
🍎 In the early hours of the morning, outside London's Leicester Square tube station,

near the *Talk Of The Town*, Paul, sporting a three-day growth of beard and dressed in a pair of dirty jeans and T-shirt, is filmed "busking", with an acoustic guitar for a scene intended for the movie *Give My Regards To Broad Street*.

Monday July 18

"Abbey Road Studios Presents The Beatles – Come and experience the magic of Number Two studio where The Beatles recorded from 1962–69. This is a unique opportunity for a limited period to see an exciting and unusual video with original sound recordings of The Beatles At Abbey Road. Recording equipment will be on display, records, books and souvenirs on sale, and refreshments provided." – EMI Promotional handout.

🍎 In London, EMI open Abbey Road's Number Two studio to the general public for a special 75-minute video programme, entitled *The Beatles At Abbey Road,* which is presented three times daily (10:30am, 3:30pm and 7:30pm) for a limited period until September 11. (Tickets are priced at £4.50 each.) The presentation includes the first public airing of two of the four tracks ('How Do You Do It?' and 'Leave My Kitten Alone') allegedly discovered by EMI just one week previously. The show also offers a chance to examine the original recording equipment used by The Beatles during their time at the studios in the Sixties. In the audience at the opening night are members of Paul's MPL staff and the parents of Olivia Harrison. As the Abbey Road show continues, Paul, once enthusiastic about the presentation, becomes distressed because Beatles fans gather outside his Cavendish Avenue home before and after the shows. As a result, Paul offers to buy up all the remaining tickets for the shows.

According to the sleeve notes on the back of the *Sessions* bootleg album: "On one particular night, after Paul McCartney had finished work at EMI's new penthouse studio, he quietly slipped into the audience after the lights had gone down and watched most of the show, making sure to disappear in time before the end. He apparently enjoyed listening to The Beatles' classic material, and alerted George and Ringo who were treated to a private viewing. After George had listened to himself recording the first take of 'While My Guitar Gently Weeps', he immediately asked EMI to release the track as soon as possible."

Saturday July 23

🍎 Linda's *Photographs* exhibition opens at the Barry Stern galleries at 12 Mary Place, Paddington, New South Wales, Australia. It will run until August 12.

Monday July 25

🍎 Paul, George and Ringo are seen enjoying a quiet drink together in the bar of the Gore Hotel in Queen's Gate, Kensington, in London.

Tuesday July 26

🍎 Paul returns to the Elstree Film Studios in Hertfordshire to supervise the brief post-production shooting of scenes for inclusion in *Give My Regards To Broad Street*.

Sunday July 31

🍎 MTV in America broadcasts an interview with Peter Brown and Steven Gaines to promote their new Beatles exposé book *The Love You Make*.

August

🍎 In America, Johnny Carson's Carson Productions announce plans for a three-hour TV film about John's life with Yoko, tentatively titled *Imagine: The Story Of John And Yoko*. American publishers Simon & Schuster announce that they will not be publishing Fred Seaman's memoirs of his life working with the Lennons. Seaman, meanwhile, announces that he will assist Albert Goldman on his biography on John.

🍎 At the start of the month, important members of the EMI staff are invited to MPL's Soho Square offices to hear Paul's new album, which will now be titled *Pipes Of Peace*. In the second week of the month, Paul and Linda visit Hampton, New Jersey, where he is seen jogging around the town. This month, an interview with Paul is published in the Liverpool music paper *Break Out* while his former musical partner Denny Laine is declared bankrupt, apparently with debts totalling $40,000.

 Ringo and Barbara are found in the Caribbean, discussing plans for a multi-million pound development to provide holiday hideaway homes for extremely rich celebrities. Also this month, Ringo joins George at the London premiere of the film *Superman III* starring Christopher Reeve.

 In England, *Titbits* magazine runs a story publicising the existence of a priceless audio tape featuring The Beatles and Elvis Presley, recorded during their famous meeting at Elvis' rented Bel Air, California, home on August 27, 1965.

Thursday August 4
 The Baldwin/Wallace college radio station BW88 in Berea, Ohio, Texas, broadcasts a Yoko Ono marathon programme, which includes an exclusive interview with the Lennons' personal assistant Elliot Mintz.

Saturday August 6
 Paul returns to Liverpool where he has lunch with his brother Mike at the Armadillo tea rooms in the city. Paul later flies on to New York where he begins legal action against bootleggers who have released The Beatles' unreleased 1964 version of 'Leave My Kitten Alone'.

Saturday August 13
 In Hawaii, George is sued for £26 million by two of his neighbours, who claim that he has ruined their reputation. After the hearing, which involves a "rights-of-way" path near his property, George screams to reporters: "Have you ever been raped? I'm being raped by all these people." Apparently, George had requested that the path in question be moved to one side of his 24-acre Hawaiian property, but the judge rules that the path, which is currently 60 feet from Harrison's residence, should be moved, but only 125 feet from George's house. After the hearing, the former Beatle remarks to the reporters: "Privacy is the single most important thing in my life!"

Monday August 22
 A rare television screening of the 1965 concert film *The Beatles At Shea Stadium* occurs when several Public Broadcasting Stations in America screen the 48-minute programme.

Friday August 26 (until Friday September 2)
 Paul joins George Martin for recordings at AIR Studios in Oxford Street, London.

Sunday August 28
 At the annual *MerseyBeatle* Convention in Liverpool, original bricks from the Cavern Club in Mathew Street are sold to raise money for the Strawberry Fields children's community home in Liverpool. At the conclusion of the convention on Monday August 29, Paul, Linda and family arrive in their car at the Adelphi Hotel where they had arranged to pick up Victor Spinetti who was a guest speaker at the convention.

September
 Exasperated by the media's addiction to scandalous tales about John, Yoko and Sean briefly settle in San Francisco, California.

 At the end of the month, Ringo and Barbara are seen in the audience at the Hard Rock Cafe in London at a benefit concert for former Small Faces and Faces bassist Ronnie Lane, who has been struck down with multiple sclerosis. To help the cause and to aid fellow MS sufferers, Ringo and Barbara bid £1,250 for a ride on the train, The Orient Express. Also in attendance this evening are Ringo's former wife Maureen and her new husband, Isaac Tigrett, the Hard Rock's co-owner.

 In Los Angeles, a few local cable stations begin screening a version of The Beatles' 1968 film *Yellow Submarine* complete with the 'Hey Bulldog' scene intact, a scene usually trimmed from US transmissions. Also this month, it is reported that the MGM/UA 1982 video documentary *The Compleat Beatles* has been certified gold, with American sales totalling over 25,000.

Thursday September 1
 In England, the children's charity single, 'The Celebrity Selection Of Children's Stories', is released by Warwick Records and features sleeve notes by Paul and Linda.

◆ At the Sotheby's auction in London, John's battered red and black Broadwood piano sells for £8,000 to an anonymous American buyer.

Tuesday September 6 (until Monday September 12)
◆ In London, Paul and Linda host their annual Buddy Holly Week extravaganza.

Friday September 9
◆ In England, *The Sun* newspaper reports that George is ready to fork out £50,000 for a greenhouse at an auction at Stanbury Park farm in Reading, Berkshire. The greenhouse was originally built in 1902 for a South African diamond millionaire.

Saturday September 10
◆ The 20th anniversary re-issue of 'She Loves You' reaches number 45 in the UK singles chart.
◆ In America, at 10pm (EST), the 1979 Concert For Kampuchea show, featuring Wings, is transmitted on MTV.

Monday September 12
◆ George, who has not been seen on UK TV since he was interviewed by the DJ Nicky Horne on February 19, 1979 (see entry), makes a very short filmed appearance on the BBC1 show *Film '83*, where he is seen on location in Henley being interviewed about his new Handmade movie *Bullshot* starring Billy Connolly.
◆ Linda's book *Photographs*, previously released in hardback in September 1982, is released in paperback in the UK by Pavilion Books.

Tuesday September 13 & Wednesday September 14
◆ A play about The Beatles called *John, Paul, George, Ringo* is staged at London's Young Vic Theatre.
◆ In America, there is a Beatle rumour that the Beverly Hills designer Sidney Altman has installed a $3,000 carved oak toilet, somewhat like a church pew, in Harrison's Hawaiian hideaway home. Apparently, the ceramic seat of the toilet has been painted with flowers, on one side of the toilet a candle holder hangs and on the other side a gold chain hangs which is connected to a bell. To top it all off, when you lift the toilet seat, it plays John's 1967 Beatles' tune 'Lucy In The Sky With Diamonds'. (During George's April 1986 *Today* show interview, he will take great pains to point out that this story was just not true!)
◆ In Liverpool on Wednesday, proposals to make The Beatles Freemen of the City is condemned as an "insult" to the previous recipients of the award, which dates back to the nineteenth century. The plan, proposed by Liberal Councillor Miss Rosemary Cooper, a former Cavern Club member, angers fellow council member Eddie Rodsrick, who says: "This is an insult to the men and women, living and dead, who hold the title of Freemen." John Chambers, chairman of the Liverpool based Beatles Appreciation Society, welcomes the move, saying: "It is a tremendous idea. The Beatles deserve it!"

Thursday September 15
◆ Ringo and Barbara are seen out socialising in London again, this time at a televised Variety Club party to celebrate Tommy Steele's 25 years in showbiz.

Monday September 19
◆ An interview with Paul, comprising pieces left out of the August *Break Out* magazine, is published today in the *Liverpool Echo*.

Thursday September 22
◆ Paul and Linda, alongside Ringo and Barbara, Eric Clapton and former Monkee Micky Dolenz, attend The Everly Brothers' comeback concert at London's Royal Albert Hall.

Wednesday September 28
◆ The war over whether or not The Beatles should be honoured with The Freeman of Liverpool rages on. Paul's brother Mike has this to offer: "The Beatles may refuse the Freeman of Liverpool offer because the honour by Liverpool City Council has been so long in coming."

Thursday September 29

🍏 In America, Rick Smulian, the founder of R/S Distribution record company, announces that he is going to release a 30-minute Beatles album entitled *John, Paul, George And Ringo,* which features the Christmas messages The Beatles sent out to their fan club members between 1963 and 1969. Smulian reveals: "The project is strictly on the level, as the tapes were acquired from Pete Bennett, who was The Beatles' promotions man." (Asked about the tapes, Bennett claims they were given to him by John.) Smulian continues: "The Christmas messages were previously released on an album called *Happy Michaelmas* in 1981 by the Adirondack Group in Houston, Texas and their release never had any problems!" The Beatles are most unhappy about this new release. Yoko, through her spokesman Elliot Mintz, releases the brief statement: "The plan to release the record is illegal." Neil Aspinall of Apple in London, has this to offer: "The Beatles' Christmas material is still licensed. EMI owns all the Capitol material, but this is *not* EMI material. The Christmas records were given away, so the copyright is still owned by Apple and therefore The Beatles." He insists: "It *cannot* be used without permission of the four individuals, with one person (Yoko Ono) representing John's estate." (Shortly after Neil's statement, it is announced that representatives of The Beatles are to sue those involved with the R/S Distribution release of *John, Paul, George And Ringo.*)

October

🍏 Back in London, Paul gives a 40-minute interview for Radio GOSH, a British hospital radio station based at the Great Ormond Street Hospital for Sick Children. He also records a one-hour special for the British Hospital Radio Association.

Paul films a cameo appearance with Tracy Ullman for the video 'They Don't Know'. He is seen driving a three-wheeled Reliant Robin, with Ullman sitting beside him. (Tracy had asked Paul to appear after she had guested in his *Broad Street* film.)

🍏 The planned ITV network premiere of the Granada TV documentary, now titled *The Early Beatles 1962–1965,* fails to materialise, even though Paul has given his "Thumbs up" to the project. Both George and Ringo remain quiet on the subject. Asked about the non-appearance, a spokesman for the station announces that the delay is due to "finding more Beatles footage in our library, which we would like to use in the programme". (Soon afterwards, the station says a Christmas screening across the ITV network is now likely.)

🍏 After a delay of a year, Thorn-EMI finally release on home video in the UK Apple's 1971 film *The Concert For Bangla Desh.* As before, Ravi Shankar's section is severely cut.

Monday October 3

🍏 Paul's single 'Say Say Say', featuring a duet with Michael Jackson, backed with 'Ode To A Koala Bear', is released in both America and the UK, along with a 12-inch single featuring 'Say Say Say' (extended remix), 'Say Say Say' (instrumental) and 'Ode To A Koala Bear'.

Tuesday October 4 (until Friday October 7)

🍏 Over four days on various locations in Los Alamos, about 70 miles from Los Angeles in California, working with the director Bob Giraldi, Paul, Linda and Michael Jackson shoot a promotional film for 'Say Say Say'. For the clip, which features a production cost of over $500,000, Paul utilises nearby locations, including the Union Hotel where Paul is seen playing pool. Heather McCartney makes a cameo appearance in the children's foster home sequence.

Wednesday October 12

🍏 In Liverpool, after much deliberating, it is announced by the City Council that Paul, George and Ringo, and Yoko, on behalf of John, are to be invited to the city to personally collect their Freeman of the City awards.

🍏 In a spoof of the *Compleat Beatles* video sleeve, Palace Video in the UK releases the home video *The Compleat Rutles,* featuring the wonderful 1978 *Rutles* TV special, starring Eric Idle and Neil Innes. Shortly after the initial copies are released, the videos have to be recalled on the insistence of MGM/UA, who feel that the similarity between their *Compleat Beatles* and the *Compleat Rutles* are too close for comfort. Palace Video subsequently issues *The Rutles* video in a totally different sleeve.

Thursday October 13

🍏 Liverpool City Council, following the initial proposal by Councillor Rosemary Cooper, passes unanimously the idea to give to The Beatles the honour of being made Freemen of the City. (It is hoped that their investiture will take place in May, 1984, to coincide with the opening of the Liverpool Garden Festival.)

Friday October 14
🎤 At BBC Broadcasting House in Portland Place, London, Paul records an interview promoting 'Say Say Say' for the BBC Radio One programme *Saturday Live Show*. He talks about the forthcoming *Give My Regards To Broad Street* film and how he loves The Beatles' *Revolver* album. (The session is transmitted on the station the following day, October 15.) Also today, blood tests carried out in London prove that Paul is not the father of Bettina Huebers. Professor Volkmar Schneider, who flew in especially to carry out the tests, confirms to reporters: "There is no mistake," adding, "Paul has been most helpful in assisting me with the tests."

Monday October 17
🎤 The release of Paul's album *Pipes Of Peace* is delayed in the UK. Sources close to Paul reveal he wishes to coincide the UK release with that in America, which is scheduled for October 31.

Tuesday October 18
🎤 In America, *The Enquirer* magazine reports that Paul has bought for Stevie Wonder, at a cost of $100,000, a huge hand-crafted bed, featuring a built-in stereo system with speakers at each of the bed's four-corners.

Thursday October 20
🎤 In London, Handmade Films' *Bullshot,* starring Billy Connolly and featuring a theme tune sung by "Legs" Larry Smith, formerly of The Bonzo Dog Doo Dah Band, opens at the Classic Cinema in the Haymarket.
🎤 Tonight's edition of *Top Of The Pops* on BBC1 had been scheduled to include 'Say Say Say' but, due to Paul being unhappy with the soundtrack of the clip, he suggests its UK TV premiere should take place on October 27. An announcement to this effect takes place during tonight's *Top Of The Pops* broadcast.

Friday October 21
🎤 Yoko is awarded a court settlement of £120,000 from a neighbour who accidentally flooded her New York Dakota apartment. The neighbour, Janet Paterson, had forgetfully left her bath water running while she went out shopping.

Saturday October 22
🎤 A pre-recorded interview with Paul is transmitted on the BBC Radio One programme *Saturday Live*.

Thursday October 27
🎤 Even though an announcement was made the previous week saying that tonight's edition of *Top Of The Pops* on BBC1 would be screening for the first time the 'Say Say Say' video, the broadcast of the clip fails to materialise because the song has slipped down the UK singles charts.

Friday October 28
🎤 The video for 'Say Say Say' is finally shown for the first time on UK TV when it is transmitted on Channel Four's *The Tube*. Meanwhile, at the Milburn Galleries, in Brisbane, Queensland, another exhibition featuring shots from Linda's *Photographs* book, is open to the public. This will run until November 19.

Saturday October 29
🎤 Paul and Linda, in an exercise aimed at getting the film of 'Say Say Say' aired on BBC TV, make their first live television studio appearance since Wednesday December 19, 1973 (see entry) by appearing on the variety show *The Late Late Breakfast Show,* hosted by the DJ Noel Edmonds and transmitted from the BBC TV Centre in Wood Lane, London, on BBC1 between 5:50 and 6:35pm. They partake in a light-hearted question and answer session with Edmonds and introduce, as planned, a screening of the 'Say Say

Say' promotional film. Unfortunately, Paul's first live television appearance in years is somewhat disappointing. Fans of McCartney blame Edmonds for asking Paul and Linda uninteresting questions, while television critics accuse Paul and Linda of ducking questions set by the host. Either way, the appearance does the trick and in the UK singles chart 'Say Say Say' rises from number 14 to number three.

Sunday October 30
 In the States, Ringo and Barbara plug the new *Princess Daisy* TV film by giving an interview for the *Dallas Morning News* newspaper.

Monday October 31
 As planned, Paul's new album *Pipes Of Peace* is simultaneously released in the UK and in America.
 EMI's 18-month-old mid-price label Fame releases The Beatles' 1966 compilation album *A Collection Of Beatles Oldies . . . But Goldies*, featuring the exact same track line-up and cover design.

November
 Paul appears in a pre-recorded interview transmitted on LBC, the London Broadcasting Company radio station.
 The children's television producer Britt Alcroft visits Ringo at his Tittenhurst Park mansion to discuss narrating the new series *Thomas The Tank Engine And Friends* for ITV. Ringo, feeling that children today are more interested in stories about "dinosaurs with handguns", initially declines the offer but finally agrees to record for Britt sample narrations of five *Thomas* stories.

Tuesday November 1
 Paul, Linda and family arrive back at Heathrow, fresh from their visit to Los Angeles, California.

Wednesday November 2
 Ringo's wife Barbara talks about Ringo being a good father in the UK magazine *Family Circle*.

Thursday November 3
 An interview with Ringo and Barbara promoting *Princess Daisy* is published in the newspaper *US Today*.

Friday November 4
 In the UK, BBC Radio Four transmits a 20-minute documentary profile on Derek Taylor. Peter Marshall presents the programme.
 In the UK, Paul Simon releases his album *Hearts And Bones*, which features 'The Late Great Johnny Ace', his tribute to John.

Monday November 7
 In America, Ringo appears in a brief interview on the CBS TV show *Entertainment Tonight* to promote *Princess Daisy*. Later, the concluding part of the two-part NBC made-for-TV film, starring Ringo and his wife Barbara, is screened on American TV.

Friday November 11
 Ringo records an interview in the gardens of his Tittenhurst Park mansion in Ascot for a special feature on Marc Bolan, for the Channel 4 music show *The Tube* in the UK. The item, which is transmitted in two weeks time on Friday November 25, also includes clips from Apple's 1972 film *Born To Boogie*.
 In America, MTV announces that Paul's next single will be 'The Man', his duet with Michael Jackson.
 The NBC TV programme *Friday Night Videos* transmits a newly re-edited promotional film for The Beatles' track 'A Hard Day's Night', which features a clever combination of the beginning and the end of the film.

Tuesday November 15
🍎 Paul writes the theme music to Richard Gere's film *The Honorary Consul*.

Saturday November 19
🍎 Tom Evans, former member of the Apple band Badfinger and half of the Ham & Evans songwriting team, is found hanged at his home in Surrey.

Monday November 21
🍎 Picture Music International and Dave Clark International release the first home video compilation from the legendary Associated Rediffusion/ITV pop series *Ready, Steady, Go!* This includes The Beatles' March 20, 1964, appearance performing 'You Can't Do That' and 'Can't Buy Me Love' and being interviewed.

Thursday November 24
🍎 An interview with Paul is published in the UK teenage pop music magazine *Smash Hits*.

Saturday November 26
🍎 The 20th anniversary reissue of The Beatles' 'I Want To Hold Your Hand' makes number 62 in the UK singles chart.

Tuesday November 29
🍎 In the early hours of the morning, Yoko and Sean arrive at Heathrow Airport from New York. It is Sean's first visit to John's homeland.

December
🍎 A low-quality CD of The Beatles' 1969 album *Abbey Road is* released in Japan by EMI-Toshiba, several years before EMI officially release The Beatles' albums on compact disc. This unapproved release, which is deleted in 1985, thus becomes the first Beatles album to be issued on CD.
🍎 Iain Johnstone interviews Paul at AIR Studios in Oxford Street, London, for the American CBS TV show *Entertainment Tonight*. Further interviews carried out by Paul this month include the 26-minute American special *MTV In London* and interviews for BBC Radio 1 with both Richard Skinner and Simon Bates, the latter for the programme *Paul McCartney Now*. During the early part of the month, Paul, working with producer Hugh Symonds, films a promotional clip for 'Pipes Of Peace' at Chobham Common in Surrey, which movingly recreates the famous Christmas Day truce of 1914 between English and German troops in France. The filming, which starts at 8am and utilises the services of 100 extras, lasts two days. On the first day, Paul, who had his hair cut especially short for the filming, arrives on the set at 6am and spends two hours in make-up. Away from the video, Paul records an interview with Capital Radio in London, in which he reveals that the mothers of both Pattie Harrison and Brian Epstein were most upset by Philip Norman's book *Shout!* Linda sends a £1,000 Fortnum & Mason Christmas hamper, and a note of encouragement, to the women anti-nuclear protesters camped outside Greenham Common air base.
🍎 Ringo signs an agreement to narrate 26 five-minute episodes of the animated children's show *Thomas The Tank Engine And Friends* for Central Television, the Midlands based area of the ITV network. An added incentive in the deal is that Ringo acquires lucrative shares in the *Thomas The Tank Engine* character.

Thursday December 1
🍎 An eight-hour meeting takes place in Yoko's eighth-floor suite at London's Dorchester Hotel with Paul, George and Ringo, reportedly in order to conclude the affairs of Apple. John's widow, in Britain for the first time since his death, has turned the plush suite into a mini fortress as she and the three former Beatles discuss how to split their multi-million pound empire. Yoko tells reporters: "I have decided I don't need all my possessions and am giving much away to charity." At the end of the meeting, at approximately 9pm, the three Beatles leave the building individually. Ringo, climbing into the back of a Rolls Royce with Barbara, is asked: "Are The Beatles going to get together again?" His reply is most direct: "Don't be daft!" Paul and Linda are the last to leave, climbing into the back of their Mercedes without uttering a word. The following

morning, Yoko and Sean travel on to Tokyo, Japan where they spend Christmas at a seaside resort.

◆ In America, the first of a two-part interview with Paul is transmitted on CBS TV's *Entertainment Tonight*. (Part two is aired on Sunday December 4.) Still Stateside, a further interview promoting *Pipes Of Peace* is aired on the WGCL Cleveland radio programme *The Source*.

Saturday December 3

◆ Paul gives a one-hour interview to the DJ Simon Bates for inclusion on his BBC Radio One morning show, where he talks about *Pipes Of Peace*, track by track. Paul reveals that he burned his copy of The Beatles' exposé book *The Love You Make* written by the former Beatles' aide Peter Brown.

Monday December 5

◆ The album *Heart Play – Unfinished Dialogue,* featuring excerpts from John's September 1980 *Playboy* interview, is released in America. (The UK release takes place on December 16.)

◆ Paul and Michael Jackson's single 'Say Say Say' reaches number one in America. Paul's single 'So Bad'/'Pipes Of Peace' is released in America. (In the UK, the single is released with the A and B-sides reversed.)

Tuesday December 6

◆ Another exhibition for Linda's *Photographs* takes place at Molly Barnes Gallery in Los Angeles, California. This will run until January 15, 1984.

Thursday December 8

◆ On the third anniversary of John's tragic death May Pang, his former lover, is a guest on TV AM, the breakfast show serving the ITV network.

Sunday December 11

◆ In America, MTV broadcasts their recently conducted interview with Paul in a 26-minute special programme called *MTV In London*.

◆ WGCL in Cleveland rebroadcasts, in a special programme called *John Lennon – A Day On The Radio*, John's February 13, 1975 radio interview with Scott Muni on the New York radio station WNEW.

Tuesday December 13

◆ In the UK, Paul appears in a pre-recorded filmed interview to promote 'Pipes Of Peace' on the Tyne-Tees children's ITV Network pop programme *Razzmatazz* (broadcast between 4:21 and 4:44pm).

Wednesday December 14

◆ Paul appears, in a pre-recorded filmed insert, on the BBC1 programme *Harty*, hosted by Russell Harty. During his appearance, Paul is seen with George Martin mixing the track 'Pipes Of Peace' at Martin's AIR Studios in Oxford Street, London.

Friday December 16

◆ Paul is interviewed by Leslie Ash on the UK TV Channel 4 pop-music show *The Tube* (broadcast between 5:31 and 6:59pm). The feature begins outside AIR Studios in Oxford Street, where Paul joins Leslie in a London cab, which arrives at Regent's Park. The interview concludes with Paul giving her a guided tour of the zoo in the park.

◆ Polydor records, in the UK, release the album *Heartplay – Unfinished Dialogue*, which features a 42-minute extract from John's marathon 22-hour *Playboy* interview in September 1980 (see entry).

Sunday December 18 (until Saturday December 24)

◆ London Wavelength's *BBC Rock Hour* broadcasts over seven days, as further promotions for 'Pipes Of Peace', a pre-recorded one-hour interview with Paul carried out by Sarah Ward of WMMS Cleveland, Ohio.

Friday December 23

In America, NBC TV broadcasts the first half of a pre-taped interview with Paul on the show *Friday Night Videos*. The programme also includes the promotional films for both 'Say Say Say' and 'Pipes Of Peace'. The second half of the interview is transmitted on Friday January 27, 1984.

Sunday December 25

A pre-recorded Christmas interview with Paul, carried out by Allan Banks, is transmitted across Europe on the German BFBS Radio station.

Monday December 26

A one-hour Boxing Day radio special entitled *The Beatles At Christmas* is transmitted in England on BBC Radio Two between 1:00 and 1:59pm.

Saturday December 31

A pre-taped 40-minute interview with Paul is transmitted on the Signal radio station.

"*Broad Street* has taken over $1.4 million at the American box office and it's currently in the top 20 of the American films. The reviews have been 50% good and 50% bad and people are going to see it, not in huge droves, but they are going to see it!"

– Paul

January
🍎 The UK press prints a report suggesting that Paul and Bill Wyman, the bass player of The Rolling Stones, will soon narrate a 12-part TV series on the history of rock music on UK TV. This does not materialise. Also this month, Paul and Linda take a memorable vacation in Barbados, West Indies. Paul's single 'Pipes Of Peace' reaches number one in the UK singles chart.

Sunday January 1
🍎 Following delays of almost a year, Granada TV in England finally broadcasts, across the ITV network between 5:41 and 6:29pm, the programme *The Early Beatles: 1962–1965*. The 45-minute documentary, which came about only because the show's producer Johnny Hamp wanted to transfer the best of Granada's archives onto videotape and stop them disintegrating, comprises fascinating Beatles interviews, TV appearances and newsreels shots. Johnny Hamp is asked why it does not feature a narrative accompaniment: "Putting together this material was more a labour of love than work. We decided we didn't need any commentary as we felt the film speaks for itself, to quote the opening credits." Johnny is also asked why Granada Television didn't use more of the unscreened four and a half hours of Beatles film discovered in their archives, and simply make the programme longer: "Naturally, we just had to use the cream of it in the time available. It would have been nice, for instance, to see the full 22-minute interview with Ken Dodd. We also found a 10-minute interview with Pete Best and his mother Mona shortly after his sacking, which is very interesting, especially as Mona does most of the talking."

Tuesday January 3
🍎 Paul, Linda and family depart from Heathrow Airport en route to New York and then Barbados for a two-week holiday. Reporters, who naturally haven't seen the *Pipes Of Peace* video, ask him why his hair had been cropped so short. "I had it cut for my *Pipes Of Peace* video, which was set in 1914, so I styled my hair to the period," he explains.

Thursday January 5
🍎 In America, an interview with Paul carried out on the set of 'Say Say Say' on Wednesday October 5, 1983, is transmitted on the WKYC News channel, a local NBC station.

Friday January 6
🍎 The first single release off *Milk And Honey* takes place when John's 'Nobody Told Me', backed by 'O'Sanity', performed by Yoko, is released in America. (The UK release takes place on January 9.)

Friday January 13
🍎 To promote his radio programme tomorrow, the DJ Andy Peebles is a guest on *BBC Breakfast Time* on BBC1. The feature also includes the first ever UK screening of the promotional film for 'Nobody Told Me'.
🍎 Paul, Linda and their children James and Stella arrive in Bridgetown in Barbados from New York. They set up base in a private home called Potter's House on the Caribbean island's west coast.

Saturday January 14
🍎 BBC Radio One broadcasts, between 1:00 and 1:59pm in FM Stereo, the programme *Life Without Lennon*, featuring Yoko Ono in conversation with Andy Peebles in Tokyo, Japan.
🍎 During the McCartneys' Barbados holiday, Paul is spotted skiing and surfing on a rubber raft.

Sunday January 15
🍎 Paul and Linda's Barbados vacation turns sour when, acting on a tip-off, their villa is raided by local police who discover 10 grams of marijuana on Paul and seven grams on Linda. The McCartneys are immediately charged with drug possession. Local police inspector Alan Long says: "We received a tip-off that they were in possession of marijuana. Four uniformed officers went round to the McCartneys holiday villa with a search warrant. Mr. McCartney freely admitted his guilt and accompanied the officers to the police station." They are ordered to appear in court the following day.

Monday January 16

♦ In the Barbados courthouse, Paul and Linda appear before Judge Haynes Blackman and plead guilty to possession of marijuana. They are fined 200 Barbados dollars ($100 dollars) each. Paul's Barbados lawyer David Simmons tells the judge: "Paul is a very talented and creative person. People who have this talent sometimes need inspiration." Following the hearing, they get ready to head back to England, the flights having been booked before their court appearance. Chief Immigration officer Kenrick Hutson is quick to point out that the McCartneys were not deported and they will be free to return. (Paul's court appearance takes place four years to the day after he was arrested in Japan.) As Paul leaves the court, he remarks to waiting reporters: "I've got absolutely no grudges and no complaints. It was a small amount of cannabis and I intended to use it, but the police came to my place and I gave them 10 grams of cannabis. Linda had another small carton of cannabis (seven grams) in her handbag."

Meanwhile in America, Paul's videotaped message to Michael Jackson is syndicated across the country on the *American Music Awards*.

Tuesday January 17

♦ The McCartneys arrive back in England at London's Heathrow airport and, following an unhindered walk through customs, Paul emerges alone to face the waiting reporters. He takes the opportunity to air his views on marijuana: "Can we get one thing straight. Whatever you think, or whatever you think I've done . . . this substance cannabis is a whole lot less harmful than rum punch, whisky, nicotine and glue, all of which are perfectly legal. I would like to see it decriminalised because I don't think, in the privacy of my own room, I was doing anyone any harm whatsoever." Joined by Linda, Paul and his family are driven a short distance to board their private aircraft, but just as they are boarding the plane customs men ask Paul and Linda to return to the customs hall where, at approximately 12 noon, they are interviewed and more marijuana is found, this time in Linda's hand baggage. She is charged with possession and arrested at Heathrow's police station on the airport's perimeter. Linda is released on unconditional bail and ordered to appear before Uxbridge magistrates court on Tuesday January 24 (see entry). News of Linda's arrest does not reach the media for another six hours. The incident at Heathrow features largely on news reports around the globe, including both BBC and ITN news bulletins in the UK and *CBS Morning News* in America.

Friday January 19

♦ John and Yoko's album *Milk And Honey – A Heart Play* is released in America. (The UK release takes place on January 23.) The album appears on compact disc in the UK, the first ever Beatles related CD to be released in the country. The original sleeve design for *Milk And Honey* was due to feature over 200 heart shaped photographs of the couple.

♦ Paul, from his Rye home, rings a national newspaper to say that Linda's recent drug bust "wasn't her fault!" He adds: "All our bags were thoroughly searched by police in Barbados after we were busted there. They told us we were clean but they obviously didn't do a thorough job. Most of the time, Linda doesn't know what's in her bag anyway. It wouldn't have been there if they'd done their job properly!"

Tuesday January 24

♦ Following her arrest at Heathrow Airport last Tuesday, Linda appears at Uxbridge Magistrates Court in Middlesex. Paul and Linda arrive early but still face massed ranks of cameramen. During the 13-minute hearing, Paul sits in the public gallery and listens while Linda pleads guilty to illegally importing a small quantity of cannabis weighing 4.9 grams, with an estimated street value of £4.90. Her defence council, Mr. Edwin Glasgow, tells the magistrates: "Linda is genuinely sorry, and wishes to make a genuine apology. I urge the court not to make an example of her just because she is famous. Linda is a thoughtful, likeable woman who has done far more for other people than those who sneer at her." After a few moments deliberation, the magistrates fine her £75 ($105). As the McCartneys leave the courts Linda, who had given her address as Soho Square in London, remarks to waiting reporters: "It's all much ado about nothing," adding, "I am unhappy about being treated as a criminal when I am just an ordinary person."

♦ In Liverpool, Yoko and Sean, who arrived in England only this morning on a *Milk And Honey* promotional visit, are on a sightseeing tour of Beatles landmarks, followed every inch of the way by a posse of photographers, reporters and television cameras. The

Lennons are seen at Penny Lane and Strawberry Fields, where Yoko promises a gift of £250,000 to the children's home.

Friday January 27
🍎 NBC TV in America broadcasts the second half of a taped interview with Paul on the programme *Friday Night Videos*. The show also screens the promotional film for 'So Bad'. Meanwhile, in the latest edition of the London entertainment magazine *Time Out,* there appears an article by Paul recommending legislation to legalise marijuana.

Tuesday January 31 (daily until Friday February 3)
🍎 In an attempt to cash in on Paul's recent drugs problem, the *Sun* newspaper prints a four-part article by his former Wings partner Denny Laine about his life and times with Paul. The TV commercial to promote the series features a ridiculously thick Birmingham accent amateurishly dubbed over Laine's moving lips.

February
🍎 The four-man Beatles committee meets at EMI's headquarters in Manchester Square to discuss plans to release an album of The Beatles' BBC recordings. The project is so far advanced that the album's artwork has already been prepared but, somewhat predictably, the album is scrapped due to legal objections from Apple just prior to release. Mike Heatley, the general manager of EMI's international department, releases this statement: "There is a possibility that the BBC material will be released in the future, but it is very much in the lap of the gods."

Thursday February 2
🍎 Humphrey Ocean's officially commissioned portrait of Paul is unveiled at The National Portrait Gallery in London. Paul and Linda miss the event as they are still engaged with work on their film *Give My Regards To Broad Street.*

Friday February 3
🍎 The French television station TF-1 screens the 1972 film of John and Yoko's *One To One Concert*, originally recorded at Madison Square Garden in New York on August 30, 1972.

Saturday February 4
🍎 George's appearance on the NBC TV show *Saturday Night Live*, originally screened in America on November 20, 1976 (see entry), receives its UK TV premiere when it is broadcast on London Weekend Television only, in the south-east area of the ITV network.

Sunday February 5
🍎 In the UK, an interview with Yoko is published in the *Sunday Times*.

Monday February 6 (daily until Thursday February 9)
🍎 The ABC TV breakfast show *Good Morning America* begins a four-day 20th anniversary celebratory look back at The Beatles' first visit to America.
🍎 In the UK, an interview with Yoko, carried out with Nicholas Wapshott, is published in *The Times.*

Tuesday February 7
🍎 The 20th anniversary of The Beatles' arrival in America is celebrated at a six-day EXPO in Miami, Florida.

Friday February 10
🍎 In America, tonight's edition of *Friday Night Videos*, features another appearance by Paul and a screening of the newly created Capitol Records 20th anniversary promo film for The Beatles' 'I Want To Hold Your Hand'.

Saturday February 11
🍎 'So Bad' reaches number one on the American singles chart.

Monday February 13
🍎 To further celebrate the 20th anniversary of both The Beatles' first visit to America and their first number one in the country, Capitol Records reissue the single 'I Want To Hold Your Hand' complete with its original black & white picture sleeve (Capitol 5112). To promote the release, Capitol mounts a massive advertising campaign, which includes 40,000 posters and 2,500 T-shirts and metal badges. In addition, over 400 American radio stations play Beatles-related programming. To coincide with the 20th anniversary celebrations, *Life* magazine features The Beatles on their cover, just as they did in 1964, as does *Rolling Stone*.
🍎 The planned Paul and Michael Jackson UK single 'The Man' (Parlophone 6066), backed with the unreleased track 'Blackpool', as featured on the unreleased film *The Backyard* (see entry for Thursday August 15, 1974), is cancelled just prior to release. The scheduled 12-inch single was due to feature an unreleased instrumental version of the A-side. The promotional film clip to accompany the song remains untransmitted.

Friday February 17
🍎 The Beatles' American 20th anniversary celebrations continue when the 10th annual *Beatlefest* convention takes place in New Jersey.

Tuesday February 21
🍎 At the annual British Rock and Pop Awards in London, transmitted live on BBC1, Paul's *Pipes Of Peace* film receives the award for Best Video of 1983. Paul, currently on a skiing holiday with Linda and the family, is unable to attend the ceremony so instead, he records a video message, which is screened during the ceremony. The director Keith MacMillan collects the award on behalf of Paul.

Friday February 24
🍎 George celebrates his 41st birthday on holiday in Hawaii with Olivia and Dhani.

Tuesday February 28
🍎 In the UK, Videoform Pictures release on home video Judith Krantz's 1983 made-for-TV film *Princess Daisy* starring Ringo and Barbara.

Wednesday February 29
🍎 In America, Paul's *Tug Of War* album is released on CD.
🍎 There are further record activities in the UK when EMI officially delete from their catalogue The Beatles' compilation albums *Rarities* and *Reel Music,* the latter being scrapped by EMI less than two years after its original release.
🍎 Also today, EMI release their first Beatles-related compact disc, in the shape of Paul's album *Pipes Of Peace*.

March
🍎 The current issue of *Playboy* magazine features an alarming report by David Sheff on the theft of many of John's personal belongings from his Dakota apartment, sadly some only days after his tragic death. These include his handwritten diary and demo tapes of unreleased songs. John's former employee Fred Seaman is charged with the theft and later arrested. Many of the stolen items are recovered. According to the story, which is entitled *The Selling Of John Lennon*, Seaman had kept 10 notebooks in which he stated his intention to use the information contained in the stolen items in a book of his memoirs. Seaman also reportedly planned to plant false stories in the news media casting doubts on Yoko's sanity, character and even of her sexual habits. He even allegedly purchased illegal drugs, claiming that they were intended for her. Seaman was ultimately convicted and sentenced to five years probation. Seaman's lucrative book deal with *Simon and Schuster* collapsed when the publisher learned of the deception and then immediately sued Seaman for $47,500, the advance already paid to him plus $1 million in punitive damages. (Seaman would eventually release a book in September, 1991, entitled *The Last Days of John Lennon*.)
🍎 John Barrett, the sound engineer at Abbey Road and one of the inspirations behind last year's *Beatles At Abbey Road* show, dies after a long illness. John, aged 31, spent many hundreds of hours going through The Beatles' tape archives at EMI, discovering the many different takes of songs used in the special Abbey Road presentations.

 In London at the end of the month, following a holiday in Switzerland, Paul films a cameo appearance for the Bob Marley promotional clip of 'One Love', where he is seen miming the title of the song and embracing the video's director Don Letts. (On May 8, the film is released on the Island Bob Marley home video release entitled *Legend*.) Paul also records at AIR Studios in London with George Martin. During one of these sessions he loans out his prized left-handed Beatles bass guitar to the group Wang Chang, who were recording in an adjacent studio. Apparently their guitarist had left his own bass guitar at home.

 After years of lying derelict, the old Apple building at 3 Saville Row, London, is sold along with the other buildings on the block to the Midlands Council Workers' Pension Fund for $3.2 million. The block soon serves as the headquarters for the Building Societies Association.

Thursday March 1

 The newspaper *The Dallas Morning News* reveals that both George and Ringo will be accepting Liverpool's Freedom of the City award and that Yoko will be accepting it on behalf of John.

Saturday March 3 & Sunday March 4

 A two-day Beatles convention takes place at Glasgow's Central Hall in Scotland, an event organised by the Paul McCartney Fan Club of Scotland.

Monday March 5

 In London, Geoff Dunbar wins the British Academy of Film and Television Award for 'Best Short Animated Film' with *Rupert And The Frog Song*. He collects the award from TV personality Rolf Harris.

Tuesday March 6

 The *Daily Mail* newspaper publishes an interview with George, by Margaret Minxman, in which he discusses Handmade Films, his current fondness for big band music and his love of movies.

Thursday March 8

 In the UK, the *Daily Express* newspaper reveals, one week after *The Dallas Morning News*, that Ringo will be accepting his Freedom of the City award.

Friday March 9

 John's single 'Borrowed Time'/'Your Hands', performed by Yoko, is released in the UK. (The American release takes place on May 11.) The single record is also available as a 12″, John's first in the UK.

Saturday March 10

 In the UK, the London Weekend Television series of selected episodes of NBC TV *Saturday Night Live* shows continues when tonight they broadcast the episode originally transmitted on October 2, 1976 which features the first ever clip of *The Rutles* (see entry).

Monday March 12

 In the UK, EMI release 15 classic oldies singles as part of a series called *Golden 45s*. Amongst the first set is John's 'Give Peace A Chance'/'Cold Turkey' and Ringo's 'It Don't Come Easy'/'Back Off Boogaloo'.

 An interview with George is published in the European editions of *Newsweek* magazine where again he talks about the rise of Handmade Films. (This interview is not featured in the American editions of the magazine.)

Thursday March 15

 John's single 'I'm Stepping Out'/'Sleepness Nights', performed by Yoko, is released in America.

Friday March 16

🍎 The promotional film for John's 'I'm Stepping Out' is premiered in America on tonight's edition of NBC TV's *Friday Night Videos*. MTV also screens the clip later this night, but trims the brief nude scenes. In England, the UK premiere of the film also takes place tonight on BBC2's *The Old Grey Whistle Test*. Also today in the UK, Polydor releases a limited edition (10,000 copies) version of 'Borrowed Time' housed in a special poster bag.

Wednesday March 21

🍎 Yoko, flanked by both Sean and Julian, officially opens Strawberry Fields, a teardrop-shaped memorial garden dedicated to John, in New York's Central Park.

🍎 After their return from a vacation in Switzerland, Paul and Linda attend a musical reception at St. James's Palace to help launch a £1 million appeal for the Aldeburgh foundation. The McCartneys are seen chatting with the Queen Mother.

Friday March 23

🍎 In the UK, *Milk And Honey* releases continue thick and fast when Polydor release a 12-inch picture disc version of the album. The issue is strictly limited to only 2,000 copies.

Saturday March 31

🍎 The 20th anniversary reissue of 'Can't Buy Me Love' peaks at number 53 in the UK singles chart.

April

🍎 During this month, several American TV stations transmit the 30 minute programme *Paul McCartney: The Man, His Music, His Movies* as part of the US series *On And Off Camera*, which focuses on the making of Paul's *Give My Regards To Broad Street* film. This month, fresh from his acting role in *Broad Street*, rumours in the industry suggest that Paul is to concentrate more on his acting career by signing with the top theatrical agent Duncan Heath. "Paul will definitely do more films," says the enthusiastic *Broad Street* producer Andros Epaninom. "Believe you me, he's amazing! I've worked with Jack Nicholson, Ryan O'Neal, Ralph Richardson and Paul's up there with them. He's absolutely superb!"

🍎 Yoko is quoted as saying: "I couldn't bear to look at Sean – he reminded me too much of John."

🍎 During the month, Paul and Ringo announce officially that they will both accept Liverpool's Freedom of the City award, while George remains noncommittal. It is now believed that Julian will collect the award on behalf of John.

🍎 Ringo and Barbara spend their Easter weekend at the Cipriani Hotel in Venice.

Monday April 2

🍎 In New York, after a trial which had lasted several days, the State Supreme Court orders that Yoko must pay the record producer Jack Douglas $2,524,809 plus three years interest for the work he carried out on the 1980 album *Double Fantasy*. The court ruling also insists that she must also pay Douglas a percentage from the royalties arising from the release of the recent *Milk And Honey* album, which contains the left-over tracks from the 1980 sessions. Yoko had maintained throughout the hearing, which she attended every day, that Douglas had agreed to a one-off fee before the recordings commenced on August 4, 1980. Also today, at the Palm Springs Spa Hotel, Yoko donates one of John's lithographs to the Barbara Sinatra celebrity art auction, an event that will benefit the family counselling service of Coachella Valley's programme for sexually abused children.

🍎 A three-part interview with Paul begins today in the Scottish newspaper the *Daily Record*. (Part two is printed tomorrow while part three appears on Wednesday April 4.)

Wednesday April 4

🍎 In the UK, an interview with Paul is published in the *Sun* newspaper.

Friday April 6
🍎 Ray Coleman promotes his upcoming two volume John Lennon biography on the BBC regional television programme *Scotland Today*.

Monday April 9
🍎 At 10:30am, the multi-million pound "multi-media experience" permanent *Beatle City* exhibition centre officially opens in Seel Street, Liverpool.

Tuesday April 10
🍎 Location filming for the promotional clip to accompany 'No More Lonely Nights' takes place today at the Old Justice Pub at the Dock Head in Bermondsey, London SE16. The shooting continues late into the night with scenes of exploding fireworks. The firecrackers annoy local residents and police receive calls of complaint. Callers are simply told: "I'm sorry, but Mr. McCartney is simply doing some filming!" In between takes, Paul and Linda chat to the regulars in the pub, one of whom is an old lady who asks Paul: "Are you famous? What groups have you been in?" Paul replies: "The Beatles?" "Nah," the lady replies. "Never heard of 'em!"

Wednesday April 11
🍎 The first of a two-part pre-recorded interview with Paul is transmitted on Capital Radio. The concluding part is aired one week later on April 18.

Thursday April 12
🍎 Lawyers acting on behalf of Mark David Chapman tell a New York court that Chapman was mentally incompetent when he pleaded guilty in 1981 and his sentence should be reduced. The appeal is turned down.

Saturday April 14
🍎 In England, *Woman's Own* magazine publishes the article "Yoko Faces The Wife Of Lennon's Killer", in which she announces: "I'm still angry – I can't forgive yet."
🍎 Linda appears alongside the legendary Sixties photographer David Bailey in a programme about photography on BBC Radio One.

Monday April 23
🍎 Pre-recorded interviews with Paul are transmitted today on BBC Radio Merseyside, in a show called *McCartney: The Man*, and on BBC Radio Northampton.

Wednesday April 25
🍎 The former "Apple Scruff" Carol Bedford, plugging her book *Waiting For The Beatles*, appears on the London radio station LBC.

Thursday April 26
🍎 Paul's brother Mike unveils the £40,000 statue of The Beatles by John Doubleday at the new £8 million Cavern Walks shopping centre in Mathew Street, Liverpool. Fans close to the statue cannot hide their disappointment. "From close up," Mike McCartney remarks, "I didn't even recognise any of them – not even my own brother!" Other guests in attendance include John's first wife Cynthia. The ribbon-cutting grand opening of the Cavern Walks complex in the Royal Life insurance complex, which includes the newly rebuilt, newly reconstructed Cavern Club, also takes place today. The three Beatles fans who started the "Beatles monument in Liverpool campaign" back in 1977 are not present. Asked about this, a spokesman for Royal Life says: "This particular statue has been commissioned and paid for by Royal Life. Our only obligation to John Chambers (one of the founders of the 'Beatles monument campaign') is to keep him informed."
🍎 Tonight's edition of *Top Of The Pops* (Thursday April 26) on BBC1 in England includes the promo film for Bob Marley's 'One Love', which features a brief cameo appearance by Paul.

Saturday April 28
🍎 Paul's video message to Michael Jackson is repeated in certain parts of America during the American Music Awards ceremony.

Monday April 30
 The Sheffield Art Gallery secures, from an auction in London, a collection of four hand painted acrylic emulsion drawings as used in The Beatles' 1968 animated film *Yellow Submarine*. The items, two of George and two of Ringo, cost £320 apiece.

Wednesday May 2
 In Liverpool, Her Majesty The Queen, Queen Elizabeth II, officially opens the Beatle Maze at the Liverpool International Garden Festival. During her visit, she steps aboard the life-size Yellow Submarine, which is a part of the exhibition.

Sunday May 6
 At the McCartneys' family home Rembrandt, in the Wirral on Merseyside, Paul and Linda are the guests of honour at a 6pm family get-together.

Tuesday May 8
 The *Art Of The Beatles* Exhibition, which portrays three decades of the group in the form of cartoons, paintings, photographs, album covers, lithographs and sculptures, opens in London. (The event runs until September 30.)

Monday May 14
 The PMI (Picture Music International) home video *Ready Steady Go! Volume 2* is released, featuring The Beatles' October 4, 1963, appearance, performing 'She Loves You', 'I'll Get You' and 'Twist And Shout', plus interviews with Dusty Springfield and Keith Fordyce.
 Ringo appears unannounced as a surprise guest on the Thames/ITV network comedy quiz show *What's My Line?*

Friday May 18
 In America, a sneak preview of Paul's film *Give My Regards To Broad Street* is shown tonight at the Phipps Plaza Cinema in Atlanta, Georgia.

Monday May 21
 George is to be found in the relative tranquillity of the annual Chelsea Flower Show in London. His appearance does not go unnoticed, and a camera crew from America's CNN (Cable News Network) interviews the former Beatle in a report on the horticultural get-together.

Thursday May 24
 The Lennons' former Tarot cards reader, John Green, releases his book on his time with the couple, entitled *Dakota Days*.

Wednesday May 30
 In the UK, Vestron Video International schedules for release, for the very first time on home video, The Beatles' 1964 cinema film *A Hard Day's Night*, featuring a new Dolby stereo soundtrack. Just prior to its issue, PMI (Picture Music International), the music video division of EMI, claims that they control the rights to the music contained on the tape, and are granted a High Court order which temporarily restrains Vestron from releasing the video. Vestron plead that they had acquired the rights from Walter Shenson, the film's producer, a point disputed by PMI who claims that the UK rights were never Shenson's to sell. The case continues.

Thursday May 31
 Just two years after it was first issued, EMI Records in the UK delete the compilation single 'The Beatles' Movie Medley'.

June
 Apple's 1971 film *The Concert For Bangla Desh* is finally released in America on home video.

Sunday June 3
 The world premiere of the MTV 26-minute programme *Milk And Honey* takes place in

America, and features the first US showings of the promotional videos for 'Borrowed Time' and 'Grow Old With Me' as well as the previously transmitted clips for 'Nobody Told Me' and 'I'm Stepping Out'. The show also features interviews with both Yoko and Sean.

Monday June 4
🍎 Stanley Paul Publishing prints the book *Tales From The Saddle,* a collection of over 40 hilarious and hair-raising encounters with horses compiled by the pop star Alvin Stardust and featuring a short anecdote by Paul and Linda.

Saturday June 9
🍎 In England, Paul and Tracy Ullman are the guests on the very first edition of the networked London Weekend Television ITV show *Aspel And Company,* hosted by Michael Aspel and recorded at the Television Studios on the South Bank in London. Following the pre-recorded interview, which was taped on Thursday June 7, in which they speak at great length about the *Give My Regards To Broad Street* film, Paul and Tracy perform a duet of 'That'll Be The Day' to close the show.
🍎 In Holland, the Dutch Beatles fan club *Beatles Unlimited* celebrates the 20th anniversary of the group's appearance at the Treslong Television Studios in Hillegom, Holland, by holding their fifth annual convention in the exact same venue. A special guest at the gathering is Jimmy Nichols, the drummer who deputised for Ringo when he had a bout of tonsillitis back in 1964.

Monday June 11
🍎 In Australia, the 20th anniversary of The Beatles' one and only visit to the country is celebrated on the television show *The Mike Walsh Show.*

Sunday June 17
🍎 Paul gives a live interview to Stuart Grundy on the BBC Radio London show *Echoes,* in which he discusses his passion for rock and roll. In October this year, the interview is syndicated around America to promote Paul's *Give My Regards To Broad Street* film.

Monday June 18 & Tuesday June 19
🍎 In America, a two-part interview with Paul is transmitted on NBC TV's *Today* show.

Sunday June 24
🍎 At an auction in New York, Yoko sells many items from her private collection. The sale is titled *Yoko's Attic Sales.*

Thursday June 28
🍎 In the UK, Sidgwick & Jackson publish Ray Coleman's biography *John Winston Lennon 1940–1966,* the first volume of a two-part account of John's life.

July
🍎 At his home studios in Sussex, Paul records a demo of 'On The Wings Of A Nightingale', a song he has written especially for The Everly Brothers to record.
🍎 At the London studios of Britt Alcroft, Ringo begins recording his narration for *Thomas The Tank Engine And Friends.*

Wednesday July 4
🍎 In America, Ringo performs as a special guest at two Beach Boys American Fourth of July concerts. During the afternoon he appears with the group on The Mall in Washington, DC, drumming on 'Back In The USSR', and later he joins the group to perform at an evening concert in Miami, Florida.
🍎 Back in England, Cynthia Lennon and Ray Coleman are the special guests on this morning's TV AM breakfast show.

Thursday July 5
🍎 The Home Theater Network in America shows the Keef & Co. television film of the December 1979 concerts for Kampuchea, entitled *Rock For Kampuchea.*
🍎 BBC Radio Merseyside transmits The Beatles tribute programme *Magical History Tour.*

Friday July 6
 Following the conclusion of the legal dispute between Vestron and PMI, The Beatles' 1964 film *A Hard Day's Night* is simultaneously released on Vestron home video cassette in America and in the UK. (In the States, the film is also released on laser disc.) In addition to the 1981 re-mastered version of the film, the tape also includes the photomontage to accompany the song 'I'll Cry Instead' which appears at the very start of the video.

Monday July 16
 John's single 'I'm Stepping Out' backed with 'Sleepless Night', performed by Yoko, is released in the UK. A 12-inch version featuring a third track, 'Loneliness' extracted from Yoko's 1982 album *It's Alright*, is also released today.

Friday July 27
 Rumoured US premiere screenings of *Give My Regards To Broad Street* in Cincinnati and various other American cities fail to take place today.

Saturday July 28
 Today at AIR Studios in London, Paul spends the day mixing the disco version of 'No More Lonely Nights'. Meanwhile, in an adjacent studio, fellow recording legends Pete Townshend and Mick Jagger are also recording, and as today is Jagger's birthday Paul takes a bottle of Scotch whisky to their session and joins them reminiscing about "The good old days".

Prior to the transmission of today's *Desert Island Discs* on BBC Radio 4, host Roy Plomley reads out an apology to Larry Parnes, stressing that Paul's comments on the programme about Parnes, two and a half years ago on January 30, 1982, were intended as a joke. (Larry Parnes was offended when Paul said that The Beatles never received any money for backing Johnny Gentle on the tour of Scotland back in 1960.)
 Today, the reissue of The Beatles' 'A Hard Day's Night' reaches number 52 in the UK singles chart and the *A Hard Day's Night* home video reaches number two in the *Music Week* video chart. It will reach the top spot one week later.

August
 In England, rumours in the record industry suggest that five unreleased Beatles tracks will soon be included on an upcoming TV-advertised EMI Beatles compilation album.

Friday August 24
 In the UK, The Everly Brothers release the single 'On The Wings Of A Nightingale', a track written and mixed by Paul.

Sunday August 26
 In Liverpool, the *1984 Beatles Convention* takes place at the St. George's Hall. Guest speakers at the one-day affair include Mike McCartney, Ray Coleman and Tony Barrow.

Thursday August 30 & Friday August 31
 A two-day Sotheby's rock and roll memorabilia auction takes place in London. The Beatles' section takes up both the morning and afternoon sessions on the first day. During the Beatles' auction, 24 out of the 356 lots are withdrawn at Paul's request before the sales begin. When the sale gets underway, "The Beatles" Ludwig bass drum skin sells for £4,200 and two of John's harmonicas go for £950 and £850. In addition, John's 1960 hand drawn unpublished 16-page manuscript called *A Treasury Of Art And Poetry*, featuring poetry, drawings and cartoons, sells for an amazing £16,000.

Saturday September 8
 In America, MTV broadcasts the short MPL Buddy Holly documentary film entitled *The Music Lives On*. The show, with a running time of only 14 minutes, also features Paul's September 14, 1979, Hammersmith Odeon in London performance of 'It's So Easy' and 'Bo Diddley'. On this date the show is also transmitted in the UK on Channel Four/ITV network at 1:30am, totally unannounced, and is repeated later this morning on the ITV region of London Weekend Television. The screening neatly coincides with the annual MPL Buddy Holly Week, which begins in London today and runs until Friday

September 14. To promote the event, MPL run a national competition, with the assistance of the ITV breakfast station TV AM, where people are asked to draw portraits, sketches or drawings of Buddy Holly.

Sunday September 9
🍎 In New York, at Forest Hills, Yoko and Sean are seen in the VIP enclosure at the United States open tennis championship final between John McEnroe and Ivan Lendl.

Thursday September 13
🍎 The album *Every Man Has A Woman* is released in America and features John's solo harmony vocal of the title track, originally recorded for Yoko's version of the song back in 1980. (The album is released in the UK on September 21.)

Sunday September 16 & Monday September 17
🍎 The two-part American TV film *Princess Daisy* receives its UK premiere across the ITV network between 7:46 and 9:28pm. (Part two is screened the following night.)

Monday September 24
🍎 Paul's single 'No More Lonely Nights' (ballad version)/'No More Lonely Nights' (playout version, featuring a running time of 3.56) is released in the UK. The 12-inch edition features 'No More Lonely Nights' (extended playout version, lasting 8.10)/'No More Lonely Nights (ballad)–Silly Love Songs'. (The American release takes place on October 5 and October 2 respectively.)
🍎 John's first electric guitar is returned to England, smuggled out of West Germany to avoid a possible export ban. It will go on display at Liverpool's Beatle City. The Hofner guitar, signed by all four Beatles, was given by the group as a prize in a talent contest at a club in Hamburg in 1962. Its owner, Frank Dorstal, reveals that he once refused a six-figure sum for the guitar.

October (onwards)
🍎 The marathon radio special entitled *Sgt. Pepper's Lonely Hearts Club Band*, featuring a history of The Beatle Years 1962–1970 is aired in America and in the UK. The series features many rare Beatles recordings, including a 1962 Cavern rehearsal, songs from the October 24, 1963, concert from Swedish radio, John's 1963 demo for 'Bad To Me' and, from the 1964 UK TV special *Around The Beatles*, a performance of the unreleased track 'Shout!' alongside a medley of their hits.

October
🍎 During the first week of this month, a secret agreement is reached by which Northern Songs, owned by the Associated Communications Corporation's company ATV, pay Paul McCartney and the estate of John Lennon approximately £2 million and increase the royalty rates to the two ex-Beatles. Due to a "no-publicity" clause in the agreement, no further details are leaked. However, it is revealed that ATV Music, the owner of the Lennon/McCartney song catalogue copyrights, has been put up for sale by Associated Communications. As this case ends, another opens in London with Paul, George, Ringo and Yoko filing a lawsuit against EMI over audit and royalty discrepancies, mainly in America.
🍎 The videotape of The Beatles' June 30, 1966, Tokyo concert at the Budokan Hall is released by The Beatles Collectors' Shop on home video, titled *The Beatles Live In Japan*.
🍎 In England, Paul's soundtrack album *Give My Regards To Broad Street* reaches number 1 in the UK album charts.
   In Poland, an exhibition of Linda's photographs opens at the ZPAF Gallery in Warsaw. Due to American *Broad Street* promotions, Paul and Linda are unable to attend. At the start of the month, Paul gives a lengthy interview to Terri Hemmert of the WXRT radio station in Chicago. Further *Broad Street* promotional interviews this month include TV appearances on news and magazine shows such as *Canada AM*, *Hollywood Happenings*, *Channel 4 LA*, *Franklin Reports*, and CNN.

Tuesday October 2
🍎 Paul's promotional film for 'No More Lonely Nights' receives its world premiere on MTV in America.

1984

Friday October 5
 Paul's single 'No More Lonely Nights' (ballad version)/'No More Lonely Nights' (playout version 3:56) is released in America. The B-side is later changed to the Arthur Baker 'Special Dance Mix'. While the labels are reworded with this information, the American picture sleeves remain unaltered. No official announcement of the change in this release is ever made to the public.
 John's single 'Every Man Has A Woman Who Loves Him'/'It's Alright', performed by Sean Ono Lennon, is released in America. (The UK release takes place on November 16.)

Tuesday October 9
 To help promote *Thomas The Tank Engine And Friends*, Ringo appears as a special guest on the TV AM show *Good Morning Britain* in the UK. Besides being interviewed, he also takes part in a cooking segment. The 13-week *Thomas The Tank Engine* series premieres across the ITV network later this day (at 12 midday and repeated again at 4pm) and, all told, features 26 five-minute segments.
 On what would have been John's 44th birthday, Yoko donates another $90,000 to the Strawberry Fields Salvation Army home in Liverpool. This brings the total to $100,000 given to the children's home.

Wednesday October 10
 A 30-minute interview with Paul, carried out by Roy Leonard, to promote *Broad Street* is transmitted on Chicago's WGN radio station.

Sunday October 14
 In England, London Weekend Television's *The South Bank Show* features a one-hour programme devoted to Paul and the making of his film *Give My Regards To Broad Street*. The 48-minute programme, shown across the ITV network between 10:31 and 11:29pm, also marks the first public broadcast of Paul's new versions of The Beatles' classics 'Eleanor Rigby', 'For No One' and 'Yesterday'. The show is transmitted later in America, with the title *The Making Of Give My Regards To Broad Street*.

Monday October 15
 Paul and Linda arrive in New York for promotional activities for *Give My Regards To Broad Street*. Their schedule includes several taped interviews and many appearances on TV shows. Paul is also honoured for his services to music at an ASCAP luncheon, held at New York's Jockey Club.
 In the UK, Charisma Records release Julian Lennon's début album, *Valotte*.

Tuesday October 16
 At the Plaza Hotel in New York, Paul and Linda take time off from *Broad Street* promotions to meet the winners of the 'Meet Paul McCartney' competition, set by Paul's London based Wings Fun Club. After which, Paul and Linda board a plane and return to Chicago.

Thursday October 18
 Paul and Linda, now based in Chicago, hold a press conference for *Broad Street*. Meanwhile, back in England, Paul's promotional film for 'No More Lonely Nights' receives a screening on tonight's edition of BBC1's *Top Of The Pops*.

Friday October 19
 Paul gives another, albeit brief, *Broad Street* promotional interview, this time to the Chicago station WLS.

Monday October 22
 Paul's soundtrack album to his film *Give My Regards To Broad Street* is released simultaneously in both the US and UK. The line-up is, side one: 'No More Lonely Nights', 'Good Day Sunshine', 'Corridor Music (incidental music)', 'Yesterday', 'Here, There And Everywhere', 'Wanderlust', 'Ballroom Dancing', 'Silly Love Songs'; side two: 'Silly Love Songs (incidental reprise)', 'Not Such A Bad Boy', 'No Values', 'No More Lonely Nights (incidental ballad reprise)', 'For No One', 'Eleanor Rigby'/'Eleanor's

Dream', 'The Long And Winding Road', 'No More Lonely Nights (playout version)'. EMI releases the album simultaneously on standard black vinyl and on compact disc, the first time that the organisation has done this. The cassette edition of *Broad Street* features additional dialogue and a new recording by Paul of his song 'So Bad'. In addition, the CD version features these and a brand new McCartney song, not included in the *Broad Street* film, entitled 'Goodnight Princess', intended to be played in cinemas when the lights go up as patrons leave the theatre. Also today in England, the second promotional video for 'No More Lonely Nights' (dance version) is prepared for television distribution. This clip, aimed purely for the influential MTV market, was shot on Saturday October 20 at the Hippodrome in London and features Jeffrey Daniels of *Starlight Express* fame, who also cameos in Paul's *Broad Street* film.

Tuesday October 23

🍎 The day begins with Paul and Linda holding another press conference for *Give My Regards To Broad Street* at the Beverly Hills Hotel, in Los Angeles, California.

🍎 Later, in Studio 1, NBC Studios, 3000 W. Almeda Avenue, Burbank, sixteen years after appearing on the show with John, Paul records an appearance on the long running NBC TV *Tonight Show* with Johnny Carson. (This is actually Paul's first appearance with Carson, as back on Tuesday May 14, 1968, Paul and John were interviewed by the major league baseball player Joe Garagiola while Carson was temporarily unavailable for duty.) Besides being interviewed about the *Broad Street* film, Paul picks up an acoustic guitar and performs a mock-drunken version of a few lines from 'Yesterday' and 'You Are My Sunshine'. Paul's 23-minute appearance is transmitted by WNBC TV later this evening.

Wednesday October 24

🍎 Promotions for *Broad Street* continue unabated with Paul appearing live for 90 minutes on the American radio call-in show *Rockline*. Then, later in the day just prior to the press screening of *Broad Street*, Paul and Linda host a party for the gathering at the Bistro Restaurant in Beverly Hills, California. Also today, a short pre-recorded interview with Paul is featured in the ABC TV programme *Rocker Special*. Paul and Linda return to New York early the following morning.

Thursday October 25

🍎 At last, following the heavy promotional tour, Paul's big-screen film *Give My Regards To Broad Street* receives its world premiere at the Gotham Theater in New York. (A further 8pm screening also takes place tonight at the Capitol 3 Cinema, situated at 820, Granville Street, in Los Angeles, California.) The following day, the film begins to run nationally, accompanied by Paul's short animated film *Rupert And The Frog Song*.

American media reviews of the film are almost totally negative. *Variety* magazine describes it as: "Characterless, bloodless and pointless!" The *Washington Post* writes: "There are only 50 shopping days till Christmas, so let's go out on a limb – *Give My Regards To Broad Street* is the worst movie of the year!" In his review of the film for CBS Television, the respected American entertainment reporter Joel Siegel states: "McCartney's performances are lifeless. He can't act and he sings like he seems he's above performing for us. This is nothing more than a $9 million home movie. Compared to The Beatles' films, *Give My Regards To Broad Street* needs *Help!*"

To coincide with *Broad Street*'s release, MTV run a competition where you can win Paul's 1955 Ford Popular as featured in the film. Out of over 200,000 entries, the winner is Annette M. Smith, who lives in Kenmore, New York.

Thursday October 25 (until Wednesday October 31)

🍎 Paul appears on five consecutive *Good Morning America* weekday shows to help promote *Broad Street*.

Friday October 26

🍎 As expected *Give My Regards To Broad Street* opens nationwide across America in 311 cinemas. Within a month, the number of theatres still running the film has dropped to just 28. According to the Hollywood Trade papers, the film, has thus far taken just $1.4 million at the box office.

Sunday October 28
 Paul gives a *Broad Street* promotional interview to the New York radio station WPLJ.

Monday October 29
 The remixed 7-inch and 12-inch versions of the 'No More Lonely Nights' singles are released in the UK, thus replacing the original September releases. Several unique mixes of 'No More Lonely Nights', such as the "Mole Mix", appear as promo releases.

Tuesday October 30
 The second part of Ray Coleman's extensive biography of John, *John Ono Lennon 1967–1980,* is published in the UK by Sidgwick & Jackson.
 In the States, a pre-recorded interview with Paul is featured in the MTV programme *Linear Notes.*
 Through a press statement, issued in Los Angeles, George announces that he has declined his Freedom of the City award in Liverpool.

November
 Reports emerge in the press that Linda has been the subject of a kidnap plot. Scotland Yard detectives believe Linda was to have been snatched from the McCartneys' Scottish farmhouse and held until Paul paid £10 million ransom.
 The long established family chain store Marks & Spencer branch out into music when, for a two-month trial period, they begin issuing a £4.99 Beatles package. This consists of a 64-page book, edited by Joyce Robbins, and a 16-track cassette, featuring an exact track-by-track replica of EMI's 1966-compilation album *A Collection Of Beatles Oldies . . .*
 At the start of the month, George re-records, at his Friar Park studios, the Bob Dylan composition 'I Don't Want To Do It', later to be released on the *Porky's Revenge* film soundtrack album. A slightly different mix of the track is released as a single in America only. During these ten day (periodical) sessions, George also records a new vocal, featuring slightly different lyrics, for 'Save The World', which is included on the 1985 charity album *Greenpeace.*

Friday November 2
 A pre-taped interview with Paul appears on the American CBS TV show *Entertainment Tonight.* Paul and Linda also appear on the radio show *A.M. Chicago.*

Monday November 5
 PMI home video in the UK releases *Ready Steady Go! Volume 3*, featuring excerpts from The Beatles' performance on November 27, 1964, which includes 'She's A Woman', 'Baby's In Black', 'Kansas City'/'Hey-Hey-Hey-Hey' and an interview with the host Keith Fordyce. (The track 'I Feel Fine', also performed on the show back in 1964, is not part of the compilation.)
 Paul's single 'We All Stand Together' (from the MPL short animated film *Rupert And The Frog Song*)/'We All Stand Together' (humming version) is released in the UK only.

Wednesday November 7
 Earlier in the day, Paul records an interview at New York's Carlyle Hotel for NBC TV's *Friday Night Videos*, a show which also features an interview with Julian Lennon. Due to Julian being caught in a traffic jam, which means he arrives later for his taping session, they accidentally meet for the first time in 10 years. Paul and Julian's separate interviews are transmitted on Friday November 16.

Sunday November 11
 The first of a two-part, pre-recorded, interview with Paul is transmitted by Capital Radio in London to promote *Broad Street.* (Part two is aired one week later on November 18.)

Monday November 12
 In America, Paul is heard on both Radio Radio's *Top 30 USA* and on *Rock Notes.*

Wednesday November 14
 George leaves Los Angeles (at 9:45pm) on flight Pan Am PA 815 en route to Sydney in Australia, where he will arrive at 7:25am on Friday November 16. Then, at 9:30am, on the

Trans Australian Airways flight TN 436 (DC9), he boards a plane to Brisbane, arriving at 9:45am.

Friday November 16
🍎 Paul appears on the American TV show *New York Hot Tracks*. Still in the States, Paul's recent meeting with Julian Lennon is featured on the NBC TV show *Friday Night Videos*.

Saturday November 17
🍎 Back in England, Paul's promotional film for 'We All Stand Together' receives its World TV premiere this morning on BBC1's *Saturday Superstore,* hosted by the DJ Mike Read.

Sunday November 18
🍎 Paul, now back in England, appears in a *Broad Street* promotional interview, transmitted this evening on Capital Radio in London.

Monday November 19
🍎 Paul, and his *Broad Street* film, appear in a pre-taped feature on the US TV show *P.M. Magazine*.

Thursday November 22
🍎 Handmade's film *A Private Function*, starring Michael Palin, premieres in London. Amongst the guests tonight are Ringo and Barbara.

Friday November 23
🍎 Paul continues with promoting his *Broad Street* film for its UK release. His first assignment, recorded this morning at BBC Broadcasting House in Portland Place, London, is with the BBC Radio One DJ Simon Bates. The session will form a three-part feature, which is broadcast over three days on the station between Monday November 26 and Wednesday November 28. Later, in the Greenwood Theatre at the BBC TV Centre, Wood Lane, in London, Paul videotapes a special programme with Russell Harty for the show, titled, *Harty With McCartney*, which is transmitted on BBC1 on Monday November 26 between 6:55 and 7:39pm. During the recording this evening, Paul also appears unannounced during BBC1's annual fundraising event *Children In Need*, where he pledges £5,000 to the cause. On the set of *Harty*, in front of an audience comprising 100 members of the Wings Fun Club, Paul and Russell record three special BBC TV trailers for the show, all of which, along with another 30 minutes of conversation, do not appear in the finished 39-minute programme. Earlier this evening, while Paul is at the Greenwood Theatre, Linda gives a nine-minute live interview, promoting *Broad Street*, on the regional news magazine programme *London Plus*.

Saturday November 24
🍎 Back in England, *Broad Street* promotions continue when a pre-recorded interview with Paul is transmitted this evening on BBC Radio Two's film magazine programme *Star Sound Extra*. Also on Radio Two this evening, Paul's *Give My Regards To Broad Street* album is featured by Howard Pearce on his radio programme *Album Time*.

Sunday November 25
🍎 Although unable to attend the recording session, Paul involves himself with the special Christmas charity single 'Do They Know It's Christmas?'/'Feed the World', proceeds of which will go to benefit the starving African drought victims. He donates two brief spoken messages on the B-side of the single. The charity release goes on to become the largest-selling record in UK history, eventually breaking the sales record held by Paul's own 'Mull Of Kintyre', back in 1977. Paul, meanwhile, is to be found with Linda, in the audience at the Odeon cinema in Marble Arch, London W1, where the first UK screenings of *Rupert And The Frog Song* and *Give My Regards To Broad Street* are taking place. These 11am showings are intended for special guests only. Across London, this time at the Empire Theatre in Leicester Square, simultaneous 11am private screenings of the two films are also taking place.

Monday November 26
🍎 A brief pre-recorded message from Paul is included in this morning's broadcast on TV AM, transmitted across the ITV network.

Tuesday November 27
🍎 In America, an interview with Paul conducted shortly before he last left the States, is transmitted on the CBS TV show *Entertainment Tonight*.
🍎 George arrives in Auckland at 08:20 on Air New Zealand flight TE-001, following a 90-minute stopover at Papeete.

Wednesday November 28
🍎 At 7:15pm, the UK gala premiere of *Give My Regards To Broad Street* takes place at the Odeon Cinema in London Road, Liverpool, where The Beatles' film *A Hard Day's Night* received its premiere back in 1964. The Odeon Cinema received over 25,000 applications for the 900 seats on offer to the public. Outside the venue, a crowd estimated at 2,000 are there to see Paul and Linda's arrival. Earlier in the day, in the Picton Library, in the centre of Liverpool, Paul accepts the Freedom of the City Council award. Originally presented to all of The Beatles by the Liverpool City Council, only Paul turns up in person to collect. The group joins only 41 other recipients, including Gladstone, the MP Bessie Braddock and the Liverpool football manager Bob Paisley, since the award was started 98 years ago. Inside the circular, book-lined room, as the guests wait for Paul to arrive, Lennon & McCartney songs are played through the building's loudspeaker system. When Paul does appear, he strolls up to the podium with his hands in his pockets to receive a gilt-edged scroll, and announces: "I'm chuffed! I would like to thank the 'Pool itself because we couldn't have made it without you."

Afterwards, at a press conference in the Picton Library, in front of journalists from as far away as Argentina, Japan, France and America, Paul speaks about the award ceremony: "I did feel very nervous, but it's a great honour. I would like to think it's the people of Liverpool giving it to me. If that's true, then it's the greatest honour." Sipping tea, Paul is asked by a reporter how long he intends to go on writing. "Until I drop," he replies. (The last time Paul appeared in this library was back in 1953 when, at the age of 11, he had been called upon to receive a prize for a school essay.)

Pre-recorded interviews with Paul concerning the Freedom of the City investiture and the *Broad Street* film, are transmitted on BBC Radio One, BBC Radio Merseyside and on Capital Radio in London, where he is interviewed by David "Kid" Jensen. In America, a pre-recorded interview with Paul to promote *Broad Street* is transmitted on the television programme *Hour Magazine*.
🍎 George joins Derek Taylor in Auckland, New Zealand, where he helps promote Taylor's limited edition book, *Fifty Years Adrift*. After a special literary luncheon, they conduct a joint 45-minute press conference to launch the book at the Hyatt Kingsgate Hotel in front of an audience of 300 reporters, photographers and television news crews. Excerpts of the event are screened this evening on TVNZ (Television New Zealand) News. Also present is Brian Roylance of Genesis Publishing, the publishers of *Fifty Years Adrift*. During George's visit to New Zealand and Australia, he will give over eighty different interviews.

Thursday November 29
🍎 Following the previous evening's UK premiere screening of *Broad Street,* the English press prints several unfavourable reviews of the film. Today's *Guardian* newspaper writes: "*Broad Street* offers an object lesson in how not to integrate musical numbers into a narrative." The *Daily Star*: "Give my goodbyes to this awful movie. You can't revive a corpse and this is a complete non-starter!" The *Sun*: "Paul's oldie is no goldie! With a gossamer thin story line, it is overblown video rubbish!" *The Times* newspaper continues with the onslaught, describing it as: "The worst film that ever cost $9 million and two years work . . ."

Unperturbed by the savaging from the critics, *Give My Regards To Broad Street* receives its London Premiere tonight at 8:30pm at the Empire Theatre in Leicester Square. Coverage of the film's premiere is featured on BBC Radio Two as well as on the major BBC and ITN news programmes. Prior to the screening, Paul and Linda are guests of honour at a premiere party at the Empire. Paul gives a live interview, at approximately 7:20pm, to the Channel Four news presenter Peter Sissons who, coincidentally used to go to school with Paul and, once the news programme is concluded, is on his way to join Paul at the premiere. During the interview, a defiant Paul does his best to defend the film and is quick to point out the following points: *"Broad Street* has taken over $1.4 million at the American box office and it's currently in the top 20 of the American films. The reviews have been 50% good and 50% bad and people are going to see it, not in huge droves, but they are going to see it."* On the subject of its budget, Paul is quick to point out: *"It's not a huge budget film. It's a very small budget so, for what it cost to make, it's doing quite well!"*

Near the end of *Broad Street*'s West End premiere screening, at the point where Bryan Brown says: "We've got the tapes", someone in the audience screams out "Thank God!" The heckler is none other than Paul himself!

In America this morning, a pre-recorded interview with Linda is transmitted on the ABC TV breakfast show *Good Morning America.*

🍎 George flies out from Auckland, en route to Sydney in Australia. Also premiered in London this week is George's Handmade Films production of *A Private Function.*

🍎 In London, Christie's hold their two-day 20th Century Entertainment's Memorabilia auction, where the highest price paid is for John's platinum disc for the American 'Let It Be' single, which raises £2,600.

Friday November 30

🍎 George and Derek Taylor attend another press conference, this time in front of 200 media representatives at the Sydney Opera House in Australia.

🍎 On the Granada Television programme *Weekend,* transmitted in north-west regions of the ITV network only, Cynthia Lennon makes her début as an interviewer. Her first subject is her only child by John, Julian. Tonight's show also includes an interview with Paul's brother Mike and a report on Wednesday's *Broad Street* premiere in Liverpool.

Saturday November 31

🍎 In the States, the CBS TV showbiz programme *Entertainment Tonight* reviews Paul's film *Give My Regards To Broad Street.*

December

🍎 EMI Records announce details of a new Beatles compilation album called *Sessions* featuring, on its cover, previously unreleased Beatles photographs (circa 1962/63). On the record itself, the tracks intended for the disc are, side one: 'Come And Get It' (1969), 'Leave My Kitten Alone' (1964), 'Not Guilty' (1968), 'I'm Looking Through You' (1965), 'What's The New Mary Jane' (1968); side two: 'How Do You Do It?' (1962), 'Besame Mucho' (1962), 'One After 909' (1963), 'If You've Got Troubles' (1965), 'That Means A Lot' (1965), 'While My Guitar Gently Weeps' (1968), 'Mailman, Bring Me No More Blues' (1969), 'Christmas Time (Is Here Again)' (1967). Within weeks of the announcement, the release is scrapped, with EMI citing the album's non-appearance as due to "unforeseen hitches!" EMI had already completed the artwork and allocated a catalogue number for the album, and further embarrassment is heaped on the label when they realise that a number of advance listening cassettes, which had already been dispatched to European EMI outlets, had not been returned despite pleas for their immediate return. EMI's fears that a bootleg release of the album will emerge soon become real when, within months, a top quality track-by-track bootleg, featuring a wonderful counterfeit sleeve, goes on sale unofficially around the world. A Parlophone/EMI single to coincide with *Sessions,* comprising 'Leave My Kitten Alone' and alternate takes of 'Ob-La-Di, Ob-La-Da' (on the American B-side) and 'Hello Goodbye' (on the UK B-side) are scheduled for release on January 18 but this does not take place.

🍎 Paul and Linda's interview with Joan Goodman, conducted at their MPL offices in Soho, London, is published in the December issue of *Playboy* magazine. Among the many topics discussed, Paul says that he resisted discussing John's death because he was in shock and felt that he could never really put his feelings about it into words. Further *Give My Regards To Broad Street* promotional interviews this month include a 55-minute cable and satellite *Music Box* television special, which is carried out by Simon Potter at his MPL offices in London.

🍎 Towards the end of the month, both Paul and George spend Christmas out of England. Paul visits America, while George again soaks up the sun in Australia.

Saturday December 1 (until Monday December 10)

🍎 Paul records the first version of 'We Got Married' during sessions co-produced by Paul and David Foster. The recordings also produce the unreleased track 'Lindiana'. (Incidentally in 1990, Foster spoke about these sessions on Canadian Television's *Much Music* programme, where he cited 'We Got Married' as the "weakest" of the songs he and Paul worked on.) 'We Got Married' is eventually released in 1989 as part of the *Flowers In The Dirt* album. In England on December 1, a pre-recorded interview with Paul is transmitted on the ITV breakfast station TV AM.

Sunday December 2

🍎 At the Sydney Opera House in Australia, George and Derek Taylor hold another press conference to launch the book *Fifty Years Adrift*.

🍎 In England, Paul's *Broad Street* film is reviewed on the ITV network tea-time show *Sunday Sunday* by the host Gloria Hunniford and guests Kenny Everett and the actress Maureen Lipman.

Monday December 3

🍎 BBC2 in England broadcasts, as part of the *Horizon* documentary series, a film about the struggle against Parkinson's Disease by 43-year-old Ivan Vaughan, the original member of The Quarry Men who first introduced John Lennon to Paul McCartney. Paul offers the production team free use of his 1968 song 'Blackbird' for inclusion in the programme.

🍎 Tonight's edition of BBC1's top-rated cinema review programme *Film '84* features Barry Norman's favourable review of Handmade Film's *A Private Function* and his most unfavourable analysis of Paul's *Give My Regards To Broad Street*. Norman, whose opinion of a film can make or break it at the UK box office, says: "In this, we discover, that the master tape for McCartney's next LP has vanished. Goodness, what a calamity! Well it is, because we have to sit through the next 108 tedious minutes while they try to find the damn thing . . ." Ringo's acting skills also come under fire, when Norman remarks: "Ringo Starr drifts in and out in a performance which suggests he should run, not walk, to the nearest acting school."

Monday December 3 (until Sunday December 16)

🍎 An interview with Paul on the Westwood One Radio programme *Star Track Profiles* is syndicated across America during these dates.

Tuesday December 4

🍎 Handmade's *A Private Function* is screened at the Glasgow Film Theatre in Scotland.

Thursday December 6

🍎 The American TV programme, *Paul McCartney: The Man, His Music, His Movies*, is premiered in certain UK areas of the ITV network late this evening, including Thames. (Further regions of the ITV network, including TVS, who serve the Southern area of the country, receive the programme on Saturday December 22.)

Friday December 7

🍎 The Band Aid Christmas single, 'Do They Know It's Christmas?'/'Feed The World', featuring Paul's brief messages on the B-side, is released simultaneously in both the US and the UK. A 12-inch edition is issued on December 14. Paul also appears today, unannounced, on Channel Four's music programme *The Tube* in the UK. In a 15-minute interview with the co-host Paula Yates he discusses his former partner John.

Saturday December 8

🍎 To commemorate the fourth anniversary of John's death, MTV in America screen a tribute entitled *Remembering John*. In the UK, the ITV network (between 11:46 and 12:28am) screen the 1983 American documentary *Yoko Ono: Then & Now*.

🍎 In England, on TV AM's *Good Morning Britain*, Paul appears in a pre-recorded 30-minute interview to remember the fourth anniversary of John's death.

🍎 In America, as 'No More Lonely Nights' reaches number six in the US singles chart, Paul is seen in a video segment recorded the previous month, on the show *Solid Gold*, where he appears giving a tongue-in-cheek introduction to the song 'Disco Duck'.

 Still in the States, Ringo becomes the latest in the line of ex-Beatles to appear on the NBC-TV show *Saturday Night Live*. Recorded at 8pm at New York's Radio City, in the RCA building (and transmitted later this evening between 11:30pm and 1:00am), the programme opens with a comedy sketch, which sends up the prices people pay for original Beatles memorabilia. At a mock Beatles auction, a guitar pick used by John on the recording of 'Eight Days A Week' and a toothbrush, used by Paul on the recording of *Rubber Soul,* are seen selling for a vast sum of money. Then, as lot 36, a real-life Ringo, dressed in his 1963 Beatles collarless jacket outfit, is wheeled in on a trolley, but the auction house cannot sell him and prospective buyers begin to leave the hall. During his stint, Ringo performs in further comedy routines with the *Saturday Night Live* regulars and reappears to perform a medley of songs with Billy Crystal, who is dressed as Sammy Davis Junior. This includes 'With A Little Help From My Friends', 'What Kind Of Fool Am I?', 'Act Naturally', 'I've Gotta Be Me', 'Octopus's Garden', 'Photograph', 'Yellow Submarine' and 'With A Little Help From My Friends' (reprise). One of the most recent re-broadcasts of the show occurs in Europe on the Paramount Comedy Channel during the early hours of Sunday October 11, 1998.
 Back in England, the 20th anniversary re-issue of 'I Feel Fine' peaks at number 65 in the UK singles charts.

Tuesday December 11
 A pre-filmed interview with Paul, at his Soho Square offices, is featured on the ITV network children's programme *CBTV,* where Paul largely takes questions from the kids about the cartoon character Rupert The Bear.

Thursday December 13
 The High Court in London finally resolves the 1979 lawsuit involving the unpaid royalties by EMI to Apple Corps Ltd. Apple had charged that The Beatles were owed $2.5 (£1.2) million in backdated royalties, unpaid from the period of 1966 to 1979. A complete audit of the accounts is immediately ordered. Meanwhile, in a separate American lawsuit, also going back to 1979, Apple had requested $42.5 million from Capitol Records, including the sum of $20 million in back royalties. This action also requests that The Beatles be released from any remaining legal ties to Capitol. Capitol, in turn, immediately file a $1.5 million countersuit claiming that The Beatles have failed in their agreement to deliver two albums required by their original contract. Capitol also state that John's 1972 album *Some Time In New York City* did not count as one of the required albums.

Friday December 14
 George, on holiday in Australia, appears as a surprise guest with Deep Purple on stage in Sydney. He is introduced to the audience as "Arnold Grove from Liverpool". (12 Arnold Grove was the Harrisons' family address at the time of George's birth in 1943.)
 In America, Paul appears on *Rick Dee's Weekly Top 40 Radio Show.* (Further excerpts from Paul's appearance are transmitted on December 15 and 16.)
 In the UK, CIC Video release on home video The Bee Gees' 1978 flop musical *Sgt. Pepper's Lonely Hearts Club Band.*

Saturday December 15
 On MTV, Paul introduces the promo film for 'No More Lonely Nights' on the *MTV Top 20* programme.
 Julian Lennon continues with his heavy round of UK promotional appearances by guesting on the ITV network programme *Tarby & Friends,* hosted by the Liverpool comic, and friend of John Lennon, Jimmy Tarbuck. During his spot, Julian mimes his début single 'Too Late For Goodbyes'.

Sunday December 16
 Still in America, Paul grants another interview to the 24-hour music station MTV. He will return to England the following day.

Friday December 21
 In the UK, a pre-recorded interview with Paul is transmitted on the ITV breakfast television station TV AM, where he is seen briefly participating in a Christmas pantomime audition with the show's puppet celebrity Roland Rat.

Tuesday December 25
 A pre-recorded Christmas day message from Paul is transmitted on the station TV AM. Later, another Christmas message from Paul appears in the ITV network show *Top Pop Videos Of 1984*, which also transmits the promotional clip for 'We All Stand Together'.

Wednesday December 26
 On Boxing Day, BBC Radio One broadcasts another pre-recorded interview with Yoko by Andy Peebles, in which they discuss the Polydor compilation album *Every Man Has A Woman*.
 On Radio Four today, with the legal threat of Larry Parnes now out of the way, the BBC repeats Paul's January 30, 1982, appearance on the programme *Desert Island Discs*.

"John was the
best collaborator
I have ever
worked with . . ."

– Paul

January

 In the UK, Argos software, with the assistance of Paul, releases the *Give My Regards To Broad Street* computer game.

 In America, the National Coalition on Television Violence recommends John belatedly and Paul for their "pro-social" music videos.

 In Liverpool, many a tear is wept when The Beatles *Cavern Mecca* museum in Mathew Street closes down due to co-proprietor Liz Hughes's ill health and various financial problems.

Wednesday January 2

 From England, Paul turns down an offer to appear in the glitzy top American TV soap opera *Dallas*. He is offered nearly £1 million to appear in just eight episodes, which works out at approximately £110,000 a show. If Paul have taken the role, he would have been cast as a wealthy British landowner who visits Dallas to look for property. Paul turns it down because he "didn't wish to be apart from his family".

Friday January 4

 Paul, Linda and family escape the arctic weather gripping Britain by flying off to New York for a holiday. His place on the Concorde flight is booked in the suitable name of "Mr. Winters".

Sunday January 6

 An interview with Paul is broadcast on MTV's repeat showing of *The Tube* in America. The segment was previously transmitted on Channel 4 in the UK the previous year.

Wednesday January 9

 BBC2 in England broadcasts (between 7:35 and 7:40pm) the British TV premiere of Linda's animated short film *Seaside Woman,* which was the 1980 Golden Palm short subject winner at the annual Cannes Film Festival in the South of France.

Friday January 11

 Paul's big-screen film *Give My Regards To Broad Street* goes on general release across London. It will open nationwide at the end of this month.

Wednesday January 16

 On the fifteenth anniversary of their seizure, eight explicit lithographs by John, which were confiscated by police from the London Arts Gallery in 1970, are put on display in Liverpool's Beatle City museum. The drawings, part of a collection of 14 called *Bag One,* show John and Yoko on their honeymoon in 1969 engaging in various acts of lovemaking.

Friday January 18

 The world premiere of the Handmade film *Water* takes place at the Odeon Cinema in London. (Because a large chunk of funding for the movie was withdrawn on the eve of filming, the production almost never took place. In order to complete the film, George and Denis O'Brien, his partner in Handmade, are forced to find extra funds in the space of a weekend.) The film features cameo appearances by George, Ringo and Eric Clapton during the performance of 'Freedom' by Billy Connolly, Christopher Tumming and The Singing Rebels Band. This clip, filmed at Shepperton Studios in London, is also used by Handmade as a promotional video. Two other songs in the film, 'Celebration' and 'Focus Of Attention', are co-written by George and performed in the film by Jimmy Helms. (George plays guitar on the soundtrack.) The tracks 'Freedom' and 'Celebration' are released as a single in the UK. *Water* will open in major provinces on January 25 and go on general nationwide release on February 22.

 Wilfred Brambell, Paul's grandfather in *A Hard Day's Night* and the co-star of BBC TV's long-running comedy series *Steptoe & Son*, dies aged 72 in a London hospital.

Saturday January 19

 In America, Paul is featured on the television programme *Night Flight.*

Tuesday January 22
🍎 In England, Ringo's eldest son Zak is married to Sarah Menikides at a private ceremony in a registry office in Bracknell, Berkshire. Both parents of the happy couple are not informed and therefore do not attend the ceremony.

Thursday January 24
🍎 At their Tittenhurst Park mansion in Ascot, Ringo and his wife Barbara, organise a small wedding reception for Zak and Sarah, two days after their wedding.

Saturday January 26
🍎 George adds slide guitar and performs backing vocals on the recording of 'Children Of The Sky', which is not released until November 7, 1986, and then only in the UK as a single and on the Mike Batt concept album *The Hunting Of The Snark*.
🍎 Tonight on BBC1 (between 11:41pm and 1:23am), the 1979 Dick Clark produced made-for-TV film *The Birth Of The Beatles* is screened for the second time.

Tuesday January 29
🍎 In order to re-appraise the Handmade film *A Private Function*, George slips in unnoticed to watch the film at a private screening in London.

Thursday January 31
🍎 The Handmade film *A Private Function* receives its grand provincial premiere in Leeds, with its co-star Michael Palin in attendance. A news crew from BBC2's *Newsnight* programme covers the event, the highlights of which are transmitted on the station tomorrow evening. (Handmade are doing very well at the box office with two of their films [*Water* and *A Private Function*] in the top five London films.)

February
🍎 In America, exploitation of The Beatles' classic music reaches an all-time low when the first licences are issued for Beatles songs to be used in television commercials. 'Help!' is used for six months by Lincoln-Mercury in America, for a fee of $100,000, and Schweppes, the soft drinks giant, pay $11,000 to use 'She Loves You' on Spanish television. In order to reduce licensing costs, cover versions of The Beatles' songs are used instead of the original Beatles' EMI recordings. (Nevertheless, The Beatles' original 1968 recording of 'Revolution' is later used in a Nike commercial.)
🍎 In Japan, VAP Video releases the home video of the televised Beatles June 30, 1966, concert at the Budokan Hall in Tokyo.
🍎 Yoko records, at her Dakota apartment, a two-hour interview with Helen Leicht for the programme *Breakfast With The Beatles*, a show celebrating its ninth anniversary on the radio station WIQQ of Philadelphia in Pennsylvania.

Friday February 1
🍎 In an extremely rare television appearance, a pre-recorded interview with George, carried out by Robin Denselow in the Handmade offices at 26 Cadogan Square, London, is transmitted in tonight's edition of BBC2's *Newsnight* programme (transmitted between 11:17 and 11:38pm). During this 19-minute extended feature, George talks about his role in Handmade films, admitting: "I don't want to be a film star, I don't even want to be a pop star. I just want to live in peace."

Monday February 4
🍎 A special 21-track home video compilation, a benefit fund-raiser for the Ethiopian Appeal, is released in the UK and features Paul's rarely screened promotional video for the disco version of 'No More Lonely Nights'.

Friday February 15
🍎 The 115-minute, 1978 film *The Last Waltz*, featuring an appearance by Ringo during The Band's farewell concert in San Francisco on Wednesday November 24, 1976, is released in the UK on Warner Home Video.

Friday February 22
🍎 Metromedia TV broadcasts the special *Visions Of Yesterday And Today*, which features

segments on The Beatles and includes a black-and-white clip of the 'Give Peace A Chance' promo-film, taken at John and Yoko's June 1969 'bed-in'.

Monday February 25
🍎 On what has been long recognised as George's birthday, it is reported that George, Ringo and Yoko, in New York's State Supreme Court, have filed a $8.6 million lawsuit against Paul for breach of contract. They allege that Paul is earning a "preferential royalty from Beatles records to the others, as an incentive for him to re-sign with Capitol as a solo artist." Lawyers on behalf of Paul are quick to point out that "although this fact is true, Capitol did not decrease royalty payments to John, George and Ringo".

Wednesday February 27
🍎 In Boca Raton, Florida, USA, 30-year-old American Michael Keith Reibel is arrested by the FBI at his parents' home, accused of stealing a master tape containing unreleased music and conversations by The Beatles. The tape in question proves to be nothing more than the previously released Beatles 1963 to 1969 Christmas fan club recordings.

Thursday February 28
🍎 In England, EMI, following the re-release of the mid-price version on MFP last September, deletes the full-price version of the 1977 album *The Beatles Live At The Hollywood Bowl.*

March (periodically until May)
🍎 At his private studios in Sussex, working with the producer Hugh Padgham, Paul begins recording tracks intended for his *Press To Play* album. (The sessions will continue in October and then again in December, concluding on the 6th.) Tracks recorded during this period include: 'Stranglehold', 'Good Times Coming'/'Feel The Sun', 'Talk More Talk', 'Footprints', 'Only Love Remains', 'Press' (including a slower version), 'Pretty Little Head', 'Move Over Busker', 'However Absurd', 'Angry', 'Write Away', 'Tough On A Tightrope' and 'It's Not True'. (Final production work is completed during January and February, 1986.) An early tape of Paul, performing several songs from the album, includes the unreleased song 'Yvonne'.

Friday March 1
🍎 The New York premiere takes place of the Handmade film *A Private Function.*
🍎 A benefit concert for Liz and Jim Hughes of Cavern Mecca is arranged by George Downey of the new Cavern Club in Mathew Street, Liverpool. Shortly after this, Paul arranges for the Hughes to visit his MPL London offices where he thanks them personally for their many years of support.

Saturday March 2
🍎 Plexus publications in the UK release the book *Beatle* by Pete Best and Patrick Doncaster.

Sunday March 3
🍎 BBC2 screens, for the third time on UK TV, the excellent 1978 Beatles spoof *The Rutles*, featuring a cameo appearance by George.

Tuesday March 5
🍎 Paul's *Give My Regards To Broad Street* film is released on CBS/Fox home video in America.
🍎 The Beatles' former drummer Pete Best appears on BBC2's *Whistle Test* programme to promote his new book *Beatle.*

Friday March 8
🍎 In tonight's edition of *The Tube*, transmitted on Channel 4, Paul, in a piece recorded at Abbey Road, gives a short interview about Little Richard.
🍎 At the BBC Television Theatre in Shepherd's Bush, London, John's first wife Cynthia appears on the BBC1 chat show *Wogan,* hosted by Terry Wogan.

Sunday March 10
🍎 At 7pm this evening, the Suffolk-based radio stations Radio Orwell and Saxon Radio transmit (between 7:00 and 8:00pm) a one-hour *Beatles Hour*, hosted by Andy Brobbin, and featuring a host of rare Beatles music.

Monday March 11 & Tuesday March 12
🍎 At Fulham Town Hall in west London, Ringo appears in a non-musical cameo role in the charity video *Willie And The Poor Boys – The Video*, an ambitious project put together by Bill Wyman of The Rolling Stones, in aid of ARMS, Action Research into Multiple Sclerosis. Ringo, who is seen without his beard and with his hair slicked back Fifties style, plays the part of the town hall caretaker and is seen, brush in hand, wearing a grey overcoat, sweeping up after the all-star band has finished playing. His wife Barbara also appears in the video, among the crowd in a concert sequence. A report of the making of *Willie And The Poor Boys* is transmitted on the TVS/ITV programme *Coast To Coast* on June 13. PolyGram Music Video in England releases the completed 30-minute film on May 25.

Wednesday March 13
🍎 In London, at the Grosvenor House Hotel, Paul receives an Ivor Novello Award for 'We All Stand Together' as Best Film Theme of 1984. Linda is not present as she is unwell.

Thursday March 14
🍎 In America, the soundtrack album *Porky's Revenge,* featuring George's version of 'I Don't Want To Do It' is released. (The album is released in the UK on July 1.)

Saturday March 30 & Sunday March 31
🍎 Michael Jackson visits Paul and Linda's Sussex farmhouse.

April
🍎 Rumours in the film industry suggest that Ringo and Harry Nilsson are to co-fund the movie *Road To Australia,* to be made in the style of the Bob Hope and Bing Crosby *Road To . . .* movies made in America between 1940 and 1952. Ringo is tipped to be playing the Bob Hope role with his wife Barbara in the role immortalised by Dorothy Lamour.
🍎 A new 56-track recording console is installed in George Martin's AIR Studios in Oxford Street, London. Unfortunately, the new equipment is too large to fit through AIR's doorway and has to be installed through an open window of the fourth floor with the aid of a crane, which disrupts busy Oxford Street traffic. Once fitted, Paul immediately books a session utilising the new recording console.
🍎 An exclusive pre-recorded interview with Paul is transmitted on the German TV station ZDF.

Thursday April 4
🍎 The *Daily Mirror* newspaper prints another completely untrue "Beatles Reunion" story, suggesting that Paul, George and Ringo will be getting together for recordings with Julian.

Monday April 8
🍎 John's eldest son Julian makes his first live concert appearance with three nights at the Beacon Theater in New York.

Sunday April 14
🍎 John Lennon's 82-year-old Aunt Mimi Smith gives her most moving ever interview in a two-part feature for the *Sunday People*, announcing: "John is always with me. Sometimes I imagine I can see him. Is it him? I like to think so." (Part two is on April 21.)

Tuesday April 16
🍎 It is revealed that the American computer group Hewlett-Packard is to pay £1,000 a week for the next year for the rights to use Lennon & McCartney's song 'We Can Work It Out' in a £1 million TV advertising campaign. The song, re-recorded at Abbey Road by a Beatles sound-a-like group, is meant to attract businessmen in their thirties who grew

up with The Beatles. Julian Appleson of ATV Music, which owns all but four of The Beatles' songs, says of the deal: "Our company is anxious not to spoil The Beatles' image. There seems to be some consternation among Beatles fans if Beatles music is used in commercials."

Saturday April 20
🍎 The 20th anniversary reissue of 'Ticket To Ride' reaches number 70 in the UK singles chart.

Monday April 29
🍎 In the UK, PMI home video releases the 20-minute tape *The Beatles Live: Ready, Steady Go Special Edition* featuring The Beatles' musical performance from their May 6, 1964, Associated Rediffusion UK TV special *Around The Beatles*. The *Midsummer Night's Dream* play, cum Beatles comedy sketch, performed on the original broadcast, is not included on the release.

May
🍎 In America, Ringo appears as the Mock Turtle performing the Steve Allen track 'Nonsense', in the CBS TV musical presentation of Lewis Carroll's *Alice In Wonderland*, a show put together by Sammy Davis Junior. The two-part show is premiered in America on December 9 and 10, across the CBS TV network. Clips from Ringo's dialogue only later appear on the soundtrack album *Alice In Wonderland*.
🍎 A single featuring a different mix of George's recording of 'I Don't Want To Do It', from the film *Porky's Revenge*, is released in the US.

Monday May 13
🍎 In a simple ceremony at Lime Street station in Liverpool, British Rail unveils a new Pullman locomotive, which has been christened *John Lennon*.

Wednesday May 15
🍎 Paul records a 17-second message of sympathy for the victims of the Bradford City football stadium fire disaster of May 11. The message is released on the B-side of Gerry Marsden's charity single 'You'll Never Walk Alone'/'Messages', credited to The Crowd and released as a single in the UK only on May 24. A 12-inch edition is released on June 7.

Friday May 24
🍎 Ringo and Barbara are among the guests present at the London charity premiere of *Wild Geese II*. Joining them tonight are Ingrid Pitt and Anthony Quayle.

Tuesday May 28
🍎 In America, an interview with Cynthia Lennon is transmitted on the CBS TV programme *Entertainment Tonight*.

June
🍎 In America, Yoko appoints the New York company *Marigold* to handle all future projects dealing with John Lennon's name.
🍎 In anticipation of imminent legal problems, Toshiba/EMI in Japan delete their compact disc version of The Beatles' 1969 album *Abbey Road*.
🍎 The Dutch Beatles Fan Club *Beatles Unlimited* sends a letter to Paul at MPL in Soho Square, London, featuring a petition signed by 782 members, all asking for the lifting of any obstacles which may prevent the release by EMI of any unreleased Beatles material.

Sunday June 2
🍎 As a tribute to Roy Plomley, who died recently, BBC2 re-screen the 1982 *Arena* documentary on *Desert Island Discs*, originally transmitted on February 23 and which features Paul's appearance on the show from January 30.

Tuesday June 4
🍎 The UK release of the special compilation album *Greenpeace*, which features George's new recording of 'Save The World'. (The American release takes place on August 19.)

Monday June 10
🍎 The Beach Boys, simultaneously in the UK and in America, release the album *The Beach Boys,* which features Ringo drumming on the track 'California Calling'.

Wednesday June 12
🍎 In America, a pre-recorded interview with Paul is transmitted on the MTV programme *Rock Of The Eighties.*

Saturday June 15
🍎 In London, John's single 'Nobody Told Me' receives a BMI (British Music Industry) award.

🍎 In the UK, as a preview to the forthcoming compilation series of *Ready Steady Go!,* Channel 4 transmits a taster for the series tonight, between 4:50 and 5:05pm, hosted by the DJ Gary Crowley and titled *The Weekend Starts Here.*

Friday June 21
🍎 In the UK, Channel 4 begins transmitting a series of seven special *Ready Steady Go!* compilations, which feature highlights of The Beatles' 1963 and 1964 appearances on the show, spread evenly over the seven weeks. (Friday evening's show is repeated the following Tuesday.)

Tuesday June 25
🍎 In America, the singer/actor Mark Lindsay is notified that he has been dropped from the lead role of John Lennon in the NBC-TV film production of *John And Yoko: A Love Story.* The news comes less than a week after he had been cast for the role. Lindsay is fired after Yoko and NBC both discover that the actor's real name is none other than Mark Chapman.

Friday June 28
🍎 A plan by Warner Brothers to release today The Beatles' 1970 film *Let It Be* is scrapped due to contractual difficulties. One of the major obstacles in its release may well have been the sleeve's original design, which surprisingly features a solo picture of John. The scheduled release today of Ringo and Frank Zappa's 1971 film *200 Motels* still materialises.

Saturday June 29
🍎 At the Sotheby's rock memorabilia auction in New York, John's psychedelically painted 1966 Phantom V Rolls Royce is sold for an amazing $2.2 million. The reserve price for this prize exhibit was only between $200,000 and $300,000.

Friday July 5
🍎 The 20th Century Fox comedy film *Porky's Revenge,* featuring on its soundtrack George's version of the Bob Dylan track 'I Don't Want To Do It', opens in London.

Saturday July 13
🍎 At Wembley Stadium in London, Paul is one of many top rock stars to perform before a crowd of 90,000, as part of the massive Live Aid concerts. The all-day event is organised by former Boomtown Rat Bob Geldof, who, only eight months previously, had arranged the 'Do They Know It's Christmas?'/'Feed The World' single. Like that, this Live Aid concert is aimed at raising funds for the starving people in Africa. Simultaneously in Philadelphia, another fundraising concert is being held and the entire event, in both England and America, is televised live around the world throughout the day and also broadcast live, simultaneously, on the radio. It attracts the largest worldwide television audience in history, estimated at over 1.5 billion people! Paul's appearance comes at the close of the Wembley concert when he performs 'Let It Be' solo at a piano. Unfortunately, due to a mishap by Queen's technicians, the lead on Paul's microphone fails to function during the first half of the song. Eventually Paul's vocals ring out loud and clear and the audience sing along with him, and as they do, Paul is joined on stage by Geldof, Pete Townshend, David Bowie and Alison Moyet. Paul, as well as Linda, remains on stage for the finale, when all the stars of the Wembley concert reappear to sing 'Do They Know It's Christmas?'

Sunday July 14
 The day after his *Live Aid* appearance, Paul records a new studio version of 'Let It Be' at the BBC TV Centre in Wood Lane, London. He overdubs a new vocal on top of his visual *Live Aid* performance for use should it ever be released officially. This never happens, although a brief clip of this new 'vocalised' *Live Aid* performance does appear in the BBC2 *Live Aid* highlights programme which is transmitted on December 31.

Thursday July 25
 Two months after its US release, CBS/Fox in the UK issue on home video Paul's film *Give My Regards To Broad Street*, priced at a hefty £55.

Saturday August 3
 John's former wife Cynthia is a special guest on this morning's TV AM breakfast show.

Tuesday August 6
 Cynthia Lennon keeps up her hectic promotional activities by appearing on the TVS/ITV network afternoon talk show *Regrets*.
 BBC1's weekly nostalgia series *Time Of Your Life*, hosted by Noel Edmunds, transmits a clip from Yoko's 1967 film *Bottoms*, a film print of which was sent personally by Yoko from New York.

Saturday August 10
 From under the noses of both Paul and Yoko, Michael Jackson purchases for $47.5 million (around £34m) ATV Music, which includes the complete Northern Songs catalogue, thereby acquiring the ownership of the Lennon and McCartney songbook. All of the Lennon and McCartney songs, with the exception of 'Love Me Do', 'P. S. I Love You' (now both owned by Paul's MPL company), 'Please Please Me', 'Don't Bother Me' and 'Ask Me Why' (all owned by Dick James) are included in the sale, along with approximately 4,000 other song titles. To obtain the catalogue, Jackson outbids stiff competition from EMI, CBS, the Lawrence Welk Group and the Coca-Cola Corporation.

Thursday August 22
 An interview with Derek Taylor, to promote his new book *Fifty Years Adrift*, is featured on the BBC Radio Two programme *The John Dunn Show*.

Thursday August 29
 At the annual Sotheby's rock and pop memorabilia auction in London, Paul's original handwritten letter to *Melody Maker* in 1970 (published on Saturday August 29 – see entry) sells for £10,000 and an audio tape of The Beatles playing at the Cavern Club in July 1961 sells for £2,100. The purchaser of these items is none other than Paul himself.

Saturday August 31 & Sunday September 1
 In America, many radio stations broadcast a special called *The Beatles – Yesterday,* a 20th anniversary tribute to Paul's classic song.

September
 During the month, at both AIR Studios in London and at his private studio in Rye, Paul records the song 'Spies Like Us', intended for inclusion in the Chevy Chase and Dan Ackroyd film comedy of the same title.
 At the end of the month, rumours in the book industry suggest that Ringo has signed a one and a half million pound deal to write a "warts and all" book on his days in The Beatles. (The stories prove to be untrue.)
 In the UK, the BMI (British Music Industry) announces that Paul's song 'Yesterday' has now been broadcast over four and a half million times in America alone.
 George is seen at the Silverstone Grand Prix, where he is interviewed by a TV news team from Brazil.
 Location filming for the American NBC made-for-TV production of *John And Yoko: A Love Story* takes place at various sites across London, Liverpool and Black Park in Berkshire. (Filming returns to the US in early October.)

Wednesday September 4

● The London traffic warden, Meta Davies, the "lovely Rita Meter Maid" who inspired Paul to compose the *Sgt. Pepper's* track 'Lovely Rita' back in 1967, retires from her duties. Fittingly, her last ticket is written out in Abbey Road, just around the corner from Cavendish Avenue where Paul had received his ticket from Meta back in 1966.

Friday September 6

● In the Bahamas, the sale of ATV Music, the holder of Northern Songs, becomes final and Michael Jackson becomes the proud owner of the works of Lennon and McCartney. Paul, naturally, is none too pleased. Part of the deal is that Jackson will go to Australia, the home of Robert Holmes A'Court, the seller of ATV Music, to take part in a two-day charity telethon in Perth on October 19 and 20.

● To coincide with this year's rather uneventful Buddy Holly Week, MCA Records in the UK re-release their 1984 box set of Buddy Holly singles.

Saturday September 7

● Ringo becomes the first Beatle grandfather when his daughter-in-law Sarah Menikides Starkey, the wife of Ringo and Maureen's eldest son Zak, gives birth to a 7lb 2oz girl, Tatia Jayne, in a private hospital in Ascot.

Wednesday September 11

● In London, Paul and Linda are the hosts of a Buddy Holly luncheon to which 30 VIP guests have been invited.

Thursday September 12

● A one minute 26 second extract from the 1958 Quarry Men acetate recording of 'That'll Be The Day' is broadcast for the very first time on the MPL/BBC TV co-production *Arena* special *Buddy Holly* on BBC2 in England. The latter part of this recording is obscured by Paul's voiceover narration, who is also seen strumming 'Love Me Do' and 'Words Of Love' on an acoustic guitar. (The scenes were shot in a barn at Paul's Sussex farmhouse.) In America, viewers have a chance to see the 65-minute programme when it is aired as *The Real Buddy Holly Story*. (An excerpt of the 'That'll Be The Day' acetate is released on *The Beatles Anthology I* compilation in 1995.)

Saturday September 14

● Paul and Linda are present at the annual Buddy Holly Week get-together in London.

Friday September 20

● In America, as part of the preparations for an upcoming American radio series, Yoko registers the copyright, posthumously, for 28 John Lennon song titles. Their "date of creation" is listed as 1980. Interestingly enough, two of the copyrights registered have nothing at all to do with John. The songs 'Lullaby For A Lazy Day' was originally recorded in 1968 as 'Lullaby' by Grapefruit and 'Have You Heard The Word' was written by Steve Kipner and Steve Groves. The confusion probably arose because the latter has appeared on numerous bootlegs over the years where it has been mistakenly listed as an unreleased track by The Bee Gees and John Lennon. The other 26 songs are home demos which are later transmitted on the American Westwood One radio series *The Lost Lennon Tapes*. These include The Beatles' 1996 "comeback" singles 'Free As A Bird' (1995) and 'Girls And Boys', which is released as 'Real Love', together with 'Dear John', 'When A Boy Meets A Girl', 'Whatever Happened To . . .?', 'She Is A Friend Of Dorothy's', 'Gone From This Place', 'The Happy Rishikesh Song', originally written in India back in 1968, 'Life Begins At Forty', a track originally given by John to Ringo to record in 1980 for his album *Can't Fight Lightning* and 'Serve Yourself'.)

Saturday September 21

● The musical tribute stage play *Lennon,* first unveiled in Liverpool at the Everyman Theatre on October 28, 1981, re-opens across England, beginning tonight at the Crucible Theatre in Sheffield. (Following its successful run in Liverpool, the play moves to New York where it fails badly.)

Wednesday September 25
♣ In London, at Hamilton's Gallery, in Mayfair, Ringo and Barbara are among the guests present at the launch party for Terry O'Neill's new book *Legends*.

October
♣ During the month, Paul re-signs with Capitol Records in America. He had been with Columbia Records since 1979.
♣ In England, Ringo re-records the narration for eight of the 26 *Thomas The Tank Engine* TV shows for a commercial release on audio cassettes in the UK only. The issue forms a part of the Pickwick Records' *Tell-a-Tale* series, produced in association with Ladybird Books.
♣ Around the middle of the month Beatle City in Seel Street, Liverpool, closes its doors for business and towards the end of the month moves its operations to Tokyo and Osaka in Japan, where it will be titled Beatle City's World Of The Beatles Exhibition. (Beatle City is scheduled to reopen in Liverpool in May 1986. (Incidentally, during its first year of business, the exhibition centre in Liverpool makes a loss of £25,000.)

Tuesday October 1 (periodically until Friday December 6)
♣ At his private home studios in Scotland, Paul resumes the recordings for his album *Press To Play*.

Monday October 7 (until Monday October 28)
♣ An exhibition of Dezo Hoffman's photographs from his book *John Lennon* is shown at the Cuts Gallery in West London.

Wednesday October 9
♣ In America, to coincide with what would have been John's 45th birthday, a section of New York's Central Park, dedicated to John and renamed Strawberry Fields is officially opened to the public, with Yoko and Sean in attendance. Yoko, who donated $1 million towards the project, also conceived the idea for the three-and-a-half-acre site. The Strawberry Fields area has been landscaped and planted with trees, shrubs and flowers from all over the world, including the Soviet Union, Jordan and Israel.
♣ At 8pm this morning, in London at Abbey Road Studios, Paul films the promotional video for 'Spies Like Us', co-starring the stars of the film, Dan Aykroyd and Chevy Chase. The white Rolls Royce used in the video is loaned from Dave Clark, of Dave Clark Five fame, who is currently at work in Studio One at Abbey Road. The 'Spies Like Us' clip, which is directed by John Landis, receives its UK premiere on November 16, as part of BBC1's *The Late Late Breakfast Show*, on which Paul and Linda also appear live. In America, the premiere of the clip takes place on MTV on November 17. Due to the insistence of the Musicians Union, and in order to get valuable UK TV screenings, Paul re-cuts the original version of the clip, which features non-Musicians Union members, such as Chevy Chase, Vanessa Angel and Donna Dixon, who are seen performing and singing on the track.

Monday October 14
♣ In the UK, principal photography commences on the Handmade film *Mona Lisa*, starring Michael Caine and Bob Hoskins.
♣ Ringo and Barbara attend the Chelsea Arts Club ball at the Royal Albert Hall in London. They are seen partying with John Hurt and George Melly.

Monday October 21
♣ At the Limehouse Television Studios, Canary Wharf, London E14, George and Ringo, before an audience of 250 specially invited guests, videotape an appearance with Carl Perkins for his TV special *Blue Suede Shoes*, which also features Eric Clapton, Roseanne Cash, Dave Edmunds and former members of The Stray Cats. During the programme George performs 'Glad All Over', shares lead vocals on 'Your True Love', contributes backing vocals and guitar on 'Blue Suede Shoes' (performing lead vocal on the encore), 'Gone Gone Gone', 'Whole Lotta Shakin' Goin' On', and a medley which includes 'That's All Right (Mama)', 'Blue Moon Of Kentucky' and 'Night Train To Memphis'. Ringo is seen performing 'Honey Don't', shares lead vocal with Carl Perkins and Eric Clapton on 'Matchbox', and plays the drums in the show and bangs the tambourine during the

medley sequence. (Two further songs, 'Right String But Wrong Yo Yo' and 'Sure To Fall', are performed and recorded but are cut from the broadcasts.) Crews from American TV, for the programmes CNN *Showbiz Today, Entertainment Tonight, Entertainment This Week*, Cinemax and TNN, tape rehearsals for the show. The programme, which sports the full title of *A Rockabilly Session With Carl Perkins And Friends*, is premiered in the UK on New Years Day, January 1, 1986 on Channel 4. In America, the show is premiered on the Cinemax station, featuring songs not included in the UK transmission, on January 5, 1986. (To accompany the Channel 4 screening, a simultaneous broadcast, this time in stereo, is aired on the Capital London radio station.) A report on the recording session, featuring interviews with both George and Ringo, is transmitted the following day, Tuesday October 22, on the BBC Radio One lunch time show *Newsbeat*.

Saturday October 26
€ The ITV network transmits the London Weekend Television programme *An Audience With Billy Connolly*, featuring Ringo and Barbara among the star-studded audience. (The show was recorded at the London Television Studios on the South Bank on October 21.)

Monday October 28
€ MTV in America premiere Yoko's promotional film clip for the song 'Hell In Paradise'.

Saturday November 2
€ The stage play *Lennon* opens at the Astoria Theatre in London. Fans are able to purchase special 'Ticket To Ride' season tickets, whereby they can obtain three tickets for the price of two.
€ In Germany, ZDF TV transmits the 45-minute documentary entitled *25 Jahre Beatles Phanomenen Und Legende*.

Tuesday November 5
€ At the Royal Albert Hall, Ringo, Barbara and Olivia Harrison, are in attendance at the *Fashion Aid* evening, an event to aid the African famine relief fund and the Band Aid trust. The former members of 10cc and now respected film makers Kevin Godley and Lol Creme capture the evening's events on film. Paul and Linda, who could not make the event, send a supportive audiotape message which is played over the hall's PA system, and includes the McCartneys singing a short improvised ditty, aptly called 'Fashion Aid'.

Wednesday November 6
€ In the States, the *New York Post* print a story about Paul, headlined "Imagine: John Tried To Steal My Songs". The article features quotations from Paul in which he was alleged to have said: "Lennon was a manoeuvring swine!" Yoko declines to comment on the accusations.

Monday November 11
€ John and Yoko's 1972 film *Imagine* is released on PMI home video in the UK, featuring an edited running time of 60 minutes. (The American release, featuring the same 60-minute version, takes place the following year.)
€ An additional two *Thomas The Tank Engine* audio cassettes, featuring a specially recorded Ringo narration, are released today in the UK.
€ The release today, in both the US and UK, of Paul's single 'Spies Like Us' fails to materialise, with a Monday November 18 release date now scheduled.

Thursday November 14
€ The Virgin home video *Rupert And The Frog Song*, which also features the short animated feature films *Seaside Woman* and *Oriental Nightfish*, is released in the UK today. Unfortunately, the clip for 'Oriental Nightfish' upsets many parents due to the cartoon representation of a naked lady. They angrily claim that no mention of this was made on the cardboard video box, which carries a "Uc" certification, meaning the video is intended "especially for young children". Subsequent video certificates on the box became simply 'U', although *Oriental Nightfish* still remains a part of the release.

Friday November 15
☀ Yoko appears on the NBC TV show *Friday Night Videos*, promoting her new *Starpeace* album.

Saturday November 16
☀ At the BBC Television Centre in Wood Lane, London, Paul appears again as a special guest on the live BBC1 Saturday Night variety show *The Late Late Breakfast Show*, where he participates in a mock question and answer session with the host Noel Edmonds. Because the questions put by Noel are quite ludicrous, the former Beatle later reveals that he did not enjoy this appearance. The short segment also features the UK premiere of the European promotional film for 'Spies Like Us'.
☀ In the UK, BBC Radio One, in FM-Stereo, repeats the special *The Beatles At The Beeb* in two one-hour parts. Part two, again between 2:00 and 2:59pm, is transmitted on the station one week later on November 23. (This is the third BBC radio programme centred around the Beatles' Sixties radio recordings.)

Monday November 18
☀ After a one week delay, the simultaneous American and UK release takes place of Paul's single 'Spies Like Us'/'My Carnival' in both 7- and 12-inch versions. In the States, the tracks become the first release under his new contract with Capitol Records. The single, when it reaches the charts, becomes Paul's 100th single in the *Billboard* Hot 100 chart, 65 of which were with The Beatles.
☀ The UK release also occurs today of John's single 'Jealous Guy'/'Going Down On Love'. The 12-inch release also included the track 'Oh Yoko'. To promote the release, a four-minute montage of various clips from the 1972 *Imagine* film is distributed to various television stations such as MTV and Channel 4 for transmission on *The Tube*.
☀ Due to the success of the first *Thomas The Tank Engine* series, Ringo today, and continuing through until December 20, begins recording the narration for 26 additional *Thomas* adventures. (The episodes are pencilled in for an end of 1986 airing.) During these sessions, Ringo also records the narration for a *Thomas Christmas Show*, also scheduled for broadcast at the end of next year.

Thursday November 21
☀ At BBC Broadcasting House, in Portland Place, London, Paul appears live on Gloria Hunniford's BBC Radio Two show in an appeal for BBC TV's annual fund-raising appeal Children In Need. During the feature, he reveals to Gloria: "I may tour to promote the new album . . . maybe starting in Liverpool."

Friday November 22
☀ In the UK, Yoko releases the record *Starpeace,* her third solo album since John's death. To coincide with its release, Channel 4's tea time rock show *The Tube,* screens the UK TV premiere of the promotional clip to accompany the song 'Hell In Paradise'.
☀ In the States, Paul promotes 'Spies Like Us' by appearing on the NBC TV show *Friday Night Videos.*

Saturday November 30
☀ The concluding part of a two-part interview with Yoko is transmitted on the CBS TV programme *Entertainment This Week*, in which she naturally talks about John, her *Starpeace* album and the recent, alleged, remarks made by Paul about John (see entry for November 6).
☀ In Belgium, a pre-recorded interview with The Beatles' former drummer Pete Best is transmitted on the BRT1 television programme *Terloops*.

December
☀ Paul officially withdraws from the ongoing legal battle between Apple and Capitol/EMI over the unpaid Beatles royalties. Media commentators further remark that his action may have been related to his new Capitol Records recording contract. George, Ringo and Yoko, though, continue with their legal action and immediately increase their demand to $30 million in compensation, $50 million in damages and the custody rights to all The Beatles' master tapes and pressings.

◆ George spends time writing with Alvin Lee. One song is the unreleased 'Shelter In Your Love'.

◆ John's white Rolls Royce is auctioned at the Christie's auction house.

Monday December 2

◆ The world premiere of the 150-minute made-for-TV Johnny Carson film *John And Yoko: A Love Story* takes place on NBC-TV in America. In New York today, the BBC disc jockey Andy Peebles interviews Yoko in her Dakota apartment for the 15-minute programme *Yoko Ono: A Life After John*, which will be transmitted on BBC1 on Friday December 6.

Thursday December 5

◆ To tie-in with the various artists *Greenpeace* compilation album, Weiner-World/Vestron Video release today in the UK the *Greenpeace: Non-Toxic Video Hits* home video compilation, which features George's song 'Save The World' set to newsreels showing *Greenpeace* ships and their activities. (The American release takes place on April 16, 1986.) Acting upon instructions from George himself to the programme's producer Ian Weiner, Harrison does not appear anywhere during the clip.

Friday December 6

◆ Paul records an interview with Alan Grimadell of the National Association of Hospital Broadcasting Organisations. The interview is titled *Paul McCartney: The Man*, and is intended purely for broadcast to UK hospital patients.

◆ BBC1 transmits (between 9:26 and 10:55pm) the drama programme *John Lennon: A Journey In His Life*, which takes a reflective look back at John's life and stars Bernard Hill, the star of *The Boys From The Black Stuff*, in the title role. As a last-minute addition to the evening's programmes immediately following the 64-minute show BBC1 screens a 15-minute programme entitled *Yoko: A Life After John*, which features the exclusive interview with John's widow at her Dakota apartment in New York last Monday. To coincide with this special John Lennon influenced programming, this week's edition of the BBC listing's magazine *Radio Times* (dated November 30 to December 6) features John on the cover.

Saturday December 7

◆ In Studio 7 at the BBC Television Centre in Wood Lane, London, Paul makes a 40-minute live appearance on the BBC1 Saturday morning children's show *Saturday Superstore,* hosted by the DJ Mike Read. During the broadcast, Paul takes part in an audience phone-in and introduces the promotional films for both 'Spies Like Us' and, to close the show, 'We All Stand Together'. In *The Times* newspaper today, an interview with Paul, conducted by Patrick Humphries, is published.

◆ Later this evening, London Weekend Television, the ITV station which serves the London based area of the ITV network, repeat the US documentary *Yoko Ono: Then And Now.*

Sunday December 8

◆ On the fifth anniversary of John's death, Paul, by way of a pre-recorded insert, is interviewed in England on TV AM's *Good Morning Britain* television show, where he calls John "the best collaborator I have ever worked with". Also appearing on the show this morning is *Shout!* author Philip Norman. In America, there is a tribute to John on the ABC TV programme *Eyewitness News*.

◆ BBC Radio One broadcasts a one-hour tribute to John, produced by Kevin Howlett and entitled *The Words And Music Of John Lennon,* which tells the story of his life through archive interviews. (The show is also syndicated to various US radio stations soon after.)

Monday December 9

◆ In America, part 1 of the CBS musical film *Alice In Wonderland,* featuring Ringo as the "Mock Turtle" who sings the Steve Allen track 'Nonsense', is premiered on CBS TV. (Part 2 of the programme, which does not feature Ringo, is transmitted the following night.)

Wednesday December 11
🍎 Ringo becomes yet another ex-Beatle to make a guest appearance on the Thames/ITV network programme *This Is Your Life*, when tonight he appears in the Thames Television studios in Euston Road, London, to honour his good friend Terry O'Neill, the show business photographer.

Wednesday December 18
🍎 One week after Ringo's appearance on the show, Paul is seen again on the Thames/ITV network show *This Is Your Life*, this time by way of a pre-recorded videotaped message, in a show honouring his fellow Liverpudlian musician, Gerry Marsden, formerly of Gerry And The Pacemakers.

Thursday December 19
🍎 Paul is seen at his MPL offices in Soho Square, London, prior to joining Linda for Christmas shopping in Regent's Street.

Sunday December 22
🍎 In London, at BBC Broadcasting House, Paul gives a lengthy interview to the DJ Janice Long for transmission on the BBC Radio One programme *Listen To What The Man Said,* transmitted this morning between 10:00am and 12:29pm.

Wednesday December 25
🍎 A previously taped video message from Paul, where he wishes viewers a "Happy Christmas" is transmitted during the *Caring Christmas Campaign* this morning on TV AM in the UK.

Thursday December 26
🍎 At 10:35pm, the Irish Television station RTE TV broadcasts, for the first time in over 22 years, an interview with The Beatles conducted with Frank Hall as they land at Dublin Airport on November 7, 1963.

Monday December 30
🍎 As part of a whole evening celebrating the 30th anniversary of Granada Television, Channel 4 in England broadcasts, for the first time in 20 years, the programme *The Music Of Lennon And McCartney*. During the 50-minute special, originally transmitted on December 17, 1965, The Beatles are seen performing their, then, latest single 'Day Tripper'/'We Can Work It Out'. John and Paul are also seen comically introducing acts, such as Marianne Faithfull, Henry Mancini and Lulu, who have recorded some of their songs. Also this evening, over on BBC2, the UK premiere takes place of the 1982 documentary *The Compleat Beatles*.

"Broad Street? I didn't like it much either!"

– Paul

January
♣ Ringo arrives in Auckland, New Zealand, to begin shooting commercials for Japanese TV on the outskirts of the Bay of Islands. He and Barbara stay at the nearby Regent Hotel.
♣ At the start of the year Capitol Records in America, as part of an attempt to streamline The Beatles' albums that are available worldwide, delete ten archive Beatles albums from their catalogue, which include the 1966 release *Yesterday . . . And Today.* Capitol announce that these records, over the next two years, will be gradually replaced by the seven British Parlophone albums from *Please Please Me* (in 1963) to *Revolver* (in 1966).

Friday January 3
♣ BBC2 in England re-screens The Beatles' 1968 film *Yellow Submarine.*

Monday January 6
♣ By the close of trading this evening, it is reported that Virgin Video have shipped out some 130,000 copies of Paul's *Rupert And The Frog Song* home video, making it the second most successful video ever released in the UK, beaten only by Michael Jackson's *Thriller.*

Sunday January 19
♣ In New York, while Yoko is in bed asleep in her Dakota apartment, an intruder lowers himself from the roof of the Dakota building and enters her apartment through an open window. He departs, leaving several scribbled notes, a photograph and a personal letter to Yoko. New York City police later arrest the intruder.

Monday January 20
♣ American TV transmits the programme *A Tribute To Martin Luther King Jnr,* which features a cameo appearance by Yoko. (The only UK TV transmission takes place on the ITV network on the evening of November 18, 1987.)
♣ In the Eastern Asia province of Macau, filming begins on the Handmade production of *Shanghai Surprise*, starring Madonna and her husband Sean Penn. (The movie is completed in the middle of March at Shepperton Studios in Middlesex.)

Thursday January 23
♣ Julian and Sean Lennon present the award commemorating Elvis Presley's induction at the first Rock And Roll Hall Of Fame induction ceremony, which is held at the Waldorf-Astoria Hotel in New York. The two also read a letter John had written praising Elvis.

Friday January 24
♣ The American release of the album and home video *John Lennon . . . Live In New York City* takes place. (The UK release eventually takes place on February 24.) The *Live In New York City* title, refers to John and Yoko's August 30, 1972, One to One Concert at Madison Square Garden in New York (see entry). For the release, Yoko deliberately mixes out her vocals and cuts several of her own songs from the performance.
♣ The Handmade film production of *A Private Function* starring Michael Palin is released on home video today in the UK.

Sunday January 26
♣ At the annual London *Evening Standard* Film Awards ceremony, held at the Savoy Hotel, George, along with his business manager Denis O'Brien, receive an award on behalf of Handmade Films for their contribution to the British film industry. He collects the award from the Duchess of Kent. When George receives the trophy he cheekily calls the Duchess "Your Majesty". She replies by giving him a kiss on the cheek, strictly against Royal protocol. BBC TV covers the event.
♣ Paul and Linda are seen at the Superbowl Party, held this evening at London's Video Cafe.

Monday January 27
♣ In Los Angeles, at the 13th annual American Music Awards, before a television audience of 50 million, Paul, in a segment pre-recorded at the London nightclub The

Hippodrome, receives a special Award Of Merit from Phil Collins, who is hosting the British segment of the show. US viewers are led to believe it is actually live by satellite from England, but Paul's appearance was, in fact, pre-taped. The accolade is in recognition of Paul's achievements over the last 20 years.

Friday January 31

✪ In the States, Ringo is featured on the CBS Radio show *Top 30 USA*.

✪ Tonight's edition of Scott Muni's one hour New York Beatles radio programme *Ticket To Ride* is dedicated to the actor Mark McGann, who was the star of last year's made-for-TV film *John And Yoko: A Love Story*. In the UK, EMI Records delete the mono version of The Beatles' 1968 double album *The Beatles*, affectionately called the *White Album*.

February

✪ At his home studio in Rye, Paul records the song 'Simple As That', for inclusion on the UK charity album *The Anti-Heroin Project: It's a Live-in World*. This month, Paul and Linda watch The Rolling Stones in performance at the 100 Club in Oxford Street where he makes a private "unauthorised" audiotape of the show.

✪ The 1972 concert film *John Lennon: Live In New York City* is screened at the library of Performing Arts at New York's Lincoln Center with Yoko, Sean and Julian in attendance.

✪ The single 'Sun City', by Artists United Against Apartheid, featuring in its all-star line-up Ringo and his son Zak, reaches number 51 in the USA singles charts and number 54 in the UK.

Saturday February 1

✪ Dick James, the original and long-time publisher of almost all of The Beatles' songs, dies of a heart attack this evening at his home in St. John's Wood, London. He was 67 years of age. His funeral takes place in Willesden on Monday February 3.

Sunday February 2

✪ A one-hour radio special about Ringo is syndicated across America.

✪ An interview with Yoko, conducted by Bob Coburn, is transmitted in America during the programme *Rockline*.

Monday February 3

✪ In the UK, DMC (the Disco Mix Club, based in Slough, Berkshire) releases the EMI and BPI sanctioned limited (3,000) copies edition of the album *The Mixes*, featuring the track *From Us To You*, which comprises segued extracts from the following original Beatles recordings: 'From Me To You', 'Day Tripper', 'I Want To Hold Your Hand', 'Please Please Me', 'She Loves You', 'A Hard Day's Night', 'Back In The USSR', 'Eight Days A Week' and 'Help!' The tracks have been "mega-mixed" by the DJ Sammy X. To coincide with the release, The Beatles are featured on the cover of this month's edition of the DMC magazine *Mixmag*.

Friday February 7

✪ The 22nd anniversary of The Beatles' arrival in America is celebrated on the children's BBC1 programme *Fax!*, hosted by the former Goodie Bill Oddie.

Saturday February 8 & Sunday February 9

✪ Paul is featured in two brief segments in the UK TV music show *Rick Dee's Weekly Top 40*. In America on Saturday, 'Spies Like Us' reaches number seven in the singles chart.

✪ On Saturday, a five-hour radio show entitled *The Beatles A–Z* is syndicated across American radio stations.

Monday February 10

✪ In the UK, the release of the PMI home video *John Lennon . . . Live In New York City* is delayed until Monday February 24.

✪ Paul and Linda are seen chatting to fans outside their MPL offices in Soho Square, London.

Friday February 14
 In the UK, the Columbia 60-minute home video entitled *British Rock: The First Wave* is released. The documentary includes various Beatles footage such as, amongst others, the colour Pathe news film *The Beatles Come To Town*, shot live in Manchester in November 1963. As well as their *Drop-In* Swedish TV appearance from October 1963, two songs from the *New Musical Express* Poll Winner's Concerts of 1964 and 1965, one song from the February 1964 Washington, DC concert and clips from the 1968 premiere of the film *Yellow Submarine*.
 In the UK, the Chevy Chase and Dan Ackroyd comedy *Spies Like Us*, featuring Paul's song tagged onto the very end of the film, receives its premiere in London.

Tuesday February 25
 At its annual general meeting, the managing director of Beatle City in Seel Street, Liverpool, announces that if a purchaser of Beatle City cannot be found by the end of March, he will auction the entire collection of Beatles' assets in New York in June.

Thursday February 27
 In Cologne, West Germany, as a prelude to her first world tour, and her first outing since 1974, Yoko and her band, which comprises Phil Ashley on keyboards, Bernie Gramm on drums, Leigh Foxx on bass and Mark Rivers and Jimmy Rip on guitars, make a live 14-minute appearance on the WDR German Television programme *Mensch Meier*. She is interviewed and performs the song 'Hell In Paradise'. To conclude the show, she is joined by the other stars on the programme to perform 'Give Peace A Chance'.
 In the UK, Channel 4 transmits the 1981 Handmade film *Time Bandits*.

Friday February 28
 Yoko begins her first solo world tour, which takes in America and Europe. The opening night tonight is in Brussels in Belgium. Due to poor ticket sales, the US leg of her tour is cancelled.
 In the States, John and Yoko's former assistant May Pang is a special guest on Scott Muni's New York radio programme *Ticket To Ride*.

Saturday March 1
 Yoko's tour rolls on with a performance at The Hague in the Netherlands.

Sunday March 2
 Yoko and her band perform in West Berlin.

Monday March 3
 In London, principal photography commences on the Handmade film *Five Corners*.

Tuesday March 4
 Yoko performs in Warsaw, Poland. Only a third of the 6,000-seater stadium is filled with fans.

Thursday March 6
 In London, at Kensington Gardens, George appears at a press conference with Madonna to smooth out relations between the press and Madonna and her husband, Sean Penn, who are currently filming the Handmade film *Shanghai Surprise*.
 Yoko performs in Munich, West Germany.

Friday March 7
 A pre-recorded four-minute interview with George by Paula Yates on the set of *Shanghai Surprise* is transmitted tonight during the Channel 4 music programme *The Tube* in the UK, an item postponed from the show on February 14. During the feature, the former Beatle discusses the problems with the press during the filming of Handmade's latest film.
 Yoko performs in Frankfurt, West Germany.

Sunday March 9
 Yoko performs in Stuttgart, West Germany.

Monday March 10

 Yoko's tour rolls on to Stockholm in Sweden.

Tuesday March 11

 Yoko and her band perform in Copenhagen, Denmark.

Wednesday March 12

 Yoko performs in Hamburg, West Germany.
 In London at the High Court, the case over backdated royalties between The Beatles and EMI begins. (See entry for March 26.)

Friday March 14

 On the Showtime cable station in America, the entire evening's viewing is billed as *The Lennon Legacy: Two Generations Of Music*. Amongst the highlights this night is the world TV premiere of *John Lennon: Live In New York City*, (the film of the 1972 One To One Concert), clips from the 1969 Montreal, Canada, "bed-in", excerpts from the 1972 *Imagine* film as well as the 1970 Beatles' film *Let It Be*. Incidentally, the Westwood One radio network joins in on the fun by simultaneously broadcasting (in stereo) the *Live In New York City* show. The Showtime cable evening begins with a 15-minute interview with Yoko who talks about the background to the *Live In New York City* video.

Saturday March 15

 In the UK at the National Exhibition Centre, in Birmingham, George joins in the all-star finale at the *Heartbeat '86* marathon charity rock concert. The event is the brainchild of the Electric Light Orchestra drummer Bev Bevan and the first in a series of different ideas to raise £1 million for the Birmingham Children's Hospital. Performing alongside former Led Zeppelin vocalist Robert Plant and former member of Wings, Denny Laine, George shares lead vocal on the tracks 'Money' and 'Johnny B. Goode'. The concert, which attracts a capacity 11,500 audience who paid gate receipts of £200,000, is videotaped by BBC Television and is transmitted on BBC1 on Saturday August 2.
 In America, the Keef & Co. television presentation of the December 1979 Kampuchea concerts, entitled *Rock For Kampuchea,* is transmitted today on cable television.
 The European leg of Yoko's tour continues with a performance at a peace festival in Budapest, Hungary, in front of a crowd estimated at 25,000.

Sunday March 16

 Yoko and her band perform in Vienna, Austria.

Tuesday March 18

 Yoko performs in Ljubljana, Yugoslavia.

Wednesday March 19

 Yoko and Sean arrive in London at Heathrow Airport and take up residence at the Dorchester Hotel in Park Lane, London. Later, the Lennons are guests of honour at the play *Lennon* at the Astoria Theatre in London. Back at the Dorchester, Yoko and Sean meet up with John's first son Julian after the show.

Thursday March 20

 Yoko and Sean are photographed outside the Dorchester Hotel, after which Yoko holds a press conference inside the hotel in the Park Suite. She is asked: "How do you feel about the response to your *Starpeace* tour." Yoko replies: "I'm very pleased. Each country has responded to me with enthusiasm, but very differently. Of course it would have been better if more people had turned up, but this is the beginning . . . the first tour. I'm not letting it go, you're going to see me again!" Later this evening, as promotion for tomorrow evening's London concert, Yoko gives a live interview to London's Capital Radio.

Friday March 21

 Yoko's tour reaches England when she and her band perform at the Wembley Conference Centre in London. A preview of the concert is featured this morning on the breakfast station TV AM.

 In America, tonight's edition of Scott Muni's New York radio programme *Ticket To Ride* features a music contest between The Beatles and their sixties contemporaries The Rolling Stones. In England, George Martin is a guest on the BBC1 chat show *Wogan*, hosted by Terry Wogan.

Saturday March 22
 Yoko makes her first appearance on Michael Aspel's live Saturday night chat show *Aspel & Company*. For her 20-minute appearance she is joined on the sofa by John Cleese and Boy George. (This show is the eleventh and final programme of the third series.) Yoko will appear again with Michael Aspel on September 17, 1988.

Monday March 24
 Julian Lennon's second solo album, *The Secret Value Of Daydreaming*, is released in the UK.

 In the UK, TV AM features a review of Yoko's concert at the Wembley Conference on Friday evening. An exclusive interview with John's widow accompanies the feature. This evening, Yoko's tour continues when she performs in Dublin, Ireland.

Wednesday March 26
 EMI agree to pay The Beatles the sum of £2,832,264.02p in back royalties. The judge, Mr. Justice Peter Gibson, insists that the group should also be entitled to review the overseas accounts. Financial analysts predict this could result in an additional £2 million in back royalties to The Beatles. (The court costs for this five-day hearing total £500,000.)

 The photographer Dezo Hoffman, who befriended The Beatles and took more pictures of the group during their early career than any other photographer, dies following a heart attack he suffered in the middle of the month, which left him in a coma. He is cremated at Golder's Green crematorium on April 1, where Dick James was also cremated. Hoffman's Beatle photo archive will eventually be acquired by Apple.

Saturday March 29
 In Russia, the first official release of Beatles' records takes place, although black-market Beatles records had been circulating among fans there for years. A unique deal struck between the Soviet recording company Melodiya and EMI results in the release of 300,000 copies of two albums, *A Hard Day's Night* and a compilation entitled *A Taste Of Honey*. The albums go on sale for 3.5 roubles (around £6). A report on these releases is featured on the BBC Radio One programme *Newsbeat* on Tuesday April 1.

April
 Ringo spends the early part of this month in America, recording a new narrative for Harry Nilsson's 1972 animated film *The Point*, which is released on home video in America during May 1986. Ringo's new narration replaces the original 1971 voice-over by Dustin Hoffman, which could not be issued on home video due to a contractual dispute.

 During the first week of the month, Paul records a spoken message, which is used later in the year on an American TV special celebrating Peggy Lee's 40 years in show business. This month, MPL announces that Paul's new album has been delayed while his producer Hugh Padgham shifts his attention to completing the new album by Genesis. The controversy over the animated naked woman in the 'Oriental Nightfish' cartoon, as featured on the *Rupert And The Frog Song* home video, rages on when the London Borough of Ilford sues Virgin Video. This results from a complaint made to them by a local resident who had bought the video for her child. This month, a pre-recorded interview with Paul is featured on the CBS *Entertainment Tonight* programme *Real Men Of Rock*.

Tuesday April 1 (until Thursday May 22)
 Planned tours of the US, Australia and Japan by Yoko and her band fail to take place due to disappointing ticket sales. Instead four low-key US shows are at the Warfield Theater, San Francisco (Thursday, May 15), Beverly Theater, Los Angeles (Friday May 16), The Forum, Montreal, Canada (Tuesday, May 20) and the Beacon Theater, New York (Thursday, May 22).

Thursday April 3

 At the very last minute, *Beatle City* in Seel Street, Liverpool, is saved by Transworld Leisure Ltd., the company which also owns the former Liverpool International Garden Festival Site. The deal is reportedly in the region of £500,000. For the initial period, Transworld will move *Beatle City* from its current Seel Street site (which will close on April 30) and move into the Festival Hall, situated on the Festival Gardens site near St. Michael's station on Docklands, south of the city centre. It is hoped that *Beatle City* will re-open to the public on May 24, with a more permanent exhibition site being ready for 1987.

Friday April 4

 In the UK, Paul turns up again on the Channel 4 music show *The Tube*, where he is seen briefly performing, on an electric guitar, an unidentified two-minute original tune for the special *Tube 100th Show* celebrations. Also appearing today on the show is Julian Lennon. (The episode is repeated on Channel 4 on Tuesday April 8.)

Saturday April 5

 In Holland, the Beatles Dutch fan club *Beatles Unlimited* holds their annual convention. Today's one-day seven-hour event, which takes place at Muziekcentrum Vredenburg Strecht, in Utrecht, features as the guest speakers, *The Beatles Monthly* magazine writer Tony Barrow, the writer/researcher Mark Lewisohn, who is there promoting his new book *The Beatles Live!* and, from America, Joel Glazier who presents his bizarre, yet fascinating slide show entitled *Is Paul Dead?*

Monday April 14, Wednesday April 16 – Friday April 18

 In his first major television interview in years, George appears in a four-part feature, recorded at his Henley-on-Thames estate, on the American breakfast show *Today*. He is originally scheduled to appear on all five shows during the week, but the April 15 interview segment is pulled due to the news coverage of a major story.
 In London at George Martin's AIR studios, between Monday April 14, and Friday April 18, Paul conducts the final mixing of his new (now delayed) studio album.

Tuesday April 22

 George and Ringo appear together briefly on the BBC1 show *Film '86*, where they discuss Handmade's latest production, *Mona Lisa*, starring Michael Caine and Bob Hoskins.

Sunday April 27

 In the US, George makes another interview appearance, this time on Scott Muni's New York radio programme *Ticket To Ride*.

Monday April 28

 The UK release takes place of the compact disc *John Lennon: Live In New York City.*

Wednesday April 30

 Yoko and Sean attend an AIDS benefit concert in New York.

May

 An exhibition entitled 'This Is My Story Both Humble And True', featuring a collection of John's humorous sketches and lithographs, opens simultaneously in San Francisco and Beverly Hills. Later, the show is transferred to the Dyansen Gallery in New York.
 Still in America, The Beatles' company Apple sign an exclusive agreement with the San Francisco company Determined Productions Inc., for exclusive marketing rights to the name 'Beatles' and associated products. The deal, Apple's first in almost two decades, ends eighteen months of negotiations with Determined. It is scheduled that the first Beatles-related product will appear in the American shops at Christmas.
 Despite the final mixings that took place between April 14 and 18, Paul again delays the release of his new album.

Friday May 2

 Paul's 1984 film *Give My Regards To Broad Street* receives its first European television screening on the cable and satellite channel Premiere this afternoon. As an introduction to the movie, in their "Star Interview" slot, the channel screens 15-minutes of highlights from Paul's December 1984 *Broad Street* interview with Simon Potter for the Music Box music channel.

Monday May 5
◆ On location in England, principal photography begins on the Handmade film production of *Withnail And I*.

Friday May 9
◆ There are numerous Beatles references tonight when BBC1 transmits *Video Jukebox*, a dazzling six and a half hour extravaganza on the history of the pop video, of which The Beatles were a main exponent. A brief interview with Paul, as well as an in-depth feature on The Beatles' promotional films of the Sixties is transmitted during the evening. These include complete colour screenings of 'Strawberry Fields Forever', 'Hello, Goodbye' (because a mute copy was delivered to the BBC, the soundtrack is dubbed at the eleventh-hour and is transmitted out of synch) and 'Penny Lane'. These broadcasts annoy Apple, who demand that the films are not included in the scheduled repeat later this year. They go as far as to threaten the BBC with legal action if: "They broadcast any more material to which we (Apple) have sole ownership, or which might be deemed to exploit the copyright name 'Beatles' in any way!" The BBC take immediate action and decide to drop any suspect Beatles footage from their archive related transmissions (i.e. *The Rock & Roll Years*) until this matter has been resolved.

Thursday May 15
◆ In the Maldive Islands, a picture of John is featured on a 70 laree postage stamp.

Sunday May 18
◆ In America, Yoko guests for the first time on the 45-minute CNN interview programme *Larry King Live*. (She will return to the programme on October 7.)

Monday May 19
◆ MTV in America begins broadcasting a 10-part, twice weekly, series entitled *In My Life: The John Lennon File*. On this day, Yoko conducts a press conference in Montreal, Canada.

Wednesday May 21
◆ Back in England, Paul and Linda meet fans who are waiting for them outside the MPL offices in Soho Square, London.

Thursday May 22
◆ The American love affair with John Lennon continues with the home video release of the 1972 John and Yoko film presentation of *Imagine*. As with the UK release, the edited 60-minute version is featured.

Monday May 26
◆ In England, on the BBC1 show *Guinness Book Of Records Hall Of Fame*, hosted by David Frost and Norris McWhirter, Paul becomes the first of six people inducted into the Guinness Book Of Records Hall Of Fame. Guinness lists Paul as the most successful musician of all time. Joining Paul tonight at the TV Centre in Wood Lane, London, are tennis player Billie Jean King, Sir Ranulph Fiennes, Vesna Vulovic, Colonel Joe Kittinger and Vernon Craig.

Wednesday May 28
◆ In Los Angeles, ASCAP presents an award to Paul for the song 'No More Lonely Nights'. The track wins the honour as the most performed song of the year since October 1, 1984. The producer and songwriter Hal David accepts the award on behalf of Paul who is still in England. Back in England, the American film and TV magazine programme *Glitter*, featuring this week the making of Paul's *Give My Regards To Broad Street* film, is transmitted on the cable station Lifestyle.
◆ George returns to Abbey Road Studios for the first time since February 3, 1971, to attend a recording session for the soundtrack of *Shanghai Surprise*. He is forced to use

the legendary St. John's Wood venue because his FPHOTS location is not big enough to cater for the large orchestra that is needed on the recording. George eventually leaves the studio at 10pm, where he happily poses for pictures and signs various Beatles artefacts for fans who were waiting outside the building, many of whom had sheltered under the tree in the car park to avoid the heavy rain.

Tuesday June 3
🍎 Cynthia Lennon is a guest on the ITV afternoon chat show *Hindsight*.

Wednesday June 4
🍎 Paul is pictured by fans leaving his MPL offices in Soho Square, London.

Friday June 6
🍎 Dick Rowe, the former head of A&R at Decca Records and the man forever tagged as "the man who turned down The Beatles", dies in London aged 64, of a diabetes-related illness. In his will (published on June 14) he leaves £6,856,839 (net), the majority going to his wife Frances. A donation is made to the British Heart Foundation.

Saturday June 7
🍎 In California at the Los Angeles Superior Court, the judge Paul Breckenridge orders the producers of the *Beatlemania* stage show and film to pay Apple Corps Ltd a total of $10.5 million in damages. Breckenridge rules that: "*Beatlemania*'s primary purpose was to commercially exploit The Beatles' popularity." The suit is settled when John's original deposition of November 28, 1980 (see entry) is heard.

Sunday June 8
🍎 The stage play *Lennon* closes at the Astoria Theatre in Charing Cross Road, London, not because of poor ticket sales but because the company that financed the production, the Lupton Theatre Company, has crashed, owing thousands of pounds to cast, staff and theatregoers who had booked tickets in advance. The actors and actresses are informed of the show's plight as they come off stage at the end of this evening's performance.

Friday June 13
🍎 The Handmade film *Mona Lisa* premieres in New York.
🍎 Linda appears live, from Broadcasting House, Portland Place, London, on the BBC Radio Four programme *Woman's Hour* in which she talks about her campaign to stop Fairlight Down, near Hastings in Sussex, from becoming an onshore oil field.

Sunday June 15
🍎 At Giant Stadium, in East Rutherford, New Jersey, in front of a sell-out 50,207 crowd, Yoko makes a brief appearance at the Amnesty International's all-star charity concert called *A Conspiracy Of Hope*, in which she sings 'I Shall Be Released'.

Monday June 16
🍎 On the Jubilee underground tube line between Charing Cross and Swiss Cottage with a short stop off at Bond Street, Paul films a most unusual promotional film for the single 'Press'. Working with director Philip Davey, Paul wanders around the underground tube stations and mimes to a tape of the song which is played on a ghetto-blaster strategically placed in an Adidas sports bag with holes punched in the sides to let the sound out. Paul, who did not seek permission from London Transport to make the film, sings while the commuters go about their day-to-day business. The UK premiere for the song occurs on Channel 4's *The Tube* on July 4 with the US premiere occurring on July 20 on the 24-hour music station MTV.

Tuesday June 17
🍎 In America, four members of the group Elephant's Memory join in a $104 million lawsuit against Yoko Ono and The Estate of John Lennon, claiming "contract fraud". Their fellow band member, Adam Ippolito, had previously filed the suit, claiming that Yoko had improperly made financial profits from the 1972 One To One Concerts, by way of a cable TV screening and the various world-wide record and video releases. Elephant's Memory, of course, had served as John and Yoko's backing band at the concert and

claim to have given their services for free. The suit also claims that during the concert, Yoko had pretended to play keyboards and that they were, in fact, being played by Ippolito. Yoko immediately asks the court to dismiss the suit. Her spokesman, Elliot Mintz issued a statement calling it: "A nuisance case, filed by tenth rate back-up musicians!" When asked about the accusation that Yoko did not play keyboards during the 1972 concert, Mintz called it "scandalous!"

🍎 Back in England, the 1978 film *I Wanna Hold Your Hand* receives its UK TV premiere this evening on BBC2.

Thursday June 19
🍎 In London, George attends a Trafalgar Square anti-nuclear rally and signs a giant white piece of paper attached to a double-decker bus, protesting the deployment of nuclear weapons. The event is covered by major news agencies around the world, notably ITN in the UK and CNN in America.

Friday June 20
🍎 At the Prince's Trust 10th Birthday Party Concert at the Wembley Arena in London, in front of Prince Charles and the Princess of Wales, Paul performs 'Long Tall Sally ', 'I Saw Her Standing There' and 'Get Back'. He is backed by an all-star line-up that includes Phil Collins, Mark King (of Level 42), John Illsley and Mark Knopfler (Dire Straits), Ray Cooper, Howard Jones, Elton John, Eric Clapton, Midge Ure, Bryan Adams and Tina Turner. BBC TV is there to videotape the proceedings and televise the results for the first time in the UK on BBC2 on June 28 between 9:15 and 10:45pm. (A repeat screening occurs on New Years Eve, December 31, later this year.) BBC Radio One transmits highlights from the concert, in stereo, on July 6. The programme is also released on video in both America and in the UK. In America, on July 23, brief excerpts from the show are included in the show *Entertainment Tonight*, which also includes an interview with Paul, carried out by Selina Scott. At the start of the evening, before going on stage, David Bowie and Mick Jagger join Paul in his dressing room.

🍎 Virgin Video in the UK releases the programme *Carl Perkins And Friends – A Rockabilly Session*, which includes George and Ringo. This video, presented in hi-fi stereo, features the extended US TV version of the programme. (See entry for October 21, 1985 for details of the show.)

Monday June 23
🍎 A short pre-taped interview with Paul is featured on the CBS TV programme *Entertainment Tonight*.

Wednesday June 25
🍎 In the UK, Channel 4 repeats the 1968 documentary film *Music!* which features a short colour film clip of The Beatles rehearsing 'Hey Jude' back on July 30, 1968.
🍎 In the UK, today's edition of the *Daily Express* newspaper features a report on George's attempts to save the Regal Cinema in Henley-on-Thames.

Friday June 27
🍎 In Europe, the Steve Blacknell Music Box programme *Off The Wall* unofficially reveals that "Paul will soon be touring!"

July
🍎 Early this month in London, Linda videotapes the second video version of 'Seaside Woman'.
🍎 At the High Court in London, Ringo is ordered to increase his annual alimony payments to his former wife Maureen from £44,000 (a sum fixed in 1981) to £70,000. Furthermore, the judge rules that this sum should be backdated to 1979. Ringo, through his lawyer, immediately issues an appeal, which results in another court case on December 19 (see entry).

Tuesday July 1
🍎 In the UK, the first audio cassettes called *Only The Beatles . . .*, featuring original Beatles music which has been licensed by EMI to the Whitbread Beer Company, are sent out to customers who have sent £2.99 and collected four lager ring pulls from the

top of the special Heineken Beatles tins. The tape contains on side one: 'Love Me Do', 'Twist And Shout', 'She Loves You', 'This Boy', 'Eight Days A Week', 'All My Loving'; side two: 'Ticket To Ride', 'Yes It Is', 'Ob-La-Di, Ob-La-Da', 'Lucy In The Sky With Diamonds', 'And I Love Her', 'Strawberry Fields Forever'. Although this piece of marketing proves popular with consumers, Beatles fans are in an uproar when they discover that they have to collect ring pulls from tins of beer in order to obtain a tape that contains two previously unavailable stereo recordings of 'This Boy' and 'Yes It Is'.

Thursday July 10
🍎 In the UK, the 192-page autobiography of Joe Brown entitled *Brown Sauce – The Life And Times Of Joe Brown* is published today by Collins Willow and features a 14-line foreword written by George.

Saturday July 12
🍎 Paul and Linda are seen chatting to fans as they leave the MPL offices in Soho Square, London. Later, the 22-minute 1984 MPL film *Blankit's First Show*, centring on Linda's Appaloosa horse, receives its UK premiere on BBC2 between 7:33 and 7:55pm. (A further screening takes place on the station in November, with a further repeat, this time unscheduled, taking place on May 10, 1989.) Of special note in the programme is the unreleased Paul McCartney track 'All You Horseriders' which is heard on the soundtrack.
🍎 At precisely the same time (between 7:31 and 8:29pm), the ITV Network begins screening the first episode in the new Granada ITV variety series *I Feel Fine* which is hosted by the Liverpudlian comedian Stan Boardman and features an appearance by Ringo.

Monday July 14
🍎 Simultaneous American and UK release takes place today of Paul's single 'Press'/'It's Not True'.

Wednesday July 16
🍎 At his MPL offices in Soho Square, London, Paul grants an interview to the former ITN news reader Selina Scott for BBC1's *Breakfast Time* show. The 14-minute feature, in which he discusses hard drugs, the making of the video for 'Press' and the Prince's Trust Gala Concert, is transmitted early the following morning, Thursday July 17, in two parts, just before and just after 8am. Of most interest is Paul's comment about his 1984 film *Give My Regards To Broad Street,* of which he says "I didn't like it much either!" a referral to the mauling it received from the critics.

Friday July 18
🍎 Paul continues promoting the album *Press To Play* by travelling to the Abbey Road Studios in London, to film the MPL/BBC co-production TV special, entitled simply *McCartney*. The programme is transmitted for the first time on BBC1 on August 29, with a repeat screening, this time an extended version, on BBC2 on December 30. During the filming, Paul also records a special studio performance version of 'Press'. A brief clip of this is included in the TV broadcasts, as well as on *Wogan* on BBC1 on August 1. (In 1989, the show is released on home video, featuring the alternative title, *The Paul McCartney Story.*)
🍎 In America, Ringo appears with Scott Muni, on the syndicated American Beatles radio show *Ticket To Ride*.
🍎 At Friar Park in Henley, George resumes work on the track 'Zig Zag', an instrumental to appear on the *Shanghai Surprise* film soundtrack. The sessions also produce the song 'Hottest Gong In Town', which will remain unreleased until 1992. Several other tracks, intended for the Madonna/Sean Penn film, remain unreleased.
🍎 Seventeen days after the release of the 12-track Beatles cassette *Only The Beatles . . .,* Apple issue a writ against Whitbread, charging that they are marketing Beatles music without their permission and that, until they read about the cassette offer in the newspapers, Apple knew nothing of the deal or the long negotiations. A spokesman for Apple comments: "We knew nothing about EMI's scheme with Heineken until then. Our lawyers contacted them and asked them to desist and they refused. We do not think this is any way for a reputable British company (Whitbread) to behave!"

Whitbread refuse to withdraw the special Heineken Beatles cans because they have filled Britain's off licences and supermarket shelves with an estimated 35 million cans advertising The Beatles tape. Whitbread will stand to lose millions of pounds by withdrawing the cans and disposing of their contents. This is in addition to the potential damage to the company's respected high standing in the highly competitive lager market while they have no product in the stores. EMI are unrepentant over the mix-up. A spokesman for the company announces: "Apple were most definitely kept informed of the Whitbread negotiations in the spring of this year before a final contract was inked. Apple made no comment at that stage and this prompted EMI to go ahead with the deal." (The row continues while fans hurriedly buy up the cassette, which is fast becoming a hot collector's item.)

Saturday July 19
 Paul's film for 'Press' receives its first showing on the cable station Music Box, appearing during today's edition of the magazine programme *Off The Wall*. In the States, a short two-minute pre-recorded interview with Paul is aired on the programme *Inside HBO*.

Saturday July 26
 'Press' enters the UK singles chart at number 32, rising to number 31 one week later.
 Yoko's recent interview on the Canadian TV music programme *The New Music* is transmitted in Europe this evening on the cable and satellite station Sky Trax.

Sunday July 27
 Ringo and Barbara are seen in the crowd at the England vs. Mexico polo match in Windsor, Berkshire. Their appearance is briefly captured in the Channel 4 coverage of the game, transmitted on August 3.

Monday July 28
 Paul is seen leaving his MPL offices in Soho Square, London.

August
 Ringo, along with the Monty Python star John Cleese and former member of The Goodies comedy team Bill Oddie, record the comical track 'Naughty Atom Bomb', which is released in the UK only on November 24, as part of the charity album *The Anti-Heroin Project: It's A Live-In World*. Ringo also records the spoken-word track 'You Know It Makes Sense', which appears also in the UK only, on a 12-inch single and on *The Anti-Heroin* album.
 Paul and George are publicly thanked by the Cystic Fibrosis Research Trust for "Their kindness and generosity in making donations to help bring closer the scientific breakthrough needed in the fight against the disease."
 In the States, Paul features in a 45-minute CBS TV *Entertainment This Week* special, entitled *An Hour With Paul McCartney,* featuring an interview recorded with the former Beatle at his MPL offices in Soho Square, London.

Friday August 1
 At the BBC Television Theatre, in Shepherd's Bush, London, Paul appears for the first time on the live BBC1 early evening talk show *Wogan*, hosted by the Irish disc jockey Terry Wogan. During Paul's 15-minute interview, (which is transmitted between 7:01 and 7:16pm) an alternative video clip of Paul performing 'Press', directed by Philip Davey and taped during the Richard Skinner Abbey Road sessions on July 18, is also transmitted.

Saturday August 2
 A telephone interview by David Jensen is featured on the children's programme *Get Fresh*, transmitted this morning across the ITV network. In the States, 'Press' enters the *Billboard* singles chart at number 66.
 This evening (between 11:06pm and 12:50am), BBC1 transmits the *Heartbeat '86* concert, featuring George, recorded on March 15 (see entry for full details).

Saturday August 9
 A four-minute pre-recorded interview with Paul, carried out with Janice Long, is transmitted on the BBC1 programme *The Saturday Picture Show*.

Sunday August 17
🍎 Paul and Linda leave Heathrow Airport en route to America to begin promotional work for the album *Press To Play*.

Monday August 18
🍎 Paul immediately begins recording a number of promotional interviews on both TV and radio, one of which is for a prestigious four-part feature on the NBC TV breakfast show *Today*, transmitted between Monday August 25 and Thursday August 28.

Friday August 22
🍎 Paul's *Press To Play* album is released in America. (The UK release takes place on September 1.) The record reaches number eight in the UK and number 30 in the US album charts.

Saturday August 23
🍎 The London Weekend Television region of ITV repeats (between 1:35 and 2:20am) the excellent 1983 Granada documentary *The Early Beatles – 1962–1965*, originally transmitted across the ITV network on New Year's Day 1984.

Sunday August 24
🍎 A pre-recorded promotional interview with Paul for *Press To Play*, recorded at BBC Broadcasting House in Portland Place, London, is transmitted today on the BBC Radio One *Simon Bates Show*.

Monday August 25 (until Friday August 29)
🍎 Whilst in New York, at the Power Station Studios, Paul records several songs with members of Billy Joel's backing band, Liberty Devitto on drums, Russell Javors on rhythm guitar, Doug Stegmeyer on bass, Mark Rivera on percussion and wind instruments and David Brown on lead guitar. These sessions, produced by Phil Ramone, include the track 'Loveliest Thing'. (Further sessions with Ramone take place in October – see entry.) Meanwhile, back in England, also on Monday August 25, a pre-recorded interview with Paul to promote his new album is transmitted on Capital Radio's *David Jensen Show*.

Tuesday August 26
🍎 In the UK, the home video of an extended version of *The Real Buddy Holly Story* is released and again includes the brief airing of the 1958 Quarry Men recording of 'That'll Be The Day'. (The tape is released in America on September 21, 1987.) This version features an additional 30-minutes of new footage and originally comes with two audiotapes featuring 28 Buddy Holly tracks. (BBC2 had screened the original, shorter version on September 12, 1985.)

Friday August 29
🍎 In New York, the world premiere takes place of the Handmade Films production *Shanghai Surprise,* starring Madonna and Sean Penn and featuring songs by George and a musical score by George and Michael Kamen. George also makes a cameo appearance in the film. (The film opens in the UK on October 17.)
🍎 Los Angeles News takes a fond look back at twenty years since The Beatles played their last scheduled concert performance at Candlestick Park on August 29, 1966.

Saturday August 30
🍎 The 20th anniversary reissue of 'Yellow Submarine'/'Eleanor Rigby' reaches number 63 in the UK singles chart.

September
🍎 During the month, Paul is interviewed by Chris Salewicz for *Q* magazine. Away from interviews, Paul composes a special song, intended only for his wife's birthday and titled simply 'Linda'. He records two versions of the track and presses only one copy of the single with both versions, one on either side. This month, interviews with Paul appear in two Italian TV programmes, namely *Vota La Voce* and *Musica E*.

Monday September 1
♦ On NBC Radio in America, Paul's *Press To Play* is featured on the programme *Album Party*.

Friday September 5
♦ In less than a week, Handmade Films premiere their second new film, the Michael Caine and Bob Hoskins film *Mona Lisa,* which opens this evening at the Odeon, Haymarket in London.
♦ In America, at the annual MTV Awards, Paul introduces Tina Turner in a pre-taped clip.

Wednesday September 10
♦ To celebrate ten years of the Buddy Holly Week, Paul and Linda host a private lunch party at the Break For The Border restaurant, just off Charing Cross Road in London. Also present are George Martin, Eric Stewart, Dave Edmunds and Jerry Allison of The Crickets. During the party, Paul presents Allison with a gold disc marking more than a million sales of 'That'll Be The Day'. Ringo and Barbara are on the guest list but are unable to attend.

Friday September 12
♦ BBC1 screens, for the first time since 1976, John's 1967 film *How I Won The War* between 11:31pm and 1:25am.
♦ BBC2 transmits the photography programme *Landscapes,* which focuses 15 of its 25 minutes duration on the work of Linda, who also appears in the show.
♦ Ringo and Barbara attend a "Bond Girls" fashion show at the Savoy Hotel in London.

Saturday September 13
♦ 'Press' reaches number 21 in the American singles charts. Also today in the States, the Westwood One radio station syndicate the 90-minute stereo broadcast of the Prince's Trust Rock Gala Concert, taped at the Wembley Arena in London on Friday June 20.
♦ A 21st birthday party for Zak Starkey is thrown by Ringo in the lodge situated in the grounds of his Tittenhurst Park mansion in Ascot. Paul and Linda are among those in attendance.

Saturday September 20
♦ MPL's *Rupert And The Frog Song* is transmitted for the first time on the Disney Channel in America.

Wednesday September 24
♦ *The Real Buddy Holly Story* is broadcast on the Cinemax television station in America.
♦ Meanwhile, in the UK, the ITV network begins transmitting the second series of 26 *Thomas The Tank Engine And Friends* episodes, again featuring Ringo's narration.

Saturday September 27
♦ Due to its recent exposure in the comedy film *Ferris Bueller's Day Off,* The Beatles' 1963 version of 'Twist And Shout' reaches number 23 in the US singles chart.
♦ A short interview with Paul is featured on the BBC Radio One programme *City To City,* a documentary on music from Liverpool. (The show is repeated on the station on Thursday October 2.)

Monday September 29 (until Sunday October 5)
♦ A one-hour show on Paul, as part of the series *Rock Today,* is syndicated across various US radio stations.

October (through month)
♦ Following their sessions in New York that lasted from August 25 until August 29 (see entry), Paul's Phil Ramone sessions resume at the start of the month at his home studios in Rye, Sussex. At the end of the month, during his return visit to the States, Paul, working again with Bob Giraldi, who directed the video for 'Say Say Say', shoots the promotional film for the track 'Stranglehold'. For the clip, which is shot at the derelict restaurant, *Halfway Station* set in the small town of Nogales, Arizona, Paul is joined by a

band which comprises Dwayne Sciacqua on guitar, Lenny Pickett on baritone sax, Jerry Marotta on drums, Alex Foster on baritone, Neil Jason on bass and Stan Harrison on alto. During the shooting, in front of 180 highly excited extras, Paul leads the band into performances of 'Fortune Teller', 'Love Is Strange', 'Tequila', 'Cactus Club' and, naturally, 'Stranglehold'. (Final editing of this rarely screened clip takes place in early November.)

🍎 At the start of the month, Yoko signs a deal with the music publishing company CBS Songs in America. The agreement allows CBS to administer songs composed by her and John in the USA and Canada. This month, also in America, the author Albert Goldman submits the first draft of his book on John. Due to its length (420,000 words), the publishers Bantam Press suggest that the text needs trimming.

🍎 The future of Beatle City is again thrown into doubt when its current owners, Transworld, are declared bankrupt with debts of over £2 million.

Friday October 3 (until Sunday October 5)
🍎 A three-hour programme about Paul, produced for the series *Rock Watch*, is syndicated across various US radio stations.

Saturday October 4
🍎 A 15-minute pre-recorded feature with Paul is transmitted on the French TV Annette 2 music programme *Les Enfants Du Rock*.

Sunday October 5
🍎 The Handmade film *Mona Lisa*, starring Michael Caine and Bob Hoskins, opens in London at the Odeon, Haymarket. The film goes on national release on October 17. A close examination of the film's credits reveals that "Richard Starkey MBE" is the "special production consultant".

Monday October 6
🍎 Ringo holds a press conference in Atlanta, Georgia, as a promotion for The Brasserie, a restaurant in which he has co-ownership, but it will not officially open until September 27, 1987.

Tuesday October 7
🍎 In the UK, an exclusive 48-minute documentary on the making of *Shanghai Surprise* is transmitted this evening on Channel 4 (between 10:56 and 11:48pm). The programme, entitled *Handmade In Hong Kong*, includes a behind-the-scenes look at the film, interviews with George and footage of him recording the soundtrack music for the film. Prior to its transmission, the stars of the film, Madonna and Sean Penn, make an attempt to stop the programme being broadcast, or, at least, insisting that certain scenes are cut from the show. At George's insistence, the documentary is screened without any cuts.

🍎 In America, Yoko makes her second appearance on the CNN interview programme *Larry King Live*. (A further feature with Yoko occurs on Friday October 10.)

Thursday October 9
🍎 The official release date for John's book *Skywriting By Word Of Mouth*, although copies had started to appear in various book shops as early as October 6.

Friday October 10
🍎 In the UK, Geffen/WEA release on CD John and Yoko's 1980 album *Double Fantasy*.

Saturday October 11
🍎 The 1965 Capitol album *The Early Beatles* re-enters the US album charts.

🍎 Denny Laine's imminent bankruptcy becomes common knowledge when a report on his problem is broadcast on the Music Box programme *Off The Wall*. (It is also revealed that his bankruptcy case has been set for Tuesday December 16 – see entry.)

Sunday October 12
🍎 Back in England, Paul makes another interview appearance on Capital Radio in London.

Tuesday October 14
🍎 In a promotional appearance for *Thomas The Tank Engine And Friends*, Ringo, alongside its writer Rev. W. Awdry, appears unannounced for four minutes live on the afternoon programme *Children's ITV*.

Thursday October 16
🍎 At the first ever British Video Awards ceremony, held at the Grosvenor Hotel in Park Lane, London, Paul receives an award for *Rupert And The Frog Song*, recognised as The Best Selling Video of 1985.

Friday October 17
🍎 The Handmade film *Shanghai Surprise*, starring Madonna, simultaneously opens at the Warner Complex in Cranbourn Street, London and nationwide in cinemas across the UK. (Scheduled to open at the cinema once this film has ended its run is the Ann Margaret movie *Twice In A Lifetime*, which features music by Paul.)
🍎 A four-hour radio programme focusing on Paul in Dick Clark's US *Rock & Roll Remembers* series, is syndicated across American radio stations until October 19.
🍎 Ron Kass, the first ever boss of Apple Records in 1968, dies of cancer in Los Angeles, aged just 51.

Thursday October 23
🍎 Yoko appears on the ABC TV breakfast show *Good Morning America*.

Monday October 27
🍎 John's posthumous compilation album, *Menlove Ave.*, is released in America, and features alternative takes from his *Walls And Bridges* album and various other previously unreleased songs. (The UK release takes place on November 3, one week ahead of its scheduled November 10 release date.)
🍎 Paul's single 'Pretty Little Head'/'Write Away' is released in the UK. Tonight, BBC1 (between 10:10pm and midnight) re-screens the 1967 film *The Family Way*, which features soundtrack music written by Paul.
🍎 Ringo's anti-heroin track 'You Know It Makes Sense' is released on a 12-inch single, but only in the UK.

Wednesday October 29
🍎 Paul's single 'Stranglehold'/'Angry' is released in America.

November
🍎 For a week-long period at the start of the month, Paul returns to his (now titled) 14-track *Hot Hitz And Kold Kutz* album. At the end of this session at AIR Studios in London, the master tape is swiftly returned to the MPL tape archives. Also this month, press reports suggest that Paul has his own plans to document The Beatles' story on film using archive films. Steven Spielberg, the legendary Hollywood film producer, is currently being mooted as the director for the project.

Sunday November 1
🍎 The lengthy compilation programme *That's Television Entertainment*, a special programme to celebrate the 50th anniversary of TV broadcasting by the BBC, features a host of Beatles and solo related clips, including a recent interview with Ringo who recalls his admiration for the Fifties science fiction series *Quatermass*.

Monday November 3
🍎 Limelight Films in Dean Street, West London, prepare for distribution the promo film for 'Pretty Little Head'. This features a cameo appearance by Paul (filmed in London on October 18) in an otherwise acted out film which centres around a young girl who runs away from home after having an argument with her father, who is played by Roger Lloyd-Pack, better known as Trig in the BBC comedy series *Only Fools And Horses*. This rarely screened clip appears in the UK on Channel 4's *The Tube*. Owing to the similarity between this and the story line in The Beatles' song 'She's Leaving Home', an 11-second clip from the track appears at the start of the video. The main bulk of filming for the clip was completed over six days, with location filming carried out in late October near Settle

in North Yorkshire, the Gower Peninsula near Swansea and in London at the Lindford House Studios. Additional scenes are also shot at the East Greenwich gasworks.

Thursday November 6
🍎 The 1984 MPL film *Blankit's First Show* is repeated on BBC1 this afternoon between 3:26 and 3:48pm.

Friday November 7
🍎 The planned screening tonight on BBC2 of the January 9, 1965, edition of Peter Cook and Dudley Moore's comedy series *Not Only . . . But Also,* featuring a cameo appearance by John, is cancelled due to a request from Dudley Moore. The programme, which was replaced by an episode of the comedy series *The Likely Lads*, was due to be screened as part of the BBC 50th anniversary celebrations.
🍎 In America, The Beatles are the subject of the one-hour syndicated radio programme called *Solid Gold Scrapbook*.

Saturday November 8 & Sunday November 9
🍎 The Beatles, alongside The Supremes, are the featured artists in the syndicated US radio show *Reelin' In The Years*.

Monday November 17 (until Wednesday November 19)
🍎 For almost three straight days, Paul commandeers the large sound stage D at Pinewood Studios in Iver Heath, Buckinghamshire, where he shoots another promotional video, this time for the track 'Only Love Remains'. During the first morning's shooting, which is directed by Maurice Phillips, an idea involving a large packet of Marlboro cigarettes is quickly shelved in favour of a second idea involving actor Gordon Jackson, best known as Hudson the butler in *Upstairs Downstairs*, and actress Pauline Yates, fondly remembered as the long suffering wife in the BBC1 comedy series *The Fall And Rise Of Reginald Perrin*. Following two days of extensive rehearsals, the shooting of the film takes place on Wednesday. In total, 24 takes are required in order to successfully pull off this unique footage. (The finished version of 'Only Love Remains' is quickly edited and prepared for distribution by the London based company of Front Row Films the following day, November 20.)

Thursday November 20
🍎 Paul and Linda fly out to West Germany for the first time in ten years to attend a reception in Munich for the annual Bambi Awards. The former Beatle is there to receive an award from the legendary West German football manager and former captain Franz Beckenbauer, who honours him with the title of Personality Of The Year. During the ceremony, Paul and Linda are visibly shaken when an explosion goes off in the studio. The McCartneys return to England the following day.
🍎 While in America at the 8th Annual *Billboard Music Awards*, held at the Sheraton Premiere Hotel in Los Angeles, California, Yoko's clip for 'Hell In Paradise' wins the award for the Most Innovative Video. (This year's event runs until Saturday November 22.)

Sunday November 23
🍎 In London, Paul and Linda attend the rehearsals for tomorrow night's Royal Variety Command Performance at London's Theatre Royal.
🍎 The first complete screening in two decades of 'All You Need Is Love' from the 1967 *Our World* live broadcast is featured during the lunch time BBC2 archive programme *Windmill* in the UK.

Monday November 24
🍎 Paul and his backing group, which now includes Linda and Tessa Niles on backing vocals, Eric Stewart on acoustic guitar, Jamie Talbot on saxophone, Graham Ward on drums, and Preston Heymen and Nick Glennie-Smith on percussion, perform the new single 'Only Love Remains' during the Royal Variety Command Performance at London's Theatre Royal in Drury Lane, an event to raise money for the Entertainment Artist's Benevolent Fund. Paul and Linda also reappear with the other stars of the cast during the show's finale. Watching Paul's performance, as she did back in 1963 when The

Beatles played at this prestigious show, is Queen Elizabeth the Queen Mother. She is accompanied tonight by Princess Alexandra, the Duchess of York, and the Hon. Mr. and Mrs. Angus Ogilvy. Following the concert, Paul, Linda and the band line up with the other stars of the performance to meet the Royal guests. Extended highlights of the show, including Paul's song, which is introduced by David Frost, is televised in the UK on BBC1 on November 29.

🍎 In the UK today, *The Anti-Heroin Project: It's A Live-In World,* an anti-drug album featuring tracks by both Paul and Ringo, is released.

Wednesday November 26
🍎 The PBS (Public Broadcasting Services) in America screen the BBC TV programme *John Lennon: A Journey In The Life,* originally screened by the Corporation on Friday December 6 last year.

Friday November 28
🍎 As a preview of tomorrow night's Royal Command Performance transmission featuring Paul, BBC1 screens a 65-minute celebration of the Royal Variety show, entitled *By Royal Command.* This includes the first screening in over two decades of John's famous "Rattle your jewellery" comment from The Beatles' 1963 appearance on the show. Also transmitted in the documentary is a short clip from their performance of 'Twist And Shout'.

Saturday November 29
🍎 On the day that Paul's Royal Variety Performance is screened by BBC1, his single 'Stranglehold' reaches a disappointing number 81 in the American chart.

Sunday November 30
🍎 The ITV network broadcasts (between 10:36 and 11:34pm) a 50-minute *South Bank Show* profile on the choreographer Christopher Bruce who has put together a new London ballet production set to John's classic solo music. The show also airs rarely seen archive film clips and a previously unheard audio interview with John from 1968.

December
🍎 Ringo travels to America, where he films several television and radio commercials for the drinks company *Sun Country Wine Coolers.* His $1 million commission also involves appearances in various magazine adverts for the product.

Monday December 1
🍎 In America, the CD release of *Wings Greatest* takes place. In the UK, Paul's single 'Only Love Remains'/'Tough On A Tightrope' is released. (The US release occurs on January 17, 1987.)
🍎 MTV in America begins re-screening selected highlights from the original Sixties cartoon series *The Beatles.*

Saturday December 6
🍎 BBC Radio One repeats (between 1:00 and 1:59pm) the documentary *The Words And Music Of John Lennon.*
🍎 In America, the three-hour radio programme *The Beatles – Twist And Shout* is syndicated across the States today and tomorrow, Sunday December 7.

Sunday December 7
🍎 Yoko and Sean are featured in the ITV 25-minute religious programme *The Human Factor,* which focuses on Captain David Botting of the Strawberry Fields home in Liverpool meeting the Lennons in New York.

Wednesday December 10
🍎 The BBC programme featuring George's March 15 appearance at the Heartbeat '86 Concert at the NEC in Birmingham is premiered on American TV. (The first BBC screening had occurred on August 2.)
🍎 This afternoon at the BBC TV Centre in Wood Lane, London, Paul drops by the studios of *Top Of The Pops* to record an "insert" performance of 'Only Love Remains' for

transmission on the show tomorrow evening, December 11. Unfortunately, due to its relatively low chart position (number 39), the clip is never screened, although the short, blink and you'll miss him, clip of Paul introducing Madonna's video of 'Open Your Heart' does appear at the close of tomorrow night's show.

Thursday December 11

🍎 On the way up to Newcastle, Tyne & Wear, to record an appearance for *The Tube* at the television studios of Tyne-Tees, Paul and Linda are lucky to escape injury when their car bursts into flames. At 4:15pm, after arriving at Studio 5 unhurt, Paul performs 'Only Love Remains' twice for the benefit of the cameras and then, following a rapturous reception to the song, he decides to play a short, impromptu, version of 'Whole Lotta Shakin' Goin' On'. (Amidst the excitement, Paul inadvertently sings the wrong lyrics, "We've got the chicken by the horn!") To close, he sings a brief snippet of 'Baby Face'. Away from the piano, Paul is also interviewed by 13-year-old Felix Howard, the teenage star of Madonna's video for 'Open Your Heart'. During the course of this feature, Howard "dries up" in front of the camera, forcing Paul to conduct the rest of the interview alone, with him turning the tables by asking Howard some questions. (The segments, which last approximately 14-minutes, are transmitted the following day, Friday December 12 with a repeat screening, again on Channel 4, on Sunday December 14.)

🍎 Meanwhile, BBC Radio One begins the first of a three-part interview with Paul. (Part two is transmitted on December 15, with the final part being aired on December 17.)

Saturday December 13

🍎 In Studio 7 at the BBC Television Centre, Wood Lane, London, Paul appears live again on the children's show *Saturday Superstore*, hosted by Mike Read. For the second December running, Paul is interviewed by Read and takes viewers' questions over the phone. (His appearance lasts approximately 28 minutes.) Over on the Music Box channel, a pre-recorded interview with Paul, carried out by the female VJ Sunie, is transmitted during the programme *Off The Wall*. (The features naturally include a screening of the 'Only Love Remains' promotional film.) During the Music Box interview, Paul also tapes a special 30-second Christmas message to be broadcast on the station at regular intervals over the festive period.

Tuesday December 16

🍎 At the London bankruptcy court, Denny Laine is finally declared bankrupt with debts now totalling £76,035, £53,000 of which is owing to the Inland Revenue in taxes. Besides revealing that he currently has no assets, it is also made known that in 1981, following his departure from Wings, he sold to Paul, for £135,000, his publishing rights to the 1977 smash-hit song 'Mull Of Kintyre'.

Wednesday December 17

🍎 MTV in America add to their video play-list Paul's rarely seen clip for 'Pretty Little Head'.

Friday December 19

🍎 In London at the Court of Appeals, three judges uphold Ringo's claim from July and declare that his backdated payments to his former wife Maureen should begin in April 1986 and not be backdated from 1979, as was originally decided. This ruling would have resulted in an extra payment from Ringo to Maureen of £260,000. His lawyer complains that the original £70,000 a year payment to Maureen was too high anyway, insisting that the Judge should take into account that Maureen's current boyfriend, Isaac Tigrett, the owner of the Hard Rock Cafe, is a millionaire himself.

Wednesday December 24

🍎 Channel 4 in the UK repeats (between 11:46 and 12:43am) the 1985 programme *Blue Suede Shoes – Carl Perkins And Friends*, previously transmitted on the station on New Year's Day this year.

Thursday December 25

🍎 A short two-minute Christmas day phone message from Paul to Noel Edmonds is featured this morning on Noel's BBC1 show.

Saturday December 27

❤ Rumours in the music industry suggest that George is to begin working on his new album at Friar Park. Insiders suggest that he will be joined by the producer Bob Rose, Ringo, Jim Keltner, and the former member of Wings, Laurence Juber. The hints prove to be true, and work begins on the album *Cloud Nine* on Monday January 5, 1987.

❤ A three-hour radio programme focusing on The Beatles and Elton John for the series *Reelin' In The Years*, is syndicated across America today and tomorrow, Sunday December 28.

Tuesday December 30

❤ BBC2 screens the extended 59-minute version of the documentary *McCartney*.

Wednesday December 31

❤ The year ends with a pre-recorded interview with Paul being transmitted on Capital Radio in London. BBC2 repeat (between 9:51 and 11:34pm) the 1986 Prince's Trust Charity Gala Concert featuring Paul.

❤ In the UK, EMI Records delete the following John Lennon singles from their catalogue, 'Cold Turkey', 'Instant Karma', 'Power To The People', 'No. 9 Dream', 'Stand By Me' and 'Love'.

"John was annoyed 'cos I didn't say that he'd written one line of 'Taxman'. But I also didn't say how I wrote two lines of 'Come Together' or three lines of 'Eleanor Rigby'.

– George

January
❦ In the UK, *Woman's Own* magazine runs a poll to find out who are the most popular Britons abroad. Paul comes in third behind Princess Diana and the Prime Minister, Margaret Thatcher.

Saturday January 3
❦ An exclusive interview with Paul, carried out at his MPL offices in Soho Square, London, is transmitted on the 24-hour music station Music Box, during the weekly pop-profile series *Private Eyes*.

Monday January 5 (until Tuesday March 31)
❦ At his Friar Park studios in Henley-on-Thames, George begins recording the tracks that will eventually form the basis of his album *Cloud Nine*. These include: 'That's What It Takes', 'This Is Love', 'When We Was Fab', 'Got My Mind Set On You', 'Fish On The Sand', 'Just For Today', 'Devil's Radio', 'Someplace Else', 'Wreck Of The Hesperus', 'Breath Away From Heaven' and the title track, 'Cloud 9'. The 11-week sessions also produce the unreleased track 'Vatican P2 Blues'.

Tuesday January 6 & Wednesday January 7
❦ A two-part interview with Paul is transmitted on Manchester's Piccadilly Radio station.

Friday January 9
❦ Following a delay from last October, the film *Twice In A Lifetime*, featuring theme music from Paul, opens in London.

Saturday January 17
❦ The Music Box programme *Off The Wall* reveals that a total of 70 "pornographic" pictures of Paul and Linda have been stolen from the McCartneys.

Wednesday January 28
❦ In America, The Beatles' 1965 film *Help!* is released on home video cassette and laser disc. (The home video is released in the UK on March 26, 1990.)

February
❦ This month, a UK CD release of John and Yoko's *Some Time In New York City* is quickly withdrawn due to sub-standard audio quality. The album is subsequently re-mastered and re-issued on August 10 this year.

Monday February 2
❦ Paul holds a recording session at Audio International Studios in London.

Wednesday February 4 & Thursday February 5
❦ At Paul's home studios in West Sussex, he plays host to Duane Eddy, who today records a cover version of Paul's 'Rockestra Theme' for inclusion on his album *Duane Eddy*. During the two-day sessions, Paul participates by producing the track and providing bass and backing vocals.
❦ In Memphis, Tennessee, at the 3 Alarm Studios of Chips Moman, Ringo begins recording songs for an album with Moman serving as producer. These sessions, which include tracks such as 'Shoo-Be-Doo-Be-Doo-Da-Dey', 'Some Kind Of Wonderful', 'Beat Patrol', 'Ain't That A Shame', 'Whiskey & Cola', 'I Can Help', do not go satisfactorily, lasting less than a week, until Tuesday February 10. A simultaneous record of the sessions is captured on videotape. (Note: In the middle of 1989 Ringo sues Moman to halt a planned release of the album. Ringo claims Moman is attempting to capitalise on Ringo's current All-Starr Band concert tour, which was then underway. Ringo also claims that the album was done under the influence of alcohol, which he had, by 1989, given up, after undergoing treatment. In his testimony on November 15, 1989, Ringo noted that he objected mostly to the timing of the release of the album, provisionally scheduled for August, 1989, and claimed that he wanted more time to overdub his own drum tracks. Ringo had not played drums during the sessions and had required help from Moman's wife, Toni, to complete his vocals.) Ringo resumes these sessions on Saturday April 25.

Tuesday February 10 & Wednesday February 11
 Eddy continues with his album *Duane Eddy* by recording the tracks 'The Trembler' and 'Theme For Something Really Important', this time at George's home studio in Henley, with George playing slide guitar on both tracks. The album is released in the UK on June 19.

Monday February 16
 George and Olivia leave Heathrow Airport, en route to Los Angeles, California.

Thursday February 19
 In America, George is to be found alongside Bob Dylan, John Fogerty and Jesse Ed Davis when they join the singer Taj Mahal on stage during his performance at the Palomino Club in North Hollywood. The two-hour performance is captured on low-quality videotape, connected to the in-house video system. Amongst the tracks George performs are 'Matchbox' (with Mahal), 'Honey Don't', 'Blue Suede Shoes' (with Fogerty), 'Watching The River Flow', 'Peggy Sue' (with Dylan) and 'Dizzy Miss Lizzy'.

Wednesday February 25
 The build-up to the release of The Beatles' albums on compact disc reaches fever pitch when a feature on their issue appears on both ITN's *News At 5:45* and *News At Ten*.

Thursday February 26
 With great anticipation, The Beatles' first four (UK) albums are, at last, officially released simultaneously around the world on compact disc. The albums, *Please Please Me, With The Beatles, A Hard Day's Night* and *Beatles For Sale,* are, for technical reasons, all in mono, which naturally results in outrage among Beatles fans and audiophile experts alike. When EMI is asked why they appear in mono, they insist that: "We had indeed prepared stereo CD releases of these albums but when George Martin was called in to review them, he found their sound quality so bad that he had no alternative but to remix all four in mono and thus reach the scheduled release date." The mono/stereo argument still rages on! To coincide with the issues, the giant HMV stores release, Apple approved, limited edition box sets, which house the CDs. This practice will continue throughout the "Beatles On CD" campaign.

Friday February 27
 As an advertisement to the opening of Linda's photograph exhibition in Bath tomorrow, flowers arranged to spell Linda's name on the grass verges on the banks of the M4 just outside Bath are quickly removed because they have distracted motorists and caused several accidents.
 To celebrate the issue of the first four Beatles albums on CD, Channel 4's rock show *The Tube* screens, according to them, some "previously unseen Beatles footage". Fans are naturally disappointed to see excerpts from the well played November 1965 Intertel Studio clips for 'Day Tripper' and 'I Feel Fine'.

Saturday February 28 (until Monday April 20)
 As scheduled, an exhibition of Linda's photographs open at the prestigious Octagon Gallery in Bath, the principal gallery of the Royal Photographic Society.

March
 At his home studios in Peasmarsh, Sussex, Paul records 'Love Comes Tumbling Down', co-produced by Paul and Phil Ramone and unreleased until December 1997 as part of the 'Beautiful Night' CD singles.
 Work on *In My Life* (later to become *John Lennon: Imagine*) officially begins when Yoko gives film producer David Wolper unlimited access to her private film and video tape archives. He sets out to make "the most definitive motion picture about the professional and private life of John Lennon ever made".

Wednesday March 4
 While the world is hurriedly buying and judging the issue of The Beatles' first four albums on compact disc, Paul and Linda are to be found on location in Moor Park, in

Hertfordshire, shooting a small scene for inclusion in the Comic Strip film production of *Eat The Rich*.

Saturday March 7
 The timeless popularity of The Beatles' music is underlined today when their four Parlophone albums, issued on CD just over a week ago, re-enter the UK album charts. *Please Please Me* reaches number 32, *With The Beatles* number 40, *A Hard Day's Night* number 30 and *Beatles For Sale* makes number 45.

Monday March 9
 In New York, John is posthumously inducted into the U.S. Songwriters Hall Of Fame. Yoko is on hand to collect the award.

Friday March 27
 In America, the footwear manufacturers *Nike* begins running commercials featuring The Beatles' 1968 recording of 'Revolution'. This angers Beatles fans around the world, even though Yoko had given her blessing to the idea.

Saturday April 4
 At a New York ceremony, Yoko presents to long-time rock promoter Bill Graham, the first *John Lennon New Age Award*.

Tuesday April 7
 Paul accompanies Linda to the all-women's luncheon at the National Rubella Council in London. Also in attendance this afternoon is the Princess Of Wales.

Wednesday April 8
 A portion of The Beatles' $80 million lawsuit against EMI is dismissed. (A further ruling occurs on May 17, 1988 when the decision is reversed.)

Monday April 13
 In the UK, John's compilation album *Menlove Ave.* is released on CD.

Saturday April 18
 At BBC Broadcasting House, George Martin is interviewed by Ian Grant for the BBC Radio 2 Programme *Sounds Of The Sixties*. The feature also includes another public airing of The Beatles' 1962 unreleased recording of 'How Do You Do It?'

Friday April 24
 The UK release takes place of the *Prince's Trust Tenth Anniversary Birthday Party* album, which includes a free bonus McCartney single. (This special freebie is not included with the US version of the album, which is released on May 11.)
 Meanwhile, at the Sadler's Wells Theatre in London, a ballet set to the music of the 1970 *John Lennon/Plastic Ono Band* album opens and features the choreography of Christopher Bruce.

Saturday April 25 (until Thursday April 30)
 Ringo resumes his recording sessions with Chips Moman in Memphis, Tennessee. The sessions, on which Ringo does not play drums, again do not go according to plan, even though Bob Dylan attends the sessions on April 29. The tapes from both this and the February sessions, which feature a total of 16 tracks, remain unreleased.

Monday April 27
 Paul's *McCartney* and *Ram* albums are released in the UK on CD.

Thursday April 30
 The second phase in the worldwide CD releases of the Beatles' original (UK) albums take place when stereo versions of *Help!, Revolver* and *Rubber Soul* all appear.

May
 In America, Goodtimes home video, release the unofficial documentary *Fun With The*

Fab Four containing a variety of interesting newsreel footage, most notably the Shakespeare sketch from *Around The Beatles* in 1964. Due to fears of a reprisal from Apple, no Beatles music is featured on the soundtrack.

Friday May 1
 In London, Paul appoints Richard Ogden as his new manager.

Thursday May 7 (and Friday May 8)
 In America, *Entertaining Tonight* run a two-part feature on the album *Sgt. Pepper's Lonely Hearts Club Band* over successive nights.

Saturday May 9
 As expected, the second batch of Beatles albums on CD enter the UK album charts. *Help!* reaches number 61, *Rubber Soul* number 60 and *Revolver* number 55.

Monday May 18
 In the UK, CD releases of George's *All Things Must Pass* and *The Best Of George Harrison* take place.

Tuesday May 26
 Simultaneously in both the US and UK, John's *Shaved Fish* album is released on CD. While in the UK, CD releases take place of Ringo's *Blast From Your Past,* John's *Rock 'N'Roll* and *Imagine,* plus Paul's *Wings Over America.*

Saturday May 30
 Geoff Baker reports in the UK papers: "Fab Three are back with a secret record". The report goes on: "Paul McCartney, George Harrison and Ringo Starr have secretly recorded an album – 25 years after their first hit. The shock news was revealed to Radio 1, according to DJ Mike Smith, by a 'very large rock star'. Last night Mike was refusing to reveal his source but a BBC spokesman has this to offer: 'I have no reason to doubt this', adding, 'The report is not a hoax'. Mike Smith says: 'The Beatles were re-united by George at his home recording studios at Henley-on-Thames. There's been a hell of a buzz in the recording industry about this, and now it's been confirmed by a very large rock star. I understand the album is at the final mixing stage.'"

Monday June 1
 To coincide with what is noted as its original 1967 release date, *Sgt. Pepper's Lonely Hearts Club Band* is officially released around the world on compact disc by EMI. (Sales of the disc are high, with 75,000 being sold before it had even reached the shops, prompting it to reach number 3 in the UK charts.) The "It was twenty years ago today" slogan is brandished around in the media more than once during this spectacular release. The fact that the album was actually rush-released by EMI on May 24 back in 1967 is conveniently overlooked! In London at Abbey Road's Number Two studio, Paul and Linda are special guests at a huge private EMI party, where he is seen cutting a *Sgt. Pepper's* cake especially made by Linda. Yoko, George and Ringo had all received invitations to the bash. John's widow declined to come, George was unable to attend and Ringo was reported to be out of the country on business. (Later in the day, he is seen at his *Startling Music* offices in Knightsbridge.) When asked about the album by a BBC reporter, Paul remarks: "I like it. I really like it as an album. I got it out a few weeks ago and listened to it and it really sounded good to me. It did sound fresh." When pushed for a favourite track on *Sgt. Pepper's*, Paul replies: "If I had to pick one track, I guess I'd pick 'A Day In The Life' . . ."

The party, also attended by stars such as Roy Orbison, features on television news bulletins throughout the world. In the UK, there are *Sgt. Pepper* themed reports on TV AM, which include an interview with Derek Taylor, *Newsround* (BBC1), the *Six O'Clock News* (BBC1), *News At 5:45* and *News At Ten* (ITN), and *London Plus* (Thames ITV). A further report on the get-together is transmitted on TV AM the following morning. Granada TV in the UK join in the celebrations by broadcasting across the ITV network tonight (between 8:01 and 9:58pm), a two-hour documentary titled *It Was Twenty Years Ago Today.* This chronicles the Sixties in general, and includes a great deal of Beatles-related footage and new filmed interviews with George and Paul. In America, PBS (Public Broadcasting Station) screens the show way past the twentieth anniversary on November 11. Also today, June 1, The Beatles' producer George Martin makes a live appearance to talk about *Sgt. Pepper* on the BBC1 early evening talk show *Wogan,* broadcast live from the BBC Television Theatre in Shepherd's Bush, London. To coincide with the album's release, ten-second *Sgt. Pepper's* television commercials begin appearing on ITV and Channel 4 this week.

In America, *Sgt. Pepper* is featured on the NBC beakfast show *Today.*

Tuesday June 2 (until Tuesday June 30)
At his home studios in Rye, Sussex, Paul holds more Phil Ramone produced sessions. During this four-week period of recording they produce 'Once Upon A Long Ago' (which is released in the UK only), 'Back On My Feet', co-written with Elvis Costello, 'I Wanna Cry', and a new arrangement for The Beatles' 1962 recordings of 'Love Me Do'/'P.S. I Love You', re-titled 'P.S. Love Me Do'. (The latter will eventually appear in Japan during March 1990 as part of a special double CD release of *Flowers In The Dirt.*) In addition, work continues on the tracks 'Beautiful Night' and 'Love Come Tumbling Down'. Further finished recordings during this month-long session produce an album's worth of material that remains unreleased. Also during this period of recording, Paul records a special version of The Beatles' track 'Sgt. Pepper's Lonely Hearts Club Band', in celebration of the UK disc jockey Alan Freeman's 60th birthday. The performance is transmitted on July 6 by Capitol Radio in London.

In America, *Sgt. Pepper* is featured on the ABC TV breakfast show *Good Morning America.*

Friday June 5 & Saturday June 6
At the Wembley Arena in London, one year after Paul graced the show, George and Ringo make an appearance, on both of these dates, at the Prince's Trust Rock Gala Concerts alongside Elton John, Bryan Adams, Dave Edmunds and Alison Moyet. George sings 'While My Guitar Gently Weeps' and 'Here Comes The Sun', while Ringo appears delivering the ever-popular 'With A Little Help From My Friends'. During the opening night of June 5, George and Ringo appear with Ben. E. King to perform 'Stand By Me'. Their performances are released on *The Prince's Trust Concert* 1987 album, released only in the UK and highlights from both shows are edited into a TV special aired in the UK, across the ITV network on June 20. The show also forms a radio special, which is transmitted on January 1, 1988, on BBC Radio One. On June 14, 1988, in the UK, a home video of the performances is released.

Sunday June 7
The Music Box music channel broadcasts (at 12:30pm and repeated later in the day) a special 48-minute celebration programme on The Beatles and their *Sgt. Pepper's Lonely Hearts Club Band* album.

Wednesday July 1
Paul returns to the Abbey Road studios in London to record overdub tracks for three songs, one of which is 'Once Upon A Long Ago', where again he works with George Martin.

Monday July 20
The UK CD release takes place today of John's *Walls And Bridges* album.

Monday July 20 & Tuesday July 21
During a two-day session of pure jamming at a large studio by the Thames in London, Paul records eighteen rock 'n' roll oldies, most of which are released in Russia in 1988 on the album *CHOBA B CCCP (Back In The USSR,* or alternatively known as *Again In The USSR).* The musicians joining him on the sessions include Mick Green (guitar), Chris Witten (drums) and Mick Gallagher (piano). The recordings include, on day one: 'Lucille', 'Twenty Flight Rock', 'That's All Right (Mama)', 'Bring It On Home', 'Summertime', 'Just Because', 'I'm Gonna Be A Wheel Someday', 'Midnight Special', 'Kansas City', 'Lawdy Miss Clawdy' and 'I'm In Love Again'. The second day of sessions produce 'Crackin' Up', 'Don't Get Around Much Anymore', 'Ain't That A Shame' and 'I Saw Her Standing There' which remains unreleased. Some of the tracks also appear as bonus tracks on various Paul singles prior to the entire album being issued on CD, with

one additional track 'I'm In Love Again', on September 30, 1991, in the UK and on October 29, 1991, in America. One further track from these sessions, 'It's Now Or Never', had appeared on the charity album *The Last Temptation Of Elvis,* which was released in the UK on March 24, 1990. This compilation was initially available only via mail order through the UK music paper the *New Musical Express,* but import copies soon started appearing in America shortly after.

Friday July 31
❦ George attends a hearing at Brentford Magistrates' Court on speeding charges.

August
❦ Paul spends most of the month between his Sussex home studios and at George Martin's AIR Studios in London, completing the mixing and editing of yet another version of his unreleased *Kold Kuts* album. He spends most of the time working with the producer Chris Thomas and engineer Bill Price. While at the end of the month, Paul's new line-up of musicians travel to his Scottish farmhouse for extensive rehearsals. Rumours in the music industry suggest that the former guitarist with The Smiths, Johnny Marr, will be amongst those present.
❦ A planned month-long booking for Ringo at the Mayfair Recording Studios in London is scrapped shortly before the sessions were due to begin. The recordings, intended to concentrate of his new album, were booked by Elton John's manager John Reid and were scheduled to feature production by Elton himself.

Monday August 3
❦ The UK CD release takes place of John's 1973 album *Mind Games.*

Friday August 7
❦ The *Beatle City* exhibition opens at the West End marketplace in Dallas, Texas, where it is scheduled to run until January 3, 1988. (It had arrived in the country from Liverpool in June.) After its stint in the States, *Beatle City* will be packed up and shipped out to Japan.

Monday August 10
❦ The UK CD re-release of John's *Some Time In New York City* takes place. Originally scheduled for February, it was withdrawn due to the poor sound quality.

Friday August 14
❦ *The Prince's Trust Concert 1987,* featuring George and Ringo in live performances from June 5 and 6, is officially released.

Friday August 21
❦ In New York, Paul records the song 'Beautiful Night'.

Monday August 24
❦ Phase four of the release of The Beatles' albums on CD continues today with the worldwide issue of both *The Beatles* (aka The *White Album* from 1968) and *Yellow Submarine.*

Tuesday August 25
❦ In America, reports on Beatles items on offer at Sotheby's auctions and the use of 'Revolution' in the Nike television commercial are featured in the programmes CNN *Showbiz Today* and CBS TV's *Entertainment Tonight.*

Wednesday August 26
❦ In California, Ringo and Barbara are pictured having a late dinner at *Le Dome Restaurant* in West Hollywood.

Friday August 28
❦ To coincide with the release of the album on CD, *Yellow Submarine,* the film, is officially released on United Artists home video in the UK. Fans are disappointed to discover that an American print of the film has been used for the release and therefore

omits the track 'Hey Bulldog' from the tape. (The American release, naturally featuring an American version of the film, occurs on October 20.)

Monday August 31
◉ The spoof TV documentary *Bruce Willis – The Return Of Bruno*, which briefly features Ringo, is transmitted this evening on BBC2 in the UK.

September
◉ In America at the end of the month, as promotions for his upcoming album *Cloud Nine*, interviews with George appear in the magazines *Newsweek, Guitar Player* and *Musician*.

Saturday September 5
◉ The CD issues of The Beatles *White Album* and *Yellow Submarine* enter the UK charts, reaching numbers 18 and 60 respectively.

Monday September 7
◉ This evening, Paul and Linda drop into the annual EMI Records sales conference at the Metropole Hotel in Brighton. Paul reveals the line-up of tracks to be featured on his upcoming greatest hits compilation, which is entitled *All The Best*. Amongst them is the unreleased recording 'Waterspout'.

Wednesday September 9
◉ At the Dolphin Brasserie, in Pimlico, London, during the annual MPL promoted Buddy Holly Week, an impromptu jam session takes place featuring Paul performing with Alvin Stardust, Mick Green (former member of Johnny Kidd and The Pirates) and the DJ Tony Prince. They perform 'What'd I Say', 'Mean Woman Blues' and 'Twenty Flight Rock'. Guests in the audience include Twiggy, Jonathan Ross, Adam Faith, Faye Dunnaway, Anne Diamond, Mike Rutherford of Genesis, Joan Collins and her husband "Bungalow" Bill Wiggins.

Sunday September 13
◉ In America, the HBO (Home Box Office) Network transmits the *1987 Prince's Trust Concerts* starring George and Ringo. This 60-minute version features extra backstage interviews with the former Beatles not included in the ITV version transmitted on June 20. (Further HBO screenings take place on September 16, 19, 21 and 25, with simultaneous FM-radio broadcasts in stereo.)

Monday September 21
◉ The worldwide release of The Beatles' albums on CD continues today, with the release of the 1967 American compilation album *Magical Mystery Tour*. The store HMV again issues a limited edition (12,500 copies) box set for the album.

Friday September 25
◉ Ringo and Barbara leave England and head off en route to Atlanta, Georgia in a specially chartered plane for the grand opening of his new restaurant, the London Brasserie. Accompanying them on their trip are various British radio personalities and competition winners.

Saturday September 26
◉ At the grand opening of his London Brasserie restaurant, situated in the Peach Tree Center, in a shopping mall in Atlanta, Ringo takes part in an all-star impromptu jam session, playing drums in a group which comprises Isaac Hayes, Jerry Lee Lewis and, amongst others, Jermaine Jackson. Among the tracks they perform are 'Whole Lotta Shakin'' and 'Mony Mony'. The following morning, Ringo and Barbara fly on to Boston, and then Los Angeles.

Monday September 28 (until Saturday October 3)
◉ The 60-minute NBC Radio programme *Legends Of Rock*, which this week focuses on Ringo, is syndicated across various US radio stations. Also this evening, pre-taped interviews with Ringo are transmitted in the television programmes *Showbiz Today* on CNN and Paramount TV's *Entertainment Tonight*.

Wednesday September 30
🍎 A pre-taped interview with George is transmitted on *Entertainment Tonight*.

September (into October)
🍎 During the *Flowers In The Dirt* recording sessions, held at Paul's Sussex recording studios, the former Beatle begins recording, with Elvis Costello, 'My Brave Face', a track co-written with Costello. The sessions also produce more Paul/Costello songs, namely 'Flying To My Home' (appearing on the 'My Brave Face' single, released in May 1989) 'Don't Be Careless Love', 'You Want Her Too' and 'That Day Is Done'. Three further co-compositions, 'Lovers That Never Were', 'So Like Candy' and 'Playboy To A Man', which Costello later records for his album *Mighty Like A Rose*, are also recorded. Other unreleased Paul/Costello tracks include 'Twenty Five Fingers' and 'Tommy's Coming Home'.

October
🍎 George's rather unusual high profile continues when interviews with him are featured on the UK breakfast stations TV AM and BBC *Breakfast Time* and in *Q* magazine.
🍎 In America, Ringo works for the first time with the world famous trumpet player, and co-founder of A&M Records, Herb Alpert when they record the track 'When You Wish Upon A Star' for inclusion on the 1988 Disney album *Stay Awake*.
🍎 A pre-recorded interview with Paul is syndicated across America in the radio series *Tim White's Rock Stars*.

Saturday October 3
🍎 The CD version of The Beatles' *Magical Mystery Tour* reaches number 52 in the UK album charts.

Monday October 5
🍎 In the UK, the CD release takes place of Paul's *Red Rose Speedway*, *McCartney II* and *Wild Life* albums.
🍎 In America at the offices of Warner Records in Burbank, California, George records a promotional 37-minute interview to assist with the sales of his new album *Cloud Nine*. During the taping, where he is occasionally seen puffing away on a cigarette, George is reminded that the interview today is taking place exactly 25 years since The Beatles signed their first EMI contract, to which he replies: "About time they gave us some royalties then!" (The exact 25th anniversary of signing their EMI contract was actually on June 4, while the anniversary today is 25 years since the release of The Beatles début single, 'Love Me Do', in England.) George denies rumours that he was booked into the Betty Ford clinic for alcohol addiction, that he is producing a television special featuring 'Every Grain Of Sand' performed by Bob Dylan, and that he didn't like his voice on the live Prince's Trust concerts.

In typical Harrison fashion, a large percentage of the interview is laden with humour. On his collection of guitars: "Some old Fenders I've got, I think, 'Oh!, that's the one that played the solo on 'Nowhere Man'. That's the one that played on 'Guitar Gently Weeps', this nice Les Paul that Eric (Clapton) gave me and the Rickenbacker 12-string, the one I just played on 'Fish On The Sand'. Oh yes, there's Betty, she was that nice blonde from back in '67' . . . it's a bit like that. The only difference is you can't have all the women hanging up by the neck on the wall."

On that he is one of the guitar greats in rock 'n' roll: "Well, I think that's a matter of opinion. Maybe to some people I am . . . to some people I'm a load of rubbish!"
🍎 In America, NBC Radio (until Sunday October 11) syndicates the 60-minute radio programme *Legends Of Rock*, which this week turns its attention to John's career.

Sunday October 11
🍎 In the UK, selected regions of the ITV network transmit the Bill Wyman produced charity video *Willie & The Poor Boys*, which features cameo appearances by both Ringo and Barbara.

Monday October 12 (September 28)
🍎 In the UK, George releases the first single off his album *Cloud Nine,* namely 'Got My Mind Set On You'/'Lay His Head'. (The release in America takes place on October 16.

The single reaches number two in the UK, Canada and Australia and the number one position in America.) A special 12-inch edition, released only in the UK, features an extended mix of the A-side. To accompany the release, George appears in two Los Angeles produced promotional film clips. The first features George playing the song set in a "what the butler saw" machine, which is standing in an amusement arcade. Apparently he was not entirely happy with this version, or an alternative re-edit, which was simply the performance without any cutaways at all, so an alternative version is quickly prepared. This second clip, directed by Gary Weiss, whom George met through his association with *Saturday Night Live* in America, features George in a haunted house, singing the song in a chair, guitar in hand, breaking out into some impressive dancing (done, of course, by a double).

Tuesday October 13
🍎 In the States, Capitol Records file a complaint in the US District Court in Los Angeles to stop Geffen Records from issuing a CD version of the 1982 album *The John Lennon Collection*.

Friday October 16
🍎 BBC Radio One begins transmitting the first of a three-part interview with George to promote his new album *Cloud Nine*. Part two is transmitted on October 29 with part three being aired on October 31. This evening on Channel 4, George appears live on the show *The Last Resort With Jonathan Ross,* where he is interviewed at the very end of the programme by Ross in a nearby pub with the BBC disc jockey John Peel. Viewers had been led to believe that George had already been and gone from the studios by the time the programme had started.
🍎 Just hours after the famous hurricane gripped Britain, Paul is to be found climbing the perilous Valley of the Rocks, near Plymouth in Devon, where he shoots the promotional clip for 'Once Upon A Long Ago'. (Subsequent footage, which is later combined with especially created animated cartoon footage, is edited to make three different promotional films, of which only version two will be transmitted.) Paul had briefly toyed with the idea of shooting the clip in Iceland, taking advantage of the country's snowy conditions.

Saturday October 17
🍎 George makes a surprise appearance with Bob Dylan on stage at his concert at the Wembley Arena in London, performing 'Rainy Day Women #12 & 35' during the encore. George, who had attended all four of Bob's Wembley shows, had been watching the show from the side of the stage.

Monday October 19
🍎 The worldwide CD release of both *Abbey Road* and *Let It Be* takes place. HMV releases a limited edition (10,000 copies) box set for each album.
🍎 In the UK, the first part of an interview with George is broadcast on BBC *Breakfast Time*. (Part two is aired the following morning.)

Tuesday October 20
🍎 In a pre-recorded interview at Friar Park with Tizianna Ferrario, George appears on the RAI UNO programme *TG1* on Italian TV. Further excerpts from the interview occur on the show *Prisma,* transmitted by the station on October 24. While in the UK, just after the BBC have finished transmitting the final part of their two-part interview with George, the rival breakfast station TV AM, which serves the ITV regions, are featuring the "quiet Beatle" as their Man Of The Week, in their regular *After Nine* slot. (The second part of their 10-minute feature is transmitted the following day.) The interviews continue thick and fast, when a two-part pre-recorded 11-minute interview with George, conducted by Rona Elliot, is transmitted on NBC TV's *Today* show in America. (Part two is aired the following morning.)

Wednesday October 21
🍎 George and Ringo visit Paul at his London home at Cavendish Avenue in St. John's Wood. The three former Beatles spend a quiet evening together, dining, relaxing and discussing their future plans, including the long-forgotten official Beatles' story *The Long And Winding Road.*

Thursday October 22

🍎 In America, *Rolling Stone* magazine features George on the front cover with an accompanying article inside, entitled "The Return Of George Harrison".

Friday October 23

🍎 The Comic Strip Productions comedy film *Eat The Rich,* featuring a cameo appearance by Paul and Linda, receives its premiere in London this evening and at several other key regional locations in the UK.

Saturday October 24

🍎 The first of a three-part interview with Paul, carried out by the DJ Mike Read, and recorded at the International Christian Community Studios, Eastbourne, Sussex, on October 12 and 13, is transmitted on BBC Radio One. Part two is broadcast on October 31, while part three is aired on November 7. During the lengthy interview, Paul gives fascinating stories behind the songs featured on the *All The Best* compilation.

🍎 In America, a pre-recorded interview with George is transmitted on the MTV programme *Week In Rock*.

Friday October 30

🍎 Australian television broadcasts the third version of The Beatles' edition of the music programme *Rage*, which features over four hours of Beatles and solo promotional film clips, television appearances, newsreels and interviews. (The first version, which ran just over three hours, had appeared in June to celebrate the 20th anniversary of *Sgt. Pepper*.)

Saturday October 31

🍎 The CD versions of *Abbey Road* and *Let It Be* enter the UK album charts. They reach numbers 30 and 50 respectively.

🍎 EMI Records in the UK delete the following Paul McCartney singles, 'Say, Say, Say', 'Spies Like Us', 'Press' and also the 1969 Plastic Ono Band single (Apple 15) 'Give Peace A Chance'.

Monday November 2

🍎 The simultaneous release in America and the UK takes place of George's album *Cloud Nine*. The cover features the guitar he bought for £75 off a sailor when he was 17 years of age. A journalist asks George about the persistent rumours that Paul and Ringo were going to play on the album. He cheekily replies: "Yeah, the only person who *wasn't* going to be on it was George!"

🍎 In the UK, Paul's second greatest hits compilation *All The Best,* is released, delayed from October 26. (The American release, featuring a different track listing, takes place on December 5 and will reach the number 62 position in the charts.) The CD version of the album omits three tracks, 'Maybe I'm Amazed', 'Goodnight Tonight' and 'With A Little Luck', which are found on the cassette and double album versions of the album. Originally scheduled as the first song on side two of the album, just before 'No More Lonely Nights', is the unreleased track 'Waterspout'. As promotion for *All The Best*, EMI release a limited edition box set comprising nine Parlophone singles, numbered PMBOX11 through to PMBOX19, which feature the tracks on the album. This evening, the first 30-second television advertisement for *All The Best* is premiered nationally across the ITV network in the UK. It is seen at approximately 7:43pm, halfway through tonight's edition of the popular Granada TV soap opera *Coronation Street*. (The commercial is directed by Derek Hayes.)

Friday November 6

🍎 The home video entitled *The Paul McCartney Story,* a repackaging of the 1986 MPL/BBC co-production *McCartney,* is released in America. (The UK release takes place on November 27.)

🍎 A pre-recorded interview with George, conducted by Geraldo Rivera, is aired on the Paramount TV show *Entertainment Tonight* in America. (The promotional film clip for 'Got My Mind Set On You' [version two] ends the show.)

Sunday November 8

 In America, promotions for *Cloud Nine* continue when George is interviewed for WNEW Radio in New York. Then, later this evening, a pre-taped interview with George is aired on the CBS programme *Entertainment Tonight*.

Monday November 16

 In the UK, the home video release containing the first 26 episodes of *Thomas The Tank Engine And Friends,* featuring a narration by Ringo is released. To add to this, collectors are also able to buy several book/audio cassette packs, which again also feature Ringo's reading of the *Thomas* stories.

 Also in the UK, Paul's single 'Once Upon A Long Ago'/'Back On My Feet' is released on a 7-inch and two separate 12-inch vinyl editions as well as on a CD. (There is no American release.)

Tuesday November 17

 In Studio 5, at the Tyne-Tees Television Studios in Newcastle, working with the director Gavin Taylor, Paul videotapes a mimed performance of 'Once Upon A Long Ago'. (Sessions last between 2:00 and 5:59pm.) This clip, in front of an audience featuring 150 school children, is intended for inclusion in the new Tyne-Tees/ITV pop show *The Roxy,* a programme hosted by the DJ David Jensen. During the taping session, Paul also performs impromptu instrumental versions of 'Ob La Di, Ob La Da', 'C Moon', 'What'd I Say' and 'Sailor's Hornpipe'. Due to a technician's dispute, the screening of Paul's performance of 'Once Upon A Long Ago' is delayed for one week, and is not transmitted across the ITV network (between 7:31 and 7:58pm) until November 24. Backstage, during a break from the afternoon taping, Paul also gives an interview to Nick Piercey of Radio Tess (T.F.M.) in dressing room number 3.

 In Holland, a 16-minute pre-recorded interview with George is broadcast on the NED TV show *Tros.*

Wednesday November 18

 Further promotions for 'Once Upon A Long Ago' take place with a rather humorous live satellite link-up from London to Japan for the programme *Yoru No Hit Studio.*

 A pre-taped six-minute interview with George, carried out by Mark Sheerer, is aired on the ABC TV programme *Good Morning America*.

Thursday November 19

 Paul and Linda return to the BBC Television Theatre in Shepherd's Bush, London, where they videotape another interview, appearing as the only guests on the popular early evening talk show *Wogan,* hosted by the genial Irish DJ Terry Wogan. Their 36-minute appearance, which includes studio performances of 'Jet', 'Listen To What The Man Said' and a screening of the promotional film for 'Once Upon A Long Ago', is transmitted on BBC1 the following day, November 20. After the taping Paul is introduced backstage to the Russian rock writer Artemy Troitsky, in town to promote his book *Back In The USSR*, a history of rock in the Soviet Union. Troitsky briefly interviews Paul for a Moscow newspaper which subsequently publishes a photograph taken by Linda of Paul and Troitsky. This is the first time in his long career that Paul has been interviewed by a Russian journalist.

 In the UK, EMI re-release twelve Beatles albums (from *Please Please Me* to *Let It Be*) on high quality XDR audio tape, taken directly from the same digital masters as used for the CD versions of the albums released this year. (The album *Sgt. Pepper* had been released on XDR tape, alongside the CD version, on the 20th anniversary on June 1.) Keeping in line with the CD releases, the first four albums (*Please Please Me, With The Beatles, A Hard Day's Night* and *Beatles For Sale*) are again issued in mono.

Friday November 20

 In the States, a pre-recorded interview with George is transmitted on the CNN programme *Showbiz Today*. (Part two of the interview is broadcast one week later, on Friday November 27.)

Sunday November 22
🍎 In the UK, George appears on the front cover of the *Observer* colour supplement. Inside, there is an interview with the previously reclusive former Beatle by Mark Lewisohn, the author of *The Beatles Live!* In the States, various US radio stations air the two-hour show *Powercuts*, which features an appreciation of the music of George and Pink Floyd.

Friday November 27
🍎 In London, Paul makes a 15-minute appearance on the programme *The Last Resort With Jonathan Ross*, transmitted live on Channel 4 this evening. Paul performs with Steve Nieve And The Playboys the songs 'Don't Get Around Much Anymore', 'I Saw Her Standing There' and 'Lawdy Miss Clawdy'. In between tracks, Ross gives Paul a pile of Beatles albums to sign, but after inscribing a few, Paul insists he is doing no more and tells him jokingly to "get out of here!" When the broadcast finishes, Paul and the band, for the benefit of the highly excited studio audience, perform a brief snippet of the 1979 Wings' track 'Spin It On'. (Highlights from Paul's appearance this evening reappear during Jonathan Ross's compilation programme *Phew! Rock 'N' Roll*, which is transmitted on Channel 4 on April 24, 1988. A further screening of the appearance is transmitted on the German television programme *Ohme Filter*, aired on March 30 and 31, 1988.)

Monday November 30
🍎 Paul and his band return to Holland where they record another appearance on the Dutch TV show *Countdown*. Their 29-minute appearance, which includes another mimed performance of 'Once Upon A Long Ago', is transmitted on Veronica TV's NED 1 on Wednesday December 2.
🍎 Release of the three-volume home video set series entitled *Queen: Magic Years,* featuring Paul in a 1986 interview on Volume 1, called *The Foundations;* while Volume 2, entitled *Live Killers In The Making,* features Ringo and Barbara.

December
🍎 In the US album charts of 1987, *Sgt. Pepper's* is placed 13th in the Best Selling CDs Of The Year and *The Beatles (White)* album is placed at number 25.

Tuesday December 1
🍎 Paul spends the day working on a new piece of music for his *Rupert The Bear* film with George Martin at the AIR Studios in London. In America, the Wings album *Band On The Run* is released on CD.

Wednesday December 2
🍎 At the BBC Television Centre in London, Paul records a performance of 'Once Upon A Long Ago' for inclusion in the following evening's edition of BBC1's *Top Of The Pops*. Following the afternoon taping session, Paul and Linda, again at BBC TV Centre, record a sketch for the BBC1 fund-raising *Comic Relief* special, which is not scheduled for transmission until February 5, 1988. At the end of the sessions, Paul and Linda drop in to see Pete Townshend at his home on Richmond Hill. During their visit, Pete remarks to the couple how lucky The Beatles are to have George Martin remixing their albums for CD, a reference to the fact that Pete is none too pleased with The Who's CD reissues.
🍎 On the European Super Channel television station, the programme *Track Record* broadcasts an excerpt from George's *Cloud Nine* promotional interview, recorded on October 5 (see entry).

Thursday December 3
🍎 Paul, Linda and the band fly to Paris to undertake more promotional work. His first assignment is a 42-minute interview with Antoine De Caunes for his French television show *Rapido*. Paul discusses his current songwriting with Elvis Costello, re-recordings of old rock 'n' roll standards which he wanted to "bootleg" into Russia and his annoyance at the use of The Beatles' 'Revolution' in the Nike television ads. He also remarks about the possibility of working next year with George. Paul is also asked about George's Handmade films company: "George has been the surprise I think," he replies, "because when we did the movies, probably the one least interested was George. He'd turn up, he'd play and didn't want to know. He was serious, he didn't like the movies. He thought

it was a bit stupid, you know, all the acting . . . 'I just want to play my guitar'. But he's turned out to be the most successful in the movies . . . they've just made *Mona Lisa* and really made some good films. They've made some bad ones too. *Shanghai Surprise* was one of them. But he's made some really good films."

During the taping session, Paul tells the crew two bad jokes, one of which is: "A man bakes a birthday cake out of baked beans . . . it's the only cake that blows its own candles out!" Paul also takes time to perform a version of 'Happy Birthday' to Antoine on an acoustic guitar. From this lengthy interview, only 10-minutes worth is used as an integral part in the *Rapido* Beatles special, transmitted the following day.

Friday December 4
❤ The French television station TF1-TV transmits a 70-minute *Rapido* Beatles special, which includes various Beatles and Paul promo films, excerpts from Ringo's films and an interview with Ray Davies of The Kinks, a neighbour of John's at the Dakota, who reveals that he "didn't like John Lennon as a person". The show, of course, also includes a 10-minute edit of Paul's interview taped yesterday.
❤ In America, until Sunday December 6, various US radio stations broadcast the three-hour syndicated radio tribute *John Lennon Remembered.*

Saturday December 5
❤ Paul, Linda and the group appears live on the *Annette 2* TV charity telethon programme on which they mime a version of 'Once Upon A Long Ago'. Earlier in the day, the group mimes another version of the song for inclusion in the programme *Sacrée Soirée,* transmitted on the French television station TFI-TV on December 23.
❤ The 20th anniversary reissue of 'Hello Goodbye' reaches number 63 in the UK singles chart.

Monday December 7
❤ The release of Paul's home video *Once Upon A Video* is issued simultaneously around the world, except for North America.

Wednesday December 9
❤ A pre-taped three-minute interview with George is transmitted on the German ZDF TV show *P.I.T.*

Friday December 11 (until Sunday December 13)
❤ Various US radio stations air the syndicated three-hour special about George, featured in the weekly series *Rockwatch.*

Saturday December 12
❤ Paul makes a surprise 15-minute appearance on the BBC1 Saturday morning children's TV show *Going Live.* During the live transmission, from the BBC TV Centre, Wood Lane, in London, Paul is joined by his son James in taking phone calls live on air. Later Paul and his band, which includes Stan Salzman and the violinist Nigel Kennedy, mime a version of 'Once Upon A Long Ago' for the studio audience. Also today, the *NME* publishes an interview with Paul where he talks about his collaboration with Elvis Costello and reveals that he would like to record some songs by John. He gives as examples 'Imagine', 'Beautiful Boy (Darling Boy)' and 'I'll Get You', adding "If I don't record it, I'll at least perform it live someday!"
❤ Of all the promotional interviews given by George to promote his new album, the most fascinating is the 14-minute feature on the American television programme *West 57th Street* which is aired in America this evening and includes George in discussion with the British celebrity journalist Selina Scott. She is seen eavesdropping on George at a photo shoot and in attendance as George oversees the editing on *Mona Lisa* with the co-star of the film Bob Hoskins. Most intriguing are the questions set by Scott, which includes her tackling George about comments made by John in September 1980.

Selina: "In an interview before his death (*Playboy*), John said he was really hurt by you, that you never mentioned in your autobiography any of the influence that he had on you."

George: "He was annoyed 'cos I didn't say that he'd written one line of this song 'Taxman'. But I also didn't say how I wrote two lines of 'Come Together' or three lines of

'Eleanor Rigby', you know, I wasn't getting into any of that. I think, in the balance, I would have had more things to be niggled with him about than he would have had with me!"

Selina: "He said, that you idolised him as a young boy . . ."

George (interrupting): "That's what he thought. I liked him very much, he was a groove. He was a good lad. But, at the same time, he misread me. He didn't realise who I was, and this was one of the main faults of John and Paul. They were so busy being John and Paul, they failed to realise who else was around at the time."

The *Shout!* biographer Philip Norman is also on hand to add comments about George's persona, remarking to Selina Scott in an interview, "The Beatles is not a normal story! It's a supernatural story. The pressure was supernatural . . . and George has recovered from it. He's the one that we're gonna have to ask about The Beatles. There's no one else left to ask now, because McCartney won't tell you, Ringo can't tell you, and John isn't here."

Selina naturally asks: "When you say Paul won't tell you, what do you mean?"

Norman: "He re-writes history all the time."

Selina: ". . . And Ringo can't tell you?"

Norman: "He doesn't know! He drank the drinks, he smoked the joints, he had the girls and he drummed the drums. That was Ringo!"

🍏 Also today, still in the States, a profile on George is featured in the CNN programme *Showbiz Today*.

Monday December 14 (until Saturday December 19)
🍏 At George Martin's AIR Studios in London, Paul again resumes work on new *Rupert the Bear* songs with Martin, intended for the soundtrack of his full-length *Rupert* film.

Friday December 18
🍏 George, Ringo and Elton John assemble at the Greenford Studios in Greenford, London, where they shoot a promotional film for George's song 'When We Was Fab'. The clip, directed by former member of 10cc, Kevin Godley, features a most elaborate collage of Beatle references.

Sunday December 20
🍏 Paul and his entourage arrive in Germany this morning for more promotional work. Their first assignment is a ten-minute appearance on the ZDF German music and game show *Wetten Dass*, where they perform another mimed version of 'Once Upon A Long Ago'.

Monday December 21 (until Thursday December 24)
🍏 Paul returns to his home in Sussex, where he continues with further recordings. This first session sees the start of the tracks 'Figure Of Eight', 'Ou Est Le Soleil?', 'How Many People' and 'Rough Ride', all eventually to appear on his album *Flowers In The Dirt* in 1989.

Tuesday December 22
🍏 In the UK, an interview with George, recorded at Broadcasting House, Portland Place, London, is transmitted on BBC Radio One.

Friday December 25
🍏 A pre-recorded three-minute Christmas message, delivered by Paul and Linda, is transmitted on the Italian RAI UNO TV programme *Canale Fantastico*. Also today, a pre-taped three-minute interview with Paul is aired on the Italian RAI TV show *Ieri Goggi Domina*. While in England, a short one-minute Christmas message from Paul and Linda is played on the BBC1 show *Christmas Morning With Noel,* hosted by Noel Edmonds.

Sunday December 27
🍏 George returns to more *Cloud Nine* promotional activities by appearing again at BBC Broadcasting House, Portland Place, London, this time on the BBC Radio One 60-minute special *On Cloud Nine*. During the show, besides being interviewed, George also plays the unreleased recording of 'Hottest Gong In Town', lifted from the 1986 *Shanghai Surprise* film soundtrack.

◆ In Italy, a 33-minute re-taped overdubbed interview appearance by Paul is aired on the Italia 1 music programme *Deejay TV*.

Monday December 28
◆ Further *Cloud Nine* promotional appearances see George and Olivia fly out from London's Heathrow Airport, en route to Los Angeles, California, where they will reside for almost two months.

Wednesday December 30
◆ George makes a live appearance on the American radio show *Rockstars,* broadcast on the Los Angeles radio station KLOS-FM.

1988

"We always had a
deal together
that The Beatles
were us four, and
that if any one of
us wasn't in the
band, The Beatles
wouldn't exist. It
can't really exist
just with the
three of us."

– George

January
◆ In America, the home video compilation *Casey Kasem's Rock'n'Roll Goldmine* is released and features a clip of The Beatles from November 1963, interviewed while cramped in the back of their van, originally broadcast that year on the Granada ITV current affairs documentary series *This Week*. In Liverpool, Cavern City Tours, the Liverpool based Beatles tourist information centre, opens its doors for business by setting up an office in Mathew Street, just above the ground floor Beatles shop. This same month, reports from America suggest that Beatle City's recent stay in Dallas, Texas, has not been a success and their planned visit to Japan is now in jeopardy. Furthermore, the plan to rehouse the Beatle City exhibition at the new Albert Dock in Liverpool has fallen through, meaning that when it returns home it will be homeless.

Saturday January 2
◆ Paul continues work, at his home studios in West Sussex, on the tracks first started on December 21, 1987.

Monday January 4
◆ In the UK, Paul's 1986 album *Press To Play* is released on mid-price CD.

Sunday January 10
◆ A feature on George is screened in tonight's edition of CBS Television's showbiz programme *Entertainment This Week*.

Monday January 11
◆ In America, George appears on the 24-hour music station VH-1.

Wednesday January 13
◆ The European TV station Sky Channel broadcasts a 55-minute exclusive interview, recorded at the MPL offices in Soho Square, London, entitled *Paul McCartney Special*.

Saturday January 16
◆ In America, in what is being described as one of the greatest comebacks in rock history, George's 'Got My Mind Set On You' reaches the number one position in the *Billboard* singles chart. His *Cloud Nine* album will reach number nine in the US and number 10 in the UK charts.

Monday January 18
◆ In America, the CD releases take place of Ringo's *Blast From Your Past,* and Paul's *McCartney, Ram, Tug Of War* and *Wings Over America*.

◆ Still Stateside, the Westwood One radio network begins syndicating the highly anticipated series *The Lost Lennon Tapes*. The first show, hosted by Elliot Mintz, a close friend of the Lennons, is a special three-hour introductory programme. The series itself is originally scheduled to run for just one year, but due to the sheer amount of archive material available (over 300 hours), the series eventually runs to over four! Every week, the programmes feature an amazing variety of unreleased John Lennon recordings, all extracted from the personal archives of Yoko Ono. These include studio outtakes, live performances, alternative mixes, home demos, plus many interesting interviews and miscellaneous clips. Among the highlights from the first few shows are extracts from John's interviews with *Rolling Stone* magazine (December 1970) and *Playboy* (September 1980), John's demo recordings from Bermuda in June 1980, the December 1970 tracks 'Make Love Not War' (which later evolved into 'Mind Games' in 1973) and 'I'm The Greatest', various studio rehearsals, for instance 'Whatever Gets You Through The Night' in 1974, and outtakes such as an eight-minute take of 'How Do You Sleep?' from 1971. The Beatles' years are covered with items such as John's Weybridge home demos of 'She Said She Said', 'Strawberry Fields Forever' (both 1966), 'You Know My Name (Look Up The Number)' from 1967 and, from George's Esher home Beatles demos of 1968, 'Revolution'. Many of the shows in the series will focus on a particular part of John's career. For instance, show 12 is dedicated to The Beatles in Hamburg, and features interviews with Paul, George, Ringo, Pete Best, Tony Sheridan, Jurgen Volmer and Klaus Voorman.

◆ To coincide with the launch of the series, the CBS programme *Entertainment Tonight* begins this evening the first of a two-part look at the series. (Part two is transmitted on Tuesday January 19.)

Wednesday January 20
 In America, during a lavish ceremony at New York's Waldorf Astoria Hotel, Mick Jagger inducts The Beatles into the third annual Rock And Roll Hall Of Fame. George and Ringo attend while Yoko, Sean and Julian are present to represent John. Paul decides not to attend and sends a prepared statement in which he cites "still-existing business differences among The Beatles" as the reason for his non-appearance, adding: "It would have been hypocritical to appear on stage with them, waving and smiling." Insiders in the industry are quick to list other reasons for Paul's non appearance, such as "He despises George Harrison and blames Yoko Ono for supporting the use of The Beatles' track 'Revolution' in the recent Nike commercial."

For his acceptance speech, George remarks: "I don't have much to say 'cause I'm the quiet Beatle. It's unfortunate Paul's not here 'cos he was the one with the speech in his pocket." He continues: "We all know why John can't be here, I'm sure he would be. It's hard, really, to stand here supposedly representing The Beatles. But er . . . It's all what's left I'm afraid. But we all loved him so much, and we all love Paul so much."

Ringo, in typical fashion, brings a sense of humour to the proceedings, by opening with the words: "You can sit down now . . . I'm gonna be here for hours!"

During the $300 a head extravaganza, Paul is on the end of a severe tongue lashing for his actions from Mike Love of The Beach Boys during their induction at the ceremony. He remarks, somewhat foolishly: "The Beach Boys are continuing to do 180 performances a year. I'd like to see the mop-tops match that!"

To close the show, George and Ringo join Bob Dylan, Mick Jagger, Bruce Springsteen and, from The Supremes, Mary Wilson, among many others in an informal all-star jam session. Songs performed during this end of evening concert include 'I Saw Her Standing There', 'All Along The Watchtower', 'Twist And Shout', 'Stand By Me', 'Stop In The Name Of Love', 'Whole Lotta Shakin' Goin' On', 'Hound Dog', 'Honey Hush', 'Barbara Ann', 'Blue Bayou' and 'Satisfaction'. (An FM Radio broadcast of the show is syndicated by CBS.) Reports of the gathering naturally feature heavily on American TV newscasts, most notably, on January 21, CNN *Showbiz Today, Entertainment Tonight,* and CBS *This Morning*. In addition, reports on the event also appear on the programme HBO's *Flipside*, aired on January 23, and in a two-part feature on MTV's *Week In Rock*, transmitted on January 24 and January 31.

Friday January 22
 Yoko and Elliot Mintz appear on the NBC TV breakfast programme *Today*.

Sunday January 24
 The premiere of George's 'When We Was Fab' video takes place on MTV in America.

Monday January 25
 Simultaneous American and UK releases take place today of George's single 'When We Was Fab'/'Zig Zag'. (The CD and 12-inch single versions are issued in the UK only with bonus tracks.)

Thursday January 28
 A feature on John is included in the American television programme *A Current Affair*.

Sunday January 31
 In the UK, EMI Records delete from their catalogue Paul's album *Red Rose Speedway* and *McCartney II*.

Monday February 1
 The Lennons' close friend Elliot Mintz appears on the CNN programme *Showbiz Today*.

Friday February 5
 Rumours in the American television industry suggest that Ringo will soon star in his first major TV comedy series, playing the role of a major rock star whose wife dies,

leaving him to bring up their children alone. (After much deliberation, he will turn down the role in July.)

⏺ In England, in a sequence videotaped at BBC TV Centre on December 2, 1987, Paul and Linda appear briefly during tonight's fund-raising *Comic Relief* extravaganza on BBC1.

Sunday February 7

⏺ During George's brief return visit to England, he attends Eric Clapton's end-of-tour gathering at Clapton's Surrey home. George returns to Los Angeles the following day.

Tuesday February 9

⏺ In Hollywood, California, George makes a live satellite link-up with the *Ray Martin Midday Show* in Australia. Due to the time difference, his 15-minute appearance will be seen 'down under' on February 10.

Wednesday February 10

⏺ George keeps up his high profile by appearing with Jeff Lynne on the American live call-in radio show *Rockline,* which originates from the KLOS-FM studios of the Global Satellite Network in Los Angeles, California, a programme transmitted on more than 200 stations across the continent. Apparently, before the broadcast, George and Jeff had consumed too much beer, which meant that, for those fortunate enough to get through on the show, they find George rude, arrogant and sarcastic. Even so, the former Beatle gives a rare live acoustic performance, with Lynne, which includes 'Drive My Car', 'Here Comes The Sun', 'The Bells Of Rhymney', 'Mr. Tambourine Man', 'Take Me As I Am', 'That's All Right (Mama)', 'Let It Be Me', 'Something' and 'Every Grain Of Sand'. A performance on the show was definitely not a part of his initial plan; his mind only changing when the radio production staff lend George a Gretsch guitar to use should he decide to perform, to which he agrees, on the condition that he keeps the instrument for his own collection.

During the transmission, George reveals that the part of the walrus in the 'When We Was Fab' video was played by Paul. But close examination of the video reveals that whoever was playing the walrus was holding a standard right-handed Rickenbacker bass and was holding it upside down in order to appear to be playing left-handed.

Thursday February 11

⏺ A stereo 35mm film print of the film *Imagine John Lennon* receives its premiere screening to Warner Brothers executives in Los Angeles. They insist that, at 122 minutes, the film is too long and order it to be re-cut. (When released later in the year, the film's running time will be reduced to 100 minutes.)

Friday February 12

⏺ From Hollywood, George again uses the satellite link-up idea to give an eight-minute appearance on the top-rated BBC1 chat show *Wogan.* During the early evening show, the promotional video for 'When We Was Fab' is also transmitted.

Monday February 15

⏺ George publishes his second limited edition book, entitled *Songs By George Harrison.* The deluxe book is priced at £235 and is available only by mail order. George signs each copy and each purchaser can decide whether they want either a 7-inch vinyl EP or a 5-inch CD containing four George Harrison songs, three of which are previously unreleased. To coincide with this, George and Olivia arrive back at Heathrow Airport in London this morning. Back in the States an interview with George, recorded shortly before his departure, is transmitted during the CNN programme *Showbiz Today.* (Additional footage from this feature is transmitted on the programme on March 2.)

Wednesday February 17

⏺ A pre-recorded 12-minute interview with George is transmitted on the German ZDF TV programme *Na Siekske*.

Thursday February 18

🍎 A five-minute interview with George, conducted during his recent stay in America, is transmitted on the Brazilian TV programme *Programa De Domingo*.

Saturday February 20

🍎 Another short pre-recorded interview with George is transmitted, this time on VH–1 in America.

Monday February 22

🍎 With perfect timing, considering his unusually high profile, George's 1970 album *All Things Must Pass* is released on CD in America.

🍎 George leaves Heathrow and flies out to Holland where he records an appearance on the Veronica Dutch television music show *Countdown* at the Con Cordia TV Studios in Bussum, during which he reads out the current Dutch Top 10 and introduces the promotional films for 'Got My Mind Set On You' and 'When We Was Fab'. (George's 19-minute appearance is transmitted on NED 1 on Wednesday February 24.) At the conclusion of the taping, as he leaves, George ignores fans who had been waiting to wish him a happy birthday. Afterwards George spends the day sightseeing in the Netherlands before heading on to Italy the following day. (Paul had also been a guest on the *Countdown* show a couple of weeks previously.)

In America today, a pre-recorded interview with George is transmitted on the CBS programme *This Morning*, where he talks about the video for 'When We Was Fab' and the current business problems with the other Beatles. "We always had a deal together that The Beatles were us four, and that if any one of us wasn't in the band, The Beatles wouldn't exist," he recalls. "It can't really exist just with the three of us, but at the same time, we could all be on stage together I suppose, like we could have done at the Rock And Roll Hall Of Fame."

Thursday February 25

🍎 In Italy, George spends the day visiting Eric Idle and Terry Gilliam on the set of their new film *Baron Munchausen*, a big-budget movie currently being produced for Columbia Pictures.

Friday February 26

🍎 George attends the San Remo Music Festival, where he receives the award of Video Of The Year for 'When We Was Fab', which is naturally screened during the transmission on the Italian TV station RAI UNO. (At the show, George also gives a five-minute interview for the programme *Il Caso Rai,* which is aired on RAI UNO on March 8.) Following his 11-minute appearance at the festival, George returns to England later this evening.

Saturday February 27

🍎 With George returning home, Paul arrives in Italy with his new band, who are unveiled when they headline the San Remo Music Festival. The group of musicians now features Hamish Stuart on guitar and bass, Chris Whitten on drums, Gary Barnacle on saxophone, Andrew Chater on violin and Linda McCartney on keyboards. In front of a large *All The Best* album banner, the group performs lip-synched versions of 'Once Upon A Long Ago' and 'Listen To What The Man Said' for the RAI UNO show. In between the two songs, Paul is interviewed by the host and announces that he has been making some new records with Elvis Costello. Reports on the San Remo Festival, and naturally the appearance of Paul and George, are featured on the news programmes *TG1, TG2* and *ORE 20:00*, this evening. (During Paul's 14-minute appearance, the first track mimed to is the standard single release, while the latter is the version specially recorded for Paul's appearance on *Wogan*, transmitted on BBC1 on November 20, 1987.) Aside from the festival, Paul gives a three-minute interview for the programme Italia 1, which is transmitted on Monday February 29. Interestingly enough, neither Paul nor George knew of each other's appearance at the festival. Even so, the UK tabloid newspaper the *News Of The World* still runs a story which claims that they had a blazing row at the festival, an event George dismisses during his *Aspel And Company* appearance with Ringo on March 3 (see entry).

Tuesday March 1
🍎 Now back in England, George and Olivia are among the guests present at the birthday party of Renata John at Brown's in Covent Garden, London.

Thursday March 3
🍎 With both George and Ringo appearing together on a television chat show, this is a historic day in the history of The Beatles. Their appearance on *Aspel & Company*, recorded at the London Television Studios on the South Bank, is the first major television interview ever given by any two former Beatles since the group disbanded. It is a wonderfully funny show, programme eight of series five, transmitted for the first, and only, time on Saturday March 5 across the ITV Network. George appears first to promote his latest release 'When We Was Fab', with Ringo joining him later to talk about subjects both amusing and Beatles related. Their appearances total a lengthy 35-minutes. Joining the two former Beatles on the show is the *Coronation Street* actress Thelma Barlow.

This unique appearance by George and Ringo leads to scores of Beatles' fans rummaging through old Beatles' encyclopaedias and reference books trying to find out the last time that any two of the ex-Beatles appeared together on a major programme since the split. The answer was December 20, 1974, when John joined George in his hotel room during a radio interview following George's final concert on his American 1974 tour, although the two are not actually interviewed at the same time.

Tuesday March 8
🍎 EMI release, simultaneously around the world, two CDs and two vinyl double albums entitled *Past Masters Vol. 1* and *Past Masters Vol. 2*. These compilations contain all of The Beatles' songs not yet officially issued on CD, the various singles, B-sides, and exclusive recordings which do not appear on the studio albums or on the *Magical Mystery Tour* compilation. Aside from the many exclusive tracks which feature different mono and stereo mixes, collectors are now able to obtain the complete Beatles EMI output on compact disc.
🍎 A five-minute pre-recorded overdubbed interview with George, recorded during his visit to Italy two weeks previously, is transmitted this evening on the Italian television programme *Il Caso Rai 1*.

Thursday March 17
🍎 In America, John's 1971 *Imagine* album is released on CD.

Saturday March 19
🍎 In the first of four payments for this tax year, George (through his Harrisongs Ltd. account) pays the Inland Revenue, the sum of £1,453. This evening, George makes an 11-minute interview appearance on the French Annette 2 television programme *Champs Elysées*.
🍎 In the UK album charts, The Beatles' compilation albums *Past Masters Vol.1* and *Vol. 2* reach numbers 49 and 46 respectively.

Monday March 21
🍎 Various Beatle home video tapes, namely *The Beatles At Shea Stadium, The Beatles In Tokyo, The Beatles In Washington D.C.* and *The Beatles Magical Mystery Tour* appear unofficially in America. Apple immediately calls for a halt on sales of these bootleg tapes.
🍎 In the UK, Sony home video releases the TV film *John and Yoko: The Complete Story*, originally transmitted in America in 1985 as a made-for-TV movie entitled *John and Yoko: A Love Story*. (The American home video release takes place on December 21, 1989, sporting the original film title.)
🍎 In America, until Monday March 27, the US radio programme *Rock Today* featuring George's music is syndicated.

Tuesday March 22
🍎 In America, the CD releases of George's *The Best Of George Harrison* and John's *Mind Games* take place.

Thursday March 24

🍎 Ringo and Barbara are seen having a late dinner at Chasen's Restaurant in Beverly Hills, California.

Saturday March 26

🍎 The 20th anniversary reissue of 'Lady Madonna' reaches number 67 in the UK singles chart.

Sunday March 27

🍎 George leaves Friar Park and heads off again to Los Angeles, California, via a flight from Heathrow and a stopover in Toronto, Canada.

Monday March 28

🍎 During George's brief visit to Toronto, he gives a press conference in front of a small team from the country's press. He is asked about Paul's recent comment that he would like to write some songs with George. "Yes, Paul has suggested that maybe, he and me should write something again. I mean it's pretty funny really. I mean, I've only been there about thirty years in Paul's life and now he wants to write with me. But maybe it would be quite interesting to do that. There's a thing with Paul, one minute he says one thing and he's really charming and the next minute, he's all uptight. We all go through that, good and bad stuff. But, by now, we've got to find the centre."

A report of the press conference, as well as an interview with George conducted by Elaine Lawren shortly after the conference, is featured on Canadian TV's *Global News* the following day. George also gives another interview, at this time, for the programme *Canada AM*, which is also broadcast the following morning. At the conclusion of these sessions, George climbs into his limousine and is driven to the MuchMusic 24-hour music TV studios in Toronto. (Such is the excitement of his 3:15pm arrival, cameras videotape the former Beatle climbing out of the car and entering the building.)

George: "Go on, show 'When We Was Fab' again . . . I haven't seen it for at least ten minutes!"

During his stay at MuchMusic, George appears unannounced live on the programme *MuchMusic Live Interview,* being interviewed by the show's host Christopher Ward. For the duration of the lengthy 34-minute interview, George talks about working with Jeff Lynne, his visit to America in 1963 to see his sister, the lyrics to 'When We Was Fab', The Beatles' studio recordings, the Rock And Roll Hall Of Fame, and the use of Beatles songs in commercials.

Ward asks George: "How did you feel when you heard the McCartney versions of the old songs on *Broad Street?*"

George: "I think they were OK. I didn't notice they were new versions. I only watched it once. I remember 'Ballroom Dancing', but I don't remember the old ones."

Ward: "He (Paul) said that he wanted to tackle some of the other old ones, including, possibly, some of John Lennon's songs, like 'Beautiful Boy' and 'Imagine'. Does that surprise you that he would do that?"

George: "Paul?"

Ward: "Yeah!"

George: "Maybe, because he ran out of good ones of his own!"

Ward: "Well . . . Now we've got that on record."

George: "Well, it's true!"

George also reveals that he bought from EMI, for £3 sterling, the big mono machine, with a replay head, that was used on The Beatles' track 'Paperback Writer' in 1966. George then aborts the interview in order to board a plane for Los Angeles. (His visit to the MuchMusic is also reported on the City TV News later this evening.)

April

🍎 At his Friar Park studios in Henley, following his return from Los Angeles, George records the song 'Ride Rajbun', a track co-written with David English for inclusion in the UK TV series *The Bunbury Tails,* and to appear during the episode entitled *Rajbun Story,* which is not scheduled for transmission until sometime in 1992. Following this session, George returns to Los Angeles where he begins recording the track 'Handle With Care', alongside Bob Dylan, Roy Orbison, Jeff Lynne and Tom Petty, a group that will soon record an album of songs together, under the name of The Traveling Wilburys. During his stay in California, George also supervises the production of the Handmade film production *Checking Out*. As in his first Handmade film, *The Life Of Brian*, he is persuaded to film a cameo appearance in the movie.

 In New York, during the early part of the month, Paul records an alternative version of 'Beautiful Night' with Billy Joel's band who are minus Billy Joel. (The track will not see the light of day until 1997 as part of the *Flaming Pie* album.)

Monday April 4 (until Sunday April 10)
 Various US radio stations in America transmit the syndicated radio programme *Classic Cuts* which features a profile of George's music.

Tuesday April 5
 The simultaneous American and UK CD release takes place of the 1970 *John Lennon/Plastic Ono Band* album.

Thursday April 7
 At the Sotheby's sale in London, an acetate of the unreleased Beatles recording '12 Bar Original', dated December 13 1965, is sold for £1,300 and another acetate, featuring a recording of 'Get Back' from 1969, sells for £450. During the sale, Paul's suit worn during the filming of *A Hard Day's Night* in 1964 sells for £2,800.

Friday April 8
 In London, George, through his Harrisongs account, issues the second of four cheques (this year) to the Inland Revenue. This time, the sum is £2,370.

Saturday April 9
 In America, *The Beatles Past Masters Vol. 1* reaches number 149 in the album charts.

Saturday April 16
 In New York, the guitar legend Les Paul presents Paul with a custom-made Les Paul Light guitar. He had originally intended to make the presentation at the January 20 Rock And Roll Hall Of Fame ceremony, but, as we know, McCartney declined to attend.
 The Beatles Past Masters Vol. 2 reaches number 121 in the American album charts.

Tuesday April 19
 In America, John's albums *Walls And Bridges* and *Rock 'N' Roll* are both released on CD.

Saturday April 23
 In the UK, a pre-recorded interview with George is featured in the 58-minute BBC Radio One programme *A Concise History Of The Frying Pan,* a fascinating documentary on the history of the Rickenbacker guitar. (The show is repeated on Thursday April 28.)

May
 During the month in Paul's Sussex studio, the former Beatle joins Johnny Cash to record the track 'New Moon Over Jamaica', which will be ultimately released on Cash's album *Water From The Wells Of Home*. (Backing vocals on the song come from Linda, June Carter and Tom T. Hall.) Paul also co-wrote and produced the record as well as, at one point, taking lead vocal.

Monday May 2
 George's single 'This Is Love'/'Breath Away From Heaven', is released in America. (The UK release takes place on June 13.) The film clip to accompany the A-side is directed by Morton Jankel.

Sunday May 8 (until Saturday May 21)
 George stays in Los Angeles to record the tracks that will ultimately be released on the Warner Brothers album *The Traveling Wilburys*. For his role in the new band, each member inherits an assumed name. George becomes Nelson Wilbury, Roy Orbison is Lefty, Bob Dylan is Lucky, Jeff Lynne is Otis and Tom Petty is Charlie T. Junior. Lynne also produces the album. George (Nelson) performs lead vocals on the track 'Heading

For The Light', shares lead on 'End Of The Line' and 'Handle With Care' and contributes backing vocals and instruments to 'Dirty World', 'Rattled', 'Last Night', 'Not Alone Any More', 'Congratulations', 'Margarita' and 'Tweeter And The Monkey Man'. Meanwhile, an unreleased film (to the general public that is) of the Traveling Wilburys recording the album is shot and subsequently titled *Whatever Wilbury Wilbury*. The Warner Brothers production premieres at the annual Warner Brothers Records convention later this year. Interestingly enough, though the short 15-minute film is shot in colour, the film is exhibited to the WB hierarchy in black and white due to a mix-up in the film prints.

🍎 Back in England, most regions of ITV network screen Ringo's 1973 film *That'll Be The Day*, also starring David Essex.

Saturday May 14
🍎 Paul's 1984 film *Give My Regards To Broad Street* receives its British television premiere as the *Drive In Movie* across most regions of the ITV network this evening between 11:06pm and 12:58am. The reviews are no better than when it was first released.
🍎 In Norway, a 10-minute pre-recorded interview with George is transmitted on the NRK programme *Pa Hengende Haret*.

Sunday May 15
🍎 For the first time ever in the UK, the original Sixties Beatles' cartoons series, produced in America between 1965 and 1967, is transmitted across most of the ITV network, the first ten minutes ('Call Your Name' and 'The Word') appearing during the late night/early morning programme Night Network. (The Beatles' cartoons will run on Night Network every weekend until October 27, 1988, when they will vanish, not appearing on any TV station anywhere in the world for the rest of the century.)

Tuesday May 17
🍎 John's 1975 compilation album *Shaved Fish* is simultaneously released in America and the UK on CD. The original release, just like with *Some Time In New York City*, had been withdrawn due to poor sound quality.
🍎 In New York, the State Supreme Court overturns the April 8, 1987, ruling that dismissed an $80 million portion of The Beatles' lawsuit against Capitol and EMI brought by George, Ringo, Yoko and Apple Records. Meanwhile, a $40 million suit which claims that Capitol Records have deliberately stalled the release of Beatles' CDs is dismissed in the Manhattan district court.

Friday May 27
🍎 In the UK, Rocket Records release the Sylvia Griffin single 'Love's A State Of Mind', which features a slide guitar contribution from George. He had recorded his track at FPHOTS, his recording later dubbed on the track at George Martin's AIR Studios in London.

Saturday May 28
🍎 Cynthia Lennon travels to Cologne, West Germany, where she opens the *Art Of The Beatles* exhibition in the city, an event which marks the start of a unique *Liverpool On The Rhine* festival, which runs until Friday June 10.

June (into early July)
🍎 In Sussex, Paul resumes home studio recordings on tracks intended for his next album. During this period, which will continue until early July, he records 'The First Stone', 'Indigo Moon', 'Put It There', 'Distractions', 'This One', 'Flying To My Home' (which will appear as the B-side to 'My Brave Face' in 1989), 'Don't Break The Promise' and 'Same Love', which are not released until 1997, as *Flaming Pie* singles.

Tuesday June 7
🍎 In London at the Savoy Hotel, George attends a private dinner for "the family and friends of Eric Clapton", an event to celebrate Clapton's 25th year as a performing musician. Later in the evening, George makes an after-dinner speech, honouring his long-time friend. Ringo and Barbara were expected to attend the all-star bash, but failed to show.

Tuesday June 14
 The home video of the 1987 *Prince's Trust Rock Gala* concert, featuring both George and Ringo, is released in the UK.

Tuesday June 21
 George is seen in public again, this time in London at the Royal Festival Hall watching a performance by Balkana, a Bulgarian choral music choir. After the concert, George goes backstage to meet the singers.

Wednesday June 22
 In America, Jesse Ed Davis, the guitarist whose work graced the solo recordings of John, George and Ringo, dies of an apparent drugs overdose at his home in Venice, California. He was just 43.

Friday June 24
 In London, Paul wins the Silver Clef Award for Outstanding Achievement in the World of British Music. The Nordoff –Robbins Music Therapy Centre sponsors the event.

Sunday June 26 & Monday June 27
 Paul and Linda travel to Liverpool where they film a brief appearance for the hit BBC1 comedy series *Bread*. Linda had been approached to appear briefly in the series as a result of her friendship with the series' writer Carla Lane. Paul's role in the programme is confined to playing Linda's driver. On the first day, June 26, sequences are shot outside the studios of BBC Radio Merseyside in Paradise Street. For the following day's shooting, additional scenes are filmed on the usual *Bread* locations, which are situated in the Liverpool suburbs. Whilst Linda is filming her part, Paul is cornered by three local DJs, Spencer Leigh, Alan Jackson and Monty Lister, for an interview. (Lister, incidentally, was the reporter who conducted The Beatles' first ever radio interview for hospital radio on the Wirral, Merseyside, on October 27, 1962.) Following additional shooting for *Bread*, which takes place at the BBC TV Centre, Wood Lane, London, on September 11, the show will premiere on BBC1 on October 30.

July
 Yoko and Sean appear in a Japanese TV commercial for KDD, the country's international telecommunications monopoly. The advert, which is meant to encourage Japanese people to use their phones more, opens with Yoko and Sean playing ball in a park to the music of John's 'Imagine'. The short item climaxes with Yoko turning towards the camera and saying, in Japanese: "People all over the world are basically the same."

Tuesday July 12
 At the Brighton Centre in East Sussex, Paul, receives from the University of Sussex, the title of Honorary Doctorate, or Doctor of the University, during a graduation ceremony. Television news crews from both BBC and ITN are on hand to cover the event.

Wednesday July 13
 Another pre-recorded interview with George is broadcast in Norway, this time on the NRK programme *Top Pop Special*.

Tuesday July 19
 In London, George, through his Harrisongs account, pays, by cheque, the Inland Revenue a sum of £1,234.

Friday July 22
 In London, the vice-chancellor of the High Court, Sir Nicholas Browne-Wilkinson, orders Charly Records to cease worldwide sales of The Beatles' Decca Records audition tape from New Year's Day 1962, until a full trial of the rights action is held in approximately twelve months time. In response to this case, Charly Records had deleted their album *Decca Sessions 1/1/62* on June 15 and, on the same day, they pulled from their catalogue the album *The Savage Young Beatles*. (Ringo is naturally not a part of this action as he does not appear on the original recordings.)

Friday July 29
 In America, a pre-taped interview with Yoko, conducted by Geraldo Rivera, is aired on the television programme *Entertainment Tonight*.

August
 Reports in Moscow announce that plans are being prepared for Paul to play eight concerts there during 1989.
 In America, reports suggest that George, Ringo and Jeff Lynne are planning an album together and may tour to promote it. The newspaper *USA Today* gives the first mention of a new mystery group who call themselves The Traveling Wilburys. The report goes on to say that "their début album will be released in October and that the group consists of a line-up of George with Roy Orbison, Tom Petty, Bob Dylan and Jeff Lynne."

Tuesday August 2
 Paul briefly directs some shooting for a promotional video at the Liverpool Institute.

Thursday August 4
 The London based Thames region of the ITV network screens Dick Clark's 1979 made-for-TV documentary *The Birth Of The Beatles*.

Monday August 22
 In America, Albert Goldman's controversial book *The Lives Of John Lennon* is published. Paul McCartney: "Boycott this book!"

Thursday August 25
 In America, Apple file in the US District Court in Newark, New Jersey, a suit against San Juan Music Group, Silhouette Music, and Ultra Sound Company, charging them with the unauthorised marketing of Beatles' material and use of the group name and image. Apple seek to remove the offensive product from the marketplace and obtain restitution.

September (during a six-week period until October)
 In Sussex, Paul resumes work on more home studio recordings. This session produces the tracks 'Good Sign', which will appear only in the UK, and 'Motor Of Love'. During this 40-day period, Paul and Linda will also spend time arranging this year's Buddy Holly Week, recording an interview with the BBC and preparing for their TV appearance on the BBC1 comedy programme *Bread*.

Friday September 2 (until Friday October 7)
 A celebration of ten years of Handmade Films takes place at the NFT (National Film Theatre) in London. During this five-week festival, all of Handmade's films will be shown, from *Monty Python's Life Of Brian*, in 1979, to their current release, the Nic Roeg film *Track 29*.
 At the BBC TV Centre in Wood Lane, London, John's sister Julia Baird appears on the BBC1 show *Wogan,* where she promotes her new book *John Lennon: My Brother*.

Monday September 5
 In the UK, Paul helps launch BBC2's *DEF II – Animation Week*, a seven-day celebration of the world of animation. During his short interview, which was taped at TV Centre last week, he expresses his fondness for animation and introduces excerpts from 'Oriental Nightfish', 'Rupert And The Frog Song', 'Seaside Woman' and 'Once Upon A Long Ago'. The Beatles' 1968 film *Yellow Submarine* is also transmitted, split into three parts, and shown this evening, tomorrow and Thursday September 8.

Tuesday September 6 & Wednesday September 7
 In the States, NBC TV's *Today* show begins a two-part interview, carried out by satellite from Frankfurt, Germany, with Albert Goldman, the author of the book *The Lives Of John Lennon*. On September 7, the interviewer Jane Pauley tells Goldman: "Paul McCartney has said boycott this book!" To which he replies: "He ought to be ashamed of himself. I mean, the generation of the Sixties. They were scathing in their

criticism of everybody. They were iconoclastic, they did everything, and now, suddenly, they've become very prissy and moralistic when someone says something they don't want to hear about themselves. They can dish it out but they sure can't take it!"

Wednesday September 7
 At Stefano's restaurant in London, Paul joins The Crickets on stage during a special Buddy Holly luncheon to launch the annual Buddy Holly Week. During The Crickets' live set, they perform their new CBS single 'T-Shirt', with Paul adding piano to the song. (Paul also produces the single.) To close the performance, Paul and The Crickets are joined on stage by Linda, Chrissie Hynde, Mike Berry and the DJs Tony Prince and Mike Read to perform the Holly song 'Rave On'. (A camera team from TV AM is there to capture the proceedings, highlights of which are transmitted on the station the following morning, September 8. Also present is a camera team from NBC TV's *Today* show. See next entry.)

Thursday September 8
 In America, an interview with Paul, conducted at the Buddy Holly luncheon in London yesterday, is transmitted on the NBC TV *Today* programme. The reporter Rona Elliot asks Paul about Albert Goldman's book *The Lives Of John Lennon* and, in particular, the revelations contained within. "Revelations? If he was homosexual I'd have thought he'd have made a pass at me in twenty years!" Asked what he would do if a book like this came out on him, Paul said: "I'd probably read that one!"
 Also aired in the feature is a live satellite interview from London with The Beatles' producer George Martin who also dismisses the Albert Goldman publication, stating that "the book has grave inaccuracies about himself", using as an example "*I* was responsible for getting rid of Pete Best. I didn't want him on record, because I didn't think he was a very good drummer. He really *wasn't* a good drummer."
 In the UK, John's sister Julia Baird appears on TV AM to promote her new book *John Lennon: My Brother*. Her feature appears alongside a report on last night's Buddy Holly party in London.

Sunday September 11
 Following five days of rehearsals, Linda tapes her final scenes for *Bread*, in front of a studio audience, at the BBC TV Centre, Wood Lane, London.
 In America, a feature on John is included in tonight's edition of *Entertainment This Week*.

Monday September 12, Tuesday September 13 & Wednesday September 14
 A three-part feature on John continues on CBS TV's *Entertainment Tonight*. The feature naturally focuses on *Imagine,* the film and book, and features an *Inside Story* report by Geraldo Rivera, including an interview with Elliot Mintz.

Wednesday September 14
 The American radio station Westwood One broadcasts a one-hour special programme entitled *Westwood One Special Report: Yoko's Response*, which allows Yoko to comment on the recent publication by Albert Goldman entitled *The Lives Of John Lennon*. The show, put together by the team who work on *The Lost Lennon Tapes*, is hosted by Elliot Mintz and features an exclusive interview with Yoko, taped at her Dakota apartment.

Friday September 16
 Yoko and Sean appear this morning on the breakfast show TV AM to promote the *Imagine* exhibition and film.

Saturday September 17
 To assist with promotions for *Imagine: John Lennon*, Yoko makes her second, and final, interview appearance with Michael Aspel for his chat show *Aspel & Company*. (The programme was recorded on September 15 at the London Television studios on the South Bank.) In America today, a 20-minute feature on Albert Goldman's book *The Lives Of John Lennon* is transmitted during the television programme *West 57th*.

Monday September 19

🍎 John's 'Jealous Guy' b/w 'Give Peace A Chance' is issued as a single in America to accompany the *Imagine: John Lennon* film and compilation soundtrack album. In London, Yoko attends a special, invitation only, *Imagine* exhibition preview event at the Business Design Centre, at 52 Upper Street, Islington, London, where she also gives a 45-minute press conference. Guests in attendance include Patti Clapton, the comedian Peter Cook, his friend Martin Shaw, the singer Sandie Shaw, and the director Kevin Godley.

Tuesday September 20 (until Sunday September 25)

🍎 In London, the exhibition entitled *Imagine*, featuring John's original art, opens at the Business Design Centre, in Islington, London.

Thursday September 22

🍎 The Handmade films *The Long Good Friday, Time Bandits* (featuring George's 'Dream Away' on the closing credits) and Monty Python's *Life Of Brian* (including a cameo appearance by George) are all released on home video in America.

Monday September 26 (until Wednesday September 28)

🍎 In the States, the CBS television programme *Good Day New York* transmits a three-part feature to celebrate the release of *Imagine: John Lennon,* which features a live (8:49am) interview with May Pang, on Monday, who naturally discusses her book *Loving John.* The rest of the features over the three days include interviews with the photographer Bob Gruen, Lennon biographer Jon Wiener, and Beatlefest organiser Mark Lapidos, who recalls his first meeting with John on April 28, 1974 at the March Of Dimes event in Central Park (see entry).

Friday September 30

🍎 Back in America, Yoko unveils a star honouring John Lennon on the Hollywood Walk Of Fame, in front of Capitol Records tower building in Los Angeles, and delivers a moving speech to a large crowd of representatives from the press and TV. (Incidentally, a star honouring The Beatles has been waiting to be put in place since 1970.)

October

🍎 At the end of the month, in Beverly Hills, California, George attends a birthday party in honour of George Michael, thrown by his managers Rob Kahane and Michael Lipman. During this month, in an undisclosed location in Los Angeles, George and the rest of the Wilburys shoot a promotional film clip for 'Handle With Care', which is produced by Limelight Films and features direction by David Leland, who also directed the Handmade film *Checking Out.*

Saturday October 1 (until Saturday December 31)

🍎 In the UK, BBC Radio Two, on the FM Wavelength, begins broadcasting a 14-part, weekly series of 30-minute programmes entitled *The Beeb's Lost Beatles Tapes.* Among its highlights are some new interviews not transmitted during the 1982 *Beatles At The Beeb* 20th anniversary radio retrospective, in particular some recently found tapes not even transmitted back in the Sixties. The programmes, which are hosted by Richard Skinner, are repeated on each following Monday evening.

🍎 Meanwhile, at Shepperton Film Studios in London on October 1, a party is held to celebrate the 10th anniversary of Handmade Films. The film of the event, which includes George's speech and a musical performance of 'Honey Don't' and 'That's Alright (Mama)', with Carl Perkins and Joe Brown, is featured in a 50-minute Granada ITV special entitled *The Movie Life Of George,* which is transmitted across the ITV network on January 8, 1989. (The American premiere occurs on the Discovery Channel on February 25, 1990, coinciding with George's 47th birthday.) The documentary also includes the clip of George, Ringo and Eric Clapton performing 'Freedom' from the 1985 Handmade film *Water.*

Sunday October 2

🍎 To talk about the film *Imagine*, which premieres in New York on Thursday, John's former companion May Pang is interviewed on the CBS programme *Entertainment This Week.* Also broadcast this evening is a 17-minute report, entitled *The Two Mrs. Lennons,* which is included in the CBS television current affairs programme *60 Minutes.* The report features in-depth interviews with Cynthia and Yoko, as well as comments from John's second son Sean.

Monday October 3
🍎 As a preview to the premiere of *Imagine,* the Paramount TV/CBS programme *Entertainment Tonight* runs a special feature on footage not included in the finished film, including John's February 12, 1970, appearance on BBC1's *Top Of The Pops,* performing 'Instant Karma', unscreened in America until tonight.

Tuesday October 4
🍎 In America, the compilation soundtrack from the film is released. (The release in the UK takes place on October 10.) The *Imagine* film is also profiled today on the American TV show *Good Day New York.*

Wednesday October 5, Thursday October 6 & Friday October 7
🍎 NBC TV in America broadcasts a three-part feature on the programme *Today,* which takes a look at the film *Imagine: John Lennon,* which opens across the country on Friday October 7. The segments include exclusive interviews with Yoko, Sean and Cynthia Lennon. Later this evening, Yoko appears live by satellite from New York being interviewed on the CNN programme *Larry King Live.* Also on October 5, at 7:30pm, *Imagine: John Lennon* receives its first screening, albeit for the press and specially invited guests, at the Paramount Theater, situated at 1577 Barrington Street, New York.

Thursday October 6
🍎 The premiere of the Warner Brothers documentary film *Imagine: John Lennon* takes place in Manhattan, New York, with Yoko in attendance. Naturally, the event features heavily on US TV newscasts, including the CBS programme *Entertainment Tonight* and NBC News. (The first UK screening of *Imagine* takes place on October 25 with the premiere opening following on October 28.)
🍎 To coincide with the release of the *Imagine* film, the American TV *Late Show* programme features the collector Colin Kaye who presents a Beatles photographic display of the work of the photographer Dezo Hoffman.

Friday October 7
🍎 The film *Imagine: John Lennon* goes on general cinema release across America. To highlight its release, the *Late Show* programme continues with its film related themes, presenting tonight a 50-minute special edition entitled *Remembering John,* which includes exclusive interviews with Yoko, Cynthia, May Pang, Julia Baird, Peter Brown, Sid Bernstein, the DJ "Cousin" Bruce Morrow, Elliot Mintz, Geraldo Rivera and Albert Goldman, who is interviewed by satellite from Germany.
🍎 In England, George pays his final tax bill for the year by sending the Inland Revenue a cheque for £357.29p.

Sunday October 9
🍎 To coincide with the release in America of *Imagine: John Lennon,* and what would have been John's 48th birthday, the cable TV network Cinemax broadcasts the D.A. Pennebaker film of John and Yoko's 1969 *Live Peace in Toronto* concert appearance from September 13, 1969. The Lennons' sequence had been cut from the film's original 1972 cinema release due to legal reasons. Also this evening, MTV in America broadcasts the 55-minute programme *Happy Birthday – John Lennon Remembered,* which features a collection of Beatles and John Lennon live clips and promotional films. The tribute show, hosted by the VJ Adam Curry, also includes interviews with Brian Wilson of the Beach Boys, David Bowie, Elton John, Bob Geldof, as well as archive interviews with Paul, Julian Lennon and Yoko.
🍎 The CBS programme *Entertainment This Week* features a profile of The Beatles' radio recordings for the BBC back in the Sixties. The item, and indeed the show, closes with the 'I Am The Walrus' sequence from *Magical Mystery Tour.*

Monday October 10

🍏 In America, Johnny Cash's album *Water From The Wells Of Home*, featuring his duet with Paul on the track 'New Moon Over Jamaica' is released. (The UK release takes place on November 14.)

🍏 Still Stateside, the one-hour special about George, produced as part of the Westwood One *Star Trak Profile* series, is syndicated across various US radio stations until Sunday October 16.

Tuesday October 11

🍏 Ringo and Barbara travel to America where they undergo an extensive six-week treatment for alcoholism in Tucson, Arizona. They spend their time cleaning ash trays and doing the laundry. Desperate for a story, newspaper reporters and photographers circle above the clinic in a helicopter.

🍏 George, who had talked to Ringo about his alcoholism, says: "I'm really glad he's sorting out his problems. Ringo's a lovely bloke and a great mate."

Saturday October 15

🍏 Channel 4 in the UK begin broadcasting a short series of Handmade films, beginning this evening with the 1983 film *Bullshot*. The series continues on Saturday October 29 with *Privates On Parade* and the 1985 film *Water* on Saturday November 12.

Monday October 17

🍏 A two-part examination of John's life, called *Lennon's Women – The Naked Truth*, begins tonight on the US TV Fox TV programme *A Current Affair*. (Part two is tomorrow night, October 18.)

🍏 The Traveling Wilburys' first single 'Handle With Care'/'Margarita' is simultaneously released in America and the UK.

Tuesday October 18

🍏 The Traveling Wilburys' first album, titled *Volume One*, is released in America. (The UK release takes place on October 24.)

🍏 Also in America, the album *Stay Awake* is released, featuring Ringo's recording with the legendary trumpet player Herb Alpert on 'When You Wish Upon A Star'. (The UK release takes place on October 24.)

Tuesday October 25

🍏 At the Cannon Cinema, Haymarket, and the Warner West End cinema in Leicester Square, London, 10:30am press screenings take place for the film *Imagine: John Lennon*.

Wednesday October 26

🍏 The Beatles' 1967 film *Magical Mystery Tour* is released in America. (The UK release takes place on March 26, 1990.)

🍏 Paul appears on the BBC1 documentary programme *The Power Of Music*, in which he is seen visiting a therapy centre for mentally retarded children operated by the Nordoff-Robbins organisation.

Friday October 28

🍏 At the Cannon Cinema, Haymarket, London, Cynthia, Yoko and Sean are in attendance at the UK premiere tonight of *Imagine: John Lennon*. Afterwards, the Lennons and invited guests attend a private party held in nearby Wardour Street.

Sunday October 30

🍏 The Traveling Wilburys are the focus of attention in the syndicated American radio programme *Power Cuts*.

🍏 Paul and Linda's appearance in *Bread* is transmitted this evening on BBC1. George misses Paul's appearance, watching the preceding programme, *Howard's Way*, by mistake. "I'd never seen the show before, and I just couldn't figure out how Paul was going to fit in with all these posh people on boats," he said later.

Monday October 31

🍏 40,000 copies of *CHOBA B CCCP* (*Back In The USSR*, or *Again In The USSR*) are pressed and released in Russia on the Melodiya label and feature Paul performing 11 rock'n'roll oldie tracks, recorded during July 1987. A second Soviet edition is issued on Christmas Eve, December 24. Meanwhile, a 14-track version is released on CD in the UK on September 30, 1991, and in America on October 29, 1991.

November
🍎 In London, Paul produces *Let The Children Play*, profits of which will go to the annual *Children In Need* fundraising event. In America, Paul's CDs *Red Rose Speedway*, *Venus And Mars* and *McCartney II* are released.

Tuesday November 1
🍎 In America, NBC TV's *Today* and *NBC News* programmes features a report, by Rona Elliot, of Paul at the annual Buddy Holly Week concert in London. The features carry an exclusive interview with Paul and footage of him joining The Crickets on stage for a performance of the track 'Everyday'.

Wednesday November 2
🍎 In America, the soundtrack album of *Porky's Revenge* is released and features George's re-recording of 'I Don't Want To Do It'. This morning, a pre-recorded videotaped interview with the Traveling Wilburys, carried out by Rona Elliot, is transmitted on the NBC TV show *Today*. (Bob Dylan does not appear because he was performing in New York when the feature was recorded.)

Friday November 4 & Monday November 7
🍎 In the UK, a two part pre-recorded interview with George and Jeff Lynne to promote the Traveling Wilburys' album, is transmitted on the breakfast station TV AM.

Saturday November 5
🍎 BBC Radio One broadcasts the music magazine programme *Saturday Sequence*, which features a pre-taped interview with George talking about the Traveling Wilburys. On this same day, an interview with George is published in the *Guardian* newspaper in the UK.

Tuesday November 8
🍎 Certain regions of the ITV Network in the UK transmit the American Television *Tribute To Martin Luther King* show, featuring a short stage appearance by Yoko.

Wednesday November 9 (until Tuesday November 22)
🍎 An exhibition of Linda's new photographic portfolio *Sun Prints,* which is published tomorrow, opens at the Victoria & Albert Museum in London.

Thursday November 10
🍎 Linda's book *Sun Prints* is published in the UK by Barrie & Jenkins, after a one week delay. The hardback, which features text written by Robert Lassam, contains 75 original prints, and a foreword written by Linda herself.

Friday, November 11
🍎 George is unusually outspoken in an interview with Gill Pringle published in today's *Daily Mirror*. "They always dubbed me the Quiet One, the Reclusive One, the Business One," he says. "Just because I wasn't in the nightclubs all the time they thought I was some kind of freak or something."

On Krishna: "After I bought the Krishna's Letchmore Heath Manor in Hertfordshire, that confirmed it for the newspapers. I was the crackers Beatle. The public had some idea of me being locked away for years on end, chanting and ringing my bells but I was never a devout Hare Krishna, although I do still chant and stuff."

On Margaret Thatcher: "She would benefit from taking the day off and sitting down and listening to the Wilburys instead of nagging everyone."

On Bob Dylan: "He has no qualms about taking 20% of the royalties but he doesn't do interviews."

On pop music: "The pop charts have changed into one big microchip . . . everyone's got the same drum sample. It dismays me, the state of the charts. They're dehumanising music as they have with our cities and buildings."

On Kylie Minogue: "It's a sorry situation when the only decent thing in the charts is Kylie Monologue [sic]. That song she did 'I Am Your U-Boat' (he actually means 'Locomotion') was all right. At least she looked nice and sang well."

Friday November 25
 Ringo and Barbara complete their six-week treatment for alcoholism in Tucson, Arizona, and return home to Tittenhurst Park in Ascot, England.

Monday November 28
 EMI Records begin another re-issue of The Beatles' entire original UK singles, this time on 3-inch CDs. Once again, EMI mistakenly use the album version of 'Love Me Do', which features Andy White and not Ringo, playing drums.
 The 3-track single 'Imagine'/'Happy Christmas (War Is Over)'/ 'Jealous Guy' is released in the UK to help promote the album and film *Imagine: John Lennon*.

December
 The planned UK radio transmissions of the Westwood One *Lost Lennon Tapes* series fail to show. The syndication company MCM Networking announces that a January or February, 1989 date for the start of UK transmissions now seems the most likely.

Friday December 2
 At the Con Cordia Television Studios in Bussum, Holland, Paul and his band reappear on the Veronica NED 2 TV music programme *Countdown*. (The appearance lasts 28 minutes.)

Saturday December 3
 John's single 'Imagine'/'Happy Christmas (War Is Over)'/ 'Jealous Guy' reaches number 45 in the UK singles chart.

Tuesday December 6
 In America, Roy Orbison, the legendary rock performer and fellow band member of the Traveling Wilburys, dies suddenly of a massive heart attack. He is only 52 years of age.

Saturday December 10
 In Los Angeles, California, George and his fellow Traveling Wilburys shoot a video clip for their next single 'End Of The Line'. By way of a tribute to Roy, an empty rocking chair is seen where he would have been sitting in the clip. The promotional film premieres worldwide on January 20, 1989.

Tuesday December 20
 Paul and Linda fly into Germany, where Paul makes a guest appearance on the ZDF TV variety programme *Wetten Dass*, being interviewed by the host Thomas Gottschalk.

Saturday December 24
 A second Soviet edition of Paul's rock'n'roll oldies album, *CHOBA B CCCP*, is released featuring two additional tracks.

Monday December 26
 Michael Jackson's film *Moonwalker*, featuring the acting début of John's youngest son Sean, is released in the UK.

"There will be no Beatles reunion so long as John Lennon remains dead."

– *George*

Friday January 6
 Ringo, accompanied by his wife Barbara, attends the taping sessions for *Shining Time Station*, the new PBS children's series, at the Travel Town Studios, in Burbank, California.
 With no scheduled UK broadcasts in sight, the American Westwood One *Lost Lennon Tapes* radio series begins transmissions in France on all of the Europe 2 stations, in the exact same running order played, almost exactly one year ago, on the Westwood One network. For the French FM stereo transmissions, the French language versions are transmitted between 7:30 and 8:30pm and hosted by Frederick Hubert. The original English language versions, hosted by Elliot Mintz, are transmitted later in the evening, between 12 midnight and 1:00am.

Sunday January 8
 In the UK, the Granada Television documentary programme *The Movie Life Of George* is transmitted across the ITV network. (See entry for Saturday October 1, 1988.)

Monday January 9
 At Chicago's Union Train Station, Ringo, following a break from videotaping, appears to promote his new PBS programme *Singing Time Station*, which is due to start broadcasting on Sunday January 29. In front of a large gathering from the American press, Ringo announces about his series: "I love to appear and disappear at will, and being miniaturised. That's the magic in the show! It's great to be 18 inches again."

Tuesday January 10
 From London, MPL issues a letter to all members of Paul's Wings Fun Club, urging them not to buy Paul's Russian album as an over-priced import. The letter states that the club is making provisions to supply the disc, restricted to one copy per member.

Thursday January 12
 Ringo again breaks from recording to promote *Shining Time Station*, appearing at 7:50am on the NBC News programme *Today*, where he is joined by the show's co-star Brian O'Connor.

Monday January 23
 The Traveling Wilburys single 'End Of The Line'/'Congratulations' is released in America. (The UK release takes place on February 20, where the 12-inch and CD versions feature an extended mix of the A-side.)

Thursday January 26
 At the BBC World Service headquarters in Bush House, in The Strand, London, Paul, aided by some of the World Service's 35 Russian speaking staff, appears live in front of an estimated 18 million short-wave listeners in the USSR on the Russian radio show *Granny's Chest*, where he answers telephone questions from the Soviet Union. The special London telephone number where you could ring Paul, in Studio S7, was printed in the Russian newspaper *Komsomolskaya Pravda* on the morning of the broadcast. As a result, the BBC station receives a total of over 1,000 calls. The last luminary to attempt this, Prime Minister Margaret Thatcher, received just under 300 calls in July 1988. Unfortunately, only 14 callers make it on to the programme. The Russian language questions are translated into English for Paul by the show's English host of *Granny's Chest*, Sam Jones. Paul's answers are then translated back into Russian for immediate transmission back behind the Iron Curtain. (The programme also features music from Paul's album *CHOBA B CCCP*, and is transmitted between 6:05 and 7:00pm GMT. Highlights from the show are transmitted to the rest of the world on the BBC World Service programme *Multi Track 3,* which is broadcast on Friday January 27, with a repeat taking place the following day. Paul's arrival at the BBC studios earlier in the day is featured on both the BBC and ITN news bulletins.)

Sunday January 29
 In America, the Public Broadcasting System (PBS), as planned, begins broadcasting, at 6:30pm ET, the new 20-part children's television show entitled *Shining Time Station*, featuring Ringo in the role of an 18-inch high Mr. Conductor who, quite conveniently,

narrates the animated stories about *Thomas The Tank Engine And His Friends*.
🍎 After finally securing the rights from Geffen Records in America, EMI and Capitol issue John and Yoko's 1980 album *Double Fantasy* on CD and LP in the US and in the UK.

February (through until April)
🍎 At his home studio in Sussex, Paul and his band are filmed rehearsing and recording several songs for inclusion in the 50-minute TV special *Put It There*. During the extensive filming, Paul and band record new versions of The Beatles' classic 'The Long And Winding Road', as well as new tracks including 'Rough Ride' and 'Party Party'. The finished show will be premiered in the UK on BBC1 on June 10 and in America on November 11 on the station *Showtime*. (An extended 65-minute version is later released on home video.)
🍎 It is officially announced that the UK radio transmissions of the *Lost Lennon Tapes* series will not now be taking place.

Thursday February 2
🍎 In Liverpool, a pre-recorded interview with Paul is transmitted on BBC Radio Merseyside.

Friday February 3 (until Tuesday February 7)
🍎 A four-hour radio special entitled *Meet The Beatles: The 25th Anniversary*, a programme celebrating the quarter of a century landmark since The Beatles first landed in the States, is syndicated across many radio stations in America.

Monday February 6
🍎 The 25th anniversary since The Beatles first landed in America is featured on the Paramount television programme *Entertainment Tonight* when this historic event is remembered during their *Inside Music* report, which includes an interview with Cynthia Lennon, and archive interviews with Paul (carried out in 1986), George (1988) and Ringo (1983).

Thursday February 23
🍎 In Los Angeles, George attends the premiere of Handmade's new film *Pow Wow Highway*, which takes place at the Director's Guild Theater, an event also organised as a benefit event for the Southwest Museum.

Friday February 24
🍎 In the UK, the home video release takes place of the 1966 film *The Family Way,* featuring a music score written by Paul.
🍎 In America, the 1969 film *The Magic Christian,* starring Ringo and Peter Sellers, as well as featuring the track 'Come And Get It' written by Paul and performed on the soundtrack by Badfinger, is simultaneously released on laser disc in the US and on home video in the UK.
🍎 Also Stateside, the Rhino compilation album *Starr Struck: Best Of Ringo Starr Vol. 2*, featuring some of Ringo's greatest hits is released. The issue marks the first outing in America of tracks originally featured on his album *Old Wave*. (*Starr Struck* is not released in the UK.)

March
🍎 During the month at FPHOTS, George, working with Jeff Lynne as producer, records a version of 'Cheer Down' for inclusion on the *Lethal Weapon 2* film soundtrack, a version later released as a single. The song was originally written in 1988 for inclusion on Eric Clapton's 1989 *Journeyman* album, but he ultimately rejected it. This month, George also attends the annual Grammy Awards at the Los Angeles' Shrine Auditorium with fellow Wilburys Petty and Lynne.
🍎 In the States, Ringo makes a cameo appearance in Jan Hammer's video for 'Too Much To Lose'.
🍎 The private German radio station in Hamburg, West Germany, called OK Radio, begins transmitting a new weekly series entitled *Beatles Forever,* which features demo tapes, rare tracks and archive interviews with the group.

Sunday March 5
 At Sarm West Studios in London, Ringo is one of many artists contributing vocals to the song 'Spirit Of The Forest', a record sold to raise funds for preservation of the planet's rain forests. The sessions, which take place in New York and Los Angeles, also include star names from the music industry, such as Dave Gilmour, Brian Wilson, Mick Fleetwood and Joni Mitchell.

Sunday March 19
 Alan Civil, the horn player who played on The Beatles' *Revolver* track 'For No One' in 1966, dies of a liver complaint in a London hospital. He was 60 years of age.

Wednesday March 22 & Thursday March 23
 On a sound stage at Pinewood Studios in Iver Heath, Buckinghamshire, George and Ringo join Tom Petty to film a promotional video for Petty's track 'I Won't Back Down'. For the second day's shoot, March 23, panic erupts when the director, David Leland, realises he still needs Ringo, who had been told not to turn up, for one long shot. Instead, a lookalike from the *Beatlemania* stage play is drafted in as a replacement, much to the annoyance of George. (The clip is prepared for television distribution on March 29.) As for the song itself, George had played guitar and sang backing vocals.

Friday March 24
 Wally Heider, the man who played host to Paul and Wings during the Los Angeles recording sessions for *Venus And Mars* in 1975, dies of lung cancer in Santa Clarita. He was 66 years of age.

Saturday March 25 (until Saturday May 13)
 BBC Radio One begins broadcasting a special eight-part series called *McCartney On McCartney*, in which Paul talks to the DJ Mike Read about his career from Beatlemania to the present day. The first part, entitled "Early Beginnings to 1962" is first transmitted on Saturday between 2:01pm and 2:59pm and then repeated the following Tuesday evening, again on Radio One, between 7:31 and 8:29pm. (The further seven parts follow suit.) Meanwhile, an edited version of the series is transmitted in America during the Memorial Day weekend of May 27 to 29.
 Ringo, meanwhile, is to be found in Paris, attending Elton John's lavish 42nd birthday party, held at the exclusive Bois De Boulogne restaurant. Due to the array of fine foods and drinks on offer, Elton's bill for the bash comes to a grand total of £265,000. Further expense is heaped on Elton when he foots the bill for his guests' accommodation, an entire floor of the nearby plush Ritz Hotel. (Not wishing to incur more expense for Elton, Ringo returns to London the following day.)

Monday March 27
 Ringo returns to the Abbey Road Studios in London where he joins Buck Owens to record a new version of 'Act Naturally'. Ringo, of course, recorded a version with The Beatles back in 1965, included on side two of their UK album *Help!*
 In the UK, Julian Lennon releases his third solo album *Mr. Jordan*.

April
 Capitol Records in America, EMI Records in London and the RIAA (the Recording Industry of America) launch an assault on the manufacturers of a new batch of high quality Beatles/solo bootleg albums that have begun to appear in Europe and across America. The titles in question, *Ultra Rare Trax, Back Track, Off White* and *Silver Wilburys*, all feature master tape quality recordings of previously unreleased studio outtakes and songs.
 Cynthia Lennon opens her restaurant Lennon's in London. Among the delights on offer are *Sgt. Pepper's Steak* and *Penny Lane Pate!*

Saturday April 1 & Sunday April 2
 John and Yoko's film *Ten For Two,* shot at the John Sinclair Benefit Concert on December 10, 1971, receives its world premiere with screenings at the Royal Oak Music Theater and the Michigan Theater in Ann Arbor.

❡ In the UK, the 60-minute home video of the 1986 BBC/MPL TV programme titled *The Paul McCartney Special*, is released. (When originally aired on BBC1 on August 29, 1986, it sported the simple alternative title of *McCartney*. A home video and laser disc version of the show is released in America on June 21.)

Tuesday April 4
❡ At the Ivor Novello Awards Ceremony luncheon in London, Paul receives a standing ovation when he receives the Outstanding Services to British Music accolade. As he collects his award, Paul delivers to the audience his very own, recently composed 'Ivor Novello Rap', as follows:
"This Ivor Novello was a pretty fine chap,
But just one thing he didn't know, was how to rap.
'Cause, if he was living in the present day,
He'd have to think of something to say.
I think I know what it might just be,
He'd say whatever happened to the melody!"

Monday April 10 & Tuesday April 11
❡ Over two days in the house at Strawberry Fields in Liverpool, Paul, Linda and his band film the promotional clips for the latest single 'My Brave Face'. Working with the director Roger Lunn, the clip features a straight (black and white) performance of the song by the group intercut with various MPL archive film clips, most notably Tony Barrow's home movies from the 1965/1966 Beatles tours that Paul acquired during the 1986 Sotheby's Auction. (Final editing on the clip, which is produced by Vanderquest Productions, takes place on Thursday April 13.) Simultaneously whilst recording the first 'My Brave Face' clip, Paul commissions a second clip for the song to be shot, featuring colour video of the group making the first version. This sports the apt title of *The Making Of My Brave Face*.

Thursday April 20
❡ At the PWL Studios in Borough, South London, Paul, along with several other artists, records vocals for a new recording of the Gerry And The Pacemakers track 'Ferry 'Cross The Mersey', a song recorded to raise money for the Hillsborough Disaster Fund, organised to help the families of the Hillsborough football stadium disaster where 90 fans tragically lost their lives. Paul completes his vocals and is seen leaving the building at approximately 2pm. (The special charity single is released in the UK only on May 8.)

Monday April 24
❡ At the annual Sony National Radio Awards show, held at the Grosvenor Hotel in London, the 14-part Radio 1 series *The Beeb's Lost Beatles Tapes* wins the award for the Best Rock & Pop Programme. On hand to collect the accolade from Alan Freeman and Michael Aspel are those responsible for the shows, namely Richard Skinner, Kevin Howlet and Mark Lewisohn.

Friday April 28
❡ The home video of *John Lennon & The Plastic Ono Band Live – Rock & Roll Revival, Toronto,* is released in the UK. (The American release takes place on May 1.) The footage derives from John and Yoko's performance at the September 13, 1969, Toronto concert. Also in America today, the 1988 film *John Lennon: Imagine* is released on American home video. (The UK release takes place on May 8.)

April (until June)
❡ During recording sessions in Henley at his private studios, George records the tracks 'Cockamamie Business' and 'Poor Little Girl', both of which appear as bonus tracks on the *Best Of Dark Horse 1976–1989* compilation album. ('Poor Little Girl' will also appear on a single in the UK.)

Monday May 1
❡ In the UK, the home video release of *Rock'n'Roll – The Greatest Years 1971* is stopped following George's objection to the inclusion of 'My Sweet Lord', which had been extracted without permission from Apple's 1971 *Bangla Desh* concert film. Harrison's

official objection will not take effect until July, which means early copies of the video still find their way into the major retailers before being withdrawn. The video also includes the 1971 Ringo promotional film for 'It Don't Come Easy', the first time that one of Ringo's promotional clips has been released commercially.

Thursday May 4
🍎 The promotional film clip for 'Spirit Of The Forest' (see entry for Sunday March 5), is premiered tonight on the BBC2 programme *Nature*.

Monday May 8
🍎 Paul's single 'My Brave Face'/'Flying To My Home' is released in the UK. (The American release takes place on May 10.) Today, the charity single 'Ferry 'Cross The Mersey', featuring Paul's vocals, is also released in the UK.

Wednesday May 10
🍎 A previously recorded appearance with Paul on the French television music show *Rapido*, appears in England on the BBC2 version of the music show. (A repeat transmission takes place on Saturday May 13, again on BBC2.) Also today, the MPL promotional film, *The Making Of My Brave Face*, which was recorded on April 10 and 11 (see entry), is distributed to selected television stations around Europe.

Saturday May 13
🍎 Paul is interviewed for nine minutes on the French television show *Champs Elysées* where he talks about his sheep, his first trip to Paris and the 'My Brave Face' promotional film. (Paul, Linda and the band return to England the following day.)

Tuesday May 16
🍎 At his home studio in Sussex, Paul records an interview with Rona Elliott for broadcast on the NBC TV *Today* show.

Wednesday May 17
🍎 In the States today, a pre-taped interview with Paul is transmitted on the NBC programme *Today*. (Part two of the interview is aired tomorrow.) Paul also crops up today in another US TV show, this time the Paramount television programme *Entertainment Tonight* where he talks about his pre-tour rehearsals and again gives his views on Albert Goldman's book on John Lennon.
🍎 George is in attendance at the opening of Bill Wyman's new London restaurant Sticky Fingers. Joining the former Beatle are other celebrities, including Tina Turner and former members of Traffic, Steve Winwood and Jim Capaldi.

Thursday May 18
🍎 Paul's European promotional tour continues with an appearance on the West German ZDF TV variety show *Mensch Meir,* where Paul and his band mime to the tracks 'Put It There' and 'Figure Of Eight'. Back home, the promotional film for 'My Brave Face' (version 1) receives a screening on tonight's edition of *Top Of The Pops* on BBC1.

Friday May 19
🍎 Paul, Linda and their band return to England and immediately head for the BBC Television Theatre in Shepherd's Bush, London, to make another appearance on the BBC1 early evening chat show *Wogan With Sue Lawley*. During the live show, transmitted between 7:00 and 7:39pm, the group mime to specially recorded new versions of 'Figure Of Eight' and 'My Brave Face'.

Earlier in the day, as Paul left his MPL offices in Soho Square, he was pushing his way through fans when a woman approached him, screaming, "Why don't you acknowledge me? Why don't you acknowledge me?" Clearly distressed by the incident, Paul requested that the running order on the *Wogan* show be changed so that he might leave early, thus avoiding more unpleasantness should the woman have followed him to Shepherd's Bush. The identity of this woman has never been established.

Saturday May 20
🍎 UK TV transmits, in certain regions of the ITV network, the annual American World

Music Awards, which feature Ringo introducing and presenting an award to the singer Tanita Tikaram.

Sunday May 21
🎸 A profile, featuring a pre-taped interview with Paul, is transmitted in America on the Paramount Television programme *Entertainment Tonight*. (Another feature on Paul is transmitted tomorrow night, this time on the show's weekday programme, *Entertainment Tonight*.)

Monday May 22
🎸 Paul, Linda and the band return to the Con Cordia TV Studios in Bussum, Holland, where they make another appearance on the NED 2 TV pop-show *Countdown*, on which Paul and his band mime to the songs 'How Many People' and 'My Brave Face'. (Their performance, alongside an interview with Paul, and a screening of the 'Mull Of Kintyre' promotional film, is transmitted on the Veronica TV station on Wednesday May 24.) During the afternoon rehearsal, watched only by a selected few, Linda plays the drums. Paul and Linda also pay a visit to the Vincent Van Gogh museum in Amsterdam where, for the benefit of a waiting cameraman, Paul poses with a strategically placed bicycle. Later in the day, Paul consents to an interview with the Belgian reporter Andre Vermeullen.

Friday May 26
🎸 A pre-recorded interview with Paul, including the first UK TV screening of the *Making Of My Brave Face* promotional film, is transmitted on the breakfast station TV AM. In Italy, Paul is a featured artist on the Italian RAI UNO television programme *Notte Rock*.

Saturday May 27
🎸 Paul and his group travel to Los Angeles, California, leaving from Heathrow Airport in London early this morning.

Monday May 29
🎸 For 90 minutes, Paul appears live on the KLOS-FM in Los Angeles radio phone-in show *Rockline*. Following this, Paul and Linda head off back to France.

Wednesday May 31
🎸 In America, Tom Petty's home video compilation entitled *A Bunch Of Videos And Some Other Stuff,* featuring the video for 'I Won't Back Down', co-starring George and Ringo is released. (The video is released in the UK on August 11.)
🎸 During their brief stay in France, Paul gives an interview to RTL Radio and makes an appearance with his band on the French Television show *Sacrée Soirée*, where they perform 'My Brave Face'. During his 23-minute appearance, which includes an interview with the host, he is reunited with George Martin and is embarrassed by a playing of 'Besame Mucho' from The Beatles' 1962 Decca Records audition tape.

June
🎸 In America, the *Tommy* album, featuring two tracks by Ringo, is released on compact disc.

Monday June 5
🎸 The 'Spirit Of The Forest' charity single, featuring brief lead vocal lines by Ringo, is released in America on a 12-inch vinyl single. (The UK release, also today, is in the form of a standard 7-inch.)
🎸 Also in the UK, Paul's *Flowers In The Dirt* album is released. (The American release occurs on June 6.) The issue features production credits by Trevor Horn, Neil Dorfsman, Chris Hughes and David Gilmour of Pink Floyd.

Wednesday June 7
🎸 At Twickenham Film Studios in Middlesex, London, before a large crowd mainly comprising 150 members from the Wings Fun Club, Paul and his band appear in a live satellite link-up with Japanese TV for the programme *Hunky Dory* (or alternatively called in Japan *Yoru No Hit Studio)*. The feature, which commences later than the scheduled 12 noon start, includes an interview with Paul carried out between mimed performances of 'This One' and 'My Brave Face'.

🍎 This evening, George and Ringo are to be found standing in the wings of Bob Dylan's concert at the NEC in Birmingham, with Eric Clapton and Jeff Lynne. Throughout Bob's UK tour, George will be seen "hanging out" with the reclusive star. Completely unnoticed, they even ride bicycles through London's Hyde Park.

Thursday June 8
🍎 Paul and his band fly to Spain and assemble at the Barcelona studios of the Spanish Television station TVE to record an appearance on the programme *La Luna*. The lengthy sessions involve the miming, two separate times, of 'My Brave Face', 'Distractions', 'We Got Married', 'This One', and a brief interview with Paul which, when transmitted, features Spanish subtitles. (As a result of the editing of their performances, the song 'Distractions' fails to appear anywhere during the transmitted show.) Shortly afterwards, the entourage return to England.

Saturday June 10
🍎 Paul's MPL documentary *Put It There* is aired tonight on BBC1 in the UK.

Tuesday June 13
🍎 Ringo appears as a guest on stage with Bob Dylan, joining him on two songs at Les Arenes in Frejus, France.
🍎 In Madrid, Spain, Yoko is a guest on the TVE programme *La Tarde*.

Thursday June 15
🍎 Paul and his group fly to Rome in Italy for further European promotions for his *Flowers In The Dirt* album. The day begins with a press conference before Paul and his band appear as guests at the Teatro Delle Vittorie in Rome on the RAI TV programme *Saint Vincent Estate '89*. During their segment, before a live studio audience, Paul and his band mime performances of 'My Brave Face' and 'This One'. (The programme is transmitted by RAI UNO the following day, June 16, just as Paul, Linda and the band are returning home.)

Saturday June 17
🍎 At BBC Broadcasting House, Portland Place, London, Paul conducts his third live radio phone-in of the year, this time on the Italian RAI station Stereo 2. During the course of the one hour broadcast, more than 500 calls are received by the BBC.

Monday June 19
🍎 Paul begins arranging a shoot for the promotional film of 'This One'. He calls for the assistance of the director Tim Pope.

Tuesday June 20
🍎 In America, Paul's albums, *Wild Life, Pipes Of Peace, London Town, Back To The Egg* and *Wings At The Speed Of Sound* are released on compact disc.
🍎 In New York at the Palladium, Ringo holds a press conference which is simultaneously broadcast on the radio station Westwood One, where he announces his plans for a live solo concert tour. Later this evening, Ringo travels to the Ed Sullivan Theater in New York, where he makes a live appearance on the top-rated *David Letterman Show* on CBS.

Wednesday June 21
🍎 Ringo continues promotions for his upcoming tour by appearing on the ABC breakfast show *Good Morning America*. (The feature had been taped at the New York press conference yesterday.)

Friday June 23 & Saturday June 24
🍎 Paul and his group assemble in the London studios of Albert Wharf to film a promotional film for 'This One', working with the director Tim Pope. This video features the song set against an Eastern, mystic backdrop with Paul and his band having eyes painted on their closed eyelids.
🍎 On June 24, Ringo and Buck Owens shoot a promotional video in America for their new recording of 'Act Naturally'.

❉ In the States on Saturday, Roseanne Cash's version of The Beatles' 1964 track 'I Don't Want To Spoil The Party' becomes the first Lennon & McCartney composition to hit the USA country & western number one spot.

Friday June 30
❉ In an out-of-court settlement in London, The Beatles' lawsuit against *Dave Clark (London) Ltd.* is finally settled. The outcome is that Clark, the one-time drummer of the Sixties group The Dave Clark Five, retains the right to market the *Ready Steady Go!* television shows which feature The Beatles' three appearances from 1963 and 1964.

Tuesday July 4 & Wednesday July 5
❉ Paul, not entirely happy with the first 'This One' video, arranges for a second version of the film to be shot, this time utilising the talents of the director Dean Chamberlain. This involves stop-motion action, a process which will take a while to complete. The clip is finally edited and prepared for television distribution on July 21.
❉ Also on July 5, the Ringo and Buck Owens' duet of 'Act Naturally' is released on a single in America. In Los Angeles, Ringo and his new band members begin rehearsals for an upcoming American tour. The band includes drummer Jim Keltner, pianist Billy Preston, saxophonist Clarence Clemmons, drummer/vocalist Levon Helm, Dr. John, guitarists Joe Walsh and Nils Lofgren, and bass player Rick Danko. Collectively they will be billed as "Ringo's All-Starr Band".

Saturday July 8
❉ 'My Brave Face' reaches number 25 in the American singles chart.

Monday July 10
❉ Paul's album *Wings At The Speed Of Sound* is released on CD in the UK.

Friday July 14 & Saturday July 15
❉ At the Cliphouse Studios in London, Paul videotapes a unique promotional film for the track 'Ou Est Le Soleil?' which largely centres around a computer game. (The clip is edited and prepared for television distribution on July 30.)

Monday July 17
❉ In the UK, Paul's single 'This One'/'The First Stone' is released. (The American release on August 2 takes place as a cassette single only.)

Friday July 21
❉ Ringo and his All-Starr band continue rehearsals in Los Calinas, Texas.

Saturday July 22
❉ On the eve of the first All-Starr Band concert tour, Ringo and Barbara attend the party at *Le Bel Age Hotel* in West Hollywood, celebrating the premiere of the latest James Bond picture *Licensed To Kill.*

*　*　*

Ringo & The All-Starr Band
First Tour Of America
Sunday July 23 – Monday September 4

Ringo and his All-Starr Band begin their first tour, a journey through North America. Besides Ringo's obvious solo turns, each member of the band performs at least one number during each show. Ringo's repertoire for the shows includes 'It Don't Come Easy', 'No No Song', 'Honey Don't', 'You're Sixteen', 'Photograph', 'Yellow Submarine', 'Act Naturally', 'Boys', 'With A Little Help From My Friends' and either, 'I Wanna Be Your Man' or 'Back Off Boogaloo'.

The tour includes performances at:

　　Park Central Amphitheater, Dallas, Texas (Sunday July 23)
　　Poplar Creek Music Theater, near Chicago (Tuesday July 25)

Deer Creek Amphitheater, Indianapolis (Wednesday July 26)
Riverfest, Minneapolis (Friday July 28)
Alpine Valley Music Theater, East Troy, Wisconsin (Saturday July 29)
Pine Knob Music Theater, Clarkston, near Detroit, Texas (Sunday July 30)
Blossom Music Center, Cuyahoga Falls, near Cleveland, Ohio (Monday July 31)
Lake Compounce Amusement Park, Bristol, Connecticut (Wednesday August 2)
Performing Arts Center, Saratoga Springs, New York (Friday August 4)
Garden State Arts Center, Holmdel, New Jersey (Saturday August 5)
Bally's Grand Hotel, Atlantic City (Sunday August 6)
Merriweather Post Pavilion, Columbia, Maryland (Tuesday August 8)
Mann Music Center, Philadelphia (Wednesday August 9)
Garden State Arts Center, Holmdel, New Jersey (Friday August 11 – return
    appearance)
Jones Beach Amphitheater, Wantaugh, New York (Saturday August 12 and Sunday
    August 13)
Great Woods Center, Mansfield, near Boston, Massachusetts (Tuesday
    August 15)
Kingston Concert Grounds, Kingston, New Hampshire (Wednesday August 16)
Memorial Auditorium, Buffalo, New York (Friday August 18)
CNE, Toronto (Saturday August 19)
Castle in Charlevoix, Michigan (Sunday August 20)
Winnipeg, Canada (Tuesday August 22)
Saskatoon, Saskatchewan, Canada (Wednesday August 23)
Olympic Saddledome, Calgary (Thursday August 24)
Northlands Coliseum, Edmonton (Friday August 25)
PNE Pacific Coliseum, Vancouver, B.C. (Sunday August 27)
Cal Expo Amphitheater, Sacramento (Tuesday August 29)
Aladdin Theater, Las Vegas (Wednesday August 30)
Shoreline Amphitheater, Mountain View, California (Friday September 1)
Pacific Amphitheater, Costa Mesa, California (Saturday September 2)
Greek Theater, Los Angeles (Sunday September 3 and Monday September 4)

Monday July 24
Ringo appears on the live American radio phone-in show *Rockline*. Ringo is also informed today that the producer Chips Moman and CRS Records are planning to release an album of recordings that Ringo made with the producer Moman back in 1987. Ringo immediately obtains a court order from Judge Ralph Hicks in Fulton County Supreme Court, preventing the release of the album for 30 days, pending a final ruling on the case.

Friday August 11
During Ringo's show at Holmdel, New Jersey, Bruce Springsteen appears on stage as a guest. He performs with Ringo on the tracks 'Get Back', 'Long Tall Sally' (both additional songs to the show's regular repertoire), 'Photograph' and 'With A Little Help From My Friends'. Ringo's son Zak is also a surprise guest on the night and plays drums on three songs, two of which ('Photograph' and 'With A Little Help From My Friends') feature the Ringo/Springsteen duet.

Saturday August 12
Paul and Linda watch from the wings at Ringo's concert at Jones Beach Amphitheater in Wantaugh, New York.

Tuesday August 22 & Wednesday August 23
Ringo's case against Moman, preventing the release of an album of recordings made back in 1987 is heard in court. Two of the tracks, 'Whisky And Soda' and 'I Can Help' are played as evidence to show that, due to his having drank alcohol during the sessions, Ringo's singing ability is below standard.

Thursday August 24
The court grants Ringo another 30 days extension barring the release by Moman of his 1987 Ringo Starr album.

Friday August 25
American TV broadcasts, for the first time, the comical *Oldsmobile* car television commercial featuring Ringo and his daughter Lee.

Sunday September 3 & Monday September 4
Four songs from Ringo's September 3 concert at the Greek Theater in Los Angeles ('No No Song', 'Honey Don't', 'You're Sixteen' and 'Photograph') and three from the September 4 show are videotaped and later included in the *Ringo Starr And His All-Starr Band* video presentation. (The sound recordings are captured on a mobile 48-track machine, which had been loaned from the Record Plant studios.) Also on September 3, the track 'Boys' is transmitted live on the long-running American TV show *The Jerry Lewis Muscular Dystrophy Telethon.*

∗   ∗   ∗

Monday July 24
🍎 In the UK, Paul's single 'This One'/'The Long And Winding Road' is released in a limited edition box. Meanwhile Paul and his band begin four days of rehearsals at the BBC Playhouse Theatre in Northumberland Avenue, London. The band now features a line-up of Paul, Linda, guitarists Hamish Stuart and Robbie McIntosh, keyboard player Paul "Wix" Wickens and drummer Chris Whitten.

Tuesday July 25
🍎 Paul and his band break from rehearsals to record appearances on several shows, including BBC1's *Top Of The Pops*, which is recorded at the BBC TV Centre and transmitted on August 3. (Footage of Paul and his band rehearsing the song on the set of *Top Of The Pops* is taped for a behind-the-scenes look at the programme, which is aired on *The O Zone* programme, broadcast on August 22.) Also on July 25, Paul tapes an interview for BBC2's *The O Zone* programme, which is aired on Friday July 28. In addition, Linda also records an appearance today for the BBC1 programme *But First This . . .* (transmitted on August 10), where she discusses ecology and vegetarianism.
🍎 At the Lumiere Cinema in London, George and Olivia attend a special preview screening of the Handmade film *How To Get Ahead In Advertising*, which opens at the cinema on Friday July 28.

Wednesday July 26 & Thursday July 27
🍎 At the Playhouse Theatre in London, Paul performs surprise 5pm concerts before an invited audience, mainly comprising staff from MPL and EMI as well as 400 members of the Wings Fun Club. Their repertoire on both days includes 'Figure Of Eight', 'Jet', 'Rough Ride', 'Got To Get You Into My Life', 'Band On The Run', 'We Got Married', 'Put It There', 'Hello, Goodbye' (ending), 'Things We Said Today', 'Can't Buy Me Love', 'Summertime', 'I Saw Her Standing There', 'This One' and 'My Brave Face'. At this point, Paul introduces his band to the audience. The shows then continue with 'Twenty Flight Rock', 'The Long And Winding Road', 'Ain't That A Shame', 'Let It Be' and, for the encore, 'Coming Up'. The shows also serve as a preview of his upcoming world tour, which is scheduled to begin on September 26. At the start of the second day of the Playhouse concerts, Paul hosts a special 1:00–3:00pm press conference to announce his upcoming world tour and performs a brief music set for the benefit of the press and TV cameras. Their performance includes 'Midnight Special', 'Coming Up', 'Twenty Flight Rock' and 'This One'. Afterwards, Paul and his band perform a second concert before an audience of Wings Fun Club members. In America, on July 26, Paul releases a 12-inch and a cassette maxi single version of 'Ou Est Le Soleil?' featuring three alternative mixes of the track.

Friday July 28
🍎 A clip from Paul's Playhouse press conference is included in tonight's edition of the BBC2 music show *The O Zone*. Further excerpts from the gathering are transmitted across Europe, including the German 3SAT music show *P.I.T.* on July 31.

Sunday July 30

🍎 A pre-recorded interview with Paul is transmitted on the Children's ITV morning show *Ghost Train*, where he promotes his new album and single, 'This One'.

August

🍎 During this month, over a few days in London, George records an appearance for the new ITV music show, entitled *Beyond The Groove*, devised and co-produced by the former Tourists and Eurythmics star Dave Stewart. The show remains unseen.

Wednesday August 2

🍎 In America, a 7-inch 45rpm vinyl promotional version of Paul's 'This One' is released. It is now thought highly likely that this will be Paul's last American vinyl single as, just prior to its issue, Capitol announces that they are discontinuing most 7-inch vinyl singles.

Thursday August 3

🍎 In the UK, the film *Porky's Revenge* is released on home video, featuring George's track 'I Don't Want To Do It' on the soundtrack.

Friday August 4

🍎 On the Italian RAI UNO TV music programme *Notte Rock*, a segment is devoted to Paul, and features excerpts from the Playhouse Theatre press conference of July 27.

Thursday August 10

🍎 The soundtrack album to *Lethal Weapon 2*, featuring George's 'Cheer Down' is released in America. (The UK release takes place on September 4.)

Monday August 21 (until Thursday August 24)

🍎 Paul and his band begin rehearsals for their upcoming world tour at the Lyceum Theater in New York. On the morning of August 24, Paul conducts a brief press conference at the Theater, which is simultaneously transmitted live (for 90 minutes) on the Westwood One Radio network in America. (Five songs from the conference, 'Blue Suede Shoes', 'Matchbox', 'Figure Of Eight', 'This One' and 'Coming Up', are included in the transmission.) During a break this afternoon at the Theatre, Paul's hectic schedule continues when he tapes a promotional video interview for Capitol Records. Later this evening, again at the Lyceum Theater, Paul and his band perform a show before a specially invited audience. Their repertoire includes 'Figure Of Eight', 'This One', 'Jet', 'Rough Ride', 'Got To Get You Into My Life', 'Band On The Run', 'We Got Married', 'Put It There', 'Things We Said Today', 'Summertime', 'Can't Buy Me Love', 'I Saw Her Standing There', 'My Brave Face', 'Twenty Flight Rock', 'The Long And Winding Road', 'Ain't That A Shame', 'Let It Be' and, as the encore, 'Coming Up'.

🍎 Still in America, George's single 'Cheer Down'/'That's What It Takes' is released.

🍎 In London at the annual Sotheby's rock and pop auction, The Beatles' former chauffeur Alf Bicknell offers for sale five Beatles reel-to-reel tapes, items personally given to him by John when Alf left his employment with the group in September, 1966. Of the five, only two of the reels sell, going for almost £12,000 to a buyer from West Germany.

Friday August 25

🍎 Paul, Linda and the band return to England where, following a day off on August 26, rehearsals resume at Paul's home studio in West Sussex on August 27.

Tuesday August 29

🍎 To capitalise on Paul's recent high profile activities, his 1978 album *London Town* is released on CD in the UK.

Friday September 1

🍎 At his Sussex studios, Paul records a completely new version of the track 'Figure Of Eight', which will appear later, released as a single in no less than eight different formats in the UK and as a cassette single in America.

Saturday September 2

🍎 In the UK, BBC2 broadcasts the *Network East* tribute programme to Ravi Shankar, which features a brief interview with George. The show is to commemorate the 50th anniversary of Ravi's first public recital. Further showings of the documentary take place on BBC2 on March 31 and then again on BBC1 on April 1, 1990.

Monday September 4 (periodically until Thursday September 21)
 Paul and his band shift rehearsals to a sound stage at the Elstree Film Studios in Borehamwood, Hertfordshire. At the end of the day, rehearsals are cut short to enable Paul and Linda to head for the BBC Television Theatre in Shepherd's Bush, London, for the programme *Wogan*. Tonight Linda will make her first solo appearance on the show to promote her cookery book, while Paul watches her interview backstage.

Thursday September 7
 Paul, Linda and the band again break from rehearsals to attend the 1989 celebrity Buddy Holly Week luncheon which, this year, is held at the Talk Of The Town in Parker Street, near Holborn, London. Afterwards, Paul's entourage of musicians returns to Elstree for more rehearsals.

Monday September 11
 Paul's single 'My Brave Face' is released on a CD in America.

Saturday September 16
 'This One' reaches a disappointing number 94 in the American singles chart, while in the UK, the single had reached number 18 the previous month.

Thursday September 21
 Following months of extensive rehearsals by Paul and his new band, the fruits of their work are finally unveiled tonight during a secret, pre-tour concert, in Studio 6 at the Goldcrest Film Studios, at Elstree in Hertfordshire. The 750 members of the audience, comprised mainly of fan club members and winners from the all-day Radio One competition, are treated to the world premiere of the 11-minute pre-concert Richard Lester-directed film, featuring many rare Beatles' film clips and the full 30-song repertoire from the band, including all of the visual effects that will be featured on the tour. The song line-up will alter periodically during the 10-month world tour. (See entry for September 26 for the full repertoire.) The show tonight, and those throughout the tour, is captured on multi-camera film and videotape and will be professionally sound recorded by Paul. Among those present is writer Barry Miles, beginning work on *Many Years From Now*, Paul's autobiography.

Monday September 25
 Paul and his band fly to Norway to begin preparations for their tour.

Tuesday September 26
 Even though the official start day of Paul's concert tour is September 28, tonight Paul and his band perform another warm-up concert, this time at the Drammenshalle in Dramen, Norway. Their repertoire for this concert, as well as for their forthcoming shows, consists of the following: 'Figure Of Eight', 'Jet', 'Rough Ride', 'Got To Get You Into My Life', 'Band On The Run', 'Ebony And Ivory', 'We Got Married', 'Maybe I'm Amazed', 'The Long And Winding Road', 'The Fool On The Hill', 'Sgt. Pepper's Lonely Hearts Club Band', 'Good Day Sunshine', 'Can't Buy Me Love', 'Put It There' (featuring the ending of 'Hello, Goodbye'), 'Things We Said Today', 'Eleanor Rigby', 'Back In The USSR', 'I Saw Her Standing There', 'This One', 'My Brave Face', 'Twenty Flight Rock', 'Coming Up', 'Let It Be', 'Live And Let Die', 'Hey Jude', 'Yesterday' and 'Get Back'. Then, as an encore, the following tracks: 'Golden Slumbers', 'Carry That Weight' and 'The End'. For the show today, September 26, the Richard Lester film does not precede the concert. (Incidentally, later in the CD booklet accompanying Paul's *Tripping The Live Fantastic* album, Paul mistakenly lists this show today in Dramen as the official start of the tour, but this is not the case.) Coincidentally, back in the UK this evening, Channel 4 is screening, for the first time on British television, the 1980 MPL concert film *Rockshow*, featuring highlights from Wings' live performance at Seattle's Kingdome on Thursday June 10, 1976.

* * *

Paul McCartney's 1989/1990 World Tour
September 28 1989 – July 29

First Leg – Europe
Thursday September 28 – Saturday November 11

Following years of unofficial stories, the rumours finally turn into fact and, after a gap of ten years, Paul goes back on the road. The first leg of his world tour opens with concerts at:

Scandinavium, Gothenburg, Sweden (Thursday September 28)

Johanneshovs Isstadion, Stockholm, Sweden (Friday September 29 and Saturday September 30)

Sportshalle, Hamburg, West Germany (Tuesday October 3 and Wednesday October 4)

Festehalle, Frankfurt, West Germany (Friday October 6 and Saturday October 7)

Palais Omnisport De Bercy, Paris, France (Monday October 9, Tuesday October 10 and Wednesday October 11)

Westfallenhalle, Dortmund, West Germany (Monday October 16 and Tuesday 17)

Olympiahalle, Munich, West Germany (Friday October 20, Saturday October 21 and Sunday October 22)

Palaeur, Rome, Italy (Tuesday October 24)

Palatrussardi, Milan, Italy (Thursday October 26 and Friday October 27)

Hallenstadion, Zurich, Switzerland (Sunday October 29 and Monday October 30)

Palacio De Sportes, Madrid, Spain (Thursday November 2 and Friday November 3)

La Halle Tony Garnier, Lyon, France (Sunday November 5)

Ahoy Sportpaleis, Rotterdam, Holland (Tuesday November 7, Wednesday November 8, Friday November 10 and Saturday November 11)

The 1989/1990 Get Back tour, as it will be fondly remembered, will travel 100,331 miles and take in 13 countries. A prop used at the start of the tour, but soon dropped, features a large aeroplane which swoops down over the audience at the start of the track 'Back In The USSR'.

A feature of the tour is the free programme, designed by the publishers of *Q* magazine to resemble a special 100-page issue of the magazine. A copy is placed on each seat in every arena, a welcome gesture in view of the prevailing trend for extortionately priced rock tour programmes with very few pages, featuring little in the way of intelligent text but plenty of adverts for tour merchandise and back catalogues.

Fans were also pleased by the accurate musical arrangements of the many Beatles' songs in Paul's repertoire. Paul and his band, Hamish Stuart in particular, had evidently taken special pains to reproduce as closely as possible the vocal harmonies and backing tracks of the original Beatles' recordings. This was particularly noticeable in 'Can't Buy Me Love', 'Sgt Pepper' and the wonderful closing sequence of *Abbey Road* songs, for which Paul played lead guitar on a Gibson Les Paul and Hamish played bass. For much of the concert Paul played an original left-handed Hofner Violin bass, just as he did with The Beatles, and the reappearance after so many years of this distinctive instrument was usually sufficient to raise a warm cheer from older fans.

Thursday September 28 (until Friday November 10)
Live tracks from several of the shows and pre-concert soundchecks, appear on the album *Tripping The Live Fantastic*. Namely, tracks from September 28 ('Put It There' and 'Live And Let Die'), October 10 ('Rough Ride'), October 17 ('Got To Get You Into My Life'), October 21 ('Can't Buy Me Love'), November 2 ('Things We Said Today'), November 8 ('Ebony And Ivory' and 'Maybe I'm Amazed') and November 10 ('Figure Of Eight'). Prior to the start of each concert on his tour, Paul's unreleased track 'Church Mice', along with several other unissued tracks, are played over each theatre's P.A. system.

Tuesday October 3
In Hamburg, Germany, Paul conducts a press conference in The Beatles' old haunt of the Kaiserkeller, in Grosse Freiheit.

Wednesday October 11

Following the last concert in Paris this evening, Paul, Linda and the band fly home to England before flying to Dortmund on Monday October 16.

Thursday October 26

Backstage at the concert in Milan, Nancy Duff, of CBS News in America, meets Paul and his manager Richard Ogden. It is during this meeting that she proposes the idea of dedicating an entire edition of CBS's news magazine programme *48 Hours* to one stop on Paul's 1989/90 world tour. (A further meeting is arranged for Tuesday November 7.) Later this evening, a live performance of 'C Moon', from today's first show in Milan, is recorded and released officially in the UK on December 3, 1990, as part of the 'All My Trials' singles.

Friday October 27

Today, during the second show in Milan, Italy, Paul performs, for the only time on this tour, the track 'All My Trials'. The performance is officially released in America on the special "record club" vinyl edition of the album *Tripping The Live Fantastic Highlights!*

Thursday November 2

A report from Paul's concert at the Palacio De Sportes in Madrid is featured in the Spanish television show *Rockopop*, transmitted on November 4. While highlights from Paul's Madrid press conference earlier in the day, naturally feature heavy on the Spanish TV news bulletins this evening.

Tuesday November 7

Further to their previous meeting on Thursday October 26, Nancy Duff again meets with Paul and his manager, this time backstage at The Ahoy in Rotterdam, Holland. At the conclusion of their meeting, she finalises a deal whereby Paul's appearance at the Rosemont Horizon in Chicago on December 3, 4 and 5, will form a special edition of *48 Hours*, to be broadcast in early 1990. As part of the conditions, Paul insists that only 15 minutes of music can be used in the completed 75 minutes show. Nancy insists that the music chosen must be an even mix between tracks from the album *Flowers In The Dirt* and classic Beatles numbers. Paul, in turn, insists that he has a say in the live concert sound used in the programme.

Saturday November 11

A film crew from the UK Channel 4 music show *Big World Cafe* videotapes excerpts from tonight's concert at The Ahoy. An accompanying interview with Paul is carried out backstage by Mariella Frostrup. The first broadcast of this footage, presented in Nicam digital stereo, takes place on November 21, but when Paul views this version he immediately orders that the video be wiped and never shown again. For the repeat transmission, scheduled for November 24, an alternative, shorter version is transmitted. Also today in Rotterdam, a team from BBC Radio One also records an interview with Paul, an item that will be edited into the revised final part of the repeated radio series *McCartney On McCartney*, which is due to start transmissions on Radio One on Christmas Day, running every day until January 4 next year.

Paul McCartney's World Tour

Second Leg – America
Thursday November 23 – Friday December 15

Paul, Linda and the band arrive in New York on Wednesday November 22 to promote their forthcoming concerts at Madison Square Garden by conducting a press conference at the Lyceum Theater. Paul also gives an interview to Scott Muni, for inclusion on his New York radio programme *World Of Rock*. An interview with Paul at the conference is also aired on the LA radio station KLOS-FM. Meanwhile, the next leg of Paul's world tour continues in the States, where they perform shows at:

Los Angeles Forum, California (Thursday November 23, Friday November 24 and Monday November 27 to Wednesday November 29)

Rosemont Horizon, Rosemont, Chicago, Illinois (Sunday December 3, Monday
December 4 and Tuesday December 5)
Skydome, Maple Leaf Gardens, Toronto, Ontario, Canada (Thursday December 7)
Montreal Forum, Quebec, Canada (Saturday December 9)
Madison Square Garden, New York (Monday December 11, Tuesday December 12,
Thursday December 14 and Friday December 15)

Thursday November 23 (until Saturday December 9)
A selection of songs from the concerts on November 23 ('Crackin' Up' and 'Sgt. Pepper's
Lonely Hearts Club Band'), December 5 (soundcheck – 'Together'), December 7
('Golden Slumbers'/'Carry That Weight'/'The End') and December 9 ('Yesterday' from
the concert and 'Don't Let The Sun Catch You Crying' from the afternoon soundcheck)
will appear on the album *Tripping The Live Fantastic*, released simultaneously around
the world on November 5, 1990.

Friday November 24
In Los Angeles, Paul tapes an interview for the music station VH-1.

Sunday November 26
In Los Angeles, during a break from concerts, Paul records an interview for the Tokyo
radio station programme *Super DJ*.

Monday November 27
The day begins with Paul holding another press conference, during which he announces
that The Beatles may get together again, adding that he has never written with George
and would like to. The press has a field day with this revelation. Highlights from Paul's
press conference in Los Angeles today at the LA Forum are included in a promotional
videotape compiled by the Visa credit card company, who are sponsoring the second leg
of Paul's tour, starting Thursday February 1. This means that, in America, Visa will be
the only credit card allowed for ticket bookings and merchandise. In addition, the Visa
Company has agreed to underwrite an $8.5 million advertising campaign to promote the
tour. Later today, at the Los Angeles Forum, the Motown legend Stevie Wonder joins
Paul on stage to perform a duet on 'Ebony And Ivory'.

Sunday December 3, Monday December 4 & Tuesday December 5
During his stay in Chicago and during the concerts at the Rosemont Horizon, Paul,
Linda and his band are followed by a CBS TV news team working on the special edition
of the current affairs programme *48 Hours*. Cameras catch a glimpse of Roger Daltrey,
the lead singer with The Who, who visits Paul backstage in 'The Green Room' on the
opening night. As a sideline to Paul, CBS cameras also follow around town the fan Joy
Waugh, who is seen preparing herself for Paul's shows at the Rosemont Horizon and
making attempts to meet Paul in person. (As a footnote to this, following the first
screening of the *48 Hours* programme, Paul's publicists, touched by her plight, contact
Joy and arrange for her to meet Paul in person, flying her and her husband Bob to see
Paul's concert at The Centrum in Worcester, Massachusetts on February 9, 1990. An
event covered by CBS and featured during the extended version of Paul's *48 Hours*
special. Paul is not aware before this meeting of Joy's failed attempts to meet the former
Beatle during his stay in Chicago, as Paul had not seen the completed *48 Hours*
programme, which Joy was most disappointed about.)
Meanwhile, back at the Rosemont Horizon venue, acting on Paul's requests, all
soundchecks from the three days, as well as the evening concerts themselves, are
preserved on digital 24-track recording equipment. Once the recordings are completed,
Paul ensures that the master tapes are dispatched to England where remixing of the live
performances is carried out by MPL staff. Once mixed, tapes of the three soundchecks
and live performances at the Rosemont Horizon in Chicago are sent to CBS in America
on quarter inch tape and suitably dubbed into the respective parts of the almost
completed *48 Hours* programme. (The special will be aired on the station for the first
time on January 25, 1990. Incidentally, all of MPL's master audio tapes, as well as the
unused CBS TV video master tapes on BETACAM and Hi8 are currently locked in a top
security area at CBS and not in the general CBS News archives. This action was taken to
prevent bootlegging.) A report from Paul's December 4 concert also features on the

NBC programme *Sirott Tonight*. Incidentally, during the show at the Rosemont Horizon on December 3, Paul, just like he did during his 1976 world tour, performs a brief snippet of the track 'Chicago'.

Monday December 11
Backstage at Madison Square Garden, Paul gives an interview to the New York radio station WNEW.

Friday December 15
Following their final concert at Madison Square Garden, in New York, Paul and Linda join Dustin Hoffman, Twiggy, and Sting for dinner at *Sardi's Restaurant* in the city.

* * *

Wednesday September 27
🍎 The Beatles' 1968 film *Yellow Submarine* is released simultaneously around the world by Warner Brothers home video, sporting a "digitally enhanced stereo hi-fi soundtrack!"

Monday October 2
🍎 The Buck Owens album *Act Naturally* is released in America, featuring his duet with Ringo on the title track. (The UK release takes place on February 19, 1990.)

Tuesday October 3
🍎 In the UK, Paul's album *Wings At The Speed Of Sound* is released on CD.

Wednesday October 4
🍎 Graham Chapman, a former member of the Monty Python comedy team, dies aged 48. Like all the members of the Python team, Graham was a good friend of George's and had appeared on stage with him on April 20, 1976 (see entry), and in the studio, when George produced the Python single 'The Lumberjack Song' in 1975.

Tuesday October 10
🍎 The 1968 film *Wonderwall,* featuring George's film score, is released on American home video.

Thursday October 12
🍎 At the MIPCOM trade fair in Cannes, France, a hastily edited video clip of Ringo and his All-Starr band live in Los Angeles on September 3 is aired to potential foreign buyers.

Tuesday October 17
🍎 George's album *Best Of Dark Horse: 1976–1989* is released in America. (The UK release takes place on October 23.) The album reaches number 132 in the American charts.

Monday October 23
🍎 The 1982 compilation album *The John Lennon Collection is* released in the UK on CD.

Thursday October 26
🍎 Ringo holds a press conference to promote his forthcoming Japanese tour in a Tokyo hotel.

* * *

Ringo and The All-Starr Band – Tour Of Japan
Monday October 30 – Wednesday November 8

Ringo, and his All-Starr band, undertake a short concert tour of Japan. Ringo's repertoire includes the following songs: 'It Don't Come Easy', 'No No Song', 'Yellow Submarine', 'Act Naturally', 'Honey Don't', 'I Wanna Be Your Man', 'Boys', 'Photograph', 'You're

Sixteen' and 'With A Little Help From My Friends'. Billy Preston, during his solo, performs The Beatles' 1969 track 'Get Back'. Concerts are performed at:

Rainbow Hall, Nagoya (Monday October 30)
Castle Hall, Osaka (Tuesday October 31)
Sun Plaza, Hiroshima (Thursday November 2)
Kitakyushu Koseinenkin Hall, Kyushi (Friday November 3)
Nippon Budokan Hall, Tokyo (Monday November 6 and Tuesday November 7)
Yokohama Arena, Yokohama (Wednesday November 8)

Monday October 30
On the opening night of the tour, Ringo is interviewed for the Japanese TV programme *11pm*, where, besides being interviewed, he is seen at the afternoon soundcheck performing 'Honey Don't'.

* * *

Friday November 3
 In the UK, the home videos of both the Handmade films *Water*, including a performance of 'Freedom', featuring George and Ringo, and *A Private Function* are released.

Wednesday November 8
 Following a case that has lasted for over 20 years, The Beatles' lawsuit against EMI/Capitol regarding unpaid royalties is finally settled. It is decided, by all the parties concerned, not to reveal to the press the exact terms of the agreement. However, sources close to The Beatles suggest that EMI/Capitol is set to pay the group approximately $100 million in back royalties. The Beatles are also given full control over the use of their EMI recordings, and a final say in any future record cover artwork.

Monday November 13
 Paul's single 'Figure Of Eight'/'Ou Est Le Soleil?' is released in the UK. (The American release takes place on November 15 as a cassette only single, featuring shorter edits of both songs.) In total, eight different 'Figure Of Eight' singles are issued in the UK.

Wednesday November 15
 In Atlanta, Ringo returns to court where he testifies that the recorded performances from the 1987 Chips Moman-produced sessions in Memphis are below standard due to the excessive use of alcohol by band members. He also charges that Moman is trying to rush release the album of these recordings to capitalise on Ringo's successful All-Starr Band tour, noting that since the 1987 sessions, no label had shown an interest in releasing the album. Ringo also claims that Moman had formed his own CRS label purely for releasing this album. The hearing ends with the court issuing a further injunction blocking the release of the record for the time being.

Saturday November 18
 In London, George attends the *Parents For Safe Foods* concert at the Albert Hall, where he is seen introducing Eric Clapton on stage. The charity features on its panel the current ex-Beatles' wives, Linda, Barbara and Olivia. Also present this evening is Jeff Lynne, Dame Edna Everage and the comedienne Pamela Stephenson. The concert is filmed but never screened.

Thursday November 23
 In the UK, the *Flowers In The Dirt* (World Tour Pack), a limited edition repackaging of Paul's album, including a bonus one-track single featuring the previously unreleased track 'Party Party' is released. (The American release takes place on January 15, 1990.)

Monday November 27
 George's single 'Cheer Down'/'Poor Little Girl' is released as a single in the UK.

Tuesday November 28
◆ From his Handmade office in Cadogan Square, London, George issues a statement replying to Paul's "The Beatles might perform together again" announcement, made in Los Angeles at a press conference the previous day. According to George there will be no reunion "so long as John Lennon remains dead!"

December
◆ In the UK, the compilation album *The Royal Concert* is released, featuring tracks from Paul and George during the 1986 and 1987 *Prince's Trust* shows, respectively. No songs from Ringo appear on the release.
◆ Also this month, Ringo takes part in the UK radio campaigns for *RADD* (*Recording Artists Against Drunk Driving*).

Tuesday December 12
◆ Ringo and his manager Hilary Gerrard are seen visiting the *Startling Music* offices in Knightsbridge, London. During his visit, Ringo delivers a Christmas message to a freelance reporter who is representing the Dutch fanzine *Beatles Unlimited*.

Thursday December 14
◆ A 24-minute interview with Paul, carried out with the DJ Anne Nightingale for the weekly series *One To One*, is transmitted in the Central region of the ITV network, just prior to a repeat screening of the 1979 film *The Birth Of The Beatles*. The One To One show receives further broadcasts on the ITV network on different days, including the London Weekend Television region on January 21, 1990.

Friday December 15
◆ In America, Paul and Linda donate a cheque for $100,000 to the Friends Of The Earth organisation, an event covered by MTV.

Tuesday December 19
◆ At Claridges Hotel in London, Paul collects a Unique Achievement Award from the PRS, the Performing Rights Society. During the lunch time ceremony, for which Paul and Linda had flown back to England especially, he is seen cutting a cake in the shape of a four string bass. The hotel's head chef, Mr. Marjan Lesnik, creates a vegetarian menu in honour of Paul and Linda. Amongst the delicacies on offer are *Hello Good Pie, Peas Please Me* and *Mash Elle*. Meanwhile, Paul's *Put It There* documentary is released in America on home videocassette and laser disc. In the UK, the video release of *Put It There* is issued as an extended 65-minute version. (When originally transmitted on BBC1, the running time was only 50 minutes.) Incidentally, the sleeve for the video lists four additional songs not featured in the TV broadcast, but, in fact, only one, 'The Fool On The Hill', is actually included. MPL refuses to comment on this mistake. The American packaging is changed to eliminate the error.

Wednesday December 20 (until Saturday December 23)
◆ Paul returns home to Sussex, where he records the music intended for the MPL film *Daumier's Law*, a short film about the artist Honore Daumier.

Thursday December 21
◆ To cash in on the lucrative Christmas market, there's more Beatles-related activity in the video market, when *John Lennon: Live In New York City* and John and Yoko's 1972 film *Imagine,* are both released on laser disc. (The UK laser disc release of *Imagine* does not take place until August of 1991.)
◆ Also released in America on laser disc today is Paul's 1980 MPL concert film *Rockshow,* as well as Paul's 1984 film *Give My Regards To Broad Street* and *Rupert And The Frog Song.*

Saturday December 23
◆ In Tokyo, Japan, newspapers begin carrying notices advertising Paul's upcoming seven concerts at the Tokyo Dome, to be held between March 2 and March 11, 1990. The reports add that the tickets will go on sale on January 7.

Wednesday December 27

🍎 In the UK on BBC2, the new Rolling Stones documentary presentation *25 × 5: The Continuing Adventures Of The Rolling Stones,* is transmitted and features miscellaneous Beatles-related footage from 1963 to 1971. (An extended home video of the programme is released on March 19, 1990.)

🍎 In the early hours of the morning, Paul's 1984 film *Give My Regards To Broad Street* is repeated on several regions of the ITV network.

"It's Greening of the World year!"

– Yoko Ono

Monday January 1
✦ In New York, Yoko starts the decade by announcing that it's *Greening Of The World* year. She announces a 12-month environmental campaign of events to mark what would have been John's 50th year.

* * *

Paul McCartney World Tour

Third Leg – The United Kingdom
Tuesday January 2 – Friday January 26

Paul kicks off the new year, and a new decade, by taking his world tour to the UK, beginning with a series of concerts at the NEC International Arena in Birmingham (Tuesday January 2, Wednesday January 3, Friday January 5, Saturday January 6, Monday January 8, Tuesday January 9) and Wembley Arena, London (Thursday January 11, Saturday January 13, Sunday January 14, Tuesday January 16, Wednesday January 17, Friday January 19, Saturday January 20, Sunday January 21, Tuesday January 23, Wednesday January 24, Friday January 26).

Tuesday January 2 (until Sunday January 21)
Live tracks from January 2 ('Inner City Madness' from the afternoon sound check), January 13 ('The Fool On The Hill' and 'Twenty Flight Rock'), January 16 ('We Got Married' and 'Band On The Run'), January 17 ('Jet'), January 19 ('My Brave Face'), January 21 ('Matchbox' and the old Gracie Fields number 'Sally' from the afternoon sound check) appear on the album *Tripping The Live Fantastic*.

Wednesday January 3
Paul performs a tree planting ceremony in Birmingham, an event exclusively covered by the newspaper the Birmingham Evening Echo. Meanwhile this evening, a report on Paul's concert at the NEC is featured on the ITV regional programme *Central News*.

Friday January 5
Backstage at tonight's concert at the NEC in Birmingham, an elderly man comes up to Paul and introduces himself as Father McKenzie (a character immortalised in The Beatles' 1966 track 'Eleanor Rigby'). Paul is heard to respond by saying: "Where's Mr. Kite and Billy Shears? Are they here too?" Today in the UK, Paul's new single 'Put It There'/'Mama's Little Girl' is released. The CD and 12-inch versions add the track 'Same Time Next Year'. (The American release, which occurs on May 1, is a cassette only single.)

Thursday January 11 to Friday January 26
The opening night's concert at Wembley is professionally recorded for a proposed BBC Radio One special programme which fails to materialise. Incidentally, it's estimated that during the 11 nights at the Wembley Arena, Paul performs to crowds totalling over 137,000.

Saturday January 13
In America, 'Figure Of Eight' reaches no higher than number 92 in the singles charts.

Tuesday January 16
Backstage at Wembley, Paul meets 21-year-old Polish teacher Agnieska Czarniecka, who for four years has run the *Paul McCartney Kindergarten* in Cracow, where 200 children are taught the English language through Paul's songs.

Wednesday January 17
BBC1 in the South East broadcasts the first of a two part interview with Paul conducted by Cathy McGowan, the famous host of the 1960s pop show *Ready Steady Go!* (Part two is transmitted on the station two weeks later on Wednesday January 31.)

Monday January 22 (until Friday January 26)
Paul appears in a (pre-taped) five-part feature, transmitted daily on the TV AM programme *Good Morning Britain*.

Monday January 22
Paul, armed simply with an acoustic guitar, films a promotional clip for 'Put It There'. Shot in black and white, without Linda or any of the band, the item features random images from a typical father-son relationship: the boy watching his father shave, the two making music and building a toy aeroplane together and more. (The clip is edited and prepared for television distribution on January 30.)

Wednesday January 24 & Tuesday January 30
A two-part report on Paul's recent US tour is featured on the Paramount Television programme *Entertainment Tonight*.

Friday January 26
At the conclusion of his series of concerts at the Wembley Arena, Paul throws a party which is attended by Elvis Costello, Neil Aspinall, George Martin, Dick Lester and Cynthia Lennon, amongst others.

* * *

Fourth Leg – Return To America
Thursday February 1 – Monday February 19

Paul's world tour returns to America, where he performs at the following venues:

Palace of Auburn Hills, Auburn Hills, near Detroit, Michigan (Thursday February 1 and Friday February 2)
Civic Arena, Pittsburgh, Pennsylvania (Sunday February 4 and Monday February 5)
The Centrum, Worcester, Boston, Massachusetts (Thursday February 8 and Friday February 9)
Rupp Arena, Lexington, Kentucky (Sunday February 11)
Cincinnati Riverfront Coliseum, Cincinnati, Ohio (Monday February 12)
Market Square Arena, Indianapolis, Indiana (Wednesday February 14 and Thursday 15)
Omni, Atlanta, Georgia (Sunday February 18 and Monday February 19)

Thursday February 1 (until Monday February 12)
Live performances from the shows on February 1 ('This One'), February 8 ('Eleanor Rigby'), February 9 ('Yesterday') and February 12 ('If I Were Not Upon A Stage' and 'Hey Jude') are released on the album *Tripping The Live Fantastic*.

Sunday February 4 & Monday February 5
His voice strained due to illness, Paul deletes several songs from both of his Pittsburgh shows.

Thursday February 8
Paul appears on the front cover of *Rolling Stone* magazine. Inside is an article containing a "Backstage Look At His Tour".

Sunday February 11
A pre-taped interview with Paul, conducted on the current US tour, is transmitted on the London based "oldies" radio station Capital Gold.

Saturday February 17
'Put It There' reaches number 32 in the UK singles chart. Also today, Paul decides to cut short his upcoming concert tour of Japan, scheduled to begin on March 2, because of his voice problems. The rearranged itinerary means that the show originally scheduled for March 2 will now take place on March 13, the show set for March 6 will now take place on March 7 and the concert due on March 8 will now be scrapped entirely. The other dates, March 3, 5, 7 and 9, are unaltered.

Tuesday February 20 (until Thursday February 22)
Paul and Linda remain in America following the conclusion of this leg of the tour to attend the Grammy Awards ceremony on February 21 (see entry).

Wednesday February 21
Following Paul's authorisation of a closed circuit broadcast of his concert in Tokyo on March 9, the Fuji Japanese television *Yoru No Hit Studio Deluxe* begins advertising the event, announcing that the limited tickets will go on sale on Saturday February 24.

*   *   *

Friday January 5
🍎 The Fulton County Superior Courts grant Ringo an injunction to prevent Chips Moman from releasing an album of recordings Ringo had recorded for him back in 1987. As part of the agreement, Ringo is ordered to pay Moman $74,354 in production costs, less than half the figure Moman had originally sought.

Tuesday January 23
🍎 The British comedy actor Derek Royle, best remembered by Beatles fans as the man who played the role of Jolly Jimmy Johnston in The Beatles' 1967 film *Magical Mystery Tour,* dies in London, aged 61.

Thursday February 1
🍎 Charlie Lennon, brother of John's father Freddie, is rushed to the intensive care unit of the Royal Liverpool Teaching Hospital after being knocked down by a car in Penny Lane. He sustains fractured ribs and broken legs.

Tuesday February 6
🍎 In New York, Yoko wins a Supreme Court Action which prevents Marilyn Goldberg, a US art dealer, from privately selling licensed reproduction prints of John Lennon's so-called erotic lithographs. Goldberg is the president of Marigold Enterprises Ltd., to whom, in 1985, Yoko granted exclusive marketing rights in John Lennon works.

Thursday February 8
🍎 The film *Lethal Weapon 2,* featuring George's 'Cheer Down', is released in America on both home video and laser disc. (The UK release takes place on March 16.)

Saturday February 10
🍎 The Traveling Wilburys album *Volume One* is featured in the second series of the BBC Radio One series *Classic Albums,* a series made and produced by the DJ Roger Scott shortly before his death in December last year. (Scott, of course, was the narrator of *The Beatles At Abbey Road* video presentation held at the studios in London in 1983.)

Monday February 19
🍎 The CD version of *The John Lennon Collection* is released in America.

Wednesday February 21
🍎 In America, Paul accepts the Lifetime Achievement Grammy Award, during the 32nd Academy Of Recorded Arts And Sciences televised award ceremony. Paul accepts the award from the actress Meryl Streep and makes a short speech.
🍎 At the same awards ceremony, the albums *The Traveling Wilburys – Volume One* and Tom Petty's *Full Moon Fever,* both featuring George, are nominated for Album of the Year. *Volume One* is also nominated for Best Rock Performance by a Duo or Group with Vocal. Ringo is even on the act when his duet with Buck Owens on 'Act Naturally' is nominated for Best Country Vocal Collaboration. Paul's *Flowers In The Dirt* and Petty's *Full Moon Fever* are also nominated for Best Engineered Album. Sadly, none of the above come away with an award.

*   *   *

Thursday March 1
Paul, Linda and the band arrived in Tokyo at Narita Airport, the New Tokyo International Airport, the previous day, February 28, at 6:40pm JST, and spent the first night in Japan socialising with Keith Richards of The Rolling Stones, who had just finished performing concerts in the country. Today, March 1, Paul's first performance, albeit brief, is part of a press conference attended by 800 people, held at the MZA Ariake Theater where besides taking a barrage of questions from the media, he sings the track 'Matchbox'. The event is broadcast live on the Japanese Fuji television programme *Super Time*. When the reporters and television crews have left the theatre, Paul and his band resume private rehearsals, performing such tracks as 'Let 'Em In', 'Don't Get Around Much Anymore', 'Twenty Flight Rock', 'Lucille', 'C Moon' and 'P.S. Love Me Do'.

Friday March 2
Paul and his band continue with further private rehearsals, this time at the Tokyo Dome, a venue fondly referred to by Japanese people as Big Egg! During the afternoon sessions, Paul leads the musicians through a complete run-through of their concert repertoire.

Paul McCartney's World Tour

Fifth leg – Tokyo, Japan
Saturday March 3 – Tuesday March 13

The re-arranged tour, which kicks off on March 3, contains six nights at the Tokyo Dome: Saturday March 3, Monday March 5, Wednesday March 7, Friday March 9, Sunday March 11 and Tuesday March 13.

Saturday March 3 (until Tuesday March 13)
Songs from the performances on March 3 ('Coming Up'), March 5 ('Back In The USSR'), March 9 ('Ain't That A Shame') and March 13 ('Get Back') appear on *Tripping The Live Fantastic* album.

Sunday March 4
Taking advantage of a day off in their tour, Paul and Linda pay a visit to Meiji Jinguu.

Monday March 5
The performance of 'Let 'Em In' from tonight's show in Tokyo appears officially as a bonus track on the CD and 12-inch versions of the 'Birthday' single, released in the UK on October 8.

Wednesday March 7
Paul gives an interview to Naoto Kine for the Japanese AM radio programme *All Night Nippon,* aired by Ippon Houson. Joining Paul is his drummer Chris Witten. Later this evening, an interview with Paul is recorded backstage in the dressing room at the Tokyo Dome, an item that will be tagged onto the closed circuit concert transmission on Friday March 9.

Thursday March 8
Paul and Linda take advantage of another day off by visiting the tourist attraction Mount Fuji.

Friday March 9
The day begins with Paul and Linda visiting the Imperial Palace Garden, a site he last visited during The Beatles' tour to Tokyo in 1966. Then, at 3:00pm JST, the McCartneys attend the Masago Primary School for a planting ceremony, an event arranged by Tetsuo Hamada of the *Japanese Beatles Cine Club*. Later, as promised, tonight's show at the Tokyo Dome is transmitted live on closed circuit TV to 10 Japanese cities, all of which is a complete sell-out! The venues who receive the broadcast are: Kyousai Hall in Sappolo, Sendai Denryoku Hall in Sendai, Ceremony

Hall Niigata in Niigata, Aichi Kousei Nenkin Kaikan in Nagoya, Suita Mei Theatre in Osaka, Takamatsu Olive Hall in Takamatsu, Matsuyama City Sougou Community Center in Matsuyama, Hiroshima Mima Koudou in Hiroshima, Papyon 24 Gas Hall in Hakata and Melpark Hall Kumamoto in Kumamoto. At each of the venues, fans who were present at the screenings are handed a free Paul McCartney CD single. During the final three Tokyo concerts (March 9, 11 and 13), Paul and his band perform the new medley track 'P.S. Love Me Do', a video tape recording of which (from March 9) is included in the fund-raising memorial concert for John Lennon, held at the Pier Head in Liverpool on May 5 this year. Paul also donates £250,000 to the Sloane-Kettering Cancer Centre and Friends Of The Earth.

Monday March 12
During a day off from the Tokyo Dome concerts, Paul and his band record a promotional clip for 'We Got Married'. The mimed performance, captured on film by Propoganda Films, is inter-cut with other miscellanous footage (i.e. Paul arriving and fans waiting etc.) from the Japanese visit. (The clip is edited and prepared for TV distribution one week later on March 19.) With filming concluded, Paul, Linda and invited guests attend a party to celebrate the McCartneys 21st wedding anniversary.

During his stay in Japan, Paul gives a 45-minute appearance on the Japanese radio programme *Super DJ On Line*. Incidentally, to coincide with Paul's concerts at the Tokyo Dome, a special limited edition telephone picture card is released.

Wednesday March 14
At 1:40pm JST, Paul, Linda and the entourage leave Tokyo at New Tokyo International Airport, en route to England, before the next leg of their world tour commences in America on Thursday March 29.

* * *

Sixth leg – Return to America
Thursday March 29 – Sunday April 15

Paul, Linda and the band arrive back in America on March 28 to prepare for the next leg of their world tour. The concerts begin again the following night, with performances at the following venues:

Seattle's Kingdome (Thursday March 29)
Berkeley Memorial Stadium, University of California, Berkeley, near San Francisco
(Saturday March 31 and Sunday April 1)
Sun Devil Stadium, Arizona State University, Tempe, near Pheonix, Arizona
(Wednesday April 4)
Texas Stadium, Irving, near Dallas, Texas (Saturday April 7)
Rupp Arena, Lexington, Kentucky (Monday April 9)
Tampa Stadium, Tampa, Florida (Thursday April 12)
Joe Robbie Stadium, Miami, Florida (Saturday April 14 and Sunday April 15)

Saturday March 31
During the afternoon soundcheck in Berkeley, Paul and his band perform the track 'Satin Doll'.

Saturday April 7
Paul gives a 45-minute interview to the DJ "Red Beard" of the Dallas radio station KTXQ.

Saturday April 14
During the Miami press conference this afternoon at Joe Robbie Stadium, Paul gives an interview for the TV programme *The Mike Duccelli Show*. Later, 'Let It Be' from tonight's show in Miami, is released on the *Tripping The Live Fantastic* album.

* * *

Paul McCartney World Tour

Brazil – Friday April 20 & Saturday April 21 1990

The tour rolls on to Brazil, where Paul and his band perform two shows at the Maracana Stadium, in Rio De Janeiro. The first concert was pencilled in for the evening of April 19 but was cancelled due to heavy rain.

Friday April 20
The opening night sees Paul perform before an estimated crowd of 80,000.

Saturday April 21
The second night at the Maracana Stadium is certified by the Guinness Book Of Records as the "largest paying audience ever to see a rock concert by a single artist." (The crowd total is estimated at approximately 184,000, beating the previous record of 175,000 set by Frank Sinatra.) A crew from the Brazilian television station GLOBO TV captures tonight's concert by Paul on videotape. Eight numbers from the performance are transmitted on April 23 as a show entitled *Paul In Rio*. The performance of 'The Long And Winding Road' from this show is released on the *Tripping The Live Fantastic* album (released simultaneously worldwide on November 5, 1990). While 'P.S. Love Me Do' from tonight's show appears as a bonus track on 12-inch and CD versions of 'Birthday', released in the UK on October 8.

* * *

March
🍎 Paul's MPL *Put It There* documentary presentation is released in America on laser disc.

Saturday March 3
🍎 In response to the increasing number of Beatles bootleg recordings which have been appearing regularly on the worldwide collectors markets, the trade paper *Music Week* publishes a notice from EMI Records which warns the UK record retailers "to be suspicious of any post-June 1962 Beatles product offered to them for sale – irrespective of how legitimate the wholesaler might claim the works to be – by any other company other than EMI". The notice concludes with the warning: "EMI Records will take legal proceedings against any person who infringes their sound copyright recordings!"

Monday March 5
🍎 In the UK, the 20th anniversary run of Beatles single re-issues concludes with the release of 'Let It Be'/'You Know My Name (Look Up the Number)' as both a picture disc and a 7-inch vinyl in a picture sleeve.

Friday March 16
🍎 Yoko and Sean arrive at Heathrow Airport for a two-week stay in London, taking up residence at the Mayfair Hotel in Stratten Street.

Monday March 19
🍎 Yoko and Sean hold a photo shoot in London to promote her new exhibition, which opens in London on Wednesday.

Tuesday March 20
🍎 As a preview to Yoko's show *In Facing*, her first major London exhibition since 1967, Yoko and Sean attend a press conference which is part of an evening which runs between 6:00 and 8:00pm.

Wednesday March 21 (until Sunday April 22)
🍎 At the Riverside Studios in Crisp Road, Hammersmith, West London, a five-week exhibition of Yoko's artwork and films, entitled *In Facing*, opens to the public. The exhibition, which will be open from Tuesday to Saturday between the hours of 1:00 and 8:00pm, features a large selection of Yoko's conceptual canvas and aural work between

1961 and 1967. To accompany the display, a small portable audio tape machine plays Yoko's unreleased 1987 album *Georgia Stone*, a collection of tracks she recorded with John Cage. Yoko's show also features some of her selected avant-garde films, presented on the next five consecutive Saturdays. (See entry for March 24.)

Friday March 23
❦ Hamlyn Books issue in paperback, Mark Lewisohn's book *The Complete Beatles Recording Sessions*.

Saturday March 24
❦ The charity compilation album *The Last Temptation Of Elvis,* featuring Paul's cover of 'It's Now Or Never' is released through the UK music paper the *New Musical Express.* (The release appears in America as an import during April.)

❦ At 2pm, at the 300-seater Riverside Studios cinema in Hammersmith, Yoko takes part in an on-stage lecture, involving a question and answer session with the audience and the show's host, Sarah Kent. Later, Yoko remains in the cinema while the films *Rape, Freedom* and *Fly* are shown to the paying public.

Monday March 26
❦ The Traveling Wilburys, namely George, Jeff Lynne, Bob Dylan and Tom Petty, assemble in Los Angeles to begin writing new songs intended for their second album. These sessions will continue until late April, when the recording sessions for the album, again in LA, will begin.

❦ VCI in the UK releases on home video The Beatles' full-length films *Help!* and *Magical Mystery Tour.*

Wednesday March 28
❦ Lynne and Petty break off from writing the new Wilburys album to join Ringo, along with Joe Walsh and Jim Keltner to record, and film, a new version of the track 'I Call Your Name', intended to be screened during the May 5 John Lennon Scholarship Concert in Liverpool.

❦ In London, Yoko holds another press conference in which she announces plans for a John Lennon musical.

Saturday March 31
❦ Yoko's *In Facing* exhibition at the Riverside Studios in Hammersmith continues when *Two Virgins, Erection* and *Fly* are shown.

Sunday April 1
❦ John and Yoko's 1972 double album *Some Time In New York City* is released on CD in America.

Saturday April 7
❦ The Riverside exhibition of Yoko's avant-garde films continues when *The Museum Of Modern Art Show 1971, Rape* and *Smile (Film No. 5)* are shown.

Monday April 9
❦ In today's *Daily Mail,* Olivia Harrison, in her first interview in fifteen years, talks about the appeal, launched by herself, Yoko and Linda, to aid the desperate plight of Romania's orphaned and abandoned children. The article carries the headline: "Beatle Wives Unite To Aid Romania's Angels With Dirty Faces."

Thursday April 12
❦ The 1972 Apple film *The Concert For Bangla Desh* is re-released on Warner Brothers home video in the UK, at the sell-through budget price of £9.99.

❦ It is announced that asteroids 4147–4150, discovered in 1983 and 1984 by Brian A. Skiff and Dr. Edward Bowell of the Lowell observatories in Flagstaff, Arizona, have been renamed *Lennon, McCartney, Harrison & Starr* by the International Astronomical Union's Minor Planet Center in Cambridge, Massachusetts, USA.

Saturday April 14
🍎 The penultimate showing of Yoko's films in the exhibition at the Riverside Studios continues with a screening of a set of silent *Fluxus* films, which pre-date her meeting with John in 1966.

Sunday April 15
🍎 The BSB (British Satellite Broadcasting) music station *Power*, premieres the TV special, *Ringo Starr And His All-Starr Band Live,* featuring Ringo's concert in Los Angeles on September 3, 1989.

Monday April 16
🍎 Shortly after returning back to England, George records an appearance with ex-Traffic drummer Jim Capaldi for inclusion in Capaldi's promotional video for 'Oh Lord, Why Lord', a track on which George also provides backing vocals. (The track also appears on Capaldi's album *Some Come Running.* This clip is also screened at the Nelson Mandela tribute concert at Wembley Stadium, but does not feature during the telecasts of the show.)

Friday April 20
🍎 At BBC Broadcasting House in London, George and Olivia appear on Simon Bates' BBC Radio One programme. Shortly after, George flies back to California to re-join the Traveling Wilburys.

Saturday April 21
🍎 The final films of Yoko's exhibition at the Riverside Studios in Hammersmith, London, take place with screenings of *Ten For Two, Sisters O' Sisters, Apotheosis, Freedom, Fly* and *Up Your Legs Forever.*

Friday April 27 (until Tuesday May 15)
🍎 At a private home studio in Bel Air, California, The Traveling Wilburys reunite to record their second album, and decide to do so without a replacement for the late Roy Orbison. The first release from these sessions is the track 'Nobody's Child', a song not too unfamiliar to George, as The Beatles had backed Tony Sheridan on a recording of it in Hamburg, Germany, during June of 1961. (The Wilburys' version also appears on the compilation album *Nobody's Child Romanian Angel Appeal,* a charity release to help raise funds for the Romanian orphanages and hospitals, a scheme organised by George's wife, Olivia. The song is also released as a single.) The Traveling Wilburys' second album is eventually released as *Traveling Wilburys Volume 3*, in response to the bootleg album, featuring unreleased tracks and alternate versions, which sported the title *Traveling Wilburys Volume 2*. The album, *Volume 3*, is produced by George and Jeff Lynne, and does not contain any George Harrison solo tracks. The only submitted Harrison composition during the sessions, 'Maxine', is ultimately rejected. The Wilburys personnel also undergo name changes. Harrison and Lynne now use the new pseudonyms Spike and Clayton Wilbury while Petty and Dylan take the names Muddy and Boo Wilbury respectively.

May (until June)
🍎 During a break in his world tour, Paul begins working with Carl Davis at the Olympic Sound Studios in Barnes, South West London, on the composition of an *Oratorio*, based on his Liverpool childhood. (It will premiere in Liverpool on June 28, 1991, and be conducted by Davis.)

Tuesday May 1
🍎 George takes a break from Wilbury happenings to join Eric Clapton live on stage this evening at his LA concert. George plays guitar on the tracks 'Crossroads' and 'Sunshine Of Your Love', both of which were originally recorded in the Sixties by Cream, Clapton's former group.

Saturday May 5
🍎 A Yoko Ono arranged, fund-raising memorial concert for John Lennon, is held at the Pier Head, on the banks of the river Mersey in Liverpool. Proceeds from the show will

go to what Yoko calls the "Greening of the World John Lennon Scholarship Fund". Artists taking part include Al Green, The Christians, Joe Cocker, Lenny Kravitz, Kylie Minogue, Natalie Cole, Wet Wet Wet, The Moody Blues, Lou Reed, Terence Trent D'Arby, Randy Travis, Cyndi Lauper, Deacon Blue, Lou Gramm, Dave Stewart, Ray Charles, Dave Edmunds, Hall & Oates and Roberta Flack. The show also features contributions from two former Beatles, albeit by way of videotape inserts. Ringo contributes his new recording of 'I Call Your Name', recorded in Los Angeles on March 28, while Paul is seen performing 'P.S. Love Me Do', taped during one of his Tokyo shows in March. Spoken word messages from both ex-Beatles are also included in their videos. (Both videos feature in the American broadcast of the show on December 8.) Short archive clips of John are also featured in the presentation, such as *Not Only . . . But Also* (transmitted on BBC2 on January 9, 1965) and *Release* (BBC2 June 22, 1968). The performances are included in a TV special, which is aired live this evening, May 5, in the UK first across the ITV network and then later on Channel 4. (Highlights from the concert are also released on home videocassette in the UK on April 15, 1991.)

Monday May 7
 In Los Angeles, with Wilburys activities still on hold, George is seen by fans shopping for a camcorder.

Tuesday May 8
 The 55-minute programme entitled *The Beatles: Alone And Together*, featuring miscellaneous archive Beatles footage is released on home video in America.

Sunday May 13
 In the UK, Granada Television networks across the ITV regions (between 10:35 and 11:33pm) a recently produced drama documentary on Stuart Sutcliffe. The 48-minute programme, which was shot in black and white, is entitled *Stuart Sutcliffe – Midnight Angel.*

Thursday May 24 & Friday May 25
 In the UK, to coincide with tickets going on sale for his Liverpool concert on Thursday June 28, a two-part interview with Paul is featured on TV AM, where he talks about his upcoming concert performances in Glasgow and Liverpool.

Saturday May 26 & Sunday May 27
 In America, the Westwood One radio network syndicates the BBC Radio One series *The Beeb's Lost Beatles Tapes* during the Memorial Day weekend. The shows were originally broadcast in the UK during late 1988 as 14 x 30-minute programmes, but now, following extensive re-editing, these new shows are presented for broadcast in a single six-hour special, re-titled *The BBC's Beatles Tapes: The Original Masters.*
 In the UK, on May 26, BBC1 repeats the 1967 film *The Family Way*, which features Paul's music on the soundtrack.

June
 In the UK, the CD *Denny Laine Featuring Paul McCartney* (previously issued as Laine's *Japanese Tears*) is released.

Thursday June 7
 The first two *Thomas The Tank Engine And Friends* home videotapes, featuring narration by Ringo, are released in America.
 In the UK, the Handmade Films production of *Checking Out,* featuring a cameo appearance by George, is released on home video.

Saturday June 9
 An international music festival called Muzeko '90, dedicated to the memory and music of John Lennon, takes place in Donetsk, Russia.

Monday June 11
 Animation City in London prepares for release the Traveling Wilburys video for 'Nobody's Child'. Derek Hayes directs the clip.

Wednesday June 13

In the Radio One headquarters in Langham Street, adjacent to the BBC Broadcasting House studios in Portland Place, London, Paul appears completely unannounced, live on the BBC Radio One programme *The Steve Wright Show*. During his surprise appearance, besides being interviewed, he takes questions over the phone, participates in the traditional disc-jockey routines of reading the weather and traffic reports and even performs short spontaneous acoustic versions of 'Matchbox' and 'Blackbird'. During the spot, host Steve Wright plays Paul's live Tokyo (March 1990) recording of the medley 'P.S. Love Me Do'. In order to perform on the show, Paul broke from work on the *Tripping The Live Fantastic* album, which is currently being mixed at George Martin's AIR Studios near Oxford Circus, close to the BBC.

Thursday June 14

Ringo and his All-Starr Band's special one-off concert at Le Zenith Indoor Arena in Paris, France, does not take place.

Monday June 18

In the UK, The Traveling Wilburys' single 'Nobody's Child' is released, backed with 'Lumiere', performed by Dave Stewart. The twelve-inch and CD versions of the single add Ringo's September 4, 1989, live version of 'With A Little Help From My Friends' at the Greek Theater in Los Angeles, California.

Tuesday June 19 & Wednesday June 20

Paul and his band rehearse at his home studios in East Sussex.

On June 20, George appears on the BBC Radio One programme *The Simon Bates Show*. Whilst at the BBC Broadcasting House studios in Portland Place, London, George and his wife, Olivia, tape an interview for inclusion in the one-hour Radio One documentary on the Romanian Appeal, entitled *Nobody's Child,* which is broadcast on BBC Radio One on August 1.

Also on June 20, Ringo's wife Barbara Bach becomes the latest in a long line of Beatles-related celebrities to appear on the BBC1 talk show *Wogan*, hosted by Terry Wogan. During her short interview, which is transmitted from the BBC TV Centre, Wood Lane, London, she talks about alcoholism.

Thursday June 21

Paul moves rehearsals with his band to Glasgow in order to prepare for their concert at the Scottish Exhibition & Conference Centre on June 23.

In the States, Ringo records an interview with the music station VH–1. During the latter half of the interview, he is joined by the guitarist Joe Walsh.

Friday June 22

George and Olivia Harrison's 15-minute appearance on *Wogan*, recorded at the BBC TV Centre, Wood Lane, London, on Wednesday June 20, is transmitted tonight on BBC1. During their interview they talk about the *Romanian Angel Appeal* and the *Nobody's Child* album, and the video for 'Nobody's Child' is shown.

* * *

Paul McCartney World Tour

Return to the UK
Saturday June 23 – Saturday June 30

Following the success of his American tour, Paul returns to the UK to play three more dates, including an emotional homecoming concert in Liverpool. The first shows take place at:

Scottish Exhibition & Conference Centre, Glasgow (Saturday June 23)
King's Dock, Liverpool (Thursday June 28)
Music Therapy Concert, Knebworth Park, Knebworth, Hertfordshire (Saturday June 30)

Saturday June 23
In front of a massive crowd gathered in the outdoor car park, Paul performs 'Mull Of Kintyre' during tonight's Get Back To Glasgow show in Glasgow, the only time this song is played during the entire world tour. This version will be officially released as a bonus track on the initial 'All My Trials' 12-inch and CD versions of the single, released on November 26. The 24-minute Granada TV/MPL documentary about Paul, entitled *Paul McCartney: Now*, is also transmitted on certain ITV regions today. The programme, which serves as a preview for the show in Liverpool on June 28, features interviews and concert footage from Paul's recent American concerts. A pre-recorded interview with Paul is also broadcast today on BBC Radio Merseyside.

Monday June 25 & Tuesday June 26
During a short break between shows, Paul, Linda and his band attend filming sessions at Twickenham Studios in Middlesex, near London.

Thursday June 28
Following his arrival at the concert site at 2:30pm, Paul's historic homecoming begins with a 5:30pm press conference, later shared with Beatles' producer George Martin, during which Paul talks about his "surprise tribute to John during tonight's show", the performing arts school, Yoko's tribute concert, the *Get Back* film and, amongst other items, Friends Of The Earth. Then later, during the concert at the King's Dock in Liverpool, which is billed as Let It Be – Liverpool, he gives the first-ever public performance of his "surprise", a "John Lennon medley" comprising 'Strawberry Fields Forever', 'Help!' and 'Give Peace A Chance'. This will be the first time ever that Paul has performed a solo John Lennon composition in public. Around 75 minutes of the concert, performed in front of 50,000 fans, is transmitted on BBC Radio One on October 27 and naturally features prominently in the MPL documentary *From Rio To Liverpool*, transmitted in the UK on Channel 4 on December 17. (The show, featuring an alternative title of *Paul McCartney – Going Home*, is aired in America on the Disney Channel on October 1991.) Media interest in this historic event looms large on the UK, and indeed worldwide, newscasts on the day. To help promote the show, if this was ever needed, Paul appears in an interview on TV AM this morning. (Paul's 'Lennon Medley' will also appear officially on the second 'All My Trials' CD single.) Following the hugely successful show, Paul and Linda host a reception for 150 guests backstage at the concert arena.

Friday June 29
Paul and his band appear on the site of the Knebworth Festival to check out the surroundings and participate in an early soundcheck performance.

Saturday June 30
At the Knebworth Festival, in front of a sell-out 120,000 spectators, Paul performs an edited 45-minute concert, in aid of the Nordoff-Robbins Music Therapy Centre and the British Recording Industry Trust School for the Performing Arts. A selection of songs from the concert ('Coming Up' and 'Hey Jude') appears on the *Knebworth: The Album* compilation, released on August 6 in both America and the UK. The soundtrack from the show is simultaneously transmitted live in both America and on BBC Radio One in the UK. Footage from the concert is aired in America on MTV on July 14 and in the UK on an ITV Network special on August 6. The performance of 'Birthday' appears officially on the *Tripping The Live Fantastic* album, and is released as a cassette single in both America (on October 16) and the UK (on October 8), which also features a live version of 'Good Day Sunshine' from the Knebworth concert.

Monday July 2
On the day that Paul, Linda and the band fly out to Washington to resume their world tour, Channel 4 in the UK screens the 1987 Comic Strip film *Eat The Rich*, which features a cameo appearance by Mr and Mrs McCartney.

*   *   *

Paul McCartney World Tour

Final leg – Return to America
Wednesday July 4 – Sunday July 29, 1990

Paul's ten-month world tour concludes with a return visit to America, which includes concerts at the following venues:

> Robert F. Kennedy Stadium, Washington, D.C. (Wednesday July 4 and Friday July 6)
> Giants Stadium, East Rutherford, New Jersey (Monday July 9 and Wednesday July 11)
> Veterans Stadium, Philadelphia, Pennsylvania (Saturday July 14 and Sunday July 15)
> University of Iowa Stadium, Aimes, Iowa (Wednesday July 18)
> Cleveland Municipal Stadium, Cleveland, Ohio (Friday July 20)
> Carter-Finley Stadium, Raleigh, North Carolina (Sunday July 22)
> Sullivan Stadium, Foxboro, near Boston, Massachusetts (Tuesday July 24 and Thursday July 26)
> Soldier Field, Chicago (Sunday July 29)

Wednesday July 4
At Paul's show today in Washington, in front of a capacity 56,000 audience, Paul replaces the 'Lennon Medley' with a performance of 'Birthday', in honour of the nation's 214th birthday.

Sunday July 8
A planned concert this evening at New York's famed Shea Stadium fails to materialise. At one time, this concert was planned to be screened as a pay-per-view event across America.

Tuesday July 24
Backstage at Sullivan Stadium, Paul is interviewed by the radio station WBCN in Boston.

Wednesday July 25
In Foxboro, Massachusetts, Paul and his band take a break from the tour to shoot additional live scenes for the concert movie *Get Back*. To help the technicians, the group, in front of an invited audience of 800, lip-synch to a recording of the previous day's concert.

Sunday July 29
The final show of the tour (concert number 102 in 45 weeks in 46 cities) takes place at Soldier Field in Chicago before an excited crowd of 53,000 fans. The press conference before the show is covered by a number of TV stations, including MTV. The planned concert today at the Yale Bowl, New Haven, was cancelled by MPL on May 24 following local hostility to the event that continued despite a 19–6 vote by the city's board insisting that it should take place.

*   *   *

Saturday June 30
🍎 In America, a 90-minute laser disc version of *Ringo Starr And His All-Starr Band*, videotaped at Ringo's September 3, 1989, show in Los Angeles, is released. (This version is released on home video in America on January 29, 1991, but UK Beatles fans only receive the 60-minute version, which is released officially on July 16. The edited version omits only one Ringo track namely 'You're Sixteen'.)

July
🍎 Rickenbacker Guitars announce they will be issuing a special *John Lennon* signature electric guitar range in America.
🍎 Still Stateside, Linda appears on the Cleveland, Ohio television programme *The Morning Exchange*, where she talks about her childhood, animals, her family, touring with Paul, and also promotes her vegetarian cookbook.

Monday July 2
🍎 Channel 4 in the UK screens the 1987 Comic Strip film *Eat The Rich*, which features a cameo appearance by Paul and Linda.

Monday July 9
🍎 The home video of the 1985 American TV documentary *Yoko Ono: Then And Now* is re-released in the UK.

Sunday July 15
🍎 The Swedish radio station Channel 3 broadcasts a special programme to celebrate Ringo's 50th birthday. The 60-minute show also includes an exclusive telephone interview with The Beatles' former drummer, carried out in Monte Carlo on June 5 by the longtime Swedish Beatles fan Staffan Olander.

Monday July 16
🍎 Another Beatles-related home video is released in the UK. This time, the American 1985 made-for-TV 2-part film *Alice In Wonderland*, featuring Ringo in a cameo role as the Mock Turtle, which is issued by Warner Brothers.

Wednesday July 18
🍎 George and Olivia, who are joined by Ringo and Barbara, attend a party at the Hyde Park Hotel in London. This all-ticket affair is part of a luncheon arranged to launch the *Romanian Angel* album.

Monday July 23
🍎 The album *Nobody's Child: Romanian Angel Appeal,* is released in the UK featuring tracks by George and Ringo, amongst others. (The album is released in America the following day, Tuesday July 24.)

August
🍎 During the month, Video Collection International releases the compilation video *Thomas The Tank Engine And Friends*, combining the previously released cassettes, featuring 17 stories narrated by Ringo.

Wednesday August 1
🍎 A pre-taped interview with George back in June 20, during which he discusses the recent release of *Nobody's Child: Romanian Angel Appeal,* is broadcast on BBC Radio One in the UK as part of a one hour documentary on the subject.

Monday August 6
🍎 *Knebworth: The Album*, featuring two of Paul's live tracks from the June 30, 1990, concert, is simultaneously released in both America and the UK.

Friday August 10
🍎 *The Beatles Revolution*, London's first permanent exhibition centre dedicated to the fab four, opens at the Trocadero shopping plaza on Piccadilly Circus, London. The showcase opens from 10am to 7pm, seven days a week.

Monday August 13
🍎 In the UK, Warner Home Video releases the bizarre 1975 film *Lisztomania*, featuring Ringo cast in the role of the Pope.

Saturday August 25
🍎 Paul and Linda host a 21st birthday party for their daughter Mary in a marquee in the grounds of their farm near Rye in Sussex. It is a fancy dress affair, with Mary arriving as Cleopatra, and Paul and Linda dressed in Chinese outfits. George Martin comes as Sir Thomas More. Music is provided by the soul band Soul Provider.

Tuesday August 28
🍎 Three weeks after the album comes *Knebworth: The Event* (Volume One), the UK home video of the concert, featuring the same four McCartney numbers, 'Coming Up',

'Birthday', 'Hey Jude' and 'Can't Buy Me Love', which appeared on the television specials of the June 30 event.

Saturday September 1
🍎 Paul and Linda arrive in New York to begin preparations for the Annual Buddy Holly bash, celebrated for the first time in New York to coincide with the November 4 launch of the Broadway musical *Buddy*.

Tuesday September 4
🍎 In New York at the Lone Star Roadhouse during the 15th annual Buddy Holly birthday celebrations, Paul jumps on stage to perform with the band, albeit briefly, the songs 'Oh Boy', 'Rave On' and 'Lucille'. Backing Paul during his live appearance are Dave Edmunds, Max Weinberg, The Crickets and many others. (The event is captured on a single camera videotape by MTV.)

Monday September 10
🍎 In the UK, the home videotapes of *Thomas The Tank Engine And Friends* are issued as part of the *Watch & Play* children's series.

Thursday September 27
🍎 The US release takes place today of two further *Thomas The Tank Engine And Friends* videocassettes, namely *Thomas And Turntables & Other Stories* and *Thomas Breaks The Rules & Other Stories*.

October
🍎 The production *My Love Is Bigger Than A Cadillac,* a new film about Buddy Holly's backing group The Crickets, including a brief appearance by Paul, is released in the UK on home video. The programme was premiered on American TV, in two parts, on August 5 and 11.

Wednesday October 3
🍎 In America, the television programme *Evening Magazine* features a report on the *Romanian Angel* appeal.

Friday October 5
🍎 A pre-recorded interview with Yoko, recorded during her brief visit to London, is broadcast on tonight's edition of the Channel 4 music series *The Word*.

Saturday October 6
🍎 In the UK, BBC Radio One begins broadcasting (between 2:00 and 2:59pm) the series *In My Life: Lennon Remembered,* a series of 10 one-hour programmes about John that feature more than 20 new interviews taped with Paul, Yoko and many other acquaintances who had either worked with, or knew, John. (Repeats of each episode, which tell the story of John's music through archive interviews and his music, are transmitted the following Tuesday on the station between 9:00 and 9:59pm.) A BBC book of the series naturally soon follows.

Monday October 8
🍎 Paul's single 'Birthday'/'Good Day Sunshine' is released in the UK in several formats. (The American release takes place on Tuesday October 16 but only as a cassette.)
🍎 The UK release takes place of the *Ringo Starr And His All-Starr Band* live concert on CD, taken from the Los Angeles shows on September 3 and 4, 1989. A bonus CD single is released with the deluxe CD version released in America on October 12 but is not issued in the UK.

Tuesday October 9
🍎 On what would have been John's 50th birthday, a special broadcast of John's 1971 recording of 'Imagine' is broadcast simultaneously by approximately 1,000 radio stations in 50 countries (or nearer to 130 according to other sources) around the world. The broadcast, which features an introduction by Marcela Perez de Cuellar, the wife of the UN secretary-general, originates from the Trusteeship Council Chamber at the United

Nations building in New York City, and also includes an excerpt from an archive John Lennon interview. To aid in this global event, special pre-recorded versions are also broadcast in both Spanish and French. Yoko says: "I wanted to provide a way for John's fans to do something together, but, at the same time, I wanted it to be original and simple."

Wednesday October 10
 In the UK, at the Salford College of Technology, George Martin presents the John Lennon Songwriting Awards to three lucky students.

Thursday October 11
 To promote their forthcoming march to save the Rye Memorial Hospital this Monday, Paul and Linda are seen distributing leaflets in their hometown centre of Rye in East Sussex.

Monday October 15
 At 12 noon, at Rye Town Hall in Sussex, Paul, Linda and a host of their friends, spearhead a campaign to save Rye Memorial Hospital by leading a march from the Town Hall to the hospital. The event is suitably called *Rye's Day Of Action*. (The demonstration naturally features on the UK TV news bulletins later this evening.) Paul has even offered to pay wages to the nurses who are willing to work in the casualty department, which has been closed since August due to the staff shortages.

Thursday October 25
 In the UK, BBC Radio One transmits a 40-minute special to celebrate the imminent release of the Traveling Wilburys' new album, which is issued in the UK next Monday.

Friday October 26
 Paul appears again on the Los Angeles radio programme *Rockline*, where he is interviewed, and performs an acoustic version of 'Matchbox'. While Paul is chatting, and singing inside, Linda is being photographed, waiting for Paul, outside the building. (Incidentally, Paul's appearance on the show reappears in America as part of the Global Satellite Network's pre-show broadcast for the FM Radio simulcast of MTV's *Unplugged* on April 3, 1991.)

Monday October 29
 The Traveling Wilburys' second album, cryptically called *Volume 3*, is released in the UK with an American release taking place the following day, Tuesday October 30.
 Still in the UK, BBC Radio One begins broadcasting a five-part pre-recorded interview with Paul. Each segment is transmitted daily, with the final part being broadcast on Friday November 2. While in the States, a radio special entitled *Paul – In The Studio*, focusing on his *Flowers In The Dirt* album and the 1989/1990 World Tour, is syndicated across America.
 The case between The Beatles' Apple Corps and the computer company Apple Macintosh reaches the High Court in London. Paul, George, Ringo and Yoko claim that Apple Macintosh have breached a 1981 agreement over use of the Apple logo and their music recording equipment. (The case is expected to last 12 weeks.)

Tuesday October 30
 After a four week delay, the John Lennon four CD boxed set, entitled simply *Lennon*, is released in the UK and features the first release on CD of many Lennon tracks. The set, comprising tracks taken from every one of his albums from *Live Peace In Toronto* in 1969, to *Milk And Honey* in 1984, is compiled to celebrate what would have been his 50th birthday. (The official American release of these 73 tracks does not take place until July 1991.)

November (into December)
 During the month at his home studios in Sussex, Paul begins recording the first demos in preparation for a new studio album. Towards the end of the month, and into December, Paul is joined at the sessions by Elvis Costello. Paul's task now is to start recording tracks properly for his next album, scheduled for release during April 1991.

 In New York during November, the case against George over his conviction for plagiarism of 'He's So Fine' on his 1970 recording of 'My Sweet Lord', is finally settled. In the US Federal Court, Judge Richard Owen rules that George will own the rights to both songs in the US, the UK and in Canada. ABKCO, Allen Klein's company, will own the rights to the song outside of those countries. George will also continue to own 'My Sweet Lord', but ABKCO will continue to receive a percentage from the song's royalties. George is also ordered to pay ABKCO a reputed net sum totalling $270,020.

Sunday November 4
 The New York premiere takes place of the Broadway musical *Buddy* with Paul and Linda naturally in attendance. The McCartneys return to England on Tuesday November 6.

Monday November 5
 The simultaneous US and UK release takes place of Paul's live concert compilation album *Tripping The Live Fantastic*.
 Also in the UK, The Traveling Wilburys' single 'She's My Baby'/'New Blue Moon' is released in the UK on a 12-inch single and a CD, which adds the bonus track 'Runaway'.

Wednesday November 7 (until Monday November 19)
 At the Cliphouse Studios in London, three artists work around the clock to complete a promotional video for Paul's track 'Party, Party'. The animation sessions, in which they are assigned to draw approximately 4,500 images, last for 12 days with the amount of man-hours labour totalling over 600 hours! Sadly, this MPL produced video is never screened on any TV station around the world in its entirety. As for the song itself, it appears only as a bonus single to be found within the *Flowers In The Dirt* limited edition world tour and as a part of an also limited edition double CD pack in Japan.

Sunday November 11
 George appears in a pre-recorded interview with Gloria Hunniford on her London Weekend Television/ITV network teatime show *Sunday Sunday*, where he promotes the new album by The Traveling Wilburys.

Monday November 12
 In the UK, BBC tapes release *John And Yoko – The Interview*, comprising excerpts from the interview with the Lennons carried out by Andy Peebles in New York on December 6, 1980.
 In the States, a pre-taped interview with Paul is aired on the programme *MTV Prime*.

Sunday November 18
 In America, Paul's original birth certificate sells for $18,000 at an auction in Houston, Texas.

Monday November 19
 Simultaneous release in both America and the UK takes place of the CD *Tripping The Live Fantastic . . . Highlights!*, which is an edited 17-track version of the tour album, which contains a different track line-up for each country. The UK edition features 'All My Trials', a track missing from the American version, which instead replaces the song 'Put It There'. (Incidentally, during the spring of 1991, the Columbia House Record Club in America releases a 12-track vinyl album entitled *Highlights*, which contains the only US release of the track 'All My Trials'.)

Sunday November 25
 In Los Angeles, Paul appears on the American version of the long running series *Desert Island Discs*. Paul recorded an appearance on the original BBC series on January 20, 1982 (see entry).

Monday November 26
 Radio spots continue when Paul appears in a special two-hour syndicated transmission of the American KLOS-FM Los Angeles radio show *Rockline*. Also today, Paul's single

'All My Trials'/'C Moon' is released in the UK in several formats. The twelve-inch and CD versions of the single add the tracks 'Mull Of Kintyre' and 'Put It There'.

Wednesday November 28
🍎 Paul appears live and answers questions during a one-hour Pan-European phone-in radio show, transmitted by 17 UK ILR (Independent Local Radio) stations as well as via outlets in 16 other countries.

Saturday December 1
🍎 Paul's album *Tripping The Live Fantastic* reaches number 26 in the American charts.

Monday December 3
🍎 The film *John And Yoko: The Bed-In,* the Lennons' self-produced film of their May/June 1969 Montreal bed-in, is released in the UK on PMI home video. It will appear later on laser disc in both the UK and in Japan. (This candid documentary will appear in America, on both home video and laser disc, sporting the alternative title of *All We Are Saying Is Give Peace A Chance.*) Amongst the most memorable items in this fascinating 60-minute documentary is John's celebrated acrimonious confrontation with the American cartoonist Al Capp.

🍎 In the UK, a second edition of Paul's CD single 'All My Trials'/'C Moon' is released, replacing the two bonus tracks with the 'Lennon Medley'. To coincide with its release, a pre-taped interview with Paul is aired on BBC Radio One's *Simon Bates Show.*

Tuesday December 4
🍎 John is the featured star of this week's edition of the BBC Radio Five show *Cult Heroes.* The programme, episode seven in a series of ten, is transmitted between 8:01 and 8:29pm.

Wednesday December 5
🍎 In the UK, a pre-taped interview with George, where he again talks about the Traveling Wilburys, is broadcast on the BBC2 version of the French television programme *Rapido.* (A further BBC2 screening of the programme takes place on Monday December 10.)

Saturday December 8
🍎 The May 5 Liverpool Lennon benefit concert is repeated in the UK on Channel 4 and syndicated throughout America. The broadcast includes video clips screened during the event, including Paul performing 'P.S. Love Me Do' in Tokyo, Japan, and Ringo, who sings a new recording of 'I Call Your Name'.

Sunday December 9
🍎 BBC2 in the UK, transmits a repeat screening of John's January 9, 1965, appearance on *Not Only . . . But Also,* starring Peter Cook and Dudley Moore. The clip is a part of the final show in this compilation series, re-titled *The Best Of . . . What's Left Of . . . Not Only . . . But Also.* This is a reference to the fact that the BBC has failed to preserve many of the shows from this historical Sixties comedy series. The transmission of this programme, as well as yesterday's Lennon tribute concert on Channel 4, is scheduled to take place near the 10th anniversary of John's death.

Monday December 10
🍎 In America, during the 1990 *Billboard* Awards, Paul receives the award for the highest grossing concert act in America during the year. The Fox Network broadcasts a special programme of the event throughout the US. Paul appears by way of a pre-recorded message, which also includes a live concert video clip for 'Sgt. Pepper's Lonely Hearts Club Band'. (The complete show receives a UK screening across the ITV network on Sunday December 30.)

Wednesday December 12
🍎 At Ronnie Scott's nightclub in London this afternoon, Paul receives the Merit Award from *Q* Magazine, in honour of his "outstanding and continued contribution to the music

industry". On BBC2, in the UK this morning, Paul's recent appearance on the US TV show *After Hours* is transmitted.

Thursday December 13

♪ In a session that was scheduled to start at 12pm but did not actually begin until approximately 4pm, Paul and his band, before a live studio audience comprising members of the Wings Fun Club, videotape various European and Japanese television appearances at the Limehouse TV studios, situated at 128 Wembley Park Drive, in Wembley, Middlesex. Their mimed performances (different versions for each country), includes the tracks 'Let It Be', 'The Long And Winding Road' and 'All My Trials', and will appear in Holland on December 18 during the NED 2 TV programme *Countdown* where he is also interviewed by Jerone Van Inkel, on December 22 in Italy on the RAI UNO television programme *Fantastico*, and in Denmark and on TVE in Spain on December 26 where it appears during the television programme *Rockopop*. One further screening takes place on Sunday January 20, 1991, on the Japanese television programme *Beat UK*. For this lengthy, overtly tiresome, five-hour session, Paul returned to the Limehouse Studios for the first time in over two decades. As a member of The Beatles, Paul had visited these premises back in the Sixties to record appearances for the legendary pop music series *Ready Steady Go!* Incidentally, by the time of this performance, drummer Chris Witten had left to join the group Dire Straits, to be replaced by Blair Cunningham, formerly with Haircut 100 and The Pretenders, which also once included Robbie McIntosh, Paul's current guitarist.

Friday December 14

♪ Paul and Linda return again to the BBC Television Centre in Wood Lane, London, where they make another guest appearance on the BBC1 chat show *Wogan*, hosted by Terry Wogan. For tonight's slot, Paul and his band mime a version of 'All My Trials'. During his time at the BBC today, Paul also records an interview for inclusion in the Saturday morning children's show *Going Live!*, which is transmitted, along with the 'All My Trials' promotional film, on Saturday December 22. In America, a pre-taped interview with Paul by Kurt Loder for the programme *Famous Last Words* is transmitted on MTV today. While in the UK newspaper the *Independent*, reports reveal that Paul has resumed writing with Elvis Costello and that three new McCartney/MacManus compositions were written this week.

Saturday December 15

♪ A special limited edition version of *Tripping The Live Fantastic* reaches number 157 in the American album charts.

Monday December 17

♪ Channel 4 in the UK broadcasts the 50-minute MPL documentary *From Rio To Liverpool*. (The American transmission takes place on The Disney Channel on October 13, 1991, where it's retitled *Paul McCartney: Going Home*. Further screenings of the programme take place on the channel on October 19, 25 and 30.) The programme, besides various interviews, also features live concert footage from the concerts in Rio, Philadelphia, Glasgow and, of course, the triumphant homecoming to Liverpool.

Friday December 21 & Saturday December 22

♪ Two John Lennon tribute concerts take place at the Tokyo Dome in Japan. Artists performing include Miles Davis, Natalie Cole and Toshionbu Kubota, Linda Rondstadt, Daryl Hall & John Oates and Sean Lennon, who performs a version of 'You've Got To Hide Your Love Away'.

Wednesday December 26

♪ MTV in America broadcast the world premiere clip of Paul's concert tour promotional video for 'Sgt. Pepper's Lonely Hearts Club Band'. (Note: This clip is a slightly different version to the one aired during the 1990 Billboard Music Awards presentation, first broadcast in America on December 10.)

December

 Paul's exciting year ends on another high point, when the American magazine *Amusement Business,* publishes a year-end survey revealing that his concert shows rate in the top-grossing bookings of the year, specifically the $3,550,560 grossed for two sell-out shows at the University of California, Berkeley on March 31 and April 1. Paul also appears at numbers 3, 6, 10, 11 and 12 in the ratings, with the shows at East Rutherford, (July 9 and 11), Philadelphia (July 14 and 15), Miami, Florida (April 14 and 15), Washington, DC (July 4 and 6) and Foxboro (on July 24 and 26).

"The Beatles don't exist, especially now as John Lennon isn't alive. The story comes around every time that Paul needs some publicity."

– *George*

January

☘ Over two years after the filming, Ringo finally narrates the film *Walking After Midnight*. A companion book is published that includes George's story behind his song 'The Art Of Dying', extracted from his 1980 publication *I Me Mine*. Ringo writes the preface to the book, which also features photos of him.

☘ Cynthia Lennon releases a limited edition reproduction set of John's 1968 cartoons on *Apple* headed notepaper.

Friday January 4

☘ Due to the outbreak of the Gulf War, Yoko, Sean and Lenny Kravitz update John's 1969 anthem 'Give Peace A Chance' with twenty other top pop personalities of the day. (It is released on January 15 and is credited to the *Peace Choir*.)

Saturday January 19

☘ In the States, a pre-taped interview with George is featured on the MTV programme *Week In Rock,* in which he talks about the war in the Middle East. The six-minute feature also includes a report on the new *Give Peace A Chance* promotional film.

Friday January 25

☘ At 6:30pm, at the Limehouse Studios, situated at 128 Wembley Park Drive, Wembley, Middlesex, Paul and his band perform live before a specially invited audience of around 200 for a videotaping of a programme in the MTV series *Unplugged*. For the show, Paul and his group perform in three separate sets: 'Mean Woman Blues', 'Matchbox', 'Midnight Special', 'I Lost My Little Girl', 'Here, There And Everywhere', 'San Francisco Bay Blues', 'We Can Work It Out' (in all attempted four times), 'Blue Moon Of Kentucky', 'I've Just Seen A Face', 'Every Night', 'Be-Bop-A-Lu-La', 'She's A Woman', 'And I Love Her', 'The Fool', 'Things We Said Today', 'That Would Be Something', 'Blackbird', 'Hi-Heel Sneakers', 'Good Rockin' Tonight' and 'Junk'. At this point, Paul switches to the drums for 'Ain't No Sunshine', featuring a lead vocal from Hamish Stuart, after which, the musicians return to how they were before for another stab at 'We Can Work It Out' and, to close the show, 'Singing The Blues'.

The 51-minute *Unplugged* programme premieres on MTV in America on April 3, with simultaneous FM stereo transmissions, networked to participating radio stations by the Global Satellite Network. The broadcast is preceded by a 15-minute radio interview with Paul in which he discusses how he came to choose some of the songs appearing on the show. (The TV programme only is repeated on MTV in America on April 7.) The first MTV Europe broadcast occurs on May 13. In the UK, on terrestrial television, the first screening takes place on the ITV channel TSW, serving the South West of England, on June 10, with a further airing, this time to a much wider audience, on Channel 4, on August 26, delayed for a week from its original August 18 scheduled airing. Incidentally, the TSW airing is hastily screened on this date to correspond with Paul's *Unplugged* gig in Cornwall, in the South West of England, which had taken place three days previously on June 7. A further scenario takes place in Denmark when, on the eve of Paul's secret concert at the Falkoner Theatre in Copenhagen, the MTV *Unplugged* show is transmitted on national Danish television on July 23.

The songs 'Here, There And Everywhere', 'And I Love Her', 'That Would Be Something', 'Junk' (instrumental) and 'I Lost My Little Girl' are sang here for the first time in public. The latter is a song that Paul wrote when he was 14 years old. 'Blue Moon Of Kentucky' is performed in both slow and fast versions. 'We Can Work It Out' is repeated, complete with false starts, when Paul forgot the lyrics. Much of the performance appears later on the album *Unplugged (The Official Bootleg)*, released in the UK on May 20 and in America on June 4 which adds the following tracks not included in the TV transmission: 'San Francisco Bay Blues', 'Hi-Heel Sneakers' and 'Ain't No Sunshine'. Although the songs 'Mean Woman Blues', 'Matchbox', 'Midnight Special', 'The Fool' and 'Things We Said Today' will remain unscreened, audio from some of these tracks will appear on singles such as the promotional CD 'Biker Like An Icon'. 'Midnight Special' and 'Things We Said Today' will appear officially in Holland on November 8, 1993, as part of a CD with 'Biker Like An Icon' (live and studio versions). (Only 'Matchbox' and 'The Fool' remain unissued in any form.)

Monday January 28

🎸 Paul is featured on *The Live Show*, syndicated in America by Radio Today, and featuring Paul's 'John Lennon Medley'. Also today, a pre-taped short interview with Paul, in which he talks about going back out on the road in 1992, is featured in the US TV programme *Pan E! Vision*.

🎸 The BBC in England announces that it is refusing to play the new version of 'Give Peace A Chance' by the Peace Choir. It claims this is down to their new policy of not playing anti-war material.

February

🎸 At the end of the month, Ringo plays drums in the Nils Lofgren promotional video for the song 'Valentine', a track featured on Lofgren's new *Silver Lining* album. The clip also features the direction of Zack Snyder and a cameo appearance by Bruce Springsteen.

Sunday February 17

🎸 George, accompanied by Rolling Stone Ronnie Wood, attends Bob Dylan's concert at the Hammersmith Odeon in London, where he presents Dylan with a bunch of flowers but declines to perform. George is reportedly seen in the audience during all eight of Dylan's concerts at this London venue.

Wednesday February 20

🎸 At the annual Grammy Awards ceremony, held at the Radio City Music Hall in New York City, John posthumously receives the Lifetime Achievement Award. (Paul received the same accolade one year previously on February 21, 1990.)

March

🎸 During a meeting of the National Association of Record Merchandisers in San Francisco, Ringo, by way of a pre-recorded videotaped message, announces that he has just signed a new recording contract with the label Private Music. During the month in California, recording commences on his *Time Takes Time* album, featuring production work by Jeff Lynne, Phil Ramone, Don Was and Peter Asher. Tracks recorded include: 'Don't Know A Thing About Love', 'I Don't Believe In You', 'Runaways', 'After All These Years', 'In A Heartbeat', 'Don't Go Where The Road Don' Go', 'Golden Blunders', 'All In The Name Of Love', 'What Goes Around', 'Don't Be Cruel' and 'Everybody Wins'. In addition, Ringo records the McCartney song 'Angel In Disguise', 'Thank You For Being A Friend' and the Jeff Lynne produced track 'Call Me'. (The sessions will continue, periodically until September this year, with the album being concluded during February of 1992 when the track 'Weight Of The World' is recorded.)

🎸 The 1972 Apple film *Born To Boogie* starring Marc Bolan & T.Rex and featuring cameo appearances by Ringo, is released in the UK on PMI home video.

Sunday March 3

🎸 In the UK, George makes another concert appearance, this time at 11:30pm during the two-day annual George Formby fan convention, held at the Winter Gardens in Blackpool. His introduction is as follows:

MC: "After some persuasion, I'd like to introduce Mr. George Harrison, who says he's nervous."

Bounding on stage, George announces to the fellow Formby worshippers: "I thought I'd retired from all this years ago. You'll have to bear with me as I'm not certain I know the right chords, but you're all welcome to join in."

Then, armed with a ukulele, he happily sings the Formby song 'In My Little Snapshot Album' and reappears to participate in a close of the evening finale. Accompanying George tonight is Olivia, Dhani, Derek Taylor, his wife Joan, and Brian Roylance of Genesis Publications. During the convention, George records an interview for BBC Radio for inclusion in their 58-minute George Formby tribute programme *The Emperor Of Lancashire*, which is first transmitted on May 26 and repeated on April 21, 1992.

Monday March 4

🎸 Ringo's 1973 self-titled album *Ringo* is released in the UK on CD. (The American release takes place on May 6.)

Thursday March 7
 In the States, Paul is named Best Bassist in the annual *Rolling Stone* reader's poll.

Monday March 25
 The simultaneous UK and US release takes place of The Traveling Wilburys' single 'Wilbury Twist'/'New Blue Moon' (instrumental). The American release takes the shape of a cassette only. Various formats take place in the UK, some adding the track 'Cool Dry Place'.

Tuesday March 26
 Ringo's 1978 *Bad Boy* album is released in America on CD.

Thursday March 28
 In Surrey, George attends the funeral of Eric Clapton's son Conor, who had been tragically killed falling from the window of a New York apartment building.

April
 In the States, the Columbia House Record Club releases the vinyl album edition of Paul's *Tripping The Live Fantastic . . . Highlights!*, featuring the only American release of Paul's live version of 'All My Trials', recorded in Milan, Italy, on October 27, 1989.
 A busy time this month for Ringo in America, when it is reported that Ringo has performed on an untitled album by Taj Mahal, which was produced by Skip Drinkwater for the Private Music label. But what is certain is that Ringo appears as a guest voice and also in the shape of an animated caricature for an episode of the hugely successful American television cartoon series *The Simpsons*. Meanwhile, it's announced that Ringo's highly successful series *Shining Time Station*, produced by the American PBS station (Public Broadcasting System), will begin production on 20 new episodes. Ringo will again be portraying Mr. Conductor and serve as the narrator for all of the *Thomas The Tank Engine And Friends* stories, contained within each programme. The new series of episodes is scheduled to begin broadcasting at the end of 1991. Reports also suggest that Ringo has yet to decide whether or not to commit himself to another series after this one.

Wednesday April 3
 Paul's appearance on MTV's *Unplugged,* recorded on January 25 this year, is transmitted today in America. The transmission is followed by an interview with Paul, subtitled *Last Word*, which also features brief interview live film clips during his 1989–90 world tour. The MTV *Unplugged* show is also simultaneously broadcast on American radio, preceded by a 15-minute exclusive interview with Paul.

Monday April 15
 The home video of *Lennon: A Tribute,* videotaped at the Liverpool tribute concert on May 5, 1990, is officially released. It includes the first official release of Ringo's new recording of 'I Call Your Name', as well as Paul's 'P.S. Love Me Do', a live video recorded in Tokyo on March 1990.

Tuesday April 30
 In London, Paul and Linda hold a press conference to launch Linda's new range of vegetarian food.

May
 In America, Yoko threatens legal action against the band EMF whose latest single, 'Schubert Dip', features a recording of Mark Chapman reading lyrics from the 1980 track 'Watching The Wheels'. Knowing that they are in a no-win situation, the group agrees to remove the offending item.

Wednesday May 1
 In the UK, Paul and Linda make another live radio appearance, this time unannounced on BBC Radio One's *The Simon Bates Show*. The McCartneys had called in because Simon Bates and his studio assistants were enjoying a live, on-air, tasting of Linda's new range of vegetarian food and playing a selection of tracks from the, as yet unreleased, album *Unplugged – The Official Bootleg*.

Friday May 3 (until Thursday May 16)

 Another season of Yoko's avant-garde films are screened at New York's Public Theater. The 14-day festival includes the following: *Two Virgins, Film No. 5 (Smile), Apotheosis, The Museum Of Modern Art Show, Film No. 4 (Bottoms), Freedom, Fly, Up Your Legs Forever, Erection, Rape, Walking On Thin Ice, Imagine, Ten For Two, Sisters O'Sisters, Woman, Goodbye Sadness* and *Bed In*.

* * *

Paul McCartney
Unplugged – six surprise concerts
Wednesday May 8 – Wednesday July 24

Paul and his band again take to the road, this time for a series of six surprise Unplugged concerts, in Europe and the UK. Their performance comes in two 45-minute halves. The first set is performed acoustically, inspired by Paul's recent appearance on MTV's *Unplugged,* while the second half is performed electrically.

Their full repertoire for the acoustic set comprises 'Mean Woman Blues', 'Be-Bop-A-Lula', 'We Can Work It Out', 'San Francisco Bay Blues', 'Every Night', 'Here, There And Everywhere', 'That Would Be Something', ('Down To The River', aka 'The River', a new McCartney song, is placed here during the final four shows on the tour), 'And I Love Her', 'She's A Woman', 'I Lost My Little Girl', 'Ain't No Sunshine' (Paul on drums), 'Hi-Heel Sneakers' (added to the repertoire on the gigs dated June 5 and 7), 'I've Just Seen A Face', 'The World Is Waiting For The Sunrise' and 'Good Rockin' Tonight'.

The electric set features 'My Brave Face', 'Band On The Run', 'Ebony And Ivory', 'I Saw Her Standing There', 'Coming Up', 'Get Back', 'The Long And Winding Road', 'Ain't That A Shame', 'Let It Be' and, as two encores, 'Can't Buy Me Love' and 'Sgt. Pepper's Lonely Hearts Club Band' (presented in the '1989/1990 World Tour' version, featuring the original version added to a jam and a reprise).

Paul's complete *Unplugged* tour itinerary is as follows:

The Zeleste Club in Barcelona, Spain (Wednesday May 8)
London's Mean Fiddler Club, Harlesden, South West London, UK (Friday May 10)
Teatro Tendo, (Tent Theatre), Naples, Italy (Wednesday June 5)
Cornwall Coliseum, St. Austell, UK (Friday June 7)
Cliffs Pavilion, Westcliffe-on-Sea, near Southend, Essex, UK (Friday July 19)
The Falkoner Theatre, Copenhagen, Denmark (Wednesday July 24)

Tuesday May 7
Details of Paul's Mean Fiddler concert on Friday evening are announced on the London station Capital Radio, with 400 tickets, at £10 each, going on sale almost immediately within the station's foyer. Such is the race for the prized items, all tickets sell within just one hour. Even so, fans are amazed to discover that almost 200 tickets for Paul's "surprise" gig are readily available this evening from the Mean Fiddler box office in South West London.

Wednesday May 8
Paul's first surprise *Unplugged!* concert takes place at the 1,800 seater Zeleste Club in Barcelona. Immediately following the show, Paul, Linda and the band return home to England.

Monday May 13
The rumoured release today of Paul's Parlophone single 'I Lost My Little Girl', extracted from the soundtrack of the MTV *Unplugged* special, fails to materialise.

Monday May 20
Paul's album *Unplugged (The Official Bootleg)* is released in the UK. (The American release takes place on June 4.) The print run is 250,000 copies worldwide.

Saturday June 1
Paul's *Unplugged – The Official Bootleg* enters the UK album/cassette/CD top 75 chart at number 7.

Wednesday June 5
During tonight's show in Italy, Paul adds to the repertoire the unreleased track 'The River', which features him playing the harmonica. Another track introduced to their set tonight is the song 'The World Is Waiting For The Sunrise', the first live rendition, albeit 30 seconds, of the song since he and John performed this as The Nerk Twins in a Berkshire pub back in 1960.

Friday June 7
Tickets for most of Paul's *Unplugged* concerts, like tonight's show at the Cornwall Coliseum in St. Austell, are priced at £16.50. Paul chose Cornwall as a venue on this tour because he has never performed a concert at any time in his career at this coastal town. (A report on this show appears in America on Wednesday June 12 during the Paramount television programme *Entertainment Tonight.*)

Friday July 19 & Wednesday July 24
For these performances, the repertoire is basically the same as that played on Wednesday May 8 except that 'Down To The River', 'Hi-Heel Sneakers' and 'Twenty Flight Rock' are added to the set, replacing 'And I Love Her' and 'My Brave Face'. An added attraction at the show, in between the acoustic and electric sets, is the poet Adrian Mitchell.

Wednesday July 24
Paul's *Unplugged* gig at the standing room only Falkoner Theatre in Copenhagen, sells out of its 3,000 tickets in just 75 minutes.

Friday July 26
The final concert of this *Unplugged* tour is due to take place this evening at the Olympia Theatre in Paris, France, but was cancelled by MPL for unspecified reasons two weeks earlier, on Friday July 12.

*   *   *

Friday May 31
◉ At the Roxy Club in Los Angeles, Ringo joins his guitarist friend Nils Lofgren on stage to play drums on his version of The Beatles' track 'Anytime At All'.

Tuesday June 4
◉ The legal dispute over the Chips Moman produced Ringo album in 1987 rolls on when Moman, at the Georgia Supreme Court, begins proceedings to seek the full $162,600 in production costs he had originally sought. The previous court judgement, on January 5, 1989, ruled that Ringo should pay only $74,354.

Tuesday June 11
◉ George's albums *Somewhere In England* and *Gone Troppo* are released on CD in America.
◉ Following the permanent closure of Rye Memorial Hospital in East Sussex, Paul writes an angry letter which is published in today's *Daily Mirror* newspaper in the UK.

Friday June 14
◉ The MPL promotional video for the live version of 'Birthday', from Paul's world tour, is released in Japan by Toshiba-EMI as the first VSD (video single disc or CD-video single) by an ex-Beatle.

Saturday June 15
◉ In the UK, Channel 4 transmits the documentary *The Man Who Moved The Beatles*, which is a profile on George Dunning, the man responsible for their 1968 film *Yellow*

Submarine, an animated classic which is repeated on the station the following day, Sunday June 16.

Tuesday June 18
⏺ In the UK, Channel 4 transmits again this evening John's 1967 film *How I Won The War*.

Thursday June 20
⏺ At the Hard Rock Cafe in Piccadilly, London, Paul and Linda host a private party to celebrate the launch of Linda's range of vegetarian dishes, including her well loved veggie burgers. Also in attendance this evening are Ringo and Barbara.

Tuesday June 25
⏺ George's album *Thirty Three And A Third* and *George Harrison* are released on CD in America.

Wednesday June 26
⏺ Linda appears live across the ITV Network on the programme *This Morning*, where she discusses her range of vegetarian foods.

Friday June 28
⏺ In the UK, *The Paul McCartney Liverpool Oratorio*, co-composed by Paul and Carl Davis, receives its world premiere in front of a capacity audience of 2,500 at the Anglican Cathedral in Liverpool. The concert is performed by the Royal Liverpool Philharmonic, conducted by Davis himself. Earlier in the day, Paul had spent the afternoon showing Michael Portillo, the Minister on Inner Cities, around his old school, now the LIPA institute. (A second *Oratorio* performance takes place at the Anglican Cathedral the following evening, Saturday June 29.)

A recording of the 90-minute Liverpool premiere show is released in the UK on October 7 and on October 22 in America. A videotape of the performance is released in the UK on October 28 with a laser disc version appearing on December 9. A single entitled 'The World You're Coming Into'/'Tres Conejos' is released in the UK only on September 20. A second single, 'Save The World'/'The Drinking Song', is issued in America on November 12 and in the UK on November 18. The television production of the Liverpool performance is transmitted in America on October 30 by the PBS network and on December 14 in the UK on Channel 4. (An accompanying special is also transmitted this night, December 14, on BBC Radio Two.)

Sunday July 7
⏺ At the Royal Festival Hall, the London premiere takes place of *The Paul McCartney Liverpool Oratorio* with Paul and Linda naturally in attendance.

Thursday July 11
⏺ After an eight-month closure, the new *Cavern Club* in Mathew Street, Liverpool, now owned by Cavern City Tours, re-opens its doors for business.

Tuesday July 23
⏺ Still in Merseyside, a plaque honouring Brian Epstein, the seventh in a series of *Harp Beat Rock Plaques* to be presented in Britain, is unveiled at 12–14 Whitechapel in Liverpool city centre, the former NEMS records store premises and now the site of the Rumbelows domestic appliances chain.

Tuesday July 30
⏺ In America, Linda's father Lee Eastman dies of a stroke in the New York Hospital. He was 81 years of age.
⏺ George's *The Concert For Bangla Desh* is released in America on compact disc. (The UK release takes place on August 19.)

August
⏺ The American television station PBS announces that Ringo will no longer appear on their children's TV programme *Shining Time Station*.
⏺ The American CD release takes place of John and Yoko's 1968 album *Two Virgins*.

Thursday August 1
 In America, George records, for promotional purposes, an interview about the CD issue of *The Concert For Bangla Desh*.

Friday August 2
 Back in the UK, Apple Corps wins a London High Court injunction which prevents EMI from issuing the *1962–1966* and *1967–1970* compilations as double CDs on October 7 this year. The judge, Mr. Justice Mummery, remarks: "It can be said with justification that EMI walked with their eyes open, or at least half-closed, into a situation which they could have avoided without difficulty by asking for written consent from Apple." (EMI immediately file an appeal which reaches the High Court on September 6 – see entry.)
 The ABC TV music series *In Concert '91*, broadcasts some brief footage from one of Paul's recent secret Unplugged concerts.

Sunday August 4
 BBC2 in the UK screens the documentary *Power Of Music*, which features footage of Paul working with mentally handicapped children.

Thursday August 29
 Christie's auction house in London presents for the first time a sale of the Cynthia Lennon archive, featuring a vast range of memorabilia and personal items.

September
 During the month, two more *Thomas The Tank Engine* home video cassettes are released in America, this time appearing on the Colortime label, each delightfully packaged with a colouring book and four pens. The titles of these releases are *Thomas Gets Tricked & Other Stories* and *James Learns A Lesson & Other Stories*, and, as always, feature Ringo's narration.

Friday September 6
 In London, the case over the proposed EMI CD releases of *The Beatles 1962–1966* and *1967–1970* compilations resumes at the High Court, where EMI appeal against the previous ruling which prevents their release. During the same trial, EMI also announces, to the court, their intention to release the two CDs in a boxed set form, which, in their opinion, does not require Apple's approval under the terms of their wide-ranging November 1989 agreement. The judge, Mr. Justice Mummery, will have none of it, ruling again in favour of Apple, upholding the previous injunction and blocking EMI's "red" and "blue" box sets.

Friday September 13
 In London, at the *Orangery* in Holland Park, Paul and Linda hold a lunch time party to celebrate the annual MPL Buddy Holly Week. This venue was used by the McCartneys for their first Buddy Holly party back in 1976.

Saturday September 14
 In Los Angeles, Ringo records the song 'You'll Never Know', which will later appear over the closing credits of the film *Curly Sue*. The track, co-written by Steve Dorff and Steve Bettis, naturally appears on the film soundtrack album, released in America on November 26 and in the UK on January 6, 1992. Produced by Peter Asher, it was recorded at the conclusion of his sessions for his next studio album, which, as yet, remains untitled. Among the musicians on the sessions are the DGC Records act from Seattle who call themselves The Posies, who apparently recorded with Ringo the track 'Golden Blunders'.

Monday September 16
 In London, at BBC Broadcasting House, in Portland Place, London, Paul gives a live interview about his *Oratorio* shows on the BBC Radio Four programme *Kaleidoscope*. (A small portion of the interview is repeated later in the day on the station during the edited highlights edition of the programme.)
 In America, a pre-recorded interview with Fred Seaman, where he talks about his book *The Last Days Of John Lennon*, is featured in the Paramount television programme *Entertainment Tonight*.

Tuesday September 17

 Paul and Linda arrive in Hamburg, Germany to prepare for the world premiere of his live concert film *Get Back*. One of his first tasks on entering the country is to play the role as a DJ on a 60-minute programme for the Antenne Bayern radio station, during which Paul delights the captive audience by speaking some German!

Wednesday September 18

 Paul's film *Get Back* receives its world premiere in Hamburg, Germany at the Passage Kino cinema. Paul holds a press conference at the start of the day at the Schmidt-Tivoli Theatre, an event covered by the station Radio Hamburg and screened on some TV stations around the world via satellite. Immediately following the screening, Paul and Linda fly back to England. (The UK premiere of *Get Back* takes places the following day, while its first American screening will not take place until October 25. Incidentally, the home video release of *Get Back* takes place in the UK on October 21 and in America on December 11.)

Thursday September 19

 Paul's *Get Back* film, receives its UK premiere at selected Odeon Cinemas in Glasgow, Leeds, Birmingham, Liverpool, and Streatham in London.

Friday September 20

 Paul's *Get Back* film opens for a week-long run in Liverpool, Leeds and Birmingham. In addition, the film begins a seven-day stretch at the London cinemas of Cannon, and at the Parkway Cinema in Camden and the Filmhouse Theatre in Richmond, Surrey.

Friday September 27

 The UK release of Paul's *Get Back* continues when the film opens for a week at the Showcase Cinemas in Derby, Peterborough and Nottingham.

Saturday September 28

 In the UK, Julian Lennon releases his fourth solo album, entitled *Help Yourself*. George is among those credited as appearing on the album, playing slide guitar on the track 'Saltwater', a song released as the first single off the album.
 Still in the UK, the 1986 Handmade film *Shanghai Surprise*, starring Madonna and Sean Penn, is aired for the first time on some regions of the ITV network.

Monday September 30

 Paul's *CHOBA B CCCP* album is released in the UK on CD. (The American CD release is delayed and will now not take place until October 29.)

Thursday October 3

 To coincide with the UK release of Paul's *CHOBA B CCCP*, humorous advertisements appear in the *Guardian* and the *Independent* newspapers, which purportedly contain a message from Alexei Itnov, the sales director of the Melodia record company in Moscow.

Saturday October 5

 In the UK, BBC Radio Two broadcasts (between 8:05am and 9:59am) the entire fifth anniversary edition of *Saturday Club*, previously transmitted on the BBC Light Programme on October 2, 1963, and recorded at the Playhouse Theatre in London on September 7, 1963. The archive tape, recently discovered during research for the 14-part Radio One series *The Beeb's Lost Beatles Tapes*, features Beatles performances of 'I Saw Her Standing There', 'Memphis, Tennessee', 'Happy Birthday Saturday Club', 'I'll Get You', 'She Loves You' and 'Lucille'.

Tuesday October 8

 BBC1 in the UK broadcasts the programme *Ghosts Of The Past,* a BBC/MPL/PMI co-produced documentary about the history from its conception to the final rehearsals of Paul's *Liverpool Oratorio*. (The American broadcast takes place on the Public Broadcasting Services station on October 30, which is immediately followed by the *Oratorio* performance production.)

Friday October 11

🍎 After a case lasting 116 days, resulting in legal bills approaching £7 million, the on-going dispute between Apple Corps and Apple Computers finally reaches its conclusion. Apple Computers agree to pay Apple Corps a sum in damages. The solicitor Gordon Pollock, representing Apple Corps, tells the High Court in London that the two parties have reached an "amicable" agreement and the settlement terms stipulate that the agreed sum should remain confidential. Experts believe that Apple Computers will be paying The Beatles' company an estimated $29 million. (Originally, it was estimated that Apple Corps were suing the computer giants for a sum in the region of $250 million!)

Sunday October 13

🍎 The MPL documentary *Paul McCartney: Going Home* is transmitted in America on The Disney Channel. (The programme originally appeared in the UK on Channel 4 on December 17, 1990, under the alternative title *From Rio To Liverpool.*) In New York City at Carnegie Hall, tickets go on sale for Paul's *Liverpool Oratorio* performance, which is scheduled for Monday November 18.

Monday October 14

🍎 Paul and Linda make a personal appearance at a food trade fair in Cologne, Germany, where they announce that her range of products will be available in most European countries by the end of 1992. (To date, it is estimated that more than five million *Linda McCartney* meals have been sold in Britain alone.)

Tuesday October 15

🍎 In Japan, official details of George's forthcoming tour of the country are released to newspapers. The former Beatle, along with Eric Clapton and his band, is set to play seven shows, which include the Osaka Castle Hall (December 2, 3, 10 and 11) and the Tokyo Dome (on December 14, 15 and 17). Tickets will go on sale on Sunday October 20.

Wednesday October 16 (until Friday October 25)

🍎 A part of John's original *Bag One* collection is displayed at the London gallery Smiths of Covent Garden. In New York City, on October 16, Yoko and Sean are among those present at a celebrity dinner given by Polygram Records at the Four Seasons restaurant. The event is arranged to launch the new various artists album *Two Rooms*, celebrating the songs of Elton John and Bernie Taupin.

Friday October 18

🍎 In the UK, Paul appears live on the London Weekend Television programme *Six O'Clock Live*, transmitted in the London and Southeast regions of ITV only. He is seen chatting with the host Michael Aspel and, by camera, to Dame Kiri Te Kanawa, who is seen signing copies of her new records at the HMV shop in nearby Oxford Street, London. (Paul, accompanied by Linda, will leave London en route to New York on Monday October 21.) In the States, Paul is featured in the ABC TV show *In Concert '91.*

Sunday October 20

🍎 As expected, tickets for George's concert tour of Japan go on sale. Such is the demand to see him perform, practically all the tickets at the venues sell out within hours. Shortly after, on November 8, and then again on November 10, following instructions from George and Eric, promoters announce that a further four shows have been added to the concert itinerary (see entry for December 1 for the full concert tour listing).

Monday October 21

🍎 Barely weeks after its first cinema screenings, Paul's live concert film *Get Back* is released in the UK on PMI home video.

Wednesday October 23

🍎 In New York, in front of approximately 150 reporters, Paul holds a press conference for his *Liverpool Oratorio* at Weill Recital Hall, situated next door to the prestigious Carnegie Hall. Before any of the reporters and classical music writers can ask Paul any questions, they are shown the documentary *Ghosts Of The Past*, the programme about the making of the *Oratorio*. Those in attendance are given a special *Oratorio* press kit, which contains a sweatshirt, emblazoned with the cover art of the *Oratorio* album. In order to retain a dignified atmosphere, the infamous New York "jock" Howard Stern is refused admission. A journalist asks Paul if writing the *Oratorio* has influenced his pop music writing at all. "It reminded me of structuring stuff, as on the second side of The Beatles' *Abbey Road* album," he replies. "I hadn't done that for a while. So now I'm writing for the next pop album, and before I record it this time, I will have written it all. Whereas normally, you go in with a few ideas, and knock 'em around in the studio. I think it'll be more satisfying to know what I'm going to go in and do." Another reporter asks Paul on how working with Carl Davis differed from writing with John Lennon. Paul laughs as he replies: "I bossed Carl around more than I bossed John!"

At the conclusion of the session, Capitol Records President Hale Milgrim presents Paul with a platinum disc for sales of *Tripping The Live Fantastic – Highlights*. Afterwards Paul, accompanied by Linda and band member Hamish Stuart, attend a reception downstairs at the Hall. (Incidentally, Paul's *Oratorio* is due to premiere in New York on Monday November 18.) Also today in the States, Paul makes interview appearances on the *Charlie Rose* television programme and the ABC TV breakfast show *Good Morning America*.

Thursday October 24

🍎 Still in New York City, Paul's *Get Back* film is premiered at the Baronet Theater, situated at 3rd Avenue and 60th Street, with the McCartneys and Stuart in attendance. At the New York premiere, Paul gives another interview to Scott Muni of the New York radio station WNEW, an item transmitted on the station the following day. During his stay in New York, Paul records several further TV appearances, including one with Bob Costas, for his show *Later With Bob Costas,* which is transmitted on November 5, 6, and 7.

Friday October 25

🍎 In America, the *Get Back* film opens in New York at the Baronet Theater. A simultaneous screening also takes place at Laemmie's Music Hall in Hollywood, Los Angeles. To coincide with the events, the ABC TV music series *In Concert '91*, features footage from the film. (At the end of its week in New York, screenings of *Get Back* shift to the Worldwide Cinema in the city.)

Paul and Linda, meanwhile, are to be found in Toronto, Canada, where they hold another press conference for the film *Get Back* at the Sutton Place Hotel, an event attended by approximately 50 photographers and reporters. At the conclusion of the conference, the McCartneys partake in a round of interviews. To reporter John Sakamoto of the *Toronto Sun*, Paul reveals that he donated a song to Ringo's latest album. "It's called 'Angel In Disguise' – which is Ringo. He was pleased." Paul adds: "Ringo wanted an extra verse, so I said, 'Let's write the extra verse together. Or you can just write it and we'll have co-written the song.' I understand he has written a third verse. If it's another 'With A Little Help From My Friends', great, if it isn't, great!"

Paul also reveals to the *Toronto Sun* reporter that the three former Beatles are moving ahead with their long mooted documentary, entitled *The Long And Winding Road,* an idea first touched upon back in 1970. Besides revealing that the director for the programme has been named as Geoff Wonfor, Paul exclusively reveals: "What I'm most excited about is getting new input into the thing. For instance, we could do voice-overs where we tell our side of the story, or put in home movies that nobody has ever seen! I've got some nice footage from Rishikesh when we went to see the Maharishi. It's interesting, seeing us looking like total wallies, wearing these little Indian things."

Paul also gives an interview to CITY TV's *Movie Television* programme, an item split into two parts and transmitted on the station on Saturday November 2 and Sunday November 3. Paul also gives a 30-minute live interview on the radio station CHUM-AM, where he also takes phone questions from the listening public. Later this evening, Paul and Linda attend the Canadian premiere of *Get Back* at the Varsity II cinema in downtown Toronto, at the Manu Life Center, but leave the cinema before the film ends. Fans present at the screening are none too pleased. Their $35 tickets (proceeds of which go to the environmental studies programme at Bishop's College School in Toronto and the Friends Of The Earth) clearly state: "Paul McCartney will be present to introduce the film." Many fans had queued all day just to see a silhouette of Paul, standing in the dark at the back of the theatre, waving to the large crowds who were straining to catch a proper glimpse of the former Beatle. Paul and Linda reappear later at the post-premiere party, which is held at Mr. Greenjean's restaurant. Diners are naturally served dishes prepared from recipes from Linda's vegetarian cookbook. (Incidentally, media coverage of Paul's visit to Toronto is shared equally with the Prince and Princess of Wales, who are also currently visiting Canada's largest city. Interestingly enough, the Toronto based newspapers claim that security at Paul's press conference on October 25 was higher than that afforded to the two Royals.)

Monday October 28
🍎 In the UK, Apple Records delay the release of the first phase of reissuing their back catalogue on CD and vinyl. The issues are re-scheduled for Monday November 11.

Tuesday October 29
🍎 Paul's recent activities in America with *Get Back* and the *Liverpool Oratorio* are featured in the MTV show *Day In Rock*.

Wednesday October 30
🍎 In England, John's uncle Norman Birch is killed as he is hit by a car near his Merseyside home, from which, just prior to his death, solicitors working on behalf of Yoko had tried, unsuccessfully, to get him evicted. The matter is swiftly dropped once news reaches the British tabloid newspapers.

November
🍎 A few weeks after Apple Corps had won their case against Apple Computers, they are back in the courts again when they file a suit in the New York Supreme Court against Sony Music Entertainments Inc. over their release in America of the two volume album *The Beatles Live At The Star Club 1962*.

Friday November 1
🍎 In the States, Paul's *Get Back* film opens at the Canada Square Cinema in Toronto for a limited run.

Saturday November 2
🍎 George comes under the spotlight today when he is featured on the Paul Gambaccini BBC Radio One programme *Appreciation*, which is also repeated on Tuesday February 11, 1992.

Monday November 4 (until Friday November 22)
🍎 In the seclusion of a large sound stage at Bray Film Studios, near Windsor in Berkshire, George begins rehearsals with Eric Clapton and his band for his upcoming concert tour of Japan. A Japanese crew from NHK TV visits the rehearsals on November 12 to preview the shows.

"It'll be special for me, because it'll be the tour which will decide whether I wanna do anymore touring or not, you see. This could be my first and last tour or it could just be something that begins a new period for me," George tells NHK TV in Japan.

For their short feature, which is transmitted on Sunday November 24, during the programme *Subarasiji Nakamatati (Beautiful Comradeship)*, George is seen arriving in his car and, knowing that the crew videoing him are from Japan, apologises by saying, "Sorry it's not a Honda!" The interview, carried out on the stage, features conversation and the songs 'While My Guitar Gently Weeps', 'Wonderful Tonight', 'Something' and 'Layla', and recalls their first meeting, which was at a Lovin' Spoonful concert at The Marquee club in London in 1966. (Different interviews carried out during the Bray Studios rehearsals also form a *Sony Music TV Special*, which is aired in Japan in November, just prior to the start of George and Eric's tour.)

Tuesday November 5 (until Thursday November 7)
🍎 A pre-recorded three-part interview with Paul is transmitted on the US TV programme *Later With Bob Costas*. Also on November 5, a pre-recorded interview with Paul is aired on the ABC TV show *Eyewitness News*.

Monday November 11
 Following the delay from October 28, Apple Records, in the UK, begin the first phase in their reissuing of their back catalogue. The first to appear on vinyl and CD are the albums *James Taylor, Postcard* by Mary Hopkin, *Is This What You Want* by Jackie Lomax, *That's The Way God Planned It* by Billy Preston and *Magic Christian Music* by Badfinger.

Tuesday November 12
 In the UK, the Granada region of the ITV network transmits the UK TV premiere of Paul's *Liverpool Oratorio* video.

Tuesday November 12 (until December 13)
 An exhibition by Bob Whittaker to accompany his book *The Unseen Beatles*, takes place at the Photographer's Gallery in Great Newport Gallery, Great Newport Street, London.

Wednesday November 13
 In America, the first Apple production in years, namely, *The Beatles: The First US Visit*, is released on MPI home video and laser disc. This wonderful 83-minute film focuses entirely on the group's first visit to America during February of 1964 and features, among many candid humorous scenes, highlights from their performances on the three *Ed Sullivan Show*s (February 9, 16 and 23) and clips from their first live concert in Washington on February 11. (The film is not released in Europe.)

Saturday November 16
 At New York's Carnegie Hall, Paul and the full orchestra have a full dress rehearsal for Paul's *Liverpool Oratorio*. This is, in fact, the first time that the boys choir and chorale have got together with Paul and the full ensemble. (On hand to capture the proceedings is CBS TV, the results of which are transmitted the following morning on the programme *CBS Sunday*.)

Monday November 18
 At New York City's Carnegie Hall, the North American premiere takes place of *The Paul McCartney Liverpool Oratorio,* with Paul, Linda and their entire family in attendance, the McCartneys having arrived at the venue in their limousine at 7:21pm. Conducted by Carl Davis, the US version features a performance by The Royal Liverpool Philharmonic Orchestra who are making their American concert début tonight. Tonight's line-up of performers is basically the same line-up as those who performed in Liverpool at the Anglican Cathedral on Friday June 28, with the exception of the soprano Dame Kiri Te Kanawa, who is replaced this evening by Barbara Bonney. At the conclusion of the premiere performance, the audience applause is timed at a most satisfactory 6 minutes 40 seconds!

Tuesday November 19
 In America, mixed reviews of the previous night's *Oratorio* performance begin appearing in the newspapers:
 "Neither McCartney's celebrity nor his fans' hysteria could diminish the power of this score . . . the piece is fervently melodic . . . a first class work that speaks in distinctly hummable tunes." *(The Chicago Tribune)*
 ". . . there are many fine melodies . . .. a work that deserves to be heard again." *(Associated Press)*
 "There's not enough variety in tempo . . . and such passages as the 'God Is Good' finale are downright sappy. Yet the majority of the musical and textual statements are strong and memorable." (*The New York Daily News*)
 "A sprawling, mawkish, excruciating, embarrassing 90-minutes of ego!" *(Newsday)*

Tuesday November 19 & Wednesday November 20
 In England, for two straight nights, a pre-recorded interview with Paul, where he discusses, amongst many other things, his *Liverpool Oratorio* and the new single 'Save A Life', is included in the Nicky Campbell show on BBC Radio 1 in the UK.

Thursday November 21
 Paul's *Oratorio* is performed for the fifth time, this time as part of the Belfast Festival at the Ulster Hall in Ireland. Paul and Linda are not present.

Sunday November 24
 Paul's *Liverpool Oratorio* is performed this evening at St. Patrick's Cathedral in Dublin, Ireland. Paul and Linda are not present, instead he is back home in Sussex preparing for studio sessions which are due to begin tomorrow.

Monday November 25 (until Friday December 6)
 At his home studios in Sussex, Paul, working with Julian Mendlesohn, begins the recording sessions for his album *Off The Ground*. This period sees the recording of the tracks: 'Peace In The Neighbourhood' and 'Biker Like An Icon'.

Saturday November 30
 A further performance of Paul's *Liverpool Oratorio* takes place at St. Anne's Cathedral in Belfast, Ireland. The concert is performed by the Northern Ireland Symphony Orchestra and Youth Chorus, and features the conduction of Alan Tonque. Again, Paul and Linda are not in attendance.

* * *

George Harrison
Tour of Japan with Eric Clapton
Billed as "Rock Legends: George Harrison And Eric Clapton And His Band"
Sunday December 1 – Tuesday December 17

George undertakes his first concert tour since 1974, visiting Japan with his close friend Eric Clapton and his eight-piece backing band. This line-up of musicians includes Nathan East (bass guitar), Steve Ferrone (drums), Chuck Leavell (keyboards), Greg Phillinganes (keyboards), Ray Cooper (percussion), Andy Fairweather-Low (guitar), Katie Kissoon and Tessa Niles (backing vocals).

This visit, George's first to the country since The Beatles' visit in 1966, will consist of just six venues and comprise the following twelve shows:

The Yokohama Arena, Yokohama (Sunday December 1- 6pm show)
Osaka Castle Hall, Osaka (Monday December 2 and Tuesday December 3 –
    both 7pm)
International Exhibition Center, Nagoya (Thursday December 5 – 7pm)
Hiroshima Sun Plaza Hall, Hiroshima (Friday December 6 – 7pm)
Fukouka Kokusai International Center Hall, Fukuoka (Monday December 9 – 7pm)
Osaka Castle Hall, Osaka (return performances on Tuesday December 10,
    Wednesday December 11 and Thursday December 12 – all 7pm)
Tokyo Dome Stadium, Tokyo (nicknamed *Big Egg*) (Saturday December 14 – 6pm,
    Sunday December 15 – 6pm, and Tuesday December 17 – 7pm).

Their repertoire, half of which features Beatles songs, includes 'I Want To Tell You', 'Old Brown Shoe', 'Taxman', 'Give Me Love (Give Me Peace On Earth)', 'If I Needed Someone', 'Something', 'Fish On The Sand' (performed on December 1 and 2 only), 'Love Comes To Everyone' (December 1 only), 'What Is Life', 'Dark Horse' and 'Piggies'. (At this stage, Eric Clapton takes over, performing 'Pretending', 'Old Love', 'Badge', a track co-written with George back in 1969, and 'Wonderful Tonight'.) George then returns to perform 'Got My Mind Set On You', 'Cloud Nine', 'Here Comes The Sun', 'My Sweet Lord', 'All Those Years Ago', 'Cheer Down', 'Devil's Radio', 'Isn't It A Pity' and an encore consisting of 'While My Guitar Gently Weeps' and 'Roll Over Beethoven'. (For the performance of 'Piggies', George adds the verse originally written by John back in 1968.) For the duration of the tour, George uses the following guitars: Roy Buchanan Bluesmaster electric guitar No. 6, Gibson J-200 custom acoustic guitar, a gold Fender 12-string electric guitar, a red Fender Stratocaster Eric Clapton model, and a Gibson Les Paul Standard '60.

"All George has got to do, essentially, is walk out on stage and strum an acoustic guitar and we'll do everything else. There's nothing for him to worry about. I put the idea to him and he was delighted and scared at the same time. He was really scared to death. He changed his mind about five different times." (Eric Clapton – *Rolling Stone* magazine.)

"We're going to Japan where the world spotlight won't be on him and he probably won't get a bad review. It's a great opportunity. If he doesn't do it now he probably never will . . . George is very paranoid about the press. There's a lot of anger in him, I don't know why. He's got his guard up before he begins . . ." (Eric Clapton on his tour with George.)

Thursday November 28
At 3:57pm Japanese Time, George and Eric arrive in Japan at New Tokyo International Airport (Narita Airport) on flight no. JAL 420. On their arrival, a waiting reporter asks George about his flight. "I had been looking forward to seeing Mount Fuji and a panoramic view of Japan from the plane, but it was really foggy and rainy," he says, adding: "I've been on the flight for 12 hours and so now I'm really sleepy. I should have gone on a different flight." After passing through customs, George, wearing a turtleneck sweater and a dark blue overcoat, appears in the airport arrivals lobby at 4:11pm, where he is greeted by a large welcoming committee of 150 screaming fans and representatives from the Japanese press and television. Immediately, George heads for the Capitol Tokyo Hotel, formerly the Tokyo Hilton Hotel, the same building used by The Beatles in 1966, where he takes a rest to recover from jet lag.

Friday November 29
Following a good night's sleep, George and Eric hold a 1pm press conference, in front of 500 reporters, in the Red Pearl room at the Capitol Tokyo Hotel. (Practically all the questions are, naturally, asked in Japanese.)

George: "A short message . . . Hello! It's very nice to be here after such a long time. It's very nice to be here, thank you."

Female reporter (speaking in English): "I'd like to ask you George a question about the reformed Beatles . . ."

George (interrupting): "No, it can't be possible because The Beatles don't exist, especially now as John Lennon isn't alive. It (the story) just comes every time Paul needs some publicity, he announces to the press that The Beatles are coming together again, but that's all. I wouldn't pay too much attention to that."

The press conference concludes with a P.A. playing George's 'Got My Mind Set On You'. Just prior to the start of the conference, George and Eric did a photo session for the Japanese press in the adjacent White Pearl room at the hotel.

Saturday November 30
At the Yokohama Arena, from 12 noon to 5pm, George, Eric and his band rehearse for the tour.

December
In the UK, *Q* magazine features an interview with Eric who talks about the tour of Japan with George. He remarks in the interview: "I don't think he's ever had the experience of playing for an audience with a great band. The Beatles played to 10-year-old kids who screamed their heads off. He's stopped smoking, he's got himself into fighting-fit shape, he's got my lighting, my sound, my band. It's a crack team."

Sunday December 1
"Hello! I hope many of you can speak much better English than I can . . . and I certainly can't speak very much Japanese . . . but this is a song which I wrote to an old friend of ours . . . whose name is John Lennon." (George's introduction to 'All Those Years Ago' in front of 13,000 fans.)

At some of the concerts during this tour, special *George Harrison Sticking Plaster* is distributed to fans. This is, according to a tour spokesman, "to aid them should they get injured in the excitement of watching the former Beatle perform!"

Monday December 2
Reviews of the first concert reach the Japanese newspapers. The *Sports Nippon* paper enthusiastically writes: "George Harrison, his guitar gently wept in Japan; a dream-come-true concert opened in Yokohama." In the *Daily Sports,* a reporter writes:

"... an impassioned performance by Harrison and Clapton." All is not rosy with *Billboard* who call it "an entertaining if unspectacular show," adding: "George looked nervous and it wasn't until 'Something' that he relaxed enough to stretch out a bit on guitar." The report goes on: "Clapton played his sideman role to the hilt, staying to the side of the stage and leaving much of the solo work to Harrison – whose slide playing was sublime!"

This evening, in front of approximately 11,000 fans, George introduces the song 'Taxman': "This next song is a very old song written in 1873!"

Wednesday December 4
George takes advantage of a day off from the tour by shopping at the Hankyu Department Store in Osaka.

Thursday December 5
To cash in on George's current tour of Japan, the albums *Living In The Material World, Extra Texture (Read All About It)* and *Dark Horse* are released in Japan on CD. The worldwide release of these albums, including both the US and the UK, takes place on January 27, 1992.

Saturday December 7
George's second day off on this tour takes him to the nearby Hiroshima Peace Park.

Sunday December 8
Day off number three sees George and Eric sightseeing in Fukouka.

Tuesday December 10
Recordings for the proposed live concert album take place tonight at the start of the concert at Castle Hall in Osaka. During George's introductions, he refers to the song 'Cheer Down' as "a song from the film *South Pacific*".

Wednesday December 11
During the performance of the song 'Piggies' in Osaka this evening, drummer Steve Ferrone walks around on stage in front of 11,000 people wearing a large pig's mask.

Thursday December 12
George is unwell due to a cold, forcing him to go to the Tanaka Clinic in Osaka. Due to this illness, George is seen taking a drink of water in between each track of his performance. (Audience attendance is estimated at 12,000.) Backstage at the concert earlier tonight, George is interviewed for the Japanese Fuji TV programme *Super Time*, an item aired the following day.

Saturday December 14
The TBS TV Network, J-Wave FM Radio Station, and Shogakkan Publishing sponsor the three shows in Tokyo at the Dome Stadium.

In America, *Billboard* magazine becomes the only national newspaper or magazine to run a story on George's tour of Japan when they print a review of his opening night concert at Yokohama on December 1.

Monday December 16
George's final free day of this tour is spent shopping at Tokyo's International Market.

Tuesday December 17
During the encore, on the final night of the tour, George's son Dhani and Nick Roylance, the son of George's good friend Brian Roylance, the proprietor of Genesis Publications, join George, Eric and the band on stage, where they perform 'While My Guitar Gently Weeps' and 'Roll Over Beethoven'.

Wednesday December 18
At 12:15pm (Japanese time), George, along with Olivia, Dhani and Eric board a plane (JAL 401) at New Tokyo International Airport and return home to England. On this day, CNN in America runs a report on George's tour, including a report in *Showbiz Today*, which shows live concert footage of the songs 'Taxman' and 'If I Needed Someone' and a

brief interview with George, recorded on Thursday December 12. Asked why he went back on the road, Harrison replies: "I had to do something when I gave up smoking!" (It is reported that the tour has grossed approximately £9.7 million.)

* * *

December
 At the start of the month, while George is on tour in Japan, a suit is filed on his behalf in the Los Angeles Superior Court for defamation of character, seeking more than $200 million in damages from the Florida-based tabloid newspaper *The Globe*. Harrison is most upset by a report, printed in an edition of the paper in September, which portrays him as a "Devotee of Adolf Hitler, a Nazi sympathiser and has a huge Nazi flag hanging in the front of his home." The article also claims that: "George parades around his little England village in a storm trooper's uniform." Bert Fields, George's solicitor, remarks to the press: "That is all totally false. George deplores Nazism and everything that Hitler stood for. He is very very upset by the story and decided to sue after *The Globe* refused to print a retraction." Incidentally, on Tuesday December 10, the Paramount television programme *Entertainment Tonight* runs a report on the suit.
 In America, reports indicate that Michael Jackson's long mooted animated film *Strawberry Fields* will be released next summer. Amongst the artists who are expected to appear on the soundtrack singing Beatles songs are Crosby Stills & Nash, Cheap Trick, Cyndi Lauper, Luther Vandross and Jackson himself.

Friday December 6
 John's Aunt Mimi, Mary Elizabeth Smith, dies at the age of 88. She passed away in the bungalow that John had bought for her in Poole, Dorset, in the south west of England. She is cremated on December 12 in a private ceremony at Poole, attended by some thirty mourners, including Yoko and Sean, who had flown in from America to attend, and Cynthia, John's first wife. Paul, George and Ringo do not attend but instead send wreaths.

Monday December 9 (periodically until July 1992)
 Paul and his band continue recording sessions for the album *Off The Ground*. These lengthy sessions, at his home studios in Sussex, feature the following songs: 'Off The Ground', 'Looking For Changes', 'Hope Of Deliverance', 'Mistress And Maid', 'I Owe It All To You', 'Golden Earth Girl', 'The Lovers That Never Were', 'Get Out Of My Way', 'Winedark Open Sea' and 'C'mon People', 'Long Leather Coat', 'Big Boys Bickering', 'Kicked Around No More', 'I Can't Imagine', 'Keep Coming Back To Love', 'Down To The River', 'Style, Style', 'Sweet Sweet Memories' and 'Soggy Noodle' plus an unlisted fade-out track entitled 'Cosmically Conscious', which Paul had originally written in India back in 1968. (These sessions will last until July of 1992.)

Saturday December 14
 Another performance of Paul's *Liverpool Oratorio* takes place this evening, this time at the Guildhall in Derry City in Londonderry. In the UK, Channel 4 transmits, between 8:00 and 9:58pm, the film of the June 28 *Liverpool Oratorio* premiere, a programme that had been issued on PMI home video on October 28. Earlier this day, between 2:00 and 3:59pm, Paul appears as part of a two hour *Oratorio* programme transmitted on BBC Radio Two.

Friday December 27
 The excellent 1988 Warner Brothers film *Imagine: John Lennon* receives its UK TV premiere, albeit in a censored form, on BBC2 this evening.

> "I saw George yesterday in California, and we're getting together, you know . . ."
>
> – Paul

January
 In quiet back street Wendell Road, near Chiswick in London, work finally recommences on another Beatles-related project, already now some twenty-two years since it was first conceived. The title of this old Beatles project is none other than their long anticipated documentary history programme . . . *The Long And Winding Road.* The director is Geoff Wonfor, a friend of Paul's who has previously worked on Channel 4's *The Tube* and has directed some of Paul's MPL produced documentaries, including *Put It There* and *Ghosts Of The Past.*

Wednesday January 29
 Paul records a classical piece of music, featuring a co-arrangement with Carl Davis and incorporating the Linda McCartney composed tune 'Appaloosa', and 'Meditation', written by Paul. The recording is used in a half-hour documentary film, entitled *Appaloosa,* which is finished during early July this year. (See entry for May 12 this year.) The piece is also performed by the Boston Pops, with Davis conducting, on May 12. A videotape of the performance is aired on PBS Television in America during August 1992.

February
 In the States, Ringo resumes the Los Angeles' recording sessions for the album *Time Takes Time.*

Wednesday February 12
 With The Beatles' history programme now at last taking shape, the fear of unofficial Beatles-related film and video footage flooding the market becomes a reality. Paul instigates proceedings against one of Europe's top collectors when a writ from the High Court in London is served today.

Monday February 17
 The dispute between Apple Corps and EMI Records over their November 1989 'wide ranging' agreement, reaches the High Court in London. Apple make known their attempts to block EMI from releasing Beatles-related product in the new formats, such as DCC (Digital Compact Disc) and MD (Midi Disc) until a new agreement has been sorted out.

Friday February 21
 At the London headquarters of the PRS (Performing Rights Society), as part of a drive towards opening a school for the Performing Arts at his old school in Liverpool, Paul hosts a fund-raising lunch for top music industry executives. He delivers a speech, as does Mark Featherstone-Witty, the full-time co-ordinator of LIPA (Liverpool Institute for the Performing Arts), in which he explains his hopes for the venture and announces that he is seeking sponsorship to the sum of £8 million. At the conclusion of this afternoon get-together, Paul is given a guided tour of the PRS building.

Tuesday February 25
 In New York, Ringo is present at the 34th Annual Grammy Awards ceremony, held at the Radio City Music Hall.

March
 A new book is published in Japan, entitled *ai: Japan Through John Lennon's Eyes*, which comprises sketches and notes taken from John's exercise book of the late Seventies when he was studying the Japanese language.

Monday March 2
 In the UK and America, Rykodisc releases the Yoko Ono six-CD box set entitled *Onobox*, comprising of 105 tracks, many of which she recorded with John between the years 1968 and 1980, and many of which are previously unreleased. Among the unreleased recordings is Yoko's album *A Story,* a selection of recordings she made during her separation from John in 1973 and 1974.
 At the Mayfair Hotel in London, George appears in the audience at a press conference given by fellow member of the Traveling Wilburys Tom Petty, who is joined by his group

The Heartbreakers. Following the conference, George and Tom go to a private party at the Hard Rock Cafe in London, at which B.B. King and Gary Moore are also in attendance.

Tuesday March 17
🍎 At London's Heathrow Airport, George joins Tom Petty on a flight to Berlin in Germany, where Petty is giving a concert later this evening.

Monday March 23
🍎 After four straight years of broadcasting in America on a regular weekly basis, Westwood One radio concludes the series *The Lost Lennon Tapes*. The series, which was originally scheduled to run for just 52 shows, concludes at show number 218, or at number 219 if you include the original two-hour preview show. One week after the finish of *The Lost Lennon Tapes* programmes, Westwood One in America begin airing the new radio series *The Beatle Years*.

April
🍎 Paul gives a private London screening of his MPL produced short animated feature entitled *Daumier's Law*.
🍎 The film *The Hours And The Times*, which focuses on the alleged relationship between John and Brian Epstein, is screened during the London gay movie festival.

Wednesday April 1
🍎 A preview of George's upcoming concert at the Royal Albert Hall in London takes place on CBS's *This Morning* in America.

Thursday April 2
🍎 In New York, at the Radio City Music Hall, a big army of reporters and TV crews gather to hear Ringo announce the release of his new album *Time Takes Time,* as well as news of a new All-Starr Band, who will tour both North America and Europe, beginning on June 2. The new band line-up retains both Joe Walsh and Nils Lofgren from the 1989 All-Starrs, and adds several new members in the shape of Dave Edmunds, Burton Cummings and Todd Rundgren who are all present at the press conference, plus Timothy B. Schmit, Tim Cappello as well as Ringo's son Zak on drums.
🍎 Back in England, at 10am, tickets for George's concert at the Royal Albert Hall in London, on Monday April 6, go on sale. Prices range from £15 to £20.

Friday April 3
🍎 To help promote both the album and forthcoming tour, Ringo begins a hectic round of personal appearances, beginning tonight with a live spot on the CBS TV programme *The David Letterman Show*, presented at the historic Ed Sullivan Theater in New York, the scene where The Beatles made their famous American television début on February 9, 1964. Following this, Ringo rushes to be a guest presenter at the annual Grammy Awards ceremony show. Also today, advance copies of Ringo's single 'Weight Of The World' are sent to various US radio stations.

Saturday April 4
🍎 In America, Ringo is interviewed on the television programme *Late Night*.

Sunday April 5
🍎 In an interview primarily to promote his concert tomorrow, George announces to the BBC, "I will be recording a new studio album in the summer and will be touring with it upon its release." He spends the day in rehearsal at the Royal Albert Hall.

Monday April 6
🍎 George performs in concert with Eric Clapton's Band at London's Royal Albert Hall in support of the Natural Law Party, a Bedfordshire based organisation which promotes transcendental meditation and a spiritual lifestyle. The show, which kicks off at 7:30pm, is promoted as "George's First UK Show Since Leaving The Beatles" and billed as "The Natural Law Party Presents George Harrison & Friends – Inspiration To The Youth Of Great Britain – Election Is A Celebration". (During the current British

elections, the Natural Law party, which was formed on March 15, has 310 candidates running for office.)

In answer to the frequently asked question as to why he is performing at the show, George issues a statement which reads: "I am performing in this concert to support the Natural Law Party. I will vote for the Natural Law Party because I want a total change and not just a choice between left and right. The system we have now is obsolete and is not fulfilling the needs of the people. Times have changed and we need a new approach. I believe this party offers the only option to get out of our problems and create the beautiful nation we would all like to have. The General Election should be a celebration of democracy and our right to vote. The Natural Law Party is turning this election into a wonderful national celebration and I am with them all the way."

Asked about The Beatles' association with Maharishi Mahesh Yogi and how he feels now about transcendental meditation, George replies: "I still practise transcendental meditation and I think it's great. Maharishi only ever did good for us, and although I have not been with him physically, I never left him."

The 105-minute set on the night consists largely of tracks performed by George and Eric during the 1991 tour of Japan, including 'I Want To Tell You', 'Old Brown Shoe', 'Taxman', 'Give Me Love (Give Me Peace On Earth)', 'Something', 'What Is Life', 'Piggies' (with the extra verse written by John back in 1968), 'Got My Mind Set On You', 'Cloud 9', 'Here Comes The Sun', 'My Sweet Lord', 'All Those Years Ago', 'Cheer Down', 'Isn't It A Pity', 'Devil's Radio' and, for the encore, 'Roll Over Beethoven' and 'While My Guitar Gently Weeps', which features Ringo. (Ringo had, in fact, started the day at 10:30am by holding a lengthy 43-minute press conference at the Dorchester Hotel in London, an event to promote his new album *Time Takes Time* and his forthcoming All-Starr Band tour.)

At the conclusion of George's set, Ringo remains on stage where he joins drummer Steve Ferrone and Ray Cooper in a spontaneous five-minute jam session. When George reappears on stage, he is accompanied by his son Dhani, who is clutching an electric guitar and joins his father and the other musicians in another performance of 'Roll Over Beethoven', which closes the show. Joining George on stage tonight are Joe Walsh, Gary Moore, Zak Starkey, Tessa Niles, Greg Phillinganes, Katie Kissoon, Steve Ferrone, Andy Fairweather-Low, Ray Cooper, Will Lee, Chuck Leavell and Mike Campbell.

In the audience is Paul and Linda's daughter Mary.

Thursday April 9
 Paul and George Martin are filmed at Abbey Road Studios in London for the TV special *The Making Of Sgt. Pepper,* which is premiered in the UK across the ITV network on June 14 and in America on the Disney Channel on September 27. The Disney Channel version is slightly different to the one broadcast in the UK, omitting a discussion between the ex-Beatles and George Martin on the use of drugs and their possible influence on the album. Alternative footage is added to fill the gaps.

Sunday April 12
 In George Martin's West London home, George Harrison films an interview for inclusion in the TV special *The Making Of Sgt. Pepper*.

Thursday April 16
 In the States, Ringo puts in a guest appearance on the CNBC show *Real Life*.

Sunday April 19
 One week after George had prepared his sequence, Ringo films his appearance for the TV special *The Making Of Sgt. Pepper* in Aspen, Colorado.

Monday April 20
 The 43-minute Japanese NHK TV children's programme *Tsukai Ningen-Den* (*Dashing Life Stories* – transmitted between 8:00 and 9:00pm) tells the story of John's life through pictures and archive film clips. Included is some amazing video footage of John, Yoko and Sean visiting Japan in August 1978 and the first ever public screening of the presumed destroyed *Double Fantasy* video footage (see entry for Monday August 18 1980). This 26-second clip, taken from day two of the taping (August 19), features scenes of only Yoko in a recording booth ready to sing and the musicians (drummer Andy

Newmark, guitarists Earl Slick and Hugh McCracken) playing in the studio. John is not seen in this extract.

The footage was directed by the New York director Jay Dubin, responsible for many pop promotional music videos. (He directed the Billy Joel video for 'Uptown Girl' in 1983.) VT recording back in August 1980 was carried out on one-inch tape using two cameras, and once the five-day sessions have been concluded, and before any copies could be made, the video master tapes are handed over personally to two of Yoko's bodyguards. A further extract of the *Double Fantasy* sessions, albeit ten seconds, appears in the 1984 American documentary *Yoko Ono: Then And Now* where, under a narrative, Yoko can be seen clearly singing 'I'm Moving On'. Sources close to Yoko and her basement archives at the Dakota in New York claim that the complete *Double Fantasy* video footage does indeed exist but it is now filed as "untouchable".

Tuesday April 21
☘ Ringo's skill as a narrator is called upon again today when he "voice-overs" the 15-minute animated story *Elbert's Bad Word*, for Shelly Duvall's *Bedtime Stories* series on the US cable station *Showtime*.

May
☘ In London, Apple Corps officially announces that the three ex-Beatles will work together again on the forthcoming official Beatles documentary film *The Long And Winding Road*. The project had originally been conceived during May 1970, but was never completed. Each Beatle, during the time of the split in April 1970, had already filmed a brief interview intended for inclusion in the first episode.
☘ At the annual, prestigious Cannes Film Festival, Paul and Linda's MPL produced film *Daumier's Law* receives its premiere. The short 15-minute animated film, directed by Geoff Dunbar, recreates the drawings of the French artist Honore Daumier. Paul wrote and produced the film's musical score and performed most of it himself, recording it during late December 1989.

Friday May 1
☘ Another Nike commercial is transmitted in America and again irritates fans. This time, John's original 1970 recording of 'Instant Karma' is featured in these "Yoko approved" commercials. (Seven years later, John's original recording of 'Instant Karma' will again appear on a television commercial. See entry for April 1999.)

Tuesday May 5
☘ Ringo appears again on the American Paramount TV show *Entertainment Tonight*.

Saturday May 9
☘ In the States, Ringo makes a guest appearance on the American one-hour NBC TV variety special *Dame Edna's Hollywood,* hosted by Dame Edna Everage. During the show, Ringo joins the host to perform a rather unique version of 'Act Naturally'.

Tuesday May 12
☘ In America, Carl Davis conducts a performance of Linda's composition 'Appaloosa', as well as Paul's piece 'Meditation' with The Boston Pops. This performance is videotaped and transmitted by PBS Television in America during August.

Saturday May 16 & Sunday May 17
☘ In America, Ringo begins shooting the promotional video for the track 'Weight Of The World'. A CNN report on the making of the clip is transmitted in the programme *Showbiz Today* on Monday May 18.

Wednesday May 20
☘ Ringo appears again on American TV to promote his new album and single, this time a guest spot on the Paramount show *Entertainment Tonight*.

Friday May 22
☘ Ringo continues the round of American TV promotional activities by being featured, with his All-Starr Band, on the ABC TV music show *In Concert '92*.

 In Barcelona, Spain, Paul's *Oratorio* receives another performance. (This is its eighth public airing.)

Tuesday May 26
 Ringo crops up again, this time on the American VH-1 TV programme *VH-1 To 1*.
 The second phase of Apple's reissue campaign takes place today when the albums *Wonderwall* by George, *Maybe Tomorrow* by The Iveys, *No Dice* by Badfinger, *Earth Song/Ocean Song* by Mary Hopkin and *Doris Troy* by Doris Troy are issued.

Wednesday May 27
 Ringo appears as a guest on the syndicated American television show *Arsenio,* hosted by Arsenio Hall. Following an interview, he joins his All-Starr Band to perform 'Weight Of The World'.

Thursday May 28
 Showing no signs of exhaustion, Ringo appears in a pre-recorded segment on the American NBC TV breakfast show *Today.* Also today, Ringo and his All-Starr Band attend a private party for them on the Paramount film studio's backlot. *Alberto VO5* and *Private Music* host the event.

* * *

Ringo and his new All-Starr Band
North American Tour
Tuesday June 2 – Friday June 26

Ringo and his new All-Starr band undertake a tour of North America, with performances at the following venues:

Sunrise Pavilion, Fort Lauderdale, Florida (Tuesday June 2 and Wednesday June 3)
Bayfront Pavilion, St. Petersburg, Florida (Friday June 5)
Blockbuster Pavilion, Charlotte, North Carolina (Saturday June 6)
Chastain Park Amphitheater, Atlanta, Georgia (Sunday June 7)
Riverbend Music Center, Cincinnati, Ohio (Tuesday June 9)
Blossom Music Center, Guyaboga Falls, Ohio (Wednesday June 10)
Deer Creek Music Center, Noblesville, Indiana, near Indianapolis (Friday June 12)
Poplar Creek Music Theater, Hofman Estates, Illinois, near Chicago
    (Saturday June 13)
Pine Knob Music Theater, Clarkston, Michigan, near Detroit (Monday June 15)
Kingswood Music Theatre in Wonderland Park, Maple, Ontario, near Toronto
    (Tuesday June 16)
Merriweather Post Pavilion, Columbia (Wednesday June 17)
Radio City Music Hall, N.Y.C. (Friday June 19 and Saturday June 20)
Garden State Arts Center, Holmdel, New Jersey (Sunday June 21)
Great Woods Amphitheater, Mansfieid, Massachusetts, near Boston
    (Monday June 22)
Jones Beach Amphitheater, Wantaugh, New York (Tuesday June 23)
Marcus Amphitheater, Milwaukee, Wisconsin (Thursday June 25)
Riverport Center, Maryland Heights, near St. Louis, Missouri (Friday June 26)

(To coincide with the tour, a special limited edition *Ringo And The All-Starr Band* promotional bubble gum is released by the concert promoters.)

Ringo and his new All-Starr Band
Tour Of Europe
Thursday July 2 – Thursday July 23

The tour moves on to Europe for a three-week period, with the following performances at:

The Gothenburg All Star Festival, Gothenburg, Sweden (Thursday July 2)
Dalarock Festival, Hedemora, Sweden (Friday July 3)
Moelleparken, Malmo, Sweden (Saturday July 4)
Empire Theatre, Liverpool, UK (Monday July 6)

Hammersmith Odeon (later renamed Hammersmith Apollo), London (Tuesday July 7)
Le Zenith, Paris, France (Wednesday July 8)
Stadtgarten, Hamburg, Germany (Friday July 10)
Tanzbrunnen, Koln, Germany (Saturday July 11)
Unterfrankenhalle, Aschaffenburg, Germany (Sunday July 12)
Montreux Jazz Festival, Montreux, Switzerland (Monday July 13)
Deutschlandhalle, Berlin, Germany (Wednesday July 15)
Pori Jazz Festival, Kirjurinluoto Park, Pori, Finland (Friday July 17)
Valby ldretspark (ITS Rock), Copenhagen, Denmark (Saturday July 18)
Lisbterg Fruespark (ITS Rock), Arhus, Denmark (Sunday July 19)
Belga Beach Festival, Belga Beach, DePanne, Belgium (Monday July 20)
Teatre Tenda, Brescia, Italy (Wednesday July 22)
Teatre La Versiliana, Marina Di Perasanta, Italy (Thursday July 23)
Foro Italico, Rome, Italy (Friday July 24 – cancelled!)

During the tour

Monday July 13
Ringo and his All-Starr Band perform at the annual Montreux Jazz Festival in
Switzerland. The following tracks appear in America and the UK on the album *Ringo
Starr And His All-Starr Band Live: Live From Montreux*, released on September 14, 1993:
'I'm The Greatest', 'Don't Go Where The Road Don't Go', 'Yellow Submarine', 'Weight Of
The World', 'Boys' and 'With A Little Help From My Friends', all performed by Ringo
and 'Desperado' and 'In The City' (performed by Joe Walsh), 'Girls Talk' (by Dave
Edmunds), 'I Can't Tell You Why' (by Timothy B. Schmidt), 'Bang The Drum All Day'
and 'Black Maria' (by Todd Rundgren), 'Walkin' Nerve' (by Nils Lofgren) and 'American
Woman' (by Burton Cummings).

Ringo and His New All-Starr Band Tour

Return to America
Saturday August 1 – Sunday September 6

Ringo's tour with his new All-Starr band continues with performances at the following
venues:

Le Champs de Brionne Summer Music Theater, George, Washington
(Saturday August 1)
Harvey's Hotel, Tahoe, California (Monday August 3)
Redwood Amphitheater in the Great American Amusement Park, Santa Clara,
California (Tuesday August 4)
Concord Pavilion, Concord, California (Wednesday, August 5)
California Mid State Fair, Paso Robles, California (Friday August 7)
Camp Pendleton Marine Base, Oceanside, California (Saturday August 8)
Pacific Amphitheater, Costa Mesa, California (Sunday August 9)
Greek Theater, Los Angeles, California (Tuesday August 11 and Wednesday August 12)
Desert Sky Pavilion, Phoenix, Arizona (Thursday August 13)
Aquafest, Austin, Texas (Saturday August 15)
Riverfront Park, Little Rock, Arkansas (Sunday August 16)
Starplex Amphitheater, Dallas, Texas (Tuesday August 18)
Ohio State Fair Celeste Center, Columbus, Ohio (Thursday August 20)
Freedom Hall, Kentucky State Fair, Louisville, Kentucky (Friday August 21)
Iowa State Fair, Des Moines, Iowa (Saturday August 22)
Star Lake Amphitheater, Pittsburgh, Pennsylvania (Monday August 24)
Finger Lakes Performing Arts Center, Canandaigua (near Rochester), New York
(Tuesday August 25)
Saratoga Performing Arts Center, Saratoga Springs, New York
(Wednesday August 26)
Taj Mahal Casino, in Atlantic City, New Jersey (Thursday August 27 – cancelled!)
Waterloo Village Amphitheater, Stanhope, New Jersey (Friday August 28)
Fiddlers Green Amphitheater, Englewood, Colorado, near Denver
(Tuesday September 1)

Park West Amphitheater, Park City, Utah in Salt Lake City (Wednesday September 2) Caesar's Palace, Las Vegas, Nevada (Friday September 4, Saturday September 5 (two shows) and Sunday September 6)

Ringo's repertoire includes the following songs: 'I'm The Greatest', 'No No Song', 'Don't Go Where The Road Don't Go', 'Yellow Submarine', 'You're Sixteen', 'Weight Of The World', 'Photograph', and encore performances of 'Act Naturally' and 'With A Little Help From My Friends'. The track 'Boys' is added during the latter half of the tour, which features the only track Ringo performs from behind his drum kit, the others being sung on centre stage. Also worth noting is that Todd Rundgren misses the shows in Englewood and Park City, while Joe Walsh is absent from the final concerts at the Caesar's Palace in Las Vegas.

Friday July 3
Ringo's All- Starr Band performance at the Montreux Jazz Festival in Switzerland is recorded and later released on the CD and home video *Ringo Starr And His All-Starr Band: Live From Montreux*. Ringo's new single 'Don't Go Where The Road Don't Go' is also scheduled for an American release today, but fails to materialise. The single does show in Germany though, featuring the otherwise unreleased track 'Everybody Wins'.

Monday July 6
Ringo returns home to Liverpool for a concert at the Empire Theatre. Highlights from the concert are included in the Disney Channel television special *Ringo Starr: Going Home*, which is transmitted in America on Sunday April 18, 1993.

Tuesday July 7
In the States, Ringo is interviewed live on CBS TV's programme *This Morning*.

Sunday August 16
A pre-recorded interview with Ringo in America is transmitted in the UK on Nicky Campbell's evening show on BBC Radio 1. Also today, to coincide with the current tour, Ringo's albums *Ringo's Rotogravure* and *Ringo The 4th* are released in the US on compact disc.

Thursday August 27
Following the cancellation of Ringo's All-Starr band concert at the Taj Mahal Casino in Jersey, he is to be found appearing on stage with his friend Joe Walsh during Walsh's charity concert at the China Club in New York City.

Friday September 4, Saturday September 5 & Sunday September 6
To coincide with Ringo's concerts at the prestigious Caesar's Palace Hotel, a special *Ringo & All-Starr Band* restaurant menu is printed. During the concert on September 6, Ringo appears live on the *Jerry Lewis Muscular Dystrophy Telethon* on US television, performing 'You're Sixteen'. The song is not aired in all areas of the States, while on the East Coast of America, it is past midnight when Ringo's appearance finally takes place.

* * *

June (through into July)
 At Paul's Mill studios in East Sussex, Aubrey Powell films Paul and his band at work, recording the album *Off The Ground*. The footage will take the shape of a 27-minute televised MPL documentary entitled *Movin' On,* which also features a behind-the-scenes look at the making of the videos for 'C'mon People' and 'Off The Ground'. (The UK premiere of the show takes place on Channel 4 on April 18, 1993, and on the Fox Network in America on June 10 featuring slightly different footage. An extended 60-minute version is later released on home video in America on October 14, 1993.)

Saturday June 6
 A 1991 film clip of George playing ukulele and singing the Cab Calloway number 'Between The Devil And The Deep Blue Sea', is featured in the Channel 4 music

documentary *Mister Roadrunner* in the UK. Hosted by the former Squeeze pianist Jools Holland, the programme is produced by the team who are currently, in West London, working on The Beatles' *Long And Winding Road* documentary series.

Wednesday June 10
◆ In the UK, additional *Anthology* interview segments with Paul are conducted today by Jools Holland, carried out whilst sailing up the Thames in a private boat.

Sunday June 14
◆ The TV special *The Making Of Sgt. Pepper* is transmitted in the UK across the ITV network, featuring separate interviews with Paul (filmed on April 9), George (April 12) and Ringo (on April 19). The show, which will premiere in America on the Disney Channel on September 27 this year, also features George Martin playing some unreleased *Sgt. Pepper's* recordings directly off the original studio 4-track master tapes.

Monday June 15
◆ George appears unannounced at the Hard Rock Cafe in Piccadilly, London, where his friend Carl Perkins is in concert. They perform 'Everybody's Trying To Be My Baby', 'Blue Suede Shoes' and 'Honey Don't'. A short clip of George's live appearance is seen on MTV's *Week In Rock*, transmitted, for the first time, on June 20.
◆ Also today, Parlophone/EMI, in the UK, release *The Beatles EP Set,* a box set of the original UK Beatles EPs on 5-inch CDs. (The American release takes place on June 30.)
◆ In Japan, Yoko makes a live studio appearance on the NHK TV programme *Tetsuko Ni Heya* to promote her new CD set *Onobox*. The entire interview is naturally carried out in the Japanese language.

Thursday June 18
◆ To celebrate Paul's 50th birthday, BBC Radio 2 in the UK, transmits a new one-hour documentary on Paul entitled *Paul McCartney – Rediscovering Yesterday*, narrated by Brian Matthew. Paul's historic landmark is also celebrated at the National Film Theatre in London, when a night of Beatles film clips from the Sixties, which include the ATV/ITV programme *The Morecambe And Wise Show* (originally transmitted on April 18, 1964), is screened. In Tokyo, Japan, Paul's *Oratorio* is played in public for the ninth time. Its tenth performance takes place at the same venue tomorrow, Friday June 19.

Sunday June 21
◆ In the UK, Paul appears briefly during the Channel 4 arts programme *This Is Tomorrow*. The programme, a special edition of the *Without Walls* series, celebrates the illustrious career of the designer Richard Hamilton, whom Paul had previously worked with on the designs for The Beatles' 1968 *White Album*.

Sunday June 28
◆ Still in the UK, Paul appears on BBC Radio 2 in a pre-recorded interview, which focuses on LIPA, the Liverpool Institute For The Performing Arts.

July
◆ MPL films a 30-minute documentary entitled *Appaloosa*. The film, directed by Barry Chattington, is the second MPL to focus attention on Linda's Appaloosa horse called Blankit (the first, of course, was *Blankit's First Show)*. As with their first film, *Appaloosa* also features new music, this time composed jointly by Paul and Linda.

Thursday July 2
◆ Paul and Linda make a flying visit to Belgium, where they host a fund-raising trip for members of the European music industry fraternity in Brussels. This fund-raising event will also help benefit LIPA. (The McCartneys return to Heathrow Airport later today.)

Monday July 13
◆ George's double album *Live In Japan,* recorded during his visit to Japan in December of 1991, is released in the UK (the American release takes place the following day, Tuesday July 14).

August
 Paul, Linda and family take their traditional, month-long, August family holiday to Long Island in New York.

Thursday August 20
 During his vacation, Paul attends a performance by the *Saturday Night Live* band at the Stephen Talkhouse in Amagansett. During the show, he needs little persuasion to jump up on stage and join in with the band on the song 'Blue Suede Shoes'. Paul and his family return home to England the following week.

Monday August 24
 George again visits Los Angeles, cutting short his holiday in Hawaii to do so. During his three-week visit, where he also meets up with Ravi Shankar in San Diego, he puts in another live appearance on the KLOS-FM radio show *Rockline*. Tonight, during the American syndicated radio series *In The Studio*, George's 1991 tour of Japan comes under the spotlight, and includes interviews and music from the shows.

September
 During the month, at his home studios in Sussex, Paul records the first demos of the tracks 'Calico Skies' and 'Great Day', songs that will ultimately appear on his 1997 album *Flaming Pie*.
 The scheduled official release in America this month of Apple's documentary *The Beatles: The First US Visit*, fails to materialise.
 Ringo makes another appearance on the US TV show *The Jerry Lewis Telethon*, where he is seen performing the track 'You're Sixteen'.

Saturday September 5
 In England, Paul and Linda arrange a 21st birthday party for Stella in a marquee in the grounds at their Rye, Sussex farmhouse, a similar affair to the party thrown for Mary when she was 21. The McCartneys request that everyone turn up in fancy dress costume. Linda dresses as Queen Elizabeth 1, while Paul comes as a highwayman. Among the guests at the party are Ringo and Barbara with music coming from The Thompson Twins and the 10-piece group Soul Provider. During the latter's 90-minute performance, Paul is persuaded to join in with the group to perform a version of the Al Green track 'Take Me To The River'.

Wednesday September 9
 The annual Buddy Holly celebrations again take place in London where Paul hosts a lunch-time Buddy Holly concert featuring The Crickets. During their performance, Paul takes to the stage to perform a medley of Holly numbers, including 'Rave On' and 'Oh Boy!' Joining Paul on stage are guitarist Big Jim Sullivan, Willie Austin, Malcolm Mortimer and Andy Crossheart. Sharing lead vocals with Paul is Seventies pop star Gary Glitter. Later in the afternoon, Paul returns to perform, again with The Crickets, the songs 'Mean Woman Blues' and 'Shake, Rattle And Roll'. This time, the line-up on stage features Gary Glitter, Leo Sayer and, from The Hollies, Allan Clarke on vocals, and Mick Green (formerly of Johnny Kidd And The Pirates), Henry Spinetti and Blair Cunningham on drums. Linda is seen joining Chrissie Hynde, Hamish Stuart and the DJ Tony Prince on backing vocals.

Thursday September 10
 In America, with his tour now over, Ringo participates in a comedy sketch as a part of the annual *MTV Music Video Awards Show*.

Friday September 11
 In the States, George features prominently during today's edition of the American ABC TV music show *In Concert '92*, where professionally shot concert film from his December 1991 Japanese concert tour is premiered. The live tracks shown include 'Taxman' and 'Piggies'. A new interview with him accompanies the five-minute item.

Saturday September 19
 Paul and Linda return to Long Island in New York to attend the wedding reception of Linda's niece, Louise Eastman. An improvised concert takes place at the reception and

again, Paul is persuaded to participate. Buddy Holly songs feature prominently in the proceedings.

Monday September 21
🍎 In Germany, Ringo's single 'Don't Go Where The Road Don't Go' b/w 'Don't Know A Thing About Love' is released as a single. (The CD version features the bonus track 'Everybody Wins'.)

Tuesday September 22
🍎 In the UK, The Beatles' unauthorised biographer Geoffrey Giuliano gives an interview, published in today's edition of the *Guardian* newspaper. He describes The Beatles as "real shits in real life", George as an "eccentric recluse" and Paul as "just shallow and vacuous". George's wife Olivia is unimpressed with the feature and decides to reply. (See entry for Monday October 5.)

Sunday September 27
🍎 The documentary *The Making Of Sgt. Pepper* is premiered in America on the Disney Channel. This screening also marks the start of a six-week Beatles Festival as part of the Disney *Sunday Night Showcase*. Over the coming weeks (starting at 9:00pm ET/PT), the series includes: *Magical Mystery Tour* (on October 4), *Paul McCartney: Going Home* (October 11), the 1990 *John Lennon Tribute Concert* (October 18), John and Yoko's 1972 *Imagine* film (October 25) and Paul's documentary film *Get Back* (on November 1). Further Disney Channel repeat screenings occur with *Paul McCartney: Going Home* being transmitted on October 17 and Paul's *Get Back* on November 7, 12, 18 and 26.

Tuesday September 29
🍎 Ringo returns to Liverpool to film additional sequences for his Disney Channel television special *Ringo Starr: Going Home*. (The show will premiere in America on Sunday April 18, 1993.) Ringo also drops in to The Beatles shop in Mathew Street, where he uses the shop's telephone which will later be auctioned at a Liverpool Merseybeatles convention.

October
🍎 During the month, over a four-day period, Paul works with the producer Youth on one of his strangest projects ever. The pair create the album *Strawberries Oceans Ships Forest,* credited to The Fireman and containing nine different mixes of the same track, with each given its own title. These are 'Transpiritual Stomp', 'Trans Lunar Rising', 'Transcrystaline', 'Pure Trance', 'Arizona Light', 'Celtic Stomp', 'Strawberries Oceans Ships Forest', '444' and 'Sunrise Mix'. These comprise samples, recorded by Paul, such as whispering, banjos, flutes and the original bass played by Bill Black on Elvis Presley's classic recording of 'Heartbreak Hotel'. To aid with the recordings, Paul sampled two of his own tracks ('The Broadcast' and 'Reception'), both of which appeared on the 1979 Wings album *Back To The Egg*. (*Strawberries Oceans Ships Forest* is released in the UK on November 15, 1993, and in America on February 22, 1994.)

This month in the UK, the publishers Secker & Warburg announce that they have signed a deal to produce the official version of Paul's life story. The book is the result of several years of negotiations and Paul will collaborate with his old friend, the writer Barry Miles.

Also this month, Paul and Linda hold a fund and awareness raising lunch at London's Groucho Club for approximately 45 potential sponsors of the Liverpool Institute for the Performing Arts. Among those present are Robert Key, the National Heritage Ministry, Peter Bounds, the chief executive of Liverpool City Council and Lord Polumbo, chair of the Arts Council.

🍎 In America, George becomes the second ex-Beatle to tape a voice-over for an episode of the top-rated TV American cartoon series *The Simpsons.* The programme, which involves Homer Simpson and his spoof-Beatles group The Bee-Sharps, is not premiered on the Fox network in America until September 30, 1993.

🍎 In the States, an interview with George, carried out by Bill Flangan, is reprinted in this month's *Rock CD* magazine. During the feature, George is quoted as saying: "*'Revolution 9'* . . . Ringo and I compiled that. We went into the tape library and looked through the entire room and pulled main selections and gave the tapes to John, and he cut them together. The whole thing 'number nine . . . number nine,' is because I pulled the box number nine. It was some kind of education programme. John sat there and decided which bits to cross-fade together, but if Ringo and I hadn't have gone there in the first place, he wouldn't have had anything." George also talks about the *Beatles Anthology* documentary series, currently in production. "This thing has been laying in cans for years," he reveals. "We did an interview for it and during the course of the questions, this thought came into my mind, which sums up the whole of The Beatles' years: How many Beatles does it take to change a light bulb? The answer is four: John, Paul, George and Ringo. Whatever history thinks, that's what it was." (The interview had previously been printed in the American publication *Musician*.)

☙ In London, the auction house Phillips begins seeking a private buyer for *The Beatles Exhibition,* which, until recently, has been on show at the Trocadero in London's Piccadilly.

Saturday October 3
☙ BBC Radio One repeats, during the programme *Archive Jukebox*, clips from John and Yoko's interview with Andy Peebles from December 6, 1980, and George's appearance on *Roundtable,* originally transmitted on February 9, 1979 (see relevant dates for further information).

☙ On the same day, this time on BBC Radio Two, the 28-minute documentary *Yesterday Forever* is broadcast, which features a profile of The Beatles and the various other acts who have recorded Paul's famous 1965 song.

Monday October 5
☙ PMI home video in the UK releases the compilation entitled *The John Lennon Video Collection.*

☙ To coincide with the 30th anniversary of the release of 'Love Me Do', an evening reception is held in Studio Two at Abbey Road in London, celebrating the release of Mark Lewisohn's book *The Complete Beatles Chronicles*. Representing The Beatles, and indeed Apple Corps, are Neil Aspinall, Derek Taylor and the photographer Tommy Hanley. Further 'Love Me Do' celebratory events take place in America today when, at the Capitol Records Tower in Hollywood, California, a special open-air Beatles party is held. Beatles fans gathering below are handed slices of a unique 'Love Me Do' birthday cake and are invited, by Capitol's president Hale Milgrim, to sign a giant Beatles birthday card and contribute to an anniversary video greeting.

☙ In England, George attends tonight's Gary Moore concert at The Royal Albert Hall in London, joining Moore briefly on stage for the encore. Meanwhile also today in the UK, the *Bunbury Tails* album, brought forward from December, is released and features George's recording of 'Ride Rajbun'.

☙ Today's *Guardian* newspaper publishes a letter from Olivia Harrison, in reply to the article on Geoffrey Giuliano, published in the paper on Tuesday September 22 (see entry). Her sharp, concise letter reads: "The sight of Geoffrey Giuliano's face is enough to make anyone a recluse. My husband once made the remark: 'That guy knows more about my life than I do.' Mr. Giuliano missed the joke and used it to endorse his book. To rate himself as the world's greatest rock'n'roll biographer (a laughable title in the first place) is nothing but delusion. He has only ever been in the vicinity of my husband for about ten minutes and considers himself an expert. He parades as a spiritual person while condemning the famous, yet without them his achievements in this life wouldn't rate one line in any newspaper. To judge Paul McCartney as 'vacuous and shallow' after all Paul has written and offered to the world is surely the judgement of an arrogant mind, especially as Giuliano's own recognition is not because he is creative, but because, like a starving dog, he scavenges from his heroes, picking up bits of gristle and sinew along the way, repackaging them for consumption by a gullible public. His life is a 'curse' to himself, and perhaps his admitted 300 acid trips by the age of 19 have something to do with it. I'm sick of this guy." The letter is signed Olivia Harrison (Mrs. George), Henley-on-Thames.

Thursday October 8
☙ Paul, George and Ringo hold a three-hour business meeting at Paul's MPL offices, in Soho, London. Afterwards they are seen leaving the building separately in the early afternoon, Paul climbing into his waiting limousine while George and Ringo jump into a

taxi. Reports suggest that they then go on for a further business meeting in London, which includes Yoko Ono.

Saturday October 10
 In the UK, the *Daily Star* newspaper runs a story headlined: "GOBSMACCA", which reports that "700 packets of Linda's vegetarian *Deep Country* pies had mistakenly been filled with a distinctly non-vegetarian steak and kidney filling." The report adds that Linda was quite rightly "fuming" and was "worried" that the slip-up could have been done deliberately. The article concludes by quoting Linda as saying: "I have instructed my solicitors to insist that from now on, none of the vegetarian products that bear my name are manufactured anywhere near any meat products."

Wednesday October 14
 George and Olivia leave Heathrow Airport en route to New York's J.F. Kennedy Airport.

Friday October 16
 At New York's Madison Square Garden, George attends the Bob Dylan Columbia Records 30th anniversary tribute concert. During the star-studded celebration of the music of Dylan, George performs the tracks 'If Not For You' and 'Absolutely Sweet Marie', and returns later, as part of the encore, to join in on the numbers 'My Back Pages' and 'Knockin' On Heaven's Door'. The event is screened live on pay-per-view cable TV in America, and broadcast live simultaneously on FM radio in stereo. (Among the many complete screenings of the show which take place around the world shortly afterwards, a broadcast of the concert takes place on the private French channel Canal Plus at 1:45am on February 26, 1993.) All of George's live performances, bar the first number, are released on the album *Bob Dylan – 30th Anniversary Concert Celebration*.

Monday October 19
 After a week's delay, Apple records in the UK re-issue John Tavener's début album *The Whale*.

Tuesday October 20
 In the States, Ringo appears in a pre-taped feature on the ABC TV breakfast show *Good Morning America*. The interview, where he appears alongside the actor Dennis Hopper, is to promote this weekend's three-day *Sierra Tucson Ringo Starr Celebrity Weekend*.
 On his Concorde flight home, George's return trip to England (BAO 44) is forced to return back to New York's J.F. Kennedy Airport when a warning light in the cockpit starts flashing. Once back at the airport, all of the passengers disembark while British Airways' staff check over the aircraft's engines. (The warning signal had been a false alarm.) To help relieve the boredom during the three-hour delay, George takes out his guitar and entertains the packed first class departure lounge with an impromptu 15-minute performance of George Formby songs. He then hands over his captive audience to the flight's other famous passenger, Norman Schwarzkopf, the commander of the allied forces, who goes on to tell his audience tales of heroic deeds and his military action in the Gulf War.

Wednesday October 21
 Ringo makes a return appearance on the American variety show *Arsenio,* hosted by Arsenio Hall, where he performs 'Don't Go Where The Road Don't Go' (announced as his new single) and 'Act Naturally', both with Nils Lofgren and the resident studio house-band. Ringo also participates in an interview with the host.

Saturday October 24
 Ringo's recent high profile in America continues with an appearance at the three-day *Sierra Tucson Foundation* fund-raising benefit concert, held at the University of Arizona's McKale Center. During the evening, which also features on the bill James Taylor and Jimmy Buffet, Ringo and members of his All-Starr Band perform several numbers. Ringo agreed to the concert because he and Barbara had undergone alcohol rehabilitation at the Sierra Tucson Alcohol and Drug Rehabilitation Center for six weeks during October/November 1988.

Sunday October 25
🍎 Yet another in a long line of surprise George Harrison live performances takes place tonight when, apparently, he and Gary Moore take part in some late-night jamming at a pub near George's home called The Crooked Billet. The event, part of a birthday celebration for Moore, angers local residents who complain about the noise to the local police, who insist that the music be turned down. When the landlord of the Crooked Billet is asked about this session, he denies that the event ever took place, adding that the music this evening was actually provided by the cockney duo Chas & Dave.
🍎 Channel 4 screens the Yorkshire Television documentary film on James Hanratty. Featured in this 65-minute film are clips from the 1969 film about Hanratty shot by John and Yoko, which has previously been screened only once, on February 17, 1972 (see entry).

Tuesday October 27
🍎 In the UK, Linda appears in a pre-taped interview for BBC2's *The Late Show*, recorded at the BBC TV Centre, Wood Lane, London, to promote her book *Sixties*.

November
🍎 In London, Apple Productions reject the original title of The Beatles' documentary series, currently in progress in Wendell Road in London. The production, in a short space of time, goes from *The Long And Winding Road* to . . . *The Beatles Anthology*. Apparently, George was against naming the entire Beatles' history after a Paul McCartney song. This new title, originally just a working title but eventually staying, suits all the parties concerned.

Sunday November 1
🍎 Paul's live-concert film *Get Back,* featuring direction by Richard Lester, receives its world television premiere on the Disney Channel in America.

Monday November 2
🍎 The Beatles' Singles Collection, a box set of all 22 original UK Beatles singles on five-inch CDs, is released in the UK. (The American release takes place on November 17.) The set has previously been released in the three-inch CD format.

Friday November 6
🍎 Work continues at Apple Productions in London on *The Beatles Anthology*. A story board is now firmly in place with certain individual tracks chosen to close each year of the programmes (i.e. 'Strawberry Fields Forever' has been designated to close the year for 1967, 'Hey Jude' for 1968, etc.). Original film sequences for 1964, currently in production this month, feature montages for tracks such as 'Things We Said Today', but are later rejected. The producer of the series, Chips Chipperfield, requests assistance in film research from the author of this book, who meets with him and researcher Nell Burley today.

Sunday November 8 (until Sunday December 20)
🍎 In America, the Disney Channel begins an *Eight Days A Week Tribute To The Beatles* campaign. This six-week event includes on-air sweepstakes, competitions, for which the prizes will be Beatles CD boxes and, as the star prize, a visit to the Abbey Road studios in London. During the period November 28 until December 6, a different Beatles film is shown on the channel every night.
🍎 In the UK tonight's edition of the LWT programme *The South Bank Show* on George Formby goes ahead across the ITV network complete with a split second silent clip of George's performance at the George Formby convention, at the Winter Gardens in Blackpool on March 3, 1991. George had written a letter requesting that the clip of him playing should not be transmitted.

Sunday November 15
🍎 The French premiere of Paul's *Liverpool Oratorio* takes place at the British Arts Festival in Lille, France. In attendance this evening is Princess Diana, who is not amused when she is forced to wait to meet Paul, who takes a full five-minute standing ovation in the centre of the concert hall.

Tuesday November 17

🍎 In the UK, the Central region of the ITV network screens Paul's MTV *Unplugged* show in glorious digital NICAM stereo.

Friday November 20

🍎 At the Mean Fiddler Club in Harlesden, North London, at approximately 8:30pm, Paul and his band videotape an appearance for a New Year's television special entitled *A Carlton New Year*. (Carlton is the new ITV franchise holder transmitting ITV programmes to London and the South East, replacing Thames ITV on January 1, 1993.) Paul's repertoire this evening includes tracks from his new album, and consists of: 'Good Rockin' Tonight', 'We Can Work It Out', 'Biker Like An Icon', 'I Owe It All To You', 'Michelle', 'Hope Of Deliverance', 'Can't Buy Me Love', 'Down To The River', and an impromptu version of 'Auld Lang Syne' with the audience. Because the television station is unhappy with some of the performance, Paul is requested to re-shoot the songs 'Biker Like An Icon', 'I Owe It All To You', 'Hope Of Deliverance' and 'Can't Buy Me Love'. (The taping concludes at approximately 10:30pm.) From the set, only three of Paul's live tracks, 'Hope Of Deliverance', 'Michelle' and 'Biker Like An Icon', find their way into the programme transmitted in the London region only, during the early hours of January 1, 1993, starting at 12:01am.

Also this evening, over in San Francisco, California, Paul's *Liverpool Oratorio* is performed. Another concert takes place there the following evening, Saturday, November 21.

Tuesday November 24

🍎 Paul's *Unplugged* show receives another screening, this time on MTV Europe at approximately 8:30am. (A one-off 30-minute edited version of the show had been aired on the station earlier this morning at 5:30am.)

Thursday November 26

🍎 In North Acton, London, Paul and his band, working with the director Andy Morahan, begin shooting the promotional film for 'Hope Of Deliverance', originally scheduled to last between 2:00 and 10:00pm. To assist with the filming, and to boost the huge cast of actors and new age travellers, there are 150 members from Paul's fan club. What is anticipated by many to be a most enjoyable day turns out to be more of an ordeal when many of Paul's fan club members are kept waiting for hours. One of the fans, Jason Hobbs, is so incensed by how the fans were treated that he writes a stinging letter to the *Beatles Book Monthly* magazine. In part, it reads: "We arrived outside the studios at 2pm and as the canteen was already packed to capacity with the other video extras, we were given a small bowl of pasta and some cheese and biscuits – instead of the meal that had been promised. We expected to be on set within the hour, but three hours passed before we had to ask what was going on. We were told that shooting would begin within 30 minutes. This went on hour after hour, until many people started to get very annoyed, and after having waited over five hours, some people even walked out in protest. Eventually, after seven-and-a-half hours of waiting, we were ushered on to the video set, which looked like a forest. Paul and the band then walked on to some disgruntled moaning from the tired and fed-up extras. Things didn't get much better, however. For the entire hour that Paul was on the set, he only spoke once, and that was in reply to a fan who called out 'Say something, Paul'. Paul's reply was 'I don't speak until tomorrow!' After running through the song a few times, the video shoot was over, and we all waited outside by Paul's car, hoping to get an autograph. But when he came out, he just got in and drove off!" Jason's letter concludes: "Although I am one of Paul's biggest fans, I felt I had to write this letter on behalf of myself and the disappointed fans that day. I don't wish to criticise Paul, but I do feel that he treated us like second-class citizens, and I would like MPL and his fan club to know how upset his fans were."

The first UK TV screening of the completed 'Hope Of Deliverance' film takes place on the ITV network *Chart Show*, transmitted on January 2 1993.

🍎 Meanwhile, away from the fuss also on November 26, The Beatles' 1964 film *A Hard Day's Night* is screened for the first time on the satellite channel TV-1000.

Sunday November 29
🍎 Paul and Linda's recent interview, on November 19 at their MPL offices in Soho, London, is transmitted in Australia on the television programme *Yana Lendt.*

Monday November 30
🍎 In the UK, Ringo's album *Goodnight Vienna* is released on CD, featuring three bonus tracks. (The American release takes place on March 23, 1993.)

November (into December)
🍎 In Sussex, as part of a Christmas present for Linda, Paul and his daughters Heather and Stella, record the unreleased song 'Ingrained Funkiness'.

December
🍎 Inside information from Apple in London, currently hard at work on *The Beatles Anthology* documentary series, indicates that the first part of The Beatles' documentary series, namely 1962, 1963 and two parts for 1964, is now completed and approved by Paul, George, Ringo and Yoko. At this stage, it is planned that at least one video will represent each year of the group's career together, with each episode now running for approximately 75 minutes. The biggest hold-up to date is over the year 1963, with Yoko asking for re-edits on John's archive film pieces.
🍎 Paul re-signs with EMI/Capitol for the whole world. The deal, according to MTV in America, is worth a cool $100 million and will keep Paul tied to the labels for the rest of his life. At the very start of the month, Paul and Linda are to be found in California.
🍎 In London, it is reported that a film based on the life of the original fifth Beatle Stuart Sutcliffe is to be made. The tentative title of the drama is *Back Beat.*

Thursday December 3
🍎 Following the conclusion of its run at the Royal Photographic Society in Bath, Linda's exhibition entitled *Sixties: Portrait Of An Era* opens at the David Fahey-Klein Gallery in West Hollywood, Los Angeles. (Paul and Linda flew in from England especially to attend the event.) To coincide with the opening, and to promote her tie-in publication, Linda later appears live on the show *Arsenio,* hosted by Arsenio Hall. Back in England, the 1967 film *The Family Way,* featuring Paul's music on the soundtrack, is screened on the cable and satellite channel Bravo.

Friday December 4
🍎 Linda is seen in a pre-taped appearance on the US TV show *Hard Copy,* where she again promotes her book *Sixties.* Also today, another promotional interview with Linda for her book is seen on the CNN programme *Showbiz Today.*

Saturday December 5
🍎 In America, George appears on the cover of the music industry magazine *Billboard.* During the interview inside, he reveals that his birthday is actually February 24 and not February 25, the date frequently published around the world for the last three decades. (Outtakes from this feature had appeared in the American magazine *Goldmine,* published on November 27.)

Tuesday December 8
🍎 In the UK, the tragic events in America leading up to John's death 12 years ago today are remembered during a BBC Radio Two documentary.

Wednesday December 9
🍎 In America, during the annual *Billboard* Music Awards ceremony, from Universal City in California, George receives the first *Billboard* Magazine Century Award. Following a short potted history of his illustrious career on videotape, George accepts his award from Tom Petty and makes a short speech. As in every other year, the Fox Television Network televises the event live across America. The event is also covered by the Paramount television show *Entertainment Tonight,* where a report of the evening, featuring an interview with George, is transmitted the following night, December 10. (Viewers in Europe have a chance to see the show when it's transmitted on Sky One on Christmas Eve, December 24.)

Thursday December 10 & Friday December 11

◆ The day begins early, with Paul meeting George briefly in California, purely for social reasons. Then, later in the day, it's Paul's turn to make an historic return to the Ed Sullivan Theater in New York City, the scene of The Beatles' historic live American TV début on February 9, 1964. (Ringo appeared at the venue a few months back when he guested on *The David Letterman Show* for CBS TV.) Paul and his band record, on videotape, at approximately 9:45pm, a concert appearance for the new MTV music series *Up Close*. During the two days, the group performs the following numbers (electrically): 'Twenty Flight Rock', 'Get Out Of My Way', 'Fixing A Hole', 'Looking For Changes' and 'Penny Lane'; (acoustically): 'Biker Like An Icon', 'I Owe It All To You', 'Big Boys Bickering', 'Michelle', an ad-lib piece of 'Jingle Bells' on the first night, and 'If I Were Not Upon The Stage' on the second night, 'Hope Of Deliverance' and 'Can't Buy Me Love', presented in a "Country Hoe-down" arrangement. Their second electric set consists of 'Peace In The Neighbourhood', 'Off The Ground', 'I Wanna Be Your Man' and 'Sgt. Pepper's'. The final set features Paul sitting at his Yamaha piano, where, accompanied by the band, he performs 'My Love', 'C Moon', 'Lady Madonna', 'C'mon People' and 'Live And Let Die'.

The programme will premiere on MTV in America on Wednesday February 3, 1993, and will include the following 13 tracks: 'Twenty Flight Rock', 'Get Out Of My Way', 'Fixing A Hole', 'Looking For Changes', 'Penny Lane', 'Biker Like An Icon', 'Michelle', 'Hope Of Deliverance', 'I Wanna Be Your Man', 'Off The Ground', 'Sgt. Pepper's', 'My Love' and 'Lady Madonna'. (The first European screening occurs on MTV on Wednesday February 24, 1993, while in the UK, the programme is transmitted on BBC1 during the Easter Weekend on Bank Holiday Monday April 12, 1993. Further worldwide 1993 transmissions include: Norway (on the NRK Channel) in two parts on January 29 and February 5, Sweden (SWT TV) on February 11, Germany (ARD Network) on February 13, Spain (Antenna 3) on February 20, Canada (The MuchMusic TV station) on March 3, Holland (Veronica TV) on March 5, Switzerland (DRF Network) on June 4. A further German TV sale, this time to N3, results in a screening taking place on March 26. In addition, the show is screened in March on Australian TV's Channel 9 and New Zealand's TVNZ to correspond with Paul's concert tour appearances.

Thursday December 10

◆ During their time in California, Linda appears live on the US TV programme *Vicki!* where she again promotes her book *Sixties*.

◆ Also today Stateside, George is featured on the Paramount Television programme *Entertainment Tonight*.

Friday December 11

◆ On the morning of the second day's shoot on *Up Close*, Paul holds another press conference in New York at The Academy, where he comments on the forthcoming Beatles television series, *The Beatles Anthology*. Paul says: "We've talked for years and years now about doing this thing – 'One of these days we'll set the story straight and do it our way.' I saw George yesterday in California, and we're getting together, you know, for this thing – so it's bringing us together. And there's a chance we might write a little bit of music for it."

◆ In Australia, news of Paul's forthcoming tour of the country is unveiled on various TV news bulletins, including the announcement that tickets for the March shows will go on sale next Monday, December 14.

Saturday December 12

◆ Paul and Linda leave New York at Kennedy Airport and return to England at Heathrow.

Monday December 14

◆ George does it again, turning up unannounced live on stage, this time at the Universal Amphitheater in Los Angeles, appearing with Eddie Van Halen during a benefit concert for the family of Jeff Porcaro, a former member of the band Toto, who died recently in mysterious drug related circumstances.

◆ In Australia, as expected, tickets for Paul's concerts in the country in March 1993 go on sale.

Tuesday December 15 & Wednesday December 16
 Following a two-day break, Paul resumes recordings at the Abbey Road Studios in London where he works on the unreleased song 'Is It Raining In London?', a track co-written by Paul and Hamish Stuart. The only public hearing of the track occurs in the 1993 MPL *Movin' On* documentary film. During the first days recording, December 15, Paul gives a live (8am) telephone interview to the BBC Radio One disc-jockey Simon Mayo, who immediately quizzes Paul over his "Beatles To Get Together Again" story, announced in New York on December 11. Unfortunately, for Simon and the millions of listeners, Paul does not give any more information away.

Saturday December 26
 BBC2 in the UK screens the *Arena* documentary on Linda's photographic career. The show is called *Behind The Lens*.

Sunday December 27
 In Europe, Ringo's 1991 appearance on the American animated *Simpsons* television show is aired on Sky One for the third time.

Monday December 28
 Paul's new single 'Hope Of Deliverance'/'Long Leather Coat', is released in the UK. (The American release takes place on January 18, 1993.)

1993

"We were recording 'C'mon People' and we were singing 'Oh yeah, oh yeah'. My guitarist Hamish Stuart and I found ourselves singing it just like John. John's spirit was in the studio with us."

– Paul

January
❦ This month in London, Paul and his band spend time filming the promotional clip for the song 'C'mon People', working with the director Kevin Godley. Also during this period, the proposed deal between Paul and ABC TV in America falls through. The planned link-up between the two organisations was scheduled to feature three exclusive Paul McCartney films or television specials.

❦ At the annual Midem music industry convention in Cannes, South of France, the television documentary *The Making Of Sgt. Pepper* wins the prestigious international visual music awards Grand Prix.

Thursday January 7
❦ With the release of a new single, it usually means another appearance on BBC TV's *Top Of The Pops*. Following rehearsals at the BBC TV Centre in Wood Lane, London, Paul and his group perform a new live vocal version of 'Hope Of Deliverance' for inclusion in tonight's live BBC1 show. Earlier in the day, prior to performing on the show, Paul videotaped another interview for the BBC2 music programme the *O Zone*. The brief five-minute interview, which will be transmitted on January 10, also includes the 'Hope Of Deliverance' video. (A short unscreened part of the interview is transmitted on the show on BBC2 on March 21.) Also on January 7, during the early hours of the morning, Paul's 1990 MPL documentary *From Rio To Liverpool,* is repeated on the Central region of ITV only.

❦ In the States, the E! (Entertainment) Channel repeats George's November 1968 appearance during the selected re-runs of the *Smothers Brothers Comedy Hour.* Due to a denial from Apple, The Beatles' performances of 'Hey Jude' and 'Revolution', also from 1968, do not figure in these repeats.

Sunday January 10
❦ John and Yoko's *Live In New York City* home video, featuring footage from the August 30, 1972, One To One concert afternoon rehearsals, is transmitted on the oldies satellite station UK Gold.

Monday January 11
❦ To help promote the rush released 12-inch version of the 'Deliverance' single issued this coming Friday, Paul begins a round of live unannounced telephone interviews with selected high-profile DJs, beginning today with a call to Steve Wright on his afternoon BBC Radio One show.

Wednesday January 13
❦ Paul's live radio phone-ins continue when the stations BRMB in Birmingham and Chiltern Radio in Milton Keynes interview him about various topics including the release of the 'Deliverance' 12-inch single.

Thursday January 14
❦ Paul puts in another live radio phone call, this time to David Jensen of Capital Gold in London.

❦ The complete uncensored version of the Warner Brothers 1988 film *Imagine: John Lennon* is transmitted on the satellite station TV1000.

Friday January 15
❦ An outtake videotape clip of Paul performing 'Big Boys Bickering' on the MTV show *Up Close,* is premiered in the UK on a special late-night edition of the ITV network *Chart Show*. This late-night screening (actually transmitted in the early hours of Saturday January 16) allows the airing of the word "fuck" in the lyrics of the song. The video clip intercuts Paul's *Up Close* performance with documentary footage of various environmental disasters. In the UK today, a 12-inch single featuring 'Deliverance'/ 'Deliverance' (Dub Mix) – 'Hope Of Deliverance' is released. The 'Deliverance' tracks are remixes by Steve Anderson of many samples from McCartney's *Off The Ground* sessions. This evening, Paul appears in a pre-recorded interview on the BBC1 programme *Entertainment Weekly* where the 'Hope Of Deliverance' video receives another airing and on the BBC Radio One programme *News '93*.

Saturday January 16

In Australia, the TV rock show *Rage* repeats their 1977 film clip featuring Wings during the *London Town* recording sessions at Abbey Road Studios. While in Pretoria in South Africa, Paul's *Liverpool Oratorio* receives another performance.

Sunday January 17

In London, at his MPL offices in Soho Square, London, Paul records an exclusive promotional interview, intended for the radio special *Paul McCartney: Off The Ground,* which will be broadcast throughout the world on January 26, including the Independent Local Radio (ILR) stations in the UK. In South Africa this evening, another performance of Paul's *Oratorio* is taking place, this time in Johannesburg.

Tuesday January 19

In New York at the MTV Studios, final editing takes place for Paul's *Up Close* programme, which is premiered in America on Wednesday February 3, at 10pm EST. (The first European screening will take place three weeks later on MTV on Wednesday February 24.)

Friday January 22

This morning, Paul makes another appearance, but this time it's unannounced and by phone during the BBCI programme *Good Morning With Anne And Nick,* where Paul puts a phone call through to the hosts and talks live on air about women's safety. Paul also appeared earlier in the day, when the first of a two-part interview, recorded on January 20, is screened on the ITV breakfast station GMTV. (The second part is broadcast on Tuesday January 26.) During rehearsals for his *New World Tour* on Stage 1 at Pinewood Studios, in Iver, Buckinghamshire, Paul is visited by Princess Diana and her two sons, William and Harry. A mutual friend David Puttnam, who has recently set up offices at the studio, had invited the Princess to the studios as his special guest. Paul begins the conversation by asking the Princes, "Are you Beatles fans?" They inform him that they are, having been introduced to their music by their father, Prince Charles, who often plays Beatles CDs in his car. Following a special performance for the Royal visitors, with Paul and his band playing the songs 'Can't Buy Me Love' and the Buddy Holly song 'Rave On', the former Beatle joins Diana and David Puttnam in the Pinewood Studios canteen where the Princess asks Paul about his various holidays. In particular, she asks about the West Indian island of Mustique.

Saturday January 23

In the UK's *Daily Mirror* newspaper, a competition is run offering fans the chance to win tickets for an upcoming "secret" Paul McCartney concert. In Germany, ZDF TV transmits a pre-taped interview with Paul.

Monday January 25

Today, a promotional campaign begins for Paul's new album *Off The Ground,* an event which involves 500 radio stations in 35 different countries. The one-hour programme, titled *Paul McCartney: Off The Ground,* is commissioned by EMI, compiled by MCM Networking, and includes the first public airing of tracks from the album. An exclusive interview with Paul, taped in London at MPL on Sunday January 17, also appears in the show.

Tuesday January 26

Besides playing host to Princess Diana, a crew from MTV Europe visits Paul at Pinewood Studios to carry out an interview. The brief segment is aired the following day on MTV News, during which he announces that he has written two letters to Michael Jackson tabling another bid to buy Northern Songs, The Beatles' publishing company. Jackson, Paul reveals, replies to neither letter. During the interview, Paul announces: "I can't blame Michael for buying the company. He needed to invest the money he made from *Thriller.*" He then goes on to disclose the royalty rate he is currently receiving from Northern Songs. "Getting 15% for a song like 'Yesterday' is hardly right, is it now?" Paul asks.

Wednesday January 27 (until Monday February 22)
🍎 Linda's exhibition Sixties: Portrait Of An Era opens at the Hamilton Gallery in Carlos Place, in Grosvenor Square, London, W1. This evening, to mark the opening of the exhibition, Paul and Linda hold a party at the gallery. Those in attendance include Paul and Linda's daughters Mary and Stella, Ringo's children Lee and Jason, Elvis Costello and the actress Koo Stark. During the get-together, Linda is interviewed for the Carlton ITV entertainment programme *Big City*, which is transmitted on the station the following evening, Thursday January 28.

Friday January 29
🍎 Not surprisingly, several American and UK radio stations including the BBC, ban Paul's track 'Big Boys Bickering', which appears as a bonus track on the 'Hope Of Deliverance' CDs. The Fox Television network videotapes an interview with Paul, who talks about his decision to use the "fuck" word in order to describe what he felt was being done to the Earth's environment.

Saturday January 30
🍎 At the Ed Sullivan Theater in New York, Ringo appears again as a guest on the hugely successful chat show *Late Night With David Letterman*, hosted by David Letterman.

February
🍎 In the UK, Music Sales, the company which handles all of The Beatles' printed sheet music in Britain, launches the book *The New Beatles Complete,* which they describe as a "landmark in music publishing". (The book is a revised and updated version of the best-selling *The Beatles Complete,* which was first published in 1973 and featured every song that The Beatles recorded, excluding their cover versions.)

Monday February 1
🍎 Taking a break from the *New World Tour* rehearsals at Pinewood Studios in Iver, Paul appears live on the BBC Radio One programme *The Simon Bates Show*. The broadcast also includes a live performance of the track 'Biker Like An Icon'.

Tuesday February 2
🍎 Paul's new album *Off The Ground*, his 18th solo effort, is released in the UK. (An American release takes place one week later on February 9.)

Wednesday February 3 & Thursday February 4
🍎 Paul shifts rehearsals from Pinewood Studios in Iver, Buckinghamshire, to the Docklands Arena in London, in preparation for the concert on February 5.

Friday February 5
🍎 At 6:30pm, at the Docklands Arena, in London, Paul conducts a 25-minute press conference, where he announces the first European leg of his New World Tour and takes questions from the gathering press, which are fielded by his publicist Bernard Doherty. This is then followed, at approximately 7:30pm, by a 90-minute rehearsal concert, before approximately 3,000 people, comprising reporters who have remained from the press conference, members of Paul's fan club and 25 winners of the *Daily Mirror* competition run in the newspaper on January 23. During the conference, Bernard Doherty goes to great lengths to point out to the press that the show tonight is "only a rehearsal and is being presented without its full complement of lighting and stage technology". (Although this gig is reported to be a "secret" event, because Paul has been rehearsing at the venue for the last couple of days, tonight's concert had become common knowledge among industry people and fans alike.) Paul's repertoire this evening, where he is joined by his regular band, includes 'Drive My Car', 'Coming Up', 'Get Out Of My Way', 'Another Day', 'All My Loving', 'Let Me Roll It', 'Peace In The Neighbourhood', 'Off The Ground' and 'I Wanna Be Your Man'. (Robbie McIntosh then performs a guitar solo while the rest of the band leave the stage for a set change.) An acoustic set then follows, including 'Good Rockin' Tonight', 'We Can Work It Out', 'And I Love Her', 'Every Night', 'Hope Of Deliverance', 'Michelle', 'Biker Like An Icon', 'Here, There And Everywhere' and 'Yesterday'. Paul then takes to his baby grand piano, which had risen centre stage from beneath the floor, where, again with the band, he performs

'My Love', 'Lady Madonna', 'Live And Let Die' and 'Let It Be'. For an encore, the band performs 'Sgt. Pepper's', a track which Paul announced before its start that he had not intended to do. (Note: For the upcoming tour, two further tracks, 'Paperback Writer' and 'Magical Mystery Tour', will be added to this set list.) Incidentally, prior to the show, a live backstage interview is carried out with Paul and transmitted on the Carlton ITV news programme *London Tonight.* The feature also includes an excerpt of Paul and his band performing 'Get Out Of My Way'. Camera teams from stations such as Meridian (ITV), CNN in America and MTV in Europe are also there to capture the proceedings. Further clips from the conference are transmitted on the ITV breakfast station GMTV the following morning, Saturday February 6.

A selection of five videotaped tracks from tonight, 'Drive My Car', 'Coming Up', 'Get Out Of My Way', 'All My Loving' and 'Hope Of Deliverance', are licensed from MPL by ABC TV of America for inclusion in the March 12 edition of US TV show *In Concert '93.* Due to a disagreement over the arrangements, the footage is never screened and instead is replaced by the official MPL promotional video for 'Get Out Of My Way'.

Saturday February 6
🍎 Paul, Linda, and the band fly out from London's Heathrow Airport en route to Los Angeles.

Sunday February 7
🍎 In LA, Paul appears live on the American syndicated radio special, titled the *Official World Premiere Special* of his *Off The Ground* album, due for release in America in two days. At the start of the day, he records an interview appearance on the syndicated radio show *Up Close.*

Monday February 8
🍎 John is featured in tonight's edition of the syndicated American radio series *The King Biscuit Flower Hour,* which includes four tracks from John and Yoko's August 1972 One To One Concert at Madison Square Garden.

Tuesday February 9
🍎 In the UK, the late night/early hours of the morning ITV network music show *The Beat*, hosted by the London DJ Gary Crowley, screens the complete performance clip for 'Get Out Of My Way'. (The show is repeated in certain ITV regions the following day, February 10.)

Wednesday February 10
🍎 Paul and his entourage fly in to New York to continue with promotional activities and a major appearance on the NBC TV show *Saturday Night Live.*

Thursday February 11
🍎 Following more promotional activities for *Off The Ground*, which include a New York press conference at The Academy where he announces details of his forthcoming New World Tour North America concert dates, Paul appears live by phone on the KLOS-FM radio phone-in show *Rockline*, in Los Angeles. (The show, of course, has played host to both Paul and George during the ex-Beatles' visits to this part of America.) Meanwhile, VH-1 in America also announces today its association with Paul's *New World Tour*, which starts on April 14 and is described by Paul's American publicists as "the biggest rock'n'roll production ever seen in the States and, in fact, Paul's life!"

Friday February 12
🍎 This evening, in Studio 8-H at 30 Rockefeller Plaza in New York City, Paul and his band perform a one-hour rehearsal for their following night appearance on NBC Television's *Saturday Night Live.* During a break from sessions, which consist of 14 tracks, three of which he will perform tomorrow, Paul consents to pre-taped interviews with both NBC *Nightly News* and NBC's *Today* show. (The complete 10-minute NBC *Nightly News* interview with Paul, conducted by Tom Brockov, will actually remain unscreened until July 11, 1997, when it appears on the NBC TV archive show *Time & Again.*)

Saturday February 13

 Returning to 30, Rockefeller Plaza in New York City, Paul and his band appear live on the long running NBC TV variety show *Saturday Night Live*, where they perform 'Biker Like An Icon', 'Get Out Of My Way' and 'Hey Jude'. Paul also reappears in several very funny comical sketches such as *The Mimic* and joins Linda to take part in a special *Saturday Night Live* song called 'I Love My Sweatshirt'. Paul is also interviewed by the spoof chat show host Chris Farley, who asks him: "Do you remember when you were in Japan and got busted?" (VH-1 in Europe screens Paul's appearance on the show on November 19.) At the start of the show, almost 17 years after the event, Paul is seen chatting to Lorne Michaels about claiming the $3,000 "Beatles reunion offer" money. To promote the show, Paul appears in a special NBC TV *Saturday Night Live* television trailer.

 In Italy, the RAI UNO television station screens a pre-taped interview with Yoko, during which she discusses her art.

Monday February 15

 Paul, Linda and the band return home to England at London's Heathrow Airport.

Wednesday February 17

 Paul and his band assemble at the BBC Television Studios in Wood Lane, London to pre-record an appearance for inclusion in tomorrow night's edition of BBC1's *Top Of The Pops*. The lip-synched performance of 'C'mon People' features a 'Hey Jude' inspired audience participation, with the studio crowd joining around Paul's piano for the song's finale. When the videotaped insert is being transmitted the following day, Thursday February 18, Paul, Linda and the band are to be found departing for Italy to begin their next world tour.

*   *   *

Paul McCartney 1993 New World Tour

First Leg – Europe
Thursday February 18 – Tuesday February 23

Paul and his band again take to the road. The first stop on this 1993 New World Tour sees performances in Italy and Germany at:

> The Forum, Assage, near Milan, Italy (Thursday February 18 and Friday February 19)
> The Festehalle, Frankfurt, Germany (Monday February 22 and Tuesday February 23)
> (The concerts in Italy are sponsored by Marshall Arts and MPL in association with D'Alssandro & Galli. In Germany, the two shows are sponsored by Marshall Arts and MPL in association with Mama Concerts.)

Their standard tour repertoire includes: 'Drive My Car', 'Coming Up', 'Get Out Of My Way', 'Another Day', 'All My Loving', 'Let Me Roll It', 'Peace In The Neighbourhood', 'Off The Ground', 'I Wanna Be Your Man', a guitar solo by Robbie McIntosh, 'Good Rockin' Tonight', 'We Can Work It Out', 'And I Love Her', 'Every Night', 'Hope Of Deliverance', 'Michelle', 'Biker Like An Icon', 'Here, There And Everywhere', 'Yesterday', 'My Love', 'Lady Madonna', 'Live And Let Die', 'Let It Be', 'Magical Mystery Tour', 'The Long And Winding Road', 'C' mon People', 'Paperback Writer', 'Fixing A Hole', 'Penny Lane', 'Sgt. Pepper's Lonely Hearts Club Band', and encore performances of 'Band On The Run', 'I Saw Her Standing There' and 'Hey Jude'.

Thursday February 18

Paul and Linda arrive in a private jet at lunchtime and head straight to The Forum, tonight's concert venue, where they join the other members of the band in a soundcheck. During which time, Paul gives two interviews for the RAI TV network in Italy, the first, just prior to his first concert in Milan, is carried out by Andrea Babrato. (The feature is transmitted on February 28 at 5:30pm.) Also today, Paul gives an interview to Rolando Giambelli of the Radio 105 Network, where he is asked if The Beatles might ever reunite? Paul replies by saying: "A documentary is being prepared in England, in ten parts. George, Ringo and I have been asked to record an instrumental piece for the soundtrack of the film. I think we're going to do it this year. But we aren't planning to get back together for a tour or anything like that, it's just for this soundtrack." The interview is also transmitted by RAI UNO on November 28. Reports from the two Milan concerts appear on the various TV news bulletins this evening, February 18. The attendance at tonight's show at The Forum is approximately 12,000.

Saturday February 20
Back in England, Paul's video for 'C'mon People' receives its UK TV premiere on the ITV network *Chart Show*. (The clip will reappear on the programme during its broadcasts on March 5 and 6.)

Sunday February 21
Still in the UK, the late night arts and magazine programme *Big E!*, transmitted this evening on the Carlton and Meridian ITV regions, screens further excerpts from Paul's February 5 Docklands press conference and clips from the MPL EPK (electronic press kit) for *Off The Ground*.

Monday February 22
Backstage, during a press conference at the Festehalle in Frankfurt, Germany, Paul is presented with a gold disc for the album *Off The Ground*. Meanwhile, back home, Paul's single 'C'mon People' is released in the UK. (The American release does not take place until July 12.)

Wednesday February 24
A special short MPL documentary entitled *The Making Of C'mon People*, is transmitted unannounced as an extra programme tonight on the Carlton and Meridian regions of the ITV network.

Thursday February 25
In America, VH-1 broadcasts the show *Inside Music,* which focuses on Paul's announcement of his upcoming American tour.

Paul McCartney 1993 New World Tour

Second Leg – Australia & New Zealand
Friday March 5 – Saturday March 27
Paul, Linda and the band had arrived in Perth, Australia, on Wednesday March 3, an event covered by the country's various news teams. They will then take up residence at a farm owned by Janet Holmes A'Court, whose financier husband, Robert, was involved in the sale of Northern Songs to Michael Jackson. (Paul and Linda's son James is also present on the tour, during which time he receives special tuition from a teacher employed by the McCartneys.) Paul's first duty down under is to appear live, for 45 minutes, on the following day's Perth Radio 96FM programme *11AM* with the Live Aid concert organiser Bob Geldof. (The programme is repeated on the station on Tuesday March 9.) Following this, he immediately joins the band for a soundcheck at the Subiaco Oval, the scene of tomorrow night's opening concert. During this exclusive performance, in scorching 95 degrees heat, the band "jam" tracks such as 'The Fool' and 'Summertime', plus improvised songs like 'Hot Enough For You', a referral to the extreme heat in the country.

Paul's tour of both Australia and New Zealand includes shows at the following dates:

Subiaco Oval, Perth, Australia (Friday March 5)
Cricket Ground, Melbourne (Tuesday March 9 and Wednesday March 10)
The Adelaide Oval (Saturday March 13)
Entertainment Centre, Sydney (Tuesday March 16, Wednesday March 17 and Saturday March 20)
Parramatta Stadium, Sydney (Monday March 22 and Tuesday March 23)
Western Springs Stadium, Auckland, New Zealand (Saturday March 27)

Thursday March 4
Paul appears live on the Radio 96FM programme *11AM,* appearing with Bob Geldof, an

event covered by the TV stations Channel 7, Channel 9 and on the Channel 10 show *Eyewitness News*. Later, during the soundcheck this afternoon at the Subiaco Oval in Perth, an outtake version of Paul's track 'Monkberry Moon Delight' is played over the Oval's PA system.

Friday March 5
The opening night's concert of Paul's Australasian tour takes place at the 40,000 seater Subiaco Oval. During an occasional performance of 'Mull Of Kintyre', Paul and the band are joined by the Blackwood Pipe Band. Incidentally, to correspond with Paul's visit "down under", EMI releases a special 4-CD box set called *The New World Collection*, which comprises the albums *Band On The Run, Wings Greatest, Unplugged* and *Tripping The Live Fantastic – Highlights*. Featured on the cover of this $75 Australian dollar box is a map of Australia and, at the very edge, New Zealand, against which the four respective album covers are cleverly merged together. The box bears the intriguing credit: Design by Stella McCartney.

Friday March 5 (and Friday March 12)
In America, a two-part feature on Paul's tour and the album *Off The Ground,* is featured on the American ABC TV show *In Concert '93*. (See entry for Friday February 5.)

Sunday March 7
Paul and Linda rent a house on Sydney Harbour at Mosman, only flying to Melbourne and Adelaide on the day of the concerts. MTV Europe designates the day *Paul McCartney Day*, by screening a non-stop supply of Macca promotional videos, interviews and programmes.

Tuesday March 9
In Melbourne, Paul records a 15-minute interview for the local radio station 3AW-AM, which is transmitted the following day.

Wednesday March 10
Paul's afternoon press conference at the Melbourne Cricket Ground is transmitted live on the television news programme *Live Eye*.

Thursday March 11
While Paul is on tour down under, his *Liverpool Oratorio* is being played in Linkoping, Sweden.

Friday March 12
Paul's *Oratorio* moves on to Stockholm in Sweden.

Tuesday March 16 & Wednesday March 17
Paul's performances on both of these dates at Sydney's Entertainment Centre are videotaped by the Sydney television station TCN 9, who transmit highlights from one of the shows. For 'Mull Of Kintyre' Paul is again joined on stage by the Blackwood Pipe Band. Incidentally, during the soundcheck, prior to the show on March 16, Paul performs a 10-minute song entitled 'Get Out Of The Rain' along with a brief segment of Paul Simon's 'Fifty Ways To Leave Your Lover'. Backstage at the show tonight, Paul and Linda are presented with several gold records and meet up with the actor Bryan Brown, who had co-starred in Paul's 1984 big-screen film *Give My Regards To Broad Street*. On Wednesday March 17, Paul gives a 30-minute interview to the Sydney based radio station 2JJJ FM.

Monday March 22
The performance of 'Here, There And Everywhere' from tonight's show in Sydney, is included on the album *Paul Is Live*. (Released in the UK on November 15 and in America on November 16.) One song from the show, 'Hey Jude', is most unlikely to see official release, as Paul gets the lyrics mixed up, singing the second verse first and getting the rest of the lyrics of the song incorrect, forcing him to keep apologising to the band.

Tuesday March 23

Two tracks from Paul's performances in Sydney today ('Magical Mystery Tour' from the concert and 'I Wanna Be Your Man' from the afternoon soundcheck) appear on the album *Paul Is Live*.

Thursday March 25

Paul, Linda and the band leave Australia this evening and head for New Zealand, arriving in Auckland at approximately 9:15pm. On his arrival, Paul meets twenty or so fans who had been waiting to greet him upon his arrival in their country. When pleasantries are concluded, Paul and Linda head for their rented home called Waimanu in Herne Bay, while the band take up residence at the Regent Hotel and Paul's roadcrew stay at the Hyatt Kingsgate Hotel.

Friday March 26

Paul and Linda spend the morning sailing and then, in late afternoon, attend a press conference and another band rehearsal. During the afternoon, Linda is interviewed for the New Zealand television show *Prime Time*, where she talks about her marriage to Paul, and reveals that she is "feeling more confident about her role in the band than she had done in the past". At the conclusion of the interview, Linda gives the interviewer a copy of her latest vegetarian book so he can pass it on to the New Zealand Prime Minister.

Saturday March 27

Prior to Paul's final show in this tour at Auckland, his 3:45pm soundcheck includes 'I Wanna Be Your Man', 'Peace In The Neighbourhood', 'C Moon', 'Hi-Heel Sneakers', 'Every Night', 'Midnight Special', 'Mull Of Kintyre' and 'My Love'. During the evening's performance, which commences at 8:30pm, Paul announces that it is Wix's birthday, and sings 'Happy Birthday' to him. (Mary McCartney is seen on stage recording the concert and scenes of the crowd on her home video camera.) 'Mull Of Kintyre' is again added to Paul's set, with the Continental Airlines Pipe Band joining the group on stage. This concert in New Zealand is Paul's first since playing with The Beatles back in 1964. At the conclusion of the show, Paul, Linda and the band travel to the Regent Hotel where they have a party which ends at approximately 3:30am. (Paul, Linda and certain members of the band return home to England later this day on a British Airways jet. Hamish Stuart does not accompany them, deciding instead to remain in New Zealand for a few more days.)

* * *

Saturday February 20

❤ In a programme scheduled to appear near George's 50th birthday, BBC Radio Merseyside broadcasts a special tribute show celebrating his career.

Thursday February 25

❤ George personally celebrates his 50th birthday by attending a private party, with Olivia, at London's Town & Country Club in Kentish Town, London.

Sunday February 28

❤ In the early hours of the morning across the ITV network, the films *A Hard Day's Night* and *Help!* are screened to celebrate George's 50th birthday.

March

❤ In the UK, George Martin is interviewed in today's edition of *The Times* newspaper. He is asked about The Beatles' tape archives at Abbey Road Studio, and the assortment of unreleased material found there. He replies: "I've listened to all the tapes. There are one or two interesting variations, but otherwise it's all junk. Couldn't possibly release it!" (Eight months later he will publicly announce that he plans to use virtually all of it in the forthcoming documentary series, *The Beatles Anthology* and release the highlights on CD.)

❤ Still in the UK, the Vegetarian Society publishes the book *Famous Vegetarians And Their Favourite Recipes* (subtitled *Lives And Lore From Buddha To The Beatles*). Amongst the 30 mouth-watering recipes contained within are contributions from George and Paul and Linda, who contribute recipes for Green Pea Soup and Savoury Mince. The £8.95 publication also profiles Paul and George's respective careers.

Saturday March 6
 Paul and Apple Corps Ltd., place a full page advert in the American *Billboard* magazine, congratulating George Martin on the opening of his new AIR Studios complex in London.

Saturday March 13
 In Ireland, RTE1 broadcasts a 45-minute radio documentary called *They Were Our Ecstasy,* which focuses on The Beatles' visit there back in 1963.

Saturday March 20
 In California, Ringo, accompanied by his wife Barbara, is pictured having an argument with a photographer at the Cicada Restaurant in Hollywood. He annoys Ringo by disturbing their evening meal.

Monday March 22
 In the UK, Apple Records begin the third phase of their Apple back catalogue reissues.

April
 In London, *Backbeat,* the film based on the life of the original fifth Beatle Stuart Sutcliffe, begins production. The unknown American actor Steven Dorf has been signed to play Stu and, apparently, the role of John has already been filled. The producers of the film, Scala Productions, who have a budget of only £3 million, announce that they are still on the lookout for actors to fill the roles of Paul, George and Ringo. Filming will take place in Liverpool, London and Hamburg.
 At a private ceremony at London's Mayfair Hotel in Piccadilly, London, Linda is presented with a Gold Dish Award (a gold plated dinner plate, knife and fork) by the frozen food company Ross Young, in recognition of 50 million sales of the Ross Young marketed Linda McCartney vegetarian food range.

Friday April 2
 In America, the television programme *Friday Night Videos* premieres the promotional clip for 'Off The Ground', an item laden with special effects and filmed by George Lucas's Industrial Light & Magic Company.

Thursday April 8
 Paul and Linda return this afternoon to the plush Mayfair Hotel in the Piccadilly district of London, where he conducts a press conference and announces his plans for the Liverpool School for the Performing Arts (LIPA), a cause in which he has recently become very active. Sharing the spotlight this morning are the Chief Executive of LIPA, Mark Featherstone-Witty, and Johan Van Splunter, the Vice President of the long established German Electronics Company Grundig. (A clip from this conference appears today on MTV News in Europe.)

Friday April 9
 Paul, Linda and the group fly out from Heathrow Airport en route to Nevada, where they begin preparations for the next leg of their world tour.
 In London, George attends the British premiere of Eric Idle's latest comedy film *Splitting Heirs.*

Monday April 12
 The Traveling Wilburys come under the spotlight during tonight's edition of the syndicated American radio series *In The Studio,* which includes exclusively recorded interviews and a selection of their music.

* * *

Paul McCartney 1993 New World Tour

Third leg – Tour Of North America
Wednesday April 14 – Tuesday June 15

Paul's world tour resumes with a two-month visit to America. The tour includes performances at the following US concert venues:

Sam Boyd Silver Bowl, Las Vegas, Nevada (Wednesday April 14)
Hollywood Bowl, Los Angeles, California (Friday April 16;
   edited performance as part of the *Earth Day* concert)
Anaheim Stadium, Anaheim, California (Saturday April 17)
Aggie Memorial, Las Cruces, New Mexico (Tuesday April 20)
Astrodome, Houston, Texas (Thursday April 22)
Louisiana Superdome, New Orleans (Saturday April 24)
Liberty Bowl, Memphis, Tennessee (Tuesday April 27)
Busch Memorial Stadium, St. Louis, Missouri (Thursday April 29)
Georgia Dome, Atlanta, Georgia (Saturday May 1)
Riverfront Stadium, Cincinnati, Ohio (Wednesday May 5)
Williams-Bryce Stadium, Columbia, South Carolina (Friday May 7)
Citrus Bowl, Orlando, Florida (Sunday May 9)
Winnipeg Stadium, Winnipeg, Manitoba, Canada (Friday May 21)
HHH Metrodome, Minneapolis, Minnesota (Sunday May 23)
Folsom Field Stadium, Boulder, Colorado (Wednesday May 26)
Alamodome, San Antonio, Texas (Saturday May 29)
Arrowhead Stadium, Kansas City, Missouri (Monday May 31)
County Stadium, Milwaukee, Wisconsin (Wednesday June 2)
Pontiac Silverdome, Pontiac, Detroit, Michigan (Friday June 4)
CNExhibition Stadium, Toronto, Ontario, Canada (Sunday June 6)
Carrier Dome, Syracuse, New Jersey (Wednesday June 9 – cancelled!)
Giants Stadium, East Rutherford, New Jersey (Friday June 11 and Saturday June 12)
Veteran's Stadium, Philadelphia, Pennsylvania (Sunday June 13)
Blockbuster Pavilion, Charlotte, North Carolina (Tuesday June 15 –
   transmitted live on the Fox Television Network)

The repertoire for these concerts is basically the same as those performed in Europe and Australia/New Zealand, except for 'Looking For Changes', which is replaced by 'Get Out Of My Way' and 'Can't Buy Me Love' which is replaced with 'I Wanna Be Your Man'.

Monday April 12
 To coincide with Paul's American concert appearances, a pre-taped interview with Paul occurs on the VH-1 television programme *Inside Music*. The feature includes clips from *Up Close* and the promotional film for 'Hope Of Deliverance'.

Thursday April 15
Excerpts of 'Drive My Car' and 'Coming Up', from Paul's previous day's concert in Las Vegas, are broadcast during tonight's edition of *Showbiz Today* on CNN.

Friday April 16
The day begins with Paul holding a special *Earth Day* press conference. Later, he performs an abbreviated show as part of the *Earth Day For The Environment Concert* at the Hollywood Bowl in Los Angeles. Paul adds the songs 'Mother Nature's Son' and 'Blackbird' to his set for this show only. The full song line-up, which runs to approximately 85 minutes, includes: 'Coming Up', 'Looking For Changes', 'Fixing A Hole', 'Band On The Run', 'All My Loving', 'We Can Work It Out', 'Hope Of Deliverance' (performed as a duet with K.D. Lang), 'Mother Nature's Son', 'Blackbird', 'Peace In The Neighbourhood', 'Off The Ground', 'Can't Buy Me Love', 'Magical Mystery Tour', 'C'mon People', 'Live And Let Die', 'Let It Be' and 'Hey Jude', where Ringo appears unannounced to join in on the all star finale. Excerpts from the show, namely 'We Can Work It Out', 'Hope Of Deliverance' and 'Hey Jude', are transmitted on VH-1 in America during a special *Earth Day* concert programme, which is aired on April 22. Viewers in the UK get a chance to see some clips from Paul's performance when excerpts turn up in the

programme *Hollywood Reports,* which is aired across some areas of the ITV network on April 30. (The Earth Day concert is an event put together to raise £250,000 for various environmental charities.) The beneficiaries of Paul's performance are Greenpeace, Friends Of The Earth and People For The Ethnical Treatment Of Animals.

Sunday April 18
Back in England, Paul's MPL documentary *Movin' On* is screened on Channel 4.

Thursday April 22
VH-1 in America screens the *Earth Day* television show, featuring excerpts from Paul's performance (see entry above for Friday April 16). Immediately following the broadcast, VH-1 shows a re-edited version of Paul's *Up Close* programme, featuring alternative interviews with Paul where he discusses "green" related issues.

Monday April 26
A behind the scenes look at Paul on tour by Pat O'Brien, is featured on the American TV show *Entertainment Tonight.* (Viewers in the UK and Europe have a chance to see this on Sky One the following day, April 27.) In England, the scheduled Parlophone single of 'Biker Like An Icon' as a 7", a cassette and a CD, fails to materialise.

Tuesday April 27
Prior to the evening's performance in Memphis, Paul 'jams' backstage with his friend Carl Perkins for the HBO (Home Box Office) programme *Go Cat Go.* Among the numbers they perform are: 'Blue Suede Shoes', 'Maybelline', 'Matchbox' and 'My Old Friend', an unreleased track written by Carl during the 1981 *Tug Of War* recording sessions.

Saturday May 1
The performance of 'Lady Madonna' from tonight's show in Atlanta, appears on the album *Paul Is Live.*

Sunday May 2
In America, Paul is featured in today's edition of *VH-1 To 1,* a primarily interview based programme intercut with various MPL archive video clips. Amongst the film that Paul has officially supplied to the station is a short colour clip of the 1971 promotional film for '3 Legs', filmed on Saturday January 2, 1971, and, except for one screening on French television's *Beatles Story* in 1976, remains unscreened in over twenty years! (Its only UK transmission occurred on BBC1's *Top Of The Pops* on June 24, 1971.)

Friday May 7
An interview is taped today with Paul, backstage prior to his concert in Columbia. (The feature is transmitted in America on the NBC show *Today* on May 19.)

Monday May 10
In America, VH-1 viewers are given the chance to enter the *Backstage With Paul Sweepstakes,* in which the grand prize winner will accompany Paul to one of his American concerts.

Tuesday May 11
A pre-taped feature on Linda, where she talks about the wide range of vegetarian food available to the crew on Paul's current American tour, is featured on the CBS TV breakfast show *This Morning.*

Friday May 21
During today's concert in Winnipeg, 'Mull Of Kintyre' is added to the set and features the Heatherbelles Ladies Pipe Band who arrive on stage to accompany Paul on the song. Prior to tonight's show, Paul consents to an interview with the Winnipeg radio station 103 UFM.

Wednesday May 26
Performances of 'Let Me Roll It', 'Peace In The Neighbourhood', 'Michelle', 'Biker Like An Icon', 'Penny Lane', 'Live And Let Die' plus, from the afternoon soundcheck, the unreleased track 'Hotel In Benidorm', all appear on the album *Paul Is Live.*

Saturday May 29
The version of 'My Love', recorded tonight in San Antonio, appears officially on *Paul Is Live*.

Monday May 31
Appropriately for tonight's show in Kansas, Paul adds to his set the song 'Kansas City'/'Hey, Hey, Hey', while 'Drive My Car', 'Looking For Changes', 'C'mon People' and the version of 'Kansas City' all appear on the album *Paul Is Live*.

Friday June 11
The following songs from tonight's show at Giants Stadium, 'All My Loving', 'We Can Work It Out', 'Hope Of Deliverance' and, from the afternoon soundcheck, 'A Fine Day', all appear on the album *Paul Is Live*.

Monday June 14 & Tuesday June 15
To help promote the live televised concert from Charlotte on June 15, the Fox Network broadcasts, over these two days, a special two-part interview with Paul. He even appears in a special TV trailer, which is transmitted on June 14, which advertises the show.

Tuesday June 15
The Fox Network Television Station broadcasts live, free of charge, Paul's concert this evening at Charlotte, North Carolina, an event presented by Blockbuster Entertainment Corps., Paul's official sponsor for the tour. Due to seven commercial breaks, several of the songs are not transmitted on television at all or appear in an edited form. The worst example is 'Hey Jude', where the middle of the encore is not seen by the American television viewers. (A much longer version of the show, complete with the missing songs and a remixed sound, is transmitted in the UK on Channel 4 on November 13.) The soundtrack of the show is transmitted simultaneously in stereo sound on the Westwood One radio network. The following songs from the show, 'Robbie's Bit (Thanks Chet)' (a guitar solo by Robbie McIntosh), 'Good Rockin' Tonight' and 'Paperback Writer' all appear on the album *Paul Is Live*.

* * *

Sunday April 18
 In America, the Disney Channel TV special *Ringo Starr: Going Home* is premiered, featuring footage from Ringo's July 6, 1992, live concert in Liverpool at the Empire Theatre, plus additional scenes shot in Liverpool in September, 1992.
 In the UK on Channel 4, a 27-minute edit of the Aubrey Powell documentary on Paul's *Off The Ground* album, entitled *Movin' On,* is premiered. (The American premiere takes place on the Fox Television network on June 10, and features slightly different footage.)

Monday April 19
 Following a delay, Paul's single 'Off The Ground' is eventually released in America.

Tuesday April 20
 The second day of new Macca issues sees the release of 'Biker Like An Icon' on a Capitol/CEMA vinyl single.

Saturday April 24
 At the Farm Aid VI concert, held at the Ames Cyclone Stadium in Iowa, Ringo appears on drums with a new group, The New Maroons. Joining him on the bill tonight are Neil Young, country star Willie Nelson, Bryan Adams, John Cooger Mellencamp and Bruce Hornsby & The Range. The event, which raises $960,000 for financially distressed American farmers, is videotaped by the Nashville Network TV channel.

Sunday May 9
 While Paul is in concert in Florida, George can be found attending the 37th Spanish Grand Prix in Barcelona, Spain. During his visit, he declines all requests for an interview.

June

 In the UK, reports suggest that George is hard at work on a new album in Henley, aiming for a release date in either late 1993 or early 1994. Delays in the recordings are, according to Warner Brothers, due to problems with newly installed DAT (digital audio tape) equipment.

 George also appears in the news this month when, agreeing with a similar statement from Paul, he announces that he is unhappy with the current production of *Backbeat*, a film based on the life of Stuart Sutcliffe. He condemns the film, announcing that he is "unhappy in the way The Beatles' younger 'wilder' days are going to be glorified on the big screen!"

Monday June 7

 In the UK, a set of completely remastered McCartney albums are issued on CD with several featuring bonus tracks. The albums in question are: *McCartney, Band On The Run, Venus And Mars, Wings Wild Life, London Town, Ram,* and *Red Rose Speedway.*

Friday June 18

 The radio station Capital Gold hosts a giant Beatles party at The Grand in Clapham, South West London. Top of the bill are The Bootleg Beatles with a Beatles disco hosted by the Capital DJs David Hamilton, Tony Blackburn, Paul Burnett and Stuart Colman. The event runs from 8:30pm to 12:30am.

Wednesday June 23

 In the States, Ringo appears at the *Together For Our Children* charity concert, held at the Royce Hall, UCLA, performing with Don Was and several other musicians who had worked on his *Time Takes Time* album. Collectively they are all part of the group who call themselves The New Maroons. (This evening's concert is syndicated across America between June 25 and July 11.) The New Maroons back the singer Jonelle Glosser and perform 'Something Wild' and 'The Dark End Of The Street', the latter being the only song transmitted during the various television broadcasts. Ringo also appears on stage to introduce singer Bonnie Raitt. During a brief press conference, carried out at the start of the day, Ringo confirms that he is indeed recording a new studio album with Don Was, but did not comment on the reports that he is intending to do a New Maroons album. The conference also reveals that Ringo will soon go back out on the road with a third All-Starr Band.

July

 Further insider reports emerge from Apple Productions regarding the long-awaited *Beatles Anthology* documentary series. The episodes up to 1967 are now completed and the company issues a call for anyone with interesting Beatles film footage to submit it to Apple for possible use in the series. They place an advert in Paul's Wings Fun Club magazine, requesting The Beatles' appearances on *Top Of The Pops* and *Juke Box Jury* and coverage of the Beatles' disastrous visit to Manilla in 1966, none of which are found.

 Exactly thirty years since his last visit, George turns up in Weston-Super-Mare where he oversees, at the printers Lawrence Allen Ltd, the final stages of his new book *Live In Japan,* which is to be published next month by Genesis Publications. During his brief visit, George is seen eating fish and chips at the local Sand's restaurant and, quite surprisingly, happily obliges in giving autographs to fellow diners in the restaurant. One recipient is most surprised when George signs the name "Barry Manilow"!

 Paul's manager Richard Ogden resigns from his position at MPL, who claim that he had left because his contract had run out. This comes in complete contrast to a story in *Music Week*'s which alleges that "Ogden's departure was linked to disagreements over the high costs and poor publicity on the New World Tour." When asked about this accusation, MPL replies in a statement, which reads "This is absolute bollocks!"

Saturday July 10

 Another playing of Paul's *Liverpool Oratorio* takes place, this time in Auckland, New Zealand, at the Aotea Centre. The Auckland Boys Choir and The Auckland Philharmonic Orchestra stage the concert. (Further performances take place at the venue on July 11 and 12.)

Wednesday July 14
♣ In England on Capitol Radio, Paul gives a live interview by phone from his Sussex home to the disc jockey Chris Tarrant.

Monday July 19
♣ The album *Bob Dylan – 30th Anniversary Concert Celebration,* featuring George's live performance of 'Absolutely Sweet Marie', is released in the UK. (The American release takes place on August 24.)

Tuesday July 20
♣ Paul appears in a brief pre-recorded interview on Carlton ITV's *London Tonight.*

Thursday July 22
♣ In London, Paul returns to the Abbey Road zebra crossing where he poses, with an Old English sheepdog, for the picture that will appear on the cover of his album *Paul Is Live.*

Wednesday July 28
♣ A brief item on *MTV News* in Europe announces that Paul is currently writing new classical pieces for piano.

August
♣ According to various published reports this month, the three surviving Beatles hold recording sessions featuring production by George Martin at an unknown location. A spokesman for the group, quite rightly, denies that this session ever took place. Paul is too pre-occupied with arrangements for the next leg of his world tour. (*Goldmine* magazine in America reports this session in a January 1994 issue and quotes someone close to The Beatles as the source of the story.) Note: The first Beatles "reunion" session will actually take place on February 11, 1994 (see entry).

Monday August 9
♣ In the UK, the next batch of completely remastered McCartney albums on CD are released, and again several feature new bonus tracks. The albums in question are *Wings At The Speed Of Sound, Back To The Egg, McCartney II, Tug Of War, Pipes Of Peace, Give My Regards To Broad Street, Press To Play, Wings Greatest,* and *Flowers In the Dirt.*

September
♣ Paul recalls the recording of 'C'mon People' in the US newspaper *The Journal*: "We were recording 'C'mon People', which is a bit 'Beatley' and we were singing the 'Oh yeah, oh yeah' part. My guitarist Hamish Stuart and I found ourselves singing it just like John. We couldn't help it. In the end, we just didn't fight it; we just went with it. John's spirit *was* in the studio with us."

*   *   *

Paul McCartney New World Tour 1993

Fourth Leg – Europe
Friday September 3 – Wednesday October 27

With rumours flying around the world of a possible Beatles' reunion recording session, Paul is to be found preparing for the start of the European leg of his world tour. Their itinerary takes them to the following concert venues:

The Waldbuehne, Berlin, Germany (Friday September 3)
Stadhalle, Vienna (Sunday September 5 and Monday September 6)
Olympiahalle, Munich (Thursday September 9)
Earl's Court, London (Saturday September 11 [extra date added],
   Tuesday September 14 and Wednesday September 15)
Westfalenhalle, Dortmund (Saturday September 18, Sunday September 19 and
   Tuesday September 21)
H.M. Schleyer-Halle, Stuttgart (Thursday September 23 and October 5)

Scandinavium, Gothenburg (Saturday September 25)
Spektrum, Oslo (Monday September 27 and Tuesday September 28)
Globen Arena, Stockholm (Friday October 1)
Maimarkthalle, Mannheim (Sunday October 3)
Festhalle, Frankfurt (Wednesday October 6)
Ahoy Sportpaleis, Rotterdam, Holland (Saturday October 9 and Sunday October 10)
Palais Omnisports de Bercy, Paris, France (Wednesday October 13 and
    Thursday October 14)
Flanders Expo, Ghent (Sunday October 17)
Metz, France (Monday October 18 – cancelled!)
Zenith, Toulon (Wednesday October 20)
Palasport, Florence (Friday October 22 and Saturday October 23)
Palau San Jordi, Barcelona, Spain (Tuesday October 26 and Wednesday October 27)

Friday September 3
The opening of the European leg of Paul's New World Tour causes much attention, as evidenced by a packed press conference he gives today in Berlin.

Saturday September 11, Tuesday September 14 & Wednesday September 15
The songs performed at the Earl's Court shows are as follows: 'Drive My Car', 'Coming Up', 'Looking For Changes', 'Jet', 'All My Loving', 'Let Me Roll It', 'Peace In The Neighbourhood', 'Off The Ground', 'Can't Buy Me Love', Robbie's Guitar Solo, 'Good Rockin' Tonight', 'We Can Work It Out', 'I Lost My little Girl', 'Ain't No Sunshine', (sung by Hamish Stuart), 'Hope Of Deliverance', 'Michelle', 'Here, There And Everywhere', 'Biker Like An Icon', 'Yesterday', 'My Love', 'Lady Madonna', 'C'mon People', 'Magical Mystery Tour', 'Let It Be', 'Live And Let Die', 'Penny Lane', 'Paperback Writer', 'Back In The USSR', 'Sgt. Pepper's' reprise and encore performances of 'Band On The Run', 'I Saw Her Standing There' and 'Hey Jude'.

Saturday September 11
Earlier in the day at Earl's Court, three acoustic tracks from the afternoon soundcheck ('Good Rockin' Tonight', 'We Can Work It Out' and 'Biker Like An Icon') are transmitted live during Johnny Walker's BBC Radio One FM programme. Paul also takes time, during the transmission, to draw out the names from a hat in a *1FM* ticket competition. This evening, prior to Paul's opening night at Earl's Court, he videotapes a spoken message to Cilla Black for inclusion in her ITV special *Cilla – A Celebration,* which is transmitted across the ITV network on September 26.

Wednesday October 13
Paul arrives in Paris 90 minutes late for a press conference just prior to the show at Bercy. As a result, the conference lasts only 15 minutes and a photo shoot a mere three minutes.

Thursday October 14
In Paris, Paul takes part in a record signing session at the FNAC Record Store; again he arrives late, this time by approximately 30 minutes. Due to this, he leaves all but 50 of the waiting fans disappointed and without an autograph. Many of the fans had been queuing for over six hours. During his brief stay at the store, Paul chats with the singer Tony Sheridan, with whom The Beatles recorded some tracks in Germany back in 1961. The troubles for Paul today continue when, during tonight's show at the Palais Omnisports, he completely forgets the lyrics to 'Penny Lane', forcing him to abort the song midway through the performance. While the crowd watch on in a stunned silence, Paul begins the song again, this time singing the lyrics correctly.

Monday October 18
Tonight's concert in Metz, France, is cancelled because Paul has recently been putting his vocal chords under immense strain.

*   *   *

Sunday September 5

 BBC2 in the UK screens, for the first time in almost three decades, excerpts from the 1964 programme *Follow The Beatles*, a documentary on the making of *A Hard Day's Night*, during the series *Hollywood UK,* a weekly look at classic British films of the Sixties. Apple, meanwhile, is none too pleased that these rare Beatles clips have been repeated.

Tuesday September 7

 At Abbey Road Studios in London, Ringo joins Paul by recording a guest appearance for the ITV special *Cilla – A Celebration*. The programme, a look back over her career, is transmitted across the ITV network on September 26. (This special also includes Paul's videotaped speech recorded backstage at London's Earl's Court on September 11.)

Thursday September 9

 Another Beatles event takes place at Abbey Road today when, in Studio Two, a press conference for American and Continental European journalists only is arranged to launch *The Beatles 1962–1966* and *1967–1970* albums on compact disc. The lunchtime session begins with introductory speeches by EMI's managing director Rupert Perry and the Abbey Road boss Ken Townsend. Beatles' producer George Martin says a few words to the press before the gathering is treated to a playback of selected remastered tracks from the two 1973 compilation albums. There is also a visual display featuring screenings of the promotional films for 'Ticket To Ride', 'Help!', 'Hello, Goodbye' and 'The Fool On The Hill', as supplied by Apple. George Martin then hosts a question and answer session with the press before being, quite unintentionally, upstaged by George Harrison, who delivers a short "Thank you" message, before joining Martin in a photo session. Also present, representing Apple, are Neil Aspinall and Derek Taylor.

Tuesday September 14

 Ringo's album *Ringo Starr And His All-Starr Band . . . Live In Montreux* is simultaneously released in both America and the UK. The recording stems from Ringo's appearance on July 13, 1992, at the Montreux Jazz Festival in Switzerland.

Saturday September 18

 To promote Monday's release of The Beatles' *Red* and *Blue* albums, the ITV Network *Chart Show* screens, for the first time ever on UK TV, the second promotional film for 'Hello, Goodbye'. The remastered clip, which has been supplied by Apple, is broadcast in glorious NICAM digital stereo.

Monday September 20

 After a lengthy delay, the digitally remastered CD versions of *The Beatles 1962–1966* (the *Red* album) and *The Beatles 1967–1970* (the *Blue* album) are released in the UK. (The American release takes place on October 5.) The *1962–1966* album also features five tracks in stereo released on CD for the very first time: 'All My Loving', 'Can't Buy Me Love', 'And I Love Her', 'A Hard Day's Night' and 'Eight Days A Week'. (These remastered versions also appear as limited edition coloured vinyl double albums on February 22, 1994, simultaneously released in both the UK and America.) To coincide with their release today, September 20, Derek Taylor talks about the albums on the BBC GLR station.

The release of the *Red* and *Blue* albums caused some controversy owing to Apple's insistence that they were released as two double CDs – and priced accordingly – despite the fact that the two *Red* CDs lasted less than 65 minutes (and could therefore fit on to one CD). Critics were quick to point out that while the *Blue* albums ran over the limit for one CD, by shuffling the tracks around and deleting one from the *Blue* album, the four CD package could easily have been issued as a two CD set at around £25 for the pair instead of around £50. EMI – and Paul via a spokesman – defended themselves against the critics as best they could but the general tone of the press coverage was that fans were being exploited. The matter even reached the Houses of Parliament where an MP suggested that fans boycott the releases as a protest.

Tuesday September 21

 The BBC1 show *Good Morning With Anne And Nick*, broadcasts the November 1965

Intertel film clip for 'Ticket To Ride' as a promotional vehicle for *The Beatles' 1962–1966* and *1967–1970* albums.

Wednesday September 22
 The 30-second television advert, featuring many archive clips, for The Beatles' *Red* and *Blue* albums begins transmissions on both the terrestrial and satellite television stations in the UK.

Saturday September 25
 A further promotion for The Beatles' *Red* and *Blue* albums occurs when British DJ and television personality Danny Baker, a self-confessed Beatles fanatic, plays on his Saturday night BBC1 show *Danny Baker After All,* the promotional film for 'Ticket To Ride', already shown on the station on the previous Tuesday.

Thursday September 30
 George's animated appearance in the hugely successful cartoon series *The Simpsons* premieres on the American Fox TV Network.

October
 In London, an Australian theatre tribute to John called *Looking Through A Glass Onion* opens to the public.
 During his annual visit to Australia, George walks into a busy Sydney high street record store, looking to purchase a CD player, when a guard at the store comes up to him. Noticing a large Beatles *Red* and *Blue* album display in the store, the guard says, "You know, you look just like George Harrison." George, finding this most amusing, turns to the guard and replies: "People say that to me all the time."

Sunday October 3
 Just days after its American premiere, the TV station Sky One broadcasts, for the first time in Europe, George's animated appearance on the American television show *The Simpsons.*

Thursday October 7
 In the UK, George appears by way of a pre-taped interview on the BBC2 motor car show *Top Gear.*

Wednesday October 13
 In the States, Ringo promotes his *Live In Montreux* CD on the NBC American breakfast show *Today.* During his appearance, excerpts from *Montreux* live home video are also screened.

Monday October 18
 In London, at 9pm, the play *John Lennon – In Music & Words,* premieres at the Criterion Theatre after which a party for the cast and selected guests is held at *Planet Hollywood* at 13 Coventry Street, London, W1. An invitation to the events had been sent to George, but he declined the offer, returning his card to the organisers with a scribbled note written across it, which simply read: "Sorry – not coming!"

Friday October 22
 Still Stateside, Beatles' photographer Harry Benson is a guest on the NBC TV breakfast show *Today.*

Saturday October 30
 Paul's promotional film clip for 'Biker Like An Icon' (version one) receives its European TV premiere during tonight's MTV programme *First Look.* (The show, including Paul's film, is repeated on the station the following day, Sunday October 31.)

November
 At a Yoko Ono art exhibition, called *Family Album (Blood Objects),* in Los Angeles, among the objects on display is a bronze replica of the shirt John was wearing when he was shot, along with his bloodstained glasses.

🍎 The Beatles' former drummer Pete Best appears twice in the Channel 4 soap *Brookside,* playing the role of the drummer in the group Scottie Dogs, which also features Gerry Marsden and two original members of The Swinging Blue Jeans.

Monday November 1
🍎 MTV Europe designates today, between 6:00am and 2:00am, a Beatles Day, by showing, at regular intervals throughout the day, brand new exclusive interviews with Paul and George, the November 1965 Intertel studio promotional film clips, plus the original films for 'Hello, Goodbye' (version two – 1967), 'Something' (the first complete television screening anywhere in the world since 1969), and the TV film *Magical Mystery Tour,* unseen in the UK since December 21, 1979. In addition, the 1990 MTV Paul McCartney *Rockumentary* is also repeated.

Sunday November 7
🍎 George attends the Adelaide Grand Prix in Australia, where he gives an interview to the local news crew of Channel 9 who are covering the race.

Wednesday November 10
🍎 In the UK, Pete Best pops up again on Channel 4, this time during a pre-recorded episode of US TV's *Oprah Winfrey Show,* in which she looks at people who "missed out on an incredible opportunity in life".

*　*　*

Paul McCartney 1993 New World Tour

Fifth & Final Leg – Tokyo, Mexico & Brazil
Friday November 12 – December 16

Paul's 1993 World Tour reaches its final stages. Firstly with shows in Tokyo, Japan, at the following venues:

> Tokyo Dome, Japan (Friday November 12, Sunday November 14 and
>   Monday November 15)
> Fukuoka Dome, Tokyo, (Thursday November 18 and Friday November 19)

Their repertoire, which again includes a mix between acoustic and electric numbers, includes: 'Drive My Car', 'Coming Up', 'Looking For Changes', 'Jet', 'All My Loving', 'Let Me Roll It', 'Peace In The Neighbourhood', 'Off The Ground', (Robbie's guitar solo), 'Good Rockin' Tonight', 'We Can Work It Out', 'I Lost My Little Girl', 'Ain't No Sunshine', 'Hope Of Deliverance', 'Michelle', 'Biker Like An Icon', 'Here, There And Everywhere', 'Yesterday', 'My Love', 'Lady Madonna', 'C'mon People', 'Magical Mystery Tour', 'Let It Be', 'Live And Let Die', 'Paperback Writer', 'Back In The USSR', 'Penny Lane', 'Sgt. Pepper's Lonely Hearts Club Band', (encore) 'Band On The Run', 'I Saw Her Standing There' and 'Hey Jude'.
The following live concerts in Brazil close the tour:

> Autodromo Hermanos Rodriquez, Mexico City (Thursday November 25 and Saturday
>   November 27)
> Pacaembu Stadium, Sao Paulo (Thursday December 3)
> Paulo Leminski Rock, Curitiba, Brazil (Saturday December 5)
> Estadio River Plate, Buenos Aires, (Thursday December 10, Friday December 11 and
>   Saturday December 12)
> Estadio Nacional, Santiago (Wednesday December 16)

Friday November 12
Video footage of nine songs, namely 'Let Me Roll It', 'We Can Work It Out', 'Biker Like An Icon', 'Lady Madonna', 'Magical Mystery Tour', 'Live And Let Die', 'Paperback Writer', 'Back In The USSR' and 'Hey Jude', from Paul's Tokyo Dome concert today is transmitted in Japan as part of a 90-minute Fuji Television special on Christmas Eve. The TV special, transmitted in "Hi-Definition Television", also features 15 other performances taken from the various afternoon soundchecks. These include Paul performing (on electric guitar) 'Matchbox', 'Just Because', 'No Other Baby' and 'Bring

It On Home To Me'. Then, with Paul on acoustic guitar, the group performs 'Good Rockin' Tonight', 'Be-Bop-A-Lula', 'Midnight Special' and 'Every Night'. Paul moves to the piano to sing 'C Moon', 'Don't Let The Sun Catch You Crying', 'Ain't That A Shame' and 'The Long And Winding Road' and finally, this time on his more familiar bass guitar, he sings 'Get Out Of My Way', 'Linda Lou' and 'Twenty Flight Rock'. (A pre-taped interview with Paul, recorded by Fuji Television earlier in the day, is also transmitted this night.)

Friday November 12 (Tokyo Dome, Tokyo)
Paul's complete afternoon soundcheck performance: 'Untitled Jam', 'Matchbox', 'Summertime', 'Untitled Jam #2', 'Let Me Roll It', 'Just Because', 'San Francisco Bay Blues', 'Midnight Special', 'Be-Bop-A-Lula', 'Every Night', 'We Can Work It Out', 'What's Going On', 'Don't Let The Sun Catch You Crying', 'C Moon', 'Ain't That A Shame', 'Untitled Jam #3', 'Twenty Flight Rock', 'Drive My Car' and 'Hey Jude'.

Saturday November 13
During a break from the tour, an alternative version of the 'Biker Like An Icon' video (featuring alternative edits) is shown on MTV in Japan on the programme *In Control*.

Sunday November 14 (Tokyo Dome, Tokyo)
Paul's complete afternoon soundcheck performance: 'Untitled Jam', 'Matchbox', 'Just Because', 'Bring It On Home To Me', 'Let Me Roll It', 'San Francisco Bay Blues', 'Midnight Special', 'All My Trials', 'Every Night', 'Untitled Jam #2', 'Don't Let The Sun Catch You Crying', 'C Moon', 'The Long And Winding Road', 'Ain't That A Shame', 'Untitled Jam #3', 'Twenty Flight Rock' and 'Robbie's Bit'.

Monday November 15 (Tokyo Dome, Tokyo)
Paul's complete afternoon soundcheck performance: 'Untitled Jam', 'Matchbox', 'Just Because', 'Summertime', 'No Other Baby', 'Be-Bop-A-Lula', 'Singing The Blues', 'Midnight Special', 'Good Rockin' Tonight', 'Untitled Jam #2', 'Ain't That A Shame', 'C Moon', 'Don't Let The Sun Catch You Crying', 'Get Out Of My Way', 'Another Day', 'Linda Lou' and 'Twenty Flight Rock'.

Thursday November 18 (Fukuoka Dome, Fukuoka)
Paul's complete afternoon soundcheck performance: 'Untitled Jam', 'Matchbox', 'Just Because', 'Crackin' Up', 'Every Night', 'Be-Bop-A-Lula', 'San Francisco Bay Blues', 'Junk', 'Midnight Special', 'All My Trials', 'Honey Don't' (performed as an instrumental), 'The Sun Is Shining', 'The Long And Winding Road', 'C Moon', 'Ain't That A Shame', 'Untitled Jam #2', 'Another Day' and 'Twenty Flight Rock'.

Friday November 19 (Fukuoka Dome, Fukuoka)
Paul's complete afternoon soundcheck performance: 'Untitled Jam', 'Matchbox', 'Bring It On Home To Me', 'Just Because', 'Honey Don't', 'Every Night', 'San Francisco Bay Blues', 'All My Trials', 'C Moon', 'Don't Let The Sun Catch You Crying', 'I'm Gonna Be A Wheel Some Day', 'Ain't That A Shame', 'Get Out Of My Way', 'Another Day' and 'Twenty Flight Rock'.

*   *   *

November
 Eight months after calling The Beatles' unreleased tape archive "junk", George Martin announces that: "EMI and Apple have asked me to look at the possibility of providing accompanying CDs for each film. That won't be in any way a film soundtrack. It will be complementary to the film. So if we're dealing with the period '66–'67, involving *Revolver* and *Sgt. Pepper,* for instance, one would look at a source of material." Referring to the long-discussed and well-documented unreleased Beatles recordings, which he had earlier called "junk", Martin replies, "Everything like that will be available. We're going to put in everything that I consider to be valid from every source, including The Beatles' own private collections, demos that they made, outtakes and alternative versions of

songs. For example, there's Take 1 of 'Strawberry Fields Forever', which is well worth people hearing now. And I don't think the famous 'How Do You Do It?' has ever been properly released, so that'll come out."

Monday November 15
 In the UK, the release takes place of the album *Paul Is Live*, recorded during Paul's 1993 world tour. (The American release takes place on November 16.) The UK release also takes place today of the album *Strawberries Oceans Ships Forest,* recorded by Paul and featuring mixing by the engineer Youth. The album is released under the pseudonym of *The Fireman*. (The American release is February 22, 1994.)

December
 In the UK, George places an order for a McClaren F1 Supercar, billed in the motoring press as, "The finest driving machine yet built for the public road." The cost of this machine is a hefty £540,000!

Sunday December 12
 George appears briefly in the ITV network documentary called *Curves, Contours And Body Horns*, a 50-minute documentary on the history of the legendary Fender Stratocaster guitar.

Monday December 27
 An excerpt from George's December 26, 1976 appearance on *Rutland Weekend Television* is repeated during tonight's BBC2 special programme *An Evening With Vic And Bob*, hosted by the comedians Vic Reeves and Bob Mortimer. George's appearance comes in the shape of his acoustic performance of 'The Pirate Song', a track co-written with Eric Idle.

1994

"As the thought of the three of us actually sitting down in a studio started to get nearer and nearer and nearer, I got cold feet about it. I thought, 'Does the world need a three-quarter Beatles record?'"

– Paul

January
🍎 Vap Video in Japan releases, on both home video and laser disc, the concert film *Paul Is Live*.
🍎 Rumours of a possible Beatles' reunion continues to gain momentum, helped by the American magazine *Goldmine* which reports that a Beatles session had taken place back in August at a secret location. Sources close to The Beatles deny the story. The *Sunday Times* newspaper gives its view on the group and their possible comeback: "The Beatles had their day. All became rich and famous. They'll remain so for the rest of their days. And some of their ditties may endure. Why can't they leave it at that?" The debate rages on in the English press when the *Independent On Sunday* reveals the results of their survey "How Good Were The Beatles?" Steve Jackson, a dance DJ from the London radio station Kiss FM said: "The Beatles don't mean anything to young people now!", while the saxophonist Mathew Winn announced: "They were extremely overrated. The early Beatles music was completely dull, a lot of their better stuff later on was down to their producer George Martin. Everything Paul McCartney has done since The Beatles with Wings has been dreadful; George Harrison has been pretty much a disaster and Ringo Starr just isn't a drummer!"

Tuesday January 11
🍎 News of a possible Beatles' reunion takes centre stage on television newscasts in the UK, with reports appearing throughout the day on both the BBC and ITN news. Ironically, as the get-together is being dismissed by sources close to the group, the first Paul, George and Ringo reunion session, scheduled to take place today at Paul's home studio The Mill, in East Sussex, is cancelled, not because of the public backlash against them reforming, but because Ringo decided to go on a skiing holiday with his wife Barbara.
🍎 Also today, special souvenir pieces from George's previous 48-track FPHOTS recording equipment, which had been in place at Friar Park between 1972 and 1992, are given to some of George's close friends. Accompanying each piece (be it a control knob, dial, switch or whatever), is a unique Friar Park certificate of authenticity. Replacing the console at FPHOTS is a brand new 96-track version.

Saturday January 15
🍎 Harry Nilsson, a close friend of both John and Ringo, dies of a heart attack in America. He was 52 years of age.

Tuesday January 18
🍎 The film *Backbeat*, which tells the story of the original "fifth Beatle" Stuart Sutcliffe, receives an advance screening at the Odeon Marble Arch cinema in London.

Wednesday January 19
🍎 In New York, at the Waldorf-Astoria, Paul makes the induction speech for John Lennon's entry as a solo artist into the Rock And Roll Hall Of Fame. Yoko accepts the award for John. Following the ceremony, in which Paul and Yoko are seen hugging each other for the first time in years, they attend a press conference where he announces that the three surviving Beatles will enter the studio next month to record together. Yoko tells the hundreds of reporters: "Give the three of them a chance!" (Incidentally, John becomes only the second artist to be twice honoured by the Rock And Roll Hall Of Fame, The Beatles, of course, having been inducted on January 20, 1988. The other double inductee is Clyde McPhatter, who entered as a solo artist and as a member of The Drifters.) Viewers in the UK are able to see highlights of the ceremony when the programme *Hollywood Report* is transmitted in certain ITV regions on February 2.
🍎 During Paul's visit to New York for the Rock And Roll Hall Of Fame event, Yoko gives him four John Lennon home demos, on which the "Beatles Comeback" recordings will be based. The songs in question are 'Free As A Bird' (from 1977), 'Real Love' (a version previously released in 1988 as 'Girls And Boys' on the soundtrack album *Imagine: John Lennon*), 'Grow Old With Me' (a version previously released on the 1984 *Milk And Honey* album) and 'Now And Then', from 1980, which is often referred to as 'Miss You' or 'I Don't Want To Lose You'.
🍎 Yoko reveals that in 1991 George and Neil Aspinall (*not* Paul) approached her with the idea of adding new instrumentation and vocals to existing John demos. According to

Aspinall, she gives Paul "two cassettes of John's songs, containing five or six tracks". (In fact, Yoko gives to Paul three tapes containing the four John Lennon demos.) As Yoko recalls: "It was all settled before then. I just used that occasion (the Rock And Roll Hall Of Fame) to hand over the tapes personally to Paul." She continues: "I did not break up The Beatles, but I was there at the time you know? Now, I'm in a position where I could bring them back together and I would not want to hinder that. It was a situation given to me by fate." Just prior to the Hall Of Fame event, Paul had asked Yoko if there was anything of John's that never came out.

Paul: "Yoko was a little surprised to get a phone call from me, because we'd often been a bit adversarial because of the business stuff. She told me she had three tracks, including 'Free As A Bird'. I'd never heard them before, but she explained that they're quite well known to Lennon fans as bootlegs!"

Paul then told Yoko: "Don't impose too many conditions on us, it's really difficult to do this. We don't know, we (George, Ringo and himself) may hate each other after two hours in the studio and just walk out. So don't put any conditions, it's tough enough. If it doesn't work out, you can veto it."

🍎 The fifth "Beatles comeback" song, 'All For Love', later cited by The Beatles as being recorded, is not a Lennon home demo at all. It is, in fact, only the second ever McCartney-Harrison composition, the first being 'In Spite Of All The Danger', originally recorded by The Beatles on a shellac acetate back in 1958. An edited version of the recording will appear on *The Beatles Anthology 1* double album in November, 1995.)

🍎 When Paul returns to England from the Rock And Roll Hall Of Fame event, he gives the audio cassettes to Jeff Lynne who spends a week, in his private studio, working on cleaning them up. He then transfers John's original mono cassettes into analogue 48-track form.

Friday January 28
🍎 Paul and Linda attend the London premiere of *Wayne's World II* on behalf of LIPA, at the Empire Leicester Square Cinema. Following the screening, they attend a reception at the Hard Rock Cafe where *Wayne's World* star Mike Myers presents them with a Hard Rock Foundation cheque for £25,000, the result of proceeds from Linda's vegetarian burgers which had been on sale at the restaurant. A report from the *Wayne's World* premiere appears on Channel 4's *Big Breakfast* the following morning, January 29.

February
🍎 *Capitol Records CEMA* division in America, release the first batch of coloured vinyl jukebox only Beatles singles. This series mainly features the standard UK versions plus special new couplings (i.e. 'Here Comes The Sun'/'Octopus's Garden' and 'Birthday'/'Taxman') especially created for this set. (The second phase, featuring four singles, is scheduled for April.)

🍎 While the world still waits for George's new album, the percussionist Ray Cooper announces in the latest issue of *Beatlefan* that George's new release is "just about completed", while Brian Roylance, the director of Genesis Publications, reveals that, "George hasn't even started the album!"

Monday February 7
🍎 A video clip for 'Drive My Car', by RAADD (Recording Artists Against Drunk Driving) is broadcast during ABC TV's showing of the annual American Music Awards and features Paul (as the main vocalist), Ringo and many other artists. Paul filmed his part of the video during the final part of January in London.

🍎 Still Stateside, the 30th anniversary of The Beatles' first visit to America is celebrated with a four-part feature, broadcast daily, on the CBS TV programme *This Morning*, during which a number of Beatles-related personnel are asked to reminisce about their time with the group. These include John's first wife Cynthia (on February 8) and their chauffeur Alf Bicknell.

Thursday February 10
🍎 In the UK, Linda visits Fakenham in Norfolk, to lay the first foundation brick of a Ross Young factory, which is dedicated exclusively to producing Linda's range of vegetarian food.

Friday February 11 (periodically until the end of the month)

🍎 Ringo: "Originally, we took the easy route, which was to do some incidental music, because, what else can we do? There were four Beatles and there are only three of us left. We were just going to do some incidental music and just get there and play the instruments and see what happened. Then we thought, well, why don't we do some new music? And then we always hit the wall and, OK, Paul had a song, or George had a song or I had a song, well, that's the three of us, why don't the three of us go in and do this. And we kept hitting the wall, because this is The Beatles; it's not Paul, George and Ringo."

🍎 Paul: "As the thought of the three of us actually sitting down in a studio started to get nearer and nearer and nearer, I got cold feet about it. I thought, 'Does the world need a three-quarter Beatles record?' But what if John was on, the three of us and John, like a real new record? If only we could pull off the impossible, that would be more fun. A bigger challenge."

🍎 The historic first Beatles reunion session, when they begin work on 'Free As A Bird', takes place at Paul's Mill Studios in Sussex. (The Mill is a converted windmill on a hill overlooking, beyond the gently rolling farmland, the English Channel.) The 48-track tapes, as prepared by Jeff Lynne the previous month are padded out with George's bluesy slide guitar riff, George and Paul on acoustic guitars, Paul's bass guitar and piano (which doubles with John's original piano) and new vocals from Paul, George and Ringo. The track begins with two beats on the snare by Ringo.

🍎 Paul: "We just got on with it and treated it like any old tune The Beatles used to do, like fixing the timing and adding some new bits. George plays some great guitar and we did some beautiful harmonies."

🍎 Following the initial recordings, Paul, George, Ringo and Jeff Lynne, who had been producing the session, visit a local public house and drop in to see one of Paul's neighbours, the former Goon comic, Spike Milligan. These Beatles reunion sessions will, according to Ringo, go so well that instead of the planned week of recordings, the sessions will continue right until the end of the month, where work also briefly commences on John's tracks 'Now And Then' and 'Grow Old With Me'.

🍎 Paul: "I played these songs to the other guys, warning Ringo to have his hanky ready. I fell in love with 'Free As A Bird'. I thought I would have loved to work with John on that. I like the melody, it's got strong chords and it really appealed to me. Ringo was very up for it and George was very up for it. I actually originally heard it as a big, orchestral forties Gershwin thing, but it didn't turn out like that. Often your first vibe isn't always the one. You go through a few ideas and somebody goes 'Bloody hell', and it gets knocked out fairly quickly. In the end we decided to do it very simply. It's crazy really, because when you think about a new Beatles record, it is impossible, because John is not around. So, I invented a little scenario; he's gone away on holiday and he's just rung us up and he says, 'Just finish this track for us, will you? I'm sending the cassette – I trust you.' That was the key thing. 'I trust you, just do your stuff on it.' I told this to the other guys and Ringo was particularly pleased, and he said 'Ahh, that's great!' It was very nice and it was very irreverent towards John. The scenario allowed us not to be to . . . ahh . . . the great fallen hero. He would never have gone for that. John would have been the first one to debunk that. A fucking hero? A fallen hero? Fuck off, we're making a record! Once we agreed to take that attitude it gave us a lot of freedom, because it meant that we didn't have any sacred view of John as a martyr, it was John the Beatle, John the crazy guy we remember. So we could laugh and say, 'Wouldn't you just know it? It's completely out of time! He's always bloody out of time, that Lennon!' He would have made those jokes if it had been my cassette."

🍎 George: "Because it was only a demo, he was just plodding along and in some places, he'd quicken up and in some places he'd slow down."

🍎 Paul: "John hadn't filled in the middle eight section of the demo, so we wrote a new section for that, which, in fact, was one of the reasons for choosing the song. It allowed us some input."

🍎 The final piece of music actually being recorded during this two-week period is George's guitar piece that closes the track 'Free As A Bird'. (The next "Threatles", Paul, George and Ringo, recording session will take place on June 22.)

Sunday February 13

🍎 In the UK newspaper, the *Mail On Sunday,* an article carries the headline: "The Beatles: Get Back", announcing that: "The Beatles are getting back together for a one-off concert that will be the biggest rock event ever staged. The three surviving Beatles are set to play alongside John Lennon's sons to a live audience of more than a million people. Paul, George and Ringo will each earn £20 million for appearing onstage on the great lawn at Central Park in New York later this year."

Monday February 14
🍎 EMI in England releases (virtually unannounced) coloured vinyl editions of the digitally enhanced versions of *The Beatles 1962–1966* and *1967–1970* in a print run of only 20,000 copies for the world. EMI officially deletes the releases just prior to them reaching the shops.

February (into March)
🍎 At the very end of the month, Paul, Linda and family travel to America for a month-long holiday. Excited by the recent Beatles reunion sessions, on the plane Paul begins a diary on what happened during the recordings. Paul: "Just to remember the facts really, before they were forgotten."

March
🍎 Yoko's off-Broadway rock opera *New York Rock* opens at the WPA Theater in the Chelsea district of New York.
🍎 In America at the start of the month, the *New York Times* reports that Paul, George and Ringo are currently "adding new vocal and instrumental lines to an unissued composition taped by John."
🍎 For the next several months, George becomes actively involved in the sale of his Handmade Films catalogue.

Tuesday March 1
🍎 At the annual Grammy Awards ceremony in America, George Martin wins his fourth Grammy for his role as the producer on the original cast album of *Tommy,* the Broadway musical written by Pete Townshend of The Who.

Wednesday March 2
🍎 In the UK, Ringo is spotted alone on London's Kensington High Street, and later at *Harrods* department store.

Sunday March 13
🍎 Still in the UK, The Beatles' former chauffeur Alf Bicknell is the centre of attention on the BBC Radio One programme *The Beatles Story – According To Alf Bicknell – The Fab Four's Driver Speaks Out!*

Monday March 21
🍎 The 85-minute film *Paul Is Live* is released in the UK on PMI (Picture Music International) home video.

Wednesday March 30 & Thursday March 31
🍎 A two-day *Bonham Entertainments* sale is held in London. Among the Beatles collectibles on offer is a complete run of 49 Apple original singles and Beatles concert posters.

April (into May)
🍎 John's first wife Cynthia talks about her life with him in a six-part, 44-page, series for the UK celebrity magazine *Hello.*

Sunday April 10
🍎 The annual survey of Britain's 500 richest people is published in the *Sunday Times.* The report suggests that Paul's fortune is estimated at £400 million while George's is reported to be a more modest £25 million.

Sunday April 17
🍎 George is to be found in Long Beach, California, joining the British racing driver Nigel Mansell at the annual Grand Prix.

May

 The American radio stations that subscribe to the Canadian network Westwood One, broadcast a marathon 12-hour Beatles documentary entitled *The Long And Winding Road*, which features 240 songs including historic BBC Radio recordings and highlights from The Beatles' legendary appearances on CBS TV's *Ed Sullivan Show*.

 Six months after placing his order, George finally takes command of his McClaren F1 supercar. The car, which set George back a cool £540,000, boasts a top speed of 235 mph!

Friday May 5

 Paul, George and Ringo take a breather from Apple's smoky viewing rooms in Wendell Road in West London, to visit a vegetarian restaurant in Chiswick High Road, near to where *The Beatles Anthology* is currently in production.

Thursday May 11

 Paul and Linda depart from London's Heathrow Airport en route to America's mid-west for the official American launch of Linda's range of vegetarian food.

Thursday May 18

 After almost three months of negotiations, George sells his complete Handmade Films catalogue to the Canadian independent film and TV company Paragon Entertainment Corporation, for $8.5 million.

Thursday June 8

 The three Beatles, this time with their respective wives, again visit the vegetarian restaurant in Chiswick, where again their conversation centres around the upcoming *Beatles Anthology* projects and their re-recordings of John Lennon's home demos.

Thursday June 22

 For the first time in almost four months, Paul, George, Ringo and Jeff Lynne, in the role of producer, return to Paul's Mill Studios in East Sussex where they attempt more work on the John Lennon demo 'Now And Then', given to them by Yoko earlier in the year at the Rock And Roll Hall Of Fame. Unfortunately, the recordings do not go well and the session is aborted early. George suggests they continue with their work tomorrow, this time at his Friar Park studios in his Henley-on-Thames mansion.

Friday June 23

 The "Threatles", as planned, resume recordings at George's FPHOTS Studios in Henley. During the day, they decide, briefly, to attempt a version of 'Let It Be' for inclusion in the finale of the forthcoming *Anthology* projects. Due to John's absence, they reject this idea and instead turn their hands to a safer collection of rock'n'roll oldies. During this session, recorded on videotape by a two-camera setup, Paul, George and Ringo perform 'Thinking Of Linking', 'Ain't She Sweet', 'Love Me Do', 'I Saw Her Standing There' and many others, including 'Blue Moon Of Kentucky'. As Ringo recalls: "It was just two acoustic guitars and me on brushes." Sadly the session fails to materialise anywhere in the finished *Anthology* series and, to date, only 'Blue Moon Of Kentucky' has seen the light of day, with a short one minute clip appearing on ABC TV's *Good Morning America* on December 4, 1996. (The idea of "The Beatles as they are now" in performance was originally planned for *The Long And Winding Road* back in 1980, as John Lennon's affidavit of November 28 testified.) Film of Paul, George and Ringo today at George's Friar Park mansion appears in the *Anthology* series, including clips such as George's new McLaren sports car, with the three Beatles getting out of the car and entering his studios. Paul is heard to say, "Nice motor, nice motor. Shall we go and make a record?" This clip introduces the first screening of 'Real Love' during the first American screening of the *Anthology* broadcasts, and sitting around the table, with Paul talking about "The Beatles getting back together", used as a clip that introduces 'Free As A Bird'. In addition, there is miscellaneous film of the three sitting on the lawn in George's grounds, reflecting on their time in India back in 1968, where George plays, on a ukulele, his unreleased song 'Dehra Dun' and Paul plays 'I Will' on an acoustic guitar. It is during this garden get-together that the idea for a 'Let It Be' finale is scrapped. (The three Beatles will not reconvene for more sessions until February 6 and 7, 1995 – see entry.)

July
♣ Even though the release has still not been officially announced, EMI prints a first batch of 180,000 copies of *The Beatles Live At The BBC* double album. The release date is still over four months away.

Tuesday July 4
♣ Two and a half years after it was first revealed, reports from America announce that Michael Jackson's $16.5 million animated feature entitled *Strawberry Fields Forever*, containing over 40 original Beatles recordings, is still due for production. (Nothing is heard of it again!)

Tuesday July 11 (Thursday July 13 and Monday July 17)
♣ Rumours circulate in the music industry that Paul, George and Ringo are to record these days at the Abbey Road Studios in London. As expected, they fail to show.

Sunday July 30
♣ In the UK, George attends the motorcycle racing at Donnington Park.

Saturday August 20
♣ In Los Angeles, California, the 30th anniversary of The Beatles' first performance at the Hollywood Bowl is celebrated by a huge fan gathering at the open-air venue. The American rare records and collectibles shop *Pepperland* sponsors the event, which runs from 11am to 8pm, and features music from The Backbeat Band.

Saturday August 27
♣ In the UK, Ringo's stepfather, Harry Graves, dies from pneumonia in Liverpool.

September
♣ EMI Records confirm that they will be moving out of their world-famous headquarters at 20 Manchester Square, London W1, and into new premises in the Brook Green area of West London between Hammersmith and Shepherds Bush during April or May of 1995. One of the historical landmarks at the old EMI House, the internal floor railings depicted on the group's *Please Please Me* and the 1973 *Red* and *Blue* albums over which The Beatles leaned, will, EMI confirm, be dismantled and re-installed at the new site. (These prized banisters will, in fact, become a memento of Paul's.)

Thursday September 15
♣ A four-minute historic audio tape recording of The Quarry Men performing 'Puttin' On The Style' and 'Baby Let's Play House', live on stage at the St. Peter's Church Fete in Woolton, Liverpool on July 6, 1957, featuring John Lennon on lead vocals, is auctioned at the annual Sotheby's sales. The tape, which has great historic significance as this was the day that John first met Paul, is bought by EMI for its own archives. David Hughes, of EMI, says: "It's obviously a poor recording, but I can assure you we didn't buy it for the sound quality! It's undeniably a piece of history." He is naturally asked why Apple, The Beatles' company, did not purchase the tape. "We did check whether Apple was proposing to buy it, they were not. But they were more than happy that we were showing an interest in doing so."

Monday September 26
♣ The Abbey Road Studios in London celebrate the 25th anniversary of The Beatles' *Abbey Road* album by holding a special reception in their car park at the front of the building.

Tuesday September 27
♣ Paul and Linda, along with 48 other celebrities, attend the launch of Little Pieces From Big Stars exhibition at the Flowers East Gallery in Hackney, North London. Linda is represented at the exhibition by one of her photographs while Paul contributes a small wooden carving entitled *Wood One*, which sells for £12,500 when auctioned at the Royal College of Art on October 4.

Wednesday September 28
❦ The Liverpool Institute For The Performing Arts (LIPA), holds its first press conference to announce that they are open for business and ready to begin auditioning its first students. Paul does not attend the conference but releases a press statement, which reads: "I want this to be the best school of its type in the world. Let's aim high with this, because I'm very optimistic of what we can do here." LIPA also reveals today that, besides Paul, donations for the institute have also been received from both George and Ringo.

October
❦ This month in the UK, due to an agreement with Apple, EMI Records are forced to increase the price of their three Beatles double albums on CD, *1962–1966, 1967–70* and the 1968 *White Album*, by a massive 40%!
❦ In the German town of Langenhagen, Yoko distributes 70,000 posters of a naked bottom. When asked for the reason behind this, she replies: "Faces can lie . . . backsides can't!"

Tuesday October 4
❦ In London, Paul films a special television advertisement for LIPA. The advert, which features 'C'mon People' on the soundtrack, is sponsored by Grundig and is scheduled to begin transmission during November and December. The satellite station MTV Europe announces that they are already booked to run the commercial.

Wednesday October 19
❦ In London, George Martin holds a press reception for the re-release of his book *The Making Of Sgt. Pepper* at Abbey Road's Studio Two. The guests present this evening include Ben Elton, Kate Bush and the comedian Bernard Cribbins. On the same day, another Beatles book launch is taking place. This time, Steve Turner's *A Hard Day's Write – The Story Behind Every Beatles Song* is receiving an unveiling in Covent Garden, London, where Melanie Coe, who inspired 'She's Leaving Home', and Lucy O'Donnell, said to be the inspiration behind 'Lucy In The Sky With Diamonds', are in attendance.

Friday October 21
❦ George Martin, plugging his new publication *The Making Of Sgt. Pepper* appears on the BBC1 lunchtime show *Pebble Mill*, alongside Victor Spinetti and The Beatles' chauffeur Alf Bicknell, who is there to promote his book *Baby, You Can Drive My Car*.

Friday October 28
❦ EMI Records in London announce the forthcoming release, on November 30, of the double album *The Beatles Live At The BBC*, featuring 56 unreleased recordings. The source for these audios comes from the widow of an avid home audiotape collector from the time, who had sold her husband's original reel-to-reel tapes directly to EMI for an undisclosed sum. This is somewhat of an embarrassment to the company as they had already paid a large sum of money to George Martin who has been remixing other tapes they had acquired previously. This new set is considerably better in quality and will feature 32 songs that were never featured on any of The Beatles original singles, EPs or albums.

Sunday October 30
❦ On NBC TV in America, George appears in a pre-recorded interview for the spiritual programme *Angel 2 – Beyond The Light*.

Thursday November 3
❦ In the UK, Paul, in his dark blue customised Mercedes, driven by his driver John Hammill, is involved in a crash involving a lorry, on a hilly country lane near to where he lives in Rye, East Sussex. Paul escaped unhurt but there was extensive damage to his car. After hearing about the incident on the news, Ringo and Yoko phone him to check that he is all right.

Thursday November 17 (until Sunday November 20)
❦ As usual, George is to be found in the pits and mixing with the drivers at the annual Adelaide Grand Prix in Australia.

Monday November 21
🍎 The press conference announcing the release of *The Beatles Live At The BBC* takes place in London with special guests including George Martin and the former BBC Radio disc jockeys Alan Freeman and Brian Matthew. Later Freeman and Matthew pose for photos alongside large cardboard cutouts of The Beatles as featured on the *BBC* album. Reports from this conference feature largely throughout the day on both the BBC and ITN news bulletins.

Tuesday November 22
🍎 The American press launch for *The Beatles Live At The BBC* album takes place today, with special guests in attendance including Carl Perkins and Chuck Berry.

Wednesday November 30
🍎 *The Beatles Live At The BBC*, the first album of new Beatles recordings since *The Beatles Live At The Hollywood Bowl* in 1977, is released today in the UK. Tower Records in Piccadilly Circus, London, strike an exclusive agreement with EMI to become the first shop in the country to sell the record by throwing open its doors in the early hours of the morning. Between 12 midnight and 2am, the store sells 250 of its initial 4,000 copies order. First in the long queue is Steven Bennett, a 33-year-old market researcher from Surrey, who becomes the first person in the UK to buy the album. He tells the waiting reporters: "I couldn't buy the first Beatles album, so I wanted to make sure I could buy the last." By the end of the first day of sales, a spokesman for Tower Records enthused: "It's the biggest album of the year for us. We've sold more than 1,000 copies . . . we've had people buying the album from Poland, Russia and many from Italy and America."
🍎 To help with the celebrations of this historic release, Ringo, at his office in London, gives a live satellite interview to ABC TV's *Good Morning America* as well as doing an interview for the *Beatles Live At The BBC* electronic press kit. In the UK today, the BBC album's release is featured in reports on the BBC and ITN news bulletins.

December
🍎 Paul records with the legendary Yardbirds guitarist Jeff Beck at his home studio in Sussex.
🍎 This month, an otherwise unreleased George song is included on an American promotional only Warner Brothers 6-CD box set, entitled *Mo's Blues,* which is presented to the company's employees to commemorate the retirement after 30 years of Mo Ostin, the Warner Brothers chief executive. George's song, written to celebrate Mo's 50th birthday, is called simply 'Mo'. The set also features John's '(Just Like) Starting Over', The Traveling Wilburys' 'Handle With Care' and George, again, with 'All Those Years Ago'. Other artists on the set include Frank Sinatra, The Kinks, Jimi Hendrix, The Smiths, Neil Young and many others.

Tuesday December 6
🍎 The album *The Beatles Live At The BBC* is released today in America.
🍎 In the UK, Alun Owens, the scriptwriter for The Beatles' first film *A Hard Day's Night* in 1964, dies after a short illness.

Saturday December 10
🍎 *The Beatles Live At The BBC* enters the UK *Music Week* top 75 album chart at number one.

Wednesday December 14
🍎 In the UK, the ITV network breakfast television station GMTV screens a clip of The Beatles' archive film sent out by Apple to promote The Beatles *BBC* album. Billed as "Previously Unseen" footage, fans are naturally disappointed to discover the "unseen" footage actually derives from the groups' concert at the Palais De Sports in France on June 20, 1965, and has been prevalent amongst Beatles collectors for many years. This promotional clip features excerpts of the songs 'Long Tall Sally', 'Rock And Roll Music', 'Can't Buy Me Love', 'I Wanna Be Your Man', 'Everybody's Trying To Be My Baby', 'Ticket To Ride' and 'A Hard Day's Night' all cleverly synched up with their audio counterparts on the *Live At The BBC* album. (The BBC2 show *TOTP2* features a complete screening of the promotional film on December 17.) Apple clears the clip for

promotional TV screenings until February 15, 1996, when all the distributed master tapes of the film are returned to the Apple Corps offices in London and America.

Thursday December 15
 EMI announces the possibility of a new Beatles single to be taken off the *Live At The BBC* album. The company announces their original choice of couplings to be 'Soldier Of Love'/'I'll Be On My Way', but this is subsequently dropped in favour of a three-track single. Capitol Records in America reveal their choice for a single to be 'Baby It's You'.

Saturday December 24
 In America, *The Beatles Live At The BBC* album enters the *Billboard* Top 200 album chart at number three.

Monday December 26
 Channel 4 in the UK joins in on the current Beatles frenzy by screening a complete version (which means 'Hey Bulldog' is included) of The Beatles' 1968 animated fantasy film *Yellow Submarine*.

Friday December 30
 Ringo's first wife Maureen dies in America after complications following a bone marrow transplant. Ringo is reported to be "devastated" by her death. (The couple had divorced on July 17, 1975, after a ten-year marriage.)

"It's a pity that there aren't more tracks like 'Free As A Bird', but then again, it's a pity that John died!"

– Paul

Sunday January 1
🍎 The New Year kicks off with The Beatles' 1965 film *Help!* being the first programme screened, just after midnight, on the Central region of ITV. (This is its eighth screening on UK TV and its first ever single regional broadcast.)

Thursday January 19
🍎 Apple Corps Ltd, with Neil Aspinall at the helm, moves its operations from Mayfair to new offices situated in a three-storey building in Ovington Square, West London. Sharing these premises are the offices of George's *Harrisongs* publishing company, which had recently moved out of its former premises in Cadogan Square, London, shared of course with George's other former business interest, Handmade Films.

February
🍎 It is reported that Apple Corps for this year have received, by their annual tax returns, a sum totalling £18.5 million.
🍎 At his AIR Studios complex in London, George Martin begins work on his compilation album *In My Life*.

Monday February 6 & Tuesday February 7
🍎 For two more days, and a full year since beginning work on 'Free As A Bird', Paul, George and Ringo reunite at Paul's Mill studios in Sussex, where recordings for 'Real Love' are started. The three Beatles work on the track in much the same way as they recorded 'Free As A Bird', with Paul, George and Ringo using John's demo as a backing track and recording guitar and drums instrumentation around it.

Unfortunately, for Jeff Lynne, there is an unwelcome technical problem with John's original demo tape, as he recalls: "The problem I had with 'Real Love' was that not only was there a 60 cycles/min hum going on but there was also a terrible amount of hiss, because it had been recorded at a low level. I don't know how many generations down this copy was, but it sounded like at least a couple. Then there were clips all the way through it. There must have been about a hundred of them. We'd spend a day on it, then listen back and still find loads more things wrong. We could magnify them, grab them, and wipe them out. It didn't have any effect on John's voice because we were just dealing with the air surrounding him in between phrases. That took about a week to clean up before it was even usable and transferable to a master."

Paul: "I don't quite like it as much as 'Free As A Bird' because I think 'Free As A Bird' is more powerful. But it's catchier. It's a pity that there aren't more tracks like 'Free As A Bird', but then again, it's a pity that John died!"

The Beatles and Jeff Lynne speeded up John's demo so that their new version is a semi-tone higher than the original and decided to incorporate as little state of the art equipment as possible in order to give the track a timeless "Beatles feel". The introduction to 'Real Love' is played by Paul on a celeste, the same instrument that John played on The Beatles' 1969 *Abbey Road* recording 'Because'. In addition, Paul adds a harmonium to the recording of 'Real Love', the exact same instrument played by John during the recording of 'We Can Work It Out' in 1965.

Jeff Lynne: "Paul used his double bass, originally owned by Elvis Presley's bassist Bill Black, and we tracked it with a Fender Jazz. Paul went direct to the desk and also used his Mega Boogie amp and we took a mixture of the two signals. George used a couple of Stratocasters, a modern Clapton style and his psychedelic Strat that's jacked up for the bottleneck stuff on 'Free As A Bird'. They also played six-string acoustics and Ringo played his Ludwig kit. When you hear George and Paul sing along with John, you go 'God, it's The Beatles!' Absolutely the greatest group ever. When they played, it was really tight playing together. Just like they'd always been playing together. 'Real Love' is a great song. A much simpler song than 'Free As A Bird', sort of a love song. And it's a bouncier song, a beautiful tune as well, and they all do harmonies with John. They all join in and have a great time."

Paul: "It was fun doing it. Unlike 'Free As A Bird', it had all the words and music and we were more like 'sidemen' to John, which was joyful, and I think we did a good job. I think George actually liked 'Real Love' a little better. It's just a matter of opinion, they are both good songs. I think it is slightly deceptive 'Real Love' because it's one of those the more you hear it, the more you go, 'Ohh, ohh!'"

During this session, work on the second day continues briefly on the unreleased track

'Now And Then'. Jeff Lynne recalls: "The song had a chorus but is almost totally lacking in verses. We did the backing track, a rough go that we didn't really finish. It was a bluesy sort of ballad, I suppose, in A minor. It was a very sweet song. I like it a lot. Should it ever be completed it would probably end up as either 'Now And Then' or 'Miss You'. I wish we could have finished it."

💣 *Anthology* documentary director Geoff Wonfor is invited by the three Beatles to tape the 'Real Love' sessions for inclusion in the 'Real Love' promotional film clip. The director Kevin Godley recalls: "It was to be a discreet fly on the wall thing and they didn't want to be lit or aware of the cameras. They just told Geoff to take along a tape machine and a Betacam and gather some footage. I suppose everybody realised what a momentous occasion it was and that it should be covered on video."
(Further sessions by Paul, George and Ringo take place on March 20 and 21 – see entry.)

Friday February 17
💣 In the States, Ringo and his All-Starr Band reappear in a pre-recorded segment on the ABC TV show *In Concert*.

Wednesday February 22
💣 In the UK, John's first wife Cynthia releases her first solo single, a cover of the 1968 Mary Hopkin track 'Those Were The Days'.

Saturday February 25
💣 On what was long thought to be George's 52nd birthday, a pre-filmed appearance by Mr. Harrison during part three of *The Peter Sellers Story* is transmitted this evening on BBC2 in the UK.

March
💣 It is reported that George is facing serious financial problems after filing a $25 million (approximately £16 million) lawsuit against his former Handmade Films partner and business adviser Denis O' Brien at the Los Angeles superior court.

💣 *The Beatles Book Monthly* in England publishes a worldwide exclusive, revealing that the American Westwood One radio station has concluded an exclusive deal with Paul to broadcast a unique 15-part radio series called *Oobu Joobu,* devoted to and starring the former Beatle. Paul, it is reported, will act out a variety of DJ roles (including one as a Jamaican), and will broadcast previously unheard tapes from his own archives such as live recordings and studio outtakes. When MPL, Paul's company, is asked about this, they reply: "Rubbish . . . never heard of it!" Even so, Paul has still found time to appear in a short home video promoting the series, intended for the private use of Norm Pattiz, the chairman of the Westwood One network. (The station was responsible for the hugely successful, long running series *The Lost Lennon Tapes*.) Meanwhile, Suzy And The Red Stripes (better known as Linda and her fellow animal rights protester, the comedy writer Carla Lane) return to the world of pop music when they contribute the song 'White Coated Man', a track first recorded in 1988, to the 13-track compilation album *Animal Magnetism*.

Monday March 6
💣 EMI in the UK releases 'Baby It's You' (from the *BBC* album), 'I'll Follow The Sun' (from the radio show *Top Gear*, transmitted on November 17, 1963), 'Devil In Her Heart' *(Pop Go The Beatles,* July 16, 1963) and 'Boys' *(Pop Go The Beatles,* June 25, 1963) as The Beatles 27th official single. EMI announces that, considering 'Baby It's You' (from the *BBC* album) is the main track of the single, they would have preferred the release to coincide with Valentine's Day on February 14.

Saturday March 11
💣 Yoko and Sean join Paul, Linda and their children Heather, Stella and James at Paul's Mill recording studios in East Sussex to record a spontaneous track called 'Hiroshima, It's Always A Beautiful Blue Sky', a song commemorating the 50th anniversary of the dropping of the atom bomb in Japan.

Monday March 20 & Tuesday March 21

❧ Again, Paul, George and Ringo assemble at The Mill Studios in Sussex, England, where further work is started, and then quickly shelved, on the track 'Now And Then'. Apple Corps' boss Neil Aspinall comments on 'Now And Then': "The song has been partly recorded in 'embryonic form' before it got put on the back burner, and that's where it stayed. The song was never intended to be released." Neil does not explain why The Beatles had bothered to record it in the first place. The idea of additional recording on 'Grow Old With Me' has now been scrapped altogether, as Paul explains: "John's original demo required too much work." The next Paul, George and Ringo session is scheduled for May 15 and 16 (see entry).

Thursday March 23

❧ At a fundraising reception held at the Royal College of Music, St. James's Palace, in St. James, London, SW1, Paul breaks from Beatles reunion sessions by premiering a new eight-minute, classical styled, piece of solo music for piano. The item, entitled 'A Leaf', is performed by the 22-year-old award-winning Russian pianist Anya Alexeyev in the presence of The Royal College's patron, Prince Charles. Following the performance by Anya, Paul takes to the stage with Elvis Costello to perform their composition 'Mistress And Maid'. Then, after a solo set from Costello, Paul sings 'For No One' and 'Yesterday' to the accompaniment of the string ensemble The Brodsky Quartet. Paul concludes the performance with a rousing uptempo version on the piano of 'Lady Madonna'. Admission is free of charge and by invitation only, although guests are expected to make their own donation, in the region of £250. (A version of 'Leaf' is released as a single by EMI's classical division, in the UK on April 24.)

Tuesday March 28

❧ MPI home video in America releases the one hour documentary *You Can't Do That – The Making Of A Hard Day's Night*. This fascinating programme, hosted by Phil Collins, who appeared in the crowd during the concert sequence of the film, features a behind-the-scenes look at the making of The Beatles' first film back in 1964, plus the first official release of 'You Can't Do That', from the concert sequence at the Scala Theatre, cut from the original film but saved due to its transmission on the May 24, 1964, edition of CBS Television's *The Ed Sullivan Show*.

Wednesday March 29

❧ In Chiswick, West London, the three Beatles, Paul, George and Ringo, take a break this morning from watching the early versions of the *Anthology* in the viewing rooms at Wendell Road and decide to drop into a nearby cafe for refreshments. So surprised at the sight of the three surviving Beatles standing in front of him, the cafe's owner screams and promptly sends a tray laden with cups and plates crashing to the floor. The Beatles laugh at the incident and settle down at a nearby table. George leaves early and heads for Cobham in Surrey, where he is seen examining a brand new Rocket Car at a private afternoon press launch.

Friday March 31

❧ The famous picture of "The Threatles", Paul, George and Ringo, taken by Apple staff photographer Tommy Hanley and published on the front cover of the *Sun* newspaper on Tuesday October 3, 1995, is taken today in a session at Apple's new Ovington Square offices in London. The candid photography lasts between 4:45 and 5:05pm.

Meanwhile, today's edition of *The White Room* on Channel 4, features the first-ever complete screening of a colour version of The Beatles' 1969 promotional film for 'The Ballad Of John And Yoko'.

April

❧ Away from *Anthology*-related business, Paul spends time this month secretly finishing off his radio series *Oobu Joobu* at his home studios in East Sussex.

❧ Apple approaches Peter Blake, the designer of the famous 1967 *Sgt. Pepper* album sleeve, for his ideas on the forthcoming *Beatles Anthology* albums and videos releases. Blake recalls the meeting: "After a few minutes I realised that they were asking me to pitch for the job. They were asking five other people as well as me, so not only was it a way for them to get some free ideas, it was also bloody insulting. I decided that I didn't want to do it, so I called back to tell them . . . I said, you either want me to do it, or you don't. And they said, well, the person we really wanted was David Hockney! So I called their bluff and gave them David Hockney's home number and said go on, call him, and if he does want to do it, then great and if not, then come back to me. So they called David and he didn't want to do it, as I suspected. I meanwhile had put my offer in writing, and the big tactical error I made was mentioning that this would be a good opportunity to recompense me for paying so little for *Sgt. Pepper*. I didn't hear anything after that. I'm not surprised, but I'm not going to start auditioning at my age."

Saturday April 1
 The Beatles' 'Baby It's You' enters the *Music Week* Top 75 singles chart at number seven. ITV's *The Chart Show* in the UK, premieres the Apple promotional film for 'Baby It's You'. Among its highlights is an amazing previously unseen colour home movie of The Beatles from 1963 taken outside the BBC's Paris Studios in London. (The alternative video clip for 'Baby It's You', compiled by Capitol Records in America, features comparatively standard Beatles archive film clips, such as excerpts from BBC TV's *The Mersey Sound* (1963) and various scenes from the *A Hard Day's Night* related show and film.)

Tuesday April 4
 The British radio and television personality Kenny Everett, whose long association with The Beatles dates back to his coverage of their American tours of the sixties, dies in his sleep at his London home, suffering from an AIDS-related illness. Kenny, of course, was responsible for the editing of The Beatles' 1968 and 1969 fan club recordings.

Thursday April 6
 Paul, Linda and over 160 building workers and VIPs, attend the "topping off" ceremony (when the last brick is placed) to mark the completion of the Rye Memorial Care Centre, a new hospital on the outskirts of the McCartneys' hometown in East Sussex. The centre has been built largely due to their efforts.

Friday May 5
 The UK press reports of the "biggest bidding war in TV history" for the upcoming *Anthology* television series. But it is Channel 4 who reveal the first concrete details of the shows, when, during their press conference at the Golden Rose TV festival in Switzerland, they announce that, "Apple are offering *The Beatles Anthology* to stations in the UK as a six-part television series," adding that "they are asking £6 million for the shows!" (The BBC and ITV have, apparently, offered only half that sum at this point.) A source close to The Beatles, reveals that they would prefer the BBC to screen the programmes because it's a national network with few regional variations and the series would be broadcast without any interruptions by commercials. However, according to the national press, it is Channel 4, run by Michael Grade, a self-confessed big Beatles fan, who are favourites to grab the UK television rights. Grade tells the *Daily Mirror*. "I don't care what it costs!", insinuating he will outbid both BBC and ITV to screen the series. In the *Evening Standard*, Grade proclaims: "Where else should the Beatles story appear on British TV but on fab four? BBC TV appears to be broke and ITV haven't had any music on their channel since Mantovani – so Channel 4 is the natural home." Elsewhere in the *Standard*, ITV boss Marcus Plantin announces: "Apple would be mad to sell the series to Channel 4. We can easily double the audience, and this is part and parcel of 20th Century history. The Beatles affected everybody. All three channels are exceptionally determined to get the show."

Wednesday May 10
 The agonising wait for any definite news on the forthcoming *Beatles Anthology* series ends when ABC TV in America holds a press conference in California to announce the first major details for the series. The press release, credited jointly to Apple Corps Ltd in London and ABC TV, is handed out after the conference and reads as follows:

"DEFINITIVE HISTORY OF THE BEATLES WILL BE TOLD IN THE BAND'S OWN WORDS IN A FIVE-HOUR SPECIAL WHICH WILL AIR OVER TWO NIGHTS IN NOVEMBER, 1995, ON THE ABC TELEVISION NETWORK."

"The definitive history of The Beatles, the most significant band in the annals of popular music, will finally be told in the band's own words, in a five-hour television special which will air on the ABC Television Network over two nights in November, 1995. The special, featuring the world premiere of two songs – the first new Beatles recordings in 25 years – was announced jointly today by ABC Entertainment president Ted Harbert, and Apple Corps Ltd.

"The unprecedented musical event will feature John, Paul, George and Ringo, with the latter three bringing additional instrumentation, voices and arrangements to two unreleased John Lennon songs on which he sings and plays.

" 'The Beatles story will be an extraordinary event on ABC,' Harbert said. 'The five-hour special is designed to provide a comprehensive look at the lives and sound of the band that changed the culture of a generation.'

"The surviving Beatles will tell their own stories in exclusive interviews, and the special will incorporate a rich archive of interviews on audio and video tape left by the late John Lennon. Together the four recall the group's formation in Liverpool and its meteoric rise, along with seminal moments from their career – such as the first trip to the United States, the making of their films, and inside stories behind specific record releases.

"The special will also reveal the impact of these developments on their private lives, including reminiscences by other key players in The Beatles' story. There will also be never-before-seen footage of the legendary musicians in their youth through home movies, film outtakes and other rarities.

"The new Beatles songs featured on the special, 'Free As A Bird' and 'Real Love', will be released by Apple Records.

"The making of the television special and associated video series has been the responsibility of Apple Productions Ltd., a company owned by the surviving Beatles and the estate of John Lennon, administered by his widow, Yoko Ono Lennon. The executive producer is Neil Aspinall, the producer is Chips Chipperfield and the director is Geoffrey Wonfor."

✪ No mention is made of the title of the series. Reporters ask if the current title, *The Beatles Anthology,* will remain. George has expressed on many occasions his desire to call the series *The Beatles By The Beatles,* as, in his words: "This will reflect the fact that it was made by the group's company and will be narrated by John, Paul, George and Ringo themselves."

✪ Aside from all the *Anthology* excitement, further details of Paul's Westwood One *Oobu Joobu* radio series is announced. Instead of running to 15 parts, as previously reported, the shows, which begin transmissions on Monday May 29 (the Memorial Day holiday in America) will run for 13 parts. The producer for the series is Eddy Pumer, a one-time member of the 1960's psychedelic pop group Kaleidoscope. He describes *Oobu Joobu* as one of McCartney's "best kept secrets" and says Paul has been working on the series since 1975! Paul had, in fact, hired Pumer for the producer's role back in 1981 when he was working at Capital Radio in London. "Paul explained to me that he wanted to do a little late-night show, then it evolved into this," Pumer tells *Billboard* magazine, adding: "Paul's former group will not be featured in the show. *Oobu Joobu* is Paul, not The Beatles!"

Monday May 15 & Tuesday May 16

✪ With the imminent release of 'Free As A Bird' and 'Real Love' now public knowledge, Paul, George and Ringo reconvene at Paul's The Mill home studio in Sussex where they complete the final parts on the track 'Real Love', which is to be released as the second "comeback single", because Paul and George feel the song is "lyrically more complete". Paul, George and Ringo also spend time recording their third "comeback single", this time the McCartney-Harrison track 'All For Love', which is only their second ever collaboration after the 1958 track 'In Spite Of All The Danger'. Unfortunately, this turns into a disaster and the sessions are aborted early. The group then decides to shelve plans for any further Beatles reunion recording sessions, with George the chief instigator behind this. Though Paul is apparently optimistic that something can be done with the recording, George is not, emphasising that he does not want it issued on *Anthology 3.* Also on May 16, Linda officially opens the new £10 million Ross Young food factory in Fakenham, Norfolk, which is dedicated to the exclusive production of Linda's range of vegetarian food.

Wednesday May 17 (until Wednesday May 24)
 Paul, Linda, their son James and the recording engineer Geoff Emerick fly to Steve Miller's studios in Seattle, Washington for a further week of recordings originally started back in 1993. These sessions now continue until Tuesday May 23, where the McCartneys invite Miller back to their studios in East Sussex to resume their work. (Songs from this period will later appear on Paul's 1997 album *Flaming Pie.)*

Monday May 22 (periodically into July)
 In the Penthouse mixing suite at Abbey Road in London, George Martin, with occasional help from Paul, George and Ringo, begins listening and mixing the tracks intended for *The Beatles Anthology* CDs. Paul: "It's *déjà vu* really. We're sitting in Abbey Road Studio Two, where we always worked, listening to the work we did when we were twenty." During one of these sessions Martin, accompanied by Paul, George and Ringo, goes on a nostalgic meander around the famous Abbey Road building, even dropping in on a recording session by Michael Nyman in Studio Three. The actor Mel Gibson, in Studio One observing the soundtrack recordings for his film *Braveheart*, is apparently overcome with emotion when he is informed that three of The Beatles are currently in the building for the first time together in 25 years. *Anthology* director Bob Smeaton shoots some video footage of the three Beatles with George Martin at the Abbey Road listening sessions; again they are intended for the *Anthology* programmes. The footage fails to appear.

Wednesday May 24
 Hours after returning from Seattle, Paul is stopped as he enters his MPL offices in London, and, rather wearily, he offers his tribute to the former prime minister Harold Wilson who had died the previous day. "He was very canny," says Paul. "The last time we met him, somebody from the press tried to put a microphone in his face and tried to get us to say something indiscreet with him. But he put the microphone in his pocket and just carried on puffing away on his pipe. I liked him a lot, he seemed like a nice man." Paul's tribute is screened in tonight's edition of *London Tonight* on the Carlton ITV station.
 In New York, Ringo begins two days of interviews to promote his forthcoming American All-Starr Band tour, scheduled to begin in St. Louis on Sunday July 2.

Thursday May 25
 In America, Ringo's promotional appearances continue when he returns to the Ed Sullivan Theater in New York City to make a return appearance on *Later Night With Letterman*, the top-rated CBS TV chat show hosted by David Letterman. During the latter half of Ringo's interview, he rather sportingly wears a "Beatle wig!"
 Back in England, at Paul's Mill home studios in East Sussex, the McCartneys return the favour by playing host to Steve Miller. Again they spend a week recording and jamming, which lasts until Thursday June 1, when Miller returns home.

Friday May 26
 Still in New York, rehearsals, originally planned for Vancouver, begin for Ringo's upcoming All-Starr Band tour of Japan and the States. During this first get-together, Ringo rehearses, and quickly shelves, the following songs from his repertoire: 'I'm The Greatest', 'Weight Of The World' and 'Octopus's Garden'. In addition, the songs 'American Woman', performed by Randy Bachman, 'Twist And Shout', by John Entwistle, 'A Beautiful Morning', by Felix Cavaliere and 'Outa-Space', by Billy Preston, are also rehearsed and subsequently scrapped from their concert set list. (Rehearsals resume in Los Angeles, where Ringo will stay before departing to Japan on Sunday June 11.)

Monday May 29
 As announced, the first part of Paul's 13-part Westwood One radio series *Oobu Joobu* begins transmissions in America with a two-hour special. (Paul reveals that the title *Oobu Joobu* is inspired by the character of Monsieur Ubu, created by the absurdist playwright Alfred Jarry.) Eleven one-hour programmes through the summer culminating in the final show, a two-hour special on September 4, which happens to be America's Labor Day, follow this first show. Over the coming weeks, with Paul as the host and DJ, listeners are

treated to many previously unheard McCartney live and studio outtakes (taken from his private archive totalling over 250 hours) in a feature called 'Rude Corner', which refers to demos recorded at his home Rude Studios in East Sussex. Other highlights of the series include Linda's cookery menus and conversations with fellow musicians such as Beach Boy Brian Wilson, Carl Perkins (who duets with Paul on 'Honey Don't'), Chrissie Hynde, Little Richard, Jeff Beck, Elvis Costello, John Entwistle, Pete Townshend, and the *Wayne's World* actor Mike Myers.

🍎 The idea for *Oobu Joobu* is already proving to be a great success for the station, with many of the advertisement slots already taken. "This is the kind of thing we had to be involved with," Westwood One chairman Norm Pattiz announces, "because it's a history-making series. I love it because it's wildly creative and breaks a lot of rules. To me, it's the height of creativity."

The US stations subscribing to the series include WXRK (In New York), KLSX (Los Angeles), WXRT (Chicago), WZLX-FM (Boston), WZGC (Atlanta), WUSA-FM (Tampa), WKLH (Milwaukee) and KGB-FM (San Diego).

May
🍎 In the States, it is announced that Paul and Linda are to follow in Ringo and George's footsteps by supplying a voice-over for the top-rated American cartoon series *The Simpsons*.

🍎 John's 1967 film *How I Won The War*, directed by Richard Lester, is released on MGM/UA home video in the UK, as a special limited edition version to commemorate the 50th anniversary of the VE Day celebrations.

🍎 Prior to the start of Ringo's Third All-Starr Band tour of America, guitarist Nils Lofgren and saxophonist Clarence Cummings drop out of the group, an item reported in the newspapers on April 7. Mark Farmer, formerly of The Grand Funk Railroad and Mark Rivera, the sax player for Billy Joel, replace them this month. Rehearsals for the impending tour are scheduled to begin in Vancouver, Canada, later this month.

* * *

Ringo & His Third All-Starr Band
Tour Of Japan and America
Wednesday June 14 – Sunday September 3
(Note: the last eight scheduled dates of the tour are cancelled)

The line-up of musicians accompanying Ringo on this tour include his son Zak, Mark Rivera (on saxophone), Mark Farner (formerly of Grand Funk Railroad), Billy Preston, Randy Bachman (Bachman Turner Overdrive), Felix Cavaliere (The Rascals) and John Entwistle (The Who). Their repertoire for the shows largely consists of the following: 'Don't Go Where The Road Don't Go', 'I Wanna Be Your Man', 'It Don't Come Easy' (all performed by Ringo), 'The Locomotion' (performed by Mark Farner), 'Nothing For Nothing' (Billy Preston), 'Taking Care Of Business' (Randy Bachman), 'People Get Ready' (Felix Cavaliere), 'Boris The Spider' (John Entwistle), 'Boys' (Ringo), 'You Ain't Seen Nothing Yet' (Randy Bachman), 'You're Sixteen', 'Yellow Submarine' (both by Ringo), 'My Wife' (John Entwistle), 'Honey Don't', 'Act Naturally' (both by Ringo), 'Groovin'', 'La Bamba' (both by Felix Cavaliere), 'Photograph' (and for the encore) 'No No Song' and 'With A Little Help From My Friends' (all by Ringo).

Monday June 12
At 3:55pm JST, Ringo, accompanied by his wife Barbara, arrives at Japan's New Tokyo International (Narita) Airport on flight Northwest 001, en route from Los Angeles. Approximately 50 Beatles fans are there at the airport to welcome them on their arrival.

Tuesday June 13
Ringo and his band assemble in Tokyo where they hold a press conference.

The tour kicks off in Japan with performances at the following venues:

Iwate Kenmin Kaikan, Morioka (Wednesday June 14)
Sendai Sun-Plaza, Sendai (Thursday June 15)

Niigata Telsa, Niigata (Friday June 16)
Osaka Castle Hall, Osaka (Sunday June 18)
Kurashiki Shimin Kaikan, Kurashiki (Monday June 19)
Hiroshima Kousel Nenkin Kaikan, Hiroshima (Tuesday June 20)
Nagoya Century Hall, Nagoya (Thursday June 22)
Bay NK Hall, Uraysu (Saturday June 24)
Nippon Budokan Hall, Tokyo (Monday June 26 and Tuesday June 27)
Hamamatu Kyouiku Bunka Kaikan, Hamamatu (Wednesday June 28)

The tour moves to America, with the performances at:

The Arch, St. Louis, Missouri (Sunday July 2)
Milwaukee Summerfest, Milwaukee, Wisconsin (Monday July 3)
Mall of America, Bloomington, Minnesota (Tuesday July 4)
Ravinia Festival Pavilion, Chicago, Illinois (Wednesday July 5)
Highland Park, Illinois (Thursday July 6)
Star Plaza Theater, Merrilville, Indiana (Saturday July 8 – two shows)
Nautica Stage, Cleveland, Ohio (Sunday July 9)
Pine Knob Music Theater, Detroit, Michigan (Monday July 10)
First of America Stage, Acme, Michigan (Tuesday July 11)
Radio City Music Hall, New York (Thursday July 13)
Bud Light Amphitheater, Harvey's Lake, Pennsylvania (Friday July 14)
Concord Hotel, Kiamesha Lake, New York (Saturday July 15)
Wolf Trap, Vienna, VA, Washington DC (Monday July 17)
Garden State Arts Center, Holmdel, New Jersey (Tuesday July 18)
Harbor Lights Pavilion, Boston, Massachusetts (Wednesday July 19)
Caesars, Atlantic City, New Jersey (Friday July 21, Saturday July 22 – two shows –
    and Sunday July 23)
Warwick Musical Theater, Warwick, Rhode Island (Tuesday July 25)
Oakdale Theater, Wallingford, Connecticut (Thursday July 27)
Starlite Music Theater, Latham, New York (Friday July 28)
Melody Fair Theater, North Tonawanda, New York (Saturday July 29)
Riverbend Music Center, Cincinnati, Ohio (Monday July 31)
Light Amphitheater, Pittsburgh, Pennsylvania (Tuesday August 1)
Orlando Centroplex, Orlando, Florida (Thursday August 3)
Sunrise Musical Theater, Sunrise, Florida (Friday August 4 and
    Saturday August 5)
Chastain Park Amphitheater, Atlanta, Georgia (Monday August 7)
Palace Theater, Louisville, Kentucky (Tuesday August 8)
Van Braun Civic Centre, Huntsville, Alabama (Wednesday August 9)
Arena Theater, Houston, Texas (Friday August 11)
Sunken Garden, San Antonio, Texas (Saturday August 12)
Starplex Amphitheater, Dallas, Texas (Sunday August 13)
Arizona Veterans Memorial Coliseum, Pheonix, Arizona (Tuesday August 15)
Humphrey's, San Diego, California (Wednesday August 16)
Greek Theater, Los Angeles, California (Friday August 18 and Saturday
    August 19)
Concord Pavilion, Concord, California (Sunday August 20)
Pier 62/63, Seattle, Washington (Tuesday August 22 and Wednesday August 23)

Dates were cancelled at:

Reno Hilton Amphitheater, Reno, Nevada (Friday August 25)
Star Of The Desert Amphitheater, Apple Valley, California (Saturday August 26)
Humphrey's, San Diego, California (Monday August 28)
MGM Grand, Las Vegas, Nevada (Tuesday August 29, Thursday August 31 until
    Sunday September 3)

Japanese television begins transmitting the Ringo Suttar commercials, Ringo being
Japanese for apple and Ringo Suttar a soft drink. On the All-Starr Band's arrival in the
country, they immediately attend a press conference.

George. *(LFI)*

February/March, 1973: Paul filming various scenes from his *James Paul McCartney* TV special. *(Rex Features)*

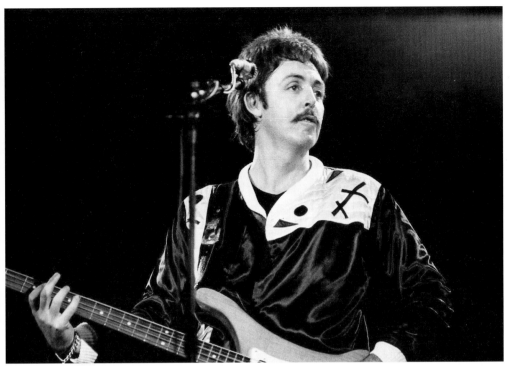

September 25, 1976: Paul performs with Wings at the UNESCO benefit concert in St. Mark's Square, Venice.
(Rex Features)

Wings on stage performing the eagerly anticipated acoustic section which usually included at least three Beatle songs, 'I've Just Seen A Face', 'Blackbird' and 'Yesterday'; left to right: Jimmy McCulloch, Denny Laine, Linda and Paul.
(Rex Features)

July 1976: Ringo shows off his shaved head look in a Monte Carlo nightclub. *(Rex Features)*

January 19, 1977: John and Yoko at Jimmy Carter's Presidential Inauguration in Washington DC. *(Associated Press)*

February 5, 1977: George takes part in a press conference in Hamburg to promote the album *Thirty-Three And A Third*.
(Redferns)

1978: Yoko, Sean and John at their apartment in New York's Dakota Building. *(Camera Press)*

September 14, 1980: John and Yoko recording *Double Fantasy* at New York's Record Plant. *(Rex Features)*

September/October/November, 1980: John and Yoko in New York, photographed during the promotional activities for *Double Fantasy*. *(Rex Features, LFI)*

Ringo. *(LFI)*

April 27, 1981: George and Olivia, Ringo and Barbara, and Paul and Linda pose for the cameras at the reception following Ringo's marriage to Barbara. This was the first time that George, Ringo and Paul had been photographed together since The Beatles split up. *(Terry O'Neill/Camera Press)*

George plays guitar while Ringo taps spoons on a table at his wedding reception. In the background are Hilary Gerard, Ringo's manager (left) and Neil Aspinall (right). *(Terry O'Neill/Camera Press)*

Paul plays piano while Ringo looks on during the reception following his wedding. *(Terry O'Neill/Camera Press)*

October 21, 1985: George, Ringo and others appear with Carl Perkins for his TV special *Blue Suede Shoes*, at the Limehouse Television Studios, London; left to right: Dave Edmunds, George, Eric Clapton, Roseanne Cash and Ringo. Perkins is in the background. *(LFI)*

June 5, 1987: Ringo and George appear on stage together at the Prince's Trust concert at London's Wembley Arena. *(LFI)*

June 7, 1996: Paul with The Queen at the opening of the Liverpool Institute Of Performing Arts. *(Rex Features)*

July 13, 1985: Paul on stage at London's Wembley Stadium immediately after his solo performance at the Live Aid concert. *(LFI)*

July 27, 1989: Paul on stage at the Playhouse Theatre, London, launching his first world tour in 13 years. *(Associated Press)*

January 20, 1988: George, Yoko, Ringo, Julian and Sean celebrate The Beatles being inducted into the Rock and Roll Hall Of Fame at a ceremony in New York. *(Redferns)*

October 16, 1992: George on stage at New York's Madison Square Garden during the concert to celebrate 30 years of Bob Dylan's recording career. *(Ron Frehm/Associated Press)*

January 19, 1994: Sean Lennon, Yoko and Paul at the Rock and Roll Hall Of Fame Induction Ceremony in New York, when John was inducted. *(LFI)*

Paul, George and Ringo in 1995 at the time of The Beatles' *Anthology* project. *(Rex Features)*

March 11, 1998: Paul and Linda, flanked by their children James and Mary, at daughter Stella's fashion show in Paris. *(Rex Features)*

March 11, 1997: Paul outside Buckingham Palace after receiving his knighthood from The Queen. *(PA News)*

May 6, 1998: George outside the High Courts in London where he gave evidence in the case of The Beatles' Hamburg tapes, recorded live at the Star Club on December 31, 1962. *(PA News)*

March 15, 1999: Paul, with his daughter Stella, at the Rock and Roll Hall of Fame Induction Ceremony at the Waldorf Astoria Hotel in New York, when he was inducted as a solo artist. (*Rex Features*)

April 10, 1999: Paul on stage with, amongst others, Tom Jones, George Michael, Elvis Costello, Eddie Izzard and Sinead O'Connor, at Linda's memorial concert at London's Royal Albert Hall. (*Rex Features*)

Wednesday June 14

A pre-taped interview with Ringo is aired on the Fuji Television programme *Super Time.*

Tuesday June 27

Almost 29 years after The Beatles last played this venue, Ringo and his band return to play at the Budokan in Tokyo, Japan. The Japanese television station NHK-TV videotapes the 7:00pm JST show.

Thursday June 29

At 4:15pm JST, Ringo, Barbara, and the band leave Japan, on flight Northwest 012, en route to Detroit.

Thursday July 13

Ringo appears on the CBS TV programme *This Morning,* promoting the current American leg of his All-Starr Band tour.

Conclusion of tour

Ringo is forced to cancel the final shows of his tour when his youngest daughter Lee is rushed into the intensive care unit at a London clinic (on August 24) suffering from hydrocephalus (fluid on the brain), a particularly dangerous illness. As Ringo leaves the hospital after visiting Lee, he tells reporters: "She had been feeling unwell and the next thing, she was here. I came as soon as I heard. We were desperately worried, but she is going to be all right. She is out of danger now. Lee had the operation (to drain the fluid from the brain) on Friday, and is now up and about. The best thing was to see her walking around." Ringo is naturally asked about his current American concerts. "We have cancelled the tour," he announces. "Family is more important, isn't it?" Ringo's rush to visit his sick daughter makes headline news around the globe in both the newspapers and on TV, where reports are featured, in the UK, on *London News Tonight* (Carlton ITV), the BBC *Evening News* (on August 28) and on GMTV the following morning, August 29.

*   *   *

June

 Early this month, Neil Aspinall contacts Klaus Voorman, the former bassist for Manfred Mann and The Plastic Ono Band, to discuss designing the covers for *The Beatles Anthology* album and video releases. (Klaus, of course, had designed The Beatles' 1966 *Revolver* album sleeve.)

Friday June 2

 Paul visits the Abbey Road Studios in London where he spends time overdubbing the tapes he has just recorded with Steve Miller. Around this time, he splashes out £48,000 on suits from the Saville Row tailor Edward Sexton, who tells reporters: "We have an association with Mr. McCartney going back many years. He orders a lot of clothes from us."

Thursday June 8

 Filming of the *Anthology* television series shifts to the Silverstone racetrack in Northamptonshire where George is filmed driving around in his red 1966 psychedelic mini. These scenes will appear during the *Magical Mystery Tour* sequence in the series.
 In the States, the drama film *Backbeat,* focusing on the relationship between Stuart Sutcliffe and Astrid Kirchner and The Beatles' days in Hamburg, Germany, is premiered on the Showtime pay cable network. (Further screenings on the station take place on June 23 and 28.)

Wednesday June 14

 ITV announces that they have outbid Britain's other television stations to secure the rights to broadcast *The Beatles Anthology.* The station have paid close to £5 million for the six-part series, while Channel 4, the long time favourites for the shows, dropped out of the bidding at £4.5 million. The BBC, The Beatles' own choice to screen the series, were apparently unimpressed with the early versions that they were shown and felt that the shows were not worth the £5 million asking price. Nevertheless, ITV announce today their success with the following (edited) press release:

THE BEATLES TELL THEIR OWN STORY ON ITV

"One of television's most long-awaited documentary series, in which The Beatles tell in their own words the story of their life and times, is to be shown on ITV this autumn. In addition to the six-part series, ITV has the rights for the UK TV premiere performance of the two new Beatles songs, 'Free As A Bird' and 'Real Love'.

"The unprecedented musical event will feature John, Paul, George and Ringo, with the latter three bringing additional instrumentation, voices and arrangements to two unreleased John Lennon songs on which he sings and plays.

"Commenting on the deal, ITV Network Director Marcus Plantin said, 'This is a coup for ITV. I'm truly delighted and proud that we are able to broadcast what must surely be one of the TV events of the decade.'

"Speaking from Apple's headquarters in West London, Neil Aspinall announced: 'The Beatles made their first television appearance on ITV, so it feels good that we should end up telling their story on ITV.' Although sales have been successfully concluded in America, the UK and other countries of the world, insiders report that a title for the series has yet to be agreed by all parties concerned."

 Early announcements for the series reveal that it is due to be screened in 41 different countries and dubbed into 20 different languages. Excitement also starts shifting towards what will be The Beatles' 28th official single 'Free As A Bird'. When asked about this 'Beatles Comeback' single, Paul issues this statement:

"We just imagined that John had gone on holiday and had said to us, 'Finish them up, lads – I trust you.' It was like he said, 'Sorry I can't make the last session, so I leave it up to you guys to finish it off. Don't get too fussy.' Once we agreed to take that attitude, it gave us a lot of freedom – because it meant that we didn't have a sacred view of John. It was John the Beatle, John the crazy guy we remember. It was something that initially sounded impossible, but we've done it."

 Paul's statement also went on to reveal why George, Ringo and himself had decided to make the documentary series: "We were fed up with every milkman's son writing books about us when they hadn't even met or talked to us."

Thursday June 22
 Paul is seen leaving the Apple Productions offices in Wendell Road, West London, clutching early copies of the *Anthology* documentary series following a meeting with the producer Chips Chipperfield and the director Geoff Wonfor.

Monday June 26
 George is due today at the Apple Productions offices to view further work on the *Anthology* series, but fails to appear. He has supplied, from his own personal archive, the following clips for use in the documentaries: *Juke Box Jury*, his solo appearance on the BBC1 show from July 25, 1964, private colour home movie footage of his wedding to Patti on January 21, 1966, and film of The Beatles' last photographic session from August 22, 1969, at Tittenhurst Park in Ascot. The collection is insured for £1 million.

July
 Reports this month indicate that *The Beatles Anthology* series has now been sold to 110 television channels around the world. Insiders on the series reveal that only two of the six parts have currently been concluded. ITV network chief Marcus Plantin announces that the station won the rights to screen The Beatles' own story "not because of the money paid, which was substantial, but because The Beatles had wanted an all-age audience only ITV could deliver." Meanwhile, Stuart Prebble, controller of ITV factual programmes, spoke about the ITV exclusive broadcasts of the 'Free As A Bird' and 'Real Love' songs: "We think the airing of these songs will be a real nation-stopping moment!" Finally, the excitement even reaches Steve Richmond, the editor-in-chief of *Music Week* magazine, when he enthuses about the group: "The Beatles will be the biggest campaign of the year . . . bigger even than Michael Jackson!"

 Debate continues within The Beatles about how the home video version of *Anthology* will be released and, for that matter, how many will appear. The original idea proposed is for ten videos at approximately 90 minutes each. George rejects this because the number ten is "karmically wrong"!

☘ Ringo meanwhile is very happy. Reports in America this month suggest that he has just been paid £500,000 to appear in a *Pizza Hut* commercial alongside three of the reformed Monkees, Davy Jones, Micky Dolenz and Peter Tork. (This is, in fact, the second time Ringo had appeared with Davy in a television advert. The two crossed paths back in 1977 for the *Simple Life* leisure commercials for Japanese Television.)

Thursday July 6
☘ In the UK, The Beatles' first manager Allan Williams, is present at the opening of the two-storey Beatles themed Pepper's Restaurant in Vernon Road, Scarborough.

Monday July 10
☘ Klaus Voorman attends a meeting at Apple Corps' London headquarters in Ovington Square, London, bringing with him a handful of sketch ideas for the *Anthology* covers. Also in attendance today is Neil Aspinall, Derek Taylor, David Saltz of ABC TV in America, and Rick Ward, the art director for the *Anthology* project.

Saturday July 15
☘ On the tenth anniversary of Bob Geldof's historic *Live Aid* concert, Paul naturally features in the commemorative programmes, which are broadcast by the BBC today. Firstly, he makes his radio acting début by appearing on the BBC Radio 4 programme *Remembering Live Aid*, which re-enacts the day's events of July 13th, 1985. Then later, this time on BBC2, a part of his concert performance is repeated in *African Summer,* a documentary about the historic show. During these tributes Paul is really to be found with Linda, leading an official victory parade through the streets of Rye, East Sussex, to celebrate the completion of the Rye Memorial Care Centre, a cause to which they had donated £800,000. The couple are joined later by their neighbour and close friend, the ex-Goon comic Spike Milligan.

☘ George, meanwhile, is to be found in the audience at this evening's Ravi Shankar concert at the Barbican Centre in London.

☘ In America, Yoko makes a brief appearance during the annual *VH-1 Honours* extravaganza.

Sunday July 16
☘ In today's *Independent On Sunday*, Paul is primarily interviewed, by Cole Moreton, about his good work for the Memorial Care Centre, but the subject of the upcoming *Anthology* series of course comes into the conversation:

"It's déjà vu really. We're sitting in Abbey Road Studio Two, where we always worked, listening to the work we did when we were 20. It is quite strange, but quite exciting as well. It's like being archaeologists. We're finding tracks that we didn't remember recording, that we didn't want, or thought, 'No, that's not too good.' Now, of course, after 30 years, they don't look too bad at all."

☘ Paul is naturally asked why 30-year-old Beatle rejects are deemed good enough to release now. He replies by saying: "I believe there will be a bunch of people interested in the George Harrison song ('You'll Know What To Do') from 30 years ago that no one to this day has heard. It's not the greatest thing George ever wrote, but it's an undiscovered nugget. If you find a little Egyptian pot, it doesn't have to be the greatest Egyptian pot. The fact that it is Egyptian is enough."

Wednesday July 19
☘ In London, George and Olivia are guests at the secret Rolling Stones gig at the Brixton Academy, but turn down the offer of going to the after-concert party. Instead they slip away to visit his Stones pal Ronnie Wood, at his home in Richmond, for a quiet get-together with Ronnie, his brother Art and other friends. Also present this evening is Ronnie's wife Jo, his son Jessie and his official biographer Terry Rawlings. Terry opens the door to George who, when ringing the buzzer requesting to be let in, announces, "Hello, it's a burglar!" George sips tea throughout the evening and talks about Formula One motor racing, Bob Dylan, and his troubles with his former business partner Denis O'Brien. (The party ends at around 6am.)

Friday July 28

✦ Paul and Linda visit the LIPA site in Mount Street, Liverpool, to survey its progress.

August

✦ The hype to the launch of *The Beatles Anthology* series begins in the UK, when the programmes are mentioned in trailers promoting the ITV autumn season. Meanwhile across the water in America, ABC TV announces that they are selling, for $300,000 a throw, a specially prepared 30-second *Anthology* TV trailer. Apparently they have been deluged with offers from TV companies to screen it. ABC's sales manager Robert Cagliero announces: "Sponsorship for the *Anthology* has sold more quickly than any special in our history!"

✦ This month, in an attempt to change his unhealthy lifestyle, Ringo admits that he has given up smoking and drinking, regularly goes jogging and lives on a strict macrobiotic diet. This may have something to do with the fact he has just signed up with American credit card giant *Discover*. As part of this lucrative deal, the company will sponsor the current All-Starr Band American tour.

Sunday August 6

✦ The song 'Hiroshima Sky Is Always Blue', as it is now called, recorded by Paul, Yoko and their respective families, receives its premiere on the television station NHK-TV as part of the programme *Good Morning Japan*. The broadcast also includes a 10-minute interview with Yoko, who is reported to be planning a performance of the song in October at Japan's Itsukushima Shrine to the victims of the atomic bomb in Mayajima, an island close to Hiroshima, where many of the Japanese World War II kamikaze pilots spent their last days preparing for their suicide missions.

September

✦ The worldwide excitement surrounding *The Beatles Anthology* continues unabated, helped by the appearance, this month, of an ABC TV five-minute promotional video tape distributed by the American station to the network's affiliated companies. For the lucky few who view this tape, it is the first glimpse anywhere of clips from the *Anthology* series.

Monday September 4

✦ At Abbey Road's Studio Two, Paul, along with Paul Weller and the Mojo Filters, who include the Oasis star Noel Gallagher, record a version of The Beatles' track 'Come Together' for inclusion on Brian Eno's War Child charity album *Help!* The track is recorded in one day, pressed the next and released, as part of the album on September 11, a process inspired by John's 'Instant Karma' back in February of 1970. Paul's re-recording of 'Come Together' is released as a single, on *Go-Discs*, on December 4. (The recordings of the War Child album are filmed for a Channel 4 television documentary.) Later Paul remarks about the session: "It reminded me a little of The Beatles' recordings, although with more drugs and booze!"

Wednesday September 6

✦ In order to gain complete access to The Beatles' photo archive at Apple, Klaus Voorman again returns to London, but this time he sets up shop downstairs at Apple's Ovington Square offices. Within two days, on Friday September 6, Klaus completes the final layouts for the *Beatles Anthology* cover designs.

Thursday September 7

✦ Paul performs during the encore on 'Rave On' at the 20th annual Buddy Holly Week concert, held over two days at the Shepherds Bush Empire in London. Among the stars on this final night are Carl Perkins, Bobby Vee, Mike Berry, DJ Tony Prince and, of course, The Crickets.

✦ Meanwhile, the latest Sotheby's auction, held in London today, is dubbed *The Cynthia Lennon Collection – Part 2*, comprising 18 items from her own private collection. Among the highlights offered for sale is John's "leather clad, metal-lined, bulbous barrel" which, according to Cynthia, John used to "stash his marijuana and cigarette papers in at home in Weybridge".

Sunday September 10

🍎 The documentary on the making of the *Help!* charity album, featuring Paul recording 'Come Together' with Noel Gallagher and Paul Weller, is transmitted tonight, in the UK, on Channel 4.

Monday September 11

🍎 The promise of unreleased Beatles recordings to accompany the *Anthology* television series sees the light of day when Rogers & Cowan, Inc. of New York, a company representing Capitol Records, issue this press release:

CAPITOL RECORDS SET TO RELEASE VOLUME ONE OF BEATLES ANTHOLOGY

"First new song in 25 years, 'Free As A Bird', along with previously unreleased music from the fab four, to be included.

"Capitol Records today put months, if not years of speculation to rest with the announcement that the first instalment of new and never-before-released music from The Beatles does exist and is slated for release worldwide on Monday November 20, 1995.

"The 40-track double CD, double cassette and triple vinyl album, entitled *The Beatles Anthology Volume One*, an unprecedented milestone in rock'n'roll history, will include previously unreleased material recorded between 1958–1964, as well as John Lennon's 'Free As A Bird', a brand new recording done earlier this year with Paul McCartney, George Harrison and Ringo Starr. The *Anthology* will contain previously unreleased material, mostly compiled from a variety of untapped sources including EMI, Polydor and Decca Records, and a variety of radio and television broadcasts.

"Songs featured include Beatles hits such as 'Love Me Do', 'Please Please Me', 'A Hard Day's Night', 'You Can't Do That', as well as never-before-heard tracks such as McCartney's 'In Spite Of All The Danger', Ray Charles' 'Hallelujah, I Love Her So' and Leiber & Stoller's 'Searchin'', among others. Another of the album's many highlights is a recording of the vintage performance of 'All My Loving' heard live from The Beatles' historic appearance on *The Ed Sullivan Show*.

"The release, set to coincide with the November airing of ABC's six-hour, three-part, three-night Beatles special, will be the first of what is anticipated to be three double CDs.

"The announcement comes on the heels of the enormous success of *Live At The BBC*, which sold nearly eight million copies worldwide."

Tuesday September 12

🍎 ITV, and its advertising sales arm Laser, throw a Beatles-theme party for over 250 people at the London Television Centre on the South Bank to launch *The Beatles Anthology* series. The get-together also marks the first official screening of footage from the series, which includes the premiere screening of a colourized version of 'All You Need Is Love' from the June 1967 *Our World* live television programme. Neil Aspinall and Derek Taylor attend on behalf of Apple, and music at the event is supplied by the group The Manfreds.

Thursday September 14

🍎 Beatles hysteria reaches the Sotheby's Auction in London today, when Paul's 1967 hand-written lyrics for 'Getting Better' sell for a world record price of £161,000!

Tuesday September 19

🍎 In the UK, London Weekend Television issues a press release concerning *The Beatles Anthology,* a release slow in coming due to the ongoing dispute over the title for the series. (Apple at this point are still keen on *The Beatles Story*, while ITV prefer the, already established, *Beatles Anthology*.) The press release, which reveals even more information on the series, and comments from key figures in the making of the programmes, reads (in part):

"The series, which traces the Beatles phenomenon, features exclusive interviews with Paul, George and Ringo – some of which were conducted by Jools Holland – and incorporates a rich archive of interviews on audio and video tape left by the late John Lennon.

"Neil Aspinall, the driving force behind *The Beatles Anthology*, tells how the series came about: 'I said to Paul, George and Ringo: "Let's do it," and I realised that the one thing that we had, that nobody else had, no third party had, was access to interviews with the three surviving Beatles and all John's interviews – with Yoko's consent.' He continues: 'What I'd decided right from the beginning was not to have some mid-Atlantic commentator telling the Beatles' story. It was better for them to tell their own story. And this included John Lennon, too.'

"Editor Andy Mathews says: 'Early on in the first programme are their own personal pictures of childhood and all that, but their home movies of when they're on holiday – things that have never been seen – I think are the best.'

"With a production team of ten, and the mammoth task of researching nearly ten thousand pieces of footage and music, the project was no mean feat. Series director and writer, Bob Smeaton, reveals, 'Originally, the idea had been to start the programme with the Beatles' first record. I said to Geoff Wonfor (the director): "Don't you know we've got a programme here before they even form a band?" We were one hour into the programme and they hadn't even picked up their instruments . . . that's when we realised how big the project was.'

"Adds producer Chips Chipperfield: 'Everybody here at Apple is very passionate about telling this story. It's a hell of a venture – it really is – and it's been quite something to be part of.'

"He admits that, while making the programme, he was overwhelmed by: 'The magnitude of it, the enormousness of the Beatles in terms of the impact they really had – not just on a generation, but on now. It really is phenomenal.' Chips continued: 'You can't pick up a paper or switch on your television without hearing about The Beatles thirty years down the line, and feel as if it's all happening over again. And it comes out in the music. Over and again- and always.'

"Director Geoff Wonfor says that while he was 'rediscovering' The Beatles, what really amazed him was the fact that: 'They were so tight – and some of the performances, the harmonies, were breathtaking.'

"Neil Aspinall explains how two new songs, featuring all four Beatles, were born out of the project: 'It was always one of Paul's things that if they were going to do it, it would be nice if they could somehow do new music, even if it was incidental music to go behind a piece of footage. And that's developed into 'Free As A Bird' and 'Real Love', which is a real bonus for everyone.' "

🍎 LWT also reveals that a November 8 date has been pencilled into their schedules for a media launch for the *Anthology,* but are unable to say where it will take place. Amongst the possibilities are the Cavern Club in Liverpool, their own LWT Studios on the South Bank or even the Abbey Road Studios in London.

Monday October 2
🍎 Paul takes a breather from the *Anthology* hysteria by joining Linda on a flight to America to promote her new cookbook *Linda's Kitchen*.

Tuesday October 3
🍎 In the UK, the *Sun* newspaper prints a "World Photo Exclusive" of Paul, George and Ringo, posing together at Apple's headquarters in London, on Friday March 31, 1995. (The last time the three appeared together in a picture was in 1981 at Ringo's wedding to Barbara Bach.) Subtitled "Got Back", the colour picture occupies almost the entire front page, with an alternative picture, this time in black and white, appearing inside the paper. With Paul appearing unsmiling, George with untidy hair and Ringo looking away from the camera, the first impression is that the photo was "sneaked" out of Apple's clutches. This hunch later proves to be true, when stories reveal that the snap actually came from long-time Apple staff photographer Tommy Hanley, who, apparently, sold the picture to the *Sun*, via its editor Stuart Higgins, for a cool £100,000!

Wednesday October 4
🍎 Location filming of the 'Real Love' promotional video begins in Liverpool and is directed by Kevin Godley. The camera team films a scene with a white piano in the air against a backdrop of the Mersey and the Liver Building. Earlier, Kevin had visited The Beatles Shop in Mathew Street to buy some props for the shoot. (Location filming for the clip then moves to London on October 11.) The final editing on the clip is carried out in several London locations, firstly at Crowe in Shepherds Bush, which just happened to be right across the road from where *The Beatles Anthology* documentary series is being

prepared. "If we needed access to any archive material at Apple, we could literally pop over the road to borrow it," Kevin remarked. He also later spoke about how the finished film came about. "I remembered seeing this extraordinary film which basically comprised John smiling for 55 minutes (Yoko's 1968 art film *Smile*). We then filmed 35mm identical contemporary film portraits of Paul, George and Ringo at 500 frames per second. When they are edited together it looked as if John was looking out from the past, from the other side, back at us. The whole semi-conscious idea of resurrection and stuff floating up came from there. Then we worked out the sequence of events for the rising of the piano and began to introduce the sessions footage, inserting specific things like the rising medals and Beatle instruments."

⚫ Due to the strict security surrounding the second Beatles comeback song, Kevin was not even furnished with the completed song to accompany the video, so he had to privately overdub his own vocal in place of the absent vocal lines for reference purposes only. "When Paul, George and Ringo looked at my first rough edit of the video they were listening to Paul, George, Ringo and Kev!" Godley also points out that Apple demanded the best for the song. "If you fuck up, you find out pretty quick," he remarks. "I think it took us just over a week to do a rough cut that was up to standard and their comments were interesting. Paul was happy with most things apart from a couple of shots. Ringo felt that the portraits should be smiling a little more. The criticism was pretty constructive. Probably the nicest thing about the video is that you actually get to see these guys working in the studio together for the first time in over 25 years, even though it's just a few glimpses. That's definitely one of the more positive attributes."

Sunday October 15
⚫ To help celebrate World Food Day, Linda's range of vegetarian food is given away free to the homeless. The campaign, organised by People For The Ethical Treatment Of Animals (PETA), centres around the cafes in London's Farringdon area and is administered by *The Big Issue*, the magazine sold in aid of the homeless.

Monday October 16
⚫ ITV reveals that the broadcast date for the first episode of *The Beatles Anthology* will be November 26, but an ITV spokesperson warns: "Network scheduling can change up to two weeks before broadcast, so that's not 100% confirmed, but it's pretty much what we'd like to go with."

⚫ At the Royal Albert Hall in London this evening, Paul joins the poet Allen Ginsberg on stage playing electric guitar for the finale, a recital of 'The Ballad Of The Skeletons', at the large poetry event entitled The Return Of The Forgotten.

Tuesday October 17
⚫ EMI issues the following press release:
"EMI Records and Apple can at last confirm the track listing for the double compact disc, double cassette and triple album *The Beatles Anthology 1*.

"The album, which will be released on 21st November, features an extraordinary 60 tracks, a combination of largely unreleased studio music, live recordings, radio and TV sessions and The Beatles' own private tapes.

"A huge amount of speculation has been building up in the media over the content of the *Anthology* project, which will also include a series of eight 75-minute videos, featuring film footage gathered from many sources, both public and private. As previously announced, the ITV network will screen the first hour of the remarkable six-hour documentary series on The Beatles on 26th November."

The Beatles Anthology 1 Track Listing (songs only)
CD1: 'Free As A Bird' (a new recording featuring John, Paul, George and Ringo), 'That'll Be The Day' (Quarry Men 1958), 'In Spite Of All The Danger' (Quarry Men 1958), 'Hallelujah, I Love Her So', 'You'll Be Mine', 'Cayenne' (all home recordings from 1960), 'My Bonnie', 'Ain't She Sweet', 'Cry For A Shadow' (all from Hamburg 1961), 'Searchin'', 'Three Cool Cats', 'The Sheik Of Araby', 'Like Dreamers Do', 'Hello Little Girl' (all from the Decca Records audition on January 1, 1962), 'Besame Mucho' (Abbey Road first session June 1962), 'Love Me Do' (first EMI version), 'How Do You Do It?' (September 4, 1962), 'Please Please Me' (September 11, 1962), 'One After 909' (sequence and complete version from March 5, 1963),'Lend Me Your Comb' (BBC Radio), 'I'll Get You'

(*Sunday Night At The London Palladium*) and 'I Saw Her Standing There', 'From Me To You', 'Money (That's What I Want)', 'You Really Got A Hold On Me' and 'Roll Over Beethoven' (all from Swedish radio in October 1963).

CD2: 'She Loves You', ''Till There Was You', 'Twist And Shout' (all from the 1963 *Royal Variety* show), 'This Boy', 'I Want To Hold Your Hand', 'Moonlight Bay' (from *The Morecambe And Wise Show*, recorded in December, 1963), 'Can't Buy Me Love' (take 2), 'All My Loving' (*Ed Sullivan Show* 1964), 'You Can't Do That' (outtake), 'And I Love Her' (outtake), 'A Hard Day's Night' (take 1), 'I Wanna Be Your Man', 'Long Tall Sally', 'Boys', 'Shout' (all from studio masters that were prepared for the *Around The Beatles* TV special in 1964), 'I'll Be Back' (takes 2 and 3), 'You'll Know What To Do' (George's second ever song from 1964), 'No Reply' (demo), 'Mr Moonlight' (*Beatles For Sale* outtake), 'Leave My Kitten Alone' (*Beatles For Sale* outtake), 'No Reply' (take 2), 'Eight Days A Week' (sequences and complete take), 'Kansas City'/'Hey-Hey-Hey' (*Beatles For Sale* outtake).

(Note: In-between the tracks, there are spoken words, introductions and comments from each of The Beatles. The Quarry Men's performance of 'In Spite Of All The Danger', The Beatles' only doo-wop ballad, appears here in an edited version, clocking in at 2′ 45″, while Paul's original priceless shellac acetate runs at 3′ 25″. The June 1962 recordings of 'Love Me Do' and 'Besame Mucho', featuring Pete Best on drums, were thought lost but were recently found at the back of a cupboard by George Martin's wife, Judy.)

George Martin: "I am trying to tell the story of The Beatles' lives in music, from the moment they met to the moment they split up in 1970. I have listened to everything we ever recorded together. Every take of every song, every track of every song, virtually everything that was ever committed to tape and labelled 'Beatles'. I've heard about 600 separate items in all. I didn't start any serious listening until early this year (May 22), when I got Paul, George and Ringo to come in occasionally and listen with me. Of course, they couldn't sit through all the sessions, so I would tend to have them come in about once a week."

Amongst tracks considered for the *Anthology* albums, but ultimately rejected were: 'Love Of The Loved' and 'To Know Her Is To Love Her' (Decca audition 1962), 'My Girl Is Red Hot' (Star Club, Hamburg 1962), 'She's A Woman' (Shea Stadium 1965), 'Paperback Writer' (EMI vocal only version), 'Nowhere Man' (Live in Tokyo 1966), 'Think For Yourself', 'Love You Too', 'Revolution', 'Hey La Le Lu'/'All Together Now' (all EMI outtakes), 'Something' (Abbey Road studios 1969 segued into a rambling piano jam) and the 27-minute version of 'Helter Skelter'.

Thursday October 19
 The cookery book *Linda's Kitchen,* featuring over 200 new recipes by Linda McCartney is released in the UK.

Friday October 20
 In London, Klaus Voorman hands his completed *Anthology 2* cover design into Apple at their offices in Ovington Square.

Monday October 23
 Location work on the 'Free As A Bird' promotional video begins in Liverpool. The director for this film, comprising titles and images gleaned from The Beatles' back catalogue from the sixties, is the American born Joe Pytka, well known in the industry for his US television commercials. The producer of the clip, Vincent Joliet, explains the shooting: "We shot the location scenes knowing that something was going to be added later. We had to find the right footage. With the accident scene, for example, we selected the best take and then looked at all the old footage for the shots of John's head and body movements that would fit best." (Further location work on the film will be carried out in London and Los Angeles, with the final editing being done alongside the ongoing location filming. Interestingly enough, among the parade of shops especially made for the 'Free As A Bird' video, a shop front called "Dylan's", a natural referral to Bob, is made but is not seen in the completed version of the film.)

Friday October 27
 The build-up to the official launch of *The Beatles Anthology* continues unabated when today in America, on the WPVI TV5 breakfast show *AM Philadelphia*, the series is

previewed with excerpts from the official *Anthology* EPK (electronic press kit) and an exclusive conversation, by phone, with the American reporter Mark Hertsgaard, who tells of how he has already heard some of the unreleased tracks to be released on *The Beatles Anthology 1* album. Joining guests in the studio during this lengthy feature is The Beatles' first manager Allan Williams who brings with him a pair of Paul's old leather trousers, as worn by him during the group's time in Hamburg in the early Sixties.

Saturday October 28
 In an exclusive interview with Thomas Quinn of the *Daily Express* newspaper, Paul speaks of his bitterness at living in the shadow of John Lennon's martyrdom: "There are those who think John *was* The Beatles. That is not true and he would be the first to tell you that."

November
 During the first part of the month, ABC TV in America begins running the trailer: "Imagine The Beatles back together again – All four! – John, Paul, George and Ringo – But how? – John left two unfinished songs – And the remaining Beatles have completed his music – It's The Beatles like you've never heard them before! – Reunited in words and music – *The Beatles Anthology* – Coming November 19 – On *A Beatles C.*"

To tie in with the *Anthology* promotions, Linda is appointed the official Beatles photographer. Her agent, Robby Montgomery, charges £2,000 per image of the three re-formed Beatles, whether in colour or black and white, posing together for the first time since 1981 at Ringo's London wedding to Barbara.

Shout! author Philip Norman reveals in the *Daily Mail* newspaper that, contrary to popular belief, it was George and Neil Aspinall and not Paul, who had originally contacted Yoko with the view of adding new instruments to John's existing demo tracks, and that Yoko merely used the 1994 Rock And Roll Hall Of Fame as an event to hand over the tapes to Paul with all the plans for the songs being concluded before then.

The three Beatles, affectionately called The Threatles, appear on the cover of this month's issue of *Q* magazine.

In the States, the E! (Entertainment) Network broadcasts a 46-minute documentary entitled *The Beatles On E!,* which is presented by Martin Lewis who is seen on location at Beatles sites in both London and Liverpool. Further Beatles reflective programmes in America this month include another unofficial version, simply called *The Beatles Story,* which is aired on the A & E (Arts and Entertainment) Channel.
 Yoko Ono makes another live appearance on CNN's *Larry King Live* in America, where she naturally discusses 'Free As A Bird'.

Friday November 10
 The first (51-minute) episode of *The Beatles Anthology* is previewed at the BAFTA (the British Academy of Film and Television Arts) Awards in London's Piccadilly. This is immediately followed by a press conference where the series director Geoff Wonfor and the director/writer Bob Smeaton, as well as Stuart Prebble, the head of ITV's factual programmes, take questions from the waiting journalists. Representing Apple are both Neil Aspinall and Derek Taylor.

In America this morning, *Anthology* promotions continue, this time on the New York television programme *Day & Date*. Besides showing the familiar clips of the *Anthology* EPK, the programme also repeats, for the first time in 17 years, fascinating colour clips of John and Paul being interviewed by the reporter Larry Kane on Tuesday May 14, 1968, during their visit to New York to launch Apple.

Also in America radio station WABC broadcasts a special entitled *Beatles '95*, including a new interview with Paul.

Saturday November 11 & Sunday November 12
 George attends the Australian Grand Prix in Adelaide. Following Damon Hill's victory in the race, on November 12, George gives a sneak preview of 'Free As A Bird' to Hill during the after-race celebration party. "I wanted Damon to be the first to hear it," George announces joyfully, adding: "After he won, I thought it was the perfect moment." During his stay in Adelaide, George also gives an exclusive interview to Frank Pengello of the Australian television programme *Today Tonight*, where, during the 10-minute feature, questions naturally take on a Beatles-related theme.

On his time with The Beatles: "The Beatles, for me, are a bit like a suit or a shirt I once wore and unfortunately, I don't mean this in a bitter way, a lot of people look at that suit and think it's me. The reality is that I'm this soul in the body, The Beatles was this thing we did for a few years and it was such a big thing. It's amazing that people keep going on about it."

On 'Free As A Bird': "I think (John) would like it, in fact I said to them (Paul and Ringo) I hope someone does this to all my crap demos when I'm dead, making them into hit songs!"

✦ ABC TV in the States transmits the trailer: "*The Beatles Anthology* – The television event of a lifetime – Two new Beatles songs – Words you've never heard before – Footage you've never seen before – How did it feel to change the world?"

✦ Also on Saturday November 11, this time in the States, NBC TV (Channel 10), during the show *Time Out,* again promotes the upcoming *Anthology* series with further clips from the *Anthology* EPK and a short clip of Yoko on the set of her first American sitcom appearance.

Monday November 13

✦ ABC TV in America screens the *Beatles Anthology* trailer: "Words you've never heard before – Footage you've never seen before – And the first new Beatles song in 25 years!"

Eager to cash in on the huge current interest in The Beatles, VCI, in conjunction with both MPI and Apple, re-releases in the UK on home video, *A Hard Day's Night* and *Help!,* both with additional newsreel clips, unavailable on the previous editions. Also today, the American documentary *The Making Of A Hard Day's Night* is released in England for the first time. (An item previously available in America as *You Can't Do That – The Making Of A Hard Day's Night.)*

Thursday November 16 (until Thursday November 30)

✦ The excitement surrounding *The Beatles Anthology* continues when huge advertising billboards for the series, bearing the slogan "You Haven't Heard Anything Yet", begin to spring up across England. (A second phase of advertising takes place on December 16 lasting until November 30.) While in America, the ABC TV breakfast show *Good Morning America* again previews *The Beatles Anthology* by featuring an interview with George Martin, who is seen playing songs from the *Anthology 1* album.

Friday November 17

✦ "Two new Beatles songs – The most anticipated event in 30 years – An event no one thought would ever happen!" – ABC TV *Beatles Anthology* trailer.

✦ An exclusive, pre-taped, interview with Yoko, in which she talks about how she helped with the current Beatles reunion, is featured on the US TV show *Inside Edition.* The item is naturally included among further promotions for *The Beatles Anthology.*

Saturday November 18

✦ The final edited version of the 'Free As A Bird' video is delivered to Apple in London. Once Neil Aspinall and Derek Taylor have given their blessings, a broadcast master is immediately dispatched to ABC TV in America for its premiere tomorrow night. Paul gave a "thumbs up" after having viewed the first edits during the previous week. (Both George and Ringo gave their blessing to the clip after being sent VHS copies to their homes.) The director Joe Pytka delivered a copy personally to Yoko at her Dakota apartment. He remarks: "Yoko absolutely loved the video!"

✦ On the eve of the great launch for the *Anthology* television series in America, VH-1 broadcasts the 23-minute programme entitled *Get Back – The Beatles Reunion,* an archive based show hosted by Anthony DeCurtis. Over this special Beatles Weekend, the station gets into the *Beatlemania* kick by broadcasting five hours of Beatles-related programming, including (broadcast straight after the previously mentioned documentary) the drama film *The Hours And The Times*, focusing on the so-called relationship between John and Brian Epstein in 1963, and the 1972 concert film *John Lennon Live In New York City.* In addition, the rest of the time is made up of Beatles-and solo-related promotional clips which include (at 4pm Eastern) back-to-back screenings of a selection of Paul's videos.

✦ ABC TV in America increases excitement by screening the television trailer: "In one day – It's the television event of our lifetime – The incredible music you've always loved – Plus two new Beatles songs – *The Beatles Anthology* – Tomorrow!"

Sunday November 19

At last, following months of extreme hype, the long awaited *Beatles Anthology* television series finally premieres on America TV on the ABC ('A Beatles C') television station. Part one this evening is transmitted between 9:00 and 10:59 EST; with an estimated audience of over 48 million watching the show! Due to an exclusive "first airing" agreement between Apple and ABC TV ('A Beatles C') in America, the first worldwide premiere playing of 'Free As A Bird', frequently advertised as the first new Beatles song in 25 years, begins at approximately 10:55 EST, rounding off part one of the series. The anticipation to the hearing of this new Beatles song is huge, to put it mildly. The excitement is further helped, during the playing of the 'Penny Lane' promotional film, by a 60 seconds "on-screen" numbered countdown. Then, in a military style manoeuvre, a Capitol Records representative in New York, who is on hand with a mobile phone, calls an EMI colleague at London's Abbey Road studios and informs him exactly when the first 'Free As A Bird' airing, and indeed the first part of the *Anthology* television series, has reached its natural conclusion. At approximately 3:59am (UK time), the excitement of hearing the first new Beatles single in a quarter of a century is about to reach England.

Meanwhile in Holland this evening, in one of the biggest security operations ever undertaken by EMI, the excitement continues when the initial printed stock of *The Beatles Anthology 1* (on CD, album and cassette), is shipped from Holland at midnight (European time) to destinations all over Europe.

Monday November 20

In the UK at approximately 4:00am, Abbey Road Studios begin to distribute to various stations around England special CD-Rs (recordable compact discs) of 'Free As A Bird'. Naturally, with a guaranteed large audience expectancy, one of the stations to receive this "Beatles Collectible" item is BBC Radio One who, at approximately 4:07am, play the single for the first time anywhere in the UK.

As the morning progresses, more and more UK radio stations play the track. The ITV breakfast station GMTV arranges for a live broadcast to take place from the new Cavern Club in Mathew Street, Liverpool, where the song is played before a large crowd of excited Beatles followers waiting in anticipation of hearing the new Beatles song.

The promotional video to accompany the song is also a major unveiling. Original plans to premiere broadcast both the song and the video at the end of this evening's ITV network special *All Together Now* (broadcast between 8:01 and 8:28pm) are soon shelved when clips of this video appear on Channel 4's *Big Breakfast Show* this morning, as well as the TV news broadcasts throughout the day on the BBC, ITN and Channel 4. The reactions to the song though are mixed.

Following the hype of the *Anthology* television series and the single 'Free As A Bird', comes the launch of the album. Described by EMI as "the most complex ship-out in the distributor's history", the day begins at 7:00am, when the huge *Anthology* stock, again under strict security, reaches the EMI distribution plant in Hayes, Middlesex from Holland. Several megastores, namely Virgin and HMV, strike a deal with EMI to receive their orders in advance and to open at midnight in order to sell copies of the album early.

The official *Beatles Anthology* press conference takes place this morning in the Lancaster rooms of London's prestigious Savoy Hotel, where, before a capacity crowd of 400 journalists and cameramen, George Martin, Derek Taylor, Jeff Lynne, Neil Aspinall and EMI's Rupert Perry, answer questions from the media and later pose for photographs. The normally shy and retiring Neil Aspinall is asked about his legendary low profile. "It's not that I've deliberately avoided interviews," he replies. "It's just that I've always felt the questions about The Beatles were better answered by themselves." Derek Taylor is asked where The Beatles are today. "They are all at home, everywhere else but here," he replies.

George Martin is naturally asked why he did not produce 'Free As A Bird'. "Jeff Lynne has done a brilliant job, and having heard it now, I wish I had produced it. Because, if anything, it would have given me 30 number ones, instead of 29. I've been working on *Anthology 1* all year, and if I had to choose between working on the single or the album, I'd have chosen *Anthology,* because it's the bigger one."

The get-together also features a press premiere of the song 'Free As A Bird' which is played twice, once accompanied by the single's picture sleeve, and the other alongside the special promotional video. On both occasions, a large round of applause greets the song's finale. Later tonight, a complete screening of the 'Free As A Bird' promo video is shown at the end of the Granada/ITV network tribute programme *All Together Now,* which features interviews with celebrities who reminisce about The Beatles.

🍎 In America, the day begins with Ringo appearing at 7:01am (EST time), by way of satellite from his home in Monte Carlo, on the ABC TV breakfast show *Good Morning America*, where he reminisces about his Beatles days, talks about the recording of 'Free As A Bird' and naturally discusses the *Anthology* project. This lengthy Beatles segment also features a live report from the radio station WZLX in Boston which is, this morning, playing Beatles music non-stop and airs another complete screening of the video for 'Free As A Bird'. The video's director, Joe Pytka, is interviewed for the programme, by satellite from Los Angeles, at 7:44am.

Tuesday November 21

🍎 The album *The Beatles Anthology 1* is finally released simultaneously worldwide. In America alone, initial orders are reported to be around 3.5 million, worth around $60–70 million.

The first week of *Anthology 1* sales reveal 121,000 copies sold in the UK, and 855,500 alone through the American Best Buy chain stores.

Due to the huge sales of *Anthology 1*, The Beatles' former drummer Pete Best receives a seven-figure royalty cheque, thanks to the ten tracks he plays on during the album. Pete is, at last, recognised for his contribution to the group, even going as so far as to review the discs in the *Sun* newspaper, where, as expected, he describes *Anthology 1* as: "The Beatles' greatest ever album," adding "and not because I'm on it!" He also goes on to write: "For me, the poignant tracks are those that I was involved in. Frankly, I'm bloody proud and believe they really stand the test of time." Further money for the sacked Beatles drummer comes in the shape of a one-off Heineken beer commercial, which is screened on ITV during the second part of the *Anthology* TV broadcasts. Original plans to screen the 15-second commercial during the opening part, in which he is featured, are scuppered by Apple because they felt this was a "piss take". (For his appearance, Pete receives a cool £10,000.)

On the subject of Pete Best's good fortune, Derek Taylor, of Apple, comments: "Pete will earn a decent amount of money, which is only right. He is a good man and he deserves it. This is a new chapter for Pete."

Wednesday November 22

🍎 The second part of *The Beatles Anthology* is transmitted on ABC TV, just like the first part, between 9:00 and 11:00 EST.

Thursday November 23

🍎 The concluding part of the *Anthology* series is screened tonight on ABC TV between 8:00 and 10:00 EST. The viewers figures have by now dropped to an estimated 25 million.

🍎 While in the UK, in an attempt to foil the bootleggers, the ITV Network (between 8:00 and 8:04pm), screens the video to accompany The Beatles' second comeback single 'Real Love', in a five-minute programme, aptly titled *The Beatles – Real Love*. The video to accompany the song was directed by the former member of 10cc Kevin Godley, and comprised archive clips from the Sixties and the Geoff Wonfor footage of Paul, George and Ringo recording the song at The Mill, East Sussex, on February 6 and 7 this year.

Saturday November 25

🍎 Derek Taylor appears as a special guest on the BBC2 late night music show *Later With Jools Holland*. Besides an interesting, Beatles-related, conversation with Derek and the host Holland, the programme transmits, for the first time anywhere in the world, a clip from the "lost" videotaped performance of 'Long Tall Sally' from The Beatles' Washington Coliseum concert on February 11, 1964. (Although promoted as a special one-off broadcast, the clip had, in fact, been prepared for a simultaneous limited release to various important music-related stations across America and Europe.)

Sunday November 26

⑥ Three days after the series had finished in America, *The Beatles Anthology* premieres in the UK across the ITV network. The first programme attracts estimated viewing figures of 14.3 million people.

Monday November 27

⑥ Channel 4, in the UK, broadcasts a most unflattering documentary on The Beatles, a controversial "warts and all" look at the history of the group's financial empire. The 50-minute profile is titled *All You Need Is Cash*.

December

⑥ In the UK, George's wife Olivia issues a statement announcing that "a seven-figure sum from the proceeds of *The Beatles Anthology* will be donated to the Romanian Angel appeal."

⑥ Ringo, at his home in Monte Carlo, personally signs the Gartlan USA limited edition Ringo Starr figurines (see entry for April 1996).

Sunday December 3

⑥ The second part of *The Beatles Anthology* is transmitted in the UK. (The viewing figures have fallen slightly to 11.6 million.)

Monday December 4

⑥ 'Free As A Bird', The Beatles' 28th official EMI single, is released on a 7-inch single, a 4-track CD and on a cassette. (120, 000 copies will be sold in its first week). Within 19 hours of its release today, it is estimated that approximately 20 million people in the UK (a third of the population) have heard the song.

⑥ EMI in America releases Yoko's first solo album in ten years, entitled *Rising,* which features her son Sean on acoustic and electric guitars, keyboards and backing vocals. (The UK release takes place on January 15, 1996.) To coincide with its release, Yoko appears this evening on the CNN programme *Larry King Live* for the third time.

Thursday December 7

⑥ In London, a routine hospital scan reveals a small malignant tumour in one of Linda's breasts. An immediate operation is recommended.

Saturday December 9

⑥ In America, Paul's 1967 soundtrack album *The Family Way* is reissued on CD and cassette.

Sunday December 10

⑥ 'Free As A Bird' enters the BBC singles music chart at number two, beaten to the top spot by Michael Jackson's 'Earth Song'. Paul, in particular, is believed to be most upset by this. When Jackson's song keeps The Beatles' single from the coveted number one slot at Christmas, the bosses at Sony, Jackson's label, celebrate their good fortune by cheekily sending the bosses at EMI a large turkey "stuffed" with The Beatles' 'Free As A Bird' CD. Meanwhile, the third part of *The Beatles Anthology* is transmitted in the UK. Sadly, the viewing figures again slump, this time to just under 10.4 million.

Monday December 11

⑥ It is publicly confirmed that Linda McCartney has been diagnosed as suffering from breast cancer. "Linda had a scan at the Princess Grace Hospital in London and was found to have a lump," Paul announces, adding, "She has had an operation to remove the lump which was performed successfully. Lucky it was caught in time!"

Friday December 15

⑥ Pauline Sutcliffe, sister of former Beatle Stuart, issues, through the Liverpool solicitors of Silverbeck Rymer, a writ against Apple Corps Ltd. in respect of the deal offered to her for the use of Stu's recorded material, which appeared on the album *The Beatles Anthology 1.*

Sunday December 17

 The fourth show of *The Beatles Anthology* is transmitted in the UK. The viewing figures slump again, this time to 8.7 million.

Monday December 25

 ABC TV (formerly 'A Beatles C' for the recent *Anthology* documentary series) broadcasts a 22-minute Christmas Day Beatles television special, entitled *With A Little Help From My Friends*. The station claimed the show was "made with no help from Apple!"

Tuesday December 26

 Due to the rearranged ITV Christmas schedule, programme planners shift part five of *The Beatles Anthology* to Boxing Day. Not surprisingly the viewing figures drop again, this time to a very poor 3.8 million.

Sunday December 31

 The concluding part of the *Anthology* is shown on ITV on New Year's Eve. Even though schedulers have returned the series to its already established Sunday night slot, the viewing figures still reach an all-time low of 2.9 million.

"The end has
finally arrived . . .
The Beatles are
no more. The
official word
is that Paul
McCartney,
George Harrison
and Ringo Starr
will never play
together again
as a group . . ."

– Apple press release

January
 In America, Capitol Records' marketing division CEMA, releases 14 more Beatles jukebox only singles.
 George spends the month in India, producing music for Ravi Shankar, specifically the album *Chants Of India* which is recorded in Madras. A 4CD Ravi Shankar retrospective, entitled *Ravi – In Celebration* is released on George's *Dark Horse* label, in association with *Angel Records*. Also this month, George wins a partial victory against his former business partner Denis O'Brien. The Los Angeles superior court awards George $11.6 million (approximately £7.25 million) against O'Brien. (Originally George had sought $25 million.)
 In London, Linda begins her gruelling course of chemotherapy sessions, usually once or twice a week.

Friday January 5
 Klaus Voorman travels to London and hands in to Apple, at their Ovington Square headquarters, his completed design for *The Beatles Anthology 3*.

Monday January 8
 Following seven years of preparation, as part of a £12 million refurbishment scheme, LIPA, the Liverpool Institute for the Performing Arts, finally opens its doors in Mount Street, for the first 200 of its planned patrons.

Monday January 22
 With the completion of *The Beatles Anthology* home video versions gaining speed, Apple Productions, from their Wendell Road offices, dispatch to Paul, at his Sussex home, VHS preview cassettes of parts one and two for his final approval.

Tuesday January 30
 In Liverpool, Paul hosts the official press launch for LIPA, alongside LIPA's chief executive Mark Featherstone-Witty and George Martin. Paul jokes: "I haven't got a speech, you're probably glad to know!" Guests include Paul and Linda's son James, Mike McCartney, Gerry Marsden and Neil Aspinall. Paul and George Martin happily pose for pictures where Paul is seen cutting into a specially baked cake. Paul's wife Linda is conspicuous by her absence.

Tuesday February 13
 A new version of the 'Real Love' video, re-edited by Jerry Chater to feature additional scenes of Paul, George and Ringo with their respective wives, is finally completed today, in West London. (The running time is again 3′ 50″.)

Wednesday February 14
 The Beatles' second comeback single 'Real Love' is beamed to UK radio stations, via satellite, for broadcast at 8:10am on St. Valentine's Day.
 Today's edition of the *Sun* newspaper carries a story with the headline: "£100,000 To Kill Macca". It reveals that two thieves, currently in custody and turned supergrass, knew of a plot to kill Paul and that a hitman had been hired to do the job. Scotland Yard dismisses the story as "totally untrue"!

Saturday February 24
 The newly edited promotional video to accompany 'Real Love' (completed in London on Tuesday February 13) is distributed to television stations around the world.

Monday February 26
 The scheduled release today of *Anthology 2* fails to materialise. EMI announces that the release has now been put back until March 18. They report that the reason for the delay was down to The Beatles' last-minute change in the album's running order. The track 'I'm Down', which had been listed as track six on the CD inlays, has been moved to track three, pushing tracks four and five back. This also means that the original two-and-a-half million CD booklets, printed to accompany the release, are now obsolete and a further batch, costing EMI an estimated £500,000, are ordered. (Rumours in the industry suggest that it is actually Paul who ends up footing this

hefty bill.) EMI also reveals that the single 'Real Love' has also been delayed until March 4.

Tuesday February 27

✦ The Beatles' announce that they have created *Apple Organic*, described as "The world's first eco-conscious merchandise label". The aim of this venture is to "promote and encourage the use of environmentally friendly fabrics and processes in Rock & Roll fashion." The first products, manufactured in Los Angeles by the US based company *O'Wear*, include T-shirts, polo shirts, jerseys and jackets etc. all sporting the *Anthology* logo. Also on this day, the United Nations nominate The Beatles for its Fashion For The Environment Award, which was set up four years previously to promote green awareness.

* * *

Yoko Ono
Mini-Tour of America
Thursday February 29 – Monday March 25

To help promote her current album *Rising,* Yoko undertakes a short tour of America on which she returns to the pioneering sounds she produced with John in the late Sixties and early Seventies. She is joined on the concerts by her son Sean Lennon's band IMA. Her seven-date tour includes performances at the following venues:

Washington DC (Thursday February 29)
New York (Wednesday March 6 where she is joined on stage by the local
    Japanese duo Cibo Matto)
Chicago (Sunday March 10 – she is joined by David Yow of the band Jesus Lizard)
Los Angeles, California (Wednesday March 13)
San Francisco, California (Monday March 18)
Seattle, Washington (Thursday March 21)
Toronto, Canada (Monday March 25)

* * *

March

✦ In stark contrast to November of last year when BBC Radio 1 rushed to become the first radio station in the UK to play 'Free As A Bird', this month "wonderful Radio 1", causes a storm of controversy by banning The Beatles' new single 'Real Love' from their playlist. "We have played 'Real Love' a few times, but no, it's not on the playlist," confirms the Radio 1 press officer Polly Ravenscroft.
✦ To cash in on the current *Anthology* excitement Lingasong Records in the UK, announce plans to reissue a remixed version of The Beatles' 1962 Star Club in Hamburg tapes, complete with four black and white photographs taken of the group backstage at the Granada Cinema in East Ham, London, in March, 1963.
✦ Ringo's career away from the fabs continues to flourish when, this month, he is reported to have been paid £500,000 to speak just one line of dialogue for a Japanese TV advert for the soft-drink product Ringo Suttar. He films his brief role over two days in Vancouver, Canada.

Monday March 4

✦ The Beatles' second comeback single 'Real Love' is released. In the press release to accompany the single, Paul says: "It was good fun doing it. Unlike 'Free As A Bird', it had all the words and music and we were more like 'sidemen' to John, which was joyful, and I think we did a good job."

The press release goes on to say: "The surviving Beatles decided to use as little state of the art equipment as possible to give a timeless Beatles feel to the single. To enhance this effect, Paul McCartney used a stand-up double bass originally owned by Elvis Presley's bassist, the late Bill Black. Both Paul and George used six-string acoustic guitars to augment the electric instruments and Ringo used his Ludwig drum kit. The result is a *bona fide* organic Beatles single with ageless appeal."

Jeff Lynne, the producer of the track, remarks: "It is much simpler than 'Free As A Bird', sort of a love song, and bouncier. It's a beautiful tune as well and they all do great harmonies."

Friday March 8
As part of the *Anthology 2* promotional tools, Apple prepares, for distribution to selective television stations in America and Europe, the following Beatles archive clips: 'Help!' (from the title sequence of the film but without the darts), 'Everybody's Trying To Be My Baby' (live in Paris, June 20, 1965) and 'Eleanor Rigby' (from the *Yellow Submarine* film 1968).

Saturday March 9
The war over BBC Radio 1 refusing to play 'Real Love' rages on when Paul writes an 800-word article on this subject for today's edition of the *Daily Mirror* newspaper: "The Beatles don't need our new single 'Real Love' to be a hit – it's not as if our careers depend on it. We've done all right over the years, and if Radio 1 feels that we should be banned now it's not exactly going to ruin us overnight . . . Is Radio 1 as important as it was? As Ringo said to me about all this, 'Who needs Radio 1 when you've got all the Independent stations?' "

The *Daily Mirror* (whose readers voted 91% in favour of hearing The Beatles' new single on the radio) back Paul and invite their readers to ring or fax Trevor Dann at Radio 1 and "Give Dann a hard day's night by telling him exactly what you think!"

Later tonight, even though it is banned from the BBC Radio 1 playlist, BBC Television screens the new version of the 'Real Love' video on the BBC2 music show *TOTP2*. (A further screening of the clip takes place the following Thursday March 14, on BBC1's *Top Of The Pops*.)

Monday March 11
Radio stations around the world receive advance copies of *The Beatles Anthology 2* album.

Saturday March 16
'Real Love' enters the *Music Week* top 75-music chart at number four, selling 50,000 in its first week. As the weeks progress, the single achieves the distinction of becoming the poorest chart-performer of an original Beatles single since 'Lady Madonna' back in 1968, which stayed in the charts for only eight weeks.

Monday March 18
EMI Records finally release the 45-track *Beatles Anthology 2*, simultaneously around the world.

The track listing is, CD1: 'Real Love', 'Yes It Is' (newly remixed and edited version), 'I'm Down' (take 1 – recorded on June 14, 1965), 'You've Got To Hide Your Love Away' (take 5 – June 18, 1965),'If You've Got Troubles' (June 18, 1965), 'That Means A Lot' (June 20, 1965), 'Yesterday' (take 1 – June 14, 1965), 'It's Only Love' (edits – takes 3 and 2 – June 15, 1965), 'I Feel Fine', 'Ticket To Ride', 'Yesterday' and 'Help!' (all from *Blackpool Night Out* – ABC TV August 1, 1965), 'Everybody's Trying To Be My Baby' (live at Shea Stadium – August 15, 1965, not included in the television documentary), 'Norwegian Wood (This Bird Has Flown)' (take 1 – October 12, 1965), 'I'm Looking Through You' (October 24, 1965), '12 Bar Original' (November 4, 1965), 'Tomorrow Never Knows' (take 1 – April 6, 1966), 'Got To Get You Into My Life' (take 5 – April 7, 1966), 'And Your Bird Can Sing' (take 2 – laughing version – April 20, 1966), 'Taxman' (take 11 – April 21, 1966), 'Eleanor Rigby' (remixed strings-only version – take 14 – April 28, 1966), 'I'm Only Sleeping' (instrumental rehearsal & take 1 – April 29, 1966), 'Rock And Roll Music' and 'She's A Woman' (both live at the Nippon Budokan Hall, Tokyo, Japan, June 30, 1966).
CD2: 'Strawberry Fields Forever' (John's home demo – November 1966, take 1 – November 24, 1966, and take 7 plus edit piece – November 29 and December 9, 1966), 'Penny Lane' (new assembled version – from outtakes recorded between December 29, 1966, and January 17, 1967), 'A Day In The Life' (new version – edited from takes 1 & 2, January 19 & 20, 1967, and February 10, 1967), 'Good Morning Good Morning' (take 8 – February 8 & 16, 1967), 'Only A Northern Song' (new version – edited from takes 3 & 12, April 13, 14 & 20, 1967), 'Being For The Benefit Of Mr. Kite' (studio dialogue – takes 1 &

2, February 17 & 20, 1967, plus take 7), 'Lucy In The Sky With Diamonds' (new version, edited from takes 8, 7 & 9; March 1 & 2, 1967), 'Within You, Without You' (remix of Indian instrumentation; March 15, 16 & 22 and April 3, 1967), 'Sgt. Pepper's Lonely Hearts Club Band' (Reprise) (take 5 – April 1, 1967), 'You Know My Name (Look Up The Number)' (restored stereo mix – from takes May 17 and June 7 & 8, 1967, plus April 30, 1969), 'I Am The Walrus' (take 16 – without overdubs – September 5, 1967), 'Fool On The Hill' (demo – September 6, 1967), 'Your Mother Should Know' (take 27 – September 16, 1967), 'Fool On The Hill' (take 4 – September 25, 1967), 'Hello, Goodbye' (take 16 – October 2 & 19, 1967), 'Lady Madonna' (new version – edited from takes 3 & 4; February 3 & 6, 1968) and 'Across The Universe' (February 3, 1968).

🍎 Paul originally wanted 'Carnival Of Light' on *Anthology 2* but George, Ringo and Yoko opposed this because they felt that the track was never originally "intended for The Beatles".

🍎 In its first week of sale in the UK, the album shifts a total of 78, 000 copies. In America, the Best Buy chain sells approximately 442,000 units.

April
🍎 In America, *The Beatles Anthology 1* is awarded three simultaneous sales awards – Gold, Platinum and six times Platinum – representing total US sales of three million (or six million single CDs) units. It's also reported that, around the world, the album has sold 12.5 million copies to date.

🍎 In the States, Ringo lends his name to a new series of ceramic collectibles, marketed by Garland USA, a New Jersey-based company which specialises in commemorative porcelain figurines. There are six in the Ringo Starr range, which include him as featured on the 1969 *Abbey Road* sleeve and, among others, Ringo behind his drums, circa 1964. Still in the States this month, Ringo undertakes a marathon four-hour signing session where he personally signs limited-edition Ringo Starr plates.

🍎 George and Ravi fly again to Madrasin India for further work on the album *Chants Of India* at the Sruthilaya Media Artists and the Swara Laya studios.

Sunday April 21
🍎 In the UK, the *Observer* newspaper writes: "In 1996, The Beatles have achieved what every group since them has failed to do – become bigger than The Beatles."

May
🍎 At the end of the month Ronnie Wood announces at a press conference in Sao Paolo that when he returns to England he'll be recording with George.

Monday May 13
🍎 Paul and Ringo are videotaped working on the song 'Beautiful Night' at the Mill Studio in Sussex. Extracts will appear in MPL's documentary *Paul McCartney In The World Tonight*.

Wednesday May 15
🍎 In the UK, ITN (the Independent Television News) transmits, in news bulletins throughout the day, a few seconds of a recently discovered colour 8mm 1962 film of The Beatles in performance at the Casanova Club in Liverpool. Apple, keen to include the film in the extended home video version of *The Beatles Anthology*, is offered the film for £30,000. They decline the offer, instead offering only £10,000.

Saturday May 18
🍎 Paul appears by phone on the BBC Radio Two programme *The Steve Wright Show,* which is transmitted today between 10am and 1pm.

June
🍎 George is voted the 16th best guitarist of all time in the current issue of *Mojo* magazine. Jimi Hendrix is placed at number one.

Wednesday June 5
🍎 Yoko Ono, in Britain to promote her European tour, is interviewed on the Sky News programme *Newsmaker*.

Thursday June 6
 Among the items on offer at the annual Christie's auction, held at their South Kensington showroom in Old Brompton Road, London SW1, are some 1966 Ringo Starr reel-to-reel audio tapes, featuring sound recordings made during The Beatles' visits to Munich in Germany and Tokyo in Japan that year. These include unreleased Ringo compositions, including 'Looking For The Lightning', 'Sitting In The Back Of My Car' and another track, which is possibly called 'Hang On To The Roll She Gave You'. (The tapes sell for £2,875.)

Friday June 7
 LIPA is officially opened by Her Majesty The Queen who, along with Paul and the Chief Executive Mark Featherstone-Witty, is shown around the building and watches, among other things, a performance by the rock band The Salvation. Paul admits later: "This is a very proud day for me. It's exciting that we have saved this fine old building of my school, and that Her Majesty has taken such an interest in our new school." Paul is naturally asked about Linda's absence. "It's a bit hectic for her, but she is well," he replies.

Saturday June 8
 Yoko and Sean, backed by IMA, play a live concert at the LA2 venue in Charing Cross Road, London WC2. For the show, Yoko makes a welcome return to the avant-garde musical style she pioneered with John back in the Sixties and early Seventies. (Shortly after, Yoko, Sean and the band fly to Japan where they resume their concert appearances. See entry for Saturday June 22.)
 A television documentary on the history of Paul's LIPA project, entitled *The Fame Game*, is transmitted on BBC1 in the UK.

Thursday June 13
 In the UK, BBC Radio 4 broadcasts a 30-minute play looking at the last troubled years of The Beatles' manager Brian Epstein. The play, entitled *With A Little Help From My Friends*, is written by Francis McNeil.

Saturday June 15
 Although Paul had been a long-time favourite to be knighted in the Queen's Birthday Honours List, the honour instead goes to The Beatles' record producer George Martin.
 In the UK, the *NME* (*New Musical Express*) publishes an interview with Yoko. When asked about her updated sound, she replies: "I like to think I'm this generation."

* * *

Yoko Ono / IMA
Tour of Japan
Saturday June 22 – Monday July 1

Yoko Ono, backed by Sean's band IMA, which consists of her son Sean, on guitar, keyboards, saw and backing vocals, Timo Ellis on drums and Andrew Weiss, on bass, play four shows in Japan. This short tour consists of the following concerts:

  Club Quattro, Tokyo (Saturday June 22)
  Akasaka Blitz, Tokyo (Tuesday June 25)
  Bottom Line, Nagoya (Friday June 28)
  Yubin Chokin Hall, Osaka (Monday July 1)

Notes on the tour:

Yoko, Sean and the band arrive in Japan on Thursday June 20, at the New Tokyo International Airport. The following day, Friday June 21, Yoko is interviewed for the NHK TV programme *News 11*, which is transmitted between 11:00 and 11:35pm. Further promotions for the tour take place on Monday June 24, when Yoko, this time accompanied by Sean, is interviewed for the TV Asahi programme *Super Morning*, which is broadcast between 8:00 and 9:55am.

* * *

Wednesday June 26
♣ In London, Paul visits Hyde Park, the site of this Saturday's Prince's Trust Concert, where he is seen chatting to Harvey Goldsmith, the promoter of the show. Rumours of a possible Beatles reunion at the concert instantly flare up in the press.

♣ In America, the *VH-1 Archive* series of classic *Dick Cavett Show*s from the Sixties and Seventies transmits the first part of John and Yoko's 1971 appearance (part two is broadcast on July 3) while on July 18, the series includes George's solo appearance from 1971, transmitted for the first time in almost 25 years. (See original 1971 dates for further information on the programmes.)

Thursday June 27
♣ In London, Geoff Baker, Paul's spokesman at MPL, is asked about the rumoured Beatles reunion at Saturday's Hyde Park concert. He instantly quashes such stories when he announces: "It's nonsense. Paul would never play on stage as The Beatles without John!"

Friday June 28
♣ Among the attractions of the auction held at the annual Silver Cleff awards lunch at the Intercontinental Hotel, Hyde Park in London, is a Paul, George and Ringo signed six-string Rickenbacker 325 V 63 vibrator guitar. (The three Beatles signed their names in silver ink in May.)

Saturday June 29
♣ The open-air Prince's Trust Concert, at London's Hyde Park, goes ahead without the rumoured Beatles onstage reunion. The story started following Eric Clapton's announcement that, during the concert, he will present a "surprise act, you've known for all these years!" The *Evening Standard* newspaper, in the UK, even got in on the act by printing the headline: "Beatles Lined Up For Hyde Park Surprise!" Present at the show though is Ringo's son Zak, who plays drums with The Who during their performance of *Quadrophenia*. In addition, Ringo's daughter Lee and Paul's daughter Mary are seen mingling with celebrities backstage.

Sunday June 30
♣ Although Ringo did not perform at Hyde Park yesterday, he does make an appearance today in Peterborough in Ontario, Canada, with the country and western star Willie Nelson, at a concert in aid of the mental illness schizophrenia, performed on the back of a flat-bed truck.

July
♣ It is revealed this month that there won't be a third Beatles reunion single after all. Jeff Lynne adds fuel to the fire by announcing: "The Beatles have not finished any of the tracks they were reported to have been working on – 'Now And Then', often referred to as 'Miss You', 'Grow Old With Me' or (the McCartney-Harrison composition) 'All For Love'."

♣ Meanwhile, in response to the planned March 1996 re-release, Apple Corps Ltd. issues a high court writ against Lingasong Music, on behalf of Paul, George, Ringo and Yoko, to prevent further manufacture of this new version of The Beatles' 1962 Star Club, Hamburg recordings.

♣ The 4CD Ravi Shankar box set *In Celebration*, featuring a written introduction by George, is issued in the UK.

Saturday July 6
♣ Yoko and Sean take to the stage for a spontaneous performance at the *Summerstage* concert held in Central Park, New York.

Sunday July 7
♣ Further recording on *Chants Of India* takes place with Ravi Shankar at George's home studio in Henley.

Thursday July 11 (until Thursday July 18)
♣ George and Ravi are joined by a small team of Indian musicians for further *Chants Of India* sessions at Friar Park.

Friday July 19 (until Thursday July 26)
 George and Ravi continue alone on *Chants Of India* sessions at Henley.

Tuesday July 23
 Apple hold a press conference at their West London headquarters to announce details of the forthcoming *Beatles Anthology* eight-volume home video box set, due for release on September 23. This get-together also features a question and answer session with Neil Aspinall, Derek Taylor and the *Anthology* producer Chips Chipperfield.

August
 Reports this month reveal that Paul has helped record a studio version of 'The Ballad Of The Skeletons' with the legendary American poet Allen Ginsberg. The song comes about after Ginsberg, in America, had sent tapes to Paul's home studios in Sussex. Meanwhile, on a more downbeat note, the LIPA chief executive Mark Featherstone-Witty announces that: "The Institute is facing a huge cash crisis which could possibly force its closure. The school is now more than £5 million in debt and must raise £2.8 million by the beginning of 1997 to stave off disaster!"
 During the month, Paul, at his Sussex farmhouse, George, at home in Henley, and Ringo, at Apple's London offices at Ovington Square, record interviews with Derek Taylor, intended for use in *The Beatles Anthology 3* EPK (electronic video press kit).

Monday August 12
 VCI home video in Britain releases a digitally enhanced version of The Beatles' 1967 film *Magical Mystery Tour*.
 George works on *Chants Of India* at his home studio with arranger John Barnham (also on August 13, 16 & 22).

September
 Paul releases a statement regarding Linda's condition: "She is doing fantastically well, all the doctors are amazingly pleased with her." During the month, Paul completes the recordings that will form his new album. (The tracks will be released in May of next year and titled *Flaming Pie*.)
 Insiders to The Beatles' activities reveal that Apple have just secured the rights to the Sixties *Beatles Cartoons* series, produced in America by King Features between 1965 and 1967.
 Figures released this month by the BPI, the British Phonographic Industry, reveal that *Sgt. Pepper's Lonely Hearts Club Band* is now the biggest selling album of all time in the UK.

Saturday September 7
 The ITV network *Chart Show* in the UK, broadcasts (for the first time ever on television around the world) a colour version of The Beatles' 1966 promotional film for 'Paperback Writer', shot at Chiswick House in London in May 1966. The following week, Saturday September 14, the same programme broadcasts an alternative colour version of 'Rain', also filmed at Chiswick House in London. The clips are naturally released by Apple to help promote the forthcoming *Anthology* video box set.

Saturday September 21
 Paul's *Liverpool Oratorio* is performed for the 100th time. This special airing takes place in Liverpool at the Philharmonic Hall.

Monday September 23
 The scheduled release today of the *Anthology* home video box set fails to show. Apple announces that the release will now take place on October 7.

Tuesday September 24
 BBC Radio 2 in the UK broadcasts a one-hour documentary entitled *The Beatles In Scotland*, which features a new interview with Paul.

Sunday September 28 & Monday September 29
 In America, Paul and Linda's short nine-minute film on the rock-group The Grateful

Dead, utilising the photofilm idea (where computer wizardry seemingly makes a still picture move) receives its premiere at the two-day New York Film Festival.

October

✪ Carl Perkins' new album *Go Cat Go*, featuring John performing 'Blue Suede Shoes' (from the 1969 *Live Peace In Toronto* concert), Paul performing 'My Old Friend' (originally recorded with Perkins back in 1981 during the *Tug Of War* sessions on the island of Montserrat), George performing 'Distance Makes No Difference' (a new Perkins' original) and Ringo with his All-Starr Band performing 'Honey Don't' (taken from his 1989 All-Starr Band concerts) is released in the UK on the Dinosaur label.

✪ The Allen Ginsberg single 'The Ballad Of The Skeletons', featuring Paul on Hammond organ, drums, guitars and maracas, is released in America on the Mercury label.

✪ In the UK, Paul again makes headlines when he begins legal proceedings against Lily Evans, the widow of The Beatles' roadie Mal Evans. The matter involves a collection of original handwritten lyrics she is trying to auction at Sotheby's, which include 'With A Little Help From My Friends' and the instrumental notes to 'Yesterday'. Paul maintains that they belong to him, George Martin and the estate of John Lennon. She insists they belong to her and is currently countersuing Paul.

✪ In Liverpool, Canon John Roberts, the vicar of St. Peter's Church in Woolton, where John met Paul back in 1957, also foments unflattering stories about Macca. Apparently, when he approached Paul about making a contribution to renovate the historical site, Paul sent him back two unsigned books to raffle. "They're no use," he stormed. "I need cash, not raffle prizes. Maybe we can persuade Paul to play a benefit gig on the 40th anniversary of their meeting. Otherwise we might as well wait until the place falls down." (The cost of the renovation has been estimated at approximately £400,000.)

Sunday October 6

✪ At Abbey Road's 65th anniversary party in London, Paul's brother Mike McCartney reveals that Linda is still having chemotherapy treatment in America, adding, "She has more stamina than all of us and Paul is there for her." Also present at the party is Sir George Martin.

Monday October 7

✪ The scheduled release today of *The Beatles Anthology 3* fails to materialise. EMI puts the release date back to October 21. What does appear today is the highly anticipated *Beatles Anthology* eight volume home video box set. Sales are brisk, especially in Liverpool where, at the HMV store, 50 copies of the £99.99 box set are sold in the first hour of business.

Friday October 11

✪ In America, Paul and Linda's short film on The Grateful Dead receives another screening at the Angelika Film Center in New York. Further showings take place this month in Santa Monica and San Francisco. In Los Angeles, the McCartneys' film is shown as support to the movie *Microcosmos*.

Monday October 14

✪ In the UK, Polygram releases, on both home video and laser disc, the legendary unreleased 1968 Rolling Stones film *The Rock & Roll Circus,* featuring John (performing 'Yer Blues') and Yoko.

Monday October 21

✪ Once again, *The Beatles Anthology 3* fails to show. EMI now insists the release will take place one week later on October 28.

✪ The pre-fab four The Rutles release, today in the UK on Virgin, their first new album in 18 years, entitled *Archaeology*.

Monday October 28

✪ *The Beatles Anthology 3*, featuring 50 songs, is finally released simultaneously around the world. The track listing for the album is:
CD1: 'A Beginning' (a short orchestral piece composed by George Martin as the original introduction to Ringo's 'Don't Pass Me By' – 1968), 'Happiness Is A Warm Gun' (John's

demo – the first of seven tracks recorded at George's Esher home in 1968), 'Helter Skelter' (Paul's R & B version – 1968), 'Mean Mr. Mustard' (John's demo – 1968), 'Polythene Pam' (John's demo – 1968), 'Glass Onion' (John's demo), 'Junk' (Paul's demo – 1968), 'Piggies' (George's demo – 1968), 'Honey Pie' (Paul's acoustic demo – 1968), 'Don't Pass Me By' (outtake – 1968), 'Ob-La-Di Ob-La-Da' (alternative version – 1968), 'Good Night' (studio outtake – 1968), 'Cry Baby Cry' (take 1 – 1968), 'Blackbird' (Paul's acoustic performance – 1968), 'Sexy Sadie' (John's slow version – 1968), 'While My Guitar Gently Weeps' (George's acoustic demo – 1968), 'Hey Jude' (alternative version – with ad libs, 1968), 'Not Guilty' (George's unreleased *White* album track – 1968), 'Mother Nature's Son' (Paul's solo demo – 1968), 'Glass Onion' (unreleased version by John – 1968), 'Rocky Raccoon' (unreleased outtake – 1968), 'What's The New Mary Jane' (unreleased track – 1968), 'Step Inside Love'/'Los Paranoias' (light-hearted jam during *White Album* sessions – 1968), 'I'm So Tired' (alternative version – 1968), 'I Will' (take one of Paul's White track – 1968), 'Why Don't We Do It In The Road?' (Paul's acoustic demo early take – 1968), 'Julia' (studio work out – 1968).

CD2: 'I've Got A Feeling' (the first of twelve selections from the January 1969 *Get Back/Let It Be* sessions, featuring Billy Preston on keyboards), 'She Came In Through The Bathroom Window' (January 1969 rehearsal), 'Dig A Pony' (*Let It Be* outtake – 1969), 'Two Of Us' (January 1969 outtake), 'For Your Blue' (January 1969 outtake of George's 12-bar blues), 'Teddy Boy' (unreleased Beatles track – January 1969- written by Paul), Medley: 'Rip It Up'/'Shake, Rattle & Roll'/'Blue Suede Shoes' (outtake from January 1969 *Get Back/Let It Be* sessions), 'The Long And Winding Road' (1969 *Let It Be* version without orchestra), 'Oh! Darling' (another January 1969 rehearsal), 'All Things Must Pass' (the first of three George demos recorded in January 1969), 'Mailman, Bring Me No More Blues' (January 1969 – *Get Back/Let It Be* outtake of a Buddy Holly song), 'Get Back' (recorded during roof top performance – January 30 1969), 'Old Brown Shoe' (George's demo – 1969), 'Octopus's Garden' (studio outtake – 1969), 'Maxwell's Silver Hammer' (studio rehearsal – January 1969), 'Something' (solo George demo 1969), 'Come Together' (first take of John's track – 1969), 'Come And Get It' (Paul's demo – completed in under an hour and released by Apple band Badfinger – 1969), 'Ain't She Sweet' (Beatles 1969 studio recording), 'Because' (new remix of John's 1969 *Abbey Road* recording), 'Let It Be' (a live studio outtake – 1969), 'I Me Mine' (last track recorded by The Beatles for 24 years, taped in January 1970 – the orginal version), 'The End' (guitar based version of the track released on *Abbey Road* in 1969).

🍎 Paul on 'Dig A Pony': "John and I sing like angels, to be modest. John and I are having such a good time on it, you can just tell in our voices."

🍎 Paul on 'Teddy Boy': " 'Teddy Boy' was considered as a Beatles song but we never got around to it. We've now put together a version, an edit of one of the takes of us trying it, which sounds interesting. But you can hear on it also that the band wasn't very interested in it. I don't know why. Maybe I hadn't finished it enough or something. Maybe it was just tension coming in. The bit I'd like to keep actually was John sort of making fun of it. He starts towards the end of it, going, 'Grab your partners, do-si-do,' so we've kept that on. And while it was, in some way, indicative of friction, it was also good humoured friction."

Again sales of *Anthology 3* are phenomenal. In America, where the album enters the charts at number one, their 18th chart-topping album in the US and their third consecutive American number one in a year – an achievement not even attained in the Sixties, the Best Buy record stores chain sells approximately 279,000 copies of the album within its first week of sales.

One week after its release, *Melody Maker* writes: "If *Anthology 2* was the parallel Beatles, stacked with portmanteau mixes which would never have existed otherwise, then *Anthology 3* is The Beatles *Unplugged*. Naked genius, no less!" *NME*: "*Anthology 3* is an enthralling glimpse between the shutters of a band in chaos!"

🍎 Yoko Ono, with the *Anthology* campaign now reaching a conclusion, is quoted as saying: "The *Anthology* albums were like a jewel. They showed how really talented they were. You get a feeling of how laid-back the Sixties were. You don't get that from groups today. Some of them are really violent. It's nice to bring back the feeling of joy of The Beatles."

Tuesday October 29
🍎 Hot on the heels of *The Beatles Anthology 3* is *The Rutles Archaeology*. The pre-fab four returns, with their first album in almost two decades, released today in America by Virgin.

November

 In London, Apple Corps sadly releases the following statement: "The end has finally arrived . . . The Beatles are no more. The official word is that Paul McCartney, George Harrison and Ringo Starr will never play together again as a group, and that they have decided that there will be no more singles issued from their back catalogue."

As The Beatles offer their swan song as an active group, figures released this month reveal that, during 1996, they sold more albums than in any one year during their time together in the Sixties. Apple announces that, by the end of the year, they expect to sell a total of 20 million *Anthology* albums. High spots this month include *Anthology 3* entering the American *Billboard* album charts at number one.

 Paul is reported to be finishing off his next album at his home studios in Sussex, with additional recordings in Los Angeles. Also during this time, Paul and Linda spend time working on a film project comprising over 4,000 Beatles photographic images between 1967 and 1969, all taken by Linda. The idea is to transform them, via computer imagery, into moving images. Reports suggest that the soundtrack to accompany the film will feature "unreleased Beatles music". (The film, at this time, is scheduled for release before the end of 1997.) Another film that Paul has been working on is *Tropical Island Hum,* a ten-minute animated film short directed by Geoff Dunbar, inspired by the character Rupert The Bear, and featuring a story centring around a frog. According to Paul's *Club Sandwich*, an unreleased Paul song will feature on the soundtrack and include Linda and himself as the voice-over artists.

 Meanwhile, at a reception towards the end of the month held in honour of his good friend the racing driver Damon Hill, George in an impromptu radio interview, begins his personal tirade against some of his contemporary pop stars. The first in line is the Oasis lead singer Liam Gallagher. "They don't actually need him," he snarls. "Noel is really good. He writes the tunes and he sings better than Liam as far as I'm concerned. They (Oasis) are a tidy band, they've written some good songs which I've enjoyed and I liked their *Unplugged* show on MTV, but that was mainly because the silly one wasn't there! I think it is proven when you see the band without him singing – they are more in tune. He's just excess baggage I think, all he does is make people think what a bunch of prannies they are." George is then asked about Liam's alleged drink and drugs abuse. "He's a bit out of date," he replies. "What's the point? It's silly and I feel sorry for him really, because he's missed the bus."

At a press launch for an Oasis biography shortly afterwards, Noel Gallagher is asked about George's comments. He replied, "He doesn't even know Liam. What can I say? I haven't heard the interview myself, but I've met George once and he's a really good bloke."

 At the annual *Q Awards* in London, George Martin collects an award for the year's Best Compilation or Reissue for *The Beatles Anthology.*

Martin collects the award from Peter Blake, who reiterates his annoyance at receiving just £200 to design the 1967 *Sgt. Pepper* album sleeve. In George's acceptance speech, he touches upon The Beatles' recent achievement of *Anthology 3* which became the 18th number one album that The Beatles have had in America. "It's the first time in 30 years that a group has had three number one albums in 12 months, and the last time that happened, it was achieved by a group called The Beatles. Of course, it represents the work of many people, faceless ones that nobody hears about, who put a great deal of work into the *Anthology* – and, of course, The Beatles themselves."

Thursday November 7

 Little Brown publishes the 176-page Linda McCartney book *Roadworks,* which features 135 black and white alongside 35 colour pictures of her life on tour with Paul's group Wings in the Seventies.

Friday November 8

 An exhibition to promote Linda's publication *Roadworks*, opens at the IPC Gallery in Manhattan, New York. Another display to tie in with the book takes place this month at the International Center of Photography in New York. During the event reporters ask Linda's brother John Eastman about the current state of Linda's health. "She is fine, and looks great," he replies, adding, "She is at the end of her treatment for cancer and she has been given a clean bill of health. She's what you call 'cancer free'."

Saturday November 9
 In the UK, to help promote *Roadworks*, Linda gives an interview in The Week section of the *Guardian* newspaper.

Monday November 11
 Still in the UK, *Anthology 3* enters the *Music Week* Top 75 album chart at number four where sales in its first week total 52,000 copies.

Friday November 15
 To assist with promotions for *Anthology 3*, most notably on VH-1, Apple prepares for television screenings the following Beatles archive film clips: 'All You Need Is Love' (*Our World* – June 24, 1967 – colourized version), 'Revolution' (alternative video-tape 1968), and 'For You Blue' and 'Two Of Us' (from the remastered *Let It Be* film 1970).
 Also today, a further Linda McCartney exhibition to promote *Roadworks* opens, this time at the Museum of Photography, Film and Television in Bradford in Yorkshire.

Wednesday December 4
 In the States, at approximately 8:54am, the ABC TV breakfast show *Good Morning America* broadcasts, for the first and only time in the world this century, a one-minute videotaped clip of Paul, George and Ringo performing 'Blue Moon Of Kentucky', recorded at George's Friar Park mansion on Friday June 23, 1994 (see entry).

Monday December 16
 In the UK, Paul is secretly notified that he has been awarded a knighthood in the forthcoming Queen's New Year's Honours List. Due to his annual traditional Christmas vacation with his family, this means that he will be out of the country when news of his knighthood reaches the press. He therefore decides to videotape an acceptance speech today to be played on television when the news breaks on January 1, 1997. The short speech, recorded in the LIPA building, goes as such: "It's a fantastic honour. I'm very grateful accepting it on behalf of all the people of Liverpool, and the other Beatles, without whom it wouldn't have been possible. So I hope I can be worthy of it. I'd like to thank my wife and kids, and wish everyone a Happy New Year." (The clip is included in most television news programmes, on BBC, ITN, Channels 4 and 5 which feature reports on the Honours List on January 1, 1997.)

Tuesday December 17
 A healthy looking Linda, appearing for the first time in public since the news of her cancer scare, appears with Paul in a video transmitted in America. She is seen sporting a new short-cropped haircut.

Sunday December 29
 BBC1 screens, for the first time in almost three decades, John's appearance as a lavatory attendant during the December 1966 edition of *Not Only . . .But Also*, as part of the programme *Spirit Of '66*, an affectionate look back at 1966, the year that England won the World Cup.

Tuesday December 31
 The recently released Rolling Stones 1968 *Rock And Roll Circus* receives its television premiere on BBC2 tonight, just months after being released on UK home video.
 In the States, Ringo and Barbara attend a party held by his sister-in-law Marjorie. While there he meets up with the 33-year-old songwriter Dean Grakal, the son of Ringo's solicitor Bruce. Ringo talks to Dean about songwriting and suggests that he and Ringo's songwriting friend, Mark Hudson, join him at his Beverly Hills home early next year and try writing as a team.

"Today is fantastic. There is blue sky and it's springtime. My mum and dad would have been extremely proud – and perhaps they are. I would never have dreamed of this day. It's a long way from a little terrace in Liverpool."

– Paul

January
☘ Ringo and Barbara travel to Aspen, Colorado for some winter skiing. (They return home in early February.)

Wednesday January 1
☘ Following much press speculation, Paul finally receives a knighthood in the Queen's New Year's Honours List, which is announced today. Paul is on holiday with Linda and the children when the news is revealed.

February
☘ In the States, The Beatles win three Grammy Awards at the 39th annual American celebration. The awards are for 'Best Vocal Group or Duo' for 'Free As A Bird', 'Best Short Form Video' for 'Free As A Bird' and 'Long Form Video' for *The Beatles Anthology*. Accepting the awards on behalf of the group is Bob Smeaton, the writer/director on *The Beatles Anthology*.
☘ Still Stateside, Ringo begins recording what is to eventually become the album *Vertical Man*. The long and winding road to the release begins when, as planned, Mark Hudson and Dean Grakal travel to Ringo's Beverly Hills home where they join him in a spot of songwriting. The first track they compose is 'My Love'. But this title is quickly shelved when Ringo points out to the others that this title has already been used by another ex-Beatle! The song title is swiftly changed to 'Everyday'. (Shortly after, the trio record a demo of the song, which also features guitarist Steve Dudas. Pleased with the results of the session, the four-piece line-up continues recordings.) At the end of February, Barbara's mother becomes ill and passes away. Ringo and Barbara leave their home in Beverly Hills and head for Europe to be by her side just before she dies.
☘ The American label Rykodisc sign a deal with Yoko to reissue her entire back catalogue on compact disc.

Friday February 14
☘ Paul arrives at Abbey Road Studios in London, where, today in studio No. 1, he oversees the massive orchestral overdubs for his track 'Beautiful Night'. Joining Paul at the session, which is videotaped and appears in the *Paul McCartney In The World Tonight* MPL documentary, is George Martin.

March
☘ Ringo and Barbara return home to Beverly Hills. He spends March 6 at home shooting publicity shots for his upcoming All-Starr Band tour with the noted photographer Henry Diltz, then rejoins Mark Hudson, Dean Grakal and Steve Dudas in writing and recording for what is to become *Vertical Man*, at Mark Hudson's Whatinthewhathe? Studios in Los Angeles, situated on the second storey of a building over the top of a Thai restaurant. The walls of this small studio are covered with frame upon frame of pictures of The Beatles, many of which are signed by the various Beatles. "I had to take some down before Ringo came the first night," Mark recalls, "otherwise he would have thought I was a stalker!" The tracks recorded by this group are 'Mr. Doubleitup' and 'One' (originally titled 'All It Takes Is One' when it first appeared on Dean Grakal's original lyric sheet). At this stage in the recordings, Ringo, instead of the 'Trap Kat' drum kit he had been using, brings into the studio his Ludwig Beatles look-a-like drum set, which features his original Beatles hi-hat cymbals and a "ride" cymbal, complete with Paul McCartney's signature still on it!

Monday March 3 & Tuesday March 4
☘ In London, Paul records demo versions of *Standing Stone* at Abbey Road Studios. These two-day sessions, featuring production by John Frazer, mark the first time the 60-minute symphony has been played by a full orchestra.

Tuesday March 11
☘ At 11am today, in a two-and-a-half hour ceremony at London's Buckingham Palace, Paul is formally invested with his knighthood for services to popular music. He is ushered into the presence of Her Majesty The Queen in the Palace ballroom where he kneels before her as she places the King George VI's Scots Guard sword on Paul's right shoulder and then on his left, before accrediting him with the title "Sir Paul", the sight of

which makes Mary McCartney start to cry. Due to strict Palace etiquette, each inductee is allowed to bring only three guests. Linda is not among them; instead he brings his three youngest children, Mary, Stella and James. Following the investiture, Paul, dressed in a black morning suit, greets the waiting army of reporters by showing his medal and saying: "Today is fantastic, there is blue sky and it's springtime. My mum and dad would have been extremely proud – and perhaps they are. I would never have dreamed of this day. If we'd had that thought when we started off in Liverpool it would have been laughed at as a complete joke. Proud to be British. A wonderful day. It's a long way from a little terrace in Liverpool."

Reporters ask him, "Have you spoken to the other Beatles about this?"

"Yep", he replies. "They make fun of me. They keep ringing me up and calling me 'Your Holiness', but they're having a good time. It seems strange being here without the other three. I keep looking over my shoulder for them."

The reporters then enquire about Linda, who is conspicuous by her absence. "She's doing fine, thanks. We drew straws, 'cos we could only get three tickets. So I've got my three youngest kids with me."

"But she's doing well?" another reporter asks.

"Linda is fine," Paul replies. "She's doing very well. I would have loved my whole family to have been here, but as we had three guest tickets, Linda and Heather decided to stay out of the limelight today."

🍎 Paul also takes time to promote, to the reporters, his new album. "I'm still heavily involved with music . . . I have a new album, *Flaming Pie*, out in May. It's mainly a solo album, but Ringo plays on it."

🍎 Paul leaves the Palace, driven away in his Mercedes to an accompaniment of screaming fans surrounding the Palace gates singing 'Hey Jude', 'A Hard Day's Night' and 'Yesterday', scenes reminiscent of when The Beatles received their MBEs back in October, 1965.

🍎 Where is George while Paul is receiving his Knighthood? He is to be found in Australia on holiday with Olivia and Dhani. Today, at 2am, George strolls into the Melbourne Casino, sits down at the house piano and plays for almost two hours. Sitting by his side throughout the performance is his 19-year-old son.

Saturday March 22
🍎 Bonham's of Chelsea, in London, present the 'Ultimate Beatles Auction' which takes place simultaneously in Tokyo.

Monday March 24
🍎 In the States, Carroll James, long recognised as being the first American disc jockey to play a Beatles record on US radio in Washington DC on December 17, 1963, dies of cancer, aged 60.

Thursday March 27
🍎 A further complete screening of the 1968 film *Yellow Submarine*, takes place today on Channel 4 in the UK.

Wednesday April 2
🍎 The first "playback" of Paul's new album *Flaming Pie*, aimed specifically for the retail trade, takes place before a gathering of 20 at 6 Hamilton Place, in Park Lane, London. The unique *Flaming Pie* press kits, given away to reporters as they enter the building and requested back as they depart, feature a message from Paul which reads: "I came off the back of *The Beatles' Anthology* with an urge to do some new music. The *Anthology* was very good for me, because it reminded me of The Beatles' standards and the standards that we reached with the songs. So, in a way, it was a refresher course that set the framework for this album.

"Watching the *Anthology* also reminded me of the time that we didn't take to make an album and of the fun we had when we did one. The Beatles were not a serious group . . . So I wanted to try and get back into some of that, to have some fun and not sweat it. That's been the spirit of making this album, you've got to have a laugh, because it's just an album. So I called up a bunch of friends and family and we just got on and did it. And we had fun making it. Hopefully you'll hear that in the songs."

🍎 Ringo meanwhile takes part in the first of two Rock 'n' Roll Fantasy Camp sessions, in which a number of artists have a chance to participate in seminars, jam sessions or simply "hang out"! Joining him at the five day get-together in Miami, Florida are former members of his All-Starr Band, including Joe Walsh, Felix Cavaliere, Mark Farmer, Nils Lofgren and Billy Preston. The cost for the session, which lasts until Sunday April 6, is a cool $695, even if you decide not to participate in any of the organised events.

Friday April 4
 Allen Ginsberg, the legendary Beat poet, with whom Paul recently collaborated on 'The Ballad Of The Skeletons', dies of liver cancer in America, aged 70.

Sunday April 6
 The first public airing of 'Young Boy', a track from Paul's new album *Flaming Pie*, occurs on *The Pepsi Chart Show*, transmitted today on ILR (Independent Local Radio). The broadcast also features a new specially recorded interview with Sir Paul.

Tuesday April 8
 In the UK, the BBC1 *Watchdog* programme reports on a scam involving the potential sale of Paul's famous Hofner bass guitar through the London auction house of Sotheby's.

Thursday April 10
 Paul ventures up onto the roof of his MPL building in Soho Square, London to play a short acoustic set ('Young Boy' and 'The World Tonight') recreating the famous Beatles January 30, 1969, rooftop concert, for inclusion in his upcoming *Flaming Pie* television documentary. (The scene, which completes the 35 hours of shooting for the *Paul McCartney In The World Tonight* documentary, does not make the final edits of the show.)

Saturday April 12
 The first version of the 'Young Boy' promotional video is prepared today for television distribution by the London-based company of Imagine Post Productions. Meanwhile, Paul is none too pleased when the *Daily Mail* newspaper publishes a four-page interview with Maggie McGivern, with whom Paul, apparently, had a secret affair between 1966 and 1969. The story is given more impetus because during the early stages, Paul was engaged to Jane Asher.

Tuesday April 15
 The press launch for *Flaming Pie*, intended purely for the benefit of international journalists, takes place this morning at Metropolis Studios in Chiswick High Road, London.

Tuesday April 15 (for almost two straight weeks until Friday April 25)
 In Los Angeles, at Studio City, Ringo and his fourth All-Starr Band begin rehearsals for his 1997 All-Starr Band tour. During the second week, Dave Mason, formerly of the Sixties group Traffic, quits the group, citing the perennial favourite of "musical differences" with Ringo and the rest of the band. He is not replaced. At this point, Ringo will spend part of the day rehearsing for the tour and the other recording *Vertical Man* with Mark Hudson at the Whatinthewhathe? Studio. The last track Ringo will record before commencing on the tour (which starts on Monday April 28 – see entry) is 'I'll Be Fine Anywhere'.

Friday April 18
 In London, the promotional video for 'The World Tonight' is prepared today for television distribution. Its first premiere screening will take place on the live VH-1 programme *McCartney's Town Hall Meeting*, transmitted on Saturday May 17.

Thursday April 24
 A party at Abbey Road Studios is held for the launch of the book *Abbey Road*, a new updated edition of which is published this week by Omnibus Press. Among those in attendance are George Martin, the vice president of the studios Martin Benge, Abbey Road managers Peter Vince and Allan Rouse (who co-authored the update section in the book) and engineers Geoff Emerick, Jeff Jarratt and John Leckle, and the former head of the studios Ken Townsend. A film on the history of Abbey Road is shown. (Note: The

original, now hard to find, book *Abbey Road: The Story Of The World's Most Famous Recording Studio*, was originally released in hardback in 1982 and in paperback in 1985, and has been out of print for years.) The new edition of the book contains the most detailed account of *The Beatles Anthology* sessions yet published.

* * *

Ringo & His Fourth All-Starr Band
Tour Of America
Monday April 28 to Sunday June 8

Ringo's current All-Starr Band, consisting of an all-British line-up of Ringo (on vocals and drums), Peter Frampton (of the sixties group The Herd, and himself a star of the Seventies on guitar), Jack Bruce (of the classic Sixties supergroup Cream on bass guitar), Gary Brooker (of Procul Harum on keyboards) and Simon Kirk (of Free and Bad Company on drums), tours America. Their repertoire includes the following songs: 'It Don't Come Easy', 'Act Naturally', 'The Devil Came From Kansas', 'Show Me The Way', 'Shooting Star', 'Boys', 'Baby I Love Your Way', 'You're Sixteen' and 'Yellow Submarine'. Then, after a short break, 'All I Want To Be (Is By Your Side)', 'Imaginary Western', 'Conquistador', 'I'm The Greatest', 'No No Song', 'I Feel Free', 'All Right Now', 'I Wanna Be Your Man', 'Do You Feel (Like I Do?)', 'White Room', 'A Whiter Shade Of Pale' and 'Photograph'.

Concerts during this tour include performances at the following venues:

The Moore Theater in Seattle, Washington (Monday April 28)
Hult Center, Eugene, Oregon (Tuesday April 29)
Arlene Schitzner Auditorium, Portland, Oregon (Wednesday April 30)
Concord Pavilion, San Francisco, California (Friday May 2)
Universal Amphitheater, Los Angeles, California (Saturday May 3)
Humphrey's San Diego, California (Sunday May 4)
Mesa Amphitheater, Phoenix, Arizona (Monday May 5)
Fiddler's Green, Denver, Colorado (Wednesday May 7)
Rosemont Horizon, Chicago, Illinois (Friday May 9)
Riverport Amphitheater, St. Louis, Missouri (Saturday May 10)
State Theater, Minneapolis, Minnesota (Sunday May 11)
Eagles Ballroom, Milwaukee, Wisconsin (Tuesday May 13)
Breslin Center, East Lansing, Michigan (Wednesday May 14)
Chastain Park, Atlanta, Georgia (Friday May 16)
Sunrise Theater, Miami, Florida (Saturday May 17)
Ruth Eckerd Hall, Tampa, Florida (Sunday May 18)
Palace Theater, Myrtle Beach, South Carolina (Tuesday May 20)
Wolftrap, Vienna, Virginia (Wednesday May 21)
Billy Bob's, Fort Worth, Texas (Friday May 23)
Six Flags, San Antonio, Texas (Saturday May 24 and Sunday May 25)
Bob Carpenter Center, Newark, New Jersey (Wednesday May 28)
I.C. Light Amphitheater, Pittsburgh, Pennsylvania (Thursday May 29)
Pine Knob Amphitheater, Detroit, Michigan (Friday May 30)
Rubber Bowl, Akron, Ohio (Saturday May 31)
Mohegan Sun Resort and Casino, Uncasville, CT (Monday June 2)
PNC Bank Arts Center, Holmdel, New Jersey (Wednesday June 4)
Harborlights Pavilion, Boston, Massachusetts (Friday June 6)
Resorts International, Atlantic City, New Jersey (Saturday June 7)
Jones Beach Amphitheater, Wantaugh, New York (Sunday June 8)

During the tour

Ringo gives an interview to the American newspaper *Orange County Register*, where he reveals that more archive Beatles projects are in the pipeline, including restored versions of the films *Yellow Submarine* and *Let It Be*, as well as CD versions of *The Beatles Live At The Hollywood Bowl* and the unreleased 1969 *Get Back* album. During the same interview, Ringo also speaks about the recent *Anthology* project. "It was great therapy for the three of us," he announces, adding: "We went over things that we thought were really big at the time, and they aren't that big at all – those little arguments that form up in your mind. It just brought back what a great time it was, and how close we all were. We tend to forget that. We did live in a box, and saved each others' lives."

Monday April 28
The opening night of the tour in Seattle is performed before a 1,400 crowd.

Friday May 30
Today's concert at the Pine Knob Amphitheater in Detroit, Michigan, is videotaped and released by MPI home video in America on July 28, 1998.

Sunday June 8
Following the conclusion of the American tour, Ringo remains in America where, at the end of July, he will continue work on his next solo album, *Vertical Man*.

* * *

Monday April 28
 'Young Boy' is released as a single in the UK today in three different formats. One 7-inch picture disc and two different CDs. Trevor Dann, the man responsible for banning 'Real Love' from Radio 1 last year, bans Paul's single from *Top Of The Pops*. He uses the "new music" argument for his decision.

Wednesday April 30
 Recordings begin on Paul's *Standing Stone* at the Abbey Road Studios in London. These sessions last until Friday May 2.

May
 In London, Paul gives an interview in the Boulevard section of the *Daily Express* newspaper. Of most significance are his recollections of the recent Beatles' reunion recording sessions and of the third "Beatles comeback" song: "There are a couple of things, which may surface at some point. You see, with The Beatles, there's always a surprise somewhere along the line. We did 'Free As A Bird' and 'Real Love', those two songs of John's. That was very exciting, very moving and very comfortable for me having his voice in my headphones in the studio again. And there was a third track, another song we had our eyes on called 'Now And Then'. I actually wanted to do it on *Anthology 3*, but we didn't all agree. But things change and the thing is that it might not go away. There was only one of us who didn't want to do it. It would have meant a lot of hard work, the song would have needed a lot of re-writing and people would have had to be very patient with us. But there are these one or two things lurking in the bushes." He adds optimistically, "The Beatles might just raise their ugly heads again . . ."
 In the UK, Corgi Toys re-launch the 1968 *Yellow Submarine* model as part of a range of six Beatles designs, manufactured under licence with Apple Corps.
 Julian Lennon rents a house in Dublin, Ireland where, at his own expense, he begins recording tracks for his next album.

Thursday May 1
 On the day of the British General Elections, Sky news broadcasts (at intervals throughout the day, with a complete round-up of the segments just before 9:00pm) an exclusive interview with Paul, carried out by the Reuters news service, which includes the first television glimpses of *The World Tonight* documentary. An extended version of the interview is transmitted on May 4 on the Sky News series entitled *Newsmakers*. Also today, the publishers Little Brown release the book *Linda McCartney's Summer Kitchen*.

Monday May 5
 Paul's new album *Flaming Pie* is released today in the UK. To commemorate its release, BBC Radio 2 transmits, this evening, the *Flaming Pie* radio special. (The American release of the album does not take place until May 20, while other territories

of the world receive the album one week previously, on May 12.) The track listing is as follows: 'The Songs We Were Singing', 'The World Tonight' (originally titled 'I Saw You Sitting'), 'If You Wanna', 'Somedays', 'Young Boy', 'Calico Skies', 'Flaming Pie', 'Heaven On A Sunday', 'Used To Be Bad', 'Souvenirs', 'Little Willow', 'Really Love You', 'Beautiful Night' and 'Great Day'. (Ringo collaborated with Paul on 'Really Love You' and 'Beautiful Night'.) In America, where the newspaper *US Today* describes it as "His Most Beatlesque Album In 30 Years", sales figures reveal that the album sells 500,000 copies in its first three days of release. To promote the release, the American video company Second Coming Productions distribute, to selected television stations across America, a 15-minute EPK (electronic press kit) for *Flaming Pie*, which includes exclusive interviews with Paul and a promotional clip for the song 'The World Tonight'.

Tuesday May 6
One day after a new offering from Paul in the UK, comes a new release from George in America, albeit on *Chants Of India*, the new CD from Ravi Shankar. George contributes acoustic guitar, bass guitar, autoharp and glockenspiel on the recordings which were carried out in London, Madras in India and at his Friar Park studios in his mansion in Henley-on-Thames. (The UK release takes place on September 1.)

Sunday May 11
In order to reach the deadline set for its first screening on Tuesday, the documentary *The World Tonight* is finally prepared for TV screenings by the Imagine Post Productions company in London today. Paul oversees the finished production.

Monday May 12
In America, VH-1 begins a week of special Paul McCartney programming, culminating in the *Town Hall Meeting* special programme, which is due to be aired this Saturday May 17.

Tuesday May 13
Paul's documentary *The World Tonight*, released to coincide with his new album, is premiered at a press launch at BAFTA in London's Piccadilly. Paul, though, is not in attendance.

Wednesday May 14
In the States, as part of the VH-1 Paul McCartney week of programming, the station transmits a show hosted by John Fugelsang entitled *The Paul McCartney Video Collection*. The 60-minute programme contains ten Macca promotional videos and gives an interesting insight into Paul's writing career through his solo years.

George arrives in New York to meet up with Ravi Shankar and various members of the press in a promotional exercise for the album *Chants Of India*. Today, George and Ravi visit VH-1's studio on 11th Avenue where they tape a two-and-a-half-hour interview with John Fugelsang for the programme *George & Ravi – Yin & Yang* (see entry for Thursday July 24 for details of the programme).

Thursday May 15
At the Plaza Hotel in New York, George and Ravi tape interviews for the American television programmes *Access Hollywood* and CNN's *Showbiz Today*, an item that will be transmitted one week later on Thursday May 22. During these lengthy sessions of interviews to promote *Chants Of India*, George and Ravi also give an interview to *People* magazine and to Robert Siegel of the NPR (National Public Radio) programme *All Things Considered*. During the latter, which is aired later this evening, Ravi recalls how he and George met at a party in 1966. "A few days later," George continues, "Ravi offered to come to my house and teach me some of the basics of sitar playing. After a few hours, we gave a small concert at my house with Alla Rakah, the tabla player, which was attended by Ringo and John Lennon."

Friday May 16
Paul's new documentary, featuring the complete title of *Paul McCartney In The World Tonight*, receives it worldwide television premiere in America tonight on VH-1.

 In New York, at the Plaza Hotel, George and Ravi continue with their *Chants Of India* promotions by giving interviews to Associated Press, Reuters, Westwood One and the New York radio station WNEW. In addition, George and Ravi also give an interview to Marc McEuen for the television programme *CBS This Morning*. When this is aired, just under a month later on Thursday June 12, McEuen notes at the end of the feature that, "George expects to begin recording a new solo album next year."

Saturday May 17
 On the day that Paul's *Flaming Pie* reaches number one in the *Music Week* Top 75 album chart, VH-1 in Europe transmits (simultaneously with VH-1 in Germany and in America) the programme *Paul McCartney's Town Hall Meeting*, a question and answer event, hosted by John Fugelsang, transmitted live from Bishopsgate Memorial Hall, in Bishopsgate, East London. (Fugelsang, a self-confessed Beatles fanatic, had met George only three days earlier, and now meets Paul, in what is his first visit to London!) During the show, Paul answers questions submitted by fans throughout the world the previous month, some asked by way of videotape, one of these being from the president of the United States, Bill Clinton! Paul also delivers, on an acoustic guitar, a short burst of the song 'Bishopsgate', a track that he claims he "wrote backstage". (Of course, Bishopsgate is a site mentioned by John in The Beatles' 1967 track 'Being For The Benefit Of Mr. Kite', which Paul point's out during the show.)

Paul arrived at the hall at 1:30pm and spent parts of the afternoon watching TV live coverage of this year's FA Cup Final. The 100 members of the audience in the Hall consists of 50 American contest winners, 25 members of Paul's Fun Club and 25 from Paul's large pool of family and close friends. The various transmission times of *Paul McCartney's Town Hall Meeting* are as follows: London – 6pm, Europe – 7pm, USA EDT – 1pm. Immediately following the 60-minute programme, Paul takes part in a 30-minute live "Netcast" chat with fans, held on the first floor of the Bishopsgate Hall.
 In America to coincide with these special shows, VH-1 transmits, for the first time in 18 years during this special *Paul McCartney Week*, the MPL programmes *Wings Over The World* (1979). This is the first time ever an almost complete uncut screening of the Wings concert film *Rockshow*, a version previously only seen in the cinemas, has been shown on TV.

Sunday May 18
 In the UK, two days after its worldwide premiere, Paul's MPL documentary *The World Tonight* receives its European premiere tonight across the ITV network between 11:01 and 11:59pm.

Tuesday May 20
 Rykodisc releases the first of its Yoko Ono back catalogue on CD. The first phase includes *Two Virgins* (1968), *Unfinished Music #2 – Life With The Lions* (1969), *The Wedding Album* (1969) and *Yoko Ono – Plastic Ono Band* (1970). All releases feature additional tracks from Yoko's own archives.

Thursday May 22
 In America, the first single off *Flaming Pie*, 'The World Tonight', is released.

Saturday May 24
 The 30th anniversary of the release of *Sgt. Pepper* passes without any official Apple or EMI celebration. The only item appearing to commemorate the landmark is on BBC Radio 2, when they broadcast the documentary *Pepper Forever*. (Although June 1, 1967, is always listed as the official release date for the album, May 24, 1967, was the date when the album was first distributed to record shops by EMI.)

June
 This month's issue of the music magazine Mojo, features an exclusive interview with Paul. Conducted over his car phone, he tells of his current "strained" relationship with George Harrison. "When we were working on 'Free As A Bird'," he announces, "there were one or two little bits of tension, but it was actually cool for the record. For instance, I had a couple of ideas that he didn't like and he was right. I'm the first one to accept that, so that was OK. We did say then that we might work together in the future, but the truth

is, after 'Real Love', I think George has some business problems. It didn't do a lot for his moods over the last couple of years. He's been having a bit of a hard time, actually, he's not been that easy to get on with. I've rung him and maybe he hasn't rung back. No big deal. But when I ring Ringo, he rings back immediately, we're quite close that way. You know, I'll write George a letter and he might not reply to it. I don't think he means not to reply to it, but it makes me wonder whether he actually wants to do it or not. And if you're not sure, you back off a little. But I love him, he's a lovely guy . . ."

🍎 Paul and Linda's youngest daughter Stella secures a £100,000 a year job as head designer at the prestigious Paris fashion house Chloe. In the UK, the National Trust wins its National Lottery bid for £47,500 to restore 24 Forthlin Road, in Allerton, Liverpool, the house where Paul lived as a teenager and wrote many of The Beatles' early songs with John.

🍎 Also this month, an exclusive interview with Paul, conducted by Des Burkinshaw, is published in *Record Collector* magazine. He is asked: "What do you think John would have thought of the National Trust buying your old house in Liverpool?" Paul replies: "If you'd ever said to me and John as kids, wandering around with guitars slung over our shoulders walking down Forthlin Road to Menlove Avenue, that one day it'd be a National Trust house . . . well – the idea is still fairly laughable!" He goes on: "The last time I was in Liverpool with the kids in the car, I drove down Forthlin Road, and pulled up outside the house and told the kids, 'That was my room, there. Dad planted a tree there. He used to have a lavender bush right there, and the ginger tom from next door used to come out and pee in the bush . . .' Then some bloke walks past, leans down to the car window and says, 'Yeah, he did used to live there!' "

🍎 Yoko briefly visits Britain where she undertakes promotional interviews to promote the Rykodisc reissues of her back catalogue.

Monday June 2
🍎 In America, approximately 12,000 schools tune in to a special radio broadcast, celebrating the 30th anniversary of the American release of *Sgt. Pepper's Lonely Hearts Club Band*.

Monday June 16
🍎 Two months four days after the version is completed, the Moving Picture Company of London prepares, for TV distribution, a second version of the 'Young Boy' promotional video, this time directed by Alastair Donald.

Monday June 23
🍎 A pre-recorded interview with Paul, conducted at his MPL offices in London, is transmitted on the programme *In Control*, on the Italian TV station RAI3.

Thursday June 26
🍎 In anticipation of his appearance on *TFI Friday* tomorrow, Paul spends the day at the Riverside Studios in Hammersmith, London, recording his guitar, drums and bass parts that will be played to "back him" on the show.

Friday June 27
🍎 Paul arrives in the early afternoon at the Riverside Studios in Hammersmith, where he rehearses the songs ('Flaming Pie' and 'Young Boy') he will be performing on the show *TFI Friday* tonight. For the transmission (on Channel 4 between 6:01 and 6:59pm, and then repeated later this night between 11:36pm and 12:29am) Paul appears at the tail-end of part two where he is interviewed by the host Chris Evans and takes questions, by fax, from various celebrities. These include Ringo, the comedian Frank Carson and the footballer George Best and then, as a climax to the programme, Paul performs, as in rehearsal, 'Flaming Pie' (aboard his psychedelic piano) and 'Young Boy', both against the backdrop of himself (videotaped the previous day) playing guitar, drums and bass. The show ends with Paul rushing out of the back of the studio with Evans to climb aboard a waiting speedboat, where they seemingly speed off down the river Thames. In fact, the pair (once live transmission on Channel 4 has been concluded) return to the studio to participate in the end of the series celebration party, with non-stop free beer until 7pm! Joining Paul at this event are his daughters Stella and Mary as well as his close friend Geoff Wonfor. Impressed with the "video screens depicting himself playing

instruments while he sings out in front" idea, Paul will resurrect this process for American television on Thursday November 20 (see entry).

July
 At the start of the month, whilst tending the garden at his Friar Park mansion, George discovers a lump on his throat and is immediately put in touch with the Princess Margaret Hospital in Windsor, Berkshire, to have it checked. As planned, George then visits Paris to promote Ravi Shankar's album *Chants Of India*, where again, he uses the world's media to launch an attack on some of the world's current top pop groups and the industry in general. In the French newspaper *Le Figaro*, George is quoted as saying: "One thing irritates me about current music, everything is based on ego. Look at a group like U2. Bono and his band are so egocentric. It's horrible . . . the more you shout, the higher you jump, the bigger your hat, the more people listen to your music. It's like that in the recording industry. It's got nothing to do with talent. Everything has got out of proportion today with the power of the record companies, the media, television, radio . . . it's staggering."

George is asked his opinion on the group Oasis. "They aren't very interesting. They're fine if you're 14 years old," he rants. "I prefer to listen to (Bob) Dylan. The Beatles still appeal to audiences aged from 7 to 77. Adolescents and children still adore *Yellow Submarine*. That gives me comfort and proves that we will last forever. Will U2 be remembered in 30 years? I doubt it." He is asked what he would do today if he were aged 20. "I would certainly produce The Spice Girls," he replies, adding, "The best thing about them is that you can watch them with the sound down!"

His ranting continues in the French Sunday paper *Le Journal Du Dimanche*: "When you are a teenager," he says, "your nervous system is able to tolerate the loudest things. Then as you get older, you consider the same things as an aggression and a pollution in your life. As far as I'm concerned, I cannot bear all sorts of pollution any more, whether it is in the food I eat, the air that I breathe or what I hear. It seems to me that music of today is a pollution and has no value at all. Rap stinks and techno is humanless music coming out of computers that bring you to madness if you listen to it for too long."

Asked if the pace of life is too fast these days, George replies philosophically: "Definitely! If you observe a monkey, it lives with quick agitated movements and its breath is very agitated. Its life is very short. Now if you consider giant turtles, they hardly breathe and move very slowly but they live many, many years. Keeping a control on your breath is respecting your spirit and assuring yourself of a long life."
 Following a holiday abroad, Ringo, at the end of the month, resumes recordings for *Vertical Man* with his second band, which he has now titled The Roundheads. (See next *Vertical Man* entry on Sunday July 20.)

Sunday July 6
 The 40th anniversary of the day when Paul first met John is celebrated today at the original venue, St. Peter's Church in Church Road, Woolton in Liverpool. Messages of support for the event are received from Paul, Yoko, The Prime Minister Tony Blair and even Her Majesty The Queen. Paul's message, recalling the historic meeting back in 1957, is sent by fax on *Flaming Pie* headed notepaper, and reads as follows:

"Ah yes, I remember it well. I do actually. My memory of meeting John for the first time is very clear. My mate Ivan Vaughan took me along to Woolton here and there were The Quarry Men, playing on a little platform. I can still see John now – checked shirt, slightly curly hair, singing 'Come Go With Me' by The Del Vikings. He didn't know all the words, so he was putting in stuff about penitentiaries – and making a good job of it. I remember thinking, 'He looks good – I wouldn't mind being in a group with him'. A bit later we met up. I played him 'Twenty Flight Rock' and he seemed pretty impressed – maybe because I *did* know all the words. Then, as you all know, he asked me to join the group, and so we began our trip together. We wrote our first songs together, we grew up together and we lived our lives together. And when we'd do it together, something special would happen. There'd be that little magic spark. I still remember his beery old breath when I met him here that day. But I soon came to love that beery old breath. And I loved John. I always was and still am a great fan of John's. We had a lot of fun together and I still treasure those beautiful memories.

"So I send you all in Woolton and Liddipool my best wishes today. And thanks for remembering – there's no way that when we met here we had any idea of what we'd be starting. But I'm very proud of what we did. And I'm very glad that I did it with John. I hope you all have a wonderful day and God bless all who sail in you."

🍎 Yoko meanwhile had telephoned the organiser Martin Lewis just prior to the event, where she left this message to the fans:

"What a sweet celebration! Yes, the meeting of John and Paul was an important event not only for those of us who loved their songs but for the whole world which went through a social change for the better as a result of their words and music. John's first thought as Paul showed what he could do was: 'Okay – this guy is good and already girls are flocking around *him*, not around me! So, if I let him in, he's going to be a tough one to handle – but I'll have a strong band.' So John took Paul in, I think this story is important in that it shows as a creator and a leader of a band, John went for getting a strong band rather than having an easy time. And John was only a teenager. What a brain! What a guy!

"By the way, it's interesting that the meeting took place at a church. Also, the main bulk of their songs were recorded at Abbey Road Studios in London. Am I the only one who thinks of these coincidences as interesting? John and Paul were travelling minstrels, who spread the word of love throughout the world. Through their songs, they brought the energy of love to the then grey world, which was still coping with the aftermath of the Second World War. With their words and music, John and Paul showed the world that law and order was not necessarily the most important force in the world. Love was the power and energy that could change the world. And it did.

"But it all started at the Woolton church forty years ago. As you celebrate this day, the world joins you in your celebration. Those who cannot come physically to Liverpool join you in spirit. It's a nice day to celebrate and I thank you for doing it. Peace."

The event, which features a musical performance by five original Quarry Men, is organised by Liverpool Beatlescene.

Monday July 7
🍎 The second single from *Flaming Pie*, 'The World Tonight', is released today in the UK. In the States, *NBC TV Today* broadcasts the first part of a three-part interview with Paul. (Parts two and three occur on Tuesday July 8, and Wednesday July 9, respectively.)

Thursday July 10
🍎 Pre-taped interviews with Paul, obviously to promote *Flaming Pie*, are transmitted in America. These include a lengthy appearance on the NBC News programme *Internight* and an extremely light-hearted conversation with Conan O'Brien for his NBC TV talk show, an item recorded at Paul's MPL offices in London a week previously.

Saturday July 12
🍎 VH-1 in Europe transmits the 50-minute Paul McCartney edition of the series *Ten Of The Best*.

Sunday July 20
🍎 In Los Angeles at the Whatinthewhathe? Studios, recordings resume with Ringo and The Roundheads writing and recording during this period 'What In The . . . World', 'La De Da' and 'Mindfield'.

Tuesday July 22
🍎 Still in the UK, Rykodisc issues the second batch of their Yoko Ono CDs, which include *Fly* (1971), *Approximately Infinite Universe* (1973), *Feeling The Space* (1973) and *A Story* (1974), originally recorded during her 1973/1974 separation from John.

Thursday July 24
🍎 The Virgin megastore in Oxford Street, London, throws a, somewhat belated, *Sgt. Pepper* 30th Anniversary Party, which features a Beatle look-a-like contest and the sound-a-like band The Paperback Beatles.

🍎 In America, VH-1 transmits the programme *George & Ravi – Yin & Yang*. This fascinating 22-minute pre-taped programme features the former Beatle and his Indian guru in conversation with John Fugelsang who, on Saturday May 17, interviewed Paul in London for the station's live *Town Hall Meeting* special. True to form, George uses the opportunity to promote his beliefs and to explain how he became friends with Ravi Shankar. "It might sound like a lofty thing to say on VH-1," George announces, "but

basically, what are we doing on this planet?" he asks. "I think, through The Beatles'
experience that we had, we had grown so many years within a small period of time,
hearing so many things and had met so many people, I realised that there was nothing
giving me a buzz anymore. I wanted something better. I remember thinking I'd love to
meet somebody who'd really impress me. That's when I met Ravi, which was funny. He
was a little feller with an obscure instrument, from our point of view, and yet he led me
into such depths. That's the most important thing, and still is, for me. I get confused
when I look around the world and I see everybody's running around and, as Bob Dylan
said, 'He not busy being born is busy dying', and yet, what's the cause of death? What
happens when you die? That to me is the only thing that is of any importance. The rest is
secondary. I believe in the thing that I read years ago that was in the Bible. It said,
'Knock and the door will be opened', and it's true. If you want to know anything in this
life, you just have to knock on the door. Whether that be psychically on someone else's
door and ask them a question or, which I was lucky to find, in meditation. You know it's
all within and that's really why, for me, this record is important (*Chants Of India*)
because it's another little key to open up within for each individual, to sit and turn off
your old mind, relax and float downstream and listen to something that has its roots in
transcendental, because even all the words of these songs carry with it a very subtle
spiritual vibration and it goes beyond intellect really, so if you let yourself be free to let
that effect have an effect on you, it can have an effect. It was a positive effect."

Naturally, excerpts from George and Ravi's 1968 meeting, captured for the 1971
released Apple film *Raga*, as well as clips from the 1971 *Concert For Bangla Desh* film, are
aired during the show. For many, a highlight of the programme is when Fugelsang asks
George to play something on an acoustic guitar which just happened to be in the studio.
"Wanna try one of The Beatles' tunes," he excitedly asks. "Wanna try 'Something'? A
Bob (Dylan) song? A Carl Perkins song? I'll take a Rick Astley song! I'll take a Spice Girls
medley, George!" A studio technician then joins in on the requests by shouting " 'All
Things Must Pass' ", which George duly obliges with a 1' 44" second version. A second
studio performance, this time 'Prabhujee', a track from the *Chants Of India* album, on
which they are joined by Ravi's wife Sukanya, closes this unique show. (Incidentally,
George's acoustic performances of two further tracks during the 150-minute recording,
namely 'If You Belong To Me', a track from the Traveling Wilburys' album *Volume 3*, and
an unreleased Harrison composition entitled 'If You Don't Know Where You're Going,
Any Road Will Take You', do not feature in the edited television transmission. The latter
track was suggested by Ravi's wife when George began wondering what song to play.
(As a footnote to this, just prior to the transmission, George writes to VH-1 requesting
that all of his performances be cut from the broadcast. His request is denied.)

Friday July 25
🍎 Back in Berkshire following his American visit, George makes a low-key appearance
in the audience at Ravi Shankar's performance at the Womad Festival concert in
Reading. Accompanying George is his 19-year-old son, Dhani, who is seen wearing dark
glasses and queuing outside a tent as part of Ravi's VIP guest list.

Monday July 28
🍎 Back in LA at the Whatinthewhathe? Studios, Ringo is to be found recording the vocal
for the track 'What In The . . . World'.

Tuesday July 29
🍎 Ringo pays a visit to see his friend Joe Walsh who is performing, for two nights, at the
club House Of Blues, on Sunset Strip in Los Angeles. He invites Joe to come and play
some new studio recordings, to which he agrees. (See entry for Thursday July 31.)

Wednesday July 30
🍎 Still at the Whatinthewhathe? Studios in Los Angeles, Ringo records the vocals for
'Without Understanding'.

Thursday July 31
🍎 The guitarist Joe Walsh drops by the Whatinthewhathe? Studios where he records a
guitar track for the songs 'La De Da', 'What In The . . . World' and 'Mindfield'.

August

 In the UK, George undergoes surgery for suspected throat cancer at the Princess Margaret private hospital in Windsor, Berkshire. To avoid publicity, George, his long hair tied in a ponytail, checks in under the name of "Sid Smith". Following the operation, in which several enlarged lymph nodes are removed from his throat, a hospital spokesman tells waiting reporters: "The operation went without a hitch, and we are all confident that it's the end of the matter. George didn't want to take any risks." He adds: "The procedure was routine and now he is home and feeling fine. The nodes were reported to be benign." (Sky news broadcast a report on George's cancer scare on August 2.) George then spends two further weeks undergoing radiation therapy at the Royal Marsden Hospital in London and is advised to return next month.

Friday August 1

 At Whatinthewhathe? Ringo records a further vocal track for the song 'Without Understanding'.

Tuesday August 5

 Recordings in Los Angeles for *Vertical Man* continue when today, at the Whatinthewhathe? Studios, Ringo and the musicians hold a session for the track 'Good News', a song originally titled 'Old Country Song'.

Thursday August 7

 Further work on Ringo's track 'Good News' takes place today when the former Stray Cat member Lee Rocker drops by the Whatinthewhathe? Studios to record a "slap-bass" track for the song.

Tuesday August 12

 Blockbuster home video in America releases *Ringo And His All-Starr Band – Volume One*, a limited edition concert CD with a price tag of only $6.

Monday August 18

 BBC1 in the UK transmits the episode of *Classic Albums*, featuring brief interviews with George, which is devoted entirely to The Band's eponymous titled 1969 album.

Friday August 22

 Paul sends a tribute message to the organisers of the Memorial Service at Liverpool Town Hall marking the 30th anniversary of the death of The Beatles' manager Brian Epstein. "Brian was a wonderful man who had an exceptional talent for guiding the careers of young people," Paul's statement read, adding: "I'm eternally grateful for the loving guide that he gave The Beatles. Brian – your show goes on!"

August

 At the end of the month, Ringo and Mark Hudson leave Los Angeles and head off to Europe, where they will remain until the autumn. (During his visit, Mark will spend September and October in England producing the young pop stars Hanson's 1997 Christmas album *Snowed In*.)

September

 It is reported that Yoko is to sign a £40 million deal with Columbia Pictures in Hollywood to make another film based on her long relationship with John Lennon. Press reports in America announce the film will, at last, enable Yoko to "tell the truth" about her relationship with John as well as her relations with the other Beatles. Production is scheduled to start sometime next year. Part of this deal also involves Columbia Pictures, to the tune of £50 million, acquiring the rights to two of John's songs, namely 'Give Peace A Chance' and 'Imagine'. Already in the frame for the lead role as John is the *Trainspotting* film star Ewan McGregor.

 Paul becomes the second Beatle to launch an attack on the group Oasis. In an interview this month with the *New Statesman* newspaper, he is quoted as saying: "They're derivative and they think too much of themselves. I hope that for their sakes they're right. But really they mean nothing to me. They're not the problem – Oasis's future is their problem. I sometimes hear their songs and think, 'That's OK', but I hope they don't make too much of it and start to believe their own legend because that can cause problems as others discovered. I wish them luck. I don't want to see them as rivals."

🍎 George returns to the Royal Marsden Hospital in London where he undergoes further radiation therapy. He remarks later: "Right through this whole period, I never felt sick. I didn't really relate to it, to be honest."

Friday September 5

🍎 Paul visits the ailing Derek Taylor at his Suffolk home.

Sunday September 7

🍎 Long time Beatles confidant Derek Taylor dies peacefully in his sleep at his home in Suffolk following his long battle with throat cancer. He is survived by his wife Joan and their six grown-up children, Timothy, Gerard, Abigail, Vanessa, Dominic and Annabel. Following his death Paul, via his spokesman Geoff Baker, releases this brief statement: "He was a beautiful man. It is time for tears and words may follow later." Respectful obituaries are published in several newspapers.

Monday September 8

🍎 The final batch of Rykodisc's Yoko Ono CDs is released today. These include: *Seasons Of Glass, It's Alright (I See Rainbows)* and *Starpeace*.

Friday September 12

🍎 In London, the private funeral of Derek Taylor takes place today. His family requests that donations should be made to the MacMillan Cancer Relief Fund. Those present at the service include Mike McCartney, Neil Aspinall, Neil Innes, Michael Palin and Jools Holland. George, wearing a baseball cap, is the only Beatle in attendance. Derek died while working on the long-planned, official *Beatles Anthology* book.

Sunday September 14

🍎 Paul and Linda send a bouquet of flowers to mark the unveiling of the English Heritage Blue Plaque in honour of Jimi Hendrix, at his former home at Brook Street in London, which is unveiled by Pete Townshend.

Monday September 15

🍎 Paul stars alongside Eric Clapton, Elton John, Phil Collins, Mark Knopfler, Sting and Carl Perkins in a charity event at the Royal Albert Hall in London, organised by George Martin to raise funds for the British Dependency of Montserrat, stricken by the recent volcanic eruptions. Martin remarks: "I am delighted that we look set to raise so much money for the long-suffering people of Montserrat. I am very grateful to all the wonderful musicians who will perform in the concert. I'm going to Montserrat in the next few weeks to see for myself where the money raised should be spent to the best effect." All the stars of the concert have, at one time or another, used George Martin's AIR Montserrat Studios on the island. Further money for the cause is raised by special pay-per-view screenings on the Sky Box Office station. The broadcast, lasting two hours 45 minutes, is transmitted daily from September 16–19. (In total, an estimated $1 million is expected to be raised from the show.) For the concert Paul, following afternoon rehearsals, performs a solo acoustic version of 'Yesterday', followed by 'Golden Slumbers', 'Carry That Weight' and 'The End' with an all-star line-up of Mark Knopfler, Eric Clapton and Phil Collins on drums. For encores he sings 'Hey Jude', duetting on piano with Elton John, and they are joined on stage by Sting, Midge Ure, Carl Perkins and others. The show closes with an all-star jam on 'Kansas City'/'Hey, Hey, Hey, Hey'. (The concert is transmitted live on the radio station Heart FM.)

Tuesday September 16

🍎 On the 20th anniversary of the death of the Seventies glam-rock star Marc Bolan, Channel 4, in the UK, transmits the 50-minute tribute programme *Dandy In The Underworld*, which features clips from the Apple 1972 film *Born To Boogie*, which Ringo directed and appeared in.

Thursday September 18

 In London, Paul and Linda's youngest daughter Stella is named as Best Young Designer at the annual *Elle* Style Awards presentation.

Wednesday September 24

 In the UK press, Paul provokes fury by calling for the decriminalisation of cannabis. "You're filling all the jails and yet it's when you're in jail that you really become a criminal. That's when you learn all the tricks!"

Monday September 29

 Paul's album *Standing Stone – A Symphonic Poem* is released in the UK. Also today, at The Mill recording studio in East Sussex, Ringo, Mark Hudson, the producer Geoff Emerick and Paul Wright, from the Sarm Hook End Studios in Henley, join Paul at his home studios where he records backing vocals and a bass line for the track 'La De Da'. Dean Grakal is also in attendance and proceeds to capture this recording session on his home video camera, clips of which appear later in the 'La De Da' promotional film and the Mercury *Vertical Man* electronic video press kit. During the afternoon get together, Paul gives Hudson, a self-confessed Beatles fanatic, a guided tour of his studio, a highlight of which is when Paul plays him a short burst of 'Strawberry Fields Forever' on the original Abbey Road Mellotron, as used on The Beatles' 1966 recording. With the excitement over, Paul begins recording the bass line for the *Vertical Man* song 'What In The . . . World', replacing the temporary one recorded in Los Angeles in July. During the playback of the song Paul turns to Ringo and says: "Whoo . . . Rich! Sounds kinda Beatle-ish!" Ringo replies, "I know! That's what I said to Mark months ago." Paul then looks back at Ringo and replies: "You are a fucking Beatle!"

October

 After more than 50 years in the music industry, George Martin, now aged 71, announces his retirement. He tells reporters: "I am an old man and don't want to do any more music. I'll go back to my Beethoven Sonatas and Chopin Etudes and start playing them again. But just for myself." George's final production will turn out to be his most successful single of all time, the re-recording of Elton John's 'Candle In The Wind', issued in memory of Diana, Princess of Wales, who died after a car crash in Paris in August.

 Peter Blake begins court proceedings against Apple to recover some of the lost royalties he insists he's still owed from the *Sgt. Pepper* album sleeve. Asked about the case, an Apple spokesman says: "That's just the way the business works. His contract said he would get a one-off payment and that is what he accepted at the time." (Blake was paid just £200 for his work back in 1967.)

 Oasis lead singer Liam Gallagher, during an interview on MTV, replies to George's criticism that he is "the silly one" in Oasis. "He doesn't know me, so what's he on about?" he snaps. "It goes to show that after all that time in The Beatles and he's still stupid! How does he know I'm silly? I've got four GCSEs; I'm not silly. If that's his personal opinion, fair enough, you know what I mean? I still love The Beatles and I still love George Harrison as a songwriter, but as a person, he's a nipple. And if I ever meet him, I'll tell him. And if you're watching George – nipple!" While U2 lead singer Bono also takes the opportunity to reply to George's attack in July. During a U2 concert in Leeds, Bono tells the audience: "Good people of Yorkshire, you are making a terrible mistake. George Harrison says you shouldn't be here. He says it's all about big hats, lemons and egos. This one's for you George," Bono concludes, making a rude gesture with his middle finger.

 The National Trust purchases Paul's old house at 20 Forthlin Road, Liverpool, on the suggestion of Sir John Birt, the Director General of the BBC, a one time Liverpool musician and a life-long Beatle fan.

Thursday October 2

 Many Years From Now, the highly anticipated 680-page authorised biography of Paul, written by Barry Miles, is published in the UK by Secker & Warburg. "I'll give it to you as I remember it. A sequence of things that did all happen within a period, so it's my recollection of then . . ." (Paul on *Many Years From Now*.)

Monday October 6

✪ Paul's second major classical work *Standing Stone*, is released today on EMI classics. Also released today in the UK is the PNE Home Video of an extended version of the MPL documentary *The World Tonight*.

Sunday October 12

✪ After waiting for more than 20 years, Paul finally succumbs to an interview with Michael Parkinson for his BBC Radio 2 show *Parkinson's Sunday Supplement*, but not his TV chat show as Parkinson would have preferred. During the course of the live interview, carried out at BBC Broadcasting House in Portland Place, London, Paul tells Michael about how privileged he was to be in the Lennon/McCartney songwriting team, and discusses the break-up of The Beatles. He also touches on delicate subjects like John's inadequacy as a father, the death of John's mother and the current health of Linda. Paul also naturally talks about his new biography *Many Years From Now*. Music from The Beatles and his latest album *Flaming Pie* are featured in the show.

Tuesday October 14

✪ In London, the day begins with an 11:30am press gathering in a Mayfair hotel for an 11:45am private screening of Paul's *Standing Stone* documentary. Afterwards, at 12:15pm, Paul conducts a press conference about the documentary and the concert itself, which opens tonight. Before departing for the Royal Albert Hall, Paul also poses for press photographers. At the Albert Hall, Paul conducts another news conference with the press and then, later on in the evening, Paul's *Standing Stone* is premiered. The evening's performance includes 'Standing Stone', 'A Leaf' and three new pieces, also being premiered, entitled 'Spiral' (performed by the London Symphony Orchestra), 'Inebriation' (by The Brodsky Quartet) and 'Stately Horn' (by the Michael Thompson Horn Quartet). Among the star-studded audience this evening are Ringo and Mark Hudson. The event is staged in aid of the Music Sound Foundation. (News clips from the show are featured on the programme *London Tonight*, transmitted the following night in the Carlton region of ITV.)

Wednesday October 15

✪ Linda reappears in public, joining Paul, as well as Ringo and Barbara, in Paris, where they attend their daughter Stella's first catwalk show for the fashion house Chloe. Backstage scenes at the show are captured on film for the ITV documentary *Clive James Meets The Super Models*, transmitted across the ITV network on Sunday September 27, 1998.

Thursday October 16

✪ Paul holds a signing session at the newly refurbished HMV store in Oxford Street, London, where he is presented with his Composer of the Century Award by HMV. Many fans had queued up all night, and Paul is asked why he returned to do this signing at the store. "Because of a bit of nostalgia," he replied. "HMV was the first place that Brian Epstein dropped off one of our records and it all happened from there. So when they asked me to do it, I thought 'Yes. Why not?' I know a lot of the kids too. I see them from event to event, but normally I don't get a chance to speak to them."

Due to London Transport, Paul's arrival at the store is delayed by 20 minutes. He is introduced at HMV by Capital Radio DJ Dr. Fox.

Adverts announcing Paul's appearance at HMV were placed in the music press and London papers by MPL. Although billed as his first album signing session in 34 years, this is not the case. Paul had recently conducted autograph sessions in Australia, at the Brash's music store, during the March 1993 Australasian tour, and at the PNAC record store in Paris, France in October that year.

Thursday October 23

✪ The George–Oasis war rages on, when tonight on BBC Radio 1FM's programme *The Evening Session*, Liam Gallagher threatens George with assault live on air. "I'm gonna shoot me mouth off here – all these snakes coming out of the closets, all these old farts, I'll offer 'em out right here on radio. If they want to fight, be at Primrose Hill, Saturday morning, at 12 o'clock. I will beat the fuckin' living daylight shit out of 'em. That goes for George, Jagger, Richards and any other cunts that give me shit. If any of them old farts have got a problem with me then leave your Zimmer frames at home and I'll hold you up with a good right hook. They are jealous and senile and not getting enough fuckin' meat pies. If they want to fight, I'll beat 'em up."

Monday October 27
 EMI releases the 20-track compilation album *Lennon Legend*, comprising John's singles and most famous solo album tracks. The tracks on the album are: 'Imagine', 'Instant Karma', 'Mother' (single edit), 'Jealous Guy', 'Power To The People', 'Cold Turkey', 'Love', 'Mind Games', 'Whatever Gets You Through The Night', '#9 Dream', 'Stand By Me', '(Just Like) Starting Over', 'Woman', 'Beautiful Boy (Darling Boy)', 'Watching The Wheels', 'Nobody Told Me', 'Borrowed Time', 'Working Class Hero', 'Happy Christmas (War Is Over)', and 'Give Peace A Chance'. (The release, which is backed by a £500,000 plus EMI press campaign, comes in the shape of a CD, cassette and double album.) *Lennon Legend* subsequently replaces on the EMI catalogue the 1982 compilation album *John Lennon Collection* which, prior to its deletion last month, had sold over 1.8 million copies in the UK alone, of which 350,000 was on CD.
 Paul is a special guest at the 21st Annual Gramophone Awards (Classical Music Awards) ceremony, held at the Alexandra Palace in London. During the event, he presents the Young Artist of the Year award to the German violinist Isabelle Faust. At the end of the get-together, Paul happily poses for pictures with the tenor, Luciano Pavarotti. (The ceremony, including Paul's presentation, is transmitted across the ITV network the following night, Tuesday October 28.)

November
 Following on from their success with their Ringo Starr range, Gartlan USA announces the launch of *The John Lennon Collection*, which includes a limited-edition "Happy Christmas" plate, featuring a Lennon drawing of stylised figures gathered around a Christmas tree.
 The National Trust begins renovating Paul's old home at 20 Forthlin Road, Liverpool. The Trust search out original Fifties' windows, doors and a fireplace to replace the modern fittings, and eventually they discover the windows in a house across the road.

Saturday November 1
 Ringo returns to Los Angeles where a collection of overdubbing sessions on previous recordings and a selection of new *Vertical Man* recordings at the Whatinthewhathe? Studios take place.

Monday November 3
 At Whatinthewhathe? Studios in Los Angeles, Ringo and his musicians record the track 'I Was Walking'.

Tuesday November 4
 Paul attends the *Q* Awards ceremony held at Park Lane Hotel in London, where he receives the Best Songwriter award for his album *Flaming Pie*. Also in attendance is the legendary American record producer Phil Spector. Paul is not pleased to see him, the antagonism stretching back to 1970 when Spector, in Paul's opinion, ruined his recording of 'The Long And Winding Road' on The Beatles' *Let It Be* album. Paul leaves when Spector gets up to deliver a speech.
 In LA, sessions begin on the track 'Puppet', a song originally titled 'The Puppet Song' and based on an expression that Ringo had come up with: "Put the puppet to bed."

Thursday November 6
 Paul and Linda fly to New York where they attend rehearsals with the St. Luke's Orchestra in preparation for their premiere performance of *Standing Stone* at Carnegie Hall. During Paul's stay in the city, he contributes an interview for the BBC2 *Arena* "warts and all" documentary on The Beatles' manager Brian Epstein, a two-part show that will receive its UK TV premiere on December 25 and 26, 1998.
 Ringo meanwhile, is still at work on recordings for the album *Vertical Man*. Today, he begins recording the track 'Sometimes', which, not knowingly, features a riff borrowed from his 1976 song 'Cryin'', recorded for his album *Ringo's Rotogravure*.

Friday November 7
🍎 Recordings at Whatinthewhathe? Studios continue with the veteran session guitarist Jeff "Skunk" Baxter, best known for his work with Steely Dan, adding steel guitar to the tracks 'One' and 'Sometimes'. Later this day, the keyboard player Jim Cox arrives at the studio to record some tracks. (Incidentally, Ringo's original choice for keyboards on the album was Billy Preston, but unfortunately, he was serving time in an American prison.)

Wednesday November 12
🍎 The first overdubs for *Vertical Man*, recorded at The Village Recorders Studios, are put to tape.

Thursday November 13
🍎 Further overdub sessions take place at The Village Recorders Studios in Los Angeles when the huge chorus, comprising 46 friends and relatives, record the backing vocals for the track 'La De Da'. This line-up includes Ringo, Barbara, Lee Starkey, Barbara's daughter Francesca and sister Marjorie, and Mark Hudson and his daughter Sarah. In addition, there are Keith Allison from the Sixties group Paul Revere & The Raiders, former All-Starr Band member Nils Lofgren as well as Van Dyke Parks and his family.

Monday November 17
🍎 The proposed release today, in the UK, of a special *Sgt. Pepper's* 30th anniversary box set fails to materialise and is cancelled altogether by Apple. EMI are reported to be "very disappointed"!

🍎 In Los Angeles, at the Whatinthewhathe? Studios, Ringo is joined by the Aerosmith frontman Steven Tyler, who had flown in from Amsterdam especially for the recordings. Tyler plays harmonica on the track 'I Was Walkin' '. Also today, Ringo begins recording a cover of The Beatles' track 'Love Me Do', an idea conceived by the former Beatle himself. "I've always loved that song," Ringo announces. "I didn't get to play on the first one (1962) – I'll show the bastards!" Steve Tyler plays a new harmonica arrangement on the track and comes up with the new "Lovemedo – lovemedo – lovemedo" ending.

Tuesday November 18
🍎 During more *Vertical Man* recordings at Whatinthewhathe?, Ringo announces that he is unsure about the re-recording of 'Love Me Do' yesterday. "It haunted me last night," he tells his line-up of musicians. The significance of a Beatle performing 'Love Me Do' is too great to allow for a change to the signature riff of the song, so Tyler is requested, by Ringo, to re-record his harmonica track, keeping true to the original.

Wednesday November 19
🍎 The Julien Temple directed promotional video for 'Beautiful Night' is prepared for TV distribution. The first (censored) copy is immediately dispatched to America for screening on tomorrow's recording of *Oprah*. In the States, Paul records an interview for the NPR Radio station at Carnegie Hall.

🍎 Back in the Whatinthewhathe? Studios in Los Angeles, the singer Alanis Morissette drops by the studio and ends up singing on the album. "We had this open-door policy," Ringo recalls, "whereby if you dropped by while we were recording, you were going to get asked to be on the record." Alanis's contribution is a beautiful strong vocal for the track 'Drift Away'.

Thursday November 20
🍎 Still in New York, Paul videotapes an appearance on the top-rated ABC TV chat show *Oprah*, hosted by the queen of the talk shows Oprah Winfrey. The 44-minute programme, first transmitted on Monday November 24, features an exclusive interview with Paul and then, as on Channel 4's *TFI Friday* on June 27, he performs the tracks 'Young Boy' and 'Flaming Pie', to an accompaniment of newly recorded videos of himself playing guitar, bass and drums, taped the previous day. The broadcast also includes the American Television premiere of the censored version of the video for 'Beautiful Night'. Following the show, ABC continues with a Beatles theme when, on an *Eyewitness News* special, they broadcast the programme *Why Is America Still In Love With The Beatles?*, examining, as the title suggests, America's great fixation with the fab four. On December

14, ABC transmits a second version of Paul's appearance on *Oprah*. This alternate show features additional scenes of Paul taking questions from the studio audience as well as the 'Beautiful Night' video being replaced with the new clip for 'Little Willow', as featured on the *Princess Diana Tribute* album. (The European premiere for the first *Oprah* show takes place on Sky One on December 23, between 4:01 and 4:58pm.)

 Ringo's recordings in Los Angeles continue, this time back at the Village Recorders Studio, with background vocals for 'Without Understanding' and 'Drift Away'. Providing their services today is the Los Angeles gospel group called Sauce.

Saturday November 22
 Yoko's latest art exhibition, entitled *Have You Seen The Horizon Lately*, co-sponsored by EMI, Virgin Atlantic, Beck's Lager and BMG Music Publishing, has a press preview at the Museum of Modern Art in Oxford. The exhibition concentrates on Yoko's London period of the late Sixties.

 On Channel 4, in the UK, the Cilla Black episode of the Granada TV series *Brit Girls*, a five-part look at British female singers from the Sixties, features pre-recorded interviews with celebrities such as Ringo Starr and George Martin.

Sunday November 23 (until March 15 1988)
 Yoko's art exhibition *Have You Seen The Horizon Lately?*, opens to the public at the Museum on Modern Art in Oxford. A fully illustrated catalogue with a text by Chriss Lles and Yoko accompanies the four-month show.

Tuesday November 25
 In Los Angeles, the sessions for *Vertical Man*, at the Whatinthewhathe? Studios, resume with the genius from The Beach Boys, Brian Wilson, dropping by to help record the song 'Without Understanding'. (The song contains the line "no good vibrations", a referral to The Beach Boys' classic, which Brian was invited to sing.) Under Mark Hudson's direction, Brian layered numerous backing vocals for the track. Later in the day, Alanis Morissette returns to the studio to record, adding backing vocals to the songs 'Mindfield' and 'I Was Walkin''. In between Brian and Alanis's recordings, Ringo's nephew Christian Phillippe Quillici, the son of Barbara's sister, drops by the studio and sings on the track 'Without Understanding'. To close the day, tape copies of the songs 'King' and 'I'll Be Fine Anywhere' are made at The Village Recorders studio by staff engineer Eric Greedy and dispatched, the following day, to George at his Friar Park home in England. (George is sent one reel of 24-track 2″ analogue tape, two mixes of each song, one with vocals, one without, along with a SMPTE time code stripe, to allow his contributions to be synchronised back with the original digital multi-tracks upon their return back to Ringo in Los Angeles.) At this point in the *Vertical Man* recordings, there are 16 finished songs waiting for the final mixing.

Friday November 28
 Throughout Europe, Sky News broadcast extracts from the *Diana Tribute* electronic press kit, which features a new clip of Paul performing his track on the album 'Little Willow'.

Sunday November 30
 With the Vertical Man album now needing a final mix, Geoff Emerick, The Beatles' studio engineer since Revolver in 1966, packs his bags in England and flies to the A&M Studios in Hollywood, just a short distance from Mark Hudson's studio. (This studio boasts the original Neve mixing console, acquired in 1985 from George Martin's AIR Montserrat Studios.) The mixing sessions for Vertical Man generally last from 11am to 11pm with each song usually taking two or three days to complete. (Ringo initially told Geoff that they had only ten days in total to mix the album. This estimation will soon prove optimistic.)

December
 The month sees two former Beatles contributing forewords to new publications. George writes a 250-word piece to the book *Skiffle – The Definitive Inside Story*, by Chas McDevitt, while Paul appears in the MPL sponsored book *A Poem For Buddy*.

Monday December 1
 In the UK, Virgin Records release the double album *Diana Tribute*, issued in honour of the late Princess of Wales and featuring Paul's recording of 'Little Willow', a track originally recorded as a tribute to Ringo's first wife Maureen.
 At the A&M Studios in Los Angeles, mixing is completed on 'One', the first track on the *Vertical Man* album.

Tuesday December 2
 At the A&M Studios, mixing work is completed on the track 'Mr. Doubleitup'.

Sunday December 7
 Paul appears in a pre-recorded interview for the BBC1 early morning show *Breakfast With Frost*, hosted by David Frost.

Thursday December 11 (until Tuesday December 16)
 At the A&M Studios in Los Angeles, mixing takes place for the *Vertical Man* track 'What In The . . . World'. At its conclusion, mixing is immediately started on 'Love Me Do', which is concluded on Tuesday December 16.

Friday December 12
 Amidst all the excitement of the *Vertical Man* recordings, Mark Hudson has not paid the rent on his room which is being used for the recordings. During activities today, a knock comes on the door. It is the landlord's secretary. "I need rent," she screams, "$450!" Ringo responds: "Do you play an instrument?" Startled by the question, the woman replies: "Yeah, cello." "Go get it," Ringo insists. Thus Nina Pieseckyj, the landlord's secretary, finds herself playing an 'I Am The Walrus'-style cello line on the album's title song 'Vertical Man'. Also today, it is announced that Ringo has signed to Guardian Records, one of EMI's newer labels, who will be releasing the *Vertical Man* album. The release date is provisionally scheduled for April 21, 1998, with the catalogue number A2-23702.

Monday December 15
 In the UK, EMI releases Paul's 'Beautiful Night', the third single to be lifted off his album *Flaming Pie*. As with the two previous releases, the single comes as a 7-inch picture disc and as two different CDs. Controversy surrounds the promotional video for the song, which features full-frontal scenes of the actress Emma Moore swimming in the River Mersey. Naturally the music station MTV bans the video, forcing Paul to order a broadcastable version of the clip to be made. The only station to quite happily play the banned version is, predictably, the American *Playboy* channel. On a less controversial note, Paul co-stars in the film with the unknown four-piece West London group Spud, who were spotted playing in a small London club by the video's director Julien Temple. Also (in whichever version of the video you see), Ringo can be seen making a cameo appearance as a night watchman, disturbed by the noise and eventually playing drums on the song.

Thursday December 18
 Just six days after the announcement that Vertical Man will be released by Guardian Records, comes the news that EMI's new president, Ken Berry, has decided to streamline the US operations of the company, which means, among many other things, the closing of the company's smaller labels, including Guardian. Ringo is again without a record label. Nevertheless, Ringo consoles himself by recording today, back at Whatinthewhathe?, his final lead vocal for the track 'Vertical Man'. Ringo, Geoff Emerick and all the musicians then take a break for the festive period.

Monday December 22
 Ringo's planned Christmas break is interrupted when he receives in the post this morning a tape from George who has, as requested, recorded guitar overdubs on to two *Vertical Man* tracks. Excited by this delivery, Ringo and The Roundheads all climb into Dean Grakal's van and drive around to The Village Recorders Studio. On their arrival, the group put on the tape and listen to George's work. Ringo, sitting back with his hands behind his head, listens to George's beautiful guitar track and announces: "You're killing

me George. You've got me crying, you bugger!" George had provided a single lead guitar for the track 'King Of Broken Hearts' while for the song 'I'll Be Fine Anywhere', he produced two guitar lines, one picked and one played with a slide, recorded on two separate tracks. The studio engineer notes: "You can hear it was a seemingly casually done track for George. He engineered it himself, and you can hear on the tape that he was at home, with people talking in the background." In the end, it is decided to use both of George's leads for 'I'll Be Fine Anywhere', the tracks playing in tandem with each other on the final mix.

There is a moment of mirth for Ringo and The Roundheads when they notice that George had accidentally wiped off the SMPTE time code from the second half of one of the songs. This means that it will now be more difficult for the engineers to synchronise this tape up with master studio recording of the song, in order to dub the guitar's track to the master tape. George, back home at Henley, had noticed this mistake and had written a note to this effect, enclosing it within the returned tapes. It read: "Well, with the rush and no engineer, I'm afraid the code has disappeared. But you're all 'smart assed jacks', I'm sure you'll be able to get it back!" George also notes that Ringo had missed a drum fill at one point in the track 'King Of Broken Hearts'. Ringo quickly puts it right before going for a European Christmas vacation with Barbara.

Thursday December 25
● On Christmas Day, Channel 5 screens throughout Europe the premiere of the television version of Paul's *Standing Stone* concert.

Friday December 26
● One day after the television version of *Standing Stone* comes the edited 51-minute *Making Of Standing Stone* documentary, shown this morning on BBC1.

Sunday December 28
● Channel 5 transmits the 58-minute programme *Paul McCartney Talks With David Frost*. Later this evening, BBC1, in the UK, begins broadcasting the three-part George Martin music documentary *The Rhythm Of Life*, which features contributions from celebrities such as Paul, The Bee Gees and Brian Wilson. (Part two is transmitted on December 29 with part three appearing on the station on January 5, 1998.)

"Paul's tragedy of losing Linda is hitting him in waves. One minute he can cope, and the next he can't. He's devastated. Paul is determined to make sure Linda's legacy will be lasting."

– Paul's MPL spokesman Geoff Baker

January
 George visits the Mayo Clinic in America, one of the top five cancer treatment centres in the world. There he meets Doctor Richard Lavelle, a friend of his for many years. George is thoroughly checked and is told that there is no recurrence of cancer. He is asked to return in the first week of May.
 Sean Lennon finishes work on his début album. Produced by his girlfriend Yuka Honda, the album is called *Photosynthesis* and is scheduled for an April release.
 Rhino Home Video in America announces plans to issue, on home video, John and Yoko's complete 1972 week-long appearance as co-hosts on *The Mike Douglas Show* (see entries for February 14 – February 18, 1972).
 OK! Magazine, in the UK, reveals that, during 1997, Paul earned £15 million, while George and Ringo earned a more modest £8 million each.

Sunday January 4
 The ITV network in the UK broadcasts the 58-minute documentary *The Story Of Abbey Road*, a programme looking at the conception and history of the world famous recording studio. Besides interviews with such pop luminaries as Paul, George Martin, Pink Floyd and The Shadows, the show also features The Beatles' former drummer, Pete Best, returning to the studios for the first time in 34 years.

Tuesday January 6
 Paul's album *Flaming Pie* is among the nominations for "The Best Album of 1997" at the 40th Annual Grammy Awards ceremony in America. Paul faces stiff competition from Bob Dylan's *Time Out Of Mind* (which eventually wins) and Radiohead's *OK Computer*.
 At the A&M Studios in Los Angeles, work resumes on Ringo's *Vertical Man* album when the mixing is started on the track 'Mindfield'. (Work on the track continues until Thursday January 8.)

Wednesday January 7
 It is reported in *The Times* newspaper that two bronze busts, worth £50,000, have been stolen from George's garden at his home in Henley. The thieves evaded security cameras after climbing a 10-foot wall and cutting the figures of two monks from their stone plinths.

Thursday January 8 (until Saturday January 10)
 Just as the mixing on 'Mindfield' is concluded, work begins on the mixing of 'The King Of Broken Hearts', which features George's guitar work recorded at his home in Henley.

Sunday January 11 & Monday January 12
 The track 'Drift Away' is mixed at the A&M Studios in Los Angeles.

Friday January 16
 Postponed from December 16 last year, BBC2, in the UK, finally transmits the Yoko Ono *O Zone* special. During the 20-minute programme, used as further promotions for the album *Lennon Legend* and subtitled *The Ballad Of John And Yoko*, Yoko discusses a wide range of subjects including the break-up of The Beatles and John's songwriting. Yoko uses this opportunity to hit back at Paul over various allegations made in his biography *Many Years From Now*. Over his claim that he was the leader of The Beatles, Yoko says: "I know Paul thinks he was leading, or something like that. The way John led the band was very high level, on some kind of magical level. Not on a daily level like Paul said. 'Oh, but I was the one who told them all to come and do it. I made the phone calls.' John didn't make the phone calls. John was not on that level of a leader. He was on a level of a spiritual leader. He was the visionary and that's why The Beatles happened."

Yoko also responds to Paul's claim in the book that he was the instigator in reconciling John and Yoko in January of 1975. "Let him say whatever he wants to say. I feel that he has to say all of those things. But if he wants to get credit about it, why not? That's fine. I know it *wasn't* true. I know that he didn't come back because Paul said a few words or something like that. He's put in a position of being Salieri to Mozart. And it's sad." (Yoko is referring to Antonio Salieri, a contemporary to Mozart, described as a "competent but uninspired composer". He is portrayed in the film *Amadeus* as being jealous of Mozart's genius and plotting to kill him.) Yoko goes on: "Because John passed away, people naturally have this strong sentiment towards him. Paul is always just encouraging people, not given the same compliment that they give John now. And naturally, they do that because he passed away. It's a high price to pay for Paul to be in the same position as John."

Saturday January 17
◆ At the A&M Studios in Los Angeles, the saxophone player Joel Peskin records his tracks for the song 'Puppet'.

Monday January 19
◆ Carl Perkins dies after a series of strokes aged 65 in a Nashville Hospital. He had been fighting throat and tonsil cancer for most of this decade. Following news of his death, Geoff Baker, on behalf of Paul, releases this statement: "Paul is saddened to hear of Carl's death. They were close friends and had the greatest respect for each other." George attends his funeral, held in America at the Lambuth University in Jackson on January 23, where he briefly performs, as a tribute, the Perkins' song 'Your True Love'. Paul sent a video message to be played at the service in which he expresses his affection and respect for Carl. Jerry Lee Lewis is also present at the funeral.

Friday January 23
◆ At the A&M Studios in Los Angeles, the track 'Puppet' is completed when the final mixing takes place this evening.

Saturday January 24
◆ Channel 4 broadcasts the 80-minute programme *Music For The Millennium*; a show based on the HMV/Channel 4 poll. (See following entry for Beatles-related placings.)

Sunday January 25
◆ *Sgt. Pepper's Lonely Hearts Club Band* is voted the "greatest album of all time" in the *Music Of The Millennium* survey, conducted by the HMV music stores and Channel 4. From the 36,000 people aged between 19 and 45 who contributed to the survey, *Revolver* made number three, *The Beatles* (aka the *White Album*) made number 10, *Abbey Road* reached number 12 and *Rubber Soul* is placed at number 39. John's 1971 album *Imagine* is placed at number 81. HMV spokesperson Gennaro Castaldo says: "We were amazed by the response, but not surprised to see The Beatles came out on top." When Paul is told of the results, he comments: "The time of *Sgt. Pepper* was a very productive period for me. Before it came out, the newspapers were saying 'The Beatles are finished. They've dried up.' But we thought, 'Ha, wait until you hear this!' "

Thursday January 29
◆ With the *Vertical Man* album now technically completed, Ringo holds a "listening party" to play the album to selected friends between 8 and 10pm at the A&M Studios. Visitors include Jeff Lynne, Timothy B. Schmidt, Peter Frampton, Gary Brooker, Geoff Emerick, The Roundheads and, of course, Mark Hudson, as well as Ringo and Barbara.

February
◆ *Q* magazine publishes the results of its reader's poll of the Greatest LPs Of All Time. *Rubber Soul* is placed at number 40, *The Beatles* (aka the *White Album*) is at number 17, *Abbey Road* is at number 12, *Sgt. Pepper's* is at number seven and *Revolver* is placed at number two. At the top is Radiohead's *OK Computer*. The Beatles also feature in the magazine's poll of the Official Worst Album Title Of All Time, with *Rubber Soul*, Paul's *Tripping The Live Fantastic* and *Ringo's Rotogravure* all on the chart.
◆ Paul pays £45,000 to have his famous Violin Hofner bass guitar worked on, in order for it to be insured to the value of £2 million. This £45,000 bill includes the hiring of a chartered jet to fly the bass, housed in a custom-made samsonite case, to New York, where a long-standing tuning problem is corrected. His insurers insisted the legendary bass guitar had to be tuned correctly to meet the requirements of their policy.
◆ During the early part of this month, the German manufacturers of the Volkswagen Beetle, the world's best-selling car, approach The Beatles to help re-promote it. VW board member Klaus Kocks announces: "The Beetle was a cult car and The Beatles also

had cult status, which fits well into the concept." VW spokesperson Martina Rudy reveals that they are seeking permission from The Beatles to use a song in a television commercial and that 'Drive My Car', is the most obvious choice. Another alternative is to use the image of the Volkswagen car as featured on the *Abbey Road* sleeve. Reports suggest that Volkswagen have originally offered $5 million to Apple, while sources close to The Beatles reveal that the figure they had in mind is nearer $50 million! Either way, if it goes ahead, industry experts predict the deal will be "one of the most lucrative in advertising history!" (The UK re-launch of the car takes place in 1999.)

 In America, Ringo completes his new album *Vertical Man*. Produced by the Los Angeles-based Mark Hudson, best known for his work with Aerosmith, and his own band the Hudson Brothers, the album features musical contribution from Paul, George, George Martin, Steven Tyler (of Aerosmith), Alanis Morissette, Tom Petty and, from The Beach Boys, Brian Wilson. The final mixing of the album has been handled by the long-time Beatles associate Geoff Emerick. (For the full list of tracks recorded during the sessions, see entry for June 16, 1998.) The title *Vertical Man* had come from a book of quotations that Ringo's stepdaughter Francesca had won at school. While flipping through the book one day, Ringo notices the line: "Let's hear it for the vertical man, there's always so much praise for the horizontal one."

Sunday February 1
 It is revealed that Pauline Sutcliffe, the sister of original fifth Beatle Stuart, has found in her archives some old Beatles' song lyrics written by Stuart and John back in 1960 and 1961. She reveals that she has given them to British band Oasis to record. Some of the lyrics read: "Everybody is getting ready, Everybody is going steady, Everybody but me. I stay home on Friday night, Go to bed at eight, On Saturday night I'm all alone, 'Cos I don't have a date."

Monday February 16
 Yoko, in a pre-taped 39-minute interview with Sir Jeremy Isaacs carried out in New York, appears in the UK on the BBC2 late-night programme *Face To Face*.

Tuesday February 17 (until Thursday February 19)
 Mark Hudson and Geoff Emerick fly to New York City where the *Vertical Man* album is mastered, under their supervision, by the engineer Greg Calbi at Masterdisk. (Emerick will finally return to England on Saturday February 21 – three months after leaving England.) During their visit to New York, Hudson and Bruce Grakal visit the Mercury Records chief Danny Goldberg who is ecstatic about the album and, on April 1, announces that Mercury will be releasing *Vertical Man* on June 16.

March
 Doctors discover that Linda's cancer has spread to her liver. This month, she gives an interview to *O.K.!* magazine, where she speaks of her relationship with Paul: "We're just like boyfriend and girlfriend again!"

 The proposed release this month of the short animated MPL film *Tropic Island Hum* fails to materialise. (The first public airing of the clip was during the 1997 MPL documentary *Paul McCartney In The World Tonight*, where production work on the featurette was seen being carried out.)

 The Beatles and Volkswagen discussion rages on. Proposed titles now submitted for the forthcoming VW TV ads include 'Day Tripper', 'Magical Mystery Tour' or 'The Long And Winding Road'. The final decision rests with Michael Jackson, the co-owner of the Northern Songs catalogue, who is reported to have accepted a $10 million offer for the use of a song. George is most annoyed when he hears of this development, saying: "Unless we do something about it, every Beatles' song is going to end up advertising bras and pork pies!"

 In London, a secret BBC document is leaked out, revealing that "The Beatles might reunite for the launch of the Millennium Dome". When asked about this rumour, Paul's MPL spokesman Geoff Baker immediately dismisses the story, saying: "It's outrageous that the BBC are using The Beatles' name for this document. I can't believe that this is the best that they can come up with! There's nothing they'd like more than to play together, but they can't – because John's dead!"

 An edited 90-minute home video version of The Concert For Montserrat, recorded at the Royal Albert Hall in London on Monday September 15 last year (see entry) is released in the UK.

🍎 The National Trust places an advert for a custodian for 20 Forthlin Road, Liverpool, in *The Big Issue*. Starting salary is £9,760 per annum.

Sunday March 1
🍎 In the States, Paul contributes a brief video message of himself singing 'Calico Skies' to the American ABC TV special *Christopher Reeve – A Celebration Of Hope*, a tribute to the Superman actor Reeves who remains paralysed after a terrible horse riding injury.

Wednesday March 4
🍎 The film documentary *Everest*, featuring George's music on the soundtrack (see entry for April) premieres at Boston's Museum of Science. (The film goes into American general cinema release on March 6.)

Wednesday March 11
🍎 Paul and Linda visit Paris where they sit hand-in-hand cheering on their fashion designer daughter Stella at a second showcase of her new Chloe fashion creations. Reporters naturally ask Linda how she is feeling: "Right now, I'm feeling great. I'm feeling fit and well and looking forward to having lunch together as a family before we go back to London." An emotional Stella proudly announces: "I'm so happy mum and dad could make it today. Families are what it's all about." Stella tells friends the show tonight is "dedicated to my mum".

🍎 In London, Ringo and Barbara visit Hyde Park where they assist in launching a £32 million Marie Curie Daffodil Appeal, a cancer fund specialising in help for nurses and assisting with medical research. For his pictures, Ringo poses with an umbrella in front of a large Help! display, made entirely from yellow daffodils. Ringo and Barbara also request that people buy a golden daffodil instead of a National Lottery ticket.

Monday March 16
🍎 After long speculation, George Martin officially retires, and to honour his achievements he throws a party this evening at his AIR Studios in London. Among his guests are Ringo and Barbara, Cilla Black and Rolf Harris. (Sky News is there to capture live the guests arriving for the party.) Also today, Echo Records in the UK release the album *George Martin – In My Life*.

Thursday March 19
🍎 Linda, with her daughter Mary, is photographed with the six-man vegetarian cycling team which she sponsors to the tune of £100,000. All the members of the team sport a shirt bearing the *Linda McCartney On Tour* logo.

March (end of the month)
🍎 At her home in Sussex, Linda poses for a series of six pictures, taken by her daughter Mary, intended for her new cookery publication entitled *Linda McCartney On Tour*. She is seen with their famous old English sheepdogs and, among others, astride her North American Appaloosa Stallion Blankit. During this period, doctors inform Linda that her cancer has now spread to her liver.

April
🍎 The scheduled release this month of Ringo's album *Vertical Man* fails to materialise when Guardian, the EMI-affiliated label who is set to distribute the album, collapses.

🍎 The restoration of Paul's old house in Forthlin Road in Liverpool, costing £47,000 of Heritage Lottery Funding, is finished and the specially chosen curator will be moving in any day now. Liverpool City Council announces that the house will eventually be open to the public from Wednesday to Sunday.

🍎 During the first week, Paul, Linda and children leave England for a holiday in America.

🍎 At the IMAX cinema in London's Trocadero, a wide-screen, high-screen, high-definition film called *Everest*, a documentary look at an attempt to climb the world's highest mountain, is currently being screened and features on the soundtrack orchestral versions of George's 'All Things Must Pass', 'Life Itself', 'This Is Love', 'Give Me Love (Give Me Peace On Earth)' and 'Here Comes The Sun' (alongside the *Live In Japan*

1991 concert version). This low-key film is screened without any advance "Harrison connection" promotions. Asked why this is so, a spokesperson for the Trocadero replies: "We've been asked not to publicise it." (For the record, the film *Everest* was premiered on March 4 and released across America on March 6, issued in Australia on March 19 and in Switzerland on March 20. Shortly after its London premiere, the film will open in Holland on April 23, Sweden on April 24 and in Belgium on May 20.)

✪ Sean Lennon gives an interview for the *New Yorker* magazine, during which he suggests that "Anybody who thinks that Mark Chapman was just some crazy guy who killed my dad for his own personal interests is insane or very naive or hasn't thought about it very clearly." Controversially, he adds, "It was in the best interests of the United States to have my dad killed. Definitely! And that worked against them because, once he died, his powers grew. They didn't get what they wanted."

Sunday April 12
✪ BBC1 in the UK broadcasts the 51-minute programme *In My Life*, a documentary on the making of George Martin's final album, featuring musical contributions by Goldie Hawn, Robin Williams and Jim Carey among others.

Monday April 13 & Tuesday April 14
✪ In Los Angeles, Ringo begins a round of press sessions to promote his new album *Vertical Man*. Also on the Tuesday, at Ringo's home in Beverly Hills, Ringo meets up again with the photographer Henry Diltz, who shoots the centrefold picture which will appear in the *Vertical Man* CD package.

Wednesday April 15
✪ During their Arizona holiday, Paul and Linda go horse riding together. As things turn out, it will be for the very last time.

Friday April 17
✪ At 5:04am (West Coast American Time), Linda McCartney, aged 56, dies from cancer in Paul's arms at their ranch home, north east of Tucson in Arizona. The news of her death is kept secret until Sunday while the location is withheld until Wednesday. Shortly after her death, Paul arranges to have her cremated and will bring her ashes back to England. Linda had bravely fought breast cancer for over two years.

Saturday April 18
✪ While Linda's tragic death remains a secret, a pre-recorded segment featuring Paul performing a unique version of 'Yesterday' merged with The Goons' 'The Ying Tong Song' is transmitted tonight on BBC2, in the UK, as part of an evening of programmes dedicated to his good friend Spike Milligan. The night is suitably titled *Spike Night*.

Sunday April 19
✪ Paul and his family arrive back in Britain and return to their farmhouse near Rye in Sussex. He immediately scatters Linda's ashes over the farm in what a close friend to the family describes as, "a quiet family occasion" involving Paul and his grieving children, Heather, Mary, Stella and James. The friend adds: "It was very moving – exactly what Linda would have wanted." Following this, Paul begins informing close friends of Linda's death, including Ringo and the comedy writer and fellow animal rights campaigner Carla Lane. Their call lasts for 45 minutes. Through his spokesman Geoff Baker, Paul tells the media of Linda's death and decides to say that she passed away on holiday in Santa Barbara, California.

At 7:44pm, Sky News, in Europe, break the news first that Linda died in California on Friday. A grief-stricken Paul also asks "anyone wishing to pay tribute to Linda should give to cancer research or animal welfare. Or the tribute that Linda would have liked best 'Go Veggie!' "

Geoff Baker speaks with great affection of Linda when he says today: "For us, her friends, the brightest light has left our lives, but she has left us a shining inspiration." He adds: "The blessing was that the end came quickly, she didn't suffer." Naturally, as news of her death begins to spread, reporters converge on the farmhouse where Paul is staying, where they face a man standing guard. "They are naturally very distressed and need some time on their own. They would like their privacy respected," he announces.

Meanwhile, the film director David Puttnam, a close friend of the McCartneys', fights back tears as he breaks news of her death at an awards ceremony in London.

Monday April 20
♦ Ringo and Barbara pay tribute to Linda by issuing, from their Monaco home, the following statement: "Both Barbara and I would like to say how sorry we are. We were privileged to have known her – her positive courage through her illness was truly inspiring. We send all our love to Paul, Heather, Mary, Stella and James. It was a blessing that she was in our lives – Ringo & Barbara."

♦ Geoff Baker announces: "Paul's tragedy of losing Linda is hitting him in waves. One minute he can cope, and the next he can't. He's devastated." He also tells of Paul's plans to issue a mini-album, comprising six unissued Linda McCartney recordings, two of which were recorded just prior to leaving for America for the last time. "Paul is determined to make sure Linda's legacy will be lasting," Baker adds. Meanwhile, the comedy writer Carla Lane reveals that Paul's son James is helping him cope with the heartbreak of losing Linda by sharing his bed. "Paul is being very brave and very positive. But Paul said that the whole family was terrified of him sleeping on his own after Linda died, so Jamie bunked in with him," Carla says. "That's just the way the family are, they are very close. Paul told me 'We will never get over this – but let's get through it.' Paul is being so very brave, at the end of the conversation he was comforting me!"

Later tonight, Linda's brother John Eastman and sisters Laura and Louise join Paul and his family in Sussex to offer their condolences. Meanwhile in New York, mourners for Linda leave bouquets of flowers on the memorial to John Lennon in Central Park.

Tuesday April 21
♦ Early this morning, Paul pens a 564-word tribute to Linda at his Sussex farmhouse.

Wednesday April 22
♦ It publicly emerges that Linda McCartney had died on Friday at their ranch in Arizona and not during their holiday in Santa Barbara, California, as the world was originally led to believe.

Thursday April 23
♦ Due to the American release today of the Columbia records film soundtrack album *Armageddon*, which features four tracks by Aerosmith, the Columbia label asks Ringo and Mercury Records to remove Steven Tyler's lead vocal on the track 'Drift Away'. Columbia fear, that with Tyler also appearing on Ringo's album, his appearance will constitute a competition.

Friday April 24
♦ At the Riverside Studios in Hammersmith, London, Julian Lennon makes a live guest appearance on the Channel 4 programme *TFI Friday*, hosted, as always, by Chris Evans. During the show Julian performs his new single 'Day After Day'.

May
♦ At the start of the month, George returns for the second time to the Mayo Clinic in America where he is given a clean bill of health. Following a tip-off, journalists catch sight of him leaving the hospital and spark new fears about his health. Within days, stations in America, including MTV and VH-1, are reporting his new cancer scare, saying that he is now suffering from "advanced lung cancer"!

♦ Paul performs a sterling rendition of the Noel Coward song 'A Room With A View', included on the EMI album *Twentieth Century Blues*, released as a tribute to the late composer, writer and actor. The album is released to raise money for the Red-Hot Aids Charitable Trust. (Paul recorded the song during early March.)

Saturday May 2
♦ At the A&M Studios in Los Angeles, additional final mastering of the *Vertical Man* album takes place. (The sessions will continue until Wednesday May 6.) In London, in Abbey Road Studio Two, Ringo, Mark and Scott Gordon, with the assistance of an ISDN telephone line connected to Tom Petty and the engineer Eric Greedy at the Village Recorders Studio in Los Angeles, record Petty's new vocal for the track 'Drift Away'. As

Ringo points out: "It's nice when you're in my position to have friends like that, who will help you out whenever you need."

Sunday May 3
❦ BBC1 in the UK repeats the 1992 BBC2 Arena documentary entitled *Behind The Scenes*, as by way of a tribute to Linda.

Monday May 4
❦ The first single from Julian Lennon's new album *Photograph Smile* is released in the UK, comprising 'Day After Day', backed with 'Don't Let Me Know'.

Tuesday May 5
❦ The case The Beatles vs. Lingasong Music opens in the High Courts of London in front of Mr. Justice Neuberger. In court is Edward "Kingsize" Taylor, who was responsible for taping The Beatles' concert back on December 31, 1962, at the Star Club in Hamburg, Germany. In evidence today he tells the court that "John Lennon gave me verbal permission to tape The Beatles' performance". Nicholas Merrimen, representing Lingasong Music, the company attempting to re-issue The Beatles' 1962 Star Club tapes, tells the court: "Mr. Taylor said he asked John Lennon and that Lennon said it was OK – as long as he got the ale in!" The case is adjourned until tomorrow when George will give evidence for the plaintiffs.

Wednesday May 6
❦ As expected, George turns up at the High Court in London. Sporting a short hair cut and wearing a grey suit, he tells reporters on his way to the courts: "I drew the short straw and was the one who had to go to court for Apple." (Ringo submitted written evidence while Paul is excused following Linda's death.) Following a brief skirmish with a photographer, George enters the packed courthouse and offers a fascinating insight into The Beatles' Hamburg years. Firstly, he is asked about Lingasong's claim that John Lennon was the leader of The Beatles and that no further permission to record them live was needed from other members of the group.

"We had a democratic thing going between us" George insists. "Everyone had to agree with everything that was done, whether it was a concert in Liverpool or to go to Hamburg." He then went on to emphasise that The Beatles' partnership was very much based on equals, telling the court how John turned to him for musical advice. "I taught John the guitar," George announced. "He had a little guitar with three strings tuned like a banjo. I had to show him all the chords. When I first met him I was very young, but so was he. He was 17 and I was maybe 14 or 15. But, by the time we were in Hamburg, I'd grown up a lot, and I could certainly hold my own against him. He was the loudest, the noisiest and the oldest. He could be wrong about something but try and win the argument just by being loud."

Turning his attention to Taylor's claim that he had The Beatles' permission to record the show that night, George states: "I have no recollection of that particular night, but I am quite certain that, to my mind, there was never any recording equipment there at all. Maybe he had it in the cupboard. Whatever he says, we didn't see it. We didn't ask him to do it, we never heard them, we never had anything to do with them – and that's the story."

Asked about what else he remembers about the Star Club, George says: "It was a really rough place, and the waiters used to let off tear-gas to get rid of the sailors if a fight started. I kept well out of it. But there were also some quite nice people who went to the club. They weren't all gangsters and transvestites – there was teenagers and art students. But by 2am on Saturday, it was hell!"

George is asked about their relationship with Teddy Taylor. "He was a leader of another group," George replies, adding: "In those days, everyone was friendly, but we only saw one another if they happened to play the same club at the same time. If we weren't, we didn't see him from one month to the next. He wasn't a friend we hung around with." George then remarked: "Even if John had given Taylor his permission to tape The Beatles' performance, that does not make it legal for the tape to be turned into an album. One drunken person recording another bunch of drunks does not constitute a business deal. It just did not happen. It certainly didn't take place in my company or my lifetime. Neither Paul nor Ringo heard it either. The only person who allegedly heard anything about it is the one who is dead; who can't actually come here and say it's a load of rubbish."

George continued: "If we had been sitting around the table and Ted Taylor was saying, 'Hey Lads, I am going to record you and I'll make this live record that will come back to haunt you for the rest of your lives', and John was saying, 'Great, you can do it', then I would have said, 'You are not recording me'. We had a record contract, and we were on a roll. The last thing we needed was one little bedroom recording to come out. The Star Club recording was the crummiest recording ever made in our name!

"There was no organised recording. It was a wild affair. We were just a whole bunch of drunken musicians grabbing guitars, and if Teddy Taylor just happened to have a tape recorder and decided to plug it in and tape us, that still doesn't constitute the right to put out a record. It's not whether he bought a pint of beer for John; it's whether people are allowed to make a recording without permission. I could go out tonight and tape Mick Jagger – but it doesn't mean I could go and sell it. The bottom line is that John didn't give permission, and even if he had, he couldn't have given it for us all. We were a democratic band."

George is also asked about various other aspects of the Beatles early career, including the sacking of The Beatles' original drummer Pete Best. "He was a loner who didn't fit in with the other Beatles, Ringo Starr was the last piece in the jigsaw puzzle."

To end his testimony, George reveals that he "maintains a healthy distance from the past. Unlike The Beatles' experts who wallow in Beatles trivia, I spend a lot of time getting the junk out of my mind through meditation, so I don't know or remember – I don't *want* to know or remember – every detail, because it is trivial pursuit."

The case was adjourned.

George's arrival, as well as departure from the courts, is featured heavily on the BBC as well as on Sky News in Europe.

Thursday May 7
* George's impressive court appearance yesterday is reflected heavily in the national newspapers, with headlines ranging from: "We Were A Bunch Of Drunk Musicians Grabbing Guitars" (the *Sun*) To "Beatles Want Bootleg Record Banned" (the *Daily Telegraph*).
* Sean Lennon plays his first solo concert in Britain and indeed one of his first solo concerts anywhere in the world tonight, when he performs at the cramped Camden Falcon rock 'n' roll pub in North London.

Friday May 8
* Today in the High Court, following a day of deliberations, Mr Justice Neuberger passes judgement in favour of The Beatles' in their court battle against Lingasong Music, who are therefore immediately barred from re-issuing the 1962 Star Club, Hamburg tapes. He also demands that the tapes be given to The Beatles' solicitor and all The Beatles' legal and court costs be paid by Lingasong Music Ltd. Lingasong, who are also liable to pay the Beatles money for damages, also agree to withdraw from sale all unsold copies of the *Star Club* CD. Mr Justice Neuberger summed up his judgement by concluding: "George's evidence is convincing while Edward (Teddy) Taylor's comments to the court had been confused and inconsistent."

Sunday May 10
* Ringo attempts to shoot a promotional video for the song 'La De Da' at New York's Shea Stadium, in between the innings of the New York Mets' baseball game, but unfortunately, due to heavy rain, he changes his plans and instead takes to the New York streets where, along with the teen sensations Hanson, and various passers-by, which include his daughter Lee, he films a video sitting on a bench holding an umbrella in the pouring rain. (The video, when edited, includes footage of Ringo and his band performing the song in the studio as well as footage of Paul singing the chorus, shot at his studio home in Sussex on Monday September 29, 1997 – see entry.) The first clips of this video appear on MTV Europe on May 19 and in America on *Entertainment Tonight* on May 25.

Tuesday May 12
* Ringo and his band, The Roundheads, perform a VH-1 *Storytellers* warm-up show at the Bottom Line Club in New York City. The show marks the first time that Ringo had

performed 'Don't Pass Me By' and 'Octopus's Garden' in public. Back at The Village Recorders Studio in LA, Greg Calbi is remastering the new version of 'Drift Away', featuring Tom Petty's vocal.

Wednesday May 13
 Ringo and his band record their edition of the VH-1 *Storytellers* show at the Bottom Line Club in New York, before a specially invited audience which includes the teen group Hanson. For the 45-minute programme (first transmitted in America on June 28 and in Europe on November 8), the group performs: 'With A Little Help From My Friends' (snippet), 'Back Off Boogaloo', 'Don't Pass Me By' (his first ever solo performance, featuring an introduction on the piano played by Ringo), 'It Don't Come Easy', 'Octopus's Garden', 'La De Da', 'The King Of Broken Hearts' and 'Love Me Do'.

Thursday May 14
 In the States, Mercury Records distribute the EPK (Electronic Video Press Kit) for Ringo's album *Vertical Man*.

Monday May 18
 The American showbiz programme *Entertainment Tonight* broadcasts an interview with both Paul and Ringo, recorded during the recent *Vertical Man* recording sessions at Paul's home studios in Sussex. (The feature was originally scheduled for May 14 but was cancelled due to a rearranged tribute programme on the death of Frank Sinatra.)
 Sean Lennon's album *Into The Sun* (previously titled *Photosynthesis* when finished in January of this year) is released on the Beastie Boys Grand Royal label. The release clashes with a new offering from Julian Lennon, his fifth album entitled *Photograph Smile*, appearing on the Music From Another Room label, a company formed by Julian and his co-producer Bob Rose.

Tuesday May 19
 Rhino Home Video in America releases a five-video box set comprising John and Yoko's five-show appearance as co-hosts of *The Mike Douglas Show*, transmitted daily between Monday February 14 and Friday February 18. (For a full index of the shows, see relevant 1972 entries.) Accompanying the set is a hardbound, 48-page, specially numbered book, featuring a visual record of the five shows, captured by resident TV photographer Michael Leshnov. "John and Yoko were on the right track, just way ahead of their time," comments Mike Douglas in 1998.

Wednesday May 20
 Ringo videotapes an appearance on the programme *Live With Regis & Kathie Lee*, where, following an interview, he joins his group to perform 'La De Da' to close the show. (The show is transmitted on July 3.)

Thursday May 21
 Ringo and his band record an appearance on the, normally live, ABC TV show *The View*. (The programme is broadcast on June 17.) During the show, Ringo performs the songs 'La De Da', 'Photograph' and 'With A Little Help From My Friends'.

Friday May 22
 Ringo and Barbara are seen at the annual Cannes Film Festival in the South of France. (They had actually flown into France the previous evening, and had spent the evening at Elton John's hotel.) Today Ringo attends the auction in aid of Elizabeth Taylor's AIDS charity, held in the Moulin De Mougins restaurant, where, during the afternoon, he jumps on stage to join Elton John and actress Sharon Stone, when a millionaire in the audience pledges £60,000 if the trio will perform the song 'Great Balls Of Fire'. With excitement at fever pitch, and with Ringo still perched behind his drums, another well-off member of the gathering offers £90,000 if the trio will perform 'Twist And Shout', which they duly oblige. Thankfully television cameras, including Sky News, are there to capture this historic one-off performance and broadcast brief highlights as part of their daily Cannes Film Festival roundup of events.

Sunday May 31

 To promote his forthcoming short visit to Europe, Ringo is interviewed in Germany for the WDR programme *Gute Nacht Gottschaulk*. To accompany the interview, a live All Starr band clip of them performing 'It Don't Come Easy' is also transmitted.

June

 An exhibition of Linda's pictures runs in New York, in tandem with a show currently on display in Switzerland.

 Promotional interviews by Ringo for *Vertical Man* this month appear in the publications *New Yorker* and *USA Today*.

Monday June 1

 Ringo's single 'La De Da' is released to American radio stations.

Saturday June 6

 VH-1 in Europe announces the results of their "Artists Top 100" poll, a survey where a wide selection of top contemporary recording artists choose their all-time favourite recording act. To no one's great surprise, The Beatles come out on top. For The Beatles' chart placing of number one, the station plays the second version of the 1996 video for 'Real Love'.

Monday June 8

 At 8:30pm, a 90-minute memorial service for Linda McCartney is held at Saint Martin-In-The-Fields Church, in London's Trafalgar Square. Paul arrives in his grey Mercedes with Heather, Mary, Stella and James. Ringo comes with Barbara while George, attempting anonymity in his green anorak and trying to keep dry from the heavy rain, arrives with his wife Olivia and their son Dhani. The order of service is as follows:

MUSIC: 'Mull Of Kintyre' – played by piper John McGeachy, Pipe Major of the Campbeltown Pipe Band who performed on the original Wings single.

WELCOME: By the Rev. Clare Herbert.

HYMN: All Things Bright And Beautiful (choir and congregation).

ADDRESS: By Ken Townsend (former head of Abbey Road Studios).

THE BRODSKY QUARTET PERFORMS SONGS WRITTEN BY SIR PAUL FOR LINDA:
'The Lovely Linda' (from the album *McCartney*)
'You Gave Me The Answer' (from *Venus And Mars*)
'Maybe I'm Amazed'
'Warm And Beautiful' (from *Wings At The Speed Of Sound*)

READING: Joanna Lumley reads Death Is Nothing At All by Henry Scott Holland (1847–1918), Canon of St. Paul's Cathedral.

Students of the Liverpool Institute of The Performing Arts sing 'Blackbird' (from the LP *The Beatles* – known as the *White Album*) and the gospel song 'His Eye Is On The Sparrow'.

ADDRESS: Brian Clarke (friend of Linda and the architectural artist with whom she recently collaborated on a revival of stained-glass photography).

THE BRODSKY QUARTET PERFORM SONGS WRITTEN BY SIR PAUL FOR LINDA:
'Golden Earth Girl' (from the album *Off The Ground*)
'Dear Boy' (from *Ram*)
'Calico Skies' (from *Flaming Pie*)
'My Love'

READING: David Bailey reads 'Lyric' by Spike Milligan.

ADDRESS: By Carla Lane.

HYMN: 'Let It Be' (choir and congregation)

ADDRESS: By Pete Townshend.

Students from LIPA and the choir of St. Martin-In-The-Fields perform 'Celebration' from Sir Paul McCartney's *Standing Stone*.

PRAYER

ADDRESS: By Sir Paul McCartney.

SONG: 'Linda', a song by Jack Lawrence written for Linda when she was a child. Sir Paul made the song into a 45rpm single recording, on which he sang, as a surprise gift for Linda's 45th birthday.

BLESSING

During his address, Paul describes Linda as: "One of the kindest people who made you feel good to be yourself. I'm privileged to have been her lover for 30 years. Except for one enforced absence, we never spent a single night apart."

To the astonishment of the congregation Paul broke off his address to lead two Shetland ponies, called Schoo and Tinsel, which he had given Linda as a Christmas present, up the aisle of the church. "She'd have loved this," said Paul, before continuing: "She was the toughest of women who didn't give a damn what other people thought. She was unique and the world is a better place for having known her. Her message of love will live on in our hearts forever. I love you Linda."

Celebrities who attended the service include Spike Milligan, Joanna Lumley, George Martin, Elton John, Sting, Peter Gabriel, Neil Tennant (of The Pet Shop Boys), Tracy Ullman, David Gilmour (of Pink Floyd), Billy Joel and Michael Parkinson.

The service is covered in the UK by Sky News, BBC, ITN, Channel 4 and Channel 5 as well as appearing on numerous television stations around the world. Witnessing the arrival of these celebrities and various friends of the McCartneys are over 4,000 fans and animal rights protesters who had congregated in the streets around Trafalgar Square.

Wednesday June 10
 The 45-minute *Vertical Man* American radio special is syndicated across America.

Monday June 15
 In the States, on the eve of the American release of his new album, Ringo appears live on the top-rated NBC TV chat show *The Tonight Show* with Jay Leno. Also joining him on the show is the actress Marilu Henner and Willie Barcena.

Tuesday June 16
 Ringo's first album in six years, *Vertical Man*, is released today in America. The thirteen tracks which appear on the release include 'One', 'What In The . . . World' (featuring Sir Paul on bass), 'Mindfield', 'King Of The Broken Hearts' (George on slide guitar and production by Sir George Martin), 'Love Me Do' (Ringo re-records The Beatles first single from 1962), 'Vertical Man', 'Drift Away', 'I Was Walkin' ', 'La De Da' (Paul on backing vocals), 'Without Understanding', 'I'll Be Fine Anywhere' (George on guitar), 'Puppet' and 'I'm Yours'.

The album's producer Geoff Emerick describes it as: "Ringo's *Sgt. Pepper*. He's got 13 number ones on it."

Four additional tracks ('Sometimes', 'Mr. Doubleitup', 'Everyday' and 'Good News') were recorded and will appear on various up-coming single B-sides, including the American retail chain Best Buy who issues a sampler single of three of these songs if you pre-order the album. This very limited CD is only issued at twenty copies per store. The UK release of *Vertical Man* takes place on August 3, brought forward from its original date of August 10.

Wednesday June 17
 In what turns out to be a very busy day promoting his new album, Ringo appears three times on the American media. Namely, live (for 45 minutes) on the Howard Stern radio show, *The View* (pre-taped on May 21) and in a pre-recorded 44-minute interview on

CNN's *Larry King Live*. This is in addition to an AOL (American On Line) Internet interview this evening between 7 and 9pm. In this he answers questions about the VH-1 *Storytellers* programme, working with the teen group Hanson, being a grandfather and George's recent cancer scare. "I had lunch with him . . . he was fine," Ringo replies. He ends the two-hour session by saying (or rather writing): "I love you all. Peace, love and bananas . . . good night."

Thursday June 18

✦ VH-1 in Europe celebrate Paul's 56th birthday by declaring the station *Paul McCartney Day* with repeat screenings of the 1997 *Town Hall Meeting, Ten Of The Best, Paul McCartney's Greatest Hits* plus a revised repeat of the 1997 VH-1 To 1 interview at Abbey Road Studios.

Friday June 19

✦ Sean Lennon makes his début on CBS TV's *Late Show With David Letterman* from the historic Ed Sullivan Theater in New York City.

Monday June 22

✦ The American memorial service for Linda McCartney takes place at the Riverside Church on Riverside Drive in New York. Among those in attendance are Chrissie Hynde, Paul Simon, Twiggy and Neil Young. During the service, Twiggy reads a poem by William Cooper, which includes the poignant line "heaven is reflected in her face". The Harlem Boys Choir sing 'Blackbird' and 'His Eye Is On The Sparrow', and The Lorma Mar string quartet performs 'The Lovely Linda' and 'My Love'. Just as at the London service two weeks ago, the congregation sings 'Let It Be'. The church, situated on Manhattan's Upper West Side, is filled with 45,000 flowers and eight blown-up colour pictures of Linda. Paul tells the congregation: "It's a very sad time for us all, but she wouldn't want it to be sad, but to count our blessings, as there are so many of them. We have four gorgeous kids and she lives on in all of them, and through them she's here. I was so lucky to be the one she chose. She was a friend, a beautiful friend to so many people. You know I love her and you all love her too – that's why we're here tonight."

✦ Sadly, much of the publicity surrounding the service dwells on the fact that Paul did not invite Yoko and her son Sean to the ceremony, although they sent a bouquet of flowers. A spokesman for John's widow remarks: "She was saddened by it." (Reports on the service are featured on numerous American news bulletins, including, among others, *Access Hollywood* and *Entertainment Tonight*.) A spokesman for Paul announces: "It was something that had been in the back of Paul's mind for a while, because of Lin' coming from New York. There were a lot of people over there who couldn't get to the first one."

Thursday June 25

✦ Sean Lennon plays only his second English concert when he appears, supporting Money Mark, at the Astoria in West London. The show is a 7pm start.

Friday June 26

✦ Almost a year to the day since Paul appeared on the show, Ringo becomes the second Beatle to appear on Channel 4's tea-time show *TFI Friday*, transmitted live (between 6:01 and 6:59pm, repeated later this evening between 11:36pm and 12:33am) from the Riverside Studios in Hammersmith, London. Ringo appears in a brief interview only but promises to perform live on the show when it returns in September, a promise he fails to keep. The segment ends just as with Paul a year ago, with Ringo joining the host Chris Evans on a speedboat for a ride down the River Thames to visit their (fictional) "Beatle Cave". The programme itself ends with the back of someone who is supposed to be George, emphasised by a sitar which just happens to be propped against the wall.

Saturday June 27

✦ The real life George, meanwhile, is to be found sitting at home in Henley watching the Eurosport World Cup coverage of Italy beating Norway 1–0 (he was cheering on Norway), when a reporter from the *News Of The World* visits his mansion. The interview is published the following day.

Sunday June 28

 A two-page feature "Beatle George: My Fight To Beat Cancer" appears in today's *News Of The World*, in which he talks about his cancer ordeal and announces that he's making a new album. When reporter Dennis Rice asks him if the events of the last year might be reflected in his new songs, George replies: "Maybe I'll record a track called 'Radiation Therapy'". (Further reports on George's cancer scares appear in the *Sun* and the *Daily Star* the following day.)

Monday June 29

 George issues a further statement about his cancer scare, saying: "The cancerous lump (which was removed from his throat) is entirely down to smoking. This is more of a warning than anything else."

July

 In the UK, Ringo causes controversy when, during an interview published this month in *The Big Issue*, he claims that: "All drugs should be legalised!" Also this month, Ringo continues with further UK *Vertical Man* promotional interviews but requests that all journalists wishing to meet him must not "smoke, drink alcohol, or eat onions or garlic for at least one hour before the session". In reply to these requests, a reporter for the *Evening Standard* remarks: "He has yet to make his position clear on salami!"

Friday July 3

 Ringo's appearance on *Live With Regis & Kathie Lee* (actually recorded on May 20) is transmitted in America. Appearing with Ringo is Joshua Jackson and Andrew Keegan.

Saturday July 4

 A clip from Ringo's 'La De Da' video is premiered across the UK on the *ITV Chart Show*.

Sunday July 5

 Julian Lennon appears at the star-studded Prince's Trust Concert at London's Hyde Park, alongside artists such as Tom Jones and All Saints.

Wednesday July 8

 Further promotions for *Vertical Man* take place in America when a brief pre-recorded interview with Ringo by Denis Michaels is included in today's edition of the CNN programme *Showbiz Today*. (The programme is also screened throughout Europe via cable and satellite.)

Thursday July 9

 George is in the audience tonight during Ravi Shankar's annual concert at the Barbican Centre in London.

Sunday July 12

 VH-1 in Europe broadcasts a short, pre-recorded, interview with Ringo promoting *Vertical Man* on the programme *Talk Music*. (The programme is repeated the following day, as well as on Thursday July 16.)

Wednesday July 15

 In the UK, rumours abound that Paul, George, Ringo as well as George Martin will be attending a bash celebrating Liverpool music, held in the dining rooms of the House of Commons in London, an event organised by Peter Kilfoyle, the Liverpudlian cabinet office minister.

 At the BBC TV Centre in London, Ringo appears live on the BBC1 show *National Lottery Live*, where he starts the lottery balls rolling and then, to close the show, he and his band mime a version of 'La De Da'.

Monday July 20

 At the BBC TV Centre, Wood Lane, London, Julian Lennon appears as a guest on the late night BBC2 talk show *Ruby*, hosted by the American comedienne Ruby Wax.

Tuesday July 21

◆ Paul's former Liverpool home at 20 Forthlin Road, is finally unveiled to the nation's media. The ITV breakfast show GMTV gets the first glimpse of the results in a live broadcast from the property this morning. In keeping with The Beatles' flavour, the programme also features a pre-recorded interview with Ringo, who again promotes his album *Vertical Man*. (The unveiling of Paul's former home also features heavily on the BBC, ITN and Channels 4 and 5 news bulletins throughout the day.) The house will be open to the public on Wednesday July 29, staying open from Wednesday to Saturday every week until October 31. The curator of this historic showpiece museum is the 50-year-old Beatles fanatic John Halliday.

Wednesday July 22

◆ BBC2 in the UK screen the programme *The Birthplace Of The Beatles*, a fascinating 25-minute programme which focuses on the history of the renovation, by the National Trust, of Paul's former home in Liverpool.

Saturday July 25

◆ Ringo makes a live appearance on the BBC Radio 2 programme *The Steve Wright Show*, transmitted from the BBC studios adjacent to Portland Place, London.

Monday July 27

◆ All of Ringo's recent promotional activities in the UK seem to have been in vain when Mercury Records announce that they will not, after all, release his single 'La De Da'.

Tuesday July 28

◆ In America, the 135-minute PMI home video *Ringo & His 4th All-Starr Band from Pine Knob Michigan*, recorded at the venue on May 30, 1997, is released on home video.

Thursday July 30

◆ It is announced that The Beatles' 1964 big screen début *A Hard Day's Night* is to be re-released to cinemas next year to celebrate its 35th anniversary. This newly restored print will include footage never seen before and a soundtrack that has been digitally re-recorded. Walter Shenson, the film's producer, says: "It will be a hit with new fans when it is shown in the UK next year."

◆ After a long-standing dispute, it's revealed that Paul has secretly paid Lily Evans, the widow of Beatles' roadie Mal, £100,000 for the handwritten lyrics to 'With A Little Help From My Friends'.

Sunday August 2

◆ In the UK, Paul appears on the front page of the *People* newspaper in a story about his plea to save monkeys.

Monday August 3 & Tuesday August 4

◆ Ringo appears as a guest on the American E! Network TV programme *The Howard Stern Show*. (Part two is aired on the station the following day, August 4.)

◆ In England, George appears completely unannounced on the BBC Radio 2 programme hosted by Paul Jones, the former lead singer of Manfred Mann. During his brief appearance, George displays an encyclopaedic knowledge of the history of blues recordings.

Wednesday August 5

◆ In his first major interview since Linda's death in April, Paul announces that he will continue with Linda's animal rights crusades. He speaks to two publications, *Viva Life* and *Animal Times*, run by animal campaigners: "Animal rights is too good an idea for the next century to be suppressed. I think it's time we got nice." He then touched upon his wife Linda, admitting that he is still "mourning her loss".

* * *

Ringo & His Fourth All-Starr Band
1998 Summer Tour
Friday August 7 – Saturday September 5

Ringo and his fourth All-Starr Band, featuring the same line-up of musicians who made up the 1997 tour, perform concerts at:

The Helsingin Jaahalli, Helsinki, Finland (Friday August 7)
Festival, Zurich, Switzerland (Saturday August 8)
Skanderborg, Festivale, Skanderborg in Denmark (Sunday August 9)
Freilichtbuehne, Killesburg, Stuttgart in Germany (Wednesday August 12)
Theatreplatz, Chemnitz, Germany (Thursday August 13)
Luxembourg City, Luxembourg (Saturday August 15 – concert cancelled, allegedly over a disagreement with the promoter)
Marktrock Festival, Leuven, Belgium (Sunday August 16)
Expo, Lisbon, Portugal (Tuesday August 18)
The Point, Dublin, Ireland (Thursday August 20)
The Shepherds Bush Empire, London (Friday August 21. A planned second concert on Saturday August 22 fails to materialise.)
Moscow Sports Complex, Moscow, Russia (Tuesday August 25)
Jubilee Complex, St. Petersburg, Russia (Wednesday August 26)
Sporting Club, Monte Carlo (Friday August 28, Saturday August 29 and Sunday August 30)
Gruga Halle, Essen, Germany (Tuesday September 1)
Stadtpark, Hamburg, Germany (Wednesday September 2)
Museumshof, Bonn, Germany (Thursday September 3)
Wintershall '98 Rock Extravaganza, Kent (Saturday September 5)

Their standard set for each concert is as follows: 'It Don't Come Easy', 'Act Naturally', 'Whiskey Train' (Gary Brooker), 'Show Me The Way' (Peter Frampton), 'Sunshine Of Your Love' (Jack Bruce), 'Love Me Do', 'I'm The Greatest', 'La De Da', 'All Right Now' (Simon Kirke), 'Boys', 'Do You Do' (Peter Frampton), 'White Room' (Jack Bruce), 'A Whiter Shade Of Pale' (Gary Brooker), 'Yellow Submarine' and 'With A Little Help From My Friends'.

Saturday August 15
The German news channel N-TV transmits a pre-recorded interview with Ringo to talk about the recent and forthcoming German All-Starr Band concerts. The feature also includes a live clip of 'It Don't Come Easy' taped at Theatreplatz Chemnitz on Thursday August 13.

Wednesday August 19
Ringo is spotted in Chelsea, London, buying a pair of army trousers. The *Sun* newspaper runs a story telling how the current all-girl hit group All Saints snubbed Ringo who wanted to meet them during their current London rehearsals.

Friday August 21
Backstage at tonight's concert at The Shepherds Bush Empire in London, Ringo gives an interview for the Australian Channel 9 programme *Today Show*, an item transmitted on Thursday July 27.

Tuesday August 25
Ringo's live concert appearance at the Moscow Sports Complex tonight marks the first live appearance by any of The Beatles in Russia.

Saturday September 5
Tonight's concert in Wintershall, Kent, is part of the Wintershall '98 open-air rock extravaganza, which is billed as a secret low-key "black collar and tie" concert in aid of a Lung Cancer Charity. Joining Ringo and the All-Starrs tonight are Rory Bremner, Roger Taylor (of Queen) and Bob Geldof, who sings a version of John's 'Working Class Hero'. Also joining Ringo tonight during their abbreviated set is Genesis guitarist Mike Rutherford.

Sunday September 6
Ringo and his band fly back to America.

Monday September 7
Ringo and his band appear on the annual American televised *Jerry Lewis Muscular Dystrophy Telethon*.

* * *

Saturday August 8
◆ In the UK, in his first major interview since Linda's death, Paul talks to the *Express* newspaper.

Sunday August 23
◆ Paul appears again in a Sunday newspaper. In today's edition of the *News Of The World*, he hits out at the pig farmers.
◆ In London, Julian makes a pre-recorded appearance on the VH-1 morning show *The Sunday Brunch*.

Monday August 24
◆ The *Sun* newspaper publishes, on its front page, a world exclusive under the headline: "I'm Lennon's Lost Sister", naming 53-year-old Ingrid Pedersen as John Lennon's long lost sister. An emotional Ingrid, given up for adoption as a baby by John's mother Julia, tells the *Sun*: "I'm just so sorry John is not here anymore. I'd have loved nothing more than to hug him and say, 'Hi bruv, gissa kiss!'" The newspaper requests John's other sisters, Julia and Jacqui, to contact them.

Tuesday August 25
◆ The *Sun* continues its coverage of John's lost sister Ingrid by publishing a story about her visit to well-known Beatle tourist spots in Liverpool, such as Strawberry Fields and Penny Lane. Ingrid also speaks about her sadness in discovering her mother's grave unmarked and overgrown. "The mother of John Lennon deserves better than this! I'm disgusted," she tells the paper. Meanwhile another of John's half-sisters Julia, aged 51, contacts the *Sun* and says: "I can't wait to meet Ingrid. It has been a very emotional day. You can imagine my feelings." John's first wife Cynthia also contacts the paper from her home in France. "John was obsessed with finding his long-lost sister Ingrid. He was convinced he would find her. Maybe if he'd lived he would have done," Cynthia says, concluding: "It's a miracle she's turned up now."

Thursday August 27
◆ There's bad news for Ringo when his album *Vertical Man* crashes out of the UK charts after selling just 2,000 copies since its release. (Its highest chart position was only number 85, just one week after its release.) A source close to Ringo announces: "He is obviously more than a little disappointed with the sales. Ringo put a lot of time and effort into the album and there was an array of talent on it too. But clearly this wasn't enough. It seems the public just didn't like it and it shows that not everything connected to the fab four is going to be popular and profitable."
◆ Meanwhile, the *Sun* reveals that a denim jacket, worn by John on the night he was thrown out of the Troubadour club in Los Angeles on Tuesday March 12, 1974 (see entry and picture section), has a reserve price of £14,000 at a London auction.

Friday August 28
◆ Four days after the appearance of John's lost sister; a trainee reporter from BBC Radio Merseyside meets an unnamed German art student who claims that she is John's illegitimate daughter. This dubious 32-year-old who wears round glasses and sports a floppy Beatles mop-top haircut, produces a birth certificate which bears the name of her father as John Lennon. She tells the reporter: "I was born in Hamburg in 1965, having been fathered by Lennon in January or February of that year, while his wife Cynthia was skiing in the Alps." John's Uncle Charlie Lennon, who breaks the story, says: "When she

leaves here she will say 'Give us a kiss Uncle Charlie' – I'm her Uncle Charlie, no messing." The Beatles' first manager Allan Williams, when told of this story says: "Her claims are rubbish. Lennon was in Switzerland when she was conceived." Meanwhile, Steve of The Beatles Shop in Mathews Street, Liverpool, storms: "The woman is not welcome in the shop and she knows it. As far as anyone who has anything to do with The Beatles in Liverpool is concerned, this woman is *persona non grata!*"

Saturday August 29
 Back in Hamburg, Germany, the mysterious woman who claimed yesterday to be the illegitimate daughter of John, is named as Kristina Hagel. She tells a *News Of The World* reporter that she was conceived as a result of a one-night stand between John and her mother Marion in an Alpine hotel room 33 years ago. Again she produces a birth certificate which names John as her father. A few hours later the *News Of The World* investigators obtain another copy of the birth certificate from the same register in Hamburg. This certificate makes no mention of John being her natural father, naming instead "worker Karl August Egon Hagel".

Tuesday September 1 (until Saturday September 5)
 John's erotic lithographs briefly go on display for the first time in almost 30 years at London's Gallery 27 in Cork Street. A spokesman for the exhibition remarks: "I do not foresee any problems with the police this time around. Things have changed quite a lot in 30 years!"

Thursday September 3
 In the States, at a press conference in Los Angeles, California, Capitol Records announces the release of the forthcoming 4-CD box set entitled *John Lennon Anthology*. They announce that the set is scheduled for worldwide release on November 3.

Sunday September 6
 The *Sunday Mail* newspaper publishes the results of the poll "The All Time Top 1,000 Albums", from the book of the same name, which is published tomorrow. The Beatles are placed at number one with *Revolver*, number two with *Sgt. Pepper's*, number three with *The Beatles* (the *White Album*), number five with *Abbey Road* and, at number 20 with *Rubber Soul*. The poll is based on the views of 200,000 people aged between nine and 62 on both sides of the Atlantic. (A further report on the poll appears in tomorrow's edition of the *Daily Mail*.)

Wednesday September 9
 The culmination of the traditional MPL promoted Buddy Holly Week takes the form of a National Rock 'N' Roll Dance Championship concert at The Empire in Leicester Square, London. Paul is in attendance but declines to take part in the end of show finale.

Thursday September 10
 VH-1 Europe hosts a press launch for their upcoming 20-part series *Ed Sullivan Rock 'n' Roll Classics*, at the Atlantic Bar & Grill, in Glasshouse Street, London. (The Beatles feature in three of the compilation shows, which is due to begin transmission on Friday October 9.) This ends a 21-month attempt by the station to screen this classic series.

Friday September 11
 Yoko issues a press release announcing her feelings about the upcoming 4-CD *John Lennon Anthology* box set.

Saturday September 12
 In the UK, the *Daily Mail* newspaper publishes the results of its "Top Ten Voices" poll, conducted from the opinions of 175 top recording stars and performers. John is placed at number four while Paul appears at number 13. Aretha Franklin is voted number one.
 While Paul's former home in Forthlin Road, Liverpool has been renovated at great expense with National Lottery money, a report in today's edition of *The Look* (free with the *Mirror* newspaper), features a report on Ringo's former home in Admiral Grove in The Dingle, Liverpool and George's former childhood dwelling in Upton Grove, Speke,

in Liverpool. The occupant of the latter property, Edna Kermode, who took over residence in 1962, remarks: "I didn't know George Harrison used to live here until I moved in. We've turned the house inside out because it was a mess! The wallpaper was hanging off all over the place and I don't think the Harrisons had much idea on how to decorate."

Sunday September 13
 Julian appears in a pre-recorded interview on the VH-1 Europe programme *Talk Music*.

Wednesday September 16
 The first of a special two-day Sotheby's sale takes place at the Hard Rock Cafe in London. The highlight is Paul's notebook featuring his original draft lyrics to the 1968 song 'Hey Jude'. The book, which also contains the lyrics to 'All You Need Is Love', is bought for £115,000 by the *Hollyoaks* actress Davina Murphy's father for her 22nd birthday. Other Beatles-related items on offer include Ringo's original customised 1965 Mini-Cooper S. (The second day of the sale takes place at the normal Sotheby's premises when the wardrobe of Geri Halliwell, formerly Ginger Spice, is put up for auction.)

Friday September 18
 The third episode of the current series of BBC2's *Rock Family Trees* focuses on the rise of The Mersey Sound, featuring Gerry And The Pacemakers, The Big Three, The Merseybeats, The Searchers and, of course, briefly The Beatles.

Saturday September 19
 Today's edition of the *Sun* newspaper features, on its front page, an exclusive story, revealing that Mel B (Sporty) and Victoria (Posh) of the Spice Girls have turned vegetarian as a tribute to Linda McCartney. They tell how they had contacted Paul's office in London and asked for advice on giving up meat and were sent a selection of Linda's cookbooks, including *Home Cooking* and *Linda's Kitchen*. A source close to the girls said Paul was "chuffed" the girls had taken his advice and sent all four of The Spice Girls a copy of Linda's new book *On Tour*. The *Sun* also reveals that Paul is teaming up with Pretenders' star Chrissie Hynde in organising a star-studded world tour as a tribute to Linda. They will call upon other acts, including George and Ringo, who support veggie causes. Other artists, including Elvis Costello, Lenny Kravitz, R.E.M. and Blur, are rumoured to be joining the shows, likely to be called The On Tour Shows. A source close to Paul says: "Chrissie was close friends with Linda and the tour was her idea. Paul thinks its a great idea and knows it could raise a lot of money for groups Linda supported. It will keep her memory alive and is just what she would have wanted. George and Ringo are keen but it is likely to be part of some sort of supergroup. The money-making potential for Linda's favourite charities is huge."

Monday September 21
 The hype surrounding the release of the *John Lennon Anthology* continues today in America, as Capitol Records announce the full listing of the tracks to be featured on the four CDs.
 In the UK, The Fireman, Paul's secret project with the producer Youth, releases the album entitled *Rushes*, on Hydra records through EMI. The press release to accompany the album reads: "The Fireman brings bison for trancing in the streets. The Fireman understands darsh walls and emerdeen sky. Do you? The Fireman knows a lemon's peal. And the power of the equinox." The track listing for *Rushes* is: 'Watercolour Guitars', 'Paloverde', 'Auraveda', 'Fluid', 'Appletree Cinnabar Amber', 'Bison', '7am', 'Fluid', 'Bison' (extended).

Wednesday September 23
 A pre-taped interview with Paul is broadcast on the station BBC Radio Merseyside.

Thursday September 24
 On what would have been Linda's 57th birthday, Paul releases the Linda McCartney cookbook *On Tour*.

Saturday September 26

 At the small 12th Century parish church of St. Peter and St. Paul in Peasmarsh, East Sussex, Paul attends the wedding of his 27-year-old daughter Mary to television producer Alistair Donald, her partner of three years. Mary's sisters Stella, who designed her wedding dress, and Heather are bridesmaids. In attendance are 100 close friends, who had arrived in a coach. Following the private 40-minute ceremony, Paul chauffeurs the couple away from the church in a vintage Rolls Royce and ignores pleas to speak to the waiting reporters.

Sunday September 27

 The *News Of The World* publishes a story about Ringo's gardener Kenny Hockley who has been caught selling drugs from a greenhouse in the grounds of Ringo's £2 million mansion.

 The ITV network screens the documentary *Clive James Meets The Super Models*, which features Paul, Linda, Ringo and Barbara backstage at Stella McCartney's Paris fashion show on October 15, 1997 (see entry for more on that event).

Wednesday September 30

 George sues the publishers Random House over an alleged libel in their book *All Dressed Up: The Sixties And The Counter Culture*, written by Jonathan Green. George is seeking £100,000 in damages over an allegation that he accepted sexual favours in exchange for a donation to charity. (See entry for Tuesday January 12, 1999.)

October

 Capitol Records in America preview the forthcoming *John Lennon Anthology* by releasing as part of a special Internet website, four full-length tracks off the album, namely 'I'm Losing You', 'Oh My Love', 'Watching The Wheels' and 'Sean's In The Sky'. The site also displays the *Anthology* artwork to accompany the release and gives a full track listing of the four CDs.

Friday October 2

 Paul attends a promotional party for his new Fireman album *Rushes* at EMI's Abbey Road Studios Studio Two. Dressed in a yellow rain hat, a black balaclava, sunglasses and headphones, he appears behind a record deck spinning discs and playing keyboards in front of a large psychedelic backdrop complete with a couch, candles and coloured lights. The get-together also forms a part of a special Fireman webcast Internet show, in which Paul appears in person, answering questions and playing snatches of the new album. Fans are requested to send e-mail questions to The Fireman, which are answered by the girl from the *Rushes* cover (who this time remains clothed) who sits next to a silent Paul on the couch. This strange spectacle is notable for the bizarre answers that fans receive during the show. One fan asks: "What inspired you to do this album?" The answer: "Night skies, flowing streams and whipped cream fire extinguishers." Another asks: "How did The Fireman get his name?" The reply: "The Fireman is no nickname – simply a warm place in the head!" Eventually fans start asking equally strange questions, such as: "How is your belly for spots?" The response: "The Fireman's belly is clear and facing towards a bright future."

Anyone unsure that the figure beneath the heavy disguise is actually Paul is left in no doubt when, at the end of the sitting, he blows his cover by giving his familiar thumbs up gesture, before thanking everyone for taking part. The broadcast ends with a note, which reads: "The Fireman Loves You".

Saturday October 3

 BBC Radio Two broadcasts a special 40th anniversary tribute to the programme *Saturday Club*. Included in the broadcast is a Beatles performance of 'Twist And Shout', originally transmitted on August 24, 1963.

Monday October 5

 With a month still to go before its official release, the American web site Hollywood & Vine previews, on its pages, four tracks to be released on the CD box set *John Lennon Anthology*, scheduled for issue on November 3.

Friday October 9

In America, to coincide with what would have been John's 58th birthday, VH-1, at 6:30pm, broadcasts the world premiere video featuring an alternative take of his song 'Working Class Hero' as featured on the *John Lennon Anthology* box set. Also today, John's birthday celebrations continue when Yoko, alongside the Lord Mayor of Liverpool, dedicates a tree in honour of him in the Strawberry Fields area of Central Park in New York. During the ceremony, the Mayor presents Yoko with the Freedom of the City award, which was awarded posthumously to John in 1984, but was never officially presented.

Saturday October 10

In Germany, Ringo and his band appear on the ZDF German TV variety show *Wetten Dass,* where they mime a performance of 'La De Da'. Ringo also takes part in a game show where a young Beatles fan is challenged to name Beatles song titles from only the briefest snatch of the song's lyrics.

Sunday October 11

The E! Network in America transmits a two-hour special entitled *John Lennon – His Final Days.*

Monday October 12

Today's 43rd Woman Of The Year lunch, at the Savoy Hotel in London, is in honour of Linda, who is honoured with an empty chair. Paul sends to every guest present a floral tribute and a message that reads: "Linda would have been chuffed at this honour", jokingly adding, "It is a shame that us blokes can't go." A spokesman for the event remarks to reporters: "Linda could have been a lady of leisure, but she pursued her own career and ideals. She was very much in the spirit of what we are celebrating."

Wednesday October 14

At a highly acclaimed fashion show in Paris, Stella McCartney dedicates her new range of spring clothes to her late mother Linda. She says: "This collection is dedicated to my mum . . . She was everything. Also, to my dad, brother and sisters, who have kept me strong. Everything. Always, Stella." She makes the dedication in the form of a statement after she receives a standing ovation for the collection which, fashion experts say, "capture the soft and feminine feel". Backstage at the event, Stella talks about her mother, Linda. "She was incredible. Everyone who met her for even ten minutes thought the same. She was strong, motherly, normal, warm. She had all the right values. People thought the animals thing was just her sympathising with a cute beagle, but it was much more intelligent than that. I'll never meet anyone like her – I just hope I have some of her qualities."

Asked about his daughter's collection, Paul remarks: "I am very proud of her because she is a serious English designer more than holding her own at the heart of Paris fashion. It is beautiful, just beautiful. It's a credit to the family. Here we are seeing real clothes for real women to look really good in." Members of the audience, at the old Paris Stock Exchange, dub the exhibition the "Yes tonight, Josephine" look. The Beatles' track 'Hey Jude' is used as background music for part of the show. The audience, which includes Mick Hucknell, of Simply Red, and Neil Tennant of The Pet Shop Boys, are also treated to highly amusing outtakes of President Clinton protesting that he did not have sex with Monica Lewinsky.

Back in London at the BBC Maida Vale studios, a 30th anniversary party is held for the release of The Beatles' film *Yellow Submarine.* Organised by TVC London, the production company which produced the animation, and Hieronimus and Co. Inc., who are currently putting together a book on the film for release next year, the party plays host to a number of celebrities and actors involved with film. Among them are Eric Segal, the film's scriptwriter, Lance Percival, the voice of "old Fred" among others, and John Clive, the cartoon voice of John.

Monday October 19

Mercury Records release, simultaneously around the world, Ringo's album VH-1 *Storytellers.* The track listing is: 'With A Little Help From My Friends', 'I Was Walkin'', 'Don't Pass Me By', 'Back Off Boogaloo', 'King Of Broken Hearts', 'Octopus's Garden',

'Photograph', 'La De Da', 'What In The World', 'Love Me Do', 'With A Little Help From My Friends' (reprise).

🍎 Also today, Paul releases to the press a set of previously unpublished pictures of Linda, taken by Paul, dated 1969. These wonderful shots are seen on Sky News this evening and reproduced in the *Mirror* newspaper the following day.

Tuesday October 20
🍎 At the Ed Sullivan Theater in New York this afternoon, Ringo tapes another appearance on the CBS TV show *Late Night With David Letterman* where, besides a brief interview, he performs 'Back Off Boogaloo'. (Viewers in Europe have a chance to see the show when it is transmitted on The Paramount Comedy Channel the following evening.) Following this, at 7pm, Ringo is to be found signing copies of his *Storytellers* and *Vertical Man* albums at the Tower Records store based at 66th and Broadway in New York. The first 250 in the queue are given a special Tower Records wristband so that they can return later to meet Ringo. Unfortunately, many of the waiting fans do not get to meet him, as the former Beatle stays at the venue for just one hour, restricting fans to just two signatures.

Wednesday October 21
🍎 Ringo makes another appearance on the American ABC TV show *Live With Regis & Kathie Lee*, where again Ringo and his band perform 'Back Off Boogaloo'.

Friday October 23
🍎 A pre-recorded interview with Paul, carried out by Des Lynam at Abbey Road in London, is broadcast in the UK on BBC Radio 2 between 5:07 and 7:00pm.
🍎 At the Grosvenor House Hotel in London this evening, George Martin is presented with an Outstanding Achievement award at the annual Music Industry Trusts' Dinner. Commenting on the award and the dinner held in his honour, Sir George replies: "This is probably the most important thing that's happened to me. I think it a bit over the top and I don't think I deserve it, but to be honoured by this kind of thing by your peers in the music industry, for me, this is a very moving occasion." Tributes to George pour in from musicians all over the world, including Paul, George and Ringo, who all sent video messages, along with the Prime Minister Tony Blair. Paul's message reads: "Congratulations on getting the man of the year, man of the minute, the man of the hour, the man for me. Thanks for everything you've done for us all. We love you."

Saturday October 24
🍎 In the UK, the BBC2 weekly archive programme *TOTP2* screens, for the first time on British television, the MPL animated promotional film clip for Linda's *Wide Prairie*.
🍎 The German TV station RTL Super broadcasts (between 8:15pm and 00:05am European time) a Beatles Night of programming, with screenings of *Hi-Hi-Hilife (Help!)*, *Yeah! Yeah! Yeah! (A Hard Day's Night)* and the recent George Martin documentary *In My Life*.

Monday October 26
🍎 Parolophone/EMI releases, simultaneously around the world, Linda's album *Wide Prairie*, containing 13 Linda McCartney tracks, many of which are previously unreleased and span 20 years of her recorded material. Paul explains the background to the album: "A couple of years ago, a fan wrote to Linda saying she had enjoyed 'Seaside Woman' and asked if there were any more tracks of hers available. That letter made us decide to gather all the music she had recorded through the years and put it on one album."

To coincide with its release, a pre-taped interview with Paul, his first since Linda's death, is released to various TV stations where he talks about cancer. The only UK TV station to screen clip's from this is the ITN News at 5:40 and 10:00pm. Meanwhile, it is reported that in some Tower Records stores around America, copies of the very last *Club Sandwich*, issue number 86, are given away free when you buy the *Wide Prairie* album.

Wednesday October 28
🍎 In the UK, The Beatles' 1969 album *Abbey Road* comes under scrutiny in the first programme of the new BBC Radio Two series *Classic Albums*, transmitted this evening between 10:02 and 10:30pm.

Friday October 30

 The proposed *White Album – 30th Anniversary* radio programme is cancelled. Producers put this down to a lack of interest from American radio stations. They claim that out of the 177 enquiries for the three-hour programme, only two stations wished to carry the show (see entry for November 1).

 The Fireman Internet website repeats (at 11pm) the exclusive interview with the Fireman, previously aired on Friday October 2 (see entry). For those who missed it again, the show is repeated on November 20 at 11pm.

November

 During the first week of the month, on a sound stage in San Francisco, Dean Carr directs a promotional film to accompany John's 'I'm Losing You', a track to be included on the upcoming *John Lennon Anthology* box set. The video features cleverly cut footage of John and his animated drawings intercut with footage of the musicians who originally played on the track back in 1980, namely Rick Nelson, Ben. E. Carlos and Tony Levin. Tony Levin: "Amazingly we all remembered our parts on the songs. The video shoot was fun and professional."

 It is announced that the publishers Little Brown have purchased, for the sum of £75,000, the rights to Danny Fields' biography of Linda McCartney. Fields had acted as a spokesman for the McCartneys after her death, and the book has received full co-operation from Paul.

Sunday November 1

 The newspaper *USA Weekend* publish an exclusive, lengthy, interview with Paul conducted by Chrissie Hynde of The Pretenders, a fellow animal-rights campaigner and close friend to the McCartneys. Paul touchingly describes Linda's final days and admits that he had to seek out professional advice to overcome his grief. "I got a counsellor because I knew that I would need some help," he recalls. "He was great, particularly in helping me get rid of my guilt. Whenever anyone you care about dies, you wish you'd been perfect all the time you were with them. That made me feel very guilty after Linda died. The guilt's a real bugger. But then I thought, hang on a minute. We were just human. That was the beautiful thing about our marriage. We were just a boyfriend and girlfriend having babies." Paul goes on to reveal that he did not let on to Linda that the treatment she was having was not going to work, and that the end was near. "I knew a week or so before she died. I was the only one who knew. One of the doctors said she ought to be told, but I didn't want to tell her because I didn't think she'd want to know."

Paul is also asked about Yoko not being invited to attend Linda's New York memorial service. He explains: "We decided to stay true to Linda's spirit and only invite her nearest and dearest friends. Seeing as Yoko wasn't one of those, we didn't invite her. People who were maybe doing it out of duty weren't asked. Everyone who went remarked that there were so many friends there and it was such a warm atmosphere. Everyone who spoke, spoke from the heart, genuinely. Linda would have hated anything else."

 The scheduled first broadcasts in America of a 30th anniversary tribute programme to The Beatles' 1968 *White Album* fails to show. The proposed 150-minute show was due to contain, over six segments, tracks like 'Birthday' (featuring alternative vocals), 'Don't Pass Me By' (unedited version), 'Revolution' (basic tracks of rock version), and various demo recordings, including 'Back In The USSR', 'Sour Milk Sea', 'Blackbird', 'I'm So Tired', 'Piggies', 'What's The New Mary Jane' and an excerpt from the legendary unreleased 27-minute version of 'Helter Skelter'. The show was due to be rounded off with clips from Kenny Everett's 1968 interviews with The Beatles, other archive interviews with John, Paul, George, Ringo and George Martin, and a selection of *White Album* songs covered by other artists, namely 'Back In The USSR' by Billy Joel, 'Blackbird' by Crosby, Stills & Nash, and 'Helter Skelter' by U2.

Monday November 2

 To preview the release of the *John Lennon Anthology* box set tomorrow, the 100-minute *Anthology* radio special is syndicated to selected American radio stations today.

Yoko: "John was a complicated man. One part of him was a hugely popular artist who loved to sell records and have hits. Meanwhile, what he was doing in private was fantastic – much more raw and unpolished. When I listen to these tracks, it's as if John is standing in the room with me."

Tuesday November 3

🍎 The 4-CD box set *John Lennon Anthology*, featuring 100 previously unreleased tracks, is released simultaneously around the world. (In the UK, the set had actually been on sale the previous day, Monday November 2. In Japan, the release will not take place until Friday November 6.)

"I hope you enjoy the box. This is the John that I knew, not the John that you knew through the press, the records and the films. I am saying to you, here's my John. I wish to share my knowledge of him with you. It was an incredible honour for me to have been with him." – Yoko's introduction to the *John Lennon Anthology*.

The four discs are individually titled *Ascot, New York City, The Lost Weekend* and *Dakota*. Also released today by EMI is a 21-track single CD "best of" *Anthology* highlights compilation album entitled *Wonsaponatime*. The release features the following tracks: 'I'm Losing You', 'Working Class Hero', 'God', 'How Do You Sleep?', 'Imagine', 'Baby, Please Don't Go', 'Oh My Love', 'God Save Us', 'I Found Out', 'Woman Is The Nigger Of The World' (live), 'A Kiss Is Just A Kiss', 'Be-Bop-A-Lula', 'Rip It Up'/'Ready Teddy', 'What You Got', 'Nobody Loves You When You're Down And Out', 'I Don't Wanna Face It', 'Real Love', 'Only You', 'Grow Old With Me', 'Sean's In The Sky', 'Serve Yourself'.

To coincide with the *John Lennon Anthology* releases, David Bowie announces plans to produce an album of John Lennon songs performed by an all-star cast. According to Bowie, this will be released on John's 60th birthday, October 9, 2000.

Wednesday November 4

🍎 In the UK, Yoko gives an exclusive interview about Linda to the newspaper the *Liverpool Echo*, where she dismisses the fact that she and Paul's late wife disliked each other. "People always portrayed us as enemies," Yoko is quoted as saying, "like boxers on opposite sides of the ring. But it was never like that. In latter life, especially, we became friends. We had an understanding of each other. We both married Beatles and we knew what that was like." Yoko also remarks about Linda's death. "It was a great loss," she admits. "She was a very passionate woman about things she believed in. I was shocked by the news of Linda's death. I am a woman who has lost my husband. I think about John every day, and talking about him is one of my last links with him."

During the interview, Yoko recalls when she first married John. "It's funny," she says, "when I first married him, I resented the fact that everything was about John. I was an established artist myself and I had my own career. I fought so hard to keep my own identity, not just to become part of John Lennon. But then John died, and that changed everything. He was taken away from me and that was a terrible shock. Of course it still hurts!"

Thursday November 5

🍎 Another exclusive interview with Yoko is published in today's edition of the *Sun*.

Friday November 6

🍎 Another exclusive in the *Sun* features Paul, in the first of a two-part interview, talking about Linda. On the question of possibly playing some vegetarian benefit concerts next year, he replies: "I don't know whether I can go up there again thinking about Linda. I'm just going to have to play it by ear. If I can manage it, then I will. But I've said that if I can't do it, she'll just have to forgive me." (Part two of the feature, published on Saturday November 7, includes Paul giving a track-by-track guide to Linda's album *Wide Prairie*.)

Saturday November 7

🍎 VH-1 in Europe, as part of their Legends Weekend, repeats the 1992 Bob Dylan Columbia Records tribute concert featuring George (see entry for October 16, 1992.) The two days of screenings also include a repeat broadcast of Paul's 1997 appearance on the VH-1 programme *Ten Of The Best*.

Sunday November 8

🍎 Ringo and The Roundheads' *Storytellers* show, recorded at the Bottom Line Club in New York on Wednesday May 13, receives its European premiere on VH-1 this evening, between 7:00 and 7:56pm.

 Also today, the *News Of The World* reports that: "George stands to make a fortune by selling the car he was sitting in when he proposed to his first wife Patti Boyd. The E-Type Jaguar car, which cost £2,300 when purchased new back in 1964, has his name on the log book and now boasts, experts believe, a six-figure price tag."

Monday November 9
 Linda's track 'Wide Prairie' is released as a single in the UK. (The American release takes place the following day.)

Tuesday November 10
 It's announced in America that both Paul and George Martin will be inducted into the annual Rock And Roll Hall Of Fame ceremony at the Waldorf-Astoria Hotel in New York, on March 15, 1999. Among the other inductees to be honoured that night will be Dusty Springfield, Billy Joel, Curtis Mayfield and Bruce Springsteen.

Thursday November 12
 The documentary programme *In My Life*, focusing on the George Martin album of the same name, is transmitted in America on the Bravo station. (Repeat broadcasts take place on December 1 and December 18. The UK premiere had taken place earlier this year on BBC1 on Sunday April 12.)

Saturday November 14
 Paul's *Liverpool Oratorio* is performed this evening at Alte Oper Frankfurt, Grober Saal, 20 Uhr Frankfurt, in Germany.

Sunday November 15
 The details of Linda's will are published. She leaves £183 million, most of it to her four children, various animal charities and towards research into breast cancer.

Tuesday November 17
 Secret unconfirmed reports leaked today reveal that a planned *Sgt. Pepper's* concert is due to take place in London next May, starring Elton John, Oasis, Chrissie Hynde, Bob Dylan and Paul Simon, among others. The event never happens.
 Another report reveals that a privately recorded concert tape of The Beatles live at the Bournemouth Gaumont in 1963, is to be auctioned at Christie's next month. (See entry for Thursday December 10.)

Wednesday November 18
 The American TV news programme *Extra* features: " . . . an interview with the sibling John Lennon searched for but never found. Hear the tragic story of lies and the secret promise that forever kept her apart from her legendary brother."

Thursday November 19
 A repeat screening of Ringo's VH-1 *Storytellers* performance is broadcast in America.

Friday November 20
 Today's edition of the American magazine *Entertainment Weekly* reports that a newly-re-mastered six-track audio version of The Beatles' 1968 film *Yellow Submarine* will get a limited cinema release next summer. Reports also reveal that both Paul and George have given their thumbs-up to this new print. To tie-in with the film's re-issue, a number of *Yellow Submarine* collectible products are also expected to be released.

Sunday November 22
 Excerpts from the American *John Lennon Anthology* EPK (Electronic video press kit) are transmitted during tonight's edition of the VH-1 music programme *Talk Music*. (The show is repeated on the station on Monday November 23, and Thursday November 26.) The EPK includes a fascinating scene where Yoko is seen returning to the 105 Bank Street apartment in Greenwich Village where John and Yoko first took up residence on Saturday October 16, 1971 (see entry).

Tuesday November 24

✝ Apple and EMI release an official 30th anniversary version of the *The Beatles (White Album)* from 1968, complete with miniaturised versions of the original poster and glossy pictures. Contrary to reports, this special release does not feature a re-mastered version of the album. There is a print run of 500,000 individually numbered copies, with 200,000 of these going to the States. In its first week of sales in the UK, the album sells 2,500 copies and enters the album charts at number 106. Sir George Martin is quoted as saying about this release: "It's a marketing thing, isn't it? It's all part of their ways of earning money. Unfortunately, the music business is in such a state that reissues and recompilations are the main way that people earn money nowadays, because new music doesn't earn much. It's a sad state of our musical life, I'm afraid."

Sir George also takes time, on the Wall Of Sound Internet website, to recall how the *White Album* came about: "They (The Beatles) presented me with 33 songs which they wanted to record at once – literally. Paul said, 'Well, you've got another studio, if George has something going in one studio, I can go in another.' I was running from one studio to another, doing a kind of executive producer role, and it was quite hectic. I actually protested to them that we shouldn't rush all these songs into print, we should be more selective and just record the good ones. But they would have none of that. They wanted to record everything, because they all wanted to be in there. I learned later that they also tried to exhaust their recording contract, which was couched in terms of number of song titles, not years."

Asked what he thinks of the *White Album*, thirty years later: "It's a good album, not one of my favourites, but it was a good album. It didn't have any real blockbusters on it, but it had some good songs. I think *Abbey Road* was better."

Wednesday November 25

✝ An interview with Paul, carried out by Edna Gundersen, is published in the newspaper *USA Today*.

Sunday November 29

✝ The *News Of The World* reveals that Paul is going to be a grandfather, as his daughter Mary is currently five months pregnant. As a tribute to her mother, Mary reveals that, if it's a girl, she will call the child Linda. A friend of the McCartneys remarks: "Mary was already starting to show at the wedding (in September), but no one said anything . . ." Meanwhile, Paul has been quoted as saying: "It will be one of the proudest moments of my life."

December

✝ The One 2 One telephone commercial, which features DJ and *TFI Friday* host Chris Evans revealing that he would like to have a "one to one" with John Lennon, begins transmissions across UK and terrestrial television stations. (Filming of the clip, which includes cleverly edited sequences featuring archive John clips, was recorded in October. Acting as a double to John in the short advert is the look-a-like Gary Gibson, who will appear personally on Evans' Channel 4 show *TFI Friday* shortly after.)

✝ Paul teams up with the *Mirror* newspaper and a group of East Sussex musicians to record the song called 'Little Children', a track written by Peter Kirkley and recorded at Paul's home studio. Proceeds from the single, which is available at the Virgin megastores, will benefit the Brazilian street children.

Meanwhile, Paul takes Gary Zimet, of the US record shop Moments In Time, to court. Zimet had been trying to sell to Paul, on behalf of another collector, his original handwritten lyrics to 'Sgt. Pepper's Lonely Hearts Club Band' for $550,000. But Paul claims that these lyrics were actually stolen from his home in late 1967 or early 1968. Zimet counterclaims that his friend had, in fact, purchased the lyrics from The Beatles' biographer Hunter Davies. Paul insists that Zimet disclose the name of the person who has the lyrics sheet and immediately puts a restraining order to prevent him from selling it. Zimet complies with Paul's demand.

✝ In Archway, North London, Ringo and Barbara make an appearance at the disabled children's project called PALACE (Play And Learn And Creative Education) to help launch a joint appeal for volunteers with the cerebal palsy charity SCOPE.

✝ The top UK dance act The Prodigy are prevented, by Apple Corps, from using a Beatles sample on a new recording. The group's Liam Howlett had originally used two verses and a chorus from the 1967 track 'Sgt. Pepper's Lonely Hearts Club Band' on his latest record *The Dirtwater Sessions – Volume 1*, but Apple had other ideas. A spokesman for Howlett says: "Liam did mix the album and one of the records that he used was 'Sgt. Pepper's', by The Beatles. It sounded great in there and we were going to include it on the commercial release of the record, but Apple would not grant us permission to license the track. Apparently, Paul didn't have any problems with it – it's simply that Apple never lets Beatles tracks appear on anything other than Beatles albums." A spokesman for Paul remarks on this matter: "Paul really liked the song, thinking it was fab. He likes The Prodigy, but it wasn't his decision, it was Apple's." (Liam Howlett will replace The Beatles' recording with snippets from Jane's Addiction's 1991 hit 'Been Caught Stealing'.)

Tuesday December 1
 In the States, Yoko recreates her and John's 1969 Peace campaign by putting up banners in New York's Times Square, which read "War Is Over! If You Want It . . . Happy Christmas From John And Yoko." Joined at the unveiling by world representatives, Yoko says of the display: "This is a billboard event John and I did 29 years ago, in Christmas of 1969. At the time it created good vibrations around the world and gave people strength. The message is 'we can do it', and it's still valid. If one billion people in the world would think peace – we're gonna get it. You may think, 'Well, how are we going to get one billion people to think?' Isn't this something we should leave to the politicians who have the power to do these things? Well, politicians cannot do anything without your support. We are the power. Visualise the domino effect and just start thinking positive, that we are all together in this. For the holiday season, I wanted this to be a gift to you from John and I. Stand in front of the billboard. Take photos of yourself, your friends and family. Send them out so the message will circulate. Above all, have fun." (For those wishing to see the "War Is Over" billboard and the live events from Times Square, a digital video camera broadcasts the happenings live on an Internet webpage.)

Wednesday December 2
 In New York, George is seen at a concert by Dave Mason and Jim Capaldi of the Sixties group Traffic. During their show they perform the track 'You Got A Hold On Me', a song that is introduced by Jim Capaldi as having been written for George's next solo album. He introduces the song by announcing: "This is something special for someone in the audience tonight. I want him to hear it live so I can get his reaction. He is one of the greatest influences of my life. This one is for you, George."

Sunday December 6
 In the UK, the *News Of The World* newspaper publishes a story headlined: "Macca Everton Sensation", in which, apparently, "Sir Paul McCartney is the key to a sensational £60 million Everton takeover. The former Beatle," the report reads, "will be asked tomorrow to help rescue the struggling Mersey giants. The dramatic plea will come from Macca's old school pal Bill Kenwright, who is desperate to bring the glory days back to Goodison . . ." A source close to Paul is reported as saying: "He will buy the football club for his dad. Jim would be so proud of his boy – coming from nothing to owning Everton FC. Paul could easily afford to buy the club. Peter Johnstone's fortune is Paul's loose change, but this is not about money." (Johnstone is Everton's current chairman.) On Monday December 7, it is revealed that Paul has turned down the chance of taking over the club.

Tuesday December 8
 At 9pm this evening, VH-1 in America premieres the special edition of the *Legends* series, which focuses on the life of John. The show, which is repeated on the station on December 9 at 8pm, December 10 at 12:00 noon, and December 12 at 11pm, includes interviews with Yoko and George Martin.

Thursday December 10
 At today's Christie's auction in South Kensington, South London, a Beatles' live concert performance tape is put up for sale and eventually raises £25,300. The 25-minute reel-to-reel tape, recorded by the chief technician at the Gaumont Theatre in Bournemouth on August 21, 1963, to check the group's sound quality, historically includes the first-ever public

performance of 'She Loves You'. Because The Beatles did not impress him, he put the tape in his workroom at home and subsequently forgot all about it. That was until his daughter, 52-year-old Irene Draper, a keen Beatles fan who saw the group every night they performed in her hometown, persuaded him to find it. Hearing this tape again, 35 years later, Irene remarks: "I nearly went through the roof when I heard it again after all these years. The sound quality is wonderful. It brought memories of those wonderful, exciting days flooding back. I knew it was really hot stuff and that we should do something with it." (Note: the tape contains the following songs: 'Roll Over Beethoven', 'Thank You Girl', 'Chains', 'From Me To You', 'A Taste Of Honey', 'I Saw Her Standing There', 'Baby It's You', 'Boys', 'She Loves You', introduced by John as "a new song for us, released on Friday. Buy your copy . . . please", and 'Twist And Shout'.)

 Also on offer at the sale is a series of lots from the personal collection of Nicola Hale who, as a 4-year-old, travelled with her mother Pam and grandmother Amy Smedley on The Beatles' *Magical Mystery Tour* bus in 1967. Included in the lots is her own copy of the *Magical Mystery Tour* EP featuring the inscription "Paul McCartney loves Nicola (True)!"

Saturday December 12
 An exhibition of Beatles photographs taken by Harry Benson is put on display at the Govinda Gallery, based at 1227 34th Street NW, in Washington DC. (The event will run until January 23, 1999.) Also today, VH-1 in Europe screens, for the first time on the station, the 1979 Dick Clark made-for-TV film *The Birth Of The Beatles*.

 While in the UK, the BBC2 archive show *TOTP2* screens, for the first time on UK TV, the promotional film clip to accompany John's 1980 recording of 'I'm Losing You', a version of the track released for the first time on the 4-CD box set *John Lennon: Anthology*.

Monday December 14
 At approximately 8:15am Eastern time, the *John Lennon Anthology* 4-CD box set is previewed on the ABC TV breakfast show *Good Morning America*.

Thursday December 17
 Paul's only public performance in 1998 takes place on the Internet, when he presents the one-hour world exclusive programme entitled *The McCartney Wide Prairie Show*, which features Paul "on line to the world" taking questions from his fans. During the broadcast, Paul tells how Linda and he made her solo album, shows his favourite pictures of her, cooks his speciality from her cookbook, and previews exclusive video clips. Paul's spokesman Geoff Baker remarks on the project: "Paul is not exactly an Internet buff, but he is very excited, and a bit nervous. He chose the format over several TV offers because he wants to go directly to the fans without the use of an interviewer." (Note: the transmissions take place at 11am in Los Angeles, 2pm in New York, 7pm in London and at 10pm in Moscow.)

Friday December 18
 In the UK, Ringo and Barbara appear in a pre-taped sequence for the Carlton ITV festive show *A Capital Christmas*, transmitted this evening across the London and South East regions of ITV only.

Sunday December 20
 VH-1 in Europe repeats the Ringo Starr & The Roundheads edition of the VH-1 series *Storytellers*.

 In the UK pop singles chart, the four-piece Spice Girls equal The Beatles' 33-year-old record by having their third consecutive Christmas number one single with the track 'Goodbye'.

Monday December 21
 To coincide with the run-up to the screening of the BBC2 two-part *Arena* profile of The Beatles' manager Brian Epstein, the UK newspaper the *Express* publishes today the first of a two-part serialisation on him. (Part two is printed the following day.)

 In the States, Yoko joins in on the live Internet webcasts by giving a SonicNet chat at 8pm this evening.

Friday December 25
 BBC2, as part of their big festive programming, transmits (between 9:06 and 10:21pm) the first of a two-part *Arena* profile on The Beatles' manager Brian Epstein. Part two is aired on the station the following day, Boxing Day. The show includes an exclusive interview with Paul carried out in New York in November 1997.

Monday December 28
 After a delay of 29 years, the star dedicated to The Beatles is placed on the Hollywood Walk Of Fame, in Los Angeles, California. The organisers announce that this is done as a "festive present to Beatles fans".

"By the way, while we're here. You've got me and you've got John in this. OK! What about George and Ringo?"

– Paul

Saturday January 2
 In Europe, during VH-1's *Top 100 Weekend,* The Beatles are placed at number 16 in the "Top 100 Artists" poll, based on nominations from the station's viewers.

Monday January 4
 Ringo's 1981 United Artists film *Caveman* receives a rare TV screening this evening on the German station TM3.

Wednesday January 6
 The delightful 1978 comedy *I Wanna Hold Your Hand,* starring Nancy Allen and Bobby DiCicco, which focuses on a group of teenagers who attempt to try to meet The Beatles when they make their début on *The Ed Sullivan Show* in 1964, is repeated on the US Bravo TV station at 4pm. (A further screening takes place the following day at 4am.)

Thursday January 7
 At a trade fair in Atlanta, Georgia, Paul attends the Homeware Designs exhibition of his daughter Heather.

Saturday January 9 (until February 27)
 In the UK, an exhibition by Yoko opens at the Minories Art Gallery in Colchester. After which, her show moves on to Helsinki in Finland.

Monday January 11
 In the UK, 21 years after appearing on the show for Barry Sheene (and 19 years after turning down an appearance for George Martin), George appears again on *This Is Your Life* (broadcast on BBC1 this evening between 7:00 and 7:29pm) where he briefly pays homage to the career of the racing driver, and his close friend, Damon Hill. (The show had been pre-taped at the BBC TV Centre in Wood Lane, London last week.)

Tuesday January 12
 In the UK, George wins his libel case over claims that he accepted sexual favours in exchange for a donation to charity. The allegation had been made in the book *All Dressed Up: The Sixties And The Counter Culture* by Jonathan Green and published last summer in the UK by Random House. The High Courts in London hear that George has now accepted an apology and an undisclosed sum in damages. In addition, Random House has agreed to pay his full legal costs. George is not in court to hear his solicitor Norman Chapman tell Mr. Justice Morland: "The allegation is untrue and the defendants now acknowledge this to be the case." Counsel Giles Crown, representing the publishers and the author, tells the judge: "They express their sincere apologies for the damage and embarrassment caused."

Monday January 25
 Advertisements concerning the banning of Linda's single 'The Light Comes From Within', appear in several UK newspapers under the headline: "Parents We Need Your Guidance". Beneath, Paul writes: "In what age are we living? Is this the Nineties or the Twenties? Should you decide that your children must not hear this record, we would be grateful for your wisdom and good sense and will put our fingers in our ears whenever we hear it played. If, on the other hand, you feel that no harm will come to your children by being exposed to this song, give the guidance so surely needed and tell them it's OK to do so. PS: By the way, young people, we know you don't listen to them anyway."

'The Light Comes From Within' falls foul of broadcasting watchdogs who object to the line: "You say I'm simple, you say I'm a hick, you're fucking no-one, you stupid Dick." As a result the track is banned by BBC radio and TV shows, *Top Of The Pops* and *Live And Kicking.*

BBC Radio 1 DJ Chris Moyles insists that the track isn't being played because of the language but because of the poor lyrics. "I feel sorry for Paul," he tells listeners. "And I was upset when Linda died. But these are stupid lyrics and we can't play it for that reason alone."

On Sky News Paul responds, saying: "I don't think Bob Geldof asking for 'fucking' money for Live Aid offended anyone."

Parlophone issues 'The Light Comes From Within' as a single with a 'Parental Guidance' sticker.

Tuesday January 26
🍎 An article on Paul is published (on page 19) in today's edition of the *Sun* newspaper, under the headline "Linda's Got A Right To Express Herself", a reference to the UK banning of Linda's single 'The Light Comes From Within'.

Wednesday January 27
🍎 In London, Paul meets Cherie Blair, the Prime Minister's wife, at 10 Downing Street, where they thrash out plans for a new campaign to fight breast cancer. Their conversation lasts just 30 minutes. Earlier in the day, Paul had rung in to the ITV breakfast station GMTV where he complained about the banning of Linda's single 'The Light Comes From Within' and made a satellite appearance on the ABC TV breakfast show *Good Morning America*, where again he vents his feelings about the banning of Linda's new single.

🍎 In Liverpool, it is announced that the Casbah, the basement coffee shop regarded by many as the birthplace of The Beatles, is set to re-open. Roag Best, the brother of The Beatles' former drummer Pete Best, is now working to prepare the venue for a special anniversary event, hoping that it will lead to the club becoming a permanent feature on the Liverpool tourist trail. (The 40th anniversary of the opening of the Casbah coffee club falls on August 29, 1999.)

Friday January 29
🍎 At 3 Saville Row in London, the old headquarters of Apple, a special celebration takes place to mark the 30th anniversary since The Beatles, on the roof of the building, gave their last live public performance. (No one mentions that the 30th anniversary of the concert is actually tomorrow!) The lunchtime event is organised by the BSA (Building Societies Association) to raise funds for their favourite charities, including Imperial Cancer Research and Shelter. The Bootleg Beatles provide the music and among the audience is Glen Matlock, a former member of The Sex Pistols. (Reports on the concert appear on both the ITN and Sky News bulletins.)

Saturday January 30
🍎 VH-1 in America broadcasts the Ringo Starr edition of *Hard Rock Live*.

🍎 In Birmingham at St. Andrews, Linda's "veggie" burgers are given away free to supporters at a Birmingham City Football Club home match. Although it is rumoured that Paul will be present at the give away, he does not appear.

🍎 The correct 30th anniversary date of The Beatles last public performance on the Apple HQ in Saville Row, London, is officially recognised when the BBC2 weekly archive show *TOTP2* screen the complete clip of 'Get Back', extracted from the remastered version of the film *Let It Be*. (Apple Corps in London supply the clip to the BBC.)

Tuesday February 2
🍎 VH-1 in Europe broadcasts for the first time the complete uncut and uncensored MPL promotional film for Linda's 'The Light Comes From Within'.

Thursday February 11
🍎 On the eve of Ringo's All-Starr Band tenth anniversary tour, Ringo takes part in another AOL (America On Line) chat with fans around the world.

* * *

Ringo & His All-Starr Band
10th Anniversary Tour of America
Friday February 12 – Sunday March 28

Ringo celebrates the tenth anniversary of his All-Starr Band by going back out on the road. His All-Starr line-up consists of Gary Brooker, Jack Bruce, Simon Kirke, Todd Rundgren, Timothy Cappello and their repertoire, which occasionally changes, features the following songs: 'It Don't Come Easy', 'Act Naturally', 'Whiskey Train' (performed by Gary Brooker), 'I Saw The Light' (by Todd Rundgren), 'Sunshine Of Your Love' (Jack Bruce), 'Shooting Star' (Simon Kirke), 'Boys', 'Love Me Do', 'Yellow Submarine', 'A Salty Dog' (Gary Brooker), 'Hammer In My Heart' (Todd Rundgren), 'I'm The Greatest', 'The

No No Song', 'Back Off Boogaloo', 'I Feel Free' (Jack Bruce), 'All Right Now' (Simon Kirke), 'I Wanna Be Your Man', 'Bang On The Drum' (Todd Rundgren), 'White Room' (Jack Bruce), 'A Whiter Shade Of Pale' (Gary Brooker) and 'Photograph'. For the encore, Ringo usually performs 'You're Sixteen' and/or 'With A Little Help From My Friends'. Gary Brooker will sometimes replace 'A Salty Dog' with another Procol Harum track, 'Conquistador', and Jack Bruce will sometimes play 'Theme From An Imaginary Western'.

Their concerts take place at the following venues:

Taj Mahal Casino, Atlantic City, New Jersey (Friday February 12, Saturday February 13 and Sunday February 14)
Beacon Theater, New York City, New York (Tuesday February 16 and Wednesday February 17)
Mohegan Sun Casino, Uncasville, Connecticut (Friday February 19 and Saturday February 20)
Westbury Music Fair, Westbury, New York (Sunday February 21)
Schottenstein Center, Columbus, Ohio (Monday February 22)
Westbury Music Fair, Westbury, New York (return performance – Wednesday February 24)
Star Plaza Theater, Merrillville, Indiana (Friday February 26)
Park West, Chicago, Illinois (Sunday February 28)
Palace Theater, Detroit, Michigan (Monday March 1)
Eureka Municipal Auditorium, Eureka (Thursday March 4)
Konocti Harbor Resort & Spa, Kelseyville, California (Friday March 5 and Saturday March 6)
Berkeley Theater, Berkeley, California (Sunday March 7)
Bank American Center, Boise, Idaho (Thursday March 11)
Dee Event Center, Ogden, Utah (Friday March 12)
The Joint, Las Vegas, Nevada (Saturday March 13)
4th & B, San Diego, California, (Sunday March 14 and Monday March 15)
Universal Amphitheater, Los Angeles, California (Thursday March 18)
Silver Legacy Casino, Reno, Nevada (Friday March 19 and Saturday March 20)
Harrah's Casino, Lake Taho, Nevada (Sunday March 21)
Horseshoe Casino, Tunica, Mississippi (Thursday March 25)
Florida Theater, Jacksonville, Florida (Friday March 26)
WMXJ Radio Show, Sunrise Musical Theater, Fort Lauderdale, Florida (Saturday March 27)
Hard Rock Cafe, Orlando, Florida (Sunday March 28)

Tuesday February 16
✦ This morning, Ringo and his All-Starr Band hold a press conference at New York City's All Star Cafe where they discuss their current tenth anniversary tour.

Saturday March 27
Tonight's show in Florida at the WMXJ Radio Show had been originally scheduled to take place at the Lockhart Stadium. Fans who had purchased tickets for the show at Lockhart were advised to exchange the tickets for ones intended for Fort Lauderdale.

* * *

Friday February 19
✦ In America, George Martin begins a tour called The Making Of Sgt. Pepper, which is billed by promoters as a "multi-media" show. Unfortunately the reviews of the shows are not good and the "multi-media" billing fails to live up to its expectations, with the video screens showing only excerpts from the Making Of Sgt. Pepper TV documentary which many of the fans had seen already. Nevertheless, the sight of The Beatles' producer talking, in person, about how these legendary songs were recorded, is enough to satisfy most fans and the tour is a great success. Patrons are requested to submit questions for Martin on index cards, which had been given to them at the start of the evening. Martin's short itinerary includes Calvin Theater, Northampton, Minnesota (February 19), Birchmere in Alexandria, Virginia (February 23), The Count Basie Theater, Red

Bank, New Jersey (February 25), Chicago's Park West (March 4) and Denver's Paramount Theater (March 5).

Sunday February 21
❦ Still Stateside, George appears in a blink and you'll miss him 10-second appeal at the conclusion of Mr. Holland's Opus on ABC TV this evening. Holding an acoustic guitar, George's short speech consists of: "I'm George Harrison. Music can make a world of difference in the life of a child, as it did mine. To find out about Mr. Holland's Opus Foundation, and to put musical instruments in the hands of children, call toll free 1-877-MrHolland. Help keep music alive in our schools." His friend Michael Kamen had recruited Harrison for the short spot.

March
❦ At the start of the month, and right up until he leaves for America to attend the Rock And Roll Hall Of Fame event, Paul is seen at Abbey Road Studios in London where he is rumoured to be working on a new set of rock'n'roll covers with David Gilmour and Mick Green. (A brief report on the sessions appears in the *Sunday People* newspaper on March 14.) An insider for Paul's label suggests that, should they ever be released, they will most probably appear next Spring. (See entry for Monday March 1.)
❦ In the States, a new range of official *Yellow Submarine* collectibles is announced, which include cruet sets and cookie jars. In addition, individual models of each Beatle, as depicted in the film, are expected to be released in stages through the year, as well as a model of the *Yellow Submarine* itself. (The releases are to coincide with the reissue of the *Yellow Submarine* film, and a documentary on the making of the film, which are expected to appear across the world later in the year.)
❦ At the funeral in Henley of Dusty Springfield, Paul sends a note which reads: "Dearest Dusty, I'm so glad I had the chance a few weeks ago to tell you what a classic you were. We love you. Paul McCartney and the kids."

Monday March 1
(until Friday March 5 and then Tuesday May 4 & Wednesday May 5)
❦ In the famed Studio 2 at Abbey Road, Paul begins a seven day series of instantaneous studio recordings, comprising three McCartney originals and some of his most memorable rock'n'roll songs from his youth. The sessions, which feature David Gilmour and Mick Green (on guitars), Ian Paice (drums), Pete Wingfield (keyboards) and, occasionally, Dave Mattacks (drums and percussion) and Geraint Watkins (keyboards), will appear on the album *Run Devil Run*, released on Monday October 4 this year.

Paul, in conversation with Patrick Humphries: "We'd spend 15, 20 minutes top whack, and everyone'd go, 'Yeah, got it.' Then, we'd go to our instruments. I'd go to bass and singing, and we'd just do it." The first session comprises 'Coquette', a Fats Domino B-side, 'I Got Stung', a 1959 number one hit for Elvis Presley and 'Fabulous', which appears later on the 'No Other Baby' single and *Run Devil Run* singles box set.

Paul on the recordings: "We did it exactly the same way The Beatles used to record. Between 10:30 (am) and 1:30 (pm), we expected to finish two songs. From 1:30 to 2:30 we had lunch. From 2:30 to 5:30, we would finish two more songs . . . It's a very comfortable way to work, and I wanted to work that way again. Actually, it's rock'n'roll, so it's play, not work."

Tuesday March 2
❦ Abbey Road Studio 2 – *Run Devil Run* recordings – 'Movie Magg' and 'Shake A Hand'.

Wednesday March 3
❦ Abbey Road Studio 2 – *Run Devil Run* recordings – 'Lonesome Town', 'Honey Hush' and the McCartney original, 'Run Devil Run', its title based on a herbal medicine shop in Atlanta, Georgia, that sells Run Devil Run products . . .

Thursday March 4
❦ Abbey Road Studio 2 – *Run Devil Run* recordings – 'Party' and the McCartney original 'What It Is'.
❦ Paul's *Liverpool Oratorio* is performed this evening at the Theatre Royal De Liege in Belgium.

Friday March 5

🍎 Abbey Road Studio 2 – *Run Devil Run* recordings – 'Blue Jean Bop', 'She Said Yeah', 'No Other Baby' and 'Brown Eyed Handsome Man'. (Recordings resume on Tuesday May 4 – see entry.)

Saturday March 6 & Sunday March 7

🍎 Further performances of Paul's *Liverpool Oratorio* take place this weekend at the Palais Des-Arts De Charleroi in Belgium. The piece is performed by the Royal Opera Company of Belgium.

🍎 In Melbourne, Australia, this weekend, George attends the Australian Grand Prix, where the *Melbourne Herald Sun* newspaper asks him when his next album will be released. "I don't know," he replies. "Maybe next month, maybe not. Maybe sometime, maybe not. I'm saving them up for when I kick the bucket. Some people will really want it then and I will sell more copies!"

Wednesday March 10

🍎 Paul appears at a political rally at Westminster Central Hall in London. During the gathering, which is titled Freedom For Tibet, Paul takes to the stage unannounced and reads aloud the lyrics to 'Blackbird'. Afterwards, he swiftly departs from the scene.

Monday March 15

🍎 At the Waldorf Astoria hotel in New York City, Paul is inducted at the 14th annual Rock And Roll Hall Of Fame ceremony. Among those in the star-studded gathering this evening are Elton John, Eric Clapton, Led Zeppelin's Jimmy Page, Lou Reed, Bonnie Raitt, Ray Charles, U2 singer Bono, and Julian Lennon. Accepting the award, following an induction speech by Neil Young, Paul remarks: "This is a brilliant night for me but it's sad too. I would have liked my baby to be with me. She wanted this." During his investiture, where he is recognised for his work with The Beatles and as a solo artist, Paul is joined on stage by his daughter Stella, who is wearing a vest adorned by the slogan: "About fucking time!" Paul also remarks: "By the way, while we're here, you've got me, you've got John in this, what about George and Ringo?"

Later, and to the delight of 1,500 guests who had paid $2,000 a head, Paul takes to the stage where, along with the evening's all-star line-up, he performs 'Blue Suede Shoes', 'What'd I Say' and, as the finale, 'Let It Be'. Paul had left the stage while Springsteen, Wilson Pickett, The Staple Singers, Mellissa Etheridge, Lauryn Hill and others performed Curtis Mayfield's 'People Get Ready'. He reappears on stage when he hears the opening chords of 'Let It Be', played by Billy Joel, and sings 'Let It Be' standing at the microphone backed by a showcase of talent including Bono, Eric Clapton, Robbie Robertson and Joel on piano. (Paul did not bring a guitar with him and, apparently, a member of the Hall Of Fame staff admitted that they "could not find him one!") At the conclusion of 'Let It Be', by which time it is now 12:45am, Paul shouts to the audience: "Thank you, it's time to go home. This is a great night, yeah?"

Backstage at the press conference, Paul is asked about his future plans. "I've just recorded some rock'n'roll songs last week," Paul confirms, "so that's coming out at some time." He does not take too kindly to his final question, whether "making the Hall Of Fame as a solo act provides a closure for him." He replies: "What closure? What am I gonna do, die next week? I'm just gonna keep on keeping on! Thank you very much, everybody, see ya." With this, he is gone. (Paul's daughter Stella had been by Paul's side only briefly at the start of the questions.)

Also inducted into the Rock And Roll Hall Of Fame this evening is the late Dusty Springfield, Billy Joel, Bruce Springsteen, Curtis Mayfield and The Beatles' producer George Martin, who remarks: "I am very honoured to be placed in a galaxy alongside many of my own heroes." The three-hour television transmission of the Rock And Roll Hall Of Fame event begins screenings on VH-1 in America on Wednesday March 17 and is repeated several times. (Coverage of the event is also featured on various news bulletins including CNN *Showbiz Today*, the following day and in the UK, on BBC, ITN and SKY, also on Tuesday March 16.)

Paul is seen leaving the Waldorf Astoria hotel at approximately 2:30am after attending a private party given by Bruce Springsteen.

Friday March 19
🍎 In London, at the Royal Albert Hall, all 4,000 tickets (priced between £25 and £75) for the Linda McCartney tribute concert sell out in just one hour. The show, which is titled Here, There And Everywhere – A Concert For Linda, is scheduled to take place at the venue on Saturday April 10 (see entry). Paul is not advertised as one of the performers.

Saturday March 20
🍎 The weekly BBC2 archive show *TOTP2* broadcasts, for the first time ever in the world, the new computer enhanced promotional film clip for 'Helen Wheels', an item released to coincide with the reissue of the album *Band On The Run* on Monday.
🍎 In Gibraltar, on the southern tip of Spain, special postage stamps are issued by the Gibraltar Philatelic Bureau and The Crown Agents Stamps Bureau to mark the anniversary of John and Yoko's marriage in the country, at just after 9am, 30 years ago today.

Sunday March 21
🍎 In the early hours of the morning (between 1:15 and 2:10am), Paul's illustrious career is featured in the ZDF German television documentary series *Pop Gallerie*.
🍎 In the UK today, the *News Of The World* runs a story about the apparent "discovery" of John Lennon's "diary tape" from 1979. Of course, this has not just been discovered – its existence has been common knowledge amongst Beatles aficionados for years. (See entry for 1979.)
🍎 Also today in the UK, BBC Radio Two, during the weekly show *Sounds Of The 60s*, begins transmitting a regular series entitled *The Beatles A–Z,* which promises to include a version of every track ever recorded and released by The Beatles. The first two songs featured today are 'A Hard Day's Night' (BBC Radio version) and 'A Day In The Life'.

Monday March 22
🍎 The 25th anniversary edition of Paul McCartney & Wings' album *Band On The Run* is released around the world by EMI, complete with previously unreleased bonus tracks, a 24-page booklet, a mini poster and interviews on the making of the album. "Catch Them Again" is EMI's press slogan.

Friday March 26 (until Sunday March 28)
🍎 In America, Beatlefest's 25th anniversary convention takes place at the (newly renamed) Meadowlands Crowne Plaza Hilton Hotel in Secaucus, New Jersey, situated four miles outside New York City. Special guests this weekend include Gordon Waller, of Peter & Gordon, the former Wings guitarist Laurence Juber, The Beatles' publicist Tony Barrow, the producer of *The Beatles* cartoon series and the full-length film *Yellow Submarine* Al Brodax and, among others, George's sister Lou Harrison. The attendance is around 7,000 over the three days, with fans coming from as far afield as Japan, Europe and many parts of America. On Friday, the opening night of the convention, a surprise guest is The Beatles' New York promoter Sid Bernstein, who cuts a big birthday cake and shares it with the thousands of Beatles fans.

Sunday March 28
🍎 In the UK, a pre-taped interview with Yoko is transmitted on BBC Radio Three.
🍎 Still in the UK, the remastered version of the 1968 film *Wonderwall*, featuring on its soundtrack a newly discovered song by George called 'In The First Place', recorded by The Remo Four, receives a screening in Southampton at the Gantry cinema. The film's director Joe Massot is also present to answer questions about the film. Shortly after, this re-edited and recently restored version of the film is released on Pilar home video in the UK.

Monday March 29
🍎 In America, tonight's edition of the two-hour A & E programme *Live By Request,* featuring Ringo and His All-Starr Band, fails to materialise. (The 9pm show was due to take place before a live studio audience from Sony Music Studios in New York City.)

Wednesday March 31
🍎 Paul's old home at 20 Forthlin Road, Liverpool, reopens for business. The museum's live-in curator John Halliday says: "I am looking forward to the new season. I enjoyed meeting the visitors to the house and showing them around last year. People have come

from all over the world, and I am pleased to be able to share the history of the house with them." (The house will be open to the public weekly from Wednesday to Saturday until October 31 and then from November 1 until December 11 on Saturdays only.)

April
- In the UK, the *Sunday Times* newspaper announces, in its annual poll, that Paul is the UK's top music millionaire with an estimated £500 million fortune. George, meanwhile, scrapes in at number 266 with an estimated fortune of just £90 million.
- In London, The Imperial War Museum holds an exhibition called *From The Bomb To The Beatles* which sets out to chronicle the change in British culture between the years 1945 and 1965. The Beatles are represented in the exhibition, which runs until May 29 2000, by stage costumes worn by John and Paul.
- In the UK, listeners to BBC Radio Two vote The Beatles' 'Yesterday' as The Song Of The Century. Also in this top 100 chart, compiled from choices by listeners, sales figures and songwriters such as Sir Elton John and Tim Rice, is John's 'Imagine', which is placed at number six. In addition, another Beatles recording, 'Hey Jude', reaches number 15.

Friday April 2
- In the UK, the *Daily Mail* newspaper prints a story which reveals that Paul has found himself a new woman, the 52-year-old designer and mother of four, Sue Timney. The report states that Sue sat near Paul at his daughter's recent fashion show in Paris. When shown this article, Paul is incensed and promptly gives an interview to the *Sun* newspaper, which appears the following day (see entry).

Saturday April 3
- "She's not my new woman. She's not even a close friend," screams an article on page nine of today's *Sun* newspaper. In response to yesterday's article in the *Daily Mail,* Paul tells the *Sun*: "This story is a pack of lies! She (Sue Timney) is not even a close friend to me or my family and it is scurrilous and mean-spirited for anyone to make any insinuations." He adds: "It is utterly out of order for a newspaper to make claims like this with no basis at all. I do wish that newspapers would check with me for the facts before they start these stupid rumours. I am now demanding a retraction."

On a more welcoming note today, Paul becomes the second Beatle grandfather when his daughter Mary gives birth to a seven-pound baby boy, who, insiders reveal, will be called Lawrence, James or Arthur. (It turns out to be the latter.) Paul drives from his Sussex farmhouse to be by her side.

Friday April 9
- Paul, along with the stars of tomorrow night's Linda McCartney tribute concert, assemble at the Royal Albert Hall in London where they begin rehearsals. As Paul is seen leaving the building, fans are saddened to hear him announce: "There'll be no more autographs . . . It's the end of an era," before he climbs into a waiting limousine, to be whisked away to a secret location in London. (Elvis Costello, incidentally, leaves the afternoon get-together and travels to Hammersmith where he appears live on the Channel 4 programme *TFI Friday*.)

Saturday April 10
- Tonight at the Royal Albert Hall in London, in a show hosted by the comic Eddie Izzard and organised by Chrissie Hynde, Paul, along with an all-star cast take part in a special tribute concert for Paul's late wife Linda. The performers include The Pretenders, Elvis Costello, Sinead O'Connor, Tom Jones, George Michael, Marianne Faithfull, Lynden David Hall, Des'ree, Johnny Marr, Neil Finn and Ladysmith Black Mambazo. At the conclusion of the show, entitled *Here, There And Everywhere – A Concert For Linda*, Paul appears on stage to perform the Ricky Nelson song 'Lonesome Town', a track that he and Linda used to listen to separately back in the Fifties, 'All My Loving' and, as part of an all-star finale, 'Let It Be'. The first highlights broadcast of the show takes place one week later on BBC Radio Two on Saturday April 17, between 7:30 and 9:00pm. The TV premiere of the show will not take place until the following day, Sunday April 18, broadcast on BBC1 between 22:35pm and 12:05am as a 90-minute show, also entitled *Here, There And Everywhere – A Concert For Linda*. (Neither programme features the finale version of 'Let It Be'.) To celebrate the show, a picture of Paul and Linda (circa

1972) appears on the front page of this week's TV and radio listings magazine, the *Radio Times* (April 17–23) in a story headlined "For The Love Of Linda", which features an exclusive interview with the comedy writer Carla Lane, a fellow animal rights campaigner and long-time friend of the McCartneys.

Thursday April 15
🍎 John is named "The Greatest Singer Of All Time" by the readers of the UK magazine *Mojo*. Paul appears in the top 100 chart at number seven.

Friday April 16
🍎 In the States, today's planned cinema reissue of The Beatles' 1964 film *A Hard Day's Night* fails to materialise. Miramax Pictures announce that the film will now open simultaneously in New York and Los Angeles on Friday September 17, with the rest of America receiving the film one week later.

Sunday April 18
🍎 In the States, George is in attendance at the Long Beach Grand Prix in California.

Monday April 19
🍎 In the States, Yoko again sues her one-time personal assistant Fred Seaman, claiming he stole priceless items after John died. The lawsuit has been prompted by Seaman's claim in a February 1999 letter to Capitol Records that a 1980 photo of John and Sean, overlooking the beach in the Bahamas, was used in last year's *John Lennon Anthology* box set without permission.

Thursday April 22
🍎 At the Bonhams rock and pop auction in London today, John's Vox stage organ, famously used during The Beatles' performance of 'I'm Down' at Shea Stadium in 1965, is put up for sale and raises £19,500. The Bonhams auction also sees one of Ringo's Beatles suits fetch £1,300, while his old Chevrolet car sells for £4,200. Among the many other Beatles items on offer, a set of Beatles Subbutteo figures sell for £420.

Monday April 26
🍎 "It's Paul McCarty". The UK newspaper the *Sun* prints a story about Paul's upcoming painting exhibition, which opens in Hamburg, Germany this Saturday.

Friday April 30
🍎 At the Kunstforum Lyz art gallery in St. Johann Street, Siegen, in Hamburg, Germany, Paul holds a press conference to launch his first exhibition of paintings, which opens at the gallery tomorrow. (European viewers can see short clips of Paul's conference on this evening's Sky News.) Paul is asked why Germany to launch his paintings. "I could have given hundreds of exhibitions with other people," he explains, "but I felt that Wolfgang was the first person who showed a real interest in my paintings." The exhibition, which is organised by Wolfgang Suttner and comprises 75 out of 500 of Sir Paul's private paintings, will run daily, between 10am and 6pm, until July 25. Wolfgang announces: "His talent completely overshadows the artistic efforts of other stars who try to paint. Paul gave me his OK to the exhibition as Siegen was the birthplace of Peter Paul Rubens." Painted since 1984, Paul's abstract artwork, in oils and acrylic, includes several paintings of Linda, John Lennon, David Bowie and the Queen of England, entitled 'A Salute To The Queen', who is painted green. (The show is expected to reach Tokyo and New York.) To accompany the exhibition is a catalogue containing 80 colour reproductions plus 20 black & white photos by Linda and articles by the artist Brian Clarke and Paul's biographer Barry Miles.

In the evening, Paul attends a private reception in the gallery for his close family, friends and associates, including his children, his brother Mike and The Beatles producer, George Martin. Paul's former Wings partner, Denny Laine, is not in attendance as previously reported. Paul's spokesman, Geoff Baker: "The launch was great. It worked really well. Paul was dead chuffed."

Late April
🍎 George is spotted at the Long Beach Grand Prix in America.

May

 The planned *Sgt. Pepper's* concert in London (revealed on November 17 last year) fails to materialise.

 Planned for release this month by the Eagle Rock label in America is a 3 CD box set featuring a compilation of live All-Starr Band recordings taken from the last ten years. Also during this time, it is reported that Ringo is recording an album in Los Angeles, intended for a Christmas 1999 release. When asked about this, Ringo replies: "It'll be very Christmassy and lots of bells, ding, ding, ding." In addition, he announces plans for another studio album in the year 2000!

 There's good news for George when reports suggest that, following a further test at a Windsor hospital, he has been given a clean bill of health, meaning his cancer has not returned.

Saturday May 1 (Sunday May 2 & Monday May 3)

 The Beatles are celebrated throughout the weekend on BBC Radio Two with their music and special programming. On the first night, there are the special programmes *The Beatles Legacy* (transmitted between 7:00 and 7:59pm) and *The Beatles Fantasy Concert* (between 8:00 and 8:59pm). The latter features a compilation of live concert performances recorded between 1963 and the Apple rooftop performance from January 30, 1969.

Sunday May 2

 At 2pm, Richard Lester is in attendance at the Philadelphia Film Festival for a special screening of The Beatles' movie *A Hard Day's Night*.

Tuesday May 4 (& Wednesday May 5)

 The seven days of *Run Devil Run* recording sessions conclude at Abbey Road in Studio No. 2 with 'All Shook Up' and then, the following day, with another McCartney original, 'Try Not To Cry'. The period of recordings also produces Jerry Leiber & Mike Stoller's 'Thumbin' A Ride' and Otis Blakewell's 'Ready Teddy'.

Thursday May 6

 George returns to Windsor Hospital in Berkshire for a checkup. He books in under the name Dylan T. Arias.

Saturday May 8

 The *Sun* newspaper prints across its middle spread a report from New York where Yoko meets, for the first time, John's lost sister, the 53-year-old hospital clerk Ingrid Pedersen. (See entry for Monday August 24, 1998.) After visiting Strawberry Fields, Lennon's memorial garden in Central Park, a tearful Ingrid remarks: "I know I'll never be closer to him than this. I was in tears of sadness and joy. Yoko never left my side and held my hand as we walked. She told me all about him. I feel that, at last, after all these years I am at peace and have reached journey's end." The report concludes by saying that when Ingrid came to say goodbye, she expected that they would never meet again. But Yoko held her hand and said, "No, no. This is not the end, it's the beginning." Yoko promises to get in touch with Ingrid when she is next in London and invited Ingrid back to New York any time. Ingrid ends by saying: "I thought one day we would be together, but fate conspired to keep us apart. In Yoko, I have the next best person."

Sunday May 9

 At this year's BAFTA awards, held at London's Grosvenor House Hotel, the two-part BBC2 *Arena* documentary called 'The Brian Epstein Story', first aired on the BBC last Christmas, wins the Hugh Wheldon Award for Best Arts Programme.

Monday May 10

 The *Sun* newspaper keeps up with its exclusive Beatles-related stories by announcing that "The Fab Four is set to release a new undiscovered single this year." The report, by Dominic Mohan of the "Bizarre" column, reveals that: "The Beatles are to release their last single *ever*. Sir Paul McCartney, George Harrison and Ringo Starr have unearthed a song they recorded but lost during sessions at Abbey Road in 1968. The as-yet-untitled track features John Lennon on vocals and will probably go on sale in September or October. The song will be the centrepiece of a Fab Four revival this summer in the run-up to the Millennium." The report continues: "The surviving Beatles are planning a summer spectacular with star acts, rumoured to include Boyzone and Robbie Williams, paying tribute to the group in front of 100,000 fans."

The article goes on to reveal that the three Beatles are currently working on a six-hour radio show, a TV special and an official Beatles biography by Paul, George and Ringo. In addition, it is confirmed that bosses at EMI want to make 1999 The Year Of The Beatles and are planning a huge range of merchandise. The revival is being dubbed The Beatlennium Project. A source close to the group says: "It is going to be a Beatles summer. They've unearthed a song that had been completely forgotten. It will be released in its original form. No new work has been done on it but Paul, George and Ringo have said this will be the last ever Beatles single – there's nothing else left. It's a perfect way to end the Millennium and it's sure to be a number one. The summer concert will see many of today's young bands paying tribute to the Fab Four. It will be the music event of the year. The revival will be based on the *Yellow Submarine* theme and they are now even talking about sailing a real yellow submarine up the River Mersey. Beatlemania looks like it's going to be back." The report concludes: "Paul, George and Ringo are likely to attend the Liverpool show, but I'm told they probably won't perform."

Paul's spokesman, Geoff Baker, has this to say: "The (unearthed) track is from the *Yellow Submarine* sessions. It's an upbeat thing, a real rocker. John is singing on it. It's not a 'Free As A Bird' job. It's something that is already there. It's good stuff!" Baker goes on to talk about the reissue of the *Yellow Submarine* album. "They've re-done the album and this is the first time that a Beatles album has been remixed. It's been re-edited in a re-fabbed way. There'll also be tons of *Yellow Submarine* merchandise in stores. Physically everything that is yellow. The whole project should be the trip of a lifetime."

The American *Ice* magazine hints that the supposedly (unearthed) "lost Beatles single" will actually be a new version of the 1968 track 'Hey Bulldog'. In reply, a spokesman for The Beatles says: "It may well be that track, but even the most die-hard Beatles fanatic will not have heard this version!" (This new version is believed to maybe feature the missing verse cut from the original version, but actually recorded and released in 1971 by the all-female rock group Fanny.)

 Also today, Paul joins the call to close down Britain's fur farm industry. Top mountaineer Sir Chris Bonnington and fellow environmental campaigner David Bellamy join Paul in an open letter to Westminster supporting the MP Maria Eagles' fur farm prohibition bill. This bill will stop the slaughter of thousands of mink and has been welcomed by the organisations Respect For Animals and the RSPCA.

 In Germany today, a VW Beetle once owned by John sells for £11,000 at a German auction.

Saturday May 15
 In the UK, the survey of the Top 100 Singles Of All Time, compiled by Guinness and based on the record's chart position and time spent at the top of the charts, is published. The Beatles feature three times in the listing; with 'She Loves You' being placed the highest, at number 19. John's 'Imagine' makes number 21. In the coveted number one spot is Bill Haley and The Comet's 'Rock Around The Clock'.

Monday May 17
 It is announced that eight British composers, including Paul, have written a classical musical tribute to Linda. The new tribute is an eight-song cycle for an unaccompanied choir with each composer contributing one song. It opens with Paul's own composition 'Nova' and other songs include 'A Good-Night', by Sir Richard Rodney Bennett, 'The Doorway Of The Dawn', by David Matthews and 'Prayer For The Healing Of The Sick', by John Tavener. The production, entitled *A Garland For Linda*, will be premiered on Sunday July 18 by the Joyful Company of Singers, alongside new choral arrangements for five Beatles songs, namely 'Lady Madonna', 'Fixing A Hole', 'And I Love Her', 'Here, There And Everywhere' and 'Let It Be'. The brainchild of Stephen Connock, chairman of the Ralph Vaughan Williams Society, the work is inspired by *A Garland For The Queen*, a 1953 tribute to the Coronation written by ten British composers.

Tuesday May 18

❦ Paul's 1984 film *Give My Regards To Broad Street* is shown in America on the FOX TV network at 4:01pm. (A further screening on the station occurs the following day, May 19, at 6:01am.)

Thursday May 20

❦ In London, at the Dorchester Hotel, Paul, on his first official UK engagement since Linda's death, attends the 1999 Pride Of Britain British Achievers awards ceremony, an event organised by Virgin and the *Daily Mirror* newspaper. Near to tears, an emotionally charged Paul, in attendance to present the Linda McCartney Award For Animal Welfare, announces: "It has been a very emotional occasion. I never expected it to be like this. What a day this has been. It has been such an inspiration. The point about these awards is that you don't usually see this side of people. You normally see the other side. I have been choked up. This shows how many good people there are in the world. Linda would have been well chuffed with the award created in her name. I have been crying all year and now I come here. I just want to thank *Mirror* readers for creating this category and dedicating it to my lovely Linda. I know she would be proud." The recipient of the first Linda McCartney Award For Animal Welfare, nominated by Paul himself, is Juliet Gellatley, the founder and director of the vegetarian charity Viva. Paul announces: "I chose Juliet because she deserves more publicity for her work. The point is that a few years ago Juliet would not have been at an awards ceremony like this, but vegetarianism is now the way of the future." Among the many other British heroes present at the ceremony today is the cancer sufferer and BBC TV sports presenter Helen Rollason, the boxer Lennox Lewis, Emma Bunton and Victoria Adams from The Spice Girls and the Prime Minister Tony Blair. At the gathering, Paul also meets the former model, Heather Mills. (Clips of the event, which do not feature Paul, are transmitted on Sky News in Europe later this evening.)

Friday May 21

❦ The British comedy star Norman Rossington, co-star of the film *A Hard Day's Night* in 1964, dies aged 70 in a Manchester hospital. The veteran character actor, believed to be the only actor to have appeared on film with both The Beatles and Elvis Presley, had been fighting cancer for the last six months. (See entry for Wednesday October 18, 2000.)

Monday May 24

❦ George and Ringo and their respective wives, attend the opening of the Annual Chelsea Flower Show in London. George, wearing a short haircut, looks extremely well, dispelling recent rumours of his poor health.

Wednesday May 26

❦ It is revealed that John is to be honoured when the Blue Plaque scheme, marking buildings' links with famous people, moves to Liverpool. Besides the former Beatle, poets, politicians and philanthropists are also among the notables selected for the scheme by the English Heritage in its first foray outside London.

June

❦ At the start of the month, in a press release, Apple announces that, " 'Hey Bulldog' will not be released as a single, but will appear as a video, designed to promote *Yellow Submarine* and the new songtrack album of re-mixed Beatles songs from the film. Geoff Baker, the Apple spokesman, announces: "In researching the *Yellow Submarine* project, Apple Corps has discovered previously unknown footage of The Beatles recording at Abbey Road Studios. It's believed to be the last unseen footage of The Beatles recording. The footage captures The Beatles recording 'Hey Bulldog', a lesser known song from the *Yellow Submarine* sessions in 1968. The footage was discovered after the screening of The Beatles *Anthology* in 1995. If it had been discovered before, it would have been included in the *Anthology*. The Beatles' recording of 'Hey Bulldog' will be issued as a video around the time of the launch of the new *Yellow Submarine* album, home video and DVD in the autumn. EMI Records recently considered issuing 'Hey Bulldog' as a new single, but it has now been decided to release the historic footage as a video instead."

(Note: The footage, excerpts of which had been seen fairly frequently over the years, was taken on February 11, 1968 when the group was required to make a promotional film for 'Lady Madonna', their new single.)

George, in conversation with Timothy White, the editor-in-chief of *Billboard* magazine: "When we were in the studio recording 'Bulldog', apparently they needed some footage for some other record and a crew came and filmed us. Then they cut up the footage and used some of the shots for something else, but it was Neil Aspinall who found out that when you watched and listened to what the original was, it was 'Bulldog'. So Neil put all the footage back together again and put the 'Bulldog' soundtrack onto it and there it was!"

🍎 Also at the start of the month, George Martin takes his Beatles orchestral show to Israel. The country had missed out on Beatlemania in the 1960s as the government in power at the time were convinced that the raucous strains of The Beatles' music would corrupt their young.

Wednesday June 2

🍎 At London's KDK Gallery in the Portobello Road, Cynthia Lennon, along with her old friend, Phyllis McKenzie, hold a launch party for their exhibition, a presentation of their favourite artwork pieces, entitled *Lennon And McKenzie*. Cynthia's work includes 14 ink-on-wash illustrations made for her 1978 autobiography, *A Twist Of Lennon*. Two pieces that did not finish in the completed publication are put up for sale at the exhibition priced at £999 each. Cynthia is quoted as saying: "I am doing this because I truly want to start afresh. I want to get all this Lennon stuff out of my life. It's a new Millennium and everything." (The show runs until Friday July 30.)

🍎 In London, later this evening, George attends a party to celebrate the Christie's charity auction of Eric Clapton's 100 guitar collection. The sale is taking place to raise, hopefully, £600,000 for the Crossroads alcohol and drug addiction centre in Antigua. Besides perusing the impressive range of guitars on offer, George joins Eric in a light-hearted jam to please the on-looking members of the press. "They were just messing around, but they looked very happy," says one partygoer. "It caused a lot of excitement." George also causes some laughter at the event when he tries to smuggle in a home-made cardboard guitar with Eric's priceless instruments. Also in attendance at the party are Olivia Harrison and Patti Boyd. (The auction takes place at Christie's in New York on Thursday June 24.)

Sunday June 6

🍎 It's announced that Paul is to spearhead a campaign exposing cruel animal practices used in testing some household cleaners. The British Union for the Abolition of Vivisection, responsible for signing up Paul, announces that: "6,000 British animals have suffered and died testing goods like washing powder in the past three years." Paul is also dedicating Linda's song 'The White Coated Man' to the cause.

🍎 In Blokker, Holland, a special ninc-foot sculpture, costing £15,000 is erected in the village to celebrate the 35th anniversary of The Beatles' performance there.

Tuesday June 8

🍎 The Beatles' 1966 track 'Tomorrow Never Knows' is named by *Musik* magazine as "one of the pioneers of modern dance music". The mag also cites the *Revolver* album track as "one of the first to avoid the standard verse/chorus/verse formats," and adds that the song "features reversed guitars and overdubs, hinting at the sampling technology of today."

Thursday June 10

🍎 Paul: "Tony Blair is wrong to support genetically modified food!"
Paul makes this comment at he announces a £3 million investment to ensure the vegetarian meal range, created by Linda, is completely GM free. During the London press conference, he announces that: "Sales of Linda McCartney Foods dropped after the BBC revealed in February that they contained a tiny trace – 0.5% – of GM Soya." He added, "The company has now removed Soya from its products and has replaced it with wheat for which there is no GM alternative grown." Paul also announces that the brand will spearhead a campaign against GM food with every pack of the 38 varieties in the range bearing the stamp "Say No To GMO". Paul then returns his attentions back to the

Prime Minister Tony Blair. "I can understand what he is doing," Paul admits. "He does not want people to panic. But I think he's wrong. I don't think there is enough evidence about the problems that might arise through GM foods. I don't think people are worrying unnecessarily. The last time they got into something like this was BSE when people did swallow it quite literally. This time we have to take time to find out exactly what the implications of GM foods are." (Footage from the ceremony is transmitted on Sky News this evening.)

As a footnote to this, it is revealed that the Linda McCartney factory at Fakenham in Norfolk, has been temporarily closed and steam-cleansed to ensure it is a GM-free zone. A new range of food has been strictly tested for any contamination and no trace of GM has been found, an exercise that has cost Paul some £3 million.

Friday June 11
 The *Daily Mail,* on its front page, prints the headline: "Why I'll Make All Linda's Foods GM Free – By Sir Paul." Inside, on page 21, in a report focusing on yesterday's news conference in London, Paul announces: "We have got to work out what the dangers of GM foods are before we put them in the public arena. How do we know what we are eating? I've got a grandson and I want him to eat good foods. As far back as 1995, Linda was saying, 'I'd rather have my own food grown by Mother Nature than by the chemical industry', and we are sticking to that benchmark." This morning, Paul appears on the UK TV breakfast show GMTV where he talks about genetically modified foods, plus Linda and his grandson, Arthur. The feature was taped in London the previous day.
 In America, George gives an exclusive interview to *Billboard* editor-in-chief Timothy White, where he reveals details of the forthcoming *Yellow Submarine* album and film, and divulges details that he is in the final stages of recording a new solo album and is compiling a boxed set of his solo demos, outtakes and previously unreleased recordings. George also reveals that ownership of Harrison's entire 1976–1992 Dark Horse/Warner Bros. catalogue has reverted back to him. This includes the two Traveling Wilburys albums. In addition, George reveals that he is contemplating re-issuing his albums with possible unreleased bonus tracks.

Sunday June 13
 Linda's photo exhibition Sixties opens at the Bruce Museum in Greenwich, Connecticut. This event marks the start of a three-year American tour for the pictures.

Monday June 14
 The Beatles beat Robbie Williams and The Spice Girls to be named Britain's greatest musical asset in a survey of people not even born when the fab four split. In the poll of under 24s, carried out by Lloyds/TSB, 52% chose The Beatles with Williams coming in at second spot with only 13% of the votes. The Spice Girls reaching fourth spot with only 11%. While in the poll of all age groups, The Beatles triumph again, collecting 44% of the votes. The Rolling Stones, who had just finished the UK leg of their tour at the weekend, receive just 3% of the votes.

Friday June 18
 Paul's 57th birthday is again celebrated by VH-1 in Europe, designating the entire day to programmes featuring the former Beatle.

Sunday June 20
 The American news station CNN broadcasts, at 9pm ET, an episode of the series *Celebrate The Century* which, this week, takes a look back at the years 1961 to 1980. The Beatles naturally feature heavily in the show. (Further airings of this programme take place on the station on Friday June 25 at 8pm ET and on Saturday June 26 at 10pm ET.)

Friday June 25
 In America, George Martin conducts the Hollywood Bowl Orchestra and an eight-piece rock band for A Tribute to The Beatles concert, held this evening at 7:30pm at the Hollywood Bowl in Los Angeles, California. At the venue, Martin tells reporters about The Beatles original feelings towards *Yellow Submarine*. "The Beatles hated both the song and the film based on it," he reveals.

July

☙ News continues to surface about the American CBS TV network's four-hour mini series based on Danny Fields' biography on the life of Linda McCartney, the details of which naturally continue to upset Paul. His spokesman, Geoff Baker, points out: "Paul has expressed his sadness at the news . . . Paul is upset at the prospect of any person or company cashing in on Linda's death. Paul accepts this sort of thing, but he is saddened by it. What man would want to see the memory of his beloved wife cheapened like this?" (The production, eventually to run to just 90 minutes, will be screened in America for the first time on Sunday May 21, 2000 – see entry.)

Monday July 5

☙ George is a surprise guest on Joe Brown's BBC Radio 2 show *Let It Rock*, where he discusses his favourite rock'n'roll records, performed by such artists as Elvis Presley, Jerry Lee Lewis, The Coasters, Eddie Cochran and Carl Perkins. George also plays the Richie Barrett version of 'Some Other Guy', a track covered by The Beatles in their Cavern Club days. "Our version's horrible," George remarks. (Harrison's piece, not originally intended for transmission, was recorded on Thursday July 1 at Joe Brown's house and began merely as a casual conversation about rock'n'roll whilst supping on a few beers!)

Joe Brown concludes the show by playing 'I Got Stung', a track recorded by Paul (on Wednesday March 1) for his forthcoming rock'n'roll oldies album (see entry). Joe Brown had obtained the McCartney track because he bumped into him during a preview of the *Yellow Submarine* film, which he attended with George. During the meeting, Paul proceeds to tell Brown that he is a big fan of his *Let It Rock* show. Brown informs Paul that the next show will be the last in the series and Paul, eager to participate, sends over to him a special mix of 'I Got Stung'. Unsurprisingly enough, fans tape the song (as well as George's interview) and the track ends up on the Internet. Two American radio stations, WRIF in Detroit and WNCX in Cleveland, download the track and proceed to air the recording, before Capitol Records force them to stop.

Sunday July 11

☙ The *Sunday People* reports that "The Beatles Get Back", revealing that "The Beatles are to get back together to where they once belonged. They will re-form and sing together for the first time in thirty years on a yellow submarine. The historic scene will be broadcast live by Channel 4's *Big Breakfast* on August Bank Holiday Monday. All three surviving members of the fab four will team up for a cruise on Liverpool's River Mersey to publicise the updated version of their 1968 film *Yellow Submarine*. A source close to the group said: 'We want to take the Yellow Submarine theme as far as we can. And there's no better way of doing this than getting the three Beatles to appear on a real submarine. They also said they were going to attend the celebrations in Liverpool on the day. But by singing 'Yellow Submarine', they are going to give fans an extra-special treat.'"

Sunday July 18

The world premiere of *A Garland For Linda,* a classical music tribute to Linda McCartney, takes place in the intimate chapel of Charterhouse School in Surrey. The piece, Paul's classical music tribute to his late wife, Linda, contains nine songs written for an unaccompanied choir and launches the Garland Appeal; a charity designed to raise money for cancer research and British music. The nine separate musical sections are written by some of the country's top composers and Paul himself. His section, called 'Nova', is a piece for a choir featuring an exchange with God, who intones: "I am here. I am here now. I am with you." Paul: "I think Linda would be very moved with most of it. I think she would be very glad that people have gone to all this bother, and I think she'd wonder what all the fuss was about." Amidst very tight security, Paul arrives at the venue in a private helicopter and lands in the school grounds about three-quarters of a mile away from the chapel. Upon his arrival, he attends a sound check, which starts at approximately 3:30pm in the chapel.

(The *A Garland For Linda* album is released by EMI Classics on Monday February 7, 2000.)

Tuesday July 20

☙ On his way to LIPA for a graduation ceremony, Paul opens a new playground in Calderstone Park, Liverpool, just yards away from his former home in Forthlin Road.

During his stay in the park, children and parents are surprised to see Paul shake hands and play with children on the roundabouts and the swings. Later, he unveils a plaque and plants an oak tree in memory of Linda.

Jean Catharell, of *Liverpool Beatlescene* recalls the event: "While standing waiting for Paul to arrive, we were all looking towards the Manor House where we expected that he would emerge. Then, all of a sudden, a black car appeared through the trees and made its way to the playground. It pulled up and Paul got out with John Hammel. Everyone moved towards him and someone said, 'We were expecting you to come from over there,' pointing to the Manor House. Paul, with a huge grin on his face, replies, 'Ah ha! I know this park better than you think.' He was wandering around the playground with kids all around him, reminiscent of the Pied Piper really, and suddenly this guy passed him a mobile phone and said, 'Paul, would you say hello to the wife?' Paul immediately took the phone and said, 'Hello wife!' and then chatted for a few minutes. Everyone was laughing their heads off. It was so funny. Paul was in a fantastic mood and up for most things.

"While Paul was walking around, there was this little kid in a Liverpool Football Club outfit. He must have been about 4 years old. He kept following Paul and walking by his side saying, 'You're Paul Cartney,' (not McCartney, just Cartney). Paul was laughing his head off and said, 'Yeah, I am.' This kid was everywhere and, at the end of the tour, Paul swiped this kid's hat off his head and put it behind his back and said to him, 'Where's your hat?' The kid stood there dumbfounded and Paul put it back on his head laughing. He picked him up and had his picture taken with him. It really was lovely stuff. At one point, the only official photographer there asked Paul to sit on the swings. Paul said no at first but was soon convinced it would be a good thing. There was a little boy on the swing and Paul jokingly said to the boy, 'Oy, get off that swing,' and promptly sat on it himself. He looked chuffed as he swung his legs around.

"When Paul performed the tree planting ceremony, it was hilarious. He was shovelling earth into the ground around the tree and there was a photographer opposite him goading him. As Paul took the next shovel of earth, he threw it at the photographer. Everyone burst out laughing and Paul stood there like the cat that had got the cream, it was a fabulous moment. The whole visit was amazing. With just John Hammel accompanying him (as it was supposed to be a private visit), it was so easy to speak to Paul and to take photographs. As I said earlier, he was in a tremendous mood and really did look like he was having the time of his life. He was wonderful with the children and looking at him, surrounded by little kids and babies, if you didn't know he was Paul McCartney, the superstar, he could have been any Dad in the park with his kids. It's very easy to see how him and Linda raised great kids with big hearts. They obviously loved raising kids and it shows. Paul was so very at ease with all the kids and babies and talked to the Mums about their offspring. At one point he sat on the roundabout and was suddenly swamped with kids. You could hardly see him, but he looked very happy. As he was walking around, he was saying to kids who were climbing, 'Hey, be careful there,' and he'd put his arms around their waists to steady them . . . It was just wonderful to see Paul like this. He was home, in Liverpool where he belongs!"

August
🍎 Scheduled to open around this time in Saitama, Japan, is the world's first John Lennon museum, featuring donations from Yoko Ono. The site will be inside a 35,000 seater sports stadium, located an hour away from Tokyo. (The museum will not actually appear until Monday October 9, 2000, John's 60th birthday.)

🍎 A remastered print of The Beatles' film *Yellow Submarine* is prepared for re-release to cinemas across the world. To coincide with the release, officially licensed *Yellow Submarine* merchandise begins to appear in stores around the world, including individual models of each of the Beatles as depicted in the film and calendars, comics, T-shirts, plates, greeting cards, limited edition cookie jars, wrist watches, model kits, silk ties, sweatshirts, hats, jewellery, bags, lighters, metal lunch boxes and, amongst other things, a limited edition Schwinn *Yellow Submarine* bike. (The latter appearing as the main prize in HMV record store competitions in the UK during September.)

Sunday August 1
🍎 In Henley-on-Thames, George upsets his neighbours when he throws a 21st birthday party for his son, Dhani. The quiet Beatle decides to mark this historic occasion by

staging a 15-minute fireworks display in the grounds of his Friar Park home. But unfortunately, local environmental health officials will soon claim that they had received a large number of complaints about the events, saying: "The show terrified children and animals for miles around." As the fireworks lit up the sky, car alarms went off, debris fell onto gardens and windows rattled. Mrs Peggy Leonard, from nearby Hop Gardens, says: "Suddenly, without warning, we were subjected to a most frightening display right overhead. Debris was falling into our gardens and one dreads to think what would have been the outcome had a spark set light to the tinder dry grass or trees. What on earth has happened to our nice, peaceful town?" The health officials write to George informing him of the complaints.

Sunday August 8

🍎 The 30th anniversary of The Beatles' photo shoot for the cover of their *Abbey Road* album is celebrated today in London. Fans are invited to cross the famed zebra crossing at the exact same time (11:35am) as the fabs did back in 1969. The event, which is marred by heavy rain, is organised by the London Beatles Fan Club.

Tuesday August 24

🍎 John's first guitar, a £10 Gallotone Champion, is bought for a staggering £155,500 by an unnamed New York investment fund manager, who bid for the instrument by telephone at the Sotheby's sale in London. The buyer remarks: "I consider John Lennon to be the most important musician of the 20th Century, and I am honoured to own something played by him." This guitar is the one played by John at the summer fete in Woolton, Liverpool, on the day he was introduced to Paul. On the guitar is a brass plaque proclaiming Aunt Mimi's legendary comment to John: "Remember, you'll never earn a living by it! September 15"

Wednesday August 25 (until Tuesday August 31)

🍎 The Liverpool based tourist organisation Cavern City Tours hold their annual international Beatles week, featuring a host of Beatle tribute bands from around the world. Due to the event's recognition from The Beatles' company Apple, this 1999 Beatles week is (besides the December 1963 Liverpool and Wimbledon fan get-togethers) the first ever official Beatles convention to be held in the world. On Saturday August 28, *Yellow Submarine* fever reaches Anfield, the home of Liverpool Football Club, when an eight-foot Blue Meanie appears on the pitch before the start of their match against Arsenal. The character, actually Paul Angelis, the voice of the original chief Meanie from the film, is also present when the city's mayor, Joe Devaney, cuts a special yellow ribbon to mark the start of the festivities. Also launched today is the new US *Yellow Submarine* postage stamp. In a written statement, Paul remarks: "It's lovely for the *Yellow Submarine* to become a postage stamp and I'm going to send lots of letters to people with little *Yellow Submarines* on them." (The stamp's first day of issue, along with the rest of the Celebrate The Century's 60s stamps, is on Friday September 17 in Green Bay, Wisconsin.)

Geoff Baker: "We wanted to bring it back to the place where they were born. Liverpool is the place where it all began."

But, for many, the highlight of the week takes place on Monday August 30, when, at the *Yellow Submarine* Mathew Street Festival, there is a *Yellow Submarine* outside stage, featuring Beatles music performed by sound-a-like bands all day long. Artists performing include Banned On The Run, The Overtures, Gary Gibson, Instant Karma, and many more. Naturally the day is dedicated to the world premiere screening this evening of the new picture enhanced and new surround sound version of the 1968 *Yellow Submarine* film at the Philharmonic Hall, an event organised by Apple in conjunction with MGM and Cavern City Tours. At the conclusion of the film, Lenny Pane from Sweden showcase the new 15-track *Yellow Submarine* songtrack album.

Friday August 27 (until Sunday August 29)

🍎 In America, the regular Beatlefest convention takes place in Orlando, Florida at the Caribe Royale Resort Suites Hotel, a venue situated eleven and a half miles from Disney World. Amongst the special guests this weekend are The Quarry Men.

September

 The Beatles appear on a list of 2,000 "Icons of the Millennium", set up by the British Prime Minister, Tony Blair. "Paul McCartney may become a lord," Blair announces. "George Harrison and Ringo Starr a Sir, but the government isn't sure about awarding John Lennon posthumously, since he's returned his MBE award."

 Hypertension Music release the single 'Little Children', which features The Peter Kirtley Band with Paul McCartney. All proceeds of the single go to Jubilee Action in aid of the Brazilian street children.

 Rumours in the Beatles fraternity suggest that, just prior to the *Yellow Submarine* releases, Apple will launch an official Beatles Internet web page.

Friday September 3 (until Wednesday September 15)

 The re-mastered version of *Yellow Submarine* is screened in San Francisco at the Castro Cinema.

Tuesday September 7

 At the Roseland Ballroom in New York City, Paul holds an invitation only Buddy Holly 'Rock'N'Roller' dance party. Accompanied by his daughter Stella, he arrives at 8:45pm, fifteen minutes later than scheduled, and makes a mad dash out of his limousine and past all the cameras and members of the press. With not one possibility of a picture, the journalists present are naturally angry. Celebrities present include the singers Chubby Checker, Neil Sedaka, Lou Christie and the record producer Tony Visconti and his wife, May Pang. Inside the venue, the crowd is treated to live music and rollerdance, with couples wheeled out to display their expertise on roller skates. Next, the singing star Bobby Vee comes out to delight the crowd, who, following more rollerdance antics, were then treated to a live performance from The Crickets. Paul and Stella spend most of the evening sitting in the balcony, and then, following a screening of a film on Buddy Holly, Paul appears on stage, where, completely unrehearsed, those around bring out to him his Sunburst Les Paul guitar. Paul then joins The Crickets for a version of 'Rave On'. But, suddenly, halfway through the number, Paul appears to change his mind about appearing and after his lacklustre performance, he promptly returns to his table in the balcony. Carl Perkins' son, Stan, and Bobby Vee, who performs with The Crickets, conclude the evening's entertainment. Also performing tonight is Nanci Griffith. (The New York radio station WCBS broadcasts the party, which is attended by 2,000 people.)

The host for the evening is Cousin Bruce Morrow. Various US TV programmes such as *Entertainment Tonight, CNN* and *Access Hollywood* cover the event. The Rogers & Cowan press release told of an all-star jam to close the evening, with rumours of surprise appearances by Elton John, Eric Clapton and Billy Joel being thrown around. The nearest we get to this is VIP area only appearances by Christopher Reeve, Phil Collins and Eric Clapton, who does not go near the stage. Fans desperate to get inside tonight to see Paul are forced to pay upwards of $500 for a ticket.

 During Paul's visit to the States, he records an interview about the Apple band Badfinger for a VH-1 *Behind The Music* documentary, which is not aired until November 2000.

Wednesday September 8

 At 11:57am, the recently painted *Yellow Submarine* Eurostar train makes its 180 miles-an-hour maiden trip, departing from London Waterloo and arriving in Paris, France, three hours later. It is reported the decoration, over 400 metres of plastic panels covering 18 carriages, and naturally featuring an assortment of Blue Meanies, Apple Bonkers and Flying Gloves, overseen by Apple's art director, Fiona Andreanelli, has cost Paul, George and Ringo, via Apple, over £100,000. A spokesman for Eurostar is quoted as saying: "It is a very interesting and exciting venture, which will see a train transformed into a *Yellow Submarine* travelling under the channel. We have been in discussion for some time with companies who want to use the marketing opportunities of the train, and this will be the first one." Before its first journey, a Jazz band struck up the 'Yellow Submarine' theme song. The head of Apple, Neil Aspinall, on hand to witness the first voyage, remarks: "I think the train looks fantastic and it's great that The Beatles' music is still listened to by the younger generation."

(The *Yellow Submarine* Eurostar train will travel, on average, three times a day between London, Paris and Brussels until the end of the year.)

Thursday September 9

 At New York's Metropolitan Opera House, Paul appears at the MTV Video Awards ceremony where, along with Madonna, he presents the "Best Video" award to Lauryn Hill. Looking at the card with the winner's name, Paul jokes: "You'll never guess who it is, man. It's some guy called Lawrence Hill . . . I love that guy!" When Paul had appeared on stage, Madonna knelt down to worship him and cited him as an example, saying: "Even famous celebrities can bring up beautiful, down-to-earth, kick-ass children." She also remarks that "his talent makes me nervous".

 The event is naturally covered by both MTV in America and Europe.

Friday September 10

 MTV in Europe broadcasts, for the first time, the 23-minute documentary *The Making Of The Beatles' Yellow Submarine*. The first repeat takes place on the station on September 14, on the same day that the show, featuring different edits, appears for the first time on VH-1 in America. The 23-minute show contains footage from the film as well as interviews with Paul, George and Ringo and many participants in the making of the movie as well as those involved with the film's restoration. To coincide with the screening, Apple release to VH-1, for a limited time of just one month, a brand new film compilation for the song 'Yellow Submarine', featuring excerpts from the animated film.

 While today in New York, on the 10th, Paul arrives at a party held for his daughter, Stella, and is seen with the cap missing from his front tooth. The story goes that he had bitten into a crusty baguette at a Big Apple delicatessen earlier in the day and it had dislodged the tooth. The story and the picture of Paul, minus the tooth, makes the front page of the *Mirror* on the following day, under the headline: "Can't Bite Me Love".

(Note: Paul originally lost the front tooth back in the spring of 1966 after an accident on his moped.)

Monday September 13

 The *Yellow Submarine* songtrack album is released in the UK as a CD and in limited edition yellow vinyl featuring the exact same tracks. Described not as a soundtrack but as a "songtrack", the album features 15 fully remixed and digitally remastered tracks, namely: 'Yellow Submarine', 'Hey Bulldog', 'Eleanor Rigby', 'Love You To', 'All Together Now', 'Lucy In The Sky With Diamonds', 'Think For Yourself', 'Sgt. Pepper's Lonely Hearts Club Band', 'With A Little Help From My Friends', 'Baby You're A Rich Man', 'Only A Northern Song', 'All You Need Is Love', 'When I'm Sixty Four', 'Nowhere Man' and 'It's All Too Much'. The Apple and MPL spokesman, Geoff Baker, is quoted as saying: "It'll be the *Yellow Submarine* album that the fans have wanted for thirty years, because this will be all The Beatles music from the film for the first time. It doesn't sound completely different, but the songs will sound like you've not heard them before." (The album is released in the States on Tuesday, September 14.)

(The album enters the UK charts at number eight, selling 19,000 copies in its first week and achieving Gold disc status by the beginning of October. While in the States, the album enters the *Billboard* chart at number 15, selling almost 68,000 copies in its first week.)

 To coincide with the 'Hey Bulldog' and *Yellow Submarine* releases, Apple distribute the recently recovered film clip of The Beatles recording 'Hey Bulldog' in Abbey Road Studios back in February 1968, clips of which originally appeared in the promotional film for 'Lady Madonna'. (See next entry for first airing.) In addition, a home video and DVD version of the *Yellow Submarine* film, which includes the 1968 documentary *A Mod Odyssey*, is issued the same day as the album by MGM Home Entertainment.

Friday September 17

 The newly edited "in the studio" promotional film clip for 'Hey Bulldog', billed as "The last video ever made of a Beatles performance", is premiered in America (at approximately 10:45pm) on the ABC TV programme, *20/20*. But fans, eagerly awaiting the first airing, are in uproar when the studio presenter, Barbara Walters, proceeds to talk throughout the song's soundtrack. Thankfully, the complete unhindered clip is repeated, this time on VH-1 in the States on Monday September 20. British Beatles fans are informed that no UK transmission for the film has yet been scheduled. (The clip eventually appears in Europe on Monday September 27 and the UK on Wednesday October 13 – see entries.)

Surprisingly, for a very limited time, the clip could be bought (unofficially) direct from ABC TV, via the station's "VHS tapes of broadcasted programmes" sales commercial arm. Apple acts quickly to stop these sales.

 Still in the States, Paul holds the first in a short series of four *Run Devil Run* listening parties. The opening event, in front of an estimated 300 crowd, takes place in Los Angeles at the House of Blues. For those already inside, the title track 'Run Devil Run' is teasingly played at 8pm, but the full programme does not begin until 9pm. By which time, Paul had arrived late (at 8:45pm), arriving in his limousine, which delivered the ex-Beatle to the backdoor. He pauses to wave to the crowd before entering the building.

Paul, wearing baggy blue jeans, a white T-shirt and a forest green jacket, arrives on stage at 9:15pm and is introduced by the president of Capitol Records. Paul then proceeds to talk about The Beatles and how he recorded *Run Devil Run* in a way similar to how they recorded in the early days. Paul concludes his seven –minute spot by saying: "I hope you enjoy the album and the listening party." The video of the making of *Run Devil Run* is played for about ten minutes before the album begins its first airing, with Paul remaining in the balcony for the duration. At the end of this, Paul reappears on stage to be given an award by the Capitol Records president for 60 million albums sold since 1970. Paul thanks the people for coming and explains the idea behind the listening party. "Instead of the usual people in suits, executive types, I decided to invite people off the street instead," he says. Paul tells everyone it was then time to go and the Capitol president tells everyone they are welcome to stay behind for a replay of the *Run Devil Run* album. Paul leaves the building with his son, James, in tow. Special guests in the VIP audience this night include Don and Phil Everly, Rod Stewart, Sheryl Crow and The Beach Boys legend, Brian Wilson. (The second *Run Devil Run* listening party takes place on Wednesday September 22 – see entry.)

 After a six-month delay, a remastered version of The Beatles' 1964 film *A Hard Day's Night* is simultaneously reissued to very selected cinemas in the UK and to choice theatres in New York and Los Angeles. This new print boasts a digitally remastered stereo soundtrack, engineered by Ron Furmanek.

Saturday September 18

 In Los Angeles, California, at the Paramount Studios in Hollywood, Paul endorses a "Party Of The Century" gala event sponsored by PETA, People for the Ethical Treatment of Animals. After a video tribute to Linda, accompanied by the moving song 'Angel', performed by Sarah McLachlan on piano, Paul returns to the stage in tears and unable to speak. But, he still manages to present the first Linda McCartney Memorial Award, which is dedicated to the fight for animal rights. Its first recipient is the actress Pamela Anderson Lee.

Later, at approximately 12:30am in an adjacent street, accompanied by his regular *Run Devil Run* band, Paul performs six tracks from the album, namely, 'Honey Hush', 'Brown Eyed Handsome Man', 'No Other Baby', 'Try Not To Cry', 'Lonesome Town' and 'Run Devil Run'. (Note: replacing Paul's regular accordion player, Chris Hall, tonight is Doug Lacy of the Los Angeles band Zydeco Party Band.) Also appearing on the bill this night are The B 52's, and Chrissie Hynde of The Pretenders.

The star studded event, which is attended by 2,000 people, is aired by the Broadcastisland.com Internet site, but they are forbidden to air any video or audio from Paul's tracks 'Honey Hush', 'Brown Eyed Handsome Man' and 'Run Devil Run'. The broadcast rights for these songs, for a short space of time, are held by VH-1 who transmit these tracks for the first time in a broadcast (in the States) at 10pm on Saturday October 16. The first complete six-track transmission will not take place until Friday January 28, 2000, when they are broadcast on Musicmax in Canada. To date, the only transmission of the PETA show in Europe (featuring Paul's complete six-song show) takes place on VH-1 on Thursday August 10, 2000 as part of their *Paul McCartney Night* (see entry as well as the entry for Saturday February 5, 2000).

Paul's appearance at the PETA awards is also featured in the American shows *Access Hollywood,* advertised cruelly as "See Paul McCartney in tears", and NBC TV's *Today* show (both aired on Monday September 20). The latter also featuring an exclusive interview with Paul conducted backstage at the venue.

Sunday September 19

 The *Mail On Sunday* cover story is on Paul, who reveals that "Linda McCartney is still my greatest inspiration".

 The Beatles' *Yellow Submarine* songtrack album enters the UK album charts at number eight.

Monday September 20
 A pre-taped interview with Paul at the PETA Awards ceremony is aired on *Entertainment Tonight* in the States.

Tuesday September 21
 An original 16mm master print of The Beatles' 1970 film *Let It Be*, is put up for sale at the Atlanta based Great Gatsby's.

Wednesday September 22
 Another *Run Devil Run* listening party takes place, this time at the Manhattan Center's Hammerstein Ballroom in New York. Celebrities in attendance, in the VIP section, include the singer Judy Collins, the actor Woody Harrelson, the record producer Tony Visconti and his wife, John Lennon's former lover, May Pang, the model Christine Brinkley, rock star Bruce Springsteen and Dia Stein from the Westwood One radio station. An hour into the evening's entertainment, a video on the making of *Run Devil Run* is played on the venue's screens and then the host for the evening, the VH-1 presenter, John Fugelsang, takes to the stage where he introduces Paul, who had arrived later than his scheduled 9pm. Paul's introduction is most memorable when Fugelsang says: "People are saying rock is dead. In a year that Ricky Martin is said to have invented Latin Pop, this man recorded 'Besame Mucho' in 1962 . . . In a year where they call The Backstreet Boys the fab five and a year where they call NSync a band, real bands write their own songs and play their own instruments . . . Well, if Madonna can introduce Paul at the VH-1 awards, I can top it . . . The only rock'n'roller to have the Queen on his speed dial . . . He is the ayatollah of rocknrolla . . . This man is said to be the only person to be kicked out of the Wu Tang Clan . . . Ladies 'n' gentlemen . . . I would like to introduce you to . . . Paul fuckin' McCartney," who then comes out on to the stage to talk about his new album.

Further *Run Devil Run* music, albeit very loud and distorted, then plays on the video screens, before Paul reappears on stage where, in a 15-minute session, he jokes with the crowd, accepts a bunch of flowers and partakes in a short question and answer session with the crowd. One young girl asks him: "Can I hold your hand?" Paul replies: "Nooooo, but I want to hold your hand." While another fan asks Paul: "When will *Let It Be* be released again on home video?" Paul replies by asking: "Isn't it already?" When he is told no, he replies: "Well, I've got one. Perhaps it will be re-released soon."

After three further *Run Devil Run* album plays, Paul leaves the building accompanied by Geoff Baker and acknowledges the fans, but does not stop to sign any autographs.

Reports of the event appear on *Fox News* (by Patrick Riley) and in *The New York Post* (by Dan Aquilante). The next *Run Devil Run* listening party takes place in Europe (see entry for Tuesday September 28).

Thursday September 23
 The *Daily Mail* lists the top 100 "Greatest British Films" ever made, with The Beatles' 1964 film *A Hard Day's Night* being listed at number 88.

Saturday September 25
 Paul makes a guest appearance on BBC Radio 2's *Tom Robinson Show*, where he, naturally, plays tracks from his forthcoming *Run Devil Run* album.

Monday September 27
 The *Making Of Yellow Submarine* documentary is transmitted on the French/Belgium channel RTBF-La Deux. The first European screening of The Beatles' brand-new 'Hey Bulldog' promotional film precedes the airing.

Tuesday September 28
 Paul's third *Run Devil Run* listening party takes place in Cologne, Germany at the Das E-Werk venue. The biggest German Beatles fan club, Beatles Club Wuppertal, has 50 pairs of tickets to give away for the event but, twenty-four hours before the party, Paul's spokesman, Geoff Baker, informs Beatles Internet webmasters to tell everyone that "everyone who shows up at the gates of the venue would get in", as 500 tickets are,

apparently, still available. Paul arrives at 6:30pm in his limousine and exits the car wearing dark glasses. Inside the venue, at 8pm, a representative from EMI Electrola comes on stage and gives his introduction to the crowd in English. "Welcome to Cologne, and welcome to this very special listening party here tonight, where we all have the chance to listen, for the very first time, to the new project by an artist who, as a musician and as a human being, has influenced the worldwide music scene like second to none during this second half of this century. Now, Paul's new album is called *Run Devil Run*, and we'd like to kick off tonight's event by giving you some inside views and background information about the production and how it all came together. Now, enjoy the music, dance if you will, and wait for the man himself. Let the tape roll first . . ." (The *Run Devil Run* EPK – Electronic Press Kit – plays.)

At the end of which, Paul appears on stage. "Deutschland . . . Guten Abend," he speaks in German, adding: "C'mon . . . Thank you, all right." Then, in a mixture of German and English languages, Paul proceeds to tell the crowd about the making of *Run Devil Run* and how its recording was influenced by the early style of recording by The Beatles. Before leaving the stage, he announces that he will be back after the album is played to take questions from the audience. As promised, Paul returns to face the German crowd. "Thank you for showing up tonight," he tells the fans. "We thank you," shouts back one fan. Someone hands Paul a stuffed toy, a Diddle mouse, and Paul proceeds to play with it. He then notices someone holding his 1982 album *Tug Of War*. "I've got that one . . . I've got hundreds at home," he tells the fan.

A fan asks Paul: "Can you imagine playing those great rock'n'roll songs live on stage in the future?" Paul replies: "Yeah, the thing is I don't know the band. Precisely, we made the record over five days and then we just did the show in LA where we did a one-day rehearsal and then one day in the show. So, I've only met this band for seven days, so I daren't ask them to go out on tour yet."

Another fan asks: "What of the songs did you write yourself and what was the inspiration for these songs?" Paul replies: "There's three of them I wrote. I wrote one called 'What It Is' and there's one called 'Run Devil Run', and there's one called 'Try Not To Cry'. The inspiration for 'What It Is' was Linda. I'd already written that for Linda, so that was the first one I wrote for the album. The second one, I was talking to the producer and he said, 'You know, it'd be a good idea if you wrote a couple of songs,' so I wrote 'Run Devil Run', because I was in a shop in Atlanta, in America, and I saw all these products. The products were called Run Devil Run and it said that if you put this in your bath it would send the devil away. I liked the title Run Devil Run, so I made a song about that. 'Try Not To Cry' was inspired by my love for rock'n'roll." Paul leaves the stage after the question and answer session had petered out. It had lasted just eight minutes. (The fourth and final *Run Devil Run* listening party takes place on Thursday September 30 – see next entry.)

Thursday September 30

 At the Equinox Club in London's Leicester Square, Paul's throws the fourth, and final, *Run Devil Run* playback launch party, arriving in a chauffeur-driven limousine, driven by John Hammel, at 6:07pm to be greeted by a large crowd of screaming, hysterically waving fans, many of whom are contained behind specially arranged metal fencing.

The first three hundred tickets for the event are available free of charge, and in order to get one, fans are invited to bring along a copy of the *Sun* newspaper. People began queuing for their tickets at 10am on the morning of the event.

Inside the Equinox club, the *Run Devil Run* EPK (Electronic Press Kit), featuring exclusive interviews with Paul and footage from the *RDR* recording sessions, receives two screenings on the large video screens set up inside the venue. Paul, who appears briefly on the stage, introduces the first screening. He returns later to take part in a short question and answer session with members of the audience, during which, one man asks, "Are there any more lost Beatles songs knocking around?" Paul responds by saying, "This isn't anything to do with *Run Devil Run*," before enigmatically admitting, "Yes, there is." During his time on stage, Paul is handed two original 45 singles, The Vipers' 'No Other Baby' and Little Richard's 'Shake A Hand', both of which are covered by Paul on his new album. The playback of *Run Devil Run* begins at 7:00pm and the get-together officially ends two hours later, at 9:00pm. (Paul is seen leaving the venue at approximately 9:10pm.) The different coloured *Run Devil Run* tickets also serve as entries to a special *RDR* competition. Special guests seen at the party, upstairs in the VIP area, include the comedian Ben Elton and the DJ, Gary Crowley.

✪ Also today, at the Christie's auction in London, John's handwritten lyrics to 'I Am The Walrus' fetches £78,500 while George's rosewood telecaster, brought to the Bonham's auction by Delaney Bramlett, remains unsold after bidding stopped halfway through the estimated price of £200,000.

September (end of month)
✪ The *Imagine* album documentary *Gimme Some Truth*, recently changed from its original *Wonsuponatime* title, is finally completed in America. The director on the 56-minute piece is Andrew Solt. (See entry for Tuesday October 5.)

October
✪ The long mooted *Project X*, the secretive EMI compilation of Beatles hit singles, is officially scrapped by the label, because EMI had missed the Christmas cutoff date, where labels have to book space in retailers racks in order that their new product is on prominent display for the lucrative festive spending spree. (See entry for August, 2000.)
✪ John's 1971 song 'Imagine' is voted Britain's favourite song lyric in a poll for National Poetry Day. John's 'I Am The Walrus' and Paul's 'Yesterday' also made the top ten of choices. (See entry for December 13.)

Saturday October 2
✪ BBC Radio 2 in the UK broadcasts a 30th anniversary special on The Beatles' final studio album, *Abbey Road*.
✪ An exclusive interview conducted with Paul by Dominic Mohan at the *Run Devil Run* listening party at the Equinox Club on Thursday is published in the *Sun*.

Monday October 4
✪ In the UK, Paul releases *Run Devil Run*; a 15-track Parlophone album comprising twelve rock'n'roll tracks and three new McCartney originals. The album is available in CD, cassette and mini disc versions. (For the tracks, see previous entry starting Monday March 1.) Also released at the same time in the UK is a limited edition two CD version in a slipcase, containing the *Run Devil Run* album alongside a special 40-minute interview CD with Paul conducted by Laura Gross. (See entries for Monday October 18 and Tuesday December 7 for further *RDR* releases information.)
   Paul on the recording of the album: "One of the great buzzes was sitting down with a cassette with a piece of paper and a pencil and getting the first line of the lyric. Then, stopping the cassette, winding it back and getting the next line. It was like, 'My God, I've not done this since I was a teenager.' Paul also reveals that Linda had encouraged him to make the LP. "We were talking about it in the last year," he announces. "She'd say, 'You've got to do that.' Unfortunately, she didn't live to see it, but it gave me an added impetus to carry on . . . She was a rocker – a major league rocker."

Tuesday October 5
✪ *Run Devil Run*, Paul's first new studio album since *Flaming Pie* in 1997, is released in the States and to coincide with the issue, Capitol Records and The MediaX Corporation, at 12 noon (EST), "fire up" an exclusive online listening bash, which features the first broadcast of an exclusive Eddie Puma McCartney interview and a promotional 5-minute making of *Run Devil Run* video, which begins airing on Wednesday October 6. Six tracks from the album, 'Run Devil Run', 'Try Not To Cry', 'No Other Baby', 'I Got Stung', 'Brown Eyed Handsome Man' and 'Lonesome Town', are streamed in their entirety at MediaX's and Capitol's site. These songs will be made available for the duration of the promotion, which lasts through until midnight on Monday October 11. In addition, the Eddie Puma produced radio interview will air in daily segments throughout the week with the final instalment slated for Sunday October 10.
✪ To coincide with the release of *Run Devil Run*, the Catalog Marketing Group of EMI Music Distribution, celebrate the millennium in "Back to the Future" style with CD album replicas and/or limited edition 180 gram vinyl re-issues of platinum titles. The set released includes the Paul & Wings album *Band On The Run*.
✪ A pre-recorded interview with Paul fails to appear this morning on the NBC TV *Today* show.
✪ While in Cannes at the Television Festival, the Yoko Ono approved *Gimme Some Truth*, the documentary on the making of John's 1971 *Imagine* album, receives its first

public screening. After its initial screening, the distributors announce that they have sold the documentary film to thirteen different countries.

Wednesday October 6
 In Paris, Paul's daughter Stella presents her fifth fashion show for the House of Chloe. Her luxurious clothing, unveiled during the fashion week in Paris, accentuates the female shape. Her inspiration for the new collection of clothing was The Beatles' 1964 song 'She's A Woman'. "It is She's A Woman, but she's a naughty little thing too." Paul, hotfoot from England, remarks on the skimpy outfits on view: "It's hot, sexy and chic. It will make all the men sweat. Stella means 'star' and she is! I'm very, very proud of her." Stella has revolutionised Chloe with teen appeal, boosting profits at the fashion house by 500% since she took over two-and-a-half years ago.

Saturday October 9
 In the States, Paul is the subject of this evening's MSNBC TV archive show *Time & Again*.
 George, Olivia and Dhani are again in the audience at Ravi Shankar's concert at the Barbican Centre in London. George is seen rushing in the side door, trying to avoid the throngs of fans who had hoped to get George to sign something. One fan, from Germany who is seen thrusting a copy of the *Abbey Road* album towards him, shouts in vein at the quiet Beatle, "But I've come all the way from Germany." George is, naturally, unimpressed, and shouts back, "I don't give a fuck about The Beatles."

Wednesday October 13
 The UK's Beatles fans wait to see the new promotional clip for 'Hey Bulldog' when it is screened (at 6:32pm) on the BBC2 archive music show *TOTP2*. A repeat screening of the complete *TOTP2* show, complete with the prized 'Hey Bulldog' clip, takes place again on BBC2 on Saturday October 16.

Thursday October 14
 VH-1 in Europe, yet again, designates the day *Paul McCartney Day*. The highlight for which, is the first European screening of an almost complete *Run Devil Run* EPK (Electronic Press Kit), which forms a 45-minute special transmitted between 8:00 and 9:00pm. The rest of the 13 hours of screenings (between 1pm and 2am) include repeats of Paul's *Greatest Hits, Ten Of The Best* and his 1993 *Live In The New World* concert in Charlotte, North Carolina.

Saturday October 16
 At 8pm, Paul is in attendance at the world premiere performance of *Working Classical*, which takes place in Liverpool at the Royal Philharmonic Hall. Paul: "*Working Classical* is a pun because I don't like to get too serious but also I'm very proud of my working class roots. A lot of people like to turn their backs especially when they get a little bit elevated in life, but I am always keen to remind other people and myself of where I'm from." On the music featured in *Working Classical*: "My favourite arrangement is 'Warm And Beautiful' . . . that always does my head in. It captures some of my innermost feelings for Linda. I'm not ashamed to be emotional. I used to be when I was younger, but I'm not anymore . . . I have heard these pieces obviously . . . they were played at Lin's memorial services in London and New York."

During a break from rehearsals on the day, Paul also gives an interview to Juliet Bremner of ITN News, where he again speaks about Linda. "She enjoyed me getting into the orchestral field," he reveals, "because she saw two of the orchestral pieces I did. She came to the premiere of those and loved them. She liked the idea of me doing something different."

Later, a specially invited 'after concert champagne reception' is held in the Rodewald Suite at the venue. Tickets are priced at £25 and donated to "The Forget Me Not" charity.

The television show of the event airs on BBC1 in the UK on Sunday April 23 (between 11:00 and 12:15am) and on PBS across America in March 2000, between the 5th and 20th. (The *Working Classical* album is released on Monday October 18 in the UK and on Tuesday October 19 in the USA.)

♣ At 10pm, VH-1 in America airs the PETA Awards ceremony, which took place on Saturday September 18 (see entry). This version features just three of Paul's six tracks, namely, 'Honey Hush', 'Brown Eyed Handsome Man' and 'Run Devil Run'.

♣ At 6:10pm on both days, today and Sunday October 17, the digitally re-mastered version of *Yellow Submarine* is screened, in NFT2, at the National Film Theatre at London's South Bank.

Monday October 18

♣ Parlophone in the UK releases the first singles from *Run Devil Run,* a two-part set limited to 15,000 copies, and featuring 'No Other Baby', 'Brown Eyed Handsome Man' and, the non album track, 'Fabulous'. The first version of the CD features the tracks in mono and the second version of the CD has, naturally, the same three tracks in stereo.

Tuesday October 19

♣ Paul's new album of classical music, *Working Classical*, is released on the EMI Classics label. The track listing is as follows: 'Junk', 'A Leaf', 'Haymakers', 'Midwife', 'Spiral', 'Warm And Beautiful', 'My Love', 'Maybe I'm Amazed', 'Calico Skies', 'Golden Earth Girl', 'Somedays', 'Tuesday', 'She's My Baby' and 'The Lovely Linda'. (A double album vinyl edition is released on Monday December 6.)

♣ While in the States, Mercury Records release Ringo's 12-track Christmas album *I Wanna Be Santa Claus*, recorded at Mark Hudson's "Whatinthewhathe?" studios and featuring a couple of guest appearances by Joe Perry of Aerosmith. The track listing is as follows: 'Come On Christmas, Christmas Come On', 'Winter Wonderland', 'I Wanna Be Santa Claus', 'Little Drummer Boy', 'Rudolph The Red Nose Reindeer', 'Christmas Eve', 'The Christmas Dance', 'Christmastime Is Here Again' (Ringo's version of The Beatles' 1967 track), 'Blue Christmas', 'Dear Santa', 'White Christmas' and 'Pax Um Biscum (Peace Be With You)'.

Wednesday October 20

♣ The BBC World Service begins broadcasting (at 10:20am UK time) Paul's four, soon to become five, part series entitled *Paul McCartney's Routes Of Rock*, which features him taking a look at some of his favourite songs and how they influenced his own music. During the 29-minute programmes, Paul reveals how the 1950's idol Buddy Holly made glasses fashionable, and saved John Lennon from years of bumping into things. "He was blind as a bat without his horn-rimmed specs, but was embarrassed to wear them in The Beatles' infancy. So when Buddy came out, he could finally stick his glasses back on and see again."

A BBC spokesman remarks on the programmes, which were recorded at Paul's home studio in Sussex: "It's a real scoop for the World Service. Paul is an international figure and we will be taking him out to an international audience." (A special two-hour compilation of *Routes Of Rock* is transmitted on BBC Radio Two on Christmas Day.) The first American radio transmissions of the series will not take place until Monday January 17, 2000 (see entry).

♣ At Abbey Road Studios in London, in Studio One, a special live broadcast takes place in honour of the 30th anniversary of The Beatles' album *Abbey Road*. Fourteen American Classic Rock stations do their morning/afternoon programming live from the studio this day, as well as on Thursday October 21 and Friday October 22. A number of special guests stop by to appear on the shows, including Rod Argent (The Zombies), Jack Bruce (Cream), Robbie McIntosh (The Pretenders and Paul McCartney's band), Chrissie Hynde (The Pretenders), Ian Paice (Deep Purple and Paul's *Run Devil Run* band) and Richard Porter of The London Beatles Fan Club. The stations taking part in the event include WVMX-FM in Cincinnati, WAAF-FM in Boston, KJQY-FM in San Diego, KUFX-FM in San Francisco and KMTT-FM in Seattle.

♣ The *Express* features an interview with Paul entitled: "Life After Linda – Why I Believe That I Could Find Love Again, By Sir Paul McCartney".

Thursday October 21

♣ Beginning today, and lasting over the coming weekend, fifty-one radio stations across America broadcast a 90-minute radio special celebrating the 30th anniversary of The Beatles' classic 1969 album *Abbey Road*. The special, produced by MJI Broadcasting, features music and interviews about the history, the recording and the effect of the album on the whole world. The show also features interviews with all four Beatles, including brand new interviews with Paul, Ringo and The Beatles producer, George Martin.

Friday October 22
❦ At the Black Island Studios in Acton, West London, Paul films a promotional clip for 'Brown Eyed Handsome Man', but the shooting runs into trouble when armed police from Scotland Yard are called following complaints that men were seen running around with guns. The first police team on the scene are forced to reverse its squad car up the road after four men came up to them with their fake guns, but they were blocked by other traffic. Paul overhears the disturbance and intervenes and explains to police that the men are only actors appearing in his new video. "It's all right," he tells the police, "these guys are with me. The guns aren't real, we're making a video."

A Scotland Yard spokesman says later: "Nobody was charged, but the extras and the management at the studio were given formal words of advice." While Paul has this to say: "You can't just sit back when you see stuff like this going on. These guys were my team and I had to look out for them." (See entry for Wednesday December 8.)

Saturday October 23
❦ Today's edition of the *Mirror* features an interview with Paul, who remarks: "When I saw Heather and Helen at the Pride of Britain Awards, I knew I needed to help." The piece, carried out during a break from yesterday's filming in London, also reveals that Paul had donated £150,000 to landmine victims.
❦ The London premiere of *A Garland For Linda* takes place at St. James's in Piccadilly.

Friday October 29
❦ Anthony Barnes, the showbusiness correspondent of PA News, exclusively reveals that: "McCartney Is To Perform Live On TV." The report continues: "Sir Paul McCartney is to play live on TV with a band for the first time in six years as he takes part in a BBC2 show, the UK début for his new outfit. The former Beatles star will perform three songs from his new rock and roll album, *Run Devil Run*, on *Later With Jools Holland* on Saturday November 6. His backing band is the same as the one for the album, featuring Pink Floyd's David Gilmour and Deep Purple's Ian Paice. The band joined him in Abbey Road's Studio 2, where he created most of The Beatles' catalogue, to create an album in just a week. Sir Paul's last appearance with a band was on *Top Of The Pops* in 1993, although he did do a solo slot on *TFI Friday* in 1997." (See entry for Friday June 27 that year as well as the entry for Tuesday November 2, this year.)

Sunday October 31
❦ Paul and Heather spend Halloween night together at his home in Sussex.

November
❦ An interview with Paul, carried out by Patrick Humphries to promote *Run Devil Run*, is printed in this month's *Record Collector* magazine.

Monday November 1
❦ An interview with Paul, conducted by the DJ Gary Crowley, is recorded at MPL in Soho Square, London, the results of which are broadcast in *The Gary Crowley Show* on GLR on Friday November 12. Later, Paul visits Gallery & Quot, situated at 6 Cork Street, London, where he watches the Tomoko Takahashi and Luke Gottelier exhibition.
❦ Paul and Ringo send wreaths to the memorial service of Bobby Willis, the late husband of Cilla Black. The private ceremony takes place in Denham, Bucks, where The Beatles producer George Martin tells the packed congregation: "Their marriage was a rock, an example to everyone."

Tuesday November 2
❦ At the BBC Television Centre in Wood Lane, London, Paul and his regular *Run Devil Run* band tape an appearance for the BBC2 live late-night music show *Later With Jools Holland*, hosted, as always, by the former Squeeze keyboards wizard Jools Holland. Paul, making his first BBC performance appearance since *Top Of The Pops* on Wednesday February 17, 1993, opens the programme with 'Honey Hush' and goes on to play, alternating between the other acts on the show, 'No Other Baby', 'Brown Eyed

Handsome Man' (joined by Chris Hall on accordion) and, to close the show, 'Party', which features piano accompaniment from Jools Holland. An excerpt from the recent Apple promotional film for 'Hey Bulldog' is also screened during Paul's interview sequence with the host. The first TV transmission of the *Later With Jools Holland* show takes place on Saturday November 6 (between 11:24pm and 12:28am), with a repeat screening on Friday September 8, 2000 (1:34 and 2:38am). A further complete screening of the show takes place in America on Saturday April 15, 2000 as part of a *Paul McCartney Night* on BBC America (see entry). Joining Paul on the show tonight are Travis, Shola Ama and The Flaming Lips. The first three tracks from Paul's appearance are repeated in *TOTP2*, transmitted on BBC2 on Wednesday November 17, 1999 with a repeat screening of the show taking place on the following Saturday, November 20.

Friday November 5
🍎 At 6:30pm, the National Film Theatre at London's South Bank premieres, in NFT1, the newly restored version of *A Hard Day's Night*. Afterwards Steven Soderbergh interviews the film's director, Richard Lester, on the stage. The event, sponsored by Carlton Cinema and the *Guardian* newspaper, is part of a brief Richard Lester season at the 43rd London Film Festival, which will also include John's 1967 film *How I Won The War*.

Saturday November 6
🍎 The Beatles are voted "Best band for a thousand years" in a "Music Of The Millennium" poll, conducted throughout the year by HMV, Channel 4 and the radio station, Classic FM. They totally dominate the results, taking four of ten titles in a massive national poll of 600,000 votes, the biggest ever survey of popular music to date. The 1967 album, *Sgt. Pepper's Lonely Hearts Club Band* comes out top in the Best Album category. John's 'Imagine' comes in at number two in the Best Song category, beaten by half a per cent by Queen's 'Bohemian Rhapsody'. Queen was second to The Beatles in the Best Band section, but they collected only a fifth of the votes cast for the fab four. The Beatles took 20% of the total votes cast in that section, as many as the rest of the top ten combined! John is also voted the 'Most Influential Musician Of All Time'. Further accolades are heaped upon him when he tops the Best Songwriter list, with Paul coming in second. The results are announced at a special event held at Elstree Studios in Hertfordshire, highlights of which are screened on Channel 4 on Saturday November 13, between 9:00pm and midnight. A planned appearance by Paul at the event fails to materialise, but a video message from Yoko, recorded in New York, is included in the special.

Sunday November 7
🍎 Jody Denberg, of the Austin, Texas based KGSR-FM radio station, webcasts a pre-recorded interview with Paul as part of the *Sunday Night News* programme. The two-hour show begins at 9pm EST. Jody announces that the interview, in raw form, ran to 25 minutes and features Paul talking about *Run Devil Run, Working Classical* and the re-mixing of The Beatles' music for the *Yellow Submarine* songtrack album.
🍎 In a front-page story of the *News Of The World* newspaper, Paul denies that he is having an affair with the British model, Heather Mills, who lost a leg in an accident caused by a policeman's motorcycle. "I have been helping Miss Mills record a charity record," he announces. "Because I have been helping Miss Mills, this does not mean that I am having anything other than a business relationship with her. Even though this story is not true, I hope it will bring attention to her worthwhile efforts for the disabled worldwide."

Tuesday November 9
🍎 The high demand for tickets for Paul's upcoming appearance on *Parkinson,* still over three weeks away, causes the BBC ticket office to announce that they have stopped accepting applications.

Thursday November 11
🍎 The *Sun* reveals: "Model Heather: I'm So Close To Paul. Model Heather Mills spoke for the first time last night about her special friendship with Sir Paul McCartney. She admitted she was close to the ex-Beatle, adding, 'I'd love to spend the Millennium with him.'"

Saturday November 13

 At the television studios in Bray, near Windsor in Berkshire, Paul and his band make a guest appearance on *Red Alert*, the first edition of BBC1's new live National Lottery game show. The show, transmitted between 7:14 and 8:04pm and hosted by the Scottish singing star Lulu, features live performances of 'Brown Eyed Handsome Man' (performed with Lulu), 'No Other Baby' and 'Party' (again performed with Lulu).

Before the show, Lulu is quoted as saying: "I am touched that Paul agreed to appear on the show. He is the greatest. I had his picture on my bedroom wall long before I met him. But I didn't imagine he would come on the show, and I didn't ask him. I'd never do that . . . It went through official channels and I was touched when he came back and said, 'Of course I'll do the show. Lulu is a mate.' I haven't seen him for years.'"

Surprisingly, Pink Floyd's David Gilmour is conspicuous by his non-appearance in Paul's band. Insiders suggest that this is down to Gilmour's disapproval of the National Lottery, citing it as being "a tax on the poor"! A member of the *Red Alert* house band replaces him.

Tuesday November 16

 Paul makes an appearance on Channel 4's *The Big Breakfast*, being interviewed in "The Shed" by Johnny Vaughan, one of the show's hosts. Paul's segments, which last approximately 22 minutes and take place between 7:54 and 8:45am, also include the first British TV screening of an excerpt from the 'No Other Baby' promotional film. (See next entry.)

Thursday November 18

 The first complete screening of Paul's video for 'No Other Baby', filmed at Pinewood Studios in Iver, Buckinghamshire, takes place on VH-1 Europe's programme *Music First*.

Saturday November 20

 Paul continues his heavy *Run Devil Run* tour of personal appearances tonight with a live appearance on Sky One's *Apocalypse Tube*, a special one-off edition of Channel 4's fondly remembered ground-breaking Eighties music series, *The Tube*. For the broadcast, which is transmitted between 9:00 and 11:58pm and comes direct from the original *Tube* television studios in Newcastle, Paul performs 'Brown Eyed Handsome Man', 'No Other Baby', 'Honey Hush' and 'Party'. The latter features Fran Healy from the Indie-pop band, Travis. A planned onstage appearance by Robbie Williams, another guest on the show, fails to materialise. The concert goes so well that Paul decides to perform another version of 'Party' and then 'Lonesome Town', which he is still playing when the end credits roll. Prior to his concert, he is light-heartedly interviewed in the studio bar by the hosts, Donna Air, of VH-1 Europe, and Chris Moyles of Radio One. David Gilmour is again absent from the band. Chester Kamen replaces him on guitar. Incidentally, the extravaganza is directed by Geoff Wonfor and edited/vision mixed by Andy Mathews, both of The Beatles *Anthology* TV and video series. (Highlights from Paul's appearance feature in a two-part edited version of the show, which are screened on Channel 4 in the UK over the Christmas holiday period. The first part is aired on Saturday January 1, 2000, between 10:00pm and midnight.)

Sunday November 21

 Extremely rare colour film of The Beatles, taken when they were in Germany in June 1966, is aired on ZDF TV in Germany (between 11:25 and 11:35pm) during the show *100 Jahre – Der Countdown*.

Monday November 22

 Paul attends the Gala Premiere of the new James Bond film, *The World Is Not Enough*, at the Odeon cinema in Leicester Square, London. Paul quips: "I've only come because I wanted to see a free film!"

Paul's appearance at the bash features briefly in the ITV special, *Premiere Bond*, which is transmitted across the ITV network on Saturday November 27. Heather Mills also attends the event, not with Paul, but with a female friend.

Tuesday November 23

❦ Heather Mills' single 'Voice' is given a press launch at the Imax Cinema in London. Following a screening of the harrowing clip to promote the single, Paul makes a brief appearance (at 11:44am) joining Heather, her sister, Fiona and pal Helen Smith to pose for the throngs of photographers. Paul on the 'Voice' video: "I saw the video (in which he makes a cameo appearance) and it is pretty shocking and I was moved by it."

The single, which features Paul on guitar and backing vocals, recorded at his home studio in Sussex, is released as a CD single in the UK on Monday December 13. Royalties from the release go to the Heather Mills Trust.

❦ Stateside, the show *Entertainment Tonight* features a one-minute report on Paul and Heather Mills, and asks: "Are they a couple?"

❦ In Montreux, at an International breast cancer conference, Stella McCartney speaks out for the first time about how she has been affected by her mother's death. "It's a really tragic thing when you experience breast cancer," she announces, "and the death of a loved one, when it's seemingly unnecessary, is very painful!"

❦ While in the States, EMI – Capitol Music Specials Market issue a new jukebox single off *Run Devil Run*, which features the two tracks 'Try Not To Cry' and 'No Other Baby'.

❦ Even though Paul or Geoff Baker will not officially announce Paul's upcoming historic concert at The Cavern Club until Friday December 3 (see entry), the *New Musical Express* pre-empts everyone by posting a message about the gig on their website today.

Saturday November 27

❦ Paul appears, by way of a pre-taped video, on ITV's *Tina Turner Special*, wishing her a happy birthday.

❦ Yoko Ono's multimedia exhibition, *Have You Seen The Horizon Lately*, has its first ever showing, in Israel at the Israel Museum in Jerusalem. To open the show, Yoko scribbles the word 'Imagine' on a white bookmark and ties it to a branch of a wishing tree. The tree is part of the exhibit and Yoko states that she hopes the tree will be filled with wishes from other visitors. Yoko: "My wish is for world peace. 'Imagine' is a song of peace." (The exhibition moves to the Arab town of Umme El-Fahm in Northern Israel shortly afterwards.)

December

❦ American sales figures confirm that The Beatles are the most successful recording act of the 20th Century, and therefore the most successful in history! According to the RIAA (the Recording Industry Association of America), the group has sold more than 106 million albums in America alone!

❦ Ringo's personal charity, The Lotus Foundation, makes a generous donation to a Liverpool school, enabling them to buy a minibus.

Thursday December 2

❦ At the BBC Television Centre in Wood Lane, London, after a wait of 25 years, Paul finally records an interview with Michael Parkinson for his top-rated BBC1 chat show, *Parkinson*. The host is quoted as saying: "I've been waiting twenty five years to do the show with Paul. It really will fulfil a dream for me. I knew Paul from the very early days of The Beatles, before they made it big, when I used to do a TV programme for Granada in Manchester called *Scene At 6:30*. The Beatles were regulars on that show. It was before they went down to London, made their début there and changed the world."

During the taping, which began for Paul at 7:44pm, he spoke about a wide range of subjects including The Beatles, his mother, John and the death of Linda. Musically, backed by his regular *Run Devil Run* band, Paul opens the show with 'Honey Hush' and also performs solo renditions of 'Twenty Flight Rock', an unreleased instrumental called 'When The Wind Is Blowing' (or 'Cohen, The Wind Is Blowing'), originally intended for Paul's unmade *Rupert The Bear* movie, and 'Yesterday'.

Moving to the piano, Paul sings 'The Long And Winding Road' and three unreleased songs, two of which were written during his recent visit to New York. The other is 'Suicide', a song written circa late 1968, intended for Frank Sinatra and jammed by The Beatles on Sunday January 26, 1969 during the *Get Back/Let It Be* sessions. (See also entry for Thursday August 15, 1974.) A brief snippet of the song had actually appeared at the end of 'Glasses' on his 1970 album, *McCartney*. In addition, a clip of 'My Love' from the *Working Classical* programme is also screened.

Before concluding the 64-minute show with a performance of 'All Shook Up', Paul announces, for the first time, that he will be playing a concert at Liverpool's Cavern Club. Later, Michael Parkinson summed up the programme by saying: "It was every bit the event I expected it to be. It was worth waiting for." (Note: for the record, the show is recorded in studio 6 in front of 200 fans, while 150 were unfortunately turned away. The taping session lasts 1 hour 35 minutes. Paul had arrived in the *Parkinson* studio at 2.55pm and, following a brief photo opportunity, leaves at 10.30pm.)

The programme is premiered on BBC1 the following evening, Friday December 3, between 9:33 and 10:37pm, with the first repeats occurring on Saturday January 15, 2000 and Saturday April 15, 2000 (see entries). Further clips, albeit brief, from the show appear in the BBC1 two-part series *History Of The Talk Show* (August 2000), and in *A Night Of A 1000 Shows* (BBC1, September 2000), where a segment of 'Yesterday' is aired.

Paul had, in fact, been at the BBC for most of Thursday December 2, beginning with an appearance on Simon Mayo's Radio 1 morning show, where he is nominated "God Of The Week". After requesting The Beatles' 1967 track 'A Day In The Life', Paul is asked, "Who would you most like on your cloud in heaven?" He replies, "My kids. Who else would I need?"

Friday December 3

🕭 Announcing Paul's forthcoming Cavern Club gig, his publicist, Geoff Baker, issues the following press release: "Paul McCartney To Rock The Cavern. Macca Returns To Root Of Where It All Began."

The release goes on to say: "Paul McCartney is to rock out the end of the century with an historic one-off rock and roll show at Liverpool's famous Cavern Club. Paul (who reveals the news tonight on *Parkinson*, on BBC1 at 9:30pm) is to return to his roots to perform a night of rock and roll on Tuesday December 14. The concert comes 12,953 days since Paul last performed in the cellar of 10 Mathew Street. The show, Paul's first at the tiny venue since The Beatles last played there on August 3, 1963, will be his 281st show at The Cavern. Paul is to rock The Cavern as a tribute to the rock and roll musical force that has so shaped the last part of the last century of the millennium. Said Paul: 'Rock and roll has shaped my life, and it changed the sound and the thinking of the century. Before The Beatles ever got big, we started out playing rock and roll at The Cavern. I'm going back, for just one night, as a nod to the music that has always, and will ever, thrill me. I can't think of a better way than to rock out the end of the century with a rock and roll party at The Cavern, singing songs of my heroes.' "

🕭 The Liverpool tourist organisation Cavern City Tours immediately brace themselves for a deluge of demands for tickets from all around the world. Due to space restrictions, it is expected that only 150–200 tickets will be available for the show. Geoff Baker: "Millions are going to want to be at this gig, and the fact is that millions are going to be disappointed. However, there are plans for the show to be broadcast on television and radio around the world. Due to the expected demand for tickets, and in an attempt to be fair to all, tickets for Paul's concert at The Cavern will be available through a national UK raffle. To apply, callers must fill in forms which will be available from Monday December 6 from HMV record stores in Liverpool, London, Birmingham, Newcastle and Glasgow." (See entry.)

🕭 An interview to promote Paul's Cavern Club gig, conducted with Dominic Mohan, is published in today's edition of the *Sun*. The piece is headlined: "Macca: I Can't Wait To Play The Cavern Again".

Saturday December 4

🕭 *A Garland For Linda* receives its US premiere at the Riverside Church in New York.

🕭 During her brief stay in London, Yoko appears, by satellite, on another edition of CNN's *Larry King Weekend*. The 45-minute programme, seen throughout the world, is screened three times in total, twice on Saturday and once on Sunday December 5.

Sunday December 5

🕭 Yoko Ono and her artist career is the subject of this evening's *South Bank Show*, transmitted across the ITV network between 11:19pm and 00:17am and hosted by Melvyn Bragg.

Monday December 6

♣ As Geoff Baker had stated in his press release on Friday December 3 (see entry), fans have a slim chance of attending Paul's Cavern concert by picking up an entry form today from one of several HMV stores nationwide. As expected, all 1,250 forms go within minutes of being made available. A spokesman for HMV remarks: "People have travelled all over the world to be in with a chance of attending the show. One fan has travelled all the way from Holland. There were stores that were nearer for him, but he decided to go to Liverpool because that's where The Beatles came from." At the front of the queue in Liverpool today is John Ono Lennon, a fan who had changed his name by deed poll, and had moved to Penny Lane from his home in Worcester. His real name is Ben Lomas. (The Cavern Club tickets draw is made on Friday December 10 – see entry.)

Tuesday December 7

♣ A special limited edition box set of *Run Devil Run* is released comprising the entire album spread over eight 7" singles. But, as there were only 15 tracks featured on *RDR*, the 16th track to make up the singles is 'Fabulous', a hit in 1957 by Charlie Gracie, and also appearing on the 'No Other Baby' CD single. The Parlophone release is confined to just 7,000 copies. The label also issues, for promotional use only, a 7" single (RDR003) comprising 'Run Devil Run' b/w 'Blue Jean Bop'.

Wednesday December 8

♣ The video for Paul's 'Brown Eyed Handsome Man' is premiered in America on VH-1 this morning between the early slot of 5:00 and 6:00am (ET/PT). The clip, directed by David Leland, features Paul leading a slowly growing mob of line-dancers. (The first UK TV screening will not take place until it is featured on the BBC2 archive show, *TOTP2* on Wednesday, December 29.)

♣ Today's Bizarre column of the *Sun* newspaper features an interview with Yoko by Dominic Mohan. In the piece, she says why "John's 'Imagine' MUST Be No. 1 This Christmas".

Friday December 10

♣ In a programme delayed from Friday November 12, Paul is the featured guest on America's National Public Radio's (NPR) *Performance Today*. He discusses, with the host Lisa Simeone, his new classical album *Working Classical*, which has been at number one in *Billboard*'s Classical Album chart for the last two weeks. Paul also introduces recordings made at the Saturday October 16 live performance premiere of *Working Classical* in Liverpool.

♣ While in Liverpool, 150 (75 pairs) of tickets for Paul's concert at The Cavern Club are drawn at the headquarters of EMI in West London. Fans from as far away as Argentina and Australia had entered their names in the raffle by sending in application forms from various HMV stores around Britain. The first name to be drawn is Kevin Reavey, 55, of the Aigburth area of Liverpool. Kevin, a regular visitor to The Cavern in the Sixties, is utterly delighted. "I stayed in this morning knowing that there was a chance I could have won," he says. "But I was very doubtful. The odds were against it with so few tickets. I have been a fan of The Beatles since the beginning. I used to go to The Cavern but I never saw them there." Another winner is John Ono Lennon, the very first person to be outside the HMV store in Liverpool last Monday. The furthest flung ticket holder picked by EMI's head of promotions, Malcolm Hill, was Tomohiri Kobayashai from Tokyo, Japan. A Beatles fan from Belgium is also lucky in the draw.

In addition, Paul announces that two further Cavern Club tickets will be given away in a telephone competition, which will aid the cancer unit of Liverpool's Alder Hey Children's Hospital. Paul's mother worked as a nurse at the hospital. The 24-hour phone line, where callers are asked to name the title of Paul's new album, will be open until the morning of Monday December 13. The money raised from the £1-a-minute calls going to the unit's fund-raising appeal.

Saturday December 11

♣ Paul and his band fly to Germany where they make an appearance on the live ZDF TV/ORF/SF DRS TV co-production celebrity game show, *Wetten Dass . . .?*, which is transmitted between 8:15 and 10:52pm, European time. Beside lip-synching a version of 'No Other Baby', and signing a painting by Klaus Voorman, he is interviewed by the show's host, Thomas Gottschalk, and shown a copy of the new deluxe book *Hamburg Days*, which features many unpublished photos by Astrid Kirchherr and drawings by Klaus Voorman, who is seen sitting in the studio audience. Before leaving the stage, Paul signs a racing car ("Paul McCartney woz ere"), which is to be sold. The proceeds of the sale going towards *Aktion Sorgenkind*, the Handicapped Children fund. (The programme is repeated two days later on ZDF, on Monday December 13.)

Sunday December 12 (until Sunday February 6, 2000)
 Linda McCartney's exhibition, *Sixties – Portrait Of An Era*, runs at the Tampa Museum of Art in Ashley Drive, Florida.

Monday December 13
 John's 'Imagine' is re-released as an enhanced CD single by Parlophone in the UK. The other tracks on the CD include 'Happy Christmas (War Is Over)' and 'Give Peace A Chance'. This CD offers the buyer a chance to view the title track, recorded at the 1972 *One To One Concert* in New York, to be played full screen or small screen, by quick-time video player.

A spokesman for the label announces: "The release is down to the incredible response we've had from the public, following the National Poetry Day poll, asking whether it would be available again." Shortly before its re-release, Yoko Ono issues a press statement about the single from her offices in The Dakota.

 'Imagine' enters the Christmas chart at number three on Sunday December 19, but had slipped to number seven on the chart published on Sunday January 2, 2000, the first of the new century.

Tuesday December 14
 In front of a crowd of just 300, Paul plays his historic concert at the new Cavern Club in Mathew Street, Liverpool. He comments: "I can't think of a better way to end the century than with a party at The Cavern, singing the songs of my heroes." Fans are naturally desperate to witness the show. "Women have been blatantly accosting me in the (Cavern) club," says an exasperated Billy Heckle, the Cavern Club's co-manager. "They've been trying to bribe me with their bodies. I've been repeatedly offered sex in exchange for a ticket!" Many people are, naturally, disappointed that they can't get in, none more so than The Beatles' former manager, Allan Williams, who blasts: "I can't believe they're not letting me in there tonight. If it wasn't for me, there would be no Beatles!" (In fact, Williams was intoxicated at the time of the concert.)

Paul arrived in Liverpool this afternoon at Speke airport at around 2pm. His flight was delayed 45 minutes before it arrived at Speke. On his arrival, after giving a couple of autographs and a quick chat with the *Liverpool Echo*, he quickly transferred to his Jaguar car, which was escorted by half a dozen policemen to the rear of The Cavern where he was driven into the completely sealed off parking area, situated under the Cavern Walks complex. Paul entered The Cavern Club via its emergency doors at the back. Afterwards Paul and his band held a two-hour rehearsal.

The press entered the building at 4pm and, at 5pm, Paul held the short press conference, which turned out to be just a small statement and photo call. When Paul arrived on the tiny stage, he kissed the "wall of fame" behind him. The statement he read to the press was as follows: "I just want to say that it's fantastic to be back at The Cavern. What better place to rock out the century? This is where it all began and, for me, the century is going to end with playing rock'n'roll. You'll remember that before The Beatles were The Beatles, they were a fabulous little rock'n'roll band, which is what held us together for so long and made us so good. I think. And I'm back here because I love Liverpool and I'm playing the music I love best in the city I love most. There is no more fantastic place to rock out the century."

Following the conference, Paul sneaked out to a nearby hotel where he was reunited with his local family for a private cup of tea and to record an exclusive interview for a BBC Radio Two special to be broadcast later this evening.

For the 45-minute evening show, which began just after 8pm, Paul's band, as expected, consists of the following: David Gilmour, Mick Green (guitars), Pete Wingfield (keyboards), Ian Paice (drums) and Chris Hall (accordion). They perform the following songs: 'Honey Hush', 'Blue Jean Bop', 'Brown Eyed Handsome Man', 'Fabulous' (with a false start), 'What It Is', 'Lonesome Town', 'Twenty Flight Rock', 'No Other Baby', 'Try

Not To Cry', 'Shake A Hand', 'All Shook Up', 'I Saw Her Standing There' and 'Party'. Paul leaves the tiny Cavern stage saying: "See you next time . . ."

VIPs in attendance include, amongst others, the Apple boss, Neil Aspinall, the old Cavern Club boss, Ray McFall, the old Cavern Club DJ, Billy Butler and Bob Wooler. Paul's immediate family is also present.

A large outdoor screen in Chavasse Park, near the Albert Dock, in Liverpool, is erected so approximately 12,000 people can also watch the show live in the freezing cold. Paul had rented the park.

After the concert, Paul, his band and friends, go to the nearby Sports Bar, Baron Pierre de Coubertin's, which is owned by Cavern City Tours. While there, Paul signs an authentic copy of his Hofner violin bass guitar, scribbling: "*Cool* Cavern! Cheers. Paul McCartney Dec 14. '99" on the scratch plate. Paul leaves the Sports Bar through a private corridor, around midnight.

🍎 Media transmission notes for the Cavern Club gig: for the Radio 2 broadcast (transmitted between 10:31 and 12:01am on the night of the concert), hosted by Richard Allinson and recorded in a BBC van parked in nearby Harrington Street, 'Shake A Hand' is omitted and for the first television transmission, on BBC1, the following night, Wednesday December 15, between 11:15 and 11:55pm, both 'Blue Jean Bop' and 'Try Not To Cry' are cut. The show is transmitted in Canada on *Much More Music* on Thursday December 16 and Saturday December 18, 1999, with all 13 songs. The first television repeat of The Cavern gig takes place on Saturday January 15 with further screenings taking place on Friday May 5, 2000, Thursday August 10, 2000 and December 2000, while further radio broadcasts of The Cavern gig occur on Thursday January 20, 2000 (see all entries). The very first television clip of Paul's Cavern gig, 'Honey Hush', actually appears on Sky News when they air a brief segment live, perhaps accidentally, during a report on the concert.

The show is also broadcast live on the Internet worldwide, on MCY.com, which features an exclusive introduction by Paul, who remarks: "This is going to be a thrilling and emotional night for me and it's fantastic that fans around the world can log on to the gig and party with us." But, because of the limitations, it is nearly impossible to get online. Ninety minutes before the start of the show, the system is already jammed to anyone trying to log on. Later, about 30 minutes after the concert has ended, EMI and MSN originally plan to make the programme available for "on demand" viewing for the following fifteen hours. But, due to the extraordinary interest in the webcast, the host MCY.com ends up re-broadcasting the concert until Sunday December 19. (Also see entries for Friday December 24 and June 30, 2000.)

Wednesday December 15

🍎 In the States, a pre-taped interview with Paul is aired on NBC TV's *Today* show.

Friday December 17 (& Saturday December 18)

🍎 An exhibition of previously unseen pictures by Tom Murray taken during The Beatles' famous 'Mad Day Out' on Sunday July 28 1968, takes place at Gallery 27 in Cork Street, London W1. (A private, invite only, screening of the pictures take place on Thursday December 16.) The event is arranged by *Not Fade Away*, one of the top archive photo libraries in London. (The build-up to the release of these pictures is covered by reports in such papers as the *Sunday Mirror* on November 7.)

Tuesday December 21 (until Sunday December 26)

🍎 Beginning tonight, Ringo is to be found hosting a brand-new three-hour American radio special called *Jingle Bell Rock*. The show, produced by MJI Broadcasting and syndicated to 75 stations across the country, features the best of Christmas rock'n'roll oldies from the Fifties to the present, including songs from Ringo's new album, *I Wanna Be Santa Claus*. Throughout the show he reminds listeners: "Please call me Santa!" The show is divided into various segments, such as a Motown set, a Phil Spector set and, of course, a Beatles set. During the latter, Ringo plays 'Christmastime Is Here Again', from his album, 'Wonderful Christmastime', by Paul, 'Ding Dong Ding Dong', by George and 'Happy Christmas (War Is Over')' by John and Yoko. In addition, as a bonus, Ringo spins The Beatles' 1964 Christmas fan club flexi disc.

Wednesday December 22
❦ George Michael, Robbie Williams and Graham Coxon of Blur are among the stars that have autographed John's 'Imagine' single to help charity. Yoko Ono has asked for the covers to be made and then auctioned for the Homeless Organisation, Shelter. "It's great to be involved in a UK charity that draws attention to such a worthwhile cause," she says. Ten customised 'Imagine' sleeves are auctioned on the WWW.MSN.co.uk website until Tuesday January 4, 2000.

Thursday December 23
❦ George's home in Maui, Hawaii, is broken into by a 27-year-old woman called Cristin Kelleher, who takes a pizza from George's freezer, cooks it and then drinks a bottle of soda. The woman is discovered by George's sister-in-law who informs the caretaker who in turn informs the police. By the time the police arrive, she is caught in the middle of doing her washing. When asked why she had broken in, she tells the police: "I thought I had a psychic connection with George." Later, bail for the woman is reduced from $10,000 to $1,500 after her attorney tells the court that she would have a place to stay on the island if she were released. The judge sets a pre-trial conference for April and, if Kelleher is convicted, she faces up to ten years in prison and a $10,000 fine. (See entry for Wednesday January 12, 2000.)

Friday December 24
❦ *The Times* newspaper prints a full-page advert by MCY.com, in which they thank Paul McCartney for "the opportunity to produce the largest music webcast in history". According to MCY, there has been over 50 million viewers worldwide who have watched Paul's Cavern Club performance (see entry for Tuesday December 14).

Saturday, December 25
❦ A two-hour edition of Paul's *Routes Of Rock* is broadcast on BBC Radio 2.

Sunday December 26
❦ On Boxing Day, VH-1 in the UK screen (between 10:00 and 10:28pm), completely unannounced, the new *VH-1 To 1* programme devoted to Paul and his *Run Devil Run* album.

Tuesday December 28
❦ A pre-recorded interview with Paul is featured on the BBC Radio 4 programme *Front Row*, which is about middle-aged rock stars and how these stars address questions of ageing in their music.

Wednesday December 29
❦ Paul's 'Brown Eyed Handsome Man' video is shown on BBC2's archive show *TOTP2* in the UK.

(Published) Thursday December 30
❦ Eerily, the scandalous *Daily Sport* newspaper asks George, via phone, for his New Year prediction. He amazingly replies: "You will all be dead!" His statement shocks the reporters as they do not know whether he is joking or not.

(The early hours of) Thursday December 30
❦ Rekindling memories of how the UK awoke to the tragic news of John's death just over nineteen years ago, the country awakes this morning to discover that a second Beatle has been seriously hurt in a violent attack. During the previous night George was stabbed by an intruder at his home, Friar Park near Henley-on-Thames. As the morning progresses, it becomes known that at around 3:30am, without the burglar alarm or sophisticated security equipment sounding first, George heard the sound of breaking glass and got up. His wife Olivia alerted the staff on the internal phone while George went downstairs in his dressing gown to investigate the noise. He found an intruder in a downstairs room, tackled him and was stabbed four times in the chest by a 6-inch knife.

A police spokesman: "As soon as he got to the bottom of the stairs, George saw the shadow of a man. He challenged him and there was a scuffle, during which a knife was pulled out."

George recalls: "I couldn't stop him from killing me."

A police spokesman: "George was stabbed in the chest and apparently let out a shout to Olivia for help."

Hearing George scream for help, Olivia ran downstairs, where she saw him locked in a struggle and proceeded to hit the intruder over the head with a table lamp, which apparently stunned him into submission. "The guy was young and strong and I couldn't stop him from stabbing George," she tells a friend. "I hit him with the lamp as hard as I could and it worked. He slumped over and George pushed him off. George was wheezing horribly. I was really worried he wouldn't make it."

A police spokesman: "She saw George fighting with the intruder and grabbed the nearest implement, which was a table lamp. She tried to use it to stop the man attacking George and in the process was cut several times on her head by the knife."

Two unarmed members of the police arrived within minutes, at approximately 3:45am, and arrested the intruder and confiscated his knife. The man, from Huyton, Liverpool, was taken to the nearby Henley police station. Later, because of injuries to his head during the skirmish, he was taken to Oxford's John Radcliffe Hospital for treatment. After his injuries had been attended to, he was moved to the St. Aldridge police station where he was detained for questioning.

Mark Gritten, executive of the Royal Berkshire Hospital: "Two ambulances arrived within fifteen minutes and four paramedics spent twenty minutes treating George's stab wounds and trying to stem the flow of blood."

Wayne Page, one of George's neighbours, who lives directly opposite the entrance to Friar Park: "I was woken by the noise of a helicopter hovering overhead at about 4am. I didn't know what was going on, but I thought it was very strange at this time of night for it to be hovering there. I can't believe he's been attacked in his own home. I thought it was like Fort Knox in there. There is security and patrol dogs to keep people out and warning signs on the gates. He's not someone who just stays behind his gates. You see him down the post office or in the local (Henley's Row Barge public house). He's just a normal guy and this is horrific."

At approximately 5am, George and Olivia are taken to the Royal Berkshire Hospital where they are admitted to a side room on the NHS Sidmouth Ward. Doctors discover that George was half-an-inch from losing his life. Medical director Andrew Pengelly says: "He has been stabbed on the right hand side of the chest, with the blade entering just below his collarbone. The knife narrowly missed a blood vessel connecting the heart and the head. If that had been ruptured, he would have perished within a matter of minutes from internal bleeding. He was extremely lucky. If the knife had gone in more than a centimetre either side, then it could have hit some very dangerous things, such as large blood vessels."

Mark Gritten, the chief executive of the hospital, later tells waiting reporters: "George is stable and there wasn't a life-threatening situation." Security at the hospital is extremely tight. Guards are seen patrolling all the entrances and exits and checking the IDs of everyone entering the building.

Apart from bruising and swelling, George has a drain in his lung to remove blood if necessary, as the lung is partially collapsed. On the right-hand side of his chest is a one-inch stab wound. George also complains to the medical staff that he is suffering breathing problems.

During the afternoon, Olivia and Dhani sit beside George's bed while he recuperates, after having twelve stitches inserted into his wound. Later, when George is reported as being stable, he is transferred to Harefield Hospital in Uxbridge, Middlesex, West London. He is transferred to a private bed at Harefield as a precautionary measure and not because doctors are concerned about his injuries. It is there that he is inundated with get well messages from friends, fans and both Paul and Ringo. With his spirits perking up, George jokingly remarks: "The attacker wasn't a burglar and he certainly wasn't auditioning for The Traveling Wilburys!" George is detained in the hospital for a further 48 hours.

William Fountain, the consultant thoracic surgeon at Harefield Hospital, a leading centre concerned with chest conditions, is quoted as saying that: "The main stab wound was a very, very small distance from a main vein and it was only by chance that his injuries were not life threatening. The second stab wound to his chest was less serious." A reporter asks him: "Was Harrison lucky not to have died?" Fountain replies: "Anyone stabbed in the chest could die," adding, "His condition is comfortable. But, it is unlikely that he will be allowed to leave hospital in time for the Millennium celebrations. I expect him to remain in hospital for at least the next few days for monitoring and is not expected to have more treatment, although he will be left with a small scar on his chest."

On the afternoon of Thursday December 30, at the request of Thames Valley Police, Merseyside Police enter the flat of George's intruder, on the tenth floor of a tower block at Woodfall Heights, Woodfall Heath, Huyton, Liverpool. After a thorough search, they leave the block thirty minutes later with a number of items in bags.

Chief Inspector Evan Read, of Thames Valley Police, the policeman leading the investigation, remarks in a rain-swept press conference held at the gates of Friar Park: "The Harrisons have been subjected to a vicious attack and it didn't appear to be a random assault linked to a simple robbery. There has been some speculation that it was a burglary that went wrong, but, my own view at present, is that it isn't a burglary that went wrong, but he probably came here on purpose."

Paul's spokesman, Geoff Baker says: "Everyone is totally shocked. Paul McCartney was told the news early today and was also shocked and anxious to hear more from the hospital. We were told George was stabbed several times with what we assume was a knife and that Olivia was hit over the head. We don't know if they were asleep when the intruder made his way into their home. God knows how he got through the security around the house. Apparently they both fought back hard against the attack. Thank God that they both appear to be stable in hospital. We are all totally shocked that a second Beatle has been attacked. Nothing like this has happened before to George to make him worried about his safety."

✉ Later, Paul will forward his own message of sympathy, which reads: "Thank God both George and Olivia are all right. I send them all my love."

✉ From California, and again through Geoff Baker, Ringo issues this statement: "Both Barbara and I are deeply shocked that this has occurred. We send George and Olivia all our love and wish George a speedy recovery."

✉ While The Beatles producer, George Martin, has this to say: "I can't imagine that this has got anything to do with the fact that George is a Beatle and the John Lennon thing. I think it's a question of a burglary that went wrong. The house is a very grand place and I know there are always people trying to get in. George leads a very quiet life and is a very down-to-earth person. He loves nothing more than doing his garden at home. It's such a large property and needed a lot of security. Somebody must have got through. If you have a large place and a determined person, there is nothing really to stop them, apart from an armed force, which is the last thing George would want . . . I can't imagine anybody picking on George. I think they must have picked on the house, rather than George."

✉ Naturally, the event features prominently on television and radio news programmes around the world. (See entry Tuesday November 14, 2000, for details of court case.)

Friday December 31

✉ George's stabbing yesterday features on the front page of newspapers around the world, thus ensuring that The Beatles dominate the news on the last day of the Millennium.

The *Daily Mail* writes: "George Saved By His Wife".

The *Express*: "Wife's Heroism Saves Beatle George".

Daily Star: "Psycho Held Over George Knifing".

✉ Magistrates at the Oxford court order 33-year-old Mike Abram, George's attacker, to be held in a secure psychiatric unit in Liverpool until after he is charged with the attempted murder of George and Olivia. Abram, who appears in court with a black eye and a blood stained face, is given bail until Friday February 11 while he undergoes psychiatric treatment. It is revealed that Abram, nicknamed "Mad Mick" by those who know him, is a heroin addict with a history of mental health problems. He was said to be obsessed with The Beatles, referring to them as "Witches". His mother, Lynda, says she has begged authorities to commit her son to a mental hospital as his condition worsened. But nothing was done.

✉ William Fountain, the consultant thoracic surgeon at Harefield Hospital, says in a press conference held in the hospital: "He is probably in quite a lot of discomfort. He is on painkillers because he has a seriously painful injury. He is breathing unaided and did not suffer a large loss of blood as far as I am aware. He has had anti-tetanus injections and antibiotics, which are normal in these circumstances, as there is always a fear of infection." He concludes: "I am reasonably confident the treatment he has had is all that he will need. Nature will do the rest."

 At Paul's home in Sussex, Heather Mills is at Paul's side to welcome in the new century. To celebrate the new Millennium, he organises a fireworks display. A friend of the couple remarks: "Heather has been a rock for Paul since Linda died and it looks like he's finally managing to rebuild his life. They were every bit the happy couple at the party and it's a sign of their deep affection for one another that they wanted to spend the start of the new Millennium together." While another remarks: "As midnight arrived, Sir Paul gave her a new year hug and a kiss as they linked arms to sing 'Auld Lang Syne' with other guests."

 While at the Millennium Dome in Greenwich, London, The Beatles' 'All You Need Is Love' is played just before the midnight celebrations begin.

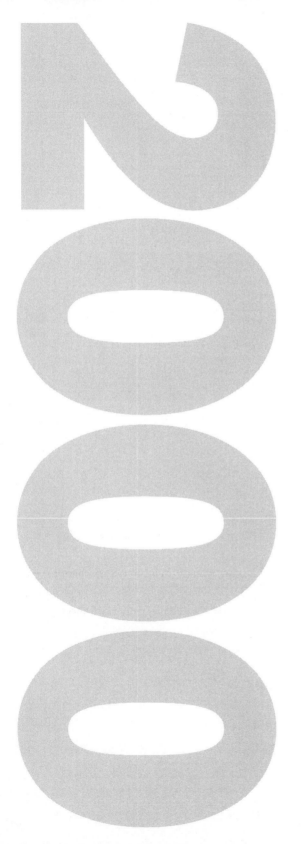

"The Beatles are dead chuffed. They are thrilled by their continued success."

– Apple spokesman

Saturday January 1
🍎 George is discharged from hospital and allowed to return home to Friar Park following his horrifying knife ordeal. He leaves Harefield Hospital in Northwest London this evening. He requests that the hospital not release the news until the following day. A spokesman for the hospital says on Sunday January 2: "He's gone home with his family and he is expected to make a full recovery. On Friday we said that George would be unlikely to be fit to leave hospital until Sunday, but he was judged to be well enough after a series of tests. He was discharged last night after an assessment of his fitness. He was delighted to go home." A reporter asks the spokesman whether George had celebrated the dawn of the new Millennium at the stroke of midnight on Friday. The spokesman briefly replies: "Hospitals are rather boring places."

George's first visitor at Friar Park is his good friend the *Monty Python* star, Eric Idle, who announces: "He's much better." Soon after Eric will tell the *National Post* in Canada: "He is recovering and it was a monstrous attack. When the trial comes out in England, you'll see how nasty that was, much nastier than reported! For once in life, it wasn't hyped."

Newspaper reports reveal that George is being kept under a 24-hour guard by two ex-SAS men, who are working 12-hour shifts and are being paid £1,000 a day. Shortly after, George will take a vacation in Ireland and then Barbados, staying at a £30,000 a week rented home with his family and his close friend, Joe Brown.

Joe Brown tells the *Daily Mail*: "I was sitting at home, the phone rang and George asked me to go to Barbados with him. It was totally unexpected, but I was pleased." He adds: "He's had a very nasty experience and he doesn't need all this hassle. The attack was a lot worse than what people realised. George struggled with the man for nearly twenty minutes before help arrived."

An onlooker in Barbados remarks: "George looked a million miles away from the troubled person of three weeks ago. He was clearly happy and relaxed. He is feeling much better and looks every inch like he is on his way to recovery. He is a picture of health and you can no longer see the scar."

George, closely watched by his ex-SAS guards, is seen taking long walks around the gardens of the island and found tucking into a feast of tropical food with his family in the evening.

George's attacker, the 33-year-old Liverpudlian Mike Abram is detained under the Mental Health Act and is due to make his next court appearance on Friday February 11.
🍎 Paul and Heather celebrate the first day of the new century having dinner together.

Sunday January 2
🍎 George's stabbing forces him to become the focus of attention in a special feature in today's *Observer* newspaper. The piece, written by Tim Adams, is called The Eccentric One.

Wednesday January 5
🍎 Paul donates $2million (£1.25m) to cancer centres in America in memory of his late wife Linda. He gives $1million to Arizona Cancer Research to establish a breast cancer research endowment. They will look at ways to treat and prevent cancer without using animals for research. Paul also gives $1million to the Memorial Sloan-Kettering Cancer Center in New York, where Linda received treatment.

Friday January 7
🍎 With John's 'Imagine' currently at number seven in the British singles chart, tonight's edition of *Top Of The Pops* (aired on BBC1 between 7:30 and 8:00pm) broadcasts the famous 1971 Tittenhurst Park, Ascot, clip of the song.

Sunday January 9
🍎 George is the subject of this week's *Time & Again*, MNNBC TV's weekly 43-minute archive news show. Among the clips on offer in this American show is his appearance on the *Today* show in 1986, *Good Morning Australia* in 1982 and reports on his recent attack at his home in Henley-on-Thames.

Wednesday January 12
🍎 Cristin Kelleher, the 27-year-old woman accused of stalking and breaking into George's home in Hawaii denies raiding his home (see entry for Thursday December 23,

1999). Although she was caught in the house eating one of George's pizzas, she pleads not guilty to theft in a Hawaii courtroom.

Friday January 14
🎸 During a vacation in the Providenciales Islands in the Bahamas, Paul and two of his children, James and Stella, decide to pay a short visit to Santiago De Cuba.

Saturday January 15
🎸 The digital only channel BBC Choice repeats Paul's recent appearance on *Parkinson* (see entry for December 2, 1999) as well as the newly re-mixed version of Paul's concert at The Cavern Club on December 14, 1999 (see entry).

Sunday January 16
🎸 George and Olivia, on holiday in Ireland, appear on the front page of the *Sunday Express*, along with a thank you to their many well-wishers. "Olivia and I are overwhelmed by the concern expressed by so many people," he says. "We thank everyone for their prayers and kindness." George and Olivia have been staying at the home of Rolling Stones' guitarist Ronnie Wood. (The syndicated picture also appears on television stations like CNN in America and CBS, where it is screened on the *CBS Evening News*.)

Monday January 17
🎸 Paul's series *Paul McCartney's Routes Of Rock*, first aired on the BBC World Service on Wednesday October 20, 1999, airs for the first time in America. It is broadcast over two successive weeks on Westwood One Network's *The Beatle Years* series.
🎸 The American Music Awards ceremony is held in the States and The Beatles win the "Artists Of The Decades" Sixties category.

Wednesday January 19
🎸 A *Yellow Submarine* reality exhibition opens in Berlin, Germany. The *Yellow Submarine Adventure* is part of Sony's Music Box theme park, a multi-million dollar music activity centre developed by the company. The amazing ride is a 30-seater *Yellow Submarine* complete with portholes and a screen that shows high definition excerpts from the film. Travellers are encouraged to sing along with tracks such as 'All You Need Is Love', 'When I'm 64', 'Only A Northern Song' and 'Sgt. Pepper'. It is expected that the ride will appear in Liverpool, at the Dome in Greenwich, London and on the West Coast of America.

Thursday January 20 (until Sunday January 23)
🎸 Paul's December 14, 1999 performance at The Cavern Club in Liverpool is broadcast by 140 radio stations across America.

Friday January 21
🎸 At midnight (ET/PT), VH-1 in America premieres a new 30-minute documentary about the making of their forthcoming drama *Two Of Us*, a fictional account of John and Paul's meeting at The Dakota in 1976, and directed by the *Let It Be* film director, Michael Lindsay Hogg. The exact details were first revealed in the August 1999 edition of this book. (Repeat screenings of the programme occur throughout the following week, except for Thursday and Friday, on the station.)

Thursday January 27
🎸 Many newspapers in the UK, including the *Mirror*, print a previously unpublished picture of John, alongside other youngsters including comedian Jimmy Tarbuck, taken in August 1952 during a school trip to the Isle of Man.
🎸 In Holborn, London, Paul joins eight other composers at St. Andrews Church in a press conference and photo opportunity to promote the classical CD *Garland For Linda*, proceeds from which will benefit the garland appeal, helping cancer research through the healing power of music. (The CD was recorded on Friday October 8, 1999, at the All Saints Church in Tooting.) This evening, Paul and his brother Mike attend the performance in the church of *Garland For Linda*, performed by the Joyful Company of Singers.

Friday January 28
🍎 The Canadian music channel Musicmax (at 9:00pm ET) broadcasts a one-off screening of the new version of the September 1999 PETA Awards ceremony, which features Paul's complete six-track performance.
🍎 Further newspapers in the UK publish the previously unseen picture of John and the comedian Jimmy Tarbuck, taken on holiday in August 1952. The agent for this picture is the *Liverpool Echo* newspaper.

Sunday January 30
🍎 Ringo appears, sitting behind his drums, in a TV commercial for the brokerage house of Charles Schwab & Co, aired in a very expensive American television slot during live coverage of Superbowl XXXIV. In the 30-second piece, he is seen suggesting a number of investing terms for a rhyme in a band song writing session. The clip reappears in the fourth quarter and again at the end of the game.
🍎 *Gimme Some Truth*, the official documentary on the making of the *Imagine* album, is aired for the first time on the European channel ARTE. The show is screened three times over the two days (Sunday January 30 and Monday January 31). The UK premiere does not take place until Sunday February 13 (see entry) while the American TV premiere is held back until Monday April 17 when it appears on the Bravo channel.

February (during the month)
🍎 Paul and Heather Mills are spotted holidaying together on the paradise Caribbean island of Parrot Cay, a hideaway on the Turks and Calcos Islands. They spend ten days at the resort, where a beachside cottage for two costs £8,000 for a week. A fellow guest at the place remarks: "Paul and Heather seemed very happy in each other's company. Parrot Cay suited them well, it's the perfect place for lovers who can have their privacy assured. It's very secure and paparazzi-proof."
🍎 Paul features in this month's *Bassist* and *Guitarist* magazines.
🍎 This month (and March) Paul features on the front of the *HMV Choice* magazine. Inside, he discusses his life, Linda, Lennon and his classical music.
🍎 The TV Shopping Channel 3-CD box set of Ringo's All-Starr Band live recordings, to be released on the Purple Pyramid label, is delayed again due to production difficulties. Reports now suggest that the release will now either take place in April or June, to coincide with the new All-Starr Band American Tour.

Tuesday February 1
🍎 At London's Mermaid Theatre, at the *NME* Premier Awards, Paul is on hand to collect, on behalf of The Beatles, the award for "The Best Band Ever". Paul: "I'm delighted! It's better than a Brit. Can I just say 'Thank you, John, George and Ringo, and thank you, God!'" Afterwards, Paul remarks: "I would much rather attend a ceremony with awards voted for by readers. I came here because it was the readers' choice, unlike the Brits, which is chosen by a committee. With these awards, you know what's going on. With the others, you don't know what's happening backstage politically. I was told we had won by a landslide, so that's why I wanted to come here today. The Beatles were a good mix of people. We were the coolest . . ." Paul's blast at The Brits comes after they had offered Paul 'The Greatest Contribution To Music' gong, but when he said he couldn't make it to the event, the organisers decided to give the award to The Spice Girls instead.
🍎 Paul's appearance at the *NME* Awards features on the front page of the paper, dated Saturday February 12.
🍎 In the States, VH-1 premiere their 90-minute drama film, *Two Of Us*, based on a fictional account of John and Paul's meeting at The Dakota in 1976. Jared Harris is in the role of John.

Saturday February 5
🍎 Excerpts from Paul's September 18, 1999 PETA Awards Ceremony (see entry) are featured in Pamela Anderson Lee's US TV show *VIP*. The programme is titled *All You Need Is Val*. (The Los Angeles transmission takes place on Sunday February 6.)

Sunday February 6
🍎 This afternoon, VH-1 in Europe screens again Paul's *VH-1 to 1* interview, made primarily to promote his *Run Devil Run* album last year.

Monday February 7
 The album *A Garland For Linda* is released by EMI Classics.

Saturday February 12
 Paul awards his personal assistant a £160,000 leaving gift. The former Beatle begged Shelagh Jones to stay after 16 years loyal service, even wining and dining her in an attempt to make her change her mind. The money ensures that Shelagh will not disclose any details about her time working for Paul. A pal of Paul's remarks: "Paul never wanted her to leave . . . They are almost like brother and sister."

Sunday February 13
 The UK TV premiere of the documentary *Gimme Some Truth*, the making of John's *Imagine* album, takes place on BBC2. But, unfortunately, due to extended live coverage of the Benson & Hedges snooker final, the preceding programme, the screening of the Yoko approved programme, begins one hour and 28 minutes later than scheduled, at 00:58am in the early hours of Monday February 14. (The original start time for the show was 11:30pm.)

Monday February 14
 As expected, considering the airing of *Gimme Some Truth* the previous night, the remastered version of John's 1971 album *Imagine* is released in the UK. Contrary to previous reports, there are no bonus tracks. Yoko: "*Imagine* is such an incredibly important album, and I wanted to keep it as close as possible to the original." (The release takes place in America, by Parlophone/EMI Music Canada, the following day, Tuesday February 15.)

Wednesday February 16 (& Thursday February 17)
 Planned screenings on VH-1 in America of the re-mixed *Yellow Submarine* film fail to materialise. Insiders suggest that the non-appearance is down to a disagreement between MGM/UA and Apple. It is an embarrassment for the station, who had been running special *Yellow Submarine* trailers for the past two weeks. The film is replaced by a made-for-TV film drama on the Jackson family.

Friday February 18
 It is announced that the piano John used to write 'Imagine' back in 1971 is to be sold. In the run-up to its auction, on the website eoffer.com on October 9, his 60th birthday, it will be stored in Liverpool's Beatles Story attraction. (See entry for Tuesday October 17, 2000.)
 On the same day, reports suggest that Paul has started work on his new studio album at his home studio in Sussex.
 This evening, Paul joins his daughter Stella at the London Fashion Week awards, where she is named "Glamorous Designer Of The Year". (The event is covered for a BBC2 special, transmitted the following evening, Saturday February 19. While Paul and Stella's arrival for the event is covered by Sky News.)
 EMI in the UK announces that The Beatles' back catalogue CDs are not being re-mastered.

Sunday February 20
 The Beach Boys legend, Brian Wilson, denies rumours that he is working on projects with Paul.

Monday February 21
 American news reports state that according to secret MI5 files, which are to be made public, John helped fund the IRA. Yoko is quick to deny the claim.

Tuesday February 22
 The producers of the new CBS TV film, based on the life of Linda McCartney, begin casting for the roles of Linda and the four Beatles.

Friday February 25
 It is announced that Ringo will tour America again this year with his All-Starr band. (See entry for Friday May 12.)

March

 According to a recently published will, filed for probate on Friday March 10, Linda's entire £138 million fortune has been left to Paul. Linda filed the will in the States to avoid the 40% death duties in Britain. The trust cash will pass to her four grown-up children when Paul dies.

 Paul and Linda are featured on the front cover of *Classical FM* magazine.

 Also this month, it is announced that Linda's first husband, Joseph Melville See Jnr, believed to be the inspiration behind the first verse of Paul's 'Get Back' in 1969, dies in Tucson, Arizona, from a self-inflicted shotgun wound. According to friends, Linda's death hit him hard and he never fully recovered. He was 62.

 Shortly after choosing a suitable cast, filming for the new CBS TV movie on the life of Linda McCartney takes place in Vancouver, Canada. Paul's spokesman, Geoff Baker remarks: "Sir Paul can't comment as he has not seen it or been asked for any input."

 In the UK, an instrumental cover version of 'Help!' appears on the soundtrack of television adverts for the Halifax building society.

Thursday March 2

 Paul, his daughter Mary and Sean Lennon are seen in the audience of Stella McCartney's Chloe fashion show in Paris, France. Sean remarks: "It's the first time I've ever seen one of her shows. It was great!"

Monday March 6

 Paul and Heather arrive in New York for the 15th annual Rock And Roll Hall Of Fame ceremony, where, this evening, he inducts the former Apple recording artist, James Taylor. After the event, Paul does not go backstage or pose for pictures. A planned traditional end-of-evening all-star jam session featuring 'Long Tall Sally' fails to materialise because of Paul's non-appearance. (The event is transmitted in America on VH1 from Wednesday March 8.) During his time in New York, Paul attends a recording session with Elvis's legendary guitarist, Scotty Moore and drummer, D.J. Fontana. The trio, calling themselves The Blue Mountain Boys, records 'That's All Right, Mama'. The session is recorded and will appear in a documentary about Memphis' Sun Studios, due to be screened by PBS in America in late 2001.

Thursday March 9

 At 1am, at the trendy Hog & Heifers bar in New York, in front of Heather Mills and over 100 drinkers, Paul, wearing a dinner jacket and braces, jumps up on stage and grooves with 28-year-old barmaid Michelle Gascoigne during the song 'Whole Lotta Shaking Going On', which is belting out from the nearby jukebox. As he does so, he waves and blows kisses to Heather.

Michelle: "I told him, 'Mr McCartney, we have a tradition that only women can dance on the bar, but we're willing to break that for one knight.' He seemed to appreciate my play on words but said he couldn't do it. Paul turned down my request at first, but agreed after I said, 'Wait a second. With all due respect Mr. McCartney, you can get up in front of 65,000 at Shea Stadium, but you're afraid to get up here with little ol' me.' He looked at me and said, 'That's it, girl,' and jumped up."

Sunday March 12

 George is seen in public – in the pits at the Australian Grand Prix – for the first time since his horrifying knife attack. In an interview with Martin Brundle, ITV's motor racing commentator, he says, "As you can see, I'm fit again. I came very close, but I'm doing OK!" He adds, "I'd like to thank everybody who sent me messages. It was overwhelming and it really helped me to recover."

 His appearance coincides with a report in the *News Of The World,* which exclusively reveals that Paul has been romancing the former model Heather Mills.

 Also today, The Beatles' authorised 1968 biographer, Hunter Davies, is a guest speaker at the first London Beatles Day of the new millennium. Aside from an impromptu appearance at a convention in Havana, Cuba, two years ago, this is Hunter's first ever scheduled appearance at a Beatles event, which takes place at its usual venue, the Bonnington Hotel in Southampton Row.

Monday March 13
 In London, Paul and Heather have dinner with Ringo and Barbara.

Wednesday March 15
 After months of speculation, Paul declares his love for Heather Mills. Naturally, the story features prominently on Sky News this evening and in the UK papers the following day.

Thursday March 16
 Paul and Heather are pictured on the front page of the *Daily Telegraph*, along with a story that reads, "Sir Paul declares his love for model." The MPL released story also takes front-page space in the *Daily Star* in a story headlined, "He Loves You, Yeah, Yeah, Yeah!" Inside, Paul confirms, "Yes, we are an item." The story also graces the pages of the *Mirror*, in a story titled, "My Love: Heather And I Are An Item, Admits Paul." In the *Sun*, the news appears in a story titled: "I'm In Love With Heather And I Feel Fine. Sir Paul McCartney opens his heart for the first time about his new romance."

Monday March 20
 Syndicated news reports suggest further that John had been secretly funding the IRA.

Wednesday March 22
 It is reported that Heather Mills has bought a £250,000 seaside home in Hove, East Sussex, a short drive from Paul's Peasmarsh estate.

Friday March 24
 It is revealed that more than nine hours of private black & white footage of John and Yoko, circa February 1970, has been uncovered in the States. The amazing videotape, shot by Yoko's ex-husband, Tony Cox, has been sold to a consortium of Beatles fans in America who are planning to issue the footage as a documentary later this year. Cox talks about the tapes: "Several scenes focus on Lennon and Ono's visit to the Black House, a centre run by Michael X, a Trinidadian counterpart of Malcolm X, who was later executed for murder. The couple (John and Yoko) shoot a promotional film for the Black House and then smoke hashish with Michael X." Other scenes in the footage describe Yoko as being stoned, and John snapping at her, "As usual, she doesn't know what we're talking about." In an intimate scene, John is seen perched on the edge of the bed, humming and strumming, trying to pick out a tune that would eventually be the song 'Mind Games' while Yoko is seen tucked up in bed, apparently asleep. In another, they are talking about Yoko's new hairstyle. "It took years off her," John remarks. "She was an old hag before I met her." Other scenes include John discussing whether he should pay for a new lake at his Ascot estate or consider "conning Apple again!" Then, during a tour of London's sights, John gives vulgar names to landmarks such as Nelson's Column and refers to piles of rubbish in the streets as "Prince Philip's mess".

Ray Thomas, a member of the consortium who is believed to have paid $1million (£625,000) for the tapes, remarks: "I have asked Yoko to be executive producer for the planned documentary, but I have had no response. Many of the scenes show her to be a very intelligent, articulate woman . . . These films capture John's creative genius in his most intimate surroundings, the couple's behaviour together, interaction with their two children, strong opinions about drugs, politics, communism, music and plans for manipulating critics, reviewers and the general press."

But before any of this footage can be made public, Yoko must sign a release form.

Monday March 27
 In the *Sun*'s "Bizarre" entertainment column, Paul exclusively reveals to the editor, Dominic Mohan, "Linda would approve of my love for Heather."
 Paul writes a letter to the *Daily Telegraph*, outlining his solution to the foxhunting debate.

Friday March 31
 In Liverpool, Paul's former home at 20 Forthlin Road, opens for its new season of business. Again, the curator is John Halliday. Coincidentally, it is also the day that Liverpool City Council win their battle to have the city named as "The Birthplace Of The

Beatles" on road signs. A sign, which reads "Liverpool Welcomes You To The Birthplace Of The Beatles", is unveiled today. John's half-sister, Julia Baird, is present at the ceremony.

April (until March 2001)

 An exhibition by the *Sgt. Pepper* designer, Peter Blake, entitled *About Collage* is staged at Liverpool's Tate Gallery and features previously unseen artwork by John and Paul. John's work, loaned from a private collection, dates back to his art school days and features portraits of the actresses Julie Christie and Edina Ronay. Paul's piece, entitled The Works, has been created specifically for the show. His work is a cross-shaped object and depicts several images including a holy cow, a husky dog, a murdered figure, a screaming man, an empty hotel corridor and a photograph of a child. Paul also compiles a 20-minute tape of non-musical audio material, some of which was recorded at his Cavern Club gig on December 14, 1999 (see entry) and during his car journey to Liverpool on the day. The sound collage also features previously unheard spoken material from Beatles recording sessions, circa 1964–69. (See entry for Monday August 21.)
 It is also announced this month that Columbia Pictures are to produce a film based on John and Yoko's colourful life together. The respected Dana Stevens is scripting the movie, which has received Yoko's blessing.
 Paul's company, MPL Communications, issues a lawsuit against My.MP3.com, an online business, which allows users to download, store and manage their CD collections on the Internet. MPL, as well as many other music organisations, including the RIAA, the American music industry organisation, claim the service breaks copyright.

Saturday April 1

 An (April Fools) story appears in today's *NME*, which claims that the Happy Monday's frontman, Shaun Ryder, will take the place of John at a Beatles reunion concert, to be held at this year's Glastonbury Festival. Ryder: "I always fancied being in The Beatles. They were top!"

Sunday April 2

 In the UK, the *News Of The World* reports: "The three surviving Beatles have joined together to write the band's official autobiography." It misleadingly continues, "Sir Paul, George Harrison and Ringo Starr have spent six years working on the book, which is expected to sell 20 million copies worldwide." The news is quickly reported around the world on both TV and radio.

Monday April 10

 Paul's girlfriend, Heather Mills makes a brief appearance on the US TV chat show *The Oprah Winfrey Show*.

Tuesday April 11

 Gimme Some Truth, the making of John's *Imagine* album in 1971 is released on both VHS home video and on DVD, extended by seven minutes. The latter DVD version also features a bonus item, a 16mm filmed record of John and Yoko being interviewed, at Tittenhurst Park, Ascot, for the BBC4 radio show, *Woman's Hour*, transmitted on Tuesday November 9, 1971.

Wednesday April 12

 Among the items on sale at Bonhams rock, pop and royalty-related items auction in London are a wooden spoon signed by John and Yoko in 1969, which sells for £345 and a 1963 roll of Beatles wallpaper, which sells for £210.

Thursday April 13

 Gimme Some Truth is transmitted in Brazil on the Fox cable channel.

Saturday April 15

 Paul's appearance on *Parkinson* (see entry for Thursday December 2, 1999) is broadcast in the States as part of a *Paul McCartney Night* on BBC America, the station available on both digital cable and satellite. *Parkinson* begins at 8pm EST and repeats at 11pm, sandwiching Paul's November 1999 appearance on *Later With Jools Holland*, which begins at 9:30pm.

Monday April 17

 Gimme Some Truth receives its American TV premiere when it is screened (at 10pm EDT) on the Bravo channel, some two and a half months after its European television premiere on Sunday February 6 on the ARTE channel. Repeat screenings on Bravo take place at 1am on Tuesday April 18 and at 7pm and 11pm on Sunday April 30.

Tuesday April 18

 The *Sun* newspaper in the UK publishes the results of its poll yesterday for readers to call in with their nominations for people to be knighted. Self-confessed 37-year-old George Harrison fanatic, Allison Devine, of Wickford, Essex, naturally nominates George, proclaiming: "George has helped put British cinema back on the map and hasn't abandoned Britain like a lot of other stars." Other popular votes for people to be knighted included the famous, but now retired, Test Match cricket umpire, Dickie Bird.

Saturday April 22

 In Holland, the Dutch fanzine *Beatles Unlimited* presents its 21st International Beatles Convention at the Vredenburg Music Centre, in the heart of Utrecht City. Special guests in attendance include Paul's former guitarist, Hamish Stuart, and one of John's sisters, Julia Baird.

Sunday April 23

 In the UK, the 75-minute television programme of Paul's *Working Classical* concert, recorded in Liverpool on Saturday October 16, 1999, is screened on BBC1 between 11:00pm and 12:15am.

Wednesday April 26

 The first of a two-part *Paul McCartney Story* is transmitted on the Satellite 10 FM radio station. (Part two is aired one week later, on Tuesday May 2.)
 In London, George Martin unveils a plaque outside HMV's landmark store at 363 Oxford Street. The plaque marks the 79 years of the famous store and its starring role in The Beatles' history, when, in 1962, a 78-rpm demo disc was cut for the group in the store's recording studio. This, of course, led to The Beatles' long-term recording contract with EMI.

Thursday April 27

 A photograph of The Beatles performing at the Liverpool Empire that hung on Brian Epstein's office wall, sells for an amazing £16,450 at Christies Rock & Pop sale in London. However, a set of 13 diaries belonging to Brian, starting from 1949, fails to reach its reserve price and the sale is aborted at just £7,500.

Friday April 28 (until Sunday May 14)

 A Beatles exhibition is held at the Seibu department store in Tokyo, Japan.

Saturday April 29

 BBC1 in the UK screens (between 9:05 and 10:00pm) *The Stars Sing The Beatles*, a 55-minute programme featuring well-known English stars singing their own versions of The Beatles' classic songs, including the news reader Anna Ford, who delivers 'Here, There And Everywhere'. Engelbert Humperdinck sings 'Penny Lane', referring to how he famously kept the 'Penny Lane'/'Strawberry Fields Forever' single from the top spot in 1967. The Bootleg Beatles close the show.
 In Detroit, Yoko Ono dedicates a wish tree to John.
 It is revealed that George Martin is bringing his *Sgt. Pepper* lecture tour to Norway.

Sunday April 30

 The *New York Post* reveals that Paul and Heather want to have children. The story is titled: "Paul McCartney Wants Baby With New Love".

Tuesday May 2

 The American scandal paper, the *National Enquirer*, features an interview with Alfie Karmal, the former husband of Heather Mills, who warns Paul about his former love. He says, "Run for your life, Paul McCartney. Your new love will break your fragile heart, just like she broke mine!" (She had married Karmal back in 1989.)

🍎 It is reported around the world that George joined Donovan for a duet in Ireland tonight. This is completely untrue, and when Donovan is told about this apparent performance he remarks: "I haven't seen George for ages. But, I'd love it to happen."

Wednesday May 3
🍎 In today's *Sun* newspaper, Heather Mills remarks: "I just wish I'd met Linda to say what an amazing job she did with her man."

Thursday May 4
🍎 In New York, Paul appears at a concert by John Tavener, the classical composer and former Apple recording artist. The event, which is held at the Church of St. Ignatius, is Tavener's first in the States and features Paul narrating a section entitled 'In The Mouth Of Athyr'. Before his appearance, Paul sits in the front row of the theatre, alongside Heather Mills.

Friday May 5
🍎 The television recording of Paul's concert at The Cavern Club in Liverpool is aired in the States on DirecTv. The programme does not appear on any network television station in America.

Saturday May 6
🍎 Ringo's edition of the VH-1 series *Storytellers,* recorded on Wednesday May 13, 1998 (see entry), is screened in France via the Canal Jimmy satellite station.

Sunday May 7
🍎 The highly acclaimed, award winning two-part BBC documentary on Brian Epstein, first aired on BBC2 on December 25 and 26, 1998, is screened on the Belgium Canvas TV channel as part of the *Het Derde Oog (The Third Eye)* series.

🍎 In the UK, the BBC1 programme, *Antiques Roadshow*, features the photographer Dezo Hoffman's granddaughter, who brings with her some familiar and rare Beatles pictures (circa 1963/1964) that he had taken. She had obtained them when she picked them up in his studio during a visit. An expert informs her that they are worth a "four figure sum". (Following Dezo's death in the mid-Eighties, Apple bought the copyright to his many Beatles photographs from his widow.)

Friday May 12
🍎 At around 11:45am, at the Strawberry Fields children's home in Liverpool, children at the home report a light blue Ford transit van parked near the entrance gates. Shortly after, they notice that the gates were being moved and inform a member of staff, who immediately went to the end of the drive to discover the gates are gone. The thieves had sawn off the distinctive red iron gates, eight feet high and ten feet wide, valued at £5,000, and thrown them into the back of their van before driving off.

* * *

Ringo and his Sixth All-Starr Band
Tour Of America
Friday May 12 (until Saturday July 1)

In America, Ringo's All-Starr Band begins its latest, David Fishof-presented, US Tour. A press conference to promote the sixth All-Starr tour had taken place on Monday May 1 at the Plaza Hotel in New York, the scene where The Beatles stayed at the start of their first US visit on Friday February 7, 1964 (see entry below). The musicians joining Ringo on the seven-week tour are Eric Carmen (on keyboards), Dave Edmunds (guitar), Jack Bruce (bass guitar), Simon Kirke (drums) and Mark Rivera (on sax).

The itinerary of shows usually features, give or take one or two tracks, the following repertoire of songs: 'It Don't Come Easy', 'Act Naturally', 'Hungry Eyes' (Eric Carmen), 'I Hear You Knocking' (Dave Edmunds), 'Sunshine Of Your Love' (Jack Bruce), 'Shooting Star' (Simon Kirke), 'I Wanna Be Your Man', 'Love Me Do' and 'Yellow

Submarine'. (Ringo leaves the stage, leaving Eric Carmen to perform 'Boat Against The Wind' and 'Go All The Way', Jack Bruce to play 'Theme From An Imaginary Western' and Dave Edmunds to play an [occasional] instrumental version of 'Lady Madonna'.) Ringo returns to sing 'I'm The Greatest', 'No No Song'/'Roll Out The Barrel' (occasionally) and then 'Back Off Boogaloo'. The rest of the concert follows with 'I Feel Free' (Jack Bruce), 'All Right Now' (Simon Kirke), 'Boys', 'I Knew The Bride' (Dave Edmunds), 'White Room' (Jack Bruce), 'All By Myself' (Eric Carmen), 'Photograph' and 'You're Sixteen' followed by 'With A Little Help From My Friends', performed as an encore.

(Note: Four of the concerts, on Monday June 5, Wednesday June 7, Monday June 19 and Tuesday June 20 are cancelled due to Ringo's bout of bronchitis.) The concerts on this tour, which begin three days earlier than planned, are as follows:

Trump Taj Mahal, Atlantic City, New Jersey (Friday May 12 & Saturday May 13)
Mid-Hudson Civic Center, Poughkeepsie, New York (Monday May 15 – the original first concert on the tour)
Westbury Music Fair, Westbury, New York (Tuesday May 16 & Wednesday May 17)
Mohegan Sun Casino, Connecticut (Friday May 19 & Saturday May 20)
I Center, Salem, New Hampshire (Sunday May 21)
The Beacon Theater, New York City (Tuesday May 23)
State Theater, New Brunswick, New Jersey (Wednesday May 24 – extra date added to tour)
Norva Theater, Norfolk, Virginia (Friday May 26)
Festival, Cleveland, Ohio (Saturday May 27)
The Riverport Amphitheater, St. Louis, Missouri (Sunday May 28 – extra gig added)
Wolf Trap, Washington, DC (Tuesday May 30)
Gaylord Entertainment Center, Nashville, Tennessee (Wednesday May 31)
Horse Shoe Casino, Robinson, Mississippi (Thursday June 1)
Sunrise Musical Theater, Fort Lauderdale, Florida (Saturday June 3)
Chastain Park, Atlanta, Georgia (Sunday June 4)
City Light Amphitheater, Pittsburgh, Pennsylvania (Monday June 5 – gig cancelled)
Casino RAMA, Ontario, Canada (Wednesday June 7 – gig cancelled)
House Of Blues, Chicago, Illinois (Thursday June 8)
Landmark Theater, Syracuse, New York (Saturday June 10)
Pine Knob Theater, Clarkston, Michigan (Sunday June 11 – replacing the gig originally scheduled at Freedom Park, Warren, Michigan)
Winery, Saratoga, California (Wednesday June 14 & Thursday June 15)
Harrahs, Lake Tahoe, Nevada (Friday June 16)
The Joint, Las Vegas, Nevada (Saturday June 17)
The Sun Theater, Anaheim, California (Monday June 19 & Tuesday June 20 – gigs cancelled)
House Of Blues, Los Angeles, California (Thursday June 22 & Friday June 23)
Humphrey's, San Diego, California (Sunday June 25 & Monday June 26)
Red Rock Amphitheater, Denver, Colorado (Wednesday June 28)
State Capitol Grounds, St. Paul, Minnesota (Friday June 30)
Summerfest, Milwaukee, Wisconsin (Saturday July 1)

Information prior to the start of the tour:

Monday May 1
Ringo drums up interest in the tour by holding a press conference at the Plaza Hotel in New York. "We're blessed to be alive," he remarks to reporters, "and that people want to come and see us. I'm still living a dream come true that I've had since I was thirteen years old. The rehearsal part is always the worst. The show is the easiest bit. It's exciting and frustrating and amazing. The format is pretty much the same as the last tours. We do all the hits, and have a lot of fun."

Ringo is then asked if he has spoken to George recently. "I haven't talked to him lately," he reveals. "But I saw him a while ago. He's doing a lot better. There's a lot of healing going on." The only mention of Paul comes when a reporter asks Ringo if he thought that Paul would marry his current girlfriend, Heather Mills. Ringo replies: "I think you should ask him that." The Beatles *Anthology* book naturally comes into the equation. "It's a very big book," he announces, "not only in size but in subject matter. I am happy with the parts I had seen or contributed. It's going to be a very worthwhile piece, because it's mainly from our lips and not from other people's."

Sunday May 7
At 8pm (EDT), Ringo has an hour-long online chat session, his first of four on the tour, on the website belonging to the real estate corporation Century 21, the sponsors of the concerts. During the session, he is asked to name three people from history with whom he would like to have dinner. Ringo replies by naming eight members of his family, Barbara, Zak, Jason, Lee, Francesca, Gianni, Tatia and Louise. He also reveals that he has five dogs and a cat, he speaks two and a half languages (English, Liverpool and half French), and he has no plans to grow his hair long, because he loves it short. Asked what goes through his mind before a concert, Ringo replies: "Most of me wants to go home. There's 15 seconds of madness there and I have to run on stage. The thoughts are, 'Do I remember the songs? Are they good?'" Further disclosures reveal that he doesn't wish to do both 'Yellow Submarine' and 'Octopus's Garden' during a show because he feels one underwater song is enough, and he takes vitamins and herbs and drinks lots of water. When asked how he would like to be remembered, he replies: "As a damn fine drummer!"
(Note: The second online chat on the tour takes place on Friday June 2.)

During the tour:

Monday May 15
The new Century 21 television commercial, featuring Ringo, airs for the first time this morning in the States on the NBC TV *Today* show. Ringo is seen as part of Century 21's "Perfect Hookups" campaign, where a couple are seen being shown a new home by their Century 21 representative who offers them some of the various services available through their connections programme. There is a choice of home entertainment including cable television, satellite TV or Ringo Starr! He obliges, pointing to the band behind him, adding, 'With a little help from my friends'. (The ad will continue to run on both satellite and cable TV after this.)

Friday May 19
At the Ed Sullivan Theater in New York, just prior to his show at the Mohegan Sun Casino in nearby Connecticut, Ringo makes another appearance on the CBS TV programme *The Late Show With David Letterman,* where he is interviewed and performs 'With A Little Help From My Friends'. (A European screening of the show occurs on the Fox TV station in Holland on Sunday May 21 and in the UK on the digital channel ITV2 on Saturday May 20.)

Wednesday May 24 (& Thursday May 25)
A two-part pre-taped interview with Ringo is aired on ABC TV's *Good Morning America.*

Wednesday May 31
During the concert at the Gaylord Entertainment Center, in Nashville, Tennessee, former Police guitarist Andy Summers joins Jack Bruce for 'Theme For An Imaginary Western'.

Friday June 2
During a break from the tour, Ringo holds his second live online chat this evening. Coming from Fort Lauderdale, Florida, the event takes place between 7:30 and 8:30pm.

Wednesday June 14
Ringo's third online chat from this tour takes place in Saratoga, California. The time is 8pm EDT (5pm Pacific) and takes place just before his show at the Winery.

Thursday June 22
During the opening night at the House Of Blues in Los Angeles, California, Micky Dolenz, the former drummer with The Monkees, Spencer Davis, Bruce Gary and George Thorogood join Ringo during the encore for 'With A Little Help From My Friends'. Ringo jokes with Micky that his was "the wrong group!"

Thursday June 29
At 8pm (EDT), on the Century 21 website, Ringo holds his fourth and final online chat from this tour, this time it comes from Denver, Colorado.

*   *   *

Sunday May 14
🎸 The *Sunday Mirror* reports that: "Paul McCartney keeps old clothes in the outbuildings at his farmhouse near Rye, East Sussex," adding that he is apparently worried that otherwise they will be auctioned off as memorabilia. The article lists the ten things he hoards, including his Hofner violin bass, his first ever guitar amplifier (an El Pico, bought from the shop Currys), his *Sgt. Pepper* suit, letters he sent to fans from Hamburg (bought at an auction), handwritten Beatles lyrics ('Hey Jude', 'She's Leaving Home' and 'Getting Better'), the balcony rail on the cover of The Beatles' first LP (*Please Please Me* – EMI gave it to Paul when they closed their London headquarters), his old school desk from the Liverpool Institute and, among other things, his old socks (a whole box of them).

Monday May 15
🎸 Paul, accompanied by Geoff Baker, makes a private appearance, visiting students at the LIPA building in Liverpool and then gives his blessing to a new cancer hospital, *The Linda McCartney Centre*, which forms part of the Royal Liverpool University Hospital.

Friday May 19
🎸 The *Daily Star* newspaper reports that Heather Mills may take over the operation of the Linda McCartney frozen food business. The report suggests that Paul has allowed Mills to revamp the packaging and test new recipes, especially cheeseless pizzas and lasagne, because of Paul's love for Italian food.

Sunday May 21
🎸 The 90-minute CBS TV Network production, *The Linda McCartney Story*, based on Danny Field's recent biography, is premiered across America and stars the unknown actress Elizabeth Mitchell in the title role and features Gary Bakewell repeating his role as Paul from the 1993 film *Backbeat*. The noted American actor George Segal appears in the role of Lee Eastman, Linda's father. (See previous entry for July 1999.) Tim Piper plays John, Chris Cound is George and Michael McMurty is Ringo.

Monday May 22
🎸 The first pictures of Leo, British Prime Minister Tony Blair and his wife Cherie's new baby boy, taken by Mary McCartney, are released to the press.

Thursday May 25
🎸 At the Ivor Novello Awards ceremony, held at London's Grosvenor Hotel, Paul receives an Academy Fellowship award by the British Academy of Composers and Songwriters (BASC), in honour of his four decades of composing. Following a lengthy standing ovation, Paul says: "I remember coming here the very first time with my mates John, George and Ringo and sitting back there. It was just fantastic to be part of this whole song writing thing. It was always just the greatest award, the greatest thing to get for songwriters and it still is many years later." Paul receives the award from Sir Tim Rice and is on hand to present Travis star, Fran Healy, with one of two gongs for 'Why Does It Always Rain On Me?' a big hit for the group. Healy remarks: "I can't believe I got my award from Paul. It's a dream. I keep pinching myself."

Friday May 26 (until Tuesday May 30)
🎸 At LIPA, Paul conducts a master recording class. The producer, Geoff Emerick, assists him.

Saturday May 27
🎸 Paul's 1984 film *Give My Regards To Broad Street* is screened in Holland on the SBS6 TV channel.

May (end of the month)

🍎 Paul makes another nostalgic trip to Liverpool where, along with his longtime friend and assistant, John Hammel, he spends hours driving around the city. Firstly, he stops at St. Peter's Church where for around twenty minutes he lingers in the adjacent field where he met John for the first time back in July 1957. The two of them then journey to Woolton swimming baths, where he signs autographs, and then visit Menlove Avenue and Strawberry Fields, where they look at the recently returned gates.

June

🍎 *Q* magazine reveals that The Beatles' 1966 album *Revolver* has been chosen, by their readers, as "The Greatest British Album . . . Ever!" In the top twenty listings, *A Hard Day's Night* is placed at number five, the *White Album* is number seven, *Sgt Pepper* is number 13 and *Abbey Road* is at number 17.

🍎 Interviews are carried out with various musicians for the *Classic Albums* television programme dedicated to George's *All Things Must Pass*. George is, apparently, not too keen to participate in the proceedings.

Friday June 2

🍎 Ben Elton's film *Maybe Baby*, featuring the Buddy Holly title track performed by Paul, is released to the cinemas in the UK. The film had received its London premiere, at the Odeon, Leicester Square, the night before. Paul was not present. The soundtrack album, featuring Paul's title track, is released in the UK on Monday June 5. The song was recorded in the studios at the Capitol Records Tower in Hollywood, working with the engineer, Geoff Emerick. Jeff Lynne produces the track.

🍎 Also on June 2, Cynthia Lennon's home in Normandy, France, is featured in the David Frost BBC1 afternoon "spot the celebrity home" quiz show, *Through The Keyhole,* transmitted between 3:00 and 3:25pm.

Saturday June 3

🍎 Paul and Heather Mills fly out from Heathrow Airport to New York City, where Paul attends a performance of *A Garland For Linda,* which takes place at the Riverside Church. (Tickets for the event, which cost between $30 for an obstructed view and $100 for the best seats, had been on sale since Wednesday March 1.)

Sunday June 4

🍎 The Diary column in the *Sunday Mirror* reports that, "The three surviving Beatles are set to return to the studio to work on new material for the first time in thirty years! Paul and Ringo have agreed to play on George Harrison's latest solo album." A friend says: "The project is in its early stages so don't expect any material to be released before 2001 at the earliest. It is in the planning phase, the album does not have a title yet."

🍎 In the *Cleveland Plain Dealer*, Ringo comments: "I had no idea that George was making an album. I had no idea that Paul might participate. Did Paul say this?" When told that it was a rumour on the Internet, Ringo replies: "Oh, yes, go on. I'm producing it then. I saw both of them last month. They're up to whatever they're up to. If you want to know what they're doing, you've got to talk to them. It's up to them to let you know what they want you to know."

🍎 The *Mail On Sunday* prints a previously unseen picture of Paul, taken at Liverpool Cathedral in 1953. In the snap, he is seen looking glum among a group of ten-year-olds gathered around a replica crown commemorating the Queen's coronation.

🍎 The front-page of the *Sunday People* features a story entitled: "Sex, Lies, Threat To Me & Macca" by Heather Mills. Inside, she is quoted as saying: "It was worse than losing my leg. I sat Paul down and told him, 'Evil liars say that I used to be a hooker.'"

🍎 Mary and Stella McCartney meet Ravi Shankar's daughter, Anouska, at the London Tibetan Peace Gardens appeal.

Tuesday June 6

🍎 George's attacker, Mike Abram pleads "not guilty" to attempted murder at Oxford Crown Court. The trail is set for Tuesday November 14. The judge rules that George will not have to give evidence in person and can supply information by written statements.

Thursday June 8
 It is revealed that Paul is buying a £2.5 million mansion for his new love, Heather. The former Beatle has been spotted weighing up the huge 13th century manor house, Wycliffe Hall, near Barnard Castle, in Co. Durham, just down the road from Heather's childhood home.

Monday June 12
 It is announced that Ringo is to retire – after one last assault on the pop charts. He says the reason for his retirement is because he wants to spend more time with his family.

Wednesday June 14
 The *Daily Star* reports: "Ringo's Joy For Paul: Ringo has given the seal of approval to the romance between Paul and Heather." Ringo: "I'm really glad that Paul is living his life and getting on with it."

Thursday June 15
 Paul inducts Beach Boy Brian Wilson into the Songwriter's Hall Of Fame at the Waldorf Hotel in New York. He praises Wilson's ability to provoke emotions in listeners. "Thank you, sir, for making me cry," Paul tells Brian. "Thank you for doing that thing you do. You got me any day." Later, Paul joins Ben E. King and James Brown on stage for a jam of 'Stand By Me' and 'Kansas City'.
 There is controversy over Paul's Concorde flight from England. Passengers are outraged because Paul had been brought onto the plane before the UN Secretary General, Kofi Annan. One passenger screams: "It was a total breach of protocol." But a British Air spokesman is quick to diffuse the situation, saying: "VIPs with the greatest security concerns are actually boarded last."

Saturday June 17 (& Sunday June 18)
 George is seen again, this time in Montreal for two days at the Canadian Grand Prix. The roving ITV cameras, in the UK, and Globo TV of Brazil, are on hand to cover his appearance.

Sunday June 18
 The 235 mile Long And Winding Road Walk from Liverpool to London, in aid of the Linda McCartney Centre begins at The Cavern Club in Mathew Street. Taking part in the walk is Dave Williams, who had suffered from bowel cancer. The walkers support vehicle for the duration of the walk is the original *Magical Mystery Tour* coach. The contingent will reach Abbey Road Studios on Sunday July 2, when the walking party is greeted by 'Sporty' Spice Girl, Mel C. The appeal will raise £3.8 million for a new cancer centre at the Royal Liverpool hospital.
 During Paul and Heather Mills' stay in New York, Paul purchases a floral sun dress at the Cynthia Rowley boutique in East Hampton.

Tuesday June 20
 Olivia and Dhani Harrison, along with Mary McCartney, are seen in the audience of Ravi Shankar's concert at the Barbican Centre in London.

Friday June 23
 Paul, wearing blue and grey trainers and a charcoal grey suit, acts as a chauffeur at his second cousin, Sally Harris's, wedding in the Wirral, Merseyside, at the Wallasey Town Hall. Sally, who is marrying her boyfriend Kevin Murphy, is the daughter of Paul's Auntie Gin. Paul's brother Mike is the official wedding photographer. Before the ceremony, Paul takes the hired black Jaguar car through an automatic car wash because, he says, "I had never done it before."

Sunday June 25
 A planned live appearance by Paul on the final day of the Glastonbury 2000 Festival fails to materialise because he feared for his life. The farmer Michael Eavis, whose land the festival takes place on, reveals: "I met Paul earlier this year and he said he would love to be asked to play Glastonbury, so I invited him. I believe Sir Paul was put off when he

saw newspaper reports saying that he might be appearing. I think it scared him. And when you think about the murder of John and the attack on George, I can see it."
 George, accompanied by Olivia, his son Dhani and his 19-year-old girlfriend, Beth, the daughter of the Planet Hollywood entrepreneur, is spotted at Goodwood's Festival Of Speed motor racing event.

Tuesday June 27
 George attends the second of Ravi Shankar's birthday concerts at the Barbican Centre in London, entering the building by a side door just as the show is about to begin and sitting in the front row. He leaves the concert just prior to the intermission. Also in attendance are Mary and James McCartney, and Olivia and Dhani Harrison.

Thursday June 29 (until Saturday July 22)
 An exhibition of Klaus Voorman's work, *Paintings From Hamburg Days*, goes on display at The John Lennon Gallery, at 31 Mathew Street, Liverpool. The opening day sees a private view, which takes place between 4pm and 8pm.

Friday June 30 (until Friday August 11)
 The webcast of Paul's December 14, 1999 concert at The Cavern Club in Liverpool is rebroadcast by MCY.com, the service which webcast it originally. Beginning at noon on the day listed, the transmission will continue for 24 hours until noon the following day. The days of broadcasts are Friday June 30, Saturday July 1, Wednesday July 5, Saturday July 8, Saturday July 15, Thursday July 20, Monday July 24, Friday August 4 and Thursday August 10.

July
 Shortly after the conclusion of his latest tour, Ringo expresses his irritation at The Beatles' classic tunes being used in TV commercials. A friend of the drummer tells the American magazine, the *National Enquirer*: "Ringo and Paul are upset that serious compositions are being turned into mere jingles. Ringo told me, 'John and Paul wrote some of the greatest songs in the history of recorded music. But, if it's left to the ad men, they'll go down as a couple of jingle writers and The Beatles will be known as hacks. I respect Michael Jackson; I just wish he'd show *us* some respect and not licence our songs for ads. It's something the band wouldn't do if it were under their control. If The Beatles could vote, they'd vote no!'"
 In England, reports suggest that Paul's latest studio album, which he had apparently started recording on Friday, February 18, is finished and ready for final mixing.
 Yoko Ono, through her Spirit Foundation, makes a £30,000 donation to Dovecotes Infants school in Liverpool. The donation, inspired by a letter by the school's headmaster Ken Williams, is intended to be used for improving the playground.
 Ringo appears in the UK TV listings paper, the *TV Times*. The interview is titled 'When I Get Older, Losing My Hair'.

Sunday July 2
 The day after the conclusion of Ringo's latest American tour, the channel AMC screens (at 10pm EDT) the movie, *Hollywood Rocks The Movies – The Early Years (1955 to 1970)*, which features Ringo's narration and focuses on the history of rock movies at the cinema. The excellent documentary is repeated on the station twice the following day, at 8pm and 11pm (EDT).
 Paul and Heather visit Iceland, arriving on a Falcon aeroplane owned by a British millionaire friend. The couple are in the country because Heather is due to attend a conference in Perlan where she is to lecture about her life. Later, the couple are seen at the Cafe Opera. A local musician, Jon Olafsson, hears that Paul is at the venue and decides to see him. Jon notices that the only available table at the restaurant is right next to Paul and Heather. Jon later tells a reporter: "McCartney is a very relaxed person. He is friendly and free from the star syndrome. After Stefan Hilmarsson (Jon's friend) and I had finished our drinks, we started to chat with him. Stefan introduced me as a 'well-respected Icelandic musician'. Paul asked what instrument I played. After I told him that I played piano, he asked me to play the piano at Cafe Opera. I smiled, but declined, and told him that I was too far out for Cafe Opera." Paul and Heather spend their first evening in the country at Hotel Borg.

Reports on their visit to Iceland are featured on RUV, the Icelandic State broadcasting service and Channel 2, the other main TV station in the country.

Monday July 3
🍎 Paul and Heather spend their second day in Iceland, by which time they have taken up residency in the honeymoon suite at the Hotel Valholl at Pingvellir, registering in the name of Mr. P. Hutchinson. They will spend the rest of the day whale watching at Keflavik, a small village on the north coast of Iceland. Before they depart from their hotel on Tuesday July 4, they breakfasted on grilled cheese sandwiches and coffee. There is an incident before Paul and Heather leave Perlan involving photographers and journalists who are waiting for the couple. Paul ignores them and heads off in his Toyota Land Cruiser car. The press immediately follow them which angers Paul, who stops his car, gets out and orders one photographer to leave.

Tuesday July 4
🍎 A live appearance by Cynthia Lennon to promote her range of John Lennon drawings is included on the Channel 5 afternoon show *Open House*, hosted by Gloria Hunniford.
🍎 This afternoon, Paul and Heather leave Iceland for London at Reykjavik Airport on the same jet that they had arrived on. As he departs, Paul refuses any chance of a quick interview with the waiting press but is seen speaking to Eirikur Einarsson, a member of The Icelandic Beatles Club. "We have waited for a long time for Paul McCartney to come to our country," she says, optimistically adding: "We want him to play at a Beatles festival this autumn."

Thursday July 6
🍎 A pre-taped feature with Ringo and Barbara at London's Battersea Dogs' Home is aired (between 6:59 and 7:28pm) on the BBC1 same titled show this evening.

Friday July 14
🍎 It is revealed that Yoko Ono is suing the Tokyo underground for £100,000 for using a picture of John on the back of their tickets. She is claiming that the image is breaking her copyright and is therefore entitled to a royalty.
🍎 Stella McCartney appears on the cover of *ES Magazine*, a free colour supplement available with the *Evening Standard* newspaper. In the piece, she talks about girls, glamour and her future with Chloe.

Sunday July 16
🍎 Lord Woodbine, the local Merseyside concert promoter, dies in a blaze, which swept through his house in Toxteth, Liverpool. Woodbine, real name Harold Phillips, aged 72, was so called because of his love for Woodbine cigarettes. He originally played with the Royal Caribbean Steel Band and occasionally booked The Beatles for his New Colony Club in Liverpool. He also travelled with The Beatles on their first visit to Hamburg in August 1960. His wife, Helen, also dies in the blaze. Geoff Baker, the Apple and MPL spokesman, remarks: "All of the guys (The Beatles) will be shocked to hear this news. It is a great loss."

Monday July 17
🍎 This evening, Paul, Heather and a group of friends, have a meal at The Wiz restaurant in Covent Garden, London. At the end of their meal, Paul leads the gathering in an impromptu sing-a-long.

Friday July 21
🍎 Paul arrives again at the Liverpool Institute (LIPA), this time wearing a grey suit and dark glasses. He speaks and jokingly kisses several students and presents degrees to 200 of them. Later, Paul, accompanied by Heather Mills, attends a reception at LIPA.

Saturday July 22
🍎 The new archive series *I Love The 70s* begins its run on BBC2 in the UK and, naturally, devotes the first show to the year 1970. A planned longer feature focusing on the break-up of The Beatles, including lengthy interviews with various Beatles-related people including the author of this book, is scrapped because Apple would not allow the BBC to use excerpts from the film *Let It Be* or The Beatles *Anthology* series.

Tuesday July 25
 In London, Paul and Heather are seen having a meal at the Pizza In The Park restaurant and then enjoying a stroll through nearby Hyde Park, during which he romantically purchases for her a red rose.

Thursday July 27
 HBO's Bob Dylan special in America goes ahead but without the rumoured guest appearance by George.

August
 In the States, the alleged track listing for the forthcoming 27-song Beatles hits CD, formerly dubbed as *Project X* last year, is published in *ICE* magazine. The line-up is scheduled to feature: 'Love Me Do', 'From Me To You', 'She Loves You', 'I Want To Hold Your Hand', 'Can't Buy Me Love', 'A Hard Day's Night', 'I Feel Fine', 'Eight Days A Week', 'Ticket To Ride', 'Help!', 'Yesterday', 'Day Tripper', 'We Can Work It Out', 'Paperback Writer', 'Yellow Submarine', 'Eleanor Rigby', 'Penny Lane', 'All You Need Is Love', 'Hello, Goodbye', 'Lady Madonna', 'Hey Jude', 'Get Back', 'The Ballad Of John And Yoko', 'Something', 'Come Together', 'Let It Be' and 'The Long And Winding Road'.

ICE magazine remarks: "The premise of the disc is simple, it will contain all The Beatles' single sides that reached number one in either England or the United States, making a total of 27 tracks contained on one 78-minute CD." (Note: George's 'Something' only made number four in the UK and number three in America. Fans are in uproar over the omission of both 'Please Please Me' and 'Strawberry Fields Forever'.)

The magazine *DVD Review* announces that the DVD versions of The Beatles *Anthology* have been delayed until next year.

 Mojo magazine reveals that 'In My Life' has been chosen as "The Greatest Song Of All Time". The result comes from a poll taken from votes by some of the world's finest songwriters, including Paul.

 Classic Rock magazine reports that George has signed a new recording contract with the Multimedia giant, DreamWorks.

 Extreme skateboarder Tony Hawk reveals that he was invited to Friar Park for dinner by George's son, Dhani, but left before Bob Dylan turned up.

 In Liverpool, it is announced that Rushworth's music store is to close. The Beatles frequently visited the shop, once the biggest musical instrument store on Merseyside, in the early Sixties.

Friday August 4
 Paul pays £450,000 for a tiny one-bedroom house next to his seaside home to stop neighbours moving in. He snaps up the property, in the exclusive East Hampton area of Long Island, New York, at an auction. One estate agent remarks: "Paul must have bought the place for privacy, as the place is only worth about £150,000."

 In London, auditions for the role of John Lennon, in the forthcoming NBC made-for-TV docu-drama on the former Beatle, take place at the Conway Hall, 25 Red Lion Square, London EC1. The London-based casting director, Beth Charkham, remarks that the most common song performed at the audition is 'Twist And Shout'. The film's executive producer, David Carson, announces: "What we are looking for is an incredible young actor who can sing, play guitar, look like John Lennon and capture the essence of his personality and wicked sense of humour on screen. Needless to say, that is a very tall order, but there is an outstanding pool of young acting talent in the United Kingdom."

Wednesday August 9
 The second audition to play the role of John in the forthcoming NBC American TV film takes place at the Elevator Music Studios, 23–27 Cheapside in Liverpool. The auditions, on both days in London and Liverpool, begin at 10am. The title of the film is confirmed as *In His Life: The John Lennon Story*.

Thursday August 10
 VH-1 in Europe features, between 6:00pm and 1:00am, an evening of Paul McCartney programming, including the first European TV screenings of the re-edited *Paul McCartney Live At The Cavern Club* show and his six song performance at the September 18, 1999 PETA Awards Ceremony (see entry). (Note: although VH-1 had all six songs,

they transmit only five, omitting 'Lonesome Town', an action taken due to time restrictions. It is a cut approved by MPL.)

Friday August 11
🍎 The *Sun* reports that Paul has forced his favourite restaurant to change its menu after he found out that ostrich and wild boar were on the menu. Strict vegetarian Paul threatened to boycott Senor Zilli in a protest letter to the owner, top chef Aldo Zilli. He writes: "I enjoyed my last visit to your wonderful restaurant but was surprised to see that you are now offering wild boar and ostrich. I was wondering if there is so much profit in including these on your menu that you feel you could not consider removing them."

Monday August 14
🍎 The *Mirror* newspaper in the UK announces that, despite previous reports to the contrary, Paul's children, especially Mary and James, are not happy with the Heather Mills relationship and worry that it's moving too fast. The *Mirror* also says the children are now avoiding family gatherings where Mills is in attendance.

Tuesday August 15
🍎 Dominic Mohan's "Bizarre" column in the *Sun* newspaper exclusively reports that: "Beatles Release New Track (And It Sounds Like The Chemical Brothers)". The article reads: "A new Beatles record has been put together by Sir Paul McCartney – 30 years after the group broke up. The psychedelic dub track is the Fab Four as you have never heard them before. Paul tells me: 'It's a new little piece of Beatles. 'Free Now' is an outbreak from my normal stuff – it's a little side dish that is not to be confused with my other work. It's more underground than what you usually hear from me but I like to be free enough to do this sort of thing.'" The *Sun* sets up a special phone line so you can hear the 'Free Now' recording.

Sunday August 20
🍎 The *News Of The World* reveals that one of The Beatles has stopped a children's author from penning a book involving the Fab Four. The report goes on to say that Anthony Brown, from St. Nicholas-at-Wade, Kent, had to stop working on the story, which was about a little girl who befriends the group, after the mystery Beatle called publishers to object.

Monday August 21
🍎 The five-track album *Liverpool Sound Collage*, featuring Paul's exclusive sound collages, mixed by The Super Furry Animals, and rare Beatles outtakes, recorded between 1964 and 1969, is released on CD. The tracks accompanied Peter Blake's *About Collage* exhibition, which is currently showing at the Liverpool Tate Gallery. The full track listing is: 'Plastic Beetle' (Paul McCartney plus The Beatles), 'Peter Blake 2000' (Super Furry Animals plus The Beatles), 'Real Gone Dub Made Manifest In The Vortex Of The Eternal Wheel' (Paul's Fireman collaborator, Youth), 'Made Up' (Paul McCartney plus The Beatles), 'Free Now' (Paul McCartney, The Beatles and The Super Furry Animals). The track 'Free Now' is also issued as a very limited promo of just five copies!
🍎 The *Daily Mail* publishes a story about The Beatles performance at Aldershot's Palais Ballroom in December 1961, which was watched by only eighteen people!

Tuesday August 22
🍎 It is announced that Ewan McGregor, the star of the film *Trainspotting*, has won the role of John in an upcoming movie about John and his love affair with Yoko Ono. The film (not to be confused with the NBC TV Lennon film *In His Life*) will portray Yoko as a peacemaker who tries to soothe tensions between John and Paul. When told of this film, a spokesman for Paul remarks: "He is watching developments in the movie with cynical interest!"

Thursday August 24 (until Tuesday August 29)
🍎 The annual, Cavern City Tours organised, Liverpool Beatles festival again takes place. Titled *Let It Be Liverpool*, the event features six days of non-stop Beatles-related activity, including the Beatles Convention, which is held, traditionally, in the Adelphi hotel on Sunday August 27, where Klaus Voorman, The Beatles' authorised biographer, Hunter

Davies, and the author of this book are guest speakers. Another highlight for many of the thousand fans present, are performances by The Overtures, who (in performances on Sunday and Monday) deliver the *Revolver* and *Let It Be* albums and the American band, The Fab Faux, who perform an amazing version of 'Tomorrow Never Knows' to open their concert at The Royal Court on Saturday August 26. Earlier this day, the original Quarry Men give a performance in the grounds of Quarry Bank High School.

Monday August 28
🍎 In an interview with Launch.com, drummer Jim Keltner announces that: "George has been pulling tracks out of his vaults and finishing them over the last couple of years. There's a tremendous amount of stuff he hadn't finished, and I put drums on a tremendous amount of that stuff. Some of the songs I played on were absolutely wonderful, brilliant. I can't wait to see what he does with them. I don't know whether he'll have somebody help him produce or what, but I'm sure he'll come out with somebody cool." Keltner also says that it is George who is the least interested in doing a new Traveling Wilbury's album. "I think it really all comes down to George. When I talk to the other guys, Tom, Jeff or Bob, they all sound like they're into it. George wants to sometimes, and other times he gets busy on other things."

September
🍎 The television advert for the Internet company Nortel Networks, which features a cover of 'Come Together' on the soundtrack, continues its run on the ITV network.
🍎 At the start of the month, George visits India where he meets up with Ravi Shankar.
🍎 The Beatles' *Revolver* is voted the number one album of all time in the *Virgin All Time Top 1,000 Albums* publication. *Sgt. Pepper* is placed at number three, the *White Album* is at number five, *Abbey Road* at number eight, *A Hard Day's Night* is at number 22 and *Rubber Soul* is placed at number 34.

Sunday September 3
🍎 The *Sunday Telegraph* scoops the world by printing extracts from the long-awaited Beatles *Anthology* book. The first part is trumpeted by leading television commercials which appear on ITV and Channel 4 up to two days before the first part is printed.
🍎 Meanwhile, the *Mail On Sunday* also publishes extracts from The Beatles *Anthology* book, also billing their piece as a "World Exclusive", adding the phrase: "The Beatles By The Beatles".
🍎 The *Sunday Times* today publish "The McCartney Interview", in which Paul gives his candid thoughts about "Lennon, Linda, Painting and Poetry".

Monday September 4
🍎 Further Beatles *Anthology* extracts, albeit much shorter, appear in the *Sun* newspaper today.

Tuesday September 5
🍎 Paul arrives at the *GQ* Man Of The Year awards ceremony in London with a woman on each arm, girlfriend Heather Mills and the wacky artist, Tracey Emin.
🍎 The *Sun* publishes the second part of their two-part Beatles *Anthology* serialisation.

Wednesday September 6
🍎 The *Daily Express* publishes the second part of their Beatles *Anthology* serialisation, which looks back at the early years of Beatlemania.

Thursday September 7
🍎 The *Daily Express* publishes the third part of their Beatles *Anthology* serialisation, focusing today on the making of The Beatles' *White* album. The paper also publishes an interview with The Beatles' authorised biographer, Hunter Davies, who writes about his two years with the group back in 1967 and 1968.

Friday September 8
🍎 The *Daily Express* concludes their four-part Beatles *Anthology* series, focusing on the *Let It Be* record and the famous January 1969 rooftop concert.

Saturday September 9
 The *Daily Express* colour supplement prints a cover story on The Beatles entitled *Get Back*, asking, "What is their legacy thirty years after their split?"

Sunday September 10
 The *Observer* newspaper prints a story by Cherri Gilham, who reveals that John's first experience of marijuana occurred in March 1964 at a London party where blue movies were shown and group sex took place. According to Ms Gilham, John was drunk and threw up in a bathroom. It had previously been thought that John had his first joint when Bob Dylan visited The Beatles' New York hotel room in August 1964.
 The *Sunday Telegraph* prints the second part of their Beatles *Anthology* serialisation.
 A recorded message by George is played at a benefit concert in honour of the late Indian tabla player, Allaraku, in Los Angeles, California.

Monday September 11
 The *Guardian* newspaper prints "The Monday Interview", featuring Paul in conversation with Simon Hattenstone. During the piece, entitled "After Linda", Paul is quoted as saying: "People say time is a healer, and time heals by erasing. That is a sad fact. When Linda died, all of us in the family expected her to walk in the door, and we don't now."
 Paul, meanwhile, is to be found in Geneva, Switzerland, at a United Nations press conference where he calls for a ban on landmines. During the gathering he presents a Nobel Peace Prize to Jody Williams. Accompanying him on the trip is Heather Mills.

Tuesday September 12
 A piece on Paul entitled: "My Fear Of Being Branded A Celebrity Painter" is published in *The Times* newspaper. The article, primarily to promote his new book *Paul McCartney: Paintings* (see Thursday December 14) also includes his "Fond Memories Of John Lennon".
 A story on Paul also appears in today's *Sun* newspaper. Headlined "Macca: I Still Talk To Linda", Paul reveals that he still talks to his late wife Linda about his romance with Heather Mills, and she is thrilled at his new love. But Linda has told him: "If I was there, you'd be dead meat, sucker!"
 Capitol/EMI release the CD *The Very Best Of Badfinger* (see entry for Sunday November 12).

Wednesday September 13
 It is revealed that gold discs presented to The Beatles to celebrate the millionth sale of *A Hard Day's Night* in 1964, seized by customs men in December 1964, are still held by the Customs and Excise Department. The ten discs, presented to the group by Capitol Records in the States, were confiscated at London's Royal Victoria Docks, having arrived by boat from America. Public Records Office documents reveal that the group failed to pay import duty and that they regularly contacted The Beatles about the discs but no cash was paid. An official memo dated 1967, revealed: "Teenagers already tell me that The Beatles are on the way out. This demands immediate action. When The Beatles craze ends, the items will be valueless." Also found in the haul are ten gold plaques presented to the group.
 Reports reveal that Ringo has played drums on a cover of John's 'Power To The People'. The track, featuring Eric Burdon, formerly of The Animals, on vocals and Billy Preston, was recorded for the soundtrack of the forthcoming film *Steal This Movie*.

Thursday September 14
 Little Brown publish the book *Paul McCartney: Paintings*, which, aside from the 1981 collection of his drawings, entitled *Composer And Artist*, is the first time that Paul has published a selection of his work. The book is an expanded version of the Siegen exhibition catalogue (see entry for Friday April 30, 1999) and features photos of Paul at work, critical essays and also a long interview with the man himself.

Sunday September 17
 The *Mail On Sunday* newspaper features an interview with Pauline Sutcliffe, Stuart's sister, who claims that, "John Lennon killed my brother", revealing that his death was probably due to John's fight with him.

❦ An interview with Paul is published in the *Electronic Telegraph*, where he reveals that it was art that helped bring him and Linda together.

Tuesday September 19

❦ NBC TV issues the following press release: "The Search For John Lennon Is Over As Phillip McQuillan Is Cast In Title Role Of NBC 2-Hour Movie *In His Life: The John Lennon Story*". The release goes on to say: "Phillip McQuillan, a 23-year-old actor/musician from Dublin, Ireland is making his television début in a very big way, starring in the title role about the formative years of Beatle founder John Lennon. Principle photography will begin on location in Liverpool on September 24. McQuillan was chosen from over 300 Lennon candidates. 'Finding John Lennon proved to be far more difficult than any of us imagined,' says writer/executive producer, Michael O'Hara. 'At one point we despaired that we would never find him. Then we met Phil. He had the edge, the personal charm and charisma as a performer that we were looking for. The fact that he is an excellent guitar player was also a major plus.' Ironically, McQuillan's first public performance was singing Beatles songs at an open fair when he was twelve years old. 'I loved Beatles music,' he says. 'I was particularly influenced by the song 'Revolution'. Being a bit of a rebel myself, John Lennon was always my favourite.' Blair Brown will star in the role of Mimi Smith, the strict aunt who raised John like her own son after Julia went off to raise another family. In addition to McQuillan and Brown, the cast of *In His Life: The John Lennon Story* is comprised of Welsh actor Daniel McGowan as Paul McCartney, London actor Mark Rice-Oxley as George Harrison, Liverpool native Kristian Ealey as Ringo Starr (and) London actor Jamie Glover as Brian Epstein . . ."

Friday September 22

❦ Mick Fleetwood, the founder of Fleetwood Mac, announces that he will be selling, via his new Internet auction site, John's vintage Ferrari and the piano on which John composed 'Imagine' in 1971. (See entry for Tuesday October 17.)

❦ Bookies in the UK place The Beatles at 25/1 for having a Christmas number one in the British singles charts.

Saturday September 23 (& Sunday September 24)

❦ George is apparently seen in the crowds at the American Grand Prix in Indianapolis. During his visit, he very reluctantly gives an interview to the Speedvision channel, and announces he came here, "just for the heck of it".

❦ On the 23rd, an interview with Ravi Shankar talking about George appears in the *Toronto Star* newspaper. "I saw him about two weeks ago . . . Sometimes he comes here and spends a few days. He's not really studying or practising sitar now but he's got much deeper into music itself, listening, understanding and getting a lot of spiritual pleasure out of it. He's very happy and he's done a lot of recordings, and we are all telling him to bring out a record soon."

Sunday September 24

❦ A pre-taped interview with Paul is aired (at midday) on the Capital Gold radio programme *UK On Air*.

❦ Later this evening, and again on Capital Gold, The Beatles are featured in the *Hall Of Fame* series, where the group's work between 1965 and 1969 is featured.

❦ In Liverpool, one week later than scheduled, filming begins on *In His Life: The John Lennon Story*, a "docu-drama" which focuses on his life from his teenage years right through to his appearance, with The Beatles, on *The Ed Sullivan Show* in the States on February 9, 1964. Based on an original screenplay by Michael O'Hara, it is expected to air on NBC TV in December. O'Hara also serves as the film's executive producer on the project, which is directed by David Carson.

❦ Robert Kellaway of the *News Of The World* reports that: "The psycho who shot John Lennon plans to tour America singing sick ballads about the murder if he is released. Mark Chapman, who is seeking parole after serving 20 years, brags of his ambition in a documentary being touted around British TV stations. But his wish to tour with a band has enraged the surviving Beatles and their families. A spokesman for Paul McCartney said, 'As far as we are concerned, this man does not exist.'"

Monday September 25

In interviews appearing around the world, John's killer, Mark Chapman, who is up for parole next week, announces that John would want him to be released if he was still alive. On hearing this, Elliot Mintz, a close friend of the Lennons, remarks: "John would have loved to have been here to speak for himself." Chapman also reveals that John's murder was because "my father didn't love me."

Today's edition of the *Daily Express* announces that George and Ringo played at racing driver Damon Hill's fancy dress 40th birthday party last week, held at his mansion in Hambleton, Surrey. Damon apparently joined them on guitar and Leo Sayer on vocals to play a number of songs recorded by The Who. An observer enthused: "The two former Beatles were brilliant!"

Today's copy of the *Guardian* newspaper features an extract from the newly updated version of *Lennon Remembers*, which has just been published by Verso, and contains brand new unpublished text recorded with John during his interview with *Rolling Stone*'s editor and publisher Jann Wenner in December 1970. The text was cut from the original 1972 paperback because of the sensitive subject matter. The interviewer, Wenner, was able to obtain these quotes because he still had the original interview tapes.

Tuesday September 26

It is reported that Paul has made his first ever political campaign contribution by donating £10,000 to the Liberal Democrats, to help its animal welfare campaign, including the ban on fox hunting.

Shooting on the NBC TV film *In His Life – The John Lennon Story* continues in various locations in Liverpool. Today, at Reynolds Park, the scene is shot when John famously meets Paul back in July 1957.

Wednesday September 27

(Transmitted between 6:00 and 6:44pm), Yoko Ono is the guest host of BBC2's archive show *TOTP2*, which, by way of celebrating John's 60th birthday, is dedicated entirely to John and his music. (The programme, which includes clips such as 'Instant Karma', from *Top Of The Pops,* and 'Stand By Me', filmed for *The Old Grey Whistle Test* in 1975, is repeated on BBC2 on Saturday September 30 between 5:09 and 5:53pm.)

Thursday September 28 (until Sunday October 1)

The first UK exhibition, albeit brief, of Paul's work opens at the Arnolfini Gallery, 16 Narrow Quay in Bristol. To celebrate the opening, Paul discusses his work with the renowned stained-glass expert, Brian Clarke, in a unique one-off event. The event kicks off at 7pm, with tickets reasonably priced between £4 and £6. Signed copies of the *Paul McCartney: Paintings* book are put up for sale in the venue's shop for a most reasonable £30! Surprisingly, some copies, complete with Macca's doodle, are still available the following day. Also, on Friday September 29, an interview with Paul, recorded at the gallery the previous day, is aired on the BBC2 *Newsnight* programme.

The Arnolfini Art Gallery sold all 120 tickets for Paul's talk very quickly, reports the *Bristol Evening Post*. Paul's spokesman, Geoff Baker, announces: "Paul has been painting since he was about 40. He held an exhibition of his work last year in Germany (see entry for April 30) and the positive response has prompted him to stage one in Britain. He decided on the Arnolfini because of its reputation within the art world. People in this country had asked him to exhibit before, but they had not seen the paintings. Paul wanted his paintings to merit an exhibition in their own right and not rely on his name."

Friday September 29

In an interview to promote the New York launch of his paintings exhibition on Thursday November 2 (see entry), Paul discusses John's famous *Rolling Stone* interview from December 1970, recently released and updated in paperback. "It hurt a lot at the time," Paul admits, "but we got back together as friends and he is on record as saying a lot of that slagging off he gave me was really just him crying for help . . . He could have been boozed out of his head, as he was during that period, he could have been crazed on this, that or the other substance."

Saturday September 30

Channel 4 in the UK broadcasts a John Lennon night featuring (at 9:00pm), a documentary entitled *The Real John Lennon*, and (at 10:35pm) *Shine On*, a celebration of John's music, performed by artists including Ronnie Wood, of The Rolling Stones, Noel Gallagher and Paul Weller. To round off the evening (at 11:40pm), the 1988 film *Imagine: John Lennon* is aired (uncensored) for the first time on Channel 4. The night had been scheduled for Saturday October 7, but was brought forward to rival Yoko's appearance on BBC2's *TOTP2* show, aired the previous Wednesday and repeated earlier tonight, at 5:09pm on BBC2.

 In America, at 8am, Atlantic area Beatles fans are requested to attend the Phillips Arena Marta station where they will appear as extras in the Cartoon Network's parody of the opening scene from the film *A Hard Day's Night*. Shooting goes on until 4pm. The Cartoon Network announces that: "There will be screaming. There will be running . . ." and invites the extras to "be pampered like all those big Hollywood extras!" Music for the parody is provided by The Lizardmen, an Atlanta based band who also appear on the upcoming McCartney tribute album, *Love In Song*.

October
 The re-release to American cinemas of the re-mastered version of *A Hard Day's Night* is cancelled.

 In the run-up to the launch of The Beatles *Anthology* book, *Mojo* features The Beatles on the cover and inside of this month's magazine.

Sunday October 1
 Total Film magazine reveals that *Monty Python's Life Of Brian* film, produced by George's Handmade Films in 1979, has been voted the funniest ever film. Handmade's film *Withnail & I* is also voted the third funniest film ever made.

Monday October 2
 A profile of Yoko Ono (screened on the Bravo station in America at 10pm ET and 7pm PT), includes the first ever interview with her daughter, Kyoko, who Yoko searched for and finally found.

Tuesday October 3
 In New York, at 3:30pm (New York Time), a parole hearing takes place for John's killer, Mark Chapman, who now believes he should be released. Yoko Ono, who had submitted an audio tape, on which she read her letter about the subject to the parole board, announces that she will not try to influence their decision. In today's the *Sun* newspaper, Dominic Mohan of the "Bizarre" column, urges fans, in a full-page plea, to tell the board, via fax or e-mail, that Chapman must not be released. Thankfully, after a hearing which lasts 50-minutes, Chapman's parole is denied. Yoko, who is in Tokyo at the press preview for the John Lennon Museum, announces: "I respect the parole's decision," she says, "but that's all I can say." At the hearing, Chapman remarks: "I deserve to stay in prison for my crime. I don't even deserve to be here . . . What I did was despicable. I don't feel it's up to me to ask to be let out." He is allowed another parole hearing in two years, in October 2002.

Wednesday October 4
 The Bloomingdale launch party for The Beatles' *Anthology* book takes place at their new Beatles shop in the men's store at 59th & Lexington Avenue, New York. The party begins at 11pm and the first copies of the book go on sale at midnight. Special guests include the Master of Ceremonies, Cousin Brucie, the Carnegie Hall and Shea Stadium promoter, Sid Bernstein and the DJ Mark Ronson, who plays Beatles tunes for the night. It is expected that there will be a further 23 Beatles shops at Bloomingdale's stores throughout America.

 The HMV store in Liverpool mirrors the New York launch by opening at midnight to sell the long-awaited publication. However, the huge anticipated crowd fails to materialise when only one punter is seen in the queue. "The fans on Merseyside have let The Beatles down," he blasts.

Thursday October 5
 After a five-year wait, the official Beatles *Anthology* book finally reaches shops around the world. Paul had told the magazine *Publishers Weekly*: "We had a good time doing it,

and it brought us closer. In truth, we had healed the wounds already when we decided we wanted to do the book." The tome ends with the scribble: "By hook or by crook I'll be last in this book – John Lennon".

🍎 Apple, The Beatles' company, insists that magazines around the world cannot review the *Anthology* book until the October 5 release date has passed.

🍎 To coincide with the release of the *Anthology* book, a Beatles celebration takes place in San Francisco when Willie Brown, the mayor of San Francisco, declares today as Beatles Day. The festivities, which take place at the city's Metreon Center at Fourth and Mission, include a live (12:30pm) performance by the tribute band, The Fab Four. (Further events, featuring further Beatles-related entertainment take place at the venue on Friday, October 6 and Saturday October 7.)

🍎 At 8:45pm, the Dutch television station, Nederland 3 transmits, on the show *Andere Tijdes*, ten minutes worth of the recently recovered footage of The Beatles visit to Holland in June 1964. (The lost film runs in total to approximately 40 minutes.) Still in Holland, the Radio 2 station designates the day, Beatles Day, with a non-stop playing of Beatles-related music.

Friday October 6 (until Monday October 9)
🍎 In the States, MJI Broadcasting syndicates a three-hour radio special entitled *John Lennon: A 60th Birthday Celebration*, which features an exclusive interview with Yoko, new interviews with Paul, George Martin, Steven Tyler, David Crosby, Brian Wilson, Don Henley and Alice Cooper as well as such close Lennon friends as Elliot Mintz and May Pang. The show, hosted by Dennis Elsas, also features 27 timeless Beatles and Lennon tracks and includes the world radio premiere of the previously unreleased Lennon track, called 'Help Me To Help Myself', which appears on the re-issue of the *Double Fantasy* album.

🍎 The *Art Of John Lennon* exhibition opens at the Royal Oak Museum in Michigan. It will run for three days only, closing on Sunday October 8.

🍎 Paul is nominated for one of the BBC's People Awards in the Lifetime Achievement Category. But he fails to win, losing out to Sir Magdi Yacoub, a renowned heart surgeon. The event is covered by BBC1 and is aired on Sunday October 8.

Monday October 9
🍎 John's 60th birthday is celebrated by VH-1 in Europe, who designate their evening programmes to the former Beatle and his music. Shows include new interview sequences with Yoko Ono, the 1988 *Imagine: John Lennon* film and a collection of John's videos compiled into the VH-1 show, *Greatest Hits*.

🍎 Digitally re-mixed versions of John's *Plastic Ono Band* album (1970) and *Double Fantasy* (1980) are also released today in the UK. The first, issued with the bonus tracks 'Power To The People' and 'Do The Oz', also contains rare photographs and reproductions of John's handwritten lyrics. The latter now contains the bonus track, 'Walking On Thin Ice', the unreleased 'Help Me To Help Myself' and a brief snippet of dialogue between John and Yoko called 'Central Park Stroll', which Parlophone claims "continues the duality of the original album and unites the two at the end of the LP". Slight problems with legal clearances for the artwork on *Double Fantasy* do not delay its release. (The two albums are released in America on the following day, Tuesday October 10.)

🍎 The world's first John Lennon museum opens at the Saitama Super Arena in Tokyo, Japan, and is divided into nine sections, each devoted to various chapters of his life. Yoko Ono is naturally present at the opening.

🍎 A major exhibition of John's work opens at the Rock And Roll Hall Of Fame in Cleveland, Ohio.

🍎 Still in the States, a six-hour John Lennon tribute show takes place on the KGSR-FM (107.1) radio station. Beginning at 6pm, in an interview recorded in New York City on Thursday September 7 by the KGSR programme director, Jody Denberg, Yoko talks about the new John Lennon re-issues. The one-piece hour is also released by Capitol Records as a promotional CD and includes six newly re-mixed/re-mastered songs from *Imagine, John Lennon Plastic Ono Band* and *Double Fantasy*. The disc is called *John Lennon: Spoken Words*. The evening continues at 7pm when (until 10pm) KGSR transmits the MJI Broadcasting *John Lennon 60th Birthday Celebration* programme (see entry for Friday October 6). And then, between 10pm and midnight, there is *Austin*

Celebrates John Lennon, a show transmitted live from the KGSR Music Lounge, where many Austin musicians perform their favourite Lennon songs live on the air. The participants include Stephen Doster, Patty Griffith, Craig Ross, Gurf Morlix, among others.

🍎 The UK radio stations, Capital Gold and Harmony FM both devote air-time to John and his music.

🍎 In Liverpool, a Civic Ceremony to celebrate John's 60th birthday takes place at Dovedale School. Among those in attendance is John's half-sister, Julia Baird.

🍎 In the States, around 200 fans gather around John's star on the Hollywood Walk Of Fame. At Strawberry Fields in New York's Central Park, fans watch five skywriters circling over Manhattan with the words "Remember Love" written repeatedly in three circles. Today is also Sean Lennon's twenty-fifth birthday.

Tuesday October 10

🍎 At the Castelli Animati Animated Film Festival in Venice, Paul unveils *Shadow Cycle*, an animated film by Oscar Grillo, featuring the music of Linda McCartney. At the unveiling, Paul claims that his late wife worked on the music for the film without telling him. Heather Mills accompanies Paul at the event, and the two are captured by photographers walking, holding hands and kissing during time away from the festival. Oscar Grillo, of course, also worked on the previous Linda McCartney cartoon film *Seaside Woman* in 1979.

Thursday October 12

🍎 John's new Internet website is unveiled at Hollywood & Vine in America. Surfers of the site have a chance to read about the recently re-mastered releases of *John Lennon/Plastic Ono Band* and *Double Fantasy,* learn about John's museum in Japan and bid on the piano used by John to write 'Imagine'. (See entry for Tuesday October 17.)

🍎 The *Art Of John Lennon* exhibition opens in Toronto at the Royal Ontario Museum.

🍎 In Russia, the Chelyabinsk City Council votes to name a street after John. The former Soviet rock star and long time Beatles fan, Valery Yarushin, was behind the move. The following day, Friday October 13, Paul e-mails his thanks to the people of Chelyabinsk for honouring John this way.

🍎 Paul attends his daughter Stella's latest Chloe fashion show in Paris. Also in attendance is the sixties fashion icon, Twiggy and the singer, Lulu.

Tuesday October 17

🍎 John's Steinway grand piano, on which he composed 'Imagine' back in 1971, sells for £1.45 million at an auction simultaneously taking place at the Hard Rock Cafe in London's West End and in New York. The buyer is the singer George Michael, who immediately donates it temporarily to The Beatles Story museum in Liverpool. A friend of Michael announces: "He feels this piano is part of Britain's music heritage. He didn't want it to go abroad and is delighted it's going to its spiritual home." The auction is broadcast through the Internet; an event organised by Mick Fleetwood's new Internet auction company. The following day, Wednesday October 18, Michael confirms his purchase, by phone, to the Capital Gold radio station. "I'm dead excited that I bought it," he says, "and I intend to keep it in the country. I'm not sure what to do with it, yet."

Wednesday October 18 (until Sunday January 14, 2001)

🍎 An exhibition comprising Yoko Ono's artwork since 1960 débuts at New York's Japan Society Gallery. Entitled *Yes Yoko Ono,* the exhibit features approximately 150 of Yoko's works and is accompanied by a book of the same name. (At its conclusion, the show will move on to Minneapolis on March 10, 2001 – see entry.)

🍎 Walter Shenson, who produced The Beatles' films *A Hard Day's Night* and *Help!* and 12 other films, dies in Los Angeles of complications from a stroke. He was 81. Shenson, who got his start in show business as a publicist for Paramount Pictures, made most of his films during an 18-year stay in England. He produced *A Hard Day's Night* in 1964 as Beatlemania swept America and produced *Help!* with the group the following year. "He had agreed to make a third film that never got off the ground," said his lifelong friend Arthur Wilde, adding that, later in life, Shenson gave talks about his time with the Fab Four. "He loved it, and The Beatles liked him and they all got along well," Wilde said, adding, "He was a wonderful, wonderful guy." Shenson, who was born in San Francisco in 1919 and educated at Stanford University, spent two years in the US Army during World War II. He worked as a publicist on the films *From Here To Eternity* and *The Caine Mutiny* before turning to producing. His other films included *The Mouse That Roared*, which featured Peter Sellers and 1983's *Reuben, Reuben*, starring Tom Conti. A sister, two sons, and four grandchildren survive Shenson, whose wife, Geraldine, died last year.

Thursday October 19
🍎 At 4:45pm GMT (11:45am EST and 8:15am PST), Paul, via Yahoo!, goes live on the Net to chat and take questions from all over the world on art and drawings. Before that, at 4:15pm GMT, a special programme called *Artcast* is broadcast, which features behind the scenes footage of the preparations for Paul's UK exhibition at Bristol's Arnolfini Gallery, and candid conversations with his friend, the artist Brian Clarke. Clarke was responsible for the cover of Paul's 1989 album *Flowers In The Dirt*. Paul's interview with Brian was recorded before Paul's art show opening in Bristol on Thursday September 28 (see entry). The exclusive *Artcast* show also includes Paul's tour of the paintings, explaining his inspirations and technique, and a page-by-page author's review of his book, *Paintings*. Paul: "For many years, I painted in private and I didn't really talk about it to anyone outside of my family. Now I'm interested in showing my paintings to anyone who is curious about them, partly to learn what people think."
🍎 In the evening Paul and Heather attend the Pantene Awards at the Albert Hall in London. During the ceremony he privately talks with *24 Hours*, a page on the ITV Teletext station. In the EIGHT-page feature, he discusses his artwork and admits involvement with a choral piece for a college in Oxford.

Friday October 20
🍎 Paul attends the VH-1/ *Vogue* Fashion Awards, held at Madison Square Garden in New York and is on hand to present the "Designer Of The Year" award to his daughter, Stella. Paul is seen wearing a T-shirt that reads "About Flippin' Time", a reference to the shirt she wore when he was inducted into the Rock And Roll Hall Of Fame last year. Accepting the award, she says, "I'd better thank him . . . And I would like to thank my mum. I give this to her." She adds an animal rights plea. "If there is anybody here thinking of buying a fur coat this year, please don't. Don't make animals fashion victims." After the ceremony, Paul joins Keith Richard of The Rolling Stones for a game of pool backstage. Besides coverage on VH-1, the show, including Paul and Stella's segment, also features on the US programme *Fashion TV*. (Reports appear on TV across America and Europe. Extended European TV coverage of the event begins on VH-1 on Friday November 3, and lasts over the weekend.)

Saturday October 21
🍎 Previews to Paul and Heather Mills' appearance on tomorrow night's ITV show *Stars In Their Lives* appear in some of today's UK tabloids. The *Sun* and *Daily Mail* both print stills from the show where they are seen kissing. The latter also features a report by Geoffrey Levy and Alison Boshof who discuss, "with Linda dead less than three years, is talk of marriage still much too premature?" Inside the colour supplement of the *Daily Mail* there is a report on Tanya Larrigan, who continues to help Paul with his stud farm. The story is titled "Linda – The friend who guards her legacy".
🍎 An exhibition of Linda McCartney's photographs open in Pontiac, Michigan.

Sunday October 22
🍎 Heather Mills is the star in the ITV programme *Stars In Their Lives*. During the 35-minute show, which is hosted by Carol Vorderman and transmitted across the ITV Network between 6:50 and 7:25pm, Heather is surprised by the appearance (in part two of the show) of Paul who had secretly rang up the show's producers asking to join in. As anticipated in the previous day's papers, the couple is seen kissing and they announce their love for each other. During the show, he also admits that he fancied her from the first time he saw her at an awards show. "When I saw her at that award show I thought, 'Wow she looks great,' he said. 'A very beautiful, true, fine woman. That was the first impression and then when I heard her speak I was very impressed. So I found out her telephone number – like you do – and rang her up and said we should talk about some charity stuff and I like what you're doing. So we had three or four meetings, all very prim

and proper. She came to the office to talk about the charity and I realised I fancied her. I did fancy her from the start but I was playing it cool.'"

♦ A short clip of the promotional video for Heather's 'Voice' single, featuring Paul, is also screened. (The programme was taped in London two weeks ago.)

Monday October 23
♦ The Beatles' 'A Day In The Life' is voted the third most popular song of all time in a phone-in poll on Capital Gold, the UK oldies station.

Friday October 27
♦ In the States, Heather Mills is interviewed on tonight's edition of ABC TVs *20/20*. The host, Barbara Walters asks Heather if she has found the love of her life, an obvious referral to Paul. Heather answers, "I hope so."

Saturday October 28
♦ A 90-second excerpt of an audio tape which lay forgotten in an attic for 26 years is broadcast by George Webley on his BBC Three Counties Radio show between 10 and 11am. The 1974 tape, which comprises further evidence of the strained relationship between John and Paul, consists of John and Ringo chatting candidly about Ringo's album *Goodnight Vienna*. But halfway through the seven-and-a-half-minute recording, Paul becomes the target of criticisms. John is heard asking Ringo, "Does Paul know who you are?" and then remarking that he would swap "two Pauls for a George anytime". The tape was sent to a record company in Britain by accident instead of the edited version of the TV and radio advert (see entry for Thursday November 14, 1974), and a replacement was sent on once the mistake was realised. But an assistant for the company kept the unedited tape in a drawer and, when she moved jobs, it was stored away in an attic. Earlier this year, the woman, who has remained anonymous, was handed a dusty box of her belongings. It was only when she played the tape, which has John and Ringo's handwriting on the box, that she realised its significance. The presenter George Webley remarks: "It is awesome to listen to John at ease with his best mate from The Beatles, having a laugh and a joke. The lady who gave me the tape wanted to remain anonymous because she is a big fan of The Beatles. She contacted me because she wanted to know what to do with it. She wants it to go to Ringo or Paul."

Sunday October 29
♦ It is announced that pictures drawn by John for his son Sean will decorate a range of children's clothes and other items to be sold in Britain next year. The range, which may be stocked by Mothercare, includes romper suits, bibs and pyjamas as well as baby chairs and toys, and will be emblazoned with elephants, monkeys and smiley faces drawn by John. They also feature a logo incorporating Lennon's signature and a self-portrait with long hair and his trademark round glasses. William Carter, an American company manufacturing children's clothing, first launched the pastel-shaded baby wear in the United States last year after signing a £10 million deal with Bag One Arts, the guardians of John's estate. The items are now on sale at over 2,000 stores across America. The range is called *Real Love*, named after one of John's songs, which was issued on The Beatles *Anthology 2* and released as The Beatles' second comeback single in March 1996.

♦ On the same day, October 29, the new forthcoming Beatles *1* album is previewed in the *Sunday Mirror* and in the *Telegraph*, where there is a report which says that the album has staggered music analysts by taking more than £10 million in advance sales.

Monday October 30
♦ It is revealed that Paul's 1983 track 'Pipes Of Peace' will appear on a forthcoming CD to benefit the Paralympic Games. The disc, *Wave To The World*, also includes contributions from Tom Petty, The Bee Gees, Ray Charles, Sting, The Police, Elton John and Smash Mouth.

November
♦ Paul and Heather Mills record a television interview with the legendary American interviewer, Barbara Walters.

 Genesis Publications release *Mania Days*, a book which features 350 pictures taken by the late Curt Gunther on The Beatles 1964 American tour. The publication is available in two editions, a regular and deluxe edition.

 The Beatles' 1964 film *A Hard Day's Night* is featured in this month's issue of the Voorhees, New Jersey *Ritz Filmbill* magazine.

Wednesday November 1
 George is invited to a benefit for the Kabbalah Centre in London's exclusive Harrington Club. Rolling Stone Mick Jagger and his former wife, Jerry Hall, stage the event.

Thursday November 2
 For one week only, a series of signed and numbered limited edition prints of Paul's paintings are made available from the Matthew Marks Gallery, at 523 W. 24th Street, New York, NY 10011. The prints, restricted to an edition of 200 numbered copies and priced at $1,750 each, feature the paintings entitled *Big Mountain Face, Egypt Station* and *Ancient Connections*, all of which feature in the *Paintings* book.

 A pre-taped interview with Paul to promote his exhibition of paintings is screened on the ABC TV show *Good Morning America*. Another pre-recorded ABC TV interview with Paul is also aired today, this time on *Primetime Live* (broadcast between 9:00 and 10:00pm.) During the five-minute sequence (recorded yesterday in New York at the Mathew Marks Gallery), Paul is seen preparing for the opening of his paintings' exhibition by signing lithographs and talking about his art and his late wife, Linda. At the conclusion, ABC viewers are promised that a longer piece of the interview with Paul will be screened the following week, on Thursday November 9. In addition, the feature will include a piece where art experts are shown Paul's paintings, some are aware that he painted them, and some are not. Part 2 goes out three weeks later on November 23.

 At 6:30pm, Paul and Heather arrive at the Mathew Marks Gallery in New York for the grand opening of his paintings exhibition. Their arrival is tagged to the start of the *Primetime Live* feature broadcast this evening.

Sunday November 5
 VH-1 in the States features the Apple recording artists Badfinger in the documentary series *Behind The Music*. The show includes an interview with Paul recorded in September 1999.

Thursday November 9
 Television crews from around the world visit the Abbey Road Studios in London for the launch of the new official Beatles website, www.thebeatles.com. The crews are shown the site separately with the event lasting all day.

Friday November 10
 As a promotion for the release of The Beatles' *1* album on Monday, the Post Office Tower in Newcastle holds a rooftop concert featuring a Beatles sound-a-like tribute band.

Saturday November 11 (to Friday November 17)
 In the States, the magazine *TV Guide* features four collector's covers, entitled *The Beatles 2000*, and each depicting one of The Beatles, taken in 1964 by the photographer Curt Gunther. A fifth collector's cover, using the *White Album* design, is available only through *TV Guide* online! Inside the magazine, between pages 21 and 33, is a series of Beatles-related features, previews and an interview with Paul carried out with Jasper Gerard and previously published in the *Sunday Times* in England.

 In the UK, the *Daily Mail* prints an interview with Louise Harrison, who recalls George's first visit to the States in 1963.

Sunday November 12
 In the UK, the first screening of the commercial for Beatles *1* takes place across the ITV Network at 7:40pm, the first advert during the break between tonight's edition of *Coronation Street*. (The three-minute advertising slot during the nation's favourite soap opera is the most expensive time to advertise on the ITV Network.) An alternative version of The Beatles' *1* commercial appears during GMTV, again across the ITV

Network, the following morning. The adverts are part of an £11 million Beatles *1* promotional budget, paid for by EMI. Incidentally, immediately following the *1* commercial on Meridian ITV on Sunday night is an advert for Linda McCartney's range of vegetarian foods.

 At midnight, the doors of the HMV record store at 360 Oxford Street, London, are thrown open for fans eager to become the first to purchase the new Beatles *1* compilation album. The first 350 buyers are presented with a certificate acknowledging their achievement. The staff in the shop wear promotional Beatles *1* T-shirts, supplied to them by EMI. On hand to cover the event are camera crews from Sky News, GMTV, ITN and, amongst others, ZDF in Germany. (Television reports naturally occur the following day.) Also present are reporters from the *Daily Express* and the *Mirror*.

 At the HMV store in Liverpool, another midnight opening for Beatles *1* takes place. Among the 100-strong crowd is the singer, Elvis Costello, who disguises himself behind a large woolly hat and scarf. Once inside, and with hat and scarf removed, he happily signs autographs. A spokesman for HMV remarks: "He was one of the first ten and would have had to wait about an hour. No one realised it was him until he filed in with everyone else. He had a woolly hat and scarf on so we think he was trying to be a bit low key, but the staff recognised him and asked him to sign copies of his albums."

Monday November 13

 After months of speculation, Parlophone and Apple finally release Beatles *1*, a 27-track collection of The Beatles' number one singles and biggest hits. (The American release takes place the following day, Tuesday November 14. For the full track listing, see previous entry for August.) Music industry insiders announce that they expect the CD to sell over 45 million copies, outstripping Michael Jackson's *Thriller* to become the biggest selling album of all time.

Ken Berry, of EMI Recorded Music, says, "The Beatles are the most influential band in popular music and no other band has had their degree of chart success. Their music has had an unprecedented impact on the lives and cultures of so many around the world. Their songs are as vibrant and contemporary today as when they were recorded. This is a must-have album for every music lover's collection, which will be supported by an innovative marketing campaign. We are proud that The Beatles spent their entire career with EMI and this album is a tribute to their genius."

Chris Windle, Sr. Vice President Marketing Recorded Music, says, "Priced as a regular album this long playing CD with over 79 minutes running time represents fantastic value to the public. Promotion on a truly global basis with hugely creative multi-media campaigns will build on The Beatles' huge fan base to emphasise the music and its importance to a contemporary audience."

Note: in selecting the tracks for *1*, EMI Records together with Capitol Records in the USA chose the songs that were either number one in the *Record Retailer* chart in the UK (the only independently audited UK chart throughout the sixties) or in the *Billboard* chart in the USA. The Beatles achieved 17 number one hits on the *Record Retailer* singles chart between May 1963 and July 1969. In the USA, The Beatles had a total of 20 number one singles between February 1964 and June 1970.

 The 79-minute Beatles *1* album, which features a brief message from George Martin in the accompanying booklet, is also released as a cassette and double vinyl album. Contrary to previous reports, the album has not been remixed, but it has been remastered by Peter Mew with the sound perfectly restored. As expected, the first three tracks on the disc, 'Love Me Do', 'From Me To You' and 'She Loves You' appear in mono, but the remaining 24 songs all appear in stereo. Inside the case is an impressive 32-page colour booklet, featuring Richard Avedon's psychedelic pictures, taken on August 17, 1967 and a range of picture covers (supplied by Joachim Noske and Bruce Spizer) for each of the songs original single releases around the world. The exception to this rule is the sleeve for 'I Want To Hold Your Hand', where the 1984, 20th anniversary American re-issue is depicted. This re-issue features Paul's "ciggie" airbrushed out from the 1963 Dezo Hoffman shot.

 It is estimated that some 8 million copies of Beatles *1* has been shipped to stores in the UK.

 On the morning of the release, a 30-second commercial for the album is aired at 8am on all the commercial radio stations in the UK. While on the ITV breakfast show GMTV, an alternative advert for Beatles *1* is screened during one of the commercial breaks.

🍎 In the UK, Capital Gold designates the day "Beatles Monday", in honour of the new album. The tribute band The Bootleg Beatles are on hand all day in the station's London studios to perform listener's requests. Then, between 6 and 7:00pm, in a show hosted by Tony Blackburn, Capital Gold plays the 'Ultimate Beatles Album', compiled from the votes given by their listeners who had rang in over the previous weekend. At number three in the Top 10 is 'Yesterday', number two is 'Hey Jude' and at number one is 'The Long And Winding Road'. (The appearance of the group and the amazing sales of *1* feature in a news report on the ITV show *London Tonight*, aired in the South East area of the country. The day of Beatles sales and footage from the HMV opening last night are featured in Sky News reports throughout the day.)

🍎 To coincide with the release, The Beatles launch their first ever official website. Designers worked on the £5 million site with Paul, George, Ringo and Yoko. Each section is based around one of the 27 tracks on the *1* album. As an example of the site, the 'Get Back' area recreates the famous January 30, 1969 rooftop concert. 'I Want To Hold Your Hand' enables you to walk around The Beatles session in Studio 2 at Abbey Road and 'Help!' is a worldwide interactive experience where participants can help each other locate instruments and "become" John, Paul, George and Ringo. In addition, there is a Beatles fan forum and an opportunity to receive the latest Beatles news. In the EMI press release for the site (issued on Thursday November 2), it reads: "The Beatles.com is a website a year in the making. Paul McCartney, George Harrison, Ringo Starr and Yoko Ono Lennon have injected their individual ideas into the project; combined with an international team of cutting-edge website designers, involving Apple Corps Ltd., Abbey Road Interactive and EMI Records, the website promises to redefine the nature of artist collaborations on the Internet. Twenty-sevem different Beatles experiences will ultimately be on the site, linking with each track on the album." (Note: The official Beatles website had been under consideration since July 1996.)

🍎 At the close of the first day of sales in the UK, a spokesman for the HMV store in Reading remarks: "*1* is outselling all the other new releases put together!" While at their prestigious stores in Oxford Street, a spokesman for HMV announces that: "*1* has sold over 600 copies. It has been our biggest first day seller for the year. The Beatles' *1* sold five times as many copies as the Irish lads [Westlife]. Even though most fans have every track, it's selling phenomenally well."

🍎 Further statistics, compiled from stores throughout the country, reveal that *1* is outselling Westlife's *Coast To Coast* by 3–1, Oasis's *Familiar To Millions*, which includes their version of 'Helter Skelter', by 4–1, The Spice Girls' *Forever* by 10–1 and the new release by Martine McCutcheon by an amazing 15–1.

🍎 The Beatles popularity comes under the spotlight in the *Drivetime* slot on BBC Radio Berkshire between 5 and 6pm, where Paul Gambaccini, The Beatles' biographer Hunter Davies and the author of this book are all interviewed.

🍎 VH-1 in Europe adds the following Beatles film clips to their visual play list, 'The Ballad Of John And Yoko', 'Paperback Writer' (Chiswick House version), 'Get Back', 'Hello Goodbye' (*Anthology* documentary edit) and 'Penny Lane'.

🍎 Yet another midnight opening for Beatles *1* takes place, this time at the Tower Records store in New York.

Tuesday November 14

🍎 At Oxford Crown Court, the trial begins of 34-year-old Michael Abram, who is charged with the attempted murder of George and Olivia Harrison in the early hours of December 30 last year (see entry). In a written statement read out in court, the former Beatle horrifyingly recalls the attack at his Friar Park mansion. "I have no doubt that this person intended to kill me and my wife. I truly believed I was dying. I shouted, 'Hare Krishna, Hare Krishna' in a vain attempt to distract the attacker." The jury heard that, on the night of the attack, George had been out to visit his brother and returned to Friar Park shortly before midnight. Olivia and his mother-in-law were also in the house. George and Olivia's 22-year-old son, Dhani, was staying in a lodge on the 30-acre estate. At approximately 3:30am, Abram broke into George's mansion by uprooting a statue of George and the Dragon and hurling it through a window of the house. Olivia Harrison awoke first; thinking that a chandelier had crashed to the floor downstairs before realising that there was an intruder inside their home.

Olivia, in her court appearance, remembers the night of their ordeal: "I feared my husband and I were going to die . . . We had gone to bed after 2am after watching a film on TV. I was awoken in my bedroom by the loudest crash of glass imaginable. After I roused my husband, I tried to summon help on the telephone while George put on a coat over his pyjamas and went in search of the intruder."

George put on boots, a zip-up jacket and ran to the first floor gallery. From the top of the stairs, he noticed a man's figure illuminated in the kitchen area. George, in his statement, which is read out by the prosecutor Simon Mayo, recalls: "I retreated hurriedly to the bedroom, shouting at my wife, 'Someone is in the house.' My wife was saying, 'Stay in the room,' but I decided to look again . . . I noticed the intruder again. As I looked down to the room below me, I saw a person run from the kitchen. He stopped in the centre of the room and looked towards me. He started shouting and screaming. He was hysterical and frightening. He said words to the effect of, 'You get down here, you know what it is.' I could see a knife in one hand and the spear from part of the statue in the other."

Olivia, fighting back tears: "I heard Abram screaming at the top of his lungs. He was demanding that my husband, 'get down here'."

George: "I decided to shout back at him, to confuse and distract him. I shouted, 'Hare Krishna, Hare Krishna.' He rushed towards me. I attempted to get into a room, but couldn't release the key from the door. I made the split-second decision to tackle this man as I had it in mind that once he passed me, both my wife and mother-in-law would be vulnerable. Armed only with the element of surprise, I ran at him."

Olivia: "Moments later the two men were grappling with each other on the balcony that runs around the first floor of the house."

George: "My first thought was to grab the knife and knock him off balance. He thrust the knife at me. I was fending off the blows with my hands and arms. He was stabbing down towards my upper body."

Olivia: "They were jabbing at each other, but my husband was just being backed up and backed up. He was trying to grab the man's wrists. I saw my husband looking very pale. He was staring at me in a very bizarre manner. I have never seen him look that way. I just raised my hand and hit the man on the back of the head as hard as I could."

George: "I was aware of my wife approaching and striking him about the head with a brass poker. It appeared to have little effect. He stood up and chased my wife."

Olivia: "The next thing I knew, I was knocked backwards. The man was up against the wall and I was on my hands and knees at his feet. I reached up and tried to grab his testicles, but I just felt a lot of fabric. I ran from the room and that's when he came after me. I felt Abram's hands on the back of my neck. Seconds later, the two of us fell to the floor as George jumped on Abram's back. I landed on cushions used for meditation and crawled away. The men carried on fighting."

George: "I feared greatly for her safety and hauled myself up to tackle him. I placed my hands around the blade. He again got the better of me and got on top of me. I felt exhausted and could feel the strength draining from me. My arms dropped to my sides and I vividly remember a deliberate thrust of the knife down into my chest. I could feel blood entering my lungs. I could feel my chest deflate. I felt blood in my mouth and air exhale from my chest. I believed I had been fatally stabbed."

Olivia: "There was blood on the walls, blood on the carpet. This was the moment I realised we were going to be murdered, that this man was succeeding in murdering us and there was no one else there to help. I turned around and grabbed a lamp, tore the shade off and brought it down on the man's head."

George: "My wife struck the man with the vase and he slumped down."

Olivia: "I struck the intruder as hard as I could, as many times as I could."

George: "I encouraged my wife to keep on hitting him."

Olivia: "I heard my husband saying, 'I've got the knife. I've got the knife.' Then I saw it lying between them. I hit Abram two or three times. He seemed to slump. I said to him, 'Stop,' because I didn't want to hit him anymore. It wasn't a pleasant experience. He was very bloody, my husband was hurt and I was exhausted. My husband said, 'Don't stop, hit him harder.' George was very weak and tried to throw the knife across the room but as he raised his arm, it fell behind him on to a cushion."

George: "With a sudden burst of energy he went towards my wife."

Olivia: "I then found myself in a tug-of-war with Abram, each of us pulling on the flex. It was then that Abram grabbed the flex of the lamp and began menacingly wrapping the cord around his hands. I thought he was going to strangle me. He whipped me with the cord on my head. Eventually I flung the lamp at him and ran out of the room. I had a big gash in my head and numerous bruises on my legs . . . My husband was fading away. I had to leave my husband there because I couldn't do any more. As I reached the last section of the stairs, I realised he wasn't following me anymore. I thought he'd gone back to inflict more harm on my husband."

🍎 George: "My wife ran to the gallery . . . He took the lamp and he rained blows down on my head. Three or four times I deflected them with my feet, but the last two struck me on my head. He stopped to chase my wife. I was lying on my back. I could see him. He stumbled and partially collapsed. I heard some voices and someone coming up the stairs. It was a uniformed police officer."

Olivia: "At that point, the police came in."

George: " I was left with serious wounds and breathing difficulties. This person has punched and kicked me in all areas of my body. I have no doubts that this person had the intention of killing me and my wife. There were times I believed I was dying."

In a statement read out to the court, PC Paul Williams, the man who arrested Abram, describes how he turned and said, 'You should have heard the spooky things he (George) was saying as he was going. Bastard! I should have got the bastard better!"

During the trial, the prosecutor, Simon Mayo, says: "Train tickets were found in the possession of the defendant and it appeared that he had travelled down from his home on Merseyside to commit the attack. It is also apparent that Abram had travelled down to Oxfordshire on a number of occasions to find out where George lived and had, on one occasion, asked a cleric about the geography of the area. There was no dispute that Abram had attacked the Harrisons. The case would centre on whether at the time of the incident, Abram was suffering from abnormality of mind. He believed that The Beatles were witches who flew around on broomsticks. Subsequently, George Harrison possessed him and that he had been sent on a mission by God to kill him. He saw George as a sorcerer and a devil. Experts conclude that, while the defendant undoubtedly intended to kill Mr. Harrison, he did not realise that to do so was wrong because of his deluded belief about being possessed. If you conclude that the defendant did the act and that he was insane, your verdict will be 'not guilty by reason of insanity'."

Accompanying Olivia in court today is Dhani, her son with George. The case, in which Abram is denying two charges of attempted murder on the grounds of insanity, continues tomorrow when it is expected to end.

🍎 On a happier note, The Beatles' *1* album sells over 350,000 copies in its first day of release in Japan.

🍎 At the Abbey Road Studios in London, the gateposts of the building are painted red with *1* yellow logos. The designs are painted over within 24 hours.

🍎 In the *Mirror*, the success of *1* leads the paper to write the story "Beatlemania 2 – New Record, Website And Book Promise £50m Pay-Day". The report, by Lucy Rock, reads: "The Beatles are set to earn £50 million for a new album, website and book, despite splitting up 30 years ago. Their first official website, also launched yesterday, could generate £15 million. A music industry source said: 'It will be a monster pay-day for them. They're still incredibly popular and blow a lot of modern acts out of the water. Hype about The Spice Girls v Westlife was everywhere last week, but this is the big one. It should spark renewed interest and many people will be curious to see what the website is like, which will boost back-catalogue sales."

Wednesday November 15

🍎 The trial at Oxford Crown Court yesterday naturally features prominently in the morning papers, with terrifying headlines such as: "Harrison: I Truly Believed I Was Dying" (*Daily Telegraph*), "Beatle Saved By Wife In Knife Terror" (*Daily Express*), "I Thought I Was Dying" (*Daily Mail*) and "My Terror" (*Mirror*).

🍎 On the second day of the Oxford Crown Court trial involving Michael Abram, the 12-member jury finds him "not guilty" of the attempted murder of George and Olivia Harrison, on the grounds of "insanity". It is a result that many secretly knew was coming. The judge, Mr. Justice Astill, says, "There was no evidence to contradict the opinion of three psychiatrists that Abram was legally insane when he attacked the Harrisons." He tells the jury, "There is only one verdict you can reach." Justice Astill, who describes the incident at Friar Park as a "horrifying attack", makes Abram the subject of a hospital order without any restrictions of time, which means he will be treated in a secure psychiatric unit.

During the second day, the consultant psychiatrist, Philip Joseph, says: "Abram believed he was the fifth Beatle. He was obsessed with George and believed he was St Michael, sent on a mission by God to kill the guitarist. And when George shouted, 'Hare Krishna' to calm him down, it enraged him even more. Because he believed it was the language of Satan, spoken backwards. He thought Mr. Harrison was cursing him in the Devil's tongue and that he was a witch. He was stabbing Mr. Harrison to kill him because he had possessed him. He had read in the Bible in the book of Exodus that sorcerers should not be allowed to live."

The Harrisons make a legal bid in court to be notified of any prospect of Abram being released from the Scott secure clinic in Rainhill, on Merseyside. Through their QC, Geoffrey Robertson, they ask the judge to recommend their request to the Home Secretary, saying they were "continuing targets". The judge replies saying, "I have no powers to make such a recommendation."

At the conclusion of the trial, George and Olivia's son, Dhani, blast the 'legal loophole' which sees Abram being found not guilty. He adds to the waiting reporters, "The prospect of him being released into society is abhorrent and we hope that the authorities will allow us to be consulted."

🍎 It is announced that The Beatles' compilation album *1* has sold 105,424 copies in the UK since its release on Monday. Meanwhile, also since Monday, the Spice Girls' new album *Forever* has shifted just 13,116 copies.

🍎 The BBC2 archive show *TOTP2* (between 6:00 and 6:44pm) screens, to close the show, the 1967 promotional film for 'Penny Lane', obviously as Apple approved promotion for The Beatles' *1* album. (This edition of *TOTP2* is aired again on the following Saturday November 18, between 3:54 and 4:39pm.)

🍎 In the States at 9pm ET, 6pm PT, Yoko gives a live interview, discussing John and his legacy, on the website MSN.COM.

🍎 One hundred and fifty bricks from John's former home in Menlove Avenue, Liverpool are auctioned on the Internet. The bricks were acquired by NBC TV during the recent filming of *In His Life – The John Lennon Story*. The current owner of John's home will get 50 per cent of the profits with some going to the nearby Strawberry Fields children's home and the rest to cover the filming costs. (The auction concludes on Monday December 4.)

Friday November 17 (until Wednesday January 10, 2001)

🍎 Linda McCartney's *Sixties – Portrait Of An Era* exhibition runs at the Palm Beach Photographic Center For The Arts, in Palm Beach, Florida.

🍎 ABC TV in America screens (between 8:00 and 10:00pm ET) *The Beatles Revolution*, a two-hour ABC Entertainment/VH-1 co-production, which looks at the most influential band in pop history. Interviews with pop celebrities such as Keith Richard, Pete Townshend, Bono, Sting, Lenny Kravitz, Garth Brooks, The Spice Girls and over fifty other guests, who all have something to say about the band that changed them forever, are included in the programme. Apple footage screened in the show includes a clip of the original 1968 Apple Records promotional film. It was repeated six days later in America on November 23 on VH-1 at 8pm ET.

Sunday November 19

🍎 An interview with Dhani Harrison where he recalls the horrifying attack on his parents at Friar Park last December is featured in today's *Sunday People* newspaper.

🍎 The *News Of The World* reports: "Macca Rescues Animal Centre". The piece reads: "Ex-Beatle Sir Paul McCartney has rescued an animal centre battered in the recent storms. Macca has sent £5,000 to the Hound Cottage Animal Sanctuary in Titchfield, Hants, to help its clean up efforts. Delighted founder, Geraldine Forehead, 62, said, 'I could not believe Sir Paul thought of us. We're such a small operation'"

🍎 Pundits cry, "It's *1* at 1" when, later in the day, and with no great surprise, it is announced that The Beatles' album *1* has gone straight in at the number one position in the UK album charts, selling 319,126 copies in its first week of release. The album also reaches the top spot today in Canada, Germany and Spain. When told of the number one position, Geoff Baker, on behalf of Paul, George and Ringo, announces: "The Beatles are dead chuffed! They are thrilled by their continued success."

Monday November 20

🎸 The Beatles reaching number one in the UK album charts again is celebrated on the breakfast ITV show, GMTV. During the short feature, the 1967 'Hello Goodbye' promotional film (*Anthology* edit) is screened. While in the *Sun* newspaper, Dominic Mohan writes: "The Beatles have shown they are still the world's top band – their new album *1* has gone straight to the top of the charts, clocking up best first week sales of the year, beating Robbie Williams' *Sing When You're Winning* by 6,000."

Tuesday November 21

🎸 Celebrating its thirtieth anniversary, George's album *All Things Must Pass* is re-issued by Capitol Records in America. The remastered package includes a bonus disc with unreleased songs. The release, which features sleeve notes on the recordings by George, fails to materialise but is rescheduled, in America, on Tuesday January 23, 2001.

Wednesday November 22

🎸 The Beatles *1* album reaches number one in the US *Billboard* charts, selling 594,666 copies in its first week.

Thursday November 23 (until Sunday November 26)

🎸 This evening, ABC TV in the States broadcasts a Beatles special.
🎸 Rhino.Com screens, via the Net, the 'Director's Cut' of the 1968 film *Wonderwall*, which features soundtrack music by George.
🎸 EMI announces that The Beatles' *1* album has gone number one in 19 countries, accumulating 35 platinum discs.

Monday November 27

🎸 *Mojo* publishes a special limited-edition version of their magazine, which features a 20th anniversary tribute to John. The issue has a limited run of 89,000 copies for the world, each individually numbered, and features exclusive interviews with Klaus Voorman and Yoko Ono, who receives the very first edition off the press.

December

🎸 In the second week of the month, John's former home at 251 Menlove Avenue in Liverpool, is honoured with a Blue Plaque. Also during this time, the twentieth anniversary of John's death is commemorated with a three-part BBC Radio 2 documentary on his life.
🎸 PBS in America air Paul's December 1999 Cavern Club performance as well as the three-part documentary *The Unknown Peter Sellers,* which features a brief interview sequence with George.
🎸 A planned TV screening of a *Classic Albums* show devoted to George's *All Things Must Pass* is scheduled for the UK and in America.

Friday December 1

🎸 Miramax Films in the States re-release The Beatles' film *A Hard Day's Night*. It is released initially in two cities, New York and Los Angeles. The film is then due to open in ten further cities on Friday December 8. *A Hard Day's Night* then rolls out to other cities in America in the future weeks.

Sunday December 3

🎸 At 9pm ET, ABC TV in America, to mark the 20th anniversary of John's passing, screens the movie *In His Life – The John Lennon Story*. In the role of John is the 23-year-old, Dublin born musician Phillip McQuillan.
🎸 VH-1 broadcasts a John Lennon special in their *Behind The Music* series, entitled "John Lennon's Last Years", at 9pm ET.

Thursday December 7

🎸 The European channel ARTE screens the tribute programme *John And Yoko*.

Friday December 8

🎸 Reports suggest that The Beatles' film *A Hard Day's Night* is to be re-released in America, while other reports suggest that the film will now not appear until sometime in 2001.

❡ A Blue Plaque honouring John is unveiled at his former home in Menlove Avenue, Liverpool. But his half-sister, Julia Baird, expresses her outrage at the timing, remarking that the event should have taken place on October 9, John's 60th birthday. (December 8 is the first day he can be honoured because the plaques honour the 20th anniversary of the honouree's death.)

Saturday December 9

❡ BBC Radio 2 commemorates the 20th anniversary of John's passing with a three-part series called *The Lennon Legacy*, which looks back at his life and career and features interviews with the many who have worked and been associated with the former Beatle. The series, which is narrated by the comedy actor Robert Lindsay, continues with Part 2 on Saturday December 16 with the third and final part being aired on Saturday December 23.

2001

Coming this year:

 Wingspan, the official MPL documentary on the career of Wings is released. It has been put together by Paul's son-in-law, Alistair Donald. "He's researched it all . . . It's all film stuff of Wings," Paul says to Patrick Humphries. "There's a version of 'Give Ireland Back To The Irish', done live in my front room . . . There's quite a lot of unreleased Wings stuff, and I'm waiting to see how much he uses in the film or the TV show or whatever it turns into . . ."

 The Beatles 1995 *Anthology* series appears on DVD and as, quite possibly, a four-video box set, edited down from its previous eight-video set.

 The re-mixed and re-mastered version of the *Let It Be* film from 1970, a home video version, on VHS and DVD, with extra footage, is likely.

 A new album by Paul is very likely, and he will appear in a documentary about Memphis' Sun Studios aired later this year on PBS. (See entry for Monday March 6, 2000.) The show also includes appearances by The Who, Bob Dylan, Robert Plant, Bryan Ferry and Jimmy Page.

 A new album by George is a slight possibility, featuring the title *Portrait Of A Leg End,* with songs, possibly, including 'Valentine', 'Pisces Fish', and 'Brainwashed'.

 Paul has a 60-paintings exhibition at the Walker Art Gallery in Liverpool, where he used to hang out with John.

 A Blue Plaque honouring the life of The Beatles' manager Brian Epstein is unveiled in Liverpool.

Saturday January 6

 Channel 4 in the UK broadcasts the show, *The 100 Greatest Number Ones Of All Time*. The extravaganza includes The Beatles' 'Hey Jude' and John's 'Imagine'.

Wednesday January 10 (until March 17)

 Linda McCartney's *Sixties – Portrait Of An Era* exhibition runs at the Delaware Art Museum in Wilmington, Delaware.

Tuesday January 23

 After a two-month delay, George's 1970 album *All Things Must Pass* is reissued in America. (European releases took place the previous day.)

February 13

 In the States, Dawn Treader Productions and Tim Ensemble Records release the *Music Of Hope* CD, issued to benefit the American Cancer Society. The ten-track collection features a contribution from Paul (an orchestral début of *Nova*) as well as Billy Joel, Andrew Previn, Kurt Masur, The New York Philharmonic and The London Symphony Orchestra.

March

 Faber publishes the book *Blackbird Singing*, an official Paul McCartney book which features poetry and lyrics dating from the 1960s to the present day.

Saturday March 10 (until June 17)

 Yoko's show *Yes Yoko Ono* opens at the Walker Art Center in Minneapolis.

Tuesday March 20

 The Beatles' film *A Hard Day's Night* is scheduled for a re-release on DVD in America.

Sunday June 10 (until August 19)

 Linda's *Sixties – Portrait Of An Era* runs at the Ackland Art Museum in Chapel Hill, North Carolina.

Friday July 13 (until September 16)
 Yoko's exhibition, *Yes Yoko Ono*, opens at the Contemporary Arts Museum in Houston, Texas.

Wednesday September 12 (until November 4)
 Linda's *Sixties – Portrait Of An Era* runs at the Dean Lester Regional Center For The Arts, in Walnut Creek in California.

Thursday October 18 (until January 6, 2002)
 Yoko's show *Yes Yoko Ono* opens at the MIT-LIST Visual Arts Center in Cambridge, Massachusetts.

Postscript

Forty years down the line and the story of The Beatles after The Beatles continues. In truth, it will never end because the musical legacy The Beatles left behind continues to entertain, enlighten and influence more than any other musical legacy from the 20th Century. Although the activities of Paul, George and Ringo will slow down as they reach their sixties and beyond, interest in them never seems to wane. More than any other pop group ever, collectively and individually, The Beatles – whether they like it or not —are still as famous as it is possible to be.

There are Beatles fans who have not yet been born, and Beatles fans will continue to be born long after the deaths of all four Beatles and all those fans who saw them perform and bought their records first time around. One hundred years from now, when everyone who is reading this book will also have died, The Beatles will still be out there in one form or another, their music long out of copyright, distributed and broadcast unchecked in some futuristic format that might seem as outrageous to us today as shiny silver CDs would have seemed to Mozart, Duke Ellington or Elvis in their day.

The Beatles will never die. Interest in them will continue for as long as the human race survives. Let it be.